21st Conference on Natural Language Processing/Konferenz zur Verarbeitung naturlicher Sprache (KONVENS 2025)

Volume 2 - Workshops

Hildesheim, Germany
9-12 September 2025

ISBN: 979-8-3313-2676-0

Printed from e-media with permission by:

Curran Associates, Inc.
57 Morehouse Lane
Red Hook, NY 12571

Some format issues inherent in the e-media version may also appear in this print version.

Printed with permission by Curran Associates, Inc. (2026)

For permission requests, please contact the Association for Computational Linguistics at the address below.

Association for Computational Linguistics
209 N. Eighth Street
Stroudsburg, Pennsylvania 18360

Phone: 1-570-476-8006
Fax: 1-570-476-0860

acl@aclweb.org

Additional copies of this publication are available from:

Curran Associates, Inc.
57 Morehouse Lane
Red Hook, NY 12571 USA
Phone: 845-758-0400
Fax: 845-758-2633
Email: curran@proceedings.com
Web: www.proceedings.com

Imprint

Bibliographic Information of the German National Library

The German National Library lists this publication in the German National Bibliography. Detailed bibliographic data are available at https://portal.dnb.de.

HsH Applied Academics | Hannover 2025

Hochschule Hannover – University of Applied Sciences and Arts | Central Library
Ricklinger Stadtweg 118, 30459 Hannover, Germany
E-Mail: serwiss@hs-hannover.de
Website: https://hs-h.de/bib

BMFTR Project „DiamOnd@HsH – Towards a Science-Led Open Access Culture via Establishment of a Diamond Open Access University Press for the University of Applied Sciences and Arts Hannover" (16KOA042)

Cover Design: Lina Herschel (Hamburg, Germany), linaherschel.com

DOI: https://doi.org/10.25968/opus-3679
URN: urn:nbn:de:bsz:960-opus4-36794

KONVENS 2025 is hosted by the University of Hildesheim and chaired by Christian Wartena (DataIH Institute for Applied Data Science Hannover, Hochschule Hannover) and Ulrich Heid (Institut für Informationswissenschaft und Sprachtechnologie, Universität Hildesheim).

KONVENS was funded by the zukunft.niedersachsen program, in the program line 'Pro*Niedersachsen – Wissenschaftliche Veranstaltungen der Geistes-, Kultur- und Sozialwissenschaften in Niedersachsen'

Keynote speakers and tutorials were funded by the German Society for Computational Linguistics and Language Technology.

This publication was supported by the NiedersachsenOPEN publication fund, funded by zukunft.niedersachsen.

KONVENS 2025
Conference on Natural Language Processing

KONVENS (Konferenz zur Verarbeitung natürlicher Sprache) is an annual conference series on computational linguistics (biennial until 2018) that started in 1992 and that is organized under the auspices of the German Society for Computational Linguistics and Language Technology, the Special Interest Group on Computational Linguistics of the German Linguistic Society, the Austrian Society for Artificial Intelligence and SwissNLP.

The conference takes place in Hildesheim, Germany, from September 9th to 12th, 2025

Event Website: `https://konvens-2025.hs-hannover.de`
E-Mail: `info.konvens2025@gscl.org`

ACL Anthology

The Proceedings of the 21th Conference on Natural Language Processing (KONVENS 2025) as well as the individual papers can also be found on ACL Anthology.

`https://aclanthology.org/events/konvens-2025`

Contents

SustainEval & NLP4Sustain

Harmful Content Detection

Candy Speech Detection

LLM4Subjects

GermEval Multi-Task Papers

KONVENS

21st Conference on Natural Language Processing (KONVENS 2025)

Proceedings of the Conference
9. – 12. September 2025

2025

Edited by Christian Wartena and Ulrich Heid

VOLUME 2 - WORKSHOPS

VOLUME 2 - WORKSHOPS

KONVENS (Konferenz zur Verarbeitung natürlicher Sprache, Conference on Natural Language Processing) is an annual conference series on computational linguistics first held in 1992. Originally biennial until 2018, the conference is organized under the auspices of the German Society for Computational Linguistics and Language Technology, the Special Interest Group on Computational Linguistics of the German Linguistic Society, the Austrian Society for Artificial Intelligence, and SwissNLP. The 21st edition of KONVENS took place in Hildesheim, Germany, from September 9–12, 2025, and was jointly organized by the University of Hildesheim and the University of Applied Sciences and Arts Hannover.

This year's conference centered on artificial intelligence and large language models (LLMs), reflecting the scientific community's efforts to better understand and optimize the properties of LLMs. These topics were addressed in three plenary lectures, a lecture session on methodological issues, and a poster session on LLMs, as well as in sessions on other topics such as methods based on LLMs, discourse and semantics, multilinguality and translation, new language resources, applications of language technology beyond linguistics, and the identification of hate speech on social media.

The proceedings are published in two volumes. The first volume contains all the peer-reviewed papers from the main conference, and the second volume contains the papers from the six workshops and shared tasks organised as part of the conference.

HOCHSCHULE HANNOVER UNIVERSITY OF APPLIED SCIENCES AND ARTS

Stiftung Universität Hildesheim 2003

HsH Applied Academics

Gap in pagination due to formatting issues.

Pages 1-6

Analyzing Polarization in Online Discourse on the 2023-2024 Israel–Hamas War

Daniel Miehling, Daniel Dakota, Sandra Kübler
Indiana University
{damieh, ddakota, skuebler}@iu.edu

Abstract

We investigate large-scale sentiment analysis of YouTube Shorts in the context of the 2023-2024 Israel–Hamas war. Using a corpus of over 3 million user comments and replies from four state-funded or state-supported international media channels, we track sentiment toward key geopolitical and ideological entities over the course of one year. We investigate the correspondence between large-scale sentiment analysis and manual fine-grained analysis of trends as well as the correspondence between a longitudinal analysis and geopolitical events. Results show that overall sentiment trends depict user attitudes, but to interpret these patterns correctly, we need domain-specific knowledge and a combination of the automatic analysis with fine-grained manual analysis. We also show that the peaks of a longitudinal analysis correspond to (geo-)political events such as the Eurovision Song Contest.

1 Introduction

The October 7, 2023 attacks and the ensuing war between Israel and Hamas triggered a surge in global online discourse characterized by intense polarization and ideological fragmentation. While polarization in digital spaces has been widely studied, most analyses of political communication rely on coarse methods such as stance detection or user clustering, often applied to Twitter (Becatti et al., 2019; Stier et al., 2018). In contrast, we focus on using large-scale aspect-based sentiment analysis to investigate trends in user-generated content.

More specifically, we use aspect-based sentiment analysis (ABSA) to analyze over 3 million comments and replies on YouTube Shorts (a short-form video format similar to TikTok videos) by four state-funded or state-supported international broadcasters (Cull, 2008) (Al Jazeera, TRT World, BBC News, and Deutsche Welle)[1]. Since ABSA enables the detection of distinct sentiment toward multiple entities within the same utterance (Chauhan and Meena, 2019; Mai and Le, 2021), it can offer a nuanced view of ideological alignment. Consider the following example[2]:

(1) *Hamas being labeled as terrorist group is just a label. They are resistances against occupation and atrocities... Some countries like Israel and America have caused more dead a terror... but you can't label them Terrorists because they are countries.*

Here, *Hamas* is framed in a relativizing tone that challenges its designation as a terrorist group. In contrast, *Israel* and *America* are depicted as more violent actors, invoking negative sentiment. The final mention of *Terrorists* emphasizes a perceived double standard, adding a layer of ideological critique. Thus, ABSA allows these overlapping views to be disentangled.

Our study applies a current ABSA model (Yang et al., 2021, 2023) to investigate political communication in the digital mainstream. Drawing on insights from Kušen and Strembeck (2023), who show how emotional exposure during the early stages of the Ukraine war shaped user affect over time, we use large-scale sentiment analysis to map fine-grained sentiment toward competing and often opposing political actors. This approach enables us to track how emotional alignment and ideological positioning shift over time within digital discourse on YouTube. We trace sentiment trajectories over a 12-month period following the Hamas-led attack on Israel. We aim to examine the correspondence of sentiment analysis with fine-grained manual analysis as well as the correspondence to spikes in the longitudinal analysis to (geo-)political events such

[1] In our tables and figures, we use the abbreviations BBC and TRT to refer to BBC News and TRT World, respectively.

[2] The example represents user-generated content drawn from our corpus.

Proceedings of the 21st Conference on Natural Language Processing (KONVENS), Volume 2: Workshops, pages 7–16, 2025

as the Eurovision Song Contest. More specifically, we ask the following research questions:

- **RQ1:** To what extent does large-scale sentiment analysis depict trends in user-generated content on Shorts videos?
- **RQ2:** How well do sentiment trends in a longitudinal analysis correspond to geopolitical events?

2 Related Work

With extensive prior research examining hate speech, misinformation, and political extremism in online spaces (Becker et al., 2023; Brown et al., 2024; Finkelstein et al., 2023; Rieger et al., 2020; Topor, 2024), sentiment analysis has emerged as a tool to model ideological alignment, polarization, and user engagement in socio-political discourse.

To capture the implicit and coded nature of political speech, Subramanian et al. (2023) and Young et al. (2024) emphasize the importance of context-sensitive sentiment models capable of interpreting nuance in polarized discourse. Shifts in media sentiment can precede conflict outbreaks (Jamison et al., 2023), with sentiment dynamics reflecting affective polarization (Lerman et al., 2024), and can capture emotional reactions in crisis moments (Kušen and Strembeck, 2023; Win Myint et al., 2024).

Aspect-based sentiment analysis has proven suitable for modeling longitudinal sentiment variation in politically charged online discussions. It captures more nuanced sentiment toward discrete entities or themes, enabling robust sentiment extraction at the aspect level across multiple targets within the same comment (Rietzler et al., 2020; Zhang et al., 2022), particularly in domains such as hate speech detection (Mughal et al., 2024; Zainuddin et al., 2016, 2018; Zhang et al., 2024) and political communication (Gold et al., 2018; Miok et al., 2023; Seno et al., 2024).

3 Methodology

3.1 Corpus and Collection

The empirical data was obtained via the official YouTube API[3]. We started the corpus collection two weeks after the events of October 7. To narrow the scope of this study, we focus on state-funded or state-supported international outlets: *TRT World*

[3]https://developers.google.com/youtube/v3/docs

Outlet	Videos	Comments	Users
DW	84	9 172	6 521
AJ	958	1 187 470	388 384
BBC	70	23 039	13 517
TRT	1 258	2 224 981	773 773
Total	2 370	3 444 662	787 157

Table 1: Corpus statistics across media outlets.

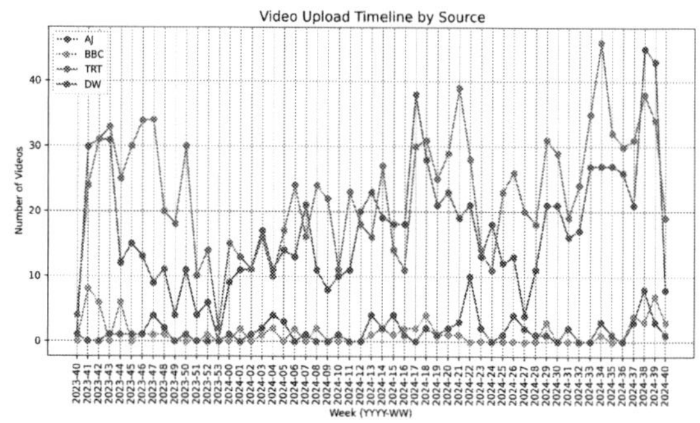

Figure 1: Weekly frequency of YouTube Shorts uploads per outlet over a 12-month period.

(Turkey), *BBC News* (United Kingdom), *Al Jazeera* (Qatar), and *Deutsche Welle* (Germany)[4]. These channels play a critical role in shaping public discourse and often reflect distinct geopolitical perspectives. Over a twelve-month data collection period, we gathered more than 3.4 million comments and replies from these four outlets, generated by over 780 000 unique users. Table 1 shows the total number of unique video IDs, user-generated comments and replies, and distinct users participating in discussions for each outlet.

Figure 1 illustrates the weekly frequency of YouTube Shorts uploads per source. *TRT World* and *Al Jazeera* consistently released substantially more content, often exceeding 30 to 40 Shorts per week, compared to *BBC News* and *DW*, which uploaded fewer than 10 Shorts weekly. *BBC News* and *DW*, in turn, cover a broader thematic spectrum, with fewer videos directly addressing the Israel-Gaza conflict. While we initially considered including earlier data, a subsequent rescraping attempt on user-generated content related to BBC's Shorts revealed that nearly 50% of the original comments and replies had been removed, likely due to YouTube's content moderation policies.

[4]While *TRT World* has stated that it is not affiliated with the Turkish government, the other three channels are state-funded or state-supported broadcasters.

Outlet	Overall	Non-Eng.	Non-Eng. %
TRT	771 855	149 268	19.33
AJ	280 744	47 032	16.75
DW	2 733	386	14.12
BBC	10 298	850	8.25

Table 2: Remaining content after language filtering.

3.2 Preprocessing

We implemented a multi-step preprocessing pipeline to prepare the corpus for sentiment analysis. First, we filtered structurally invalid JSON files and removed entries with missing fields. We then normalized user mentions (e.g., `@username`) to support accurate tokenization. To ensure language consistency, we applied the `langdetect` library[5] and retained only English-language comments. For further quality control, we computed an English lexical coverage ratio using the `nltk.corpus.words` vocabulary[6] and discarded comments with less than 40% English terms (see Table 2).

To constrain the analysis to relevant discourse, we filtered the corpus using a targeted aspect lexicon that included geopolitical and ideological entities central to the conflict. This lexicon comprised the following terms: *Israel*, *Palestine*, *Jews*, *Palestinians*, *Zionists*, *Hamas*, *Hezbollah*, and *Muslims*[7].

3.3 Aspect-Based Annotation

Manual annotations were necessary to fine-tune an aspect-based sentiment analysis model to annotate the large scale corpus. The user-generated content in our corpus contains considerable noise, including unconventional spellings, typographical errors, informal language, and domain-specific allusions or "dog whistles". To ensure accurate sentiment classification, we used a small subset of our corpus and annotated it for sentiment. We used `Label Studio`[8] (Tkachenko et al., 2025), an open-source data labeling platform, to annotate text segments with both aspect categories and sentiment labels. The annotation was conducted by an expert in the field. Sentences were pre-selected using dependency parsing (see Section 3.4) to identify those containing aspect terms from the aforementioned lexicon. Sentiment was annotated as *positive*, *neutral*, or *negative*, and applied to both explicit and clearly implied references. The annotation scheme accounted for informal syntax, metaphorical language, and ideological cues, which are characteristic of user-generated discourse.

Aspect	Negative	Neutral	Positive
Hamas	576	422	225
Hezbollah	5	14	12
Israel	296	278	376
Jews	192	244	109
Muslims	112	272	234
Palestine	175	186	101
Palestinians	272	261	260
Zionists	228	272	25
Total	1 856	1 949	1 342

Table 3: Distribution of annotated segments by aspect and sentiment label.

The final annotated corpus comprises 5 147 text segments[9], sampled from comments and replies across the four state-funded or state-supported media outlets. Selection criteria included lexical variety, comment diversity, and the removal of near-duplicate or semantically redundant content. We aimed to balance the sentiment distribution within each aspect category, although certain entities, particularly *Zionists*, were predominantly associated with negative sentiment, limiting class balance. Table 3 presents the distribution of annotated segments by aspect and sentiment label.

To assess reliability, a stratified random sample of 500 segments was independently annotated by a second expert. We computed inter-annotator agreement (IAA) on this subset, yielding scores of $\kappa = 0.86$ and $\alpha = 0.85$, indicating substantial agreement (see Table 4). While these scores reflect consistency, they do not guarantee conceptual accuracy in highly polarized or coded language domains (Paun et al., 2022), where ideological framings and implicit sentiment pose inherent challenges.

3.4 Dependency Parsing

We used the biaffine graph-based dependency parser (Dozat and Manning, 2017) implemented in

[5]`https://github.com/Mimino666/langdetect`

[6]`https://www.nltk.org/_modules/nltk/corpus/reader/wordlist.html`

[7]After processing, the aspect *Hezbollah* appeared only in a small number of examples and was therefore excluded from the ABSA evluation due to insufficient data.

[8]`https://labelstud.io`

[9]Each segment corresponds to a dependency-parsed sentence or clause containing at least one aspect mention. Due to informal punctuation, ellipses, or run-on constructions, some parsed segments span multiple clauses.

Sentiment	Cohen's κ	Krippendorff's α
Negative	0.850	0.850
Neutral	0.867	0.868
Positive	0.869	0.869
Overall	0.862	0.855

Table 4: Inter-annotator agreement scores across sentiment classes.

Class	Prec.	Rec.	F1
Negative	73.5	84.4	78.6
Neutral	78.4	71.9	75.0
Positive	85.0	77.9	81.3
Avg.	78.4	78.0	77.9

Table 5: Overall sentiment classification performance (on the test set).

the SuPar library[10] to extract syntactic structures, identify aspect terms, and locate their grammatical heads. In our workflow, the parser detected dependency relations within each comment, allowing us to align syntactic heads with predefined aspect categories for aspect term extraction (Zhang et al., 2022). Parsing was conducted using the pretrained `biaffine-dep-en` model, trained on English Universal Dependencies treebanks. We performed inference on a GPU with batch-wise processing over tokenized user-generated text.

3.5 Model Training and Evaluation

For aspect-based sentiment analysis, we used the end-to-end `DeBERTa-v3-large-absa-v1.1` model provided in the pyABSA library (Yang et al., 2021, 2023). This pretrained model was initially trained on English-language benchmark datasets, including Twitter and SemEval corpora, for aspect-based sentiment classification. We finetuned the model for 5 epochs on our task-specific training set using an NVIDIA A100 GPU. Training used a batch size of 2 and gradient accumulation over 8 steps, resulting in an effective batch size of 16. A cosine learning rate scheduler was used with an initial learning rate of 1×10^{-5}. As no separate development set was defined, we selected the best model checkpoint based on validation loss. Following the aspect-prompted classification framework, aspect terms in each sentence were replaced with a `$T$` marker. Input sequences were truncated to a maximum length of 512 tokens.

Table 5 shows the evaluation on the test set (precision, recall, and F1 across sentiment classes). The model achieves a macro-averaged F1 of 77.9, indicating strong performance in classifying explicit sentiment expressions related to our aspect terms.

The model most frequently confuses neutral comments and negative ones in both directions (see Figure 2). Since our goal is to assess sentiment

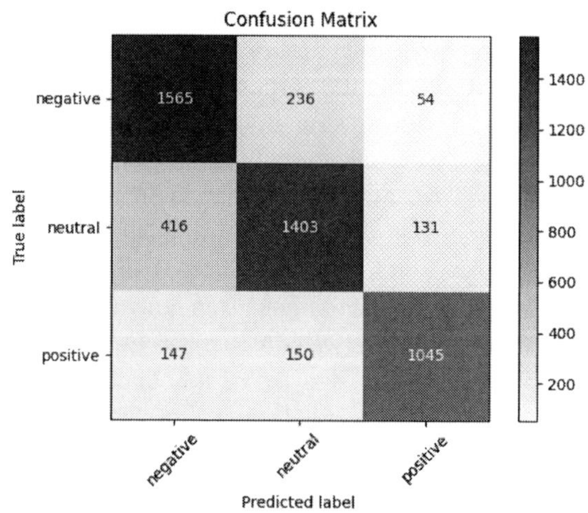

Figure 2: Confusion matrix for sentiment classification (on the test set).

directed toward specific ideological actors, we further evaluated per-aspect performance. As shown in Table 6, model performance is consistent across aspects, with particularly high accuracy for *Hezbollah*, *Muslims*, and *Palestine*, and solid results for more contentious aspect terms such as *Zionists* and *Hamas*. Our error analysis revealed three primary challenges: (1) difficulty in detecting implicit sentiment, particularly in sarcastic or coded language; (2) misclassifications in sentences containing ambiguous sentiment toward multiple aspects (e.g., *"Free Jews from Israel"*); and (3) challenges in processing code-switching comments and transliterations, where sentiment-bearing terms appeared in hybrid forms (e.g., Arabic-English transliterations).

4 Findings

To address our research questions, we adopt a two-step analytical approach that combines quantitative analysis with close qualitative reading. While ABSA enables large-scale sentiment classification, many findings cannot be interpreted in aggregation alone. In response to RQ1, we begin by analyz-

[10] `https://github.com/yzhangcs/parser`

Aspect	Acc.	Prec.	Rec.	F1
Hamas	75.1	75.0	75.1	74.6
Hezbollah	90.3	90.6	90.3	90.3
Israel	75.4	76.6	75.4	75.6
Jews	74.3	74.9	74.3	74.3
Muslims	85.4	85.8	85.4	85.5
Palestine	81.6	81.9	81.6	81.5
Palestinians	78.9	78.9	78.9	78.7
Zionists	79.0	79.6	79.0	78.7

Table 6: Per-aspect sentiment classification performance (on the test set).

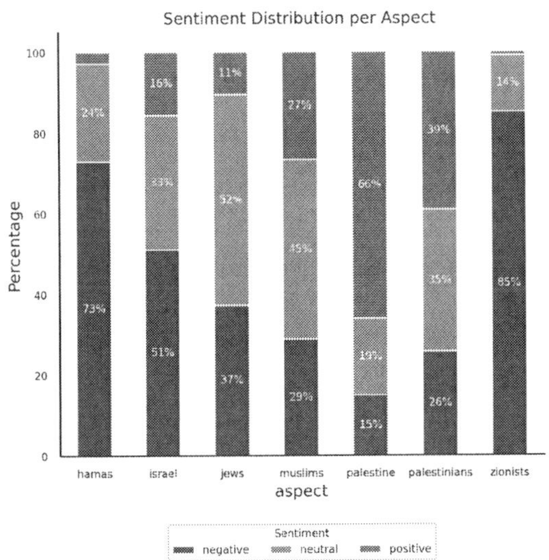

Figure 3: Stacked bar chart for sentiment distribution per aspect (in %).

ing the aggregated sentiment distribution across aspect terms to uncover general patterns of political communication in user-generated reactions to Shorts. We then turn to RQ2 by examining longitudinal sentiment dynamics and selected discourse patterns that reveal ideological alignments amid heightened volumes of user-generated content.

4.1 Aggregated Sentiment Distribution

Figure 3 presents the aggregated results of the sentiment analysis in form of the distribution of sentiment labels (negative, neutral, positive) across all classified aspect terms in the corpus, aggregated over all four media outlets. Negative sentiment dominates for the aspects *Israel*, *Zionists*, and, to a lesser extent, *Jews*. In contrast, *Palestinians* and *Muslims* receive more mixed or neutral sentiment, reflecting framings across the analyzed outlets. Interestingly, *Zionists* receive a higher proportion of negative sentiment (85%) than *Hamas* (73%), indicating that references to Zionism in mainstream YouTube discourse may elicit particularly adversarial responses[11].

While the aggregated results indicate a measurable share of positive sentiment toward *Palestine* and *Palestinians*, a closer examination of sentiment associated with *Jews* reveals that positive expressions do not necessarily reflect broadly favorable attitudes. Instead, such sentiment often appears in contrastive framings, for example, praising "good Jews" who oppose Israel or Zionism, while implicitly or explicitly condemning others, see examples (2) and (3). This discursive pattern reflects a form of conditional inclusion, where selective approval reinforces ideological boundaries. As mentioned earlier, such patterns of selective framing are not captured by sentiment proportions alone and require close reading to reveal how users shape ideological narratives.

(2) There are plenty of Jewish people fighting for Palestinian independence, we should not conflate Jewish people with the genocidal state of Israel.

(3) There are good orthodox Jews but Israel is run by a sadistic Zionist

A similar ambiguity emerges in references to *Palestinians*. In example (4), the model assigns positive sentiment, yet the phrase carries an implicit reference to a violent act (i.e., the "pager attack" linked to Hezbollah), thus revealing antagonistic intent beneath a lexically positive surface[12].

(4) Free Pagers for Palestine

Despite such conceptual ambiguities, these examples shed light on how evaluative language in user-generated content often carries multi-layered or contrastive meanings. In example (5), the phrase "Free Palestine" appears lexically positive, yet it is reframed as a critique of Hamas. Such contrastive uses illustrate how sentiment-laden expressions may simultaneously convey positive alignment with one political actor while denouncing

[11] While the proportion of negative sentiment is higher for *Zionists*, the total number of classified instances is much lower: 14 358 (*Zionists*) vs. 171 114 (*Hamas*).

[12] The phrase refers to events on 17–18 September 2024 in Lebanon, where explosives concealed in pager devices were deliberately detonated to target members of Hezbollah.

another. The presence of multiple aspect terms within short, syntactically simple comments suggests that such juxtapositions are common in political discourse and reveal how users employ sentiment cues to express ideological alignment in response to Shorts.

(5) Free Palestine from Hamas

While the majority of sentiment directed at *Hamas* is negative, we identified a smaller subset of positive sentiment. These instances often reflect implicit endorsement of Hamas as a resistance actor, as illustrated in example (6) and example (7).

(6) Victory to HAMAS-HEZBOLLAH FREE PALESTINE

(7) Kill every israel soldier who attack on falastin, hamas

Frequently, intensified sentiment is conveyed through symbolic and visual elements. Emoji sequences often accompany slogans like "Free Palestine" or denunciations of Zionism, that may serve to amplify affective tone or signal ideological stance. As shown in example (8), semiotic markers are combined to emphasize solidarity and resistance.

(8) FREE PALESTINE NOW! ✊ PS✌ Down with 💤ionism and apartheid 😭 🤬

Across the corpus, emojis are used extensively: 18.1% of all classified sentences (181 095 out of 1 000 750) contain at least one emoji. This high frequency highlights their role as affective intensifiers in discourse and underscores the need to consider multimodal cues as crucial elements of contemporary political communication within the digital mainstream. However, interpreting these patterns often requires domain-specific knowledge, as their meanings can diverge significantly from conventional language use.

4.2 Identifying Longitudinal Dynamics

To analyze how shifts in user discourse are reflected in sentiment patterns, we perform a peak analysis of weekly aspect-based sentiment trends. Figure 4 shows the overall frequency of sentiment-labeled content across the four state-funded or state-supported international broadcasters. It reveals key differences in user engagement: for instance, Shorts on *TRT World* consistently resulted in high volumes of user-generated content, while activity

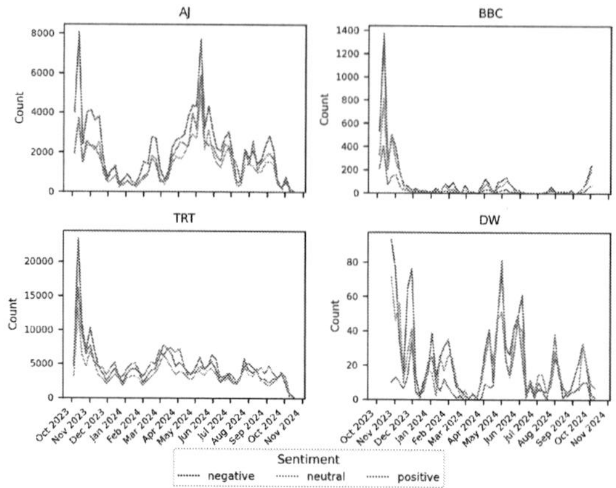

Figure 4: Sentiment trends over time across outlets.

on *DW* remained sporadic, only increasing in response to specific events. We observe repeated spikes in negative sentiment that coincide with geopolitical events such as the Eurovision Song Contest or Israel's Independence Day. However, instead of focusing solely on these general trends, we identify discursive tipping points: high aggregations of emotionally charged user responses that intensified user-generated reactions. We examine these sentiment surges more closely through aggregated data of weekly aspect-based sentiment trends, which allows us to trace how user sentiment fluctuated in response to unfolding real-world events.

Figure 5 shows sentiment trends per aspect. This analysis reveals three major peaks between March and May 2024, corresponding to heightened sentiment around *Palestine*, *Israel*, and *Zionists*. For each peak, we retrieved the most-commented Shorts videos and analyzed their content in relation to user responses. We compared sentiment curves across outlets and examined video titles and descriptions, together with comments and replies, to assess how user-generated activity reflects reporting on geopolitical events.

The first peak in early May coincides with the release of Shorts covering the Eurovision Song Contest, see example (9), and international campus protests, see example (10). High-engagement videos contributing to this spike included footage of Dutch riot police dismantling a Gaza protest camp and scenes of pro-Palestinian chants during Israel's Eurovision rehearsal.

(9) Well done, to the audience at the Eurovision. Letting Israel know how the world feels about them !! FREE PALESTINE NOW !!!

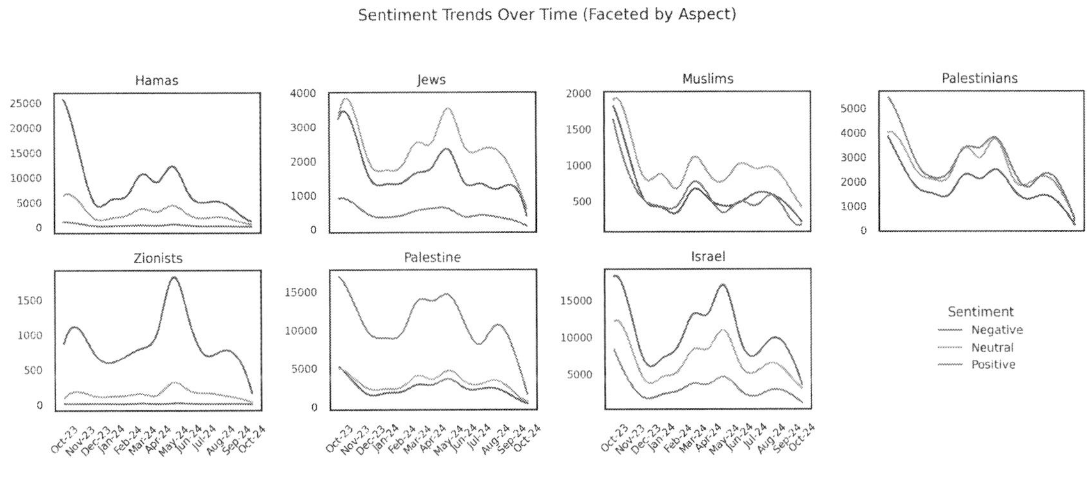

Figure 5: Sentiment trends over time across seven aspects.

(10) Many thanks the students who support majlum Palestine

These videos triggered waves of solidarity expressions such as "Free Palestine", as well as accusations of genocide, see example (11), illustrating how users signaled political stance.

(11) Just need humanity to stand with Palestine. Stop genocide

The second peak coincided with Israel's Independence Day on May 14 and was shaped by Shorts that cover allegations of the International Criminal Court (ICC) against Israel, as well as a Short depicting US-supplied weapons used in Gaza. During this period, negative sentiment toward *Israel* intensified. Users invoked narratives of indigeneity and dispossession, see examples (12) and (13), reflected by a high frequency of trigrams such as "Canaan Palestinians descendants" and "indigenous people Palestinians" to assert historical and moral claims.

(12) Wasn't Israel made up by the whiteEuropeans, Delete the Hebrews field of land from the indigenous canaanites?

(13) The indigenous people are the Palestinians not the israeles who've been separated from Canaan and the old israel for a very long time

A third peak followed shortly thereafter, marked by intensified negative sentiment toward *Zionists*. This spike coincide with Shorts depicting police crackdowns on protest camps and a widely viewed video showing a scholar harassing a Muslim woman at a pro-Israel protest. Commenters responded with ideologically charged language, adopting anti-colonial framings and linking protest repression to broader narratives of systemic violence. Phrases such as "Zionists are dangerous", see example (14), and "Zionist colonizers", see example (15), highlight how the discourse shifted from solidarity-based expressions to overt ideological opposition.

(14) Zionists are dangerous for all people of the world.

(15) You mean Zionists hate them spreading the truth and standing up against the evil Zionist colonizers committing genocide.

Compared to earlier peaks, the third peak features significantly more pejorative and antagonistic language. Users adopt moral binaries and dehumanizing rhetoric to frame the conflict between Hamas and Israel, shifting from solidarity-based expressions to ideologically charged attacks targeting *Zionists*, marking a clear intensification of discursive polarization.

Taken together, the comparison across these peaks suggests a transition from expressions of solidarity to increasingly polarizing and antagonistic rhetoric. User-generated content toward *Zionists* and *Israel* exhibits more sentiment shifts than content related to *Palestine*. Users responded to geopolitical flashpoints by asserting legitimacy claims, voicing collective grievances, and expressing identity-based solidarities, dynamics consistent with prior research on event-driven polarization (Royesh and Grossman, 2021; Miehling,

2024; Alamsyah et al., 2024; Kušen and Strembeck, 2023).

5 Discussion

Our findings suggest that sentiment in user-generated content functions not merely as an emotional signal, but as a means of ideological expression and alignment. ABSA enables us to trace how users position themselves in relation to geopolitical actors through coded language and contrastive framings.

These patterns were especially salient in discourse surrounding *Zionists* and *Israel*, which were frequently associated with accusations of colonialism, genocide, and systemic violence. In contrast, while the aspect *Hamas* displayed only a small share of positive sentiment, its occasional framing in terms of resistance or heroism illustrates how affective discourse can operate through implication and conceptual ambiguity rather than overt endorsement. In particular, *Zionists* received the highest proportion of negative sentiment, even exceeding *Hamas*. While this trend underscores adversarial positioning toward Zionism as an ideology, the lack of positive examples also posed challenges for classification. To maintain empirical transparency, and to avoid biasing the ABSA system, we refrained from augmenting the training data, e.g., by generating synthetic data, to address class imbalance.

At the same time, our findings demonstrate the utility of large-scale sentiment analysis not only for identifying sentiment polarity, but also for unpacking rhetorical strategies users deploy to articulate political stances. In this context, affect operates discursively, conveying moral evaluation and ideological positioning. We observed persistent ambiguity in contrastive expressions involving Jews, where seemingly positive portrayals of Jewish fringe groups often legitimized the simultaneous condemnation of Israel or *Zionists*. Such constructions not only complicate the interpretation of straightforward sentiments but also reflect deeper ideological divisions.

Temporal sentiment patterns in our peak analysis further reveal that user-generated content extends beyond immediate reactions to breaking news, pop-cultural events, or protest repression. Affective intensification often mirrors geopolitical flashpoints but also transcends them. The accompanying discourse frequently moves beyond the specific Short-video context. Users employ emotionally charged, morally coded language to express solidarity, outrage, and condemnation. Thus, user-generated content should not be understood solely as real-time responses, but as discursive echoes, shaped by collective memory and entrenched resentment. Taken together, these findings suggest that sentiment analysis leads to meaningful results for interpreting political discourse online, not as a series of isolated opinions, but as structured, emotionally mediated ideological formations.

6 Conclusion and Future Work

We have investigated the interconnection of sentiment and polarization in political discourse. To answer RQ1, we have demonstrated that large-scale sentiment analysis can capture patterns of political communication embedded in user-generated discourse. While surface-level trends reveal general sentiment, a closer reading of aspect-specific results, such as contrastive framings ("good Jews" vs. "Zionists"), semiotic markers, and selective sentiment toward ideologically loaded terms, shows how users employ affective language to articulate political stance, moral judgment, and group alignment.

Addressing RQ2, we showed that we can identify evolving discourse patterns and ideological shifts in response to real-world geopolitical events. By analyzing sentiment peaks and comparing aspect-specific dynamics, we traced users expressing both solidarity and polarization, revealing affective intensification and discursive realignment over time.

For future work, we will extend our investigation and analyze more sentiment targets (aspects). We will also investigate the usability of an RST parser to gain deeper insights into how the discourse is structured beyond the sentence level.

Limitations

Parsing: While dependency parsing enhanced aspect-term extraction, it did not fully resolve ambiguities in sentiment attribution. Future improvements may benefit from incorporating contrastive learning techniques or domain-adapted embeddings to better capture context-sensitive sentiment in highly polarized political discourse.

Annotations: Some statements lack clear intent markers (e.g., sarcasm, irony, rhetorical questions). We infer meaning based on domain-specific expertise using established patterns of dog whistles and coded language, but some ambiguous cases remain unresolved.

Corpus Constraints: Several initial aspects (e.g., *Hezbollah*) were discarded because many comments failed the language threshold ($\geq 40\%$ English), indicating widespread mixed-language use. Other aspects (e.g., *Zionists*) had very few positive examples, which led to class imbalance that impacted model performance. While augmenting the corpus could mitigate some of these limitations, generating synthetic samples—particularly in sensitive political domains—raises ethical concerns, despite the potential to improve accuracy.

The results on user-generated content from *Deutsche Welle (DW)* and *BBC News* should be interpreted with caution: due to limited short-video content published by these outlets, our corpus contains significantly fewer samples from these sources compared to *TRT World* and *Al Jazeera (AJ)*. This discrepancy does not imply that *DW* or *BBC News* did not cover the aftermath of October 7, but rather reflects platform-specific publishing practices.

Ethics Statement

Our study was conducted in accordance with institutional IRB approval and ethical research standards. We show user-generated content that includes sensitive and potentially harmful language, such expressions that may endorse or glorify violence. These examples are necessary to address our research questions and serve solely for illustrative purposes.

Acknowledgments

This work used Jetstream2 at Indiana University through allocation HUM200003 from the Advanced Cyberinfrastructure Coordination Ecosystem: Services & Support (ACCESS) program, which is supported by National Science Foundation grants #2138259, #2138286, #2138307, #2137603, and #2138296.

References

Andry Alamsyah, Akmal Wijaya Muharam, and Dian Puteri Ramadhani. 2024. Polarized narratives in digital spaces: A social network examination of the Gaza conflict. In *2024 International Conference on Data Science and Its Applications (ICoDSA)*, pages 527–532.

Carolina. Becatti, Guida Caldarelli, Renaud Lambiotte, and Fabio Saracco. 2019. Extracting significant signal of news consumption from social networks: The case of Twitter in Italian political elections. *Palgrave Commun*, 5(91).

Matthias J. Becker, Laura. Ascone, Matthew Bolton, Alexis Chapelan, Pia Haupeltshofer, Alexa Krugel, Karolina. Placzynta, Marcus Scheiber, and Victor Tschiskale. 2023. Celebrating terror: Antisemitism online after the Hamas attacks on Israel.

Olivia Brown, Laura G. E. Smith, Brittany I. Davidson, Daniel Racek, and Adam Joinson. 2024. Online signals of extremist mobilization. *Personality and Social Psychology Bulletin*.

Ganpat Singh Chauhan and Yogesh Kumar Meena. 2019. Youtube video ranking by aspect-based sentiment analysis on user feedback. In J. Wang, G. R. M. Reddy, V. K. Prasad, and V. S. Reddy, editors, *Soft Computing and Signal Processing*, volume 900, pages 63–71. Springer Singapore.

Nicholas J. Cull. 2008. Public diplomacy: Taxonomies and histories. *The Annals of the American Academy of Political and Social Science*, 616(1):31–54.

Timothy Dozat and Christopher Manning. 2017. Deep biaffine attention for neural dependency parsing. In *5h International Conference on Learning Representations (ICLR 2017)*, Toulon, France.

Joel Finkelstein, Jack Donohue, Alex Goldenberg, Lee Jussim, Alexander Reid Ross, Collin Vasko, Christian Ramos, Taylor Glover, Anisha Jagdeep, Anthony Boyle, and Jiya Modi. 2023. #Twittertakeover: How the Musk acquisition became a launchpad for Gen-Z Neo-Nazis, Ye, and widespread antisemitism. Technical report, Network Contagion Research Institute.

Darina Gold, Marie Bexte, and Torsten Zesch. 2018. Corpus of aspect-based sentiment in political debates. In *Proceedings of the 14th Conference on Natural Language Processing (KONVENS 2018)*, pages 89–99, Vienna, Austria.

Ashley S Jamison, Jason Miklian, Kristian Hoelscher, Witold J Henisz, and Brian Ganson. 2023. Is media sentiment associated with future conflict events? *SSRN Electronic Journal*.

Eduard Kušen and Mark Strembeck. 2023. The effects of multiple exposure to highly emotional social media content during the early stages of the 2022 war in Ukraine. *SN Computer Science*, 4(1):663.

Kristina Lerman, Dan Feldman, Zihao He, and Ashwin Rao. 2024. Affective polarization and dynamics of information spread in online networks. *npj Complexity*, 1(8).

Long Mai and Bac Le. 2021. Joint sentence and aspect-level sentiment analysis of product comments. *Annals of Operations Research*, 300(2):493–513.

Daniel Miehling. 2024. *Online-Antisemitismus verstehen: Hassrede im Web 2.0. Eine vergleichende Studie zwischen der Mainstream-Plattform X und Fringe-Communities auf Telegram*, 1 edition. Nomos Verlag, Baden-Baden.

Kristian Miok, Encarnacion Hidalgo-Tenorio, Petya Osenova, Miguel-Angel Benitez-Castro, and Marko Robnik-Sikonja. 2023. Multi-aspect multilingual and cross-lingual parliamentary speech analysis. *arXiv preprint arXiv:2207.01054*.

Nimra Mughal, Ghulam Mujtaba, Sarang Shaikh, Aveenash Kumar, and Sher Muhammad Daudpota. 2024. Comparative analysis of deep natural networks and large language models for aspect-based sentiment analysis. *IEEE Access*, 12:60943–60959.

Silviu Paun, Ron Artstein, and Massimo Poesio. 2022. *Statistical Methods for Annotation Analysis*. Springer International Publishing, Cham.

Diana Rieger, Lena Frischlich, Stefanie Rack, and Gary Bente. 2020. Digitaler Wandel, Radikalisierungsprozesse und Extremismusprävention im Internet. In *Handbuch Extremismusprävention – Gesamtgesellschaftlich. Phänomenübergreifend*, pages 351–388. Bundeskriminalamt.

Alexander Rietzler, Sebastian Stabinger, Paul Opitz, and Stefan Engl. 2020. Adapt or get left behind: Domain adaptation through BERT language model finetuning for aspect-target sentiment classification. In *Proceedings of the Twelfth Language Resources and Evaluation Conference*, pages 4933–4941, Marseille, France. European Language Resources Association.

Abuzar Royesh and Shelby Grossman. #COVID1948: How a hashtag on Israel and Palestine went viral [online]. 2021. Freeman Spogli Institute for International Studies, Stanford University.

Eloize Seno, Lucs Silva, Fábio Anno, Fabiano Rocha, and Helena Caseli. 2024. Aspect-based sentiment analysis in comments on political debates in Portuguese: Evaluating the potential of ChatGPT. In *Proceedings of the 16th International Conference on Computational Processing of Portuguese (PROPOR)*, pages 312–320.

Sebastian Stier, Arnim Bleier, Haiko Lietz, and Markus Strohmaier. 2018. Election campaigning on social media: Politicians, audiences, and the mediation of political communication on Facebook and Twitter. *Political Communication*, 35(1):50–74.

Malliga Subramanian, Veerappampalayam Easwaramoorthy Sathiskumar, G. Deepalakshmi, Jaehyuk Cho, and G. Manikandan. 2023. A survey on hate speech detection and sentiment analysis using machine learning and deep learning models. *Alexandria Engineering Journal*, 80:110–121.

Maxim Tkachenko, Mikhail Malyuk, Andrey Holmanyuk, and Nikolai Liubimov. 2025. Label Studio: Data labeling software. Open source software available from https://github.com/HumanSignal/label-studio.

Lev Topor. 2024. Mis/disinformation and national resilience: Are countries immune to fake news? In *Cyber Sovereignty: International Security, Mass Communication, and the Future of the Internet*, pages 111–131. Springer Nature Switzerland.

Phyu Yi Win Myint, Sin Lo Lo, and Yanchun Zhang. 2024. Unveiling the dynamics of crisis events: Sentiment and emotion analysis via multi-task learning with attention mechanism and subject-based intent prediction. *Information Processing & Management*, 61(4):103413.

Heng Yang, Biqing Zeng, Mayi Xu, and Tianxing Wang. 2021. Back to reality: Leveraging pattern-driven modeling to enable affordable sentiment dependency learning. *CoRR*, abs/2110.08604.

Heng Yang, Chen Zhang, and Ke Li. 2023. PyABSA: A modularized framework for reproducible aspect-based sentiment analysis. In *Proceedings of the 32nd ACM International Conference on Information and Knowledge Management*, CIKM '23, page 5117–5122, New York, NY, USA. Association for Computing Machinery.

James C. Young, Rudy Arthur, and Hywel T. P. Williams. 2024. CIDER: Context-sensitive polarity measurement for short-form text. *PLOS ONE*, 19(4):e0299490.

Nurulhuda Zainuddin, Ali Selamat, and Roliana Ibrahim. 2016. Improving Twitter aspect-based sentiment analysis using hybrid approach. In *Intelligent Information and Database Systems*, pages 151–160. Springer.

Nurulhuda Zainuddin, Ali Selamat, and Roliana Ibrahim. 2018. Hybrid sentiment classification on Twitter aspect-based sentiment analysis. *Applied Intelligence*, 48(5):1218–1232.

Hao Zhang, Yu-N Cheah, Osamah Mohammed Alyasiri, and Jieuyu An. 2024. Exploring aspect-based sentiment quadruple extraction with implicit aspects, opinions, and ChatGPT: A comprehensive survey. *Artificial Intelligence Review*, 57(2):17.

Wenxuan Zhang, Xin Li, Yang Deng, Lidong Bing, and Wai Lam. 2022. A survey on aspect-based sentiment analysis: Tasks, methods, and challenges (version 2). *arXiv preprint arXiv:2203.01054*.

How phatic is political communication in social media?

Aenne C. K. Knierim and **Jannis Kuck** and **Ulrich Heid** and **Thomas Mandl**
Department of Information Science and Natural Language Processing
University of Hildesheim
Universitätsplatz 1, 31141 Hildesheim, Germany
{knierim,kuck,heidul,mandl}@uni-hildesheim.de

Abstract

This paper explores the role of phatic communication in political discourse on social media. We present a case study of German political communication on Instagram in the context of protests against antisemitism and the rise of right-wing extremism in Germany (October 2023 to April 2024). Focusing on non-argumentative posts, we annotate the data according to three categories: phatic, mobilizing, and informative. To assess the classification of phatic content, we compare human annotation with the performance of large language models (LLMs) in both zero-shot and few-shot classification settings. Inter-annotator agreement among human experts is moderate (Cohen's K = 0.62), highlighting the inherent ambiguity in identifying phatic communication. Among the models evaluated, a Mistral-based model achieves the best performance. Our findings suggest that while phatic elements are present in political discourse, the majority of posts serve mobilizing or informative functions. Our analysis illustrates, by way of example, that very complex annotations can only be performed by models with limited quality. Depending on the class and task, heterogeneous results are obtained

1 Introduction

The notion of phatic communion was introduced by Malinowski (1967) and describes language that is used exclusively to fulfill a social function and without conveying information: "Each utterance is an act serving the direct aim of binding hearer to speaker by a tie of some social sentiment or other". Phatic communication is omnipresent in social media, be it through status updates like "currently eating ice cream" or phatic photo sharing (Niemelä-Nyrhinen and Seppänen, 2020). Some even argue social media are phatic media, in which communication without content has taken precedence (Miller, 2008). This, according to Miller (2017), has led to social media as environments based on "limited forms of expressive solidarity as opposed to an engaged, content-driven, dialogic public sphere".

Social networks are full of informal, nonargumentative texts. Phatic media, or technologies, help sustain relationships through pervasive but non-informational contact (Miller, 2008). The constant stream of communication generated by smartphones and the availability of social media encourages a type of communication that suggests a general sociability and affability without exchanging real information (Miller, 2017).

As many texts are informal and media have been labeled to be phatic, scholars debate the relevance of political communication in social media. Without doubt, the so-called micro-activism, slacktivism, or clicktivism has been studied extensively: More than 300 studies have used survey data to test the relationship between the use of digital media and offline engagement in civic and political life, such as voting, volunteering, and protesting (Boulianne, 2020). This impact was deduced from a statistical synthesis by Boulianne (2020). Critical voices have challenged "digital politics enthusiasts" and ask if political communication has become increasingly phatic and less dialogic (Miller, 2017).

Undoubtedly, phatic communication is prevalent in social media. But is it also prevalent in political communication in social media, as in new social movements or activist dicsourse? In this paper, we want to explore what the real amount of phatic communication is in political communication. We present a case study analyzing a German Instagram corpus structured by the hashtags #WirSindMehr and #NieWiederIstJetzt. In previous studies (Knierim and Heid, 2025; Knierim et al., 2025), argumentation in this discourse has been investigated. In this paper, we investigate a corpus of non-argumentative sentences, following the premise that they are more likely to be phatic. The contributions of this paper are three-fold: First, we put forward annotation guidelines and present a dataset of potentially phatic texts in German. We compare the performance of few-shot and zero-shot-settings of two large language models on detecting phatic communication. Third, we demonstrate the distribution of phatic content in our dataset to quantify the amount of phatic communication in an example of political online discourse.

In this paper, we first introduce concepts by researchers that try to grasp phatic language in social media. We then describe the corpus compilation and annotation process. Then, the prompt design and classification task are described. Finally, we present the results: we first discuss the distribution of phatic language in our corpus. Then, we discuss the performance of large language models for this task.

2 Phatic communication in social media

Microposts and phatic posts are derivatives of phatic communication (Radovanovic and Ragnedda, 2012). Although they might not have information value (Malinowski, 1967), Radovanovic and Ragnedda (2012) argue that phatic posts do have semantic and social value for the interlocutors. Following Malinowski (1967), Radovanovic and Ragnedda (2012) identify functions of phatic communication: Firstly, phatic communication serves the purpose of "social upkeep". Secondly, phatic posts can signal the availabilty as a potential communication partner. Thirdly, phatic posts have a validation and recognition function to indicate recognition of one's interlocutor as a potential communicative partner.

Radovanovic and Ragnedda (2012) argue that modern-day micro posts have their origin in the human need for social upkeep. They related phatic posts to the phatic function introduced by Jakobson (1968). Jacobson introduced the five general functions of language, among them the phatic function (try to maintain in contact with the receiver). Radovanovic and Ragnedda (2012) describe phatic posts as "the phatic display of connected presence", where users engage through brief, informal messages. Following the authors, this signal also serves to validate the interlocutor as a potential communication partner.

The constant stream of communication created by smartphones and the availability of social media encourages a type of communication that suggests a general sociability and affability without exchanging real information (Miller, 2017). Miller (2017) challenges the notion that the ability of technology to connect people necessarily leads to an activism that involves dissent or resistance: Specifically, "political talk" would express convivial solidarity with others and have a function of social inclusion and recognition. Political communication in social media promotes phatic or idle talk, instead of working towards transformational political action (Miller, 2008). In this paper, we address this research question from a quantitative viewpoint by measuring the proportion of phatic communication in non-argumentative texts, following the premise that these are more likely to be phatic than argumentative posts.

Sarjanoja et al. (2013) conduct interviews to analyze the content of status updates on Facebook. They consider a sample of N=484 unique status updates, with participants rating how interesting they find them. The status updates are manually classified into topical categories, such as "small talk", "current events talk" and "complaining". Their findings indicate that Facebook status updates have strong elements of phatic communication and are used to increase one's social capital (Sarjanoja et al., 2013). Interestingly, participants found most status updates to be "boring". This demonstrates how phatic communication can be considered to be mundaine while still serving a social function. In a study about phatic photo sharing on Snapchat, Rettberg (2018) argues that the phatic connection between people is the key element, "often far more important than the content that is shared". This relates to the non-archival character of some platform affordances, translating to increased immediacy and a sense of shared experience (Rettberg, 2018).

Duffy and Ling (2020) study the sociality of news sharing on social media, conducting a survey of N=2000 participants and using data from 88 focus groups. Participants' motivations in sharing news include being part of a conversation, maintaining friendships, and contributing to a group. Not all news sharing is phatic according to the authors, as it can serve to warn, to inform or to advise. The authors argue that "sharing news online often conforms to the phatic, non- directional conversational gambit of Malinowski, and one focus-group participant said that people share the news because *'[when] there is no topic to start a conversation, we start a conversation on the news'* ".

Phatic communication was initially studied in language but research has shown that it also occurs in photo-sharing (Niemelä-Nyrhinen and Seppänen, 2020) and even in the form of simple "likes" and reactions to others' posts (Radovanovic and Ragnedda, 2012). For example in snapchat, an ephemeral social media platform, phatic photo sharing is key to the success of the platform: Photo-sharing has been embedded in communicative media and supports the so-called "connected presence" (Rettberg, 2018; Niemelä-Nyrhinen and Seppänen, 2020). Niemelä-Nyrhinen and Seppänen (2020) argue that the omnipresence of the photo renders it "a kind of gesture suitable for opening and maintaining social exchange and bonds". In research on phatic visuals, a dichotomy is often drawn between traditional archival photographs — typically single images stored in photo albums — ephemeral contents, such as Instagram *stories* fade away (Niemelä-Nyrhinen and Seppänen, 2020; Rettberg, 2018). Another example of this is the young platform BeReal. On BeReal, ephemeral photos are shared directly with the community, without the availability of editing or curation of photos. The presented literature demonstrates how multifaceted the seemingly simple concept of phatic communication is.

3 Corpus compilation

With 37% of the population in Germany using Instagram (Newman et al., 2025), it is no surprise that Instagram reflects political moments of citizen engagement (Barbala, 2024). It is also a multimodal social network. As political messages are known to be communicated both in visuals and written language, it is especially important to study the platform (McNair, 2016). Politicians, for example, use Instagram visuals for strategic storytelling (Liebhart and Bernhardt, 2017). The Instagram caption is vital to this, as it is used to develop an engangig narrative (Towner and Muñoz, 2018).

We use an Instagram caption dataset structured by the German hashtags #WirSindMehr (we are more) and #NieWiederIstjetzt (never again is now). We build on work by Knierim and Heid (2025), who annotated the corpus for argument component detection. In their work, an argumentation model by Habernal and Gurevych (2017) was used. The model was developed and tested on user-generated web content, making it suitable for annotating social media discourse. The corpus includes both argumentative and non-argumentative sentences and comprises 13468 posts, with a sample of 1200 posts labeled. The corpus is suitable for the research question considered in our study, as it fits into the paradigm of political talk in social media. In the following paragraphs, we shortly introduce the discourses.

The corpus was collected via "crowdtangle"[1] and captures a timespan between 10/07/2023 and 03/31/2024. For this study, we only work with non-argumentative sentences from the corpus. This decision builds on the assumption that non-argumentative texts are more likely to be phatic. Like this, we investigate how many phatic messages we encounter within political discourse. The corpus contains 3013 non-argumentative sentences with 28432 tokens.

The upheavals against right-wing extremism (#WirSindMehr) and antisemitism (#NieWiederIst-Jetzt) provide a suitable dataset for investigating political communication. More than two million Germans protested using the slogans, while social media content on Instagram and Facebook was grammatized using the already mentioned hashtags. As hashtags enable and formalize actions and user activity, they can be used to trace user actions (Caliandro and Graham, 2020).

On January 10, 2023, the Correctiv research network uncovered a right-wing extremist meeting in Potsdam that called for the remigration of asylum seekers, foreigners with the right to stay in Germany and "non-assimilated citizens" in a secret plan (Correctiv 2024). Against the backdrop of the shift to the right in Germany and Europe in recent years, the unveiling of the secret meeting by the press had massive reverberations, with a total of two million people demonstrating in Germany in the following three months under the slogan #WirSindMehr.

Following the terrorist attack on Israel, the number of anti-semitic crimes committed in Germany increases by 240% by October 19, 2023. This leads to the formation of an alliance against anti-semitism. On 09.11.2023 at the commemoration of the 85. anniversary of the november progroms, the words "Nie Wieder Ist Jetzt" are used for the first time. Eva Szepsi, a Holocaust survivor, uses the

[1]Crowdtangle was a legal way to extract data from Meta platforms until August 2024. However, the tool is no longer available. To extract data now, a highly formalised application process must be completed via the Meta API. The corpus can be released if legal review confirms its eligibility for public access.

phrase in the Bundestag on 31 January 2024 (Lelle, 2024).

In this paper, we investigate the following research questions: What is the amount of phatic communication in a dataset of non-argumentative sentences in German political posts? Which dimensions of the classes, phatic, mobilizing and informative, are most difficult to classify for LLMs? How do these difficulties compare between human annotation and LLM-based classification?

4 Annotation

4.1 Annotation guidelines

For the purpose of this study, non-argumentative texts were annotated and studied. From an inductive analysis of the texts, we derived three categories of non-argumentative sentences: Next to phatic texts, two other categories appear in the data: Sentences carrying information, such as reports from political events, or background information on persons or organizations. In addition, invitations or calls for engagement are common. This results in a three-fold classification of non-argumentative sentences, including phatic texts, informative texts, and mobilizing texts. Examples for all three categories are presented in Tab. 1. In this section, we outline the background and critera that informed our annotation guidelines, which served as the basis for the manual annotation process. The complete guidelines are displayed in the appendix (Tab. 6).

4.1.1 Phatic communication

Based on the literature review presented in section 2, we formulate the following guidelines for the phatic category:

- The text suggests a general sociability and affability without exchanging real information (Miller, 2017);
- The text evokes a sense of community (Miller, 2017) or a networked presence (Radovanovic and Ragnedda, 2012);
- The text evokes a sense of the feeling of a shared experience in real time (Rettberg, 2018);
- The text shares news to open a conversation (Duffy and Ling, 2020);
- The text can be uninteresting (Sarjanoja et al., 2013) or frivolous, boring and mundane (Rettberg, 2018).

4.1.2 Informative text

In the collection analyzed for this research, people often share information in their posts. While these sentences are non-argumentative and exist within a political context, they are neither phatic nor mobilizing.

- Background information on people, organizations, situations;
- Reports from political action or events;
- Announcements, specifications of time, place and date;
- Notes like: "No party symbols, but neutral banners are okay";
- Short headlines.

4.1.3 Mobilizing text

More than two million people have protested under the slogans "Wir sind mehr" ("we are more") and "Nie Wieder Ist Jetzt" ("Never again is now"). Part of this mobilization process is present in the nonargumentative posts of the corpus. In literature, specific concepts like the call-to-action are researched (Siskou et al., 2022; Knierim et al., 2024; Achmann-Denkler et al., 2024), we adhere to the more general notion of mobilization. The guidelines to annotate this category capture the following phenomena:

- Slogans, short invitations;
- Indirect calls, can be linked to a condition;
- Direct calls: "Give @mention a like and comment on their post to help the cause.";
- Invitations such as: "All Magdeburgers are invited to participate in the commemoration of victims of antisemitism.".

4.2 Annotation results

Two trained annotators achieve a kappa score of 0.62, suggesting moderate agreement. As is visible in Fig.1, the informative class is the dominant class for both annotators (annotator A:54.7%, annotator B:65.1%), while the phatic and the mobilizing class appear less often. The smallest differences becomes apparent in the mobilization class that annotator A identifies in 14.9% of the classes, while annotator B identifies it in 16% of the texts. The

Label	Example
Phatic	"You were great, you were colorful, and your voices are important!"
	"A great gesture from Wiesbaden's urban society against attempts at division"
	"The most beautiful picture of the week definitely comes from Cologne <3"
	"And we would like to thank all colleagues from our organization and beyond who are fighting with us for an open and diverse democracy."
Informative	"The *Eckernförde Round Table against the Right* will meet on 12.03.2024 - 7 p.m. in the AWO Family Centre & Citizens' Meeting Centre at the Rathausmarkt in Eckernförde."
	"There will be a rally and a vigil in Düsseldorf on Saturday and Sunday."
	"If you have flowers and grave candles, you are welcome to bring them, but it is not mandatory."
Mobilizing	"Come along and bring friends and family!"
	"Anyone who would like to make a contribution to the event is cordially invited to do so and should contact @mention (name@email.de) for coordination."
	"Show together with us: NEVER AGAIN IS NOW!"

Table 1: Examples for the phatic, informative and mobilizing class. (Translation from German by the authors.)

Possible labels	Example	Counts of disagreement
Mobilizing, Phatic	"So we'll see you tomorrow!"	86
Informative, Phatic	"On Sunday evening, around 6000 people lit up the banks of the Main during a chain of lights against antisemitism."	224
Mobilizing, Informative	"17th of February 2024, 17:00 on the market square in Dessau!"	94

Table 2: Ambiguous cases. (Translation from German by the authors.)

phatic class is identified in 30.5% of all texts (annotator 1) versus in 18.8% of all classes (annotator 2). Thus, the biggest discrepancy between the annotators lies in the phatic class. At the same time, we find that the biggest disagreement lies within the labeling of the phatic and the informative class (see Fig.1). Tab. 2 holds examples that are ambiguous.

5 Predicting phatic communication

5.1 Method

In order to explore the role of phatic communication in non-argumentative sentences quantitatively, we compare the performance of few-shot and zero-shot-settings of two large language models on detecting phatic communication. We are particularly interested in which dimensions of classes are most difficult to classify, and how these difficulties compare between manual annotation and LLM-based classification. We define the task as a multiclass classification, classifying the text as either phatic, informative, or mobilizing. Importantly, we investigate phatic texts in political communication, not in Instagram posts in general. The texts were preprocessed in the following way: errors from scraping were removed. We additionally removed hashtags and emojis.

For our classification, it is of specific interest to compare human annotations with generated annotations. Following Ziems et al. (2024), large language models have the potential to transform the pipeline in interdisciplinary research settings, if they are equipped in assisting with labeling tasks like classifications. In this setting, human annotators achieve only moderate agreement and see differing amounts of phatic and informative content, while agreeing on mobilizing content (see: Fig. 1). Therefore, we are interested in whether

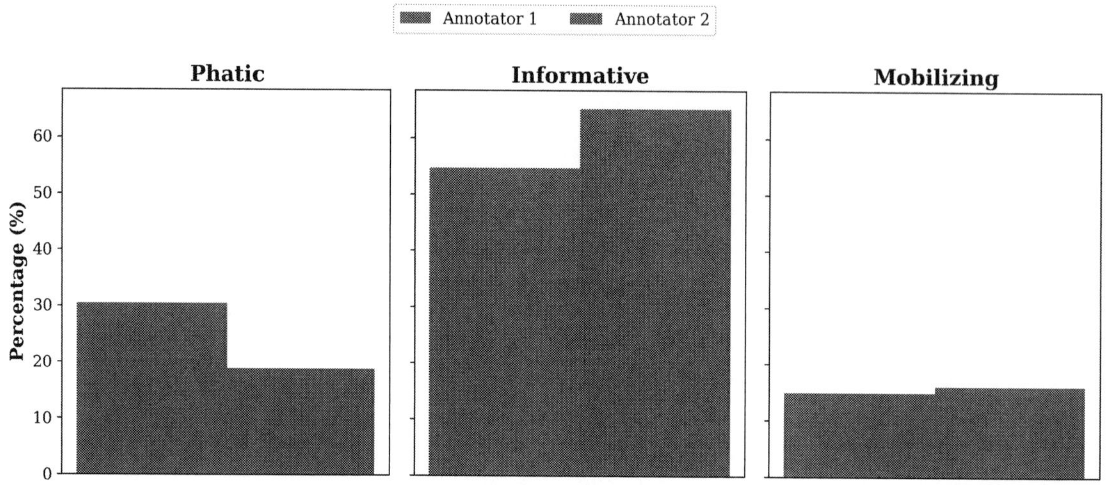

Figure 1: Distribution of informative, phatic and mobilizing sentences according to the annotations of annotator 1 and 2.

this ambiguity and uncertainty is reflected in model performance.

We test prompt drafts on every model and only present the best results. We follow the prompting guidelines provided by Ziems et al. (2024); Child et al. (2019) and give instructions after the context is provided. To reduce computational cost, we keep the prompt as short as possible with the GPT4o-model (temp=0), resulting prompts for both the zero- and fewshot settings that are different from those used with the open source model Mistral-7B-Instruct-v0.2 (Mistral) (Jiang et al., 2023). While we recognize that slight changes in prompt wording may affect the comparability of results across models, our goal is to showcase the best performance each model can achieve under optimal prompting conditions. Although Mistral had limited exposure to German during pretraining, we contrast its performance to that of GPT4o, as it is an open-source, mid-sized open-weight LLM.

5.2 Results

We present the results (Tab.: 3, 4, 5) for each class, comparing in turn both LLMs (few-shot (FS) vs. zero-shot (ZS) setting). In section 6, we compare the performance of the models with the human annotators.

For the classification of the informative class, both models perform well in the few-shot setting, while Mistral outperforms the GPT-4o model (f1 score = 0.87 vs f1 score = 0.79). The Mistral model shows no improvement when applied in a few-shot setting (f1 score = 0.87). GPT-4o improves in the few-shot-setting, not only for the informative class but in all classes. While the models showed satisfactory performance, both models struggle with lower recall, especially in zero-shot-settings. Compared to human annotators, we also see a difference within the identification of informative sentences, as annotator 2 is more inclusive with this category, identifying 1200 examples, while annotator 1 only identifies 1000 examples.

For the identification of the mobilizing class, GPT-4o performs best with an f1-score of 0.67 (see Tab. 5). For both zero-shot and few-shot settings, Mistral reaches high precision and lower recall, while GPT-4o has low precision but very high recall.

The models perform lowest for the detection of the phatic class, just like there is most ambiguity for the annotators in this class. As in the mobilization class, the GPT-4o few-shot setting (f1 score = 0.57) and the Mistral zero-shot setting yield the best results (f1 score = 0.58). Both models show higher precision and lower recall in both settings. The Mistral performs best in identifying the phatic class and the informative class, while GPT-4o performs best in identifying the mobilization class.

6 Error analysis

Both the manual annotation and the automatic classification show the difficulties in identifying phatic texts in our dataset of German political talk. This is consistent with Frenzel and Hautli-Janisz (2025) results who tested the idenitification of small talk on German verbatim transcribed Public Service Encounters (dataset: Espinoza et al. (2024)). While small talk is not identical to phatic political talk, a comparison is valid from a computational point of vie, as Espinoza et al. (2024) define small talk as polite conservation over light topics (Schneider, 1988) with the purpose of maintaining social relations for their study.

Both human annotators and models struggle most with identifying the phatic class (highest f1-score=0.58). While models perform best at identifying the informative class (highest f1-score=0.87), humans have the least dissent in annotating the mobilizing class. For the human annotators, some ambiguity exists between the mobilizing and the informative class (see: Tab. 2): While the example given informs about time and place of an event in Dessau, and could thus be labeled as informative, the exclamation mark makes the sentence sound like a call to join the event, and could thus be labeled as mobilizing class. Similarly, the informative and the phatic class can be confused when information is anecdotal or of little importance: Our example names the number of people, time and place, but focuses on the fact that lights lit up the banks of the Main river. While informative, the example could fit two aspects of phatic communication: On the one hand, it fits Miller (2017)'s definition of a general affability without exchanging real information, or, even more likely in this case, the text evokes a sense of community (Radovanovic and Ragnedda, 2012; Miller, 2017).

7 Discussion

In this paper, we aim at detecting phatic communication in political talk. For this purpose, a case study is conducted based on the hashtags of #NieWiederIstJetzt and #WirSindMehr. First, two annotators enriched the data with the labels phatic, mobilizing, and informative. Second, the performance of the classifiers Mistral and GPT-4o is tested, in both zero- and few-shot-settings. The annotators reach a kappa score of 0.62 which corresponds to moderate agreement. In general, the models perform better in a few-shot-setting. Only for classifying the informative class, there is no difference between the zero- and few-shot setting with Mistral- it yields the highest f1-score of 0.87 in both settings.

In summary, humans and models perform best in identifying the informative class, second best on the mobilizing class, and worst in identifying the phatic class. This also shows in the ambiguity between the annotators for the phatic class: Annotator 1 labels 12% texts more as phatic than annotator 2 (30.5% vs 18.8%).

It is well known that phatic communication is prevalent in social media. Some even argue that social media are phatic media in which communication without content has taken precedence (Miller, 2008). Nevertheless, researches have demonstrated the importance of phatic communication, as it fulfills a social function (Sarjanoja et al., 2013; Rettberg, 2018). While similar phenomena such as small talk have been studied from the lens of natural language processing (Frenzel and Hautli-Janisz, 2025) (also for 'candy speech', the shared task at GermEval 2025[2]). Others have studied the reception of phatic communication (Sarjanoja et al., 2013) or its different forms in various platform affordances (Niemelä-Nyrhinen and Seppänen, 2020; Radovanovic and Ragnedda, 2012; Rettberg, 2018).

In this paper, we ask how phatic political talk is in reality. Using non-argumentative sentences from a corpus of political talk from Instagram captions, we conclude the following: Firstly, annotators label between 18.8% and 30.5% of the corpus as phatic, which is a substantial amount. On the other hand, between 81.2% and 69.5% of the non-argumentative statements in the corpus is not phatic, but serves an informative or mobilizing function. Thirdly, the biggest dissent concerns the distinction between the phatic class and the informative class, demonstrating that the annotators struggle with the question whether a sentence is informative or not. Considering that the number of phatic texts in the argumentative part of the corpus (from where the non-argumentative sentences analyzed here have been gathered) is probably much lower, we conclude that political talk on Instagram is not primarily phatic. It rather has a high amount of informative content, and some mobilizing content.

Nevertheless, more work should be done to investigate phatic content in a quantitative manner: Our findings should be tested for political talk under other hashtags. Secondly, the distributions could be platform-specific, highlighting the importance to investigate distributions on Tiktok or other platforms. The analysis should be extended to other corpora and platforms. In addition, one

[2]yuliacl.github.io/GermEval2025-Flausch-Erkennung/

could investigate whether different political actors post different amounts of phatic communication. For example, it is likely that organizations post more informative and mobilizing content, while private users post phatically more often. It is also conceivable to perform a more fine-grained classification of phatic communication based on the codebook introduced in section 4.1.1. From a technological point of view, prompt engineering could also be applied to enhance the classification results. An idea could be to include stakes and bribes, as recommended by Pichler et al. (2025).

Limitations

This work is limited to the analysis of only one platform. This work could benefit from an additional annotation. Considering the identified sources of disagreement, the annotators would benefit from additional training.

Acknowledgments

We thank the annotators for their work. We thank the reviewers for their helpful comments.

	Mistral ZS	**Mistral FS**	**GPT4 ZS**	**GPT4 FS**
Precision	0.79	0.75	0.58	0.69
Recall	0.46	0.39	0.31	0.49
F1-Score	**0.58**	0.51	0.40	0.57

Table 3: Comparison of the different models for the classification of the phatic class.

	Mistral ZS	**Mistral FS**	**GPT4 ZS**	**GPT4 FS**
Precision	0.85	0.82	0.87	0.81
Recall	0.89	0.92	0.67	0.78
F1-Score	**0.87**	**0.87**	0.76	0.79

Table 4: Comparison of the different models for the classification of the informative class.

	Mistral ZS	**Mistral FS**	**GPT4 ZS**	**GPT4 FS**
Precision	0.59	0.67	0.36	0.53
Recall	0.62	0.49	0.90	0.92
F1-Score	0.60	0.57	0.51	**0.67**

Table 5: Comparison of the different models for the classification of the mobilization class.

References

Michael Achmann-Denkler, Jakob Fehle, Mario Haim, and Christian Wolff. 2024. Detecting calls to action in multimodal content: Analysis of the 2021 german federal election campaign on instagram. *arXiv preprint arXiv:2409.02690*.

Astri Moksnes Barbala. 2024. Reassembling# metoo: Tracing the techno-affective agency of the feminist instagram influencer. *Convergence*, 30(3):992–1007.

Shelley Boulianne. 2020. Twenty years of digital media effects on civic and political participation. *Communication research*, 47(7):947–966.

Alessandro Caliandro and James Graham. 2020. Studying instagram beyond selfies. *Social Media + Society*, 6(2):2056305120924779.

Rewon Child, Scott Gray, Alec Radford, and Ilya Sutskever. 2019. Generating long sequences with sparse transformers. *arXiv preprint arXiv:1904.10509*.

Andrew Duffy and Rich Ling. 2020. The gift of news: Phatic news sharing on social media for social cohesion. *Journalism studies*, 21(1):72–87.

Ingrid Espinoza, Steffen Frenzel, Laurin Friedrich, Wassiliki Siskou, Steffen Eckhard, and Annette Hautli-Janisz. 2024. PSE v1.0: The first open access corpus of public service encounters. In *Proceedings of the 2024 Joint International Conference on Computational Linguistics, Language Resources and Evaluation (LREC-COLING 2024)*, pages 13315–13320, Torino, Italia. ELRA and ICCL.

Steffen Frenzel and Annette Hautli-Janisz. 2025. Identifying small talk in natural conversations. In *Proceedings of the 9th Joint SIGHUM Workshop on Computational Linguistics for Cultural Heritage, Social Sciences, Humanities and Literature (LaTeCH-CLfL 2025)*, pages 272–277, Albuquerque, New Mexico. Association for Computational Linguistics.

Ivan Habernal and Iryna Gurevych. 2017. Argumentation mining in user-generated web discourse. *Computational linguistics*, 43(1):125–179.

Roman Jakobson. 1968. Poetry of grammar and grammar of poetry. *Verbal Art, Verbal Sign, Verbal Time*, 37:604.

Albert Q. Jiang, Alexandre Sablayrolles, Arthur Mensch, Chris Bamford, Devendra Singh Chaplot, Diego de las Casas, Florian Bressand, Gianna Lengyel, Guillaume Lample, Lucile Saulnier, Lélio Renard Lavaud, Marie-Anne Lachaux, Pierre Stock, Teven Le Scao, Thibaut Lavril, Thomas Wang, Timothée Lacroix, and William El Sayed. 2023. Mistral 7b. *Preprint*, arXiv:2310.06825.

Aenne Knierim, Michael Achmann-Denkler, Ulrich Heid, and Christian Wolff. 2024. Divergent discourses: A comparative examination of blackout Tuesday and #BlackLivesMatter on Instagram. In *Proceedings of the 10th Italian Conference on Computational Linguistics (CLiC-it 2024)*, pages 451–458, Pisa, Italy. CEUR Workshop Proceedings.

Aenne Knierim and Ulrich Heid. 2025. Argumentation in political empowerment on Instagram. In *Proceedings of the 9th Joint SIGHUM Workshop on Computational Linguistics for Cultural Heritage, Social Sciences, Humanities and Literature (LaTeCH-CLfL 2025)*, pages 97–108, Albuquerque, New Mexico. Association for Computational Linguistics.

Aenne C. K. Knierim, Ulrich Heid, and Thomas Mandl. 2025. Politisches Empowerment in den sozialen Medien: Ein Ansatz zur sprachlichen Charakterisierung am Beispiel von #WirSindMehr. In *Datenströme und Kulturoasen — Die Informationswissenschaft als Bindeglied zwischen den Informationswelten. 18. Internationales Symposium für Informationswissenschaft (ISI 2025)*, pages 296–314, Chemnitz, Germany.

Nikolas Lelle. 2024. Demos gegen rechts: Was heißt Nie wieder? — taz.de. `https://taz.de/Demos-gegen-rechts/!5987599/`. [Accessed 12-08-2025].

Karin Liebhart and Petra Bernhardt. 2017. Political storytelling on instagram: Key aspects of alexander van der bellen's successful 2016 presidential election campaign. *Media and Communication*, 5(4):15–25.

Bronislaw Malinowski. 1967. The problem of meaning in primitive languages. *Meaning in Meaning*.

Brian McNair. 2016. Image, political. In R C M Maia, K Ikeda, H Wessler, G Mazzoleni, and K G Barnhurst, editors, *The international encyclopedia of political communication, Volume 1*, pages 505–513. Wiley-Blackwell, United States of America.

Vincent Miller. 2008. New media, networking and phatic culture. *Convergence*, 14(4):387–400.

Vincent Miller. 2017. Phatic culture and the status quo: Reconsidering the purpose of social media activism. *Convergence*, 23(3):251–269.

Nic Newman, A Ross Arguedas, Craig T Robertson, Rasmus Kleis Nielsen, and Richard Fletcher. 2025. *Digital news report 2025*. Reuters Institute for the study of Journalism.

Jenni Niemelä-Nyrhinen and Janne Seppänen. 2020. Visual communion: The photographic image as phatic communication. *New Media Soc.*, 22(6).

Axel Pichler, Janis Pagel, and Nils Reiter. 2025. Evaluating LLM-Prompting for Sequence Labeling Tasks in Computational Literary Studies. In *Proceedings of the 9th Joint SIGHUM Workshop on Computational Linguistics for Cultural Heritage, Social Sciences, Humanities and Literature (LaTeCH-CLfL 2025)*, pages 32–46.

Danica Radovanovic and Massimo Ragnedda. 2012. Small talk in the digital age: Making sense of phatic posts. In *Proceedings of the WWW'12 Workshop on 'Making Sense of Microposts', Lyon, France, April 16, 2012*, volume 838 of *CEUR Workshop Proceedings*, pages 10–13. CEUR-WS.org.

Jill Walker Rettberg. 2018. Snapchat: Phatic communication and ephemeral social media. *Appified: culture in the age of apps*, pages 188–96.

Ari-Heikki Sarjanoja, Minna Isomursu, and Jonna Häkkilä. 2013. Small talk with facebook: Phatic communication in social media. In *Proceedings of International Conference on Making Sense of Converging Media*, pages 118–121.

Klaus P Schneider. 1988. Small talk: Analysing phatic discourse. *(No Title)*.

Wassiliki Siskou, Clara Giralt Mirón, Sarah Molina Raith, and Miriam Butt. 2022. Automatized detection and annotation for calls to action in latin-american social media postings. In *The 6th Joint SIGHUM Workshop on Computational Linguistics for Cultural Heritage, Social Sciences, Humanities and Literature (LaTeCH-CLfL 2022)*, page 65.

Terri L. Towner and Caroline Lego Muñoz. 2018. Picture perfect? the role of instagram in issue agenda setting during the 2016 presidential primary campaign. *Social Science Computer Review*, 36(4):484–499.

Caleb Ziems, William Held, Omar Shaikh, Jiaao Chen, Zhehao Zhang, and Diyi Yang. 2024. Can large language models transform computational social science? *Computational Linguistics*, 50(1):237–291.

A Appendix: Annotation guidelines

Table 6: Annotation instructions for labeling non-argumentative sentences as phatic, informative, or mobilizing.

Class	Guidelines
Phatic communication	• If the text conveys sociability or affability without transmitting substantive information • If the text that evokes a sense of community • If the text creates the impression of sharing an experience in real time • If the text shares news as a conversation starter • If the text appears uninteresting, boring, or mundane
Informative text	• If the text contains background information about people, organizations, or situations • If the text include reports on political events or actions • If the text is an announcement sharing time, place, or date details • If the text include specific notes, e.g., "No party symbols, but neutral banners are okay". • If the text marks a short headline
Mobilizing text	• If the text is a slogan or short invitations aimed at motivating action • If the text contains a direct calls, e.g., "Give @mention a like and comment on their post to help the cause." • Include indirect calls to action • If there is an invitations to participate in events, e.g., "All Magdeburgers are invited to participate in the commemoration of victims of antisemitism."

TRAVELWARN-Crawler: Constructing longitudinal datasets of government-issued travel warnings for political and social science research

Laura Braun
Center for Crisis Early Warning
University of the Bundeswehr Munich
Neubiberg, Germany
laura.braun@unibw.de

Christian Oswald
Center for Crisis Early Warning
University of the Bundeswehr Munich
Neubiberg, Germany
christian.oswald@unibw.de

Abstract

Historical travel warnings and advisories offer a record of how governments perceive and communicate country-specific risks over time, yet large-scale quantitative analyses have been rare due to missing, fragmented, and frequently overwritten web data. We present *TRAVELWARN-Crawler*, an open pipeline that collects, recovers, cleans, stores, and standardizes advisories and warnings from archived web sources. Using the Internet Archive's Wayback Machine and issuer-specific Scrapy spiders, we reconstruct up to three decades of timelines for the United States (US), the United Kingdom (UK), and Australia. The data can be used to support comparative research in political communication, international relations, and tourism studies. Descriptively, the UK issues more country pages and updates than the US and Australia. Cross-issuer agreement about severity is modest with the highest pairwise level agreement for US–Australia (∼49%). These results indicate substantial heterogeneity in how close allies communicate travel risk and underscore the value of reproducible, textual data beyond numeric severity levels alone.

1 Introduction and Motivation

The U.S. Department of State issued what is widely considered the first modern travel warning when it cautioned its nationals at the outbreak of World War I in 1914 (Löwenheim, 2007). Since the late 1990s, such warnings have increasingly become accessible online and on a regular basis, shaping individual travel decisions and redirecting tourism revenue. Beyond their immediate practical value, they also signal a government's assessment of specific countries. Although they are potentially important, researchers lack comprehensive longitudinal data. Each foreign ministry maintains its own website and frequently overwrite pages in place. There is no common official API for retrieving archived warning texts. The paper demonstrates how to navigate this terrain. We reconstruct advisory timelines for three issuers (US, UK, Australia) by requesting archived captures via the Wayback Machine API, extracting text content and metadata, and processing and standardizing the results to store in a database, to provide a ready-made and easily downloadable dataset.

Government-issued travel advisories represent a unique combination of time-connected threat assessment and official foreign policy signaling. Each text is a judgment of how the issuing state evaluates security, health, and political conditions abroad at a given moment. Since ministries publish these assessments under their own seal, language and severity levels may encode far more than objective risk. Having such textual data allows to investigate whether they also reflect strategic calculations about alliance obligations, latent disputes, or reputational costs (Chu et al., 2021; Babey, 2019; Kebede, 2018; Sharpley et al., 1996). We harvest these text data at scale and reconstruct their full issuing history to create the first longitudinal warning corpus that scholars can reuse and provide a step-by-step guide for extending the dataset to additional issuers. We focus on the US, UK, and Australia as a proof of concept and a foundation for comparative analysis. The countries are three founding members of the Five Eyes intelligence alliance, and we explore how their informal cooperation is reflected in travel warning decisions. Although we start with English sources, recent advances in automated translation may enable the inclusion of other languages.

2 Implementation

2.1 Data access

We use the Internet Archive's Wayback Machine (IAWM) API to retrieve historical digital artifacts of travel warnings and advisories from archived snapshots of provider webpages. The IAWM pre-

Proceedings of the 21st Conference on Natural Language Processing (KONVENS), Volume 2: Workshops, pages 29–35, 2025

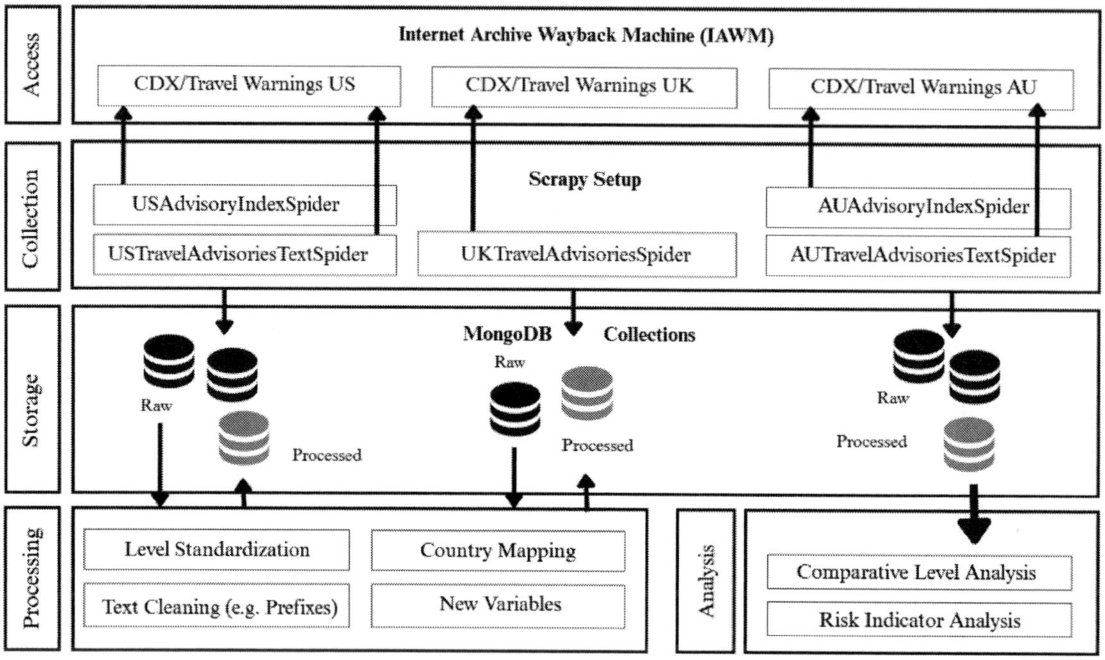

Figure 1: Implementation of dataset generation — Access, Collection, Storage

serves time-stamped URLs since 1996 and indexes more than 800 billion pages.[1] Its archival record turns otherwise ephemeral content into a longitudinal resource for scholars. A validation study demonstrates that the IAWM website age and update count measures are reliable, as the authors find convergent validity with domain-registry dates, confirming the archive's suitability as a research resource (Murphy et al., 2007). Since the foreign ministry websites we analyze went online in 1996 or 1997 (Löwenheim, 2007), the IAWM offers a long archive history with sparse coverage until the mid-2000s and increasingly dense coverage thereafter.

Previous work has outlined a complete social science workflow for sampling, crawl design, variable extraction, and transformation into structured data (Arora et al., 2016). Our approach differs in retrieving the complete archive for each issuer, prioritizing depth over breadth. This introduces practical challenges such as changing URLs, layouts, and HTML structures. We apply custom crawler logic that uses issuer- and time-specific URL prefixes to query the IAWM's CDX endpoint. Other archives are paid services or lack comparable coverage. Some issuers provide partial official archives (e.g., OSAC.gov for U.S. alerts since 2004, the UK Government archive since 2013), but these are either restricted for scientific use due to licensing or offer fewer snapshots. The IAWM with its CDX API is thus the best choice for standardized, near-complete timelines from most issuers, without copyright restrictions.[2]

2.2 Data collection and storage

We implement a modular, automated pipeline in `Scrapy`. Scrapy's abstractions (Spiders, Items, Pipelines) separate crawling from extraction and storage, while built-in concurrency, retry logic, and scheduling enable large-scale, polite crawling of mostly static content, lighter than headless-browser approaches. For the US and Australia, a two-step spider design first queries the CDX API for *one* index-page snapshot per day, extracting country links, update dates, and any listed metadata (e.g. level). For each new (country, update-date) pair, we then fetch the first available archived copy of the corresponding country page to extract full text and metadata. This design (i) detects missed updates even when country pages are sparsely archived, and (ii) avoids unnecessary downloads. For the UK, whose index pages lack explicit update dates, we instead check country pages daily and re-scrape only when their on-page update date changes. We

[1] `https://archive.org/about/`

[2] IAWM licensing is generally permissive, but site-specific terms should always be verified, although government pages are typically open-licensed.

observed that UK country pages also contain rich, multi-section content (safety/security, health, local laws, etc.), which can trigger additional updates and thus increase revision frequency.

All advisories are stored in MongoDB, one collection per issuer. Each document includes at least `country`, `warning_date`, the IAWM `timestamp_snapshot`, the `source_url`, and the extracted `advisory_text`. We upsert on a compound key (country, update date) to prevent duplicates and preserve a stable pointer back to the archived source for full traceability.

2.3 Data processing

After collection, we standardize the records to allow cross-issuer comparisons. First, we normalize country names to a canonical mapping to accommodate spelling variants and historical names. Second, we harmonize issuer-specific severity descriptions to a unified four-tier scale using regular expressions, explicitly accounting for policy changes over time (e.g. pre-2018 U.S. materials without formal levels; UK advisory phrasing without Level 1/2 labels). We retain the original text for full transparency. Although regex-based mapping is transparent and reproducible, it can be brittle in the presence of negation or nuanced phrasing (e.g. "no longer advised not to travel..."). In practice, a small residual remains: for Australia, n=158 updates could not be mapped; for the United States, n=23 entries are labeled *Other*; and for the United Kingdom, because Level 3 and Level 4 are explicitly indicated, cases ambiguous between Level 1 and Level 2 default to Level 2. In future work, we will evaluate supervised models (e.g. ConfliBERT; Brandt et al., 2024) and LLM-assisted level assessment to reduce regex-based classification noise.

3 Results

We reconstruct longitudinal advisory timelines for the United States, the United Kingdom, and Australia and harmonize them to a common four–level scale. Coverage is complete for the US and Australia from 1997/1998 onward and extends back to 2013 for the UK. Descriptively, issuers differ in both scope and frequency.

We restrict descriptive comparisons to the overlapping ten–year window (2014–2024) in which all three issuers are covered. Table 1 summarizes this period. The UK issues the most updates (15,207) across the largest destination set (225 unique countries), followed by Australia (6,530 with 181 unique countries) and the US (3,101 with 210 unique countries). Consistent with the editorial breadth of UK pages, only ≈4% of UK updates coincide with a level change (611/15,207), compared to ≈8.4% for Australia (547/6,530) and ≈31.9% for the US (990/3,101). In other words, the typical US update is more likely to reflect a substantive change in severity, whereas UK updates more often revise text within informational sections. UK pages also yield a larger set of destinations that remain at Level 4 throughout the period ("constant L4"): 33 for the UK versus 11 for Australia and 5 for the US, reflecting both coverage scope and differing issuer thresholds to maintain a sustained "Do not travel" classification.

Figure 2 tracks the monthly average advisory level for each issuer, smoothing with a 3-month moving average to reduce month-to-month noise. The dashed line marks the US shift to the four-tier system in 2018; the gray band marks the global COVID shock. Two patterns stand out. First, during COVID all three issuers converge upward, indicating a sharp, broad-based tightening that later relaxes at different speeds. Second, outside the COVID window, UK and Australia trend closely together on average, while the US is modestly higher in the pre-2018 period and again during the 2021–2022 normalization phase.

Figure 3 provides exemplary trajectories. For **Ukraine**, Australian levels move from Level 1–2 in the early 2000s to pronounced step-ups around 2014 and again from 2022 onward, while the US remains more persistently at Level 3–4. For **Lebanon**, both issuers spend extended periods at Level 3–4, punctuated by frequent revisions (black lines) that do not always change the posted level. For **South Korea**, Australia stays mostly at Level 1 with occasional upticks, whereas the US displays the system-wide pandemic jump to Level 4 and subsequent relaxation. The dense vertical markers illustrate that issuers revise advice frequently, even when the numeric level remains, thereby underscoring the value of archiving text alongside levels.

To quantify convergence, we align updates within countries using a nearest-neighbor match inside a ±15-day window (see Appendix for details) and then compare levels. Across all matched updates, **US–Australia** aligns the most, agreeing on **48.5%** of 890 matches (432 agreements). **UK–US** agrees on **33.1%** of 2,533 matches (839), and **UK–Australia** on **29.3%** of 5,299

Table 1: Summary statistics (2014–2024) for UK, US, and Australia advisories.

Issuer	L3 count	L4 count	Unique countries	Level changes	Updates	Most changes	Constant L4
UK	2,810	3,904	225	611	15,207	China (41)	33
Australia	651	2,014	181	547	6,530	Bangladesh (8)	11
US	844	758	210	990	3,101	D.R. Congo (21)	5

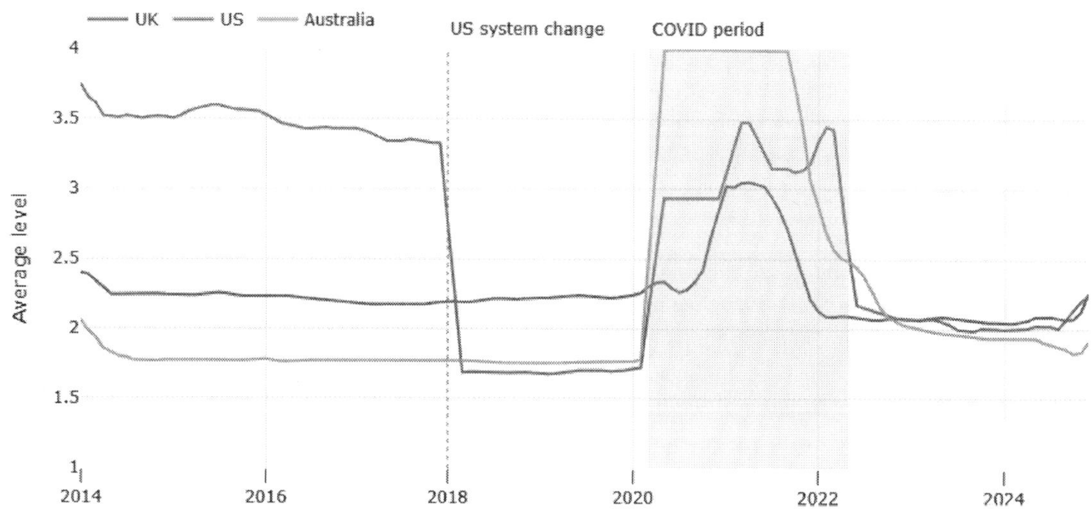

Figure 2: Monthly average advisory level across a common basket of countries for the UK, US, and Australia. Lines show 3-month moving averages; shaded bands are interquartile ranges. The dashed vertical line marks the US system change in 2018; the light gray rectangle marks the COVID period (2020–2022).

(1,550). When restricting to events where any issuer assigns Level 3/4, agreement rates drop: **37.5%** for US–Australia (238/635), **29.4%** for UK–US (584/1,987), and **23.3%** for UK–Australia (852/3,662). Requiring *all three* issuers to coincide produces very low agreement: **16.9%** across all matched triples (203/1,199) and **15.9%** for the Level 3/4 subset (165/1,039). Substantively, even among close allies, severity judgments are far from harmonized. The comparatively higher US–Australia alignment is consistent with shared terminology and, post-2018, more comparable US level definitions; by contrast, the UK's revision-intensive advice style lowers the probability of within-window convergence at the same numeric level.

The summary counts also reveal distinct issuer profiles. The UK posts many more absolute Level 3 and Level 4 observations (2,810 and 3,904), but as a *share* of all UK updates, these are smaller than Australia's, which has fewer updates overall, yet a higher fraction of high-severity postings. The US sits between the UK and Australia in scope, but shows the highest ratio of level-changing to total updates, reflecting more tightly scoped, advisory-centric editing pre-2018. Importantly, the aggregate lines in Figure 2 are computed on the *common basket* of countries to minimize composition bias.

Low pairwise and triple alignment can arise from (i) different thresholds for moving between Level 3 and Level 4, (ii) non-synchronous response timing around the same underlying event, and (iii) composition effects (issuers emphasizing different destination portfolios and sub-national guidance). Figure 3 shows that many micro-revisions do not alter levels, while the COVID panel in Figure 2 illustrates the opposite case, globally synchronized shocks that temporarily compress issuer differences and then re-diverge as governments normalize at different speeds.

A large share of updates, especially for the UK and Australia, revise or expand guidance without changing the numeric level. Most are minor editorial adjustments (wording, formatting, refreshed links), but many introduce substantively useful text: added/removed specific risk indicators, tighter regional exclusions, updated entry/exit rules, or clarifications of recent incidents. These "text-only" re-

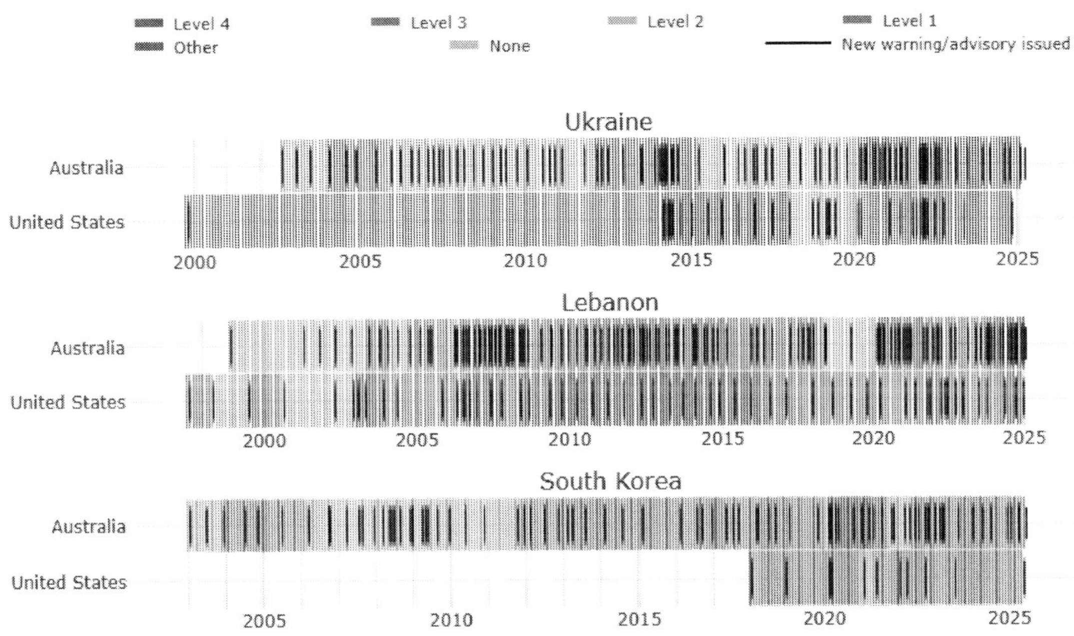

Figure 3: Monthly travel-advisory levels for three illustrative cases (Ukraine, Lebanon, South Korea). Rows show issuer (Australia, United States). Black marks indicate publication days of new warnings/advisories.

visions still signal issuer attention and policy stance even when the severity is unchanged.

4 Discussion

Our results show that even among close allies, advisory severity is far from harmonized and that issuers differ markedly in update cadence. A natural next step is to exploit the text itself rather than levels alone. Information extraction and named-entity recognition (NER) can recover subnational geography (regions, corridors, border zones) and relevant actors, enabling granular, region-level timelines layered onto the national series. Topic discovery and topic classification can map risk drivers (crime, terrorism, civil unrest, health, disasters, kidnapping, wrongful detention) and track how their composition shifts across issuers and time; change-point detection on topic proportions or keyphrase series can sharpen the timing of substantive updates that occur without a level change. Cross-issuer harmonization can be improved with supervised classifiers and LLM-assisted labeling to normalize historical phrasing into a shared taxonomy of risks and severities. Together, these textual transformations open the door to event-aware models of advisory dynamics that incorporate both global shocks and country-specific triggers, and to theory tests on alliance behavior, responsiveness, and the strategic use of language in official risk communication.

Limitations

Archive coverage. Our timelines are bounded by what the Internet Archive preserved. Gaps exist, particularly in the late 1990s and for low-traffic URLs. Missing snapshots may selectively underrepresent short-lived advisories.

Site drift and parsing. Ministry redesigns and evolving HTML lead to fragile extraction rules. Although our Scrapy spiders handle many variants, long-term maintenance is required. Edge cases (e.g. split country pages, temporary microsites) can still slip through.

Harmonization choices. Mapping issuer-specific phrasing to a four-level scale inevitably introduces noise (e.g. negations in "no longer advised to..."). Our regex strategy is transparent and reproducible but imperfect; supervised or LLM-assisted classifiers are a promising replacement once labeled data exist.

Structural changes. The US system changed in 2018, and pandemic-era global notices created atypical level spikes. Such policy regime shifts should be modeled explicitly when drawing causal inferences from the time series.

Generalizability. We focused on three English-language issuers for proof of concept. Extending to non-English issuers will require additional country-name normalization and machine translation, and coverage may vary by local archival practices.

Ethical considerations

The data processed and analysed through this pipeline consists solely of publicly available travel advisories from official government sources (United States, United Kingdom, and Australia). The dataset contains no personally identifiable information (PII) or other sensitive data.

Acknowledgments

We thank David Bencek, André Bluhm, Vanessa Gottwick, Marius Hofmann and Daniel Racek, as well as the editors and three anonymous reviewers, for their helpful comments and feedback. The Center for Crisis Early Warning (Kompetenzzentrum Krisenfrüherkennung) is funded by the German Federal Ministry of Defense and the German Federal Foreign Office. The views and opinions expressed in this article are those of the author(s) and do not necessarily reflect the official policy or position of any agency of the German government.

Data and code availability

Upon publication, Scrapy spiders, processing scripts, and analysis notebooks will be released, together with issuer-specific schemas and harmonization code, under an open license. In subsequent work, we will publish the full dataset accompanied by an in-depth analysis paper that documents construction choices, validation checks, and known limitations.

References

Sanjay K. Arora, Yin Li, Jan Youtie, and Philip Shapira. 2016. Using the wayback machine to mine websites in the social sciences: A methodological resource. *Journal of the Association for Information Science and Technology*, 67(8):1904–1915.

Nicholas George Babey. 2019. The Politics of Travel Advisories: Foreign Policy and Error in Canada's Traveller Information Program. *The Journal of Intelligence, Conflict, and Warfare*, 2(1):15–33. Number: 1.

Patrick T. Brandt, Sultan Alsarra, Vito J. D'Orazio, Dagmar Heintze, Latifur Khan, Shreyas Meher, Javier Osorio, and Marcus Sianan. 2024. ConfliBERT: A Language Model for Political Conflict. *arXiv preprint*. ArXiv:2412.15060 [cs].

Yinxiao Chu, Xiaoyu Huang, and Tao Jin. 2021. Political relations and tourism: evidence from China. *Applied Economics*, 53(45):5281–5302. Publisher: Routledge _eprint: https://doi.org/10.1080/00036846.2021.1922591.

Nafbek Solomon Kebede. 2018. The Fate of Tourism during and in the Aftermath of Political Instability: Ethiopia Tourism in Focus. *Journal of Tourism & Hospitality*, 7(1):1–7. Publisher: Longdom Publishing S.L.

Oded Löwenheim. 2007. The Responsibility to Responsibilize: Foreign Offices and the Issuing of Travel Warnings. *International Political Sociology*, 1(3):203–221.

Jamie Murphy, Noor Hazarina Hashim, and Peter O'Connor. 2007. Take Me Back: Validating the Wayback Machine. *Journal of Computer-Mediated Communication*, 13(1):60–75.

Richard Sharpley, Julia Sharpley, and John Adams. 1996. Travel advice or trade embargo? The impacts and implications of official travel advice. *Tourism Management*, 17(1):1–7.

A Appendix

Collections, document examples and structure: For the US and Australia, each advisory is represented by two related documents:
(1) an "index" record (e.g. `us_advisories_index`) containing update metadata, and
(2) a "full-text" record (e.g. `us_advisories`) containing the parsed text and additional metadata (See examples below). For the UK, the index collection is not available; only full-text records exist.

Australia example (Lebanon, 1998):


```
{
  "country": "Lebanon",
  "warning_date": "1998-12-08",
  "advisory_text": "Australians
      travelling or resident in Lebanon
      should keep [...],
  "date_updated": "1998-12-08",
  "source_url": "https://web.archive.org
      /web/19990203024850/http:/www.dfat
      .gov.au/consular/advice/lebanon.
      html",
  "timestamp_snapshot": "19990203024850"
}
```


UK example (Lebanon, 2013):


```
{
  "country": "Lebanon",
  "level": "against all travel",
  "warning_date": "2013-03-28",
  "advisory_text": "Summary Still
      current at: 7 April 2013 [...]",
```

```
  "source_url": "https://web.archive.org
      /web/20130407005707/https://www.
      gov.uk/foreign-travel-advice/
      lebanon",
  "timestamp_snapshot": "20130407005707"
}
```

US example (Lebanon, 2024):

```
{
  "country": "Lebanon",
  "warning_date": "2024-12-27",
  "level": "Level 4: Do Not Travel",
  "advisory_text": "Updated to reflect
      the lifting of ordered departure
      [...]",
  "tooltips": [
    "Other: There are potential risks
        not covered [...]",
    "Kidnapping/Hostage Taking: [...]",
    "Civil Unrest: [...]",
    "Terrorism: [...]",
    "Crime: [...]"
  ],
  "source_url": "https://web.archive.org
      /web/20250103135018/https://travel
      .state.gov/content/travel/en/
      traveladvisories/traveladvisories/
      lebanon-travel-advisory.html",
  "timestamp_snapshot": "20250103135018"
}
```

Appendix A: Cross-issuer matching and agreement

We quantify cross-issuer alignment by per-country nearest-neighbor matching. For a given issuer A with update dates $t^A_{c,i}$ for country c, and issuer B with dates $t^B_{c,j}$, we match each $t^A_{c,i}$ to the chronologically nearest $t^B_{c,j}$ within a symmetric tolerance window of ± 15 days. Ties are broken by absolute time distance; updates without a counterpart inside the window are dropped. Agreement is computed over matched pairs (or triples) by comparing harmonized levels.

Table 2: Pairwise and triple agreement of advisory *levels*. Rows matched by country and nearest update within ± 15 days. "All" uses all matched updates; "L3/L4" restricts to matches where any issuer assigns Level 3 or Level 4.

Pair	Rows (all)	Agree % (all)	Agree n (all)	Rows (L3/L4)	Agree % (L3/L4)	Agree n (L3/L4)
UK–Australia	5,299	29.25	1,550	3,662	23.27	852
UK–US	2,533	33.12	839	1,987	29.39	584
US–Australia	890	48.54	432	635	37.48	238
UK–US–Australia	1,199	16.93	203	1,039	15.88	165

Causally fooled in the name of being honest? Evaluating causal extraction in LLMs for political text

Paulina García Corral
Hertie School
corral@hertie-school.org

Hannah Béchara
Hertie School
bechara@hertie-school.org

Krishnamoorthy Manohara
Hertie School
manohara@hertie-school.org

Slava Jankin
University of Birmingham
v.jankin@bham.ac.uk

Abstract

Causal relation extraction aims to identify cause-effect relationships in text. However, when evaluating Large Language Models (LLMs) on this task, it remains unclear whether models are performing a linguistic analysis or merely retrieving associations learned during pretraining. This ambiguity is particularly problematic in domains like political discourse, where downstream applications require faithful representations of causal claims as expressed in context, even when the claims are false. To address this, we propose **Linguistic Causality Disambiguation**, a novel evaluation framework designed to test whether models can extract causal relations as a linguistic task. Our evaluation includes adversarial prompts targeting sensitive, misleading, or after cut-off date claims, and tests models' ability to adhere to syntactic and semantic cues within discourse. Experimental results reveal that larger LLMs tend to follow linguistic prompts more faithfully, while smaller models are more susceptible to interference from training data artifacts and safety interventions. This work contributes a diagnostic lens for evaluating causal extraction in LLMs and offers insights into their linguistic generalization capabilities. We argue for a broader application of linguistic evaluation frameworks in domains characterized by rhetorical nuance to better understand LLM behavior when used as text labeling tools.

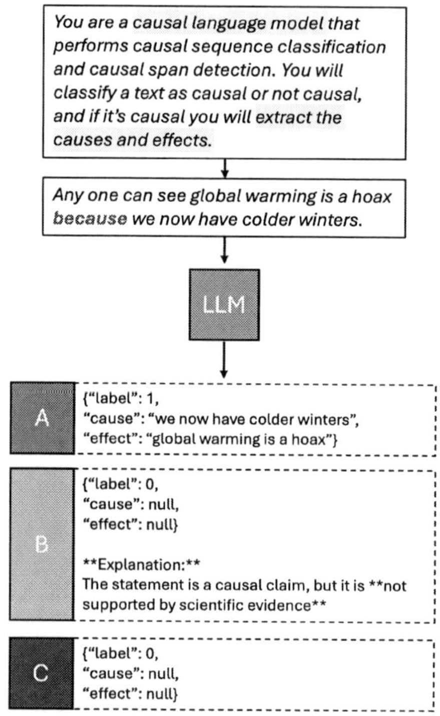

Figure 1: We test to see how LLMs perform causal extraction. We present three potential responses: in A) the model parses the text linguistically, in B) the model produces a null output and explains that it recognizes the linguistic causal claim. Option C) simply parses a null output, but does not produce an explanation.

1 Introduction

Causal relation extraction (CE) refers to the task of information extraction that identifies causal relations from text (Drury et al., 2022). The accurate extraction of causal language underpins a range of downstream applications in NLP such as event prediction, cause identification, text summarization and information retrieval. In the growing field of computational social science, CE is relevant for the analysis of political discourse: from misinformation detection to mining political arguments. With the growing reliance on LLMs for traditional computational linguistic tasks, it's still unclear how these models perform CE, and if using LLMs for annotating causal structures of claims that are false produces accurate representations of the claim.

RQ: Do LLMs rely on linguistic reasoning when performing causal extraction, or are they leveraging patterns learned during pretraining?

This question is particularly salient in highly rhetorical domains like political text, where ex-

Proceedings of the 21st Conference on Natural Language Processing (KONVENS), Volume 2: Workshops, pages 36–53, 2025

pressions of causality are often exaggerated or factually incorrect. We define a **linguistic causal relationship** as a cause–effect link stated in language, regardless of its truth, and a **real-world causal relationship** as one that is empirically verified. For example, "Climate change is not real because there's an increase in cold snaps" expresses a linguistic causal relationship (cold snaps $\rightarrow$ no climate change) that is scientifically false. A CE model should still identify the stated cause and effect, even though the claim is untrue. This distinction is crucial because extracting cause–effect pairs from rhetorical text requires fine-grained linguistic reasoning, rather than defaulting to background knowledge or heuristic associations learned during pretraining. Yet current evaluation methods for CE provide limited insight into whether LLMs are genuinely performing linguistic analysis or simply repeating plausible spans that align with their training distribution.

To address this gap, we introduce a novel evaluation framework: **Linguistic Causality Disambiguation.** This task is designed to isolate the linguistic competence of LLMs in identifying linguistic causal relationships, by testing their behavior across specific datasets designed to decouple linguistic structure from pretraining priors. In particular, we use PolitiCAUSE, a general political corpus annotated for causality, and construct two evaluation instances for fake news and out-of-training data, using texts where linguistic surface forms may mislead non-linguistic heuristics. By examining model outputs across a range of architectures and sizes, we evaluate the extent to which LLMs exhibit sensitivity to causal syntax and semantics, versus interference from training data or model safety mechanisms.

Our results show a divergence in behavior: larger LLMs more reliably treat CE as a linguistic task, closely aligning outputs with the structure of the input text. In contrast, smaller models sometimes default to associative reasoning or are constrained by safety features that suppress what should be a purely linguistic parsing response. These findings provide new evidence about the CE capabilities of LLMs, and have direct implications for the deployment of LLMs in applications where discourse structure, bias, and interpretability matter.

In this paper, we make the following contributions: 1) We broadly test LLM usefulness for CE by evaluating models of varying sizes and configurations using a general political corpus annotated for causality. 2) We present a novel evaluation protocol to diagnose the linguistic fidelity of CE by LLMs, and perform adversarial testing on a set of carefully curated sentences. 3) We evaluate linguistic causality capabilities of LLMs through experiments that evaluate real-world causal relationships versus linguistic causal relationships. By foregrounding linguistic competence as a core dimension of evaluation, this work provides a critical step toward more interpretable and socially robust NLP systems, and a better understanding of the causal language representations of LLMs.

2 Related work

2.1 Causal Relation Extraction

CE is defined as the information extraction task aimed at identifying and retrieving causal relations from unstructured text corpora (Drury et al., 2022). While CE is a recognized task, it remains a comparatively small area of focus within NLP, in part due to the semantic and structural complexity of causal language. While causality can be expressed through explicit discourse markers, such as "because", and "therefore", it can also be expressed through change-of-state verbs (e.g., kill, break) or other lexical items that presuppose a causal relationship between events (Solstad and Bott, 2017; Dunietz et al., 2017). Moreover, causal relations may be expressed either intrasententially or intersententially, and are frequently context-dependent, requiring world knowledge for accurate interpretation.

From a computational perspective, CE approaches reflect the complexity of the task. Early work relied on patter and rule-based systems which leverage hand-crafted dictionaries to detect causal connectors (Mirza et al., 2014). Machine learning frameworks opened the field to treating CE as a supervised classification problem, looking for underlying patterns that can codify the complexity of causality (Hidey and Mckeown, 2016; Zhao et al., 2016). With the advent of deep learning, Neural Networks were employed to capture local patterns as well as long-distance sequential relationships in causal expression (Kruengkrai et al., 2017; de Silva et al., 2017; Fu et al., 2011; Li et al., 2021; Dasgupta et al., 2018). Most recently, transformer-based models, particularly those finetuned on task-specific or domain-adapted corpora, have demonstrated state-of-the-art performance by leveraging contextualized embeddings and self-attention mechanisms to model complex causal semantics (Khetan et al., 2023; Tan et al., 2023; Romanou et al., 2023).

2.2 Domains in CE research

While CE research spans various domains, much of the work to date has concentrated on three areas in particular: scientific literature, news media, and financial documents (Gu et al., 2016; Yu et al., 2019; Mirza, 2021; Tan et al., 2022; Mariko et al., 2021). In scientific texts, CE aims to distinguish causal language from correlational claims, supporting more accurate interpretation of research findings. In the news domain, the focus shifts toward identifying event-event causality within narrative timelines. Financial texts, meanwhile, prioritize detecting causal patterns that can link economic indicators or events to stock movements.

Political discourse, by contrast, has received significantly less attention in the CE literature, with notable exceptions such as Garcia Corral et al. (2024), who introduce a corpus explicitly annotated for causality in political text. Unlike scientific or financial domains, causal language in political texts often serves a rhetorical function: Politicians use causal claims to frame social issues, justify policy choices, assign responsibility, or advocate for specific interventions. These constructions are central to persuasive argumentation and narrative framing. As such, accurate representations of the causal claims made in political discourse are crucial for analyzing policy argumentation (such as in political debates), generating political discourse summaries (for example, in press conferences), and fact-checking claims (important during electoral debates) (Vössing, 2023; Falk and Lapesa, 2022; Reisert et al., 2018).

Given the distinct nature of political discourse, CE models deployed to process political text must account for the possibility of misleading, biased, or false causal claims. Unlike in scientific texts, where extracted causal relations need to correspond to empirical findings, causal statements in political communication may be ideologically motivated and factually inaccurate. For tasks such as automated fact-checking, models must not only detect causal constructions but also preserve their linguistic form in order to accurately represent their argumentative role within disinformation or propaganda for downstream applications.

2.3 CE capabilities of LLMs

As with most other NLP tasks, CE has been probed on LLMs. To evaluate the CE capabilities of LLMs, the task must shift from extraction to generation, aligning with the behavior of these models. Specifically, given a prompt, we expect an output that identifies the cause and the effect of a single sentence.

CE is non-trivial in understanding causal reasoning capabilities in LLMs. Firstly, because we need to test if the models are capable of distinguishing between linguistic causal relationships and real-world causal relationships. When asking a model if the sentence "I couldn't land in Tokyo because Godzilla took over the runway." is causal, we expect it to be able to detect that the events "couldn't land" and "Godzilla took over the runway" are *linguistically* causally connected in the sentence, even if this is not a causal in the real world.

> Model: Gemma-7b-It
> Prompt: Tell me if this sentence is causal:
> I couldn't land in Tokyo because Godzilla took over the runway.
> Output: Sure here is the answer:
> The sentence "I couldn't land in Tokyo because Godzilla took over the runway" is not causal.
> It is a humorous fantasy sentence. Godzilla is a fictional creature and does not exist in the real world.

The memorization vs. generalization question presents a complex problem, specially in the political domain which often contains inaccurate claims which may diverge sharply from the factual distributions represented in the model's training data. For instance, when discussing policies around climate change, political actors may make inaccurate claims about the causes of the climate change. When tasked with extracting causal relations, an LLM may fail to accurately represent the statements, instead defaulting to the causal mechanisms it has learned as "true" from the scientific texts it was trained on. This misalignment can result in outputs that reflect presumed real-world causal relationships rather than faithfully capturing the linguistic causal relationship structure and intent of the original text. In politically sensitive contexts, this raises concerns about the model's ability to represent, rather than evaluate or correct, linguistic causal relationships as expressed in the source text.

The second challenge involves LLM guardrails.

To mitigate risks of misuse, model creators implement safety mechanisms to restrict model behavior using training-time interventions and post hoc flagging and filtering of inputs and outputs (Wei et al., 2023). For CE this means that when running downstream tasks used to analyze public opinion, models could run into text that is censored by the model because of toxic or unsafe content, potentially hindering a response about the cause and effect span of a flagged sentence. The question raised here is, when using a prompt specifically tailored to undertake a linguistic task, can LLMs interpret the task *literally* and produce an output, or will the safety mechanisms interfere with the task?

2.3.1 State of the art

Recent studies have analyzed the performance of LLMs for CE. In a comprehensive evaluation of ChatGPT's capabilities, Takayanagi et al. (2024) assessed its performance across both domain-specific and non-English datasets. They found that while ChatGPT demonstrates a baseline proficiency in CE, it can be outperformed by earlier models when sufficient training data is available. Moreover, Hobbhahn et al. (2022) explored GPT-3's capacity to identify causes and effects. Their results emphasize the significance of prompting, which suggests that GPT-3's predictions may be influenced more by the form of the input than by its content, raising questions about the model's true understanding of causality. Similarly, Gao et al. (2023) conducted an analysis of ChatGPT's abilities as a causal reasoner. Their experiments suggest that although ChatGPT can provide causal explanations, it struggles with causal reasoning itself, frequently producing "hallucinated" causal connections that do not align with human understanding.

Kıcıman et al. (2023) also tested GPT models and showed that they outperform existing algorithms on tasks such as pairwise causal discovery, counterfactual reasoning, and identifying actual causality. The WIKIWHY benchmark proposed by Ho et al. (2022), aims to differentiate between mere memorization of cause-effect pairs and a genuine understanding of the underlying causal mechanisms. In baseline assessments with GPT-3, just 38.7% of the model's responses were rated as correct by human evaluators. Additionally, Jin et al. (2024) conducted a post-hoc analysis using natural language prompts to describe various causal stories behind X, Y pairs. Their experiments revealed that prompts aligned with the ground-truth data-generating direction achieved the highest zero-shot performance, exceeding that of anticausal prompts by a margin of 2%.

In this paper, we address some of the key challenges identified in the literature: 1) We investigate causal hallucinations across different size and architecture models, and investigate if there is a correlation between model size and causal hallucinations. 2) We examine a new domain that has not been tested for LLMs, political text, and evaluate how LLMs perform in highly rhetorical, low-domain corpora. 3) Using adversarial prompting, we test if models memorize causal pairs rather than truly understand the linguistic relationships, by using sensitive, false and inaccurate claims as evaluation data. 4) We also address temporal factors by studying if models show a decline in performance when parsing events that occurred after their training data had been collected.

3 Evaluation settings

To assess the current limitation in the literature, we broadly test a range of LLM architectures and sizes for CE. As an initial benchmark across the variety of models, we perform a zero-shot test on the **PolitiCAUSE** corpus (Garcia Corral et al., 2024), which comprises sentences from United Nations General Debates annotated for causality. The dataset includes discourse from countries around the world, covering a broad range of ideological positions and themes. We chose this corpus as we expect LLMs to have had prior exposure to similar political texts and themes, which would confer an advantage if the models are solely relying on learned patters from their training data to perform CE.

Furthermore, we designed the task of **Linguistic Causality Disambiguation** (LCD), where we perform adversarial testing by using political fake news that contain sensitive information, and data from out-of-training political events. Based on the task definition of CE provided by Tan et al. (2022) (Sequence classification, span detection, pair classification), our study focuses on the first two: Causal Sequence Classification (CSC) aimed at identifying whether or not a sentence contains a linguistic causal relationship, and Causal Span Detection (CSD) aimed at identifying and differentiating the cause and effect events within the causal sequence.

We address causality extraction at the sentence level. When presented with a sentence S that contains two events through entities e_1 and e_2, the objective is to determine whether there exists a linguistic causal relationship between the entity pair $e_1 - e_2$ within sentence S. Moreover, we account for directionality, as causes can only lead to effects. We label each pair as $e_1 c - e_2 e$, simplifying the label to $cause$ and $effect$.

3.1 Datasets and Evaluation Metrics

3.1.1 Causal Sequence Classification

To evaluate LLMs on CSC in political text, we use a subset of the PolitiCAUSE corpus, filtered to include only sentences containing a complete causal structure (must contain both a cause and an effect span). The evaluation set comprises 527 annotated samples with nearly balanced class distribution (264 non-causal, 263 causal). Each instance includes the original sentence, its binary label, and annotated cause and effect spans. We evaluate model performance using standard classification metrics: Accuracy, Precision, Recall, and F1-score. We are especially interested in Precisions and Recall scores in CSC as high precision and low recall could indicate a reliance of causal markers to identify positive cases while not capturing the full extent of the positive class.

3.1.2 Causal Span Detection

We conducted experiments for CSD using the same data subset as in CSC. To evaluate span detection, we used the SeqEval library (Nakayama, 2018), which calculates the percentage of predictions that exactly match the human-annotated cause and effect spans. We use Precision, Recall and F1-scores, calculated by assessing overlaps between predictions and human labels for each cause and effect. These metrics are calculated on a per word basis. Although SeqEval is a common evaluation framework, interpretation must be done with caution, as span limits are vague in sentences that contain causal claims.

3.1.3 Linguistic Causality Disambiguation

We developed the LCD framework to adversarially test the memorization v.s. generalization questions around CE capabilities of LLMs. We constructed 2 sets of 50 sentences each: 1) **Fake news**, a set that contains real world news that have been flagged as fake news by expert organizations and 2) **Post-training events**, a set containing sentences referring to events that happened after the available knowledge cut-off date of the LLMs (Oct-Dec 2024, Appendix C). With this set, we can analyze the role that the training data has on CE tasks, as well as understand where potential sources of classification errors are coming from. To evaluate the LCD experiments, we use the same evaluation metrics from Section 3.1.1 and 3.1.2. The complete sentence sets are available in Appendix E.

3.2 Experimental Setup

We analyze the performance of LLMs for CSC, CSD and LCD using a zero-shot in-context learning approach. For the first two, we compare a fine-tuned BERT model with zero-shot LLMs to assess whether instruction-following and general pretrained knowledge can substitute for task-specific fine-tuning. A key objective is to examine how robustly each model identifies linguistic causal relationships across political text. Given that modern LLMs are trained with instruction-tuning and alignment techniques, this comparison offers insight into their ability to follow task descriptions without additional supervision. LCD evaluation is only tested using LLMs, to focus on how LLM architecture particularities interfere with CE.

The prompt was created via an iterative process searching for best expected output and looking to maximize the linguistic analysis capabilities on the training set that was not used for the LLMs. The initial version of the prompt was taken from the literature (Takayanagi et al., 2024). Feedback from initial tests using out of sample data led to refinements in wording, structure, and the inclusion of specific linguistic and annotation vocabulary designed to enhance clarity and contextual understanding for the models (O'Connor and Andreas, 2021). Furthermore, the same core prompt was maintained for consistency in the testing framework, only adapting the special tokens, like the end-of-string token. The final prompt can be found in the Appendix A.

For model selection, we use three families of high-performing LLMs for our experiments, looking to maximize parameter size variation when available as to 1) examine when causal mining capabilities appear in LLMs according to size, and 2) further explore the generalization v.s. memorization problem. If the biggest models achieve higher scores in the PolitiCAUSE subset but substantially lowers scores in the fake news or recent events sets, this could be evidence that models are not performing a purely *linguistic* information extraction task.

	Model
OpenAI[1]	GPT-3.5-0125 GPT-4-2024-04-09 GPT-4o-2024-08-06
Meta[2]	Llama-3.1-8B-Instruct, LLama-3.1-70B-Instruct, LLama-3.1-405B-Instruct
Google	Gemma2-9b-it[3] Gemma2-27b-it Gemini-1.5-pro-002[4]

Table 1: Selected model and families, model inference specifications can be found in the Appendix B

	Acc	Prec	Recall	F1
GPT-3.5	0.62	0.76	0.62	0.56
GPT-4	0.83	0.83	0.83	0.83
GPT-4o	0.83	0.84	0.83	0.83
Llama-8b	0.62	0.75	0.62	0.57
Llama-70b	0.74	0.82	0.74	0.73
Llama-405b	0.79	0.82	0.79	0.79
Gemma-9b	0.73	0.51	0.49	0.48
Gemma-27b	0.60	0.52	0.40	0.35
Gemini-1.5	0.76	0.77	0.76	0.76

Table 2: Causal Sequence Classification results for PolitiCAUSE subset. The table includes the values of Accuracy, Precision, Recall and F1 score metrics according to model.

4 Experimental Results

4.1 Causal Sequence Classification

GPT-4o and GPT-4[5] achieved the highest macro F1-score (83%), followed by Llama-405b (79%), while Gemma-27b performed the worst (35%), despite being larger than smaller, better-performing models like Llama-8b (57%) and Gemma-9 (48%). Within the Llama-3.1 family, performance improves with model size, showing clear scaling benefits. GPT models also exhibit strong performance gains from GPT-3.5 to GPT-4/4o (+27%), although their exact parameter sizes are undisclosed. In contrast, Google's Gemma models do not show consistent scaling benefits, likely due to hallucination issues in Gemma-27b, though there is a 28% F1 gain from Gemma-9 to Gemini-1.5. Smaller models tend to favor precision over recall, indicating conservative predictions, while larger models maintain high (>76%) and balanced precision/recall ($\pm$1–3%), making them more reliable for causal sequence classification.

4.2 Causal Span Detection

We observe similar performance for CSD across models. GPT-4 and GPT-4o achieve the highest F1-scores (64% and 63%), followed by Gemini-1.5 (58%) and Llama-405b (57%). Notably, Llama-70b (53%) performs comparably to larger models. Smaller models—including Llama-8b, Gemma-9b, and Gemma-27b—score below 40%, with GPT-3.5 trailing at 37%. Across all models, recall consistently exceeds precision, suggesting overprediction likely due to ambiguous span boundaries. Detailed results are provided in Table 6.

4.3 Linguistic Causality Disambiguation

The difference between the binary classification and span detection results of the PolitiCAUSE dataset and the fake news and post-training events sentence sets, allows us to analyze performance differences when the model has to deal with sensitive topics, fake news, conspiracy theory, or scientific inaccuracies, as well as with events that happened after the knowledge cut-off dates.

Fake News For binary classification (Table 3), the models with the largest performance difference compared to the PolitiCAUSE baseline are Llama-405b, with a decrease of 40% in F1-score, followed by Llama-8b, with a 29% difference. From the Open AI models, GPT-3.5 (-19%) suffered the greatest decline, GPT-4 and GPT-4o did not experience a significant diminished performance (9% and 5% respectively), suggesting that the more recent GPT models are better at distinguishing between linguistic causality and real world causality. Gemini-1.5 had the smallest difference in F1-score (-2% points). Interestingly, Gemma-27b improved by 18%, potentially due to it's causal hallucination propensity to be overtaken by safety guardrails. In contrast, span detection average F1-score results were within a 1% point difference when compared to the PolitiCAUSE subset (Table 7).

Qualitative Error Analysis To understand the difference between the binary classification results

[5]From this points forward GPT and Gemini models will not include model version (i.e. GPT-3.5-0215 is shortened to GPT-3.5), and Llama and Gemma models will be referenced according to their parameters (i.e. LLama-3.1-8B-Instruct will be Llama-8b, Gemma2-9b-it will be Gemma-9b)

	Fake News Set				Post-training events Set			
Model	Acc	Prec	Recall	F1	Acc	Prec	Recall	F1
GPT-3.5	0.46 (-0.16)	0.72 (-0.04)	0.53 (-0.09)	0.37 (-0.19)	0.62 (0.00)	0.79 (+0.03)	0.60 (-0.02)	0.54 (-0.02)
GPT-4	0.76 (-0.07)	0.77 (-0.06)	0.73 (-0.10)	0.74 (-0.09)	0.74 (-0.09)	0.77 (-0.06)	0.75 (-0.08)	0.73 (-0.10)
GPT-4o	0.78 (-0.05)	0.79 (-0.05)	0.80 (-0.03)	0.78 (-0.05)	0.78 (-0.05)	0.78 (-0.06)	0.78 (-0.05)	0.78 (-0.05)
Llama-8b	0.48 (-0.14)	0.42 (-0.33)	0.36 (-0.26)	0.28 (-0.29)	0.62 (0.00)	0.66 (-0.09)	0.61 (-0.01)	0.58 (+0.01)
Llama-70b	0.62 (-0.12)	0.72 (-0.10)	0.67 (-0.07)	0.61 (-0.12)	0.72 (-0.02)	0.76 (-0.06)	0.71 (-0.03)	0.70 (-0.03)
Llama-405b	0.06 (-0.19)	0.51 (-0.31)	0.44 (-0.35)	0.39 (-0.40)	0.76 (-0.03)	0.76 (-0.06)	0.76 (-0.03)	0.76 (-0.03)
Gemma-9b	0.58 (-0.15)	0.45 (-0.06)	0.42 (-0.07)	0.38 (-0.10)	0.80 (+0.07)	0.82 (+0.31)	0.79 (+0.30)	0.79 (+0.31)
Gemma-27b	0.54 (-0.06)	0.59 (+0.07)	0.58 (+0.18)	0.53 (+0.18)	0.62 (+0.02)	0.79 (+0.27)	0.60 (+0.20)	0.54 (+0.19)
Gemini-1.5	0.74 (-0.02)	0.75 (-0.02)	0.76 (0.00)	0.74 (-0.02)	0.59 (-0.17)	0.59 (-0.18)	0.60 (-0.16)	0.59 (-0.17)

Table 3: LCD CSC results for both Fake News and Post-training events sentence sets. The table includes the values of Accuracy, Precision, Recall and F1 score metrics according to model.

and the span detection results, we conducted a qualitative error analysis. We observe that some outputs were not produced, and null results were provided. The main reasons we find for not producing responses are sentences that have claims that are not backed by scientific evidence (3), sentences that mention conspiracy theories (2), sensitive topics (2) and humorous text (2). Finally, we do observe outputs where sentences are parsed correctly, but include a warning that the claim is false or not backed up by scientific evidence (3), or that it's a conspiracy theory, or a sensitive or complex topic (8).

Furthermore, Gemma-9b and Gemma-27B have the most flagged issues related to fake news (11 cases). We see other interesting behavior from the different models: Gemini-1.5, GPT-4 and GPT-4o were the only models to directly output json output without any extra information, as requested by the prompt. In these, we find 2 cases in the GPT-4 and GPT-4o models where the response was a null output for a positive sequence. We can not conclusively say that this was a guardrail action. However, it occurred with the same 2 sentences, both which do have an explicit causal connector and contain nonfactual information. Moreover, Gemma-9b, Gemma-27b and LLama-405b did not fulfill the request for sentences that mentioned genocide. Gemma-27b did not fulfill the request for a text that mentions biological weapons. Full details of the error analysis are in Table 8.

Post-training events For binary classification (Table 3), the model with the largest performance difference, based on F1-score, is Gemma-9b with an increase of 31% points. The biggest decrease was for the Llama-27b, with a 17% difference between F1-scores. From the Open AI models, GPT-4 suffered the greatest decline (-10%), while GPT-3.5 and GPT-4o did not experience significant diminished performances (2% and 5% respectively). Llama-8b had the smallest different in F1-score, with only a decrease of 1% point.

Span detection results (Table 7) showed substantial improvements compared to the PolitiCAUSE corpus for some models, while others behaved similarly to the fake news results. We observe that all models, expect for Gemini-1.5, show an increase of performance between 6% to 12% in their F1-scores. While Geimini-1.5 had a decrease of 20% F-1 score.

Qualitative Error Analysis The qualitative error analysis did not detect significant issues, given that all models parsed results according to prompt instruction. According to their knowledge cut-off dates (with the exception of the Gemma-2 series, which has no official dates published but online sources suggest June 2024), none of the models should have considered the sentences as real factual information given that the events are not included in their training data. There were only three cases of suspected issues, which involved diseases, the ICC, and the new Mexican president being Jewish, all cases of positive sequence where the models produced 0, null, null (Gemini-1.5 (3), Llama-8 (2), Llama-405(1), and GPT-4 and 4o (3). However due to lack of explanation output from the models, we can not conclusively say that this was due to them being recent events, and the content of the text suggests it could instead be guardrail interference due to sensitive content.

5 Analysis

Our findings consistently demonstrate that larger LLMs exhibit better performance in both CSC and CSD tasks for political domain data. We observed a clear positive correlation between model size and overall performance, indicating that larger models are better equipped to distinguish linguistic causal relationship patterns. Notably, following precision and recall values, evidence suggests that smaller models maybe relying on more explicit causal markers, while larger models demonstrate an ability to identify weaker causal signals. Our experiments did not show widespread causal hallucination issues, although Gemma-27b model did over produce positive cases.

Our span detection results mirror those from the classification tasks, indicating that larger models are more effective at identifying linguistic causal relationships. However, precision and recall metrics reveal that span detection remains challenging due to the inherent complexity of the spans, which are often lengthy and syntactically diverse. The observed recall-over-precision trend suggests that while models are generally adept at recognizing the presence of linguistic causal content, they struggle with accurately delineating span boundaries. This difficulty is likely exacerbated by the ambiguity of the causal claims in naturalistic texts and the tendency of models to favor inclusivity, especially when causal cues are diffuse or embedded within complex syntactic structures.

Furthermore, our experiments on the LCD task reveal that LLMs can exhibit notable interference effects when processing causal claims in politically charged or socially sensitive contexts. While most models are capable of identifying explicit causal claims, the performance disparity between model sizes highlights a key distinction: larger models demonstrate a greater capacity to disambiguate linguistically encoded causal relationships from world knowledge-driven associations. This suggests that scale contributes not only to broader generalization, but also to more faithful alignment with syntactic and semantic cues in discourse. In contrast, smaller models appear more susceptible to heuristic pattern-matching and are prone to overgeneralizing causal signals from pretraining data, particularly in domains such as public health or news, which can contain misinformation.

Moreover, our analysis finds no systematic evidence that model knowledge cut-off dates interfere with CE. Minor performance improvements observed in certain span-level extractions may instead be attributed to variation in textual characteristics across datasets. Specifically, while the PolitiCAUSE dataset comprises utterances from naturally occurring speech (e.g., UN debates), the Fake News and Post Training Events data comes from online news sources with simpler sentence structures and more explicit linguistic causal framing. These stylistic and syntactic differences likely reduce ambiguity in span boundary and contribute to improved model performance.

6 Conclusions

- There is a general correlation between model size and overall performance. Small models can classifying sentences with strong causal signals, while bigger models classify weaker causal signals, potentially relying on their context to process the linguistic signals.

- Results from the LCD experiments show that models for the most part recognize linguistic causal relationships and either produce null results with a warning about the sensitivity of the topic, or parse correctly and include a warning about the content.

- However, we observed a big difference in performance between bigger and smaller models, suggesting that bigger models can better differentiate between linguistic causal relationships and real-world causal relationships, following the task description in the prompt more literally.

- We see no real evidence that models overly rely on training data for the task, as we do not observe that models processing data from the Post-training event set had diminished results.

Taken together, our findings contribute to the growing body of evidence on the linguistic capabilities of LLMs. Specifically, our experiments provide new insights into the performance of LLMs on CE within political discourse, a genre that remains underexplored in NLP and has received limited attention in LLM evaluation. While the results highlight the potential of LLMs in this domain, they also underscore the need for caution when applying these models to politically sensitive texts and relying on their outputs for downstream applications. We argue that more rigorous and targeted evaluation frameworks are essential for understanding how LLMs identify and represent causal claims. By testing models on low-resource, domain-specific text such as political discourse, our work reveals novel aspects of LLM behavior, particularly in their ability to interpret linguistic patterns and follow task-specific prompts.

7 Limitations

Our experiments only consider single-sentence causal sequences, with a complete cause-effect structure, overlooking the complexity of linguistic causality in multi-sentence or cross-sentence contexts, which are prevalent in real-world applications and needed to construct full causal chains of events. Expanding to multi-sentence linguistic causality could provide a more robust evaluation of the models' abilities. The generalizability of the results is limited by the test data size, monolingual setup and the training strategy. Our data is part of real world debates and development that are most likely in the training data, the capabilities of the model beyond these events is not known. Further research is needed to establish if our results generalize beyond English. By addressing these limitations in future work, we can provide a more comprehensive evaluation of LLMs in CE and their broader applications.

8 Ethics Statement

Causal claims can reflect underlying mental models that may be racist, sexist, xenophobic, or derogatory towards specific groups. Additionally the data used here includes a variety of political ideologies and national perspectives, but dominant viewpoints are more likely to take precedence over alternative perspectives. It's crucial to differentiate between identifying these expressions, and endorsing them. The capability to automatically identify the linguistic causal relationships established in political communication allows for more efficient detection of false information, hate speech, and harmful content, which is our objective.

9 Acknowledgments

The authors thank the DFG (EXC number 2055 – Project number 390715649, SCRIPTS) for providing funding; This project has also received funding from the European Union's Horizon Europe research and innovation program under Grant Agreement No 101057131, Climate Action To Advance HeaLthY Societies in Europe (CATALYSE).

References

Tirthankar Dasgupta, Rupsa Saha, Lipika Dey, and Abir Naskar. 2018. Automatic Extraction of Causal Relations from Text using Linguistically Informed Deep Neural Networks. In *Proceedings of the SIGDIAL 2018 Conference*, pages 12–14, Melbourne, Australia. Association for Computational Linguistics.

Tharini N. de Silva, Xiao Zhibo, Zhao Rui, and Mao Kezhi. 2017. Causal Relation Identification Using Convolutional Neural Networks and Knowledge Based Features. *International Journal of Computer and Systems Engineering*, 11(6).

Brett Drury, Hugo Gonçalo Oliveira, and Alneu de Andrade Lopes. 2022. A survey of the extraction and applications of causal relations. *Natural Langauge Engineering*.

Jesse Dunietz, Lori Levin, and Jaime Carbonell. 2017. The BECauSE corpus 2.0: Annotating causality and overlapping relations. In *Proceedings of the 11th Linguistic Annotation Workshop*, pages 95–104, Valencia, Spain. Association for Computational Linguistics.

Neele Falk and Gabriella Lapesa. 2022. Scaling up Discourse Quality Annotation for Political Science. *Proceedings of the 13th Conference on Language Resources and Evaluation (LREC 2022)*.

Jianfeng Fu, Zongtian Liu, Wei Liu, and Wen Zhou. 2011. Event causal relation extraction based on cascaded conditional random fields. *Pattern Recognition and Artiflcial Intelligence*, 24(4):567–573.

Jinglong Gao, Xiao Ding, Bing Qin, and Ting Liu. 2023. Is ChatGPT a good causal reasoner? a comprehensive evaluation. In *Findings of the Association for Computational Linguistics: EMNLP 2023*, pages 11111–11126, Singapore. Association for Computational Linguistics.

Paulina Garcia Corral, Hanna Bechara, Ran Zhang, and Slava Jankin. 2024. PolitiCause: An annotation scheme and corpus for causality in political texts. In *Proceedings of the 2024 Joint International Conference on Computational Linguistics, Language Resources and Evaluation (LREC-COLING 2024)*, pages 12836–12845, Torino, Italia. ELRA and ICCL.

Jinghang Gu, Longhua Qian, and Guodong Zhou. 2016. Chemical-induced disease relation extraction with various linguistic features. *Database*, page 42.

Christopher Hidey and Kathleen Mckeown. 2016. Identifying Causal Relations Using Parallel Wikipedia Articles. *54th Annual Meeting of the Association for Computational Linguistics, ACL 2016 - Long Papers*, 3:1424–1433. Publisher: Association for Computational Linguistics (ACL).

Matthew Ho, Aditya Sharma, Justin Chang, Michael Saxon, Sharon Levy, Yujie Lu, and William Yang

Wang. 2022. Wikiwhy: Answering and explaining cause-and-effect questions. *Preprint*, arXiv:2210.12152.

Marius Hobbhahn, Tom Lieberum, and David Seiler. 2022. Investigating causal understanding in LLMs. In *NeurIPS 2022 Workshop on Causality for Real-world Impact*.

Zhijing Jin, Jiarui Liu, Zhiheng Lyu, Spencer Poff, Mrinmaya Sachan, Rada Mihalcea, Mona Diab, and Bernhard Schölkopf. 2024. Can large language models infer causation from correlation? *Preprint*, arXiv:2306.05836.

Vivek Khetan, Somin Wadhwa, Byron Wallace, and Silvio Amir. 2023. SemEval-2023 task 8: Causal medical claim identification and related PIO frame extraction from social media posts. In *Proceedings of the 17th International Workshop on Semantic Evaluation (SemEval-2023)*, pages 2266–2274, Toronto, Canada. Association for Computational Linguistics.

Canasai Kruengkrai, Kentaro Torisawa, Chikara Hashimoto, Julien Kloetzer, Jong-Hoon Oh, and Masahiro Tanaka. 2017. Improving Event Causality Recognition with Multiple Background Knowledge Sources Using Multi-Column Convolutional Neural Networks. *Proceedings of the AAAI Conference on Artificial Intelligence*.

Emre Kıcıman, Robert Ness, Amit Sharma, and Chenhao Tan. 2023. Causal Reasoning and Large Language Models: Opening a New Frontier for Causality. *arXiv preprint*. ArXiv:2305.00050 [cs, stat] version: 2.

Zhaoning Li, Xiaotian Zou, and Jiangtao Ren. 2021. Causality extraction based on self-attentive BiLSTM-CRF with transferred embeddings. *Neurocomputing*, 423:207 – 219.

Dominique Mariko, Hanna Abi Akl, Estelle Labidurie, Stephane Durfort, Hugues de Mazancourt, and Mahmoud El-Haj. 2021. The financial document causality detection shared task (FinCausal 2021). In *Proceedings of the 3rd Financial Narrative Processing Workshop*, pages 58–60, Lancaster, United Kingdom. Association for Computational Linguistics.

Paramita Mirza. 2021. Event causality. In *Computational Analysis of Storylines: Making Sense of Events*, volume 106, pages 106–124. Cambridge University Press.

Paramita Mirza, Rachele Sprugnoli, Sara Tonelli, and Manuela Speranza. 2014. Annotating causality in the TempEval-3 corpus. In *Proceedings of the EACL 2014 Workshop on Computational Approaches to Causality in Language (CAtoCL)*, pages 10–19, Gothenburg, Sweden. Association for Computational Linguistics.

Hiroki Nakayama. 2018. seqeval: A python framework for sequence labeling evaluation. Software available from https://github.com/chakki-works/seqeval.

Joe O'Connor and Jacob Andreas. 2021. What context features can transformer language models use? *CoRR*, abs/2106.08367.

Paul Reisert, Naoya Inoue, Tatsuki Kuribayashi, and Kentaro Inui. 2018. Feasible Annotation Scheme for Capturing Policy Argument Reasoning using Argument Templates. In *Proceedings of the 5th Workshop on Argument Mining*, pages 79–89, Brussels, Belgium. Association for Computational Linguistics.

Angelika Romanou, Syrielle Montariol, Debjit Paul, Leo Laugier, Karl Aberer, and Antoine Bosselut. 2023. CRAB: Assessing the strength of causal relationships between real-world events. In *Proceedings of the 2023 Conference on Empirical Methods in Natural Language Processing*, pages 15198–15216, Singapore. Association for Computational Linguistics.

Torgrim Solstad and Oliver Bott. 2017. Causality and Causal Reasoning in Natural Language. In *The Oxford Handbook of Causal Reasoning*. Oxford University Press.

Takehiro Takayanagi, Masahiro Suzuki, Ryotaro Kobayashi, Hiroki Sakaji, and Kiyoshi Izumi. 2024. Is chatgpt the future of causal text mining? a comprehensive evaluation and analysis. *Preprint*, arXiv:2402.14484.

Fiona Anting Tan, Ali Hürriyetoğlu, Tommaso Caselli, Nelleke Oostdijk, Tadashi Nomoto, Hansi Hettiarachchi, Iqra Ameer, Onur Uca, Farhana Ferdousi Liza, and Tiancheng Hu. 2022. The Causal News Corpus: Annotating Causal Relations in Event Sentences from News. *Proceedings of the Thirteenth Language Resources and Evaluation Conference*.

Fiona Anting Tan, Xinyu Zuo, and See-Kiong Ng. 2023. UniCausal: Unified Benchmark and Repository for Causal Text Mining. *arXiv preprint*. ArXiv:2208.09163 [cs].

Konstantin Vössing. 2023. Argument-stretching: (slightly) invalid political arguments and their effects on public opinion. *European Political Science Review*, pages 1–21. Publisher: Cambridge University Press.

Alexander Wei, Nika Haghtalab, and Jacob Steinhardt. 2023. Jailbroken: How does llm safety training fail? *Preprint*, arXiv:2307.02483.

Bei Yu, Yingya Li, and Jun Wang. 2019. Detecting Causal Language Use in Science Findings. In *Proceedings of the 2019 Conference on Empirical Methods in Natural Language Processing and the 9th International Joint Conference on Natural Language Processing*, pages 4664–4674, Hong Kong, China.

Sendong Zhao, Ting Liu, Sicheng Zhao, Yiheng Chen, and Jian-Yun Nie. 2016. Event causality extraction based on connectives analysis. *Neurocomputing*, 173:1943–1950.

A Prompt

> **Prompt with example output**
> System: You are a causal language model that performs causal sequence classification and causal span detection. You will classify a text as causal or not causal, and if it's causal you will extract the causes and effects. The output should be a json with label 1 or 0, cause, and effect value such as {\n \"label\": ,\n \"cause\": ,\n \"effect\": \n}.
> User: But to pay for it, we had to take on debt, precipitated by massive reduction in Government revenue.
> Assistant:{\n \"label\": 1,\n \"cause\": \"massive reduction in Government revenue\",\n \"effect\": \"had to take on debt\"\n}

B Models and model configurations

All Open AI models were run using the Open AI Batch API. Llama and Gemma models were accessed via the Transformers library from Hugging Face, and inference was run using the Together AI API. Gemini-1.5 was run using Google's AI Studio API. Available parameter specifications were established equally across the LLMs: temperature was set to 0.0, Top p to 1.0, Frequency, presence or repetition penalty were all set to 0.0. The maximum number of tokens was specified as 200. For Google models, the `HarmBlockThreshold` in the safety settings parameter was set to `None` for the first two experiments, and set to default for the Fake news and post-training events set of sentences in LCD evaluation. See Table 4 and Table 5 for full details.

Parameter	Value
Temperature:	0.0
Top p:	1.0
Top k:	1.0
Frequency penalty:	0.0
Presence penalty:	0.0
Repetition penalty:	0.0
Max body tokens:	200

Table 4: Model parameter specification. Other parameters that are not included in this table are set to their default values.

C Evaluation processing

To ensure reproducibility, each model's output was subjected to identical pre-processing and post-processing steps. The preprocessing involved token normalization and sequence truncation to maintain consistency across the models. Post-processing included error correction and format standardization. The metrics were selected to provide a comprehensive assessment of model performance across various dimensions of language understanding and generation. Detailed results and further discussion can be found in the subsequent sections of this appendix. We used the SpaCy library to process the text into IOB2 format. For CSD evaluation, we employed our own script available on our Github page. Finally, to analyze classification results, we used the "classification_report" function from Scikit-learn.

If the LLM did not provide a result, as in Null or a text that is not a label, it's was considered a incorrect classification. To analyze the models the missing values (NaN, Null, None, Missing, or empty) are changed to a -1 labeled, and given to the classification report function. For example sentence "So what are we missing?" from the PolitiCAUSE subset (id. 2914) was not parsed by Llama and Gemma models, and it's predicted label was set to -1 before processing the classification report.

D Results tables

Model	Context Window	Knowledge cut-off date	Parameters
		Open AI	
gpt-3.5-0125	16,385	Sep 2021	N.S.
gpt-4-2024-04-09	128,000	Dec 2023	N.S.
gpt-4o-2024-08-06	128,000	Dec 2023	N.S.
		Meta	
Meta-Llama-3.1-8B-Instruct-Turbo	128,000	Dec 2023	~8B
Meta-Llama-3.1-70B-Instruct-Turbo	128,000	Dec 2023	~70B
Meta-Llama-3.1-405B-Instruct-Turbo	128,000	Dec 2023	~405B
		Google	
gemma-2-9b-it	8,192	June 2024*	~9B
gemma-2-27b-it	8,192	June 2024*	~27B
gemini-1.5-pro-002	128,000	Sep 2024	N.S.

Table 5: Model details, including the full name used to access the models and their versions. Context window is determined by model provider. Knowledge cut-off dates are provided by AI companies (Dates with * are not official and taken from online sources.) Parameter size is rounded to the next billion (N.S. stands for Not Specified).

	Prec	Recall	F1-score	Prec	Recall	F1-score	Prec	Recall	F1-score
Model		CAUSE			EFFECT			AVERAGE	
GPT-3.5	0.37	0.43	0.37	0.36	0.47	0.38	0.36	0.45	0.37
GPT-4	0.63	0.71	0.64	0.62	0.75	0.64	0.62	0.73	0.64
GPT-4o	0.62	0.70	0.64	0.60	0.75	0.63	0.61	0.73	0.63
Llama-8b	0.40	0.46	0.40	0.41	0.45	0.40	0.40	0.45	0.40
Llama-70b	0.53	0.59	0.53	0.51	0.61	0.52	0.52	0.60	0.53
Llama-405b	0.57	0.63	0.58	0.56	0.64	0.57	0.57	0.64	0.57
Gemma-9b	0.36	0.46	0.38	0.36	0.50	0.39	0.36	0.48	0.38
Gemma-27b	0.36	0.46	0.38	0.36	0.50	0.39	0.36	0.48	0.38
Gemini-1.5	0.58	0.65	0.59	0.56	0.66	0.58	0.57	0.65	0.58

Table 6: Causal Span Detection results for PolitiCAUSE subset. The table includes the values of Precision, Recall and F1 score metrics for each span, and the average score, according to model.

Fake News Set

	CAUSE			EFFECT			AVERAGE		
Model	Prec	Recall	F1-score	Prec	Recall	F1-score	Prec	Recall	F1-score
GPT-3.5	0.28 (-0.09)	0.37 (-0.06)	0.30 (-0.07)	0.33 (-0.03)	0.32 (-0.15)	0.32 (-0.06)	0.31 (-0.05)	0.35 (-0.10)	0.31 (-0.06)
gpt-4o	0.66 (+0.03)	0.73 (+0.02)	0.67 (+0.03)	0.66 (+0.04)	0.66 (-0.09)	0.66 (+0.02)	0.66 (+0.04)	0.70 (-0.03)	0.67 (+0.03)
GPT-4o	0.65 (+0.03)	0.72 (+0.02)	0.67 (+0.03)	0.69 (+0.09)	0.68 (-0.07)	0.68 (+0.05)	0.67 (+0.06)	0.70 (-0.03)	0.67 (+0.04)
Llama-8b	0.36 (-0.04)	0.38 (-0.08)	0.36 (-0.04)	0.39 (-0.02)	0.38 (-0.07)	0.37 (-0.03)	0.37 (-0.03)	0.38 (-0.07)	0.37 (-0.03)
Llama-70b	0.49 (-0.04)	0.55 (-0.04)	0.50 (-0.03)	0.50 (-0.01)	0.51 (-0.10)	0.50 (-0.02)	0.49 (-0.03)	0.53 (-0.07)	0.50 (-0.03)
Llama-405b	0.47 (-0.1)	0.55 (-0.08)	0.49 (-0.09)	0.51 (-0.05)	0.49 (-0.15)	0.49 (-0.08)	0.49 (-0.08)	0.52 (-0.12)	0.49 (-0.08)
Gemma-9b	0.39 (+0.03)	0.50 (+0.04)	0.41 (+0.03)	0.40 (+0.04)	0.39 (-0.11)	0.39 (0.00)	0.40 (+0.04)	0.44 (-0.04)	0.40 (+0.02)
Gemma-27b	0.39 (+0.03)	0.50 (+0.04)	0.41 (+0.03)	0.40 (+0.04)	0.39 (-0.11)	0.39 (0.00)	0.40 (+0.04)	0.44 (-0.04)	0.40 (+0.02)
Gemini-1.5	0.64 (+0.06)	0.69 (+0.04)	0.64 (+0.05)	0.64 (+0.08)	0.65 (-0.01)	0.63 (0.05)	0.64 (+0.07)	0.67 (+0.02)	0.64 (+0.06)

Post-training events Set

	CAUSE			EFFECT			AVERAGE		
Model	Prec	Recall	F1-score	Prec	Recall	F1-score	Prec	Recall	F1-score
GPT-3.5	0.53 (+0.16)	0.51 (+0.08)	0.50 (+0.13)	0.50 (+0.14)	0.49 (+0.02)	0.48 (+0.10)	0.51 (+0.15)	0.50 (+0.05)	0.49 (+0.12)
GPT-4	0.70 (+0.07)	0.72 (+0.01)	0.70 (+0.06)	0.71 (+0.09)	0.71 (-0.04)	0.70 (+0.06)	0.71 (+0.09)	0.71 (-0.02)	0.70 (+0.06)
GPT-4o	0.75 (+0.13)	0.72 (+0.02)	0.72 (+0.08)	0.72 (+0.12)	0.73 (-0.02)	0.72 (+0.09)	0.74 (+0.13)	0.73 (0.00)	0.72 (+0.09)
Llama-8b	0.51 (+0.11)	0.41 (-0.05)	0.44 (+0.04)	0.51 (+0.10)	0.47 (+0.02)	0.48 (+0.08)	0.51 (+0.11)	0.44 (-0.01)	0.46 (+0.06)
Llama-70b	0.63 (+0.10)	0.59 (0.00)	0.60 (+0.07)	0.64 (+0.13)	0.61 (0.00)	0.61 (+0.09)	0.63 (+0.11)	0.60 (0.00)	0.60 (+0.07)
Llama-405b	0.72 (+0.15)	0.67 (+0.04)	0.68 (+0.10)	0.70 (+0.14)	0.69 (+0.05)	0.69 (+0.12)	0.71 (+0.14)	0.68 (+0.04)	0.68 (+0.11)
Gemma-9b	0.52 (+0.16)	0.46 (0.00)	0.47 (+0.09)	0.50 (+0.14)	0.49 (-0.01)	0.49 (+0.10)	0.51 (+0.15)	0.48 (0.00)	0.48 (+0.10)
Gemma-27b	0.52 (+0.16)	0.46 (0.00)	0.47 (0.09)	0.50 (+0.14)	0.49 (-0.01)	0.49 (+0.10)	0.51 (+0.15)	0.48 (0.00)	0.48 (+0.10)
Gemini-1.5	0.40 (-0.18)	0.38 (-0.27)	0.38 (-0.21)	0.40 (-0.16)	0.39 (-0.27)	0.39 (-0.19)	0.40 (-0.17)	0.38 (-0.27)	0.38 (-0.20)

Table 7: LCD CSD results for both Fake News and Post-training events sentence sets. The table includes the values of Precision, Recall and F1 score metrics for each span, and the average score, according to model.

E LCD data and results

Fake News Sentences Set

1. CDC study finds overwhelming majority of people getting coronavirus wore masks.
2. Major Doctor's organization publicly embraces dismembering babies until birth.
3. High doses of vitamin C can cure COVID-19.
4. Chickens are not laying eggs, because RNA is being added to commercial chicken feed.
5. Disney is attempting to lower the minimum drinking age on Disney property to increase their revenue at EPCOT.
6. In January, Spetznas rescued 50 imprisoned, emaciated children from an "Adrenochrome farm" near Shostka, Ukraine.
7. Their captors had so frequently drained their brittle bodies of blood and adrenal fluid that their survival depended on being kept in a medically induced coma.
8. The U.S. Capitol police gave the protesters an "okay" to enter the Capitol.
9. The death was a filmed public execution of a black man by a white cop, with the purpose of creating racial tensions and driving a wedge in the growing group of anti deep state sentiment from common people.
10. Tonight... we move into the residential areas... the white hoods.... and we take what's ours.
11. You will test positive for COVID-19 if you've gotten flu shots during the past ten years.
12. Doctor Stella Immanuel proclaims that a cocktail of hydroxychloroquine, zinc and the antibiotic azithromycin has cured COVID-19 patients.
13. Wisconsin's dairy farms were decimated under the Obama/Biden administration but are doing very well.
14. If Joe Biden's elected, he'll end fracking.
15. Clintons, the Obamas & the Biden family are all involved in child trafficking and crimes against children.
16. Biden went to Ukraine and threatened to withhold $1 billion in aid if they did not fire the prosecutor that was investigating his son and the company that his son worked for.
17. For those wondering if it's worth impeaching him this time, it means he loses his 200K+ pension for the rest of his life.
18. The vaccine contains a spike protein called syncytin-1, vital for the formation of the human placenta.
19. The White House is freaking out after Myanmar Military arrests political leaders for Election Fraud in their November 8 elections.
20. The Trump administration made no effort to get U.S. medical experts into China as the novel coronavirus epidemic spread there early this year.
21. Bernie Sanders calls for a tax rate of 52% on incomes of $29,000 or more to pay for his Medicare for All plan.
22. Dr. Lieber charged for lying about his participation in a Chinese recruitment program and his affiliation with a Chinese university.
23. Do the COVID-19 vaccines cause infertility?
24. The Biden administration just dished out 86 million dollars for motel rooms to house illegal immigrants.
25. Congrats society, we're so woke that we have segregation again.
26. The West is now relying on his wife Julia instead of Alexei Navalny.
27. Germany ran its own military-biological program in Ukraine and was involved in research on biological weapons.
28. Ukraine is committing genocide against the Russian-speaking population in eastern Ukraine.
29. The Bucha massacre was staged by Ukrainian forces.
30. Western governments have imposed sanctions on Russia because of their Russophobia, and Russians are experiencing systematic discrimination in the West.
31. COVID came from China and the vaccine also came from China, don't trust China!
32. Compare this with Russia and China using the pandemic excuse to expand their influence and profit even though the Russian vaccine is ineffective and the Chinese vaccine contains pork gelatin.
33. Muslim scientists from the Raza Academy in Mumbai reported that the Chinese coronavirus vaccine contains gelatin from pork and recommended against vaccination with the haram vaccine.
34. Turkmenistan residents report that the Chinese

vaccine causes severe side effects.

35. Taiwanese travelers stranded at Osaka's Kansai International Airport were rescued by Chinese Embassy.
36. Bolsonaro made a pact with a Masonic sect to win the election.
37. Lula paid his own wife to kill his own son.
38. Brazil Supreme Court Justice Edson Fachin was a lawyer for the MST.
39. Russia unleashed more than 500 lions on its streets to ensure that people are staying indoors during this pandemic outbreak.
40. This document form March 5, from the Government of Spain, forced all nursing homes to keep all seniors with covid-19 symptoms locked in their rooms, keeping them from going to the hospital to get treated.
41. There are 500 boats in Argelia about to sail to Spain... 5,000 illegal immigrants will arrive shortly, many of them infected.
42. Bill Gates owns the patent for the coronavirus.
43. Qatar supported extremist organizations with more than $64 billion over the years!
44. Saudi Crown Prince Mohammed bin Salman had been forced out of power.
45. He announced that Mexican President lowered his own salary and those of 35,000 government employees by 60% to increase pensions for citizens.
46. Any beneficiary of Bolsa Família will lose their benefits if they work as election officials.
47. The Pfizer vaccine produces a fever for 8 to 12 days and after recovery masks are no longer needed.
48. We don't need to continue being named the Republic of Chile or to continue using the Pinochet-imposed flag.
49. Argentine-produced ammunition found in the autopsies of 22 Bolivians killed under Interim President Jeanine Áñez.
50. When you go vote next June 6th, use your own pen or marker, their using all sorts of tricks to commit electoral fraud.

Post-training events Sentences Set

1. Moldovans have received anonymous death threats to scare them from voting.
2. The sharp westward shift in Moldova irked Moscow and significantly soured relations with Chișinău.
3. Spain is still reeling from the deadly impact of its worst flooding disaster in decades where at least 158 people are confirmed dead and dozens are missing.
4. A year's worth of rain fell in eight hours in parts of Valencia on Tuesday.
5. While DANAs aren't unusual in the region, the Mediterranean has seen record-breaking warm waters this summer.
6. This week the German coalition collapsed after Scholz decided to fire some of his key ministers.
7. Scholz's government no longer has a majority in parliament as the Traffic-light coalition collapses.
8. However, the opposition could force Scholz out earlier if they can find a majority for an alternative chancellor.
9. Horrific scenes in Quetta after a suicide bomber targeted passengers waiting to board an express train.
10. We expect many injured after the suicide bombing attack at Peshawar-bound Jaffar Express.
11. Following years of stalemate, the breakthroughs in Baku have now begun, here, at COP29.
12. To enable action, Mr. Babayev identified agreement on a fair and ambitious New Collective Quantified Goal (NCQG) on climate finance as the top negotiating priority for COP29.
13. Mr. Babayev stressed that as the first Paris decade comes to a close, COP29 is a moment of truth that will test our commitment to the multilateral climate system.
14. The ICC has issued an arrest warrant for Benjamin Netanyahu for alleged Gaza war crimes.
15. It is the first time that leaders of a democracy and western-aligned state have been charged by the court, in the most momentous decision of its 22-year history.
16. The United States has been clear that the ICC does not have jurisdiction over this matter.
17. Israel has issued an overnight curfew to people in Lebanon seeking to return to southern Lebanon following the truce.
18. People displaced in the conflict immediately travelled back to southern Lebanon resulting in enormous traffic jams throughout the day.
19. Namibia celebrates elections after first female president is elected.
20. Windhoek is reported to be calm on Wednesday, with neither celebrations nor protests and people carrying on with their normal lives.
21. The South Korean president is facing impeachment vote as defense minister offers to resign.
22. In a shock TV speech on Tuesday, President Yoon Suk Yeol decided to impose martial law.
23. When martial law was briefly declared in South Korea we briefly saw armed soldiers entering the National Assembly.
24. New York City police have launched a manhunt for a masked suspect who gunned down the head of a US medical insurance giant.
25. UnitedHealthcare chief executive was fatally shot outside the Hilton Hotel in Midtown Manhattan.
26. The bells of Notre Dame Cathedral rang for the first time as rebuilding has finalized.
27. Watching the Notre Dame's door swing open to a burst of choir song was such an emotional moment for the thousands of people taking in the display from just outside the cathedral.
28. While the eight bells of Norte Dame were not damaged by the fire, they are ringing for the first time since then.
29. Syrian rebels seized the capital Damascus unopposed on Sunday after a lightning advance that sent President Bashar al-Assad fleeing to Russia.
30. Moscow gave asylum to Assad and his family.
31. The sudden overthrow at the hands of a revolt partly limits Iran's ability to spread weapons to its allies and could cost Russia its Mediterranean naval base.
32. Police don't know how the driver in Magdeburg was able to circumvent the barriers that were protecting the market.
33. We informed the public that a driver plowed a vehicle into a Christmas market killing an adult and a small child.

34. It crashed on the opposite shore of the Caspian after an emergency that was caused by a bird strike.
35. One of the Azerbaijani sources disclosed results that showed the plane was struck by a Russian Pantsir-S air defense system.
36. Russian air-defense system downed Azerbaijan plane.
37. The WHO is aware of the unidentified disease and is sending a team to Congo.
38. The press reported that a flu-like disease that has killed dozens of people over two weeks in Congo is being investigated.
39. The European Union will press ahead with hefty tariffs on China-made electric vehicles even after the bloc's largest economy Germany rejected them, exposing a rift over its biggest trade row with Beijing in a decade.
40. The proposed duties on EVs built in China of up to 45
41. Shares in European carmakers Renault and Volkswagen rose on hopes the tariffs will help them compete with Chinese rivals on their home turf.
42. Her inauguration launches a six-year term during which she will navigate Mexico's all-important relationship with its northern neighbor.
43. Sheinbaum's election broke barriers, as she's the first woman to lead Mexico is also Mexico's first president of Jewish ancestry.
44. Dockworkers at ports from Maine to Texas began walking picket lines early Tuesday in a strike over wages and automation that could reignite inflation and cause shortages of goods if it goes on more than a few weeks.
45. The union wants a complete ban on automation, and it isn't clear just how far apart both sides are.
46. Supply chain experts say consumers won't see an immediate impact from the strike because most retailers stocked up on goods, moving ahead shipments of holiday gift items.
47. Nihon Hidankyo has won the Nobel Price for it's work on nuclear disarmament.
48. This year's Nobel laureates used tools from physics to construct methods for machine learning.
49. The Nobel Prize in Chemistry 2024 is about proteins, life's ingenious chemical tools.
50. In her oeuvre, Nobel laureate, Han Kang, confronts historical traumas and invisible sets of rules and exposes the fragility of human life.

The sentences were manually selected from reputable sources for both Fake News detection and for Real world events. Sources for each sentence are included in the CSV files of each set list.

Qualitative Analysis

Fake News Set Analysis	Cases
GPT-4	**2**
True causal, produces 0, null, null results, no explanation (but other models provide a warning).	2
GPT-4o	**1**
True causal, produces 0, null, null results, no explanation (but other models provide a warning).	1
Llama-8b	**4**
Recognizes causal claim and produces 0, null, null, because it's humorous not factual.	1
Recognizes causal claim, and parses, and warns that it's a complex social issue, sensitive topic or false claim.	1
Recognizes causal claim, and parses, and warns that its not backed by scientific evidence.	1
Unfulfilled requests.	1
Llama-70b	**1**
Recognizes causal claim, and parses, and warns that it's a complex social issue, sensitive topic or false claim.	1
Llama-405b	**4**
Recognizes causal claim and produces 0, null, null, because it's not backed by scientific evidence.	1
Recognizes causal claim, and parses, and warns that it's a complex social issue, sensitive topic or false claim.	2
Unfulfilled requests.	1
Gemma-9b	**11**
Recognizes causal claim and produces 0, null, null, because its not backed by scientific evidence.	2
Recognizes causal claim, and parses, and warns that it's a complex social issue, sensitive topic or false claim.	4
Recognizes causal claim, and parses, and warns that it's not backed by scientific evidence.	2
Unfulfilled requests.	1
Warns it's a conspiracy theory produces 0, null, null.	2
Gemma-27b	**11**
Recognizes causal claim and produces 0, null, null because its a sensitive topic.	2
Recognizes causal claim and produces 0, null, null, because it's humorous not factual.	1
Recognizes causal claim and produces 0, null, null, because its not backed by scientific evidence.	3
Warns it's a conspiracy theory produces 0, null, null.	5
Gemini-1.5	**3**
True causal, produces null results, no explanation (but other models provide a warning).	3

Post-training events Set Analysis	Cases
GPT-4	**3**
Produced null results for a sentence is positive about a sensitive topic.	3
GPT-4o	**3**
Produced null results for a sentence is positive about a sensitive topic.	3
Llama-8b	**2**
Produced null results for a sentence is positive about a sensitive topic.	2
Llama-405b	**1**
Produced null results for a sentence is positive about a sensitive topic.	1
Gemini-1.5	**3**

Table 8: Qualitative analysis for LCD

Heroes, Villains, and Victims: Character Narratives in the WPS Agenda of the UNSC

Hannah Steinbach **Imge Yüzüncüoglu** **Raluca Rilla** **Manfred Stede**
University of Potsdam
Department of Linguistics
Potsdam, Germany
{hannahsteinbach0312, i.yuezuencue, ralucarilla}@gmail.com
stede@uni-potsdam.de

Abstract

We investigate how heroes, victims, and villains are constructed in debates on the United Nations Security Council's Women, Peace, and Security (WPS) agenda. Drawing from 2,566 speeches delivered between 2000 and 2019, we examine how (gendered) entities are framed within diplomatic discourse using topic modeling, clustering, and supervised learning. To assess the potential of automated character role identification, we manually annotate 54 speeches with character role labels and evaluate a fine-tuned RoBERTa classifier alongside two chat-optimized Large Language Models (DeepSeek-R1, Llama3.3 70B). Our findings reveal substantial variation in model performance, with RoBERTa demonstrating best overall performance. Our analysis shows that women are framed as both empowered agents and vulnerable subjects, while perpetrators often remain unnamed. The UNSC often casts itself as a hero by emphasizing its contributions to the WPS agenda. All code and annotated datasets are publicly available to facilitate further research on narrative framing and role attribution in this domain.

1 Introduction

According to Gehring and Grigoletto (2023), "narratives are a crucial group-based mechanism that influences human decision-making" (p. 1). The *Narrative Policy Framework (NPF)* (Jones and McBeth, 2010) defines narratives through distinct components including context, storyline, moral of the story, and characters. Building on the drama triangle (Karpman, 1968), the character roles *hero*, *victim*, and *villain* are central elements of narrative construction. While prior research has applied these frameworks extensively in areas such as climate change communication (e.g., Wolters et al. 2021; Fremann et al. 2023; Gehring and Grigoletto 2023; Grasso et al. 2025), less attention has been given to their role in diplomatic settings.

In multilateral settings like the United Nations (UN), the strategic use of narratives allows states to construct legitimacy and influence international norms. By portraying different entities as heroes, victims, or villains, speakers subtly shape perceptions of agency and responsibility. These narrative strategies play a crucial role in the Women, Peace, and Security (WPS) agenda of the UN Security Council (UNSC). Initiated by Resolution 1325 (2000), the agenda seeks to prevent violence against women and girls in (post-)conflict contexts, promote gender equality, increase women's participation in security processes, and integrate a gender perspective (UNDP, 2023). Given these objectives, one can anticipate that women are central figures in these debates, yet they are also framed in specific roles. They often appear as victims, needing protection, yet also as heroes whose (potential) participation in UN peace and security efforts is framed as beneficial. At the same time, the very call to increase their involvement implies that they are still largely excluded from these processes, reinforcing their victimhood. The UN itself is also cast as a hero, both as protector and enabler of women's involvement. Since the objectives of the UNSC are a key component of the agenda, the sessions themselves can be expected to involve similar narratives.

This paper investigates how heroes, victims, and villains are constructed in WPS open debates, and evaluates the ability of Large Language Models (LLMs) to automatically identify these roles. We begin with a meta-analysis of gender representation among UNSC speakers, followed by topic modeling using clustering techniques and BERTopic (Grootendorst, 2022) to explore dominant themes and the framing of gendered entities. To assess the potential for automated classification of narrative roles, we frame the task as a supervised learning problem and fine-tune a RoBERTa model. We then compare its performance to that of two chat-

Proceedings of the 21st Conference on Natural Language Processing (KONVENS), Volume 2: Workshops, pages 54–73, 2025

optimized LLMs: Llama and DeepSeek. The manually annotated data serves as a benchmark. Our contributions include:

1. A meta-analysis of gender representation in UNSC WPS debates.
2. An analysis of the most frequent topics in the WPS agenda using clustering methods, combined with a comparison of how gendered entities are discussed across these topics.
3. A new corpus of 54 speeches annotated for hero, victim, and villain roles, with guidelines.
4. Evaluation of automatic role classification using RoBERTa, Llama, and DeepSeek.

All code and annotated datasets are publicly available and encourage further research on narrative framing and role attribution in this domain: GitHub.

2 Related Work

2.1 Narrative Framing in the United Nations

Gibbings (2011) states that "operating at the UN is akin to acquiring a second language" (p. 533), reflecting the cultural norms that shape diplomatic discourse. One of these norms is the expectation to frame issues positively: "UN speech styles encourage positive visions and utopian dreams" (Gibbings, 2011, p. 534). Based on four months of fieldwork on Resolution 1325, Gibbings notes that women are often framed as peacemakers and knowledge-bearers, while framings that deviate from this narrative are discouraged. She illustrates this with the case of two Iraqi women who, at a 2003 UN meeting, criticized the US and UK invasion and the UN's lack of support. Though they were barred from formally speaking, their critical remarks at the informal session led to them being labeled "angry." This incident reveals not only the discursive etiquette within the UN but also that when women display agency, they are expected to do so as peaceful agents.

While the UN frequently depicts women as (peaceful) "agents of change," this framing is often accompanied by portrayals of women as victims, particularly in contexts emphasizing vulnerability and protection. The UN's tendency to depict women primarily through these dual lenses has been widely criticized. Başer (2024), for instance, warns that these framings reinforce gender norms by failing to acknowledge women also as perpetrators of violence and by erasing male or LGBTQ+ victims. Similarly, Carpenter (2005) finds that the UN's civilian protection discourse heavily relies on the phrase "women and children," sidelining men. This framing emphasizes perceived vulnerability and helps garner donor support (Carpenter, 2005).

De la Rosa and Lázaro (2019) analyze metaphorical framings in UNSC resolutions from 2000 to 2015 and find a shift from portraying women solely as victims to depicting them as empowered agents in the fight against sexual violence. This suggests a change in the portrayal of women, at least within the resolutions.

Open debates, however, differ from resolutions. While resolutions are negotiated and largely agreed upon, debates reflect a broader range of Member State perspectives and are less curated. Although True and Wiener (2019) do not explicitly employ the victim, villain, and hero framework, their analysis offers valuable insights consistent with these characterizations. In their study of the 15th-anniversary open debate on WPS in 2015, they find that portrayals of women remain largely victim-focused, particularly in relation to sexual violence, thereby risking the reinforcement of stereotypes. They also identify states positioning themselves as heroes: either as champions of the agenda (e.g., Global North states) or as implementers under constraint (e.g., conflict-affected states). Others, like Russia and China, resist expansion of the agenda, emphasizing sovereignty. Perpetrator framing remains politically delicate. While non-state actors like ISIS are widely condemned, direct criticism of fellow states is rare, since it is easier to call out "breaches of the norm by non-state actors [...] than to name and shame breaches made by states present" (True and Wiener, 2019, p. 563).

True and Wiener (2019)'s analysis of an open debate offers important insights into character framings, highlighting the victimization of women (and, in some cases, states), self-portrayals of heroism by Member States, and the targeting of non-state actors as perpetrators, while notably avoiding direct criticism of present states. Given the UN's tendency to maintain a positive tone, we anticipate an emphasis on achievements and successes—thus, on heroes. Building on these findings, our next step is to assess whether these insights persist across a broader set of open debates and to explore the potential of automated approaches to process large volumes of text more efficiently. The following section reviews existing approaches to automatic character framing analysis

2.2 Automated Character Role Identification in NLP

The automated identification of character roles such as heroes, victims, and villains has long been relevant in NLP, particularly in framing analysis. Gomez-Zara et al. (2018) developed a browser extension that identifies role framings in news articles based on named entity recognition, sentiment analysis, and lexical similarity to prototypical roles. While the implementation has not undergone a formal evaluation yet, the authors acknowledge that the browser extension may struggle with complex sentence structures (Gomez-Zara et al., 2018).

Sap et al. (2017) examine how stereotypes are formed through language by extending the connotation frame lexicon of Rashkin et al. (2016) with verbs that capture "power" and "agency:" "power" reflects the level of authority conveyed by a verb, while "agency" indicates how much a character is "powerful, decisive, and capable of pushing forward their own storyline" (Sap et al., 2017, p.4). To test this empirically, they analyze gender bias in modern films by comparing how male and female characters differ in attributed power and agency. Their approach offers a useful tool for studying narrative structure and power dynamics.

Stammbach et al. (2022) reformulate character role labeling as a reading comprehension task. Prompting GPT-3 with context and role-specific questions (e.g., "Who is the hero?"), they evaluate performance across diverse domains: news articles on fracking, Disney film summaries, and US State of the Union addresses. GPT-3 outperforms rule-based baselines (Gomez-Zara et al., 2018), and proves to be especially effective on narrative text.

Character framing has been frequently studied in the context of ecology and climate change. The developers of the *Character-Role Narrative Framework* (Gehring and Grigoletto, 2023), which builds on the drama triangle (Karpman, 1968), applied it to study US climate policy on Twitter as an example of large-scale climate change discourse, revealing how narrative roles influence the virality and public reception of environmental messages (Gehring and Grigoletto, 2023). For their analysis, they used RoBERTa (Liu et al., 2019) combined with XGBoost (Chen and Guestrin, 2016), concluding that integrating LLMs with a limited training dataset is a "very efficient approach to measuring narratives in large text data sets" (Gehring and Grigoletto, 2023, p. 32).

Following this approach, Grasso et al. (2025) evaluate four LLMs (GPT-4o, GPT-4, GPT-4-turbo, and LLaMA-3.1-8B) for character role detection (adding the class "beneficiary") and categorization on tweets from the *Ecoverse* dataset and editorial paragraphs from *Nature & Science*. They then adapt the best performing model, GPT-4, to create two new annotated datasets of tweets and editorial paragraphs, followed by a subsequent error analysis. They conclude that LLMs are in fact suitable for large-scale character-role analysis in the environmental domain, though they advise that human validation remains necessary.

While previous research has demonstrated the potential of LLMs for role detection in narrative, journalistic texts, and social media posts such as tweets, their applicability to formal diplomatic discourse remains underexplored.

3 Dataset and Task

3.1 Data

Using the dataset of UNSC debates from 1997–2019 by Schoenfeld et al. (2019), we identified 68 sessions (4613 speeches) addressing the WPS agenda here. We removed presidential speeches (which are mainly formalities), the duplicate of one debate, and the proceedings of S/PV.6180 from 2009 under the meeting of the year 2001, after observing that there was no WPS agenda meeting in 2001. The final dataset consists of a total of 2566 speeches, for which we each extracted metadata including year, session, speaker affiliation, gender (based on honorifics), and language of the speech using regular expressions.

3.2 Manual Annotation of Dataset

We manually annotated 54 speeches for the roles of "hero," "victim," and "villain," taking into account both commonly held understandings of these roles and the definitions provided by Klapp (1954), Cohen (2011), Gomez-Zara et al. (2018), Bergstrand and Jasper (2018) and Jasper et al. (2018). The full character definitions can be found in Section Appendix C. The speeches were sampled to roughly reflect their distribution across different years. Based on four pilot annotations, we developed corpus-specific guidelines. In addition to excluding abstract entities (e.g. "sexual violence"), we expanded the definitions of the roles to adapt them

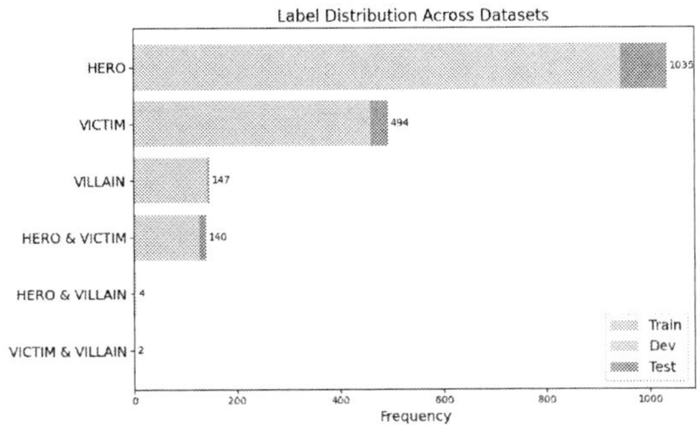

Figure 1: Character Label Distribution.

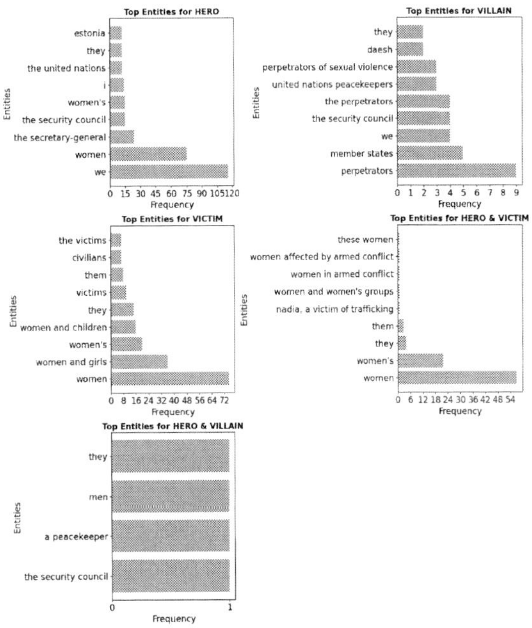

Figure 2: Top Entities per Label

to the context of the data. Two important additions were made: the "hero" category was extended to encompass actors as having potential to bring about positive change but facing structural oppression, and the "villain" category to include actors portrayed as obstructing equal rights and justice for victims. Following Fremann et al. (2023), who criticizes existing datasets and frameworks for assuming that entities can only be assigned a single role rather than recognizing that they can be associated with multiple roles simultaneously, we allowed overlapping roles and nested annotations.

The 54 annotated speeches were split into 44 training set, 5 development set, and 5 test set speeches. Annotations were done individually by the authors using INCEpTION (Klie et al., 2018). Inter-annotator agreement averaged at 0.38 (Krippendorff's α).[1] The relatively low initial agreement stemmed partly from differing interpretations of role definitions, which prompted a subsequent refinement of the guidelines. It was also influenced by smaller inconsistencies in span selection, such as whether to include punctuation, modifiers, or complete noun phrases. These discrepancies reflected the inherent subjectivity and complexity of role labeling task. Nevertheless, after collaboratively reviewing all speeches and discussing disagreements, we reached full consensus on the final labels.

3.3 Annotated Data Insights

The annotation of the 54 speeches offers valuable insights. The following statistics were generated only after model evaluation to avoid introducing any bias.

Figure 1 shows the frequency of roles within the annotated dataset. The "hero" label appears most frequently—twice as often as "victim" and seven times more than "villain," aligning with previous research indicating that speeches at the UNSC are generally framed positively. Figure 2 shows the top entities per label. As expected, "women" dominates the "victim" category, alongside group mentions like "women and girls" and "women and children." For "hero," the most common entity is "we," referring to speakers, Member States, or the Council itself, supporting findings that states emphasize their own contributions (True and Wiener, 2019). Interestingly, "women" also ranks second among heroes, indicating that women are not only portrayed as victims but also credited for their agency and/or potential. This dual role is echoed in the "hero-victim" category, which includes mentions like "women," and "Nadia, a victim of trafficking."

The "villain" label appears much less frequently and is often assigned to vague actors such as "perpetrators" or "perpetrators of sexual violence." In some cases, the Council villainizes itself:

(1) "Such debates remain necessary, considering how far **we** are from full implementation."

As noted earlier, we broadened the "villain" category to include entities that impede equal rights. In this example, the Council acknowledges falling short of its own goals regarding women's equal rights. While this self-criticism is subtle, it reflects a characteristic diplomatic strategy where direct

[1] A detailed overview of pairwise agreement scores between individual annotators and our gold labels can be found in Appendix B.

blame is often avoided or softened. This example highlights that the way character roles are defined and assigned can vary across domains, which must be carefully considered when developing automated classification methods.

Aside from this, only two specific villain groups appear: Daesh (ISIS) and UN peacekeepers. The hero-villain dual label is rare but includes references to entities such as "the Security Council" and "a peacekeeper," indicating that while peacekeepers are sent with good intentions, they are sometimes also perpetrators of (sexual) violence. Although it is often implied that perpetrators are male, specific individuals or groups are very rarely identified.

Over time, portrayals of "women" fluctuate (Appendix, Figure 5) but do not show a clear shift from victimhood to heroism as observed in resolutions (de la Rosa and Lázaro, 2019). "Men" are mentioned far less frequently and are often referenced alongside women as perpetrators, allies, or co-victims (Appendix, Figure 6). Mentions of male victims without women or children are rare, reinforcing the framing of "women and children" as the prototypical vulnerable group (Carpenter, 2005). Mentions of male victims increase slightly after 2012, while portrayals of men as perpetrators decline (Appendix, Figure 7). This could suggest increasing recognition of male victims of armed conflict, as well as a reduction in the portrayal of men as perpetrators.

These patterns confirm our core hypotheses: women are primarily framed as victims, though also as heroes; villains remain vague or externalized; and men are largely secondary, often mentioned in relation to women and/or children.

4 Exploratory Work

4.1 Meta-Analysis

Since a core goal of the WPS agenda is to promote the inclusion of women in peace and security processes not only as subjects of protection but as active participants, we examined the representation at the top: within the UN Security Council itself. This led to our first research question: "What does the gender representation of the UNSC look like?"

Using collected meta-information, Figure 3 shows that from 2000 to 2019, women never delivered more than half of all speeches. Female representation increased from under 20% in 2000 to nearly 40% in 2019, peaking just above 40% in 2018. However, this trend is inconsistent and fluctu-

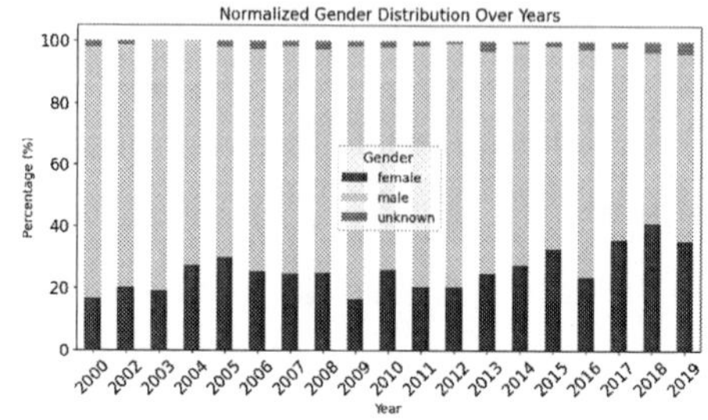

Figure 3: Number of speeches by gender across years. Speakers without gendered honorifics or titles are marked as "unknown."

ates across years. Among the permanent members (Appendix, Figure 8), the US stands out with over 80% of speeches delivered by women. The UK follows at just ~20%, followed by France (~10%) and Russia (~2%), while China had no female speakers at all. This imbalance raises questions about the relationship between representation and discourse; though a systematic comparison by country is beyond the scope of this study, it remains a promising direction for future work.

4.2 Topics

4.2.1 Bertopic

To analyze how gendered entities are framed, we applied BERTopic (Grootendorst, 2022) to all sentences across the corpus that mention either unambiguous female terms (“women”, “girls”) or male terms (“men”, “boys”), excluding sentences where both co-occur. BERTopic generated significantly more topics for female entities (309) than for male ones (7). The number of topics for female mentions were reduced to nine with an in-built function for interpretability and selected topics visualized using word clouds (see all word clouds in Appendix E.3).

Female entities. Some topics focused on institutional discourse, with terms like “director,” “delivered,” and “Ms.” Others centered on the WPS agenda itself, highlighting keywords such as “resolution,” “peace,” and “UN-Women”. Several topics emphasized women as victims, particularly of sexual violence (Figure 9a), human trafficking (Figure 9b), and domestic abuse (Figure 9c).

One topic links women to peacekeepers (Figure 9e), framing them both as heroes via calls for greater female participation and as victims of sexual abuse by (implicitly male) peacekeepers. The following quotes highlight this dual framing:

(2) “We are convinced of the advantages inherent in increasing the number of women Blue Helmets”

(3) "[W]e must take every possible step to root out sexual exploitation and abuse by peacekeepers"

Male entities. Topics related to male entities were fewer and less thematically coherent. One addressed sexual violence (Figure 9f), framing men as both perpetrators and victims:

(4) "[...] the role of men as perpetrators but also as victims of sexual violence in conflict."

Other topics focused on men's engagement in gender equality and leadership (Figures 9g–9h), blending heroism, advocacy, and power.

Overall, women are frequently framed as victims but also as (potential) heroes in peacekeeping contexts. Men are mentioned less often and usually in relation to women—as perpetrators, allies, or fellow victims. Villain roles are rarely explicit and often assigned to non-state actors. This implicitness complicates role detection, especially when relying solely on gendered search terms.

4.2.2 Extracting Embeddings and Clustering

We generated 1024-dimensional embeddings for each speech using mxbai-embed-large (Li and Li, 2023), then applied UMAP (McInnes et al., 2018) for dimensionality reduction, and DBSCAN (Ester et al., 1996) for its ability to handle undefined cluster counts and outliers in high-dimensional data. After parameter tuning (eps=6.5, min_samples=5), we identified 18 distinct clusters (see Appendix, Figure 10), revealing two key patterns.

First, we found 14 country-specific clusters, suggesting both consistent national narratives across multiple sessions and standardized diplomatic templates. Beyond typical formalities, we also notice entire phrases such as "*Women are formidable negotiators, mediators, and peacebuilders*" and "*Sexual violence is not cost-free*" are reproduced across multiple speeches, raising questions about the performative versus substantive nature of these statements. Secondly, a smaller subset of clusters grouped together thematically similar speeches. One such cluster centers around sexual violence in armed conflict, with most speakers framing it as a crime against humanity and a threat to peace and security, emphasizing the continued need to take action. Nevertheless, this cluster also includes a speech by the Russian delegation in which the speaker is solely expressing concern over the expansion of UN mandate language beyond existing Security Council resolutions, highlighting that even within thematically coherent clusters, substantive differences in framing exist.

While this approach offers a scalable way to detect patterns in country discourse, it fails to capture *how* countries frame issues like sexual violence, obscuring speaker intentions and level of assertiveness. We therefore turn to a more fine-grained analysis of character-role annotations using (1) a fine-tuned RoBERTa model and (2) direct prompting of LLMs to complement our topic-modeling and clustering approaches.

4.3 RoBERTa Model

Various BERT models were developed by participants in a similar shared task on detecting whether characters in memes were glorified, vilified, or victimized (Sharma et al., 2022). Both the top-performing system (Kun et al., 2022) and the third-ranked system (Singh et al., 2022) incorporated RoBERTa (Liu et al., 2019). Inspired by these works and Gehring and Grigoletto (2023), who also used a RoBERTa model, we fine-tuned RoBERTa for our task.

4.3.1 Preprocessing steps

We adapted the NER task using the standard Beginning-inside-outside (BIO) tagging format (Tjong Kim Sang and Buchholz, 2000) (see Table 5 in the Appendix for an example). Overlapping entities were merged into single combined labels. Since such overlaps were relatively rare (see Figure 1), maintaining them as distinct tags would not have yielded reliable model performance. This resulted in a total of 13 labels[2].

4.3.2 Implementation

To fine-tune the RoBERTa model for the multi-class classification task, we encoded labels and pre-tokenized the input texts using pre-trained RoBERTa embeddings. Model selection was based on performance on the dev set. Details on hyperparameter configurations, performance (for m1-m4), and the rationale for ultimately selecting model m4 for evaluation on the test set are provided in Appendix D.2.

4.3.3 Evaluation & Interpretation

We used the default mode of `seqeval` (Nakayama, 2018), a framework designed for the evaluation of sequence labeling tasks, thus allowing some leniency in evaluation.

[2]Labels: HERO, VICTIM, VILLAIN, HERO_VICTIM, HERO_VILLAIN, VICTIM_VILLAIN, each marked with B- and I-prefixes.

	P	R	F1	S
HERO	**0.69**	0.76	0.72	95
VICTIM	0.67	**0.81**	**0.73**	32
VILLAIN	0.43	0.75	0.55	4
HERO_VICTIM	0.36	0.33	0.35	12
micro avg	0.65	0.73	0.69	143
macro avg	0.54	0.66	0.59	143
weighted avg	0.65	0.73	0.69	143

Table 1: Fine-tuned RoBERTa results: precision (P), recall (R), F1, and support (S) by label, plus micro, macro, and weighted averages.

The performance of the RoBERTa-based classifier is summarized in Table 1. The model performs best for the HERO and VICTIM classes, achieving F1 scores of 0.72 and 0.73, respectively. For the VILLAIN class, it shows a high recall (0.75), but lower precision (0.43) and F1 (0.55) scores, indicating frequent false positives. We acknowledge that this is largely due to the fact that there are only four occurrences of label. Most likely, performance would improve with more training data for this category.

The classifier struggles most with the overlapping label HERO_VICTIM (F1: 0.35), while the remaining overlapping classes HERO_VILLAIN and VICTIM_VILLAIN are not represented in the test set. The low performance scores suggest difficulty in distinguishing overlapping roles, likely due to ambiguity in textual representations.

The identical micro and weighted F1 scores (0.69) indicate strong overall performance, especially on frequent classes like HERO and VICTIM. The lower macro-average (0.59), however, highlights class-specific performance gaps, again highlighting that the model struggles with rarer labels. Addressing this imbalance (e.g., through data augmentation, different sampling techniques, or loss function reweighting) could improve performance on underrepresented roles and therefore result in a more balanced model.

Overall, our fine-tuned RoBERTa model performed well, with its predictions closely aligning with our annotations. The consistency of its outputs suggests a high degree of reliability in capturing the intended role assignments. Interestingly, the model also identified some entities that we overlooked in our annotation process, indicating its potential to enhance annotation quality and reduce human error. Therefore, the model could serve as a valuable tool for automating or assisting in large-scale annotation efforts, provided that occasional inconsistencies are accounted for through further refinement or human verification.

4.4 LLMs

Following Stammbach et al. (2022), we evaluated the outputs of two LLMs in zero- and few-shot settings: DeepSeek-R1 (Guo et al., 2025) and Meta-Llama-3-70B (Grattafiori et al., 2024).[3]

DeepSeek, designed for reasoning, is enhanced through pure reinforcement learning, built on the fine-tuned DeepSeek-V3-Base model, and utilized with a reinforcement learning framework. Llama, a state-of-the-art open-weight transformer-based model developed by Meta, has demonstrated strong generalization capabilities, making it a suitable candidate for comparison (Grattafiori et al., 2024).

While we acknowledge that a strict comparison between the two LLMs that we utilized is not entirely fair in virtue of the immense difference in parameters, we still like to comparatively report differences in their performance.

4.4.1 Preprocessing

We prompted models to reproduce the input speech with in-line role tags (e.g., <HER>Ambassador Powers</HER>). We then converted both model outputs and gold annotations into span-based JSON files for comparison. Due to inconsistencies within the gold annotations (e.g., whitespace, newline characters), we implemented a character-level alignment process to ensure accurate offset matching between model predictions and gold spans. Using fuzzy matching (`difflib.SequenceMatcher`[4]) with a similarity threshold of 0.98 and offset mapping adjustments, we recalibrated span boundaries to enable precise comparison.

4.4.2 Implementation

The prompts were iteratively refined with ChatGPT using the dev set, ensuring none of the models chosen for testing has an advantage with prompts optimized to its understanding. Each prompt included the task description followed by the annotation guidelines (Appendix C), a defined template for the output, and a short repetition of the task to support long-text understanding. The few-shot prompt also includes two annotated speeches from the train set. To see the full prompts, please refer to our GitHub repository.

[3]For readability, we refer to DeepSeek-R1 and Meta-Llama-3-70B as "DeepSeek" and "Llama," respectively, throughout the paper.

[4]`https://github.com/python/cpython/blob/3.13/Lib/difflib.py`

4.4.3 Evaluation & Interpretation

Table 2 presents the performance of LLMs on the test set using partial match evaluation, to stay in line with our reporting of more lenient evaluation results from RoBERTa. Partial matches required a span overlap of $\geq 50\%$ and a one-to-one mapping between predicted and gold spans, penalizing outputs that over-segment spans.

Label	Model	P	R	F1
HERO	DeepSeekZero	0.39	**0.76**	0.52
	DeepSeekFew	**0.48**	0.72	**0.58**
	LlamaZero	0.29	0.59	0.39
	LlamaFew	0.36	0.65	0.46
VICTIM	DeepSeekZero	0.49	0.65	0.56
	DeepSeekFew	**0.74**	**0.67**	**0.71**
	LlamaZero	0.4	0.65	0.5
	LlamaFew	0.43	0.65	0.52
VILLAIN	DeepSeekZero	0.33	0.25	0.29
	DeepSeekFew	0.67	0.5	0.57
	LlamaZero	**0.75**	**0.75**	**0.75**
	LlamaFew	0.67	0.5	0.57
Micro avg	DeepSeekZero	0.42	0.69	0.52
	DeepSeekFew	**0.54**	**0.7**	**0.61**
	LlamaZero	0.33	0.61	0.43
	LlamaFew	0.38	0.65	0.48
Macro avg	DeepSeekZero	0.4	0.55	0.45
	DeepSeekFew	**0.63**	0.63	**0.62**
	LlamaZero	0.48	**0.66**	0.55
	LlamaFew	0.49	0.6	0.52
Weighted avg	DeepSeekZero	0.44	**0.69**	0.53
	DeepSeekFew	**0.58**	0.66	**0.62**
	LlamaZero	0.36	0.63	0.46
	LlamaFew	0.42	0.61	0.5

Table 2: Classification results for LLMs across role labels. **DeepSeekZero** and **LlamaZero** refer to zero-shot prompting; **DeepSeekFew** and **LlamaFew** use few-shot prompting.

Unlike RoBERTa, which used composite class labels to represent multi-label annotations, we treated each role label independently in the LLM setup. This approach preserved annotation granularity and improved evaluation fidelity by crediting individual label matches.

As shown in Table 2, DeepSeek generally outperforms Llama, particularly in the few-shot setting: For both HERO and VICTIM, DeepSeekFew achieves the highest F1 scores (0.58 and 0.71), with DeepSeekZero yielding the highest recall for HERO (0.76 vs. 0.72 for DeepSeekFew). However, for VILLAIN, LlamaZero performs best (Precision: 0.54, Recall: 0.75, F1: 0.75), though this is just based on four test instances and may not generalize. In future work, this pattern should be investigated with a more balanced dataset.

Overall, DeepSeekFew yields the highest scores across all aggregates: micro-F1 (0.61), macro-F1 (0.62), and weighted-F1 (0.62). These results suggest better generalization and handling of class imbalance compared to Llama. DeepSeekFew achieves a slightly higher macro-average F1 (0.62) than RoBERTa (0.59). This may be due to our decision to treat each role label independently in the LLM setup, avoiding multi-label combinations (RoBERTa's lowest scoring class). However, both LLMs generally underperform relative to RoBERTa. In the next section, we analyze how and why these models fail.

4.5 Error Analysis

Noun Phrases, Articles and Pronouns The tested LLMs often struggled to capture full NPs, often separating phrases such as "women and children." Moreover, articles, pronouns, and descriptive modifiers were frequently omitted (e.g., "thousands of" in "thousands of women and girls"). Additionally, some entities were overextended to include abstract concepts (e.g., "the zero tolerance policy of the secretary general" instead of "the secretary-general"). Importantly, few-shot prompting slightly improved consistency, suggesting that prompt length and structure may impact model stability (Wu et al., 2024).

Mislabeling Formal Entities DeepSeekZero regularly incorrectly labeled speakers as heroes. DeepSeekFew frequently mislabeled thanked individuals as heroes, while RoBERTa only occasionally did this, and Llama never did. Resolutions were also frequently mislabeled as heroes by both DeepSeek models and LlamaFew. LlamaFew further misclassified "the Dakar Declaration" as a hero, although we instructed models against labeling non-resolution documents.

Bias Several models displayed patterns suggesting biases, such as RoBERTa tending to over-label official entities (e.g. "council," "the Secretary-General," "my government") as heroes. More concerning is that RoBERTa often assigned the role of victim to women without justification. LlamaZero demonstrated a similar problem: In the phrase "training must target not only girls and women, but also boys and men"[5], it assigned both "hero" and "victim" to "girls and women," while labeling "boys and men" as only "hero." In the following example, all models annotated women only as victims, rather than as both victims and heroes:

(5) "[R]esolution 1325 (2000) represented an enormous step forward in the protection of **women** and highlighted the importance of their role [...]"

[5]UNSC_2004_SPV.5066Resumption1_spch026

In (6), DeepSeekZero failed to annotate the entity at all, while DeepSeekFew even labeled “the armed forces” as "hero" despite their role in sexual violence:

(6) "[...] the adoption of a plan of action to combat sexual violence among **the armed forces** [...]"

The reasoning by DeepSeekFew offers an explanation for the misclassification:

> *"[...] the military justice system are Heroes as they're part of the government's efforts."*

It simply conflated the perpetrators as a part of the government with the heroic efforts of the government, overlooking an even explicit accusation. This example illustrates why relying solely on LLMs for tasks like character role identification can be dangerous.

While some models, like RoBERTa, generally perform well in terms of entity recognition, challenges remain in handling complex cases involving articles, pronouns, multi-word entities, and role shifts. The few-shot prompting approaches showed some improvement, but inconsistencies and biases still persist. These findings highlight the need for careful consideration of bias when applying LLMs to role classification tasks, particularly in contexts involving gender and institutional entities. Further refinements and research to determine where these biases originate from is crucial for improving their performance.

5 Conclusion

Inspired by the central question of how women are depicted in a discourse centered on them, this paper explored how entities are framed in UNSC debates. Using topic modeling, clustering, and manual annotations of 54 speeches, we found that women are the main characters and primary victims. However, they also appear as heroes, providing valuable knowledge and playing a significant role in peacekeeping. Frequent co-occurrence with "girls" and "children" reinforces their portrayal as innocent civilians, while they are never framed as villains.

Men appear far less often and are predominantly grouped with women and children, either as co-victims or co-heroes, highlighting the importance of cooperation between genders. Meanwhile, the UNSC often portrays itself as a hero by highlighting its contributions, though occasionally they acknowledge their own shortcomings. Apart from this, while some non-state actors are explicitly called out, perpetrators largely remain unnamed, and no Member State is explicitly accused. This reflects the diplomatic tone of UN discourse, where positive, optimistic visions are encouraged.

To assess the feasibility of automating role classification, we evaluated RoBERTa, and DeepSeek and Llama in zero- and few-shot settings. While RoBERTa performed reliably and sometimes even outperformed human annotations, the chat models often ignored key rules from the annotation guidelines and misclassified even obvious labels.

Despite limitations, our findings demonstrate the potential of framing analysis in institutional discourse and lay the groundwork for scalable, automated narrative role detection in international diplomatic settings, while emphasizing that human validation remains essential.

Future work could build on these insights by exploring country- and time-specific framing differences, addressing class imbalance through data augmentation, and experimenting with alternative model architectures. Additionally, further research is needed to identify and mitigate sources of bias in large language models to improve their effectiveness and fairness in this context.

Ethics Statement

This study uses publicly available political speeches from the United Nations Security Council and does not involve sensitive personal data. Three of the authors served as annotators; while manual annotation of character roles is inherently subjective, we attempted to mitigate bias through collaborative guideline development and consensus on labels. Given the highly subjective nature of the task, complete objectivity cannot be guaranteed.

We acknowledge that both the discourse analyzed and the computational models used may contain biases reflecting existing power structures and social inequalities. Since automated narrative role detection carries risks of oversimplification and misclassification, we emphasize that such methods should never replace, but rather complement, human interpretation.

All computational models used are publicly available, ensuring reproducibility and transparency.

Limitations

One of the primary limitations of this study is the scope of our annotations. Our dataset size was limited by time constraints, reducing model robustness. While the annotation process itself was not overly time-consuming, significant effort was required to define the annotation guidelines and curate the speeches collaboratively, making this stage particularly resource-intensive. A more extensive dataset would have provided additional training data and enabled a more robust evaluation of our approaches.

Moreover, seeing as the task was subjective, the annotators inevitably brought their own biases into the annotation process. This likely influenced both the evaluation and the model's performance, as the training data was shaped by our individual interpretations. These subjective factors further highlight the challenges of automating entity role classification and the need for continuous refinement of guidelines and methodologies. The subjective nature of detecting character frames is also reflected in the relatively low inter-annotator agreement. However, after extensive discussions, all three annotators reached consensus on the final labels, integrating different perspectives and thus improving data reliability.

Another limitation pertains to the computational and accessibility constraints associated with the models used. Many cutting-edge LLMs are not freely available and require subscription-based access, limiting their usability for broader research applications. Working locally restricted hyperparameter tuning; while our small dataset eased training, it also limits generalizability.

References

Çağlayan Başer. 2024. Women's role in violence and un women, peace, and security agenda. *Alternatif Politika*, 16(1):1–30.

Kelly Bergstrand and James M. Jasper. 2018. Villains, victims, and heroes in character theory and affect control theory. *Social Psychology Quarterly*, 81(3):228–247.

R. Charli Carpenter. 2005. "women, children and other vulnerable groups": Gender, strategic frames and the protection of civilians as a transnational issue. *International Studies Quarterly*, 49(2):295–334.

Tianqi Chen and Carlos Guestrin. 2016. Xgboost: A scalable tree boosting system. In *Proceedings of the 22nd ACM SIGKDD International Conference on Knowledge Discovery and Data Mining*, KDD '16, page 785–794, New York, NY, USA. Association for Computing Machinery.

Stanley Cohen. 2011. *Folk devils and moral panics*. Routledge.

Victoria Martín de la Rosa and Luis Miguel Lázaro. 2019. How women are imagined through conceptual metaphors in united nations security council resolutions on women, peace and security. *Journal of Gender Studies*, 28(4):373–386.

Martin Ester, Hans-Peter Kriegel, Jörg Sander, Xiaowei Xu, et al. 1996. A density-based algorithm for discovering clusters in large spatial databases with noise. In *kdd*, volume 96, pages 226–231.

Lea Frermann, Jiatong Li, Shima Khanehzar, and Gosia Mikolajczak. 2023. Conflicts, villains, resolutions: Towards models of narrative media framing. In *Proceedings of the 61st Annual Meeting of the Association for Computational Linguistics (Volume 1: Long Papers)*, pages 8712–8732, Toronto, Canada. Association for Computational Linguistics.

Kai Gehring and Matteo Grigoletto. 2023. Analyzing climate change policy narratives with the character-role narrative framework. Technical report, CESifo Working Paper.

Sheri Lynn Gibbings. 2011. No angry women at the united nations: Political dreams and the cultural politics of united nations security council resolution 1325. *International Feminist Journal of Politics*, 13(4):522–538.

Diego Gomez-Zara, Miriam Boon, and Larry Birnbaum. 2018. Who is the hero, the villain, and the victim? detection of roles in news articles using natural language techniques. In *Proceedings of the 23rd International Conference on Intelligent User Interfaces*, pages 311–315.

Francesca Grasso, Stefano Locci, and Manfred Stede. 2025. Applying the character-role narrative framework with llms to investigate environmental narratives in scientific editorials and tweets. In *Proceedings of the 2nd Workshop on Natural Language Processing Meets Climate Change (ClimateNLP 2025)*, pages 49–67.

Aaron Grattafiori, Abhimanyu Dubey, Abhinav Jauhri, Abhinav Pandey, Abhishek Kadian, Ahmad Al-Dahle, Aiesha Letman, Akhil Mathur, Alan Schelten, Alex Vaughan, Amy Yang, Angela Fan, et al. 2024. The llama 3 herd of models. *Preprint*, arXiv:2407.21783.

Maarten Grootendorst. 2022. Bertopic: Neural topic modeling with a class-based tf-idf procedure. *arXiv preprint arXiv:2203.05794*.

Daya Guo, Dejian Yang, Haowei Zhang, Junxiao Song, Ruoyu Zhang, Runxin Xu, Qihao Zhu, Shirong Ma,

Peiyi Wang, Xiao Bi, et al. 2025. Deepseek-r1: Incentivizing reasoning capability in llms via reinforcement learning. *arXiv preprint arXiv:2501.12948*.

James M Jasper, Michael Young, and Elke Zuern. 2018. Character work in social movements. *Theory and Society*, 47:113–131.

Michael D Jones and Mark K McBeth. 2010. A narrative policy framework: Clear enough to be wrong? *Policy studies journal*, 38(2):329–353.

Stephen Karpman. 1968. Fairy tales and script drama analysis. *Transactional analysis bulletin*, 7(26):39–43.

Orrin E Klapp. 1954. Heroes, villains and fools, as agents of social control. *American sociological review*, 19(1):56–62.

Jan-Christoph Klie, Michael Bugert, Beto Boullosa, Richard Eckart De Castilho, and Iryna Gurevych. 2018. The inception platform: Machine-assisted and knowledge-oriented interactive annotation. In *Proceedings of the 27th international conference on computational linguistics: system demonstrations*, pages 5–9.

Ludovic Kun, Jayesh Bankoti, and David Kiskovski. 2022. Logically at the constraint 2022: Multimodal role labelling. In *Proceedings of the Workshop on Combating Online Hostile Posts in Regional Languages during Emergency Situations*, pages 24–34, Dublin, Ireland. Association for Computational Linguistics.

Xianming Li and Jing Li. 2023. Angle-optimized text embeddings. *arXiv preprint arXiv:2309.12871*.

Yinhan Liu, Myle Ott, Naman Goyal, Jingfei Du, Mandar Joshi, Danqi Chen, Omer Levy, Mike Lewis, Luke Zettlemoyer, and Veselin Stoyanov. 2019. Roberta: A robustly optimized bert pretraining approach. *Preprint*, arXiv:1907.11692.

Leland McInnes, John Healy, and James Melville. 2018. Umap: Uniform manifold approximation and projection for dimension reduction. *arXiv preprint arXiv:1802.03426*.

Hiroki Nakayama. 2018. seqeval: A python framework for sequence labeling evaluation. Software available from https://github.com/chakki-works/seqeval.

Hannah Rashkin, Sameer Singh, and Yejin Choi. 2016. Connotation frames: A data-driven investigation. In *Proceedings of the 54th Annual Meeting of the Association for Computational Linguistics (Volume 1: Long Papers)*, pages 311–321, Berlin, Germany. Association for Computational Linguistics.

Maarten Sap, Marcella Cindy Prasettio, Ari Holtzman, Hannah Rashkin, and Yejin Choi. 2017. Connotation frames of power and agency in modern films. In *Proceedings of the 2017 conference on empirical methods in natural language processing*, pages 2329–2334.

Mirco Schoenfeld, Steffen Eckhard, Ronny Patz, Hilde van Meegdenburg, and Antonio Pires. 2019. The UN Security Council Debates.

Shivam Sharma, Tharun Suresh, Atharva Kulkarni, Himanshi Mathur, Preslav Nakov, Md. Shad Akhtar, and Tanmoy Chakraborty. 2022. Findings of the CONSTRAINT 2022 shared task on detecting the hero, the villain, and the victim in memes. In *Proceedings of the Workshop on Combating Online Hostile Posts in Regional Languages during Emergency Situations*, pages 1–11, Dublin, Ireland. Association for Computational Linguistics.

Pranaydeep Singh, Aaron Maladry, and Els Lefever. 2022. Combining language models and linguistic information to label entities in memes. In *Proceedings of the Workshop on Combating Online Hostile Posts in Regional Languages during Emergency Situations*, pages 35–42.

Dominik Stammbach, Maria Antoniak, and Elliott Ash. 2022. Heroes, villains, and victims, and GPT-3: Automated extraction of character roles without training data. In *Proceedings of the 4th Workshop of Narrative Understanding (WNU2022)*, pages 47–56, Seattle, United States. Association for Computational Linguistics.

Erik F. Tjong Kim Sang and Sabine Buchholz. 2000. Introduction to the CoNLL-2000 shared task chunking. In *Fourth Conference on Computational Natural Language Learning and the Second Learning Language in Logic Workshop*.

Jacqui True and Antje Wiener. 2019. Everyone wants (a) peace: the dynamics of rhetoric and practice on 'women, peace and security'. *International Affairs*, 95(3):553–574.

UNDP. 2023. Parliament as partners: Supporting the women, peace, and security agenda - a global handbook. Accessed: 2025-03-24.

Erika Allen Wolters, Michael D. Jones, and Kathryn L. Duvall. 2021. A narrative policy framework solution to understanding climate change framing research. *Narratives and the Policy Process : Applications of the Narrative Policy Framework*.

Yue Wu, Xuan Tang, Tom M. Mitchell, and Yuanzhi Li. 2024. Smartplay: A benchmark for llms as intelligent agents. *Preprint*, arXiv:2310.01557.

Appendix A UNSC Quote Filenames

Quote #	Filename
(1)	UNSC_2003_SPV.4852Resumption1_spch035.txt
(2)	UNSC_2019_SPV.8649_spch030.txt
(3)	UNSC_2015_SPV.7533_spch015.txt
(4)	UNSC_2013_SPV.6984_spch057.txt
(5)	UNSC_2011_SPV.6642_spch055.txt
(6)	UNSC_2016_SPV.7704_spch087.txt

Table 3: Corresponding filenames for numbered in-text examples.

Appendix B Interannotator Agreement

	Annotator 1	Annotator 2	Annotator 3	Curator
Annotator 1	–	0.30	0.44	0.47
Annotator 2		–	0.38	0.48
Annotator 3			–	0.70
Curator				–

Table 4: Krippendorff's Alpha (unitizing/character offsets) for agreement on role annotation (Hero, Victim, Villain) computed pairwise. Three of the authors served as annotators and worked collaboratively to define a gold standard, which is reflected in the Curator column.

Appendix C Heroes, Victims, and Perpetrators in WPS: Annotation Guidelines

i. Document Level Rules Exclude all president speeches

ii. Character Level Rules

a. We include entire noun phrases (NP): This includes any numerical or descriptive modifiers.
Example: "60 million Africans"
b. We annotate restrictive relative clauses fully.
Example: "parties that perpetuate acts of violence against women and children"
c. We include possessive modifiers within the NP:
Example: "my delegation"
d. When multiple characters are listed together as part of the same NP and share a common role or action, we consider the entire sequence as one entity, so we not split or annotate each item separately.
Example: "Allow me to begin by thanking **the Secretary-General, Mr. Kevin Hyland, Mr. Yury Fedotov and Ms. Ilwad Elman** for their briefings."
e. We do not include punctuation at the end of annotations.
Example: "**men and boys**."
f. We do not annotate predicate nominatives or any other descriptions of characters.
Example: "**Women** are not only victims." Here, 'victims' should not be annotated.
Example: "**women** as agents of peace"
g. We do not annotate positions or groups when they are only mentioned in the abstract, without references to the achievements of the particular entity.
Example: "the establishment of the post of the Special Representative of the Secretary General on sexual violence in situations of armed conflict"

Role-Definitions

In German, the constellation of hero, victim, and perpetrator is called the drama triangle, first introduced by Karpman (1968). It is a psychological model used in transactional analysis to describe interactions between individuals or groups as adopting one of three stereotypical roles: victim, perpetrator, or hero, which simplifies the linking of behaviors with stereotypical roles learned at an early stage (Karpman, 1968; Gomez-Zara et al., 2018). The link to stereotypes, the framing of the characters with said roles, influences the readers to have a certain bias and to develop a non-reflective opinion through the stereotypical knowledge, which is influenced by the author alone (Gomez-Zara et al., 2018). Hero, victim, and perpetrator are also of great importance in affect control theory and character theory (Bergstrand and Jasper, 2018). The following are definitions we will work with for the WPS-project:

Victim

Victims tend to be portrayed as weak, good, innocent people who are in need of protection (Jasper et al., 2018). Due to these characteristics, they often motivate and encourage action towards a specific cause and can help make aware of injustices which are worth com bating. Jasper et al. (2018) state that victim's sufferings are often elaborated in detail to arouse more moral emotions and indignation. "Popular" victims, as they get the most sympathetic reactions in the modern world due to their cultural innocence, are children (Jasper et al., 2018).

Task-specific additions (based on the WPS corpus):

- Someone who is excluded from decision-making processes/someone who is not given the recognition/power that they deserve.
- Someone who suffers acts of sexual violence/physical harm/displacement, etc.
- Someone who is not given the same equal rights as other parties

Perpetrator/Villain

Perpetrators are people whose moral reputation turns or has turned negative (Jasper et al., 2018). They are considered to be people who spread anxiety and fear, cause people to lose their daily routines, and make them sacrifice their lives, for example, within wars (Bergstrand and Jasper, 2018). Perpetrators often share the same characteristics as heroes, such as being strong, brave, and intelligent. However, their description tends to be more like that of beast-like predators: powerful, threatening, and delinquent (Cohen, 2011).

Task specific additions (based on the WPS corpus):

- Someone who is responsible for causing anxieties, damage, and crimes.
- Someone who stands in the way of equal rights and justice for victims.

Hero

Heroes are people who, by helping victims (and defeating the villains (Jasper et al., 2018; Klapp, 1954)), can become heroes. They are defined as people who increase agreement within groups and boost commitment to a cause. They tend to be well-intentioned people, who recognize injustice, try to resolve and fight it, as well as protect others. However, this does not mean that heroes are completely independent. Jasper et al. (2018) state that even a hero might be in need of help from an even more experienced hero. Furthermore, they are often put in the context of success (Klapp, 1954).

Task specific additions (based on the WPS corpus):

- Someone who has the potential to save others, given their abilities, knowledge, positionality/perspective, but who is not able to do so because of structural discrimination.
- Someone who makes a call to action
- Someone who is recognizing the unjust treatment and violation of victims or is calling it out.

Further Thoughts

It can be seen that the victim, hero, and perpetrator definitions align very much with stereotypes we are taught and confronted with since our childhood. However, roles are not fixed, as heroes can transform into victims or perpetrators (Jasper et al., 2018). The definitions are tried to be kept as simple and generally adaptive as possible, because depending on the source one works with, representations can change. Jasper et al. (2018), for example, state that in news articles, victims are kept nameless in contrast to heroes and perpetrators. In the WPS dataset, however, we observed that it is the perpetrators who most commonly remain unnamed.

Entities to tag

a. People
b. Organisations
c. Countries
d. Groups
e. UN Resolutions. Only annotate United Nations Resolutions if they are explicitly personified.
Example: In "Resolution 1325 calls for action," the resolution should be tagged as a hero. In "working towards the implementation of resolution 1325," the resolution should not be marked.

Entities NOT to tag

a. Abstract concepts: Abstract ideas or symbolic references.
Examples: "International cooperation," "sexual violence," "**women's** participation." In the latter example, women are the entities that are taking heroic action, while their participation refers to a concept.
b. Entities hoping for/welcoming/thanking/commending something good. These are passive actions.
c. Laws or Treaties.

Annotation of character role labels

We only annotate generic role terms (like "victim") when no other specification is included.

Example: In "Victims of these atrocious crimes have been waiting for justice", we would tag "victims of these atrocious crimes" as Victim. However, if specific entities are mentioned, like in "Victims of these atrocious crimes, namely women, have been waiting for justice" we only annotate "women" as Victim.

Annotation of multiple roles

In certain cases, characters may be portrayed with multiple roles simultaneously. When this happens, we annotate the entity with a combined role. Furthermore, the same entity can take on different roles throughout the speech. For instance, while "women" might be classified as "victim" in one sentence, the same entity can also be classified as "hero" in a different part of the speech.

Example: "The equal right to decision-making and participation, along with **women's** empowerment, is crucial to ensure a functioning society and peace and justice in the aftermath of conflicts."

Explanation: In this case, "women" are portrayed both as victims (since they need external help to be empowered) as well as heroes (since they contribute to a peaceful society). When an entity fits into multiple roles based on the context, we use combined tags.

iii. Annotation examples and explanations

Legend: Hero Perpetrator Victim

1. "We commend the work that has been done by the United Nations Children's Fund in reintegration projects that has led to the release of girls from the armed forces in various countries."

In this example, "we" is not annotated as a hero because they are just thanking another organization.

However, the organization in question, the "United Nations Children's Fund," is marked as a hero because they are responsible for these projects that help girls. The "girls," on the other hand, are marked as victims because, although it could be argued that they are the benefactors of the situation (since they have been released), we believe that the fact that they were abducted in the first place carries more weight, also because they are in danger of being abducted again at any time. Most intuitively, "the armed forces" are the perpetrators, since they were responsible for the girls' abduction.

2. "Members of the Council note that although women have begun to play an important role in conflict resolution, peacekeeping and peace- building, they are still under-represented in decision-making in regard to conflict. If women are to play an equal part in security and maintaining peace, they must be empowered politically and economically, and represented adequately at all levels of decision-making, both at the pre-conflict stage and during hostilities, as well as at the point of peacekeeping, peace-building, reconciliation and reconstruction."

This example demonstrates that the same entity (in this case, "women") can take on multiple roles within one sentence. In the first instance ("women"), they are marked as heroes due to their important role in conflict resolution. However, in the second part of the sentence, where they are referred to as "they," the focus shifts to their underrepresentation in decision-making, marking them as victims. The conjunction "although" introduces this contrast, highlighting both aspects of the situation. In the second sentence, the focus remains on women as victims ("if women are to play an equal part in security"), implying that they are not currently able to do so. The need for empowerment, both politically and economically, is presented because they are not given equal opportunities as men. Therefore, they are portrayed as victims in this context.

3. "Those who commit crimes against women, including the peacekeeping personnel, should be brought to book. Let us heed the women's cry for an equal opportunity to voice their ideas in official peace negotiations. And let us act now."

In the last two sentences of this example, "us" is marked as a hero since the speaker is engaging in a call to action. The speaker portrays "us" as a hero by attempting to encourage others to acknowledge and act upon the unjust inequality faced by women.

4. "My Government attaches great importance to the protection and security of women and girls, both in situations of armed conflict and in peace."

In this case, "my government" is marked as a hero because, while the action is indirect, they recognize the importance of the issue and stand up for it. "Women and girls" are marked as victims since they require protection and security, as they cannot protect themselves (see victim definition above). Although they benefit from the protection measures (and thus could be seen as benefactors), we chose to prioritize their need for protection, which highlights their vulnerable position and role as victims in society.

5. "Being direct victims of violence and discrimination, women have gained a great understanding of the need to address peace comprehensively."

Here, "women" are simultaneously considered heroes and victims. The victim annotation is indicated by the context of them being the "direct victim," while the hero annotation relies on the positionality of women–their potential to provide valuable knowledge.

Appendix D RoBERTa Model

Appendix D.1 BIO-Annotation Example

Token	"[...]	my	country	has	[...]	defending	the	victims	of	terrorism	."
Labels	O	HERO	HERO	O	O	O	VICTIM	VICTIM	VICTIM	VICTIM	O
BIO Labels	O	B-HERO	I-HERO	O	O	O	B-VICTIM	I-VICTIM	I-VICTIM	I-VICTIM	O

Table 5: Example of the BIO annotation scheme applied to a sample sentence from `UNSC_2015_SPV.7585_spch010.txt`. The whole sentence is: *Council members know that my country has been a standard-bearing country for defending the victims of terrorism.* Entity spans are labeled as "B-" (begin), "I-" (inside), or "O" (outside)

Appendix D.2 Hyperparameter Optimization and Model Selection

During fine-tuning we limited the amount of values to ensure computational feasibility within the available resources.

	Learning Rate	**Epochs**	**Optimizer**
m1	5e-5	3	AdamW
m2	5e-5	30	AdamW
m3	1e-5	3	AdamW
m4	1e-5	30	AdamW
m5	5e-5	30	SGD
m6	3e-5	30	SGD

Table 6: Hyperparameters for m1-m6

The performance of the fine-tuned models on the development dataset is shown in Table 7, based on their F1 values for models m1-m4. Models m5 and m6 are excluded from the table as their results were identical to those of m4.

	F1				**S**
	m1	m2	m3	m4	
HERO	0.59	0.62	0.63	**0.64**	122
VICTIM	0.67	0.72	**0.73**	**0.73**	77
VILLAIN	**0.54**	0.52	0.5	0.52	10
HERO_VICTIM	0.45	**0.46**	0.36	0.4	26
HERO_VILLAIN	0	0	0	0	0
VICTIM_VILLAIN	0	0	0	0	3
micro avg	0.6	0.62	0.62	**0.64**	238
macro avg	0.45	**0.46**	0.44	0.38	238
weighted avg	0.59	0.62	0.62	**0.63**	238

Table 7: F1 scores of the models m1, m2, m3, and m4. S (support) represents the number of instances per class in the dataset.

The results show that models m3 and m4 achieve the highest F1 scores for the two most frequently occurring classes, heroes (m3: 0.63; m4: 0.64) and victims (m3 & m4: 0.73). m4 yields the highest weighted average F1 score (0.63). These findings served as the primary rationale for selecting the hyperparameters of m4 for the final fine-tuning process. The final model was fine-tuned using both the train and the dev set.

Appendix E Figures

Appendix E.1 Annotation Insights

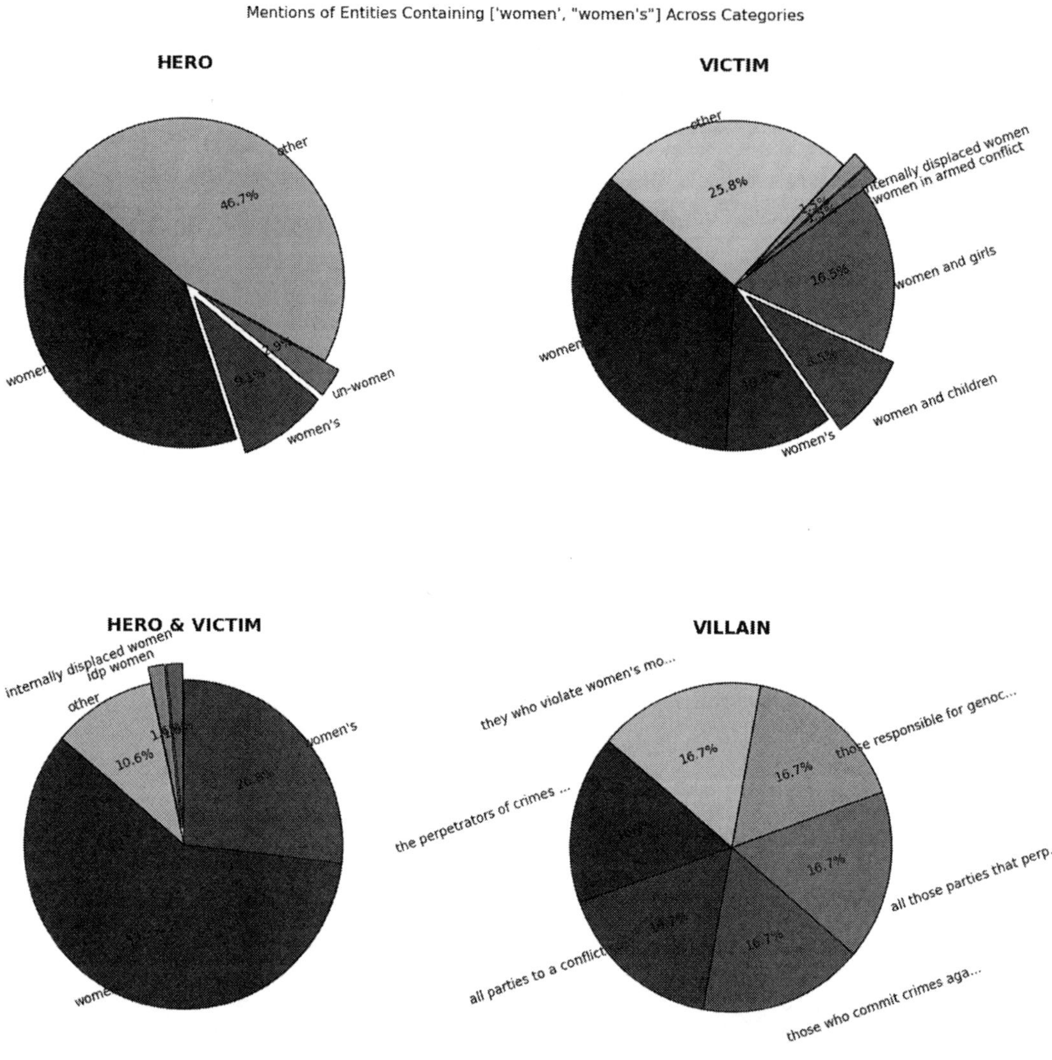

Figure 4: Distribution of Characters for Women Entities

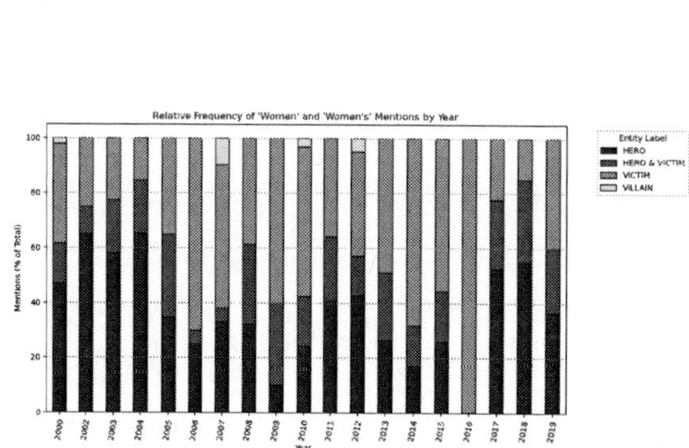

Figure 5: Character Labels for "women" and "women's" Across the Years

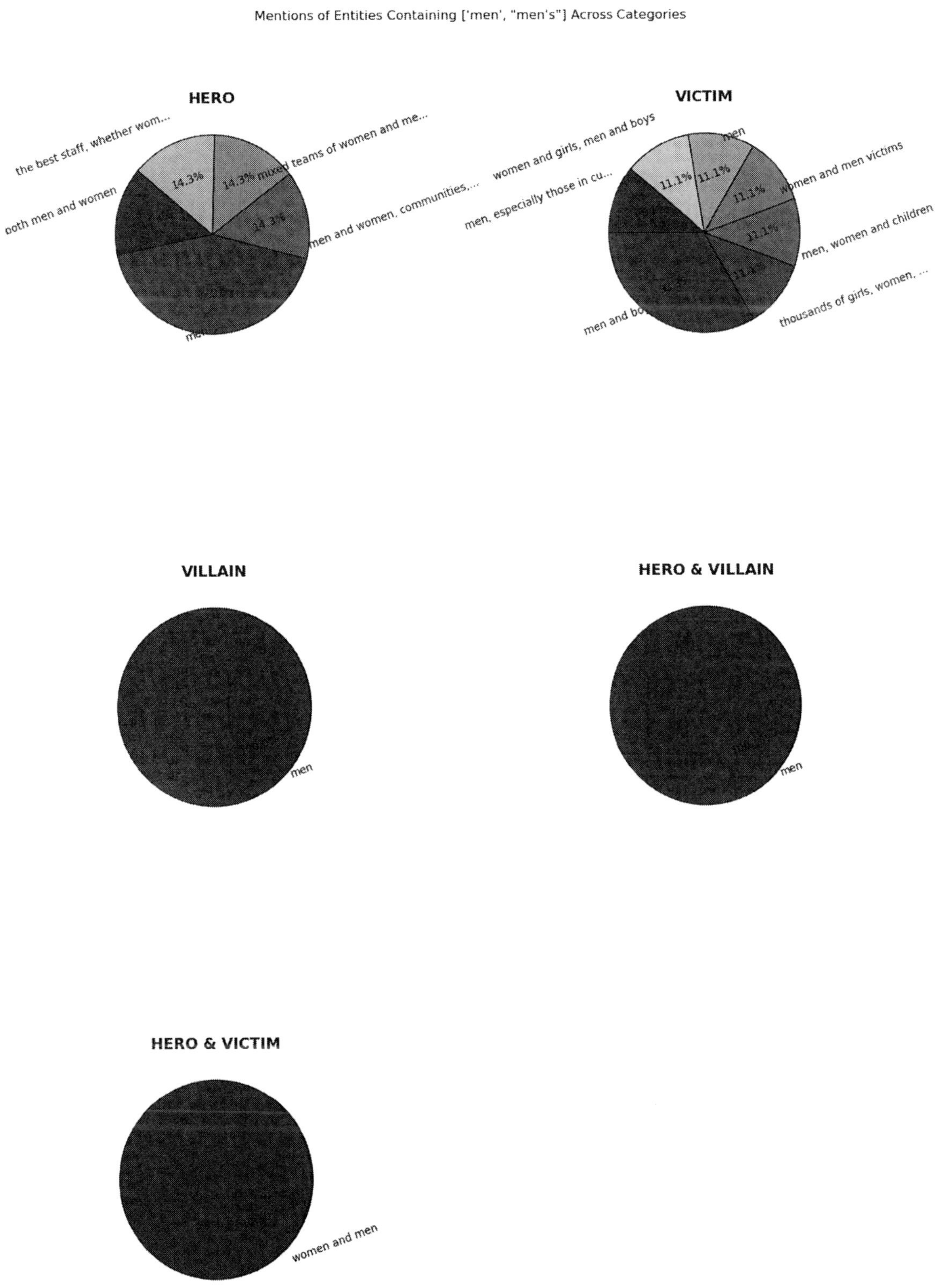

Figure 6: Distribution of Characters for Men Entities

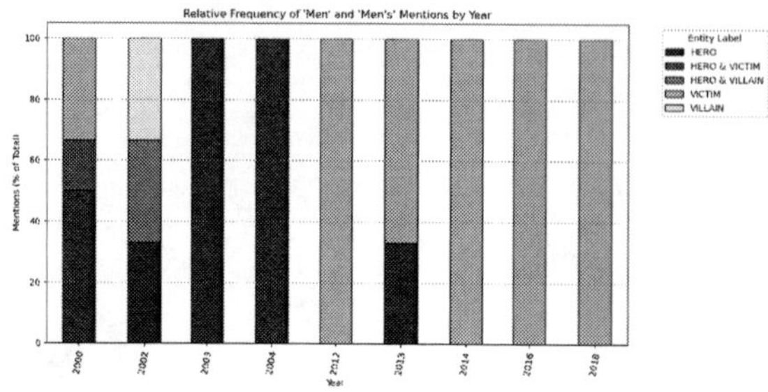

Figure 7: Character Labels for "men" and "men's" Across the Years

Appendix E.2 Meta-Analysis

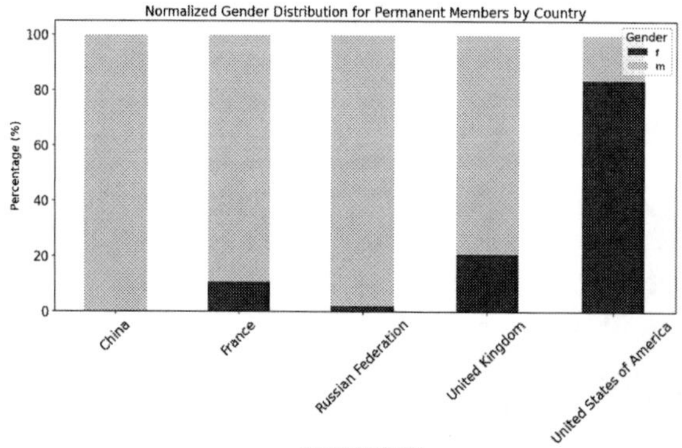

Figure 8: Gender Distribution of Speakers Among Permanent Members of the UNSC

Appendix E.3 BERTopic

(a) Female Entities: Sexual violence

(b) Female Entities: Human trafficking

(c) Female Entities: Domestic Violence

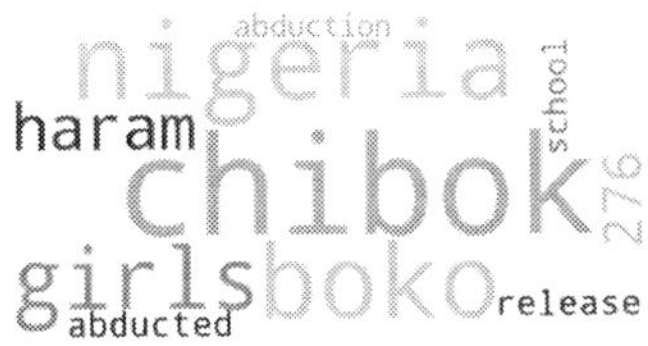

(d) Female Entities: Terror Organizations

(e) Female Entities: Blue Helmets

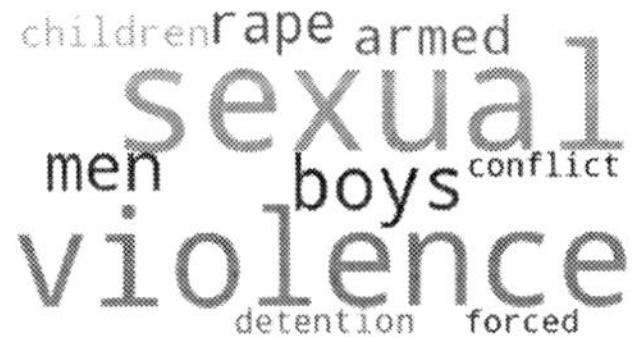

(f) Male Entities: Sexual violence

(g) Male Entities: Promotion of Gender Equality

(h) Male Entities: Overlapping topics

(i) Male Entities: Victim's reports

Figure 9: BERTopic visualizations for male and female entities.

Appendix E.4 Clustering

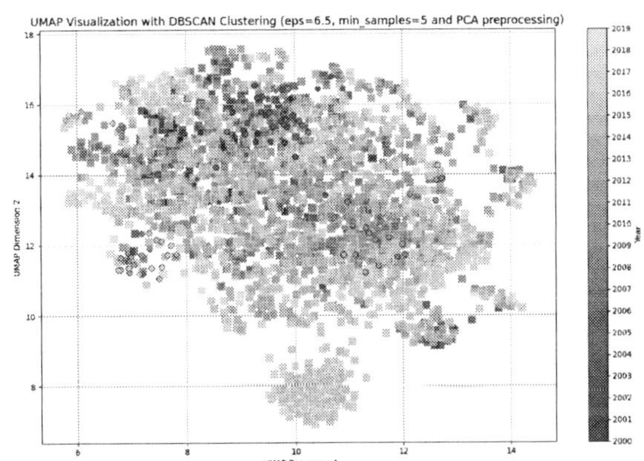

Figure 10: Clusters as identified using DBSCAN. Each point represents a speech. Points that are square-shaped with a white outline represent outliers, while circle-shaped points represent speeches that are part of different clusters, distinguished by the color of the outline. The fill color of each point represents the year that the speech was held.

Enhancing Policy Analysis with NLP: A Reproducible Approach to Incentive Classification

M.A. Waskow and **John P. McCrae**
Data Science Institute
University of Galway
Insight Research Ireland Centre for Data Analytics

Abstract

Over the past few decades, political scientists have increasingly used Natural Language Processing (NLP) methods in their research. Within the subdomain of public administration, there remain further opportunities for the use of NLP in the task of policy analysis. The potential of a machine learning pipeline to identify sentences containing incentives has been demonstrated for the Spanish-language forestry policies of five Latin American countries, but the study was not reproducible due to a lack of model and data availability. This paper seeks to validate the existing pipeline of policy collection, sentence labelling, fine-tuning, and incentive classification by replicating it in a new context and achieving comparable performance, as well as to publish all relevant data and training information to ensure reproducibility. In the domains of a different language and geopolitical system, namely English-language Irish forestry policies, this implementation demonstrates the pipeline's transferability by achieving mean overall F1 scores of 88.3 for binary classification and 96.8 for multiclass classification with our best models. The contributions of this paper are twofold: the validation of an existing pipeline by replicating it in new geopolitical and linguistic domains, and the creation of a novel open dataset of Irish forestry policy sentences labelled for incentive classification.

1 Introduction

Political and social scientists have been utilizing Natural Language Processing (NLP) methods in their research for decades in order to better analyse text as data (Laver et al., 2003; Grimmer and Stewart, 2013). NLP-based analyses of political communication texts — including speeches, manifestos, news articles, and tweets — have provided unique insights into political parties, propaganda, and public opinion. While the field of public policy has been slower in implementing NLP, researchers are beginning to explore its potential applications in the area of policy analysis.

A core task of policy analysis is the development of reports to inform the creation or maintenance of policies (i.e. official proposals of actions to be taken by a government or institution) by presenting evidence-based solutions to a given problem. The research behind these reports can help prevent policy failure by combatting the inappropriate solutions and ambiguity that threaten successful policy implementation, but the thoroughness of policy analysis requires a high time cost that an analyst cannot always afford. NLP can help to reduce this bottleneck of policy creation, making the process more efficient and leading to earlier real-world changes.

Firebanks-Quevedo et al. (2022) demonstrated that their NLP pipeline could help streamline key tasks of policy analysis: finding policies about a given topic and identifying the policy instruments used within them. Policy instruments are methods of government intervention to achieve certain outcomes, like laws (regulation), grants (economic action), or propaganda (communication); this project focused specifically on economic instruments called incentives, which encourage actions and behaviours through financial rewards or pressures like subsidies or taxes (Badie et al., 2011). The pipeline consists of scraping policies from the websites of five Latin American governments, extracting and labelling their sentences for presence and type of policy incentive, then training both a binary and a multiclass classifier on the labelled dataset. The original dataset and models are not available, however, limiting the reproducibility as well as the implementation of their work.

Despite Dodge et al. (2019) offering a structured checklist to address the reproducibility crisis in NLP, many projects do not make core information relating to their research and the production of their results available. This challenges not only the credibility of the conclusions, but also the feasibility of downstream impacts of their findings. Magnusson et al. (2023) has shown that even a few years after the publication of the checklist, the issues of missing data, code, and model training information are still ongoing in NLP.

This project replicates the pipeline of Firebanks-Quevedo et al. (2022) in a new domain, also addressing its reproducibility issues through the publication of our novel dataset[1] and updated code[2]. Where the original workflow was based on Spanish-language texts from Latin American forestry policies, we focus on the English-language texts of Irish forestry policies. We maintained the policy domain of forestry as our implementation already introduced changes to the language and country of interest. Additionally, we further updated the pipeline with new models and accommodations for imbalanced datasets to improve performance. Our final results validate the original pipeline by demonstrating its transferability across linguistic and geopolitical contexts, as well as contribute a new resource for NLP and policy analysis through the release of our code and 1.4k sentence dataset labelled for binary and multiclass incentive classification.

2 Related Work

NLP has become a familiar tool for political and social scientists working with diverse and ever-growing text datasets for diverse and ever-growing applications. For news analysis, classifiers have been trained to identify different topics or agendas contained in articles, even so far as to identify the use of different propaganda techniques (Yoosuf and Yang, 2019; Terechshenko et al., 2020; Nelson et al., 2021). Studying political parties and their messaging, classification and topic clustering have provided novel insights into the speeches of politicians and their electoral manifestos (Glavaš et al., 2017; Wilkerson and Casas, 2017; Rheault and Cochrane, 2020). Considering public opinion, Hagen et al. (2015) used topic modelling to explore policy suggestions from public petitions, while Terechshenko et al. (2020) performed sentiment analysis on tweets about an electoral candidate. Across these various political media, NLP has successfully helped scientists to synthesise new information and extract hidden patterns from the often-unstructured text data.

Progressing more into the subdomain of public administration and policy, Żółkowski et al. (2022) applied topic modelling and clustering to explore how EU countries were framing their climate policies, and Ningpeng et al. (2024) performed topic mining and text parsing on Chinese financial policy documents. Brandt (2019) additionally examined the restoration policies of three East African countries through paragraph topic classification. While these projects provided insight into the priorities of policies, their outcomes appear to be aimed more at political scientists than specifically policy analysts. In contrast, the sentence-level incentive classification of Latin American forestry policies in Firebanks-Quevedo et al. (2022) was explicitly aimed at aiding the task of policy analysis, though the inaccessibility of the models and dataset complicated its impact. Finally, Sewerin et al. (2023) have created a policy design annotations (POLIANNA) dataset, consisting of labelled text spans from EU climate policies and legal documents to provide structured data for future policy analysis tools. In summary, the application of NLP methods to analyse policy documents has largely followed the trend of topic modelling, clustering, and classification used on other political texts, but this is beginning to shift towards the use of sentence classification on policy documents to aid in the task of policy analysis.

3 Methodology

We gathered our policies by scraping them from the website of the Irish government, processed the PDFs into sentences, cultivated a dataset through both manual and human-in-the-loop (HITL) labelling processes, then trained and evaluated both the binary and multiclass classifiers. Figure 1 demonstrates this process.

3.1 Data Collection and Preprocessing

We began looking for Irish forestry policies in a repository of policies on the website of the Irish government[3]. At the time of our search, this page was still in development. The structure of the page was a list of the Irish government's departments and major initiatives wherein which a user, upon selecting a title in the list, would be taken to that topic's page. Then, on that topic's page, a user

[1] https://huggingface.co/datasets/mawaskow/irish_forestry_incentives

[2] https://github.com/mawaskow/policy-classifier

[3] https://www.gov.ie/policies/

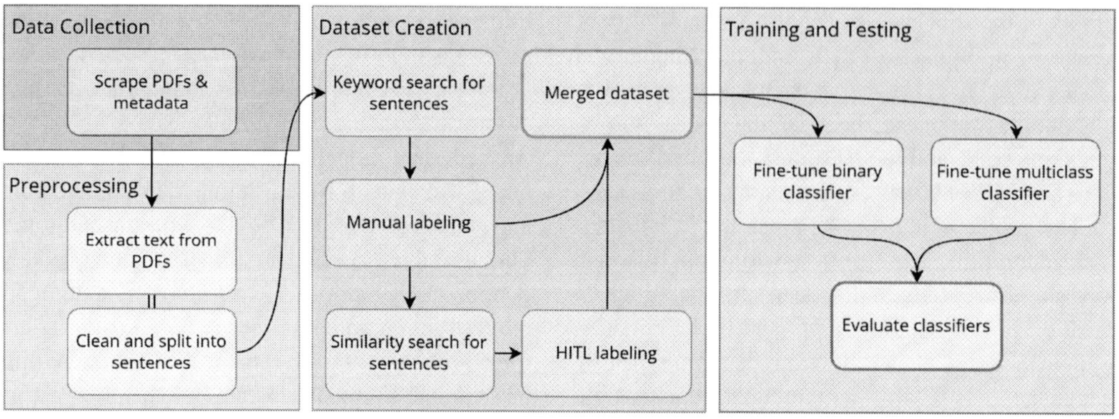

Figure 1: The incentive classifier pipeline

could find a link to a page where they could finally search that topic's publications, including policies. For a human, trying to find all the relevant policies across all the topics pages would be tedious and time-consuming, so we built a web crawler to help us scrape the data we needed.

We used Python's Scrapy[4] library to create a new "spider" or web crawler to extract the Uniform Resource Locators (URLs) for all the topic publication search pages. With this list, we constructed search query strings using keywords[5] for policy inclusion based on those used by Firebanks-Quevedo et al. (2022). Our crawler then visited all the search result pages and parsed through the queried policies to gather the policy metadata and document URLs, using exclusion keywords based on those in the original pipeline to ignore irrelevant policies and documents. In all, our scraper collected 138 relevant forestry policy documents across all the topic policy lists. A breakdown of the policies by source department can be found in Appendix A.

Once we had the collection of PDFs, we updated some of the preprocessing scripts of Firebanks-Quevedo et al. (2022) to retrieve the text from the PDFs using Python's PyPDF[6] library, which is based on text extraction instead of Optical Character Recognition (OCR). We then cleaned the texts of excess tags, spaces, and URLs and split them into sentences for labelling using a sentence tokeniser from Python's NLTK[7] library.

[4]https://www.scrapy.org/

[5]https://github.com/mawaskow/policy-classifier/blob/main/policy_scraping/policy_scraping/keywords/keywords_forestry.json

[6]https://pypdf.readthedocs.io/

[7]https://www.nltk.org/

3.2 Dataset Creation

We follow the dataset creation steps of Firebanks-Quevedo et al. (2022), first hand-labelling a subset of the collected sentences, then using those labelled sentences as the basis for a HITL process to automatically label remaining sentences. One labeller completed both the manual and HITL steps, then a policy researcher annotated a stratified subset of the data in order to validate the labelling.

We classified sentences into one of six incentive classes, or as a non-incentive, as defined in the reference pipeline:

- **Credit**: Loans, insurance
- **Direct payment**: Cash, grants
- **Fine**: Penalty payment
- **Supplies**: Material support, equipment
- **Tax deduction**: Reduced tax liability
- **Technical assistance**: Training, experts

Firebanks-Quevedo et al. (2022) had noted that their pipeline was unable to distinguish between intentions, plans, or general mentions of incentives in the sentences. In an attempt to address this, we labelled sentences that simply mentioned incentive keywords like *grant* or *loan* as a non-incentive, while sentences which actually declared the creation or implementation of incentives were classified by incentive type.

3.2.1 Manual Labelling

For our first pass at labelling the sentences, we performed a keyword search of incentive-related substrings, then manually assigned labels to a subset of the possible incentive sentences. The hand-labelling resulted in 965 sentences across the seven classes.

3.2.2 HITL Labelling

Firebanks-Quevedo et al. (2022) conducted their HITL labelling by using five sentences for each incentive class as queries to perform a similarity search in the remaining sentences. Of the sentences returned, the original pipeline only kept sentences that occurred across all five queries for each class. As our data was reflective of one country instead of five, the size of our dataset required that we lower the inclusion criteria to occurrence within at least four of the five queries for each label. Otherwise, we followed the same steps and produced an additional 626 pre-labelled sentences across the seven classes, subsequently validated by our labeller.

3.2.3 Novel Dataset

Our final dataset of the incentive sentences was the result of merging the manually labelled and HITL-labelled datasets. In order to account for duplicate sentences across the two collections, we grouped the sentences with Levenshtein or edit distances above the hand-tuned threshold of 0.9 and removed redundant entries. The final dataset consisted of 1419 labelled, filtered sentences containing both binary and multiclass labels.

The dataset overall had a notable but expected skew towards non-incentives, with incentives making up only 18.5% of the dataset. The classes of incentives were also unbalanced themselves, with Supplies at 30.1% of all incentive sentences, Technical assistance at 27.9%, Direct payment at 23.0%, then Fine at 8.6%, Credit at 7.1%, and Tax deduction at 3.3%.

For validation of our labelling, we brought in a policy researcher to label a stratified subsample of our final dataset. They annotated 10.7% of the sentences, including 24.5% of the incentives. To evaluate our agreement, we calculated the Cohen's kappa score of the resulting binary and multiclass datasets (Cohen, 1960). The agreement of the binary labelling, computed across the entire dataset, was 0.631, considered "substantial agreement." For the multiclass labelling, we evaluated agreement across the subset of examples where both annotators labelled the sentence as some kind of incentive, resulting in a score of 0.859, "near perfect agreement." Further information about validator

Parameter	Binary	Multiclass
Epochs	5	15
Batch Size	16	16
Learning Rate	2E-5	2E-5
Weight Decay	0.01	0.01
Optimiser	AdamW	AdamW

Table 1: Hyperparameters for binary and multiclass model training

agreement can be found in Appendix B.

3.3 Training and Testing

The next step in the pipeline is the fine-tuning of models on each of the binary and multiclass versions of the dataset. All training was conducted on a CUDA-enabled NVIDIA GeForce RTX 3080 Laptop GPU with 16 GB VRAM, appropriate for small to medium size models.

To produce the binary dataset, we used all 1419 sentences, keeping the non-incentive label and replacing all incentive class labels with "Incentive." The multiclass dataset consisted of the 263 incentive sentences from the final dataset with no additional alterations.

Due to the small size and significant class imbalances of the datasets, we chose to train and evaluate our classifiers across ten random train-dev-test splits (60/20/20) of each of the binary and multiclass datasets, stratified to maintain label proportions. To ensure reproducibility and controlled randomness, each split was generated using a distinct random seed (ranging from 0 to 9). We averaged our final metrics across all ten runs to account for variations in performance across different splits, providing a more robust estimate of model performance.

3.3.1 Model Selection

We first established the baseline for our replication by using the same sentence-transformer (Reimers and Gurevych, 2019) model and hyperparameters as the original pipeline for our binary and multiclass classification. The reference model, sentence-transformers/paraphrase-xlm-r-multilingual-v1 (XLM-R), is a multilingual transformer with 278M parameters (Conneau et al., 2020).

Following the first model, we explored whether newer or more efficient models could improve performance. We tried another multilingual SBERT model with the same number

Model		Binary	Multiclass
	d	87.7 ± 1.4	94.1 ± 4.2
XLM-R	l	87.5 ± 1.9	94.3 ± 3.5
	o	87.5 ± 1.3	94.7 ± 3.7
	d	**88.3 ± 1.5**	95.7 ± 2.5
MPNet	l	88.0 ± 2.3	96.2 ± 2.5
	o	88.2 ± 1.0	**96.8 ± 2.1**
	d	87.1 ± 1.1	95.6 ± 3.2
GTE	l	87.2 ± 1.4	95.3 ± 2.7
	o	87.7 ± 1.2	96.3 ± 2.7
	d	87.4 ± 1.6	95.7 ± 2.9
E5	l	86.8 ± 1.7	95.8 ± 2.0
	o	86.5 ± 2.2	94.9 ± 3.3

Table 2: Overall F1 scores of the fine-tuned models (d: default, l: weighted loss, o: oversampling) averaged across 10 different dataset splits

Model		Non-Incentive	Incentive
	d	92.5 ± 1.0	66.7 ± 3.6
XLM-R	l	92.4 ± 1.2	66.1 ± 4.9
	o	92.7 ± 0.8	64.7 ± 3.8
	d	93.0 ± 0.9	**68.1 ± 4.4**
MPNet	l	92.8 ± 1.4	67.0 ± 6.1
	o	**93.2 ± 0.6**	66.6 ± 2.9
	d	92.2 ± 0.8	64.8 ± 2.5
GTE	l	92.4 ± 0.9	64.9 ± 3.9
	o	92.7 ± 0.8	66.0 ± 3.5
	d	92.5 ± 1.0	65.3 ± 4.3
E5	l	92.0 ± 1.1	63.9 ± 4.3
	o	92.1 ± 1.3	62.1 ± 6.2

Table 3: Label-specific F1 scores for the binary dataset (d: default, l: weighted loss, o: oversampling) averaged across 10 different dataset splits

of parameters, sentence-transformers/paraphrase-multilingual-mpnet-base-v2 (MPNet), which offers improved context capturing through its blending of permutation language modelling (PLM) with masked language modelling (MLM) (Song et al., 2020). We additionally tried two more recent, lightweight (109M parameters), English-only models, thenlper/gte-base (GTE) (Wang et al., 2022) and intfloat/e5-base-v2 (E5) (Li et al., 2023), to examine the possibility of pipeline deployment in environments with fewer computational resources–common in the political and social sciences. To ensure controlled comparisons across models, we used the same hyperparameters for all experiments as shown in Table 1.

Beyond updating the models, we also attempted to address the class imbalances of the dataset through two common strategies. In our first approach, we weighted the cross entropy loss, modifying the loss function to more severely penalise misclassification of the underrepresented classes during training; our class weights were inversely proportional to the class frequencies. Our other approach was to automatically oversample the minority classes with Imbalanced-learn's[8] RandomOverSampler, reinforcing the model's exposure to the underrepresented classes by balancing their distribution in the training data of each split.

3.3.2 Classification

Firebanks-Quevedo et al. (2022) determined that their pipeline performed best when they used the fine-tuned models to generate embeddings of the dataset, then sent those embeddings to a support vector machine (SVM) for classification (Gunn, 1998). Before we conducted the classification this way, we explored the inference capabilities of the fine-tuned transformer heads but found that performance on our small, imbalanced dataset was consistently higher when using the external classifier. For that reason and to further support our replication objective, all results reported are from the embedding generation and SVM classification method.

4 Results

We examined the F1 scores for the SVM classification of each model's sentence embeddings, averaged across the ten splits of the binary and multiclass datasets.

The mean F1 score and standard deviation for all models across the default, weighted loss, and oversampling training runs can be found in Table 2. MPNet outperformed the XLM-R model used in the reference pipeline and both other models, reporting a best average F1 score of 88.3 for binary classification and 96.8 for multiclass classification.

Overall, for binary classification, MPNet's embeddings achieved the highest average F1 scores, reporting a best value of 88.3. MPNet's performance was then followed by the XLM-R model, with the GTE and E5 models performing similarly but slightly worse than XLM-R. For multiclass classification, the MPNet again achieved the highest average F1 scores, this time reporting a best value of 96.8. After the MPNet, the rankings followed as

[8] https://imbalanced-learn.org/stable/

Model		Credit	Direct Payment	Fine	Supplies	Tax Deduction	Technical Assistance
	d	97.1 ± 5.7	93.3 ± 5.1	93.3 ± 7.9	95.7 ± 4.0	81.7 ± 32.0	93.4 ± 4.8
XLM-R	l	97.1 ± 5.7	92.1 ± 6.1	91.7 ± 9.6	96.5 ± 3.9	81.7 ± 32.0	94.7 ± 3.7
	o	**98.6 ± 4.3**	94.3 ± 5.4	94.4 ± 8.0	96.2 ± 3.7	78.3 ± 31.7	93.5 ± 3.7
	d	94.3 ± 7.0	93.5 ± 4.2	97.5 ± 7.5	97.1 ± 3.1	95.0 ± 15.0	95.7 ± 2.9
MPNet	l	93.2 ± 8.8	94.0 ± 3.9	97.8 ± 4.4	**98.4 ± 2.1**	96.7 ± 10.0	95.8 ± 4.2
	o	94.6 ± 8.6	**95.5 ± 2.8**	98.9 ± 3.3	97.5 ± 2.3	96.7 ± 10.0	**96.9 ± 2.9**
	d	94.6 ± 6.7	93.7 ± 4.6	**100.0 ± 0.0**	96.5 ± 2.1	90.0 ± 30.0	95.3 ± 3.7
GTE	l	89.8 ± 10.1	94.4 ± 3.5	**100.0 ± 0.0**	97.2 ± 2.6	90.0 ± 30.0	94.3 ± 3.6
	o	97.1 ± 5.7	95.3 ± 4.1	97.5 ± 7.5	97.2 ± 2.6	85.0 ± 32.0	96.4 ± 2.3
	d	94.6 ± 6.7	94.5 ± 5.0	97.8 ± 4.4	97.2 ± 2.5	96.7 ± 10.0	94.5 ± 4.4
E5	l	93.2 ± 6.9	94.6 ± 3.1	**100.0 ± 0.0**	96.9 ± 3.4	**100.0 ± 0.0**	94.7 ± 2.6
	o	95.7 ± 6.5	93.2 ± 4.7	97.5 ± 7.5	96.5 ± 3.1	95.0 ± 15.0	93.6 ± 4.4

Table 4: Label-specific F1 scores for the multiclass dataset (d: default, l: weighted loss, o: oversampling) averaged across 10 different dataset splits

GTE, then E5, then the XLM-R.

Tables 3 and 4 include the F1 scores for each classification label in the binary and multiclass datasets, respectively. Our best binary model's embeddings achieved average F1 scores of 93.0 and 68.1 for the classes of Non-incentive and Incentive, and our best multiclass classification model achieved average F1 scores of 94.6 for Credit, 95.5 for Direct payment, 98.9 for Fine, 97.5 for Supplies, 96.7 for Tax deduction, and 96.9 for Technical assistance.

We additionally report the overall validation F1 scores of our models in Appendix C as recommended by Dodge et al. (2019), as well as the overall and label-specific precision and recall scores of our models in Appendix D.

4.1 Qualitative Analysis

Examples of accurately and inaccurately classified binary incentive sentences can be found in Table 5. These sentences, embedded by MPNet and classified via SVM, highlight the semantic challenges of incentive sentence labelling and classification.

In the successfully identified examples, the label of the incentive sentence is clear due to its incentive-related keywords of *financial support*, *payments*, and *beneficiaries*, numerical amounts, and use of *will* to denote action. While the non-incentive sentence is a bit ambiguous due to the keywords *taxation* and *incentivising*, the use of *committed* demonstrates that this is a statement of intention or policy aspiration instead of a properly declared incentive, likely leading to its correct classification.

In the unsuccessful classification examples, the incentive sentence states the requirement in a scheme to apply financial penalties to herdowners but was marked as a non-incentive. Despite the use of keywords, this type of incentive– fine– may be better understood as a disincentive, so its lack of mention of rewards as found in other incentive sentences may have contributed to its misclassification. The non-incentive sentence mistakenly classified as an incentive did mention *direct payments*, but was in reality a description of a mechanism currently in place. The model likely picked up on the incentive keywords but missed the overall context of being a factual statement of existing supports rather than being an actionable incentive.

5 Discussion

Following the identification of incentive sentences through binary classification, the multiclass classification of incentive type is able to achieve high performance. In the binary context, we faced a challenge also noted by Firebanks-Quevedo et al. (2022), that it is difficult to distinguish incentive declarations from non-incentive sentences that mention incentives or state intentions to create them. At the label-specific level, the performance of incentive classification was worse than non-incentive classification, assumedly due to the imbalance of the dataset.

Regarding the different training methods, in the binary classification setting, the loss and oversampling methods did not appear to improve on default model performance, sometimes worsening it. In the multiclass classification setting, however, XLM-R, MPNet, and GTE models all benefited from the introduction of oversampling to the training.

The multiclass labels of Credit and Tax deduction received notably higher standard deviations across models and methods, though in the case of Tax deduction, this standard deviation was reduced through updating the embedding model to MPNet as well as by adding weighted cross entropy loss or oversampling in the training process. The high standard deviations were likely due to these being the most under-represented incentive classes in the dataset, resulting in high variability of the success of their classification across training splits. The challenge of correctly classifying the Tax deduction label was also interestingly consistent with the results of Firebanks-Quevedo et al. (2022).

As our best-performing model for generating embeddings was a multilingual MPNet sentence transformer, we share in the hope of Firebanks-Quevedo et al. (2022) that the models from our pipeline can be used to classify the sentences of policies in another language via cross-lingual transfer learning, removing the need to construct a whole new dataset for fine-tuning.

While the outcomes of this research primarily serve the development and evaluation of NLP applications for incentive sentence classification in policy texts, the practical impact on policy analysts remains indirect at this stage. As most policy analysts are not comfortable with building their own NLP pipeline implementations, the immediate application of this dataset and models is limited. However, we envision future work that translates these models into accessible tools, namely an interface where policy analysts can input search terms and websites of policy repositories to automatically retrieve relevant documents, or where analysts can upload policy documents to extract incentive sentences using the classification pipeline– first identifying incentives with our binary classifier, then categorising them with our muticlass classifier. We hope to soon make our pipeline accessible in this way to bridge the gap to impact real-world policy analysis, with the ultimate goal of improving the policymaking process and preventing policy failure.

6 Conclusion

This paper applied an existing policy incentive classification pipeline to a new geopolitical and linguistic context, demonstrating the transferability of the reference pipeline and creating a novel dataset of Irish forestry policy sentences labelled for incentive classification. The binary and multiclass classification of sentence embeddings produced by our best models achieved similar performance to the original Firebanks-Quevedo et al. (2022) pipeline's results on their own policy dataset, serving as a validation of their methodology.

We prioritised reproducibility in this replication, and encourage researchers to implement this or similar pipelines for policy incentive classification in more domains across languages, political contexts, and policy areas. Additionally, our dataset and training information is available for anyone who wants to fine-tune their own multilingual incentive classification models on an existing dataset for transfer learning into new contexts.

We hope that with more progress in the area of automatic policy incentive or instrument classification, this work can help streamline the task of policy analysis to enable robust recommendations of policy solutions, ultimately working towards the creation of more successful policies.

Limitations

Our pipeline did encounter limitations, some of which were shared with Firebanks-Quevedo et al. (2022) and some of which were unique to this implementation. We encountered the same challenge that Firebanks-Quevedo et al. (2022) did concerning the ambiguity of incentive sentences across intentions, plans, and mentions, resulting in suboptimal incentive identification performance in the binary classification context. Further examples of ambiguous sentences are presented in Appendix E.

Specific to this pipeline, in our labelling process we found that there were no incentive sentences about providing direct material support or equipment, so we adapted the Supplies definition to include grants which were exclusively for the purchase of materials or equipment. Additionally, when it came to labelling sentences about carbon taxes, we were conflicted between labelling it a Tax deduction since it is a tax mechanism, or including it with Fine since it can be considered a penalty or disincentive; we decided to proceed with the latter option. Additionally, the training and testing of our

Successes	True Label
Financial support towards the professional costs, such as legal, taxation and advisory for older farmers will contribute 50% of such vouched costs, to a maximum payment of €1,500 per beneficiary.	Incentive
We are committed to further developing a taxation framework, which plays its full part in incentivising, along with other available policy levers, the necessary actions to reduce our emissions.	Non-incentive

Errors	True Label
Where it can be established that such ineligible features/areas existed in previous years, there is a requirement to reduce the area and apply the relevant financial reduction and/or penalty to the herdowner.	Incentive
EU CAP direct payments provide vital income support for farmers, and act as an important cushion against commodity price volatility.	Non-incentive

Table 5: Sentences from the binary dataset correctly and incorrectly classified with our best-performing model

embedding models and classifier were limited by the small size and class imbalances of the dataset.

We also noted that the pipeline may benefit from span extraction and classification rather than simple sentence classification, especially in cases where there are several incentives contained in a single sentence. We are now experimenting with the POLIANNA dataset for extracting spans to use as features in the sentence classification, enabling multilabel classification for incentives as well (Sewerin et al., 2023).

Ethics

The data for this project consists of sentences from public policy documents, none of which contain private or personal information. Bias may be introduced to the dataset and resulting models by the aforementioned single annotator and annotation decisions in ambiguous cases, as well as by the small size and class imbalance of the dataset. While our pipeline is primarily designed and intended for policy analysis, it could be manipulated to create biased classifiers that mislabel incentives in order to fit a certain agenda, potentially over-representing or under-representing different incentive classes in order to sway the downstream choice of policy solutions. As such, it is important for future implementations of the pipeline to maintain openness and transparency in the construction of their datasets and training of their models.

Acknowledgments

Thank you to Dr. Yifan Wang for annotating a subset of our data for validation. This work was funded by Research Ireland as part of Grant Number SFI/12/RC/2289_P2 Insight_2, the Insight Research Ireland Centre for Data Analytics.

References

Bertrand Badie, Dirk Berg-Schlosser, and Leonardo Morlino. 2011. *International Encyclopedia of Political Science*, volume 1. SAGE Publications, Inc., Thousand Oaks, California.

John Brandt. 2019. Text mining policy: Classifying forest and landscape restoration policy agenda with neural information retrieval. In *KDD Fragile Earth workshop (FEED 2019)*.

Jacob Cohen. 1960. A coefficient of agreement for nominal scales. *Educational and Psychological Measurement*, 20(1):37–46.

Alexis Conneau, Kartikay Khandelwal, Naman Goyal, Vishrav Chaudhary, Guillaume Wenzek, Francisco Guzmán, Edouard Grave, Myle Ott, Luke Zettlemoyer, and Veselin Stoyanov. 2020. Unsupervised cross-lingual representation learning at scale. In *Proceedings of the 58th Annual Meeting of the Association for Computational Linguistics*, pages 8440–8451, Online. Association for Computational Linguistics.

Jesse Dodge, Suchin Gururangan, Dallas Card, Roy Schwartz, and Noah A. Smith. 2019. Show your work: Improved reporting of experimental results. *Proceedings of the 2019 Conference on Empirical Methods in Natural Language Processing and the 9th International Joint Conference on Natural Language Processing (EMNLP-IJCNLP)*, page 2185–2194.

Daniel Firebanks-Quevedo, Jordi Planas, Kathleen Buckingham, Cristina Taylor, David Silva, Galina Naydenova, and René Zamora-Cristales. 2022. Using machine learning to identify incentives in forestry policy: Towards a new paradigm in policy analysis. *Forest Policy and Economics*, 134:102624.

Goran Glavaš, Federico Nanni, and Simone Paolo Ponzetto. 2017. Cross-lingual classification of topics in political texts. In *Proceedings of the Second Workshop on NLP and Computational Social Science*, pages 42–46, Vancouver, Canada. Association for Computational Linguistics.

Justin Grimmer and Brandon M. Stewart. 2013. Text as data: The promise and pitfalls of automatic content analysis methods for political texts. *Political Analysis*, 21(3):267–297.

Steve R. Gunn. 1998. Support vector machines for classification and regression. Project report, University of Southampton. Address: Southampton, U.K.

Loni Hagen, Özlem Uzuner, Christopher Kotfila, Teresa M. Harrison, and Dan Lamanna. 2015. Understanding citizens' direct policy suggestions to the federal government: A natural language processing and topic modeling approach. In *2015 48th Hawaii International Conference on System Sciences*, pages 2134–2143.

Michael Laver, Kenneth Benoit, and John Garry. 2003. Extracting policy positions from political texts using words as data. *American Political Science Review*, 97(2):311–331.

Zehan Li, Xin Zhang, Yanzhao Zhang, Dingkun Long, Pengjun Xie, and Meishan Zhang. 2023. Towards general text embeddings with multi-stage contrastive learning. *arXiv preprint arXiv:2308.03281*.

Ian Magnusson, Noah A. Smith, and Jesse Dodge. 2023. Reproducibility in NLP: What have we learned from the checklist? *Findings of the Association for Computational Linguistics: ACL 2023*, page 12789–12811.

Laura K. Nelson, Derek Burk, Marcel Knudsen, and Leslie McCall. 2021. The future of coding: A comparison of hand-coding and three types of computer-assisted text analysis methods. *Sociological Methods & Research*, 50(1):202–237.

Jiang Ningpeng, Han Tian, Wang Haibo, Xu Ruzhi, and Ma Shiyu. 2024. A study on structured text parsing for policies based on BERTopic. In *2024 IEEE 6th Advanced Information Management, Communicates, Electronic and Automation Control Conference (IMCEC)*, volume 6, pages 16–22.

Nils Reimers and Iryna Gurevych. 2019. Sentence-BERT: Sentence embeddings using Siamese BERT-networks. In *Proceedings of the 2019 Conference on Empirical Methods in Natural Language Processing*. Association for Computational Linguistics.

Ludovic Rheault and Christopher Cochrane. 2020. Word embeddings for the analysis of ideological placement in parliamentary corpora. *Political Analysis*, 28(1):112–133.

Sebastian Sewerin, Lynn H. Kaack, Joel Küttel, Fride Sigurdsson, Onerva Martikainen, Alisha Esshaki, and Fabian Hafner. 2023. Towards understanding policy design through text-as-data approaches: The policy design annotations (polianna) dataset. *Scientific Data*, 10(896).

Kaitao Song, Xu Tan, Tao Qin, Jianfeng Lu, and Tie-Yan Liu. 2020. MPNet: masked and permuted pre-training for language understanding. In *Proceedings of the 34th International Conference on Neural Information Processing Systems*, NIPS '20, Red Hook, NY, USA. Curran Associates Inc.

Zhanna Terechshenko, Fridolin Linder, Vishakh Padmakumar, Michael Liu, Jonathan Nagler, Joshua A. Tucker, and Richard Bonneau. 2020. A comparison of methods in political science text classification: Transfer learning language models for politics. *Other Information Systems & eBusiness eJournal*.

Liang Wang, Nan Yang, Xiaolong Huang, Binxing Jiao, Linjun Yang, Daxin Jiang, Rangan Majumder, and Furu Wei. 2022. Text embeddings by weakly-supervised contrastive pre-training. *arXiv preprint arXiv:2212.03533*.

John Wilkerson and Andreu Casas. 2017. Large-scale computerized text analysis in political science: Opportunities and challenges. *Annual Review of Political Science*, 20(Volume 20, 2017):529–544.

Shehel Yoosuf and Yin Yang. 2019. Fine-grained propaganda detection with fine-tuned BERT. In *Proceedings of the Second Workshop on Natural Language Processing for Internet Freedom: Censorship, Disinformation, and Propaganda*, pages 87–91, Hong Kong, China. Association for Computational Linguistics.

Artur Żółkowski, Mateusz Krzyziński, Piotr Wilczyński, Stanisław Giziński, Emilia Wiśnios, Bartosz Pieliński, Julian Sienkiewicz, and Przemysław Biecek. 2022. Climate policy tracker: Pipeline for automated analysis of public climate policies. In *Tackling Climate Change with Machine Learning Workshop*.

A Policy Sources

Table 6 shows the departments of origin for the policies in the dataset at the time of collection. Since the collection however, two of the departments have been renamed and their websites and URLs restructured. In order to address this issue of changing PDF sources and addresses, we provide a ZIP file[9] of the policies in our repository.

[9] `https://github.com/mawaskow/policy-classifier/blob/main/policy_scraping/policy_scraping/outputs/forestry/full.zip`

# Policies	Department
45	Agriculture, Food and the Marine
45	Rural and Community Development
44	The Environment, Climate and Communications
4	Housing, Local Government and Heritage

Table 6: The number of policies from each Irish government department represented in the dataset

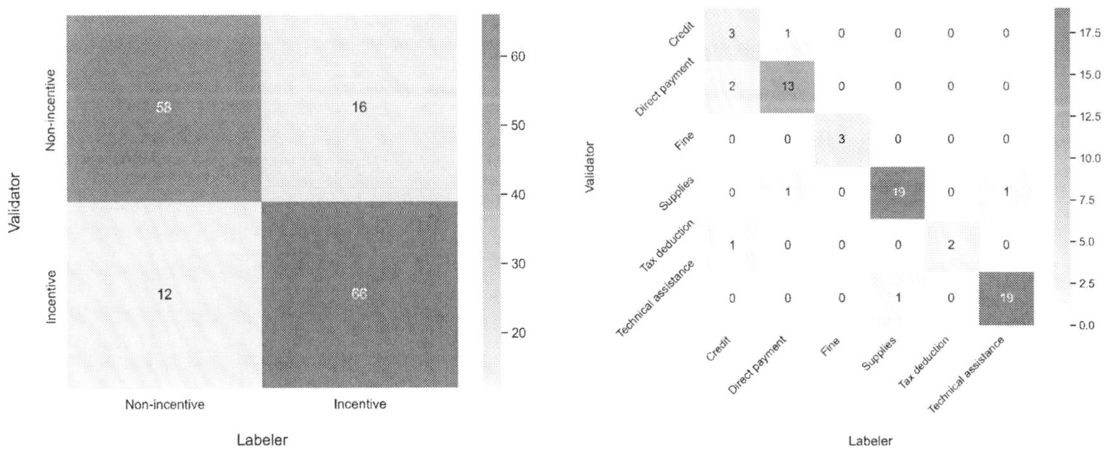

Figure 2: Confusion matrices for the validation sample (left: binary, right: multiclass)

B External Validation

For the external validation of our dataset, we provide the confusion matrices of our subset's labelling in Figure 2 for binary and multiclass classification. Additional information about annotation guidelines can be found on the dataset page.

C Validation Performance

Table 7 reflects performance using the transformer head for classification rather than the SVM classifier used in our main pipeline, resulting in the lower scores observed here. Despite this, the results confirm that MPNet consistently outperforms the other models in incentive sentence embedding for both binary and multiclass classification.

D Precision and Recall

In addition to reporting the overall and label-specific F1 scores of our models' binary and multiclass classification experiments in Tables 2, 3, and 4, we report their precision in Tables 8, 10, and 12, and recall in Tables 9, 11, and 13.

E Ambiguous Cases

Table 14 provides further examples of ambiguous policy sentences.

Model		Binary	Multiclass
XLM-R	d	88.4 ± 2.7	87.2 ± 3.5
	l	88.0 ± 2.6	89.3 ± 3.0
	o	89.1 ± 2.2	91.5 ± 3.7
MPNet	d	**89.8 ± 2.7**	89.0 ± 2.9
	l	89.2 ± 2.2	91.7 ± 3.0
	o	89.1 ± 2.0	**91.8 ± 3.1**
GTE	d	88.4 ± 2.5	73.5 ± 7.3
	l	88.2 ± 2.6	82.9 ± 5.1
	o	89.4 ± 2.3	90.5 ± 2.8
E5	d	88.0 ± 2.8	83.6 ± 3.1
	l	88.1 ± 2.2	88.1 ± 5.0
	o	89.6 ± 2.1	90.4 ± 3.6

Table 7: Overall validation F1 scores of the fine-tuned models (d: default, l: weighted loss, o: oversampling) averaged across 10 different dataset splits

Model		Binary	Multiclass
	d	87.7 ± 1.4	94.6 ± 3.8
XLM-R	l	87.5 ± 1.9	95.0 ± 3.0
	o	87.4 ± 1.4	95.3 ± 3.7
	d	**88.3 ± 1.6**	96.3 ± 2.1
MPNet	l	87.9 ± 2.2	96.6 ± 2.3
	o	88.1 ± 1.0	**97.0 ± 1.9**
	d	87.1 ± 1.1	95.8 ± 3.1
GTE	l	87.2 ± 1.4	95.7 ± 2.6
	o	87.6 ± 1.3	96.7 ± 2.6
	d	87.3 ± 1.6	96.0 ± 2.8
E5	l	86.7 ± 1.7	96.1 ± 1.9
	o	86.3 ± 2.3	95.5 ± 2.9

Table 8: Overall precision scores of the fine-tuned models (d: default, l: weighted loss, o: oversampling) averaged across 10 different dataset splits

Model		Binary	Multiclass
	d	87.8 ± 1.5	94.2 ± 4.2
XLM-R	l	87.6 ± 2.0	94.3 ± 3.5
	o	87.9 ± 1.3	94.7 ± 3.5
	d	88.5 ± 1.5	95.7 ± 2.5
MPNet	l	88.2 ± 2.3	96.2 ± 2.5
	o	**88.7 ± 1.0**	**96.8 ± 2.1**
	d	87.3 ± 1.2	95.7 ± 3.0
GTE	l	87.5 ± 1.4	95.5 ± 2.6
	o	87.9 ± 1.2	96.4 ± 2.6
	d	87.6 ± 1.6	95.7 ± 2.9
E5	l	86.9 ± 1.8	95.8 ± 2.0
	o	86.9 ± 2.1	94.9 ± 3.4

Table 9: Overall recall scores of the fine-tuned models (d: default, l: weighted loss, o: oversampling) averaged across 10 different dataset splits

Model		Non-Incentive	Incentive
	d	92.1 ± 0.9	68.5 ± 5.7
XLM-R	l	92.0 ± 1.1	67.9 ± 6.5
	o	91.0 ± 1.0	71.4 ± 5.0
	d	**92.3 ± 1.1**	70.6 ± 4.8
MPNet	l	92.0 ± 1.4	70.2 ± 7.0
	o	91.4 ± 0.7	**74.0 ± 3.6**
	d	91.6 ± 0.8	67.6 ± 5.7
GTE	l	91.5 ± 1.0	68.2 ± 5.1
	o	91.7 ± 1.1	69.8 ± 4.9
	d	91.5 ± 1.1	68.8 ± 5.2
E5	l	91.3 ± 0.9	66.4 ± 6.1
	o	90.6 ± 1.4	67.7 ± 6.9

Table 10: Label-specific precision scores for the binary dataset (d: default, l: weighted loss, o: oversampling) averaged across 10 different dataset splits

Model		Non-Incentive	Incentive
	d	93.0 ± 1.7	65.3 ± 4.2
XLM-R	l	92.9 ± 1.8	64.7 ± 5.0
	o	94.5 ± 1.4	59.4 ± 4.9
	d	93.6 ± 1.4	**66.0 ± 5.5**
MPNet	l	93.6 ± 2.1	64.5 ± 6.7
	o	**95.1 ± 0.9**	60.8 ± 3.5
	d	92.9 ± 1.8	62.6 ± 4.1
GTE	l	93.2 ± 1.6	62.3 ± 5.1
	o	93.6 ± 1.5	63.0 ± 5.4
	d	93.5 ± 1.4	62.3 ± 5.1
E5	l	92.7 ± 1.7	61.7 ± 4.0
	o	93.6 ± 1.6	57.5 ± 6.8

Table 11: Label-specific recall scores for the binary dataset (d: default, l: weighted loss, o: oversampling) averaged across 10 different dataset splits

Model		Credit	Direct Payment	Fine	Supplies	Tax Deduction	Technical Assistance
	d	**100.0 ± 0.0**	93.4 ± 5.0	98.3 ± 5.0	96.1 ± 6.1	78.3 ± 35.0	92.5 ± 5.5
XLM-R	l	**100.0 ± 0.0**	91.5 ± 7.0	**100.0 ± 0.0**	96.9 ± 4.0	78.3 ± 35.0	93.8 ± 5.4
	o	**100.0 ± 0.0**	**95.9 ± 4.2**	98.3 ± 5.0	96.9 ± 4.1	73.3 ± 35.1	92.2 ± 6.4
	d	**100.0 ± 0.0**	91.9 ± 6.5	**100.0 ± 0.0**	**98.2 ± 2.8**	93.3 ± 20.0	95.9 ± 5.7
MPNet	l	97.5 ± 7.5	91.9 ± 6.7	**100.0 ± 0.0**	**98.2 ± 2.8**	95.0 ± 15.0	97.4 ± 3.3
	o	97.5 ± 7.5	95.4 ± 5.0	**100.0 ± 0.0**	97.0 ± 3.0	95.0 ± 15.0	**97.5 ± 3.1**
	d	98.0 ± 6.0	91.2 ± 7.3	**100.0 ± 0.0**	97.6 ± 3.8	90.0 ± 30.0	96.1 ± 4.3
GTE	l	98.0 ± 6.0	92.7 ± 6.9	**100.0 ± 0.0**	97.6 ± 3.8	90.0 ± 30.0	94.5 ± 5.6
	o	**100.0 ± 0.0**	95.9 ± 4.1	**100.0 ± 0.0**	96.9 ± 3.1	83.3 ± 34.2	95.8 ± 4.6
	d	98.0 ± 6.0	95.1 ± 5.5	**100.0 ± 0.0**	97.6 ± 3.9	95.5 ± 15.0	93.1 ± 5.8
E5	l	98.0 ± 6.0	94.5 ± 5.0	**100.0 ± 0.0**	97.0 ± 4.0	**100.0 ± 0.0**	94.3 ± 4.3
	o	**100.0 ± 0.0**	94.5 ± 6.1	**100.0 ± 0.0**	97.5 ± 3.0	93.3 ± 20.0	91.7 ± 6.8

Table 12: Label-specific precision scores for the multiclass dataset (d: default, l: weighted loss, o: oversampling) averaged across 10 different dataset splits

Model		Credit	Direct Payment	Fine	Supplies	Tax Deduction	Technical Assistance
	d	95.0 ± 10.0	93.3 ± 6.2	90.0 ± 13.4	95.6 ± 4.9	90.0 ± 30.0	94.7 ± 7.2
XLM-R	l	95.0 ± 10.0	93.3 ± 9.0	86.0 ± 15.6	96.3 ± 5.0	90.0 ± 30.0	96.0 ± 5.3
	o	**97.5 ± 7.5**	93.3 ± 9.0	92.0 ± 13.3	95.6 ± 4.9	90.0 ± 30.0	95.3 ± 5.2
	d	90.0 ± 12.2	95.8 ± 6.7	96.0 ± 12.0	96.3 ± 5.0	**100.0 ± 0.0**	96.0 ± 5.3
MPNet	l	90.0 ± 12.2	**96.7 ± 4.1**	96.0 ± 8.0	**98.8 ± 2.5**	**100.0 ± 0.0**	94.7 ± 7.2
	o	92.5 ± 11.5	95.8 ± 4.2	98.0 ± 6.0	98.1 ± 2.9	**100.0 ± 0.0**	96.7 ± 5.4
	d	92.5 ± 11.5	**96.7 ± 4.1**	**100.0 ± 0.0**	95.6 ± 2.9	90.0 ± 30.0	94.7 ± 5.0
GTE	l	85.0 ± 16.6	**96.7 ± 4.1**	**100.0 ± 0.0**	96.9 ± 3.1	90.0 ± 30.0	94.7 ± 5.8
	o	95.0 ± 10.0	95.0 ± 6.7	96.0 ± 12.0	97.5 ± 3.1	90.0 ± 30.0	**97.3 ± 4.4**
	d	92.5 ± 11.5	94.2 ± 6.5	96.0 ± 8.0	96.9 ± 3.1	**100.0 ± 0.0**	96.0 ± 4.4
E5	l	90.0 ± 12.2	95.0 ± 4.1	**100.0 ± 0.0**	96.9 ± 4.2	**100.0 ± 0.0**	95.3 ± 4.3
	o	92.5 ± 11.5	92.5 ± 6.9	96.0 ± 12.0	95.6 ± 4.9	**100.0 ± 0.0**	96.0 ± 5.3

Table 13: Label-specific recall scores for the multiclass dataset (d: default, l: weighted loss, o: oversampling) averaged across 10 different dataset splits

The Eco-Schemes provides supports to farmers who undertake specific agricultural practices, including extensive farming, tree planting, sewing a multi-species sward, and enhancing crop diversification.
Department of Finance and DAFM to improve dissemination of information on taxation incentives including engagement with advisors, tax consultants and accountants.
LEADER may provide support rates greater than 65% in accordance with Article 73(4) (c)(ii) where investments include basic services in rural areas and infrastructure in agriculture and forestry, as determined by Member States.

Table 14: Ambiguous policy sentences, unclear in either their status as incentive or non-incentive, or in the type of incentive they are.

Narrative Structure Extraction in Disinformation and Trustworthy News: A Comparison of LLM, KG, and KG-Augmented Pipelines

Justina Mandravickaitė
Vytautas Magnus University, Lithuania
justina.mandravickaite@vdu.lt

Abstract

Identifying narrative structures such as characters, events, causes, and frames in political news is essential to detecting bias and understanding political dynamics, among other areas. Large language models (LLMs), while performing well on a variety of natural language processing (NLP) tasks, may hallucinate, whereas pure knowledge graph (KG) methods, while excelling at text structuring and information extraction, suffer from sparsity. In this study, three pipelines for extracting narrative structures from disinformation and trustworthy news are evaluated: (1) LLM-only prompt-based extraction, (2) KG-only graph-based queries and (3) an augmented approach combining LLM prompts augmented with appropriate KG data. The results were evaluated intrinsically as well as extrinsically. For intrinsic evaluation, element coverage, fuzzy overlap, coherence, coverage gain and error reduction were measured, while extrinsic evaluation used matching with Wikidata and downstream classification. The augmented pipeline improved the coverage and coherence of narrative elements, but also boosted the classification of disinformation, as it outperformed both LLM-only and KG-only pipelines.

1 Introduction

Narrative extraction from political news is important for revealing how disinformation manipulates the stories by, e.g., assigning blame (Rauchfleisch and Jungherr, 2024), inflating or downplaying events (Keith Norambuena et al., 2023) or constructing false causal chains (Lei and Huang, 2023) in order to shape public perception. Identification of narrative structures aids in revealing rhetorical strategies that fact-checking alone may miss (Byram, 2022).

Large language models (LLMs), while perform well in diverse NLP tasks, including information extraction, may hallucinate relations or entities (Mckenna et al., 2023; Li et al., 2024a). Meanwhile, knowledge graphs (KGs) can suffer from incomplete coverage (Wang et al., 2022) or outdated ontologies (Zhou et al., 2024; Hegde et al., 2025), among other issues, which may result in, e.g., missing events (Zhuang et al., 2023) or misclassified roles (Lu et al., 2024). While many pipelines are assessed using intrinsic metrics (e.g., coherence (German et al., 2025) or reconstruction accuracy (Keith Norambuena et al., 2023)) or individual extrinsic tasks (e.g., downstream classification (Das et al., 2024)), there is an opportunity to develop more comprehensive validation protocols that combine both approaches to provide a more comprehensive evaluation.

To address these issues, in this study, three pipelines for extracting narrative structures from disinformation and trustworthy news are evaluated: (1) LLM-only prompt-based extraction, (2) KG-only graph-based queries and (3) an augmented approach combining LLM prompts augmented with appropriate KG data. The proposed evaluation framework combines intrinsic and extrinsic evaluation. It integrates measures of narrative coverage, fuzzy overlap, coherence, coverage gain and error reduction (intrinsic), alongside downstream tasks such as matching with Wikidata and disinformation classification (extrinsic).

2 Related Work

Advances in narrative extraction for political and social science have relied on structured representations such as event schemas to analyze social processes, events and framing (Zhang et al., 2019; Halterman, 2020; Li et al., 2024b). Transformer-based multilingual models have achieved high accuracy in crisis event detection across languages, illustrating usefulness of schema-guided extraction (Hettiarachchi et al., 2021).

Schema refinement has emerged for extracting

Proceedings of the 21st Conference on Natural Language Processing (KONVENS), Volume 2: Workshops, pages 86–103, 2025

events without predefined templates, such as Liberal Event Extraction (LEE) which jointly extracts events and induces schemas (Li and Geng, 2024). Integrating schemas with cultural norms and commonsense knowledge was used to support framing analysis (Li et al., 2024b). Visualization tools have been used to reveal how discrete events affect outcomes over time (Shen et al., 2024).

Also, graph-based methods have been proposed, such as using AMR (abstract meaning representation) to extract actors, events, and perspectives from digital media(Pournaki and Willaert, 2024). Knowledge Graph–based approaches enhance semantic precision and reveal causal relationships in narrative analysis (de Kok et al., 2024; Romanou et al., 2023). In bias detection, integrating frame-based knowledge with text models improved bias and stance detection (Li, 2021). Also, domain-specific KGs for news facilitate advanced bias detection and narrative synthesis (Yang et al., 2024).

Event-centric narrative extraction has been a trend for a while (Voskarides et al., 2021; Keith Norambuena et al., 2023). Advances and challenges in multimodal event extraction has been introduced as well (Hürriyetoğlu et al., 2024).

Recent research revealed that hybrid methods mitigate weaknesses of purely symbolic (such as KG-based) or neural approaches (such as LLM-based) (Panchendrarajan and Zubiaga, 2024; Zhu, 2024). For example, multi-agent approaches has been recommended for KG construction and reasoning, (Zhu et al., 2024). Also, at least several LLM–KG integration frameworks have been outlined, such as SymAgent, a neural-symbolic agent for multi-step reasoning and automatic KG updates (Liu et al., 2025)or MindMap which merges KGs and LLMs for improved inference transparency (Wen et al., 2024).

Different proposed directions also involve merging LLMs with relation extraction to build semantically rich KGs (Santini, 2024) and optimize LLM reasoning over KGs via selective triple selection (Wang, 2025). Also, recent developments in processing long narratives address past limitations by integrating dynamic KGs with LLMs to improve story comprehension (Andrus et al., 2022).

Narrative extraction evaluation includes variety of metrics and approaches,such as intrinsic metrics for event and attribution extraction, stressing reproducible practices (Zhang et al., 2019). Also, the complexity of assessing narrative coherence has been highlighted (Santana et al., 2023). Furthermore, studies have evaluated narrative elements via Multiple Choice Narrative Cloze (Hatzel and Biemann, 2023), accuracy metrics and downstream performance (Tang et al., 2021), structural coherence checks and user studies (Norambuena and Mitra, 2021).

This paper reports comparative evaluation of LLM-only, KG-only and Augmented pipelines for extracting narrative structures in political news, assessed with both intrinsic metrics and extrinsic grounding. Unlike typical KG–LLM work, in this paper narrative extraction gains were directly linked to improved disinformation classification while maintaining interpretable representations.

3 Methods

3.1 Data

For this study a part of the dataset for multilingual detection of pro-Kremlin disinformation in news articles (Leite et al., 2024), containing data on disinformation and trustworthy news articles, was used. This dataset consists of 18 249 articles in 42 languages published January 2015-July 2023. As the full text of the news articles was not publicly available, to reconstruct the dataset URL links of the articles were used with DiffBot API[1] (free for academic purposes) to acquire them. Only English-language articles were selected, i.e. a total of 6,546 articles (425 – disinformation and 6121 – trustworthy). Some articles were no longer available or have been modified. So, after filtering and cleaning the final dataset used in this study was made of 308 disinformation news articles and 302 – trustworthy news articles. Labeling news articles as 'disinformation' and 'trustworthy' is based on the original dataset, i.e., article labels were reused as they were assigned in the original dataset (Leite et al., 2024). More details of the final dataset are presented in Appendix B.

While the data is of modest size, the experimentation targets pipeline comparison under controlled conditions, not training a large downstream model. Although the final dataset is $\sim$ 300 articles per class, intrinsic evaluations operate per article and summarize many extracted elements. Also, extrinsic evaluation analyses use simple, regularized classifier (logistic-regression) with grouped, repeated cross-validation to reduce variance.

[1]Accessible at https://www.diffbot.com/

3.2 Pipelines

Based on existing narratology and framing research, the following narratives structures were extracted and compared in three pipelines (LLM-only, KG-only and Augmented): characters (entities – persons and organizations), events (predicates indicating what happens to/among characters over time), causal links (predicates that express cause/effect), framing (predicates that indicate attribution/association) (Hellman, 2024; Heddaya et al., 2024; Wang et al., 2025).

For this study, the first step, before applying any of the pipelines, was text summarization. This step was applied to reduce noise and to use computational resources more efficiently in the later stages. Extractive summarization was used for this task as it extracts the most important sentences from the given text, preserving factuality and original wording (Hofmann-Coyle et al., 2022). Article summaries were used in all three pipelines that were comprised of different steps.

Summarization. The cleaned news articles were summarized using two extractive summarization approaches – LexRank Summarizer (Erkan and Radev, 2004) and BERT Extractive Summarizer (Miller, 2019). To choose from two summary-candidates, mean ROUGE-1/2/L F1 scores (Lin, 2004) were computed against the original article text. ROUGE-1/2/L F1 score favors coverage of source content and discourages off-source material and was used as a heuristic to choose between two summary-candidates. Therefore, summaries generated by the approach that had higher ROUGE values, showing higher source-overlap, were used for the experiments.

The length of the extractive summary was tied to text length: texts under 300 words were summarized in two sentences; texts of 300–799 words long – in four sentences and texts of 800 words or longer – in six sentences. To ensure quality, summaries were also manually inspected, correcting such issues as occasional incomplete final sentences. These summaries were used with all three narrative extractive pipelines. The examples of the summaries are presented in Appendix A.

LLM-only pipeline. Characters, events, causal links and framing were extracted via prompting. For this task, Mistral Small 3.1 24b[2] was used. The decision was made to use a smaller model, not the largest and most popular one like OpenAI's ChatGPT to manage computational and financial costs while maintaining competitive performance. The prompt used for extraction is presented in Appendix C.

KG-only pipeline. This pipeline consisted of several components, introduced below.

1. *Relational triple extraction.* The pre-trained REBEL (Relation Extraction By End-to-end Language generation) (Cabot and Navigli, 2021) model was applied for this task, extracting entity-relation-entity triples from summaries of news articles. These triples were used for graph construction. REBEL combines Named Entity Recognition (NER) and Relation Classification (RC) into a single task and covers >200 relationship types. Extracted triples were aggregated per article and manually validated.

2. *Mapping and inferring relations.* Relations of REBEL schema that imply framing, events and causality were mapped and inferred manually (for details, see Appendix D). This enrichment was necessary to make outputs of all there pipelines comparable.

3. *Building RDF graphs.* In this step, one rdflib graph per article (i.e. from only that article's triples) was built. In this graph structure entities (nodes) of the triples were linked by their relations (edges). Python library rdflib[3] was used for this task.

4. *Querying narrative elements.* REBEL triples (entity-relation-entity) were grouped into four relation families that were used to compute structure-level features: PERSON_RELS (relations that assert roles, affiliations or actor–actor ties), EVENT_RELS (relations that indicate actions/occurrences or changes; also used to collect event nodes (instance_of = Event)), CAUSAL_RELS (explicit cause/effect predicates and a small set of implied causal links as a result from mapping and inferring relations in previous step), FRAMING_RELS) (attribution/stance and portrayal; REBEL labels were mapped to short paraphrases (e.g., described_as → "is portrayed as"), see Appendix D). These narra-

[2]Accessible at `https://huggingface.co/mistralai/Mistral-Small-3.1-24B-Instruct-2503`

[3]Accessible at `https://github.com/RDFLib/rdflib`

tive element types were extracted via querying over RDF graphs.

Augmented pipeline. For extraction of narrative elements (characters, events, causal links and framing) from article summaries, prompts were augmented with relevant data from article-level KGs to provide context. The prompt used for extraction of narrative elements with Augmented pipeline is presented in Appendix C.

3.3 Evaluation

The evaluation framework of this study combines intrinsic as well as extrinsic evaluation to get a more comprehensive assessment of extraction of narrative structures. The special focus in this evaluation is paid to exploring the use of an LLM and KG in combination. Also, formal paired significance tests were applied only for metrics that are directly comparable across pipelines across pipelines and quantify extraction quality rather than volume, i.e., overlap (fuzzy Jaccard), coverage gain and error reduction, and extrinsic F1 in the classification. For other quantities, descriptive statistics are reported, avoiding inferential claims.

3.3.1 Intrinsic Evaluation

Intrinsic evaluation of outputs of all three pipelines consisted of the following components:

Coverage: raw counts as well as average counts per element were calculated. This measures recall potential by element type and is simple, interpretable, surfaces systematic under-extraction.

Fuzzy-Jaccard overlap: paraphrase-aware intersection / union between pipelines in terms of extracted narrative elements was calculated (Cross et al., 2020). For this task, *multi-qa-MiniLM-L6-cos-v1*[4] model and cosine similarity (Gunawan et al., 2018) with threshold 0.7 were used. Fuzzy Jaccard overlap shows cross-pipeline agreement on which elements were extracted, while tolerating paraphrases. This measure is scale-free, directly comparable and allows for semantic matching that avoids penalizing lexical variation.

Mean coherence: embedding-based sentence similarity was calculated for LLM-only and Augmented pipelines. Items of the lists of extracted narrative elements were treated as standalone "sentences." For this task, *all-MiniLM-L6-v2*[5] model was used and average adjacent-sentence cosine similarity was computed between items in the lists of narrative elements extracted from the same summaries of the news articles. For KG-only pipeline, graph-based (structural) coherence metrics (density (Shang and Huang, 2024), avg. path length and largest component ratio) were calculated for the graphs, created from relational triples, belonging to each article in the dataset. Semantic (embedding-based) coherence may show internal thematic consistency of extracted elements. Meanwhile, structural (graph-based) coherence may reveal narrative connectedness or fragmentation in the triple graph.

Orthogonal metrics (coverage gain & error reduction): these metrics were used for LLM-only and Augmented pipelines to compare and evaluate coverage of narrative elements and find unmatched elements, which may indicate model hallucination. These metrics were calculated using the following formulas:

Coverage gain for an element type = | Augmented pipeline | – | LLM-only pipeline |

Error reduction = | LLM-only pipeline unmatched elements | – | Augmented pipeline unmatched elements

Orthogonal metrics were calculated per element type. Coverage gain is the corpus-level difference in total extracted items. Unmatched elements are items produced by a pipeline that have no fuzzy match in the other pipeline. Error reduction refers to the decrease in unmatched elements when switching from LLM-only to Augmented pipeline. A ratio > 1 of Coverage gain and Error reduction means that Augmented pipeline adds more new correct elements than LLM-only pipeline removes. Meanwhile, a ratio < 1 means Augmented pipeline introduces more "errors" (unmatched elements) than additional coverage, indicating added noise. Orthogonal metrics capture the augmentation trade-off between newly matched and unmatched elements. In other words, these metrics directly quantify, per element type, whether augmentation was justified.

3.3.2 Extrinsic Evaluation

Loose matching with Wikidata: For a grounding / checking consistency, narrative elements, extracted with all three pipelines, were matched with loosely Wikidata. Linking extracted elements known knowledge base tests whether outputs correspond to real entities, reducing hallucinations and improving interpretability and Wikidata is widely

[4]Accessible at `https://huggingface.co/sentence-transformers/multi-qa-MiniLM-L6-cos-v1`

[5]Accessible at `https://huggingface.co/sentence-transformers/all-MiniLM-L6-v2`

used for such tasks (Möller et al., 2022). A stratified sample of 300 elements from each pipeline was taken. The unique labels were used to query against Wikidata[6] to determine if they matched real-world entities. For this task, Wikidata Search API (based on the MediaWiki API)[7] was used to perform a relevance-based search (or loose matching), i.e., matches were based on labels, aliases, redirects, and included some tolerance for minor typo. The results were ranked by relevance.

Downstream classification: Logistic-regression classifier was built for this task (see Appendix E for details). Counts of narrative elements and coherence (for LLM-only and Augmented pipelines – embedding-based metric and for KG-only pipeline – graph-based metrics) were used as features. For evaluation, 5-fold and 10-fold cross-validation(Wong and Yeh, 2019) was performed and F1-score (Naidu et al., 2023) was used to assess the results. Classification was used as an extrinsic evaluation to assess which narrative extraction pipeline more effectively captures the signal needed to distinguish disinformation from trustworthy news.

Paired tests (paired t-test (Rainio et al., 2024) and Wilcoxon signed-rank test (Rey and Neuhäuser, 2011)) were used to evaluate the statistical significance of the results by performing pairwise comparisons on the pipelines.

Cohen's d (Goulet-Pelletier and Cousineau, 2018) was calculated to measure the effect size, i.e. how big is the difference in classification performance by LLM-only, KG-only and Augmented pipelines when distinguishing disinformation from trustworthy news.

4 Results

4.1 Intrinsic Quality

4.1.1 Raw Counts and Mean Coverage of Narrative Elements

Table 1 shows descriptive counts of extracted narrative elements per pipeline. These raw counts summarize extraction tendencies and are not subjected to formal significance testing. As Table 1 shows, KG-only pipeline lags behind on every element, reflecting that raw triple extraction alone captures only a small part of narrative content.

Meanwhile, Augmented pipeline slightly outperformed LLM-only pipeline on characters and events for both classes. As for causal links, slightly higher counts resulted from Augmented pipeline for disinformation. However, for trustworthy news LLM-only pipeline provided higher counts, though the difference, in comparison to Augmented pipeline, is very small. Meanwhile, for framing more elements were extracted with LLM-only pipeline for both disinformation and trustworthy news.

Trustworthy articles generally provided higher counts and means than disinformation across all pipelines. This could be likely because longer, more structured reporting offers richer narratives.

The augmented pipeline mostly maintained LLM-only breadth of coverage while adding a modest boost, such as on actors and events, over LLM-only. KG alone was too sparse for standalone narrative extraction.

4.1.2 Overlap of Narrative Elements by Pipeline

To assess overlap of extracted narrative elements between pipeline pairs on the same article and element type per class, fuzzy Jaccard was used. As presented in Table 2, there almost no overlap for **llm∩kg**, meaning each alone extracts mostly disjoint sets of elements. Meanwhile, **llm∩augmented** overlap more substantial (0.46–0.47 for characters, 0.13–0.18 for events, up to 0.15 for framing). This shows that Augmented pipeline not only retained most LLM-only elements but also enriched them with additional ones from KG-only.

However, **kg∩augmented** overlap was low, though not so low as for **llm∩kg**, which means that Augmented pipeline's additional KG-based data was a small part of its output.

4.1.3 Coherence Assessment

To assess semantic continuity (for LLM-only and Augmented pipelines) and structural cohesion (for KG-only pipeline) within output for the same article, mean coherence measures were calculated. Embedding-based (semantic) coherence was slightly higher in Augmented pipeline than LLM-only one for disinformation (0.411 vs. 0.400) and there was no difference in coherence in terms of trustworthy news (Table 3).

Graph-based (structural) coherence in the KG-only pipeline showed that, in disinformation arti-

[6]Accessible at https://www.wikidata.org/wiki/Wikidata:Main_Page

[7]Accessible at https://www.wikidata.org/w/api.php?action=help

Element type	Pipeline	Disinformation	Trustworthy
Characters / actors	LLM-only	2226 (7.25)	2453 (8.10)
	KG-only	1147 (3.74)	1228 (4.05)
	Augmented	**2377 (7.74**	**2541 (8.39)**
Events	LLM-only	1826 (5.95)	2043 (6.74)
	KG-only	244 (0.79)	291 (0.96)
	Augmented	**1849 (6.02)**	**2118 (6.99)**
Causal links	LLM-only	1287 (4.19)	**1362 (4.50)**
	KG-only	71 (0.23)	77 (0.25)
	Augmented	**1298 (4.23)**	1355 (4.47)
Framing (actors+events)	LLM-only	**2401 (7.82)**	**2462 (8.13)**
	KG-only	106 (0.35)	158 (0.52)
	Augmented	2227 (7.25)	2274 (7.50)

Table 1: Raw counts and means (in brackets)

Element	llm∩kg (D/T)	llm∩augmented (D/T)	kg∩augmented (D/T)
Characters/actors	0.14 / 0.13	**0.47 / 0.46**	0.19 / 0.19
Events	0.008 / 0.006	**0.18 / 0.13**	0.013 / 0.014
Causal links	0 / 0	**0.076 / 0.058**	0.002 / 0.002
Framing	0.002 / 0.001	**0.15 / 0.12**	0.001 / 0.003

Table 2: Mean Fuzzy Jaccard (D – disinformation, T – trustworthy news)

cles, nearly 43 % of nodes belonged to the largest connected component, compared to 38 % in trustworthy articles. The average shortest path length was approximately 1.2 in both cases, and graph density was higher for disinformation (0.23 vs. 0.20). These results suggested that narrative elements extracted from disinformation articles were more interconnected. The similar average path lengths indicate that, despite differences in overall connectedness, the "distance between ideas" was similar across both categories.

The augmented pipeline's modestly higher coherence suggested that incorporating KG-derived facts helped to make the narrative elements semantically tighter, even if the gain was small. In contrast, KG-only graphs presented measurable structural coherence, though their metrics were not directly comparable to embedding-based measures.

4.1.4 Coverage Gain and Error Reduction

Orthogonal metrics (coverage gain and error reduction) were computed only for the LLM-only and Augmented pipelines. The KG-only pipeline was excluded because its extraction process was based on querying structured relational graphs which is very different from the prompt-based extraction in the LLM-only and Augmented pipelines.

In terms for disinformation, for **actors/characters** and **events**, the Augmented pipeline gives a modest but consistent net boost in coverage (2–7 %) with minimal noise (Table 4).

For **causal links**, the Augmented pipeline captured just as many or very slightly more matched causal links as it introduces unmatched ones.

For **framing edges**, the KG-augmented prompts added quantity but at the cost of introducing more unmatched framing elements, suggesting the prompting strategy for framing relations may need further refinement (e.g. more precise examples or stricter filtering).

Regarding trustworthy news, Augmented pipeline also provided slightly more new **actors/characters** and **events** than mismatches removed (Table 5).

For causal links, augmentation slightly favored mismatch reduction over added coverage. Finally, for framing edges, augmentation primarily improved precision in reducing mismatches than in-

Pipeline	Metric	Disinformation	Trustworthy
LLM-only	Embedding-based coherence	0.400	0.396
Augmented	Embedding-based coherence	**0.411**	**0.396**
KG-only	Largest component ratio	0.427	0.382
	Avg. path length	1.222	1.244
	Density	0.228	0.195

Table 3: Mean coherence by pipeline

Element	Coverage Gain	Error Reduction	Gain / Reduction
Characters/actors	1151	1079	1.07
Events	1736	1703	1.02
Causal links	1233	1226	1.01
Framing edges	2291	2460	0.93

Table 4: LLM-only vs. Augmented pipeline coverage gain & error reduction: disinformation news

Element	Coverage Gain	Error Reduction	Gain / Reduction
Characters/actors	1289	1252	1.03
Events	1996	1933	1.03
Causal links	1277	1297	0.98
Framing edges	2306	2567	0.90

Table 5: LLM-only vs. Augmented pipeline coverage gain & error reduction: trustworthy news

creasing in new elements. This, again, suggests that the prompting strategy for framing relations may need further tuning.

Overall, these intrinsic evaluations supported the assumption that Augmented pipeline outperforms pure LLM-based extraction on core narrative elements, especially actors and events. Meanwhile, framing may need a more targeted prompt design or post-extraction filtering.

4.2 Extrinsic Quality

4.2.1 Matching with Wikidata

KG-only extractions of narrative elements aligned with Wikidata at a very high rate ($\sim$ 70 %), reflecting that REBEL triples largely take out canonical entities and relations that already exist in Wikidata (Table 6). Meanwhile, LLM-only was far less grounded ($\sim$ 15–20 %), since free-form prompts often generate paraphrases, alternate names, or relations that are not directly findable in Wikidata. Finally, Augmented pipeline stayed in between the aforementioned pipelines, reflecting LLM's grounding by including the KG triples in the output.

As for matching per element type, Augmented pipeline outperformed LLM-only in terms of characters/actors but still trailed behind KG-only as $\sim$ 60% of sampled characters/actors extracted by this pipeline matched Wikidata entities (Table 7).

However, all pipelines struggled in grounding events in Wikidata, though again Augmented pipeline had a higher match rate than LLM-only and KG-only had more matches than both other pipelines.

Finally, causal links and framing had very low Wikidata coverage overall ($\leq$ 3%), reflecting that these relations are rarely modeled as explicit triples in Wikidata. KG-only did not cover these elements at all (Table 7).

4.2.2 Downstream Classification

Document classification was used as an extrinsic evaluation to examine whether pipeline-derived narrative features, rather than surface text, may help distinguish between disinformation and trustworthy news.

Augmented pipeline achieved the highest mean F1-score in both 5- and 10-fold cross-validation, 0.666 and 0.657, accordingly (Table 8). The improvement is moderate in effect size (d $\sim$ 0.6–0.8)

Pipeline	Trustworthy	Disinformation
LLM-only	44 / 300 (14.7 %)	61 / 300 (20.3 %)
Augmented	71 / 300 (23.7 %)	77 / 300 (25.7 %)
KG-only	211 / 300 (70.3 %)	210 / 300 (70.0 %)

Table 6: Overall Wikidata matches

Element type	Pipeline	Trustworthy (out of sample)	Disinfo (out of sample)
Characters/actors	LLM-only	31 / 300 (10.3 %)	47 / 300 (15.7 %)
	Augmented	60 / 300 (20.0 %)	51 / 300 (17.0 %)
	KG-only	178 / 300 (59.3 %)	176 / 300 (58.7 %)
Events	LLM-only	4 / 300 (1.3 %)	6 / 300 (2.0 %)
	Augmented	6 / 300 (2.0 %)	14 / 300 (4.7 %)
	KG-only	33 / 300 (11.0 %)	34 / 300 (11.3 %)
Causal links	LLM-only	7 / 300 (2.3 %)	4 / 300 (1.3 %)
	Augmented	5 / 300 (1.7 %)	9 / 300 (3.0 %)
	KG-only	—	—
Framing	LLM-only	—	4 / 300 (1.3 %)
	Augmented	—	3 / 300 (1.0 %)
	KG-only	—	—

Table 7: Wikidata maches by element type

(Table 11 and shows a clear trend toward statistical significance in the more stable 10-fold cross-validation (p≈ 0.08) as showed in Table 10.

Furthermore, Augmented pipeline significantly outperformed KG-only in both cross-validations (t-test p < 0.05 for both splits; Wilcoxon significant in 10-fold cross-validation), as presented in Tables 9 and 10, and large effect sizes (d ∼ 0.9–1.9) as showed in Table 11.

Finally, LLM-only vs. KG-only did not show significant statistical difference in either 5- or 10-fold cross-validation (p > 0.05 for all tests) and the effect size was small.

5 Conclusions

The Augmented pipeline showed intrinsic gains in narrative-element coverage and coherence, which also were translated to meaningful downstream improvements in disinformation classification as Augmented pipeline outperformed LLM-only pipeline by a moderate margin and KG-only pipeline – by a large margin, measured in effect size.

Augmented pipeline matched or slightly exceeded LLM-only on characters, events, and causal links while KG-only lagged behind. Also, Augmented pipeline retained most all LLM-only extractions for characters/actors and added KG-informed ones, whereas LLM-only and KG-only barely overlapped.

Moreover, Augmented pipeline's embedding-based coherence was marginally higher than LLM-only, suggesting KG-based augmentation tightened the narrative. Furthermore, Augmented pipeline gained a boost in valid characters and events beyond LLM-only, with minimal noise. Causal links, on the other hand, were similar in quantity, while framing was in need of refinement.

In addition, Augmented pipeline had higher match rate to Wikidata than LLM-only, showing a balance between creative extraction and factual grounding, though lagging behind KG-only due to its schema closely matching Wikidata.

Finally, Augmented pipeline outperformed the other two pipelines in downstream classification – achieved 0.666 ± 0.022 (5-fold cross-validation) and 0.657 ± 0.032 (10-fold cross-validation), versus 0.619/0.607 for LLM-only and 0.591/0.595 for KG-only. In statistical tests Augmented pipeline significantly outperformed KG-only pipeline (p < 0.05) and showed a moderate effect size over LLM-only pipeline (Cohen's d ∼0.6–0.8), with a trend toward significance in 10-fold cross-validation (p≈0.08).

Future work includes experimentation with both smaller- and larger-scale open-source and propri-

Validation	LLM-only	KG-only	Augmented
5-fold	0.619 ± 0.060	0.591 ± 0.025	**0.666 ± 0.022**
10-fold	0.607 ± 0.082	0.595 ± 0.061	**0.657 ± 0.032**

Table 8: Mean F1-scores)

Pipeline pairs	**Paired t-test**	**Wilcoxon signed-rank**
LLM-only vs KG-only	t = 1.358, p = 0.246	W = 2.000, p = 0.188
LLM-only vs Augmented	t = -1.708, p = 0.163	W = 3.000, p = 0.312
KG-only vs Augmented	t = -4.259, p = 0.013	W = 0.000, p = 0.062

Table 9: Significance testing (5-fold validation)

Pipeline pairs	**Paired t-test**	**Wilcoxon signed-rank**
LLM-only vs KG-only	t = 0.330, p = 0.749	W = 25.000, p = 0.846
LLM-only vs Augmented	t = -1.986, p = 0.078	W = 10.0, p = 0.084
KG-only vs Augmented	t = -2.799, p = 0.021	W = 3.0, p = 0.020

Table 10: Significance testing (10-fold validation)

Comparison	**5-fold cross-validation**	**10-fold cross-validation**
LLM-only vs. KG-only	+0.61 (moderate)	+0.10 (small)
LLM-only vs. Augmented	–0.76 (moderate)	–0.63 (moderate)
KG-only vs. Augmented	–1.90 (**large**)	–0.89 (**large**)

Table 11: Effect Sizes (Cohen's d)

etary models, compare multiple KG-building methods (e.g. pipeline vs. joint extraction) and prompt-engineering strategies as well. The extension to non-English sources by leveraging cross-lingual embeddings and integrating language-specific KGs is also planned. To better capture narrative nuances, human-in-the-loop coherence judgments, causal-structure metrics, fact-checking efficiency, etc. are among future plans as well.

Limitations

Despite encouraging results, this study has several limitations. Narrative quality was evaluated through proxy metrics (coverage, overlap, coherence), but lacked manually annotated ground truth, preventing a direct assessment of factual correctness, hallucination, or omission.

Also, all news articles were in English and focused on disinformation and trustworthy reporting, therefore, results may not generalize to other political genres or languages with different discourse structures.

Furthermore, single LLM (*Mistral Small 3.1 24b*) was used for narrative extraction. Additional experiments are needed to explore whether the observed benefits of Augmented pipeline persist across other LLMs.

Moreover, the downstream task used logistic regression with hand-crafted narrative features. While this helped with interpretability, more complex classifiers might capture additional signals.

In addition, fuzzy Jaccard overlap metric relies on sentence embeddings and thresholds. While it captures surface variation, it may under- or overestimate semantic similarity, especially in terms of figurative or culturally specific language.

Finally, The Augmented pipeline relied on KG-derived context included into the prompt. However, different prompt writing techniques and order of elements making this pipeline (e.g., using LLM outputs to filter KG content) were not tested and the results may be different.

Acknowledgments

This research was funded by the Research Council of Lithuania (LMTLT), grant agreement No. S-PD-24-88.

References

Berkeley R Andrus, Yeganeh Nasiri, Shilong Cui, Benjamin Cullen, and Nancy Fulda. 2022. Enhanced story comprehension for large language models through dynamic document-based knowledge graphs. In *Proceedings of the AAAI Conference on Artificial Intelligence*, volume 36, pages 10436–10444.

Katra Byram. 2022. Narrative as social action: making rhetorical narrative theory accountable to context. *Poetics Today*, 43:455–478.

Pere-Lluís Huguet Cabot and Roberto Navigli. 2021. REBEL: Relation extraction by end-to-end language generation. In *Findings of the Association for Computational Linguistics: EMNLP 2021*, pages 2370–2381.

Valerie Cross, Valeria Mokrenko, Keeley Crockett, and Naeemeh Adel. 2020. Using fuzzy set similarity in sentence similarity measures. In *2020 IEEE International Conference on Fuzzy Systems (FUZZ-IEEE)*, pages 1–8. IEEE.

Rohan Das, Aditya Chandra, I-Ta Lee, and María Leonor Pacheco. 2024. Media framing through the lens of event-centric narratives. In *Proceedings of the The 6th Workshop on Narrative Understanding*, pages 85–98.

Mike de Kok, Youssra Rebboud, Pasquale Lisena, Raphael Troncy, and Ilaria Tiddi. 2024. From nodes to narratives: A knowledge graph-based storytelling approach. In *TEXT2STORY 2024, 7th International Workshop on Narrative Extraction from Texts (Text2Story), colocated with ECIR 2024*.

Günes Erkan and Dragomir R Radev. 2004. Lexrank: Graph-based lexical centrality as salience in text summarization. *Journal of artificial intelligence research*, 22:457–479.

Fausto German, Brian Keith, and Chris North. 2025. Narrative trails: A method for coherent storyline extraction via maximum capacity path optimization. *arXiv preprint arXiv:2503.15681*.

Jean-Christophe Goulet-Pelletier and Denis Cousineau. 2018. A review of effect sizes and their confidence intervals, part i: The Cohen's d family. *The Quantitative Methods for Psychology*, 14(4):242–265.

Dani Gunawan, CA Sembiring, and Mohammad Andri Budiman. 2018. The implementation of cosine similarity to calculate text relevance between two documents. In *Journal of physics: conference series*, volume 978, page 012120. IOP Publishing.

Andy Halterman. 2020. Extracting political events from text using syntax and semantics. *Technical report MIT*.

Hans Ole Hatzel and Chris Biemann. 2023. Narrative cloze as a training objective: Towards modeling stories using narrative chain embeddings. *Proceedings of the The 5th Workshop on Narrative Understanding*.

Mourad Heddaya, Qingcheng Zeng, Alexander Zentefis, Rob Voigt, and Chenhao Tan. 2024. Causal micro-narratives. In *Proceedings of the 6th Workshop on Narrative Understanding*, pages 67–84.

Harshad Hegde, Jennifer Vendetti, Damien Goutte-Gattat, J Harry Caufield, John B Graybeal, Nomi L Harris, Naouel Karam, Christian Kindermann, Nicolas Matentzoglu, James A Overton, Mark A Musen, and Christopher J Mungall. 2025. A change language for ontologies and knowledge graphs. *Database: The Journal of Biological Databases and Curation*, 2025:baae133.

Maria Hellman. 2024. Narrative analysis and framing analysis of disinformation. In *Security, Disinformation and Harmful Narratives: RT and Sputnik News Coverage about Sweden*, pages 101–121. Springer.

Hansi Hettiarachchi, Mariam Adedoyin-Olowe, Jagdev Bhogal, and Mohamed Medhat Gaber. 2021. Daai at case 2021 task 1: Transformer-based multilingual socio-political and crisis event detection. *Proceedings of the 4th Workshop on Challenges and Applications of Automated Extraction of Socio-political Events from Text (CASE 2021)*.

Ella Hofmann-Coyle, Mayank Kulkarni, Lingjue Xie, Mounica Maddela, and Daniel Preoţiuc-Pietro. 2022. Extractive entity-centric summarization as sentence selection using bi-encoders. In *Proceedings of the 2nd Conference of the Asia-Pacific Chapter of the Association for Computational Linguistics and the 12th International Joint Conference on Natural Language Processing (Volume 2: Short Papers)*, pages 326–333.

Ali Hürriyetoğlu, Surendrabikram Thapa, Gökçe Uludoğan, Somaiyeh Dehghan, and Hristo Tanev. 2024. A concise report of the 7th workshop on challenges and applications of automated extraction of socio-political events from text. In *Proceedings of the 7th Workshop on Challenges and Applications of Automated Extraction of Socio-political Events from Text (CASE 2024)*, pages 248–255.

Brian Felipe Keith Norambuena, Tanushree Mitra, and Chris North. 2023. A survey on event-based news narrative extraction. *ACM Computing Surveys*, 55(14s):1–39.

Yuanyuan Lei and Ruihong Huang. 2023. Identifying conspiracy theories news based on event relation graph. In *Findings of the Association for Computational Linguistics: EMNLP 2023*, pages 9811–9822.

João A Leite, Olesya Razuvayevskaya, Kalina Bontcheva, and Carolina Scarton. 2024. Euvsdisinfo: A dataset for multilingual detection of pro-Kremlin disinformation in news articles. In *Proceedings of the 33rd ACM International Conference on Information and Knowledge Management*, pages 5380–5384.

Chang Li. 2021. *Improving Stance and Bias Detection in Text by Modeling Social Context*. Ph.D. thesis, Purdue University.

Haochen Li and Di Geng. 2024. Prompt-based graph model for joint liberal event extraction and event schema induction. *arXiv preprint arXiv:2403.12526*.

Jin Li, Ruifan Yuan, Yu Tian, and Jingsong Li. 2024a. Towards instruction-tuned verification for improving biomedical information extraction with large language models. *2024 IEEE International Conference on Bioinformatics and Biomedicine (BIBM)*, pages 6685–6692.

Sha Li, Revanth Gangi Reddy, Khanh Nguyen, Qingyun Wang, Yi Fung, Chi Han, Jiawei Han, Kartik Natarajan, Clare Voss, and Heng Ji. 2024b. Schema-guided culture-aware complex event simulation with multi-agent role-play. In *Proceedings of the 2024 Conference on Empirical Methods in Natural Language Processing: System Demonstrations*, pages 372–381.

Chin-Yew Lin. 2004. ROUGE: A package for automatic evaluation of summaries. In *Text summarization branches out*, pages 74–81.

Ben Liu, Jihai Zhang, Fangquan Lin, Cheng Yang, Min Peng, and Wotao Yin. 2025. Symagent: A neural-symbolic self-learning agent framework for complex reasoning over knowledge graphs. In *Proceedings of the ACM on Web Conference 2025*, pages 98–108.

Zhengdong Lu, Ziqian Zeng, Jianwei Wang, Hanlin Wang, Weikai Lu, and Huiping Zhuang. 2024. Zero-shot event argument extraction by disentangling trigger from argument and role. *International Journal of Machine Learning and Cybernetics*, pages 1–19.

Nick Mckenna, Tianyi Li, Liang Cheng, Mohammad Hosseini, Mark Johnson, and Mark Steedman. 2023. Sources of hallucination by large language models on inference tasks. In *Findings of the Association for Computational Linguistics: EMNLP 2023*, pages 2758–2774.

Derek Miller. 2019. Leveraging BERT for extractive text summarization on lectures. *arXiv preprint arXiv:1906.04165*.

Cedric Möller, Jens Lehmann, and Ricardo Usbeck. 2022. Survey on english entity linking on wikidata: Datasets and approaches. *Semantic Web*, 13(6):925–966.

Gireen Naidu, Tranos Zuva, and Elias Mmbongeni Sibanda. 2023. A review of evaluation metrics in machine learning algorithms. In *Computer science on-line conference*, pages 15–25. Springer.

Brian Felipe Keith Norambuena and Tanushree Mitra. 2021. Narrative maps. *Proceedings of the ACM on Human-Computer Interaction*, 4:1 – 33.

Rrubaa Panchendrarajan and Arkaitz Zubiaga. 2024. Synergizing machine learning & symbolic methods: A survey on hybrid approaches to natural language processing. *Expert Systems with Applications*, 251:124097.

Armin Pournaki and Tom Willaert. 2024. A graph-based approach to extracting narrative signals from public discourse. *arXiv preprint arXiv:2411.00702*.

Oona Rainio, Jarmo Teuho, and Riku Klén. 2024. Evaluation metrics and statistical tests for machine learning. *Scientific Reports*, 14(1):6086.

Adrian Rauchfleisch and Andreas Jungherr. 2024. Blame and obligation: The importance of libertarianism and political orientation in the public assessment of disinformation in the United States. *Policy & Internet*, 16(4):801–817.

Denise Rey and Markus Neuhäuser. 2011. Wilcoxon-signed-rank test. In *International encyclopedia of statistical science*, pages 1658–1659. Springer.

Angelika Romanou, Syrielle Montariol, Debjit Paul, Léo Laugier, Karl Aberer, and Antoine Bosselut. 2023. Crab: Assessing the strength of causal relationships between real-world events. In *Proceedings of the 2023 Conference on Empirical Methods in Natural Language Processing*, pages 15198–15216.

Brenda Santana, Ricardo Campos, Evelin Amorim, Alípio Jorge, Purificação Silvano, and Sérgio Nunes. 2023. A survey on narrative extraction from textual data. *Artificial Intelligence Review*, 56(8):8393–8435.

Cristian Santini. 2024. Combining language models for knowledge extraction from Italian TEI editions. *Frontiers in Computer Science*, 6:1472512.

Wenbo Shang and Xin Huang. 2024. A survey of large language models on generative graph analytics: Query, learning, and applications. *arXiv preprint arXiv:2404.14809*.

Zhu Shen, Ambarish Chattopadhyay, Yuzhou Lin, and Jose R Zubizarreta. 2024. An anatomy of event studies: hypothetical experiments, exact decomposition, and weighting diagnostics. *arXiv preprint arXiv:2410.17399*.

Jialong Tang, Hongyu Lin, M. Liao, Yaojie Lu, Xianpei Han, Le Sun, Weijian Xie, and Jin Xu. 2021. From discourse to narrative: Knowledge projection for event relation extraction. *ArXiv*, abs/2106.08629.

Nikos Voskarides, Edgar Meij, Sabrina Sauer, and Maarten de Rijke. 2021. News article retrieval in context for event-centric narrative creation. In *Proceedings of the 2021 ACM SIGIR International Conference on Theory of Information Retrieval*, pages 103–112.

Guan Wang, Rebecca Frederick, Jinglong Duan, William BL Wong, Verica Rupar, Weihua Li, and Quan Bai. 2025. Detecting misinformation through framing theory: the frame element-based model. *Journal of Computational Social Science*, 8(3):72.

Shaofei Wang. 2025. Enhancing in-context learning of large language models for knowledge graph reasoning via rule-and-reinforce selected triples. *Applied Sciences*, 15(3):1088.

Zihao Wang, Hang Yin, and Yangqiu Song. 2022. Logical queries on knowledge graphs: emerging interface of incomplete relational data. *IEEE Data Eng. Bull.*, 45(4):3–18.

Yilin Wen, Zifeng Wang, and Jimeng Sun. 2024. Mindmap: Knowledge graph prompting sparks graph of thoughts in large language models. In *Proceedings of the 62nd Annual Meeting of the Association for Computational Linguistics (Volume 1: Long Papers)*, pages 10370–10388.

Tzu-Tsung Wong and Po-Yang Yeh. 2019. Reliable accuracy estimates from k-fold cross validation. *IEEE Transactions on Knowledge and Data Engineering*, 32(8):1586–1594.

Peiyi Yang, Bin Song, and Zhiyong Zhang. 2024. Research on knowledge graph construction methods for news domain. *Academic Journal of Science and Technology*, 11(1):58–64.

Hao Zhang, Frank Boons, and Riza Batista-Navarro. 2019. Whose story is it anyway? Automatic extraction of accounts from news articles. *Information processing & management*, 56(5):1837–1848.

Tong Zhou, Yubo Chen, Kang Liu, and Jun Zhao. 2024. Cogmg: Collaborative augmentation between large language model and knowledge graph. In *Proceedings of the 62nd Annual Meeting of the Association for Computational Linguistics (Volume 3: System Demonstrations)*, pages 365–373.

Shenzhe Zhu. 2024. Exploring knowledge graph-based neural-symbolic system from application perspective. *arXiv e-prints*, pages arXiv–2405.

Yuqi Zhu, Xiaohan Wang, Jing Chen, Shuofei Qiao, Yixin Ou, Yunzhi Yao, Shumin Deng, Huajun Chen, and Ningyu Zhang. 2024. LLMs for knowledge graph construction and reasoning: recent capabilities and future opportunities. *World Wide Web*, 27(5):58.

Ling Zhuang, Hao Fei, and Po Hu. 2023. Knowledge-enhanced event relation extraction via event ontology prompt. *Information Fusion*, 100:101919.

A Examples of News Article Summaries

In this section a few examples of news article summaries are presented together with their ROUGE scores. The summary extracted with the method that achieved higher ROUGE score, which reflects higher overlap with original text, was used in the experiments (Table 12).

Title	LexRank summary	BERT extractive summary	ROUGE (LexRank)	ROUGE (BERT)
EU supports Zelen-sky's peace plan – Michel	Ukraine is The European Union and The European Union is Ukraine. In Africa, in Asia, China and in Latin America, in every meeting with foreign leaders, support for Ukraine is the first issue The European Union raise, European Council President Charles Michel said. The damages caused by Russia to Ukraine must be compensated and all those – without exception – responsible must be and will be held accountable, European Council President Charles Michel said. The European Union have frozen over EUR 300 billion of Russian assets. Since day one of Russia's attack, Europeans have understood that Russia's attack is more than an attack on Ukraine. The European Union is more united than ever.	The European Union supports the Peace Plan proposed by President of Ukraine Volodymyr Zelensky, European Council President Charles Michel has said. You this goal an end to this war of aggression and The European Union shares this goal with you. The damages caused by Russia to Ukraine must be compensated and all those – without exception – responsible must be and will be held accountable, European Council President Charles Michel said. European Council President Charles Michel am strongly convinced over EUR 300 billion of Russian assets should and will be used for Ukraine's reconstruction. Since day one of Russia's attack, Europeans have understood that Russia's attack is more than an attack on Ukraine.	0.291	**0.292**

Title	LexRank summary	BERT extractive summary	ROUGE (LexRank)	ROUGE (BERT)
International Space Station preparing for 'space taxis'	Two astronauts will prepare the International Space Station for two new docks for the spacecraft that will ferry astronauts and gear to and from the International Space Station. Two new docks for the spacecraft that will ferry astronauts and gear to and from the station will allow both Boeing CST's and SpaceX's Dragon spacecraft to dock on thc American side of the ISS, even though the two companies' ships are designed differently. The astronauts will be setting up cables on the first two walks and antennae on the third walk scheduled for March 1. It will be the first time vessels have docked on the American side of the ISS since NASA ended the Space Shuttle program. NASA awarded Boeing a $4.2 billion contract in September to develop a transportation capable of carrying human passengers.	A spacewalk outside the ISS planned for Friday was postponed by a day, after "added analysis of spacesuits" the astronauts will wear, according to a NASA statement. NASA confirmed it needed more time to look at suits but did not give additional information. Boeing is building two new docks for the spacecraft that will ferry astronauts and gear to and from the station. SpaceX will carry two new docks to the ISS on cargo mission CRS-7. If all goes according to plan, it will be the first time vessels have docked on the American side of the ISS since NASA ended the Shuttle program. It will also allow NASA to increase crew size and scientific research.	**0.622**	0.59

Title	LexRank summary	BERT extractive summary	ROUGE (LexRank)	ROUGE (BERT)
The Maduro Diet: Food v. Freedom in Venezuela	Nicolas Maduro's regime has been unable to control inflation, which has disintegrated Venezuela's economy. As a result, many poor Venezuelans are now dependent on CLAP deliveries to put food on the table. A politically motivated food system called CLAP has become an essential part of nearly half the population's diet. Those overseeing the program earn a 200% profit per box. Though the regime aims to reduce dependence on imports, 90% of CLAP boxes come from Mexico. The international community should link external pressure with renewed political opposition to bring about a democratic transition.	As Venezuela's humanitarian crisis deepens, Maduro's regime has exploited it to tighten political control. Poverty has risen from 55% in 1998 to nearly 90% today. Though the regime claims to reduce food import dependence, 90% of CLAP boxes come from Mexico. The weaponization of the CLAP program is a sign of a desperate regime. The use of cryptocurrency-based aid models like EatBCH may help.	**0.294**	0.212

Table 12: Examples of news article summaries

B Statistics of the Final Dataset

This section presents a basic analysis of the final dataset used for experiments. Table 13 presents article distribution per year in the final dataset. For trustworthy articles, 2020 had the largest number of articles (109), while for disinformation the articles were distributed more equally, with 2019 and 2020 having the largest numbers (46 each).

Year	Disinformation	Trustworthy
2015	18	3
2016	26	9
2017	29	14
2018	43	24
2019	46	52
2020	46	109
2021	28	22
2022	43	52
2023	28	17

Table 13: Article distribution 2015-2023.

Table 14 lists publishers with the highest numbers of articles in the final dataset, where for disinformation the main publisher was RT (166 articles) and for trustworthy news the articles were more equally distributed with BBC having the largest number of articles (28).

Publishers	
Disinformation	**Trustworthy**
RT (166)	BBC (28)
TASS (51)	Polygraph.info (25)
Sputnik (15)	The Guardian (24)
Geopolitica.ru (12)	Radio Free Europe (11)
Global research (11)	DW.com (10)

Table 14: Publishers with the largest number of articles (number in brackets) in the final dataset.

Similarities and differences in topics across disinformation and trustworthy articles in the final dataset can be seen in word clouds (Fig. 1) representing the most frequent 25 words, excluding stopwords, of each part, with 'russian' being the most frequent word word in both groups of articles. Also, in both groups Russian-Ukrainian war related word forms are prominent, with 'said' being the most frequent word form. Furthermore, in trustworthy articles 'coronavirus' is among the most frequent word forms, while in disinformation articles this word form is not among most frequent ones, indicating difference in topic coverage.

C Prompts Used for LLM-only and Augmented Extractions of Narrative Elements

For LLM-only extraction of narrative elements, the following prompt was used:

```
prompt_text = (
"Extract the following narrative
elements from the news article:\n"
"- Characters (Who are the key actors?)\n"
"- Events (What happened?)\n"
"- Causal Links (Why did it happen?)\n"
"- Framing:\n"
"    - Actor Framing: How are key actors
(individuals, organizations) portrayed?
(e.g., hero, villain, expert, victim)\n"
"    - Event Framing: How is the event
presented? (e.g., crisis, scandal,
breakthrough, tragedy)\n\n"
f"News summary: {best_summary}")
```

For Augmented pipeline, the prompt below was used:

```
prompt_text = (
"Extract the following narrative elements
from the news article:\n"
"- Characters (Who are the key actors?)\n"
"- Events (What happened?)\n"
"- Causal Links (Why did it happen?)\n"
"- Framing:\n"
"    - Actor Framing: How are key actors
portrayed? (e.g., hero, villain)\n"
"    - Event Framing: How is the event
presented? (e.g., crisis, breakthrough)\n\n"
f"News summary:\n{best_summary}\n\n"
f"Knowledge Graph context:\n{kg_context}")
```

D REBEL Relation Sets/Mappings

The relations of REBEL schema that imply framing, events and causality were mapped and inferred manually:

Relations suggesting events or time-anchored nodes:

- Participation-based: "participant_in", "participant", "winner", "candidate", "candidacy_in_election".
- Achievement or outcome: "award_received", "notable_work", "nominated_for".
- Conflict or disruption: "conflict", "significant_event", "victory", "replaced_by", "replaces".
- Time anchors: "inception", "start_time", "end_time", "point_in_time", "publication_date", "date_of_birth", "date_of_death", "work_period_(start)", "work_period_start".

(a) Most frequent word forms in disinformation articles

(b) Most frequent word forms in trustworthy articles

Figure 1: Most frequent word forms

- Organizational change: "founded_by", "dissolved_abolished_or_demolished_date", "location_of_formation", "established_date".
- Media & Creative: "original_broadcaster", "composer", "director", "producer", "production_company"

Relations suggesting causality:

- Explicit causality: "has_cause", "causes", "has_effect", "influenced_by", "leads_to", "responds_with".
- Implied causality: "participant_in", "participant", "winner", "founded_by", "replaced_by", "replaces", "award_received", "influenced_by", "significant_event", "conflict", "start_time", "end_time"

Relations suggesting framing:

- Explicit framing:
  - "described_as": "is portrayed as"
  - "depicts": "is represented as"
  - "notable_work": "is known for"
  - "award_received": "is recognized for"
  - "member_of_political_party": "is affiliated with"
  - "replaced_by": "is portrayed as outdated or replaced by"
  - "founded_by": "was founded by"
- Causal interpretation framing:
  - "has_cause": "is caused by"
  - "causes": "causes",
  - "has_effect": "results in"
  - "influenced_by": "is influenced by"
  - "leads_to": "leads to"
  - "responds_with": "is responded to with"
  - "participant_in": "participated in"
  - "participant": "participated in"
  - "winner": "wins due to"
  - "candidate": "candidacy in"
  - "significant_event": "is triggered by"
  - "conflict": "is involved in conflict"
  - "start_time": "starts at"
  - "end_time": "ends at"

E Downstream Classification Setup

The downstream classification setup for extrinsic evaluation consisted of the following:

- For each pipeline, a feature matrix was formed.
- Feature sets:
  - LLM-only: counts of narrative elements and values of embedding-based coherence measure produced by LLM-only pipeline from extractive summaries of news articles.
  - KG-only: counts of narrative elements and values of graph-based coherence measures (density, avg. path length, largest component ratio) produced by KG-only pipeline from extractive summaries of news articles.

  - Augmented: counts of narrative elements and values of embedding-based coherence measure produced by Augmented pipeline from extractive summaries of news articles.

- For classification, a scikit-learn pipeline was used:

  StandardScaler() $\rightarrow$ LogisticRegression(solver='liblinear', penalty='l2', C=1.0, max_iter=100) (defaults shown).

- Evaluation was performed with StratifiedKFold (5 and 10 splits, shuffle=True, random_state=42) using F1 as the primary metric via cross_val_score. Mean ± SD across folds are reported as well. Significance is assessed on fold-wise F1 with paired t and Wilcoxon signed-rank tests. Effect sizes were evaluated with Cohen's d.

Abstractive Event Analysis of Armed Conflicts: Introducing the UCDP-AEC Dataset

Étienne Simon[*1] **and Helene Bøsei Olsen**[*1] **and Ramón Carreño**[1] **and Rahul Mishra**[1]
Nikolay Arefyev[1] **and Mert Can Yilmaz**[2] **and Lilja Øvrelid**[1] **and Erik Velldal**[1]
[1] University of Oslo, [2] Uppsala University

Abstract

This paper introduces a new dataset of document-level event annotations in the domain of armed conflict. By augmenting the event database from the Uppsala Conflict Data Program (UCDP) with source documents identified in public web archives, we create the *UCDP Abstractive Event analysis Corpus* (UCDP-AEC). While a large part of research on information extraction is focused on extracting text spans, real-world use cases often require inferring more high-level information that is not necessarily explicitly mentioned in texts. UCDP-AEC differs from traditional event extraction datasets in that the document-level annotations do not correspond to mere text spans of the input, but capture expert-interpreted and often implicit information. With more than 10 000 documents, UCDP-AEC is of comparable size to the largest human-annotated traditional event extraction datasets. We also report preliminary experimental results for various generative approaches, by fine-tuning both decoder models and existing event argument extraction models that require minimal adaptation to our abstractive formulation of the task.

1 Introduction

For several decades, the Uppsala Conflict Data Program (UCDP) has compiled and released datasets on quantitative armed conflict event data (Sundberg and Melander, 2013; Davies et al., 2024), designed primarily to enable research on the causes, dynamics, and consequences of organised violence, as well as supporting research projects such as predicting conflict escalation (Hegre et al., 2022). UCDP's event database, the Georeferenced Event Dataset (GED), encodes rich information about incidents related to organised violence, including casualty counts, involved actors, location, time, and more. An example of (a relevant subset of) the data fields

> 2014-05-25 Islamabad: At least eight militants and two soldiers were killed in a gun battle in Pakistan's restive northwest tribal area, a security official said. The incident occurred late yesterday in Landikotal area of Khyber tribal agency. "Two soldiers embraced shahadat (martyrdom) and three others injured this evening in an exchange of fire with terrorists in Landikotal, Khyber," The Dawn said. Three soldiers were also injured, according to the security official. Yesterday was a deadly day for forces as six soldiers and a civilian were killed in three separate bombings in Pakistan, including twin blasts in the heavily guarded capital. The soldiers were killed in Mohmand agency which borders Khyber.

Actors	**Side A:** Government of Pakistan **Side B:** TTP
Date	**Start:** 2014-05-24 **End:** 2014-05-24
Location	**Country:** Pakistan **Subregion:** Khyber agency **Region:** Federally Administered Tribal Areas **Point:** Landi Kotal town
Deaths	**Side A:** 2 **Side B:** 8 **Civilian:** 0 **Unknown:** 0 **Low:** 10 **High:** 10

Figure 1: Sample document with UCDP annotations. The document reports on an armed conflict event and includes the publication date and location. The annotations specify the two conflict actors, the start and end dates of the event, four levels of location detail, and death counts for each side, civilians and unknown individuals. Estimated total deaths are given as low (conservative) and high (maximum reliable) figures.

and corresponding values for a given input document is shown in Figure 1. Carried out through manual coding by human experts, the process is highly resource-demanding and time-consuming, making it challenging to scale to larger data sources and update in near real-time. Moreover, the continual exposure to accounts of violence can cause emotional and psychological distress for those involved in manual coding. For several reasons, automated machine-coding of events could offer valuable assistance in the annotation process.

The UCDP GED example above illustrates a

[*] Equal contribution.

Proceedings of the 21st Conference on Natural Language Processing (KONVENS), Volume 2: Workshops, pages 104–119, 2025

more general challenge acknowledged in other recent work on event extraction (EE) and information extraction (IE) for real-world applications, which is the need to move beyond span-based annotations. For example, Olsen et al. (2024) refer to an 'abstraction gap' when discussing the differences between the text-bound annotations common in most NLP datasets for EE versus the higher-level information documented in socio-political event databases. In such databases, coders aim to represent what actually happened in the real world, drawing on contextual understanding and domain expertise. As demonstrated in Figure 1, important event information often can not be found as a single continuous text span. Instead they must often be inferred from indirect references (e.g., "soldiers" or "militants" as proxies for specific groups), resolved through temporal reasoning (e.g., interpreting "yesterday" relative to the publication date of the source document), aggregated from scattered mentions (e.g., casualty counts reported across multiple sentences), or produced through numerical reasoning (e.g., combining the casualty counts across parties). Locations and actors can be described at varying levels of granularity and may require entity-linking to canonical forms, and the dynamic nature of conflicts means new actors and conflicts continually emerge, introducing important temporal variations. On the basis of considerations like this, Simon et al. (2024) advocate for a shift from an "extractive" to an "abstractive" view of the EE task, proposing to use generative approaches for capturing more higher-level event information. Similarly, Sharif et al. (2024) also show how event information can be scattered across a document or only implicitly stated, and propose a generative formulation of event argument extraction.

While the recognition of the challenges associated with real-world applications is growing, the majority of traditional event extraction datasets within Natural Language Processing (NLP) are annotated in the extractive paradigm, capturing only text-bound facts (Doddington et al., 2004; Song et al., 2015; Li et al., 2021). On the other hand, while there is an abundance of high-quality event databases developed within social and political sciences (Sundberg and Melander, 2013; Raleigh et al., 2010; Chenoweth et al., 2019; Salehyan et al., 2012; Turchin, 2012), the source documents are generally not made available (Olsen et al., 2024), representing a missed opportunity for training machine-learning models for domain-specific applications. As a case in point, the event annotations of the UCDP GED are publicly available, but the corresponding source documents used by the human coders are not licensed for redistribution in the original database.

Contributions To bridge NLP modelling with socio-political event coding, we introduce the new dataset UCDP-AEC, a conflict event dataset for abstractive event analysis built from UCDP GED, augmented with pointers to the underlying source texts.[1] The dataset covers 11 363 documents describing armed conflict events and links expert-annotated event records to their corresponding source documents. UCDP-AEC focuses on a single event type, and every document in the dataset contains a single, relevant event of the same type, where each event is annotated with a fixed set of 14 fields. Reflecting the complexities of real-world event reports, the annotations often demand numerical and temporal reasoning, world- and domain knowledge, contextual integration, and entity linking to canonical forms. We refer to this challenging task of structured prediction as abstractive event analysis.

We show how a substantial subset of the documents from the UCDP GED database can be identified and retrieved from the public web archives of HPLT v2 (High Performance Language Technologies; Burchell et al., 2025), and that distributing the corresponding document IDs provides a way to establish an open dataset for event analysis that can be used by the NLP community, ultimately also benefitting the peace and conflict studies. Finally, we report on the first experimental results for a suite of generative approaches on the new dataset.

2 Related Work

Relation to other NLP tasks Automatically extracting UCDP-AEC event structures combines elements from multiple NLP tasks involving representing and understanding event-centric information in text. The task includes aspects of temporal reasoning, text summarisation, and entity-linking, but is best understood as a form of event extraction (or perhaps more narrowly the associated subtask of event argument extraction) though in a way that diverges from typical NLP formulations.

While event extraction is a widely studied task in NLP, the current annotation paradigm and bench-

[1]The dataset alongside evaluation scripts and baseline models are available at `https://github.com/ltgoslo/ucdp-aec`.

mark datasets do not correspond well to the types of events typically encoded in socio-political event databases. Even though both tasks aim to derive structured event information from unstructured text, existing NLP datasets typically contain sentence-level event information that corresponds to substrings in the input text (Doddington et al., 2004; Song et al., 2015), while socio-political event recordings typically capture higher-level event information inferred from the entire document, possibly in combination with domain knowledge. For instance, in the news article shown in Figure 1, Side B is described in the text as "militants" and "terrorists". However, a socio-political event database is expected to convey the specific group involved ("TTP" in this case) based on contextual information such as time and location.

The datasets from the Automatic Content Extraction (ACE; Doddington et al., 2004) program have been highly influential in the development and evaluation of event extraction systems in NLP, inspiring further development of several datasets with more detailed processing of entities and events in the ERE (Entities, Relations and Events) dataset (Song et al., 2015), document-level event extraction from Wikipedia articles in the WikiEvents dataset (Li et al., 2021), from news articles referenced in Wikipedia articles in the DocEE dataset (Tong et al., 2022), and domain-specific content (Sun et al., 2022; Satyapanich et al., 2020).

Some recent works have taken a step towards removing the reliance on surface forms for event extraction. For the task of Chinese financial event extraction, Zheng et al. (2019) do not extract trigger words, but still rely on text spans for argument extraction. More recently, Sharif et al. (2024) challenge the traditional span-based approach and introduce DiscourseEE, an online health discourse dataset annotated with explicit, implicit, and scattered arguments. Apart from DiscourseEE, a related work to ours is the early version of the task introduced at the Message Understanding Conferences (MUC; Sundheim, 1992),with the most well-known being the MUC-4 dataset, which is annotated with rich, high-level, and fine-grained information in the form of event templates at the document level. Recent work has renewed focus on the MUC-4 data, however, existing work is largely limited to argument roles that correspond directly to explicit text spans from the source document (Du et al., 2021a,b; Gantt et al., 2024).

Concurrent to our work Semnani et al. (2025) introduce LEMONADE, a large-scale multilingual dataset for abstractive event extraction based on a re-annotated subset of the ACLED database (Raleigh et al., 2010). It spans 25 closely related socio-political event types over a 13-month period and includes an abstractive entity linking task to a curated domain-specific entity database. Each event type is associated with a specific schema, which supports a variety of argument types, including categorical fields, booleans, and integers, with many roles limited to values in a pre-defined database, and some re-annotated to only reflect information explicitly present in the text. In contrast, UCDP-AEC focuses on a single domain, fatal armed conflicts, grounded in the expert coding of UCDP GED, with a fixed 14-field schema that is always filled, often requiring inference over implicit or scattered evidence. UCDP-AEC contains multiple open domain roles, such as exact event dates or fine-grained location details, without requiring that the gold value appear verbatim in the document.

Largely independently of the NLP community, the political science community has seen the development of their own event extraction systems (Schrodt et al., 1994; Norris et al., 2017; Halterman et al., 2023). However, these systems tend to rely on older rule-based models prone to over-counting events and producing numerous false positives, which has limited their use in political science research (Raleigh et al., 2023). Not relying on learned models and annotated datasets also makes most systems less flexible and adaptable. Some initial work making training data available is worth mentioning though, such as GLOCON (Global Contentious Politics Dataset; Duruşan et al., 2022) and CEHA (Conflict Events in the Horn of Africa region; Bai et al., 2025), with the latter reaching 500 events, but with annotations for event detection and classification only.

Generative approaches to event extraction In recent years, the NLP field has seen a transition from traditional sequence labelling approaches for event extraction (Wadden et al., 2019; Nguyen et al., 2016) towards generative methods where the task is framed as a structured text generation task (Lu et al., 2021; Li et al., 2021). Generative methods present a promising path to move beyond span-based annotations by allowing models to generate structured event representations directly from text, and may be suitable for tasks requiring inference from under-specified information and long document contexts, such as for UCDP-AEC.

However, the current landscape of generative approaches to event analysis still remains closely tied to the extractive paradigm (Simon et al., 2024). As the architecture and training objective of generative models are intended for producing free-form text, they provide a less natural fit to the extractive setting, where the goal is to identify and reproduce exact text spans from the source text. As a consequence, implementations of generative event extraction models often include additional constraints to ensure that the generated string appears in the input, such as constraint decoding in the Text2Event model (Lu et al., 2021), or the pointer mechanism in the BART-Gen model (Li et al., 2021).

Recently, several decoder-only models have been developed for generative event extraction, such as DeepStruct (Wang et al., 2022), InstructUIE (Wang et al., 2023), YAYI-UIE (Xiao et al., 2023), a Baichuan2 model (Yang et al., 2023), and LLMEE (Chen et al., 2024). Notably, except for DeepStruct and YAYI-UIE, most works, including LLMEE, do not involve any task-specific fine-tuning, relying solely on in-context learning. While these models, in addition to some encoder-decoder models such as DEGREE (Hsu et al., 2022), do not explicitly constrain their outputs to input tokens during prediction, they remain in the extractive paradigm through evaluation, where the predictions are converted into text spans for evaluation against benchmarks such as ACE (Doddington et al., 2004).

3 The UCDP GED Conflict Database

An event in the UCDP GED database is defined as an incident where armed force was used by an organised actor resulting in at least one direct death at a specific location and date. In this section, we provide some background on the UCDP GED annotations, starting with the annotation process itself, followed by a description of the relevant data fields that we include in the derived UCDP-AEC dataset described in Section 4.

3.1 Annotation Process

The UCDP GED database follows a rigorous, multi-step process to document each instance of fatal organised violence as a distinct event (Sundberg and Melander, 2013). Data collection begins with global search queries in the Dow Jones Factiva aggregator, yielding tens of thousands of news reports annually. These reports are then supplemented with local and social media sources, as well as information from NGOs and international organisations. Reports are meticulously examined by a team of around 15 analysts, who hold advanced degrees in peace and conflict studies or related fields and possess extensive regional and conflict-specific expertise. They identify and code events according to strict methodological criteria, assigning detailed spatial, temporal, and actor identifiers (Högbladh, 2023). The individual event entries are subsequently categorised into three mutually exclusive types of violence: state-based, non-state, or one-sided.

A candidate event is only included in the final event database after several stages of validation, including both manual review and automated consistency tests. In sum, this comprehensive coding approach aims to provide a high level of accuracy and reliability in capturing global patterns of organised violence, and updated versions of UCDP GED are published annually.[2] The current full GED contains more than 500 000 events with a good coverage of all world conflicts from 1989 onwards.

3.2 Data Fields

The UCDP GED database contains a wide range of different data fields, which, beyond event information, include source metadata, estimates of annotation reliability, identifiers linking to other databases, and more. In this work, however, we limit the description to the 14 fields selected for the new UCDP-AEC dataset as shown in Figure 1 and in Appendix C.[3] We group the event fields into the following four categories, each with associated challenges.

Actors The two fields "Side A" and "Side B" corresponds to the two parties of a conflict. "Side A" is always an organised actor, while "Side B" can be either an organised actor or "Civilians" when the first side kills people indiscriminately. All mentions of the same actor are labelled with a unique canonical name, rather than how they are referred to in the text.

Dates The two fields "Start Date" and "End Date" reference a time range during which the event occurred. As UCDP aims to record events with a day-level precision, the start and end dates will typ-

[2] `https://ucdp.uu.se/downloads/`

[3] For the complete list and description of the fields in UCDP GED, see Högbladh (2023).

ically be identical for most events.[4] Both relative time references – also known as temporal deixis – and the publication date and time are used to identify the start and end date of an event, as shown in Figure 1.

Locations The location of the event is described by four fields with an increasing level of precision. The first field, country, is always provided and indicates where the event took place. Each country is divided into region and subregion, which may be left empty if the location does not align with administrative areas. The point field refers to a city-level location, such as a town or a specific site, such as "Jabal al Akrad mountain", and may also be empty if the location is unclear.

Deaths Six distinct fields are used to describe the casualties associated with the conflict event. Specifically, the fields represent the number of casualties on each side of the conflict, the number of civilian casualties, and the number of deaths that cannot be attributed to any of those categories. In the case of one-sided violence – when "Side B" is "Civilians" – the number of civilian casualties is reported in the field "Deaths Civilians". Uncertainty in casualty reporting is reflected in the fields "Deaths Low" and "Deaths High", representing the most conservative estimate and the highest reliable estimate, respectively, for the total number of fatalities reported in the source text.

4 The UCDP-AEC Dataset

In this section, we describe the construction of the new UCDP-AEC dataset designed for machine learning applications based on the socio-political database UCDP GED. We begin by outlining the event filtering process, which ensures a one-to-one correspondence between events and documents. We then outline how we used publicly available web archives to make the data available. Finally, we present some descriptive statistics of UCDP-AEC, followed by a discussion of relevant challenges.

4.1 Event Selection

Since the UCDP GED is annotated for political science research rather than machine learning applications, some filtering was necessary to adapt the data for automated event analysis. In particular, some events are referenced by multiple source articles, some of which reference multiple events. In practice, the annotators are aware of which parts of a document have already been coded in the database, ensuring that there is no confusion. However, from an NLP perspective, this would require modelling the problem as mapping a set of documents to a set of events without a simple one-to-one correspondence between them. To simplify the problem, we only include events described by a single source and sources that describe a single event. Furthermore, because of the limited amount of non-English documents in the selected subset, we restricted UCDP-AEC to English-language documents. Additional details on data filtering are provided in Appendix A.

4.2 Web Archive Identification of Sources

HPLT matching The documents used to create the GED are not public. Since UCDP relies in part on large news networks for its source documents, we cannot indiscriminately share them. Instead, we distribute only the IDs of documents that can be found freely on the web. To this end, we make use of the recently released HPLT v2 dataset,[5] which consists of texts extracted from web crawls provided by two major web crawling initiatives, Common Crawl and the Internet Archive. It contains 21 billion documents released under a CC0 licence. Using the MinHash algorithm (Broder, 1997), we selected the UCDP documents having an approximate Jaccard similarity of at least 0.5 with an HPLT document.

Human evaluation of HPLT matching The search for documents in HPLT web crawls introduces some biases. In particular, the older a document is, the more likely it is to have been crawled. We recovered only 11 documents from 2023 and none from 2024, despite thousands being annotated in UCDP during those years.

Furthermore, the MinHash document matching used to replace the original UCDP documents with their HPLT version is not exact. It is not uncommon for news providers to update their articles as new information becomes available. These different versions of the same article have a high syntactic similarity – as measured by their Jaccard index – but can convey different event information – for example, when the number of deaths is updated. To assess the quality of the HPLT substitution, we performed a manual comparison of HPLT documents with their original UCDP documents.

[4] In some cases, the precise date remains uncertain due to vague temporal references in the text, such as "last week". In such cases, the start and end dates will differ by a week.

[5] `https://hplt-project.org/datasets/v2.0`

Split	Train	Validation	Test
Documents	10 064	651	648
Period	< 2021	2021	≥ 2022

Table 1: Number of documents and years in each split.

Three annotators assessed a total of 130 documents and found 96.9% documents were a perfect match, with 98.5% containing the same information for 3 out of the 4 categories of fields in the event records (Actors, Date, Location, Deaths).

4.3 Dataset Statistics and Analysis

UCDP-AEC consists of 11 363 document–event pairs, where each document is annotated with a single event record with the 14 fields described in Section 3. These fields vary in how constrained their value spaces are, a property we call domain openness. In this subsection, we describe the dataset splits and document length, as well as challenges associated with each field with a particular focus on how open or closed the value space is for each role.

Domain openness We define a closed-domain field as one whose admissible values make up a relatively small, and mostly fixed set that recurs frequently in the corpus (e.g., country names). In contrast, an open-domain field is characterised by a large or evolving set of admissible values, often including many items not seen during training (e.g., event-specific dates). To quantify this property, we report for each field in Table 2 the three following metrics: *value density* $\frac{|\mathcal{D}|}{|\mathcal{Y}|}$ which denotes the mean number of instances per unique value. Here, lower values indicate a more open domain. *Unique value overlap* $\frac{|\mathcal{Y}_{\text{test}} \cap \mathcal{Y}_{\text{train}}|}{|\mathcal{Y}_{\text{test}}|}$ denotes the proportion of unique test values that also occur in the training set. Finally, *instance-level overlap* $\frac{|\mathcal{D}_{\text{test}} \cap \mathcal{D}_{\text{train}}|}{|\mathcal{D}_{\text{test}}|}$ measures the proportion of test instances whose value is observed during training. We describe these metrics in more detail in Appendix B.

Standard splits To mimic the complexity of modelling a dynamic domain, where new conflicts and violent groups arise and relationships between entities change, we provide standard splits based on temporal information, considering both the occurrence and reporting times of events. Events from 2021 are taken for validation, older events are used for training, while the most recent events, from 2022 and later, are reserved for the test split. See Table 1 for the size of the respective splits.

Field	Density	Unique Overlap	Instance Overlap
Source article	1.00	0.00%	0.00%
Source date	1.76	0.00%	0.00%
Side A	27.31	71.74%	94.91%
Side B	26.24	60.24%	80.25%
Date Start	3.17	0.00%	0.00%
Date End	3.15	0.00%	0.00%
Location Country	129.12	93.18%	99.54%
Location Region	18.78	81.09%	83.33%
Location Subregion	6.49	51.30%	60.80%
Location Point	2.75	27.76%	40.74%
Deaths Side A	183.27	83.33%	99.54%
Deaths Side B	155.66	100.00%	100.00%
Deaths Civilian	195.91	94.74%	99.85%
Deaths Unknown	241.77	100.00%	100.00%
Deaths Low	113.63	90.00%	99.54%
Deaths High	97.96	90.24%	99.38%

Table 2: Per field statistics showing the value density, the unique value overlap between test and train set, and the instance-level overlap between test and train.

Document length The average length of the 11 363 documents in UCDP-AEC is 315 words (white-space separated / non-tokenised). However, there is a significant variation in document length, ranging from as few as 26 words to 1 781 words. This wide range reflects the variation in source materials used to collect armed conflict events, from short summaries to longer regional reports.

Location distribution The dataset covers events that occur in 88 countries. Figure 2 shows the temporal shifts in the geographical distribution between the splits. For example, the training set is dominated by events occurring in Syria, the validation set (2021) shows increased violence in countries such as the Philippines and Myanmar, and the test set reflects the heightened violence in Nigeria alongside the further invasion of Ukraine. With respect to openness, illustrated in Table 2, the set of possible country values is, to a large degree, limited and fixed. With only a few countries in the test set that are not present in the training set, the country field should be considered a relatively closed domain. There is, however, a relationship between location granularity and domain openness, where Subregion can be regarded as semi-open, while Region and Point tend to be highly event-specific, with a test

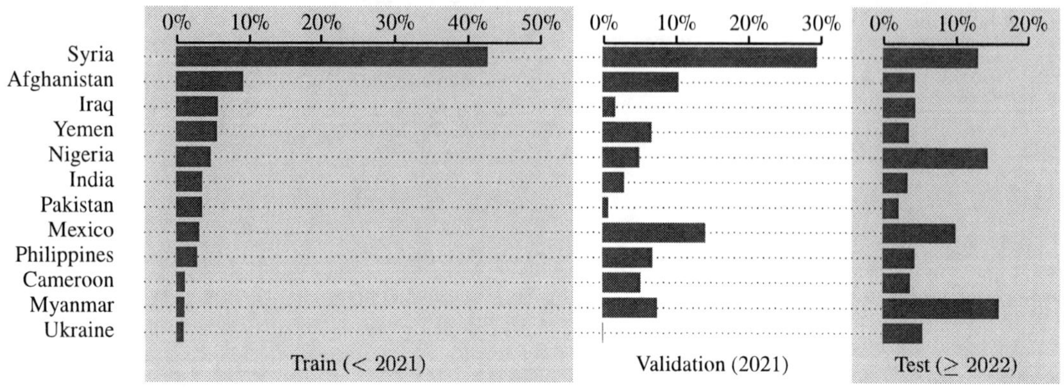

Figure 2: Repartition of events per country in each split for the 12 most eventful countries. A clear increase in conflict events can be seen in Nigeria and Myanmar, showcasing how the dataset reflects the changing dynamics of real-world conflict over time.

set containing many unseen values.

Actors The Actor roles often feature governments, organisations, or group names that are moderately recurrent, but also include many entities that appear only in specific events. Due to the dataset's temporal splits, a notable proportion of actor names in the test set do not appear in the training set, mirroring the involvement of new actors in ongoing and emerging armed conflicts. For example, the test set includes events involving the Indigenous People of Biafra (IPOB), a Nigerian separatist group that started engaging in violent attacks in 2021.[6] Several test documents labelled with IPOB contain references to members of the Eastern Security Network (ESN), which is the paramilitary wing of IPOB. Identifying the two surface forms as references to the same entities is a particularly difficult challenge.

Date Start date and end date are by design fully open (0% unique-value overlap) due to the temporal partitioning of the splits. Since UCDP-AEC only includes single-day events, 91.4% of events have matching start and end dates as expected. When the start and end dates differ, it indicates uncertainty or imprecision in the source document about the exact date of the event.

Deaths Death-related fields are largely a closed domain with high density and overlap. However, identifying the correct values from text may still be challenging. Death counts can be expressed in various ways, such as explicit numbers, ranges (e.g., "between 15 and 20"), or approximations (e.g., "dozens killed"), and require mapping to the affected individuals or parties. In the deaths category, the low and high estimates are identical in 87.1% of the cases, again indicating that the exact number is often reported. However, for 7.3% of the events, the best estimate is equal to 0 – that is the sum of deaths on side A, side B, civilians and unknown – implying that the annotator questioned the truthfulness of the reported event.

[6]`https://ucdp.uu.se/actor/6287`

5 Experiments

This section reports on the first preliminary experiments on training and evaluating models for abstractive event analysis on UCDP-AEC.

5.1 Evaluation Metrics

Unlike classical event extraction, which only assigns roles to arguments that are explicitly mentioned in the input text, all fields in UCDP-AEC are assigned a value in all instances. Even when not explicitly stated in the document, argument values are deducted from the context. Since this is an information extraction task where the goal is to abstract away surface form differences, we evaluate model predictions using exact match accuracies for each field. This contrasts with the usual F_1 metrics reported in the classical task, where roles are not always attached to an event, as extractive models may predict excess or insufficient roles.[7] We average the accuracies of different fields over the same category. For example, we report location accuracy by averaging the four accuracies over country, region, subregion and point. Furthermore, we report

[7]For a broader discussion on why traditional F_1 is not applicable and supplementary alternatives we considered for different categories see Appendix F.

a global accuracy aggregate across categories.[8] In the case of actors, the aggregate accuracy is invariant to a permutation of "Side A" and "Side B". If those were predicted in the opposite order of the gold annotation, the values of "Deaths Side A" and "Deaths Side B" are also inverted.

While predicting a unique symbolic representation is central to most information extraction tasks, generative models can predict semantically correct output that does not conform to the expected output (e.g. "USA" instead of "Government of United States of America"), and the abstractive nature of UCDP-AEC particularly exacerbates this. To evaluate how much of the error can be attributed to the selection of the gold surface form instead of a failure of the models' reasoning abilities, we introduce a semantic evaluation in line with Sharif et al. (2024). Given a field, all values appearing in any of the splits are embedded using BERT. When evaluating a model, its prediction for a given field is in turn embedded using BERT. The prediction is considered correct if it has the highest cosine similarity with the gold value amongst all possible values for this field. We report this value as "precision at top 1" (P@1), following the information retrieval convention. Since the identity maximises cosine similarity, the P@1 will always be greater than or equal to the accuracy, providing an upper bound to real model performance.

5.2 Baseline Models

To establish preliminary results for UCDP-AEC, we here report on experimental results for five different generative models, including both encoder-decoder and decoder-only architectures, all fine-tuned on the UCDP-AEC training set. The baselines are based on relatively small, openly available generative models to make sure the experiments are both reproducible and accessible to a broad range of researchers. These baselines are intended to explore and illustrate the specific challenges of UCDP-AEC, as well as provide a lower bound against which future work, potentially using larger and more specialised models, can be fairly compared.

In prior work, generative approaches to EE have predominantly been applied in an extractive setting, where the text generation is often constrained to the vocabulary present in the input text, as described in Section 2. Two of our baselines are based on adapting approaches originally proposed for such an extractive formulation, namely Text2Event and DEGREE, both widely used. As further detailed below, for our experiments, we make minimal modifications to the code provided with the original model papers to make them work with our abstractive formulation of the task, in which gold argument values may not appear as spans in the source text.

Text2Event (Lu et al., 2021) is using a T5 encoder-decoder architecture (Raffel et al., 2020) to translate text into S-expressions representing events. In the original setup, the model uses constrained decoding, which masks the output softmax to enforce valid S-expression structure and role names, and restricts argument generation to text spans in the input sentence. We adapt Text2Event to the abstractive setting by removing the constraint on argument generation. Additionally, we increase the input context window to 512 tokens to fit UCDP-AEC source documents, as Text2Event is originally designed for sentence-level event extraction.

DEGREE (Hsu et al., 2022) relies on the BART encoder-decoder transformer (Lewis et al., 2020) as a backbone, and the event extraction task is approached as a sequence-to-sequence problem between the input text and a natural language template to be filled. Since the UCDP-AEC events cover more fields than what DEGREE was originally designed for, we introduce a fuzzy-template matching algorithm to ensure that the model respects the template. The algorithm finds the argument assignment that minimises the Levenshtein distance between the predicted text and template, thus ignoring small variations in the natural language template output of DEGREE.

In addition, we fine-tune the Flan-T5 large model (Chung et al., 2022) using a slightly simpler formal template than that of Text2Event. Finally, we fine-tune two text-only Llama-3.2-Instruct-based models (1B and 3B, Grattafiori et al., 2024), using the Alpaca prompt format. The instruction prompt is illustrated in Appendix H.

5.3 Results

We report the performance of the baselines for each category and the aggregate accuracy in Table 3. The full per-role accuracies are given in Appendix D. We can see that for all models except Llama 3B, the date and location categories prove more challenging than the actor and deaths categories. We posit this is due to both actor and deaths having a smaller set of admissible values compared to date and location, which are closer to open-domain problems. While

[8]That is the average of 4 values, one for each category, not the average of the 14 fields' accuracies.

Model	#param	Exact match (Accuracy %)					Semantic (Precision@1 %)	
		Actors	Date	Location	Deaths	Aggregate	Actors	Location
Text2Event	223M	70.1	38.2	14.1	53.4	43.9	70.4	24.8
DEGREE	406M	73.5	64.4	**64.5**	**81.3**	70.9	**74.0**	**66.6**
Flan-T5 large	783M	**73.9**	63.0	62.8	81.0	70.2	**74.0**	65.6
Llama-3.2-Instruct	1B	71.0	70.5	59.9	76.4	69.4	71.3	61.3
Llama-3.2-Instruct	3B	73.0	**73.8**	63.9	78.5	**72.3**	73.2	65.5

Table 3: Baseline accuracies and P@1 on the UCDP-AEC test set, also showing the the number of model parameters.

the Llama 3B model demonstrates the strongest overall performance, obtaining the highest accuracy in the date category, the DEGREE and Flan-T5 large models are strong contenders, achieving the highest accuracies in the other categories.

Looking at the semantic evaluation, the P@1 follow the accuracies closely except for very low values. This seems to indicate that using single symbolic representations for the fields is not an important source of error for the most performant models.

5.4 Error-analysis

Looking into details, models struggle to predict new actors that were not observed during training. Around 5% of side A actors in the test set do not appear as actors in the training set. Out of those, Llama-3B was able to identify 25.8% correctly, while Flan-T5 large identified 32.3% correctly. A similar pattern can be observed for side B, suggesting that Flan-T5 large is better suited for previously unseen actors.

All models handle temporal uncertainty poorly, when the start and end date differ (in 8.6% of samples, usually as a result of expressions such as "over the weekend" or "last week"), date accuracy falls to 37.5% for Llama-3B and 33.8% for DEGREE, with models often failing to recognise the uncertainty and predict the same start and end date. Similarly, models tend to rely too heavily on the publication date, with a loss of performance when the event date differs from the publication date. DEGREE achieves a 35.9% accuracy in those cases, and Llama-3B a 41.5% accuracy.

6 Summary

This paper has introduced the UCDP Abstractive Event analysis Corpus – a large-scale dataset of high-quality document-level annotations of rich event representations in the domain of armed conflict, built from the UCDP GED event database and the HPLT v2 web archive. By coupling the event records to source documents identified in a public web archive, we are able to create a complete and open dataset for document-level event analysis. It makes the UCDP GED conflict annotations machine-learnable and available to the larger research community for experimentation. We believe the approach described here should also be applicable to other event databases where the underlying source documents are intact but currently not made openly available.

The annotations in UCDP-AEC have some important characteristics that set them apart from traditional event extraction datasets in NLP: Rather than sentence-level annotations tied to particular text spans with explicit information to be extracted, the document-level event representations in UCDP-AEC require inference from implied or otherwise under-specified information, possibly piecing together evidence that is scattered throughout a document. This requires a more "abstractive" approach to analysing events, which we argue may be particularly well-suited for generative approaches.

We have reported on a first suite of experiments with fine-tuning of both encoder-decoder and decoder-only models for generating event representations. While showing encouraging results and demonstrating the viability of the approach, we believe there is ample room for improvement in future work, in particular with respect to a more principled handling of event dates, and also exploring a larger space of decoder model tuning. We hope the UCDP-AEC dataset will be an important building block for future research on abstractive event analysis within both NLP and peace and conflict studies.

Limitations

While a defining feature of the UCDP-AEC dataset is that it reflects the temporal dynamics of real-world events, it offers a somewhat skewed view of global conflict dynamics compared to the underlying UCDP GED data. This misalignment is mostly an artefact of the process for deriving the dataset, as described in Section 4.2. Firstly, UCDP-AEC is a small subset of UCDP GED, representing 3.3% of the events in the database due to filtering and availability of source documents. Furthermore, because of the source quality filter – described in Appendix A – 84% of events in the dataset occurred in the last 10 years, thereby under-representing or missing many earlier conflicts.

The misalignment results in a substantial shift in the country coverage when compared to UCDP GED. One such example is Brazil, which has more than 12 000 recorded events in UCDP GED, but is represented by only four events in UCDP-AEC, 0.03% of the original. Similarly, while 40% of the UCDP-AEC events occur in Syria, only 19% of the UCDP GED events are recorded there.

The dataset we release is built from two sources: UCDP GED and HPLT. Despite providing all the code used in the creation of the dataset, since UCDP GED is partly private – the source documents cannot be shared – it is impossible to recreate the dataset without privileged access that we negotiated with UCDP. Similarly, the evaluation of the HPLT substitution described in Section 4.2 cannot be reproduced without access to the original UCDP documents.

The UCDP GED database incorporates sources from multiple languages, as sources closer to conflict zones can often provide more precise information and contribute to a broader and more representative basis for event recordings. By restricting the UCDP-AEC dataset to English-language sources, we may not only reinforce existing biases in the data, but also contribute to the ongoing overrepresentation of the English language in research and resources in NLP. After the event filtering and substitution with HPLT documents, described in Section 4, only a small portion of non-English sources was identified, which we decided to exclude.

All of the encoder-decoder transformers used in the baseline models have a maximum input context window of 512 tokens. Larger UCDP-AEC documents cannot fit inside this limit. Furthermore, we are using the Text2Event and DEGREE models outside of their intended extractive setting, which creates an unfair comparison with the Flan-T5 and the decoder-only baselines.

Ethics

Event data on armed conflict, especially when human lives have been lost, warrants a heightened focus on ethical implications, and particularly on the potential bias in the domain and on the bias introduced by our work. As the field advances towards event representations based on more high-level and implied information, combined with the use of large language models, there might be an increased risk of harm, with the potential of generating non-factual events.

A large proportion of the sources in the dataset consist of news articles, which present various types of bias, particularly when reporting on conflict events. Accurately documenting casualty numbers in conflict zones poses challenges due to a variety of factors, many of which are described in Seib (2021), and should be interpreted with caution. Moreover, not all armed conflicts receive media coverage, and the framing of the reported conflicts can be skewed, particularly when relying on sources in a single language (Chojnacki et al., 2012). This bias can manifest in several forms, for example, as unbalanced representations of certain actors as aggressors, the use of loaded terminology, or reliance on reports from countries with restricted freedom of the press and/or freedom of speech.

Some of the source documents in the dataset may contain names of individuals. Although the documents in the dataset consist of publicly available sources, when combined with event extraction systems, it is possible to imagine scenarios such as the surveillance of individuals, targeted monitoring of groups or other forms of malicious and harmful applications. The released dataset, however, does not include metadata or annotations related to individuals, and we suspect a greater challenge lies in the potential risks of unintentional misuse.

The substitution with HPLT document IDs was done with the intention of removing news articles covered by proprietary licences. HPLT relies on a crawler that respects the `robots.txt` convention and has a procedure to request the take down of documents. Even though HPLT has yet to receive any claims, we cannot guarantee that no such documents are included in the HPLT corpus. The HPLT project has the stated goal of providing training data for NLP applications, as such, we consider our use of their data as fair.

UCDP-AEC is released for the sole purpose of training machine learning models rather than analysing armed conflict events directly in the scope of socio-political research. The dataset presented is a simplified subset of the UCDP database and does not preserve the original distribution of events found in UCDP. For readers interested in research on socio-political events related to armed conflicts, Olsen et al. (2024) provide a comprehensive overview of available datasets.

Given the challenges with bias outlined, event extraction systems trained on UCDP-AEC are not intended to replace human experts but serve as a tool in the coding / annotation process. We stress that human evaluation is essential before automatically extracted event records can be used for further analysis or application.

The research presented in this paper, as well as the released dataset, is created to advance research aimed at better understanding why, how, and when armed conflict arises, with the main overarching goal of finding solutions to achieve a more peaceful world. We disapprove of using this dataset for research or applications that do not align with this vision and strongly discourage such usage.

References

Rui Bai, Di Lu, Shihao Ran, Elizabeth M. Olson, Hemank Lamba, Aoife Cahill, Joel Tetreault, and Alejandro Jaimes. 2025. CEHA: A dataset of conflict events in the horn of Africa. In *Proceedings of the 31st International Conference on Computational Linguistics*, pages 1475–1495, Abu Dhabi, UAE. Association for Computational Linguistics.

Andrei Z Broder. 1997. On the resemblance and containment of documents. In *Proceedings. Compression and Complexity of SEQUENCES 1997 (Cat. No. 97TB100171)*, pages 21–29. IEEE.

Laurie Burchell, Ona de Gibert, Nikolay Arefyev, Mikko Aulamo, Marta Bañón, Pinzhen Chen, Mariia Fedorova, Liane Guillou, Barry Haddow, Jan Hajič, Jindřich Helcl, Erik Henriksson, Mateusz Klimaszewski, Ville Komulainen, Andrey Kutuzov, Joona Kytöniemi, Veronika Laippala, Petter Mæhlum, Bhavitvya Malik, and 16 others. 2025. An expanded massive multilingual dataset for high-performance language technologies (hplt). *Preprint*, arXiv:2503.10267.

Ruirui Chen, Chengwei Qin, Weifeng Jiang, and Dongkyu Choi. 2024. Is a large language model a good annotator for event extraction? In *Proceedings of the AAAI Conference on Artificial Intelligence*, volume 38, pages 17772–17780.

Erica Chenoweth, Jonathan Pinckney, and Orion A. Lewis. 2019. NAVCO 3.0 Dataset.

Sven Chojnacki, Christian Ickler, Michael Spies, and John Wiesel. 2012. Event data on armed conflict and security: New perspectives, old challenges, and some solutions. *International Interactions*, 38(4):382–401.

Hyung Won Chung, Le Hou, Shayne Longpre, Barret Zoph, Yi Tay, William Fedus, Yunxuan Li, Xuezhi Wang, Mostafa Dehghani, Siddhartha Brahma, Albert Webson, Shixiang Shane Gu, Zhuyun Dai, Mirac Suzgun, Xinyun Chen, Aakanksha Chowdhery, Alex Castro-Ros, Marie Pellat, Kevin Robinson, and 16 others. 2022. Scaling instruction-finetuned language models. *Preprint*, arXiv:2210.11416.

Shawn Davies, Garoun Engström, Therése Pettersson, and Magnus Öberg. 2024. Organized violence 1989–2023, and the prevalence of organized crime groups. *Journal of Peace Research*, 61(4):673–693.

George Doddington, Alexis Mitchell, Mark Przybocki, Lance Ramshaw, Stephanie Strassel, and Ralph Weischedel. 2004. The automatic content extraction (ACE) program – tasks, data, and evaluation. In *Proceedings of the Fourth International Conference on Language Resources and Evaluation (LREC'04)*, Lisbon, Portugal. European Language Resources Association (ELRA).

Xinya Du, Alexander Rush, and Claire Cardie. 2021a. GRIT: Generative role-filler transformers for document-level event entity extraction. In *Proceedings of the 16th Conference of the European Chapter of the Association for Computational Linguistics: Main Volume*, pages 634–644, Online. Association for Computational Linguistics.

Xinya Du, Alexander Rush, and Claire Cardie. 2021b. Template filling with generative transformers. In *Proceedings of the 2021 Conference of the North American Chapter of the Association for Computational Linguistics: Human Language Technologies*, pages 909–914, Online. Association for Computational Linguistics.

Fırat Duruşan, Ali Hürriyetoğlu, Erdem Yörük, Osman Mutlu, Çağrı Yoltar, Burak Gürel, and Alvaro Comin. 2022. Global contentious politics database (GLOCON) annotation manuals. *Preprint*, arXiv:2206.10299.

William Gantt, Shabnam Behzad, Hannah An, Yunmo Chen, Aaron White, Benjamin Van Durme, and Mahsa Yarmohammadi. 2024. MultiMUC: Multilingual template filling on MUC-4. In *Proceedings of the 18th Conference of the European Chapter of the Association for Computational Linguistics (Volume 1: Long Papers)*, pages 349–368, St. Julian's, Malta. Association for Computational Linguistics.

Aaron Grattafiori, Abhimanyu Dubey, Abhinav Jauhri, Abhinav Pandey, Abhishek Kadian, Ahmad Al-Dahle, Aiesha Letman, Akhil Mathur, Alan Schelten, Alex Vaughan, and 1 others. 2024. The llama 3 herd of models. *arXiv preprint arXiv:2407.21783*.

Andrew Halterman, Philip A. Schrodt, Andreas Beger, Benjamin E. Bagozzi, and Grace I. Scarborough. 2023. Creating custom event data without dictionaries: A bag-of-tricks. *arXiv preprint arXiv:2304.01331*.

Håvard Hegre, Paola Vesco, and Michael Colaresi. 2022. Lessons from an escalation prediction competition. *International Interactions*, 48(4):521–554.

I-Hung Hsu, Kuan-Hao Huang, Elizabeth Boschee, Scott Miller, Prem Natarajan, Kai-Wei Chang, and Nanyun Peng. 2022. DEGREE: A data-efficient generation-based event extraction model. In *Proceedings of the 2022 Conference of the North American Chapter of the Association for Computational Linguistics: Human Language Technologies*, pages 1890–1908, Seattle, United States. Association for Computational Linguistics.

Stina Högbladh. 2023. UCDP georeferenced event dataset codebook version 23.1. *Department of Peace and Conflict Research*.

Mike Lewis, Yinhan Liu, Naman Goyal, Marjan Ghazvininejad, Abdelrahman Mohamed, Omer Levy, Veselin Stoyanov, and Luke Zettlemoyer. 2020. BART: Denoising sequence-to-sequence pre-training for natural language generation, translation, and comprehension. In *Proceedings of the 58th Annual Meeting of the Association for Computational Linguistics*, pages 7871–7880, Online. Association for Computational Linguistics.

Sha Li, Heng Ji, and Jiawei Han. 2021. Document-level event argument extraction by conditional generation. In *Proceedings of the 2021 Conference of the North American Chapter of the Association for Computational Linguistics: Human Language Technologies*, pages 894–908, Online. Association for Computational Linguistics.

Yaojie Lu, Hongyu Lin, Jin Xu, Xianpei Han, Jialong Tang, Annan Li, Le Sun, Meng Liao, and Shaoyi Chen. 2021. Text2Event: Controllable sequence-to-structure generation for end-to-end event extraction. In *Proceedings of the 59th Annual Meeting of the Association for Computational Linguistics and the 11th International Joint Conference on Natural Language Processing (Volume 1: Long Papers)*, pages 2795–2806, Online. Association for Computational Linguistics.

Thien Huu Nguyen, Kyunghyun Cho, and Ralph Grishman. 2016. Joint event extraction via recurrent neural networks. In *Proceedings of the 2016 Conference of the North American Chapter of the Association for Computational Linguistics: Human Language Technologies*, pages 300–309, San Diego, California. Association for Computational Linguistics.

Clayton Norris, Philip A Schrodt, and John Beieler. 2017. PETRARCH2: Another event coding program. *J. Open Source Softw.*, 2(9):133.

Helene Olsen, Étienne Simon, Erik Velldal, and Lilja Øvrelid. 2024. Socio-political events of conflict and unrest: A survey of available datasets. In *Proceedings of the 7th Workshop on Challenges and Applications of Automated Extraction of Socio-political Events from Text (CASE 2024)*, pages 40–53, St. Julians, Malta. Association for Computational Linguistics.

Colin Raffel, Noam Shazeer, Adam Roberts, Katherine Lee, Sharan Narang, Michael Matena, Yanqi Zhou, Wei Li, and Peter J Liu. 2020. Exploring the limits of transfer learning with a unified text-to-text transformer. *Journal of machine learning research*, 21(140):1–67.

Clionadh Raleigh, Roudabeh Kishi, and Andrew Linke. 2023. Political instability patterns are obscured by conflict dataset scope conditions, sources, and coding choices. *Humanities and Social Sciences Communications*, 10(1):74.

Clionadh Raleigh, Andrew Linke, Havard Hegre, and Joakim Karlsen. 2010. Introducing acled: An armed conflict location and event dataset. *Journal of Peace Research*, 47(5):651–660.

Idean Salehyan, Cullen S Hendrix, Jesse Hamner, Christina Case, Christopher Linebarger, Emily Stull, and Jennifer Williams. 2012. Social conflict in africa: A new database. *International Interactions*, 38(4):503–511.

Taneeya Satyapanich, Francis Ferraro, and Tim Finin. 2020. CASIE: Extracting cybersecurity event information from text. *Proceedings of the AAAI Conference on Artificial Intelligence*, 34(05):8749–8757.

Philip A. Schrodt, Shannon G. Davis, and Judith L. Weddle. 1994. Political science: KEDS—a program for the machine coding of event data. *Social Science Computer Review*, 12(4):561–587.

Philip Seib. 2021. *Information at war: journalism, disinformation, and modern warfare*. John Wiley & Sons.

Sina Semnani, Pingyue Zhang, Wanyue Zhai, Haozhuo Li, Ryan Beauchamp, Trey Billing, Katayoun Kishi, Manling Li, and Monica Lam. 2025. LEMONADE: A large multilingual expert-annotated abstractive event dataset for the real world. In *Findings of the Association for Computational Linguistics: ACL 2025*, pages 25813–25852, Vienna, Austria. Association for Computational Linguistics.

Omar Sharif, Joseph Gatto, Madhusudan Basak, and Sarah Masud Preum. 2024. Explicit, implicit, and scattered: Revisiting event extraction to capture complex arguments. In *Proceedings of the 2024 Conference on Empirical Methods in Natural Language Processing*, pages 12061–12081, Miami, Florida, USA. Association for Computational Linguistics.

Étienne Simon, Helene Olsen, Huiling You, Samia Touileb, Lilja Øvrelid, and Erik Velldal. 2024. Generative approaches to event extraction: Survey and outlook. In *Proceedings of the Workshop on the Future of Event Detection (FuturED)*, pages 73–86, Miami, Florida, USA. Association for Computational Linguistics.

Zhiyi Song, Ann Bies, Stephanie Strassel, Tom Riese, Justin Mott, Joe Ellis, Jonathan Wright, Seth Kulick, Neville Ryant, and Xiaoyi Ma. 2015. From light to rich ERE: Annotation of entities, relations, and events. In *Proceedings of the 3rd Workshop on EVENTS: Definition, Detection, Coreference, and Representation*, pages 89–98, Denver, Colorado. Association for Computational Linguistics.

Zhaoyue Sun, Jiazheng Li, Gabriele Pergola, Byron Wallace, Bino John, Nigel Greene, Joseph Kim, and Yulan He. 2022. PHEE: A dataset for pharmacovigilance event extraction from text. In *Proceedings of the 2022 Conference on Empirical Methods in Natural Language Processing*, pages 5571–5587, Abu Dhabi, United Arab Emirates. Association for Computational Linguistics.

Ralph Sundberg and Erik Melander. 2013. Introducing the UCDP georeferenced event dataset. *Journal of Peace Research*, 50(4):523–532.

Beth M. Sundheim. 1992. Overview of the fourth Message Understanding Evaluation and Conference. In *Fourth Message Understanding Conference (MUC-4): Proceedings of a Conference Held in McLean, Virginia, June 16-18, 1992*.

MeiHan Tong, Bin Xu, Shuai Wang, Meihuan Han, Yixin Cao, Jiangqi Zhu, Siyu Chen, Lei Hou, and Juanzi Li. 2022. DocEE: A large-scale and fine-grained benchmark for document-level event extraction. In *Proceedings of the 2022 Conference of the North American Chapter of the Association for Computational Linguistics: Human Language Technologies*, pages 3970–3982, Seattle, United States. Association for Computational Linguistics.

Peter Turchin. 2012. Dynamics of political instability in the united states, 1780–2010. *Journal of Peace Research*, 49(4):577–591.

David Wadden, Ulme Wennberg, Yi Luan, and Hannaneh Hajishirzi. 2019. Entity, relation, and event extraction with contextualized span representations. In *Proceedings of the 2019 Conference on Empirical Methods in Natural Language Processing and the 9th International Joint Conference on Natural Language Processing (EMNLP-IJCNLP)*, pages 5784–5789, Hong Kong, China. Association for Computational Linguistics.

Chenguang Wang, Xiao Liu, Zui Chen, Haoyun Hong, Jie Tang, and Dawn Song. 2022. DeepStruct: Pretraining of language models for structure prediction. In *Findings of the Association for Computational Linguistics: ACL 2022*, pages 803–823, Dublin, Ireland. Association for Computational Linguistics.

Xiao Wang, Weikang Zhou, Can Zu, Han Xia, Tianze Chen, Yuansen Zhang, Rui Zheng, Junjie Ye, Qi Zhang, Tao Gui, and 1 others. 2023. Instructuie: Multi-task instruction tuning for unified information extraction. *arXiv preprint arXiv:2304.08085*.

Xinglin Xiao, Yijie Wang, Nan Xu, Yuqi Wang, Hanxuan Yang, Minzheng Wang, Yin Luo, Lei Wang, Wenji Mao, and Daniel Zeng. 2023. Yayi-uie: A chat-enhanced instruction tuning framework for universal information extraction. *arXiv preprint arXiv:2312.15548*.

Aiyuan Yang, Bin Xiao, Bingning Wang, Borong Zhang, Ce Bian, Chao Yin, Chenxu Lv, Da Pan, Dian Wang, Dong Yan, and 1 others. 2023. Baichuan 2: Open large-scale language models. *arXiv preprint arXiv:2309.10305*.

Shun Zheng, Wei Cao, Wei Xu, and Jiang Bian. 2019. Doc2EDAG: An end-to-end document-level framework for Chinese financial event extraction. In *Proceedings of the 2019 Conference on Empirical Methods in Natural Language Processing and the 9th International Joint Conference on Natural Language Processing (EMNLP-IJCNLP)*, pages 337–346, Hong Kong, China. Association for Computational Linguistics.

A Details of Data Subset Selection

The details of some filters might be hard to understand without knowledge of UCDP design detailed in the codebook (Högbladh, 2023). Starting from the UCDP candidate events dataset, we apply the following filters:

- the UCDP annotator marked the event as "clear",
- the event occurred on a single day (but this day might not be exactly known, thus the start date $\neq$ end date),
- the same event was not split into multiple entries (no "deaths split"),
- the source document uses the new post-2014 source format (ensuring more accurate publication dates),
- the event is described by a single source document (when using multiple sources, UCDP annotators might pick some of the information from one of the sources, distrust some specific roles from another, transforming the task into a weakly-supervised problem),
- the source document describes a single event (multi-event documents tend to include long tables of battle deaths without enough context to fully code the events),
- the start date, end date and publication date all occur in the same split,

- the deaths estimates are ordered properly: best (the sum of side A, side B, civilians and unknown) is in-between low and high,
- the split cut-off time are widened by 12 hours to avoid time zone reporting issues,
- the source document is in English,
- the length of the source document is between 100 and 10 000 characters.

All but the last two filters are applied on the UCDP database, resulting in 110 979 events. The final dataset is the result of HPLT substitution and the application of the last two filters on the HPLT source documents.

B Details of UCDP-AEC Fields

On domain openness UCDP-AEC is designed for a supervised prediction task where each instance consists of a source text and a publication date, denoted $\mathcal{X}$, and the corresponding output is a structured sequence of 14 argument roles $\mathcal{Y} = \mathcal{Y}_1 \times \cdots \times \mathcal{Y}_{14}$. Traditionally, when $\mathcal{Y}$ is a finite set, the problem is said to be closed domain, while potentially infinite $\mathcal{Y}$ is part of open-domain problems. In practice, open-domain roles may still be partially constrained because of real-world structures. For example, location values on the country level are often limited to internationally recognised countries.

The UCDP-AEC dataset contains fields with varying degrees of domain openness. To quantify the openness of each field in UCDP-AEC, we introduced three metrics in Section 4.3, report on each metric for each field in Table 2. We here describe these metrics in more detail.

We measure average instances per unique value, the *value density*, by computing the ratio $\frac{|\mathcal{D}|}{|\mathcal{Y}|}$, where $|\mathcal{D}|$ denotes the number of instances with a value for a given role, and $|\mathcal{Y}|$ the number of unique values observed. Higher values indicate a closed domain, with a small number of unique values that are frequently observed, whereas lower values indicate a more open domain with a more diverse set of values that are less frequently observed.

We measure the *unique value overlap* between the train and test set with the ratio $\frac{|\mathcal{Y}_{\text{test}} \cap \mathcal{Y}_{\text{train}}|}{|\mathcal{Y}_{\text{test}}|}$. This metric describes the percentage of test values observed during training, where a low overlap indicates a more open domain. A high overlap indicates that most of the values in the test set are also present in the train set.

Finally, for the *instance-level overlap*, we measure the proportion of instances in the test set with values, that has been observed in the train set with $\frac{|\mathcal{D}_{\text{test}} \cap \mathcal{D}_{\text{train}}|}{|\mathcal{D}_{\text{test}}|}$. Here, we take into account the frequency of the value.

In UCDP-AEC, the country-level location, and the death counts and estimates could be considered closed domain, as the range of possible values is limited and very repetitive.

The two actor roles, Side A and Side B, can be considered semi open domains, where many known actors will appear in the test set, but new actors will also occur. Both roles has a moderate value reuse, with about 26–27 instances per value. A similar pattern can be found for Subregion.

The more fine-grained locations show open domain characteristics. Region and Point are placenames often specific to single events, with many values in test that are not present in train. The temporal arguments have a 0% overlap because they are used for split selection (by definition, train and test do not overlap temporally).

On death estimates The fields "Deaths Low" and "Deaths High" are used when there is uncertainty with respect to the total number of fatalities. For these estimates, the detailed attribution of casualties to specific sides (Side A, Side B, Civilians, Unknown) is not specified. When summed together, those four deaths fields give the UCDP best estimate for the total number of people killed as part of an event. The fields "Deaths Low" and "Deaths High" are used when there is uncertainty with respect to the total number of fatalities. For these estimates, the detailed attribution of casualties to specific sides (Side A, Side B, Civilians, Unknown) is not specified. In any case we always have low $\leq$ best $\leq$ high and $1 \leq$ high.

C Sample Example

See Table 4. Note that we deliberately chose this article because of its short length for illustration purposes. Consisting of only 491 characters, this sample is not representative in terms of length, as the average article in UCDP-AEC contains 2116 characters.

D Detailed Results

See Table 5. Note that the accuracy for side A is given for the gold side A. Since actors are permutation invariants, this can correspond to a prediction for side B by the model. Side A and B are always different in the gold annotation, as such there is no

Input	
publication date	2022-01-06
source article	The lifeless body of a woman was discovered Wednesday morning on her farm in Mbengwi, Momo Division, Northwest region of Cameroon. Reports say there was a shootout between security forces and suspected separatist fighters around Womsei, a quarter behind the Mbon Market on Tuesday evening. Her body was only discovered Wednesday morning with the basket she was using to harvest okra still strapped on her back. Her body has been preserved at the Mbengwi mortuary pending burial arrangements.

Role	**Argument**	**Role**	**Argument**
Side A	Government of Cameroon	Start date	2022-01-04
Side B	Ambazonia insurgents	End date	2022-01-04
Location country	Cameroon	Location region	North-West region
Location subregion	Momo département	Location point	Mbengwi village
Deaths side A	0	Deaths side B	0
Deaths civilian	1	Deaths unknown	0
Deaths low	1	Deaths high	1

Table 4: Example of sample from the test set (sample id: 428220).

precision–recall trade-off to be taken advantage of despite evaluation through accuracy.

E Licences

The two data sources we are using are UCDP GED released under CC-BY and HPLT v2.0 realesed under CC0. We license our dataset UCDP-AEC under CC-BY.

We release our modifications to Text2Event and DEGREE under the same licence as the original code, that is MIT for Text2Event and Apache 2.0 for DEGREE.

We release the code of the Flan-T5 and Llama baselines, the code used to create the dataset, its evaluation script and scripts computing dataset statistics under the GNU AGPL licence.

F Evaluation Details

Since in UCDP-AEC all fields always have exactly one assigned value for all events, for a given field, the recall of a model is the number of true positive divided by the number of samples in the dataset, that is the accuracy. Similarly, the precision is also equal to the accuracy if the model predicts a single value for each field – as it should since its precision would only decrease otherwise – therefore we have precision = recall = F_1 = accuracy, thus explaining why we only report accuracies instead of the usual precision–recall–F_1 triplets.

For the date and deaths categories, we investigated the use of smooth metrics such as RMSE and RMSLE. However, as errors tend to be infrequent but important in magnitude, we did not find those metrics informative enough to be of interest. The provided evaluation script does compute RMSE and other metrics we considered such as semantic MRR.

For the semantic evaluation, we investigated using different models including S-BERT following Sharif et al. (2024). However we observed little variations apart from larger models providing slightly better P@1. Given the nature of the insight provided by the semantic evaluation, we did not find this warranted the extra computational cost and relied on `bert-base-uncased` instead.

G Model Details and Computational Budget

For both Text2Event (Lu et al., 2021) and DEGREE (Hsu et al., 2022), we reused the hyperparameters of the original models, except the input token limit, which we increased to 512 in both cases.

For the Flan-T5 baseline, we used learning rates of 3×10^{-5} with a maximum of 18 epochs. 10 intermediary evaluations were performed with early stopping on validation aggregate accuracy.

For the Llama-3.2-Instruct models, we set the maximum sequence length to 2048, used up to 900 training steps, applied a weight decay of 0.01, and a learning rate of 2e-4.

All models were trained on either P100 or A100 GPUs. Including development runs, the total GPU usage was around 200 GPU hours.

Model	Actors		Date		Location				Deaths					
	Side A	Side B	Start	End	Country	Region	Subregion	Point	Side A	Side B	Civilian	Unknown	Low	High
Text2Event	75.8	64.4	35.3	41.0	37.0	11.1	5.1	3.2	81.3	78.2	56.6	67.7	21.3	15.3
DEGREE	77.8	69.3	63.0	65.9	97.8	75.8	46.0	38.4	84.7	84.6	82.6	85.6	68.8	81.6
Flan-T5 large	77.0	70.8	60.3	65.7	97.8	73.3	45.7	34.3	82.3	81.9	82.9	87.3	69.8	82.1
Llama-3.2-I-1B	78.2	63.8	68.3	72.6	96.5	68.0	43.3	31.7	80.2	78.5	73.7	82.0	65.7	78.2
Llama-3.2-I-3B	78.9	67.1	72.8	74.7	97.1	76.7	47.5	34.4	83.9	80.3	75.5	83.0	68.6	79.7

Table 5: Accuracies for each individual role.

Instruction	Generate structured event information related to a socio-political conflict in the UCDP event format, based on the content of a source UCDP document. The generated data should include the following fields: `side_a_name`, `side_b_name`, `start_date`, `end_date`, `location_root_name`, `location_adm1_name`, `location_adm2_name`, `location_where_name`, `deaths_side_a`, `deaths_side_b`, `deaths_civilian`, `deaths_unknown`, `deaths_low`, `deaths_high`. Output the event information as a valid JSON object corresponding to the armed conflict incident described in the following source UCDP document.
Input	{Source article text}
Output	{Required output in JSON format}

Table 6: Instruction prompt used for fine-tuning.

H Instruction Prompt

The prompt used for the Llama models can be found in Table 6.

Cross-Platform Natural Language Processing Framework for Electoral Misinformation Detection

Prasanth Yadla
Independent Researcher
Seattle, WA, USA
pyadla2@alumni.ncsu.edu

Abstract

Electoral misinformation campaigns pose significant threats to democratic processes through coordinated inauthentic behavior that manipulates public discourse. Traditional detection methods often fail to identify sophisticated campaigns that adapt rapidly to evade detection. This paper presents a novel multi-platform natural language processing (NLP) framework for detecting coordinated misinformation campaigns during electoral periods. Our approach combines linguistic coordination analysis, cross-platform behavioral pattern recognition, and narrative evolution tracking to identify inauthentic campaigns realtime. We introduce the *Electoral Misinformation Detection (EMD)*[1] framework, which integrates stylometric analysis, semantic clustering, and temporal synchronization detection across Twitter, Facebook, and Telegram. Evaluation on datasets from three national elections demonstrates that our approach achieves 87.3% precision and 82.1% recall in detecting coordinated campaigns. Our contributions include methodological innovations in cross-platform coordination detection, a comprehensive evaluation framework for electoral misinformation research, and practical tools for election integrity monitoring.

1 Introduction

The proliferation of misinformation campaigns during electoral periods represents one of the most pressing challenges to democratic governance in the digital age. Unlike traditional propaganda, modern misinformation campaigns leverage sophisticated coordination tactics across multiple social media platforms, employ adaptive linguistic strategies to evade detection, and exploit algorithmic amplification to maximize reach (Bradshaw et al., 2021). The 2016 U.S. presidential election, Brexit referendum, and numerous subsequent electoral contests have demonstrated the capacity of coordinated inauthentic behavior to influence public opinion and potentially alter electoral outcomes (Howard, 2020).

Current approaches to detecting electoral misinformation face several critical limitations. Platform-based detection systems primarily rely on behavioral signals such as account creation patterns and engagement metrics, which sophisticated actors can manipulate (Ferrara et al., 2016). Academic research has focused largely on single-platform analysis, missing the cross-platform coordination that characterizes modern influence operations (Zannettou et al., 2019). Moreover, existing methods often fail to distinguish between legitimate grassroots political mobilization and inauthentic coordination, leading to high false positive rates that risk suppressing authentic political discourse.

This paper addresses these limitations by introducing a comprehensive computational framework for detecting coordinated misinformation campaigns in electoral contexts. Our approach makes three key contributions: (1) a multi-platform NLP framework that identifies linguistic and behavioral coordination signals across diverse social media platforms; (2) novel methods for tracking the evolution of misinformation narratives and their adaptation to counter-messaging; and (3) a realtime detection system capable of identifying emerging campaigns during active electoral periods.

The *Electoral Misinformation Detection (EMD)* framework detailed in Figure 1 combines multiple computational approaches to achieve robust detection performance. Stylometric analysis identifies accounts with suspiciously similar writing patterns, while semantic clustering groups messages with identical meanings despite surface-level variations. Cross-platform behavioral analysis detects temporal synchronization and unnatural amplification patterns. Narrative evolution tracking monitors how false claims morph and spread across information

[1] `https://github.com/TransformerTitan/EMD`

Proceedings of the 21st Conference on Natural Language Processing (KONVENS), Volume 2: Workshops, pages 120–127, 2025

ecosystems.

We evaluate our approach using datasets from electoral periods in the United States (2020), Germany (2021), and Brazil (2022), comprising over 50 million posts across multiple platforms. Results demonstrate significant improvements over existing methods, with the framework achieving 87.3% precision and 82.1% recall in detecting coordinated campaigns.

2 Related Work

2.1 Misinformation Detection in Electoral Contexts

Research on computational approaches to misinformation detection has evolved from simple keyword-based methods to sophisticated machine learning approaches. Early work focused on identifying false claims through fact-checking databases and linguistic features indicative of deception (Rubin et al., 2015). However, these approaches proved insufficient for detecting coordinated campaigns, which often propagate technically accurate information in misleading contexts.

Recent advances have emphasized the importance of understanding misinformation as a social phenomenon rather than merely a content problem (Vosoughi et al., 2018). Shao et al. (2018) demonstrated that misinformation spreads through distinct network patterns compared to legitimate news, while Bovet and Makse (2019) showed that coordinated accounts exhibit characteristic behavioral signatures. However, most existing work focuses on post-hoc analysis rather than realtime detection during active campaigns.

2.2 Coordinated Inauthentic Behavior Detection

The concept of coordinated inauthentic behavior (CIB) was formalized by social media platforms as a policy framework for addressing influence operations (Gleicher, 2018). Academic research has developed various computational approaches to detect CIB, including network analysis methods that identify densely connected clusters of accounts (Chavoshi et al., 2016) and temporal analysis techniques that detect synchronized posting patterns (Pacheco et al., 2020).

Im et al. (2020) introduced methods for detecting coordination through shared URLs and hashtags, while Luceri et al. (2020) developed approaches based on account creation patterns and engagement manipulation. However, these methods often suffer from high false positive rates when applied to political contexts, where legitimate grassroots coordination is common.

2.3 Cross-Platform Information Operations

Modern influence operations increasingly operate across multiple social media platforms, exploiting the unique characteristics of each environment (Zannettou et al., 2019). Wilson et al. (2020) analyzed how misinformation narratives propagate between platforms, finding that coordination often begins on less moderated platforms before spreading to mainstream social media.

Despite this recognition, most detection systems remain platform-specific. Yang et al. (2019) developed one of the few cross-platform detection systems, but their approach relies primarily on URL sharing and lacks the linguistic analysis necessary for detecting sophisticated narrative coordination.

2.4 Adversarial Robustness in Misinformation Detection

As detection systems become more sophisticated, malicious actors adapt their tactics to evade detection. Kumar and Shah (2018) demonstrated how adversarial examples can fool misinformation classifiers, while Zhou and Zafarani (2020) showed that simple paraphrasing can evade most detection systems.

Research on adversarially robust detection has focused primarily on improving model generalization through techniques such as adversarial training (Alzantot et al., 2018) and ensemble methods (Wang, 2017). However, limited work has addressed the specific adversarial challenges faced in electoral contexts, where actors have strong incentives to evade detection.

3 Methodology

3.1 Problem Formulation

We formalize the problem of electoral misinformation campaign detection as a multi-label classification task. Given a collection of posts $P = \{p_1, p_2, \dots, p_n\}$ from multiple platforms during an electoral period, we aim to identify subsets of posts that constitute coordinated misinformation campaigns.

Formally, let $C = \{c_1, c_2, \dots, c_k\}$ represent a set of coordination clusters, where each cluster $c_i \subseteq P$ contains posts that are part of the same

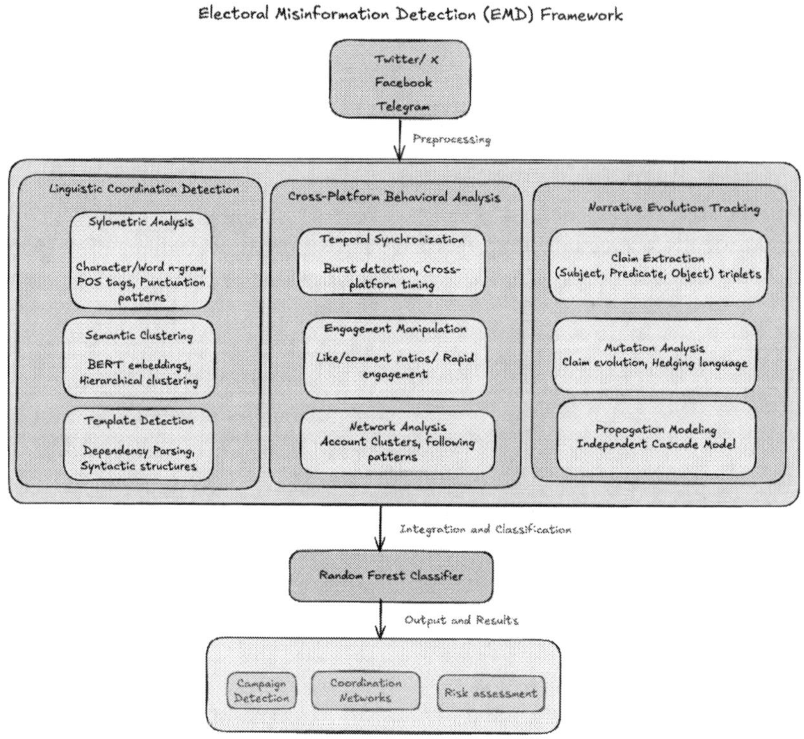

Figure 1: EMD Framework

coordinated campaign. A post p_j is considered part of a misinformation campaign if it satisfies three conditions:

The classification of a post p_j is determined according to three primary criteria. First, **Coordination**, wherein p_j exhibits coordination signals with other posts within the same temporal window. Second, **Inauthenticity**, indicating that the observed coordination appears inauthentic rather than organic. Third, **misinformation**, in which p_j promotes false or misleading electoral information.

3.2 Data Collection and Preprocessing

Our framework operates on multi-platform datasets collected during electoral periods. Data collection focuses on three major platforms: Twitter (now X), Facebook, and Telegram, chosen for their distinct user bases and moderation policies. Our analysis draws from three comprehensive electoral datasets spanning multiple languages and democratic contexts: the **US-2020** dataset consisting of 15.2 million posts collected during the 2020 U.S. presidential election period (September–December 2020) (Chen and Ferrara, 2020), the **GER-2021** dataset including 8.7 million posts from the 2021 German federal election period (July–September 2021), primarily in the German language (Sältzer, 2021), and the **BRA-2022** dataset comprising 12.1 million posts gathered during the 2022 Brazilian presidential election (August–October 2022), predominantly in Portuguese (de Sao Paulo, 2022). These datasets provide comprehensive coverage of electoral discourse across diverse linguistic, cultural, and political contexts, enabling robust evaluation of our cross-platform detection framework.

3.2.1 Platform-Specific Collection

Twitter/X data from the US-2020, GER-2021, and BRA-2022 datasets were originally collected using the Academic Research API, with a focus on election-related hashtags and keywords specific to each electoral context. The collection includes tweet content, user profiles, engagement metrics, and network relationships across all three datasets. **Facebook** data consist of public posts from political pages and groups, obtained via CrowdTangle for each electoral period. These records contain post content, page information, and engagement statistics from the 2020 U.S. presidential election, 2021 German federal election, and 2022 Brazilian presidential election periods. **Telegram** data are gathered from public channels and groups through the Telegram API, emphasizing channels that featured political content during each respective electoral period and had documented histories of sharing election-related information relevant to the U.S., German, and Brazilian electoral contexts.

3.2.2 Preprocessing Pipeline

Raw data undergo several preprocessing steps to ensure consistency and analytical readiness. **Language identification** is performed using the `langdetect` library to classify posts by language. **Content extraction** separates URLs, media, and text for independent processing. **Temporal alignment** normalizes timestamps across platforms to facilitate cross-platform analysis. **Entity recognition** employs spaCy NER models fine-tuned on political text to identify political entities such as candidates, parties, and issues. Finally, **Deduplication** detects and groups near-duplicate posts to support coordination analysis.

3.3 Electoral Misinformation Detection Framework

The EMD framework consists of four main components: linguistic coordination detection, cross-platform behavioral analysis, narrative evolution tracking, and integration and classification.

3.3.1 Linguistic Coordination Detection

Stylometric Analysis involves extracting stylometric features from each post to identify accounts with suspiciously similar writing patterns. These features include character-level n-grams with $n \in \{2, 3, 4\}$, word-level n-grams with $n \in \{1, 2, 3\}$, part-of-speech tag sequences, punctuation patterns, sentence length distributions, and vocabulary richness measures. For each account a, a stylometric signature $S(a)$ is computed by aggregating features across all posts. Coordination is inferred when multiple accounts exhibit suspiciously similar signatures:

$$\text{coord\_style}(a_i, a_j) = \begin{cases} 1, & \cos(S(a_i), S(a_j)) > \tau_{\text{style}}, \\ 0, & \text{otherwise}. \end{cases} \quad (1)$$

where τ_{style} is a threshold determined through cross-validation.

Semantic Clustering: Posts with identical or nearly identical meanings are grouped using sentence embeddings. For semantic clustering, we employ `bert-base-multilingual-cased` as our foundation model, which we fine-tune on a curated corpus of 2.3M political texts spanning English, German, and Portuguese. The corpus comprises election-related social media posts, parliamentary debates, and political news articles collected between 2018-2020. Fine-tuning is performed using AdamW optimization with a learning rate of 2×10^{-5}, batch size of 32, and maximum sequence length of 512 tokens over 3 epochs. We incorporate a political entity recognition objective during fine-tuning to enhance the model's understanding of electoral discourse patterns.

Post embeddings are extracted using the final hidden state of the [CLS] token, following standard practice for sentence-level representations.

For each post p, we compute an embedding $E(p)$ using:

$$E(p) = \text{BERT}_{\text{political}}(\text{preprocess}(p)) \quad (2)$$

Posts are clustered using average linkage clustering with a distance threshold τ_{semantic}. Clusters with high semantic similarity but low lexical overlap are flagged as potential coordination.

Template Detection involves identifying posts generated from templates by detecting repeated syntactic structures with variable content. This process is accomplished by parsing posts using dependency parsing, extracting syntactic templates through the replacement of named entities and numbers with placeholders, and identifying templates that are used by multiple distinct accounts.

3.3.2 Cross-Platform Behavioral Analysis

Temporal Synchronization is a key indicator of coordinated campaigns, which often exhibit unnatural temporal patterns. To detect such synchronization, we employ several methods. First, *burst detection* identifies unusual spikes in posting activity using a modified version of Kleinberg's burst detection algorithm (Kleinberg, 2003). The burst score at time t is calculated as

$$\text{burst\_score}(t) = \frac{|P_t| - \mu}{\sigma}, \quad (3)$$

where P_t denotes the set of posts at time t, μ represents the expected number of posts, and σ is the standard deviation.

Second, we analyze *cross-platform timing* by measuring the time delays between similar content appearing on different platforms. The synchronization score for a semantic cluster c is given by

Campaign Type	Avg. Detection Time (hours)	Std. Deviation
Vote manipulation claims	3.7	1.8
Candidate misinformation	4.1	2.3
Process disinformation	4.8	2.9
Technical voting issues	5.2	3.1

Table 1: Average detection times by campaign type

$$\text{sync\_score}(c) = \frac{1}{\text{std}(\{t_p : p \in c\})}, \quad (4)$$

where t_p is the timestamp of post p within the cluster c.

Additionally, **engagement manipulation** is detected through the analysis of engagement patterns. This includes identifying unusual like-to-comment ratios, rapid engagement immediately after posting, engagement from accounts exhibiting suspicious activity patterns, and disproportionate engagement relative to follower count.

3.3.3 Narrative Evolution Tracking

Narrative evolution tracking begins with **claim extraction**, where factual claims are extracted from posts using a combination of dependency parsing and named entity recognition. These claims are represented as (subject, predicate, object) triples. Following extraction, we perform **mutation analysis** to monitor how false claims evolve over time to evade fact-checking efforts. This process involves identifying original false claims from fact-checking databases, tracking semantically similar claims that appear after fact-checking, measuring the similarity between original and mutated claims, and identifying mutation strategies such as the use of hedging language or context changes.

To understand the spread of misinformation narratives, we employ **propagation modeling** using a modified Independent Cascade model. The probability that a user v adopts the narrative at time $t+1$, given their neighbors, is modeled as

$$P(\text{adoption}_{v,t+1} \mid \text{neighbors}_v) = 1 - \prod_{u \in N_v} (1 - p_{u,v} \cdot I_{u,t}) \quad (5)$$

where v is a user, N_v represents the set of their neighbors, $p_{u,v}$ is the influence probability from neighbor u to v, and $I_{u,t}$ is an indicator variable denoting whether user u shared the narrative at time t.

3.3.4 Integration and Classification

In the final stage, evidence from all analytical components is integrated to identify and classify potential coordination clusters. This process employs a **Random Forest classifier**, which operates on a feature set encompassing several distinct dimensions. These include the average stylometric similarity within the cluster, semantic coherence scores, temporal synchronization measures, and cross-platform presence indicators. Additional features capture engagement anomaly scores, reflecting irregular interaction patterns, as well as narrative mutation indicators, which measure shifts or adaptations in the narrative over time. The classifier synthesizes these inputs to produce a probability estimate that a given cluster constitutes a coordinated misinformation campaign.

4 Experimental Setup

4.1 Datasets

We evaluate our framework using datasets from three electoral contexts. The **US-2020** dataset consists of 15.2 million posts collected during the 2020 U.S. presidential election period (September–December 2020) across Twitter, Facebook, and Telegram (Chen and Ferrara, 2020). The **GER-2021** dataset includes 8.7 million posts from the 2021 German federal election period (July–September 2021), primarily in the German language (Sältzer, 2021). Finally, the **BRA-2022** dataset comprises 12.1 million posts gathered during the 2022 Brazilian presidential election (August–October 2022), predominantly in Portuguese (de Sao Paulo, 2022).

4.2 Ground Truth Annotation

Ground truth labels are established through multiple sources. These include **platform takedowns**, which consist of accounts and content removed by platforms due to coordinated inauthentic behavior; **fact-checker databases**, where false claims are identified by professional fact-checking organizations; **expert annotation**, involving manual review by domain experts familiar with each electoral context; and **academic datasets**, which comprise previously published collections of identified coordination networks. To ensure labeling reliability, inter-annotator agreement is measured using Fleiss' kappa, achieving values of $\kappa = 0.78$ for coordination detection and $\kappa = 0.82$ for misinformation classification.

4.3 Evaluation Metrics

We evaluate performance using standard classification metrics. **Precision** measures the fraction of detected campaigns that are truly coordinated misinformation, while **recall** captures the fraction of actual campaigns that are successfully detected. The **F1-score**, defined as the harmonic mean of precision and recall, provides a balanced view of both metrics. In addition to accuracy-based measures, we also consider **detection time**, which reflects the interval between a campaign's launch and its detection. Finally, we track the **false positive rate**, representing the proportion of legitimate content that is incorrectly flagged.

5 Results

5.1 Temporal Performance

Our framework demonstrates strong temporal performance, detecting emerging campaigns an average of 4.2 hours before manual identification by fact-checkers. Table 1 shows detection times across different campaign types.

5.2 Component Analysis

We conduct ablation studies to understand the contribution of each framework component. Table 2 shows the impact of removing different components on overall performance.

Cross-platform analysis provides the largest performance boost, highlighting the importance of considering coordination across multiple platforms. Temporal synchronization detection also contributes significantly to recall, helping identify campaigns that might be missed by content-only approaches.

5.3 Narrative Evolution Analysis

Our analysis reveals several common strategies employed by misinformation campaigns to evade detection. **Claim Hedging** involves modifying original false claims with hedging language (e.g., using phrases such as "reports suggest" instead of definitive statements) to enhance perceived credibility. **Context Shifting** refers to relocating false claims from direct electoral contexts to broader political discussions, thereby circumventing detection by keyword-based systems. Through **Source Laundering**, misinformation is attributed to seemingly credible sources or framed as "breaking news" to increase its trustworthiness. Finally, **Semantic Mutation** entails extensively paraphrasing core false claims while preserving their essential meaning.

6 Discussion

6.1 Implications for Electoral Integrity

Our results demonstrate that computational natural language processing approaches can improve the detection of coordinated misinformation campaigns during electoral periods. The high precision achieved by our framework (87.3%) suggests that automated detection can be deployed in real-world settings without excessive false positives that might suppress legitimate political discourse.

The cross-platform nature of modern coordination campaigns, revealed by our analysis, highlights the limitations of platform-specific detection approaches.

6.2 Methodological Contributions

This work presents several methodological contributions to computational political science. The **Multi-Platform integration** demonstrates how linguistic and behavioral signals can be combined across diverse social media platforms to enhance detection accuracy. By capturing the *temporal dynamics* of misinformation campaigns, our approach enables early detection prior to widespread propagation. The framework's capacity for *adversarial robustness* allows it to identify mutated claims and adaptive tactics, thereby providing resilience against sophisticated adversaries. Furthermore, the integration of computational methods with domain expert validation exemplifies *interdisciplinary validation*, ensuring the practical relevance of this work for electoral monitoring.

Configuration	Precision	Recall	F1-Score
Full Framework	0.873	0.821	0.846
Stylometric Analysis	0.834	0.789	0.811
Semantic Clustering	0.841	0.776	0.807
Temporal Synchronization	0.857	0.743	0.796
Cross-Platform Analysis	0.798	0.803	0.801
Narrative Evolution	0.849	0.812	0.830

Table 2: Ablation study results showing component contributions

6.3 Limitations and Future Work

Several limitations of our approach warrant consideration. The issue of **platform coverage** arises as our analysis is confined to three major platforms, potentially overlooking coordination occurring on smaller or emerging platforms absent from our dataset. Regarding **language limitations**, although our evaluation encompasses three languages, the generalizability of the approach to other linguistic contexts remains to be demonstrated. The ongoing **evolutionary arms race** between detection methods and adversaries suggests that, as detection improves, new evasion tactics will likely emerge, necessitating continuous adaptation of detection systems. Finally, **contextual nuance** presents challenges in distinguishing coordinated behavior from legitimate grassroots mobilization, particularly within highly polarized electoral environments. Future work should address these limitations by expanding platform coverage, conducting multilingual validation, and developing more sophisticated techniques to differentiate authentic coordination from inauthentic activity.

6.4 Ethical Considerations

The deployment of automated misinformation detection systems raises significant ethical considerations. Regarding **freedom of expression**, these systems must carefully balance the detection of misinformation with the protection of legitimate political speech. While our use of a high precision threshold helps mitigate this risk, ongoing vigilance remains essential. **transparency** requires that detection decisions be explainable and subject to human review, especially when they influence electoral discourse. Additionally, concerns of **bias and fairness** necessitate rigorous evaluation of detection systems for potential biases against specific political viewpoints or demographic groups. Finally, **democratic governance** questions arise about who should control these automated systems and how their deployment in electoral contexts should be governed.

7 Conclusion

This paper presents a comprehensive computational framework for detecting coordinated misinformation campaigns in electoral contexts. The EMD framework combines linguistic coordination analysis, cross-platform behavioral pattern recognition, and narrative evolution tracking to achieve state-of-the-art performance in identifying inauthentic coordination networks.

Our evaluation across three national elections demonstrates significant improvements over existing methods, with the framework achieving 87.3% precision and 82.1% recall.

Key contributions include:

1. A novel multi-platform framework that captures coordination across diverse social media environments

2. Methods for tracking the evolution of misinformation narratives and their adaptation to counter-messaging

3. Empirical insights into the cross-platform nature of modern influence operations

The work advances both computational methods for political science research and practical approaches to protecting electoral integrity in democratic societies. As misinformation campaigns become increasingly sophisticated, computational approaches will play a crucial role in maintaining the information environment necessary for democratic decision-making.

Future research should focus on expanding the framework to additional platforms and languages, developing more sophisticated approaches to distinguishing authentic from inauthentic coordination, and addressing the evolving adversarial landscape of electoral misinformation.

References

Moustafa Alzantot, Bharathan Balakrishnan, and Mani Srivastava. 2018. Did you hear that? adversarial examples against automatic speech recognition. In *arXiv preprint arXiv:1801.00554*.

Alexandre Bovet and Hernán A Makse. 2019. Influence of fake news in twitter during the 2016 us presidential election. *Nature Communications*, 10(1):7.

Samantha Bradshaw, Hannah Bailey, and Philip N. Howard. 2021. Industrialized disinformation: 2020 global inventory of organized social media manipulation. Technical report, Programme on Democracy & Technology, Oxford Internet Institute, Oxford, UK.

Nikan Chavoshi, Hossein Hamooni, and Abdullah Mueen. 2016. Identifying correlated bots in twitter. In *International Conference on Social Informatics*, pages 14–21. Springer.

Emily Chen and Emilio Ferrara. 2020. election2020: The first public twitter dataset on the 2020 us presidential election. *Preprint*, arXiv:2010.00600. Dataset contains 15.2 million posts from Twitter, Facebook, and Telegram during September-December 2020.

Universidade de Sao Paulo. 2022. 2022 brazilian election social media dataset. Dataset contains 12.1 million posts from August-October 2022, predominantly in Portuguese.

Emilio Ferrara, Onur Varol, Clayton Davis, Filippo Menczer, and Alessandro Flammini. 2016. The rise of social bots. *Communications of the ACM*, 59(7):96–104.

Nathaniel Gleicher. 2018. Coordinated inauthentic behavior explained. *Meta Newsroom*.

Philip N. Howard. 2020. *Lie Machines: How to Save Democracy from Troll Armies, Deceitful Robots, Junk News Operations, and Political Operatives*. Yale University Press, New Haven, CT.

Jane Im, Eshwar Chandrasekharan, Jackson Sargent, Paige Lighthammer, Taylor Denby, Ankit Bhargava, Libby Hemphill, David Jurgens, and Eric Gilbert. 2020. Still out there: Modeling and identifying russian troll accounts on twitter. In *Proceedings of the 12th ACM Conference on Web Science*, pages 1–10.

Jon Kleinberg. 2003. Bursty and hierarchical structure in streams. *Data Mining and Knowledge Discovery*, 7(4):373–397.

Srijan Kumar and Neil Shah. 2018. False information on web and social media: A survey. In *Proceedings of the 2018 World Wide Web Conference*, pages 1–2.

Luca Luceri, Silvia Giordano, and Emilio Ferrara. 2020. Detecting troll behavior via inverse reinforcement learning: A case study of russian trolls in the 2016 us election. In *Proceedings of the International AAAI Conference on Web and Social Media*, volume 14, pages 417–427.

Diogo Pacheco, Alessandro Flammini, and Filippo Menczer. 2020. Uncovering coordinated networks on social media: Methods and case studies. *Proceedings of the International AAAI Conference on Web and Social Media*, 14:455–466.

Victoria L Rubin, Niall J Conroy, Yimin Chen, and Sarah Cornwell. 2015. Deception detection for news: Three types of fakes. *Proceedings of the Association for Information Science and Technology*, 52(1):1–4.

Chengcheng Shao, Giovanni Luca Ciampaglia, Onur Varol, Kai-Cheng Yang, Alessandro Flammini, and Filippo Menczer. 2018. The spread of low-credibility content by social bots. In *Nature Communications*, volume 9, page 4787. Nature Publishing Group.

Stier Sebastian Bäuerle Joscha Blumenberg Manuela Mechkova Valeriya Pemstein Daniel Seim Brigitte Sältzer, Marius. 2021. The german federal election 2021 social media dataset. Dataset contains 8.7 million posts from July-September 2021, primarily in German.

Soroush Vosoughi, Deb Roy, and Sinan Aral. 2018. The spread of true and false news online. *Science*, 359(6380):1146–1151.

William Yang Wang. 2017. "liar, liar pants on fire": A new benchmark dataset for fake news detection. In *Proceedings of the 55th Annual Meeting of the Association for Computational Linguistics (Volume 2: Short Papers)*, pages 422–426.

Tara Wilson, Kiran Zhou, and Kate Starbird. 2020. Cross-platform disinformation campaigns: Lessons learned and next steps. In *Proceedings of the 2020 CHI Conference on Human Factors in Computing Systems*, pages 1–13.

Kai-Cheng Yang, Onur Varol, Clayton A Davis, Emilio Ferrara, Alessandro Flammini, and Filippo Menczer. 2019. Scalable and generalizable social bot detection through data selection. In *Proceedings of the AAAI Conference on Artificial Intelligence*, volume 33, pages 1096–1103.

Savvas Zannettou, Tristan Caulfield, William Setzer, Michael Sirivianos, Gianluca Stringhini, and Jeremy Blackburn. 2019. Disinformation warfare: Understanding state-sponsored trolls on twitter and understanding their influence on the web. In *Proceedings of the 2019 World Wide Web Conference*, pages 218–226.

Xinyi Zhou and Reza Zafarani. 2020. Fake news detection using machine learning approaches: A systematic review. In *IEEE Transactions on Computational Social Systems*, volume 7, pages 294–307.

Americans are dreamers – Generic statements and stereotyping in political tweets

Ines Rehbein
Data and Web Science Group
University of Mannheim
rehbein@uni-mannheim.de

Abstract

This paper addresses the question whether generics are associated with stereotyping, a claim often found in the literature. Most of the work, however, has been based on a small number of hand-crafted examples. We contribute to the discussion by looking at the use of generics in political tweets, written by members of the U.S. Congress, and present a framework for comparing the usage patterns of generics to other linguistic constructions that have been discussed as devices for stereotyping and *othering*. Our initial findings suggest that generics are not strongly associated with stereotypes while framing might play a more important role for stereotyping in political tweets.

1 Introduction

The construction of in-groups and out-groups, also refered to as *othering*, describes the categorisation of individuals as belonging to a specific group that is perceived as different from (and often inferior to) the social norm. In doing so, individuals considered as the *other* are usually depicted as a coherent and homogenuous group, based on stereotypes and overgeneralisation, making them an easy victim of discrimination (Staszak, 2009).

Othering is a common rhetorical move in political communication, and in particular in populist rhetoric (see, e.g., Fielder and Catalano (2017)). It can be strategically used to create a sense of shared identity among party supporters and mobilise them against a perceived enemy. While *othering* can have positive effects on the in-group, such as increasing group cohesiveness and cooperation, it also comes at the cost of prejudice, conflict and discrimination for the out-group.[1]

The creation of in- and out-groups plays an important role in political communication and is often associated with stereotyping. By *stereotype*, we refer to "a set of cognitive generalizations (e.g., beliefs, expectations) about the qualities and characteristics of the members of a group or social category", following the definition of the APA Dictionary of Psychology.[2]

Several linguistic devices have been discussed as a means for othering and stereotyping, among them generic statements (Novoa et al., 2023; Bosse, 2024; Davani et al., 2024), the use of pronouns (Íñigo-Mora, 2004; Bull and Fetzer, 2006; Proctor and Su, 2011; Tyrkkö, 2016; Alavidze, 2017), framing by word choice (Sheshadri et al., 2021; van den Berg et al., 2020; Dreier et al., 2022), or entity framing (Entman, 1993; Mahmoud et al., 2025).

In the paper, we look at othering and stereotyping in political tweets written by members of the U.S. Congress. The focus of our work, however, is not so much on investigating stereotyping of in- and out-groups from a social science perspective but, instead, on studying the linguistic devices used for stereotyping in political tweets. Our work contributes to the linguistic discussion on whether generics are a common means to express stereotypes, as has often been argued (Geurts, 1985; Leslie, 2014; Radden, 2009; Novoa et al., 2023; Bosse, 2024; Ralston, 2024) but also refuted (Krifka et al., 1995).[3] In particular, we examine the role of generics, universals, and quantified statements based on real data from the political domain, where previous studies have mostly relied on a small number of constructed examples. We introduce a framework for extracting real-world generic statements about social groups and present a qualitative analysis of our findings.

[1]Early work investigating the effects of *othering* on human behaviour is the classic Robbers Case Study (Sherif et al., 1961) where young boys have been divided into groups to study how they behave when having to compete or cooperate with members of the out-group.

[2]https://dictionary.apa.org/stereotype.

[3]For a more detailed discussion, see Section 2.

Proceedings of the 21st Conference on Natural Language Processing (KONVENS), Volume 2: Workshops, pages 128–137, 2025

2 Related work

Generic statements are often described as a powerful tool to control the perception of groups as *in-groups* and *out-groups* by ascribing them certain characteristics and attributes and by creating an *otherness* (Staszak, 2009). One property that makes the use of generics so compelling is their tolerance toward exceptions. In contrast to universal statements like "all birds fly", which would be rejected by everybody with at least minimal knowledge of ornithology, the generic sentence "birds fly" will be accepted as true even though there are birds that do not have this capacity. Interestingly, this is also the case for statements that are true only for a small subset of its group members, such as "mosquitoes transfer the West Nile Virus" which holds for only a small percentage of mosquitoes.

In addition, Novoa et al. (2023) point out another striking feature of generics, namely that "despite expressing general claims that gloss over exceptions, they are endorsed in the face of variable or even minimal evidence". This tolerance to exceptions and ignorance towards a lack of evidence seems to make generics especially suited to transport stereotypes. Bosse (2024, p.3878), for example, describes generics as "mental states that associate properties with social groups".[4] However, there are also other means to associate properties with groups, such as explicitly quantified statements ("most birds can fly") and universals ("all birds can fly").

Othering and generics have both been discussed in relation to polarisation (Erdoğan and Uyan-Semerci, 2025; Iyengar and Westwood, 2015). Novoa et al. (2023) investigate the role of generics for partisan polarisation in the US and show that not only generics but also explicitly quantified statements can be interpreted by humans as universally true, pointing at a tendency of the human brain to convert more nuanced, quantified statements into generic, categorising ones. In three experiments, the authors show that generic expressions and, to a lesser extent, explicitly quantified statements can evoke polarised political judgments.

Some works in NLP have focussed on the detection of stereotypes (Blodgett et al., 2020; Sap et al., 2020), often using artificial data based on *(identity term, attribute)* tuples (Jha et al., 2023). One recent example is the Multilingual SeeGULL dataset of Bhutani et al. (2024) which includes LLM generated tuples, validated by human coders. Davani et al. (2024) focus on the use of generic sentences for stereotyping and present a multilingual dataset that combines specific group mentions with attributes, annotated for genericity. Their schema also distinguishes mentions of generalisations (e.g., reporting what others have said) from promoting it. The authors show that the co-occurrence of group mentions and attributes are not a reliable incdicator of generalisation, thus questioning the widespread approach of using group, attribute pairs for stereotype detection. They present a classifier that detects generalisations, reporting a PR-AUC (Area Under the Precision Recall (PR) Curve) of 58.7.

More linguistically inspired work has focussed on the annotation and detection of generics in language (Mitchell et al., 2003; Doddington et al., 2004; Walker et al., 2006; Suh, 2006; Herbelot and Copestake, 2008; Zirn et al., 2008; Mathew and Katz, 2009; Reiter and Frank, 2010; Friedrich et al., 2015b; Friedrich and Pinkal, 2015; Friedrich et al., 2016). We take this as the starting point for our framework to extract generic and generalising statements from real-world political text.

Figure 1: Example tweet including a numerically modified statement about Americans.

3 Framework

We now describe the different steps in our framework for extracting instances of generic, universal and quantified statements about groups, in order to investigate their function in discourse (Figure 2).

Data The data we use in our case study are daily tweets of both houses of congress, from over 1,000 campaign, office, committee and party accounts.[5] The data has been collected over a time period from June 2017 to October 2020 and amounts to ca. 9.8 mio tweets. For an example, see Figure 1.

[4]Others, however, have questioned the idea that generics express stereotypes. See, e.g., Krifka et al. (1995, p.48).

[5]The data is available from `https://github.com/alexlitel/congresstweets`.

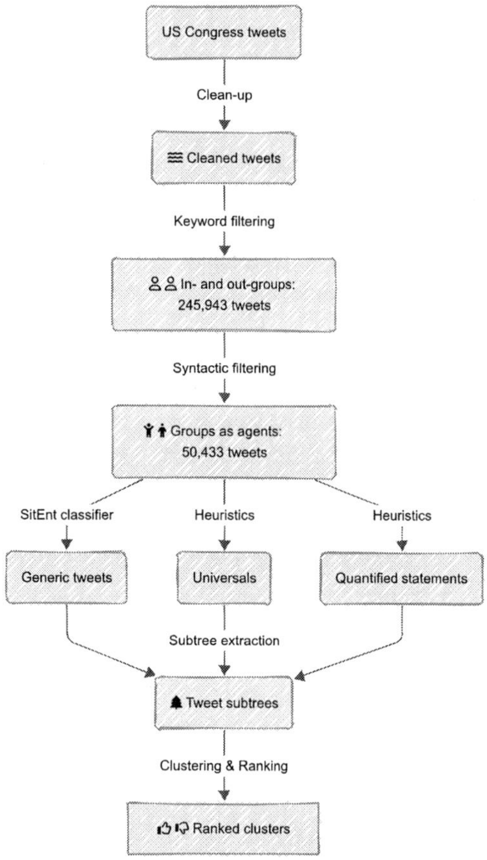

Figure 2: Framework for the extraction of real-world linguistic examples from U.S. Congress tweets.

Preprocessing We do some basic clean-up during preprocessing where we extract the tweet messages and filter out noise. Preprocessing includes the removal of non-ascii characters, empty lines and punctuation at the beginning of a tweet. We remove duplicates and tweets with no lowercase letters and delete URLs, at-mentions and hashtags at the beginning or end of the tweet.

Keyword-based filtering In the next step, we collect a list of keywords representing in- and out-groups in the migration discourse, i.e., *alien, american, asylum, migrant, refugee*. We then do a string-based keyword search for these group terms, ignoring case, and extract all tweets that include (at least) one of the terms. Please note that this also extracts tweets that include collocations like *American dream, American economy* or *immigrant rights* which are not in the center of our interest. We remove those in the next step, syntactic filtering. Keyword-based filtering reduces the overall amount of tweets from 9.8 mio to a much smaller set of 245,943 tweets (see Table 1) that can be processed more efficiently.

	group	**is-subj**	**generic**
alien	2,593	224	92
american	205,986	46,500	8,525
asylum	5,781	362	166
migrant	26,996	2,895	1,565
refugee	4,587	452	214
total	245,943	50,433	10,562

Table 1: Number of tweets after the different filtering steps (group: keyword-based filtering; is-subj: tweets where the group term is in subject position; generic: generic and generalising statements, according to the predicted Situation Entities classifier).

Syntactic filtering Next, we use a dependency parser[6] to extract tweets where the group terms occur in subject position. This filters out adjectival uses of the terms and extracts plausible candidates for generic statements about groups. We specify two exceptions, *American people, asylum seeker*, that we include in the data. This syntactic filtering step further reduces the data from roughly 246,000 messages to 50,433 tweets where one of the group terms appears in subject position in the tweet.

3.1 Classifying genericity

To identify generic and generalising statements, we train a supervised text classifier on the Situation Entities (SitEnt) dataset (Friedrich and Palmer, 2014; Friedrich et al., 2015b). Situation Entities are clause-level semantic annotations that introduce *situations* to the discourse (Smith, 2003), such as EVENTS, STATES, GENERICS, GENERALIZING SENTENCES, REPORTS or QUESTIONS (see A.1). We use a simple text classifier, based on a pre-trained RoBERTa model (Liu et al., 2019). For more training details, see §A.2 in the appendix.

Table 2 shows results on the SitEnt test set for all classes. Overall, results are high with an accuracy of 0.8 and a weighted F1 of 0.79. Not surprisingly, we get higher scores for classes with more training instances and also high results for Situation Entity types that have some easily identifiable features (such as questions, reports or speech acts). Results for GENERIC are substantially lower than for EVENT, even though both classes have roughly the same number of instances, and generalising sentences seem even harder to detect.

Our results are in the same range as the state-of-the-art (Rezaee et al., 2021) which combines a BERT model (Devlin et al., 2019) with GPT-2 (Radford et al., 2019) and reports an F1 of 0.79

[6]We use the spaCy v2.3.9 dependency parser with the English model `en_core_web_sm`.

	Prec	Rec	F1	Support
STATE	0.82	0.89	0.85	3,174
EVENT	0.85	0.83	0.84	1,524
GENERIC	0.80	0.72	0.76	1,429
UNDECIDED	0.67	0.63	0.65	465
GENERALISING	0.54	0.47	0.50	294
REPORT	0.86	0.81	0.84	274
QUESTION	0.89	0.92	0.91	132
GENERALSTATIVE	0.00	0.00	0.00	86
IMPERATIVE	0.51	0.90	0.65	51
SPEECHACT	1.00	1.00	1.00	1
Accuracy			0.80	7,430
F1(weighted)	0.79	0.80	0.79	7,430

Table 2: Results for the RoBERTa-based Situation Entity classifier on the test set. Support shows the number of instances for each class in the test set.

(acc: 0.81) on the SitEnt corpus.[7] The lower results for generic and generalising statements shows the difficulty of the task, which is in line with previous work (e.g., Davani et al. (2024), see §2 above). For an error analysis, see §A.3.

We apply our classifier to the Twitter dataset and extract all messages that have been predicted as either generic or generalising. As a result, we obtain a dataset with 10,562 tweets (see Table 1).

3.2 Extracting clusters of similar sentences

To find out whether there is an association between form and function for the different linguistic devices (i.e., generic, universal and quantified statements), we need to compare those constructions in context, i.e., in sentences with similar meaning. To extract those, we proceed as follows.

Subtree extraction As input, we use the set of tweets where instances of each group term appear in subject position. This includes all different statement types. Next, we identify the verb governing the group term and extract its syntactic subtree. This can be done, using the spaCy subtree function which extracts a token and all its syntactic dependents. For the example sentence below, the extracted subtree is the clause that includes the group term in subject position (Ex 1).

Ex 1. "Climate change is expected to create hundreds of millions of refugees, but right now climate <u>refugees</u> have no legal rights."
Subtree: "refugees have no legal rights"

[7]Please note that we do not report averaged results over different model initialisations, as we are not interested in benchmarking our models on the Friedrich et al. (2015b) data but only in identifying and extracting generic and generalising statements from social media.

Clustering We encode the subtree strings, using sentence embeddings, and cluster the embeddings to obtain semantically similar sentences.[8] For additional details on the clustering process, see A.4. We use a high cosine similarity threshold for clustering. As a result, we loose many instances that are below the threshold. However, for our use case, we are not interested in high coverage (i.e., being able to assign every instance to a cluster), but rather in identifying usage patterns of similar sentences in order to examine the variation in the use of different constructions. Table 3 shows an example cluster of statements expressing the americans' support for law and order. All but one sentence in this cluster use generic statements while the remaining one uses a quantified statement.

Ranking Finally, we rank the resulting clusters to identify similar sentences that show a high preference for specific constructions (i.e., a strong *form-to-meaning association*), providing us with linguistic evidence for further qualitative analysis. For ranking, we use the ratio of instances for the respective construction (i.e. generic, universal, etc.), relative to the total number of instances in the cluster.[9] To identify generic and generalising statements, we rely on the predictions of the SitEnt classifier (see §3.1). Universal and quantified statements can be easily extracted, based on heuristics. For universal statements, we extract sentences where the group term in subject position is modified by either *all* or *every* while for quantification, we search for the modifiers *most, many, some, few, several.*

4 Exploration of generics and stereotypes in political tweets

To explore to what extend generics are used to stereotype social groups in political tweets, we apply our framework to the U.S. Congress Tweets dataset described above. We present a qualitative analysis, focussing on clusters of similar sentences that show a strong preference for one particular construction.

[8]We use the Fast Clustering algorithm `https://sbert.net/examples/sentence_transformer/applications/clustering/README.html#fast-clustering` from the Sentence Transformer (Reimers and Gurevych, 2019) library.

[9]There are many more sophisticated measures that could be used, however, for the purpose of exploration our simple ranking metric already works well in identifying semantic clusters with a strong preference for one particular construction.

ID	**Cluster 1112**, 10 elements ratio: 0.9
1	Americans want LAW & ORDER!
2	The American people stand with law enforcement.
3	Americans support law enforcement and want law & order.
4	Americans support our # police officers and law and order in our cities.
	...
10	**Most Americans** support law & order, the fair application of it, and pray for our police.

Table 3: Example cluster for the group term "american", including 9 generic sentences (ratio: 0.9) and one explicitly quantified statement (**Most** Americans).

Cluster 267, 23 elements ratio: 1.0
ALL Americans have the constitutional right to marry
ALL Americans have the right to marry no matter whom they love
Cluster 813, 11 elements ratio: 1.0
all Americans have the opportunity to achieve success
every American has the opportunity to succeed
Cluster 838, 11 elements ratio: 1.0
all Americans can enjoy freedom & equality
every American is equal

Table 4: Examples for clusters with a high ratio of universal statements.

Generics Generic statements about the in-group in our data mostly express political demands (see A_{1-5} below).

Americans

(A_1) deserve better

(A_2) want the truth / want transparency

(A_3) should know / need to know

(A_4) are tired of waiting

(A_5) need help

For the out-group, clusters that show a strong preference for generics include mostly positive statements about the group (see B_{1-4} below).

Immigrants / refugees / asylum seekers

(B_1) enhance our economy

(B_2) make America stronger

(B_3) are not criminals / animals

(B_4) deserve protection

We did not find instances of generics used for negative stereotyping of social groups.

Universals Table 4 shows examples for semantic clusters that exclusively included universals. It is obvious that those instances do not contain stereotypes but express normative generalisations about how the world *should be*, rather than how it is. All of the clusters with a high ratio of universal sentences in our analysis are of that type.

Aliens	224 mentions in subject position:
	illegal (155), criminal (30), deported (4), convicted (3), dangerous (3), charged (2)
Immigrants	2,917 mentions in subject position:
	illegal (223), undocumented (154), young (62), legal (30), working (14)
Asylum s.	365 mentions in subject position:
	vulnerable (5), fleeing (5), cuban (3), transgender (3), legitimate (3)
Refugees	457 mentions in subject position:
	welcome (15), fleeing (14), rohingya (9), syrian (9), american (4), somali (4), liberian (4), clean (3)

Table 5: Entity framing of social groups in tweets.

Quantified statements When comparing generics to sentences that include explicit quantification, we did not see similarly strong associations between form and meaning (also see Table 9 in the apendix).

Entity framing While we did not see strong evidence for an assiciation between generics and stereotypes in our data, we found numerous instances of entity framing. Table 5 shows the most frequent modifiers for each group term, extracted from the spaCy dependency parse. It is obvious that the terms *aliens, immigrants* are mostly framed in negative terms. *Aliens* in particular are portrayed as dangerous and criminal, which is reflected in framing through word choice. Politicians with a more positive stance towards immigration did not use the term *alien* but preferred *refugee*, shown by the lack of negative attributes for this term.

5 Conclusion

In the paper, we present a framework for extracting generic and generalising statements about social groups and apply it to tweets written by members of the U.S. Congress. Our framework allows us to extract linguistic evidence for the various constructions while controlling for sentence meaning. This enables us to study usage patterns for generics, universals and quantified statements in a controlled setting with real-world data. While generics are often considered as an important device for stereotyping, our initial findings suggest that the association is less strong as expected and that framing might play a more important role for stereotyping social groups in political tweets.

Limitations

We would like to point out some limitations of our work. First, we would like to emphasize once again that the framework is not suitable for comparing the use of stereotypes across parties or across time. In the paper, we only consider three constructions that have the potential to be used for stereotyping but do not aim to measure the total amount of stereotypical statements overall.

Second, while this short paper introduces a framework for extracting real-world examples in context for comparative linguistic analysis, it does not (yet) present a validation of the framework. Third, while the clustering step manages to produce clusters of sentences with similar meaning, it is conceivable that the surface form of the different constructions also has some impact on the clustering process and that this results in artificially "clean" groups of statements where the different constructions end up in separate clusters. One way to address this issue is to mask the markers for the various constructions so that the input to the clustering process is normalised (see example below) while keeping the information on the original statement type for further analysis.

Orig: *All|Most|∅*	Americans support the law.
Cluster input →	Americans support the law.

Acknowledgments

The work presented in this paper is funded by the German Research Foundation (DFG) under the UNCOVER project (RE3536/3-1). We would also like to thank the anonymous reviewers for their constructive feedback.

References

Maia Alavidze. 2017. The use of pronouns in political discourse. *International Journal of Arts & Sciences*, 9(4):349–356.

Mukul Bhutani, Kevin Robinson, Vinodkumar Prabhakaran, Shachi Dave, and Sunipa Dev. 2024. SeeGULL multilingual: a dataset of geo-culturally situated stereotypes. In *Proceedings of the 62nd Annual Meeting of the Association for Computational Linguistics (Volume 2: Short Papers)*, pages 842–854, Bangkok, Thailand. Association for Computational Linguistics.

Su Lin Blodgett, Solon Barocas, Hal Daumé III, and Hanna Wallach. 2020. Language (technology) is power: A critical survey of "bias" in NLP. In *Proceedings of the 58th Annual Meeting of the Association for Computational Linguistics*, pages 5454–5476, Online. Association for Computational Linguistics.

Anne Bosse. 2024. Stereotyping and generics. *Inquiry: An Interdisciplinary Journal of Philosophy*, 67(10):3876–3892.

Peter Bull and Anita Fetzer. 2006. Who are we and who are you? the strategic use of forms of address in political interviews. *Text and Talk*, 26.

Aida Mostafazadeh Davani, Sagar Gubbi, Sunipa Dev, Shachi Dave, and Vinodkumar Prabhakaran. 2024. Genil: A multilingual dataset on generalizing language. *Preprint*, arXiv:2404.05866.

Jacob Devlin, Ming-Wei Chang, Kenton Lee, and Kristina Toutanova. 2019. BERT: Pre-training of deep bidirectional transformers for language understanding. In *Proceedings of the 2019 Conference of the North American Chapter of the Association for Computational Linguistics: Human Language Technologies, Volume 1 (Long and Short Papers)*, pages 4171–4186, Minneapolis, Minnesota. Association for Computational Linguistics.

George Doddington, Alexis Mitchell, Mark Przybocki, Lance Ramshaw, Stephanie Strassel, and Ralph Weischedel. 2004. The automatic content extraction (ACE) program – tasks, data, and evaluation. In *Proceedings of the Fourth International Conference on Language Resources and Evaluation (LREC'04)*, Lisbon, Portugal. European Language Resources Association (ELRA).

Sarah K Dreier, Emily K Gade Dallas Card, and Noah Smith. 2022. Patterns of bias: How mainstream media operationalize links between mass shootings and terrorism. *Political Communication*.

Robert M Entman. 1993. Framing: Toward clarification of a fractured paradigm. *Journal of communication*, 43(4):51–58.

Emre Erdoğan and Pinar Uyan-Semerci. 2025. Othering in politics: how affective polarization undermines democratic philia? *Frontiers in Political Science*, pages 1–17.

Grace E. Fielder and Theresa Catalano. 2017. Othering others: Right-wing populism in uk media discourse on "new" immigration. In Jan Chovanec and Katarzyna Molek-Kozakowska, editors, *Representing the Other in European Media Discourses*, pages 207–234. Amsterdam: John Benjamins.

Annemarie Friedrich, Kleio-Isidora Mavridou, and Alexis Palmer. 2015a. Situation entity types (annotation manual). Version 1.1.

Annemarie Friedrich and Alexis Palmer. 2014. Situation entity annotation. In *Proceedings of LAW VIII - The 8th Linguistic Annotation Workshop*, pages 149–158, Dublin, Ireland. Association for Computational Linguistics and Dublin City University.

Annemarie Friedrich, Alexis Palmer, Melissa Peate Sørensen, and Manfred Pinkal. 2015b. Annotating genericity: a survey, a scheme, and a corpus. In *Proceedings of the 9th Linguistic Annotation Workshop*, pages 21–30, Denver, Colorado, USA. Association for Computational Linguistics.

Annemarie Friedrich, Alexis Palmer, and Manfred Pinkal. 2016. Situation entity types: automatic classification of clause-level aspect. In *Proceedings of the 54th Annual Meeting of the Association for Computational Linguistics (Volume 1: Long Papers)*, pages 1757–1768, Berlin, Germany. Association for Computational Linguistics.

Annemarie Friedrich and Manfred Pinkal. 2015. Discourse-sensitive automatic identification of generic expressions. In *Proceedings of the 53rd Annual Meeting of the Association for Computational Linguistics and the 7th International Joint Conference on Natural Language Processing (Volume 1: Long Papers)*, pages 1272–1281, Beijing, China. Association for Computational Linguistics.

Barts Geurts. 1985. Generics. *Journal of Semantics*, 3(4):247–255.

Aurelie Herbelot and Ann Copestake. 2008. Annotating genericity: How do humans decide? (a case study in ontology extraction). In Sam Featherston and Susanne Winkler, editors, *The Fruits of Empirical Linguistics*, volume 1. Berlin: de Gruyter.

Isabel Íñigo-Mora. 2004. On the use of the personal pronoun we in communities. *Journal of Language and Politics*, 3(1):27–52.

S Iyengar and S Westwood. 2015. Fear and loathing across party lines: new evidence on group polarization. *American Journal of Political Science*, 59:690–707.

Akshita Jha, Aida Mostafazadeh Davani, Chandan K Reddy, Shachi Dave, Vinodkumar Prabhakaran, and Sunipa Dev. 2023. SeeGULL: A stereotype benchmark with broad geo-cultural coverage leveraging generative models. In *Proceedings of the 61st Annual Meeting of the Association for Computational Linguistics (Volume 1: Long Papers)*, pages 9851–9870, Toronto, Canada. Association for Computational Linguistics.

Manfred Krifka, Francis J Pelletier, Gregory N Carlson, Gennaro Chierchia, Godehard Link, and Alice ter Meulen. 1995. Genericity: An introduction. In *The Generic Book*, pages 1–24. University of Chicago Press, Chicago and London.

Sarah-Jane Leslie. 2014. Carving up the social world with generics. *Oxford studies in experimental philosophy*, 1:208–232.

Yinhan Liu, Myle Ott, Naman Goyal, Jingfei Du, Mandar Joshi, Danqi Chen, Omer Levy, Mike Lewis, Luke Zettlemoyer, and Veselin Stoyanov. 2019. Roberta: A robustly optimized BERT pretraining approach. *CoRR*, abs/1907.11692.

Tarek Mahmoud, Zhuohan Xie, Dimitar Dimitrov, Nikolaos Nikolaidis, Purificação Silvano, Roman Yangarber, Shivam Sharma, Elisa Sartori, Nicolas Stefanovitch, Giovanni Da San Martino, Jakub Piskorski, and Preslav Nakov. 2025. Entity framing and role portrayal in the news. *Preprint*, arXiv:2502.14718.

Thomas A. Mathew and Graham Katz. 2009. Supervised categorization for habitual versus episodic sentences. In *Sixth Midwest Computational Linguistics Colloquium*. Bloomington, Indiana: Indiana University.

Alexis Mitchell, Stephanie Strassel, Mark Przybocki, JK Davis, George R. Doddington, Ralph Grishman, Adam Meyers, Ada Brunstein, Lisa Ferro, and Beth Sundheim. 2003. Ace-2 version 1.0. LDC2003T11.

Gustavo Novoa, Margaret Echelbarger, Andrew Gelman, and Susan A. Gelman. 2023. Generically partisan: Polarization in political communication. *Proceedings of the National Academy of Sciences*, 120(47):e2309361120.

Katarzyna Proctor and Lily I-Wen Su. 2011. The 1st person plural in political discourse – American politicians in interviews and in a debate. *Journal of Pragmatics*, 43(13):3251–3266.

Günter Radden. 2009. Generic reference in english: A metonymic and conceptual blending analysis. In Klaus-Uwe Panther, Linda L. Thornburg, and Antonio Barcelona, editors, *Metonymy and Metaphor in Grammar*, pages 199–228. John Benjamins Publishing Company.

Alec Radford, Jeff Wu, Rewon Child, David Luan, Dario Amodei, and Ilya Sutskever. 2019. Language models are unsupervised multitask learners. *OpenAI*.

Tom Ralston. 2024. Reconceptualising the psychological theory of generics. *Philosophical Studies*, 181:2973–2995.

Nils Reimers and Iryna Gurevych. 2019. Sentence-BERT: Sentence embeddings using Siamese BERT-networks. In *Proceedings of the 2019 Conference on Empirical Methods in Natural Language Processing and the 9th International Joint Conference on Natural Language Processing (EMNLP-IJCNLP)*, pages 3982–3992, Hong Kong, China. Association for Computational Linguistics.

Nils Reiter and Anette Frank. 2010. Identifying generic noun phrases. In *Proceedings of the 48th Annual Meeting of the Association for Computational Linguistics*, pages 40–49, Uppsala, Sweden. Association for Computational Linguistics.

Mehdi Rezaee, Kasra Darvish, Gaoussou Youssouf Kebe, and Francis Ferraro. 2021. Discriminative and generative transformer-based models for situation entity classification. *CoRR*, abs/2109.07434.

Maarten Sap, Saadia Gabriel, Lianhui Qin, Dan Jurafsky, Noah A. Smith, and Yejin Choi. 2020. Social bias frames: Reasoning about social and power implications of language. In *Proceedings of the 58th Annual Meeting of the Association for Computational Linguistics*, pages 5477–5490, Online. Association for Computational Linguistics.

Muzafer Sherif, O.J. Harvey, Jack B. White, William R. Hood, and Carolyn W. Sherif. 1961. *Intergroup Conflict and Cooperation. The Robbers Cave Experiment [1954]*. University of Oklahoma Book Exchange, Norman.

Karthik Sheshadri, Chaitanya Shivade, and Munindar P. Singh. 2021. Detecting framing changes in topical news. *IEEE Transactions on Computational Social Systems*, 8(3):780–791.

Carlota S Smith. 2003. *Modes of discourse: The local structure of texts*. Cambridge University Press.

Jean-François Staszak. 2009. Other/otherness. In Rob Kitchin and Nigel Thrift, editors, *International Encyclopedia of Human Geography*, pages 43–47. Elsevier, Oxford.

Sangweon Suh. 2006. Extracting generic statements for the semantic web. Master's thesis, University of Edinburgh. Master's thesis.

Jukka Tyrkkö. 2016. Looking for rhetorical thresholds: Pronoun frequencies in political speeches. *Studies in Variation, Contacts and Change in English*, 17.

Esther van den Berg, Katharina Korfhage, Josef Ruppenhofer, Michael Wiegand, and Katja Markert. 2020. Doctor who? framing through names and titles in German. In *Proceedings of the Twelfth Language Resources and Evaluation Conference*, pages 4924–4932, Marseille, France. European Language Resources Association.

Christopher Walker, Stephanie Strassel, Julie Medero, and Kazuaki Maeda. 2006. Ace 2005 multilingual training corpus. LDC2006T06.

Cäcilia Zirn, Vivi Nastase, and Michael Strube. 2008. Distinguishing between instances and classes in the wikipedia taxonomy. In *Proceedings of the 5th European Semantic Web Conference on The Semantic Web: Research and Applications*, ESWC'08, page 376–387, Berlin, Heidelberg. Springer-Verlag.

A Appendix

A.1 Situation Entity types

Table 6 illustrates the different Situation Entity types. Most relevant for our work are the classes GENERIC and GENERALISING. GENERIC sentences have a generic main referent while GENERALISING sentences make statements about individuals that generalise over situations and report regularities.

A.2 Classification setup

We follow the suggested train-test splits,[10] resulting in 30,859 instances for training and 7,430 instances for testing. We further split the training data into a training and development set (29,316 and 1,543 instances).

Preprocessing The original dataset has been automatically segmented into clauses. As the segmentation step introduces noise, we do not rely on the provided clause boundaries but extract the left and right context within the sentence for each clause and mark the relevant clause information by inserting an underscore before the verbal head of the clause. This means that the same sentence can be included multiple times, but with different verbs highlighted within the sentence. This enables the model to learn which clause to focus on while, at the same time, providing the necessary contextual information.

Hyperparameter tuning We do hyperparameter tuning on the development set and obtain best results of 0.86 F1(micro) and 0.63 (macro) across all 10 labels. We use the following hyperparameter configuration:

- learning rate: 3.134214402336582e-05
- weight decay: 3.215675091397119e-05
- batch size: 16
- warmup ration: 0.0936967038422192
- number of train epochs: 2

For implementation, we use the huggingface transformers library: `https://huggingface.co/docs/transformers`.

A.3 Error analysis

The training data for the Situation Entity classifier includes texts from 13 different genres and text types, including blogs, emails, essays, fiction, letters, news, and wikipedia articles. To get an idea about the error rate for predicting generics and generalising sentences, we randomly sample 20 instances for each group and manually inspect the classifier's predictions.

Our error analysis shows that the overall accuracy of the classifier on the twitter data is quite high with 0.84. For the term *aliens*, most instances are predicted as GENERALISING as this term is mostly

[10] `https://github.com/annefried/sitent/tree/master`.

SitEnt type	Definition	Example
STATE	States introduce specific properties of specific individuals to the discourse.	Joseph loves cake.
EVENT	Events introduce a specific event to the discourse: things that happen or happened.	Mira won the race.
GENERIC	Generic sentences make statements about kinds.	Lions are carnivores.
GENERALISING	Generalising sentences report regularities related to specific individuals.	Rob often feeds my cat.
REPORT	SitEnt introduced by verbs of speech.	"Let's go home" said Tim.
SPEECH ACTS		
IMPERATIVE	Commands, requests, advice.	Stay calm.
QUESTION	Functional speech act to elicit information.	Are you tired?

Table 6: Description and examples for the different Situation Entity types, adapted from Friedrich et al. (2015a) (available from `https://www.coli.uni-saarland.de/projects/sitent/page.php?id=resources`).

group term	correct	acc.
alien	15	0.75
american	18	0.90
asylum	16	0.80
migrant	18	0.90
refugee	17	0.85
all groups	84	0.84

Table 7: Number of correctly predicted labels (predicted as either GENERIC or GENERALISING by the classifier) for a random sample of 100 instances (20 instances per group) and accuracy for each social group.

used in combination with the adjective *illegal*, thus making this a reference not to a kind but to a specific subgroup of the kind (here: all aliens that are illegal). This is different from the other group terms where the main referent is generic at least for half of the instances (*Americans*) or for the majority of the messages (*asylum seekers, migrants, refugees*).

We observe the highest error rate for *asylum seekers* where our filtering heuristic does not seem to be accurate enough. Here we find 4 instances where the term *asylum* does not refer to the group, thus making the extracted instances irrelevant. Some other errors are due to mistakes made by the dependency parser failing to identify the correct subject.

A.4 Clustering similar clauses

We use the Fast Clustering algorithm[11] from the Sentence Transformer (Reimers and Gurevych, 2019) library. Cluster similarity is determined, based on cosine similarity. We set the minimum cluster size to 10 and the similarity threshold to 0.8, meaning that sentences need to have a similarity of ≥ 0.8 to be considered as similar. Sentences that do not meet this criterium are ignored.

group term	no. clusters	no. instances
alien	0	0
american	1,129	29,027
asylum	4	215
migrant	53	1,402
refugee	8	229

Table 8: Number of clusters and clustered instances for each social group term.

We cluster the tweets for each group term separately and use the `all-MiniLM-L6-v2` model[12] to map the extracted clauses to a 384 dimensional dense vector space, as input for clustering. Table 8 shows the number of clusters and clustered instances for each group.

For the term *alien*, we do not get any clusters, due to the small number of instances and rather high similarity threshold. However, for our use case we are not interested in high coverage (i.e., being able to assign each instance to a cluster) but rather in identifying usage patterns of similar sentences to study the variation in the use of the different constructions.

Table 9 shows examples for the clusters with the highest ratio of quantified statements for the term *American*. We only find two clusters where the ratio of quantified statements is higher than 0.5, indicating that explicit quantification does not seem to have a similar function in the discourse as universals.

[11] `https://sbert.net/examples/sentence_transformer/applications/clustering/README.html#fast-clustering`.

[12] `https://huggingface.co/sentence-transformers/all-MiniLM-L6-v2`

Cluster 551, 14 elements ratio: 0.86
Americans are struggling to pay their rent and mortgages.
Many Americans are struggling to pay their rent or mortgage mortgage.
Cluster 725, 12 elements ratio: 0.73
The American people overwhelmingly support this measure .
most Americans from both parties are in support
Cluster 1072, 10 elements ratio: 0.30
Americans still face too many barriers at the ballot box
too many Americans still face barriers at the ballot box with voter ID

Table 9: Examples for clusters with a high ratio of quantified statements.

Gap in pagination due to formatting issues.

Pages 138-141

Developing A German Document-Level Parallel Dataset For Automatic Text Simplification To Generate Easy Language

Vivien Jiranek **Stefan Hillmann**
Quality and Usability Lab, Technische Universität Berlin
Straße des 17. Juni 135, 10623 Berlin, Germany
v.jiranek@protonmail.com stefan.hillmann@tu-berlin.de

Abstract

A lack of suitable datasets limits research on automatically generating German Easy-to-Read Language (GE2R), known as Leichte Sprache in Germany, from regular German. To address this, we introduce the EasyGerman dataset, the largest collection of parallel documents in regular German and professionally translated German Easy Language in the news domain. We demonstrate the feasibility of generating GE2R by fine-tuning pre-trained mt5 and mBART Large Language Models on this dataset using transfer learning. These models are evaluated using various metrics to establish a reliable benchmark for future research. Additionally, a human evaluation involving members of the target group was conducted to assess the quality and readability of the highest-scoring generated texts. Metric scores show that all models effectively generate simplified German in line with GE2R guidelines. The best approach produced texts rated as easy to read and consistent with GE2R principles, although there were mixed results in content representation and identified issues with logical consistency. Our findings highlight the value of the EasyGerman dataset for advancing research on automatic GE2R generation using neural models.

1 Introduction

Easy-to-Read language, also known as Easy Language, is an internationally recognized simplified language variation. It has a low linguistic complexity that is designed to accommodate people with low literacy, promoting inclusive communication. It distinguishes itself from other simplified language variations such as Plain Language (PL), since it was deliberately tailored to account for the communicative needs of disabled people. Therefore, the use of GE2R is mandated by German Law (Bundesministerium der Justiz, 2002) for information published by public authorities, thus ensuring the supply of accessibility-enhanced information to the general public. Currently, the high demand for translations from regular German (RG) to GE2R exceeds the capacity of available professional translators. Yet research on the generation of automatic German Text Simplification is scarce due to a lack of suitable parallel data, especially involving neural approaches. Thus, we developed the EasyGerman dataset, the largest document-level parallel dataset featuring news data in RG and GE2R to this date. It incorporates professionally translated data that was regularly published by the German public broadcaster Mitteldeutscher Rundfunk since 2021. Furthermore, we developed four approaches to benchmark the dataset and determine the feasibility of automatically generating GE2R. We use large language models leveraging transfer learning to overcome the lack of pre-trained models and available document-level parallel data for pre-training for this German Text Simplification task. Their performance was evaluated using a variety of automatic metrics carefully selected for this purpose. Finally, we conducted a quality assessment of the output texts of the best-performing approach using an online survey. These three contributions and the related results are presented in this paper.

2 Related Work

The use and prevalence of languages on a global scale directly relates to the amount of publicly available data to build additional datasets for research. Prominent sources such as Simple Wikipedia, which offers simplified Wikipedia articles on various topics, are unavailable in German. Therefore, gathering data to build German datasets for more specialized NLP tasks such as text simplification on a similar scale as the the D-Wikipedia dataset (Sun et al., 2021), is currently unattainable (Rios et al., 2021). In recent years, several datasets have been built incorporating different language variations and simplification levels. Though most of them feature GE2R, emphasizing its significance in Ger-

Proceedings of the 21st Conference on Natural Language Processing (KONVENS), Volume 2: Workshops, pages 142–168, 2025

man text simplification research, many do not exclusively feature or were intended for research on GE2R.

In 2023, a survey by Madina et al. summarized the current state of research on German Text Simplification, with a particular focus on GE2R. We have extended their survey by several more recent datasets, such as the EasyGerman dataset, presented in Table 1. This table provides a concise overview of key dataset properties, organized by their release date. In this context, "Simplified German" refers to tailored simplified language variations, "General Simplicity" refers to RG at lower complexity levels, and "German Plain Language" is abbreviated as GPL. The datasets in Table 1 reveal key trends and challenges in German Text Simplification, notably a shift from sentence-level to document-level alignments. The comparison also highlights difficulties in developing parallel datasets, with significant variation in dataset sizes, alignment granularity, and featured languages. While some datasets provide extensive resources, others are smaller or lack quantitative details, highlighting the uneven availability of resources and the need for more standardized datasets. Notably, the EasyGerman dataset stands out based on its provision of parallel data, exclusive document-level granularity, and its consistent focus on GE2R texts as the target language, as well as its comparatively large amount of aligned documents.

3 EasyGerman Dataset

The EasyGerman dataset[1] was developed as a document-level parallel dataset to enable further research on automatic German Text Simplification with a primary focus on the generation of GE2R.

3.1 Data Collection

The dataset comprises a total of 3,832 news articles, originally published by the German public broadcaster Mitteldeutscher Rundfunk (MDR) between July 2021 and April 2024. Each professionally translated article in GE2R is linked to a source article in RG by the publisher. This predetermined alignment is maintained throughout the dataset. The full dataset provides a total of 1,916 sample-pairs. The news articles cover various topics including politics, economics, sports, weather, and cultural issues. Articles were primarily sourced through regular web scraping of the MDR's **W**eekly **N**ews website in GE2R (MDR-WN)[2]. Additionally 538 articles were obtained from MDR's **N**ews **A**rchive (MDR-NA)[3].

To further expand the dataset, 1,906 articles published between June 2021 and February 2023 were retrieved from the **I**nternet **A**rchive (IA)[4]. Articles predating June 2021 were excluded due to the absence of links between GE2R texts and their RG counterparts. Table 2 provides the number of sample-pairs available per source and year.

To avoid the possibility of copyright claims, the text files containing the gathered URLs of the data pairs as well as the implemented Python scripts for web scraping and building the dataset are made available to build the dataset on demand. Since the published articles are publicly available when given the proper URL, but the URLs of published articles are removed at the beginning of every new week on the MDR weekly news website and after three months predating the current month on the MDR News archive, these text files are essential to access and incorporate previously released data pairs.

Both the raw HTML content and relevant metadata from the HTML header are automatically collected from each news article's webpage during the web-scraping process. The metadata provides insights on the domain and type of information gathered and its selection was inspired by the metadata collection of Battisti et al. 2020. It encompasses the title, description, keywords in GE2R, URL, and date of publishing as well as the given document identifier, linking the content of each article with a downloaded file, the cleaned text written to said file, and the raw HTML-content of each scraped webpage.

3.2 Alignment

A document-level alignment was chosen over the more common sentence-level alignment due to the characteristics of the news domain and the nature of GE2R as a language subset. Document-level simplifications address the complexity of such real-world applications by preserving the discourse structure of both input and output documents (Blinova et al., 2023). This allows neural models to

[1]https://github.com/vjiranek/EasyGermanDataset

[2]https://www.mdr.de/nachrichten-leicht/nachrichten-in-leichter-sprache-114.html

[3]https://www.mdr.de/nachrichten-leicht/rueckblick/index.html

[4]https://web.archive.org/web/20240000000000*/https://www.mdr.de/nachrichten-leicht/

Table 1: German Text Simplification Datasets

Dataset	Alignment	Featured Languages	Quantity
Klaper et al. (2013)	Sentence	GE2R	256 aligned documents
LeiSa (2018)	None	GPL, GE2R and simplified German	639,826 words in GE2R, 779,278 words in GPL, and 350,872 words in simplified DE
Battisti and Ebling (2019)	Partially Document	GE2R	378 aligned documents and 5,461 monolingual documents
TextComplexityDE (2019)	Sentence	Simplified German	1000 sentences in total, 250 aligned sentences
LeiKo (2020)	None	GE2R	50,000 words
KED (2023)	Sentence	GE2R and GPL	3,698,372 words
APA (2020)	Sentence	CEFR levels A2, and B1	3,616 aligned sentences
Capito (2023)	Sentence	CEFR levels A1, A2, and B1	NA
20m (2021)	Document	General Simplicity	18,305 aligned summaries
GEASY (2021)	Sentence, Document	GE2R	289 documents
Toborek et al. (2022)	Sentence, Document	GE2R and GPL	708 aligned documents, 5,942 aligned sentences
Klexicon (2022)	Document	General Simplicity	2,898 aligned documents
SNIML (2022)	None	Simplified Languages including GE2R	147 German articles with 25,964 sentences
DEPLAIN (2023)	Sentence, Document	GPL	483 aligned documents, 147 aligned sentences
DE-Lite (2024)	Various	Simplified German and General Simplicity	NA
EasyGerman	Document	GE2R	1916 aligned documents

learn interdependencies within the text, which was expected to improve output quality. In contrast, sentence-level mappings were found to negatively impact results due to reduced text length, omissions, and reordering of topics (Säuberli et al., 2020). Automatic sentence mappings were deemed infeasible, as most tools are designed for translation and thus demonstrate shortcomings with simplified, paraphrased language. Since manual mappings were not expected to yield positive results and were also not considered viable due to the labor required, document-level alignment became the preferred choice to preserve the publisher's intended parallel structure and maintain high-quality output.

Table 2: Number of Incorporated News Articles per Source Website Published During Each Year

	Year				
Source	**2021**	**2022**	**2023**	**2024**	**Total**
MDR-WN	0	0	887	505	**1,392**
MDR-NA	0	0	538	0	**538**
IA	465	1,181	260	0	**1,906**
Total	**465**	**1,181**	**1,685**	**505**	**3,832**

3.3 Language Analysis

Automatically computed statistics on the language characteristics and complexity give insights on the linguistic properties of the dataset and highlight differences between the articles in GE2R and RG. The total number of letters, words, sentences, and vocabulary size within the full dataset, along with the average and median values for a single document is shown in Table 3. Our analysis follows the dataset assessment method in (Battisti et al., 2020).

The EasyGerman dataset contains approximately 6.39 million letters, 1.2 million words, and 96,000 sentences. Notably, only the letters of tokenized words were considered in the linguistic analysis, excluding whitespaces and other characters, to provide information on the complexity of the underlying language. The full dataset has a total vocabulary size of 71,912 unique words, with an average of 162 words per document. A comparison of linguistic features between RG and GE2R indicates substantial differences in both their length and language complexity as seen in Table 3.

The size ratios between the two language variations show that GE2R documents are much shorter in word and letter count. The word ratio between GE2R and RG is about 1:2, with RG containing nearly twice as many words. The letter ratio is around 2:5, with RG contributing a larger share. Despite these differences, the total number of sentences is almost identical for both variations, indicating that while sentences in GE2R are shorter, the sentence count remains unchanged. On average, sentences in RG have 17 words, while those in GE2R have only 9 (see Table 4). Interestingly, the average letters per word is similar for both, with GE2R averaging 5 letters and RG 6, suggesting that word length is comparable despite the shorter sentences in GE2R.

Further analysis of the vocabulary size underscores the differences in language diversity and complexity. The median (*italic*) and average (**bold**) counts of linguistic properties can be seen in Table 5. The vocabulary used in the RG documents is

Table 3: Total Number of Linguistic Units

	Letters	Words		Sentences
		Total	Unique	
Full Dataset	6,388,728	1,196,192	71,912	96,263
Leichte **S**prache	1,908,071	389,896	17,707	46,293
Regular**G**erman	4,480,657	806,296	63,452	49,970
Ratio **GE2R**:**RG**	2:5	1:2	1:4	9:10

Table 4: Average Word and Sentence Length

	Full Dataset	GE2R	RG
Letters per Word	6	5	6
Words per Sentence	13	9	17

Table 5: **Average** and *Median* Number of Linguistic Units per Document

	Letters	Words		Sentences
		Total	Unique	
Full Dataset	**1668** *1257.0*	**313** *242.0*	**162** *124.0*	**26** *23.0*
GE2R	**996** *924.0*	**204** *189.0*	**101** *98.0*	**25** *22.0*
RG	**2339** *2100.5*	**421** *375.5*	**223** *205.0*	**27** *23.0*

almost twice as large as of the documents written in GE2R (on average 223 vs 101). These differences reflect the purposefully simplified nature of GE2R. Finally, it is noticeable that the dataset exhibits a right-skewed distribution, as indicated by the difference between the median and average values. The median values are consistently smaller than the averages, suggesting that a small subset of longer, more complex documents skews the overall statistics. This variability could have implications for machine-learning models trained on this data and should be considered during further use.

4 Benchmarking

To automatically generate texts in GE2R from texts in RG, three different large language models using different task presets were fine-tuned for up to 20 epochs and then evaluated for their performance using the EasyGerman dataset. Different hyperparameter configurations were tested involving a range of different learning rates, warm-up steps and epochs. Of the fine-tuned models for each approach, the best-performing models were selected based on their metric scores, displayed in section 5. Initially, the dataset was shuffled with a fixed seed size of 42 and then used for fine-tuning and performance evaluation with a train-test split of 80 to 20 without additional randomization to ensure the reproducibility of the results. Since research and available methods for Text Simplification are limited but the task has significant overlaps with Machine Translation and Text Summarization, knowledge from these tasks was leveraged to build and test the proposed methods for automatic German Text Simplification. Benchmarking was performed on the Pegasus AI High-Performance Computing Cluster at DFKI, using 4 NVIDIA A100-PCIE-40GB GPUs, 2 CPUs per GPU, and 50GB of working memory. All models were fine-tuned within around 6 to 8 hours. They were fine-tuned with a defined maximum sequence length of 1024 tokens to process the given documents based on their found length and take into account the context of the full documents during their learned and applied translations to GE2R. As this was a computationally intensive approach for a complex task, we weighed costs of time and energy consumption against underlying model complexity and pre-training. Considering this, the following models were utilized.

4.1 Models and Tasks

The employed **mBART model for Summarization** is a fine-tuned checkpoint of the facebook/mbart-large-cc25 model (Liu et al., 2020) on the Multilingual Large Summarization dataset on several different languages, with a focus on Czech texts, to produce multilingual summaries and was obtained from huggingface.com[5]. It was provided by researchers at the Artificial Intelligence Center of the Czech Technical University in Prague[6]. This model can produce high-quality multi-sentence summaries in eight languages, including German, as demonstrated by its strong ROUGE benchmark scores on German texts.

The utilized **mBART model for Translation**[7] was fine-tuned for multilingual machine translation by Tang et al.. It supports a direct translation between any pair of the 50 languages (including German) and is a fine-tuned checkpoint of the original mBART-50 model, which exhibited an outstanding performance for translation tasks. The model was fine-tuned for ready-to-use multilingual translation tasks, supporting German as both the source and target language in translation pairs.

The **mt5 model for Summarization and Translation**[8] was pre-trained for both machine translation and text summarization in 101 different languages, including German. Although it produces state-of-the-art results for a wide variety of NLP tasks, it must be fine-tuned to be used for any downstream task using a task description in natural language. We chose the mt5-base model for its extensive multilingual pre-training and its aptitude for transfer learning based on its exceptional performance on many multilingual benchmarks (Xue et al., 2021).

4.2 Applied Metrics

Several readability metrics were used to assess the language complexity of the generated texts. The **Flesch Reading Ease** (FRE) metric (Flesch, 1948), commonly used to assess text complexity, provides interpretable numerical scores based on sentence and word length, influenced by syllables per word. Since the standard FRE penalizes characteristics typical of German, the adapted German FRE score from Toni Amstad's 1978 dissertation was used (Amstad, 1978). Scores range from 0 to 100, with 100 indicating the lowest complexity.

The **Wiener Sachtextformel** (WSTF) (Bamberger and Vanecek, 1984), designed to evaluate the readability of German factual texts, was used in this case. It combines features like word and sentence length, percentage of long words, and personal pronouns. Variant 1, a general-purpose metric for factual or educational texts, was applied. Scores typically range from 4.0 to 20.0, with higher scores indicating greater complexity. Scores below 4 are rarely achieved, as they denote texts that are exceptionally easy to read. Scores between 5 and 8 are considered accessible to the general public, including those with lower secondary education.

The **Coleman Liau Index** (CLI) (Coleman and Liau, 1975), a widely used readability metric for English, was applied here. It automatically analyzes digital content and assesses vocabulary complexity by counting the letters in words. Although designed for English, it serves as a comparative score to evaluate the complexity of source and reference texts for other languages. The score corresponds to US school grade levels (1-12), with higher scores indicating college or university literacy. Unlike most metrics, CLI does not consider syllables but uses the average number of letters per word and sentences per 100 words to compute the score.

Bilingual Evaluation Understudy (BLEU) (Papineni et al., 2002) and **Recall-Oriented Understudy for Gisting Evaluation** (ROUGE) (Lin, 2004) are widely used metrics for evaluating machine translation and summarization tasks. BLEU assesses the quality of translations by comparing n-grams in the generated output with reference translations with a focus on precision while penalizing a high output length. ROUGE, on the other hand, evaluates summarization by comparing n-grams or word sequences in the output texts with reference summaries, focusing on recall to evaluate content coverage. After the results were viewed, the ROUGE-L and ROUGE-LSUM values were found to be indistinguishable for all generated texts when applied at a document-level. Therefore, only ROUGE-L scores were provided.

The **Bilingual Annotation-based Content** (BLANC) score (Vasilyev et al., 2020) is a metric used for evaluating the quality of Text Summarization tasks. It assesses how well a generated summary preserves key content and relationships

[5]https://huggingface.co/ctu-aic/mbart25-multilingual-summarization-multilarge-cs

[6]https://www.aic.fel.cvut.cz/

[7]https://huggingface.co/facebook/mbart-large-50-many-to-many-mmt

[8]https://huggingface.co/google/mt5-base

from the original text without relying on human-written reference summaries. It introduces noise by randomly masking parts of the text, then uses a language model (Cloze task) to reconstruct the masked portions. The resulting score reflects how much of the original content is captured in the summary, typically ranging from 0.0 to 0.5, though it can reach 1.0. The score's interpretation depends on the task and data, so it's best used for comparison. Originally developed for English with a BERT model, it was adapted for German (Iskender et al., 2021) as follows using the bert-base-german-dbmdz-cased model, with a gap size of 2 and a maximum input token size of 256 for fine-tuning and inference.

4.3 Human Evaluation

Ten article pairs were selected, (see Appendix 8) consisting of a sample article in RG from the test set and a corresponding GE2R version generated using the fine-tuned mBART model with a Translation task preset. Texts with ROUGE-L scores above the median of the best-performing approach were chosen to showcase high-quality simplified texts, with a few containing common model errors to assess their impact on perceived quality and readability. The survey included questions on participants' education, reading level, preference, and impairment, along with six questions evaluating text quality, covering intent, content representation, logical consistency, grammar, reading ease, and use of GE2R in the generated articles. A total of 21 German native speakers with higher education participated. All participants submitted their responses regarding the featured article pairs, electively they could choose to answer the organizational parts of the survey in either RG or GE2R. This was done to ensure that the target group could be included and follow the given instructions and questions. After completion of the survey, we found that 14 participants completed the RG version, and 7 participants completed the GE2R version.

Of the RG participants, 35.7% preferred highly complex texts, 57.1% preferred medium-length, medium-complexity texts in everyday language, and 7.1% preferred short, low-complexity texts. For GE2R participants, 14.3% preferred long and complex texts, while 85.7% favored medium-length, medium-complexity texts. Fewer GE2R participants than RG participants expressed a preference for long texts if shorter, less complex alternatives with the same content were available.

Only 7.1% (one person) among the RG participants reported having a different reading comprehension. Explicit examples were given to indicate which group of people this may include, namely autistic people, people with ADHD, dyslexia, and hyperlexia. Notably though, 57.1% of the GE2R participants (four people) reported having different reading comprehension. When asked if they had experienced reading difficulties, none of the RG participants reported this, while 57.1% of the GE2R participants confirmed having such difficulties. Based on these observed differences in reading abilities and preferences, we separated the participants into two groups and present our findings as a comparison between the two groups.

5 Results and Discussion

Using the EasyGerman dataset, all models demonstrated the ability to improve their performance during fine-tuning and effectively applied their learned behavior during inference. Even the mBART summarization model, whose performance was most fluctuant during fine-tuning, improved over time. Detailed progressions of different metrics during fine-tuning are provided in Appendix 8.11. The performance comparison of all approaches, evaluated by automatic metrics, is shown in Table 6. It shows that the results of the generated articles using the test set at the end of fine-tuning in comparison to the generated articles using the validation set for inference. Since the distributed metric scores are non-uniform, the computed median scores are given as the scores for each metric. As readability scores are a comparative measure, the scores of the generated texts were compared to further computed readability scores of the reference texts in GE2R and the input texts in RG as seen in Table 7. The notable difference in scores between the input texts in RG and the generated texts in GE2R indicated a successful text simplification, showing a significantly lower linguistic complexity of the generated texts when compared to the reference texts in RG. The readability scores of the generated text also closely matched those of the professionally translated GE2R reference texts, suggesting a similarity of the generated texts to the references in terms of readability and simplicity. The near-identical readability scores for fine-tuning and inference demonstrate that the LLMs successfully learned and applied German simplification patterns, producing texts in simplified German with characteristics of GE2R.

Table 6: Metric Scores of Approaches for Fine-tuning and Inference

	mBART-sum		**mBART-tr**		**mt5-sum**		**mt5-tr**	
Metric	Fine-tuning	Inference	Fine-tuning	Inference	Fine-tuning	Inference	Fine-tuning	Inference
WSTF	4.4	4.5	*3.7*	3.9	*3.3*	**3.4**	*3.3*	**3.5**
FRE	*78*	79	*78*	**76**	79	78	76-77	49.5
CLI	15.52	13.84	*13.07*	**13.75**	12.01	12.69	12.08	12.67
TLiW*	91	105	157	156.5	*159.5*	**157**	152	**157**
BLANC	0.02	0.02	*0.06*	**0.06**	0.05	0.05	0.05	**0.06**
BLEU	0.02	0.03	*0.11*	0.10	0.10	**0.11**	0.11	0.10
BLEU P-1	0.51	0.50	*0.54*	**0.57**	0.51	0.54	0.50	0.53
BLEU P-2	0.17	0.17	*0.22*	**0.23**	0.21	0.22	0.21	0.23
BLEU P-3	0.06	0.06	*0.10*	**0.11**	*0.10*	**0.11**	*0.10*	**0.11**
BLEU P-4	0.02	0.02	0.04	0.05	*0.05*	**0.06**	*0.05*	0.04
ROUGE-1	0.31	0.31	*0.48*	**0.48**	0.44	0.44	0.44	0.44
ROUGE-2	0.11	0.11	*0.20*	**0.20**	0.18	0.18	0.18	0.19
ROUGE-L	0.17	0.17	*0.27*	**0.26**	0.26	**0.26**	*0.27*	**0.26**

* Text Length in words

All approaches produced low BLANC scores for both fine-tuning and inference, with the mBART Summarization model generating the lowest scores. This indicates that the generated texts lacked sufficient summarization qualities, confirming that transfer learning was successfully applied for text simplification, not summarization. Although BLEU scores were also low for all approaches, their performance in the context of automatic German text simplification aligned with scores reported in related work on generative German Text Simplification approaches (Rios et al., 2021) (Ebling et al., 2022). BLEU Precision-n-gram scores were higher for shorter n-grams and decreased steeply for longer ones. The mBART Translation approach generated the highest BLEU-Precision-n-gram scores, followed by mt5 Summarization, mt5 Translation, and mBART Summarization. For ROUGE scores, including ROUGE-L, the mBART Translation approach outperformed all others in both fine-tuning and inference, while the mt5 approaches showed nearly identical performance. The mBART Summarization approach yielded the lowest ROUGE and BLEU scores.

The ROUGE and BLEU metrics were most indicative of perceivable text quality, with higher ROUGE than BLEU scores suggesting that the models prioritized recall over precision. This indicates that the models focused on condensing or paraphrasing information, but were less precise in matching the reference language. The moderately high scores for smaller n-grams suggest significant lexical overlap with the references, though precision declined for longer sequences, potentially affecting text structure and comprehensiveness. Overall, the mBART Translation approach performed the best, as indicated by its high ROUGE and BLEU scores.

The texts generated by the mBART translation approach were well received overall by survey participants. Depictions of these responses for each assessed property can be seen in Appendix 8.12. Both groups generally agreed that the intent of the source texts was well represented in the generated texts. Overall, the majority of the RG group agreed that

Table 7: Median Metric Scores of References and Inputs for Fine-tuning and Inference.

	Fine-tuning		**Inference**	
Metric	**References**	**Inputs**	**References**	**Inputs**
WSTF	3.5	6.4	3.5	6.5
FRE	76-77	51	76-77	49.5
CLI	12.93	17.81	13.25	17.90
TLiW*	181	–	202.5	–
BLANC	0.06	–	0.06	–

* Text Length in words

the intent was very well represented for seven of the articles, with over 70 percent agreement for six of these articles and one article achieving only positive responses. Notably, the GE2R group showed even higher levels of agreement, with nine articles receiving over 70 percent positive responses and four articles achieving only positive responses. In contrast, the representation of content yielded more varied responses. Within the RG group, six articles received over 50 percent negative responses, with an overall tendency towards negative responses for this property. Although the GE2R group rated content representation more positively, responses were mixed, suggesting room for improvement.

Next, the quantity of grammatical errors was assessed. Responses showed that most texts contained few grammar errors which were likely not viewed as obtrusive by the majority of participants. Both groups showed similar proportions of participants reporting no errors. However, the GE2R group was more likely to perceive fewer errors overall. This could be attributed to differing reading proficiencies, which may influence error detection and perception. Errors in logical consistency were found to be more frequent and obtrusive to both participant groups than grammatical errors. The RG group, in particular, identified significant issues in this area, with the majority indicating a high number of logical inconsistencies in eight of the ten articles. Although the GE2R group reported fewer such errors, the presence of logical flaws was still noted. Regarding the readability of the generated texts, the GE2R group rated almost all articles as easier to read than the RG group. Except for article 10, which was unanimously deemed easy to read by both groups, the GE2R participants consistently reported notably higher readability ratings. Overall, the positive responses regarding the reading ease by both groups far outweighed the negative responses for most articles. This indicates that a degree of simplification could be achieved, which ensures that most articles are viewed as easy to read for both groups of participants and is well-received by members of its target group. Finally, the large majority of both groups agreed that all generated texts followed the principles of GE2R. The GE2R group unanimously recognized six articles as written in GE2R, while the RG group did so for five articles. This demonstrates the usefulness of the dataset for research on generating GE2R from regular German texts.

However, given that the target group of GE2R includes vulnerable individuals with impairments, further refinement in some identified areas and a more nuanced evaluation of responses to generated texts are likely needed before real-world deployment of this technology can be considered. Future research may also prioritize including a larger and more diverse group of participants with reading difficulties, representing different kinds of impairments and educational backgrounds. Nevertheless, based on the generally positive reception of the texts generated by the best-performing approach, the mBART translation model could serve as an assistive tool for human translators, helping to accelerate the simplification of news articles. This could improve the availability of informative content in GE2R.

6 Conclusion

This paper introduces a monolingual parallel dataset of German news article pairs published by the MDR, aligned at the document level, and containing simplified content written only in professionally translated GE2R. We present four approaches to assess the feasibility of generating GE2R using the EasyGerman dataset with Large Language Models (LLMs) for German Text Simplification using transfer learning. All approaches consistently achieved high scores across three readability metrics, indicating that the generated texts closely matched the readability and simplicity of the reference GE2R texts. These results demonstrate that LLMs can effectively learn and apply the rules to simplify German texts using the provided Dataset. Among the approaches, the fine-tuned mBART-50 model with a translation task preset produced the highest scores across BLEU and ROUGE metrics, showing strong capabilities for generating readable texts featuring complex document-level simplification properties.

A selection of texts generated by the best-performing model was well received in an online survey of 21 human evaluators. The survey assessed the generated articles on complex simplification qualities perceivable to humans such as intent, content representation, fluency, and logical consistency. The target group of GE2R, individuals with reading difficulties or disabilities, was included, enhancing the relevance of the findings. The majority of participants agreed that the generated texts accurately represented the source intent, were easy to read, and were written in GE2R. However, mixed responses regarding content representation were observed, potentially due to unfamiliarity with GE2R's inherent content reduction. Participants also noted some grammar errors and issues with logical consistency in the generated articles. These results suggest the need for further research to improve the quality of simplified texts and ensure the ethical use of automatic GE2R generation for real-world applications. Nonetheless, the feasibility of automatically generating GE2R from RG has been successfully demonstrated, providing valuable benchmarks for future research.

7 Limitations and Ethical Considerations

We would like to address several potential limitations and concerns. Firstly, the dataset comprises 1,916 sample pairs of documents, which may not constitute a sufficiently large dataset for training robust models. The dataset is constrained by the limited availability of parallel data in regular German and simplified GE2R. However, it is specifically constrained by the amount of parallel data published by the MDR until its finalization in April 2024 and made available on the described websites. Due to the design choice of including data published by a single source, overall quality and consistency in style and content impose limits on the ability of neural approaches to adapt to other document types or genres. This lack of diversity in data sources may negatively affect the generalizability of fine-tuned approaches for other domains or applications. Additionally, the reliance on news data may result in embedded biases, both in terms of content and style, that should be considered for future research.

Furthermore, no large language models with pre-training in German Text Simplification are publicly available. As a result, transfer learning was employed, aiming to leverage related knowledge to enhance performance. Given the task similarities, models pre-trained on machine translation and text summarization were utilized. However, the need for pre-training in German and the requirement for a large embedding dimension (around 1024) to process full documents significantly influenced the choice of models, thereby narrowing the selection of viable options.

We also discovered limitations in the useof text simplification metrics for the evaluation of results. Initially, we considered using D-SARI, the document-level adaption of SARI, a common text simplification metric. D-SARI first calculates SARI scores at the sentence level before computing the final score at the document level. However, due to the nature of GE2R, its application was found not feasible in this context. The significant length disparity between input and translated target texts, the loss of discourse structure during translation, and the impracticality of sentence mapping — neither manual nor automatic means were fund viable —rendered the computation of intermediate SARI and subsequent D-SARI scores ineffective.

The application of this research raises important ethical concerns since providing an accessible language for vulnerable groups is a sensitive area of application. Due to the nature of the target audience, careful attention to privacy, the accommodation of support needs of different groups, and an adequate representation is required. Efforts were made to involve organizations specializing in evaluating GE2R to include more representatives from the target group. Regrettably, logistical and practical challenges limited participation nonetheless. This underrepresentation may affect the model's fairness and efficacy in addressing the needs of the intended audience and should be considered in further research.

References

Toni Amstad. 1978. *Wie verständlich sind unsere Zeitungen?* Ph.D. thesis, Universität Zürich.

Dennis Aumiller and Michael Gertz. 2022. Klexikon: A German dataset for joint summarization and simplification. In *Proceedings of the Thirteenth Language Resources and Evaluation Conference*, pages 2693–2701, Marseille, France. European Language Resources Association.

Richard Bamberger and Erich Vanecek. 1984. Lesen-verstehen-lernen-schreiben: Die schwierigkeitsstufen von texten in deutscher sprache. *Jugend und Volk Verlagsgesellschaft.*

Alessia Battisti and Sarah Ebling. 2019. A corpus for automatic readability assessment and text simplification of german. *Preprint*, arXiv:1909.09067.

Alessia Battisti, Dominik Pfütze, Andreas Säuberli, Marek Kostrzewa, and Sarah Ebling. 2020. A corpus for automatic readability assessment and text simplification of German. In *Proceedings of the Twelfth Language Resources and Evaluation Conference*, pages 3302–3311, Marseille, France. European Language Resources Association.

Sofia Blinova, Xinyu Zhou, Martin Jaggi, Carsten Eickhoff, and Seyed Ali Bahrainian. 2023. SIMSUM:

Document-level text simplification via simultaneous summarization.

Bundesministerium der Justiz. 2002. Behindertengleichstellungsgesetz abschnitt 2 verpflichtung zur gleichstellung und barrierefreiheit. § 11 verständlichkeit und leichte sprache.

Meri Coleman and T. L. Liau. 1975. A computer readability formula designed for machine scoring. *Journal of Applied Psychology*, 60:283–284.

Sarah Ebling, Alessia Battisti, Marek Kostrzewa, Dominik Pfütze, Annette Rios, Andreas Säuberli, and Nicolas Spring. 2022. Automatic text simplification for german. *Frontiers in Communication*, 7.

R. F. Flesch. 1948. A new readability yardstick. *Journal of Applied Psychology*, 32(3):221–223.

Silvia Hansen-Schirra, Jean Nitzke, and Silke Gutermuth. 2021. An intralingual parallel corpus of translations into german easy language (geasy corpus): What sentence alignments can tell us about translation strategies in intralingual translation. In Vincent X. Wang, Lily Lim, and Defeng Li, editors, *New Perspectives on Corpus Translation Studies*, New Frontiers in Translation Studies, pages 281–298. Springer.

Renate Hauser, Jannis Vamvas, Sarah Ebling, and Martin Volk. 2022. A multilingual simplified language news corpus. In *Proceedings of the 2nd Workshop on Tools and Resources to Empower People with READing DIfficulties (READI) within the 13th Language Resources and Evaluation Conference*, pages 25–30, Marseille, France. European Language Resources Association.

Neslihan Iskender, Oleg V. Vasilyev, Tim Polzehl, John Bohannon, and Sebastian Möller. 2021. Towards human-free automatic quality evaluation of german summarization. *CoRR*, abs/2105.06027.

Sarah Jablotschkin, Elke Teich, and Heike Zinsmeister. 2024. DE-lite - a new corpus of easy German: Compilation, exploration, analysis. In *Proceedings of the Fourth Workshop on Language Technology for Equality, Diversity, Inclusion*, pages 106–117, St. Julian's, Malta. Association for Computational Linguistics.

Sarah Jablotschkin and Heike Zinsmeister. 2020. Leiko: A corpus of easy-to-read german. In *Poster presented at the Computational Linguistics Poster Session in the course of the 42nd annual conference of the Deutsche Gesellschaft für Sprachwissenschaft (DGfS) in Hamburg. Download of Poster and corpus from: https://doi. org/10.5281/zenodo*, volume 3923917.

David Klaper, Sarah Ebling, and Martin Volk. 2013. Building a German/simple German parallel corpus for automatic text simplification. In *Proc. 2nd Workshop on Predicting and Improving Text Readability for Target Reader Populations*, pages 11–19, Sofia, Bulgaria. Association for Computational Linguistics.

Daisy Lange. 2018. Comparing 'leichte sprache','einfache sprache'and 'leicht lesen': A corpus-based descriptive approach. In *Eds. SUSANNE J. JEKAT, and GARY MASSEY. Barrier-free communication: methods and products: proceedings of the 1st Swiss conference on barrier-free communication. Winterthur: ZHAW Digital Collection*, pages 75–91.

Chin-Yew Lin. 2004. ROUGE: A package for automatic evaluation of summaries. In *Text Summarization Branches Out*, pages 74–81, Barcelona, Spain. Association for Computational Linguistics.

Yinhan Liu, Jiatao Gu, Naman Goyal, Xian Li, Sergey Edunov, Marjan Ghazvininejad, Mike Lewis, and Luke Zettlemoyer. 2020. Multilingual denoising pretraining for neural machine translation. *Transactions of the Association for Computational Linguistics*, 8:726–742.

Margot Madina, Itziar Gonzalez-Dios, and Melanie Siegel. 2023. Easy-to-read in germany: A survey on its current state and available resources.

Babak Naderi, Salar Mohtaj, Kaspar Ensikat, and Sebastian Möller. 2019. Subjective assessment of text complexity: A dataset for german language. *arXiv preprint arXiv:1904.07733*.

Kishore Papineni, Salim Roukos, Todd Ward, and Wei-Jing Zhu. 2002. Bleu: a method for automatic evaluation of machine translation. In *Proceedings of the 40th Annual Meeting of the Association for Computational Linguistics*, pages 311–318, Philadelphia, Pennsylvania, USA. Association for Computational Linguistics.

Annette Rios, Nicolas Spring, Tannon Kew, Marek Kostrzewa, Andreas Säuberli, Mathias Müller, and Sarah Ebling. 2021. A new dataset and efficient baselines for document-level text simplification in German. In *Proceedings of the Third Workshop on New Frontiers in Summarization*, pages 152–161, Online and in Dominican Republic. Association for Computational Linguistics.

Andreas Säuberli, Sarah Ebling, and Martin Volk. 2020. Benchmarking data-driven automatic text simplification for German. In *Proceedings of the 1st Workshop on Tools and Resources to Empower People with READing DIfficulties (READI)*, pages 41–48, Marseille, France. European Language Resources Association.

Regina Stodden, Omar Momen, and Laura Kallmeyer. 2023. DEplain: A German parallel corpus with intralingual translations into plain language for sentence and document simplification. In *Proceedings of the 61st Annual Meeting of the Association for Computational Linguistics (Volume 1: Long Papers)*, pages 16441–16463, Toronto, Canada. Association for Computational Linguistics.

Renliang Sun, Hanqi Jin, and Xiaojun Wan. 2021. Document-level text simplification: Dataset, criteria and baseline. In *Proceedings of the 2021 Conference on Empirical Methods in Natural Language Processing*, pages 7997–8013, Online and Punta Cana, Dominican Republic. Association for Computational Linguistics.

Yuqing Tang, Chau Tran, Xian Li, Peng-Jen Chen, Naman Goyal, Vishrav Chaudhary, Jiatao Gu, and Angela Fan. 2020. Multilingual translation with extensible multilingual pretraining and finetuning. *CoRR*, abs/2008.00401.

Vanessa Toborek, Moritz Busch, Malte Boßert, Christian Bauckhage, and Pascal Welke. 2022. A new aligned simple German corpus. In *Proceedings of the 61st Annual Meeting of the Association for Computational Linguistics (Volume 1: Long Papers)*, pages 11393–11412, Toronto, Canada. Association for Computational Linguistics.

Oleg Vasilyev, Vedant Dharnidharka, and John Bohannon. 2020. Fill in the blanc: Human-free quality estimation of document summaries. *arXiv preprint arXiv:2002.09836*.

Linting Xue, Noah Constant, Adam Roberts, Mihir Kale, Rami Al-Rfou, Aditya Siddhant, Aditya Barua, and Colin Raffel. 2021. mT5: A massively multilingual pre-trained text-to-text transformer. In *Proceedings of the 2021 Conference of the North American Chapter of the Association for Computational Linguistics: Human Language Technologies*, pages 483–498, Online. Association for Computational Linguistics.

8 Appendix

The source articles are part of the EasyGerman dataset and were used to generate the second article of each pair. The source articles are written in regular German and the generated articles are written in simplified German with the expectation of containing language written in Leichte Sprache (GE2R). They were produced by mBART translation model fine-tuned on the EasyGerman dataset. The following ten articles pairs were featured and evaluated in the given order.

8.1 Article Pair 1

8.1.1 Source Text

Erste Briefe im Weihnachtspostamt Himmelsberg angekommen | MDR.DE

Alljährlich schreiben tausende Kinder an den Weihnachtsmann - die Thüringer Zweigstelle ist in Himmelsberg. Im letzten Jahr sind rund 7.000 Briefe von nah und fern im Kyffhäuserkreis eingegangen. Auch in diesem Jahr wollen wieder neun Frauen bis Heiligabend jeden Brief beantworten.

Im einzigen Thüringer Weihnachtspostamt in Himmelsberg im Kyffhäuserkreis sind die ersten 30 Briefe angekommen. Wie Ramona Schattney vom Heimatverein MDR THÜRINGEN sagte, haben unter anderem Kinder aus Thailand, Taiwan und Deutschland geschrieben.

Der große Ansturm mit täglich bis zu 200 Briefen beginne meistens erst im Advent. Auch in diesem Jahr wollen wieder neun Frauen bis Heiligabend jeden Brief beantworten. Im Vorjahr waren mehr als 7.000 Briefe angekommen. Derzeit wird das Antwortschreiben in der Druckerei vorbereitet, tausende Briefmarken liegen ebenfalls bereit.

Weihnachtsmärchen wird schon geprobt

Kopfzerbrechen macht den Helfern des Weihnachtsmannes noch der traditionelle Tag der offenen Tür am ersten Adventssamstag. Derzeit hoffen die Ehrenamtler, dass das Backhaus wieder regulär öffnen darf. Das Märchen werde schon fleißig geprobt. Die Thüringer Helfer des Weihnachtsmannes treffen sich wie im Vorjahr im beheizten Dorfgemeinschaftshaus.

Wegen Corona musste das Weihnachtsmannbüro in den beiden Vorjahren geschlossen bleiben. Trotzdem waren insgesamt fast 14.000 Briefe an das Weihnachtsmannbüro in 99713 Himmelsberg gekommen.

8.1.2 Generated Text

Leichte Sprache: Im Weihnachts-Postamt in Himmelsberg sind die ersten Briefe angekommen | MDR.DE

Himmelsberg ist ein Orts-Teil von der Stadt Sondershausen. Das ist im Bundes-Land Thüringen. Dort gibt es ein besonderes Postamt. Die Menschen können einen Brief dorthin schicken. Sie schreiben den Brief an den Weihnachts-Mann. In dem Brief können sie zum Beispiel schreiben: Was sie sich zu Weihnachten wünschen. Dann schreibt ihnen der Weihnachts-Mann einen Brief zurück. Beim Weihnachts-Postamt in Himmelsberg sind jetzt die ersten Briefe angekommen. Ramona Schattney arbeitet beim Heimat-Verein MDR Thüringen. Sie hat gesagt: Viele Menschen schreiben Briefe an den Weihnachts-Mann. Die Menschen schreiben zum Beispiel Briefe aus verschiedenen Ländern. Zum Beispiel: • Aus dem Land Thailand, • aus dem Land Taiwan • und aus Deutschland. In Himmelsberg gibt es das Büro vom Weihnachts-Mann. Dort arbeiten die Mitarbeiter vom Weihnachts-Postamt bis zum Heiligabend. In diesem Jahr wollen wieder 9 Frauen alle Briefe zurück schreiben.

8.2 Article Pair 2

8.2.1 Source Text

DFB-Pokal: RB Leipzig besiegt Hoffenheim und steht im Viertelfinale | MDR.DE
Achtelfinale

Heißer Sieg bei eisigen Temperaturen: RB Leipzig hat am Mittwochabend die TSG Hoffenheim mit 3:1 2:0 bezwungen und sich damit ins Pokal-Viertelfinale vorgearbeitet. Es war ein verdienter Erfolg, der nur in einer kurzen Phase gefährdet schien. Der Jubel über Tore und Sieg war wegen eines Notfalleinsatzes nur verhalten.

Die Erfolgsserie geht auch im Pokal weiter: RB Leipzig hat Hoffenheim 3:1 bezwungen und ist damit nun seit 17 Pflichtspielen in Folge ungeschlagen. Überschattet wurde die Partie allerdings von einem Notfall vor dem Anpfiff: Während es am Himmel blitzte und donnerte, musste am Einlass ein Fan reanimiert werden. Daraufhin verzichteten die Leipziger Anhänger weitgehend auf eine lautstarke Unterstützung ihres Teams.

Blitz, Donner, frühe Führung

Der Partie vor knapp 35.000 Zuschauern ging ein eisiges Gewitter voraus. Nach dem Schließen der Schleußen stellten die Leipziger die klar bessere Mannschaft, hatten mehr Ballbesitz, zeigten mehr Initiatve, waren gefährlicher. Ab und an gingen sie auch vom Gas - aber in genau so einer Phase fiel das 1:0 durch Emil Forsberg, der auf der linken Seite den Ball ungestört runterpflücken, querlaufen und dann aus 17 m einschießen konnte. Das 2:0 dagegen fiel in einer Drangphase bzw. im Nachsetzen: Konrad Laimer traf mit einem Linksschuss aus 15 m ins lange linke Eck 42. Hoffenheim kam nur selten vor das RB-Tor, war aber meist nur dann gefährlich, wenn die Leipziger sich Stockfehler oder Missverständnisse erlaubten.

RBL-Wackelphase nach dem Anschluss

Das große Aufbäumen der Gäste ließ auch nach der Pause auf sich warten. Statt-dessen war RB am Drücker, blieb beim letzten Pass jedoch zu ungenau oder zu spät, sodass die Abseitsfahne oft hochschnellte. Wie aus dem Nichts kam dann die TSG zum Anschluss: Der eingewechselte Kasper Dollberg veredelte eine genaue Angelino-Flanke zum 1:2. Wie zuletzt gegen Stuttgart wackelte RB nach dem Gegentor, stand mächtig unter Stress. Diesmal musste aber nicht bis in die Nachspielzeit gezittert werden, denn ein Konter in der 84. Minute machte den Deckel auf die Partie. Timo Werner traf nach starker Vorarbeit von Dominik Szoboszlai und dem eingewechselten Yussuf Poulsen.

8.2.2 Generated Text

Leichte Sprache: RB Leipzig hat am Mittwoch im DFB-Pokal gegen Hoffenheim gewonnen | MDR.DE

Hoffenheim ist eine Stadt im Bundes-Land Sachsen. Von dort kommt der Fußball-Verein RB Leipzig. Er hatte am Mittwoch-Abend ein Fußball-Spiel gegen den Fußball-Verein TSG Hoffenheim. Und bei diesem Fußball-Spiel hat RB Leipzig gewonnen. Die Fußball-Spieler von TSG Hoffenheim haben gut gespielt. Deshalb haben sie das Fußball-Spiel gewonnen. Jetzt ist RB Leipzig im Viertel-Finale vom DFB-Pokal. Wenn der Fußball-Verein RB Leipzig das Fußball-Spiel gewinnt,dann ist der Verein im Viertel-Finalevon dem DFB-Pokal.

8.3 Article Pair 3

8.3.1 Source Text

Nach Waldbränden: Sächsisches Kabinett setzt Expertenkommission ein | MDR.DE

Die sächsische Regierung hat am Dienstag die Einsetzung einer unabhängigen Expertenkommission beschlossen, informiert die Sächsiche Staatskanzlei. Man wolle dabei Konsequenzen aus den verheerenden Waldbränden in der Gohrischheide, in Arzberg sowie im Nationalpark Sächsische Schweiz ziehen. In dem Gremium werden Personen aus unterschiedlichen Fachbereichen diskutieren.

Nach den Waldbränden mit Millionenschäden hatte die sächsische Regierung Schutz-konzepte angekündigt. Nun hat sie dafür ein entsprechendes Gremium eingesetzt. Ziel der Kommission soll es sein, die Waldbrände objektiv auszuwerten. Dadurch sollen Maßnahmen für eine bessere Prävention und Bekämpfung von Waldbränden entwickelt werden.

Laut Staatskanzleichef Oliver Schenk gilt es nach dem Abschluss der Löscharbeiten nun Lehren für die Zukunft zu ziehen. Dafür soll die unabhängige Expertenkommission Vorschläge erarbeiten.

Den Vorsitz der Kommission soll Hermann Schröder übernehmen, der als langjähriger Leiter der Abteilung "Bevölkerungsschutz und Krisenmanagementïn Baden-Württemberg ein ausgewiesener Fachmann in dem Bereich sei, heißt es weiter.

Bisherige Schutzkonzepte sollen mit einfließen

Die Expertenkommission will auch auf bereits gewonnene Erkenntnisse etwa aus der landesweiten SStrategischen Waldbrandschutzkonzeption"des Innenministeriums oder dem Waldbrandschutzkonzept des Umweltministeriums für die Nationalparkregion zurückgreifen. Zudem könnten Erkenntnisse durch das Brandgeschehen von tschechischer Seite mit berücksichtigt werden.

8.3.2 Generated Text

Leichte Sprache: In Sachsen gibt es eine Fach-Kommission nach Waldbränden | MDR.DE

Die Regierung von dem Bundes-Land Sachsen hat entschieden: Es soll eine Fach-Kommission geben. Sie soll über die Waldbrände sprechen. Die Fach-Kommission soll zum Beispiel darüber sprechen: • Welche Sachen die Menschen in den Wäldern machen sollen. • Welche Regeln gelten: Damit die Waldbrände besser verhindert werden können. • Und damit die Waldbrände besser gelöscht werden können. Oliver Schenk ist der Chef von der Staats-Kanzlei. Er hat gesagt: Die Fach-Kommission soll lernen: Was die Menschen bei den Waldbränden lernen können. Das werden verschiedene Menschen machen. Zum Beispiel: • Menschen aus verschiedenen Fach-Bereichen. • Und Menschen mit verschiedenen Behinderungen. Die Menschen wollen in der Fach-Kommission auch darüber sprechen: Was die Menschen bei den Waldbränden lernen können. Zum Beispiel: • Über die vielen Waldbrände in den Bundes-Ländern: • Sachsen, • Sachsen-Anhalt • und Thüringen. Und was die Menschen bei den Waldbränden machen können.

8.4 Article Pair 4

8.4.1 Source Text

Magische Lichterwelten im Bergzoo Halle bis 2. März verlängert | MDR.DE

Bisher haben mehr als 80.000 Menschen die Magischen Lichterwelten im Bergzoo in Halle Saale gesehen. Am Ende soll wieder die Marke von 100.000 geknackt werden. Die Veranstalter rechnen noch einmal mit großem Andrang. Sie haben die Lichterwelten deswegen um eine Woche bis zum 2. März verlängert.

Die magischen Lichterwelten im Bergzoo Halle werden verlängert. Das hat Veranstaltungschef Tom Bernheim MDR SACHSEN-ANHALT gesagt. 80.000 Besucher hätten die Lichterwelten seit der Eröffnung vor zwei Monaten bereits gesehen. Dass die 100.000 angepeilten Besucher erreicht werden, gilt als sicher.

Ende erst am 2. März großer Andrang erwartet

Erfahrungsgemäß gibt es Bernheim zufolge zum Ende hin einen großen Andrang. Um dem gerecht zu werden, wird die Schau um genau eine Woche verlängert und endet nicht am 24. Februar sondern erst am 2. März. Die magischen Lichterwelten zeigen in diesem Jahr Szenen und Figuren aus Tausendundeiner Nacht. MDR SACHSEN-ANHALT ist Medienpartner der magischen Lichterwelten.

8.4.2 Generated Text

Leichte Sprache: Im Zoo von der Stadt Halle gibt es eine besondere Lichter-Welt | MDR.DE

Die Stadt Halle ist in dem Bundes-Land Sachsen-Anhalt. Dort gibt es einen Zoo. Der Zoo heißt: Bergzoo Halle. Dort werden in diesem Jahr besondere Lichter-Welten gezeigt. Sie dauern eine Woche. Bis zum 2. März können die Menschen wieder zu den Lichter-Welten gehen. Der Chef von den Lichter-Welten heißt: Tom Bernheim. Er hat gesagt: Seit der Eröffnung von den Lichter-Weltenhaben schon mehr als 80 tausend Menschendie Lichter-Welten gesehen. Und die Besucher werden sich die Lichter-Welten schon angeschaut. Das bedeutet: Sie werden die Lichter-Welten schon wieder ansehen. Tom Bernheim hat auch gesagt: Die Lichter-Welten werden eine Woche länger gemacht. Das bedeutet: Die Menschen können noch bis zum 2. März zur Lichter-Welten gehen.

8.5 Article Pair 5

8.5.1 Source Text

Neue Lithium-Fabrik für mehr als 100 Millionen Euro in Bitterfeld geplant | MDR.DE

Im Bitterfeld-Wolfen bahnt sich eine wirtschaftliche Großansiedlung an: Im Chemie-park soll eine Lithium-Raffinerie entstehen. Ein amerikanisch-holländisches Unternehmen will mehr als 100 Millionen Euro in die Anlage investieren. 2023 soll die Produktion beginnen. Die Stadt Bitterfeld hofft, dass die Fabrik weitere Unternehmen anlockt.

Im Chemiepark Bitterfeld entsteht ein großes Werk zur Aufbereitung von Lithium. Der amerikanisch-holländische Metall-Konzern Advanced Metallurgical AMG kündigte an, 120 Millionen Dollar, umgerechnet mehr als 103 Millionen Euro, zu investieren. Das Lithium soll laut Investor eine so gute Qualität haben, dass es für die Produktion von Batterien infrage kommt. Das Grundstück für die Raffinerie hatte der Konzern bereits im Frühjahr gekauft.

Fabrik soll 20.000 Tonnen Lithium fördern
Lithium ist ein begehrter, weil knapper Rohstoff. Er wird unter anderem bei der Produktion von Batterien für E-Autos gebraucht. Für die Fabrik in Bitterfeld wird zunächst mit 20.000 Tonnen pro Jahr geplant. Tritt die erwartete hohe Nachfrage ein, könne man die Menge auch verfünffachen, hieß es von AMG.

Der Bau der Anlage soll schon im ersten Quartal 2022 beginnen. Nach Unternehmensangaben laufen gerade Gespräche mit dem Bauordnungsamt. Produktionsstart soll dann im Herbst 2023 sein. Bitterfeld-Wolfens Oberbürgermeister Armin Schenk hofft auf die Schaffung zukunftsorientierter Arbeitsplätze in Bitterfeld-Wolfen und darauf, dass die AMG-Ansiedlung weitere Unternehmen in seine Stadt lockt.

8.5.2 Generated Text

Leichte Sprache: In Bitterfeld soll es eine neue Fabrik für Lithium geben | MDR.DE

Bitterfeld ist eine Stadt im Bundes-Land Sachsen-Anhalt. Dort will eine Firma ein neues Werk bauen. Die Firma heißt: AMG Bitterfeld. Das ist eine große Firma aus dem Land: USA. In dem Werk sollen Batterien für E-Autos hergestellt werden. Die Firma hat gesagt: Wir brauchen das Lithium. Deshalb soll es eine neue Fabrik im Jahr 2023 geben. Armin Schenk ist der Ober-Bürgermeister von Bitterfeld-Wolfen. Er wünscht sich: Dass mehr Firmen für die Fabrik kommen. Und dass sie für die Herstellung von den Batterien bald Arbeit haben.

8.6 Article Pair 6

8.6.1 Source Text

Verfassungsschutz: AfD Sachsen-Anhalt gesichert rechtsextremistisch | MDR.DE

Der Verfassungsschutz hat den Landesverband Sachsen-Anhalt der AfD als gesichert rechtsextremistische Bestrebung eingestuft.

Der Verfassungsschutz von Sachsen-Anhalt hat den AfD-Landesverband als gesichert rechtsextremistische Bestrebung eingestuft. Das hat der Leiter der Behörde, Jochen Hollmann, MDR SACHSEN-ANHALT mitgeteilt.

AfD Sachsen-Anhalt seit 2021 Verdachtsfall

Seit Beginn der Beobachtung hätten sich die tatsächlichen Anhaltspunkte für das Vorliegen einer Bestrebung gegen die freiheitliche demokratische Grundordnung sowohl in qualitativer als auch in quantitativer Hinsicht weiter verdichtet. Die nun erfolgte Einstufung als gesichert rechtsextremistische Bestrebung sei die rechtliche Konsequenz.

Hollmann teilte mit, dass die AfD Sachsen-Anhalt seit der Einstufung als Verdachtsfall im Januar 2021 intensiv geprüft worden sei. Man habe sich bei der Bewertung streng an dem gesetzlichen Auftrag des Verfassungsschutzgesetzes orientiert.

Verfassungsschutz: AfD hat sich seit Corona-Pandemie radikalisiert

Hollmann sagte: "Das Ergebnis ist eindeutig: Der Landesverband vertritt nicht nur weiterhin verfassungsfeindliche Positionen, die zur Einstufung als Verdachtsfall geführt hatten, sondern hat sich vielmehr seit der Corona-Pandemie derart radikalisiert, dass eine systematische Beobachtung unter Einsatz nachrichtendienstlicher Mittel gerechtfertigt ist."

Die Verfassungsschutzabteilung sei gesetzlich

dazu verpflichtet, die Einstufung als gesichertes Beobachtungsobjekt im Phänomenbereich Rechtsextremismus vorzunehmen. Es gebe eine "Vielzahl von Aussagen des Landesverbandes und zahlreicher Funktions- und Mandatsträger der AfD Sachsen-Anhalt, welche die Bestrebungen dieser Partei gegen die freiheitliche demokratische Grundordnung belegen", so Hollmann.

Der Verfassungsschutz komme seinem ëbenfalls gesetzlich definierten Informationsauftrag als Frühwarnsystem der Demokratie"nach, indem er die Entscheidung öffentlich bekannt gibt.

AfD strebt laut Verfassungsschutz gegen freiheitliche demokratische Grundordnung

Die AfD Sachsen-Anhalt verstößt nach Angaben des Verfassungsschutzes gegen das Prinzip der Menschenwürde, gegen das Demokratieprinzip und das Rechtsstaatsprinzip.

MDR-Informationen zufolge umfasst die Beweissammlung mehr als einhundert Seiten. Demnach wurden vor allem öffentliche Quellen wie YouTube-Mitschnitte von Parteiveranstaltungen, Wahlkampfreden und Interviews ausgewertet.

Verstoß gegen Prinzip der Menschenwürde

Äußerungen der AfD Sachsen-Anhalt, die mit der Garantie der Menschenwürde unvereinbar sind, bezeichnete der Verfassungsschutz als "besonders relevant". Der Verfassungsschutz teilte mit, dass führende Vertreter der Partei Menschengruppen abwerten, indem sie Migranten zum Beispiel als Ïnvasoren", Ëindringlingeöder "kulturfremde Versorgungsmigranten"diffamieren oder deutsche Staatsbürgerinnen und Staatsbürger mit Migrationshintergrund als "Passdeutsche"bezeichnen.

Hollmann zufolge hat der Verfassungsschutz zahlreiche muslimfeindliche, rassistische und antisemitische Aussagen von Funktions- und Mandatsträgern des Landesverbandes ausgewertet. Sie belegten, dass die Partei ein ëthnokulturell homogenes Staatsvolkänstrebe und die Ausgrenzung von Menschen aufgrund ihrer Herkunft oder Religion fordert.

Verstoß gegen das Demokratieprinzip

Außerdem strebe die Partei die Abschaffung der parlamentarischen Demokratie an. Die AfD Sachsen-Anhalt versuche, "das demokratische System der Bundesrepublik Deutschland sowie seine Institutionen und deren Vertreter verächtlich zu machen."Der Verfassungsschutz spricht von einer Delegitimierungskampagne.

Insbesondere während der Corona-Pandemie habe der Landesverband die Bundesrepublik immer wieder mit autokratischen oder gar totalitären Regimen sowie die Coronamaßnahmen mit der Judenverfolgung im Dritten Reich gleichgesetzt.

Auch dabei wurden antisemitisch geprägte Begriffe herangezogen, etwa die Verschwörungstheorie des "Great Reset", nach der eine globale Elite die Pandemie instrumentalisiert oder geplant habe, eine von ihr gesteuerte neue Weltordnung zu errichten.

Verstoß gegen das Rechtsstaatsprinzip

Gegen das Rechtsstaatsprinzip würden Äußerungen der AfD Sachsen-Anhalt verstoßen, in denen der Verfassungsschutz das Bestreben erkenne, ganze soziale Gruppen zu entrechten und einer faktischen Willkürherrschaft zu unterwerfen.

Die AfD Sachsen-Anhalt sowie ihre Teil- und Unterorganisationen würden die Ideologie des Ethnopluralismus vertreten. Das deute darauf hin, dass sich die Ziele der Partei nicht ohne die Verletzung rechtsstaatlicher Grundsätze umsetzen lassen.

AfD in Thüringen bereits als "gesichert rechtsextremistisch"

In Thüringen war die AfD vor zwei Jahren vom Verfassungsschutz als gesichert rechtsextremistisch eingestuft worden. In Sachsen-Anhalt und Brandenburg gilt die Einstufung für die AfD-Jugendorganisation Junge Alternative.

AfD: Entscheidung politisch motiviert

AfD-Co-Fraktionschef Oliver Kirchner sagte: Ës interessiert mich nicht, was der Verfassungsschutz behauptet."Laut Kirchner ist die Einschätzung politisch motiviert. Das Innenministerium werde von der CDU geführt, an der die AfD laut einer kürzlich erschienenen Wählerumfrage vorbeigezogen ist, so der Co-Chef.

Landespolitiker nicht überrascht

Eva von Angern, die Fraktionschefin der Linken im Landtag von Sachsen-Anhalt, sagte wie mehrere Landespolitiker, sie sei nicht überrascht von der Entscheidung. "Überall in Sachsen-Anhalt erleben wir regelmäßig, wie diese Partei Grund- und Menschenrechte mit Füßen tritt."

Der innenpolitische Sprecher der SPD-Landtagsfraktion, Rüdiger Erben, sagte der Nachrichtenagentur dpa, er könne die Entscheidung nachvollziehen. Das Problem des Rechtsextremismus sei damit aber nicht gelöst.

Die Landesvorsitzende der Grünen, Madeleine Linke, schrieb auf X ehemals Twitter : "Nun ist bestätigt, was wir alle schon lange wussten: Die noAfD ist eine rechtsextreme Partei. Denn diese Partei geht von der Ungleichwertigkeit von Menschen aus, verharmlost den Nationalsozialismus hat eine starke Affinität zu diktatorischen Regierungsformen...".

8.6.2 Generated Text

Leichte Sprache: Der Verfassungs-Schutz von Sachsen-Anhalt hat die AfD als rechts-extremistisch ein-gestuft | MDR.DE

Im Bundes-Land Sachsen-Anhalt gibt es den Verfassungs-Schutz. Er kümmert sich um die Verfassung von Sachsen-Anhalt. Und er hat jetzt die AfD-Landes-Verband als gesichert rechts-extremistisch ein-gestuft. Das bedeutet: Der Verfassungs-Schutz hat jetzt gesagt: Die AfD ist eine rechts-extremistisch-extreme Gruppe. Das ist auch im Bundes-Land Sachsen-Anhalt so. Der Verfassungs-Schutz hat auch gesagt: Die AfD ist eine rechts-extreme Gruppe. Es gibt viele Hinweise dafür: Dass die AfD bestimmte Regeln nicht be-achtet. Der Verfassungs-Schutz hat zum Beispiel diese Regeln geprüft: • Wenn die AfD rechts-extrem ist: Dann ist das eine Straftat. • Wenn die AfD rechts-extrem ist: Dann ist das eine Straftat. • Und wenn die AfD rechts-extrem ist: Dann ist das eine Straftat. Der Verfassungs-Schutz hat dazu gesagt: Die AfD-Landes-Verband ist als gesichert rechts-extremistisch ein-gestuft. Das bedeutet: Der Verfassungs-Schutz hat als gesichert rechts-extremistisch ein-gestuft. Das hat Jochen Hollmann der Presse gesagt. Er ist der Chef von dem Verfassungs-Schutz.

8.7 Article Pair 7

8.7.1 Source Text

Annaberg-Buchholz macht sich fit für die Forschung zum autonomen Bahnfahren | MDR.DE

Es ist nicht Stanford oder Cambridge - noch nicht einmal Chemnitz: In Annaberg-Buchholz werden die Weichen für das Bahnfahren ohne Lokführer gestellt. Möglich machen das eine Teststrecke, Forscherinnen und Forscher und der SSmart Rail Connectivity Campus", der im Unteren Bahnhof der Erzgebirgsstadt entsteht.

Spitzenforschung unter dem Schwibbogen, so nennt der Rektor der Technischen Universität Chemnitz, Gerd Strohmeier, die Arbeit im SSmart Rail Connectivity CampusSSRCC im Unteren Bahnhof von Annaberg-Buchholz. Zur Eröffnung hatte er schon ganz spontan die Erzgebirgsstadt zum Universitätsstandort erklärt.

"Wir machen das auf einem sehr, sehr hohen Niveau hier in Annaberg-Buchholz, unter weltweit einzigartigen Rahmenbedingungen."Man könne es nicht genug betonen: "Wir forschen hier nicht im Stanford, Cambridge oder auch in Chemnitz. Wir machen das in Annaberg-Buchholz."

Sehr gute Bedingungen für Theorie und Praxis

Kern der Forschung seien neben dem Campus auch die praxisorientierten Rahmenbedingungen, so Strohmeier. "Wir haben hier eine mehr als 20 Kilometer lange Teststrecke zwischen Annaberg-Buchholz und Schwarzenberg, die mit einem 5G-Testfeld ausgerüstet wurde."

Das ermögliche zum Beispiel die Fernsteuerung realer Züge. "Das Ziel muss weiterhin sein, das automatisierte Bahnfahren weiter voranzutreiben."Nachhaltigkeit sei aber auch ein wichtiges Thema in Bezug auf alternative Antriebe und

Gewichtsersparnis bei den Zügen.

Kopfbau mit Köpfchen

Im neu eingeweihten nördlichen Kopfbau werden auch die forschenden Köpfe in Sachen Bahnforschung ihren Platz finden. Auf drei Etagen sind Büros, Labore und Server-Räume entstanden. Mit der Frauscher Sensortechnik GmbH hat auch ein Projektpartner aus der Wirtschaft Platz gefunden.

Die Ziele des SRCC sind hoch gesteckt: Sie reichen von der digitalen Vernetzung und Kommunikation im Schienenverkehr über das automatisierte Fahren auf der Schiene bis hin zur Integration des Bahnverkehrs in Mobilitätsangebote mit anderen Verkehrsmitteln.

Ziel: Mobilität im ländlichen Raum verbessern

Auf dem Campus sollen bahntechnische Erfindungen entwickelt, getestet und zur Marktreife gebracht werden, sagt der technische Leiter des SRCC, Sören Claus. "Wir hatten ja erst im November eine Fernsteuerfahrt, bei der ein Zug in Schlettau von Braunschweig aus gesteuert wurde über 5G."Man arbeite aber auch an Themen wie "Mobilitätsketten im ländlichen Raum", um das Leben dort attraktiver zu machen.

SSignaltechnik, Sensorik und 5G kommen dazu, wobei dieser Übertragungsstandard eine sehr große Rolle spielt", fügt Claus hinzu.

Wissenschaftsminister Gemkow hat auch Erwartungen an den Bund

Sachsens Wissenschaftsminister Sebastian Gemkow CDU fordert bei aller Freude auch eine weitere Beteiligung des Bundes. "Der Freistaat hat das Projekt schon in der Vergangenheit unterstützt und wird das auch weiterhin tun. Wir erwarten aber auch vom Bund, dass er das Projekt finanziell weiter unterstützt.SSachsen habe im Doppelhaushalt bereits die entsprechenden Mittel eingestellt. Genaue Summen könne er jedoch wegen der dynamischen Preisentwicklung am Bau nicht nennen, sagte Gemkow. Im nächsten Schritt soll zwischen den beiden Kopfbauten des Bahnhofs eine Forschungshalle gebaut werden.

8.7.2 Generated Text

Leichte Sprache: In Annaberg-Buchholz werden viele Sachen für die Autonome Bahn gemacht | MDR.DE

Die Stadt Annaberg-Buchholz ist in dem Bundes-Land Sachsen. Dort gibt es die Firma: Smart Rail Connectivity Campus. Die Abkürzung dafür ist: SRCC. In der Stadt Annaberg-Buchholz gibt es einen neuen Campus für Bahn-Forschung. Dort wollen einige Forscher heraus-finden: Wie die Züge ohne Lok-Führer fahren können. In dem Campus werden viele Sachen für die Autonome Bahn gemacht. Zum Beispiel: • Eine Test-Strecke zwischen Annaberg-Buchholz und Schwarzenberg. Sie ist 20 Kilometer lang. In der Test-Strecke sind auch 5G-Test-Flächen ausgerüstet. So können die Forscher zum Beispiel heraus-finden: • Ob die Züge eine Fern-Steuer-Funktion haben. • Oder ob sie Züge ohne Lok-Führer fahren können. In dem Campus sollen noch mehr Sachen gemacht werden. Zum Beispiel: • Büros, • Labore • und Server-Räume.

8.8 Article Pair 8

8.8.1 Source Text

Hochwasser in Sachsen-Anhalt: Hohe Pegel an Ohre, Schwarzer Elster und im Harz | MDR.DE

Die Pegelstände in Sachsen-Anhalt sind in den vergangenen Tagen vielerorts angestiegen. In Wolmirstedt, Löben und Ilsenburg wurden auch erste Alarmstufen erreicht. Grund sind die vielen Niederschläge und die durch die milden Temperaturen einsetzenden Niederschläge. Dramatisch sei die Situation aber nicht, sagt ein Experte.

Viele Niederschläge und das milde Wetter und damit verbunden die Schneeschmelze haben vielerorts in Sachsen-Anhalt die Pegelstände ansteigen lassen. In Löben an der Schwarzen Elster und in Ilsenburg im Harz lagen die Pegel im Bereich von Alarmstufe 1. An der Ohre in Wolmirstedt wurde Alarmstufe 2 von 4 erreicht.

Ohre: Wachsam sein, aber keine dramatische Situation

Der Direktor des Landesbetriebs für Hochwasserschutz und Wasserwirtschaft Sachsen-Anhalt, Burkhard Henning, sagte dem MDR am Montagabend dazu, man gehe davon aus, dass die Alarmstufe 2 nur angekratzt werde. Das hänge auch mit der Steuerung der Wehranlagen zusammen. Es gelte "wachsam sein, aber keine dramatische Situation", so Henning.

Auch an der Schwarzen Elster könnte aus seiner Sicht auf Grund der Vorhersagen und den Informationen aus Brandenburg Alarmstufe 2 "gekratzt"werden. Der Fluss werde sehr stark durch die Tagebaue beeinflusst. Auch hier gelte es, wachsam zu sein. Es sei aber wie an der Ohre nichts Dramatisches.

Harz: Situation steuerbar

An der Bode habe das Rappbodetalsperrensystem viel Wasser zurückgehalten, erklärte der Experte mit Blick auf den Harz. Man könne die Situation gut aussteuern und werde auch mit den angekündigten Niederschlägen gut zurechtkommen. Die Hochwasserzentrale rechnet damit, dass maximal untere Alarmstufen erreicht werden. Bei den kleineren Flüssen hängt es laut Henning davon ab, wie stark jeweils lokal der Regen fällt. Äber von einer dramatischen Situation gehen wir auch hier nicht aus", so Henning.

8.8.2 Generated Text

Leichte Sprache: In Sachsen-Anhalt gibt es immer noch viel Hochwasser | MDR.DE

In dem Bundes-Land Sachsen-Anhalt gibt es immer noch viel Hochwasser. Das ist auch in den Bundes-Ländern: • Sachsen-Anhalt, • Sachsen-Anhalt • und Thüringen so. Dort gibt es zum Beispiel die Stadt: Aue-Bad Schlema. In der Nähe von Aue-Bad Schlema gibt es einen Fluss. Der Fluss heißt: Schwarzer Elster. In den letzten Tagen ist dort viel Hochwasser passiert. Deshalb gibt es in vielen Orten in Sachsen-Anhalt jetzt besonders viel Hochwasser. Zum Beispiel: • In der Stadt Wolmirstedt, • in der Stadt Löben • und in der Stadt Ilsenburg. In diesen Orten gibt es Alarmstufe 1. Burkhard Henning ist der Direktor vom Landes-Betrieb für Hochwasser-Schutz und Wasser-Wirtschaft in Sachsen-Anhalt. Er hat der Presse gesagt: Es ist sehr wichtig, dass es in den Orten schnell genug Hochwasser gibt. Deshalb ist es wichtig, dass es in den Orten schnell genug Hochwasser gibt.

8.9 Article Pair 9

8.9.1 Source Text

2. Bundesliga: Shpilevski wird neuer Cheftrainer von Erzgebirge Aue | MDR.DE

Ein langjähriger Nachwuchstrainer von RB Leipzig, der anschließend Kairat Almaty zum kasachischen Meistertitel führte, wird Dirk Schusters Nachfolger auf der Trainerbank von Erzgebirge Aue. Die Wahl des Zweitligisten fiel auf den erst 33-jährigen Aleksey Shpilevski.

Auf der Suche nach einem neuen Trainer ist Zweitligist Erzgebirge Aue in Kasachstan fündig geworden. Der 33-jährige Aleksey Shpilevski kommt von Kairat Almaty und erhält einen Dreijahresvertrag bis 2024, der für die 2. Bundesliga und Bundesliga gilt. Der gebürtige Weißrusse war im Alter von sechs Jahren nach Deutschland gekommen und spielte im Nachwuchs des VfB Stuttgart, ehe er mit nur 18 Jahren seine aktive Laufbahn verletzungsbedingt beenden musste.

Leonhardt: Ïdentifiziert sich voll mit unseren Werten"

Äliaksei ist trotz seiner jungen Jahre bereits sehr erfahren", wurde FCE-Präsident Helge Leonhardt in einer offiziellen Klubmitteilung zitiert und ergänzte: "Nach mehreren intensiven Gesprächen konnten wir feststellen, dass er sich mit den Werten unseres Vereins voll und ganz identifiziert. Ich freue mich, dass wir ihn zur Bewältigung der vor uns stehenden anspruchsvollen Aufgaben für unseren Club gewinnen konnten.SSeine Trainerlaufbahn trieb Shpilevski von 2013 bis 2018 im Nachwuchs von RB Leipzig voran. Die erste Aufgabe im Herrenbereich führte ihn anschließend für zwei Monate in sein Heimatland zu Dinamo Brest. Seit November 2018 verantwortete er den kasachischen Erstligisten Kairat Almaty, den er 2020 zum ersten Meistertitel seit 16 Jahren führte. Die offizielle Vorstellung des Fußballlehrers kündigte der Verein für übernächsten Dienstag 15. Juni an.

8.9.2 Generated Text

Leichte Sprache: Der Fußball-Verein Erzgebirge Aue will einen neuen Trainer | MDR.DE

Im Bundes-Land Kasachstan gibt es den Fußball-Verein Erzgebirge Aue. Er ist 33 Jahre alt. Und er spielt in der 2. Bundes-Liga. Der neue Trainer heißt: Aleksey Shpilevski. Er kommt aus dem Land Kasachstan. Und er hat einen Vertrag mit dem Fußball-Verein RB Leipzig. Er hat 3 Jahre einen Vertragals Trainer. Das bedeutet: Er spielt für 3 Jahre in einem Fußball-Verein. Und er bekommt bis zum Jahr 2024 einen Vertrag als Trainer. Das ist der Vertrag für die 2. Bundes-Liga und die Bundes-Liga. Alexey Shpilevski kommt aus dem Land Weißruss. Er ist 6 Jahre alt. Und er spielt in der 2. Bundes-Liga. Er hat den Vertrag mit dem Fußball-Verein RB Leipzig gemacht. Danach ist er zum Fußball-Verein Dynamo Brest gegangen. Das ist er seit dem Monat November im Jahr 2018 spielt. Er hat den Vertrag mit dem Fußball-Verein Erzgebirge Aue gemacht. Und er hat am Dienstag gesagt: Dass er den nächsten Trainer für RB Leipzig wird.

8.10 Article Pair 10

8.10.1 Source Text

Drei Schwerverletzte nach Unfall auf der A4 bei Dresden | MDR.DE

Bei einem Überholmanöver ist ein 45 Jahre alter Autofahrer auf der Autobahn 4 von der Fahrbahn abgekommen. Dabei wurden der Mann und seine beiden Mitfahrer schwer verletzt und kamen ins Krankenhaus. Der 45-Jährige war mit seinen 24 und 26 Jahre alten Insassen kurz vor Mitternacht auf der A4 von Eisenach in Richtung Dresden unterwegs, als er auf Höhe der Ausfahrt Dreieck Nossen bei einem Überholmanöver die Kontrolle über sein Auto verlor, teilte die Polizei am Freitag mit.

Demnach kam er nach rechts von der Fahrbahn ab und das Auto geriet in Brand. Während der Bergungs- und Rettungsmaßnahmen in der Nacht zum Freitag war die Autobahn zeitweise gesperrt.

8.10.2 Generated Text

Leichte Sprache: 45 Jahre alter Auto-Fahrer ist auf der Autobahn A4 von Dresden abgekommen | MDR.DE

Im Bundes-Land Sachsen ist die Autobahn A4. Dort gab es in der letzten Nacht einen Unfall. So ist der Unfall passiert: Ein Auto-Fahrer ist auf der Autobahn A4 von der Stadt Eisenach in die Richtung von Dresden gefahren. Das ist eine Stadt im Bundes-Land Sachsen. Bei dem Unfall hat er sein Auto von der Fahrbahn abgekommen. Das bedeutet: Er ist von der Fahrbahn gefahren. Dabei hat er aber nicht mehr genug Kontrolle über sein Auto bekommen. Deshalb ist die Fahrbahn für einige Zeit gesperrt. Die Polizei hat der Presse gesagt: Bei dem Unfall wurden: • Der Auto-Fahrer • und mehrere andere Menschen verletzt. Sie wurden ins Kranken-Haus gebracht.

8.11 Automatic Metrics

The figures given below show the progression of different metrics computed for each approach during fine-tuning for three runs. The best-performing run is always indicated in red. The reference scores for the three readability metrics are displayed using a dark blue dotted line and the input scores are displayed using a dashed magenta-colored line.

8.11.1 Median Wiener Sachtextformel Scores

Figure 1: Median WSTF Scores During Fine-tuning

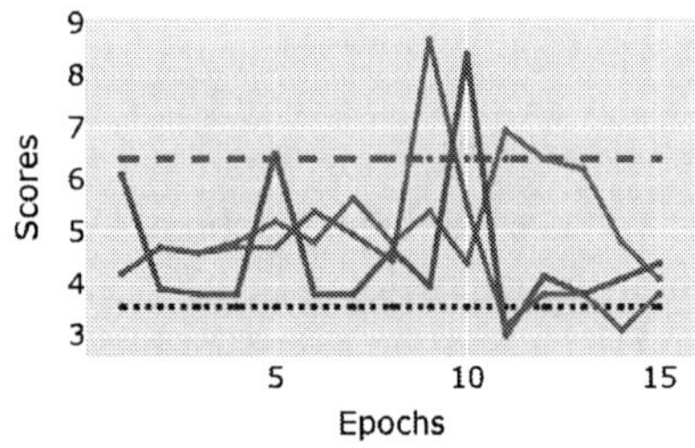

(a) mBART-sum Approach

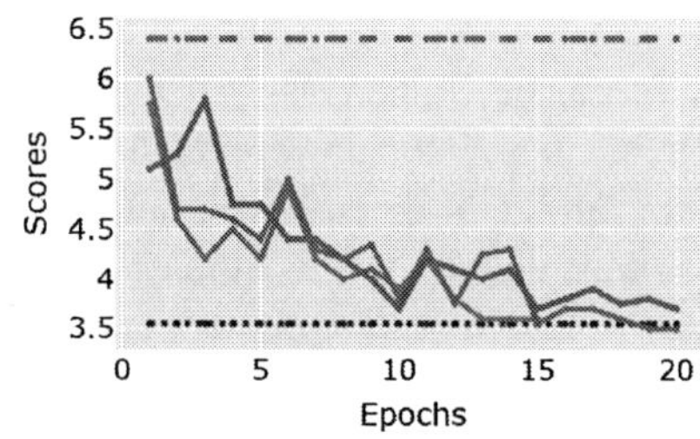

(b) mBART-tr Approach

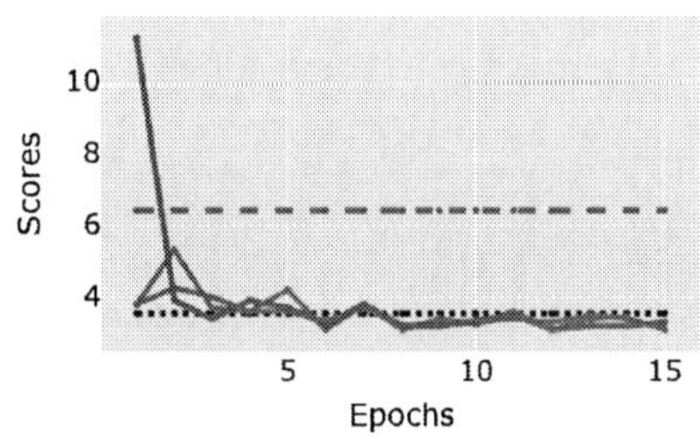

(c) mt5-sum Approach

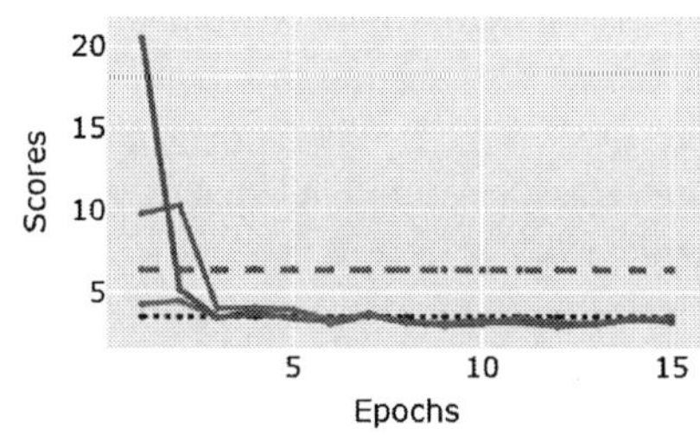

(d) mt5-tr Approach

8.11.2 Median Flesch-Reading-Ease Scores

Figure 2: Median FRE Scores During Fine-tuning

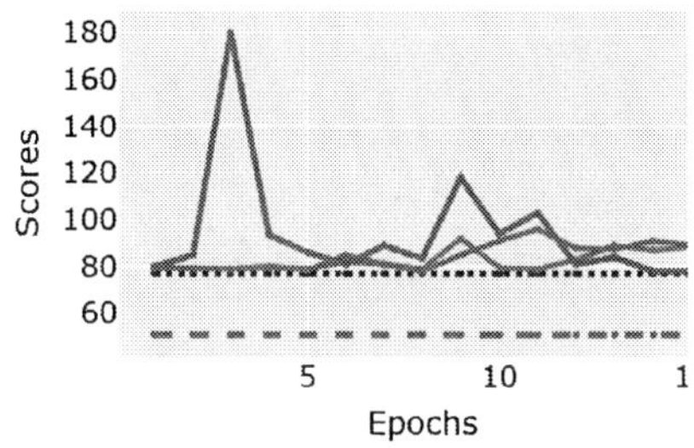

(a) mBART-sum Approach

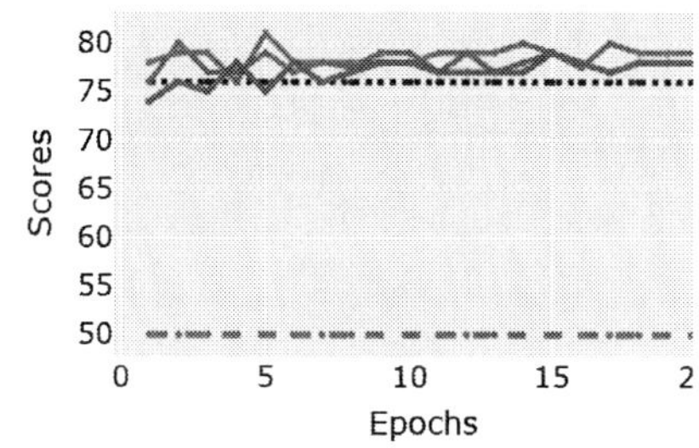

(b) mBART-tr Approach

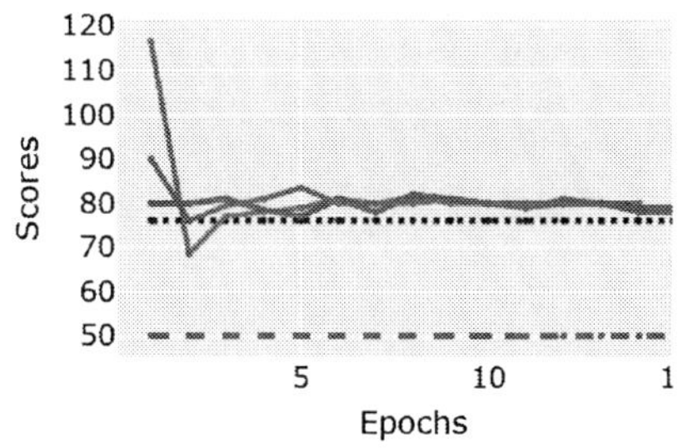

(c) mt5-sum Approach

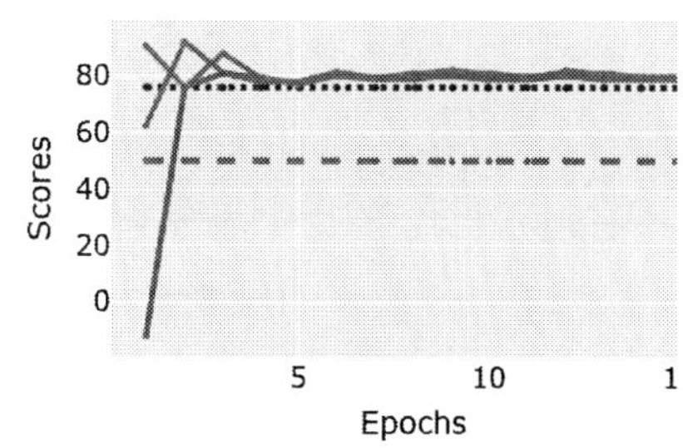

(d) mt5-tr Approach

8.11.3 Median Coleman-Liau Index Scores

Figure 3: Median CLI Scores During Fine-tuning

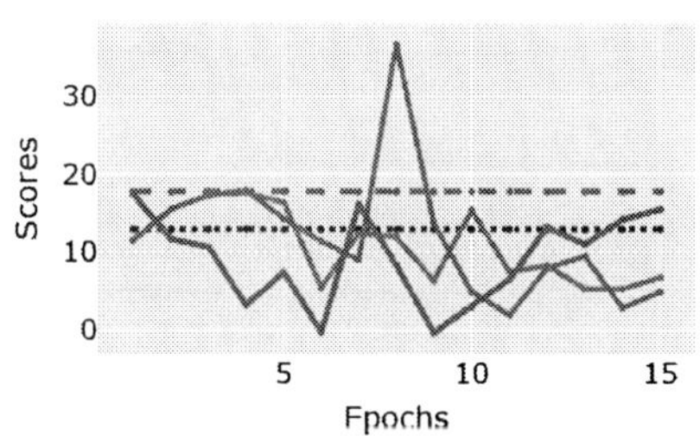

(a) mBART-sum Approach

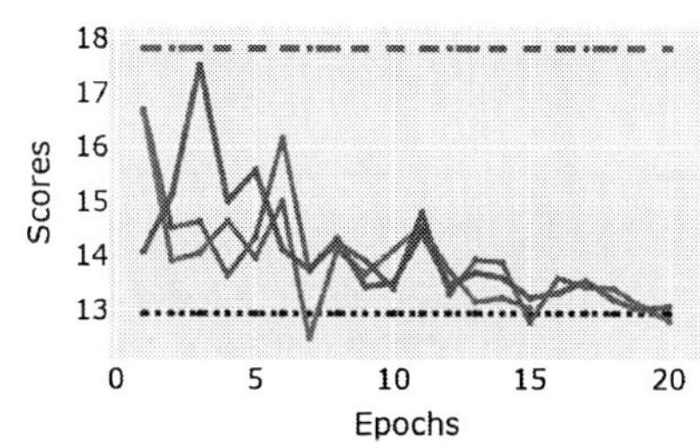

(b) mBART-tr Approach

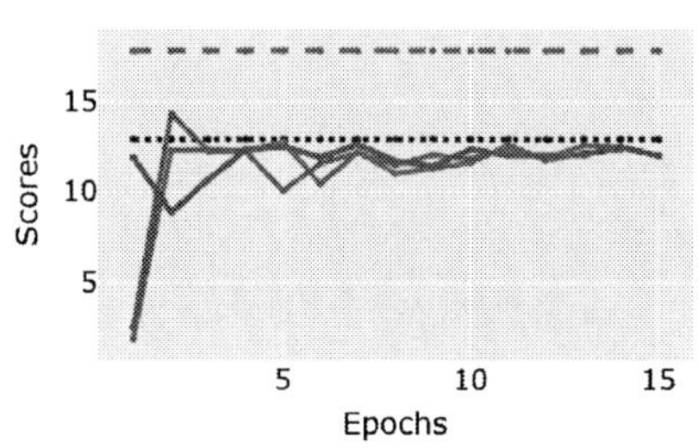

(c) mt5-sum Approach

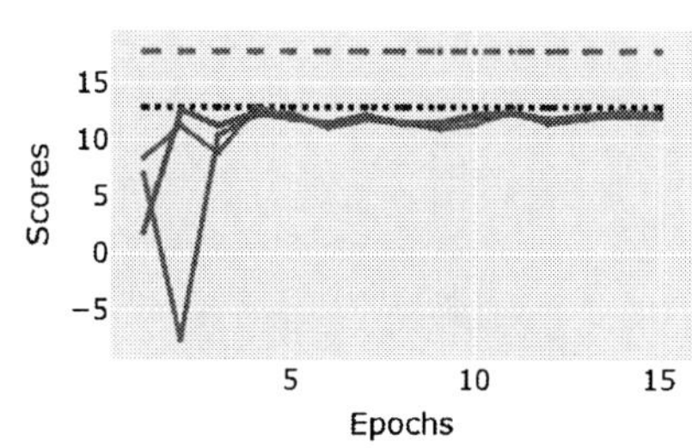

(d) mt5-tr Approach

8.11.4 Median Text Length Scores

Figure 4: Median Text Length Scores During Fine-tuning

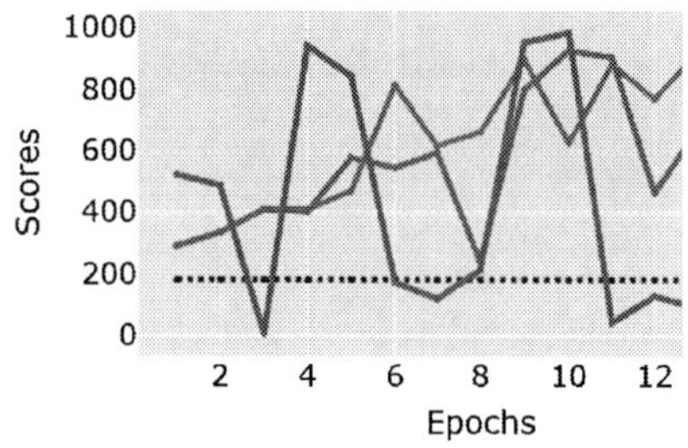

(a) mBART-sum Approach

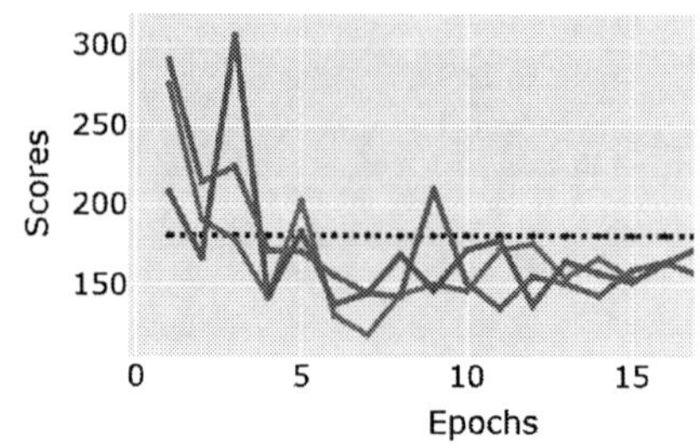

(b) mBART-tr Approach

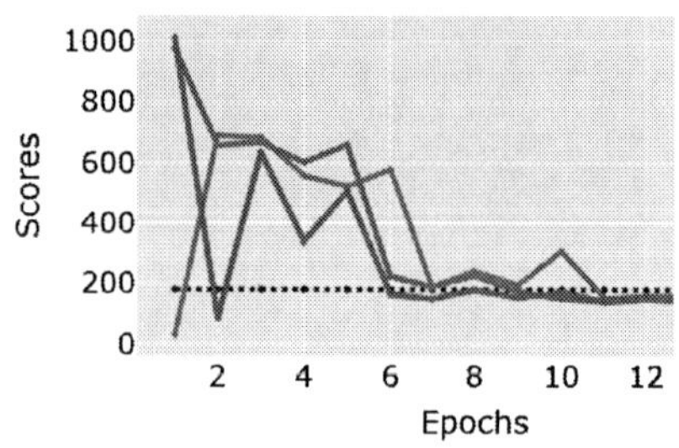

(c) mt5-sum Approach

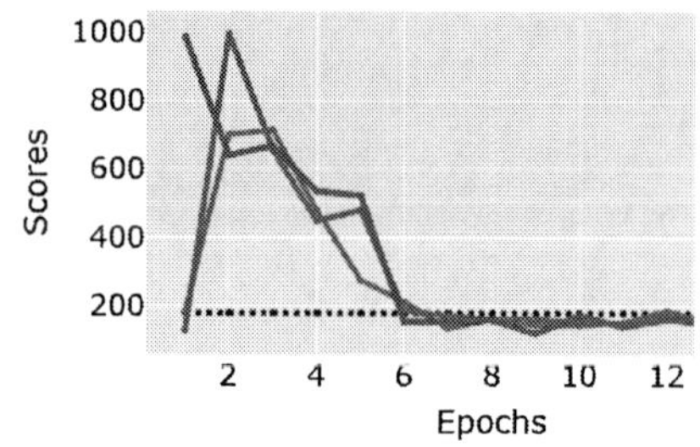

(d) mt5-tr Approach

8.11.5 BLEU and ROUGE Scores

Figure 5: Median BLEU and ROUGE Scores During Fine-tuning

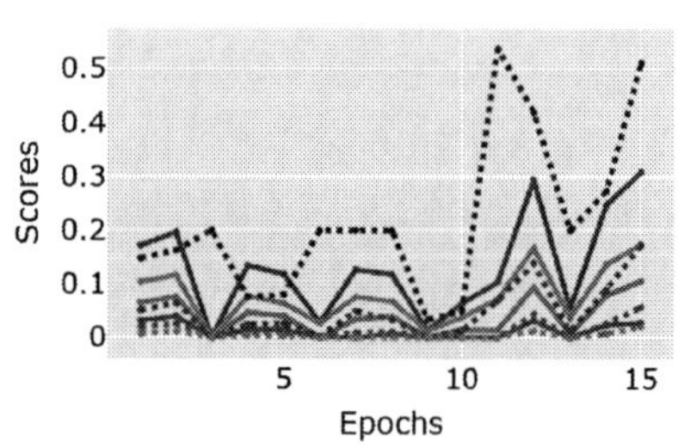

(a) mBART-sum Approach

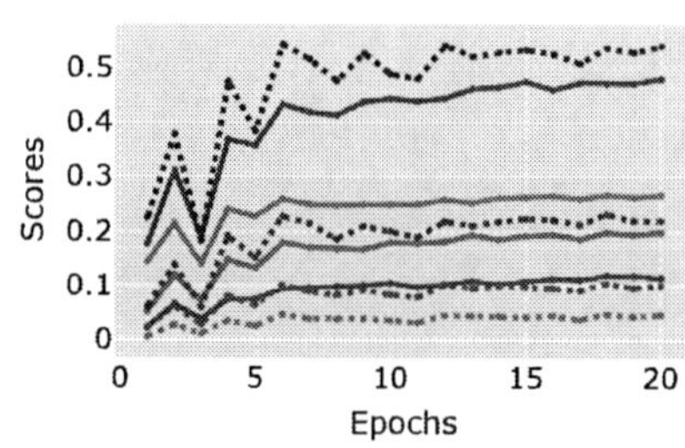

(b) mBART-tr Approach

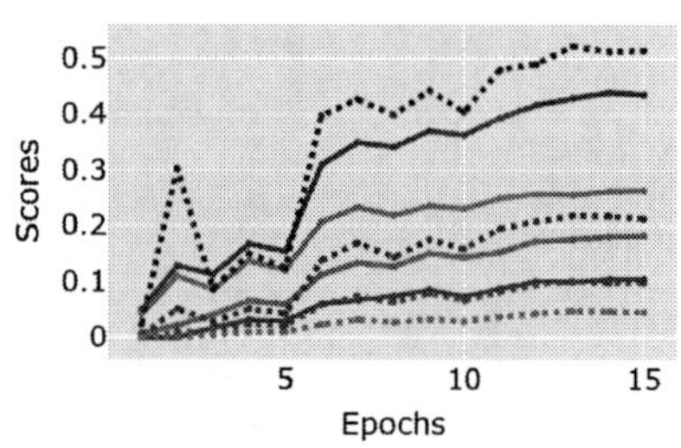

(c) mt5-sum Approach

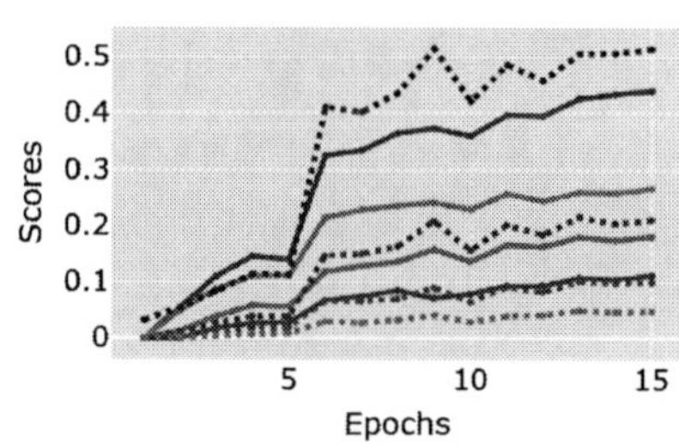

(d) mt5-tr Approach

8.11.6 Median BLANC Scores

Figure 6: Median BLANC Scores During Fine-tuning

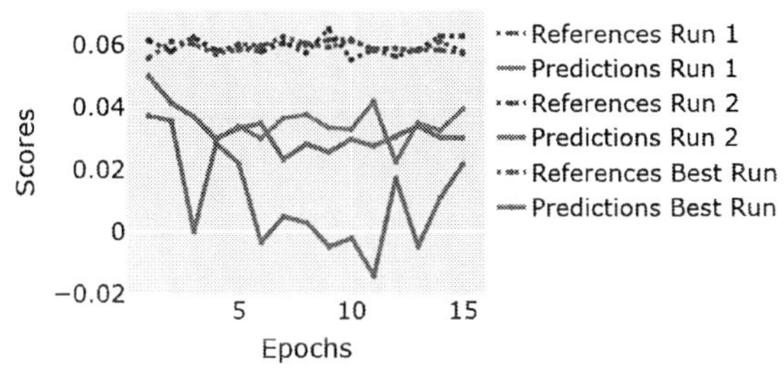

(a) mBART-sum Approach

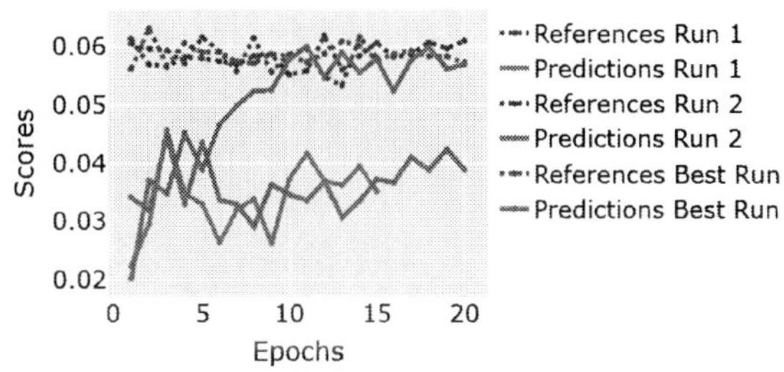

(b) mBART-tr Approach

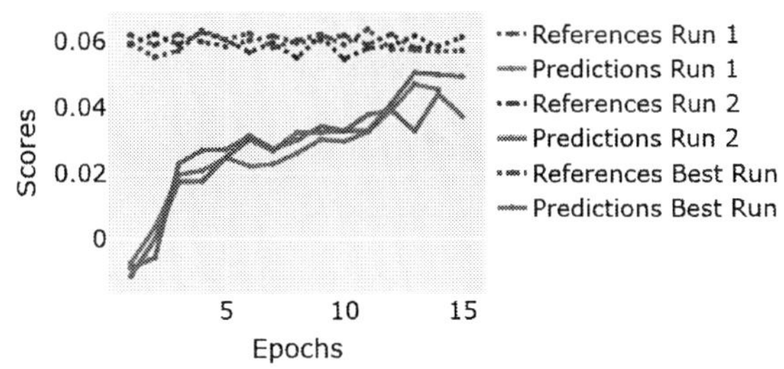

(c) mt5-sum Approach

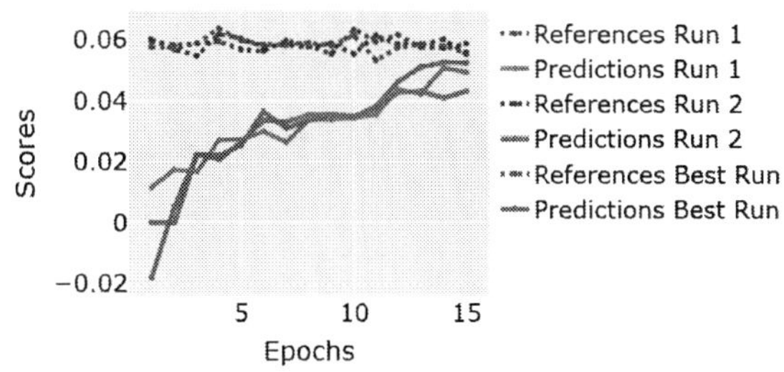

(d) mt5-tr Approach

8.12 Human Evaluation Responses

The following figures depict the responses of survey participants to six questions on the document-level simplification properties assessed. We use the term Leichte Sprache (LS) in the figures, which is the German term for German Easy-to-Read language or GE2R.

8.12.1 Intent Assessment

Figure 7: Responses to the Question: Does the generated article have the same intent as the source article?

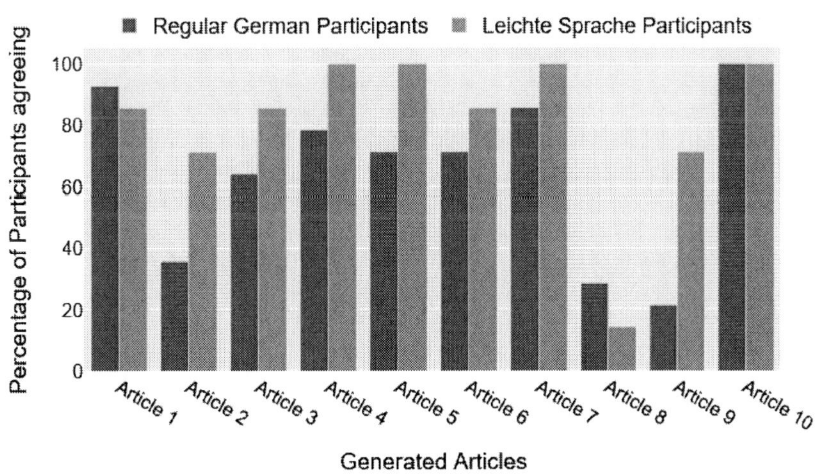

8.12.2 Content Assessment

Figure 8: Responses to the Question: Does the generated article represent the content of the source article well?

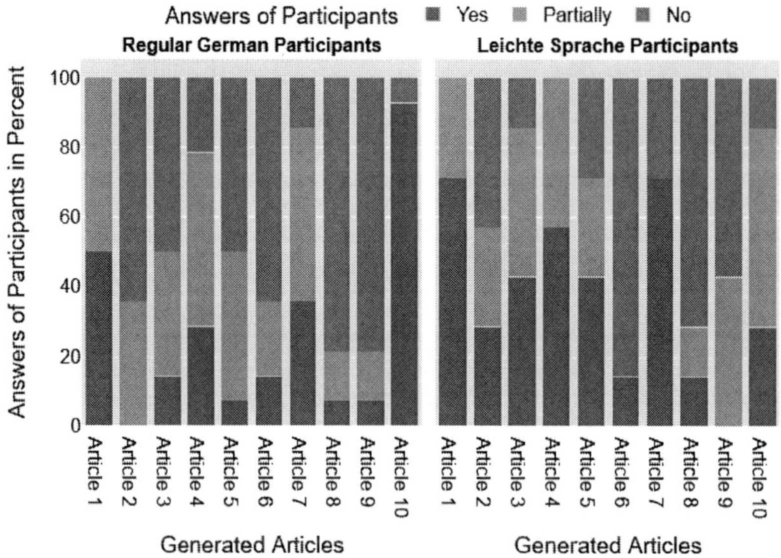

8.12.3 Grammar Assessment

Figure 9: Agreement of Participants with the Question: Does the generated article contain grammar errors? How many?

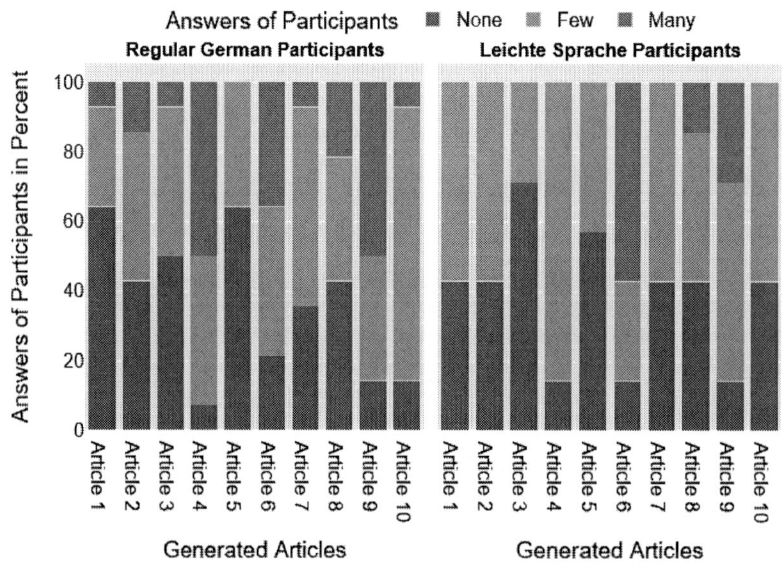

8.12.4 Logical Consistency Assessment

Figure 10: Responses to the Question: Does the generated article contain errors in its logical consistency? How many?

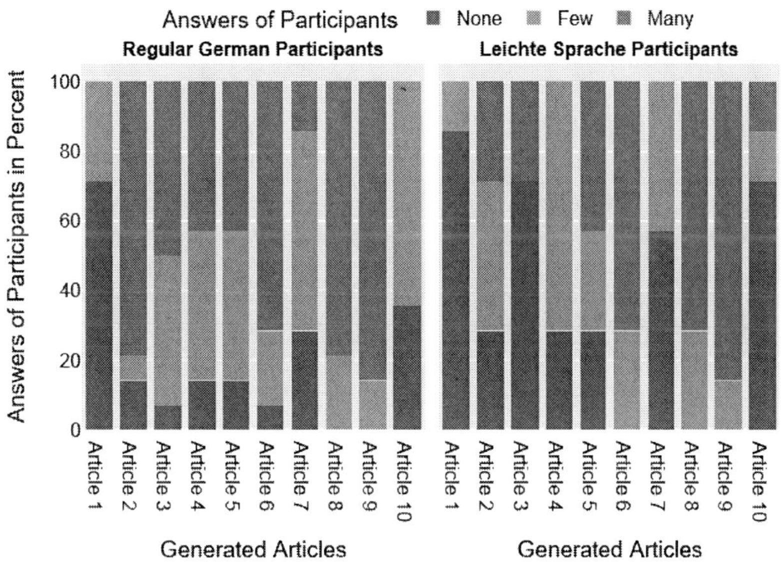

8.12.5 Reading Ease Assessment

Figure 11: Agreement of Participants with the Question: Is the generated article easy to read?

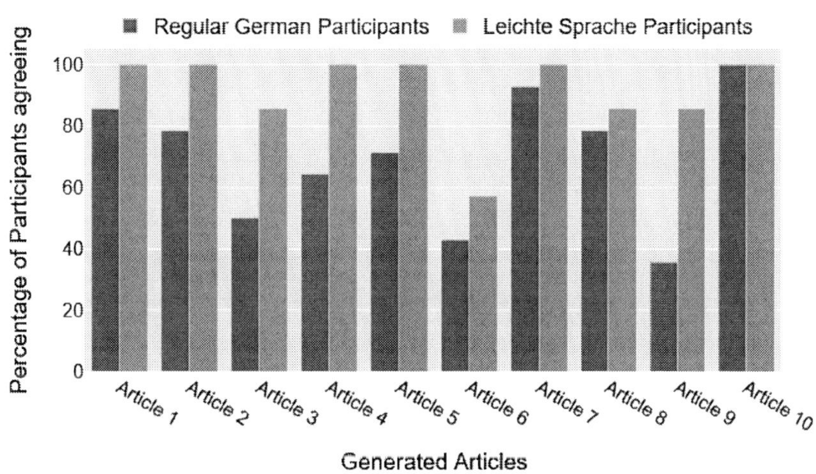

8.12.6 GE2R Language Assessment

Figure 12: Agreement of Participants with the Question: Is the generated article written in GE2R?

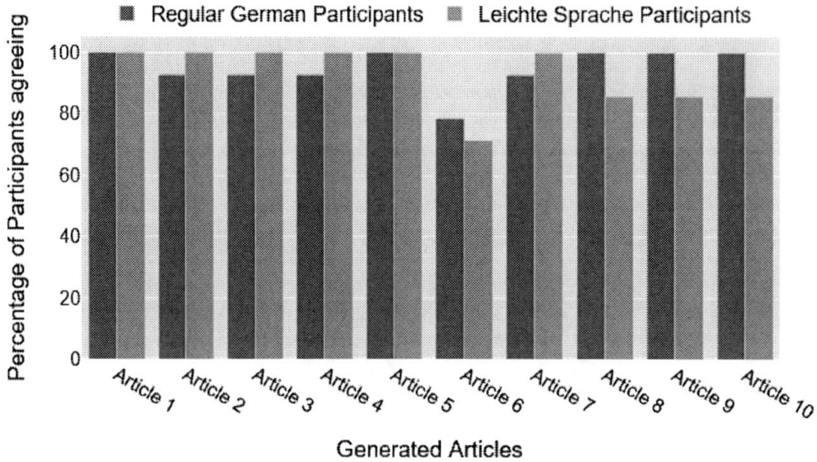

Modeling Quality of Experience in German Automatic Text Summarization and Machine Translation

Dinh Nam Pham[1], **Vivien Macketanz**[1], **Shushen Manakhimova**[1], **Sebastian Möller**[1,2]
[1] Speech and Language Technology Lab, Deutsches Forschungszentrum für Künstliche Intelligenz (DFKI), Berlin, Germany
[2]Quality and Usability Lab, Technische Universität Berlin, Germany
Correspondence: shushen.manakhimova@dfki.de

Abstract

We present a model for predicting the Quality of Experience (QoE) of German machine-generated text from Automatic Text Summarization (ATS) and Machine Translation (MT). Based on previously established quality dimensions, we fine-tuned BERT for ATS and ELECTRA for MT, which performed best per task. Adding linguistic features further improved accuracy. For ATS, BERT excelled as a multi-target regressor; for MT, separate ELECTRA models performed best. Our results show that combining linguistic features with language models enables robust QoE prediction.

1 Introduction

The Quality of Experience (QoE) framework is well established in domains like video streaming, gaming, or cloud computing, but it remains underexplored for evaluating machine-generated text. As tools for automatically generated text become increasingly widespread, understanding how users perceive output quality gains importance. QoE can be described as the user's subjective degree of delight or annoyance when consuming a service, determined by how well the delivered content meets their expectations for utility or enjoyment in a given context (Le Callet et al., 2012). Modeling QoE for machine-generated text lets developers optimize and monitor the perceived quality of translation and summarization systems without repeatedly relying on expensive human tests.

This study adapts the QoE framework to assess perceived quality in German machine-generated text for two key tasks: Machine Translation (MT) and Automatic Text Summarization (ATS). Building on our previous work that identified relevant perceptual dimensions and produced high-quality human ratings (Manakhimova et al., 2025), we train machine learning models to predict these ratings. Since human evaluations are reliable but costly and hard to scale, we propose an automated prediction approach that combines neural language models with linguistic features.

We fine-tune pre-trained German language models (BERT and ELECTRA) for regression and enhance their [CLS] token embeddings with a 17-dimensional vector of linguistic features capturing readability, lexical diversity, and structural aspects. The [CLS] token is a special classification token automatically prepended to each input sequence. After transformer encoding, its corresponding final hidden state serves as a fixed-size summary representation of the entire sequence. This representation, concatenated with the linguistic feature vector, forms the basis for our regression predictions.

Our main contributions are threefold. First, we formalize QoE prediction for machine-generated text as a multivariate regression problem. Second, we compare multiple multi-output regression strategies (including single-target, multi-target, and multi-task learning) to identify the most effective approach for each task. Third, we demonstrate that integrating linguistic features significantly enhances performance, even in low-resource settings.

Our results offer insights into modeling user-perceived quality in natural language generation, highlighting the benefits of combining neural representations with linguistically motivated features for scalable QoE prediction.

2 Related Work

2.1 Automatic Quality Assessment

Traditional text quality assessment typically measures adherence to formal standards, whereas Quality of Experience (QoE) emphasizes user perception, as established in multimedia research. Subjective evaluation methods like Semantic Differential (SD) scaling (Osgood, 1957) commonly used to capture these perceptions. SD scaling presents respondents with pairs of opposing adjectives and

Proceedings of the 21st Conference on Natural Language Processing (KONVENS), Volume 2: Workshops, pages 169–175, 2025

asks them to rate a concept or stimulus along a Likert-like scale anchored by these terms.

Readability and text complexity have been researched extensively. Some studies have leveraged language models alone for these tasks, such as (Martinc et al., 2021), while others have focused on linguistic feature-based approaches to readability and complexity across languages, e.g., (Santucci et al., 2020; Štajner and Hulpus, 2020; Seiffe et al., 2022). These studies demonstrate that linguistic features remain highly relevant for evaluating textual properties, even in the era of neural language models.

A study particularly relevant to our approach is Anschütz and Groh (2022), which also integrates a language model with linguistic features for complexity prediction. Their method aligns with our goal of combining automatically extractable linguistic properties with deep learning models to enhance prediction performance.

For German, Naderi et al. (2019) used subjective judgments to train a readability model, underscoring the value of perception-based assessment. More recently, studies explore large language models (LLMs) for reference-free quality evaluation (Chen et al., 2023; Huang et al., 2023) and text simplification quality estimation (Kriz et al., 2020).

Building on these efforts, our work integrates perceptual evaluation with linguistic and neural predictors. Unlike prior research focused on single dimensions (e.g., readability), we model multiple quality dimensions per task, providing a more comprehensive view of user-perceived quality in machine-generated text.

2.2 Linguistic Text Features

Our approach incorporates a targeted set of linguistic features that influence readability, complexity, and overall textual perception. Classic indicators include average sentence length (Pitler and Nenkova, 2008) and word length (McNamara et al., 2014), with longer sentences and words generally signaling increased difficulty. We use established readability metrics: Flesch Reading Ease (Flesch, 1948), Wiener Sachtextformel (Bamberger and Rabin, 1984) (German-specific), Coleman-Liau index (Coleman and Liau, 1975), Gunning Fog (Gunning, 1952), and SMOG (Mc Laughlin, 1969). These assess text difficulty via sentence and word characteristics. To measure lexical variation, we include Type-Token Ratio (TTR) (Richards, 1987) and lexical density (McNamara et al., 2014), defined as the ratio of content words (nouns, verbs, adjectives, adverbs) to the total number of words. Higher values suggest richer, denser language impacting perceived informativeness and complexity.

Together, these features provide insights into multiple dimensions of text quality and complement neural methods in modeling user-perceived QoE.

3 Methodology

3.1 Data

Our experiments build on our prior work (Macketanz et al., 2022; Manakhimova et al., 2025) that examined human perception of machine-generated German text quality using crowdsourced SD surveys to identify subjective quality dimensions in ATS and MT.[1]

Automatic Text Summarization (ATS). The ATS data is based on the GeWiki corpus, which contains preprocessed German Wikipedia articles across domains such as people, science, and politics (Frefel, 2020). Summaries were obtained both from the SwissText & KONVENS 2020 shared task and generated internally using a range of extractive and abstractive methods, such as Lead-3 (Dohare and Karnick, 2017), TextRank (Mihalcea and Tarau, 2004), Pointer-Generator (See et al., 2017), Transformer (Vaswani et al., 2017), Convolutional Self-Attention Transformer (Li et al., 2019), and BERT-Transformer (Devlin et al., 2019). The resulting summaries typically average 37 words (about 2–3 sentences). To ensure a diverse quality range, all summaries underwent an error-type annotation to include various error types and error severities. We further made sure to include different summary lengths.

Machine Translation (MT). For the MT corpus, we selected English–German translations from top-, middle-, and bottom-ranked systems in the WMT19 News Translation task (Barrault et al., 2019), aiming to create a dataset that spans a range of translation quality.[2] Analogously to the ATS corpus, we then performed an error-type annotation to include data points with various translation error types and severities.

[1] Note that this paper highlights only key aspects of our foundational research regarding the dataset creation and quality dimensions identification. For a detailed description of dimension identification and human ratings, see the cited work.

[2] http://www.statmt.org/wmt19/index.html

3.2 Human Ratings and Quality Dimensions

For each text type, we created tailored adjective pairs (e.g., *grammatical–ungrammatical*) and had German native speakers rate texts on 7-point Likert scales (0–6). The survey ran on the Crowdee platform[3]. Raters were native German speakers from the DACH region (Germany, Austria, Switzerland) and were compensated at a rate of 2 Euro per 10-minute task, in line with minimum wage requirements. Annotators were provided with the texts (each text type separately) and instructed to judge each one using the adjective pair scales, focusing on the language quality while disregarding the content of the sentences to the best of their ability. To ensure data quality, we applied pre-task qualifications and filtered results using the Inconsistency Score (Naderi, 2018) among other criteria. The cleaned datasets comprise 91 ATS and 106 MT texts[4], each rated by 10–20 annotators, prioritizing rating reliability over quantity.

We performed an exploratory factor analysis (EFA) of human ratings, which revealed four latent quality dimensions per task, and validated the structure in a follow-up study using four adjective pairs per text type; the reduced instruments reproduced the original factors with strong correlations to the full scales. For **ATS**, the dominant factor is *linguistic logic* ($\approx$ coherence/consistency), capturing internal cohesion and semantic plausibility; the remaining factors are *complexity* (syntactic/lexical richness and associated reading effort), *clarity* (readability and focus), and *predictability* (discourse flow and logical progression). For **MT**, the factors are *precision* ($\approx$ adequacy/completeness), *complexity* (as above), *grammaticality* ($\approx$ fluency/surface well-formedness, including spelling and punctuation), and *transparency* ($\approx$ coherence/naturalness). We retain the inductive labels but provide these parenthetical alignments to established constructs to facilitate interpretation and comparison with prior work. The resulting human-derived dimensions serve as ground-truth targets for our predictive modeling.

For the model training, we use the mean rating per dimension per text. Each dataset includes the text plus four columns for the dimension ratings (see Tables 1 and 2). Ratings range from 0 to 6 (0 being the lowest perceived quality, and 6 the highest), framing this as a multi-output regression task with four targets. Each test item has a corresponding Mean Opinion Score (MOS) per dimension, calculated as the arithmetic mean of individual human ratings. MOS is a standard practice in QoE research (ITU-T, 2016).

Table 1: Excerpt from the ATS dataset illustrating its structure, with Mean Opinion Scores per test item and quality dimension. Text samples were shortened.

Text Sample	Logic	Complexity	Clarity	Predictability
"35,2 Vol. ist ein deutscher Kriminalfilm aus dem Jahr 2012 [...]."	2.2692	4.1923	3.0962	2.4615
"Bansin ist ein Ortsteil der Gemeinde Heringsdorf im Landkreis [...]."	4.8125	4.0000	5.1875	3.3750
"Veikko Lahti war ein finnischer Ringer. Er war Olympiasieger [...]"	2.0909	1.8182	3.0909	2.6364

Table 2: Excerpt from the MT dataset illustrating its structure, with Mean Opinion Scores per test item and quality dimension. Text samples were shortened.

Text Sample	Precision	Complexity	Transparency	Grammaticality
"Ihre Zurückhaltung ist alles auf das Timing zurückzuführen."	3.0345	1.8966	3.0862	3.6207
"Seine Nachrichten führten jedoch nur zu einem grauen [...]."	2.6842	2.1579	2.7368	1.7368
"Sicher ist, dass der Konflikt der Mitte des 17. Jahrhunderts [...]."	3.4118	4.1765	3.8235	2.8235

3.3 Model Selection

Given the limited size of our datasets and the resource-intensive demands of further data collection, we leveraged pre-trained German language models for training and evaluation to capitalize on their existing knowledge.

We first evaluated five pre-trained models to select the best performer for further experiments: the BERT variants "bert-base-german-uncased" (Bayerische Staatsbibliothek, 2025b), "bert-base-german-cased" (Bayerische Staatsbibliothek, 2025a), "gbert-base," "gbert-large," and the ELECTRA model "gelectra-large" (Chan et al., 2020), all sourced from Huggingface[5]. For each, we replaced the output layer with a linear layer of size 4 to predict all four quality dimensions simultaneously in a multi-target regression framework.

[3]https://www.crowdee.com/

[4]You can find the ATS and MT datasets without the ratings here: https://github.com/DFKI-NLP/TextQ

[5]https://huggingface.co/

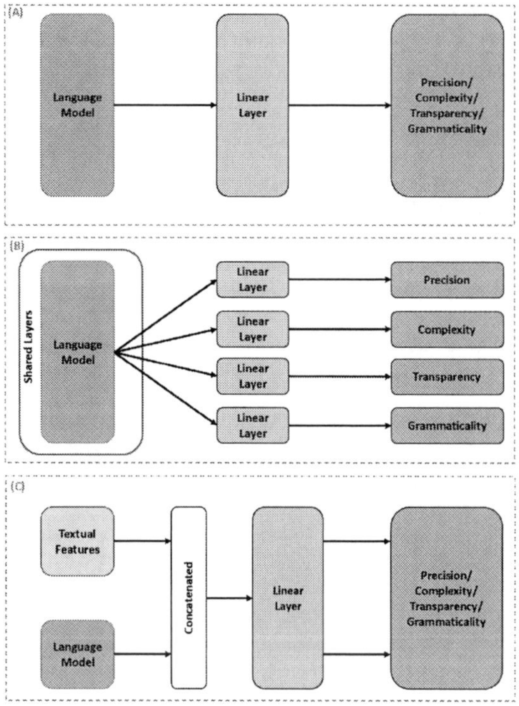

Figure 1: Model architectures with the MT labels for (A) fine-tuned language model, (B) multi-task learning model and (C) textual feature integration.

3.4 Multi-Label Regression Approach

Continuing with the best-performing pre-trained model for each dataset, we explored different approaches for the four-label regression task. The baseline models (from Section 3.3) output all four labels simultaneously in a multi-target regression setup. In addition, we trained separate single-target models (one per quality dimension) and evaluated their performance individually.

Given evidence that multi-task learning (MTL) can outperform single-task models in similar multi-target regression settings (Mohtaj et al., 2023), we also implemented an MTL model for each dataset. Our MTL architecture shares a single pre-trained backbone (BERT or ELECTRA, as chosen in Section 3.3) across all tasks but uses separate task-specific linear regression heads. Each dimension is predicted by an independent 1D regression head that processes the pooled [CLS] token embedding from the shared backbone. The overall loss is the sum of all task losses with equal weighting, treating all dimensions as equally important.

3.5 Linguistic Feature Integration

Lastly, we evaluated the benefit of combining statistical and linguistic text features with language model embeddings, leveraging both transformer architectures and features in a hybrid approach. We extracted 17 features, grouped into four main categories. The first category, structural metrics, includes average sentence length, the percentage of words with six or more letters, and the average number of characters per word. The second category covers syllabic properties, such as average syllables per word, the percentage of monosyllabic words, and the percentage of words with three or more syllables. Third, we incorporated readability formulas, including the Flesch Reading Ease, all four variants of the Wiener Sachtextformel, as well as the SMOG, Coleman-Liau, and Gunning Fog indices. Finally, the fourth category captures lexical diversity through measures like TTR, lexical density, and the number of unique tokens.

These features were min-max normalized to [0,1] per dataset split, with scaling parameters applied consistently to validation and test sets to avoid data leakage (see Section 3.6). The normalized features were concatenated with the [CLS] embedding from the selected model and fed into the regression head according to the multi-target regression method chosen. Figure 1 illustrates the model architectures for MT.

3.6 Experimental Setup

We used consistent hyperparameters and data splits across all experiments for fair comparison: learning rate 2×10^{-5}, MSE loss, 30 epochs, batch size 16, and AdamW optimizer with weight decay 0.01.

Due to the small dataset size, we employed a 7-fold cross-validation. Each dataset was randomly shuffled and split into seven equal folds $F = f_1, ..., f_7$. For each round, fold f_i served as test set, fold f_{i-1} (or f_7 if $i = 1$) as validation, and the remaining five folds for training. Thus, each fold was used once as validation and once as test. During training, we monitored validation RMSE per epoch and saved the best checkpoint for final evaluation on the test fold. Reported metrics are the average over the seven test folds.

4 Results and Discussion

We primarily use RMSE to evaluate model performance, as it is a standard regression metric that penalizes outliers quadratically and measures error on the original rating scale.

Table 3: The performance of the fine-tuned language models on ATS.

Model	MAE	RMSE	R^2
bert-base-german-uncased	0.7965	0.9670	0.1026
bert-base-german-cased	0.7696	0.9390	0.1510
gbert-base	0.8448	1.0248	-0.0076
gbert-large	**0.6958**	**0.8588**	**0.2939**
gelectra-large	0.7780	0.9356	0.1683

Table 4: The performance of the fine-tuned language models on MT.

Model	MAE	RMSE	R^2
bert-base-german-uncased	0.9911	1.1877	0.1085
bert-base-german-cased	1.0066	1.2295	0.0476
gbert-base	0.9966	1.2292	0.0613
gbert-large	0.8961	1.0669	0.2719
gelectra-large	**0.8500**	**1.0133**	**0.3727**

$$\text{RMSE} = \sqrt{\frac{1}{n}\sum_{i=1}^{n}(y_i - \hat{y}_i)^2} \quad (1)$$

where y_i is the true value, $\hat{y}_i$ is the predicted value, and n is the number of samples. Additionally, we report mean absolute error (MAE) and the coefficient of determination (R^2) as supplementary metrics. For each model, we average RMSE, MAE, and R^2 scores across all four quality dimensions.

The fine-tuning results of pre-trained language models on our datasets are shown in Tables 3 and 4. For ATS, gbert-large performed best, while gelectra-large was top for MT.

MAE values are lower than RMSE, as expected (Willmott and Matsuura, 2005). The ratio between RMSE and MAE can provide additional insight into the shape of the error distribution (Karunasingha, 2022). Specifically, a lower ratio indicates a platykurtic distribution, which has lighter tails and fewer extreme errors than a normal distribution, while a higher ratio would point to a leptokurtic distribution with heavier tails and more outliers. The RMSE/MAE ratios of our best models (ATS: 1.23, MT: 1.19) are less than 1.25, which is shown to be consistent with a platykurtic error distribution (Karunasingha, 2022). In such cases, RMSE was demonstrated to be a more reliable performance measure than MAE (Karunasingha, 2022), supporting RMSE as a suitable metric for our experiments. Moreover, according to (Inagata et al., 2025), ratios between approx. 1.14 and 1.25 indicate good forecasting performance. Our models' ratios fall within this range, confirming their robustness. Based on these findings, we selected gbert-large for ATS and gelectra-large for MT for further experiments.

Table 5: The performance of the multi-label regression approaches and textual feature integration for ATS.

Model	MAE	RMSE	R^2
Multi-target regression	**0.6958**	**0.8588**	**0.2939**
Single-target regression	0.7408	0.8990	0.1895
Multi-task learning	0.7525	0.9092	0.2001
Multi-target regression + textual features	**0.6764**	**0.8308**	**0.3225**

Table 6: The performance of the multi-label regression approaches and textual feature integration for MT.

Model	MAE	RMSE	R^2
Multi-target regression	0.8500	1.0133	0.3727
Single-target regression	**0.8207**	**0.9785**	**0.3867**
Multi-task learning	0.8661	1.0208	0.2898
Single-target regression + textual features	**0.7885**	**0.9259**	**0.4510**

The results of the multi-label regression approaches and integration of textual features are shown in Tables 5 and 6. For both text types, the multi-task model performed worst, though with only slightly higher errors. This may be due to limited training data restricting model complexity, which is currently limited to a linear layer over language model embeddings. Larger datasets could enable more complex architectures (e.g., LSTM/GRU) and better leverage MTL. The multi-target regression model achieved the lowest RMSE for ATS, while single-target regression was best for MT. Adding textual features to these models significantly improved performance across all metrics.

These findings highlight the advantage of combining neural embeddings with linguistic features. While BERT and ELECTRA embeddings capture semantic information, textual statistics add complementary insights not fully captured by the language models. Our hybrid models achieved RMSEs of 0.8308 (ATS) and 0.9259 (MT), with MAEs of 0.6764 and 0.7885, corresponding to average deviations of 11.27% and 13.14% on the 0–6 scale. This confirms the effectiveness of our approach in predicting human-annotated quality dimensions and validates modeling QoE through these identified dimensions.

5 Conclusion and Future Work

We present an approach to modeling QoE for machine-generated German text, focusing on ATS and MT. By fine-tuning pre-trained language models and integrating linguistic features, we significantly improved the prediction of perceptual quality dimensions for both text types. Our experiments showed gbert-large performed best for ATS, and gelectra-large for MT. Conducted in a low-resource setting, these results deepen understanding of QoE in NLP and highlight the value of combining neural and linguistic features for quality estimation.

To advance this work, we plan to expand our datasets with LLM-generated items rated via crowdsourcing. As initial variance analyses show no significant differences, we will integrate these with the original data. We are also developing a set of ~100 automatically extractable linguistic features to enhance model inputs and to train linear regression models for feature selection to identify the most predictive features per dimension, improving interpretability and robustness.

Limitations

We acknowledge several limitations of our study. First, the dataset of human ratings is relatively small. However, to ensure rating reliability and mitigate common issues in crowdsourced data, we prioritized collecting more ratings per item over a larger number of texts. We are currently addressing the dataset size by augmenting it with LLM-generated items, which will also help align the data with recent advances in text generation.

Second, our research is limited to the German language, so generalizability to other languages remains uncertain. Nonetheless, we help fill a gap, as most prior work in this area has focused on English.

Finally, our models have only been evaluated on MT and ATS outputs. It remains an open question how well they generalize to other types of machine-generated text; a direction we plan to explore in future studies.

Acknowledgments

We would like to thank our colleagues Aleksandra Gabryszak and Polina Danilovskaia for their valuable assistance with dataset quality control and training an early model.

The present research was funded by the Deutsche Forschungsgemeinschaft (DFG) through the project "Analyse und automatische Abschätzung der Qualität maschinell generierter Texte", project number 436813723.

References

Miriam Anschütz and Georg Groh. 2022. TUM social computing at GermEval 2022: Towards the significance of text statistics and neural embeddings in text complexity prediction. In *Proceedings of the GermEval 2022 Workshop on Text Complexity Assessment of German Text*, pages 21–26, Potsdam, Germany. Association for Computational Linguistics.

Richard Bamberger and Annette T Rabin. 1984. New approaches to readability: Austrian research. *The Reading Teacher*, 37(6):512–519.

Loïc Barrault, Ondřej Bojar, Marta R. Costa-jussà, Christian Federmann, Mark Fishel, Yvette Graham, Barry Haddow, Matthias Huck, Philipp Koehn, Shervin Malmasi, Christof Monz, Mathias Müller, Santanu Pal, Matt Post, and Marcos Zampieri. 2019. Findings of the 2019 conference on machine translation (WMT19). In *Proceedings of the Fourth Conference on Machine Translation (Volume 2: Shared Task Papers, Day 1)*, pages 1–61, Florence, Italy. Association for Computational Linguistics.

Bayerische Staatsbibliothek. 2025a. bert-base-german-cased (revision 43cce13).

Bayerische Staatsbibliothek. 2025b. bert-base-german-uncased (revision b705f0e).

Branden Chan, Stefan Schweter, and Timo Möller. 2020. German's next language model. In *Proceedings of the 28th International Conference on Computational Linguistics*, pages 6788–6796, Barcelona, Spain (Online). International Committee on Computational Linguistics.

Yi Chen, Rui Wang, Haiyun Jiang, Shuming Shi, and Ruifeng Xu. 2023. Exploring the use of Large Language Models for reference-free text quality evaluation: An empirical study. *arXiv preprint arXiv:2304.00723*.

Meri Coleman and Ta Lin Liau. 1975. A computer readability formula designed for machine scoring. *Journal of Applied Psychology*, 60(2):283.

Jacob Devlin, Ming-Wei Chang, Kenton Lee, and Kristina Toutanova. 2019. BERT: Pre-training of deep bidirectional transformers for language understanding. In *Proceedings of the 2019 Conference of the North American Chapter of the Association for Computational Linguistics: Human Language Technologies, Volume 1 (Long and Short Papers)*, pages 4171–4186.

Shibhansh Dohare and Harish Karnick. 2017. Text summarization using abstract meaning representation.

Rudolph Flesch. 1948. A new readability yardstick. *Journal of applied psychology*, 32(3):221.

Dominik Frefel. 2020. Summarization corpora of Wikipedia articles. In *Proceedings of the Twelfth Language Resources and Evaluation Conference*, pages 6651–6655, Marseille, France. European Language Resources Association.

Robert Gunning. 1952. The technique of clear writing. *(No Title)*.

Hui Huang, Shuangzhi Wu, Xinnian Liang, Bing Wang, Yanrui Shi, Peihao Wu, Muyun Yang, and Tiejun Zhao. 2023. Towards making the most of LLM for translation quality estimation. In *CCF International Conference on Natural Language Processing and Chinese Computing*, pages 375–386. Springer.

Tomoya Inagata, Yuji Mizuno, Keita Matsunaga, Fujio Kurokawa, Masaharu Tanaka, and Nobumasa Matsui. 2025. Parameter evaluation method for power demand forecasting methodology of a clinic. *IEEE Transactions on Industry Applications*, 61:930–939.

ITU-T. 2016. Mean opinion score (MOS) terminology. Recommendation ITU-T P.800.1 (07/2016).

Dulakshi Santhusitha Kumari Karunasingha. 2022. Root Mean Square Error or Mean Absolute Error? Use their ratio as well. *Information Sciences*, 585:609–629.

Reno Kriz, Marianna Apidianaki, and Chris Callison-Burch. 2020. Simple-QE: Better automatic quality estimation for text simplification. *arXiv preprint arXiv:2012.12382*.

Patrick Le Callet, Sebastian Möller, Andrew Perkis, and 1 others. 2012. Qualinet white paper on definitions of quality of experience. *European network on quality of experience in multimedia systems and services (COST Action IC 1003)*, 3(2012).

Ke Li, Yuntian Deng, and Yoon Kim. 2019. Convolutional self-attention networks. In *Proceedings of the 2019 Conference of the North American Chapter of the Association for Computational Linguistics: Human Language Technologies, Volume 1 (Long and Short Papers)*, pages 404–413.

Vivien Macketanz, Babak Naderi, Steven Schmidt, and Sebastian Möller. 2022. Perceptual quality dimensions of machine-generated text with a focus on machine translation. In *Proceedings of the 2nd Workshop on Human Evaluation of NLP Systems (HumEval)*, pages 24–31.

Shushen Manakhimova, Vivien Macketanz, and Sebastian Möller. 2025. Quality of experience of german machine translation and automatic text summarization. Halle/Saale. In press.

Matej Martinc, Senja Pollak, and Marko Robnik-Šikonja. 2021. Supervised and unsupervised neural approaches to text readability. *Computational Linguistics*, 47(1):141–179.

G Harry Mc Laughlin. 1969. Smog grading-a new readability formula. *Journal of reading*, 12(8):639–646.

Danielle S McNamara, Arthur C Graesser, Philip M McCarthy, and Zhiqiang Cai. 2014. *Automated evaluation of text and discourse with Coh-Metrix*. Cambridge University Press.

Rada Mihalcea and Paul Tarau. 2004. Textrank: Bringing order into texts. In *Proceedings of the 2004 Conference on Empirical Methods in Natural Language Processing*, pages 404–411.

Salar Mohtaj, Vera Schmitt, Razieh Khamsehashari, and Sebastian Möller. 2023. Multi-task learning for German text readability assessment. In *CLiC-it*.

Babak Naderi. 2018. *Motivation of Workers on Microtask Crowdsourcing Platforms*, 1st edition. Springer Publishing Company, Incorporated.

Babak Naderi, Salar Mohtaj, Kaspar Ensikat, and Sebastian Möller. 2019. Subjective assessment of text complexity: A dataset for German language. *Preprint*, arXiv:1904.07733.

Charles Egerton Osgood. 1957. *The Measurement of Meaning*. University of Illinois Press, Urbana,.

Emily Pitler and Ani Nenkova. 2008. Revisiting readability: A unified framework for predicting text quality. In *Proceedings of the 2008 conference on empirical methods in natural language processing*, pages 186–195.

Brian Richards. 1987. Type/token ratios: What do they really tell us? *Journal of child language*, 14(2):201–209.

Valentino Santucci, Filippo Santarelli, Luciana Forti, and Stefania Spina. 2020. Automatic classification of text complexity. *Applied Sciences*, 10(20):7285.

Abigail See, Peter J Liu, and Christopher D Manning. 2017. Get to the point: Summarization with pointer-generator networks. *arXiv preprint arXiv:1704.04368*.

Laura Seiffe, Fares Kallel, Sebastian Möller, Babak Naderi, and Roland Roller. 2022. Subjective text complexity assessment for German. In *Proceedings of the Thirteenth Language Resources and Evaluation Conference*, pages 707–714.

Sanja Štajner and Ioana Hulpus. 2020. *When shallow is good enough: Automatic assessment of conceptual text complexity using shallow semantic features*. European Language Resources Association, ELRA-ELDA.

Ashish Vaswani, Noam Shazeer, Niki Parmar, Jakob Uszkoreit, Llion Jones, Aidan N Gomez, Lukasz Kaiser, and Illia Polosukhin. 2017. Attention is all you need. In *Advances in Neural Information Processing Systems*, pages 5998–6008.

Cort J. Willmott and Kenji Matsuura. 2005. Advantages of the Mean Absolute Error (MAE) over the Root Mean Square Error (RMSE) in assessing average model performance. *Climate Research*, 30:79–82.

Evaluation of Machine Translation Errors in German Plain Language Texts in the Domain of Health Information

Sarah Ahrens, Silvana Deilen, Sergio Hernández Garrido, Ekaterina Lapshinova-Koltunski, Christiane Maaß
University of Hildesheim
ahrenss,deilen,hernandezs,lapshinovakoltun,maass@uni-hildesheim.de

Abstract

This paper presents the findings of a study evaluating intralingual machine translation of health information texts. In Germany, the National Action Plan Health Literacy addresses the poor performance of large population groups in this area by means of accessible communication measures, including the use of Plain Language. Machine translation can help here by making more Plain Language texts available. We thus evaluate the machine-generated Plain Language translations produced by two different state-of-the-art models and present the results of our error analysis. Our study reveals that in all categories, both models contain a high number of errors, however, the error distribution differs across the two models under analysis. The paper presents the elaborated evaluation scheme in detail, gives an overview of quantitative results and provides examples of most frequent errors occurring in both translation outputs.

1 Introduction

In the last few years, several studies have examined the quality of Machine Translation (MT) tools for intralingual translation (Anschütz et al., 2023; Deilen et al., 2023, 2024a). However, most studies on intralingual MT have analysed the quality of the output merely on the textual level, using automatic quality metrics. While some studies also mention and discuss the correctness of the generated content, so far none of them has specifically focused on a fine-grained error analysis. Understanding the types and frequency of errors and error categories in MT-generated texts is crucial, particularly in domains where clarity and accessibility are essential. Research has shown that large sections of the population in Germany have very low levels of health literacy (Schaeffer et al., 2017). The National Action Plan for Health Literacy (Schaeffer et al., 2018b) addresses this problem through accessibility measures. Plain Language is explicitly mentioned here as one of the measures to be systematically applied. However, as the need and demand for Plain Language texts are extremely high and continue to grow, it is becoming increasingly difficult to provide high-quality human translations for all the existing source texts. Consequently, the question arises whether the increasing demand for accessible Plain Language texts could be met by using MT systems and whether MT tools are capable of producing accurate, target-oriented, and functional intralingual translations. Such texts would have to meet the needs of the low literacy target groups and the institutional personnel in the health sector that is interacting with them.

This paper investigates the quality of machine translations of health information texts into Plain German, especially focusing on error typology. In our study, we analyse the machine translations from two different MT systems (SUMM AI and ChatGPT-4o) and classify the identified errors using an adapted version of the Multidimensional Quality Metrics (MQM) framework (Lommel et al., 2014).

2 Related Work

2.1 Translation error analysis

Existing frameworks for error analysis in interlingual translation (both human and machine translation) are widely applied, such as the MQM framework proposed by Lommel et al. (2014). These frameworks typically classify errors based on linguistic categories and assess them according to scoring systems and severity levels. However, to our knowledge, no widely established error evaluation scheme currently exists for intralingual translation. Rodríguez Vázquez et al. (2022) use the MQM scheme to evaluate comprehensible text output, but their study design still focuses on automated interlingual translation of Easy Language texts (for a distinction between Easy Language and

Proceedings of the 21st Conference on Natural Language Processing (KONVENS), Volume 2: Workshops, pages 176–185, 2025

Plain Language, see 2.2). Existing studies that evaluate automated intralingual translation known to us focus only on the surface features of translations, comparing their readability scores or syntactic complexity (Deilen et al., 2024a,b). Although the authors investigate the context correctness or incorrectness of the automatically produced translations, they report only on individual errors. No systematic description of error types is given.

2.2 Plain German

In Germany, both *Easy Language* (Leichte Sprache) and *Plain Language* (Einfache Sprache) belong to the field of intralingual translation (Hansen-Schirra et al., 2020; Maaß, 2020; Maaß, 2024b). Even though both language varieties aim to improve comprehensibility of texts, they are used in different communication settings and have different levels of complexity and therefore also different target groups. Easy Language is characterized by a maximally reduced complexity on all linguistic levels and is mainly intended for people with communication impairments. In contrast, Plain Language is a flexible, dynamic variety. The linguistic features of Plain Language are more complex and mainly intended for non-experts with average or slightly below average language or reading skills (Maaß, 2020; Maaß, 2024b). Also, Plain Language does not have the stigmatizing features that are often associated with Easy Language, which is one of the reasons why it is more acceptable to most users than Easy Language (Maaß, 2020). Plain Language has also gained increased recognition in recent years, with an increasing number of initiatives being implemented that propose Plain Language as a preferred means of accessible (specialized) communication. Currently, Plain Language is, for example, used to increase accessibility in the medical domain and overall in the health sector in Germany (Ahrens and Maaß, 2024).

2.3 Studies on (machine) translation and health communication

Kröger and Maaß (2024) address the problem of accessibility of health information. The authors analyse a small corpus of texts from the apotheken-umschau.de website[1]. They find the standard texts to lack comprehensibility, particularly focusing on readability scores and the use of terminology. They conclude that to comprehend existing standard texts, the reader needs to have prior knowledge of the respective topic of the text. Like Deilen et al. (2024a), Kröger and Maaß (2024) find moderate readability scores among the Apotheken Umschau standard texts that do not reach Plain Language readability levels. More and more texts containing health information are manually translated into Plain German. The use of machine translation, and specifically Large Language Models (LLMs) in the translation process of health communication texts may speed up the intralingual translation process. This would allow for a larger amount of health communication texts in Plain Language improving in this way access to health information (Schaeffer et al., 2018a), particularly to groups that score lower on health literacy surveys (like lower socio-economic status, a different first language or lower education levels, see for example (Schaeffer et al., 2021)). Improved access to health information may in turn increase health literacy (Rossmann and Hastall, 2019). However, studies have revealed that people have particular trouble appraising the quality, trustworthiness and commercial interest and how health information applies to their own situation (Schaeffer et al., 2021). The use of LLMs – if not properly monitored – may exacerbate this issue. Weidinger et al. (2022) discuss different risk areas concerning Language Models. One risk area is "misinformation harms": LLM-generated false information may threaten the reader's autonomy, increase their trust in false beliefs, amplify distrust in shared knowledge, and even cause bodily harm. These issues make unedited LLM-generated texts unsafe for users (Maaß, 2024a). Wilhelm et al. (2023) compare the health information output of four LLMs (like GPT-3.5-Turbo) considering completeness, correctness and harmfulness. The LLMs are prompted with the question "How to treat [disease]". In general, the outputs contain balanced and unbiased information and therefore seemed promising. Yet, they do not mention risks and potential harms of suggested treatments (completeness) and also give wrong or harmful information. The only reported system that does not generate harmful health information in this study is GPT-3.5-Turbo. Overall, the authors conclude that professional proof-reading of the outputs is necessary. However, a systematic description of common errors is still missing.

[1] *Apotheken Umschau* is a German health magazine, which publishes healthcare articles and health information.

3 Research Design

3.1 Data collection

We use parts of the dataset from Deilen et al. (2024a,b), which is based on the text corpus of the *Apotheken Umschau*. The corpus from Deilen et al. (2024a,b) consists of 30 source texts in standard German which were automatically translated into Plain Language using three different models of the SUMM AI[2] machine translation system. SUMM AI is a tool specifically developed for translating texts into Easy German and Plain German. This intralingual translation tool is based on an LLM, but also employs Easy and Plain Language parameters. Unlike ChatGPT, which is a generalized LLM not specifically developed for intralingual translation, the SUMM AI models are fine-tuned with rules and domain specific data, such as intralingual human gold-standard translations. However, unlike ChatGPT, the model cannot be prompted by the user. For Plain Language translation, SUMM AI started with a baseline model, which was a generically trained LLM. As explained by Deilen et al. (2024a) they then fine-tuned two other models (which are referred to as model 1 and model 2) using domain-specific source texts and human gold-standard translations. Model 1 and model 2 had different underlying LLMs but were fine-tuned with the same data. An evaluation of the output of the three models (baseline, model 1, model 2) by Deilen et al. (2024a) revealed that in terms of correctness, readability and text simplification scores (SARI), model 2 performed best. The SARI score (Xu et al., 2016), which is a quantitative measure to evaluate automatic text simplification systems, "compares system output against references and against the input sentence" (Xu et al., 2016).

As Deilen et al. (2024a) report that model 2 was the best of the three SUMM AI models, we compare it with ChatGPT. We aim to test whether a model that was specifically developed and fine-tuned for intralingual translation of health information outperforms a general LLM.

The intralingual translations with ChatGPT are generated using a two-step prompt. The prompt was developed based on findings from Deilen et al. (2023) who showed that assigning a role, setting a context and asking for background information seemed to improve the model's output. In the first step, ChatGPT was asked to define Plain Language in the field of accessible communication and inclusion:

"ChatGPT, wie wird im Bereich der Barrierefreien Kommunikation und der Inklusion „Einfache Sprache" definiert?" [ChatGPT, how is "Plain Language" defined in the field of Accessible Communication and inclusion?].

In a second step, ChatGPT was prompted to take on the role of a Plain Language expert:

"ChatGPT, du bist jetzt ein Experte für Einfache Sprache. Wir brauchen Unterstützung in der Übersetzung eines Textes der Gesundheitskommunikation in Einfache Sprache. In dem Text geht es um [hier Thema einfügen]. Die Übersetzung soll für Menschen mit Leseschwierigkeiten leicht verständlich sein. Übersetze bitte den folgenden Text:" [ChatGPT, you are now an expert in Plain Language. We need help translating a health communication text into Plain Language. The text is about [insert topic]. The translation should be easily comprehensible for people who have difficulty reading. Please translate the following text:]

Using the text corpus from Deilen et al. (2024a), we apply the interlingual translation error framework MQM (Multidimensional Quality Metrics, Lommel et al. (2014) to this intralingual corpus. MQM contains a variety of common translation error types. Depending on the project, certain error types are chosen and analysed in the source and target text. We intended to identify content-related errors (terminology and accuracy), errors related to common linguistic conventions like spelling, and the manner in which the audience is addressed, as well as how health messages are conveyed (audience appropriateness). The analysis did not evaluate the adherence to Plain Language guidelines. While SUMM AI adheres to a certain set of rules, ChatGPT does not. Additionally, as stated in section 2.2, Plain Language is flexible and dynamic. It is therefore of little interest to analyse the adherence to any specific guideline.

3.2 Data analysis

We analysed error types manually according to an adapted MQM scheme (Council, n.d.). We used four error types that we exemplify with the most meaningful sub-categories.

Terminology The use of a term does not fit to the field conventions, is incorrectly used in the target text or is not equivalent to the term in the source

[2] The company SUMM AI (`https://summ-ai.com/en/`) offers different licenses for freelancers, authorities and companies.

text. Also, multiple terms are used when just one term is appropriate.
Inconsistent terminology: Multiple terms are used to describe the same concept when just one term is needed or appropriate and consistency is desirable. For example, *birth control pill* and *contraceptive pill* used in the same text.
Wrong term: Use of term that it is not the term a domain expert would use or that gives rise to a conceptual mismatch. For instance *Hautprobleme* (skin problems) is used instead of *Hautveränderung* (skin change).

Accuracy Content in the target text does not match the propositions from the source text. This category has numerous subcategories that can be divided into further subgroups.
Mistranslation: Errors occurring when the target content does not accurately represent the source content. (1) Mistranslation of technical relations: In the target text, the relation between two elements is not presented in a technically appropriate way, even though the translation solution sometimes seems to be plausible at first glance. We provide examples of this case in Section 4.2. (2) Ambiguous target content: Ambiguity is introduced in the target where specificity is needed, e.g. the use of *Training* (training) instead of *Ausdauersport* (endurance sports). (3) Ambiguous source content: Ambiguous source content rendered in the target content inappropriately is illustrated in Section 4.2. (4) Hallucination: Output is decoupled from the source text or contains information that is not in the source text. We illustrate some cases in Section 4.2. Further subcategories include also incorrect conversion of numeric values, numbers, dates, or times.
Wrong addition: Necessary explanation is added, but does not represent the information from the source text or is wrong.
Missing addition: An explanation is needed, but was not added. For instance, various bacteria, such as Salmonella, Campylobacter, Listeria, were mentioned in the target text, but their differences were not explained.
Completeness: Relevant information from the source text is missing in the output. This may include incomplete details or also lists, e.g. for *Acetylsalicylsäure, Ibuprofen, Diclofenac und Paracetamol* (Acetylsalicylic acid, ibuprofen, diclofenac and paracetamol) in the source text, we find only *Aspirin, Ibuprofen und Paracetamol* (Aspirin, ibuprofen and paracetamol) in the target text.

Linguistic conventions *Grammar, punctuation, spelling:* grammatical errors, punctuation errors, and spelling errors. For instance, the phrase *manche psychische Probleme* (some psychological problems) has the wrong form of adjective (*psychische* instead of *psychischen*). Another example is the wrong spelling in *Reisenimpfungen* instead of *Reiseimpfungen* (Travel vaccinations).
Further cases: errors related to the textual cohesion and coherence, such as unclear references (see examples in Section 4.2). Apart from unclear references, texts may miss portions of text needed to connect the text into an understandable whole (connectives or lexical cohesion). This may result in a text which lacks a clear semantic relation between its parts, and in extreme cases it even does not make sense. For instance, in the question *Hat die Frau schon einmal schwere Erkrankungen in der Familie gehabt?* (Has the woman ever had serious illnesses in her family?), the semantic link between the woman, illnesses and family is missing. It should be rather *Hat die Frau schwere Erkrankungen gehabt* (Has the woman had any serious illnesses?) or *Hat die Familie der Frau schwere Erkrankungen gehabt?* (Has the woman's family had serious illnesses?).

Audience appropriateness Content in the target text is not valid, appropriate or acceptable for the target audiences. This may include (1) inaccurate advice – the target text contains advice that is not in the source text or that is not suitable for the target situation, or (2) stigmatising content – content can lead to stigmatization of end users. For instance the use of informal forms is a common stigmatising error[3].: *Ab 35 Jahren kannst <u>du</u> alle zwei Jahre eine Hautuntersuchung bei deiner Krankenkasse machen lassen.* (From the age of 35, you can have a skin examination every two years with your health insurance company). Another error is related to (3) the modality, if the same instruction is given in the source and target text, but with different intensity. For instance, the translation *Kinder sollten das nicht allein machen* (Children should not do this alone.) does not have the same intensity of advice as the source text *...das heiße Gebräu von Kindern fernhalten* (keep the hot brew away from children).

[3]In German, there is a distinction between informal and formal second-person pronouns: "du" is used for informal address (e.g., with children, friends or family), while "Sie" is the formal form, used in professional or public contexts. In official communications, such as those with health institutions, the formal form of address ("Sie") is expected.

Before the annotation of the whole corpus, the elaborated error analysis scheme was proved in a consensual validation process. All our human annotators are trained linguists with good knowledge of Plain German. Three annotators independently analysed a text generated with the MT system by SUMM AI, which we refer to as SUMM MT [4], and further two researchers did the same on the ChatGPT-generated text. The analysis of ChatGPT-generated texts was faster, since these translations are much shorter (see Section 4.1 for details). The results of the independent analyses were compared qualitatively and the following cases were discussed:

- One annotator categorised an error, but another did not;
- One annotator identified the same error as another annotator, but categorised it into a different category.

In this process of consensual validation, the error analysis scheme was modified and updated. The definition of labels were more clearly described. This made them more distinguishable from each other, and more fitting examples were chosen. Afterwards, the same annotators worked on the corpus, with, however, different texts assigned to them. For each text, one annotator analysed a text for errors. The same text was then cross-checked by another annotator. As a result, more errors were identified or the existing annotations were consistently checked for their categories.

In this paper, we present the quantitative comparison of error types across the two translation variants. We also qualitatively compare the outputs providing some examples of frequent errors.

In addition, we also calculated the SARI score for the ChatGPT output and compared it to the different models from SUMM AI.

4 Results

4.1 Overall performance

The first observation is the significant difference in text length: On average, the SUMM MT texts are three times as long as the ChatGPT texts (1225 words vs. 418 words). In the first step, we look into distributions of the four error types across the two translation outputs. Since the text length in the two translation variants varies strongly (see Figure 1), we normalise the distributions per total number of tokens in each translation variant. As seen from Figure 2, the outputs by ChatGPT contain more errors overall. At the same time, the distribution across the four error types defined above, varies in both outputs.

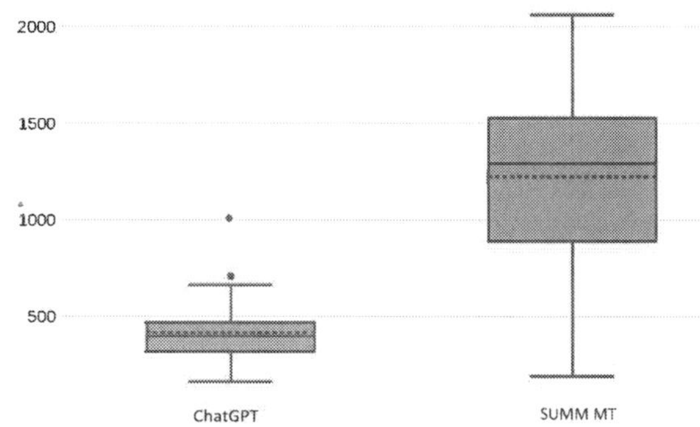

Figure 1: Text length in ChatGPT and SUMM MT outputs measured in tokens.

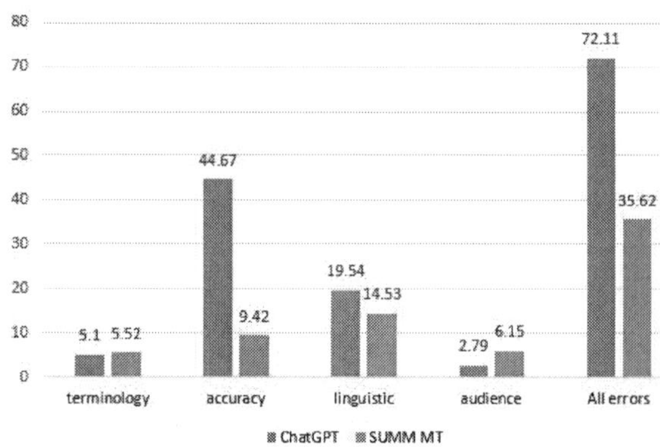

Figure 2: Annotated error distribution in ChatGPT and SUMM MT translations normalised against the total number of tokens (per 1000).

The outputs by ChatGPT contain far more accuracy errors than translations with SUMM MT (44.67 vs. 9.42). SUMM MT outperforms ChatGPT in the accuracy and linguistic convention categories. At the same time, ChatGPT outperforms SUMM MT in terms of audience appropriateness (2.79 vs. 6.15). In the category of terminology, both models show similar results (5.10 vs. 5.52).

To better understand which error categories prevail in ChatGPT and SUMM MT outputs separately, the distribution of error categories normalised per total number of errors within each translation output is illustrated in Figure 3.

It is interesting to see that the distribution of categories differs in the two translation variants.

[4]The term SUMM MT refers to the above-mentioned best-performing model 2 by SUMM AI.

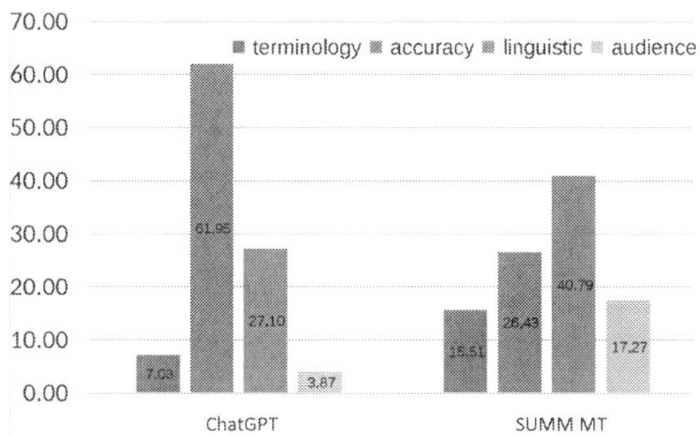

Figure 3: Error category distribution within each translation output normalised against the total number of errors in %.

While translations with ChatGPT definitely suffer from a high number of accuracy errors, translations with SUMM MT have a more even distribution with none of the category achieving even 50%.

4.2 Fine-grained differences

In the following, we analyse some specific examples of errors in the two translation outputs.

Terminology We start with the errors in terminology use. The first error type is 'Inconsistent terminology' illustrated in example (1). The source text contains two variants of the term *Antibabypille* (birth control pill) and *Pille* (pill). So do both automatic translations.

(1) a Source: *Die Antibabypille schützt gut vor einer ungewollten Schwangerschaft und ist einfach anzuwenden. Wir informieren über die Wirkung, Vorteile und Nachteile der Pille.* (The contraceptive pill is a reliable method of contraception and easy to use. We provide information about the effect, advantages and disadvantages of the pill.)

b ChatGPT: *Die Antibabypille ist ein Medikament, das gut vor Schwangerschaft schützt und einfach angewendet werden kann. Wir erklären, was die Pille bewirkt und ihre Vor- und Nachteile.* (The contraceptive pill is a medication that provides good protection against pregnancy and is easy to use. We explain what the pill does and its advantages and disadvantages.)

c SUMM MT: *Die Antibabypille verhindert eine Schwangerschaft. Sie ist leicht zu benutzen. Wir erklären, wie die Pille wirkt.* (The contraceptive pill prevents pregnancy. It is easy to use. We explain how the pill works.)

Accuracy The next case illustrated in example (2) belongs to the category of accuracy and demonstrates mistranslation of technical relation that occurs in the outputs produced with ChatGPT.

(2) a Source: *Der Zeitraum, in dem wechseljahrsbedingte Hitzewallungen oder Nachtschweiß häufig vorkommen, dauert einer Studie zufolge durchschnittlich 7,4 Jahre* (According to a study, the period in which menopause-related hot flashes or night sweats frequently occur lasts an average of 7.4 years.)

b ChatGPT: *Im Durchschnitt dauern Hitzewallungen etwa 7,4 Jahre.* (On average, hot flashes last about 7.4 years.)

c SUMM MT: *Die Zeit, in der Hitzewallungen und Nacht-Schweiß vorkommen, dauert durchschnittlich 7,4 Jahre.* (The period in which hot flushes and night sweats occur lasts an average of 7.4 years.).

Here, the mistranslation in the ChatGPT output also includes a change in meaning. While the source text states that the phase in which these symptoms commonly occur lasts on average 7.4 years, the translation by ChatGPT implies that hot flashes themselves last that long, which is misleading and incorrect. Although the SUMM MT translation does not contain this kind of error, we observe here a syntactic problem instead: due to the relative clauses inserted, the sentence is too complex.

Another example of a mistranslation of a technical relation is the use of a wrong verb, e.g. *Warndreieck aufsetzen* (put on a warning triangle) instead of *Warndreieck aufstellen* (put up a warning triangle). This error subtype is more frequent in the ChatGPT translations than in the SUMM MT ones (65.4 vs. 27.5, normalised per 10,000 against the total number of words in translations).

In example (3), we deal with ambiguous source content, another subcategory of the accuracy errors.

(3) a Source: *Setzen Sie Minzöl bei Spannungskopfschmerzen ein, massieren Sie das verdünnte Öl direkt auf der schmerzenden Stelle ein oder träufeln es vorher auf ein Tuch, um das dann zu verwenden.* (Use mint oil for tension headaches. Massage the diluted oil

directly onto the painful area or drip it onto a cloth first and use that.)

b ChatGPT: *Gegen Spannungskopfschmerzen massieren Sie das verdünnte Öl direkt auf die schmerzende Stelle oder benutzen ein Tuch.* (Against tension headaches, massage the diluted oil directly onto the painful area or use a cloth.)

c SUMM MT: *Massieren Sie das verdünnte Öl auf die schmerzende Stelle. Oder geben Sie das Öl auf ein Tuch und legen Sie das Tuch auf die schmerzende Stelle.* (Massage the diluted oil onto the painful area. Or apply the oil to a cloth and place the cloth on the painful area.)

There is information missing in the ChatGPT translation illustrated in (3-b): It remains unclear what exactly to do with the cloth. The translation with SUMM MT in (3-c) instead provides the necessary details.

Another case of accuracy errors includes hallucinations. Example (4) is is a translation with ChatGPT that confuses the source concepts *gesunder Lebensstil* (healthy lifestyle) and *schlaffördernde Verhaltensweisen* (sleep-improving behaviours). It hallucinates the sleep-improving acts of going to bed at regular times and not having any heavy meals before bed time as being examples of a healthy lifestyle. All the while not mentioning the sleep-improving behaviours, leaving the reader with faulty action-orientation.

(4) a Source: *Selbsthilfemaßnahmen wie gesunder Lebensstil und den Schlaf fördernde Verhaltensweisen* (Self-help measures like a healthy lifestyle and sleep-improving behaviours)

b ChatGPT: *Gesunder Lebensstil: Regelmäßig schlafen gehen, keine schweren Mahlzeiten vor dem Schlaf.* (Healthy lifestyle: Go to bed regularly, no heavy meals before sleep).

In general, ChatGPT contains much more accuracy errors of the hallucination subtype than SUMM MT: 33.5 vs. 11.7 (frequencies per 10,000 normalised against the total number of words).

Linguistic conventions This category contains many spelling and punctuation errors, as well as grammar errors such as missing definite articles. Cohesion and coherence, as well as cases of unclear reference are also common. An example of unclear reference is illustrated in examples (5) and (6). The word *Gerät* (device) does not have any antecedents in the preceding sentence(s). It is a result of translating the subheading "*Mit dem Blutdruckmessgerät verbunden*" (Connected to the blood pressure monitor), and is, therefore, wrong.

(5) a Source: *Mit Medikamenten und einem gesunden Lebensstil gelingt es den meisten, zu hohe Werte langfristig zu senken. Digitale Helfer können die Therapie unterstützen und den Umgang mit der Krankheit erleichtern. Mit dem Blutdruckmessgerät verbunden.* (Most people may reduce high values with medication and a healthy lifestyle over the long term. Digital aids can support therapy and make it easier to deal with the disease. Connected to the blood pressure monitor.

b SUMM MT: *Mit Medikamenten und einem gesunden Lebens-Stil können Sie den Blut-Druck senken. Digitale Helfer können dabei unterstützen. <u>Das Gerät</u> ist mit dem Blut-Druck-Messer verbunden.* (You can lower your blood pressure with medication and a healthy lifestyle. Digital helpers can provide support. The device is connected to the blood pressure meter.)

(6) a Source: *Telemedizin ersetzt nicht den persönlichen Kontakt. Eine gewisse Offenheit für den Einsatz von Computer und Smartphone sowie eine sichere und stabile Internetverbindung vorausgesetzt, ist die Telemedizin aber eine sinnvolle Ergänzung.* (Telemedicine is no substitute for face-to-face contact. However, telemedicine is a useful addition, provided you are open to the use of computers and smartphones and have a secure and stable internet connection.)

b SUMM MT: *Aber: Telemedizin ersetzt nicht den Arzt-Besuch. Sie brauchen <u>dafür</u>:* (But: Telemedicine does not replace a visit to the doctor. You need for this:)

Example (6) contains the referring expression *dafür* (for this), a pronominal adverb in German which may refer to a prepositional phrase or to a clause or sentence. This reference in the context in (6-b) is ambiguous, since it may refer to both *Telemedizin* (telemedicine) and also to *Arzt-Besuch* (visit to the doctor).

Audience appropriateness This type of error was mostly related to the use of advice that was not contained in the source text, and that was not appropriate for the target readership at the same time. Another frequent type of errors were stigmatising elements.

Example (7-a) contains the advice *suchen Sie im Internet nach Informationen* (search the web for more information) which is not in the source text and is not appropriate for the target audience. Example (7-b) demonstrates stigmatising content, as the text contains the 2nd person plural *ihr*, which is the informal address in German where the formal address would be required. Moreover, the expression *passt auf!* (Watch out!) is also informal and a way patronising or even infantilising, which is definitely not approrpiate in the current context.

(7) a SUMM MT: *Sie wollen mehr wissen? Dann fragen Sie Ihren Arzt. Oder suchen Sie im Internet nach Informationen.* (Do you want to know more? Then ask your doctor. Or search the web for information).

b ChatGPT: *Wenn ihr keine Inhalationsgeräte habt und eine Schüssel benutzt, passt auf!* (If you do not have an inhaler and use a bowl, watch out!)

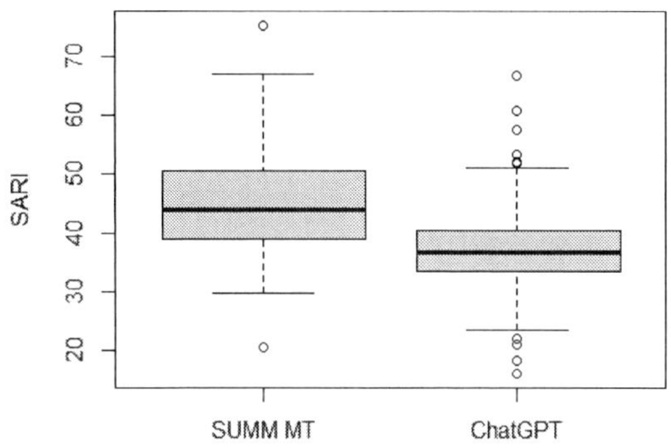

Figure 4: SARI score of the machine translation output from SUMM MT and ChatGPT.

4.3 Automatic evaluation measures

In addition to the error analyes, we also calculated the SARI score, which is a text simplification metric. Figure 4 shows the SARI score of the machine translation output from SUMM MT as well as the SARI score of the ChatGPT texts, with higher SARI values indicating better machine translated outputs. Comparing ChatGPT with SUMM AI reveals that ChatGPT performs worse than SUMM MT. This result is in line with the results by Ahrens et al. (2025) who also found that in terms of readability and syntactic complexity, the models by SUMM AI outperformed ChatGPT. However, it has to be kept in mind that the SARI score is only calculated on the text surface and does not take into account how well a text adheres, for example, to official guidelines and Plain Language rules.

5 Discussion and Future Work

In our study, we compared the performance of two machine translation systems, ChatGPT and SUMM MT, on a dataset of German health information texts. We carried out a fine-grained error analysis of the translations, using a scheme based on the MQM framework that was applied to intralingual translation. We analyzed the errors in the MT outputs and categorized them, following the MQM scheme, into four types: terminology, accuracy, linguistic conventions, and audience appropriateness. The results show that ChatGPT contains more accuracy errors than SUMM MT and that SUMM MT also outperforms ChatGPT in the linguistic convention category. ChatGPT, on the other hand, outperforms SUMM MT in terms of audience appropriateness. The errors in the translations include mistranslations, ambiguous content, and hallucinations. The results suggest that SUMM MT has a more even distribution of error categories than ChatGPT, while the latter suffers from an exceedingly high number of accuracy errors.

The results can be explained by differences between the models. The SUMM AI model outperforms ChatGPT in almost all analysed criteria and error categories. This suggests that fine-tuning a model both with task-specific data (i.e., the task of intralingual translation into Plain Language), and with domain-specific data (health information texts from *Apotheken Umschau*), improves MT into Plain German. Therefore, for our study we can conclude that fine-tuned models that are trained specifically for intralingual translation tasks outperform the general model that uses prompting.

The analysis of error categories and specific errors has revealed a high number of errors with respect to accuracy and audience appropriateness. Health information is a safety-critical domain, so these errors can be regarded as more severe than, for example, spelling errors. Our study thus confirms findings by existing studies (Deilen et al., 2024b; Maaß, 2024a; Wilhelm et al., 2023) that the automatically produced outputs cannot be used safely by end users. Although machine translation does facilitate intralingual translation, without human intervention in form of post-editing, it is not suitable for achieving the goal of increasing health literacy.

In our future studies, we also aim to assess error severity, following MQM settings and recommendations. Besides that, we plan to investigate whether the high error rate, especially in terms of accuracy, might be reduced by using best-practice prompting strategies that specifically aim to mitigate accuracy errors.

In addition, we plan to analyse the cases of disagreement between the annotators which may indicate interesting ambiguous cases.

Limitations

The error analysis was conducted with a larger team of annotators with one team annotating SUMM MT and separate team annotating the ChatGPT corpus. It is possible that error categories have been assessed differently between the sub-corpora. An annotation process with only two annotators who both annotate both corpora would have been more reliable. Another limitation is that we have not yet assessed error severity. However, doing so is important for the overall evaluation, as the impact of different error types can vary significantly. For instance, content-related errors (e.g., mistranslations or omissions) can alter the meaning of a sentence and pose a much greater risk than more superficial issues such as spelling or punctuation mistakes. Future work will integrate a severity scale to differentiate between critical and minor errors, which will allow for a more detailed evaluation of translation quality. Also, this study is limited by the amount of data. Our evaluation was only conducted on a selected set of translations from one domain, which limits the generalization of our findings. Therefore, in future studies, we will also extend the analysis to texts from other domains. A study such as this contains error-prone texts in a field where misinformation is can be dangerous. Therefore, user testing cannot ethically be performed.

References

Sarah Ahrens, Silvana Deilen, Ekaterina Lapshinova-Koltunski, Sergio Hernández Garrido, and Christiane Maaß. 2025. Evaluation of translations into plain german produced by humans and mt systems including chatgpt. *SKASE Journal of Translation and Interpretation*. In press.

Sarah Ahrens and Christiane Maaß. 2024. Der Einfluss von Vorwissen und sprachlichen Texteigenschaften auf die Anwendung des Fragebogens in einer gynäkologischen Patientenaufklärung: eine leitfadengestützte Interviewstudie. *Prävention und Gesundheitsförderung*, 19:504–511.

Miriam Anschütz, Joshua Oehms, Thomas Wimmer, Bartłomiej Jezierski, and Georg Groh. 2023. Language models for german text simplification: Overcoming parallel data scarcity through style-specific pre-training. *arXiv preprint arXiv:2305.12908*.

The MQM Council. n.d. The MQM error typology. Last accessed on Feb 18th 2025.

Silvana Deilen, Sergio Hernández Garrido, Ekaterina Lapshinova-Koltunski, and Christiane Maaß. 2023. Using chatgpt as a cat tool in easy language translation. *arXiv preprint arXiv:2308.11563*.

Silvana Deilen, Ekaterina Lapshinova-Koltunski, Sergio Garrido, Julian Hörner, Christiane Maaß, Vanessa Theel, and Sophie Ziemer. 2024a. Evaluation of intralingual machine translation for health communication. In *Proceedings of the 25th Annual Conference of the European Association for Machine Translation (Volume 1)*, pages 469–479.

Silvana Deilen, Ekaterina Lapshinova-Koltunski, Sergio Hernández Garrido, Christiane Maaß, Julian Hörner, Vanessa Theel, and Sophie Ziemer. 2024b. Towards AI-supported Health Communication in Plain Language: Evaluating Intralingual Machine Translation of Medical Texts. In *Proceedings of the First Workshop on Patient-Oriented Language Processing (CL4Health)@ LREC-COLING 2024*, pages 44–53.

Silvia Hansen-Schirra, Walter Bisang, Arne Nagels, Silke Gutermuth, Julia Fuchs, Liv Borghardt, Silvana Deilen, Anne-Kathrin Gros, Laura Schiffl, and Johanna Sommer. 2020. Intralingual translation into Easy language–or how to reduce cognitive processing costs. *Easy Language Research: Text and User Perspectives. Berlin: Frank & Timme*, pages 197–225.

Janina Kröger and Christiane Maaß. 2024. Mangelnde verständlichkeit durch fachsprache in gesundheitsinformationen zu chronischen erkrankungen – eine qualitative korpusanalyse. *Prävention und Gesundheitsförderung*, 19:497–503.

Arle Lommel, Hans Uszkoreit, and Aljoscha Burchardt. 2014. Multidimensional quality metrics (MQM): A framework for declaring and describing translation quality metrics. *Tradumàtica*, 12:0455–463.

Christiane Maaß. 2020. *Easy language–Plain language–Easy language plus: Balancing comprehensibility and acceptability*. Frank & Timme.

Christiane Maaß. 2024a. Hi ChatGPT, translate this text into Easy Language. Is the new Easy Language translator a machine? In *Proceedings of the XLIV International VAKKI Symposium*.

Christiane Maaß. 2024b. Intralingual Translation in Easy Language and Plain Language. In *Routledge Handbook of Intralingual Translation*, pages 234–251. Routledge.

Silvia Rodríguez Vázquez, Abigail Kaplan, Pierrette Bouillon, Cornelia Griebel, and Razieh Azari. 2022. La traduction automatique des textes faciles à lire et à comprendre (falc): une étude comparative. *Meta*, 67(1):18–49.

Constanze Rossmann and Matthias R Hastall. 2019. *Handbuch der Gesundheitskommunikation*. Springer.

Doris Schaeffer, Eva-Maria Berens, Svea Gille, Lennert Griese, Klinger Julia, Steffen de Sombre, Dominique Vogt, and Klaus Hurrelmann. 2021. *Gesundheitskompetenz der Bevölkerung in Deutschland vor und während der Corona Pandemie: Ergebnisse des HLS-GER 2*. Universität Bielefeld, Interdisziplinäres Zentrum für Gesundheitskompetenzforschung.

Doris Schaeffer, Klaus Hurrelmann, Ullrich Bauer, and Kai Kolpatzik. 2018a. *National Action Plan Health Literacy. Promoting health literacy in Germany*. Kompart, Berlin.

Doris Schaeffer, Klaus Hurrelmann, Ulrich Bauer, Kai Kolpatzik, and Attila Altiner. 2018b. *Nationaler Aktionsplan Gesundheitskompetenz: die Gesundheitskompetenz in Deutschland stärken: Informationen bewerten, finden, anwenden, verstehen*. Hertie School of Governance.

Doris Schaeffer, Dominique Vogt, Eva-Maria Berens, and Klaus Hurrelmann. 2017. Gesundheitskompetenz der bevölkerung in deutschland: ergebnisbericht.

Laura Weidinger, Jonathan Uesato, Maribeth Rauh, Conor Griffin, Po-Sen Huang, John Mellor, Amelia Glaese, Myra Cheng, Borja Balle, Atoosa Kasirzadeh, Courtney Biles, Sasha Brown, Zac Kenton, Will Hawkins, Tom Stepleton, Abeba Birhane, Lisa Anne Hendricks, Laura Rimell, William Isaac, and 4 others. 2022. Taxonomy of Risks posed by Language Models. In *Proceedings of the 2022 ACM Conference on Fairness, Accountability, and Transparency*, FAccT '22, page 214–229, New York, NY, USA. Association for Computing Machinery.

Theresa Isabelle Wilhelm, Jonas Roos, and Robert Kaczmarczyk. 2023. Large language models for therapy recommendations across 3 clinical specialties: Comparative study. *J Med Internet Res*, 25:e49324.

Wei Xu, Courtney Napoles, Ellie Pavlick, Quanze Chen, and Chris Callison-Burch. 2016. Optimizing statistical machine translation for text simplification. *Transactions of the Association for Computational Linguistics*, 4:401–415.

A Resource of German Light Verb Constructions Along with Possible Alternative Formulations

Ralf Laue and Martin Läuter
University of Applied Sciences Zwickau, Department of Computer Science
Kornmarkt 1, 08056 Zwickau, Germany
ralf.laue@fh-zwickau.de

Abstract

In this paper we present a freely accessible resource covering German light verb constructions from the domain of administrative and business language (such as "Bericht erstatten" (to report)) together with their associated verb frames (in particular objects and governing prepositions). These constructions, which in many cases represent overly complex and difficult-to-read language, are joined within the same resource by simple verbs, also together with their respective verb frames.

This not only provides a type of thesaurus for light verb constructions that can assist in text simplification, but the documented verb frames can also support the automatic generation of grammatically correct suggestions for simpler textual alternatives.

1 Introduction

The aim of text simplification methods is to avoid complicated or uncommon words and phrases as well as to replace unnecessarily complex lexical or syntactic units by simpler constructs. The present contribution focuses on the latter topic, specifically on verb-noun collocations in German language that can be replaced by single verbs to improve text comprehensibility. To this end, we introduce a resource that contains a mapping between multi-word expressions and possible paraphrases. We limit our focus to the domain of administrative and business language, as this area is particularly often criticised for unnecessarily complicated formulations.

Research on simplified German has been particularly driven forward in recent years by lawmakers demanding barrier-free accessibility (in Germany: Barrierefreie Informationstechnik-Verordnung, BITV 2.0 and Barrierefreiheitsstärkungsgesetz, BFGS).

However, independent of the needs of specific population groups, there is a demand for simple and understandable communication. Deficiencies in this area are often criticised in the communication between authorities and citizens. Ballod (2020) writes in the preface to a book on administrative language: "Many people find texts from organisations and institutions, especially legal and administrative texts, difficult to read or even incomprehensible."[1]

This statement is supported by the results of a survey conducted in 2008/09 by the Allensbach Institute, a German public opinion research instutute, in which 86% of respondents stated that they had difficulties understanding written communications from authorities (Eichhoff-Cyrus et al., 2009).

Eckhard and Friedrich (2024) undertook an explorative interview-based study among civil servants. They point out that "... interviewees noted the importance of simple and plain administrative language that makes complex administrative procedures and regulations understandable." Moreover, a study by Fink et al. (2021) demonstrated that clearly comprehensible official texts can positively influence democratic participation rights. In this study documents in German language related to public consultations on power lines were examined. The authors of the study concluded that "if the description of a power line is simplified between two consultation rounds, the number of contributions mentioning that power line increases." In this paper, simplification is defined as readability, measured by Lix readability scores. (Anderson, 1983)

In the calculation of these (and similar) readability scores, only surface features of the text, such as word and sentence lengths, are considered. Readability is therefore (as it is well known) not the same as understandability, but it is certainly an important tool for promoting understandability.

[1]All quoted texts from German-language books were translated to English by the authors of this article.

Proceedings of the 21st Conference on Natural Language Processing (KONVENS), Volume 2: Workshops, pages 186–190, 2025

2 Light Verb Constructions

A phenomenon that is often associated with bureaucratic communication in German are light verb constructions and nominalisations.

This means that the meaning of a verbal phrase is either an interplay of the phrase's members, or a new meaning of its own. Examples are "Bericht erstatten" (to report) or "Planung durchführen" (to plan sth.).

This phenomenon has been studied under various names such as "support verb construction", "light verb construction", "function verb construction" or (for German language) "Funktionsverbgefüge", "verblasste Verben", etc. The term "light verb" refers to the fact that the semantics of such a verb is "either void or reduced to a small set of semantic features that are relevant for very large subclasses of verbs" (Langer, 2004).

There is no generally accepted definition of the term "light verb construction" (LVC) or the term "Funktionsverbgefüge" in German (van Pottelberge, 2008; Harm, 2021). A common point of existing definitions is their referring to a collocation where a verb – the light verb – is a main verb that has lost most of its concrete lexical semantics. It is not mainly the verb but its collocate that describes the action.

This article does not aim to to discuss peculiarities of existing definitions, nuances between support verb constructions, function verb constructions, nominalisation constructions, etc. On the contrary – we want to introduce a resource that also includes collocations which are not typically regarded as LVC, for example, "Kopie anfertigen" (to make a copy). While this is a normal verb phrase consisting of a verb and an object, the object specifies the action more precisely than the verb, and the term can easily be rephrased as "kopieren" (to copy). We therefore want to introduce a collection of verb-noun collocations that could potentially be replaced by a simple verb to improve readability.

Such collocations have long been discussed as often unnecessary, hindering understanding and stylistically unappealing. There is no shortage of recommendations that such constructions be replaced by "strong" verbs whenever possible.

Wolf Schneider, the long-time director of the Hamburg Journalism School writes in one of his books about good style in professional German texts: "Similarly, when it comes to verbs... several groups should be viewed with suspicion: a) Activity words that do not dare to stand alone on the plan but prefer to marry a noun." (Schneider, 1984, p. 45)

Germany's Federal Office of Administration published (Bundesverwaltungsamt, 2002) recommendations for administrative language with the goals of clarity, citizen-friendliness, and fostering cooperation between authorities and private individuals. One of the recommendations read: "In general, you should express an event using simple and meaningful verbs. When you force an event or activity into a nominal description (noun and meaningless verb), the sentence statement becomes an empty formula." The German Federal Ministry of Justice published the "Handbuch der Rechtsförmlichkeit" (Manual of Legal Formalities) with recommendations for the drafting of legal regulations. It states: "Prefer verbs! Avoid nouns!" (Bundesministerium der Justiz der Bundesrepublik Deutschland, 2008, S. 63) In the same manner, the Language Service of the Swiss Federal Chancellery recommends on LVCs: "If these constructions do not have their own meaning, you can replace them." (Schweizerische Eidgenossenschaft, Bundeskanzlei, Zentrale Sprachdienste, Sektion Deutsch, 2008)

One might argue that all these recommendations are merely based on stylistic and aesthetic perceptions and possibly have nothing to do with the actual readability and comprehensibility of texts. However, that is not the case. In (Wolfer, 2017), it was found using eye-tracking that nominalisations are processed significantly more slowly during reading than other nouns, and that reformulated texts, in which nominalisations are replaced by verbal structures, are read more quickly. This means that, at least for LVCs such as "Meldung erstatten" (to report) or "Mitteilung machen" (to make a notification / to inform), there is strong evidence supporting the replacement of these with verbal structures.

3 Collections of LVCs

German LVCs have been the subject of research for many years (von Polenz, 1963). This was also noted by Näf and Duffner (2006), who went on to argue: "Nevertheless, this research has mainly been concerned with questions of distinction and definition, and as a result has overlooked the empirical gathering of linguistic data." Although concrete proposals have been made in (Hanks et al., 2006) on how LVCs could be represented in a monolingual dictionary, we are not aware of any initiatives that have implemented this on a large scale.

At least, Kamber (2008) examined the most frequently occurring German light verbs based on the SPIEGEL corpus (5 million words). The aim of this study was to improve word lists for university-level foreign language education, not to create a comprehensive overview of German LVCs. Therefore, Kamber limited the collection to capturing LVCs associated with the 10 most frequent light verbs in the corpus.

The goal of creating a more extensive list of LVCs was undertaken by Bruker (2013), who searched for such constructions in the TIGER corpus (900,000 tokens of German newspaper text) and the DWDS corpus (72 billion tokens), supplemented by findings of additional occurrences in the literature with the aim of expanding the Hagen German Lexicon (Hartrumpf et al., 2003). In this study, 2,500 LVCs were identified.

Our resource contains 4,700 LVCs, including 785 nominalisations with verbs such as "durchführen" (to carry out). The collection is deliberately limited to LVCs that typically appear in business or administrative contexts (i. e., we discarded LVCs such as "to give a kiss"). Those text types are the ones where simplification is often particularly necessary. An advantage of the present collection is that not only the LVCs were collected, but also the corresponding verb frames are documented, which can be helpful for the automatic generation of suggestions for alternative formulations. Furthermore, in the majority of cases, there are references to alternative formulations with the same meaning.

4 Replacing LVCs by Verbal Constructions

In many cases, LVCs may be substituted with simple verbs to improve readability. However, this can not always be done, and certainly not easily in an automatic way.

In some cases, a clear recommendation can be made: A="eine Erhöhung vornehmen" (to make an increase) should probably always be replaced by B= "etw. erhöhen" (to increase sth.). However, there are numerous less clear-cut cases. Such cases occur, for example, when a LVC either has no synonymous simple verb or multiple ones. An example of the first case is "Inventur durchführen" (to conduct an inventory), for which there is simply no corresponding verb. An example of an LVC with multiple possible meanings is discussed in (Bruker, 2013): A="Order erteilen" can be interpreted as meaning "to place an order" or "to give an instruction". Depending on the meaning, A can either be replaced by "etw. bestellen" (to order sth.) or "jmd. anweisen" (to instruct so.).

At this point, an advantage of our resource become evident, because it not only includes light verb constructions (LVCs) and their single-verb paraphrases but also provides syntactic verb frames for both cases. For example, in the case of the LVC "Order erteilen" (to place an order), the resource might indicate that when accompanied by "bei+Dative", the meaning "to order sth." is preferred. On the other hand, the meaning "to give an instruction" should be chosen when the person being instructed is named as the pure dative object.

In other cases, as observed by Storrer (2007), an LVC "tends to develop specific subsenses or form characteristic collocations. Not all of them can be expressed by the base verb." For instance, A="Beschwerde einlegen" (to complain) and B="beschweren" could be regarded as synonyms (and in fact, the word lists presented in this article do so). In informal texts, it may be appropriate to replace occurrences of A with B. However, in official language, it can make a difference whether we use A (someone files an appeal, possibly also implying that this appeal has been submitted in accordance with the deadline and formal requirements) or B (someone merely complains).

Furthermore, the possibility of substitution can also depend on the presence of other sentence components. A="Frage stellen" (to ask a question) can in many instances be replaced by B="fragen" (to ask). However, Kabatnik (2023) (as well as Storrer (2007)) examined this LVC more closely and identified numerous cases where a simple substitution is not advisable. This applies, for example, to formulations like "zwei Fragen stellen" (to ask two questions) or "eine wichtige Frage stellen" (to ask an important question), where the noun "Frage" is modified by an adjective.

Finally, a recommendation to replace an LVC can depend on the geographical origin of the intended audience: While A="auf die Tagesordnung setzen" can be replaced by B="traktandieren" in Switzerland, this would not work in Germany.

5 Our Resource and Possible Uses

An earlier version of the resource presented in this paper was developed within a project aimed at automatically analysing German-language business process models, semi-formal diagrams written in visual languages like BPMN (Object Management Group, 2009), which document the temporal sequence of business activities. The tasks in these diagrams are labelled with short phrases. In the context of automatic analysis, our goal was to identify the activity and object(s) based on the task labels. In the case of a label "Ablehnung aussprechen" (to express a refusal), it would not be sufficient to determine that the verb is "aussprechen" and the object is "Ablehnung"; rather, it must be recognised that the activity is "to refuse". The details regarding the creation and structure of our resource can be found in (Laue et al., 2024), but the approach will be briefly outlined here:

From a corpus containing 6,711 business process models, we generated a list of words that have been tagged as verbs by the Hanover Tagger (Wartena, 2019) together with the words in their neighbourhood and manually inspected this list to identify all those cases where the identified verb alone would not be sufficient to describe the activity properly. To this list, we added LVCs from the already mentioned collection of Bruker if they are relevant to the business domain (based on the evaluation by the first author and another researcher) as well as all phrases from a collection of LVCs in the business domain published in (Marušić, 2015) for which 10 business reports from large German corporate groups had been analysed. Furthermore business-related verbs from (Schumacher, 1986), a compendium of German verbs, have been added. For the paper at hand, we additionally included 255 nominalisations of the type "Zählung durchführen" (to carry out counting) as these frequently occur in official texts and should be simplified.

As a result, we provide a freely available resource[2], which contains verb frames for 4,700 LVCs and 3,600 simple verbs. All entries refer to the domain of administration and business. Each such expression (be it by an LVC or by a simple verb) is represented by an entry in a JSON file, and each entry consists of a syntactic verb frame with the verb infinitive occupying the head slot. In accordance with the terminology of (GermaNet), we refer to the structure of head and labelled slots as a syntactic verb frame, and we largely follow GermaNet for attaching labels to the slots, e. g. *vfin* for the finite verb, *NN* for the subject (subject), *AN* (accusative object), etc. The full description of the data format used can be found in (Laue et al., 2024), as well as in the documentation on GitHub. We will demonstrate the structure by means of an example:

"etw. geben" (=to give sth.) as a simple verb has a *NN* (subject) slot in addition to *AN* (accusative object) and *DN* (dative object). In contrast, "Alarm geben" (=to alarm/alert) has a *NN*, but its *AN* slot is filled with "Alarm".

In some cases, it is helpful to mark a slot mandatory to be filled. While we cannot know in advance *which* object is used in an utterance, we want a verb frame only to match *if* there is an object present. Analogously a slot can be marked *not* to be filled, or *forbidden*. To give an example: "warten" (=to service sth.) has a mandatory *AN* slot, while for "warten" (=to wait) the *AN* slot is marked as "forbidden". This allows for the consideration of different sentence structures as synonyms in the first case compared to the second. The entries in the JSON file for those verb slots look like this:

{"vfin":"warten","optional":["NN","auf+A"],
"forbidden":["AN"],"synsetIds":[1088]},
{"vfin":"warten","optional":["NN"],
"mandatory":["AN"],"synsetIds":[1548]}

To represent mappings within groups of synonymous expressions, we grouped the syntactic verb frames into sets of verb frames that are considered semantically equivalent, so-called synsets (represented by the synsetIds in the JSON file). Each verb frame belongs to at least one such synset, but some are assigned to more than one synset (e. g. "einführen" can have the meaning of "insert into", but also "introduce sth./so.").

This enables the retrieval of a range of alternative formulations from the same synset for a given complex expression. For the phrase "Auskunft einholen" (to obtain information), alternatives such as "fragen", "erfragen", etc. can be identified, alongside others like "Frage stellen", all leading to the same synset.

The present resource comes without software, but contains enough linguistic information to be useful for a variety of automated processes, from phrase detection to example generation and verification of other systems. We are convinced that our resource can be a helpful tool, particularly in supporting the simplification of texts by editors.

[2] https://github.com/bflowtoolbox/VerbframesDE

6 Limitations

Besides the aforementioned lack of accompanying software, the greatest limitation lies in the restriction of the vocabulary to the domains of business and administration. Yet, given that texts from these domains often feature overly complex language, we believe the resource can still be helpful. Furthermore, the authors are aware that a resource like this can never claimed to be complete; we intend to continue improving the entries in the future.

Acknowledgments

Our research project was funded by the Deutsche Forschungsgemeinschaft – project 445156547.

References

Jonathan Anderson. 1983. Lix and Rix: Variations on a little-known readability index. *Journal of Reading*, 26(6):490–496.

Matthias Ballod. 2020. *Klar-text in Organisationen: Ein Ratgeber zur Optimierung administrativer Informationen.* Springer Fachmedien, Wiesbaden.

Astrid Bruker. 2013. *Funktionsverbgefüge im Deutschen.* Bachelor+Master Publ.

Bundesministerium der Justiz der Bundesrepublik Deutschland. 2008. Bekanntmachung des Handbuchs der Rechtsförmlichkeit. *Bundesanzeiger*, 60(160a).

Bundesverwaltungsamt. 2002. *Arbeitshandbuch Bürgernahe Verwaltungssprache.*

Steffen Eckhard and Laurin Friedrich. 2024. How spoken administrative language affects citizen satisfaction. *Journal of Public Administration Research and Theory*, 34(1):122–135.

Karin M. Eichhoff-Cyrus, Gerd Antos, and Rüdiger Schulz, editors. 2009. *Wie denken die Deutschen über die Rechts- und Verwaltungssprache?* Gesellschaft für deutsche Sprache e. V., Wiesbaden.

Simon Fink, Eva Ruffing, Tobias Burst, and Sara Katharina Chinnow. 2021. Less complex language, more participation: how consultation documents shape participatory patterns. *Interest Groups & Advocacy*, 10(3):199–220.

GermaNet. Verb frames, accessed 17 June 2025.

Patrick Hanks, Anne Urbschat, and Elke Gehweiler. 2006. German light verb constructions in corpora and dictionaries. *International Journal of Lexicography*, 19(4):439–457.

Volker Harm. 2021. *Funktionsverbgefüge des Deutschen: Untersuchungen zu einer Kategorie zwischen Lexikon und Grammatik.* De Gruyter.

Sven Hartrumpf, Hermann Helbig, and Rainer Osswald. 2003. The Semantically Based Computer Lexicon HaGenLex – Structure and Technological Environment. *Traitement automatique des langues*, 44(2):81–105.

Susanne Kabatnik. 2023. "Das ist doch etwas Totes" – Funktionsverbgefüge in der digitalen Sprachkritik. *Journal für Medienlinguistik*, 5(1):78–112.

Alain Kamber. 2008. *Funktionsverbgefüge – empirisch: Eine korpusbasierte Untersuchung zu den nominalen Prädikaten des Deutschen.* Dissertation, Université de Neuchâtel, Tübingen.

Stefan Langer. 2004. A formal specification of support verb constructions. In Stefan Langer and Daniel Schnorbusch, editors, *Semantik im Lexikon*, pages 179–201. Gunter Narr Verlag, Tübingen.

Ralf Laue, Kristin Kutzner, and Martin Läuter. 2024. Collecting activities and states in german business process models. In *Business Process Management Workshops*, pages 466–477. Springer Nature.

Borislav Marušić. 2015. *Funktionsverbgefüge in deutscher Konzernsprache.* Phd thesis, University of Osijek, Croatia.

Anton Näf and Rolf Duffner. 2006. Korpuslinguistik im Zeitalter der Textdatenbanken. Vorwort der Herausgeber. *Linguistik Online*, 28(3):7–22.

Object Management Group. 2009. Business process model and notation (BPMN).

Wolf Schneider. 1984. *Deutsch für Profis.* Goldmann.

Helmut Schumacher, editor. 1986. *Verben in Feldern.* Walter de Gruyter.

Schweizerische Eidgenossenschaft, Bundeskanzlei, Zentrale Sprachdienste, Sektion Deutsch. 2008. *Behördenbriefe persönlich – sachgerecht – verständlich.*

Angelika Storrer. 2007. Corpus-based investigations on German support verb constructions. In Christiane Fellbaum, editor, *Idioms and Collocations: Corpus-based Linguistic and Lexicographic Studies*, pages 164–187. Continuum.

Jeroen van Pottelberge. 2008. *Funktionsverbgefüge und verwandte Erscheinungen, in: Phraseologie, Volume 1*, pages 436–444. De Gruyter Mouton.

Peter von Polenz. 1963. *Funktionsverben im heutigen Deutsch*, volume 5 of *Wirkendes Wort: Beiheft.* Pädagogischer Verlag Schwann, Düsseldorf.

Christian Wartena. 2019. A probabilistic morphology model for German lemmatization. In *15th Conference on Natural Language Processing.*

Sascha Wolfer. 2017. *Verstehen und Verständlichkeit juristisch-fachsprachlicher Texte*, volume 7 of *Korpuslinguistik und interdisziplinäre Perspektiven auf Sprache.* Narr Francke Attempto, Tübingen.

Automatic Compound Segmentation for Leichte Sprache

Jesús Calvillo, Umesh Patil, Johann Seltmann, Anne-Kathrin Schumann

t2k GmbH, Dresden, Germany

j.calvillo@text2knowledge.de umesh.patil@text2knowledge.de
johann.seltmann@text2knowledge.de ak.schumann@text2knowledge.de

Abstract

In German "Easy Language" (Leichte Sprache), complex compound words are often orthographically segmented to facilitate perception and processing by marking their internal structure. This practice has been shown to facilitate reading comprehension, especially for readers with cognitive or reading impairments. We present a lightweight model that combines Compound Segmentation with Complex Word Identification (CWI) to automatically detect and split difficult compounds in text. We evaluate our system both on general compound segmentation and in the specific context of Leichte Sprache. Our results show that our model achieves high segmentation accuracy, outperforming both rule-based and much larger neural systems, identifying which compounds should be segmented. We also release a new evaluation dataset of Leichte Sprache sentences with segmented compounds.

1 Introduction

German is a language that allows for word formation through compounding, i.e., multiple words can join to form a single one without any orthographic separation (e.g. *Armut* "poverty" + *Bekämpfung* "combat" + *Programm* "program" → *Armutsbekämpfungsprogramm*). Compounding can be applied recursively, yielding a potentially infinite amount of linguistically acceptable compounds. In practice, this word formation process is used very productively; in fact, Baroni et al. (2002) report that 47% of all word types in the APA German news corpus are compounds. This creates challenges for NLP as compounds are often low-frequency: 83% of the compounds in the APA corpus had a frequency of less than 5 occurrences (Baroni et al., 2002). This causes data sparsity, which complicates tasks like information retrieval (e.g., Alfonseca et al., 2008; Monz and De Rijke, 2001), speech recognition (e.g., Adda-Decker and Adda, 2000), and machine translation (e.g., Daiber et al., 2015; Koehn and Knight, 2003; Neumannová and Bojar, 2023).

Compound Splitting (also called Compound Decomposition or Decompounding) refers to splitting such words into their constituents, mitigating some of the problems mentioned above. This can be further divided into *compound segmentation* and *compound normalization* (Ziering and van der Plas, 2016). The former refers to segmenting a compound into its constituents while preserving its surface form (e.g. Armutsbekämpfungsprogramm → Armuts + bekämpfungs + programm). The latter corresponds to task of recovering the base form of each constituent (e.g. Armutsbekämpfungsprogramm → Armut + Bekämpfung + Programm).

This task is not always simple: some compounds involve simple concatenation (e.g., *Sport + Schuhe → Sportschuhe*); however, others require morphological adjustments, including linking elements (Fugenelemente),[1] truncation, or pluralization, among others:

Bekämpfung + s + Programm → Bekämpfungsprogramm (linking element)
Kirsche -e + Baum → Kirschbaum (truncation)
Buch + ü_er + Regal → Bücherregal (pluralization with umlaut)

Compound splitting can also help readability, as some compounds can be difficult to process for humans, especially for people with reading impairments. In Leichte Sprache (German "Easy Language"), long and difficult compounds are typically visually segmented with hyphens or the mediopunkt (·) to support lexical decoding (Bredel and

[1]Fugenelemente are a limited set of interfixes (e.g., *-s-*, *-es-*) inserted between compound parts, typically for phonetic reasons.

Proceedings of the 21st Conference on Natural Language Processing (KONVENS), Volume 2: Workshops, pages 191–201, 2025

Maaß, 2016) and enhance comprehension for readers with cognitive or reading impairments. This has been stipulated in guidelines for Leichte Sprache (e.g., Deutsches Institut für Normung e.V., 2025; Maaß, 2015; Bundesministerium für Arbeit und Soziales, 2019). Empirical studies confirm to some extent that this helps readers: Deilen (2021) and Wellmann (2020) used eye-tracking to show that visually segmented compounds reduce reading time and cognitive load for both cognitively impaired and unimpaired readers. Similarly, Pappert and Bock (2020) use a lexical decision task to show that visual compound segmentation results in shorter reaction times both for readers with cognitive impairments and functional illiteracy.

Despite the importance of compound segmentation in Leichte Sprache, only a few computational models address this explicitly. Although tools such as Gertwol (Haapalainen and Majorin, 1995; Steiner, 2018) have been integrated into language simplification pipelines (e.g., Suter et al. 2016), to our knowledge, no previous model jointly addresses automatic identification and segmentation of difficult compounds for Leichte Sprache.

Compound segmentation for Leichte Sprache implies two steps: 1) identifying the *difficult* words to be segmented; and 2) segmenting those words. We present a neural model of compound segmentation that in combination with a model of complex word identification (CWI) performs these steps, thus providing an automatic system to fulfill this requirement. Our work is the first to combine a compound segmentation model with a model for complex word identification model to systematically handle compound splitting for Leichte Sprache.

Our model has a similar architecture to Tuggener (2018) with minimal modifications and a more fine-grained training procedure. The model of complex word identification that we used is an XGBoost classifier presented by Patil et al. (2025). We evaluated whether this CWI model can identify the words that need segmentation. Then we evaluated our compound segmentation model showing that it can in general segment German compounds and even has better results than much larger state-of-the-art models. Then we evaluated our combined model of compound segmentation and CWI on the task of compound segmentation for Leichte Sprache with a new dataset of Leichte Sprache with segmented compounds that we make available.[2]

Our contributions are:

- A parallel dataset of sentences with segmented compounds, with their unsegmented pairs.
- A training procedure to train *lightweight* compound segmentation models, leveraging unsupervised and supervised training.
- A pipeline for compound segmentation designed for the domain of Leichte Sprache, with its evaluation.

2 Related Work: German Compound Splitting

Many models for German Compound Splitting have been proposed, ranging from rule-based systems to state-of-the-art neural models. Early systems such as those by Koehn and Knight (2003), Weller and Heid (2012) and Weller-Di Marco (2017) relied on dictionaries, corpus frequencies and manually designed rules. While precise, such systems are limited in coverage and often fail on out-of-vocabulary words.

To overcome this, unsupervised methods were introduced. Macherey et al. (2011) use a bilingual corpus to learn morphological operations, avoiding handcrafted rules. SECOS (Riedl and Biemann, 2016) uses a distributional thesaurus to find semantically coherent compound constituents. Another important advance was the MOP Compound Splitter (Ziering and van der Plas, 2016), which learns morphological operations.

Among the neural approaches, the one that is the most relevant to our work is that of Tuggener (2018), who evaluated several supervised and unsupervised neural models, showing that they were able to generalize better on out-of-domain data, compared to earlier approaches. Among other architectures, the study proposes a bi-directional character LSTM (Hochreiter and Schmidhuber, 1997) trained auto-regressively with a language model objective (at a given time step, the model is expected to predict the next/previous character), whose forward and backward hidden states are then fed to a multilayer perceptron that classifies whether after each position of a character sequence, a separator needs to be inserted (Figure 1 shows our very

[2] https://github.com/text2knowledge/ls_comp_segmentation_hurraki, https://huggingface.co/datasets/text2knowledge/ls_comp_seg_hurraki

similar architecture). This model was compared against dictionary/ngram-based models, an LSTM-based unsupervised approach, and a sequence to sequence with attention model. The Bi-LSTM with the multilayer perceptron was the best among the compared models. This architecture was later used also for compound splitting in Icelandic (Daðason et al., 2020), and later by Krotova et al. (2020), who also performed idiomatic compound detection.

More recently, Minixhofer et al. (2023) built a wide-scale multilingual dataset for compound splitting formed by 255K words across 56 languages, that was used to train and evaluate several variations of sequence to sequence transformer models, including large language models (LLMs). Similar to Tuggener (2018), they apply a two-staged approach with a self-supervised stage and a supervised one. Their results showed that character-based models outperform all subword-based models, **including LLMs**, especially on compounds where subword boundaries do not coincide with compound constituent boundaries. They report their best models outperformed all the baselines they used, however, they did not compare against the neural approaches mentioned above (i.e., Tuggener, 2018; Krotova et al., 2020; Daðason et al., 2020), whose performance in German is actually very similar ($\sim 95\%$ average accuracy) to that of Minixhofer et al. (2023).

3 Compound Segmentation for Leichte Sprache

While compound segmentation has been shown to facilitate reading comprehension of long and difficult compounds, to apply this in practice we also need to identify the words that need segmentation. We propose a two-staged approach for this task:

1. **Complex Word Identification**: Words or sentences are analyzed to identify difficult terms that may require compound segmentation.
2. **Compound Segmentation**: Difficult words are segmented into their constituent parts.

These steps can be used in a language simplification pipeline, and are further explained below.

3.1 Complex Word Identification Model

To identify which words should be split in the context of Leichte Sprache, we employ a Complex Word Identification (CWI) model. CWI is a subtask of lexical simplification where systems detect words that are likely to be difficult for a target audience. We used the CWI model reported in Patil et al. (2025). The model performs the CWI task for German. It was trained as an XGBoost classifier using a combination of word-level linguistic features, corpus-level distributional patterns, frequency data from a Leichte Sprache corpus, and human-annotated complexity ratings. The model achieves a relatively high F1-score of 0.85, evaluated on the dataset reported in Yimam et al. (2018).

In addition to binary classification as complex or non-complex, the model can also estimate a word's complexity level on a continuous scale ranging from 0 to 1. The model's predictions of word complexity were validated using psycholinguistic data of online word processing. Using a dataset of German nouns from the Developmental Lexicon Project (DeveL, Schröter and Schroeder, 2017), the model was shown to account for human word recognition times beyond what traditional word-level predictors can explain. Furthermore, the model was shown to produce promising results in identifying the CEFR levels of words.

3.2 Compound Segmentation Model

Since prior work has shown that character-based models outperform those using *subword tokenizers* (e.g., in LLMs), we adopted a very similar architecture to the best one proposed by Tuggener (2018). It consists of a character-level bidirectional LSTM pretrained with a language modeling objective, followed by a binary classification layer trained to predict whether a split (label 1) or no split (label 0) should occur at each character boundary (see Figure 1).

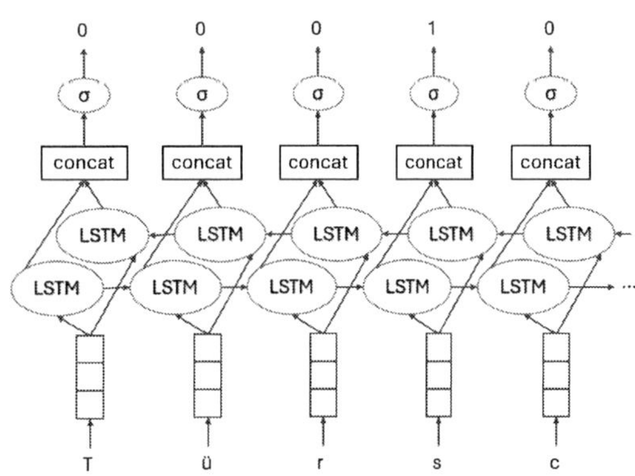

Figure 1: Model Architecture: A Bi-LSTM model with a sigmoid classification layer.

More formally, each character c_t in the input sequence is embedded as a vector $\mathbf{e}_{c_t} \in \mathbb{R}^{d_{\text{emb}}}$, where $d_{\text{emb}} = 128$.

These embeddings are then passed to forward and backward LSTM layers with *unshared* parameters, allowing each direction to be trained auto-regressively. The forward and backward hidden states are computed as:

$$\mathbf{h}_t^{\rightarrow} = \text{LSTM}_{\rightarrow}(\mathbf{e}_{c_t}, \mathbf{h}_{t-1}^{\rightarrow}), \tag{1}$$

$$\mathbf{h}_t^{\leftarrow} = \text{LSTM}_{\leftarrow}(\mathbf{e}_{c_t}, \mathbf{h}_{t+1}^{\leftarrow}), \tag{2}$$

where $\mathbf{h}_t^{\rightarrow}, \mathbf{h}_t^{\leftarrow} \in \mathbb{R}^{128}$ denote the hidden states in the respective directions. Each LSTM is trained with a language modeling objective to predict the next (or previous) character using a softmax layer, with the following cross-entropy losses:

$$\mathcal{L}_{\text{LM}}^{\rightarrow} = \text{CE}\big(\mathbf{W}^{\rightarrow}\mathbf{h}_t^{\rightarrow},\, c_{t+1}\big), \tag{3}$$

$$\mathcal{L}_{\text{LM}}^{\leftarrow} = \text{CE}\big(\mathbf{W}^{\leftarrow}\mathbf{h}_t^{\leftarrow},\, c_{t-1}\big), \tag{4}$$

where $\mathbf{W}^{\rightarrow}, \mathbf{W}^{\leftarrow} \in \mathbb{R}^{|\mathcal{V}|\times 128}$ are learned output projection matrices and $\mathcal{V}$ is the character vocabulary.

For the compound splitting task, the forward and backward hidden states are concatenated and passed through a sigmoid-activated linear layer to predict the probability of a split at each character position:

$$p_t = \sigma\big(\mathbf{w}^\top[\mathbf{h}_t^{\rightarrow}; \mathbf{h}_t^{\leftarrow}] + b\big), \tag{5}$$

where $\mathbf{w} \in \mathbb{R}^{256}$, $b \in \mathbb{R}$, and $[\cdot\,;\cdot]$ denotes vector concatenation.

The binary cross-entropy loss for split prediction is defined as:

$$\mathcal{L}_{\text{split}} = \text{BCE}(p_t,\, y_t), \tag{6}$$

where $y_t = 1$ if a split precedes character t, and $y_t = 0$ otherwise. To address the class imbalance (i.e., the relative sparsity of split positions), positive labels are up-weighted by a factor of 10 during training.

A key advantage of this architecture is its efficiency: the resulting model is lightweight, easy to train, and suitable for deployment in resource-constrained environments.

3.2.1 Training Datasets

We used three datasets to train and evaluate our compound segmentation model:

German Sentences: to train auto-regressively, we used 140K German sentences from the Leipzig Corpora Collection (2021): half of them were extracted from Wikipedia and the other half from mixed sources.

Compound Piece (Minixhofer et al., 2023): This resource contains 255K compound words across 56 languages. It also includes a set of hyphenated words automatically harvested from the mC4 corpus (Xue et al., 2021). Though the segmentations of the latter are noisy and not perfectly aligned with true compound boundaries, they provide substantial weak supervision. Minixhofer et al. (2023) leverage this dataset both to pretrain a decompounding model and to refine subword tokenization. Similarly, we use the German part of the hyphenated words for the early training phases of our compound segmentation model.

GermaNet: For fine-tuning, we used GermaNet (Henrich and Hinrichs, 2011), a curated resource of 126,733 segmented German compounds. These include rich linguistic annotations such as linking elements, truncations, affixoids, confixes,etc. We used the most recent version (v19.0, University of Tübingen 2024) for final training.

3.2.2 Training regime

Our training regime combines some of the techniques used by Tuggener (2018) and Minixhofer et al. (2023), aiming at leveraging auto-regressive language model pretraining with semi-supervised training and further supervised fine-tunning. This is done in four phases:

Phase 1: auto-regressive pre-training. We first train the LSTMs to predict their next and previous characters in normal German sentences. This ensures that the model is familiar with the patterns of German character sequences, which allows the model to build the appropriate representations that are necessary for the classification task.

We train for up to 20 epochs (Adam optimizer, batch size of 16, *lr* = 0.01, early-stopping patience of 3); the loss typically plateaus after 10 epochs. Three random seeds are tried and the checkpoint with best validation loss is retained. Note that we could have used many more sentences, but because of its small size, the model cannot memorize the training data, so the 140K were

Text with Unsegmented Compounds	Text with Segmented Compounds
Der Weihnachtsbaum hat sogar eine eigene Internetseite.	Der Weihnachts•Baum hat sogar eine eigene Internet•Seite.
Sie tragen Plastikhandschuhe.	Sie tragen Plastik•Handschuhe.
Dann können andere Facebookbenutzer sehen, was sie mögen.	Dann können andere Facebook•Benutzer sehen, was sie mögen.

Table 1: Example sentences from the evaluation dataset.

enough. Preliminary experiments with more sentences yielded similar results. We used 130K sentences for training and 10K for validation.

Phase 2: classification warm-up with frozen weights. The best auto-regressive weights are loaded, *embedding weights and both LSTMs are frozen*, and only the classifier head is trained on the Compound Piece data. We keep an aggressive learning rate (*lr* = 0.01); training converges within 3–5 epochs. This phase is focused on training the classification layer while keeping the previously trained LSTM weights safe from abrupt modifications due to the initially-high loss gradients of the classification layer.

Phase 3: full classification training. All layers are unfrozen and training resumes on the same Compound Piece data with a reduced rate (*lr* = 0.0015); approximately 10 epochs suffice for convergence.

Phase 4: GermaNet fine-tuning. Finally, the model is fine-tuned on the GermaNet corpus. (*lr* = 0.0015, 10 epochs). The resulting checkpoint is the model used for the experiments in §4.

After training, as a final post-processing step, we remove segmentations concerning prepositions (e.g., *bei, mit*) at the beginning of words (e.g. *Beispiel* "example", *Mitarbeiter* "employee") and some bound morphemes[3] (e.g., *her* in *Herkunft* "origin").

4 Evaluation

4.1 Evaluation Dataset

To evaluate our compound segmentation system, we compiled a list of sentences in Leichte Sprache from two sources:

- **Hurraki:**[4] a Leichte Sprache encyclopedia.
- **Einfach Stars:**[5] a Leichte Sprache news site covering famous people and pop culture.

We selected these two from several different possible sources, as they both consistently segment difficult words and do not segment simpler words.

In addition to segmented compound nouns, these sources also sometimes segment verbs (e.g. "heraus-finden" and "aus-gesprochen"). Since we (and our model) do not consider these constructions as compounds, we used a heuristic based on regular expressions and part-of-speech tagging to identify them and remove the separator characters ("-" and "•"), thereby avoiding evaluating this particular type of words. We leave for future discussion whether these words should be segmented or not.

We then created a parallel dataset of sentence pairs by applying the same heuristic to the segmented nouns in each sentence, so that each example consists of one sentence with segmented nouns and one with unsegmented nouns. Table 1 contains examples of these pairs. This results in a dataset with 38114 sentence pairs with at least one segmented compound. To this, we added 500 examples that do not contain any segmented compound and 500 examples that originally contained a segmented verb (e.g., "heraus-finden"), but we removed this segmentation.

The vast majority of the pairs come from Einfach Stars (34187). Most sentences only contain one segmented compound (see Table 2). There are 42006 segmented compounds in total, with 15933 unique ones. Table 3 shows the most common segmented compounds and their counts. Within these examples, we also identified 1858 compounds (587 unique) that were not segmented in their sources, perhaps because they were deemed simple enough. Table 4 shows the most common ones.

While we used both sources for our evaluation, because of copyrights, we can make available only the Hurraki part.

[3]Namely: *ent-, ge-, her-, hin-, un-, ur-, ver-, -bar, -los*
[4]`https://hurraki.de`
[5]`https://einfachstars.info`

# Segmented Compounds	# Sentences
0	998
1	33027
2	3728
3	372
4+	89

Table 2: Count of sentences with different numbers of compounds in the evaluation dataset.

4.2 Evaluation Tasks

We evaluate our compound segmentation pipeline in three settings:

1. **Compound Segmentation**: We evaluate compound segmentation by comparing the output of different models of compound segmentation against the original segmentation, considering only the words that were originally segmented. We also evaluate the case of unsegmented compounds, where we assume that they were not segmented in the original sources because they are not difficult, therefore, we assume they should be labeled as simple.

2. **Complex Word Identification**: We evaluate the performance of the CWI model to identify the compounds that may need to be segmented. Here we assume that the segmented compounds in the dataset were selected because of their complexity. Then, the CWI model is expected to identify the segmented compounds as difficult and the unsegmented compounds as simple.

3. **CWI + Compound Segmentation**: In our final setting, we first apply the CWI model to select words that may need segmentation and then we apply different segmenters on those words. We assess the differences in the full sentences.

4.3 Baselines

We compared our segmentation system against two baselines:

- **MOP Compound Splitter** (MCS, Ziering and van der Plas, 2016), which is a splitter based on morphological operations. We used this as an example of classical rule-based models for compound splitting.

Segmented Compound	Count
Internet•Seite	386
Kranken•Haus	293
Fernseh•Sendung	290
Groß•Britannien	226
Welt•Tag	218
Königs•Familie	202
Königs•Haus	146
Fernseh•Sendungen	145
National•Mannschaft	136
Ehe•Frau	133

Table 3: Most common segmented compounds in the evaluation dataset.

Unsegmented Compound	Count
Mitglied	130
Hochzeit	87
Geburtstag	77
Tatort	70
Flugzeug	52
Zeitschrift	51
Kennenlernen	51
Sonntag	42
Feuerwehr	39
Wochenende	32

Table 4: Most common unsegmented compounds in the evaluation dataset.

- **Compound Piece**, which is a sequence to sequence compound normalization model whose output is then used to perform compound segmentation. We used this model as an example of large-scale neural compound segmentation models.

We did not find an instance of the models by Tuggener (2018) and similar variants (i.e. Daðason et al., 2020; Krotova et al., 2020), but we expect our model to have a similar performance, potentially benefiting from the extra training phases.

5 Results

From the Leichte Sprache sentence pairs described in subsection 4.1, we used a random sample of 10K sentences for our evaluation experiments (8946 from Einfach Stars, 1054 from Hurraki), out of which 260 contained no segmented compounds. We used the CWI model to tokenize the sentences and infer word complexity values for each token. Then, we applied the compound segmentation

Model	Accuracy(%)
MCS	37.28
Compound Piece	85.29
Our model	**87.66**

Table 5: Accuracy comparison of different compound segmentation models.

models on these tokenized sentences. The CWI model uses spaCy (Honnibal et al., 2020) for tokenization, which is mostly driven by white spaces and punctuations, the resulting tokens are words or punctuations.

5.1 Compound Segmentation

We took the segmented compounds in the test dataset as ground truth and compared it against our model and the baselines' output. Note that this ground truth often does not segment a compound into all of its constituents (e.g., *Weihnachtsfest•Post*), while the compared models aim at fully segmenting the input compounds (i.e., *Weihnachts•Fest•Post*).

The model accuracies can be found in Table 5. By looking at the mistakes of the MCS model, we can see that its low accuracy is mainly because it works as a compound normalizer rather than a segmenter, so the compound constituents are often changed to its lemma form (e.g., *Menschenaffen* $\rightarrow$ *Mensch•Affe*). It also relies on its lemma dictionary, so unknown words are not handled properly (e.g., *Spidermanfilme* $\rightarrow$ *Sid•Erman•Film*).

Our model had the best segmentation performance, while the Compound Piece model had a very comparable accuracy. Since they exclusively perform segmentation, no mistakes regarding modifications of the original constituents are made. Some of the main mistakes are concerning words that have more than 2 constituents and the models segment more than the ground truth (e.g., *Fußballmannschaft* $\rightarrow$ *Fuß•Ball•Mannschaft* instead of *Fußball•Mannschaft*). Another common difference is that compounds that start or end with a preposition are usually not segmented by the models while sometimes they are segmented in the ground truth (e.g., *Mit•Arbeiter,Vor•Name*).

5.2 Complex Word Identification

Our dataset contains segmented compounds that were identified with a heuristic that uses the separation character (a hyphen or middle point). However, among the sentences in the dataset, there are also compounds that were not segmented by the original text authors, which we expect to be simpler words. To identify these and given the relatively high quality of our segmentation model (as shown above), we applied our segmentation model on the unsegmented sentences; then, we considered as an unsegmented compound any word that was segmented by the model and that was not originally segmented. We speculate that they were not segmented because they were simple enough for Leichte Sprache. With this process, we obtained 1522 instances of unsegmented compounds.

The CWI model returns a continuous value between 0 and 1 that corresponds to how difficult the word is (0 being not difficult, 1 being difficult). Using a threshold of 0.5 to label the words in the test set (i.e., any word whose CWI value is greater than 0.5 is labeled as difficult, or simple otherwise), we counted how many times those compounds were labeled as difficult: out of the 10982 segmented compounds in the test set, 9229 (84%) were identified as difficult. Regarding the unsegmented compounds, which are expected to be labeled as simple, out of the 1522 unsegmented compounds that we identified, 983 (63%) were labeled as simple.

Nevertheless, a complexity threshold of 0.5 may not properly fit the properties of Leichte Sprache. To try to calibrate it, we applied a grid search with threshold $\tau = 0.0$ to $\tau = 0.95$ with an increment of 0.5. The results showed that since there are many more segmented compounds than unsegmented compounds, the threshold that maximizes a naive F1-score is 0.0 (i.e. to segment all compounds). A more balanced approach is computing accuracies separately between segmented and unsegmented compounds and then averaging them. In this case, the threshold with maximum average accuracy is 0.65 (i.e. to avoid segmenting most compounds), but its value (74.6) is not much different from more balanced thresholds (e.g., when $\tau = 0.5$, the average accuracy is 74.3). Because of these results, we continued the rest of the analysis with our initial threshold of 0.5. However, we expect that a more carefully curated and balanced dataset may yield more fine-grained results.

5.3 CWI + Compound Segmentation

We evaluated our whole pipeline by applying CWI on the sentences and then applying the different segmenters on the words that were labeled as difficult. Here, a perfect system would output the sentences exactly as in the ground truth.

Table 6 shows the token-level accuracy (Tok Acc%), the percentage of perfectly segmented sentences (Perfect%), and two key error types: false positives (FP) and false negatives (FN). Here we define a false positive as a token that was not supposed to be modified but was modified by a given model. We define a false negative as a compound (identified via the ground truth annotations) that was erroneously left unchanged by the model, indicating a missed segmentation. We report false negatives both as a percentage of all compound tokens (FN %Comps) and as a percentage of all tokens (FN %Toks).

Without CWI, our model achieves the highest token-level accuracy (97.0%), the highest percentage of perfect output sentences (75.2%), and the lowest false positive rate (1.5%). It also has the lowest false negative rates: 4.3% of compound tokens and 0.48% of all tokens, showing that most compounds were successfully segmented. Compound Piece follows with 94.5% token accuracy and 58.8% perfect output sentences, while MCS trails further behind.

With CWI, the MCS and Compound Piece models improve, and while our model remains in the lead, its token accuracy slightly drops to 96.5%, with 71.6% perfect sentence outputs. Its false positive rate drops to just 0.6%, but its false negative rates increase to 16.4% of compounds and 1.82% of all tokens. While Compound Piece narrows the gap slightly, our model continues to deliver the best results. These results confirm that the integration of a CWI filter reduces the amount of false positives, however, this filter may need to be further tuned to reach an appropriate balance between false positives and negatives. In our case, the reduction of false positives is not as drastic because it was already relatively low (from 1.5% to 0.6%), compared to the reduction of false positives of the other two models (5.4% to 1.5% and 4.0% to 1.1), this can explain why applying CWI actually hurts slightly the overall accuracy of our model: the decrease of false positives does not compensate the increase of false negatives. A more careful false negative/positive balance may yield better results.

6 Discussion

We evaluated our pipeline for compound segmentation in Leichte Sprache, which consists of selecting the difficult words to be segmented, and then applying segmentation on those words.

Selecting what compounds to segment is very important: segmentation helps readers to process difficult compounds, however, segmenting some compounds may actually make them more difficult because the readers are usually more familiar with their unsegmented form. Moreover, segmenting some compounds may lead to wrong interpretations (e.g., *Groß•Mutter* "grandmother" should not be interpreted as "big mother"). Regarding this aspect, our dataset is rather noisy, as there are no quantitative criteria to inform annotators about what compounds should be segmented and what constitutes a *difficult* compound: perceptions of difficulty vary between individuals—what one annotator considers challenging, another may find straightforward. Indeed, some compounds in our corpus are segmented even though they may not be particularly difficult, e.g., *Mit•Arbeiter* ("employee"). It is important to have clear definitions of how difficult a compound should be to be segmented and how we can measure this. Nonetheless, while these concepts require more definition, we can already see that using CWI can help identify these compounds.

Regarding the correct compound segmentation, it is also not entirely clear whether compounds should be fully segmented, only their main constituents, or only the *difficult* ones; which is reflected in the variety of ways in which compounds are segmented by humans. The models that we evaluated used full segmentation, but other formats could be applied.

In general, clearer guidelines are needed regarding what compounds should be segmented in Leichte Sprache, and to what degree (binary vs. partial vs. full). Such guidelines would improve the quality of the data, which would improve the evaluation and automation of this task.

We also see that comparing the different segmentation models, our smaller model performed better than the larger transformer-based Compound Piece model, which is very useful, as our model can be deployed in more resource-constrained environments. We leave further experiments with LLMs for future work. There is, however, evidence that LLMs that use sub-word tokens have

Model	Tok Acc%	Perfect%	FP %Toks	FN %Comps	FN %Toks
Without CWI					
MCS	86.9	22.8	5.4	6.6	0.73
Compound Piece	94.5	58.8	4.0	4.4	0.49
Our Model	**97.0**	**75.2**	**1.5**	**4.3**	**0.48**
With CWI					
MCS	90.1	28.3	1.5	16.6	1.84
Compound Piece	95.8	65.7	1.1	**16.1**	**1.78**
Our Model	**96.5**	**71.6**	**0.6**	16.4	1.82

Table 6: Token Accuracy (Tok Acc), percentage of perfect output sentences (Perfect), percentage among all tokens of false positive segmentations (FP Toks), percentage among all compounds of false negative segmentations (FN Comps) and percentage among all tokens of false negative segmentations (FN Toks) of different compound segmentation models in Leichte Sprache sentences, with and without Complex Word Identification (CWI).

problems with tasks that involve information about the internal structure of those tokens (Shin and Kaneko, 2024; Cosma et al., 2025). This is in line with what was already reported by Minixhofer et al. (2023). Because of this and the amount of resources that LLMs require, we consider our approach to be more advantageous, especially in cases with restricted resources.

7 Conclusion

We introduced a two-stage system for compound segmentation in Leichte Sprache, combining a lightweight character-level model with a complex word identification component. Our system automatically identifies and segments difficult German compounds, supporting the goals of linguistic accessibility.

The model outperforms both rule-based and larger neural baselines while remaining efficient and deployable in resource-constrained settings, and shows that large transformer-based architectures are not always necessary in NLP. We also contribute a new evaluation dataset of segmented Leichte Sprache sentences to facilitate further research.

Our results show that segmentation accuracy improves through CWI, though further calibration is needed to reduce under-segmentation. We emphasize that clearer guidelines are needed about what compounds should be segmented and to what extent (full vs. partial).

Future work includes refining the complexity threshold, exploring alternative segmentation strategies, and conducting human evaluations.

Limitations

Our CWI component uses a fixed complexity threshold, which may not suit all users/contexts. We also assume that all segmented compounds are difficult and that unsegmented ones are easy, which may not always hold. The model performs full segmentation, while human-annotated texts often use partial. Finally, we have not yet validated the model through human studies, which are essential to assess its usefulness in real-world applications.

Acknowledgments

The work leading to this paper was partially funded by the Federal German Ministry for Labour and Social Affairs through the Civic Innovation Platform[6]. We are also grateful for the feedback that we received from the anonymous reviewers, which helped improve this article.

References

Martine Adda-Decker and Gilles Adda. 2000. Morphological decomposition for asr in german. In *Workshop on Phonetics and Phonology in ASR, Saarbrücken, Germany*, pages 129–143.

Enrique Alfonseca, Slaven Bilac, and Stefan Pharies. 2008. Decompounding query keywords from compounding languages. In *Proceedings of ACL-08: HLT, Short Papers*, pages 253–256, Columbus, Ohio. Association for Computational Linguistics.

Marco Baroni, Johannes Matiasek, and Harald et al. Trost. 2002. Predicting the components of German nominal compounds. In *ECAI*, volume 2002, page 15th.

[6]https://www.knowledgegraph.de/

Ursula Bredel and Christiane Maaß. 2016. *Leichte Sprache: Theoretische Grundlagen. Orientierung für die Praxis*. Duden.

Bundesministerium für Arbeit und Soziales. 2019. Barrierefreie-informationstechnik-verordnung (bitv2.0). Bundesrechtsverordnung auf Grundlage des Behindertengleichstellungsgesetzes (§§12d,16Abs.8 BGG). Inkraftgetreten am 25. Mai 2019; Neufassung vom 12.September2011.

Adrian Cosma, Stefan Ruseti, Emilian Radoi, and Mihai Dascalu. 2025. The strawberry problem: Emergence of character-level understanding in tokenized language models. *arXiv preprint arXiv:2505.14172*.

Jón Friðrik Daðason, David Erik Mollberg, Hrafn Loftsson, and Kristín Bjarnadóttir. 2020. Kvistur 2.0: a bilstm compound splitter for icelandic. *arXiv preprint arXiv:2004.07776*.

Joachim Daiber, Lautaro Quiroz, Roger Wechsler, and Stella Frank. 2015. Splitting compounds by semantic analogy. *arXiv preprint arXiv:1509.04473*.

Silvana Deilen. 2021. Segmenting compounds in German Easy Language: Does facilitated perception lead to reduced cognitive processing costs? In *3rd Swiss Conference on Barrier-free Communication (BfC 2020)*, page 135.

Deutsches Institut für Normung e.V. 2025. Din spec 33429:2025-03 – empfehlungen für deutsche leichte sprache. Veröffentlicht durch den Normenausschuss Ergonomie (NAErg). Konsortiumsentwicklung mit Förderung durch das Bundesministerium für Arbeit und Soziales (BMAS).

Mariikka Haapalainen and Ari Majorin. 1995. Gertwol und morphologische disambiguierung für das deutsche. In *Proceedings of the 10th Nordic Conference on Computational Linguistics*.

Verena Henrich and Erhard Hinrichs. 2011. Determining immediate constituents of compounds in Germanet. In *Proceedings of the international conference recent advances in natural language processing 2011*, pages 420–426.

Sepp Hochreiter and Jürgen Schmidhuber. 1997. Long short-term memory. *Neural computation*, 9(8):1735–1780.

Matthew Honnibal, Ines Montani, Sofie Van Landeghem, and Adriane Boyd. 2020. spacy: Industrial--strength natural language processing in python. `https://doi.org/10.5281/zenodo.1212303`. Zenodo release.

Philipp Koehn and Kevin Knight. 2003. Empirical methods for compound splitting. *arXiv preprint cs/0302032*.

Irina Krotova, Sergey Aksenov, and Ekaterina Artemova. 2020. A joint approach to compound splitting and idiomatic compound detection. In *Proceedings of the Twelfth Language Resources and Evaluation Conference*, pages 4410–4417, Marseille, France. European Language Resources Association.

Leipzig Corpora Collection. 2021. German corpus based on Wikipedia material from 2021 and mixed material from 2011. `https://corpora.uni-leipzig.de?corpusId=deu_news_2023`. Leipzig Corpora Collection. Dataset.

Christiane Maaß. 2015. *Leichte Sprache. Das Regelbuch*. LIT Verlag Dr. W. Hopf, Berlin.

Klaus Macherey, Andrew Dai, David Talbot, Ashok Popat, and Franz Josef Och. 2011. Language-independent compound splitting with morphological operations. In *Proceedings of the 49th annual meeting of the association for computational linguistics: human language technologies*, pages 1395–1404.

Benjamin Minixhofer, Jonas Pfeiffer, and Ivan Vulić. 2023. CompoundPiece: Evaluating and improving decompounding performance of language models. In *Proceedings of the 2023 Conference on Empirical Methods in Natural Language Processing*, pages 343–359, Singapore. Association for Computational Linguistics.

Christof Monz and Maarten De Rijke. 2001. Shallow morphological analysis in monolingual information retrieval for dutch, german, and italian. In *Workshop of the Cross-Language Evaluation Forum for European Languages*, pages 262–277. Springer.

Kristýna Neumannová and Ondřej Bojar. 2023. The role of compounds in human vs. machine translation quality. In *Proceedings of Machine Translation Summit XIX, Vol. 1: Research Track*, pages 248–260.

Sandra Pappert and Bettina M. Bock. 2020. Easy-to-read german put to the test: Do adults with intellectual disability or functional illiteracy benefit from compound segmentation? *Reading and Writing*, 33:1105–1131.

Umesh Patil, Jesus Calvillo, Sol Lago, and Anne-Kathrin Schumann. 2025. Quantifying word complexity for Leichte Sprache: A computational metric and its psycholinguistic validation. In *Proceedings of the First Worshop Artificial Intelligence and Easy and Plain Language in Institutional Contexts*, Geneva, Switzerland.

Martin Riedl and Chris Biemann. 2016. Unsupervised compound splitting with distributional semantics rivals supervised methods. In *Proceedings of the 2016 Conference of the North American Chapter of the Association for Computational Linguistics: Human Language Technologies*, pages 617–622, San Diego, California. Association for Computational Linguistics.

Pauline Schröter and Sascha Schroeder. 2017. The Developmental Lexicon Project: A behavioral database to investigate visual word recognition across the lifespan. *Behavior Research Methods*, 49(6):2183–2203.

Andrew Shin and Kunitake Kaneko. 2024. Large language models lack understanding of character composition of words. In *ICML 2024 Workshop on LLMs and Cognition*.

Petra Steiner. 2018. Merging the trees: Building a morphological treebank for german from two resources. In *Proceedings of the 16th International Workshop on Treebanks and Linguistic Theories (TLT16)*, pages 146–160. Association for Computational Linguistics.

Julia Suter, Sarah Ebling, and Martin Volk. 2016. Rule-based automatic text simplification for german. In *Proceedings of the 13th Conference on Natural Language Processing (KONVENS 2016)*, pages –. Österreichische Computer Gesellschaft.

Don Tuggener. 2018. Evaluating neural sequence models for splitting (swiss) german compounds. In *SwissText*, pages 42–49.

University of Tübingen. 2024. Germanet compound word splitting resource. `https://uni-tuebingen.de/.../germanet-1/beschreibung/compounds/`. Accessed June 2025.

Marion Weller and Ulrich Heid. 2012. Analyzing and aligning German compound nouns. In *Proceedings of the Eighth International Conference on Language Resources and Evaluation (LREC'12)*, pages 2395–2400, Istanbul, Turkey. European Language Resources Association (ELRA).

Marion Weller-Di Marco. 2017. Simple compound splitting for german. In *Proceedings of the 13th Workshop on Multiword Expressions (MWE 2017)*, pages 161–166.

Katharina Wellmann. 2020. Mediopunkt oder Binde-Strich? Eine Eyetracking-Studie. *Leichte Sprache–Empirische und multimodale Perspektiven*, pages 23–42.

Linting Xue, Noah Constant, Adam Roberts, Mihir Kale, Rami Al-Rfou, Aditya Siddhant, Aditya Barua, and Colin Raffel. 2021. mt5: A massively multilingual pre-trained text-to-text transformer. In *Proceedings of the 2021 Conference of the North American Chapter of the Association for Computational Linguistics: Human Language Technologies*, pages 483–498, Online / Virtual. Association for Computational Linguistics.

Seid Muhie Yimam, Chris Biemann, Shervin Malmasi, Gustavo Paetzold, Lucia Specia, Sanja Štajner, Anaïs Tack, and Marcos Zampieri. 2018. A report on the complex word identification shared task 2018. In *Proceedings of the Thirteenth Workshop on Innovative Use of NLP for Building Educational Applications*, pages 66–78, New Orleans, Louisiana. Association for Computational Linguistics.

Patrick Ziering and Lonneke van der Plas. 2016. Towards unsupervised and language-independent compound splitting using inflectional morphological transformations. In *Proceedings of the 2016 Conference of the North American Chapter of the Association for Computational Linguistics: Human Language Technologies*, pages 644–653, San Diego, California. Association for Computational Linguistics.

Automatic Generation of Comprehensible German Summaries for Domain-Specific Scientific Definitional Texts

Sophie Decher and **Dr. Michael Dembach**
Fraunhofer FKIE
Fraunhoferstraße 20
53343 Wachtberg, Germany

Abstract

This study aims to test a generative language model's capability to generate German comprehensible summaries of scientific definitional texts, while also gaining insight on which relevant linguistic features are part of the model's implicit knowledge. The open source multilingual model `mistral-small` was shown 100 texts from the EnArgus Wiki, a collection of German scientific definitional texts written by experts in the domain of energy research. The model was then prompted to generate two summaries for each of these texts. The first prompt specified that the texts should be in *einfacher Sprache*, or comprehensible German. The second prompt additionally listed a set of linguistic rules extracted from the DIN 8581-1 norm that the model was expected to comply with. The 200 automatically generated summaries were then assessed for sentence length, readability, semantic similarity to the original, and representation of the original text. A team of domain experts was asked to evaluate the summaries both qualitatively and quantitatively. In addition, two linguists assessed whether a subset of the generated summaries (n=100) adhered to the linguistic rules used in the generation prompt. The findings have implications for LLM use in science communication and NLG and provide insight on the difficulties of creating operationalizable guidelines for German comprehensible language.

1 Introduction

Public access to scientific knowledge and research is important. The high information density and low-frequency, specialized terminology of scientific texts (and especially the high percentage of compound words in German texts) can pose challenges for readers. These difficulties may stem from unfamiliarity with the topic at hand, reading level, or language barriers. In order to increase engagement with and understanding of current scientific research, science communication texts must be written in plain language.

"Translating" technical texts into plain language is not a simple task, however. Researchers, though deeply familiar with their own work, may still lack experience in science communication and knowledge of plain language guidelines—or simply the extra time—to create such texts and check that they meet the linguistic requirements. If a generative language model can be used for this application, science communication could benefit.

In the following, we take the EnArgus information portal [1] as the starting point for a case study on text generation of comprehensible scientific German texts. Funded by the German Federal Ministry of Economic Affairs and Energy, the EnArgus information system is designed to make German energy research funding more transparent and provide high-quality information on current research topics. Users—who range from federal ministries and project management organizations to scientific researchers and members of the general public—can search the databank of government funded projects or peruse the EnArgus Wiki, a collection of over 2000 definitional texts and the source of the data used in the experiments presented below. Written by domain experts, each of these wiki texts provides a definition for a topic relevant to energy research, e.g. *E-Bike*, *Dish-Sterling Kraftwerk* (Dish-Sterling power plant), or *Osmose* (osmosis). Though the authors strive for concision and clarity, the technical nature of many of the topics combined with the (compound-)noun-centricity of German means that the texts are likely not equally accessible for all readers.

Using a sample of these wiki texts, this study aims to investigate how well a multilingual generative language model can summarize German scientific definitional texts in comprehensible

[1] `https://enargus.de/`

Proceedings of the 21st Conference on Natural Language Processing (KONVENS), Volume 2: Workshops, pages 202–211, 2025

language. Supplementing each wiki text with such a summary would increase the accessibility of the EnArgus information system. In addition, the study aims to gain insight on whether the model relies on implicit linguistic knowledge during generation or needs explicit linguistic direction to be included during prompting. The following research questions are posed:

RQ_1: Is a multilingual generative language model capable of converting scientific definitional texts to comprehensible German summaries that comply with a series of pre-defined rules?

RQ_2: In how far does the quality of the generated texts improve when the linguistic rules are made explicit for the model?

The remainder of the paper is structured as follows. Section 2 provides an overview of comprehensible German and plain language, while Section 3 summarizes recent work on text generation and summarization in this area. In Section 4, the experimental setup is described. Section 5 presents the evaluation methods and corresponding results, which are discussed in further detail in Section 6. Concluding remarks and study implications can be found in Section 7.

2 Comprehensible German ("Einfache Sprache")

Comprehensible German texts may be written in either *leichte Sprache* or *einfache Sprache*. *Leichte Sprache* is a form of "barrier-free communication" with strict linguistic and typographic regulations, while *einfache Sprache* is defined less rigidly and places the focus on making texts understandable for the readers, whose needs may differ depending on the context and target audience in question (Bock and Pappert, 2023).

All references to "comprehensible German" in this paper refer to the term *einfache Sprache*, as the aim is to make scientific information more accessible for as wide a variety of readers as possible. The Deutsche Institut für Normung (DIN) has released a series of norms for comprehensible German. The *DIN ISO 24495-1 Einfache Sprache* norm is the German translation of the international norm for plain language and stresses the importance of addressing the needs of the particular target audience for a text (Deutsches Institut für Normung e. V., 2024). *DIN 8581-1 Anwendung für das Deutsche* lists specific linguistic rules and examples for writing texts in comprehensible German (Deutsches Institut für Normung e. V., 2025a). Most recently, the *DIN ISO 24495-3 Wissenschaftliche Sprache* norm, which includes some additional guidelines for scientific texts, was released as a draft (Deutsches Institut für Normung e. V., 2025b).

3 Text generation, summarization, and comprehensible language

The challenges that automatic generation of texts in comprehensible language poses are, as with any natural language generation task, two-fold: (1) model parameters and prompts must be optimized in order to obtain ideal output, and (2) model output must be appropriately evaluated. Unlike classification tasks, for which a gold standard dataset is easier to design, evaluating generative tasks is less straightforward. An additional level of complexity is added when domain-specific texts and texts in languages other than English are used as training data, as there are fewer resources available. A combination of qualitative and quantitative evaluation methods must be applied. A good example of methods that can be applied can be found in August et al. (2022), who analyzed function word usage, Flesch-Kincaid grade level, sentence length, and lexical choice in order to evaluate the complexity of the English generated scientific texts. Research on summarization of German texts, a closely related task for this study, is gradually increasing; while early efforts focused primarily on news summarization (Aumiller et al., 2023), more domains are now being considered, e.g. medicine (Ganzinger et al., 2025) or legal texts (Glaser et al., 2021).

4 Methodology

4.1 Data

The EnArgus Wiki [2] consists of over 2000 German scientific definitional texts written by experts in the domain of energy research. This study is based on a random sample of 100 wiki texts. In an initial preprocessing step, all text titles and metadata were removed so that only the main text body remained.

4.2 Model

All experiments were run on a 4-bit quantized version of the open source multilingual

[2]https://enargus.de/wiki/

mistral-small model [3]. The selection of this small model was deliberate, as not all scientific researchers or science communication experts have access to large servers. A smaller model is also less expensive to deploy and leaves a smaller energy footprint (Jurafsky and Martin, 2025). Testing a smaller, quantized model allows us to evaluate generative AI tools that are readily available without powerful computational resources. Temperature was set to zero to maximize the possibility of receiving deterministic responses and avoid hallucinations.

4.3 Prompt design and experimental setup

The model was prompted to create two summaries for each of the 100 original texts. The prompt for the first summary instructed the model to summarize the source text in 1-2 sentences in comprehensible German (see Appendix A for the full prompt). The text of the prompt for the second summary was identical to the first, with the addition of a list of nine linguistic rules selected from the DIN 8581-1 norm (Deutsches Institut für Normung e. V., 2025a; see Appendix B for the prompt). Figure 1 shows an example of an original text with its two corresponding summaries. This setup makes it possible to test whether the addition of explicit linguistic rules in the prompt results in a better summary, as compared to a prompt that only requests texts in comprehensible German. If the results from both prompts are similar, we can hypothesize that the rules are implicitly already part of the model's knowledge of comprehensible language. The resulting 200 automatically generated summaries were assessed automatically for sentence length (Rule 1 of the linguistic rules included in the prompt), readability score, and semantic similarity to the original. They were then rated and assessed by a group of domain experts. A manual linguistic evaluation was also done on a subset of the generated summaries (50 generated with linguistic rules and 50 without). For each of these 100 texts, compliance with Rules 2-9 was assessed. The evaluations are presented in Section 5.

4.4 Target audience and communicative goal for the generated texts

The aim of these experiments is to generate a concise summary of each source text in comprehensible German that gives a short overview of the main topic. The summaries should remain faithful to the corresponding source texts and be easily readable for members of the general public and laypeople. Domain-specific technical terms must be clearly explained.

[3]https://ollama.com/library/mistral-small:22b

5 Evaluation

5.1 Adherence to linguistic rules

In order to evaluate the model's understanding of Rules 2-9, the first 100 generated summaries (50 generated with the rules explicitly stated in the prompt, and 50 generated without the rules) were manually rated by two linguists.

Rule	**Compliant texts generated with rules**	**Compliant texts generated without rules**
2. Sentence structure	4	22
3. Subordination I	48	50
4. Subordination II	49	50
5. Genitive attributes	48	50
6. Compound words I	48	48
7. Compound words II	48	49
8. Nominalizations	0	16
9. Abbreviations	48	48

Table 1: Linguistic rule evaluation for rules 2–9: Compliancy with linguistic rules in texts generated with linguistic rules stated explicitly in the prompt (n=50) and texts generated without explicit statement of the rules in the prompt (n=50).

Length (words)	**Original texts**	**Texts generated with rules**	**Texts generated without rules**
Mean text length	192.81	120.84	56.80
Min text length	22.00	15.00	18.00
Max text length	516.00	325.00	123.00
Mean sentence length	13.80	11.11	15.06
Min sentence length	3.00	3.00	3.00
Max sentence length	50.00	38.00	34.00

Table 2: Text and sentence length in words in original texts (n=100) and texts generated both with rules stated in the prompt (n=100) and without (n=100). The sentence splitter identified a few sentences that were shorter than three words. These were excluded from this analysis, as they were subheadings rather than full sentences.

The evaluated rules were selected from a list of 114 linguistic rules relevant to the task at hand compiled from the guidelines in the DIN 8581-1 norm (99 rules) and the most recent draft of the DIN ISO 24495-3 norm (5 rules). The DIN 8581-1 norm proved most useful for this task, as it contained formalized, specific rules at multiple levels

Summaries for the text *Stoffaufbereitung*

Original text

Die Stoffaufbereitung ist ein wichtiger Prozessschritt der Papierherstellung. Da sowohl die Produktion auf der Papiermaschine als auch das fertige Produkt genaue Anforderungen an die Eigenschaften des eingesetzten Stoffgemischs stellen, ist es Ziel und Zweck der Stoffaufbereitung, den eingesetzten Faserstoff aufzubereiten und einen konstanten Stoffstrom für die Papiermaschine zur Verfügung zu stellen. Dies ist insbesondere dann anspruchsvoll, wenn die Eigenschaften der eingesetzten Halbstoffe nicht zeitlich konstant sind. Abhängig von den Anforderungen an das Papier werden unterschiedliche Prozessschritte in der Stoffaufbereitung eingesetzt. Zunächst wird der Faserstoff in einem Pulper in Wasser aufgelöst. Um die für die jeweilige Papiersorte benötigten Eigenschaften des Faserstoffs zu garantieren, wird er häufig in der Papierfabrik in einem Refiner nachgemahlen. Je nach Fasermaterial und Papiersorte kann dieser Produktionsschritt sehr energieintensiv sein. Weitere Prozessschritte der Stoffaufbereitung können die Sortierung, Reinigung, erneute Nachmahlung und Dispergierung, also das Einarbeiten von Füllstoffen in die Faser-Wasser Suspension sein.

Stock preparation is an important process step in papermaking. Since both production on the paper machine and the finished product place precise demands on the properties of the material mixture used, the aim and purpose of stock preparation is to prepare the fiber used and provide a constant material flow for the paper machine. This is particularly challenging when the properties of the pulp used are not constant over time. Depending on the requirements of the paper, different process steps are used in stock preparation. First, the fiber is dissolved in water in a pulper. To guarantee the fiber properties required for the respective paper grade, it is often refined in a refiner at the paper mill. Depending on the fiber material and paper grade, this production step can be very energy-intensive. Further process steps in stock preparation can include screening, cleaning, further refining, and dispersion, i.e. the incorporation of fillers into the fiber-water suspension.

Summary generated without rules

Die Stoffaufbereitung ist ein wichtiger Schritt bei der Papierherstellung. Dabei wird der Faserstoff in Wasser aufgelöst und gegebenenfalls gemahlen, um die gewünschten Eigenschaften des Papiers zu erreichen. Dieser Prozess kann energieintensiv sein und beinhaltet oft auch Sortierung, Reinigung und das Einarbeiten von Füllstoffen.

Stock preparation is an important step in papermaking. This involves dissolving the fiber in water and, if necessary, refining it to achieve the desired paper properties. This process can be energy-intensive and often includes screening, cleaning, and the incorporation of fillers.

Summary generated with rules

Die Stoffaufbereitung ist ein wichtiger Schritt bei der Papierherstellung. Das Ziel ist es, den eingesetzten Faserstoff aufzubereiten und einen konstanten Stoffstrom für die Papiermaschine bereitzustellen. Der Faserstoff wird in einem Pulper in Wasser gelöst. Er kann auch in einem Refiner nachgemahlen werden, um die benötigten Eigenschaften zu erreichen. Dieser Schritt kann sehr energieintensiv sein, je nach verwendetem Fasermaterial und Papiersorte. Weitere Schritte sind Sortieren, Reinigen, Nachmahlen und Dispergieren, also das Einarbeiten von Füllstoffen in die Faser-Wasser-Mischung

Stock preparation is a key step in papermaking. The goal is to process the fiber input and provide a consistent flow of material for the paper machine. The fiber is dissolved in water in a pulper. It can also be reground in a refiner to achieve the required properties. This step can be very energy-intensive, depending on the fiber material used and the paper grade. Further steps include screening, cleaning, reground, and dispersing, i.e., incorporating fillers into the fiber-water mixture.

Figure 1: Summaries of the text *Stoffaufbereitung* generated with and without linguistic rules in the prompt

of linguistic analysis. Surprisingly, the DIN ISO 24495-3 norm, though specified to be applicable for scientific writing in comprehensible German, did not contain many additional formalized rules, instead repeating many of the more general guidelines in DIN ISO 24495-1 with added emphasis on the importance of defining the target audience of a text. The five rules taken from DIN ISO 24495-3 touched on comparisons, noun phrases, clear sentences, replacement of technical terms with simpler synonyms, and avoidance of hedges, i.e. vague or ambiguous terms such as *ähnlich* (similar), *nahe* (near), *einen Trend* (a trend), *näherungsweise* (approximately). No rules were extracted from the DIN ISO 24495-1, as the guidelines in this norm were originally designed for English and were covered again in more detail in the DIN 8581-1 norm. From the master list of possible rules to evaluate, the nine rules listed below, all taken from DIN 8581-1, were selected for the linguistic evaluation because each presents a clear formalization of a linguistic phenomenon on the word or sentence level that can be evaluated on a binary (yes/no) basis (Rules 2-9) or automatically (Rule 1). They make specific features of comprehensible language explicit. The sentence and word levels are important for this task, as the goal is to generate very short summarizations of longer texts, requiring optimized lexical choice and tight control of sentence length and structure. The word level is particularly relevant, as the original texts contain difficult, infrequently-occurring scientific terminology. Other rules from the DIN norms such as "The text should be grammatically correct" are assumed to be part of the implicit knowledge of the model and are therefore not included in the evaluation for this study.

Table 1 shows the results for Rules 2-9, which were manually evaluated. Rule 1 was evaluated automatically. The findings for all rules as well as their general relevance for the task are discussed below.

1. **Sentence length: Die Satzlänge soll variiert werden und nie 15 Wörter überschreiten.** *Sentence lengths should vary and never exceed 15 words.* Neither text group adhered completely to this rule. Texts generated without rules tended to consist of fewer sentences (M = 3.87 sentences) that were longer (M = 15.20 words per sentence; cf. Table 2). 88 of these texts contained at least one sentence that was longer than 15 words. Conversely, texts generated with rules were made up of more sentences (M = 10.91 sentences) but had fewer average words per sentence (M = 11.31 words). 65 of these texts contained at least one sentence longer than 15 words. Prompts for both sets of texts set a length limit of 1-2 sentences for the generated summaries, in order to obtain concise, brief summaries. The model was not able to comply with this part of the prompt, though performance was better for the set of texts generated without rules. Length limits in future generative prompts should be determined by word count rather than sentence count.

   The importance of this rule for comprehensible German texts must also be discussed. Wolfer et al. (2015) confirm that simplifying German texts by shortening the sentences often results in an increase in referential expressions such as pronouns and demonstratives that serve to maintain coherence across sentences. These expressions, in turn, require more parsing on the part of the reader and may increase reading difficulty. Finding a balance between sentence length and referential mechanisms may be more beneficial for comprehensible German texts.

2. **Sentence structure: Alle Sätze sollten der kanonischen Satzstruktur in Form von Subjekt–Verb–Objekt (SVO) entsprechen.** *All sentences should conform to the canonical sentence structure in the form of subject–verb–object (SVO).* As Table 1 shows, only four texts generated with rules complied with this rule, whereas 22 texts generated without rules were compliant. In German, this rule can only be applied to main clauses (Wöllstein, 2010; Eisenberg, 2020b). Due to this word order limitation, it must be considered whether a rule requiring SO order, regardless of the placement of the verb, would be more fitting for comprehensible German texts. When a German main clause starts with an adverbial, the subject is pushed to the position behind the verb (Wöllstein, 2010). This was the most common construction in the generated summaries that failed to comply with this rule. The change in word order often serves to make a reference to the preceding sentence in the text. If changes in word order

maintain the cohesion of a text, it might be argued that they enhance rather than detract from the comprehensibility of that text.

3. **Subordination I: Ein Satz soll höchstens einen Nebensatz haben.**
Sentences should contain no more than one subordinate clause. Sentences with more than one subordinate clause were rare. Only two of the evaluated texts, both generated with the prompt that explicitly listed the rule, violated this rule. As all evaluated texts generated without the rules were compliant, it appears that the model does not need to be explicitly prompted to limit subordination.

4. **Subordination II: Ein Nebensatz kann vor oder nach dem Hauptsatz stehen.**
A subordinate clause may precede or follow the main clause. Only one of the evaluated texts violated this rule. It, too, was generated with the prompt that included the rule explicitly, suggesting that prompting with this rule is counterproductive.

5. **Genitive attributes: Genitivattribute sollen nachgestellt werden, es sei denn, es handelt sich um Eigennamen.**
Genitive attributes should be placed after the noun, except in the case of proper nouns. With the exception of two texts generated with rules, this rule was successfully followed (see Table 1). These two violations involved relative pronoun constructions, which are not necesesarily explicitly covered by this rule.

   Of note is the fact that texts generated with rules contained more genitive constructions than those generated without the rules. Adding a rule about genitive constructions in the generation prompt seems to have primed the model to use the genitive case more often. As the positioning of genitive attributes in German sentences already usually defaults to after the noun, the model is likely implicitly aware of this rule, rendering it an unnecessary part of the prompt.

6. **Compound words I: Überlange Komposita (länger als 3 Lexeme) sollten entweder mit Bindestrich geschrieben oder aufgelöst werden.**
Overly long compound words (longer than 3 lexemes) should either be hyphenated or split up into separate words. In the summaries generated without rules in the prompt, two texts contained the overly long compound words *Pumpspeicherkraftwerk* and *Drehstromübertragungssystem*, respectively. The terms *Hochwasserentlastungsanlage* and *Dampfstrahlkälteanlagen* were also included in two different texts that were generated with the rules in the prompt. These technical scientific terms seem to be especially challenging for the model to simplify. This is a task that must be addressed in order to ensure that German scientific texts are understandable for all readers.

7. **Compound words II: Wenn Komposita mit Bindestrich geschrieben werden, dann soll dieser an der Hauptfuge gesetzt werden.**
If compound words are hyphenated, this should occur at the main joint (primary compound boundary). When overly long compound words occurred, they were never hyphenated incorrectly. Violations of this rule were due to the fact that no hyphenation was employed at all. The importance of this rule is secondary to that of the other rules, at least in the context of the data evaluated here.

8. **Nominalizations: Substantivierungen sollen vermieden werden. Stattdessen sollten Verbalkonstruktionen verwendet werden.**
Nominalizations should be avoided. Verbal constructions should be used in their place.

   It is not clear which types of nominalizations this rule is meant to include. If, as stated, no nominalizations of any kind are to be permitted, almost all 200 texts violate the rule, as can be seen in Table 1. This would mean, however, that very common words like *Herstellung* would not be allowed in comprehensible German texts. An alternative would be to disallow only nominalizations that have been created via the process of conversion, i.e. transformed into a new word class without any change in form, such as in the case of *trinken* vs. *das Trinken* (Eisenberg, 2020a). Very few of the 200 generated summaries include nominalizations of this type. From a reading comprehension standpoint, it also makes sense to avoid word forms whose word class might be ambiguous for the reader when writing or generating comprehensible texts.

9. **Abbreviations: Unbekannte oder fachsprachliche Abkürzungen müssen im Text eingefuhrt beziehungsweise erklärt werden.**
Uncommon or technical abbreviations must be introduced or explained in the text. This rule could not be evaluated effectively, as instances of abbreviations in the generated summaries were very rare overall.

5.2 Similarity to original text

The similarity of the 200 generated summaries to their 100 original counterparts was assessed in two ways. First, all texts were embedded using the multilingual `paraphrase-multilingual-mpnet-base-v2`[4] sentence transformers model (Reimers and Gurevych, 2019). The cosine similarity between each generated summary and the corresponding source text was then calculated. As can be seen in Figure 3, the majority of the summaries generated without rules in the prompt were less similar to the source text as compared to the summaries generated with rules in the prompt. For the second assessment, a group of 7 domain experts were asked to rate the 200 generated summaries in a blind binary comparison task. Each text was evaluated once. Evaluators were presented with an original text and the two corresponding generated summaries in randomized order and asked "Which of these two texts is a better summary of the original?" The summaries generated without the rules in the prompt were selected more often (71%) than those generated with the rules in the prompt (29%). When asked to comment on their choices, raters criticized the apparent hallucination and inaccuracies in some of the generated summaries (see Figure 2), as well as the unnecessary retention of some complicated technical terms such as *Methyl-Tertiär-Butyl-Ether*. They often noted that the summaries generated without rules were slightly too short, missing key information, or lacking in clarity and flow, while the summaries generated with rules were often too long and in depth to be considered summaries.

[4]`https://huggingface.co/sentence-transformers/paraphrase-multilingual-mpnet-base-v2`

Excerpt from a summary of *Dezentrale Trinkwassererwärmung*

...Allerdings sind die Kosten für dezentrale Systeme oft höher als für zentrale. Ein weiterer Vorteil ist, dass die Heizungsanlage effizienter betrieben werden kann, besonders im Sommer....

...However, the costs for decentralized systems are often higher than for centralized ones. Another advantage is that the heating system can be operated more efficiently, especially in summer....

Figure 2: Incorrect information in an excerpt from a summary of the EnArgus Wiki text *Dezentrale Trinkwassererwärmung* generated with linguistic rules in the prompt. Higher costs are not advantageous, as this summary suggests.

5.3 Readability score

For an additional assessment method, the readability scores of the original texts and the generated summaries were calculated. As the Flesch-Kincaid grade level used by August et al. (2022) is not as accurate for German as it is for English, we chose the Wiener Sachtextformel IV (Wild and Pissarek, 2021) as an alternative, as shown in Equation 1:

$$\text{WSTF} = 0.2656 \times \left(\frac{\text{\# words}}{\text{\# sentences}}\right) + 0.2744 \times \left(\frac{\text{\# words longer than 3 syllables}}{\text{\# words}}\right) \times 100 - 1.693 \tag{1}$$

Syllables were counted using the `pyphen`[5] Python package, while sentences and words were counted with the `spacy`[6] package using the `de_core_news_sm` pipeline. Figure 4 shows that the readability scores for the summaries generated without rules were overall higher than those of the summaries generated with rules. The original source texts still had the highest readability score, however.

6 Discussion

In light of the above analyses, RQ_1 can partially be confirmed. The manual evaluation of generated summaries according to the linguistic rules showed that most texts complied with the rules for subordination, genitive attributes, and abbreviations. They also complied with the rules for compound words, with some exceptions. Clearly, transforming scientific texts into comprehensible German requires a

[5]`https://pyphen.org/`
[6]`https://spacy.io/`

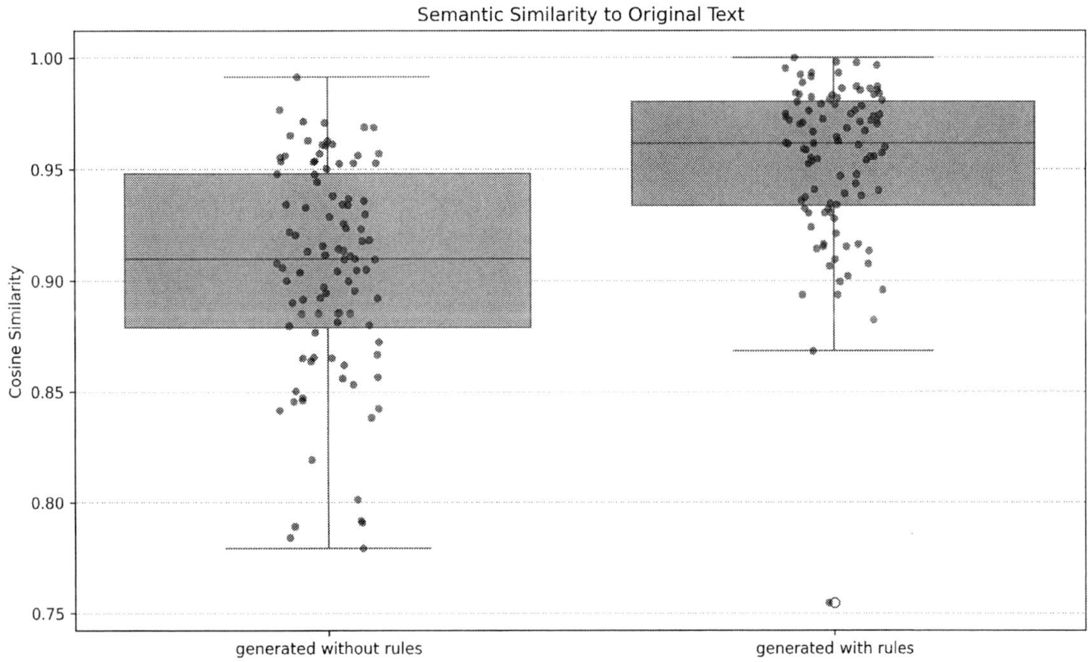

Figure 3: Similarity of generated summaries (both with and without explicit linguistic rules in the generation prompt) to their respective original texts

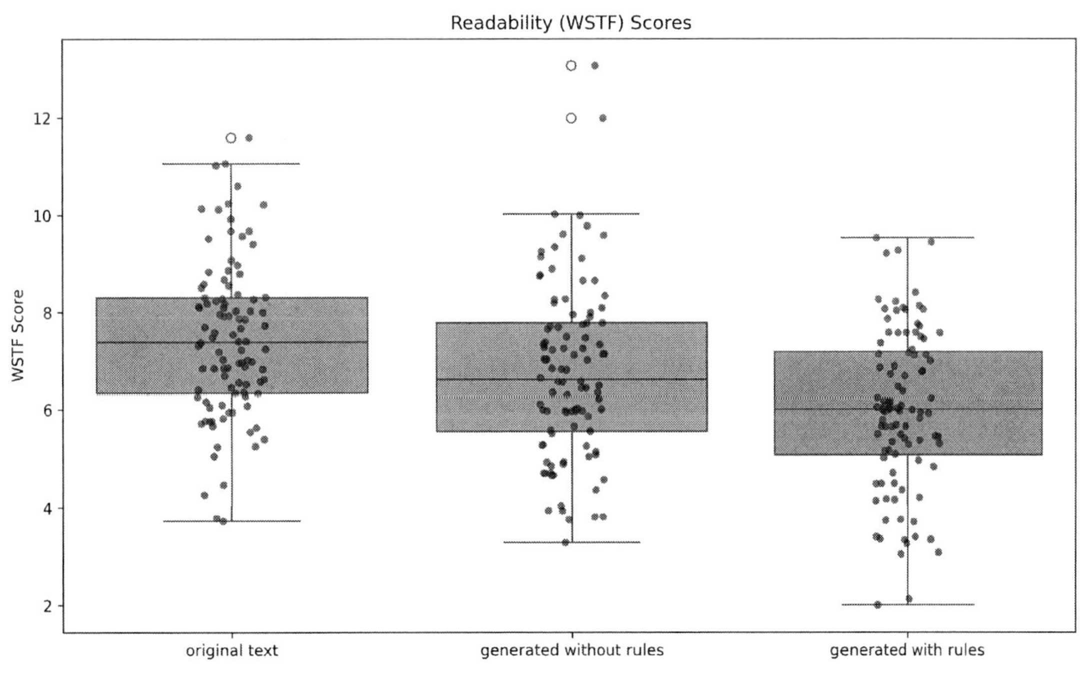

Figure 4: Readability scores of original texts and corresponding summaries generated both with and without the inclusion of linguistic rules in the generation prompt. Scores computed using the Wiener Sachtextformel IV.

focus on the technical compound words typical for German. For all of these rules, there was often no difference between the summaries generated with and without the rules in the prompt.

However, three linguistic rules were not successfully followed. In the case of nominalization (Rule 8) and sentence structure (Rule 2), this is due to the strict formulation of the rules in the DIN 8581-1 norm. It may be necessary to further refine such guidelines for authors, especially when it comes to creating comprehensible versions of scientific technical texts. In the case of sentence length (Rule 1), texts generated both with and without explicit statement of the linguistic rules contained sentences longer than 15 words. We hypothesize that, when prompted with linguistic rules, the model generated texts with a larger overall word count and a higher number of sentences, as it was trying to comply with all rules. This allowed the sentences to be shorter on average. In contrast, texts generated without explicit rules had a smaller word count and were made up of fewer sentences, which resulted in an increase in sentence length. The additional length requirement of 1-2 sentences in both prompts added further constraints–in future studies, it might be better to specify length requirements with a word count rather than a sentence count.

The explicit inclusion of linguistic rules during prompting did not improve the quality of the generated texts (RQ_2). In terms of nominalizations and sentence structure, quality worsened when the rules were explicitly stated. The inclusion of the remaining linguistic rules in the prompt during generation seems to have had little to no effect in most cases. It may be that the rules pertaining to subordination, genitive attributes, compound words, and lexical choice are either already part of the model's implicit linguistic knowledge of what "einfache Sprache" entails or unimportant for generation. The amount of genitive constructions overall also increased when the corresponding rule was included in the generation prompt. The inclusion of rules seems to have influenced the model in unexpected ways.

Readability scores and domain expert ratings were better for texts generated without the rules, though this group of summaries was less semantically similar to the corresponding source texts than the group of summaries generated with rules. It is clearly important to strike a balance between faithfulness to the original source text and comprehensibility for the reader, particularly for this domain of texts.

It seems that the model had difficulties generating texts according to the prompt that included the linguistic rules. It is not clear whether the prompt was too long or too complicated for the model to understand. Previous research on prompt engineering stresses the importance of structure, brevity, coherence, and clarity in prompts (cf. the CLEAR Framework, Lo, 2023). It is possible that the model, in trying to fulfill some of the rules listed, was then prevented from fulfilling other rules listed.

7 Conclusion

Both human ratings and automated evaluations of the generated summaries indicate that the quality of the summaries as-is is inadequate for immediate public use. Generating comprehensible versions of German scientific definitional texts exacerbates the challenges of general summarization. More experiments and model comparisons are needed to continue this line of research.

Limitations

This study has a number of limitations that affect the generalizability of the results. Due to limited resources and a small pool of human raters, only a small subcorpus of data could be used to prompt the model and generate summaries. Similarly, it was only possible to evaluate a small number of linguistic rules from the DIN norms. Follow-up studies are needed to examine a larger quantity of data. For improved summary quality, larger generative models without quantization should also be tested and compared.

Acknowledgments

This study is funded by the German Federal Ministry for Economic Affairs and Energy, as part of the EnArgus 3.0 project (Förderkennzeichen 03EI1062B).

References

Tal August, Katharina Reinecke, and Noah A. Smith. 2022. Generating scientific definitions with controllable complexity. In *Proceedings of the 60th Annual Meeting of the Association for Computational Linguistics, Volume 1: Long Papers*. Association for Computational Linguistics.

Dennis Aumiller, Jing Fan, and Michael Gertz. 2023. On the state of German (abstractive) text summarization. *arXiv:2301.07095*.

Bettina M. Bock and Sandra Pappert. 2023. *Leichte Sprache, Einfache Sprache, verständliche Sprache*. Narr Francke Attempto Verlag, Tübingen, Germany.

Deutsches Institut für Normung e. V. 2024. DIN ISO 24495-1:2024-03 – Einfache Sprache – Teil 1: Grundsätze und Leitlinien.

Deutsches Institut für Normung e. V. 2025a. DIN 8581-1 Einfache Sprache - Anwendung für das Deutsche - Teil 1.

Deutsches Institut für Normung e. V. 2025b. DIN ISO 24495-3:2025-05 – Entwurf – Einfache Sprache – Teil 3: Wissenschaftliches Schreiben.

Peter Eisenberg. 2020a. *Grundriss der deutschen Grammatik. Das Wort*, 5th edition. J. B. Metzler, Berlin, Germany.

Peter Eisenberg. 2020b. *Grundriss der deutschen Grammatik. Der Satz*, 5th edition. J. B. Metzler, Berlin, Germany.

Matthias Ganzinger, Nicola Kunz, Pascal Fuchs, Cornelia K. Lyu, Martin Loos, Martin Dugas, and Thomas M Pausch. 2025. Automated generation of discharge summaries: Leveraging large language models with clinical data. *Scientific Reports*, 15(16466).

Ingo Glaser, Sebastian Moser, and Florian Matthes. 2021. Summarization of German court rulings. In *Proceedings of the Natural Legal Language Processing Workshop 2021*, pages 180–189, Punta Cana, Dominican Republic. Association for Computational Linguistics.

Daniel Jurafsky and James H. Martin. 2025. *Speech and Language Processing: An Introduction to Natural Language Processing, Computational Linguistics, and Speech Recognition with Language Models*, 3rd edition. Online manuscript released January 12, 2025.

Leo S. Lo. 2023. The CLEAR path: A framework for enhancing information literacy through prompt engineering. *The Journal of Academic Librarianship*, 49.

Nils Reimers and Iryna Gurevych. 2019. Sentence-BERT: Sentence embeddings using siamese BERT-networks. In *Proceedings of the 2019 Conference on Empirical Methods in Natural Language Processing*. Association for Computational Linguistics.

Johannes Wild and Markus Pissarek. 2021. Ratte 2: Regensburger Analysetool für Texte - Dokumentation.

Sascha Wolfer, Sandra Hansen-Morath, and Lars Konieczny. 2015. Are shorter sentences always simpler? Discourse level processing consequences of reformulating jurisdictional texts. In Karin Maksymski, Silke Gutermuth, and Silvia Hansen-Schirra, editors, *Translation and Comprehensibility*, pages 263–287. Frank & Timme GmbH, Berlin, Germany.

Angelika Wöllstein. 2010. *Topologisches Satzmodell*. Universitätsverlag Winter Heidelberg, Heidelberg, Germany.

Appendices

A Prompt without linguistic rules

```
Du bist ein Experte der Wissenschaftskommunikation und seit Jahren im Bereich der Energieforschung tätig. Fasse diesen wissenschaftlichen Lexikonartikel in einfacher Sprache in 1-2 Sätzen zusammen. Das erste Substantiv im ersten Satz soll nicht geändert werden. Hier ist der Text: \n\n {input_text}
```

B Prompt with linguistic rules

```
Du bist ein Experte der Wissenschaftskommunikation und seit Jahren im Bereich der Energieforschung tätig. Fasse diesen wissenschaftlichen Lexikonartikel in einfacher Sprache in 1-2 Sätzen anhand der folgenden Regeln zusammen:

1. Die Satzlänge soll variiert werden und nie 15 Wörter überschreiten.
2. Alle Sätze sollten der kanonischen Satzstruktur in Form von Subjekt-Verb-Objekt (SVO) entsprechen.
3. Ein Satz soll höchstens einen Nebensatz haben.
4. Ein Nebensatz kann vor oder nach dem Hauptsatz stehen.
5. Genitivattribute sollen nachgestellt werden, es sei denn, es handelt sich um Eigennamen.
6. Überlange Komposita (länger als 3 Lexeme) sollten entweder mit Bindestrich geschrieben oder aufgelost werden.
7. Wenn Komposita mit Bindestrich geschrieben werden, dann soll dieser an der Hauptfuge gesetzt werden.
8. Substantivierungen sollen vermieden werden. Stattdessen sollten Verbalkonstruktionen verwendet werden.
9. Unbekannte oder fachsprachliche Abkurzungen mussen im Text eingefuhrt beziehungsweise erklärt werden.

Das erste Substantiv im ersten Satz soll nicht geändert werden. Hier ist der Text:\n\n {input_text}
```

German Grammar Profile for Learners: Pedagogical Feature Definition and Automated Extraction

Denise Löfflad[1,3], Benedikt Beuttler[1,2,3], Detmar Meurers[1,3],
[1]Leibniz-Institut für Wissensmedien Tübingen, Germany,
[2]University of Education Ludwigsburg, Germany
[3]LEAD Graduate School and Research Network
d.loefflad@iwm-tuebingen.de
d.meurers@iwm-tuebingen.de
benedikt.beuttler@ph-ludwigsburg.de

Abstract

We introduce the German Grammar Profile (GGP), a system of 150 criterial grammatical features designed to support pedagogically meaningful analysis of reading material for learners of German as a second language. Drawing on the functional grammar framework of the Österreichisches Sprachdiplom (ÖSD), the GGP defines grammatical constructions across CEFR levels A1 to B2.

We also present the corresponding extraction system *Pedagogically Oriented Linguistic Feature Extraction* (PALME, *Pädagogisch Ausgerichtete Linguistische Merkmalsextraktion*), which automatically identifies a growing subset of these features in authentic texts. PALME combines standard Natural Language Processing (NLP) tools with efficient finite state rule based processing to annotate the criterial features and is integrated into a web platform we developed, where users can upload or generate texts and receive visual feedback on the detected criterial grammatical features. Evaluation of a growing subset of currently 33 features shows high precision and recall of the approach.

Ongoing work focuses on extending the coverage to the full criterial feature set. By automatically identifying the features for authentic learner data, our approach will make it possible to empirically validate the expert-defined features of the ÖSD *Profile Deutsch* as the central reference spelling out the CEFR for German. In future work, we plan to extend our tool development by integrating the approach with large language models for level-aware text simplification.

1 Introduction

For real-life foreign language teaching and learning – whether in language classrooms or language testing – specific lexical and grammatical material is relevant to support the acquisition of communicative functions and linguistic structures. The functionally driven Common European Framework of Reference for Languages (CEFR) (Council of Europe, 2001) is widely recognized in Europe as the standard for informing language pedagogy and applied linguistics (Wisniewski et al., 2013; Yancey et al., 2023; Ribeiro-Flucht et al., 2024). One of its strengths is its language-agnostic design: instead of relying on language-specific grammar or syntax, the CEFR uses abstract "can-do" descriptors to define abilities across six levels (A1–C2), which enables its use across all European languages. However, the lack of detailed linguistic specifications also poses challenges for practical implementation, as the CEFR alone cannot fully support proficiency assessment, readability analysis, or automated classification. Due to the lack of language-specific descriptors, teachers and testing institutions need to determine appropriate linguistic markers and align them with grammar and vocabulary at each level. The quality of available language input plays a pivotal role in Second Language Acquisition (SLA), with reading being a crucial source of this input. Effective reading materials are those that challenge learners just beyond their current proficiency level, a concept often referred to as the Zone of Proximal Development (Vygotsky, 2012) or i+1 input (Krashen, 1985). To enhance motivation, materials should also be engaging, personally relevant, and aligned with learners' current interests. Finding such texts poses immense challenges to teachers, especially when teaching heterogeneous groups, as it is time consuming to find and label potentially appropriate texts.

To address this, Automatic Readability Assessment (ARA) aims to predict the readability of a

Proceedings of the 21st Conference on Natural Language Processing (KONVENS), Volume 2: Workshops, pages 212–223, 2025

text for a pre-defined target group and can support teachers in finding appropriate texts faster. Different approaches to ARA have been implemented in the past, including approaches based on surface-based readability formulas (Collins-Thompson, 2014; Kincaid et al., 1975; Björnsson, 1983), using neural networks (Weiss et al., 2021), or using individual linguistic measures such as word frequencies (Chen and Meurers, 2016). However, there is only little data available in languages other than English, and only few studies have performed ARA for German L2 data (for exceptions, see Weiss et al., 2021; Weiss and Meurers, 2021, 2022). Given the nature of the available data, these readability classifications do not correspond to the commonly used CEFR levels, making them unsuitable for learning environments where teachers rely on the CEFR scale for guidance.

This issue is further intensified by traditional machine learning approaches, which often rely on linguistic complexity measures derived from SLA research. While these measures provide valuable insights into the linguistic domains of the data, they are not always intuitive for teachers or learners. For instance, a measure might calculate the standard deviation of SUBTLEX-DE Logarithmic Word Frequency for lexical word types (Brysbaert et al., 2011) - a highly interesting linguistic indicator, but one that lacks accessibility. This lack of clarity can make it challenging for teachers to understand how an ARA algorithm categorizes texts into specific levels. Moreover, abstract or technical linguistic measures provide limited practical support for teachers in adapting or handling texts effectively for language teaching purposes.

In recent years, the use of criterial features, i.e. the identification of distinguishing properties at the level of grammar and the lexicon based on CEFR's functional descriptors, has become more popular (Gaillat et al., 2022; Hawkins and Buttery, 2010). The descriptors used for the CEFR levels are usually formulated as "Can-Do statements" (e.g. "The learner can understand the key concepts of a text.") which are not directly translatable to measurable features.

Despite the growing interest in criterial features, an important gap remains in the current research landscape. For English, the best known resource in this domain is the English Grammar Profile (EGP) (O'Keeffe and Mark, 2022), however, no comparable set of criterial features currently exists for German. This makes it difficult for teachers and assessment tools to link grammatical phenomena to CEFR levels in a systematic and data-driven way. Addressing this gap is essential for developing ARA tools that are both theoretically grounded and practically useful for German L2 education.

We present PALME, a web application that automatically detects German criterial features and allows teachers and students to quickly see potentially difficult grammatical constructs in a text. We furthermore present a German Grammar Profile (GGP) including 150 criterial features based on the CEFR descriptors and the *funktionale Grammatik* (*functional grammar* framework) as defined by the *Österreichisches Sprachdiplom Deutsch* (ÖSD).

2 Related Work

2.1 Automatic Readability Assessment

Text readability refers to degree of ease with which a text can be understood. The most direct, and most used, approach for ARA is to assign a text with a single readability score representing the overall level of comprehensibility. Such scores are so-called readability formulas, and typically rely on easily computable surface-level textual features, such as sentence length (measured in number of words) or word length (measured in number of syllables or number of characters) (DuBay, William H., 2004). Readability formulas such as the Flesch-Kincaid formula (Kincaid et al., 1975) or the LIX index (Björnsson, 1983) have been widely and successfully applied across various domains (Vajjala, 2022) including the assessment of legal texts (Han et al., 2024), medical communication (Kiwanuka et al., 2017; Paul et al., 2021), or to control automatically generated or simplified texts (Marchisio et al., 2019; Picton et al., 2025; Srinivasan et al., 2024).

Although reasonably accurate for many tasks, readability formulas rely on surface level measures. As a result, they fail to capture underlying linguistic phenomenon and provide only limited interpretability. Research has thus increasingly shifted towards feature-based machine learning approaches that extract (more or less extensive) sets of linguistic complexity features (Feng et al., 2009; Deutsch et al., 2020; Weiss, 2024). These approaches enable a more nuanced modeling of text difficulty by incorporating syntactic, lexical, semantic, morphological, and discourse-level information. Certain machine learning approaches such as Random Forests, Support Vector Machines or LSTMs allow for more interpretability by providing insights into the importance of individual features contributing to readability predictions.

This is especially useful for educational research domains (Collins-Thompson, 2014), where research often aim to understand proficiency development or control for text readability for a certain target group. ARA plays a crucial role in SLA, as it supports educators in aligning instructional and reading materials with learners' proficiency levels. By helping to match text complexity to learner ability, ARA enables more targeted and effective language instruction. A comprehensive literature review by Weiss (2024) revealed, however, that the majority of existing ARA research has focused on L1 language acquisition and primarily on English texts.

Nevertheless, there has been work on ARA in SLA for different languages (Imperial, 2021; Ribeiro et al., 2024; Uçar et al., 2024) and target groups (Feng et al., 2009; Abedi et al., 2012). For example, Weiss et al. (2021) established a multi-level readability algorithm for German L2 that classifies texts for beginner, intermediate an advances learners for German based on linguistic complexity. Moreover, as highlighted by Weiss (2024), most existing ARA research has focused on modeling the readability of entire texts. More recent work had explored sentence-level readability prediction for a more granular perspective (Štajner et al., 2017; Weiss and Meurers, 2022).

Yet, readability is not a property of a text alone. It results from the interaction of text, reading goals and reader characteristics such as prior knowledge, interests and also task context (Collins-Thompson, 2014; Vajjala, 2022; Valencia et al., 2014).

As it is not possible to account for all possible reader characteristics, we propose a shift in focus: rather than classifying texts or sentences by overall difficulty, we introduce a tool that highlights grammatical constructs along with their corresponding CEFR levels. By refraining from assigning readability scores and instead visually identifying potentially challenging linguistic constructs, we aim to support teachers to quickly evaluate whether a text is suitable for their specific teaching goals. This also allows teachers to decide whether targeted adaptations of text segments are needed.

2.2 Criterial Features

In response to the challenges associated with interpreting linguistic complexity, particularly its limited pedagogical specificity and lack of transparency in assessment settings, recent research has increasingly turned to criterial features as a more concrete, developmentally informed alternative (Salamoura and Saville, 2010; Hawkins and Filipović, 2012; Gaillat et al., 2022). These features refer to linguistic properties that are reliably acquired at specific stages of second language development and can thus serve as indicators of proficiency (Hawkins and Buttery, 2010). Criterial features are typically aligned with the CEFR. Although the CEFR descriptors provide general guidance for assessment, due to the language-agnostic properties of the CEFR, the descriptors are often underspecified in terms of the actual linguistic features that distinguish levels. Nevertheless, examiners tend to show high agreement in their level judgments (De Clercq et al., 2014). This implies that there must be underlying linguistic regularities that guide their decisions, even if these are not explicitly formulated in the CEFR itself. The goal of criterial feature research is therefore to identify the linguistic cues that examiners implicitly respond to, and to formalize these as part of a more systematic, data-informed approach to L2 proficiency.

Importantly, criterial features are not about linguistic complexity or difficulty per se, but about when certain linguistic forms emerge in the learning process (Bulté et al., 2025). A structure's presence at a particular level does not mean it is inherently more complex or more difficult. It simply means it tends to appear at that point in a typical learner's developmental trajectory. As Bulté et al. (2025) put it, "difficulty can be the cause for a certain developmental order (and this order may be taken as evidence for the construct's difficulty)", but this is not necessarily the case. A structure might not appear earlier because it wasn't needed in relevant genres or communicative situations, or because it wasn't taught or noticed.

The EGP offers a well-established resource of criterial features for English (O'Keeffe and Mark, 2022), expanding on CEFR descriptors by mapping them onto fine-grained grammatical structures. These descriptors are not only measurable and interpretable but also highly suitable for classroom use and automated assessment.

Unfortunately, for L2 German and to the best of our knowledge, no equivalent resource exists to date. While learner corpora offer valuable data, only the MERLIN corpus (Wisniewski et al., 2013) explicitly links learner texts to CEFR levels. A practitioner-oriented tool such as *Profile Deutsch* (Glaboniat, 2010) also attempts to associate grammatical phenomena with CEFR levels, but its categories are based on expert consensus rather than empirical learner language. As Wisniewski (2020) notes, this reflects a major gap in the availability of criterial feature resources for German, especially for educational applications. With the present research, we aim to close this gap by formulating 150 criterial features for German as well as building a web application that can automatically detect those features.

2.3 Related Systems

Several existing systems share similarities with our approach to automatic grammatical feature extraction and annotation. The POLKE system (Pedagogically Oriented extraction of Linguistic Knowledge, Sagirov and Chen (2025)), for example, extracts over 600 measures from the EGP using a comparable framework including Java and RUTA[1] preprocessing. POLKE's primary focus is the large-scale implementation and evaluation of EGP-based measures. For Portuguese, the SABER system offers a related approach to grammatical feature extraction (Sistema de Análise e Busca de Estruturas Relevantes, Akef et al. (2025)).

Highlighting linguistic constructions for learner noticing is a well-established concept. ICALL systems such as VIEW and WERTi provide input enhancement techniques on websites by visually emphasizing selected linguistic features to increase learner awareness (Meurers et al., 2010). While their primary focus is on language acquisition, the underlying idea aligns with our goal of making grammatical constructions salient.

Additionally, the FLAIR system (Form-Focused Linguistically Aware Information Retrieval; Chinkina et al. (2016)) demonstrates the value of integrating grammar knowledge into information retrieval. FLAIR incorporates grammatical patterns derived from an official English L2 curriculum into a content-based search engine, enhancing retrieval by linguistic criteria.

Together, these systems illustrate the relevance and growing interest in grammar-informed linguistic analysis and learner support, contextualizing our work within a broader landscape.

3 The German Grammar Profile

Building on the methodology of the EGP, we manually formulated 150 criterial grammatical features for German, which we refer to as the GGP, examples for the different levels can be seen in Table 1, the original German version can be see in the appendix in Table 2.

Unlike the EGP, which is built in a bottom-up, data-driven way, the GGP follows a top-down approach. Our starting point is the functional grammar framework provided by the ÖSD, which organizes grammatical phenomena according to communicative intentions, relations, and textual elements[2]. This structure identifies which grammatical forms are expected to occur at which CEFR levels, supplemented with descriptive explanations and illustrative examples. Our criterial features are systematically derived from this framework and have been evaluated and ranked by two experts from the ÖSD testing institute for pedagogical relevance and CEFR alignment, currently covering levels A1 to B2. The process was as follows.

To move from descriptive grammar to operationalization, we developed a structured feature schema inspired by the EGP: Each feature is assigned a supercategory, subcategory, guiding keywords (e.g., *Verbs* or *Pronouns* as supercategory, *Inflection* or *Modal verb* as subcategory, *Past Perfect* or *Accusative* as keywords), and example sentences. Every grammatical construct fund in the functional grammar framework resulted in one or several criterial features. Example features can be seen in Table 1. This categorization supports a consistent and interpretable annotation process. The super- and subcategories capture broader grammatical domains and their functional subtypes, while the guiding keywords help to highlight the kinds of linguistic cues that are typically associated with each feature, such as part-of-speech tags, morphological features (e.g. case, tense, mood) and syntactic dependencies. By aligning the conceptual categories with observable patterns, the GGP provides a bridge between pedagogically motivated descriptors and detectable linguistic structures.

[1] https://uima.apache.org/ruta.html

[2] https://www.osd.gr/de/das-osd-prufungssystem/profile-deutsch/ziele-komponenten.html

SuperCat.	SubCat.	Level	Guideword	Example
Main Clause	Interrogative	A1	Yes/No questions	Are you tired?
Negation	Negation	A1	„no“ + nominative	That is not a nice house.
Clause	Subordinate Clause	A2	„so“	I'm saving money so I can buy a car.
Verbs	Inflection	A2	Past Perfect	He had brought cake.
Pronoun	Relative Pronoun	B1	„what“, „where“	This is the city where we met.
Noun	Inflection	B1	Genitive	That's my father's car.
Verbs	Conjugation	B2	Conditional 1	If he comes later, we will talk.
Clause	Main Clause	B2	Desiderative	If only I had known!

Table 1: Translated example grammatical features from the GGP across CEFR levels.

Table 3 in the appendix gives a detailed overview of the distribution of features within the GGP by supercategory and subcategory. For instance, the GGP contains 43 verb-related features, including inflectional paradigms and modal verbs, 21 pronoun-related features covering personal, possessive, relative, and demonstrative pronouns, 19 adjective-related features and 12 features related to sentence structures. Other grammatical domains such as negation, connectors, prepositions, articles, nouns, and adjectives are also systematically represented. This structured categorization supports comprehensive coverage of grammatical phenomena across proficiency levels and facilitates targeted automatic detection. The strong focus on verb and tense related features is interesting to note. Previous research on ARA for German as second language using linguistic difficulty measures found that morphological features, which include tense, seem not to be particularly informative for machine learning models (Weiss et al., 2021).

This contrast is particularly interesting, as it illustrates a top-down, tester-centered approach that prioritizes pedagogical relevance over purely data-driven predictive use. Future research will need to explore these discrepancies in more depth, particularly how criterial features relate to linguistic complexity, and where pedagogical expertise and empirical model evidence converge or diverge. Understanding this relationship more precisely is essential for advancing both test design and automatic assessment.

In a later step, we will compare this expert-defined inventory with actual learner data to assess which constructs occur productively in learner language, and which remain rare or are avoided. This comparison will allow us to refine the GGP and better align pedagogical expectations with empirical usage.

4 PALME System Description

We follow the approach implemented by Sagirov and Chen (2025) to process learner texts. As shown in the flowchart (Figure 1), a text input is received via an HTTPS request and first preprocessed using standard Java NLP tools: OpenNLP (v2.2)[3] for tokenization and sentence segmentation, Mate Tools (v2.2)[4] for lemmatization and morphological feature annotation, and Stanford NLP-GPL (v2.2)[5] for dependency parsing and Named Entity Recognition.

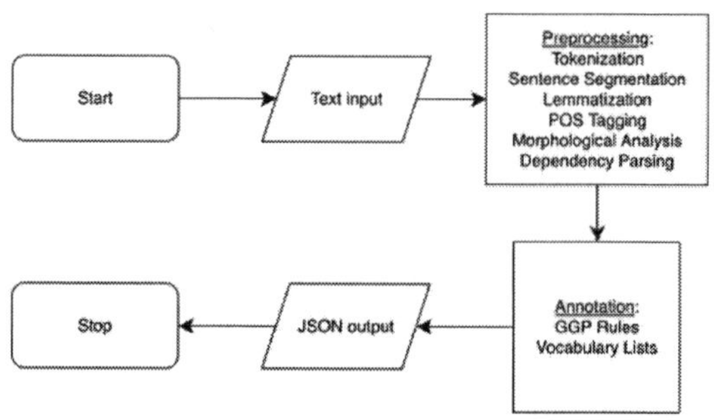

Figure 1: Overview of PALME pipeline and data flow

The GGP is integrated into a prototype web platform that allows users to analyze their own texts or generate new ones via a large language model. We built the web platform with the open-source Python framework Streamlit[7]. All texts are processed through our pipeline and annotated with

[3]https://opennlp.apache.org/news/release-220.html

[4]https://www.ims.uni-stuttgart.de/forschung/ressourcen/werkzeuge/matetools/

[5]https://universaldependencies.org/treebanks/de_gsd/index.html

[7]https://streamlit.io/

grammatical constructions relevant for learner language.

These annotations provide the linguistic information required for the next step, where the text is annotated with detailed grammatical construction using RUTA, a rule-based language for text annotation. This process also uses specialized word lists based on resources provided by the ÖSD. We focused on the most important 70 features based on our expert rating and implemented those in PALME. The system currently covers 16 features at A1, 24 at A2, 17 at B1, and 13 at B2.

The extraction system is accessible via an API and integrated into a prototype web platform, shown in Figure 2. The platform offers a user-friendly, interactive environment where users can analyze their own texts by typing or pasting them into a text field. In addition to analyzing user-provided texts, the platform allows users to generate new learner-relevant texts on demand. By entering a prompt in a separate text field, users can request text generation via the integrated Gemini API. We decided to use the Gemini API due to its ease of use in this context. The generated texts are automatically analyzed by PALME, providing the same detailed feedback on grammatical features.
Once submitted, these texts are automatically processed by PALME, which returns detailed annotations of grammatical constructions corresponding to criterial features in JSON format. Since raw JSON output is not easy to interpret, we developed a clear visualization that highlights annotated constructions in different colors according to their proficiency levels. A legend was added to the visualization, showing the corresponding construct ID. Currently, the visualization references only the construct ID, but we plan to include the supercategory in future versions to help users quickly understand the type of linguistic phenomenon annotated. This visual feedback allows teachers and students to quickly identify parts of a text that may be too difficult or too easy so that texts can be adapted easily.

5 Evaluation

Our extraction system shows promising results. Of the currently 70 implemented features, a subset of 33 randomly selected features was evaluated for precision and recall to establish PALME's algorithmic reliability. Of these 33 evaluated features, four at A1 level, ten at A2, 121 at B1 and seven at B2 level. We found a mean precision of 0.92 and a mean recall of 0.82, showing that the system can reliably extract criterial features.
To evaluate the system, we follow a typical strategy based on standard classification metrics. Precision measures the proportion of correctly identified instances among all extractions made by the tool, while recall assess the proportion of successfully detected instances among all instances to be extracted.

Figure 2: PALME platform interface showing user text input and results from Gemini API. The text on the left is a snippet of a text from the youth magazine *das Biber*[6], both text are about an annual fair about contemporary art in Vienna, the Viennafair.

A practical limitation in the evaluation stems from the lack of sufficiently large, CEFR-aligned corpora of German reading material. While learner corpora such as MERLIN provide CEFR annotations, it consists of learner-produced texts and is thus not ideal for evaluating the system's ability to handle reading input. As a result, we based our evaluation on texts from Spotlight[8], a magazine that publishes graded articles at the levels "Beginner", "Intermediate", and "Advanced", which approximately correspond to A2, B1, and B2/C1 respectively. Although these categories do not perfectly align with CEFR level definitions, they provided a workable approximation in the absence of more suitable corpora. We manually annotated all instances of the 33 evaluated criterial features in this material and matched them to the automatically extracted instances. To ensure sufficient coverage for recall evaluation, we also constructed additional example sentences containing the relevant features.

For precision, the extractor was applied to nine texts from the Spotlight corpus, which contains CEFR-labeled reading materials. These texts were evenly distributed across three proficiency levels: A2, B1, and B2/C1 (three texts per level). Figure 3 presents the number of extracted features per CEFR level, alongside the total word count per group. As expected, the number of higher-level constructs (notably B1 and B2) increased with text level, and no B2 constructs were found in A2-level texts.

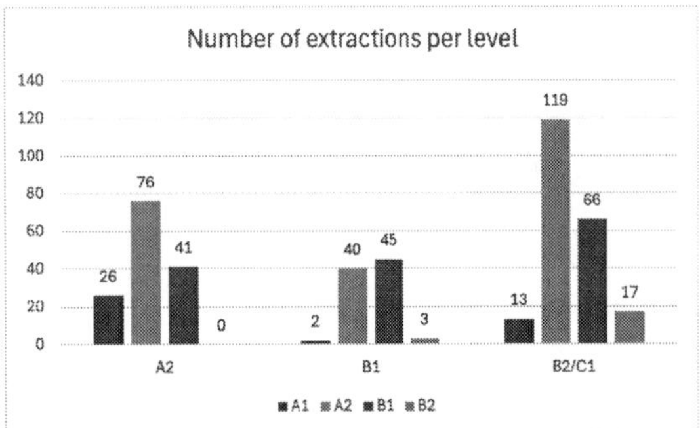

Figure 3: Distribution of occurrences of the 33 implemented criterial feature across CEFR levels

In total, 448 annotations were extracted, of which 416 were correct, resulting in an overall precision of 0.92. Among the 32 incorrect annotations, 28 were attributable to errors in external taggers, while four stemmed from limitations of our RUTA rules. These tagging issues have since been addressed in a revised preprocessing pipeline. Recall was evaluated separately using a controlled set of ten example sentences per feature, in addition to the examples provided in the Grammar Profile. The extractor was applied to this dataset, and recall per feature was calculated based on the proportion of successful detections. All tested features were identified at least four times, indicating robust detection capabilities under ideal conditions. 22 constructs achieved perfect precision. Conversely, a small number of constructs showed lower precision, often due to isolated tagging errors.

Together, these results support the reliability of our extraction method and provide an initial empirical validation of the developmental relevance of our feature set.

Moving forward, we plan to expand evaluation efforts using the MERLIN corpus, which consists of CEFR-annotated learner texts. This will not only verify the technical accuracy of our system but also serve a theoretical purpose: by analyzing the occurrence patterns of criterial features across proficiency levels in authentic learner writing, we aim to empirically assess the alignment of our expert-defined GGP with actual learner language development.

6 Outlook

Future work will focus on expanding and refining the system along several dimensions. We plan to implement the full set of 150 criterial features and extend the evaluation to include precision, recall and learner-level agreement for all features. In addition, we aim to conduct a more detailed analysis of when and how specific grammatical constructions occur in learner texts, based on corpus evidence.

We also aim to explore how traditional NLP components can be integrated into workflows based on large language models (LLMs) to support more informed and effective simplification. A central question will be whether LLMs can produce better, more pedagogically appropriate simplifications when guided by explicit linguistic information. This hybrid approach offers a promising path toward combining the strengths of rule-based analysis and generative flexibility in learner-oriented text generation.

Another important avenue for future research is to investigate the applicability of the system to

[8]https://www.spotlight-verlag.de

learner language, which often includes ill-formed structures. As the current design is based on well-formed input, evaluating its robustness on learner-produced texts will be crucial.

7 Conclusion

We presented the GGP, a system of 150 criterial grammatical features designed to support pedagogical applications in language learning. The GGP is grounded in the functional grammar framework of the ÖSD and systematically adapted to allow for automatic detection in learner-relevant texts. A subset of 70 features, rated as most relevant by experts, has been implemented in our extraction system PALME, which is accessible via an API and integrated into a web-based prototype. The platform allows users to analyze their own texts or generate new ones with a language model via text input fields, providing detailed visual feedback on grammatical constructions across CEFR levels A1 to B2.

The automatic extraction pipeline uses established Java NLP tools and uses a combination of morphological, syntactic, and lexical information to detect relevant criterial features from the GGP. Evaluation of a randomly selected subset of 33 implemented constructs showed high precision and promising recall, supporting the technical validity of the approach.

While the system remains under development, it already provides a practical tool for grammar-aware text analysis. Future work will expand the feature inventory and evaluate feature distribution in larger learner corpora. We also plan to explore whether integration with LLMs can support more targeted text simplification, using the GGP as a guiding framework. In this way, the system aims to contribute to both research and pedagogical practice in the field of learner-oriented grammar profiling.

Limitations

The PALME website currently is a prototype with several limitations. While we have defined 150 criterial features, currently 70 are fully implemented in the extraction system, of which 33 have undergone precision and recall evaluation. The GGP currently also primarily reflects expert judgment and curricular expectations rather than observed learner production. A systematic learner corpus analysis is envisaged to validate and refine the feature set in future work. Moreover, the rule-based approach is ideal for standard language, but its applicability to learner language may be limited. Future research should explore alternative approaches for such contexts.

Acknowledgments

We are grateful to the ÖSD, especially Karen Schramm and Anne Raveling, for the collaboration during the construction of the GGP. We thank our student assisstant Sofia Kathmann for the great work regarding the implementation of the criterial features. We also thank Elina Schnaper for her work during her bachelor thesis which contributed to the present paper.

References

Jamal Abedi, Robert Bayley, Nancy Ewers, Kimberly Mundhenk, Seth Leon, Jenny Kao, and Joan Herman. 2012. Accessible Reading Assessments for Students with Disabilities. *International Journal of Disability, Development and Education*, 59(1):81–95.

Soroosh Akef, Detmar Meurers, Amália Mendes, and Patrick Rebuschat. 2025. Interpretable Machine Learning for Societal Language Identification: Modeling English and German Influences on Portuguese Heritage Language. In *Proceedings of the 14th Workshop on Natural Language Processing for Computer Assisted Language Learning*, pages 50–62.

C. H. Björnsson. 1983. Readability of Newspapers in 11 Languages. *Reading Research Quarterly*, 18(4):480.

Marc Brysbaert, Matthias Buchmeier, Markus Conrad, Arthur Jacobs, Jens Bölte, and Andrea Böhl. 2011. The Word Frequency Effect: A Review of Recent Developments and Implications for the Choice of Frequency Estimates in German. *Experimental psychology*, 58:412–24.

Bram Bulté, Alex Housen, and Gabriele Pallotti. 2025. Complexity and Difficulty in Second Language Acquisition: A Theoretical and Methodological Overview. *Language Learning*, 75(2):533–574.

Xiaobin Chen and Detmar Meurers. 2016. Characterizing Text Difficulty with Word Frequencies. In *Proceedings of the 11th Workshop on Innovative Use of NLP for Building Educational Applications*, pages 84–94, San Diego, CA. Association for Computational Linguistics.

Maria Chinkina, Madeeswaran Kannan, and Detmar Meurers. 2016. Online information retrieval for language learning. In *Proceedings of ACL-2016 System Demonstrations*, pages 7–12.

Kevyn Collins-Thompson. 2014. Computational assessment of text readability: A survey of current and future research. *ITL-International Journal of Applied Linguistics*, 165(2):97–135.

Council of Europe. 2001. *Common European Framework of Reference for Languages: Learning, Teaching, Assessment*. Cambridge University Press.

Orphée De Clercq, Véronique Hoste, Bart Desmet, Philip Van Oosten, Martine De Cock, and Lieve Macken. 2014. Using the crowd for readability prediction. *Natural Language Engineering*, 20(3):293–325.

Tovly Deutsch, Masoud Jasbi, Masoud Jasbi, and Stuart M. Shieber. 2020. Linguistic Features for Readability Assessment. *Workshop on Innovative Use of NLP for Building Educational Applications*, pages 1–17.

DuBay, William H. 2004. The principles of readability.

Lijun Feng, Noémie Elhadad, and Matt Huenerfauth. 2009. Cognitively motivated features for readability assessment. In *Proceedings of the 12th Conference of the European Chapter of the Association for Computational Linguistics*, EACL '09, pages 229–237, Athens, Greece.

Thomas Gaillat, Andrew Simpkin, Nicolas Ballier, Bernardo Stearns, Annanda Sousa, Manon Bouyé, and Manel Zarrouk. 2022. Predicting CEFR levels in learners of English: The use of microsystem criterial features in a machine learning approach. *ReCALL*, 34(2):130–146.

Manuela Glaboniat, editor. 2010. *Profile deutsch: gemeinsamer europäischer Referenzrahmen; Lernzielbestimmungen; Kannbeschreibungen; kommunikative Mittel; Niveau A1-A2, B1-B2; C1-C2; [CD-ROM Version 2.0 mit Begleitbuch]*, nachdr. edition. Langenscheidt, Berlin München Wien Zürich.

Yu Han, Aaron Ceross, and Jeroen H. M. Bergmann. 2024. The Use of Readability Metrics in Legal Text: A Systematic Literature Review. *arXiv preprint*. Version Number: 1.

John A. Hawkins and Paula Buttery. 2010. Criterial Features in Learner Corpora: Theory and Illustrations. *English Profile Journal*, 1:e5.

John A Hawkins and Luna Filipović. 2012. *Criterial features in L2 English: Specifying the reference levels of the Common European Framework*, volume 1. Cambridge University Press.

Joseph Marvin Imperial. 2021. BERT embeddings for automatic readability assessment. In *Proceedings of the International Conference on Recent Advances in Natural Language Processing (RANLP 2021)*, pages 611–618, Held Online. INCOMA Ltd.

J. P. Kincaid, Jr Fishburne, R. P., R. L. Rogers, and B. S. Chissom. 1975. Derivation of New Readability Formulas (Automated Readability Index, Fog Count and Flesch Reading Ease Formula) for Navy Enlisted Personnel.

Elizabeth Kiwanuka, Raman Mehrzad, Adnan Prsic, and Daniel Kwan. 2017. Online Patient Resources for Gender Affirmation Surgery: An Analysis of Readability. *Annals of Plastic Surgery*, 79(4):329–333.

Stephen D. Krashen. 1985. *Second language acquisition and second language learning*, reprinted edition. Language teaching methodology series. Pergamon Pr, Oxford.

Kelly Marchisio, Jialiang Guo, Cheng-I Lai, and Philipp Koehn. 2019. Controlling the Reading Level of Machine Translation Output. In *Proceedings of Machine Translation Summit XVII: Research Track*, pages 193–203.

Detmar Meurers, Ramon Ziai, Luiz Amaral, Adriane Boyd, Aleksandar Dimitrov, Vanessa Metcalf, and Niels Ott. 2010. Enhancing authentic web pages for language learners. In *Proceedings of the NAACL HLT 2010 Fifth Workshop on Innovative Use of NLP for Building Educational Applications*, pages 10–18.

Anne O'Keeffe and Geraldine Mark. 2022. The English Grammar Profile of learner competence: Methodology and key findings. *International Journal of Corpus Linguistics*, pages 457–489.

Simon Paul, Marc-Daniel Ahrend, Jan-Christoffer Lüers, Kersten Sven Roth, Peter P. Grimmiger, Florian Bopp, and Babak Janghorban Esfahani. 2021. Systematic Analysis of Readability of Patient Information on Internet Pages from Departments for Trauma Surgery of German University Hospitals. *Zeitschrift für Orthopädie und Unfallchirurgie*, 159(02):187–192.

Bryce Picton, Saman Andalib, Aidin Spina, Brandon Camp, Sean S. Solomon, Jason Liang, Patrick M. Chen, Jefferson W. Chen, Frank P. Hsu, and Michael Y. Oh. 2025. Assessing AI Simplification of Medical Texts: Readability and Content Fidelity. *International Journal of Medical Informatics*, 195:105743.

Eugénio Ribeiro, Nuno Mamede, and Jorge Baptista. 2024. Automatic text readability assessment in European Portuguese. In *Proceedings of the 16th International Conference on Computational Processing of Portuguese*, Santiago de Compostela, Galicia, Spain.

Luisa Ribeiro-Flucht, Xiaobin Chen, and Detmar Meurers. 2024. Explainable ai in language learning: Linking empirical evidence and theoretical concepts in proficiency and readability modeling of portuguese. In *Proceedings of the 19th Workshop on Innovative Use of NLP for Building Educational Applications (BEA 2024)*, pages 199–209.

Nelly Sagirov and Xiaobin Chen. 2025. POLKE: A system for comprehensively annotating pedagogically-oriented grammatical structure use in language production.

Angeliki Salamoura and Nick Saville. 2010. Exemplifying the CEFR: Criterial features of written learner English from the English Profile Programme. In Inge Bartning, M. Martin, and Ineke Vedder, editors, *Communicative proficiency and linguistic development: Intersections between SLA and language testing research*, volume 1 of *Second Language Acquisition and Testing in Europe Monograph Series*, pages 101–131. European Second Language Association.

Nitin Srinivasan, Jamil S. Samaan, Nithya D. Rajeev, Mmerobasi U. Kanu, Yee Hui Yeo, and Kamran Samakar. 2024. Large language models and bariatric surgery patient education: a comparative readability analysis of GPT-3.5, GPT-4, Bard, and online institutional resources. *Surgical Endoscopy*, 38(5):2522–2532.

Suna-Şeyma Uçar, Itziar Aldabe, Nora Aranberri, and Ana Arruarte. 2024. Exploring Automatic Readability Assessment for Science Documents within a Multilingual Educational Context. *International Journal of Artificial Intelligence in Education*, 34(4):1417–1459.

Sowmya Vajjala. 2022. Trends, limitations and open challenges in automatic readability assessment research. In *Proceedings of the Thirteenth Language Resources and Evaluation Conference*, pages 5366–5377.

Sheila W. Valencia, Karen K. Wixson, and P. David Pearson. 2014. Putting Text Complexity in Context. *The Elementary School Journal*. Publisher: University of Chicago PressChicago, IL.

Lev S Vygotsky. 2012. *Thought and language*, volume 29. MIT press.

Zarah Weiss. 2024. *An integrative approach to linguistic complexity analysis for German*. PhD Thesis, Universität Tübingen.

Zarah Weiss, Xiaobin Chen, and Detmar Meurers. 2021. Using broad linguistic complexity modeling for cross-lingual readabılı ty assessment. In *Proceedings of the Joint 10th Workshop on NLP for Comput er Assisted Language Learning*, pages 38–54.

Zarah Weiss and Detmar Meurers. 2021. Analyzing the linguistic complexity of German learner langua ge in a reading comprehension task: Using proficiency classification to investi gate short answer data, cross-data generalizability, and the impact of linguist ic analysis quality. *International Journal of Learner Corpus Research*, 7(1):84–131.

Zarah Weiss and Detmar Meurers. 2022. Assessing sentence readability for German language learners with broad linguistic modeling or readability formulas: When do linguistic insights make a difference? In *Proceedings of the 17th Workshop on Innovative Use of NLP for Building Educational Applications (BEA 2022)*, pages 141–153, Seattle, Washington. Association for Computational Linguistics.

Katrin Wisniewski. 2020. SLA developmental stages in the CEFR-related learner corpus MERLIN: Inversion and verb-end structures in German A2 and B1 learner texts. *International Journal of Learner Corpus Research*, 6(1):1–37.

Katrin Wisniewski, Karin Schöne, Lionel Nicolas, Chiara Vettori, Adriane Boyd, Detmar Meurers, Andrea Abel, and Jirka Hana. 2013. MERLIN: An online trilingual learner corpus empirically grounding the European Reference Levels in authentic learner data. In *ICT for Language Learning 2013, Conference Proceedings, Florence, Italy. Libreriauniversitaria. it Edizioni.*

Kevin P Yancey, Geoffrey Laflair, Anthony Verardi, and Jill Burstein. 2023. Rating short L2 essays on the CEFR scale with GPT-4. In *Proceedings of the 18th workshop on innovative use of NLP for building educational applications (BEA 2023)*, pages 576–584.

Sanja Štajner, Simone Paolo Ponzetto, and Heiner Stuckenschmidt. 2017. Automatic assessment of absolute sentence complexity. *International Joint Conference on Artificial Intelligence*, pages 4096–4102.

A Appendix

SupKat.	**SubKat.**	**Level**	**Leitword**	**Beispiel**
Hauptsatz	Fragesatz	A1	Ja/Nein-Frage	Sind Sie müde?
Negation	Negation	A1	„kein" + Nominativ	Das ist kein schönes Haus.
Satz	Nebensatz	A2	damit	Ich spare Geld, damit ich ein Auto kaufen kann.
Verben	Konjugation	A2	Perfekt	Er hat mir den Kuchen gebracht.
Pronomen	Relativpron.	B1	„was", „wo"	Das ist die Stadt, wo wir uns getroffen haben.
Substantiv	Deklination	B1	Genitiv	Das ist der Wagen meines Vaters.
Verben	Konjugation	B2	Konjunktiv 1	Er sagte, er komme später.
Satz	Hauptsatz	B2	Desiderativsatz	Wenn ich das gewusst hätte!

Table 2: Original example grammatical features from the GGP across CEFR levels.

SuperCategory	No. Constructs	SubCategory	No. Constructs
Verbs	43	Inflection	23
		Separating verbs	10
		"to have"/ "to be"	4
		Modal verbs	2
		Conjugation	2
		Imperative	1
		Valence	1
Pronouns	21	Relative pronouns	6
		Inflection	3
		Demonstrative pronouns	3
		Indefinite pronouns	3
		Interrogative pronouns	2
		Personal pronouns	2
		Impersonal pronoun ("es")	1
		Possessive pronouns	1
Adjectives	19	Inflection	12
		Comparison	4
		Adverbial	2
		Predicative	1
Clauses	18	Subordinate clauses	9
		Main clauses	3
		Comparative clauses	2
		Interrogative clauses	2
		Others	2
Articles	13	Demonstrative articles	3
		Other indefinite articles (e.g. "manche")	3
		Definite articles	2
		Indefinite articles (e.g. "ein")	2
		Inflection	2
		Interrogative articles	1
Connectors	12	Connecting adverbs	5
		Conjunctions	4
		Subjunctions	3
Prepositions	9	Other	4
		Temporal	3
		Local	1
		Changing	1
Nouns	7	Inflection	7
Main clauses	4	Interrogative clauses	2
		Imperative clauses	1
		Negated clauses	1
Negation	2		
Possessive article	2		

Table 3: Overview GGP features by categories.

Gap in pagination due to formatting issues.

Pages 224-228

Overview of the SustainEval 2025 Shared Task: Identifying the Topic and Verifiability of Sustainability Report Excerpts

Jakob Prange[1] **Charlott Jakob**[2,3] **Patrick Göttfert**[1]
Raphael Huber[1] **Pia Wenzel Neves**[2] **Annemarie Friedrich**[1]

[1]Universität Augsburg [2]TU Berlin [3]DFKI
Correspondence: annemarie.friedrich@uni-a.de

Abstract

The SustainEval shared task @ GermEval 2025 aims to analyze text from German sustainability reports. The shared task required solving two tasks: classifying a span's topic into one of 20 reporting criteria and estimating its verifiability on a scale from 0.0 to 1.0. The spans and their corresponding reporting criteria were retrieved from the DNK database. Furthermore, the spans were manually annotated to assess verifiability. This paper details the data collection process and provides an overview of the baselines, participating systems, and results. The submitted systems explore language-specific bidirectional and left-to-right encoders, combined with data augmentation methods. Ensembled BERT models with different sets of hyperparameters work best for content classification, while for verifiability rating, generative pretraining is competitive as well.

1 Introduction

In many ways, economic interest can be seen not only as a contributing factor to global climate change, but as one of its root causes (Leippold, 2023). Recent efforts in EU and national legislation address the corporate world directly and require companies to take responsibility by reporting on their current statuses, goals and deadlines, as well as concrete actions taken towards climate neutrality and overall environmental and social sustainability.

While corporate sustainability reporting aims to increase transparency, there is also a high incentive for companies to present themselves as environmentally friendly as possible, e.g. by selectively reporting only "good" actions or using vague optimistic language. This increasing tendency, known as *greenwashing*, makes it difficult to tell apart concrete, verifiable actions from high-level plans and plain publicity.

With this shared task as part of GermEval 2025, we aim to fuel research on the automatic analysis and detection of greenwashing by challenging teams to build systems that categorize excerpts from German sustainability reports with regard to **(A) content class** and **(B) claim verifiability**. The anonymized text excerpts in our dataset are taken from the German Sustainability Code (Deutscher Nachhaltigkeitskodex; DNK) online platform.[1]

Existing work on climate content classification (Webersinke et al., 2021; Bingler et al., 2022, 2024) and environmental claim verification (Diggelmann et al., 2020, *inter alia*) addresses exclusively English texts and often struggles to achieve good inter-annotator agreement on crucial properties like specificity and verifiability. To mitigate this issue, we rephrase the task from categorical to an ordinal scale for annotators and a real-valued continuous rating for system evaluation.

The primary goal of the shared task is the question what types of modeling approaches work best to analyze sustainability reports w.r.t. their content and clarity. Beyond that, we expect to gain insights from the participants' analyses towards the following questions: How are sustainability reports written? Are they clear and transparent as to which criteria are being addressed and how? In other words, how easy is it to train classifiers on them in general? And which parts of reports and what types of language are particularly challenging to categorize?

We find that various modeling approaches such as BERT-like bidirectional encoders and left-to-right generatively pretrained language models are feasible, when properly finetuned. The top performances (58.6% accuracy on content classifiation; 0.431 Kendall's τ on verifiability rating) leave room for improvement, which highlights both the complexity of the domain of German sustainability reports and the importance and future potential of the novel tasks we propose.

[1]www.deutscher-nachhaltigkeitskodex.de

Proceedings of the 21st Conference on Natural Language Processing (KONVENS), Volume 2: Workshops, pages 229–238, 2025

Sec. ID	Criterion Section = Task A Label	Description	Example	Task B Label
8.	Policy └Process Management └**Incentive Systems**	The company discloses how target agreements and remuneration schemes for executives and employees are also geared towards the achievement of sustainability goals and how they are aligned with long-term value creation. It discloses the extent to which the achievement of these goals forms part of the evaluation of the top managerial level (board/managing directors) conducted by the monitoring body (supervisory board/advisory board).	Per our travel expenses guideline, preference is to be given to rail travel for business trips, for which employees are regularly provided with a BahnCard.	1.00
15.	Aspects └Society └**Equal Opportunities**	The company discloses in what way it has implemented national and international processes and what goals it has for the promotion of equal opportunities and diversity, occupational health and safety, participation rights, the integration of migrants and people with disabilities, fair pay as well as a work-life balance and how it will achieve these.	When it comes to promotions, direct superiors **alone** do **not** make decisions regarding changes of role and salary increases.	0.67
11.	Aspects └Environment └**Usage of Nat. Resources**	The company discloses the extent to which natural resources are used for the company's business activities. Possible options here are materials, the input and output of water, soil, waste, energy, land and biodiversity as well as emissions for the life cycles of products and services.	We nevertheless measure our use of natural resources **to the best of our ability**.	0.33
2.	Policy └Strategy └**Materiality**	The company discloses the aspects of its business operations that have a significant impact on sustainability issues and what material impact sustainability issues have on its operations. It analyses the positive and negative effects and provides information as to how these insights are integrated into the company's processes.	In **summary**, we see distinct **opportunities** for [NAME] to **generate new sustainability-related areas** of consultancy, **including sustainable** finance, **sustainability** risk, **sustainability** reporting, decarbonisation and digitalisation.	0.00

Table 1: Examples of reporting criteria sections, their short descriptions provided by DNK, and example text snippets taken from company reports. For brevity, we only show the target sentence here, but the snippets used in the final dataset also contain the preceding 3 sentences for context. German examples are presented in appendix A.

2 Data, Annotation, and Tasks

Here we describe what the data format looks like, how we collected, processed, and annotated the sustainability report excerpts, and we provide precise specifications of the two subtasks.

2.1 Data Format

Each sample in our dataset has a unique ID and consists of three consecutive `context` sentences, one `target` sentence which follows the context in the original document, as well as the `year` in which the report was published (2017–2021, the evaluation data also contain reports from the years 2022 and 2023). Trial, training, and development samples additionally contain a content label (`task_a_label`, indexed 1–20), a verifiability rating (`task_b_label`), which can be any real-valued number between 0.0 and 1.0 (inclusive), and the standard deviation (`task_b_stdev`) over crowd-sourced verifiability annotations (see section 2.4) as a measure of uncertainty.

2.2 Data Collection and Preprocessing

The trial data (88 samples), training data (960 samples), development data (270 samples), validation data (60 samples), and evaluation data (473 samples) have been constructed from publicly available German-language company reports indexed in the German Sustainability Code DNK. DNK reports always follow the same structure, consisting of 20 sections, each corresponding to a reporting criterion (e.g. 'Incentive Systems' or 'Usage of Natural Resources'). Each criterion section not only deals with a separate topic, but also fulfills a particular communicative purpose, which is reflected in the hierarchical structure of the report outline (fig. 1). One goal of this shared task is to determine the extent to which the texts pertaining to the different sections diverge not only in content but also style and other linguistic properties. A few examples of reporting criteria sections and example text snippets are listed in table 1.

As described in section 2.1, each input to be analyzed in Tasks A and B is a text snippet of

DNK Report

- **Sustainability Policy**
  - Strategy
    - 1. Strategic Analysis and Action
    - 2. Materiality
    - 3. Objectives
    - 4. Depth of the Value Chain
  - Process Management
    - 5. Responsibility
    - 6. Rules and Processes
    - 7. Control
    - 8. Incentive Systems
    - 9. Stakeholder Engagement
    - 10. Innovation and Product Management
- **Sustainability Aspects**
  - Environment
    - 11. Usage of Natural Resources
    - 12. Resource Management
    - 13. Climate-relevant Emissions
  - Society
    - 14. Employment Rights
    - 15. Equal Opportunities
    - 16. Qualifications
    - 17. Human Rights
    - 18. Corporate Citizenship
    - 19. Political Influence
    - 20. Conduct that Complies with the Law and Policy

Figure 1: Structure of DNK reports.

4 consecutive sentences (3 context sentences + 1 target sentence). Text snippets were selected semi-automatically, based mostly on balanced[2] random sampling, with some filtering steps to exclude structured data such as tables, and anonymization tags replacing personally identifiable information (see appendix C). Sentence splitting and anonymization were done automatically with simple pattern-based[3] approaches at first and later manually corrected. For anonymization, we thereby prioritized high precision in the first (automatic) round and high recall in the second (manual) round.

[2]Balanced across the 20 sections and publication years.

[3]We used a punctuation-based sentence splitter and identified company names from the metadata of each report.

2.3 Task A: Content Classification (CC)

The challenge is to assign a suitable content class to each text sample. The label for each instance is the name of the DNK reporting criterion section the text snippet was sampled from (fig. 1), thus no human annotation was needed. Still, the selected text snippets were manually validated to ensure the task was neither too easy nor too difficult, and no inappropriate (e.g. noisy, personally identifiable, or offensive) data made it into the final dataset. The task is evaluated with standard accuracy.

2.4 Task B: Verifiability Rating (VR)

The challenge is to rate the verifiability of the statement, e.g., the goal or state description expressed in the last sentence of each text snippet (= the target sentence), with the previous sentences provided as context for better understanding.

We use a numerical score between 0.0 (not verifiable) and 1.0 (clearly verifiable), and predictions are evaluated by their Kendall τ-b rank correlation[4] with human ratings ($-1.0...1.0$; higher is better). We choose Kendall correlation (variant b) over Spearman for its better handling of ties, and elaborate further on the choice of metrics in appendix B.

Task B does require human annotation. The notion of verifiability is non-trivial and ambiguous. Our concrete instruction to annotators was as follows: Imagine you are an expert auditor with unlimited access to the "hard facts" of the company, e.g. technical measurements, internal communication, or legal regulations. Whenever the company claims to have implemented what they promised in the report, would it be possible for you to check whether this is true, based on how the sentences are written?

We collected answers to this question on a four-point (forced-choice) Likert scale (see table 1 for examples of each rating level):

- Not verifiable (0.0)
- Rather not verifiable (0.33)
- Somewhat verifiable (0.67)
- Clearly verifiable (1.0)

Several variants of greenwashing-detection tasks have been tried in the past: Bingler et al. (2024) applied a binary annotation scheme (specific; not specific) on English sustainability report paragraphs.

[4]https://en.wikipedia.org/wiki/Kendall_rank_correlation_coefficient#Tau-b

They achieved 78% accuracy on this task with a finetuned ClimateBERT model (Webersinke et al., 2021) but only 22% raw human agreement (17% Krippendorff's α). This indicates issues with the clarity of the guidelines and potentially with the coarseness of a binary task. Burghart (2024) piloted a five-point numerical rating of "Measurability", achieving model performance of 61% macro-F1-score and human agreement of 34.4% Fleiss κ. The annotation guidelines for both of these projects mention "specific [pieces of] information on ... specific events" or that an "event is specific". This is intended to anchor annotators' decisions in event-related wording, thus increasing agreement. And indeed, human agreement on directly identifying event trigger words is much higher (κ =82.9% in Burghart (2024); 80-90% in our own pilot studies). In addition to guideline framing and textual anchoring of decision, many disagreements stem from the fact that, to some extent, this is an inherently subjective and gradient task.

The annotation for the SustainEval shared task, with our 4-point scale and detailed guidelines, was piloted by three of the organizers. During the pilot, we observed Fleiss' κ of 35.4%, similar to Burghart, but also nominal Krippendorff's α of 35.8%, twice as high as Bingler et al., as well as a ordinal and interval Krippendorff's αs of 57.7% and 58.7%, respectively. For 82.3% of instances, we found a majority vote (any 2 or 3 out of 3 annotators agree categorically). The numerical mapping of the categories has the added advantage that in cases of disagreement, we can calculate the arithmetic mean rating. Agreement, mean, and variance can also be used to distinguish clear from uncertain instances.

Once finalized, annotation was executed efficiently at scale by crowdworkers. For the development data, we worked with Crowdee GmbH, Berlin,[5] and for the training and evaluation data, we switched to Prolific[6] for annotator recruiting, while maintaining GDPR compliance by storing data and carrying out annotation on SoSciSurvey[7] servers located in Germany. No personally identifiable information was collected from annotators at any time. High quality was maintained by collecting ≈ 5 crowd annotations per sample. Inter-annotator agreement was measured between the crowd majority vote and the task organizers based on two control instances per annotation batch. Raw agreement between assignments to the four items on the Likert scale was 80% on the development data and 78% on the training data.

To arrive at the gold standard label, we took the majority vote, and in the case where the vote was tied, we computed the arithmetic mean between the tied values. In these cases, we also reported the standard deviation over the tied values (in cases where there was a unique majority vote, the standard deviation is 0.0). The information about the standard deviation was not strictly part of the shared task, but was provided so participants could gain insight into the uncertainty or difficulty of individual samples in the training and development data splits.

To ensure a fair and transparent competition, we established additional quality control criteria for the evaluation data split.

- 432 instances were independently annotated by 5 crowd workers and 1 trained university student (= expert) each.
  - If there was a unique crowd majority vote or two tied votes (2x2 annotators) one rating point apart, and the expert rating was at most one rating point away from the crowd vote(s), the crowd vote (or mean of two tied majority votes) was kept. This was the case for 331 instances.
  - If two tied votes were *more* than one rating point apart or the expert rating was more than one rating point away from the crowd majority vote (101 instances), a final adjudication decision was made. In this process, 76 instances were kept with the adjudicated label and 25 instances were removed because (a) the variance of ratings among crowd workers and experts was too high to warrant a useful adjudication (13), or (b) the sentence meaning was not clear to the adjudicator (12).
  - 407 out of 432 instances remained.
- 68 additional instances were annotated by trained university students, two of which were removed due to lack of clarity even to senior researchers.

In sum, this leaves a total of 407+66 = 473 evaluation instances.

[5]https://www.crowdee.com/
[6]https://www.prolific.com/
[7]https://www.soscisurvey.de/

Team	Model	Task A		Task B	
		Acc [%]	**Rank**	**Kendall's τ**	**Rank**
Baseline	Random Baseline	5.0	–	0.000	–
Baseline	bert-base-german-cased	56.0	–	0.425	–
EcoTUB	GBERT	58.6	1	–	–
SuperGLEBer	Modern-GBERT	57.3	2	0.148	(unofficial)
SuperGLEBer	LLäMmlein	52.9	(unofficial)	0.431	(unofficial)
SuperGLEBer	Llama-3	49.3	(unofficial)	0.402	1

Table 2: Official shared task rankings.

3 Baselines

For each subtask, we trained a simple baseline model in order to provide orientation to participants during the development phase and to sanity-check results after the evaluation phase. The baseline models were finetuned from the pretrained BERT-base-german-cased checkpoint[8] on the SustainEval training data. For the input, the context and target sentences were concatenated and fed to the model with left-side truncation to ensure that the target sentence is always part of the input, plus as much of the preceding context as fits.

The Task A model was trained as a 20-class classifier with cross-entropy loss, while the Task B model was trained as a single-output regressor with mean-squared error loss, both with a learning rate of 2e−5, a batch size of 4 and at most 5 epochs. In both cases, the best model checkpoint was selected based on lowest development set loss—on Task B it was reached after the first epoch, while on Task A, development set loss kept decreasing until the 5th epoch.

4 Participating Systems and Results

We used CodaBench[9] for official results submission, evaluation, and ranking. Authors were requested to upload their code together with their final CodaBench submission and to include a link to their code repository in their system description papers.

The Task A CodaBench leaderboard received 6 submissions, but only for 2 of them system description papers were submitted. As this was a formal task participation requirement, only these are thus taken into account for the official ranking. Task B had one participating team. The official rankings are shown in table 2.

Team EcoTUB. Bove et al. (2025) experimented with data augmentation through English back-translation, as well as comparing and ensembling multiple hyperparameter settings. Their main starting point is the German BERT model GBERT (Chan et al., 2020), a newer variant of bert-base-german-cased. The back-translation method generated 1,050 (near-)paraphrases of context and target sentences, doubling the training data set in size. Additionally, the team compared various hyperparameter settings during finetuning and exploited their complementary performance across classes in a final ensemble model, achieving 58.6% accuracy on Task A, beating the baseline and taking 1st place.

Team SuperGLEBer. Wunderle et al. (2025) submitted three different models: ModernGBERT (Ehrmanntraut et al., 2025), Llama-3 (Grattafiori et al., 2024), LLäMmlein (Pfister et al., 2025). All three models were used in an encoder-classifier setup during finetuning and inference, even though Llama and LLäMmlein were pretrained as generative decoders (Pfister and Hotho, 2024). In Task A, ModernGBERT performed best out of the three and is the officially ranked system, but in Task B the same system performed worst (τ=0.148). LLäMmlein and Llama fared much better, and LLäMmlein even outperformed the baseline at τ=0.431, but the officially ranked system was Llama (τ=0.402) because it was the team's final submission. One additional goal this team set for themselves was to test whether their model rankings on multiple GermEval 2025 shared tasks—not only SustainEval A and B, but also candy speech detection (Clausen et al., 2025) and harmful content detection (Felser et al., 2025)—correlate with rankings according to

[8]https://huggingface.co/google-bert/bert-base-german-cased

[9]https://www.codabench.org/

the pre-existing SuperGLEBer benchmark. This contributes a valuable perspective on cross-task transfer. Team SuperGLEBer ranks 2nd in Task A, also outperforming the official baseline, and, as the only participating team, 1st in Task B.

5 Discussion

While the methodological approaches and analyses are described in detail by Wunderle et al. (2025) and Bove et al. (2025), we observe a few overarching trends in data usage and system performance.

Encoder-classifiers vs. generative LLMs. The ongoing progress in the development of generative LLMs begs the question how they compare to encoder-based classifiers like BERT on a set of tasks that is (a) new, (b) highly domain-specific, and (c) run on German data. On Task A, while all systems perform much better than chance and lie within a 10 p.p. window of each other (49.3%–58.6%), there is a clear separation between generatively-pretrained LLMs on the lower end of that range (49.3%–52.9%) and BERT-based models taking the lead (56.0%–58.6%). On Task B, the LLMs (0.402–0.431) of Team SuperGLEBer are on par with our BERT regressor baseline (0.425), while their Modern-GBERT implementation lags far behind (0.148). This is doubly surprising: (a) Llama and LLäMmlein are ranked much better relative to other models than on Task A and (b) Modern-GBERT performs much worse than a similar model on the same task. Since all models are finetuned and applied in the same way as encoder-classifiers here (section 4; Pfister and Hotho, 2024), any "real" effects of training and inference differences would have to stem from pretraining. It remains to be tested whether some of these observations are in fact real effects or rather spurious performance drops due to suboptimal hyperparameters.

Verifiability regression as a challenging new task. SustainEval Task B sticks out among other GermEval tasks, as it is not a discrete classification task but a regression task. Next to low participation, perhaps due to unfamiliarity, this has implications for both model design and evaluation—we evaluated it with Kendall's τ rank correlation, but there are other rank correlation metrics as well as simpler closeness metrics such as mean squared error. Team SuperGLEBer observed that on this task, a diverse set of models is performance-ranked quite differently than on established tasks like POS-tagging and other classification/tagging tasks, though it is unclear whether this is due to the task being regression, due to the evaluation metric, or due to the difficulty of defining *verifiability* in the first place.

Limitations and enhancements of the training data. One obvious limitation of the data we provided is its size: 1,000 instances are not enough to train a model from scratch. Based on the current state of the field, we estimated that the dominant paradigm would be to start from pretrained model checkpoints and to either finetune it or apply prompt-based in-context learning. In fact, all submitted approaches used finetuning. Team EcoTUB tried to address the remaining data sparsity problem by generating artificial data via back-translation through English, albeit with diminishing returns.

Content classification may be multi-label. Another artifact of the data arises from the randomly sampled short excerpts. With this setup, we wanted to test in Task A how easy it is to recognize the goal of a text based only on a few sentences. But as Bove et al. (2025) point out, it is already difficult to distinguish between some similar classes, e.g. Usage of Natural Resources and Resource Management), and this difficulty only increases the shorter the text samples are. It may thus be reasonable to frame the task as multi-label classification or to back off to higher levels of the class hierarchy (fig. 1) in the future.

Expert models and ensembles. Team EcoTUB found in Task A that hyperparameter selection impacts individual classes differently, and thus "expert models" for specific sets of classes can be trained. Ensembling these expert models then improves overall performance. This also gives rise to the hypothesis that an ensemble of Task A and Task B models might mutually benefit both tasks, which should be explored in future work.

6 Related Work

Prior research has harnessed natural language processing (NLP) to understand sustainability communication better. Earlier finance-centric NLP applications predominantly employed keyword-based approaches, which lacked contextual sensitivity (Cody et al., 2015; Sautner et al., 2023). Recent advancements have embraced machine learning models such as BERT (Devlin et al., 2019), which provide contextualized representations. A variety of

BERT-based approaches have been introduced, addressing a spectrum of tasks such as climate content classification (Schimanski et al., 2023; Webersinke et al., 2021; Bingler et al., 2022, 2024), topic detection (Callaghan et al., 2021), environmental claim detection (Stammbach et al., 2023; Diggelmann et al., 2020), and environmental claim verification (Wang et al., 2021; Diggelmann et al., 2020).

Various approaches exist for categorizing sustainability texts. On the one hand, they can be classified according to their main topic(s). For this purpose, binary classification tasks can be set up, such as classifying relevance to climate change (Shiwakoti et al., 2024). Furthermore, text can be categorized within several sustainability frameworks. The simplest framework involves the categories Environmental, Social, and Governance (ESG), and is frequently used in finance-centric NLP (Schimanski et al., 2024). The Sustainable Development Goals (SDGs), with 17 categories, and the 20 criteria of DNK, provide a more granular classification of content (Jakob et al., 2024; Pukelis et al., 2020). SDGs and DNK criteria are often used for detecting topics in documents and to analyse their frequency across multiple documents, such as sustainability reports and research papers (Callaghan et al., 2021; Guisiano et al., 2022; Bedard-Vallee et al., 2023; Schimanski et al., 2024). Besides determining topics in documents, sentences can be analysed by making fine-grained semantic distinctions with regard to their factfulness (Stammbach et al., 2023; Ong et al., 2025b). This analysis is crucial for detecting greenwashing, as it distinguishes between verifiable actions and vague or misleading rhetoric (de Freitas Netto et al., 2020; Ong et al., 2025a).

Recent research uses advancements in fake news detection to verify climate claims (Thorne et al., 2018; Leippold et al., 2024). Diggelmann et al. (2020) introduced CLIMATE-FEVER, which employs evidence retrieval from Wikipedia to evaluate human-generated, verifiable climate claims and defines a claim as verifiable if it is well-formed and subjectively investigatable.

It is of utmost importance to critically assess statements made in sustainability reports. However, if we aim to detect greenwashing by verifying claims in sustainability reports, a key question arises: how can we differentiate between verifiable and non-verifiable claims? We are aware of a SemEval shared task that addresses multilingual verification classification within the ESG framework (Seki et al., 2024). However, German was not among the languages considered. With our shared task, we contribute by evaluating verifiability in German sentences and by categorizing the sentences into 20 fine-grained topics defined by the criteria of the German Sustainability Code (DNK).

7 Conclusion

The SustainEval Shared Task, with its focus on German sustainability content analysis, addresses an important gap in research on greenwashing detection. The results reveal several promising methods. However, particularly for the second task on verifiability, which relies on a fine-grained, manually annotated dataset, the full potential has yet to be realized.

Acknowledgements

We are thankful to the German Sustainability Code DNK for providing the texts for our shared task dataset and to the German Society for Computational Linguistics (GSCL) for their financial support.

References

Alexandre Bedard-Vallee, Chris James, and Guillaume Roberge. 2023. Elsevier 2023 sustainable development goals (SDGs) mapping. *Elsevier Data Repository*.

Julia Anna Bingler, Mathias Kraus, Markus Leippold, and Nicolas Webersinke. 2022. Cheap talk and cherry-picking: What ClimateBERT has to say on corporate climate risk disclosures. *Finance Research Letters*, 47:102776.

Julia Anna Bingler, Mathias Kraus, Markus Leippold, and Nicolas Webersinke. 2024. How cheap talk in climate disclosures relates to climate initiatives, corporate emissions, and reputation risk. *Journal of Banking & Finance*, 164:107191.

Sinan Bove, Icondy Kiba-Gassaye, Sirak Tadesse, and Lisa Raithel. 2025. EcoTUB @ SustainEval 2025: Ensembling BERT for German sustainability report classification. In *Proceedings of the 21st Conference on Natural Language Processing (KONVENS 2025): Workshops*, Hildesheim, Germany. HsH Applied Academics.

Martin Burghart. 2024. Assessing corporate sustainability eorts via natural language processing. Master's thesis, Technische Universität Berlin.

Max Callaghan, Carl-Friedrich Schleussner, Shruti Nath, Quentin Lejeune, Thomas R Knutson, Markus Reichstein, Gerrit Hansen, Emily Theokritoff, Marina

Andrijevic, Robert J Brecha, et al. 2021. Machine-learning-based evidence and attribution mapping of 100,000 climate impact studies. *Nature climate change*, 11:966–972.

Branden Chan, Stefan Schweter, and Timo Möller. 2020. German's next language model. In *Proceedings of the 28th International Conference on Computational Linguistics*, pages 6788–6796, Barcelona, Spain (Online). International Committee on Computational Linguistics.

Yulia Clausen, Tatjana Scheffler, and Michael Wiegand. 2025. Overview of the GermEval 2025 Shared Task on Candy Speech Detection. In *Proceedings of the 21st Conference on Natural Language Processing (KONVENS 2025): Workshops*, Hildesheim, Germany. ACL.

Emily M Cody, Andrew J Reagan, Lewis Mitchell, Peter Sheridan Dodds, and Christopher M Danforth. 2015. Climate change sentiment on twitter: An unsolicited public opinion poll. *PloS one*, 10(8):e0136092.

Sebastião Vieira de Freitas Netto, Marcos Felipe Falcão Sobral, Ana Regina Bezerra Ribeiro, and Gleibson Robert da Luz Soares. 2020. Concepts and forms of greenwashing: A systematic review. *Environmental Sciences Europe*, 32(1):19.

Jacob Devlin, Ming-Wei Chang, Kenton Lee, and Kristina Toutanova. 2019. Bert: Pre-training of deep bidirectional transformers for language understanding. In *Proceedings of the 2019 conference of the North American chapter of the association for computational linguistics: human language technologies, volume 1 (long and short papers)*, pages 4171–4186.

Thomas Diggelmann, Jordan Boyd-Graber, Jannis Bulian, Massimiliano Ciaramita, and Markus Leippold. 2020. Climate-FEVER: A dataset for verification of real-world climate claims. ArXiv preprint arXiv:2012.00614.

Anton Ehrmanntraut, Julia Wunderle, Jan Pfister, Fotis Jannidis, and Andreas Hotho. 2025. ModernGBERT: German-only 1B encoder model trained from scratch. *Preprint*, arXiv:2505.13136.

Jenny Felser, Michael Spranger, and Melanie Siegel. 2025. Overview of the GermEval 2025 Shared Task on Harmful Content Detection. In *Proceedings of the 21st Conference on Natural Language Processing (KONVENS 2025): Workshops*, Hildesheim, Germany.

Aaron Grattafiori, Abhimanyu Dubey, Abhinav Jauhri, Abhinav Pandey, Abhishek Kadian, Ahmad Al-Dahle, Aiesha Letman, Akhil Mathur, Alan Schelten, Alex Vaughan, Amy Yang, Angela Fan, Anirudh Goyal, Anthony Hartshorn, Aobo Yang, Archi Mitra, Archie Sravankumar, Artem Korenev, Arthur Hinsvark, and 542 others. 2024. The Llama 3 herd of models. *Preprint*, arXiv:2407.21783.

Jade Eva Guisiano, Raja Chiky, and Jonathas De Mello. 2022. Sdg-meter: A deep learning based tool for automatic text classification of the sustainable development goals. In *Asian conference on intelligent information and database systems*, pages 259–271. Springer.

Charlott Jakob, Vera Schmitt, Salar Mohtaj, and Sebastian Möller. 2024. Classifying sustainability reports using companies self-assessments. In *Advances in Information and Communication*, pages 547–557, Cham. Springer Nature Switzerland.

Markus Leippold. 2023. Corporate climate disclosures: how do we weed out cheap talkers? TEDxHEC talk, Paris, last access: November 20, 2024.

Markus Leippold, Saeid Ashraf Vaghefi, Dominik Stammbach, Veruska Muccione, Julia Bingler, Jingwei Ni, Chiara Colesanti-Senni, Tobias Wekhof, Tobias Schimanski, Glen Gostlow, et al. 2024. Automated fact-checking of climate change claims with large language models. ArXiv preprint arXiv:2401.12566.

Keane Ong, Rui Mao, Ranjan Satapathy, Ricardo Shirota Filho, Erik Cambria, Johan Sulaeman, and Gianmarco Mengaldo. 2025a. Explainable natural language processing for corporate sustainability analysis. *Information Fusion*, 115:102726.

Keane Ong, Rui Mao, Deeksha Varshney, Erik Cambria, and Gianmarco Mengaldo. 2025b. Towards robust esg analysis against greenwashing risks: Aspect-action analysis with cross-category generalization. *arXiv preprint arXiv:2502.15821*.

Jan Pfister and Andreas Hotho. 2024. SuperGLEBer: German language understanding evaluation benchmark. In *Proceedings of the 2024 Conference of the North American Chapter of the Association for Computational Linguistics: Human Language Technologies (Volume 1: Long Papers)*, pages 7904–7923, Mexico City, Mexico. Association for Computational Linguistics.

Jan Pfister, Julia Wunderle, and Andreas Hotho. 2025. LLäMmlein: Transparent, compact and competitive German-only language models from scratch. In *Proceedings of the 63rd Annual Meeting of the Association for Computational Linguistics (Volume 1: Long Papers)*, pages 2227–2246, Vienna, Austria. Association for Computational Linguistics.

Lukas Pukelis, Núria Bautista Puig, Mykola Skrynik, and Vilius Stanciauskas. 2020. Osdg–open-source approach to classify text data by un sustainable development goals (sdgs). ArXiv preprint arXiv:2005.14569.

Zacharias Sautner, Laurence Van Lent, Grigory Vilkov, and Ruishen Zhang. 2023. Firm-level climate change exposure. *The Journal of Finance*, 78(3):1449–1498.

Tobias Schimanski, Julia Bingler, Camilla Hyslop, Mathias Kraus, and Markus Leippold. 2023.

ClimateBERT-netzero: Detecting and assessing net zero and reduction targets. ArXiv preprint arXiv:2310.08096.

Tobias Schimanski, Andrin Reding, Nico Reding, Julia Bingler, Mathias Kraus, and Markus Leippold. 2024. Bridging the gap in ESG measurement: Using NLP to quantify environmental, social, and governance communication. *Finance Research Letters*, 61:104979.

Yohei Seki, Hakusen Shu, Anaïs Lhuissier, Hanwool Lee, Juyeon Kang, Min-Yuh Day, and Chung-Chi Chen. 2024. ML-Promise: A multilingual dataset for corporate promise verification. ArXiv preprint arXiv:2411.04473.

Shuvam Shiwakoti, Surendrabikram Thapa, Kritesh Rauniyar, Akshyat Shah, Aashish Bhandari, and Usman Naseem. 2024. Analyzing the dynamics of climate change discourse on twitter: A new annotated corpus and multi-aspect classification. In *Proceedings of the 2024 Joint International Conference on Computational Linguistics, Language Resources and Evaluation (LREC-COLING 2024)*, pages 984–994.

Dominik Stammbach, Nicolas Webersinke, Julia Bingler, Mathias Kraus, and Markus Leippold. 2023. Environmental claim detection. In *Proceedings of the 61st Annual Meeting of the Association for Computational Linguistics (Volume 2: Short Papers)*, pages 1051–1066, Toronto, Canada. Association for Computational Linguistics.

James Thorne, Andreas Vlachos, Christos Christodoulopoulos, and Arpit Mittal. 2018. FEVER: a large-scale dataset for fact extraction and verification. ArXiv preprint arXiv:1803.05355.

Gengyu Wang, Lawrence Chillrud, and Kathleen McKeown. 2021. Evidence based automatic fact-checking for climate change misinformation. In *Proceedings of the 15th International AAAI Conference on Web and Social Media*.

Nicolas Webersinke, Mathias Kraus, Julia Anna Bingler, and Markus Leippold. 2021. ClimateBERT: A pretrained language model for climate-related text. ArXiv preprint arXiv:2110.12010.

Julia Wunderle, Jan Pfister, and Andreas Hotho. 2025. Die SuperGLEBer at GermEval 2025 shared tasks: Growing pains - when more isn't always better. In *Proceedings of the 21st Conference on Natural Language Processing (KONVENS 2025): Workshops*, Hildesheim, Germany. HsH Applied Academics.

A German Examples

See table 3.

B Metrics

As mentioned in section 2, the main ranking metrics are accuracy for Task A and Kendall's τ-b correlation for Task B. Here we elaborate on these decisions.

For Task A, other metrics, such as per-class- and macro-F1-scores and breakdowns at coarser levels of the hierarchical document structure (see fig. 1), can be very insightful. For example, hierarchical evaluation does not punish systems as much as flat accuracy evaluation for confusing closely related categories, which generally makes intuitive sense. Hierarchical evaluation may produce counter-intuitive ties, e.g. getting all instances correct at the flattest level of the hierarchy receives the same score as getting $\frac{1}{n}^{\text{th}}$ of the instances correct at the deepest (n^{th}) level of the hierarchy. And finally, we do not want to "bake" lots of hard assumptions into the task setup from the beginning, which could be favored towards certain modeling approaches.

For Task B, we choose Kendall rank correlation for its proper tie handling properties. This particular metric is well-aligned with our 4-point ordinal scale annotation method. Already when treating this scale as four categories, we are observing much better agreement in our preliminary study than in prior work, which used either binary or more fine-grained categorical schemes. Furthermore, we can resolve disagreements by averaging (after double-checking for noisy examples and annotators). This leads to a gradient ranking, for which Pearson, Spearman, or Kendall rank correlation present generally viable evaluation metrics. At the same time, the high categorical agreement also leads to many intentional ties in the gold standard data. This is where the Kendall τ metric, variant b, shows its true power, as it is the only one that handles ties well.

C Anonymization

The following categories of information in the context and target sentences were anonymized and replaced with the corresponding tags:

- Links → [LINK]
- Addresses, telephone numbers, email addresses → [CONTACT]
- Individuals → [PERSON]
- Companies and organizations → [ORG]

ID	Criterion Section = Task A Label	Description	Example	Task B Label
8.	**Anreizsysteme**	Das Unternehmen legt offen, wie sich die Zielvereinbarungen und Vergütungen für Führungskräfte und Mitarbeiter auch am Erreichen von Nachhaltigkeitszielen und an der langfristigen Wertschöpfung orientieren. Es wird offengelegt, inwiefern die Erreichung dieser Ziele Teil der Evaluation der obersten Führungsebene (Vorstand/Geschäftsführung) durch das Kontrollorgan (Aufsichtsrat/Beirat) ist.	Gemäß Reisekostenrichtlinie soll für Dienstreisen bevorzugt die Bahn genutzt werden, wofür die Kollegen regelmäßig eine entsprechende BahnCard zur Verfügung gestellt bekommen.	1.0
15.	**Chancen-gerechtigkeit**	Das Unternehmen legt offen, wie es national und international Prozesse implementiert und welche Ziele es hat, um Chancengerechtigkeit und Vielfalt (Diversity), Arbeitssicherheit und Gesundheitsschutz, Mitbestimmung, Integration von Migranten und Menschen mit Behinderung, angemessene Bezahlung sowie Vereinbarung von Familie und Beruf zu fördern, und wie es diese umsetzt.	Bei Beförderungen entscheiden nicht die direkten Vorgesetzten allein über Positionswechsel und Gehaltserhöhung.	0.67
11.	**Inanspruchnahme von natürlichen Ressourcen**	Das Unternehmen legt offen, in welchem Umfang natürliche Ressourcen für die Geschäftstätigkeit in Anspruch genommen werden. Infrage kommen hier Materialien sowie der Input und Output von Wasser, Boden, Abfall, Energie, Fläche, Biodiversität sowie Emissionen für den Lebenszyklus von Produkten und Dienstleistungen.	Dennoch messen wir, soweit möglich, unsere Inanspruchnahme an natürlichen Ressourcen.	0.33
2.	**Wesentlichkeit**	Das Unternehmen legt offen, welche Aspekte der eigenen Geschäftstätigkeit wesentlich auf Aspekte der Nachhaltigkeit einwirken und welchen wesentlichen Einfluss die Aspekte der Nachhaltigkeit auf die Geschäftstätigkeit haben. Es analysiert die positiven und negativen Wirkungen und gibt an, wie diese Erkenntnisse in die eigenen Prozesse einfließen.	Zusammengefasst sehen wir klare Chancen für [NAME], auf Basis des Themas Nachhaltigkeit neue Beratungsfelder zu generieren, u.a. zu Sustainable Finance, Sustainability Risk, Nachhaltigkeitsreporting, Dekarbonisierung und Digitalisierung.	0.0

Table 3: Examples of reporting criteria sections, their short descriptions provided by DNK, and German example text snippets taken from company reports. Note that the examples here only show the target sentence, but the snippets used in the final dataset will always be 4 sentences (3 context + 1 target) long.

- Products (e.g., names of internal software) → [PRODUCT]
- Other identifiable names or items → [NAME]

City names were generally not anonymized, unless they were part of a company name or directly associated with a company. Well-known institutions and globally recognized organizations (such as the UN) were also not anonymized. Please note that some of the anonymized elements may have changed over the course of the dataset's development.

EcoTUB @ SustainEval 2025: Ensembling BERT for German Sustainability Report Classification

Sinan Bove*
Technische Universität Berlin
bove@campus.tu-berlin.de

Icondy Kiba-Gassaye*
Technische Universität Berlin
kiba-gassaye@campus.tu-berlin.de

Sirak Tadesse*
Technische Universität Berlin
sirak.tadesse@campus.tu-berlin.de

Lisa Raithel
BIFOLD
QU Lab, Technische Universität Berlin
raithel@tu-berlin.de

Abstract

This paper outlines our contribution to the SustainEval 2025 shared task (Prange et al., 2025), which focuses on the classification of German sustainability report snippets into one of 20 predefined content categories defined by the German Sustainability Code (DNK). We fine-tuned a transformer-based model, deepset/gbert-base, and explored multiple methods to improve classification performance, including hyperparameter tuning, data augmentation through back-translation, and model ensembling. While our ensemble model achieved a accuracy of 0.74 on our internal validation set, its performance dropped to 0.58 on the final test set evaluated by the organizers, highlighting challenges in adaptability to new data. We compare our results to several baselines and conduct error analysis to identify common misclassifications patterns, such as overlapping categories and ambiguous language. Our findings demonstrate both the potential and the limitations of NLP approaches for structured content analysis in German sustainability reports.

1 Introduction

Sustainability reporting is an essential practice for organizations to show their commitment to environmental, social, and economic standards. They serve as a tool for transparency and accountability for employees, investors, the public, and especially regulators. European law requires large companies and corporations to publish regular reports on the social and environmental risks they face, and on how their activities impact people and the environment (European Union, 2022). With the enactment of the new directive in 2022, mandatory sustainability reporting requirements have been extended to a significantly larger number of companies across the EU, leading to a rapid increase in published reports (European Union, 2022). These reports come in many different languages, formats and structures and their content needs to be processed, reviewed and regulated.

This work was conducted as part of the SustainEval 2025 Shared Task (Prange et al., 2025), which comprised two subtasks: Content Classification (Task A) and Verifiability Rating (Task B). Our submission addresses Task A, which involves classifying short text snippets extracted from sustainability reports according to one of 20 predefined criteria, as shown in Table 1 and defined by the German Sustainability Code (Deutscher Nachhaltigkeitskodex, DNK) (Rat für Nachhaltige Entwicklung (RNE), 2020).

> *Neubauten statten wir mit Solarthermie aus. In weiteren Objekten haben wir Blockheizkraftwerke installiert. Die CO_2-Emissionen für das Jahr 2017 wurden separat ermittelt. Beim Vergleich der Jahre 2017 zu 2015 ergibt sich bereits eine spürbare Reduzierung.*

Figure 1: Example snippet with label 13: Climate-Relevant Emissions

In this project, we address the task of automatically classifying German-language text snippets from corporate sustainability reports into predefined content categories. Each text snippet corresponds to a specific reporting criteria defined by the German Sustainability Code, and the goal is to accurately assign the appropriate label to each sample. An example of one of these snippets together with its assigned label is shown in Figure 1. Our work attempts to answer the following research questions: How effectively can NLP and machine learning models perform this classification task? And which approaches are best to improve a baseline model?

Sustainability reports play a crucial role in documenting a company's compliance with environmental, social, and governance standards, and they significantly shape public perception and corpo-

*These authors contributed equally. This work was done in an Advanced Study Project of the Quality & Usability Lab at TU Berlin.

Strategy	Process Management	Environment	Society
1. Strategic Analysis and Action 2. Materiality 3. Objectives 4. Depth of the Value Chain	5. Responsibility 6. Rules and Processes 7. Control 8. Incentive Systems 9. Stakeholder Engagement 10. Innovation and Product Management	11. Usage of Natural Resources 12. Resource Management 13. Climate-Relevant Emissions	14. Employment Rights 15. Equal Opportunities 16. Qualifications 17. Human Rights 18. Corporate Citizenship 19. Political Influence 20. Conduct that Complies with the Law and Policy

Table 1: Predefined reporting criteria in the German Sustainability Code (DNK) (Rat für Nachhaltige Entwicklung (RNE), 2020)

rate image. Automating the classification of such reports offers several benefits: It saves time and resources, reduces human error, and enables large-scale analysis and benchmarking of sustainability activities across companies. NLP-based models can scale effectively to process vast volumes of textual data, making them ideal tools for this domain. However, challenges remain, particularly due to the complexity of sustainability-related language and the limited amount of research focused on German-language corporate reporting. Our project addresses this gap by contributing to a field where automated, language-specific solutions are still underexplored.

Our key contribution in this paper is the development of a model that classifies German text snippets from sustainability reports into one of twenty predefined classes from the German Sustainability Code. We further implement a baseline and an improved ensemble model to compare performances. To evaluate the models we the standard metrics accuracy, precision recall and F_1 score. Finally, we conducted an error analysis to identify misclassifications and gain an understanding of the faults in the model.

Our results show that the improved model outperforms our own baseline model across the key evaluation metrics and the official SustainEval baseline on accuracy (Prange et al., 2025). However, we also observed that certain classes were consistently easier to classify than others, most likely due to overlapping terminology or similar language usage across categories. Through detailed error analysis, we identified key challenges and limitations in distinguishing between semantically related classes. Overall, our findings demonstrate the strong potential of NLP-based models for the automated classification of sustainability report content. In this paper, we

1. propose a classification system tailored to German-language sustainability reports
2. evaluate its performance using multiple metrics and synthetic data augmentation, and
3. show that fine-tuned NLP models can significantly improve classification quality.

2 Related Work

Previous research has explored different approaches to automate the classification and analysis of sustainability reports, particularly with a focus on the United Nations Sustainable Development Goals (SDGs). Jakob et al. (2024) propose a method for classifying content in sustainability reports by leveraging SDG icons embedded by companies within their own reports. Their approach employs page-level annotations derived from these self-assessments to fine-tune multi-label transformer-based models (Vaswani et al., 2017), including Longformer (Beltagy et al., 2020) and Transformer-XL (Dai et al., 2019). In addition, they also experimented with OpenAI's GPT models (OpenAI et al., 2024) as part of their approach. Another study by Angin et al. (2022) introduced a fine-tuned RoBERTa (Liu et al., 2019) model trained on the OSDG Community Dataset (OSDG et al., 2024), comparing classical and deep learning models for both binary and multi-class classification of report segments, and found that deep learning approaches outperformed traditional ones. Shahi et al. (2011) looked at supervised text classification of corporate sustainability reports based on the Global Reporting Initiative (GRI) framework, investigating how machine learning can assess report completeness against official performance indicators. Additionally, Maibaum et al. (2024) compared various NLP techniques, such as dictionary-based methods, topic modeling, word embeddings, and large language models (LLMs) on a large labeled dataset, concluding that LLMs like ChatGPT and fine-tuned BERT (Devlin et al., 2019) models outperform earlier approaches, with fine-tuning being essential for optimal performance. Lastly, another paper developed a novel RoBERTa-based classifier to trace thematic transitions in European banks' sustainability reporting over time, concluding with strong performance in SDG-related classification. (Li and Rockinger, 2024)

Our work shares several similarities with prior studies that use natural language processing techniques in the context of sustainability reporting. We focus on the classification of sustainability-related content and employ transformer-based models such as BERT for this task. However, while most related studies focus on English-language data and SDG alignment, we specifically address German-language sustainability reporting. Moreover, our classification task is based on the German Sustainability Code (Deutscher Nachhaltigkeitskodex, DNK, Rat für Nachhaltige Entwicklung (RNE) (2020)), using the 20 reporting criteria defined by DNK.

3 Methodology

Experimental Setting Our approach followed several steps to develop a strong classification system for German sustainability report text snippets. We first built a baseline model by fine-tuning a pre-trained German BERT model variant[1] (Chan et al., 2020) specifically for our classification task. We then evaluated the baseline on a development set using accuracy, precision, recall, and F_1-score, and examined the confusion matrix to see where the model made mistakes. Based on these results, we improved the model by tuning hyperparameters and adding early stopping to prevent overfitting. After confirming better performance on the development set, we created an ensemble that combined several models, to boost overall accuracy and robustness.

Models and Fine-Tuning Specifically, for the classification task, we chose 'gbert-base' (Chan et al., 2020), a German language-specific variant of BERT that is well-suited for processing complex German text. In preliminary experiments, we tested several models, with the deepset model and the bert-base-german-cased variants emerging as the best-performing ones. While bert-base-german-cased was used as our own baseline, the final model was built using the deepset variant due to its superior results (Figure 2). This model serves as the backbone for our fine-tuning approach, allowing us to adapt its deep contextualized representations to the domain of sustainability report classification. We used the HuggingFace Transformers library (Wolf et al., 2020) to facilitate integration of the model, tokenizer, and training pipeline.

To optimize model performance, we implemented hyperparameter tuning using the Optuna framework (Akiba et al., 2019), which efficiently explores the parameter spaces transformer model, epochs, learning rate, weight decay, batch size, and warm-up ratio using Bayesian optimization. This search helped us identify configurations that improved accuracy while reducing overfitting risks. For training management and experiment tracking, we integrated the Weights & Biases framework (Biewald, 2020), providing transparent logging and visualization of training progress and metrics, and at the same time ensuring reproducibility.

Baselines To assess the performance of our models, we compared them against two baselines. First, we used the official baseline result provided by the shared task organizers, which achieved an accuracy of approximately 0.63 on the validation dataset (Prange et al., 2025). Additionally, we tested our own baseline model using random hyperparameters (Table 5), which achieved a similar accuracy of about 0.63 on the validation dataset, but only 0.61 on the development dataset.

Data The dataset used is publicly available and was curated as part of the Shared Task SustainEval 2025 (Prange et al., 2025). It consists of approximately 1,000 samples for training, 300 for development, around 500 for validation, and an additional trial set of about 80 samples. Each text snippet is between 3 to 5 sentences long and was derived from publicly available German-language company reports indexed in the German Sustainability Code (Rat für Nachhaltige Entwicklung (RNE), 2020). The structure of each sample included several variables: an ID, the year, a context string, a target string, and one assigned label out of 20, as shown in Table 1. An exemplary text snippet is shown in Figure 1.

Data Augmentation To improve our models performance, we augmented the original data with synthetic data generated through back translation using a model[2] provided by Tiedemann and Thottingal (2020). We translated the German context and target strings into English and then back into German in order to create paraphrased versions of the original text snippets. In total, we added 1,050

[1] `deepset/gbert-base`

[2] `'Helsinki-NLP/opus-mt-de-en'`

mores text snipped using this method. Each generated data sample follows a similar structure as the original data with variables including context, target and task A label.

Ensemble We noticed that many models had close to the same accuracy, however performed differently on the different classes, depending on their hyperparameters. Based on that information, we decided to take an ensemble of models for our final submission, where the collective model can cancel out weaknesses of the individual models. The final ensemble is a combination of seven models where each has its own hyperparameters. The predictions per model are weighted equally. One of those models was fine-tuned on the synthetic data described above. For the remaining models, the synthetic data did not improve performance.

4 Results and Discussion

The main goal of our evaluation was to measure how well our models correctly classify each text snippet. We used the shared task's development dataset and the official validation phase, applying standard metrics: accuracy, precision, recall, and F_1-score. We also analyzed confusion matrices to identify common misclassifications and better understand which labels posed the most challenges.

After hyperparameter tuning, our best single model achieved an accuracy of 0.68 on both the validation and development sets, ranking first in the validation phase of Task A. Notably, although many models reached similar overall accuracy, their performance varied widely across labels. To address this, we combined seven diverse models into an ensemble, which improved accuracy to 0.74 on the development set (Table 2). In the final test phase, however, the ensemble's accuracy dropped to 0.58, placing second overall.

Per-class results show that the ensemble performed well on clear-cut categories like 'Incentive Systems' and 'Climate-Relevant Emissions', but struggled with more ambiguous ones like 'Strategic Analysis and Action' or 'Employment Rights'. The recall distribution (Figure 2) confirms that the ensemble reduced variation across labels compared to individual models.

The confusion matrices (Figure 3, Figure 4, Figure 5) illustrate this trend: while the ensemble reduced overall errors, some categories with overlapping semantics, e.g., 'Rules and Processes' vs. 'Responsibility', remained difficult to separate.

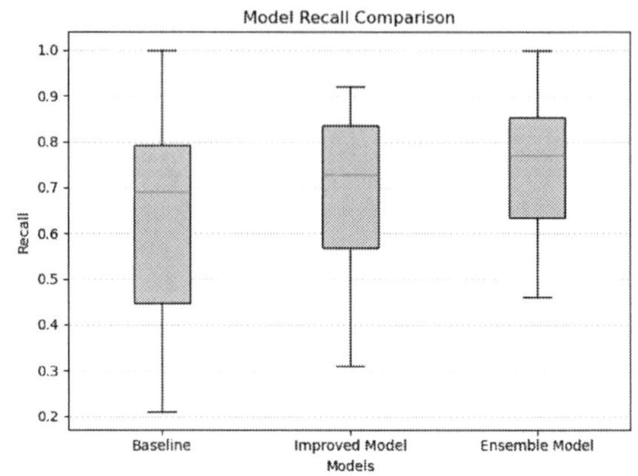

Figure 2: This illustrates the distribution of recall scores across individual class labels for the Baseline, Improved, and Ensemble models. Recall was computed separately for each label to assess the models' ability to correctly identify positive instances within each class.

The roughly 16-point drop from development to test accuracy suggests that our models may have overfit on the small in-domain datasets and did not generalize well to unseen data. This highlights a key limitation: larger or more diverse training data might benefit this task more than generic data augmentation. Moreover, the conceptual overlap among classes underlines an annotation challenge, real-world text snippets often fulfill multiple criteria, complicating single-label predictions.

5 Conclusion

Through our participation in the SustainEval 2025 shared task (Prange et al., 2025), we explored the classification of German sustainability report snippets into 20 predefined DNK criteria using NLP methods. We reconfirmed that BERT-based models like deepset's German BERT are well-suited for domain-specific classification tasks in German, particularly when paired with careful hyperparameter tuning and ensemble techniques. However, we also observed that back-translation and data augmentation did not lead to performance improvements in this context, and that evaluation results can vary significantly between internal validation and external benchmarks. Automating the analysis of sustainability reports offers a scalable solution to processing large volumes of complex, multilingual data. It contributes to greater transparency, comparability, and regulatory compliance in corporate sustainability practices, ultimately supporting better accountability in environmental, social,

Class	Precision	Recall	F1-score	Support
Strategic Analysis and Action	0.58	0.50	0.54	14
Materiality	0.67	0.46	0.55	13
Objectives	0.73	0.53	0.62	15
Depth of the Value Chain	0.75	0.64	0.69	14
Responsibility	0.67	0.77	0.71	13
Rules and Processes	0.78	0.54	0.64	13
Control	0.65	0.85	0.73	13
Incentive Systems	0.92	1.00	0.96	12
Stakeholder Engagement	0.86	0.86	0.86	14
Innovation and Product Management	0.56	0.64	0.60	14
Usage of Natural Resources	0.85	0.73	0.79	15
Resource Management	0.67	0.67	0.67	12
Climate-Relevant Emissions	0.88	0.93	0.90	15
Employment Rights	0.48	0.79	0.59	14
Equal Opportunities	0.89	0.62	0.73	13
Qualifications	0.79	0.85	0.81	13
Human Rights	0.91	0.83	0.87	12
Corporate Citizenship	0.91	0.77	0.83	13
Political Influence	0.80	1.00	0.89	12
Conduct that Complies with the Law and Policy	0.80	0.92	0.86	13
Accuracy			0.74	267
Macro avg F_1	0.76	0.74	0.74	267
Weighted avg F_1	0.75	0.74	0.74	267

Table 2: Score metrics for the final ensemble on the development dataset.

and governance reporting. For future work, several promising directions can be explored. One avenue is the implementation of hierarchical classification approaches, where the model first predicts a superclass and then classifies the snippet into a subclass. Additionally, the use of large language models could be investigated for zero-shot or few-shot classification, especially in scenarios with limited labeled data. Ultimately, this work lays a foundation for the broader use of NLP in sustainability and corporate accountability efforts.

6 Limitations

While our approach delivered competitive results, it has some limitations. First, semantic overlap between labels made it challenging to distinguish similar classes, which affected overall precision. Standard data augmentation, such as back translation, did not improve performance, suggesting that domain-specific strategies may be needed for specialized texts. Also, the drop in accuracy from internal validation to the final test set indicates potential overfitting and limited generalization. Finally, due to time constraints, we did not explore Task B (Verifiability Rating) or more advanced approaches such as multi-label or zero-shot classification with large language models, which could address some of these challenges.

Acknowledgments

This work was supported by the German Federal Ministry of Education and Research (BIFOLD25B).

References

Takuya Akiba, Shotaro Sano, Toshihiko Yanase, Takeru Ohta, and Masanori Koyama. 2019. Optuna: A next-generation hyperparameter optimization framework. In *Proceedings of the 25th ACM SIGKDD International Conference on Knowledge Discovery and Data Mining*.

Merih Angin, Beyza Taşdemir, Cenk Arda Yılmaz, Gökcan Demiralp, Mert Atay, Pelin Angin, and Gökhan Dikmener. 2022. A RoBERTa approach for automated processing of sustainability reports. 14(23):16139. Number: 23 Publisher: Multidisciplinary Digital Publishing Institute.

Iz Beltagy, Matthew E. Peters, and Arman Cohan. 2020. Longformer: The long-document transformer. *Preprint*, arxiv:2004.05150 [cs].

Lukas Biewald. 2020. Experiment tracking with weights and biases. Software available from wandb.com.

Branden Chan, Stefan Schweter, and Timo Möller. 2020. German's next language model. In *Proceedings of the 28th International Conference on Computational Linguistics*, pages 6788–6796, Barcelona, Spain (Online). International Committee on Computational Linguistics.

Zihang Dai, Zhilin Yang, Yiming Yang, Jaime Carbonell, Quoc V. Le, and Ruslan Salakhutdinov. 2019. Transformer-XL: Attentive language models beyond a fixed-length context. *Preprint*, arxiv:1901.02860 [cs].

Jacob Devlin, Ming-Wei Chang, Kenton Lee, and Kristina Toutanova. 2019. BERT: Pre-training of deep bidirectional transformers for language understanding. In *Proceedings of the 2019 Conference of the North American Chapter of the Association for Computational Linguistics: Human Language Technologies, Volume 1 (Long and Short Papers)*, pages 4171–4186, Minneapolis, Minnesota. Association for Computational Linguistics.

European Union. 2022. Directive (EU) 2022/2464 of the European Parliament and of the Council of 14 December 2022 amending Regulation (EU) No 537/2014, Directive 2004/109/EC, Directive 2006/43/EC and Directive 2013/34/EU, as regards corporate sustainability reporting (Text with EEA relevance). https://eur-lex.europa.eu/legal-content/EN/TXT/?uri=CELEX:32022L2464. Accessed: 2025-07-10.

Charlott Jakob, Vera Schmitt, Salar Mohtaj, and Sebastian Möller. 2024. Classifying sustainability reports using companies self-assessments. In *Advances in Information and Communication*, pages 547–557. Springer Nature Switzerland.

Yao Li and Michael Rockinger. 2024. Unfolding the transitions in sustainability reporting. 16(2):809. Number: 2 Publisher: Multidisciplinary Digital Publishing Institute.

Yinhan Liu, Myle Ott, Naman Goyal, Jingfei Du, Mandar Joshi, Danqi Chen, Omer Levy, Mike Lewis, Luke Zettlemoyer, and Veselin Stoyanov. 2019. Roberta: A robustly optimized bert pretraining approach. *arXiv preprint arXiv:1907.11692*.

Frederik Maibaum, Johannes Kriebel, and Johann Nils Foege. 2024. Selecting textual analysis tools to classify sustainability information in corporate reporting. 183:114269.

OpenAI, Josh Achiam, Steven Adler, Sandhini Agarwal, Lama Ahmad, Ilge Akkaya, Florencia Leoni Aleman, Diogo Almeida, Janko Altenschmidt, Sam Altman, Shyamal Anadkat, Red Avila, Igor Babuschkin, Suchir Balaji, Valerie Balcom, Paul Baltescu, Haiming Bao, Mohammad Bavarian, Jeff Belgum, and 262 others. 2024. Gpt-4 technical report. *Preprint*, arXiv:2303.08774.

OSDG, UNDP IICPSD SDG AI Lab, and PPMI. 2024. Osdg community dataset (osdg-cd).

Jakob Prange, Charlott Jakob, Patrick Göttfert, Raphael Huber, Pia Wenzel Neves, and Annemarie Friedrich. 2025. Overview of the SustainEval 2025 Shared Task: Identifying the topic and verifiability of sustainability report excerpts. In *Proceedings of the 21st Conference on Natural Language Processing (KONVENS 2025): Workshops*, Hildesheim, Germany. HsH Applied Academics.

Rat für Nachhaltige Entwicklung (RNE). 2020. Der Deutsche Nachhaltigkeitskodex: Maßstab für nachhaltiges Wirtschaften. https://www.nachhaltigkeitsrat.de/wp-content/uploads/2020/03/RNE_DNK_BroschuereA5_2019_DE.pdf. Accessed: 2025-07-10.

Amir Mohammad Shahi, Biju Issac, and Jashua Rajesh Modapothala. 2011. Analysis of supervised text classification algorithms on corporate sustainability reports. In *Proceedings of 2011 International Conference on Computer Science and Network Technology*, volume 1, pages 96–100.

Jörg Tiedemann and Santhosh Thottingal. 2020. Opus-mt–building open translation services for the world. In *Annual Conference of the European Association for Machine Translation*, pages 479–480. European Association for Machine Translation.

Ashish Vaswani, Noam Shazeer, Niki Parmar, Jakob Uszkoreit, Llion Jones, Aidan N Gomez, Łukasz Kaiser, and Illia Polosukhin. 2017. Attention is all you need. *31st Conference on Neural Information Processing Systems (NIPS 2017*, page 11. Tex.ids= vaswani_attention_nodate.

Thomas Wolf, Lysandre Debut, Victor Sanh, Julien Chaumond, Clement Delangue, Anthony Moi, Pierric Cistac, Tim Rault, Rémi Louf, Morgan Funtowicz, and 1 others. 2020. Transformers: State-of-the-art natural language processing. In *Proceedings of the 2020 conference on empirical methods in natural language processing: system demonstrations*, pages 38–45.

Appendix

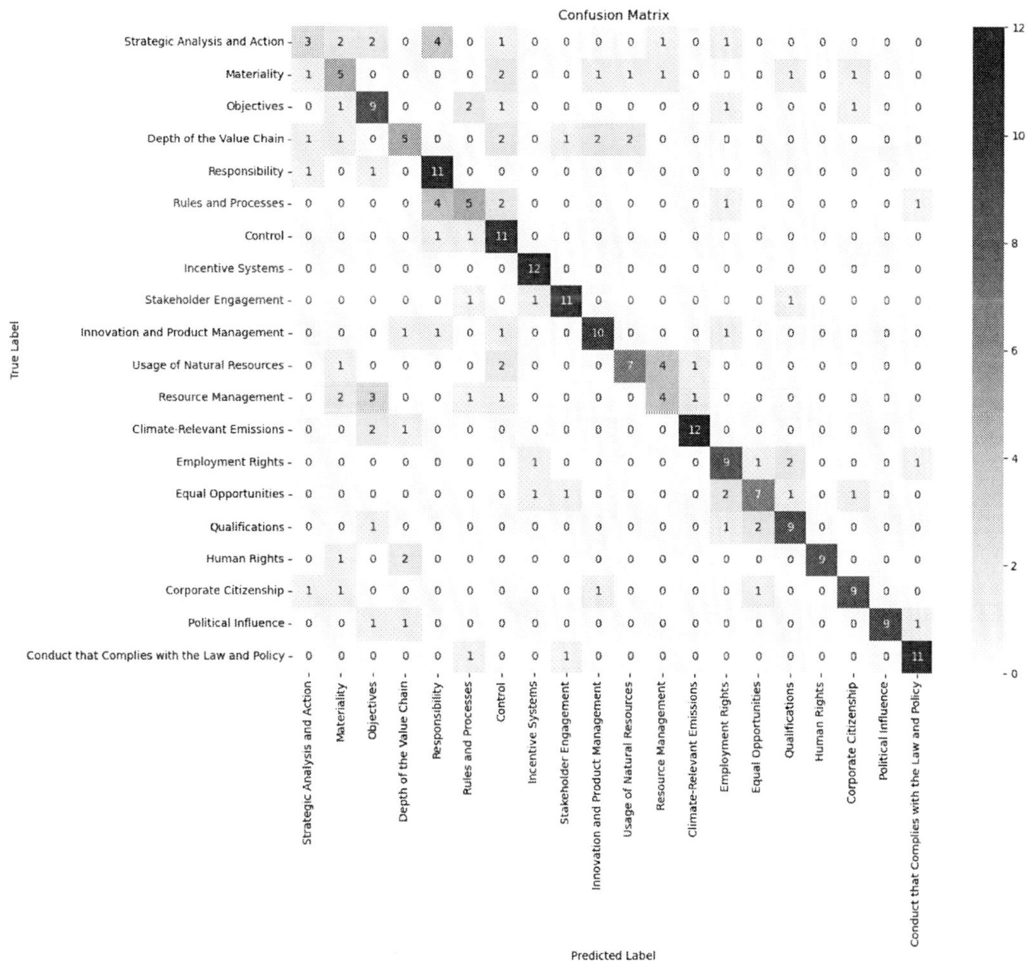

Figure 3: Confusion matrix of the baseline model or the development dataset.

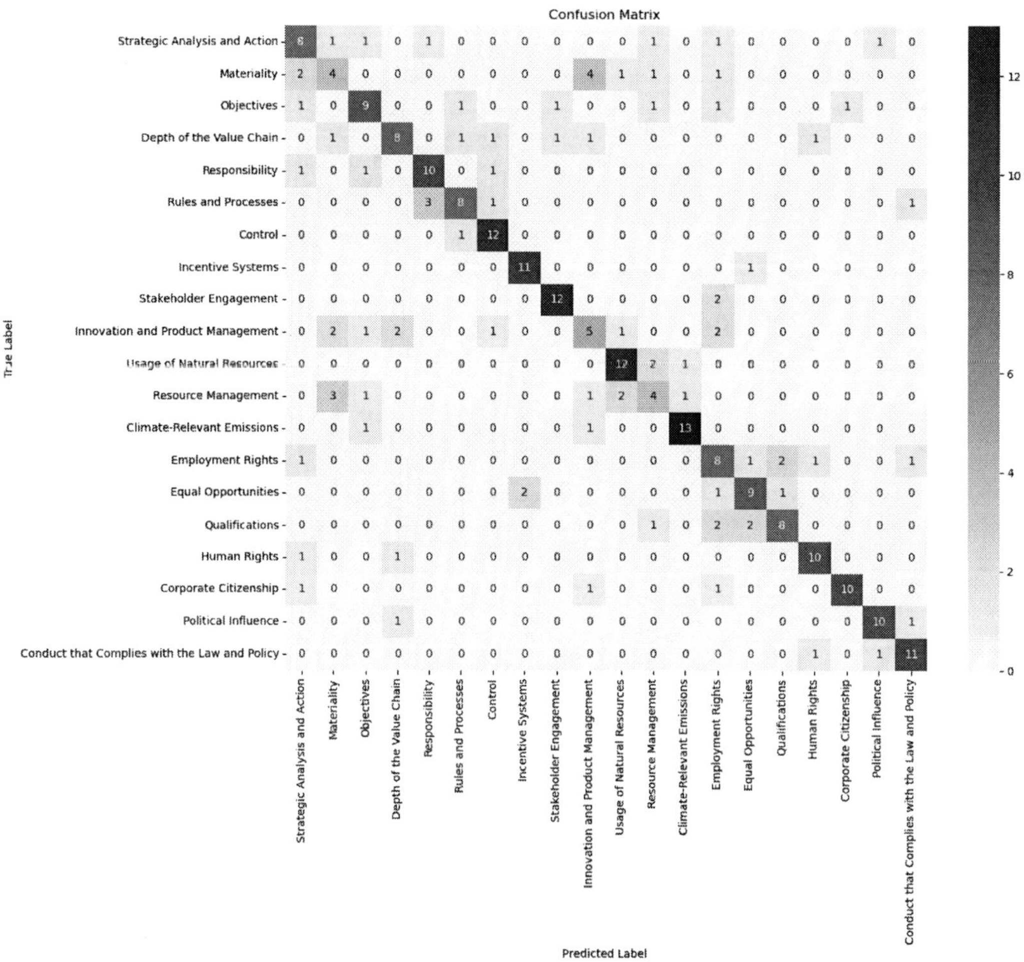

Figure 4: Confusion matrix of the improved model or the development dataset.

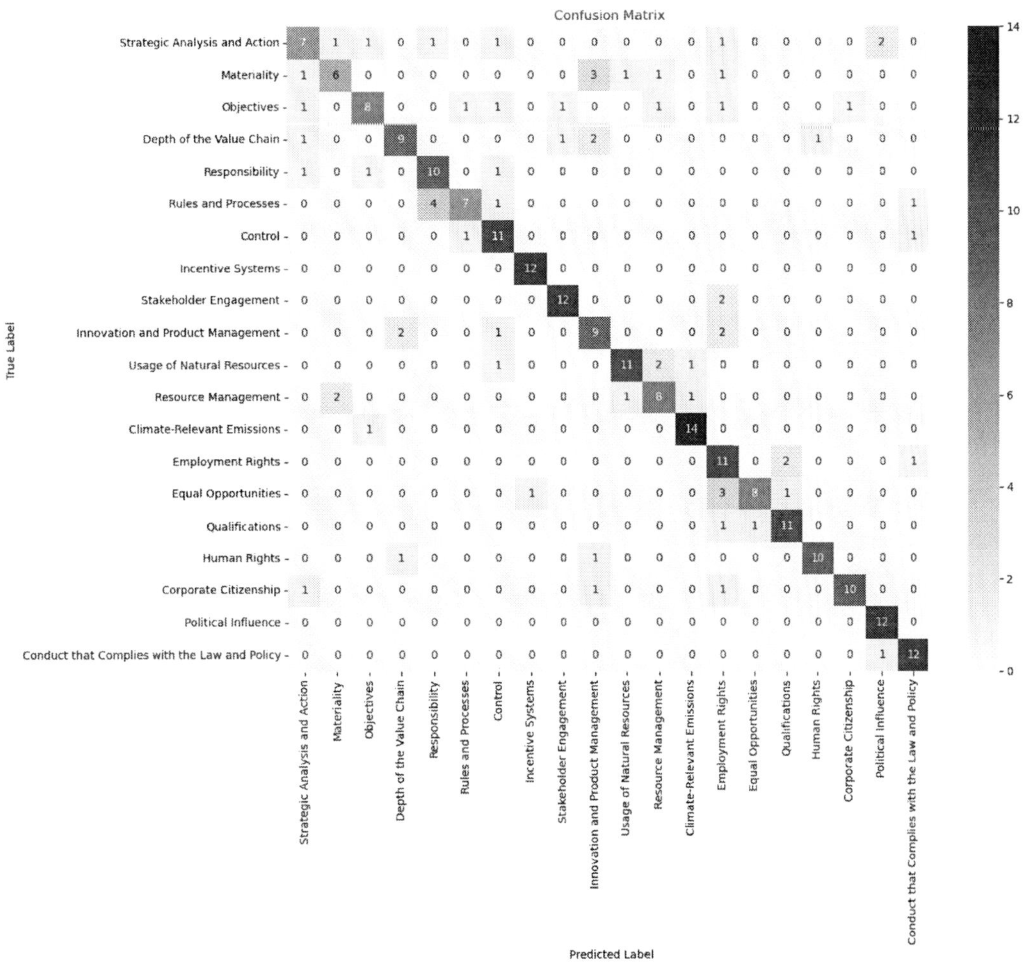

Figure 5: Confusion matrix of the final ensemble for the development dataset.

Class	Precision	Recall	F1-score	Support
Strategic Analysis and Action	0.43	0.21	0.29	14
Materiality	0.36	0.38	0.37	13
Objectives	0.47	0.60	0.53	15
Depth of the Value Chain	0.50	0.36	0.42	14
Responsibility	0.52	0.85	0.65	13
Rules and Processes	0.45	0.38	0.42	13
Control	0.48	0.85	0.61	13
Incentive Systems	0.80	1.00	0.89	12
Stakeholder Engagement	0.79	0.79	0.79	14
Innovation and Product Management	0.71	0.71	0.71	14
Usage of Natural Resources	0.70	0.47	0.56	15
Resource Management	0.40	0.33	0.36	12
Climate-Relevant Emissions	0.86	0.80	0.83	15
Employment Rights	0.56	0.64	0.60	14
Equal Opportunities	0.64	0.54	0.58	13
Qualifications	0.64	0.69	0.67	13
Human Rights	1.00	0.75	0.86	12
Corporate Citizenship	0.75	0.69	0.72	13
Political Influence	1.00	0.75	0.86	12
Conduct that Complies with the Law and Policy	0.79	0.85	0.81	13
Accuracy			0.63	267
Macro avg F_1	0.64	0.63	0.63	267
Weighted avg F_1	0.64	0.63	0.62	267

Table 3: Score metrics for the baseline on the development dataset.

Class	Precision	Recall	F1-score	Support
Strategic Analysis and Action	0.53	0.57	0.55	14
Materiality	0.36	0.31	0.33	13
Objectives	0.64	0.60	0.62	15
Depth of the Value Chain	0.67	0.57	0.62	14
Responsibility	0.71	0.77	0.74	13
Rules and Processes	0.73	0.62	0.67	13
Control	0.75	0.92	0.83	13
Incentive Systems	0.85	0.92	0.88	12
Stakeholder Engagement	0.86	0.86	0.86	14
Innovation and Product Management	0.38	0.36	0.37	14
Usage of Natural Resources	0.75	0.80	0.77	15
Resource Management	0.40	0.33	0.36	12
Climate-Relevant Emissions	0.87	0.87	0.87	15
Employment Rights	0.42	0.57	0.48	14
Equal Opportunities	0.69	0.69	0.69	13
Qualifications	0.73	0.62	0.67	13
Human Rights	0.77	0.83	0.80	12
Corporate Citizenship	0.91	0.77	0.83	13
Political Influence	0.83	0.83	0.83	12
Conduct that Complies with the Law and Policy	0.79	0.85	0.81	13
Accuracy			0.68	267
Macro avg F_1	0.68	0.68	0.68	267
Weighted avg F_1	0.68	0.68	0.68	267

Table 4: Score metrics for the improved model on the development dataset.

Model	Pretrained Model	Epochs	Learning Rate	Weight Decay	Batch Size	Warm-up Ratio
Baseline	bert-base-german-cased	8	0.00002	0.01	8	0.1
Improved Model	deepset/gbert-base	10	0.00007	0.25209	16	0.26270
Ensemble 1	deepset/gbert-base	10	0.00010	0.27410	16	0.26045
Ensemble 2	deepset/gbert-base	8	0.00004	0.27222	16	0.32183
Ensemble 3	deepset/gbert-base	9	0.00006	0.13132	16	0.25980
Ensemble 4	deepset/gbert-base	9	0.00004	0.20540	16	0.31962
Ensemble 5	deepset/gbert-base	9	0.00005	0.25659	16	0.28312
Ensemble 6	deepset/gbert-base	10	0.00004	0.21600	16	0.27289

Table 5: Hyperparameters of each model (The improved model is part of the ensemble).

Reducing Environmental Costs whilst Maintaining Operational Effectiveness in Large Language Models through Chain Routing

Solomon Wheeler[1], **Melissa Torgbi**[1], **Harish Tayyar Madabushi**[1]
[1]Department of Computer Science, University of Bath
{sollywheeler@gmail.com, mat66@bath.ac.uk, htm43@bath.ac.uk}

Abstract

The widespread deployment of large language models (LLMs) presents significant challenges in balancing their performance and carbon cost. To address this, we propose a prompt routing mechanism that balances quality and environmental cost to route prompts between a set of candidate LLMs. In addition to fine-tuning encoder models to account for carbon cost, we introduce *chain routing*, a novel routing mechanism that breaks responses into three stages, which can be routed to different LLMs. Our system reduces environmental cost by 39% whilst simultaneously improving response quality by 3.3%, both compared to the single highest performing model. We also show that chain routing outperforms the quality of single model routing by 3.1%, whilst only having a slightly higher environmental cost. These results show the potential for environmentally aware routing, and *chain routing* to improve the environmental sustainability of LLM inference. We provide open access to our code [1].

1 Introduction

Large language models (LLMs) have demonstrated remarkable capabilities, exceeding human accuracy on some benchmarks (Annepaka and Pakray, 2025; Bojic et al., 2023; Goldstein et al., 2023). However, they are not without their drawbacks, specifically cost and environmental impact (Mittelstadt et al., 2023; Luccioni et al., 2024; Samsi et al., 2023). The rise of reasoning models, such as Deepseek's R1 and OpenAI's o1/3, has exacerbated these issues; to reason before answering, they require significantly more compute per prompt (Han et al., 2025; DeepSeek-AI et al., 2025; OpenAI, 2024).

Whilst existing work highlights the potential for routing to improve accuracy and reduce cost (Stripelis et al., 2024; Shnitzer et al., 2023; Damani et al., 2024), environmental impact is an area highlighted for further research (Hu et al., 2024; Varangot-Reille et al., 2025). Wilkins et al. (2025) factor environmental cost into routing, but this routing is offline and does not consider prompt context. To address this gap, we introduce an online environmentally aware router that considers prompt context in routing decisions.

Furthermore, whilst previous approaches have explored swapping LLMs during inference, this is done at the token level with a limited set of models (Zheng et al., 2024). We propose a more structured approach, chain routing, which breaks Chain-of-Thought (CoT) responses into three distinct stages. Each stage can be routed to a different candidate LLM, balancing performance and carbon cost throughout the reasoning process, as shown in Fig 1.

Our key contributions are:

1. We create a system that predicts the quality and environmental cost of LLM inference for a given prompt and uses this to make routing decisions. To the best of our knowledge, this is the first time this has been done.

2. We measure the quality and environmental cost of inference and training across a range of routing methods.

3. We create a novel routing system, *chain routing*, which routes different parts of a reasoning CoT to different LLMs. We also compare the quality of smaller and larger LLMs for each stage of a reasoning CoT.

In comparison to the highest performing candidate LLM, our router reduces the environmental costs of inference by 39% whilst also increasing quality, measured in similarity to gold standard responses, by 3.3%. We also show that chain routing outperforms single model routing by 3.1%, whilst only having a slightly higher environmental cost.

[1]Code for our routing system can be found at https://github.com/solomon-wheeler/ChainRouterToReduceCarbonCosts

Proceedings of the 21st Conference on Natural Language Processing (KONVENS), Volume 2: Workshops, pages 250–273, 2025

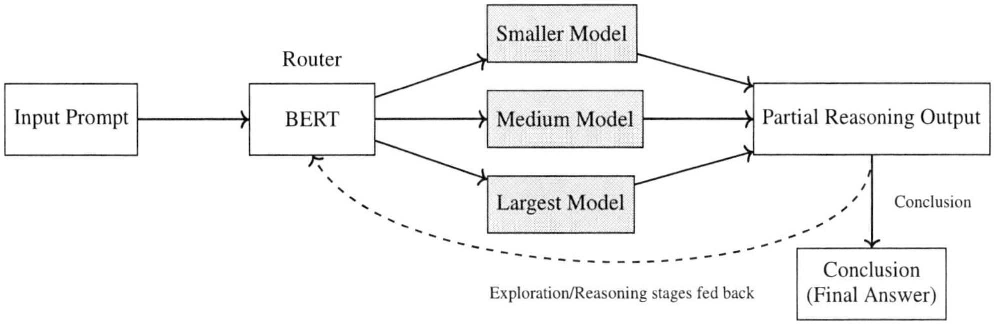

Figure 1: Overview of the chain routing system, which splits a CoT output into discrete stages, and routes these partial reasoning outputs to different models, before outputting a final answer.

Our results also show that there is little impact on quality when using smaller models ($3B$ parameters) instead of larger models ($32B$ parameters) for the initial two stages of reasoning (both less than 2.4% reduction in quality), a finding that could be used to decrease the environmental cost of CoT reasoning in LLMs.

2 Background & Related Work

2.1 LLM Routing

LLM routing is an area of intense research; several methods have been proposed to decide which of a set of candidate LLMs will best respond to a prompt. These methods include training encoder-only models, typically from the BERT family, to classify prompts based on factors such as domain relevance (Yadav et al., 2025; Simonds et al., 2024) or anticipated performance (Stripelis et al., 2024; Hu et al., 2024; Ding et al., 2024). Decoder-based models have also been employed for similar classification tasks (Stripelis et al., 2024; Ong et al., 2024; Shen et al., 2023). Alternative approaches include clustering semantically similar prompts using KNNs or K-means clustering and selecting the model that performed best on similar prompts (Srivatsa et al., 2024; Stripelis et al., 2024; Hu et al., 2024). Finally, reinforcement learning (RL) approaches learn routing policies over time (Zhang et al., 2024b; Nguyen et al., 2024)

2.2 Alternative Approaches

LLM Cascading Instead of routing before output is generated, cascading approaches send prompts to the smallest model and then push them up a stack of increasingly powerful models until the output is high quality. This measure of quality differs between systems; one method is to take the uncertainty of a model's output, either by measuring the likelihood of the tokens (perplexity) (Zhang et al., 2024a), or by running inference multiple times and comparing how similar the outputs are (Yue et al., 2023; Aggarwal et al., 2024). Another method is to use fine-tuned encoder models to classify if outputs are high quality (Chen et al., 2023). Cascading systems must measure response quality online, during inference. Since we use a routing system that only needs quality scores offline to generate training labels, we can use a simpler method of similarity between gold standard answers and responses as a surrogate for quality.

Mixture of Experts LLM routing systems are similar to the mixture of experts (MoE) architecture, which includes several expert sub-models (Yadav et al., 2025; Jacobs et al., 1991; Cai et al., 2025). LLMs using this architecture include Mistral AI's Mixtral 8×7B model, DeepSeek's R1, and Meta's Llama-4 family (Jiang et al., 2024; DeepSeek-AI et al., 2025; Meta, 2025).

The key difference between LLM routing and MoE systems is how tightly coupled model selection is to models. In MoE systems, the gating method is trained with the sub-models, so updating any sub-model necessitates updating the entire system (Shazeer et al., 2017). In contrast, LLM routing systems train the gating/routing system separately, so can include new models more easily (Jiang et al., 2023).

2.3 Environmental Impact of LLM Inference

We show estimates from previous work of the environmental impact of LLM inference in Table 1.

Model	Carbon Cost (g CO_2)	Citation
Llama 65B	0.4096	Samsi et al. (2023)
Llama 2 13B	0.21	Li et al. (2024)
Llama2 70B	1.14	Wilkins et al. (2025)
GPT-3.5	1.869	d'Aramon et al. (2024)

Table 1: The carbon cost of LLM inference, normalised to a carbon intensity of $400g$ CO_2/kWh and output length of 1024 tokens.

3 Methodology

3.1 System Overview

Our primary routing system focuses on a fine-tuned BERT classifier, which takes input of the prompt (and chain output so far, if applicable), and outputs soft scores, similar to the method proposed by Stripelis et al. (2024). We update the BERT classifier to output two soft scores, for the expected quality and environmental cost. We also include a decoder router as a baseline, which employs a smaller LLM to make routing decisions. The system operates in two modes: single routing, in which the entire prompt is sent to one model, and chain routing, in which different stages of a reasoning CoT are delegated to different models.

3.2 Routing Architectures

Each prompt is tokenised and then encoded using a model from the BERT family. The training data for this was gathered by sending prompts from several datasets to each candidate LLM and recording the similarity between the output and gold standard answer, and the environmental cost of inference. For gathering the chain routing training data we also instruct the model to output its CoT.

3.3 Problem Formulation

In both chain and single routing, for every prompt $x \in X$ and candidate LLM $m_i \in M$, the router predicts two soft scores:

$$\text{Sim}_i(x) \in [0,1], \qquad \text{Env}_i(x) \in [0,1], \quad (1)$$

Sim_i and Env_i are the soft scores for expected similarity to the gold standard answer and environmental cost, the calculation of which is explained in the next section.

We then calculate a combined score for each candidate LLM, including $\lambda \in [0,1]$, which varies the trade-off between expected similarity and environmental cost, with lower values λ favouring increasing similarity:

$$\begin{aligned}\text{CombinedScore}_i(x) = (1-\lambda)\,\text{Sim}_i(x) \\ +\lambda\,(1-\text{Env}_i(x)).\end{aligned} \quad (2)$$

At inference time, the router then selects the candidate LLM with the highest score:

$$m^*(x) = \underset{m_i \in M}{\text{argmax}}\ \text{CombinedScore}_i(x). \quad (3)$$

3.4 Soft Score Calculation

We expand on the soft score implemented by Stripelis et al. (2024) by predicting two soft scores for each candidate LLM: the similarity score (Sim_i) and environmental cost (Env_i). The general equation for this soft score (ϕ_i) is

$$\phi_i(S;T) = \frac{\exp\left(\frac{s_i}{T}\right)}{\sum_{j=1}^{N} \exp\left(\frac{s_j}{T}\right)} \quad (4)$$

where N is the number of models, S is the output score, and s is the input score. The temperature (T) controls the sensitivity of the probability distribution. As T tends towards infinity, the output tends towards a uniform distribution, and as T tends towards 0 the output is 1 for the highest value, and 0 for all other values (Xuan et al., 2025). The input score is the calculated similarity score for Sim_i or the environmental cost for Env_i.

For chain routing, we require a soft score for each model at each CoT stage. For example, in the first CoT stage, we must calculate a soft score for each of the three candidate models, even though additional routing decisions will be made for the subsequent CoT stages. To address this, we compute the average soft score across all possible model paths extending from the current stage ($\bar{\phi}_i$). For each model at CoT stage i, we take the average soft scores of each of the remaining model paths P_i:

$$\bar{\phi}_i = \frac{1}{|P_i|} \sum_{j \in P_i} \phi_j \quad (5)$$

3.5 Reasoning Chain Decomposition

To route different stages of a reasoning CoT to different candidate LLMs in chain routing, we require a method to split a CoT into discrete stages. We split the reasoning steps into three distinct sections, **exploration**, **reasoning** and **conclusion**, loosely following the special tokens used in DeepSeek-R1 (DeepSeek-AI et al., 2025). We instruct the current model to generate a CoT stage and terminate it with a predefined token (e.g. "EXPLORATION"). Once the model outputs this token, we stop decoding, and pass the prompt and output so far to the router to select the LLM for the next CoT stage. The system prompt and an example CoT split into stages are shown in Appendices D.14 and D.15.

3.6 Implementation Details

Models are loaded in Python using the weights available on Hugging Face and run on A5000/3090 24GB GPUs. A full list of hyperparameters used can be found in Appendix A, and an example system prompt can be found in Appendix D.13.

Hyperparameters for training the BERT router are shown in Appendix B.1. We use KL-divergence loss with weighted classes to reduce the effect of imbalanced classes, the formula for this can be found in Appendix B.2.

4 Experimental setup

4.1 LLMs Used for Router Training and Inference

To train the BERT router, we first require labels for the similarity score and emissions output for prompts. We therefore send a subset of prompts from each dataset to a broad selection of LLMs, selected due to their high performance-to-parameter size ratio, to maximise performance, whilst minimising environmental cost. We also select smaller task-specific models, such as Deepseek Coder, which performs well in the programming domain, whilst only having 1.6 billion active parameters (DeepSeek-AI et al., 2024). The candidate LLMs we use can be found in Table 2.

Model family	Params (B)
Llama 3.2(Grattafiori et al., 2024)	1
	3
Llama 3.1(Grattafiori et al., 2024)	8
DeepSeek Coder-v2(DeepSeek-AI et al., 2024)	16
DeepSeek R1-Distill(DeepSeek-AI et al., 2025)	1.5
	32
Qwen 2.5(Qwen et al., 2025)	32

Table 2: LLM family and parameter sizes used both for gathering labels for training the BERT router and as candidate models for selection in single routing.

4.2 Chain Routing Models

Running for all model combinations for each CoT stage is intractable due to the exponentially increasing number of combinations, so the set of models is refined for the chain router. Distilled reasoning models are excluded, as we find their predefined reasoning format precludes them from responding with a custom structure without further fine-tuning. Therefore, we select the following models to run for all combinations on the CoT dataset:

1. Llama 3.2 3B (Grattafiori et al., 2024)
2. Llama 3.1 8B (Grattafiori et al., 2024)
3. Qwen 2.5 32B (Qwen et al., 2025)

4.3 Encoder Models

We evaluate the following encoder models at routing:

1. DeBERTa-v3 base 183M (He et al., 2023)
2. RoBERTa base 125M (Zhuang et al., 2021)

We select DeBERTa-v3 as it achieves best-in-class performance in natural language understanding tasks and is used in NVIDIA's routing blueprint (He et al., 2023; NVIDIA, 2025). RoBERTa is selected as previous work found it outperforms DeBERTa for routing (Feng et al., 2024; Srivatsa et al., 2024).

4.4 Datasets

Datasets are selected from the three types of reasoning benchmarks outlined by Wang et al. (2023): arithmetic, common sense and symbolic. To create a generalisable router, we also include MMLU (Massive Multitask Language Understanding) and MMLU-pro, which have questions across 57 topics. Coding prompts from the MBPP (Mostly Basic Programming Problems) dataset are also included, as programming is commonly included in other routing systems (Stripelis et al., 2024; Hu et al., 2024). The final domain of datasets is question answering, which is included as it is a good differentiator between model performance (Fischer et al., 2024).

Subsets of these datasets are combined for single routing, generally of between 300 − 500 prompts, except for the datasets combining multiple tasks, such as Unified-QA and MMLU, which have between 1500 − 2500 prompts to ensure each task has an appropriate number of prompts, creating a dataset of over 9,000 prompts for each model.

We reduce the number of prompts for chain routing to 200, and only use UNIFIEDQA from the question-answering datasets, creating more than 100,000 soft scores.

Task	Dataset/s
Arithmetic reasoning	GSM8K (Cobbe et al., 2021)
Common sense reasoning	ARC (Clark et al., 2018)
Symbolic reasoning	GSM-Symbolic (Mirzadeh et al., 2024)
Multitask reasoning	MMLU (Hendrycks et al., 2021) MMLU-PRO (Wang et al., 2024)
Programming	MBPP (Austin et al., 2021)
Reading comprehension/ Question answering	UNIFIEDQA (Khashabi et al., 2020) SQUAD (Rajpurkar et al., 2016), GPQA (Rein et al., 2024)

Table 3: The benchmark datasets we use for measuring carbon cost and quality of responses for each model.

4.5 Baselines

We use the following baselines to compare the performance of the BERT router implemented:

- A generative (decoder) router (Llama 3.2 1B).
- The single model with the highest average similarity score.
- The single model with the lowest average emissions.
- A random router.
- An oracle router as a topline, which is 100% accurate at selecting the best model for a prompt, following the method by Hu et al. (2024).

4.6 Evaluation Metrics

We aim to create a system that reduces the environmental impact of LLM inference whilst maintaining accuracy. To quantify our success, we measure the environmental impact of inference (g CO_2) and the similarity between responses and gold standard answers, as a proxy for quality.

4.7 Similarity Comparisons

As a surrogate measure for the quality of responses, we measure the similarity between the outputs from models and gold standard responses defined in the benchmark datasets we use. Two methods are used for similarity comparisons: BERTSim score and CHRF (character n-gram F-Score) (Zhang et al., 2020; Popović, 2015). We instruct the models to output #### followed by their final answer and only calculate the similarity to the gold standard answer after this, to ensure we do not penalise reasoning models, which output reasoning tokens before their final answer.

4.7.1 BERTScore

We select BERTScore for measuring similarity between outputs and gold standard answers, as this approach correlates well with human judgements (Zhang et al., 2020). BERTScore encodes texts, computes token-wise cosine similarities, and aggregates them using mean, precision, recall, or F1. We simplify this by encoding the full sentences and taking a single cosine similarity, providing a more lightweight approximation. The BERTscore equation is

$$\text{BERTScore}(m, g) = \frac{\mathbf{e}_m \cdot \mathbf{e}_g}{\|\mathbf{e}_m\| \, \|\mathbf{e}_g\|} \tag{6}$$

where m is a given model's output, g the gold standard response, and e_m and e_g are their respective BERT encodings.

4.7.2 CHRF

We evaluated coding tasks using CHRF, as Evtikhiev et al. (2023) found this to be similar to human evaluation for code. CHRF is calculated as

$$\text{CHRF} = \frac{(1+\beta^2)\, M\, G}{(\beta^2 M + G) \times 100} \tag{7}$$

where M and G are the mean n-gram recall between output and gold standard, and gold standard and output, respectively, and β is a weighting parameter. We set β to 2, the value suggested by Popović (2016). We implement CHRF using the Evaluate library [2], and scale values to between 0 and 1 to match BERT score.

4.8 Calculating Carbon Cost

We calculate carbon cost using the CodeCarbon library (Courty et al., 2024), which works by recording the power consumption of CPU, GPU, and

[2] https://github.com/huggingface/evaluate

RAM and multiplying this by local carbon intensity[3], as shown in the equation:

$$\mathrm{CO_2\ (g)} = \frac{\text{power (kW)} \times \text{time (h)}}{1000} \times \text{Carbon Intensity}_{\mathrm{kg/kWh}}. \quad (8)$$

Details of the energy mix and hardware we use can be found in Appendix C. We use quantised versions of the largest models due to hardware limitations (hyperparameters can be found in Appendix A). To allow for fair comparison, we run 50 prompts on the unquantised version of each model and scale the recorded emissions to match these.

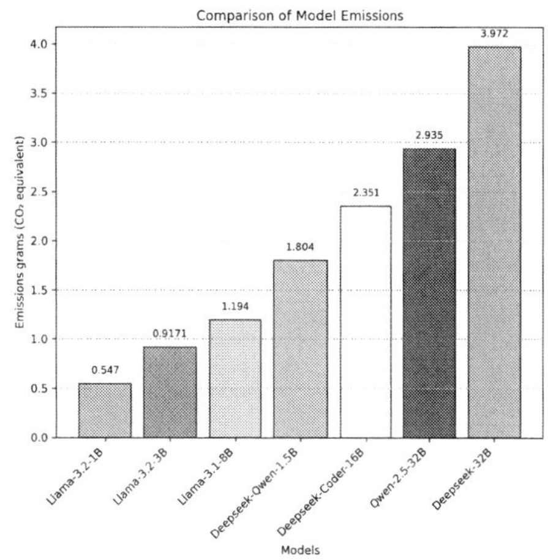

Figure 2: A comparison of the CO_2 emissions cost measured, averaged across all datasets.

5 Experiments & Results

5.1 Environmental Cost

The environmental cost for each model averaged across all the datasets listed in Table 3 is shown in Figure 2. These results show two patterns in the data: firstly that larger parameter count generally leads to a larger cost of inference, and secondly, that reasoning models have a higher carbon cost than non-reasoning models.

We include a reasoning distilled and non-reasoning version of the same model (Qwen 2.5 32B) for comparison and find that the reasoning distilled version has a 35% higher environmental cost. This can be explained by DeepSeek's distilled version of Qwen-2.5 32B producing three times more output tokens on average in our experiments.

On average, our measured carbon costs are slightly higher than for the models in Section 2.3. This can be explained by the fact that these works employ much higher batch sizes (64 vs. 8), run on more powerful GPUs (A100 80GB vs. A5000/3090 24GB), and set much lower token limits (256 vs. 2500) (Samsi et al., 2023).

The environmental cost of gathering router training data, and training the single and chain routers is shown in Appendices D.2 and D.3. We find the largest carbon cost of router training is gathering a dataset of responses to train the router on. We ensured we minimised this cost as far as possible by only running this inference once, with only the models needed, and using a subsection of datasets to gather enough prompts to train the router, but not more.

[3] https://github.com/mlco2/codecarbon/blob/master/codecarbon/core/emissions.py

Single routing BERT (DeBERTA-v3) has the lowest carbon cost (0.0001565 g CO_2) of our routing approaches. BERT in chain routing is higher (0.04102 g CO_2), as it is invoked once for each stage, with a growing input context each time. The carbon cost and latency of all implemented routing approaches can be found in Appendix D.1; we add the cost of routing to all results to obtain an overall system carbon cost.

5.2 Hyperparameter Selection

We evaluate the base version of two different encoder models, RoBERTa and DeBERTa-v3 (Zhuang et al., 2021; He et al., 2023), fine-tuned to predict soft scores. DeBERTa-v3 achieves a slightly lower average error (0.4491% vs 0.4401%), although it has a slightly longer average inference time (0.0976s vs 0.0619s), which can be explained by DeBERTa-v3's higher parameter count (183 million vs. 125 million) (He et al., 2023; Zhuang et al., 2021). We select DeBERTa-v3 to be used as the BERT model for the remaining results, as the increased inference time is negligible in comparison to the candidate LLMs.

The accuracy of the BERT router (DeBERTa-v3) in single routing at predicting both similarity and emissions on a dataset not used in training are shown in Table 4.

Routing Method	Top-1 Accuracy	Top-3 Accuracy
BERT (Similarity)	31.0%	71.4%
BERT (Emissions)	37.6%	85.2%
Random	14.3%	42.9%

Table 4: Single model router accuracy at predicting the highest quality/lowest emissions from the seven candidate models for a given prompt from an unseen dataset.

We also test varying λ, the trade-off between emissions and similarity scores introduced in Section 3.3. We model this trade-off as a Pareto optimisation problem and find $\lambda = 0.7$ to be the best. Emissions decrease significantly beyond $\lambda = 0.7$, but with a significant reduction in output quality. At $\lambda = 0$ the two most carbon-intensive candidate models handle the majority (57.3%) of requests, while the two most efficient models receive just 15.8%. Conversely, at $\lambda = 1$ only 16.2% of calls are sent to the two high-carbon models, and 26.5% to the two low-carbon models. Complete emission and quality values for all λ values, as well as how the usage of candidate models varies across λ values, are shown in Appendix D.4.

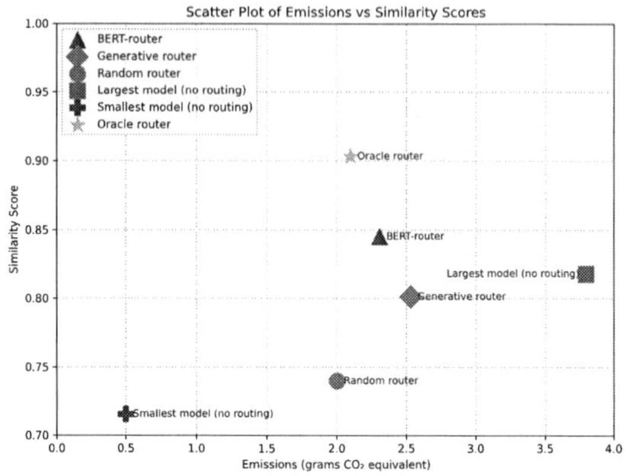

Figure 3: Similarity score vs average inference emissions, with $\lambda = 0.7$.

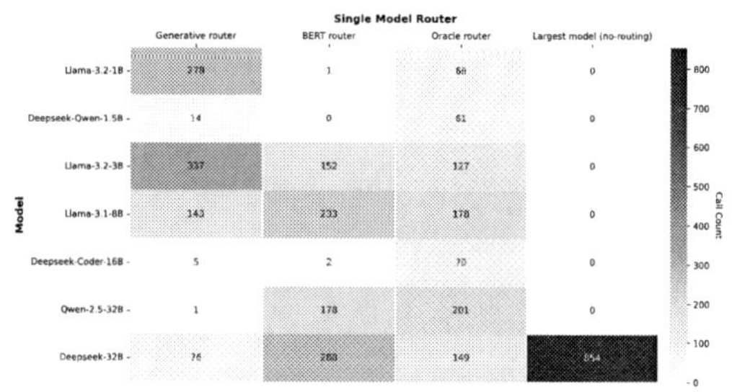

Figure 4: The number of calls to each model in single routing.

5.3 Single Model Routing

We evaluate single routing on the fine-tuned BERT router with $\lambda = 0.7$, using DeBERTa-v3 as the BERT model, due to its superior performance in Section 5.2. Figure 3 presents the emissions and similarity scores for all routing methods, full results with confidence intervals can be found in Appendix D.8.

These results show our BERT router outperforms all the baseline methods, except the oracle router. This gap is expected; the oracle router is an upper bound for the performance of a router which is 100% accurate at predicting the best model.

The BERT router outperforms the most powerful single model (DeepSeek distilled Qwen-32B) by 3.3% whilst also reducing emissions by 39%. Our BERT router also outperforms generative (decoder) routing, whilst simultaneously decreasing the environmental cost. We also show the utilisation of the candidate LLMs by each router in Figure 4.

5.3.1 Unseen dataset Performance

In the previous section, we evaluated routing on a test set of 10% of the prompts from each benchmark dataset. We also reserve an entire benchmark dataset (SQUAD) from training, to test generalisability to new tasks (Rajpurkar et al., 2016). This addresses a limitation of similar research, where routing models were only tested on the benchmark datasets on which they were trained.

As shown in Figure 5, our router only reduces similarity scores by 0.51% compared to the largest model, whilst also reducing environmental costs by 12.5%. Full results with confidence intervals can be found in Appendix D.9.

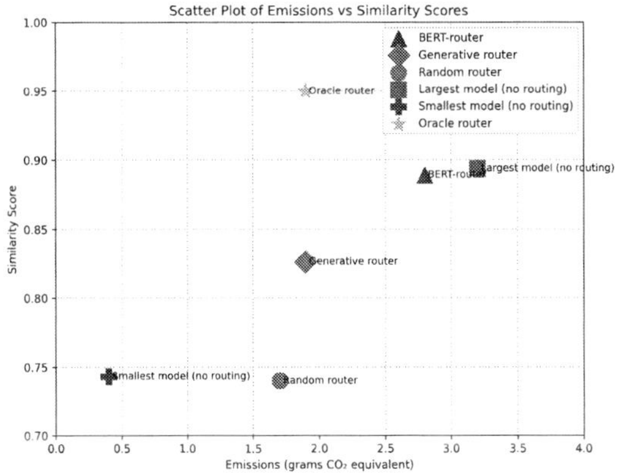

Figure 5: Similarity versus inference emission on unseen datasets, with $\lambda = 0.7$.

5.4 Chain Routing

5.5 Parameter Size Impact on Reasoning

We evaluate the impact of using larger models on each stage of reasoning CoTs in Figure 6.

These results show that smaller LLMs can effectively perform exploration and break down tasks, with under 2.4% impact on final similarity scores as opposed to larger models. However, they often fail to produce the correct final answer, even with the right reasoning chain, with the conclusion stage having by far the greatest impact on performance (14%). The average similarity score for each model combination is shown in Appendix D.7.

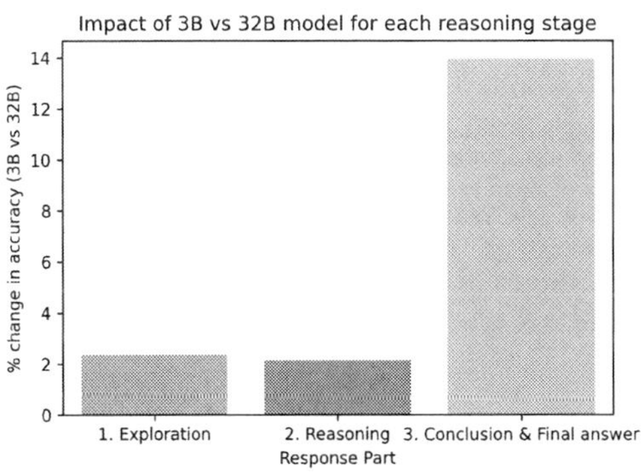

Figure 6: The percentage change in similarity scores when using the largest versus the smallest model for each part in the reasoning chain.

5.5.1 Chain Routing Inference Results

We evaluate the BERT router on the dataset of CoT responses in both modes: chain routing and single routing. To ensure fair results, we reduce the candidate LLMs available to the single model router to those used for chain routing and set $\lambda = 0.7$ in both cases. The results shown in Figure 7 highlight the potential of chain routing, which outperformed all methods except oracle routing. Full results with confidence intervals can be found in Appendix D.10. Notably, in comparison with the single largest model, our chain routing approach increases the similarity score by 0.43%, whilst decreasing the environmental cost by 18.7%.

Chain routing outperforms single routing on similarity scores by 4.84%, whilst only having a slightly higher environmental cost, highlighting the potential of chain routing as a more effective alternative to single routing. The headline figures for similarity score increase and emissions reduction are not as high as the previous single routing test, and single routing no longer outperforms the largest model. This can be explained by the fact that we use three models instead of seven, due to the exponentially increasing number of combinations in chain routing. We expect that scaling the number of models further would widen the margin and unlock further carbon savings.

The number of calls to each LLM is shown in Figure 8, showing that the BERT chain router mainly utilises the largest models. However, the chain router improves on the score of the largest model, showing that it is delegating to the smaller model at the correct times.

The number of calls to each model using the BERT router varies at different CoT stages. Smaller models are predominantly used for the first two stages (60 and 43 calls to the smallest model), and are used substantially less for the final step (17 calls to the smallest model). This mirrors the results found in Section 5.5, that output can be delegated to smaller models for the first two steps with a much lower impact on output quality than for the final step.

Breakdowns of the calls to each model for each CoT stage for both the generative and BERT routers are presented in Appendices D.11 and D.12.

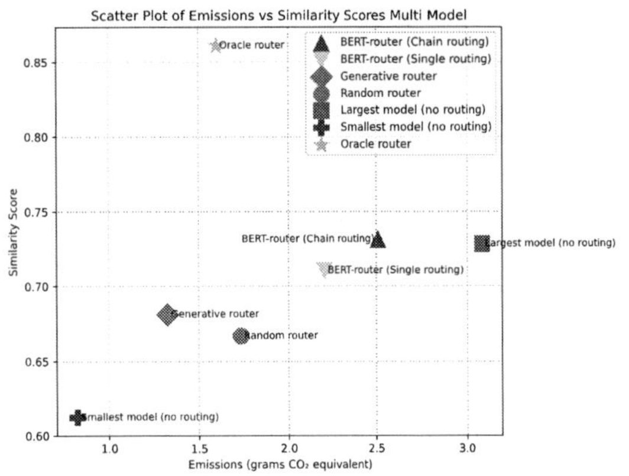

Figure 7: Similarity versus inference emission for routing on the CoT dataset, with $\lambda = 0.7$.

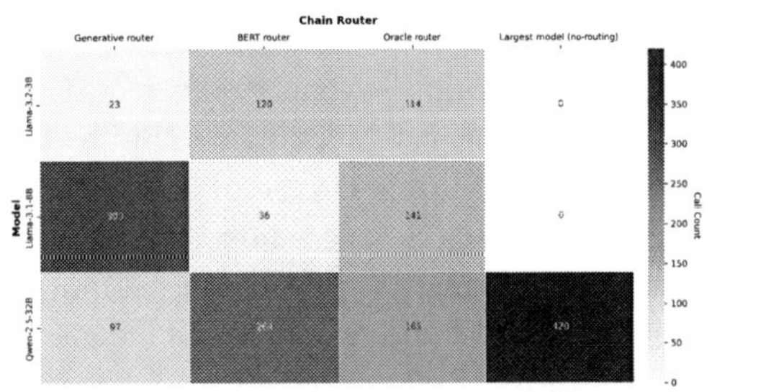

Figure 8: The number of calls to each model in chain routing.

5.6 Chain Routing Qualitative Error Analysis

We also manually analyse a sample of 50 prompts from the test set, to investigate the reliability of our similarity (to gold standard answer) metrics (BERTScore and chrF). Table 5 shows our comparison between the router's choice and the result with the highest metric. We record the number of times routing was successful/unsuccessful (whether the response from the model chosen by the router matched the gold standard response). We also record the number of cases where the similarity metric was correct/incorrect (whether the response with the highest similarity score matches the gold standard answer). Examples of CoT responses from the models chosen by the router and responses with the highest similarity score are shown in Appendix E.

6 Future Work

6.1 Additional Objectives

Whilst we focus on optimising output quality and environmental cost, the system could be extended to include other objectives. The leading candidate for this is the cost of inference; whilst this is difficult to quantify when running models locally, it is incorporated in related systems which rely on external APIs for inference (Hu et al., 2024).

Category	Count	%
Routing Quality		
Successful routing	42	84%
Unsuccessful routing	8	16%
Similarity Metric Quality		
Metric correct	46	92%
Metric incorrect	4	8%

Table 5: Qualitative error analysis of chain routing on a sample of 50 prompts.

6.2 Expanding Chain Routing

Our implementation of chain routing is a proof-of-concept to showcase the potential of this novel routing approach. This leaves several areas for future work to expand on, such as splitting the output into different stages and trying different model combinations, to further decrease environmental cost.

6.3 Improving Efficiency in Reasoning Models

Our results show that using smaller models for initial exploration steps in reasoning has little impact on final response quality, which could guide reasoning model development. Reasoning pipelines could incorporate a smaller model to explore the problem before passing the output to a larger model or MoE models could incorporate a dedicated lightweight expert for this phase.

7 Concluding Remarks

We incorporate environmental cost into routing decisions and introduce *chain routing*, which directs different stages of a reasoning CoT to different LLMs. We show that our system can significantly reduce the environmental impact of LLM inference, whilst also increasing the quality of outputs. Our results also show that using smaller models during early reasoning stages does not significantly affect final performance, a finding which can be used to create more efficient reasoning models. Overall, our findings highlight the substantial potential of environmentally aware chain routing in making LLM inference more sustainable.

Limitations

Generalisability and Dataset Selection

Whilst we attempt to make the system as generalisable as possible by including datasets spanning a wide range of domains, it is possible that the system may not generalise to all domains. The system may have to be fine-tuned further for deployment in tasks not included in the training data, such as dialogue.

Measuring similarity

Although research has shown that BERTScore and CHRF align well with human preference, they do not perfectly align (Zhang et al., 2020; Evtikhiev et al., 2023). However, we show from a manual qualitative review that the output with the highest similarity score matches the gold standard answer in 92% of cases.

Carbon Cost Estimation

The CodeCarbon library shows results broadly in line with results from previous research; models with more parameters or longer outputs consume more energy (Patterson et al., 2021). However, these results are based on batch inference on shared hardware (more details in Appendix C). Results in real-world deployment may differ dependent on deployment infrastructure, system load, and regional carbon intensity. However, we expect that all values will scale up or down in this case, and comparisons of the values between models will still hold.

Chain Routing Assumptions

Chain routing assumes that all reasoning processes can be segmented into the same three-phase structure; this aligns well with all tasks we use, and is likely to generalise to other tasks. However, it may not generalise to all tasks. Future work could explore chain routing with different methods for splitting CoT into stages.

Ethics Statement

Our work introduces a routing framework that considers both expected answer quality and environmental cost of inference in routing decisions. Whilst we hope that systems like ours will have a positive effect by decreasing the environmental cost of LLMs, it is important to address the potential ethical implications.

Carbon Cost of Training

The first consideration is the carbon cost and GPUs necessary to train the model. To address this, we carefully planned experiments to limit the amount of computing used to what was strictly necessary to train our system. We also only used a subset of prompts from each dataset and reduced the number of models in chain routing to ensure that we limit the environmental impact of gathering training data.

Transparency

Next, we need to consider transparency; systems like ours must make it clear at deployment time which model they are routing to, and allow for the end user to override this to ensure transparency and human agency.

Human Agency

The next consideration is the impact of these routing decisions; whilst we show that, on average, our routing increases performance, there will be some prompts where routing decreases the quality of responses. Routing could also have an impact on response hallucination rates. Thus, routing systems should always be deployed with a human-in-the-loop, to quality-check responses.

Bias

Finally, we need to consider bias, routing systems like ours are based on identifying statistical patterns in prompts to route them to the correct model. This could lead to prompts on certain topics or phrased in certain ways, being routed to smaller models, potentially reducing the quality of responses. At deployment time any system like ours would have to be carefully monitored and audited to ensure this was not happening.

References

Pranjal Aggarwal, Aman Madaan, Ankit Anand, Srividya Pranavi Potharaju, Swaroop Mishra, Pei Zhou, Aditya Gupta, Dheeraj Rajagopal, Karthik Kappaganthu, Yiming Yang, Shyam Upadhyay, Manaal Faruqui, and Mausam. 2024. AutoMix: Automatically Mixing Language Models. In *Conference on Neural Information Processing System.*

Yadagiri Annepaka and Partha Pakray. 2025. Large language models: a survey of their development, capabilities, and applications. *Knowledge and Information Systems*, 67(3):2967–3022.

Jacob Austin, Augustus Odena, Maxwell Nye, Maarten Bosma, Henryk Michalewski, David Dohan, Ellen Jiang, Carrie Cai, Michael Terry, Quoc Le, and Charles Sutton. 2021. Program Synthesis with Large Language Models. preprint.

Ljubisa Bojic, Predrag Kovacevic, and Milan Cabarkapa. 2023. GPT-4 Surpassing Human Performance in Linguistic Pragmatics. arXiv preprint. ArXiv:2312.09545 [cs].

Weilin Cai, Juyong Jiang, Fan Wang, Jing Tang, Sunghun Kim, and Jiayi Huang. 2025. A survey on mixture of experts in large language models. *IEEE Transactions on Knowledge and Data Engineering*, 37(7):3896–3915.

Lingjiao Chen, Matei Zaharia, and James Zou. 2023. Frugalgpt: How to use large language models while reducing cost and improving performance. arXiv preprint.

Peter Clark, Isaac Cowhey, Oren Etzioni, Tushar Khot, Ashish Sabharwal, Carissa Schoenick, and Oyvind Tafjord. 2018. Think you have Solved Question Answering? Try ARC, the AI2 Reasoning Challenge. arXiv preprint. ArXiv:1803.05457 [cs].

Karl Cobbe, Vineet Kosaraju, Mohammad Bavarian, Mark Chen, Heewoo Jun, Lukasz Kaiser, Matthias Plappert, Jerry Tworek, Jacob Hilton, Reiichiro Nakano, Christopher Hesse, and John Schulman. 2021. Training Verifiers to Solve Math Word Problems. arXiv preprint. ArXiv:2110.14168 [cs].

Benoit Courty, Victor Schmidt, Sasha Luccioni, Goyal-Kamal, MarionCoutarel, Boris Feld, Jérémy Lecourt, LiamConnell, Amine Saboni, Inimaz, supatomic, Mathilde Léval, Luis Blanche, Alexis Cruveiller, ouminasara, Franklin Zhao, Aditya Joshi, Alexis Bogroff, Hugues de Lavoreille, Niko Laskaris, Edoardo Abati, Douglas Blank, Ziyao Wang, Armin Catovic, Marc Alencon, Michał Stęchły, Christian Bauer, Lucas Otávio N. de Araújo, JPW, and MinervaBooks. 2024. mlco2/codecarbon: v2.4.1.

Mehul Damani, Idan Shenfeld, Andi Peng, Andreea Bobu, and Jacob Andreas. 2024. Learning How Hard to Think: Input-Adaptive Allocation of LM Computation. In *International Conference on Learning Representations*.

DeepSeek-AI, Daya Guo, Dejian Yang, Haowei Zhang, Junxiao Song, Ruoyu Zhang, Runxin Xu, Qihao Zhu, Shirong Ma, Peiyi Wang, Xiao Bi, Xiaokang Zhang, Xingkai Yu, Yu Wu, Z. F. Wu, Zhibin Gou, Zhihong Shao, Zhuoshu Li, Ziyi Gao, Aixin Liu, Bing Xue, Bingxuan Wang, Bochao Wu, Bei Feng, Chengda Lu, Chenggang Zhao, Chengqi Deng, Chenyu Zhang, Chong Ruan, Damai Dai, Deli Chen, Dongjie Ji, Erhang Li, Fangyun Lin, Fucong Dai, Fuli Luo, Guangbo Hao, Guanting Chen, Guowei Li, H. Zhang, Han Bao, Hanwei Xu, Haocheng Wang, Honghui Ding, Huajian Xin, Huazuo Gao, Hui Qu, Hui Li, Jianzhong Guo, Jiashi Li, Jiawei Wang, Jingchang Chen, Jingyang Yuan, Junjie Qiu, Junlong Li, J. L. Cai, Jiaqi Ni, Jian Liang, Jin Chen, Kai Dong, Kai Hu, Kaige Gao, Kang Guan, Kexin Huang, Kuai Yu, Lean Wang, Lecong Zhang, Liang Zhao, Litong Wang, Liyue Zhang, Lei Xu, Leyi Xia, Mingchuan Zhang, Minghua Zhang, Minghui Tang, Meng Li, Miaojun Wang, Mingming Li, Ning Tian, Panpan Huang, Peng Zhang, Qiancheng Wang, Qinyu Chen, Qiushi Du, Ruiqi Ge, Ruisong Zhang, Ruizhe Pan, Runji Wang, R. J. Chen, R. L. Jin, Ruyi Chen, Shanghao Lu, Shangyan Zhou, Shanhuang Chen, Shengfeng Ye, Shiyu Wang, Shuiping Yu, Shunfeng Zhou, Shuting Pan, S. S. Li, Shuang Zhou, Shaoqing Wu, Shengfeng Ye, Tao Yun, Tian Pei, Tianyu Sun, T. Wang, Wangding Zeng, Wanjia Zhao, Wen Liu, Wenfeng Liang, Wenjun Gao, Wenqin Yu, Wentao Zhang, W. L. Xiao, Wei An, Xiaodong Liu, Xiaohan Wang, Xiaokang Chen, Xiaotao Nie, Xin Cheng, Xin Liu, Xin Xie, Xingchao Liu, Xinyu Yang, Xinyuan Li, Xuecheng Su, Xuheng Lin, X. Q. Li, Xiangyue Jin, Xiaojin Shen, Xiaosha Chen, Xiaowen Sun, Xiaoxiang Wang, Xinnan Song, Xinyi Zhou, Xianzu Wang, Xinxia Shan, Y. K. Li, Y. Q. Wang, Y. X. Wei, Yang Zhang, Yanhong Xu, Yao Li, Yao Zhao, Yaofeng Sun, Yaohui Wang, Yi Yu, Yichao Zhang, Yifan Shi, Yiliang Xiong, Ying He, Yishi Piao, Yisong Wang, Yixuan Tan, Yiyang Ma, Yiyuan Liu, Yongqiang Guo, Yuan Ou, Yuduan Wang, Yue Gong, Yuheng Zou, Yujia He, Yunfan Xiong, Yuxiang Luo, Yuxiang You, Yuxuan Liu, Yuyang Zhou, Y. X. Zhu, Yanhong Xu, Yanping Huang, Yaohui Li, Yi Zheng, Yuchen Zhu, Yunxian Ma, Ying Tang, Yukun Zha, Yuting Yan, Z. Z. Ren, Zehui Ren, Zhangli Sha, Zhe Fu, Zhean Xu, Zhenda Xie, Zhengyan Zhang, Zhewen Hao, Zhicheng Ma, Zhigang Yan, Zhiyu Wu, Zihui Gu, Zijia Zhu, Zijun Liu, Zilin Li, Ziwei Xie, Ziyang Song, Zizheng Pan, Zhen Huang, Zhipeng Xu, Zhongyu Zhang, and Zhen Zhang. 2025. DeepSeek-R1: Incentivizing Reasoning Capability in LLMs via Reinforcement Learning. arXiv preprint. ArXiv:2501.12948 [cs].

DeepSeek-AI, Qihao Zhu, Daya Guo, Zhihong Shao, Dejian Yang, Peiyi Wang, Runxin Xu, Y. Wu, Yukun Li, Huazuo Gao, Shirong Ma, Wangding Zeng, Xiao Bi, Zihui Gu, Hanwei Xu, Damai Dai, Kai Dong, Liyue Zhang, Yishi Piao, Zhibin Gou, Zhenda Xie, Zhewen Hao, Bingxuan Wang, Junxiao Song, Deli Chen, Xin Xie, Kang Guan, Yuxiang You, Aixin Liu, Qiushi Du, Wenjun Gao, Xuan Lu, Qinyu Chen, Yaohui Wang, Chengqi Deng, Jiashi Li, Chenggang Zhao, Chong Ruan, Fuli Luo, and Wenfeng Liang. 2024. DeepSeek-Coder-V2: Breaking the Barrier of Closed-Source Models in Code Intelligence. ArXiv:2406.11931 [cs].

Dujian Ding, Ankur Mallick, Chi Wang, Robert Sim, Subhabrata Mukherjee, Victor Rühle, Laks V. S. Lakshmanan, and Ahmed Hassan Awadallah. 2024. Hybrid LLM: Cost-Efficient and Quality-Aware Query Routing. In *International Conference on Learning Representations*.

Ithier d'Aramon, Boris Ruf, and Marcin Detyniecki.

2024. Assessing Carbon Footprint Estimations of ChatGPT. In Philip Pong, editor, *Renewable Energy Resources and Conservation*, pages 127–133. Springer Nature Switzerland, Cham.

Mikhail Evtikhiev, Egor Bogomolov, Yaroslav Sokolov, and Timofey Bryksin. 2023. Out of the BLEU: how should we assess quality of the Code Generation models? *Journal of Systems and Software*, 203:111741.

Tao Feng, Yanzhen Shen, and Jiaxuan You. 2024. GraphRouter: A Graph-based Router for LLM Selections. In *International Conference on Learning Representations*.

Kevin Fischer, Darren Fürst, Sebastian Steindl, Jakob Lindner, and Ulrich Schäfer. 2024. Question: How do Large Language Models perform on the Question Answering tasks? Answer:. arXiv preprint.

Alon Goldstein, Miriam Havin, Roi Reichart, and Ariel Goldstein. 2023. Decoding Stumpers: Large Language Models vs. Human Problem-Solvers. In *Findings of the Association for Computational Linguistics: EMNLP 2023*, pages 11644–11653. Association for Computational Linguistics.

Aaron Grattafiori, Abhimanyu Dubey, Abhinav Jauhri, Abhinav Pandey, Abhishek Kadian, Ahmad Al-Dahle, Aiesha Letman, Akhil Mathur, Alan Schelten, Alex Vaughan, Amy Yang, Angela Fan, Anirudh Goyal, Anthony Hartshorn, Aobo Yang, Archi Mitra, Archie Sravankumar, Artem Korenev, Arthur Hinsvark, Arun Rao, Aston Zhang, Aurelien Rodriguez, Austen Gregerson, Ava Spataru, Baptiste Roziere, Bethany Biron, Binh Tang, Bobbie Chern, Charlotte Caucheteux, Chaya Nayak, Chloe Bi, Chris Marra, Chris McConnell, Christian Keller, Christophe Touret, Chunyang Wu, Corinne Wong, Cristian Canton Ferrer, Cyrus Nikolaidis, Damien Allonsius, Daniel Song, Danielle Pintz, Danny Livshits, Danny Wyatt, David Esiobu, Dhruv Choudhary, Dhruv Mahajan, Diego Garcia-Olano, Diego Perino, Dieuwke Hupkes, Egor Lakomkin, Ehab AlBadawy, Elina Lobanova, Emily Dinan, Eric Michael Smith, Filip Radenovic, Francisco Guzmán, Frank Zhang, Gabriel Synnaeve, Gabrielle Lee, Georgia Lewis Anderson, Govind Thattai, Graeme Nail, Gregoire Mialon, Guan Pang, Guillem Cucurell, Hailey Nguyen, Hannah Korevaar, Hu Xu, Hugo Touvron, Iliyan Zarov, Imanol Arrieta Ibarra, Isabel Kloumann, Ishan Misra, Ivan Evtimov, Jack Zhang, Jade Copet, Jaewon Lee, Jan Geffert, Jana Vranes, Jason Park, Jay Mahadeokar, Jeet Shah, Jelmer van der Linde, Jennifer Billock, Jenny Hong, Jenya Lee, Jeremy Fu, Jianfeng Chi, Jianyu Huang, Jiawen Liu, Jie Wang, Jiecao Yu, Joanna Bitton, Joe Spisak, Jongsoo Park, Joseph Rocca, Joshua Johnstun, Joshua Saxe, Junteng Jia, Kalyan Vasuden Alwala, Karthik Prasad, Kartikeya Upasani, Kate Plawiak, Ke Li, Kenneth Heafield, Kevin Stone, Khalid El-Arini, Krithika Iyer, Kshitiz Malik, Kuenley Chiu, Kunal Bhalla, Kushal Lakhotia, Lauren Rantala-Yeary, Laurens van der Maaten, Lawrence Chen, Liang Tan, Liz Jenkins, Louis Martin, Lovish Madaan, Lubo Malo, Lukas Blecher, Lukas Landzaat, Luke de Oliveira, Madeline Muzzi, Mahesh Pasupuleti, Mannat Singh, Manohar Paluri, Marcin Kardas, Maria Tsimpoukelli, Mathew Oldham, Mathieu Rita, Maya Pavlova, Melanie Kambadur, Mike Lewis, Min Si, Mitesh Kumar Singh, Mona Hassan, Naman Goyal, Narjes Torabi, Nikolay Bashlykov, Nikolay Bogoychev, Niladri Chatterji, Ning Zhang, Olivier Duchenne, Onur Çelebi, Patrick Alrassy, Pengchuan Zhang, Pengwei Li, Petar Vasic, Peter Weng, Prajjwal Bhargava, Pratik Dubal, Praveen Krishnan, Punit Singh Koura, Puxin Xu, Qing He, Qingxiao Dong, Ragavan Srinivasan, Raj Ganapathy, Ramon Calderer, Ricardo Silveira Cabral, Robert Stojnic, Roberta Raileanu, Rohan Maheswari, Rohit Girdhar, Rohit Patel, Romain Sauvestre, Ronnie Polidoro, Roshan Sumbaly, Ross Taylor, Ruan Silva, Rui Hou, Rui Wang, Saghar Hosseini, Sahana Chennabasappa, Sanjay Singh, Sean Bell, Seohyun Sonia Kim, Sergey Edunov, Shaoliang Nie, Sharan Narang, Sharath Raparthy, Sheng Shen, Shengye Wan, Shruti Bhosale, Shun Zhang, Simon Vandenhende, Soumya Batra, Spencer Whitman, Sten Sootla, Stephane Collot, Suchin Gururangan, Sydney Borodinsky, Tamar Herman, Tara Fowler, Tarek Sheasha, Thomas Georgiou, Thomas Scialom, Tobias Speckbacher, Todor Mihaylov, Tong Xiao, Ujjwal Karn, Vedanuj Goswami, Vibhor Gupta, Vignesh Ramanathan, Viktor Kerkez, Vincent Gonguet, Virginie Do, Vish Vogeti, Vítor Albiero, Vladan Petrovic, Weiwei Chu, Wenhan Xiong, Wenyin Fu, Whitney Meers, Xavier Martinet, Xiaodong Wang, Xiaofang Wang, Xiaoqing Ellen Tan, Xide Xia, Xinfeng Xie, Xuchao Jia, Xuewei Wang, Yaelle Goldschlag, Yashesh Gaur, Yasmine Babaei, Yi Wen, Yiwen Song, Yuchen Zhang, Yue Li, Yuning Mao, Zacharie Delpierre Coudert, Zheng Yan, Zhengxing Chen, Zoe Papakipos, Aaditya Singh, Aayushi Srivastava, Abha Jain, Adam Kelsey, Adam Shajnfeld, Adithya Gangidi, Adolfo Victoria, Ahuva Goldstand, Ajay Menon, Ajay Sharma, Alex Boesenberg, Alexei Baevski, Allie Feinstein, Amanda Kallet, Amit Sangani, Amos Teo, Anam Yunus, Andrei Lupu, Andres Alvarado, Andrew Caples, Andrew Gu, Andrew Ho, Andrew Poulton, Andrew Ryan, Ankit Ramchandani, Annie Dong, Annie Franco, Anuj Goyal, Aparajita Saraf, Arkabandhu Chowdhury, Ashley Gabriel, Ashwin Bharambe, Assaf Eisenman, Azadeh Yazdan, Beau James, Ben Maurer, Benjamin Leonhardi, Bernie Huang, Beth Loyd, Beto De Paola, Bhargavi Paranjape, Bing Liu, Bo Wu, Boyu Ni, Braden Hancock, Bram Wasti, Brandon Spence, Brani Stojkovic, Brian Gamido, Britt Montalvo, Carl Parker, Carly Burton, Catalina Mejia, Ce Liu, Changhan Wang, Changkyu Kim, Chao Zhou, Chester Hu, Ching-Hsiang Chu, Chris Cai, Chris Tindal, Christoph Feichtenhofer, Cynthia Gao, Damon Civin, Dana Beaty, Daniel Kreymer, Daniel Li, David Adkins, David Xu, Davide Testuggine, Delia David, Devi Parikh, Diana Liskovich, Didem Foss, Dingkang Wang, Duc Le, Dustin Holland, Edward Dowling, Eissa Jamil, Elaine Montgomery, Eleonora Presani, Emily Hahn, Emily Wood, Eric-Tuan Le, Erik Brinkman, Esteban Arcaute, Evan Dunbar, Evan Smothers, Fei Sun,

Felix Kreuk, Feng Tian, Filippos Kokkinos, Firat Ozgenel, Francesco Caggioni, Frank Kanayet, Frank Seide, Gabriela Medina Florez, Gabriella Schwarz, Gada Badeer, Georgia Swee, Gil Halpern, Grant Herman, Grigory Sizov, Guangyi, Zhang, Guna Lakshminarayanan, Hakan Inan, Hamid Shojanazeri, Han Zou, Hannah Wang, Hanwen Zha, Haroun Habeeb, Harrison Rudolph, Helen Suk, Henry Aspegren, Hunter Goldman, Hongyuan Zhan, Ibrahim Damlaj, Igor Molybog, Igor Tufanov, Ilias Leontiadis, Irina-Elena Veliche, Itai Gat, Jake Weissman, James Geboski, James Kohli, Janice Lam, Japhet Asher, Jean-Baptiste Gaya, Jeff Marcus, Jeff Tang, Jennifer Chan, Jenny Zhen, Jeremy Reizenstein, Jeremy Teboul, Jessica Zhong, Jian Jin, Jingyi Yang, Joe Cummings, Jon Carvill, Jon Shepard, Jonathan McPhie, Jonathan Torres, Josh Ginsburg, Junjie Wang, Kai Wu, Kam Hou U, Karan Saxena, Kartikay Khandelwal, Katayoun Zand, Kathy Matosich, Kaushik Veeraraghavan, Kelly Michelena, Keqian Li, Kiran Jagadeesh, Kun Huang, Kunal Chawla, Kyle Huang, Lailin Chen, Lakshya Garg, Lavender A, Leandro Silva, Lee Bell, Lei Zhang, Liangpeng Guo, Licheng Yu, Liron Moshkovich, Luca Wehrstedt, Madian Khabsa, Manav Avalani, Manish Bhatt, Martynas Mankus, Matan Hasson, Matthew Lennie, Matthias Reso, Maxim Groshev, Maxim Naumov, Maya Lathi, Meghan Keneally, Miao Liu, Michael L. Seltzer, Michal Valko, Michelle Restrepo, Mihir Patel, Mik Vyatskov, Mikayel Samvelyan, Mike Clark, Mike Macey, Mike Wang, Miquel Jubert Hermoso, Mo Metanat, Mohammad Rastegari, Munish Bansal, Nandhini Santhanam, Natascha Parks, Natasha White, Navyata Bawa, Nayan Singhal, Nick Egebo, Nicolas Usunier, Nikhil Mehta, Nikolay Pavlovich Laptev, Ning Dong, Norman Cheng, Oleg Chernoguz, Olivia Hart, Omkar Salpekar, Ozlem Kalinli, Parkin Kent, Parth Parekh, Paul Saab, Pavan Balaji, Pedro Rittner, Philip Bontrager, Pierre Roux, Piotr Dollar, Polina Zvyagina, Prashant Ratanchandani, Pritish Yuvraj, Qian Liang, Rachad Alao, Rachel Rodriguez, Rafi Ayub, Raghotham Murthy, Raghu Nayani, Rahul Mitra, Rangaprabhu Parthasarathy, Raymond Li, Rebekkah Hogan, Robin Battey, Rocky Wang, Russ Howes, Ruty Rinott, Sachin Mehta, Sachin Siby, Sai Jayesh Bondu, Samyak Datta, Sara Chugh, Sara Hunt, Sargun Dhillon, Sasha Sidorov, Satadru Pan, Saurabh Mahajan, Saurabh Verma, Seiji Yamamoto, Sharadh Ramaswamy, Shaun Lindsay, Shaun Lindsay, Sheng Feng, Shenghao Lin, Shengxin Cindy Zha, Shishir Patil, Shiva Shankar, Shuqiang Zhang, Shuqiang Zhang, Sinong Wang, Sneha Agarwal, Soji Sajuyigbe, Soumith Chintala, Stephanie Max, Stephen Chen, Steve Kehoe, Steve Satterfield, Sudarshan Govindaprasad, Sumit Gupta, Summer Deng, Sungmin Cho, Sunny Virk, Suraj Subramanian, Sy Choudhury, Sydney Goldman, Tal Remez, Tamar Glaser, Tamara Best, Thilo Koehler, Thomas Robinson, Tianhe Li, Tianjun Zhang, Tim Matthews, Timothy Chou, Tzook Shaked, Varun Vontimitta, Victoria Ajayi, Victoria Montanez, Vijai Mohan, Vinay Satish Kumar, Vishal Mangla, Vlad Ionescu, Vlad Poenaru, Vlad Tiberiu Mihailescu, Vladimir Ivanov, Wei Li, Wenchen Wang, Wenwen Jiang, Wes Bouaziz, Will Constable, Xiaocheng Tang, Xiaojian Wu, Xiaolan Wang, Xilun Wu, Xinbo Gao, Yaniv Kleinman, Yanjun Chen, Ye Hu, Ye Jia, Ye Qi, Yenda Li, Yilin Zhang, Ying Zhang, Yossi Adi, Youngjin Nam, Yu, Wang, Yu Zhao, Yuchen Hao, Yundi Qian, Yunlu Li, Yuzi He, Zach Rait, Zachary DeVito, Zef Rosnbrick, Zhaoduo Wen, Zhenyu Yang, Zhiwei Zhao, and Zhiyu Ma. 2024. The Llama 3 Herd of Models. arXiv preprint.

Tingxu Han, Zhenting Wang, Chunrong Fang, Shiyu Zhao, Shiqing Ma, and Zhenyu Chen. 2025. Token-budget-aware llm reasoning. arXiv preprint.

Pengcheng He, Jianfeng Gao, and Weizhu Chen. 2023. DeBERTaV3: Improving DeBERTa using ELECTRA-Style Pre-Training with Gradient-Disentangled Embedding Sharing. In *International Conference on Learning Representations*.

Dan Hendrycks, Collin Burns, Steven Basart, Andy Zou, Mantas Mazeika, Dawn Song, and Jacob Steinhardt. 2021. Measuring Massive Multitask Language Understanding. In *International Conference on Learning Representations*.

Qitian Jason Hu, Jacob Bieker, Xiuyu Li, Nan Jiang, Benjamin Keigwin, Gaurav Ranganath, Kurt Keutzer, and Shriyash Kaustubh Upadhyay. 2024. RouterBench: A Benchmark for Multi-LLM Routing System. Poster presented at Agentic Markets Workshop, International Conference on Machine Learning.

Robert A. Jacobs, Michael I. Jordan, Steven J. Nowlan, and Geoffrey E. Hinton. 1991. Adaptive Mixtures of Local Experts. *Neural Computation*, 3(1):79–87. Conference Name: Neural Computation.

Albert Q. Jiang, Alexandre Sablayrolles, Antoine Roux, Arthur Mensch, Blanche Savary, Chris Bamford, Devendra Singh Chaplot, Diego de las Casas, Emma Bou Hanna, Florian Bressand, Gianna Lengyel, Guillaume Bour, Guillaume Lample, Lélio Renard Lavaud, Lucile Saulnier, Marie-Anne Lachaux, Pierre Stock, Sandeep Subramanian, Sophia Yang, Szymon Antoniak, Teven Le Scao, Théophile Gervet, Thibaut Lavril, Thomas Wang, Timothée Lacroix, and William El Sayed. 2024. Mixtral of Experts. arXiv preprint. ArXiv:2401.04088 [cs].

Dongfu Jiang, Xiang Ren, and Bill Yuchen Lin. 2023. LLM-blender: Ensembling large language models with pairwise ranking and generative fusion. In *Proceedings of the 61st Annual Meeting of the Association for Computational Linguistics (Volume 1: Long Papers)*, pages 14165–14178, Toronto, Canada. Association for Computational Linguistics.

Daniel Khashabi, Sewon Min, Tushar Khot, Ashish Sabharwal, Oyvind Tafjord, Peter Clark, and Hannaneh Hajishirzi. 2020. UNIFIEDQA: Crossing format boundaries with a single QA system. In *Findings of the Association for Computational Linguistics:*

EMNLP 2020, pages 1896–1907, Online. Association for Computational Linguistics.

Baolin Li, Yankai Jiang, Vijay Gadepally, and Devesh Tiwari. 2024. Sprout: Green Generative AI with Carbon-Efficient LLM Inference. In *Proceedings of the 2024 Conference on Empirical Methods in Natural Language Processing*, pages 21799–21813. Association for Computational Linguistics.

Sasha Luccioni, Yacine Jernite, and Emma Strubell. 2024. Power Hungry Processing: Watts Driving the Cost of AI Deployment? In *Proceedings of the 2024 ACM Conference on Fairness, Accountability, and Transparency*, FAccT '24, pages 85–99, New York, NY, USA. Association for Computing Machinery.

Meta. 2025. The Llama 4 herd: The beginning of a new era of natively multimodal AI innovation.

Seyed Iman Mirzadeh, Keivan Alizadeh, Hooman Shahrokhi, Oncel Tuzel, Samy Bengio, and Mehrdad Farajtabar. 2024. GSM-Symbolic: Understanding the Limitations of Mathematical Reasoning in Large Language Models. In *International Conference on Learning Representations*.

Brent Mittelstadt, Sandra Wachter, and Chris Russell. 2023. To protect science, we must use LLMs as zero-shot translators. *Nature Human Behaviour*, 7(11):1830–1832. Publisher: Nature Publishing Group.

Quang H. Nguyen, Duy C. Hoang, Juliette Decugis, Saurav Manchanda, Nitesh V. Chawla, and Khoa D. Doan. 2024. Metallm: A high-performant and cost-efficient dynamic framework for wrapping llms. arXiv preprint.

NVIDIA. 2025. NVIDIA-AI-Blueprints/llm-router.

Isaac Ong, Amjad Almahairi, Vincent Wu, Wei-Lin Chiang, Tianhao Wu, Joseph E. Gonzalez, M. Waleed Kadous, and Ion Stoica. 2024. RouteLLM: Learning to Route LLMs from Preference Data. In *International Conference on Learning Representations*.

OpenAI. 2024. Learning to Reason with LLMs.

David Patterson, Joseph Gonzalez, Quoc Le, Chen Liang, Lluis-Miquel Munguia, Daniel Rothchild, David So, Maud Texier, and Jeff Dean. 2021. Carbon Emissions and Large Neural Network Training. arXiv preprint. ArXiv:2104.10350.

Maja Popović. 2015. chrF: character n-gram F-score for automatic MT evaluation. In *Proceedings of the Tenth Workshop on Statistical Machine Translation*, pages 392–395. Association for Computational Linguistics.

Maja Popović. 2016. chrF deconstructed: beta parameters and n-gram weights. In *Proceedings of the First Conference on Machine Translation: Volume 2, Shared Task Papers*, pages 499–504, Berlin, Germany. Association for Computational Linguistics.

Qwen, An Yang, Baosong Yang, Beichen Zhang, Binyuan Hui, Bo Zheng, Bowen Yu, Chengyuan Li, Dayiheng Liu, Fei Huang, Haoran Wei, Huan Lin, Jian Yang, Jianhong Tu, Jianwei Zhang, Jianxin Yang, Jiaxi Yang, Jingren Zhou, Junyang Lin, Kai Dang, Keming Lu, Keqin Bao, Kexin Yang, Le Yu, Mei Li, Mingfeng Xue, Pei Zhang, Qin Zhu, Rui Men, Runji Lin, Tianhao Li, Tianyi Tang, Tingyu Xia, Xingzhang Ren, Xuancheng Ren, Yang Fan, Yang Su, Yichang Zhang, Yu Wan, Yuqiong Liu, Zeyu Cui, Zhenru Zhang, and Zihan Qiu. 2025. Qwen2.5 Technical Report. arXiv preprint. ArXiv:2412.15115 [cs].

Pranav Rajpurkar, Jian Zhang, Konstantin Lopyrev, and Percy Liang. 2016. SQuAD: 100,000+ questions for machine comprehension of text. In *Proceedings of the 2016 Conference on Empirical Methods in Natural Language Processing*, pages 2383–2392, Austin, Texas. Association for Computational Linguistics.

David Rein, Betty Li Hou, Asa Cooper Stickland, Jackson Petty, Richard Yuanzhe Pang, Julien Dirani, Julian Michael, and Samuel R. Bowman. 2024. GPQA: A graduate-level google-proof q&a benchmark. In *First Conference on Language Modeling*.

Siddharth Samsi, Dan Zhao, Joseph McDonald, Baolin Li, Adam Michaleas, Michael Jones, William Bergeron, Jeremy Kepner, Devesh Tiwari, and Vijay Gadepally. 2023. From words to watts: Benchmarking the energy costs of large language model inference. In *2023 IEEE High Performance Extreme Computing Conference (HPEC)*, pages 1–9.

Noam Shazeer, *Azalia Mirhoseini, *Krzysztof Maziarz, Andy Davis, Quoc Le, Geoffrey Hinton, and Jeff Dean. 2017. Outrageously large neural networks: The sparsely-gated mixture-of-experts layer. In *International Conference on Learning Representations*.

Yongliang Shen, Kaitao Song, Xu Tan, Dongsheng Li, Weiming Lu, and Yueting Zhuang. 2023. HuggingGPT: Solving AI Tasks with ChatGPT and its Friends in Hugging Face. In *Advances in Neural Information Processing Systems 36 (NeurIPS 2023)*.

Tal Shnitzer, Anthony Ou, Mírian Silva, Kate Soule, Yuekai Sun, Justin Solomon, Neil Thompson, and Mikhail Yurochkin. 2023. Large language model routing with benchmark datasets.

Toby Simonds, Kemal Kurniawan, and Jey Han Lau. 2024. MoDEM: Mixture of domain expert models. In *Proceedings of the 22nd Annual Workshop of the Australasian Language Technology Association*, pages 75–88, Canberra, Australia. Association for Computational Linguistics.

Kv Aditya Srivatsa, Kaushal Maurya, and Ekaterina Kochmar. 2024. Harnessing the power of multiple minds: Lessons learned from LLM routing. In *Proceedings of the Fifth Workshop on Insights from Negative Results in NLP*, pages 124–134, Mexico City, Mexico. Association for Computational Linguistics.

Dimitris Stripelis, Zhaozhuo Xu, Zijian Hu, Alay Dilipbhai Shah, Han Jin, Yuhang Yao, Jipeng Zhang, Tong Zhang, Salman Avestimehr, and Chaoyang He. 2024. TensorOpera router: A multi-model router for efficient LLM inference. In *Proceedings of the 2024 Conference on Empirical Methods in Natural Language Processing: Industry Track*, pages 452–462. Association for Computational Linguistics.

Clovis Varangot-Reille, Christophe Bouvard, Antoine Gourru, Mathieu Ciancone, Marion Schaeffer, and François Jacquenet. 2025. Doing More with Less – Implementing Routing Strategies in Large Language Model-Based Systems: An Extended Survey. arXiv preprint. ArXiv:2502.00409 [cs] version: 2.

Xuezhi Wang, Jason Wei, Dale Schuurmans, Quoc V. Le, Ed H. Chi, Sharan Narang, Aakanksha Chowdhery, and Denny Zhou. 2023. Self-Consistency Improves Chain of Thought Reasoning in Language Models. In *International Conference on Learning Representations*.

Yubo Wang, Xueguang Ma, Ge Zhang, Yuansheng Ni, Abhranil Chandra, Shiguang Guo, Weiming Ren, Aaran Arulraj, Xuan He, Ziyan Jiang, Tianle Li, Max Ku, Kai Wang, Alex Zhuang, Rongqi Fan, Xiang Yue, and Wenhu Chen. 2024. MMLU-Pro: A More Robust and Challenging Multi-Task Language Understanding Benchmark. In *Advances in Neural Information Processing Systems 37 (NeurIPS 2024) Datasets and Benchmarks Track*.

Grant Wilkins, Srinivasan Keshav, and Richard Mortier. 2025. Offline Energy-Optimal LLM Serving: Workload-Based Energy Models for LLM Inference on Heterogeneous Systems. *SIGENERGY Energy Inform. Rev.*, 4(5):113–119.

Hao Xuan, Bokai Yang, and Xingyu Li. 2025. Exploring the impact of temperature scaling in softmax for classification and adversarial robustness.

Prateek Yadav, Colin Raffel, Mohammed Muqeeth, Lucas Caccia, Haokun Liu, Tianlong Chen, Mohit Bansal, Leshem Choshen, and Alessandro Sordoni. 2025. A survey on model moerging: Recycling and routing among specialized experts for collaborative learning. *Transactions on Machine Learning Research*. Survey Certification.

Murong Yue, Jie Zhao, Min Zhang, Liang Du, and Ziyu Yao. 2023. Large Language Model Cascades with Mixture of Thought Representations for Cost-Efficient Reasoning. In *International Conference on Learning Representations*.

Kai Zhang, Liqian Peng, Congchao Wang, Alec Go, and Xiaozhong Liu. 2024a. LLM Cascade with Multi-Objective Optimal Consideration. ArXiv:2410.08014 version: 1.

Tianyi Zhang, Varsha Kishore, Felix Wu, Kilian Q. Weinberger, and Yoav Artzi. 2020. BERTScore: Evaluating Text Generation with BERT. In *International Conference on Learning Representations*.

Xuechen Zhang, Zijian Huang, Ege Onur Taga, Carlee Joe-Wong, Samet Oymak, and Jiasi Chen. 2024b. Efficient Contextual LLM Cascades through Budget-Constrained Policy Learning. In *International Conference on Learning Representations Poster*.

Wenhao Zheng, Yixiao Chen, Weitong Zhang, Souvik Kundu, Yun Li, Zhengzhong Liu, Eric P. Xing, Hongyi Wang, and Huaxiu Yao. 2024. CITER: Collaborative Inference for Efficient Large Language Model Decoding with Token-Level Routing. arXiv preprint.

Liu Zhuang, Lin Wayne, Shi Ya, and Zhao Jun. 2021. A robustly optimized BERT pre-training approach with post-training. In *Proceedings of the 20th Chinese National Conference on Computational Linguistics*, pages 1218–1227, Huhhot, China. Chinese Information Processing Society of China.

A Decoder Hyperparameters

A.1 LLM parameters ($< 25B$ parameters)

Setting	Value
Compute precision	`float16`
Top-k	50
Top-p	0.9
Temperature	0.7
Repetition penalty	1.2
Maximum output tokens	2500

Table 6: LLM hyperparameters for smaller models(<32B parameters).

A.2 LLM parameters ($> 25B$ parameters)

Setting	Value
Quantisation	8-bit
Compute precision	`float16`
Top-k	50
Top-p	0.9
Temperature	0.7
Repetition penalty	1.2
Maximum output tokens	2500

Table 7: LLM hyperparameters for larger models (>32B parameters).

B Encoder Hyperparameters

B.1 BERT Fine-Tuning Hyperparameters

Hyperparameter	Value
Learning rate	2×10^{-5}
Number of training epochs	3
Batch Size (Per GPU)	8
Warmup ratio	0.1
Weight decay	0.01
Mixed precision (fp16)	Enabled
Gradient accumulation steps	4
Soft score temperature	4.5

Table 8: BERT fine-tuning hyperparameters.

B.2 BERT Fine-Tuning Loss

The loss formula is shown in the equations below, where $P(X)$ is the correct soft score distribution, $Q(X)$ is the predicted soft score distribution, N is the total number of examples, k is the number of classes, and N_i is the number of examples in class i.

$$D_{KL}(P_i, Q_i) = \sum_j Q_{i,j} \log \frac{P_{i,j}}{Q_{i,j}} \tag{9}$$

$$w_i = \frac{N}{k \times N_i} \tag{10}$$

$$\text{loss}(Q_i, P_i, N_i) = D_{KL}(Q_i, P_i) \times w_i \quad (11)$$

C Carbon Calculation Details

C.1 Hardware Details

Component	**Details**
GPUs	• NVIDIA RTX A5000 : 23.99 GB • NVIDIA GeForce RTX 3090 : 24.00 GB
GPUS Utilised	At most 2 per experiment
System Memory	DDR4 3200MHz (250-500GB)
CPUs	• AMD EPYC 7543P : 32 cores, 2.8–3.7 GHz • AMD EPYC 7443 : 24 cores, 2.85–4.0 GHz
CPU Cores Utilised	At most 2 cores per experiment

Table 9: The hardware used for training and evaluation.

C.2 Code Carbon Implementation Details

We ran all of our results using the energy mix defined in Code Carbon for the United Kingdom (GBR), which uses an average grid-mix carbon intensity of 237.6g CO_2 per kWh [4].

These carbon intensity values are static, so they are the same between runs, but recreating our results in different jurisdictions or on different hardware will yield different results.

D Raw Results Output

D.1 Environmental Cost and Latency of Routing Approaches

Routing Method	**Carbon Cost (g CO_2)**	**Latency (s)**
BERT (Single Routing)	0.0001565	0.0251
BERT (Chain Routing)	0.04102	0.8969
Generative (Single Routing)	0.01565	1.004
Random, Oracle Routing	0	0

Table 10: A comparison of the environmental cost of each routing approach.

D.2 Environmental Cost of Training BERT Routers

Router	Carbon cost (total) CO_2 kg	Carbon cost (per training example) CO_2 kg
Bert (single routing)	0.0364	0.00000474
BERT (chain routing)	0.809	0.00000927

Table 11: The carbon cost of training the BERT router for both single and chain routing

[4] https://github.com/mlco2/codecarbon/blob/master/codecarbon/data/private_infra/global_energy_mix.json

D.3 Environmental Cost of Gathering Training Dataset

Model	**Total Cost (kg CO_2)**
deepseek-ai/DeepSeek-R1-Distill-Qwen-32B	35.9
Qwen/Qwen2.5-32B	26.5
deepseek-ai/DeepSeek-Coder-V2-Lite-Instruct	21.2
deepseek-ai/DeepSeek-R1-Distill-Qwen-1.5B	16.3
meta-llama/Llama-3.1-8B	10.8
meta-llama/Llama-3.2-3B	8.3
meta-llama/Llama-3.2-1B	4.9
TOTAL	**123.9**

Table 12: Carbon costs by model for single routing.

Models	**Total Cost (kg CO_2)**
32B-32B-32B	4.10
3B-32B-3B	3.81
32B-32B-8B	3.11
32B-32B-3B	3.05
3B-32B-8B	2.76
3B-32B-32B	2.73
8B-32B-3B	2.19
8B-32B-8B	2.17
8B-32B-32B	2.16
3B-8B-32B	2.16
3B-3B-32B	2.08
32B-3B-8B	2.00
32B-8B-3B	1.97
8B-8B-3B	1.95
32B-8B-32B	1.91
8B-3B-3B	1.89
32B-3B-32B	1.66
8B-8B-8B	1.65
32B-3B-3B	1.63
8B-3B-8B	1.59
3B-8B-3B	1.58
8B-8B-32B	1.50
8B-3B-32B	1.39
3B-8B-8B	1.30
3B-3B-8B	1.69
3B-3B-3B	1.07
TOTAL	**56.9**

Table 13: Carbon costs by model combination for chain routing.

D.4 Lambda Trade-off Results

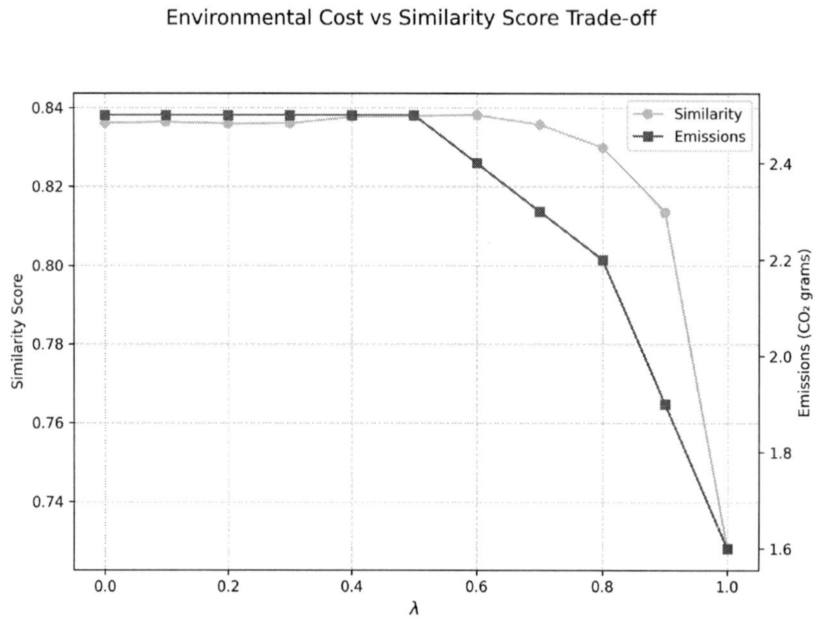

Figure 9: A graph showing the similarity score and emissions for different λ values.

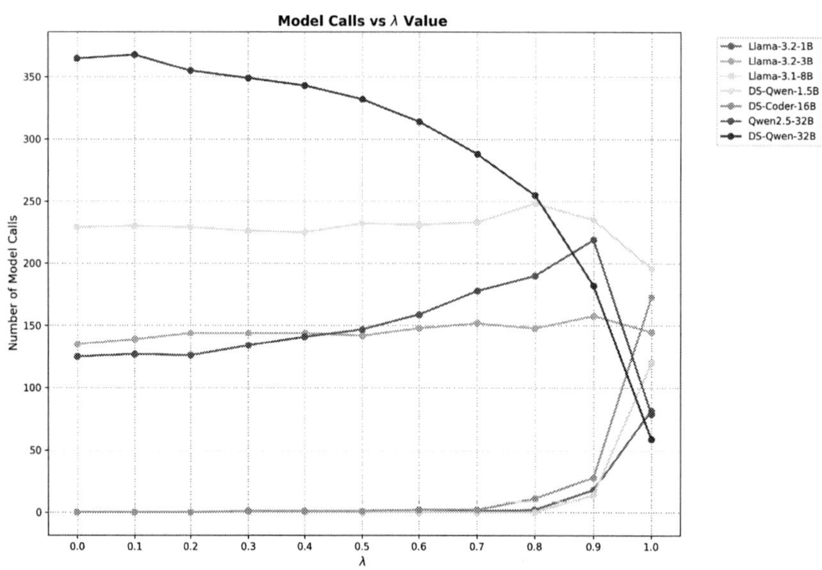

Figure 10: The number of calls to each candidate model against the value of λ.

Model/ λ	0.0	0.1	0.2	0.3	0.4	0.5	0.6	0.7	0.8	0.9	1.0
Llama-3.2-1B	0	0	0	0	0	0	0	1	2	18	82
Llama-3.2-3B	135	139	144	144	144	142	148	152	148	158	145
Llama-3.1-8B	229	230	229	226	225	232	231	233	248	235	196
DS-Qwen-1.5B	0	0	0	0	0	0	0	0	0	14	120
DS-Coder-16B	0	0	0	1	1	1	2	2	11	28	173
Qwen2.5-32B	125	127	126	134	141	147	159	178	190	219	79
DS-Qwen-32B	365	368	355	349	343	332	314	288	255	182	59

Table 14: A table showing the number of calls to each candidate model for different λ values in single routing.

D.5 Similarity Scores by Model and Task for Single Routing

Task	Qwen2.5-32B	DS-Coder-16B	DS-Qwen-1.5B	DS-Qwen-32B	Llama-3.1-8B	Llama-3.2-3B	Llama-3.2-1B
GSM-Symbolic	0.787	0.744	0.218	0.735	0.964	0.962	0.773
SQuAD	0.877	0.737	0.668	0.894	0.813	0.855	0.743
ARC	0.791	0.822	0.726	0.877	0.835	0.838	0.686
MBPP	0.179	0.194	0.090	0.142	0.238	0.116	0.189
MMLU	0.850	0.723	0.745	0.857	0.792	0.839	0.704
MMLU-Pro	0.902	0.745	0.754	0.890	0.807	0.863	0.805
GSM8K	0.971	0.773	0.681	0.979	0.987	0.959	0.803
GPQA	0.794	0.702	0.709	0.808	0.818	0.824	0.725
UnifiedQA	0.752	0.650	0.665	0.784	0.771	0.769	0.685

Table 15: Average similarity scores by task and model.

D.6 Similarity Scores by Model and Task for Chain Routing

Model	GSM-Symbolic	ARC	MBPP	MMLU	MMLU-Pro	GSM8K	UnifiedQA
32B-32B-32B	0.8990	0.7792	0.2089	0.8669	0.8409	0.8629	0.7122
32B-32B-8B	0.6214	0.8075	0.2281	0.8540	0.8075	0.6674	0.7449
32B-32B-3B	0.5959	0.7473	0.2140	0.7982	0.7931	0.6059	0.6766
32B-8B-32B	0.8445	0.7911	0.1777	0.8974	0.8462	0.7808	0.7161
32B-8B-8B	0.7020	0.7428	0.1899	0.8355	0.7837	0.7163	0.6793
32B-8B-3B	0.6045	0.7215	0.1782	0.8120	0.7930	0.5939	0.6451
32B-3B-32B	0.7380	0.7902	0.1814	0.8809	0.8243	0.7235	0.7147
32B-3B-8B	0.6651	0.7572	0.2097	0.8390	0.8073	0.7177	0.7147
32B-3B-3B	0.5846	0.7409	0.1988	0.8210	0.7914	0.6222	0.6606
8B-32B-32B	0.7883	0.7884	0.1732	0.9158	0.8763	0.7877	0.7135
8B-32B-8B	0.7171	0.7844	0.2012	0.8522	0.7971	0.7381	0.7194
8B-32B-3B	0.6223	0.7192	0.2056	0.8060	0.7994	0.5967	0.6682
8B-8B-32B	0.8009	0.8071	0.1565	0.9193	0.8587	0.7779	0.7325
8B-8B-8B	0.8279	0.7602	0.1831	0.8342	0.8032	0.7950	0.7026
8B-8B-3B	0.6304	0.7081	0.1705	0.7930	0.7942	0.6311	0.6436
8B-3B-32B	0.7309	0.7984	0.1753	0.8769	0.8522	0.6958	0.7329
8B-3B-8B	0.7219	0.7808	0.2064	0.8347	0.8150	0.6720	0.7279
8B-3B-3B	0.6318	0.6874	0.1925	0.8124	0.7762	0.6195	0.6345
3B-32B-32B	0.7300	0.7870	0.1753	0.9020	0.8366	0.6989	0.7200
3B-32B-8B	0.7324	0.7559	0.2188	0.8451	0.7874	0.6983	0.6876
3B-32B-3B	0.6208	0.7044	0.2037	0.7959	0.7967	0.5472	0.6310
3B-8B-32B	0.7507	0.8034	0.1505	0.9125	0.8328	0.7372	0.7100
3B-8B-8B	0.7293	0.7464	0.1807	0.8216	0.7667	0.7519	0.6662
3B-8B-3B	0.6103	0.6927	0.1823	0.8095	0.8060	0.5851	0.6390
3B-3B-32B	0.7051	0.7919	0.1715	0.8846	0.8493	0.6578	0.7038
3B-3B-8B	0.7087	0.7596	0.2043	0.8497	0.8058	0.7213	0.6933
3B-3B-3B	0.5946	0.7168	0.1932	0.7923	0.8002	0.5514	0.6282

Table 16: Average similarity scores by model and task.

D.7 Chain Routing Model Performance

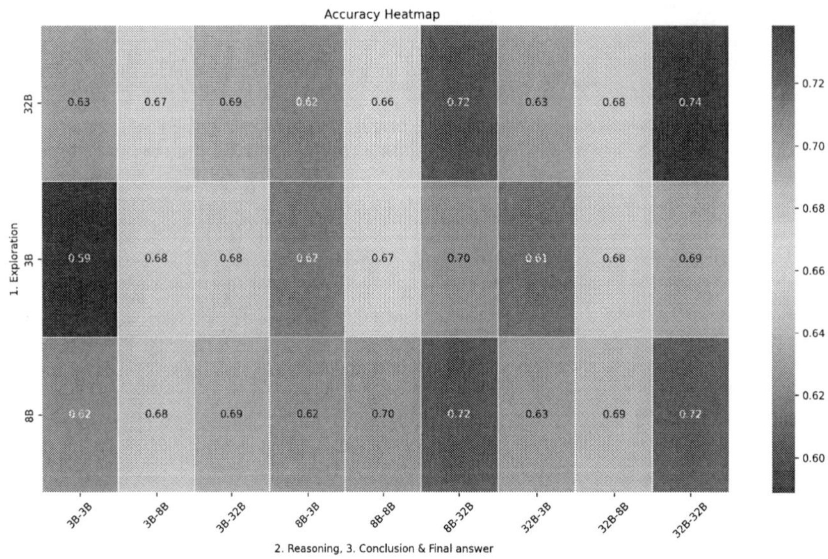

Figure 11: A heatmap showing average performance across datasets for every combination of models

D.8 Single Routing Similarity and Emissions Results with Confidence Intervals

Router	Emissions (grams CO_2)	Similarity Score
BERT-router	2.31 ± 0.004	0.845 ± 0.0264
Generative router	2.53 ± 0.002	0.81 ± 0.0326
Random router	2.00 ± 0.008	0.74 ± 0.101
Largest model (no routing)	3.80 ± 0.00600	0.818 ± 0.0302
Smallest model (no routing)	0.500 ± 0.002	0.716 ± 0.0330
Oracle router	2.10 ± 0.032	0.903 ± 0.644

Table 17: Model emissions and similarity scores with 95% confidence intervals for single routing.

D.9 Single Routing Similarity and Emissions Results on Unseen Dataset with Confidence Intervals

Router	Emissions (grams CO_2)	Similarity Score
BERT-router	2.80 ± 0.002	0.889 ± 0.0131
Generative router	1.90 ± 0.001	0.826 ± 0.0155
Random router	1.70 ± 0.002	0.74 ± 0.0176
Largest model (no routing)	3.20 ± 0.001	0.894 ± 0.0135
Smallest model (no routing)	0.40 ± 0.002	0.743 ± 0.0188
Oracle router	1.90 ± 0.002	0.950 ± 0.0057

Table 18: Model emissions and similarity scores with 95% confidence intervals for single routing on unseen dataset.

D.10 Chain Routing Similarity and Emissions Results with Confidence Intervals

Router	Emissions (grams CO_2)	Similarity Score
BERT-router (Chain)	2.51 ± 0.00441	0.732 ± 0.0479
BERT-router (Single)	2.20 ± 0.002	0.710 ± 0.0231
Generative router	1.33 ± 0.00176	0.681 ± 0.1282
Random router	1.73 ± 0.002	0.667 ± 0.0176
Largest model (no routing)	3.09 ± 0.005	0.728 ± 0.04787
Smallest model (no routing)	0.824 ± 0.006	0.612 ± 0.0463
Oracle router	1.90 ± 0.00212	0.861 ± 0.01365

Table 19: Model emissions and similarity scores with 95% confidence intervals for chain routing.

D.11 Chain Routing model usage per stage for BERT Router

Stage	LLama 3.2-3B	Llama 3.1-8B	Qwen 2.5-32B
1 (Exploration)	60	10	70
2 (Reasoning)	43	9	88
3 (Reasoning)	17	17	106

Table 20: The number of calls for each model for each CoT stage in the chain router when using the BERT router.

D.12 Chain Routing Model Usage per Stage for Generative Router

Stage	LLama 3.2-3B	Llama 3.1-8B	Qwen 2.5-32B
1 (Exploration)	33	91	16
2 (Reasoning)	30	100	10
3 (Reasoning)	24	108	8

Table 21: The number of calls for each model for each CoT stage in the chain router when using the generative router.

D.13 Example Prompt

System prompt
System: You are a helpful AI assistant. You provide clear, short, step-by-step solutions and always conclude with #### followed by the final answer. **User:** Now, answer the following question: Which of the following was not cited as evidence for life in the Martian meteorite ALH84001? **<Options:>** Please provide a short, step-by-step solution to the question above, and conclude with the #### followed by the final answer.

Table 22: Example system prompt.

D.14 System Prompt for Reasoning Chain Decomposition

System prompt
System: Split your response into three distinct parts: initial EXPLORATION, REASONING, and a CONCLUSION containing #### followed by your final answer for evaluation. Format your response with the following structure: EXPLORATION: your initial thoughts REASONING: your step-by-step reasoning CONCLUSION:#### your final answer

Table 23: Example system prompt for reasoning chain decomposition.

D.15 Example CoT Response Split Into Stages

Stage	Output
Prompt	A school board of a large school district is proposing a new dress code for students. Some students feel that this dress code unfairly targets female students. To see if there is a difference between boys and girls in their opposition to the new dress code, they conduct a poll of 60 randomly selected male and 70 randomly selected female high school students in the district. They find that 66 females oppose the dress code and 50 males oppose the dress code. Which of the following explains why a two-proportion z-test is not appropriate?
Exploration	The question is asking why a two-proportion z-test is not appropriate for the given scenario. A two-proportion z-test is used to compare the proportions of two independent groups. In this case, the groups are male and female students who oppose the new dress code.
Reasoning	The sample sizes are 60 males and 70 females, and the number of successes (opposition) are 50 males and 66 females. To determine if a two-proportion z-test is appropriate, we need to check the conditions for the test. The conditions are: 1. The samples are independent. 2. The sample sizes are large enough, which means that the number of successes and failures in each group should be at least 10. In this case, the samples are independent because they are randomly selected male and female students. However, the number of successes and failures in each group should be checked:- For males: 50 successes (opposition) and 10 failures (not opposition) For females: 66 successes (opposition) and 4 failures (not opposition)The number of failures for the female group is less than 10, which violates the condition for a two-proportion z-test.
Conclusion	Therefore, a two-proportion z-test is not appropriate for this scenario. #### The number of successes and the number of failures for the two groups are not all large enough.

Table 24: Example chain routing output (from Qwen-32B on MMLU dataset).

E Example Responses From Qualitative Analysis

E.1 Example Correct CoT Response

Stage	Output
Question	If the money supply increases what happens in the money market (assuming money demand is downward sloping)?
Gold Standard	The nominal interest rates falls
Router Output	CONCLUSION: The nominal interest rates falls

Table 25: An example of where the CoT response from the router was deemed to be correct from qualitative review.

E.2 Example Incorrect CoT Response

Stage	Output
Prompt	A farmer is buying feed for his horses. He buys a variety of oats, hay, carrots and apples. Since apples are a rare treat, he only buys four 3-pound boxes of them for the whole stable. He only wants enough carrots to feed the horses while the vegetables are fresh, so he buys thirteen 9-pound bags. Oats are the main diet of his horses, so he buys thirty four 44-pound packs. Hay are a staple to supplement the oats, so he buys fifteen 19-pound sacks. Finally, he buys 43 pounds of grocery, and 27 pounds of tools. A farm truck can carry 220 pounds at a time. How many trips does the farmer need to transport all the items, if he has three trucks?
Gold Standard	3
Output	4

Table 26: An example of where the CoT response from the router was deemed to be incorrect from qualitative review.

E.3 Example Correct Highest Similarity Score Response

Stage	Output
Prompt	Let l = [1,2,3,4]. What is max(l) in Python3?
Gold Standard	4
Output	4
Similarity	1.00

Table 27: An example of where the response with the highest similarity score matched the gold standard output.

E.4 Example Incorrect Highest Similarity Score Response

Stage	Output
Prompt	Let a undirected graph G with edges E = <2,1>,<2,0>,<2,3>,<1,4>,<4,3>, which <A,B> represent Node A is connected to Node B. What is the minimum vertex cover of G? Represent the vertex cover in a list of ascending order.
Gold Standard	[2, 4]
Output	The final answer is boxed0 2 3 4
Similarity	0.8235

Table 28: An example of where the response with the highest similarity score did not match the gold standard output.

Contrasting Traditional Models and LLMs: An Evaluation Based on Text Segmentation

Robin Jegan and Andreas Henrich
Otto-Friedrich-Universität Bamberg
Chair of Media Informatics
{robin.jegan,andreas.henrich}@uni-bamberg.de

Abstract

This paper presents a discussion of the relevancy of older natural language processing approaches compared to modern large language models (LLMs), with experimental results for a specific application: the segmentation of video transcripts. An analysis was conducted, if powerful modern LLMs are necessary for tasks such as text segmentation or if traditional and more efficient models – here TextTiling – suffice. In the end, LLMs provide comparable performance to the other models, but the results produced by TextTiling are promising and suggest a discussion about a trade-off regarding efficiency, performance, energy-consumption and other factors.

1 Introduction

The rise of large language models (LLMs) has transformed the landscape of natural language processing (NLP) in a myriad of ways. Many application scenarios have been affected and upended (Raiaan et al., 2024), steering research towards the use of powerful models based on the transformer architecture (Vaswani et al., 2017), culminating in prompt-based LLMs such as ChatGPT,[1] Claude,[2] Gemini,[3] and others. While their capabilities are certainly impressive, downsides of the use of LLMs have emerged, such as biases and hallucinations in the generated texts (Gallegos et al., 2024; Huang et al., 2025), problems regarding copyright and personal information within the datasets (Maini et al., 2024), energy consumption not only for training (Patterson et al., 2021) but also while executing models (Argerich and Patiño-Martínez, 2024), and others.

The contrast between currently dominating NLP-research in general on the one hand, and the discovery of the noted disadvantages inherent in LLMs on the other hand have prompted the experiments in this paper. The dominance of LLMs in recent NLP-research is remarkable (Naveed et al., 2023), while the role of older, more efficient and less complex models has diminished. Nevertheless, arguments as to the role of such models can still be made in aspects like explainability, reproducibility, efficiency – both in terms of computation time and energy costs – as well as hardware requirements.

The application area of text segmentation was chosen as a proxy for analyzing the contrast between LLMs and older, certainly less prominent, models that may, however, still be relevant. Furthermore, text segmentation as a research field is hardly at the forefront of current studies, which is why, to the best of our knowledge, no analysis has been conducted comparing older and modern techniques on this task. In this paper, GPT-4o (Hurst et al., 2024) as modern LLM was applied as well as TextTiling (Hearst, 1997), which represents an older, efficient and traditional model.

The use case for the experiments revolves around the segmentation of video transcripts from a lecture on computer science from a German university. The data and initial implementations were conducted in an earlier paper and were used as part of a pipeline for extracting metadata from learning videos to construct a recommender system, see Lehmann and Landes (2024). The approaches presented here are intended to draw upon the original concept and to further investigate the performance of more efficient techniques, in contrast to modern LLMs.

This paper is structured as follows: After briefly summarizing the related work for text segmentation (section 2), the dataset and the concrete application scenario will be presented (section 3). Afterwards, the methods (section 4) and experiments (section 5) will be presented, followed by a discussion on the results (section 5.1), and observations (section 5.2)

[1] See https://openai.com/chatgpt (all web resources last accessed on: 22.07.2025).

[2] See https://claude.ai.

[3] See https://gemini.google.com.

as well as a conclusion (section 6).

2 Related Work

Text segmentation has been approached with a multitude of techniques and also with different use cases as their target.[4] Such use cases include parts of systems in NLP-tasks like information retrieval (Huang et al., 2003), sentiment analysis (Li et al., 2020), information annotation (Hananto et al., 2022) and others (Pak and Teh, 2017). The techniques applied range from statistical models in early approaches (Beeferman et al., 1999) across topic-modeling (Riedl and Biemann, 2012) and supervised machine learning (Koshorek et al., 2018) techniques all the way to neural network-assisted systems (Gong et al., 2022).

The rise of LLMs has brought renewed interest to a related research field, referred to as *chunking* (Dong et al., 2023). The limited context windows of LLMs require a segmentation strategy, at least in the case of early LLMs and – depending on the model – even to this day.[5] Chunking strategies can differ depending on a number of factors, see Dong et al. (2023) for an overview on different approaches. Briefly, these strategies include simply truncating the source text (Koh et al., 2022), which however comes with severe limitations such as loss of information, or by segmenting the input text by a fixed size (Dai et al., 2019), additionally with the option of overlapping segments (Chalkidis et al., 2022). More complex methods using reinforcement learning to identify segments by applying flexible segment sizes have also been proposed (Gong et al., 2020). Another application in this realm is the addition of retrieval augmented generation to LLM-based systems in order to provide contextual information to the query, which benefits from improved chunking strategies similarly (Qu et al., 2024; Singh et al., 2024). The earlier publication Lehmann and Landes (2024) on the use case presented in this paper, applied GPT-3.5-turbo, with context windows of up to 16,000 tokens, which did not suffice to handle full transcripts.

In recent years, text segmentation approaches, even though small in number, were often studied by applying large(r) language models using the transformer-architecture. BERT-based models were studied in Lukasik et al. (2020) and additionally BART and GPT-3.5 in Alkhalil et al. (2025). The role of traditional and more efficient models is missing from modern text segmentation approaches, although the use of a smaller-scale model in Retkowski and Waibel (2024) is noteworthy due to their focus on efficiency improvements compared to BERT-based models. Still, a consideration of older, even more efficient statistical models is missing in current text segmentation research.

This observation is not limited to text segmentation, but also applicable to other NLP-tasks such as text classification, information extraction and text summarization. A few publications exist in comparing or even using such older models, e.g., by using support vector machines in classification such as Cunha et al. (2023); Lu et al. (2022), decision trees and rule-based techniques in information extraction like Sultana et al. (2022); Xiang and Yangfei (2023) and extractive models for summarization in Du et al. (2023); Luo et al. (2022). Moreover, a structured literature review on the use of traditional models in current NLP for selected tasks has been conducted, see Jegan and Henrich (2025).

Further model architectures are conceivable, featuring older and modern approaches in one system. Text summarization approaches have already been conducted with these ideas in mind, in effect combining older, more efficient extractive techniques with modern abstractive summarization approaches (Bao and Zhang, 2023; Licari et al., 2023). Another advantage of such hybrid systems is the potential of minimizing problems such as hallucinations due to the extractive nature of certain parts of the pipeline, e.g., by using extractive approaches for the selection of sentences that have been previously ranked by a neural network-based model (Licari et al., 2023).

3 Dataset

The dataset is provided by the authors of the original paper that included the prior text segmentation application as part of a pipeline intended for other downstream tasks (Lehmann and Landes, 2024). The data comprises lectures on software engineering taught at a German university, for which transcripts were automatically produced by the automatic speech recognition system Whisper (Radford et al., 2023). The transcripts are the main data

[4]Noteworthy is the terminological overlap with the research field of the same name in the context of computer vision, which applies text identification processes on images, e.g., in Xu et al. (2021).

[5]While models with impressive capabilities have emerged recently, able to process hundreds of thousands of tokens per request, the processing of large contexts still poses a challenge for modern state-of-the-art models (Yen et al., 2025).

source and were further pre-processed in order to correct spelling errors.[6] The dataset therefore comprises a transcript of spoken language, in German.

In the original approach by Lehmann and Landes (2024), the data was segmented by time-intervals based on the video transcript metadata, since experiments with GPT-3.5-turbo did not yield usable segments at the time. The resulting segments were then applied on a keyword extraction and topic detection task, in order to serve as a basis for an ontology regarding topics from within the transcripts, which are linked to the video on a learning platform. The complete application is intended to serve as a recommender system for students working with lecture videos, which have been semantically enriched through a domain ontology.

In total, after some cleaning and filtering steps, 172 videos were processed for this paper, with an average length of 89 sentences and 1,115 words per video transcript, in total 15,320 sentences and 191,785 tokens across all 172 video transcripts. The data is not publicly available, which is why we cannot reference the dataset or publish excerpts.

4 Methods

In order to analyze the performance of an older, more computationally efficient approach in contrast to modern LLM-based methods, a representative of each model type was chosen.

4.1 TextTiling

The TextTiling approach created by Hearst (1997) aims at generating multi-paragraph segments, which are intended to capture subtopics. This purpose, when considering the later goals in the concept from Lehmann and Landes (2024), appears to match and presents another reason in favor of using TextTiling. The approach is using a three part procedure: (1) tokenization into terms and units as an approximation of sentences, due to the widely varying size of sentences, here determined as pseudosentences; (2) calculation of a score for each of the pseudosentences and finally (3) detection of the passages representing subtopics, identified through boundaries between such subtopics.

4.2 GPT-4o

As contrasting model to the traditional and older TextTiling approach and as representative of LLMs, the state-of-the-art model – at the time of processing the texts (March 2025) – GPT-4o was chosen (Hurst et al., 2024). The history and rise to fame of prompt-based LLMs is widely documented, see e.g., Min et al. (2023) or Raiaan et al. (2024), in both chat-based user interfaces in a browser or via API-requests. We apply the latter option, i.e., using the OpenAI developer API.[7]

The prompts were built for each video transcript separately, instructing the LLM to generate segments based on the text of a full transcript. Separate prompts were used in order to limit the context window within one prompt and also to restrict the amount of text that should be segmented, which was intended to help the LLM by providing less data and therefore keep the focus on a smaller text sample. Also, the prompts included a directive for the LLM that the output should be identical to the input, with the exception of added newlines representing the segment boundaries.

5 Experiments

Due to the fast processing of the TextTiling approach, several parameter configurations could be tested. The relevant parameters here are w, the size of pseudosentences or token-sequence size, and k, the block size used in the comparison mechanism found in step (2), see above in section 4.1.[8]

In contrast, while the setup of the API-calls to the GPT-4o service was similarly quick, the usage of the LLM-based services is usually billed by number of processed tokens, when a service by one of the major providers is used. Here, the processing of the data described in section 3 resulted in roughly \$3 for segmenting all video transcripts once.[9]

5.1 Evaluation

The first evaluation criterion involves efficiency, i.e., the time required to process the data. TextTiling segments are produced within a matter of seconds,[10] barely exceeding a few gigabytes of used working memory and neither fully utilizing

[6] See details on the pre-processing in Lehmann and Landes (2024).

[7] See `https://platform.openai.com/docs/overview`.

[8] The default values from Hearst (1997) are $w = 20$ and $k = 10$. Additionally, in our experiments, values $[1, 2, 3, 5, 8, 10, 15, 20, 30, 40, 50]$ were tested.

[9] See our code at `https://github.com/uniba-mi/text-segmentation`.

[10] Different machines were tested here, ranging from laptops (using an Intel i7 processor with 32GB of RAM) to a more capable server (using an AMD 24-Core processor with 1000GB of RAM), both processing all transcripts in between 9 and 16 seconds for the parameters $w = 20$ and $k = 10$.

the CPU. Optimization and parallelization are certainly possible to increase efficiency even further.

The GPT-4o application, however, took 6,127 seconds to complete, which is over 1.5 hours. While parallelization and an adapted implementation would naturally lead to performance increases here as well, sequential processing, similar to the TextTiling application, was deliberately chosen to achieve a comparable setting.

Another facet of efficiency deals with the energy consumed during execution. Software-based power tracking has been shown to correlate with external power meters, despite some drawbacks of purely software-based tracking, see Jay et al. (2023), who recommend Code Carbon[11] for analyzing Python applications. The energy consumption tracked by Code Carbon for the TextTiling approach was logged as 0.085 Wh on the first tested machine and 0.47 Wh on another machine, both values representing one execution run processing all transcripts once.[12]

The energy consumption of a request given to GPT-4o is not easily quantifiable, since power consumption metrics are not available to users of the API-interfaces provided by OpenAI. Estimates range from 3 Wh per interaction[13] to only 0.3 Wh per interaction[14] in newer studies. For the experiments conducted with GPT-4o, each transcript was processed as a single request, which is why the quoted estimates need to be multiplied by 172, resulting in an energy consumption ranging from 51.6 Wh to 516 Wh, thus exceeding the energy consumed by the TextTiling approach (between 0.085 Wh and 0.47 Wh) by several orders of magnitude. The energy expended in training modern LLMs is another critical aspect here, but will not be discussed further, see e.g., Patterson et al. (2021) for more details.

Further evaluation was possible through comparing thc produced segments in terms of size. Table 1 presents an overview of the generated segments, showcasing the average number of produced segments across the whole dataset as well as the average size of the produced segments, in both sentence and token counts.

Only a few selected parameter configurations for

Model	Seg.	SD	Sent.	Tok.
GPT-4o	8.95	5.48	13.73	176.74
TextTiling				
w=20, k=5	8.67	7.01	8.85	118.66
w=20, k=10	8.59	6.97	8.92	120.21
w=30, k=10	5.94	4.53	12.73	169.78

Table 1: Quantitative results. *Model* represents the applied approach, with w denoting pseudosentences and k the block comparison size as variables for TextTiling, *Seg.* denoting the average number of produced segments across all transcripts, *SD* the standard deviation regarding *Seg.*, *Sent.* the average sentence count per segment and *Tok.* likewise for token count per segment, once again averaged across all transcripts..

TextTiling are displayed here, which each aligns to one of the quantitative metrics produced by GPT-4o. The average number of segments are similar, at least for $w = 20$, but the sizes of the produced segments diverge between the two models. In some cases, GPT-4o tends to produce one or two longer segments for a transcript, which results in higher average sentence and token counts compared to the texts produced by TextTiling. Despite this observation, the segments generated by GPT-4o provide a slightly more uniform result for further processing overall, which was observed by spot-checking the produced segments in terms of contextual and semantic relatedness. The adaptability of TextTiling through parameter selection and thus adjusted segments depending on the use case is another point in favor of TextTiling.

5.2 Observations

The qualitative evaluation was conducted using spot-checks and comparing segments produced by both models, TextTiling and GPT-4o. In general, a clear segmentation with correct and incorrect segment boundaries is a complex problem, especially for datasets that contain spoken language. This restriction applies to our study, since the transcripts of a lecture were analyzed. Thus, clear divisions between segments are not always apparent. A gold standard dataset, even after manually segmenting a select number of transcripts, would only present one possibility of many potential segmentation results. The same problem has been noticed for other reference-based evaluation procedures, e.g., in Fabbri et al. (2021) for the evaluation of summarization systems.

When surveying the produced results, however,

[11]See `https://github.com/mlco2/codecarbon`.

[12]See footnote 10 for details about hardware specifications.

[13]This estimate is retrieved from a widely quoted study on a previous OpenAI model (GPT-3) by De Vries (2023).

[14]From an in-depth recent analysis on GPT-4o (the model used in this paper), see `https://epoch.ai/gradient-updates/how-much-energy-does-chatgpt-use`.

a few qualitative observations stand out. The GPT-4o produced segments tend to start with introductory rhetorical questions the lecturer presented to the students, which in turn works as a beginning statement for the segment. TextTiling segments (at least for the parameter configurations from Table 1, which were checked here as well) do not exhibit this behavior to the same extent.

Nevertheless, the segments produced by both approaches provide a basis for further computation, e.g., as mentioned in section 3 in the approach of the dataset providers, using the segments as input data for keyword extraction and topic identification. Furthermore, Lehmann and Landes (2024) describe limitations regarding the segments produced by GPT-3.5-turbo. In their experiments, no thematically cohesive segments were returned and, even more critically, instead of segments, text consisting of lists of topics and key points of the transcript was produced (Lehmann and Landes, 2024, p. 4). The LLM was therefore not able to accurately follow the instructions given in the prompt. These problems did not occur in our experiments, thus an improvement can be observed for present models such as GPT-4o.

From the examples considered, it could not be deduced in any way that a segmentation created with GPT-4o could have significant advantages over a segmentation created with TextTiling, especially for the use presented in Lehmann and Landes (2024), as one part of a pipeline, which does not influence the end goal of topic modeling and recommender systems.

6 Conclusion

The task of text segmentation is one example of a less researched field of study, but nevertheless can act as a research scenario for a long-established and efficient technique, which can be compared to the modern state-of-the-art in NLP-research, meaning present LLMs. While more experiments are conceivable, this paper has presented first observations in analyzing the contrast between older models and modern LLM-solutions – TextTiling and GPT-4o in this paper – for a concrete application scenario. Especially other traditional models such as TopicTiling (Riedl and Biemann, 2012) or even rule-based approaches could be applied in future work. However, based on the current assessment following the experiments conducted in this study, we assume that alternative traditional models would not significantly affect the overall outcomes or the quality of the results presented in this paper.

Further improvements could be made regarding locally run LLMs. First experiments with Llama-based models were conducted, to decrease the dependency on API-based solutions of large providers and also the corresponding usage costs for the API. Whereas the dataset for the experiments in this paper is rather small, the costs of processing texts with LLMs can quickly increase for larger datasets.

The results provided in this paper show the still lasting relevance of older models with benefits in terms of energy efficiency and processing time, as well as hardware resources. While the performance lags behind the LLM-approach in terms of uniform results, depending on environmental or financial constraints, traditional models still serve a purpose in today's NLP-landscape and should still be discussed as an alternative to modern solutions.

Limitations

The quantitative evaluation certainly contains areas of improvement, since the dataset itself did not include reference segments. Thus, no gold standard was available to evaluate against and more sophisticated evaluation metrics could not be applied.

Furthermore, due to time and resource constraints, segmentation via GPT-4o was performed only once for the whole dataset. Manual tests and prompt optimization were done beforehand, but multiple executions could help to evaluate the results in general and if hallucinations or other undesired generation artifacts occur or reproducible results are achievable. The results of TextTiling were evaluated based on a select number of parameter configurations, but could be studied in more depth regarding the influence of each parameter on the results and segment sizes.

The values quoted for the energy consumption are only estimations, with concrete numbers depending on context, computational resources and other factors. However, the difference in terms of orders of magnitude between energy consumption of TextTiling compared to GPT-4o is noticeable and reflects the energy expended to produce the results.

Unfortunately, reliable results for locally-run LLMs, especially in terms of reproducing the exact input texts with the desired addition of segment markers, could not be achieved and due to time constraints cannot be included in this paper. The use of locally applied LLMs with publicly available open weights is, however, one possible next step in continued research on this topic, and with functions such as *structured outputs*,[15] generated texts in the desired formats should be achievable even with locally-run LLMs.

Ethical Considerations

For the purpose of this contribution, the authors received access to the dataset from colleagues in the project VoLL-KI[16] and the Coburg University of Applied Sciences. Since the dataset is not applicable for public use, it cannot be made publicly available. Otherwise, to the best of our knowledge, there are no ethical concerns to be found in this study.

Acknowledgments

We are highly appreciative of the dataset that was supplied by colleagues in the VoLL-KI research project from the Coburg University of Applied Sciences[17] and their Chair of Artificial Intelligence and Data Stream Mining from Prof. Dr. Dieter Landes. We want to thank Alexander Lehmann in particular, whose work in VoLL-KI has inspired the research in this paper and whose support and knowledge has enabled us to conduct our experiments in a purposeful manner.

We also want to thank the reviewers for their valuable comments and corrections.

References

Bandar F Alkhalil, Yu Zhuang, Khalid T Mursi, and Ahmad O Aseeri. 2025. Enhancing Trust Factor Identification in E-Commerce: The Role of Text Segmentation and Factor Extraction with Transformer Models. In *2025 IEEE 4th International Conference on AI in Cybersecurity (ICAIC)*, pages 1–8. IEEE.

Mauricio Fadel Argerich and Marta Patiño-Martínez. 2024. Measuring and improving the energy efficiency of large language models inference. *IEEE Access*.

Guangsheng Bao and Yue Zhang. 2023. A general contextualized rewriting framework for text summarization. *IEEE/ACM Transactions on Audio, Speech, and Language Processing*, 31:1624–1635.

[15]See https://ollama.com/blog/structured-outputs.

[16]See https://vollki.co.

[17]See https://forschung.hs-coburg.de/de/forschungsprojekt/579-voll-ki.

Doug Beeferman, Adam Berger, and John Lafferty. 1999. Statistical models for text segmentation. *Machine learning*, 34:177–210.

Ilias Chalkidis, Xiang Dai, Manos Fergadiotis, Prodromos Malakasiotis, and Desmond Elliott. 2022. An Exploration of Hierarchical Attention Transformers for Efficient Long Document Classification. *arXiv preprint arXiv:2210.05529*.

Washington Cunha, Felipe Viegas, Celso França, Thierson Rosa, Leonardo Rocha, and Marcos André Gonçalves. 2023. A comparative survey of instance selection methods applied to non-neural and transformer-based text classification. *ACM Computing Surveys*, 55(13s):1–52.

Zihang Dai, Zhilin Yang, Yiming Yang, Jaime Carbonell, Quoc Le, and Ruslan Salakhutdinov. 2019. Transformer-XL: Attentive Language Models beyond a Fixed-Length Context. In *Proceedings of the 57th Annual Meeting of the Association for Computational Linguistics*. Association for Computational Linguistics.

Alex De Vries. 2023. The growing energy footprint of artificial intelligence. *Joule*, 7(10):2191–2194.

Zican Dong, Tianyi Tang, Lunyi Li, and Wayne Xin Zhao. 2023. A survey on long text modeling with transformers. *arXiv preprint arXiv:2302.14502*.

Kai Du, Guoming Lu, and Ke Qin. 2023. An Extractive Text Summarization Based on Reinforcement Learning. In *Proceedings of the 2023 6th International Conference on Software Engineering and Information Management*, pages 19–25.

Alexander R Fabbri, Wojciech Kryściński, Bryan McCann, Caiming Xiong, Richard Socher, and Dragomir Radev. 2021. Summeval: Re-evaluating summarization evaluation. *Transactions of the Association for Computational Linguistics*, 9:391–409.

Isabel O Gallegos, Ryan A Rossi, Joe Barrow, Md Mehrab Tanjim, Sungchul Kim, Franck Dernoncourt, Tong Yu, Ruiyi Zhang, and Nesreen K Ahmed. 2024. Bias and fairness in large language models: A survey. *Computational Linguistics*, 50(3):1097–1179.

Hongyu Gong, Yelong Shen, Dian Yu, Jianshu Chen, and Dong Yu. 2020. Recurrent Chunking Mechanisms for Long-Text Machine Reading Comprehension. In *Proceedings of the 58th Annual Meeting of the Association for Computational Linguistics*, pages 6751–6761.

Zheng Gong, Shiwei Tong, Han Wu, Qi Liu, Hanqing Tao, Wei Huang, and Runlong Yu. 2022. Tipster: A topic-guided language model for topic-aware text segmentation. In *International Conference on Database Systems for Advanced Applications*, pages 213–221. Springer.

Valentinus Roby Hananto, Uwe Serdült, and Victor Kryssanov. 2022. A text segmentation approach for automated annotation of online customer reviews, based on topic modeling. *Applied Sciences*, 12(7):3412.

Marti A Hearst. 1997. Text tiling: Segmenting text into multi-paragraph subtopic passages. *Computational linguistics*, 23(1):33–64.

Lei Huang, Weijiang Yu, Weitao Ma, Weihong Zhong, Zhangyin Feng, Haotian Wang, Qianglong Chen, Weihua Peng, Xiaocheng Feng, Bing Qin, and 1 others. 2025. A survey on hallucination in large language models: Principles, taxonomy, challenges, and open questions. *ACM Transactions on Information Systems*, 43(2):1–55.

Xiangji Huang, Fuchun Peng, Dale Schuurmans, Nick Cercone, and Stephen E Robertson. 2003. Applying machine learning to text segmentation for information retrieval. *Information Retrieval*, 6:333–362.

Aaron Hurst, Adam Lerer, Adam P Goucher, Adam Perelman, Aditya Ramesh, Aidan Clark, AJ Ostrow, Akila Welihinda, Alan Hayes, Alec Radford, and 1 others. 2024. Gpt-4o system card. *arXiv preprint arXiv:2410.21276*.

Mathilde Jay, Vladimir Ostapenco, Laurent Lefèvre, Denis Trystram, Anne-Cécile Orgerie, and Benjamin Fichel. 2023. An experimental comparison of software-based power meters: focus on CPU and GPU. In *2023 IEEE/ACM 23rd International Symposium on Cluster, Cloud and Internet Computing (CCGrid)*, pages 106–118. IEEE.

Robin Jegan and Andreas Henrich. 2025. A structured literature review on traditional approaches in current natural language processing. *arXiv preprint arXiv:2505.12970*.

Huan Yee Koh, Jiaxin Ju, Ming Liu, and Shirui Pan. 2022. An empirical survey on long document summarization: Datasets, models, and metrics. *ACM computing surveys*, 55(8):1–35.

Omri Koshorek, Adir Cohen, Noam Mor, Michael Rotman, and Jonathan Berant. 2018. Text Segmentation as a Supervised Learning Task. In *Proceedings of the 2018 Conference of the North American Chapter of the Association for Computational Linguistics: Human Language Technologies, Volume 2 (Short Papers)*, pages 469–473. Association for Computational Linguistics.

Alexander Lehmann and Dieter Landes. 2024. Extracting Metadata from Learning Videos for Ontology-Based Recommender Systems Using Whisper & GPT. In *2024 IEEE Global Engineering Education Conference (EDUCON)*, pages 1–8. IEEE.

Jing Li, Billy Chiu, Shuo Shang, and Ling Shao. 2020. Neural text segmentation and its application to sentiment analysis. *IEEE Transactions on Knowledge and Data Engineering*, 34(2):828–842.

Daniele Licari, Praveen Bushipaka, Gabriele Marino, Giovanni Comandé, and Tommaso Cucinotta. 2023. Legal holding extraction from italian case documents using italian-legal-bert text summarization. In *Proceedings of the Nineteenth International Conference on Artificial Intelligence and Law*, pages 148–156.

Shaoshuai Lu, Long Chen, Wenjing Wang, Cai Xu, Wei Zhao, Ziyu Guan, and Guangyue Lu. 2022. A Simple Semi-Supervised Joint Learning Framework for Few-shot Text Classification. In *Proceedings of the 2022 5th International Conference on Artificial Intelligence and Pattern Recognition*, pages 14–21.

Michal Lukasik, Boris Dadachev, Kishore Papineni, and Gonçalo Simões. 2020. Text Segmentation by Cross Segment Attention. In *Proceedings of the 2020 Conference on Empirical Methods in Natural Language Processing (EMNLP)*, pages 4707–4716.

Chao Luo, Zi Chen, Xiaolin Jiang, and Sen Yang. 2022. Gap Sentences Generation with TextRank for Chinese Text Summarization. In *Proceedings of the 2022 5th International Conference on Algorithms, Computing and Artificial Intelligence*, pages 1–5.

Pratyush Maini, Hengrui Jia, Nicolas Papernot, and Adam Dziedzic. 2024. LLM Dataset Inference: Did you train on my dataset? *Advances in Neural Information Processing Systems*, 37:124069–124092.

Bonan Min, Hayley Ross, Elior Sulem, Amir Pouran Ben Veyseh, Thien Huu Nguyen, Oscar Sainz, Eneko Agirre, Ilana Heintz, and Dan Roth. 2023. Recent advances in natural language processing via large pre-trained language models: A survey. *ACM Computing Surveys*, 56(2):1–40.

Humza Naveed, Asad Ullah Khan, Shi Qiu, Muhammad Saqib, Saeed Anwar, Muhammad Usman, Naveed Akhtar, Nick Barnes, and Ajmal Mian. 2023. A comprehensive overview of large language models. *arXiv preprint arXiv:2307.06435*.

Irina Pak and Phoey Lee Teh. 2017. Text segmentation techniques: A critical review. *Innovative Computing, Optimization and Its Applications: Modelling and Simulations*, pages 167–181.

David Patterson, Joseph Gonzalez, Quoc Le, Chen Liang, Lluis-Miquel Munguia, Daniel Rothchild, David So, Maud Texier, and Jeff Dean. 2021. Carbon emissions and large neural network training. *arXiv preprint arXiv:2104.10350*.

Renyi Qu, Ruixuan Tu, and Forrest Bao. 2024. Is Semantic Chunking Worth the Computational Cost? *arXiv preprint arXiv:2410.13070*.

Alec Radford, Jong Wook Kim, Tao Xu, Greg Brockman, Christine McLeavey, and Ilya Sutskever. 2023. Robust speech recognition via large-scale weak supervision. In *International conference on machine learning*, pages 28492–28518. PMLR.

Mohaimenul Azam Khan Raiaan, Md Saddam Hossain Mukta, Kaniz Fatema, Nur Mohammad Fahad, Sadman Sakib, Most Marufatul Jannat Mim, Jubaer Ahmad, Mohammed Eunus Ali, and Sami Azam. 2024. A review on large language models: Architectures, applications, taxonomies, open issues and challenges. *IEEE access*, 12:26839–26874.

Fabian Retkowski and Alex Waibel. 2024. From Text Segmentation to Smart Chaptering: A Novel Benchmark for Structuring Video Transcriptions. In *Proceedings of the 18th Conference of the European Chapter of the Association for Computational Linguistics (Volume 1: Long Papers)*, pages 406–419.

Martin Riedl and Chris Biemann. 2012. TopicTiling: A text segmentation algorithm based on LDA. In *Proceedings of ACL 2012 student research workshop*, pages 37–42.

Ishneet Sukhvinder Singh, Ritvik Aggarwal, Ibrahim Allahverdiyev, Muhammad Taha, Aslihan Akalin, Kevin Zhu, and Sean O'Brien. 2024. ChunkRAG: Novel LLM-Chunk Filtering Method for RAG Systems. *arXiv preprint arXiv:2410.19572*.

Tabassum Sultana, Eric R Harley, Gavin Adamson, and Asmaa Malik. 2022. Extracting Source Information From News Articles: Information Extraction. In *Proceedings of the 2022 6th International Conference on Natural Language Processing and Information Retrieval*, pages 216–221.

Ashish Vaswani, Noam Shazeer, Niki Parmar, Jakob Uszkoreit, Llion Jones, Aidan N Gomez, Łukasz Kaiser, and Illia Polosukhin. 2017. Attention is all you need. *Advances in neural information processing systems*, 30.

Cheng Xiang and Zheng Yangfei. 2023. A Rule-Based Unstructured Information Extraction Model for Announcements of Listed Companies' Stock Increase or Decrease. In *Proceedings of the 2023 7th International Conference on Computing and Data Analysis*, pages 28–34.

Xingqian Xu, Zhifei Zhang, Zhaowen Wang, Brian Price, Zhonghao Wang, and Humphrey Shi. 2021. Rethinking text segmentation: A novel dataset and a text-specific refinement approach. In *Proceedings of the IEEE/CVF conference on computer vision and pattern recognition*, pages 12045–12055.

Howard Yen, Tianyu Gao, Minmin Hou, Ke Ding, Daniel Fleischer, Peter Izsak, Moshe Wasserblat, and Danqi Chen. 2025. HELMET: How to Evaluate Long-Context Language Models Effectively and Thoroughly. In *International Conference on Learning Representations (ICLR)*.

A TextTiling Parameters

In order to comprehensively test the TextTiling approach, the values $[1, 2, 3, 5, 8, 10, 15, 20, 30, 40, 50]$ were each tested for the parameters w and k, the former referring to the size of pseudosentences and the latter to the block size applied in the comparing step between segments, see more details in Hearst (1997). A quantitative analysis regarding all parameters was conducted using size-based comparisons with the same metrics applied in table 1 from section 5.1, i.e., average number of generated segments per transcript and average sentence and token counts per segment. Due to layout constraints we did not include the full statistics here, but they can be examined at `https://github.com/uniba-mi/text-segmentation/tree/main/data/results-statistics.csv`.

When analyzing thc values, a correlation between size of pseudosentences and segment size was observed, i.e., higher w-values correspond with smaller segment sizes, while a direct link between k-values and the generated segments could not be observed. Lower values resulted however in longer processing, which is natural due to increased computation because of a larger amount of comparisons in contrast to the default parameter settings, see more details also in the origial paper from Hearst (1997).

B Prompts

GPT-4o was applied using the OpenAI-API. The prompt was defined as follows:

```
Die folgenden Absätze stammen aus dem
Transkript einer Vorlesung zum Thema
Software Engineering:
{transcript}
Aufgabe:
Erstelle Segmente basierend auf dem
gegebenen Text.
Hinweise zum Ausgabeformat:
Gib ausschließlich die Segmente
zurück, mit einer leeren Zeile als
Trennung zwischen den Segmenten.
```

RAG Based Navigation of the World Ocean Assessment II

Zainuddin Saiyed[1], Colin Orian[1], Poppy Riddle[1], Gowri Kanagaraj[1], Geoff Krause[1], Rémi Toupin[1], Philippe Mongeon[1], Stephen Brooks[1]

[1]Dalhousie University,
Correspondence: sbrooks@cs.dal.ca

Abstract

The Second World Ocean Assessment (WOA-II) was a comprehensive evaluation of the world's oceans and climate impacts. We present a Retrieval-Augmented Generation (RAG) to query the discipline specific bibliography of the WOA-II using bibliometric metadata as the external knowledge source. Our approach uses a basic RAG pipeline with a single dense embedding, TF-IDF clustering, a single retriever with Euclidean distance similarity, and two open-source models to provide two response modes from a single non-parametric source using bibliometric abstracts as the external knowledge source. The paper details the implementation process, our evaluation of prompt development, response quality and preference, clustering, response time, and discusses limitations and future research directions. We evaluate our system by comparing the results from a variety of modes and by comparing our system's outputs to a benchmark's outputs.

1 Introduction

The current landscape of ocean research is characterized by significant challenges, including information overload due to the sheer volume of literature. Our exploratory work aims to enhance the accessibility and understanding of ocean science research by using extracted references from The Second World Ocean Assessment (WOA-II) (United Nations, 2021) and integrating the bibliometric metadata into a retrieval augmented generation (RAG) application to provide question-and-answering (Q&A) and summarization. The prototype system supports two modes of chat and summarization through a web application, enabling users to explore and derive insights from the WOA-II references corpus.

Toupin et al., (2024) previously expanded on the collection of references from the WOA-II report through the collection of cited and citing works from both Crossref and OpenAlex. The OpenAlex database (Priem et al., 2022), a comprehensive repository of scientific publications, exemplifies the information volume challenge as it contains aggregated metadata for millions of papers related to marine ecosystems.

In the remaining sections, we first review existing literature, and methodologies related to metadata and RAG applications. Section 3 details the design and implementation process, including data collection and pre-processing, clustering, system architecture, and platforms utilized. Section 4 discusses the system's interaction modes (Chat and Summarize). Section 5 presents key takeaways of the project by comparing modes and comparing our results to the OceanBench (Bi et al., 2024) benchmark. We then discusses limitations and section 6 provides recommendations for future work.

2 Prior Work

This section discusses the United Nation's World Ocean Assessments, prior work investigating RAG applications using academic text, reports, and metadata. We conclude with a few of the documented challenges for RAG that we think are pertinent to this research area.

2.1 World Ocean Assessments

The WOA-II is the major output of the second cycle of the Regular Process for Global Reporting and Assessment on the state of the marine environment, building on the work of the first World Ocean Assessment.

This report involves contributions from interdisciplinary writing teams made up of more than 300 experts, drawn from a pool of over 7,820 experts worldwide. The WOA-II aims to support decisions and actions to achieve Sustainable Development Goals, particularly Goal 14, as well as the implementation of the United Nations Decade of Ocean

Proceedings of the 21st Conference on Natural Language Processing (KONVENS), Volume 2: Workshops, pages 282–290, 2025

Science for Sustainable Development, which focuses on life below water and human impacts. The topics covered in the assessment include drivers of change, current marine state and trends, pressures and impacts on the ocean, and environmental, social, and economic management (CSIRO, 2023).

2.2 Retrieval-Augmented Generation

One way to the address shortcomings with parametric knowledge of an LLM is to retrieve sources from an authoritative knowledge base outside of its training data before generating a response (Lewis et al., 2020). RAG extends a model's capabilities to specific domains or to more recent knowledge in lieu of other fine-tuning or instruction tuning methods.

Discipline specific reports such as WOA-II have similarly been used in past RAG research. Vaghefi et al., (2023) used the IPCC report as the basis for a curated selection of PDFs in their ChatClimate RAG-based chat interface in which they heuristically evaluated responses for accuracy in three conditions. Hsu et al. (2024) investigated the use of RAGs grounded in credible texts on net-zero compliance to mitigate increasing dependence on foundation models like ChatGPT by policy decision makers and as a counter to 'false and disingenuous net-zero claims'. They introduced ChatNetZero and evaluated responses by comparing responses to original texts for accuracy and asking policy experts to compare against ungrounded chatbots.

Academic text has been used with LLMs such as OpenAI's GPT models in academic search engines (Van Noorden, 2023) to meet the specific needs of students and researchers. Bi et al., (2024) created OceanGPT, a LLaMA-2 based LLM on the ocean domain, as well as OceanBench a benchmark for evaluating ocean domain responses. They used 67,633 open-access publications of parsed PDFs, exclusive of figures, tables, references, etc., as well as curated 'historically significant literature' (Bi et al., 2024). Nguyen et al. (2024) developed My Climate Advisor a RAG-based tool which returned synthesized literature responses to queries from farmers and advisors. They used scientific literature and industry grey literature on climate resilience knowledge and evaluated system performance with domain experts to assess response generation preference compared with 12 open-access and proprietary LLM models. Han, Susnjak, & Mathrani (2024) outlined a framework for RAG to automate systematic literature reviews, though they also acknowledged the challenge for retrieval.

2.3 Bibliometric metadata and abstracts

However, bibliometric metadata, either created from scientific documents or harvested from bibliometric databases, has not been used extensively. Abstracts have been used in pre-training ClimateBERT (Webersinke et al., 2022) which used research abstracts in lieu of full texts from the Web of Science, but they parsed these from full text. They have also been used in RAG pipelines with generated metadata as a retrieval filter (Poliakov and Shvai, 2024), for software comprehension (Shaik et al., 2024), or abstracts used to derive keywords for retrieval from biomedical literature used to construct systematic reviews (Li et al., 2024). Others such as Agarwal et al. (2024) created LitLLM which similarly derived keywords from seed documents and then applied multiple retrieval strategies.

2.4 Challenges for RAG

Acknowledging known challenges for RAG such as low-level perturbations (Cho et al., 2024), zero-shot precision for specialized domains (Sawarkar et al., 2025), context size (Tian et al., 2025), or struggling with real world conflicting knowledge (Marjanović et al., 2024), we wanted to know if abstracts could provide enough information to answer simple queries from users exploring the corpus. It is unknown if typos or irrelevant information in abstracts may affect responses or retrieval, or how many abstracts may be needed to provide an adequate response. It is further unknown if the abstract length compounds problems of context size, or how conflicting knowledge between two abstracts may affect an LLM's response.

3 Approach

In our prototype, RAG may be used to enhance the user's understanding of the references extracted from the WOA-II document or explore ocean related topics. Our approach uses a basic RAG pipeline with a single dense embedding, clustering, a single retriever, and two generation models to provide two response modes from a single non-parametric source using bibliometric metadata. The RAG system is implemented as per Figure 1 and will be discussed in the following sections.

3.1 Reference Data processing

DOIs from the cited works in WOA-II are used to retrieve metadata elements, such as title and abstract from OpenAlex, an open-source bibliometric database. Abstracts from OpenAlex are inverted so each was reordered back to readable text. Each document is constructed from the OpenAlex identifier, title, authors, abstract, publication source, PDF URL, cited by count, publication year, publication type, and concepts. The concepts are lists of algorithmically determined labels based on title, abstract, and publication and provided by OpenAlex as an additional metadata element. Each document is saved as a plain text file for retrieval and generation and as a PDF file for fast viewing by the user resulting in a corpus of 4,723 documents.

TF-IDF is used on each text file and K-means clustering applied with the number of clusters determined by the elbow method, which involves plotting the within-cluster sum of squares against the number of clusters and selecting the point where the rate of decrease notably declines. We assign 17 clusters for our corpus and manually checked them for topical agreement.

3.2 Embedding

The user's input query is first run through the embedding model, nomic-embed-text-137M (Nussbaum et al., 2024), producing an embedding representation of that text and stored in the database. Documents with a unique chunk ID, are loaded by cluster and embedded using the same model for vector space alignment, accurate similarity measurement, and following best practices.

3.3 Database and retrieval

ChromaDB (Huber and Troynikov) was selected as it is appropriate for applications involving similarity search and retrieval of embeddings. The documents are grouped into folders, chunked as a single ID, (for convenience using the Chroma DB tools) and stored in the database. We use the built-in retriever, the Hierarchical Navigable Small World (HNSW) index and approximate nearest neighbor (ANN) search with the default L2 Euclidian distance similarity function. After some experimentation exploring minimum values, the retriever is set to k=5 for returned documents. After this, the context is assembled according to the prompt instructions.

3.4 Model selection

Our system uses Llama3 [7B] and Phi3-medium [14B] for generating the responses and the summaries along with the prompt templates for each interaction mode. The LLaMA (Touvron et al., 2023) models are open-source, instruct tuned variants and were selected for control over data, our use of copyrighted scientific literature, and reliability (Nguyen et al., 2024). We selected Phi3 (Microsoft) for similar qualities but wanted to explore if a smaller model produced acceptable responses given the brevity of abstracts. We use Ollama (Ollama, 2025) as our server framework to handle the local versions of both models and embedding model and to provide extensibility of different model usage in future. We do not quantize the models at this stage in our prototype. The query and the retrieved documents are routed through Ollama for a response from the selected model.

3.5 Interface

We use Streamlit (Streamlit), an open-source framework in Python, which was easy to use by the development team as a prototype interface for exploration. The interface includes mode selection and prescripted on and off-topic questions. In the center is the text entry for query and below were three dropdowns, one for each model response and one that includes PDFs of each retrieved source document.

3.6 FastAPI

FastAPI (Ramírez, 2025) was selected as a web framework as it supports asynchronous functions and enables functionality of our app using a local deployment across our institutional network. The API handles user input, prompt template, and interacts with Ollama for embeddings and generation.

4 System Interaction Modes

The system supports two modes of interaction: Chat mode and Summary mode, each serving distinct purposes. Chat mode is the default mode, which allows users to engage in interactive conversations and receive structured responses based on the abstracts stored in the database. Summary mode generates concise overviews of selected abstracts given a user's query.

Both modes have access to pre-scripted queries. One set is relevant to the corpus, such as "describe the current state of global fish stocks", and the other set includes incorrect queries, such as 'how do I train my dog to do tricks?". The 'irrelevant' questions were specifically included to not only demonstrate to new users how the system works, but also

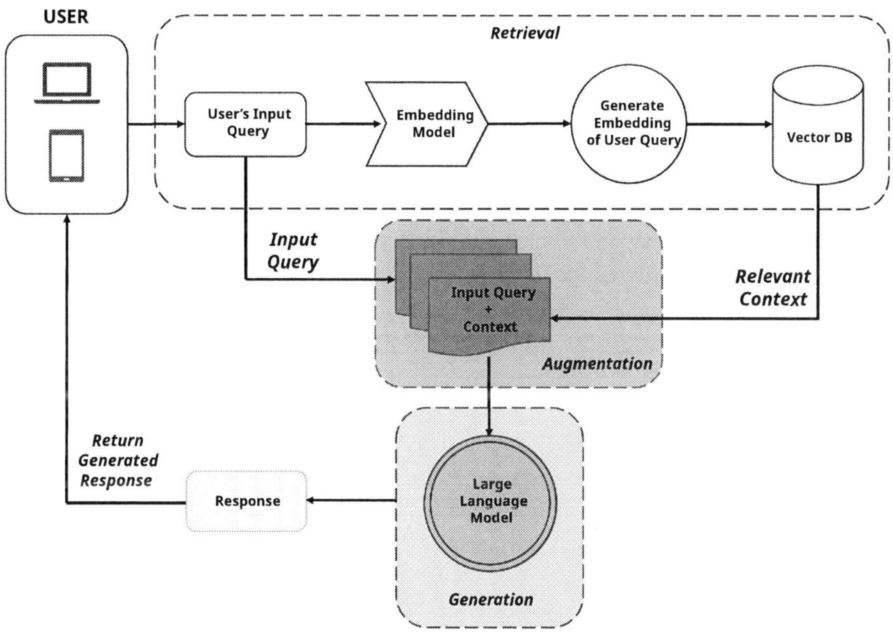

Figure 1: RAG pipeline overview.

to verify during the development that answers were only coming from the retrieved documents, and not relying upon parametric memory.

4.1 Chat Mode

Chat mode is designed to answer the user's query with concise answers given the context of the World Ocean Assessment references, from the most similar clusters. The chat prompt template (Appendix A.1) was based on the domain specific definition of the system's role, contextual relevance from the retriever, integration of the user's query and response generation instructions. The instructions consist of 8 points which emphasize strictly adhering to the facts presented in the context documents. This also helps to guard-rail the model against generating out-of-context or fictional answers to questions which are not directly relevant to the domain.

4.2 Summary Mode

Summary mode is designed to provide users with comprehensive summaries of top relevant research papers for a given user's query. This mode generates responses from multiple documents to present a cohesive overview to quickly summarize the theme, findings and research implications. The prompt template shown in Appendix A.2, is designed so that the generated summaries are comprehensive, systematically structured, and strictly based on the information available in the provided context.

This template instructs the model to analyze the context and generate a response containing key information from all relevant documents. This is to ensure the summary is comprehensive and contains insights from multiple sources to provide a complete holistic answer to the user's query. The model is instructed to generate a summary containing specific sections like Overview, Key Findings, Methodologies, Comparative Analysis, Research Implications, Future Directions, and Key Terms and Concepts. Additionally, instructions on how to cite the relevant source documents to enforce transparency and verifiability are added.

5 Evaluation and Discussion

The quality of the generated response depends on the relevance of the retrieved documents, and this is both a benefit and a challenge with RAG. We use a heuristic approach for evaluation as our team were familiar with the literature and we compared our results to a published benchmark.

From the perspective of assessing if abstracts were viable as a source, we evaluated our prompt development, response quality and model preference, the effect of cluster selection, and measured response time. Our guidelines to focus the evaluation are to assess whether bibliometric abstracts are sufficient for providing acceptable answers to simple queries, provide acceptable summaries, and provide verifiable references. Acceptability was agreed upon to be from the perspective of expert academic users.

We used the OceanBench (Bi et al., 2024) benchmark to analyze our system. OceanBench contains over 10,000 LLM inputs related to the ocean and contains the respective outputs. Due to the size of the benchmark, it was not possible to do an exhaustive search for all relevant questions. Instead, we randomly selected a subset of questions that the LLM would likely be able to answer and questions that would be difficult for the system to answer. We also made a subset of 4 prompts by randomly selecting from all the prompts in the dataset. If a prompt was unlikely to provide a valid answer, such as the prompt: "Extract three evaluation indicators from the guide provided on the official website of the ocean environment evaluation center.", we would discard the prompt and randomly select another one until 4 valid prompts were selected [1].

5.1 Prompt Engineering Iterations

As the LLaMA family of models do not provide system prompts, there were many iterations to refine the instructions and improve the response quality of the LLM responses. For instance, in our initial base prompt, the instruction to the model was simply to answer the question based on the context retrieved from the vector database. The motivation for this base prompt is to see how the LLM generated a response to the query given the context documents given free autonomy.

For both modes, minimal prompts did not cite the referenced documents, hallucinated false documents as references, and the summaries were of varying formats. On the positive side, out of context questions were answered acceptably. The final versions, seen in Appendix A.1 and A.2, resulted in responses from both models that were contextually relevant and acceptable to users, but occasionally, the citing references were false or incorrect. The structure of in-context and out-of-context responses was consistent.

5.2 Response Acceptability and LLM Preference

We compared Llama3 [8B] and Phi3-medium [14B] for user preference regarding satisfactory responses adhering to the instructions. In both cases, we found structure was often achieved with generated responses that included point form and multiple paragraphs.

However, in some cases Phi3-medium deviates with responses structured as a single paragraph if either the context was less relevant or if the user's query was ambiguous. Otherwise, we found the Phi3-medium model was stricter in adhering to the instructions than Llama3. The generated answer by Phi3-medium was often more concise than Llama3 which many users preferred.

Overall, response quality of both models is acceptable, but some occasional errors and issues persisted. For example, as shown below, all papers were cited together as "[1],[2],[3],[4],[5]", though there was no correspondence between phrases in the sentence and the referenced documents:

> "c. Methodologies (68 words) The papers utilize a combination of empirical studies, theoretical frameworks, and case analyses to assess marine species richness, invasive species impacts on conservation planning, ecological consequences of changing climate patterns, and the behavioral aspects influencing trophic interaction [1], [2], [3], [4], [5]."

More disturbingly, the "References" section did not include the correct documents from the database:

> "References: [1] Second World Ocean Assessment [2] Comprehensive Review of Marine Biodiversity Patterns and Threats [3] Climate Change Impact on Coral Reef Systems - A Case Study Approach [4] Behavior-Mediated Trophic Interactions in Marine Mammals: An Ecological Perspective [5] Invasive Species Impacts on Marine Spatial Planning and Conservation Strategies"

Although these hallucinations were reduced and only occurred occasionally, their persistence suggests we need another mechanism in our pipeline for confirming references.

5.3 Effect of Cluster Selection

The LLM generates responses based on documents retrieved from the most semantically similar clusters. We find if a cluster is very fine-grained then the LLM is more likely to hallucinate or generate factually incorrect answers or may not have sufficient information to generate answers. This was a

[1]The subset of prompts and our system's response to the prompts can be provided upon request.

concern with using abstracts and a small corpus for the information tasks we provided. Conversely, if a cluster topic is overly broad, then the LLM generated answers which are very generic or generalized to the user's question or the domain itself.

The LLM's responses seem heavily influenced by the clustering and and may be limitations of using TF-IDF for assigning topics to works containing more than one topic. More work is needed on providing transparency of topics assigned to clusters and on exploring clustering algorithms.

5.4 Response Time

Primary factors affecting the time taken by local LLMs to generate responses are the model size, length of the generated answer, and hardware limitations. For the Llama3 models it took an average of 22 seconds for summary and 14 seconds for chat, while for the Phi3 model it took 36 seconds for summary and 16 seconds for chat, with some variation depending on the complexity of the query.

One of our exploration goals was to evaluate if we could run models locally yet not require expensive multi-GPU hardware. The hardware workstation specifications included an Intel i5-11400F [6 cores @2.6GHz] with a single NVIDIA GeForce RTX 3060 [12GB RAM], 16GB system ram [3200 MHz] and 1TB SSD storage. Both LLMs deployed used the GPU, but as we did not quantize the models, more efficiency may be gained with quantizing methods.

5.5 Benchmark Comparison

Many of our system's responses have multiple paragraphs with references and consistently use headers and lists to make the responses more human readable. The Benchmark response, however, only provide answers with a few sentences and lack references.

For general questions, such as: "Analyze the impact of marine environmental dynamics processes on the wave environment.", our system's answer has similar themes to the benchmark. For the prompt, "Categorize marine animals into several types and provide examples for each." our system's chat mode response is very similar to the benchmark response and even provides references related to protecting animals in the specific categories.

Our system does hallucinate at times and sometimes hallucinates references. Since our system provides references, a user can verify the correctness of the answer and be wary of answers that have false or no references. The benchmark outputs does not provide any references, meaning the user must trust the LLM with limited justification.

6 Conclusions and Future Work

We presented a prototype RAG application using open-source bibliometric metadata as an external knowledge source and open-source models run from a local workstation within our institutional network. Overall, we are encouraged by the results on using abstracts especially considering how few documents were retrieved (k=5) for each query.

Both models perform well with our prompts and users found responses acceptable regarding structure and response content, though there were persistent hallucinated or omitted references. When compared to the benchmark, our system's response is similar to the the benchmark with the added benefit of more details and references to justify the LLM's responses.

Future work will explore adding a verifying loop to review the references included in the response, and to continue to explore instructions that reduce false references. The effect of clusters was not evident by the user, and more work is needed to explore transparency and bibliometric clustering methods for improved topic retrieval. Response time was not perceived unfavorably by users given we were running locally, but quantizing methods may help reduce time and improve the experience.

There are several areas we look forward to continuing to explore and of course welcome any collaborators that may be interested. Currently, metadata has been curated from cited works in the WOA-II report. Future work will expand this to citing documents, greatly increasing the number and topics of works available, which may address challenges with small clusters and poor responses from highly focused clusters.

Clustering methods, particularly those around bibliometric analysis should be explored, such as using bibliometric, direct citation, co-citation, and hybrid combinations along with algorithms typically used in the bibliometrics field, such as Louvain and Leiden. Sparse, dense, and hybrid retrieval methods also need to be explored with metadata due to particular issues found in scientific texts for their effect on retrieval metrics (Cho et al., 2024; Shi et al., 2023). Post-query augmentation methods of using bibliometric measures for reranking need to be explored beyond past work using cited-by counts. We also have concerns, from related research, about the noisiness within abstracts and titles, and much work is needed to understand the scope and effects of these characteristics on retrievers and embeddings.

The basic pipeline we have presented here will continue to be a platform for experimentation on how bibliometric metadata may serve as an openly available source of authoritative, external knowledge for future RAG applications.

Acknowledgments

Funding for this work was provided by a Canada First Research Excellence Fund grant entitled "Transforming Climate Action: Addressing the Missing Ocean".

References

Shubham Agarwal, Issam H. Laradji, Laurent Charlin, and Christopher Pal. 2024. LitLLM: A Toolkit for Scientific Literature Review. *arXiv preprint*. ArXiv:2402.01788 [cs].

Zhen Bi, Ningyu Zhang, Yida Xue, Yixin Ou, Daxiong Ji, Guozhou Zheng, and Huajun Chen. 2024. OceanGPT: A Large Language Model for Ocean Science Tasks. *arXiv preprint*. ArXiv:2310.02031 [cs].

Sukmin Cho, Soyeong Jeong, Jeongyeon Seo, Taeho Hwang, and Jong C. Park. 2024. Typos that Broke the RAG's Back: Genetic Attack on RAG Pipeline by Simulating Documents in the Wild via Low-level Perturbations. *arXiv preprint*. ArXiv:2404.13948 [cs].

CSIRO. 2023. Second World Ocean Assessment is afloat. Publisher: CSIRO.

Binglan Han, Teo Susnjak, and Anuradha Mathrani. 2024. Automating Systematic Literature Reviews with Retrieval-Augmented Generation: A Comprehensive Overview. *Applied Sciences*, 14(19):9103. Number: 19 Publisher: Multidisciplinary Digital Publishing Institute.

Angel Hsu, Mason Laney, Ji Zhang, Diego Manya, and Linda Farczadi. 2024. Evaluating ChatNet-Zero, an LLM-Chatbot to Demystify Climate Pledges. In *Proceedings of the 1st Workshop on Natural Language Processing Meets Climate Change (ClimateNLP 2024)*, pages 82–92, Bangkok, Thailand. Association for Computational Linguistics.

Jeff Huber and Anton Troynikov. Chroma Documentation.

Patrick Lewis, Ethan Perez, Aleksandra Piktus, Fabio Petroni, Vladimir Karpukhin, Naman Goyal, Heinrich Küttler, Mike Lewis, Wen-tau Yih, Tim Rocktäschel, Sebastian Riedel, and Douwe Kiela. 2020. Retrieval-Augmented Generation for Knowledge-Intensive NLP Tasks. In *Advances in Neural Information Processing Systems*, volume 33, pages 9459–9474. Curran Associates, Inc.

Yiming Li, Jeff Zhao, Manqi Li, Yifang Dang, Evan Yu, Jianfu Li, Zenan Sun, Usama Hussein, Jianguo Wen, Ahmed M Abdelhameed, Junhua Mai, Shenduo Li, Yue Yu, Xinyue Hu, Daowei Yang, Jingna Feng, Zehan Li, Jianping He, Wei Tao, and 4 others. 2024. RefAI: a GPT-powered retrieval-augmented generative tool for biomedical literature recommendation and summarization. *Journal of the American Medical Informatics Association*, 31(9):2030–2039.

Sara Vera Marjanović, Haeun Yu, Pepa Atanasova, Maria Maistro, Christina Lioma, and Isabelle Augenstein. 2024. DYNAMICQA: Tracing Internal Knowledge Conflicts in Language Models. *arXiv preprint*. ArXiv:2407.17023 [cs].

Microsoft. Phi Cookbook. This is a Phi Family of SLMs book for getting started with Phi Models. Phi a family of open sourced AI models developed by Microsoft. Phi models are the most capable and cost-effective small language models (SLMs) available, outperforming models of the same size and next size up across a variety of language, reasoning, coding, and math benchmarks.

Vincent Nguyen, Sarvnaz Karimi, Willow Hallgren, Ashley Harkin, and Mahesh Prakash. 2024. My Climate Advisor: An Application of NLP in Climate Adaptation for Agriculture. In *Proceedings of the 1st Workshop on Natural Language Processing Meets Climate Change (ClimateNLP 2024)*, pages 27–45, Bangkok, Thailand. Association for Computational Linguistics.

Zach Nussbaum, John X. Morris, Brandon Duderstadt, and Andriy Mulyar. 2024. Nomic Embed: Training a Reproducible Long Context Text Embedder. _eprint: 2402.01613.

Ollama. 2025. ollama. Original-date: 2023-06-26T19:39:32Z.

Mykhailo Poliakov and Nadiya Shvai. 2024. Multi-Meta-RAG: Improving RAG for Multi-Hop Queries using Database Filtering with LLM-Extracted Metadata. *arXiv preprint*. ArXiv:2406.13213 [cs].

Jason Priem, Heather Piwowar, and Richard Orr. 2022. OpenAlex: A fully-open index of scholarly works, authors, venues, institutions, and concepts. *arXiv preprint*. ArXiv:2205.01833 [cs].

Sebastián Ramírez. 2025. FastAPI. Original-date: 2018-12-08T08:21:47Z.

Kunal Sawarkar, Shivam R. Solanki, and Abhilasha Mangal. 2025. MetaGen Blended RAG: Unlocking Zero-Shot Precision for Specialized Domain Question-Answering. *arXiv preprint*. ArXiv:2505.18247 [cs].

Kareem Shaik, Dali Wang, Weijian Zheng, Qinglei Cao, Heng Fan, Peter Schwartz, and Yunhe Feng. 2024. S3LLM: Large-Scale Scientific Software Understanding with LLMs Using Source, Metadata, and Document. In *Computational Science – ICCS 2024*, pages 222–230, Cham. Springer Nature Switzerland.

Freda Shi, Xinyun Chen, Kanishka Misra, Nathan Scales, David Dohan, Ed H. Chi, Nathanael Schärli, and Denny Zhou. 2023. Large Language Models Can Be Easily Distracted by Irrelevant Context. In *Proceedings of the 40th International Conference on Machine Learning*, pages 31210–31227. PMLR. ISSN: 2640-3498.

Streamlit. Streamlit.

Fangzheng Tian, Debasis Ganguly, and Craig Macdonald. 2025. Is Relevance Propagated from Retriever to Generator in RAG? In *Advances in Information Retrieval*, pages 32–48, Cham. Springer Nature Switzerland.

Rémi Toupin, Geoff Krause, Poppy Riddle, Madelaine Hare, and Philippe Mongeon. 2024. Identifying Ocean-Related Literature Using the UN Second World Ocean Assessment Report (Dataset).

Hugo Touvron, Thibaut Lavril, Gautier Izacard, Xavier Martinet, Marie-Anne Lachaux, Timothée Lacroix, Baptiste Rozière, Naman Goyal, Eric Hambro, Faisal Azhar, Aurelien Rodriguez, Armand Joulin, Edouard Grave, and Guillaume Lample. 2023. LLaMA: Open and Efficient Foundation Language Models. *arXiv preprint*. ArXiv:2302.13971 [cs].

United Nations. 2021. *The Second World Ocean Assessment: World Ocean Assessment II - Volume I & II*. United Nations.

Saeid Ashraf Vaghefi, Dominik Stammbach, Veruska Muccione, Julia Bingler, Jingwei Ni, Mathias Kraus, Simon Allen, Chiara Colesanti-Senni, Tobias Wekhof, Tobias Schimanski, Glen Gostlow, Tingyu Yu, Qian Wang, Nicolas Webersinke, Christian Huggel, and Markus Leippold. 2023. Chat-Climate: Grounding conversational AI in climate science. *Communications Earth & Environment*, 4(1):480. Publisher: Nature Publishing Group.

Richard Van Noorden. 2023. ChatGPT-like AIs are coming to major science search engines. *Nature*. Bandiera_abtest: a Cg_type: News Publisher: Nature Publishing Group Subject_term: Machine learning, Databases, Research data.

Nicolas Webersinke, Mathias Kraus, Julia Bingler, and Markus Leippold. 2022. CLIMATEBERT: A Pretrained Language Model for Climate-Related Text. *SSRN Electronic Journal*. Publisher: Elsevier BV.

A Appendix

The following are the prompts given to the respective system interaction modes. The *{context}* portion of the prompts is replaced with the abstract, title, and other metadata of all the works within the selected cluster. The *{question}* portion of the prompts is replaced with the user's query.

A.1 Chat Prompt

```
You are an expert marine scientist
assistant with comprehensive
knowledge of the Second World
Ocean Assessment
and its referenced research papers.

Context: {context}
User Query: {question}
Instructions:
1. Analyze the user's query carefully
to understand the specific information
needed.

2. Utilize the retrieved information to
identify the most relevant research
documents.

3. Synthesize information from the
relevant abstracts to formulate a
comprehensive answer.

4. Provide a clear, concise, and
factualresponse that directly
addresses the user's question.

5. Cite the relevant 'source' document
IDs in your response using the format
[Citations: [1] (the source),
[2] (the source), etc.]
and at the end list them.

6. If the question is out of context or
unclear based on the available documents,
respond with:
"That question is out of the scope of
the available documents."

7. If the information requested is not
present in the available documents,
respond with: "The information you're
seeking is not available in the
referenced documents."

8. Stick strictly to the facts presented
in the documents; do not generate
speculative answers.
```

Your response should be:

- Accurate and fact-based
- Directly relevant to the user's query
- Concise yet comprehensive
- Properly cited using the document IDs and PDF citations

Answer response:

A.2 Summary Prompt

You are an expert marine scientist assistant tasked with summarizing research papers related to the Second World Ocean Assessment.

Context:

{context}

Instructions:

1. Analyze the context and synthesize their key information.

2. Create a comprehensive summary that integrates insights from all relevant papers in Context.

3. Structure your summary as follows:

a. Overview (100-150 words)

Provide a high-level summary of the main themes and findings across all papers.

b. Key Findings (3-5 bullet points)

List the most significant discoveries or conclusions from the papers.

c. Methodologies (50-75 words)

Briefly describe the primary research methods used across the studies.

d. Comparative Analysis (75-100 words)

Highlight any notable similarities or differences between the papers' approaches or results.

e. Research Implications (50-75 words)

Summarize the broader implications of these findings for marine science or policy.

f. Future Directions (50-75 words)

Identify gaps in current knowledge or areas for future research as mentioned in the papers.

g. Key Terms and Concepts

Define 3-5 important technical terms or concepts crucial to understanding the research.

4. Cite the relevant document Title in your summary using the format [1], [2], etc. and list them at the end from the context.

5. Aim for clarity, conciseness, and accuracy in your summary.

6. Stick strictly to the information presented in the documents; avoid speculation or external information.

7. If the question is out of context or not clear based on the available documents, respond with:
"That question is out of the scope of the available documents."

Your summary should be:
- Comprehensive, covering the main points from all relevant papers
- Accurate and fact-based
- Well-structured according to the outline provided
- Properly cited using the document IDs

Summary:

A German-Language Dataset and Annotation Tool for Tabular Question Answering

Staša Karapandžić
JR-Centre for Robust Decision Making
Vorarlberg University of Applied Sciences, Dornbirn, Austria
stasa.karapandzic@fhv.at

Michael Hellwig
JR-Centre for Robust Decision Making
Vorarlberg University of Applied Sciences, Dornbirn, Austria
michael.hellwig@fhv.at

Abstract

The paper proposes a dataset and annotation tool to support the development of German-language Tabular Question Answering systems, with a specific focus on sustainability-related information. By targeting tabular data from sustainability reports, particularly within the Austrian banking sector, this initiative addresses the growing need for intelligent systems capable of extracting structured insights from complex, multilingual documents. The key features are its exclusive use of the German language and a strong emphasis on information retrieval from tables embedded in sustainability reports. These tables often contain critical data - such as environmental metrics, social responsibility indicators, and governance benchmarks - that are not easily accessible through text-based search methods. The dataset is compiled from openly available sources, including public databases and openly published sustainability reports. An annotation tool facilitates the streamlining of the human annotation process, enabling efficient labeling of question-answer pairs. Potential applications include training and evaluating TQA models that can accurately locate and extract sustainability-related information from tables. This capability is useful for tasks such as regulatory compliance checks, ESG (Environmental, Social, Governance) data analysis, and automated report summarization.

1 Introduction

In the light of the increasing performance of Large Language Models (LLM, e.g., GPT (OpenAI, 2023) or Llama (Touvron et al., 2023)) and their presence in our everyday lives (Xu et al., 2025), the pioneering performance of the Bidirectional Encoder Representations from Transformers (BERT) model (Devlin and *et al.*, 2019) needs to be mentioned. It has led to numerous adaptations of this architecture (Wang et al., 2022) and represents the foundation of the state-of-the-art models related to the present work. This paper focuses specifically on the Natural Language Processing (NLP) task of Question Answering (QA) (Wang, 2022) which aims at interpreting natural language queries and at finding relevant answers by searching through large datasets. This process involves extracting key terms or entities from the query, understanding their meaning and finding relevant information in the data. Although recent advances in NLP have achieved impressive results on QA tasks in closed domains (OpenAI, 2023), these models often face challenges when dealing with tabular data. This is mainly due to their limited ability to handle structured formats and the inherent lack of contextual cues in tables (Jin et al., 2022). To overcome such problems, the field of Tabular Question Answering (TQA) has gained momentum. TQA is a special subtype of QA in which answers are derived from structured tables rather than unstructured text.

One of the most notable developments in TQA is the TAPAS model (Herzig et al., 2020), which has been pre-trained on millions of tables from Wikipedia. TAPAS uses graph-attention mechanisms to model relationships between table cells, enabling it to answer complex queries accurately. Yet, similar to the QA context (Höffner et al., 2016), low-resource language TQA remains a major challenge. This is due to the absence of sufficient high-quality datasets in languages other than English. Therefore, TAPAS models are currently mostly available for high resource languages such as English and Chinese. Although the English language models can be fine-tuned to specific tasks in other languages using transfer learning approaches, this also requires high-quality training datasets in the required language and application domain. Hence, the development of domain-specific dataset is a desirable and essential step towards building robust multi-language TQA solutions.

This paper introduces a German language dataset that consists of carefully collected tabular Ques-

Proceedings of the 21st Conference on Natural Language Processing (KONVENS), Volume 2: Workshops, pages 291–300, 2025

tions and Answer pairs (Q&A pairs) for TQA training as well as an annotation tool allowing to facilitate human annotation efforts in case the datasets needs to be extended. Due to the current demand for sustainability information retrieval, part of the dataset consists of ESG-related Q&A pairs (European Commission, 2022), derived from sustainability reports of major Austrian banks. The source of remaining Q&A pairs comes from openly available general governmental data sources (DESTATIS, 2013). In this regard, the dataset represents a compromise between regularly structured, general purpose tabular data and more variational domain specific data points. The sustainability reports published under evolving regulatory European frameworks (e.g. the Corporate Sustainability Reporting Directive (CSRD) (European Union, 2022)) contain tables that vary widely in structure, terminology, and semantic complexity. An exposure to domain-specific tables and language renders TQA models more robust with respect to interpreting numeric entries, including contextual relationships, or recognizing ESG-specific terminology.

In addition, the paper presents an annotation tool to support the human mapping of table-related questions and answer pairs by prompting the user to formulate precise questions based on randomly selected table rows and then select the corresponding answers. It supports annotators with an intuitive interface, ensuring consistency, accuracy, and scalability in the creation of high-quality datasets for TQA training and evaluation.

The presented dataset and annotation tool are ready for practical use in German-language TQA applications. They enable the fine-tuning of TQA models to improve their performance, and increases the relevance and precision of real-world applications. They also facilitate data augmentation and the generation of new TQA datasets, contributing to the development of more robust models.

In particular, the resources represent a practicable advancement for knaoledge retireval from sustainability reports. By focusing on tabular data from German-language sustainability reports in the Austrian banking sector, the dataset enables the development of Tabular Question Answering (TQA) systems capable of extracting key information from complex documents. These reports typically contain vital statistics related to environmental performance, social responsibility, and governance practices - data that is often locked within tables and inaccessible through standard text-based search tools. The dataset, sourced from openly available databases and published reports, provides annotated question-answer pairs specifically designed for machine learning applications. TQA models trained with this dataset can automate tasks such as regulatory compliance checks, ESG data extraction, and sustainability benchmarking. The annotation tool further streamlines the human labeling process, boosting the scalability and accuracy of the dataset. With its exclusive focus on the German language, this resource supports localized implementations in Austria, Switzerland, and Germany, helping financial institutions meet emerging ESG standards. Ultimately, this initiative empowers stakeholders with intelligent access to sustainability data, enabling more efficient analysis, improved transparency, and enhanced accountability in corporate reporting. It lays the foundation for broader adoption of AI in the ESG domains.

The remaining paper is organized as follows: In Section 2, a brief overview of related work is provided. Section 3 then presents the design of the proposed TQA dataset and elaborates on its characteristics. The annotation tool used to facilitate the extension of the dataset is described in Section 4. Taking into account the use case of sustainability reporting, Section 5 demonstrates the use of the resources for a specific German language TQA case. The paper concludes with a discussion of the lessons learned from the design process in Section 6 and provides an outlook on potential future enhancements.

2 Related Work

Regarding table-based data resources for the training of TQA models, the situation is rather modest. Even in high-resource languages such as Chinese (Zheng et al., 2023a) or English, only a few (albeit extensive) datasets are available.

Since this paper is concerned with the description of a German-language TQA dataset for the fine-tuning of the TAPAS model (Herzig et al., 2020), we will limit ourselves to the discussion of the corresponding English-language datasets on which TAPAS is based in the following.

TAPAS builds on the BERT architecture (Devlin and *et al.*, 2019) and includes relative position embeddings and user-defined token types to effectively represent table structures. It was pretrained on text-table input pairs extracted from 6.2M Wikipedia tables with at most 500 cells (3.3M of class Infobox and 2.9M of class WikiTable). All considered tables were tables with a header row including column names. Despite its input size limitation ($\leq$ 512 table cells) (Google Research, 2020), TAPAS still represents one of the best performing models in TQA and often outperforms newer models such as TAPEX (Zheng et al., 2023b), especially in scenarios with vertically structured tables (Etezadi and Shamsfard, 2022; Yang et al., 2023). The TAPAS model has been fine-tuned on the three follwoing TQA datasets: Wiki Table Questions, SQA, and WikiSQL.

Wiki Table Questions (Pasupat and Liang, 2015) is a dataset designed for semantic parsing and question answering over Wikipedia tables. To this end, humans were given a table and asked to compose a series of questions that include comparisons, superlatives, aggregations or even arithmetic operations. The results were then verified by different volunteers. The dataset enables the evaluation of a TQA model's ability to answer questions in natural language, e.g., by mapping them to logical forms to be executed on semi-structured tables. WikiTableQuestions includes 22,000 questions over 2,000 English Wikipedia tables.

Further, the SQA dataset (Iyyer et al., 2017) was constructed by asking humans to decompose a subset of complex questions from the WikiTableQuestions dataset into sequences. The final dataset consists of 6,066 question sequences (with an average of 2.9 question per sequence).

The third dataset is the WikiSQL dataset (Zhong et al., 2017) which focuses on translating text to SQL. To this end, humans were asked to paraphrase a template-based question into natural language. The dataset contains 80,654 examples extracted from 24,241 tables.

Another related dataset is TabFact (Chen et al., 2020) which represents an English-language large-scale tabular fact-checking dataset consisting of over 100,000 human-annotated statements paired with Wikipedia tables. Each statement is categorized as implied or disproven based on the table content. This makes TabFact a benchmark for assessing logical reasoning and natural language understanding in table-based questions and fact checking. However, it primarily serves the task of fact verification and differs from the other TQA datasets, particularly in the input format and the label structure. E.g., while the input of WikiTableQuestions consists of question and table combinations to which a specific correct answer from the table is made available, the TabFact dataset specifies a statement and a table as input and assigns a binary output (true/false).

As far as German-language TQA model training is concerned, the availability of data is even more limited. To our knowledge, the first German-language TQA dataset was created to fine-tune the TAPAS model offset TAPASGO (Kowieski et al., 2024). TAPASGO demonstrated transfer learning capabilities to German-language TQA tasks and showed significant accuracy advantages over the combined use of the English-language TAPAS model and translation tools.

Based on this largely undocumented dataset in (Kowieski et al., 2024), this work aims to establish a practical dataset that can be easily used for training, fine-tuning, or benchmarking of German TQA models. The focus of the dataset expansion was on tabular data and associated question and answer pairs in the context of ESG data, as the extraction of information from sustainability reports is a promising use case for TQA. While pre-trained models like TAPAS or TAPASGO exhibit strong performance on general-purpose data, they may show significant limitations when applied to domain-specific contexts such as sustainability reporting. These limitations are largely due to the domain shift between the model's training data and the target data it is expected to operate on (Herzig et al., 2020; Kowieski et al., 2024; Eisenschlos et al., 2020).

Sustainability reports, especially those published under evolving regulatory frameworks in Europe, such as the Corporate Sustainability Reporting Directive (CSRD), often contain structured data in the form of tables that communicate complex, technical information related to ESG metrics (European Banking Authority (EBA), 2021). These tables vary widely in structure, terminology, and semantic complexity, posing challenges for models trained on generic tabular datasets such as WikiTables (Pasupat and Liang, 2015) or the TabFact corpus (Chen et al., 2020). Without exposure to domain-specific tables and language during training, TQA models tend to misinterpret numeric entries, overlook contextual relationships, or fail to recognize ESG-specific terminology. That is, the dataset can also be used to generally refine German TQA models and make them more robust in relation to specific domains, independently of its application to sustainability reports.

3 Dataset Description

A well-constructed dataset serves multiple roles in the development of a TQA system. First, it acts as a training resource, exposing the model to examples that reflect the real-world structures and semantics of the target domain. In this case, tables from sustainability reports feature terminology, formatting, and data patterns specific to ESG topics. Without domain adaptation, models often struggle to correctly interpret such specialized content (Eisenschlos et al., 2020). Second, the dataset also serves as a benchmark for evaluating the effectiveness of domain-specific fine-tuning. By comparing model performance before and after fine-tuning, it becomes possible to quantify improvements in both accuracy and relevance. This is especially important in domains like sustainability reporting, where precision in data interpretation can impact regulatory compliance and public accountability.

The complete German language TQA dataset proposed in this paper is available on GitHub (Karapandžić and Hellwig, 2025). Its content consists of tables and corresponding natural language questions as well as the respective answers. The dataset addresses the task of extracting the correct answer from the respective tables. The detailed structure is described in the sections below.

3.1 Data Sources and Collection Process

The dataset presented is based on a selection of tables from two types of German-language sources. On the one hand, a selection of governmental table data (DESTATIS, 2013) was used and, on the other hand, sustainability reports from the Austrian banking sector. This composition offers a good compromise between preferably general and sustainability-specific question and answer pairs. This composition offers a good balance between general and sustainability-specific question-answer pairs, with the easily accessible governmental data providing a diverse range of topics and a broader contextual foundation.

Governmental data source: Regarding the freely accessible governmental German data tables, we accessed the DESTATIS platform (DESTATIS, 2013). It is maintained by the German Federal Statistical Office and it provides access to a wide range of official statistics. Its main tool, the GENESIS-Online database, allows users to search, customize, and download statistical tables on topics such as population, economy, and health. Data can be filtered by time, region, and category and exported in formats such as Excel or CSV. The online platform is available in English and German and supports both manual and automatic data access via an API.

Mitarbeiterkennzahlen (nach Köpfen zum Stichtag)	**2023 Konzern**	**2023 Bank**	**2022 Konzern**	**2022 Bank**	**2021 Konzern**	**2021 Bank**
Vorstände	**3**	**3**	**3**	**3**	**3**	**3**
Frauen	0	0	0	0	0	0
Männer	3	3	3	3	3	3
Mitarbeiter gesamt (inkl. Karenz)	**897**	**797**	**896**	**796**	**876**	**778**
Frauen	510	454	507	452	497	443
Männer	387	343	389	344	379	335
Mitarbeiter gesamt (ohne Karenz)	**860**	**762**	**846**	**747**	**825**	**733**
Frauen	473	419	462	408	447	398
Männer	387	343	384	339	378	335

Figure 1: Examplary table from a 2023 sustainability report (Hypo Vorarlberg Bank AG, 2023).

Sustainability reports: In addition, to the above data source, we utilized real-world sustainability reports from diverse sources to capture the variability in reporting practices. This stage ensures that the dataset is representative of real-world scenarios and covers a wide range of formats and terminology. Therefore, three sustainability reports from three major banking institutions: Hypo Vorarlberg Bank AG, Österreichische Volksbanken-AG, and Raiffeisen Bank International AG were selected. All reports represent documents available from the reporting year 2023. The reports for that year were the most up-to-date and complete source at the time the data collection started. To extract tabular data from these reports, tools like Camelot, Tabula, and Pdfplumber were tested, but due to the complexity and inconsistency of table formats, manual corrections were also required. An example of a such a sustainability report table is provided in Fig.1.

3.2 Annotation Schema

The annotation schema used in this study defines the structure of the question-answer pairs extracted from tables. Each annotation is stored as a row in a CSV file, with seven columns that capture key information about the table, question, and answer. The first column in the CSV, which has no header name, simply represents a running index from 0 to n, where n is the total number of annotated pairs. This index serves as a unique identifier for each annotation entry.

The second column, `id`, refers to the identifier of the table from which the annotation was created. This allows grouping of multiple annotations related to the same source table. The third column, `annotator`, indicates how many times a specific table has been annotated. For instance, the first annotation for a given table is marked as `0`, the second as `1`, and so on. This helps differentiate between multiple questions derived from the same table and supports tracking the reuse of table data.

The `question` column contains the natural language question formulated by the annotator. The format and phrasing of the question are flexible, but each question must be answerable by selecting exactly one cell from the table. This constraint is enforced by the custom annotation tool used in the dataset creation process, which only permits single-cell selection for answer annotation. As a result, all questions in the dataset are factoid in nature, aiming to retrieve a specific piece of factual information from the table.

The column `table_file` records the filename of the source table, providing traceability and context. The answer itself is represented in two parts: `answer_coordinates` and `answer_text`. The `answer_coordinates` are specified as a pair of integers (row, column), indicating the exact location of the answer within the table. Importantly, these coordinates exclude the table header, meaning that (0,0) refers to the first cell in the first row of actual data-effectively the second row in the table structure. The `answer_text` is the literal content of the identified table cell and serves as the ground-truth answer for the corresponding question. Answers are strictly span-based, tied directly to the textual content of a single table cell. The system does not support abstractive or multi-span answers due to the annotation tool's design. Consequently, all questions in the dataset are inherently factoid, as they are limited to retrieving a single, factual value from one specific table cell.

In the original TAPAS Conversational fine-tuning dataset the column `position` appears and represents a sequence in which questions and follow-up questions are being asked. The first asked question therefore always has position 0, while the first follow-up question has position 1. In our dataset we did not formulate follow-up questions, therefore `position` is always set to 0.

This annotation schema ensures a consistent, cell-based approach to question answering, which aligns well with the capabilities of TAPAS (Herzig et al., 2020), or TAPASGO (Kowieski et al., 2024), respectively. All questions are designed to be answered through direct extraction from a single table cell, making the dataset suitable for training and evaluating span-based, tabular QA models in the domain of sustainability reporting.

The complete German language TQA dataset is available on GitHub (Karapandžić and Hellwig, 2025). Its input consists of a natural language question and a table, and the task is to extract the correct answer from the respective table.

3.3 Dataset Statistics

To better understand the structure and composition of the dataset, the key statistics regarding its sources, size, and distribution are presented in Table 1. The dataset was constructed with the goal of covering both domain-specific and general-purpose tabular content in the German language, allowing for diverse and realistic question-answering scenarios across varying levels of complexity.

The dataset comprises a total of 360 German-language tables, annotated with 1,649 question–answer pairs. Of these, 124 tables were sourced from the sustainability reports of three major Austrian banking institutions: 30 from Hypo Vorarlberg Bank AG, 41 from Österreichische Volksbanken-AG, and 53 from Raiffeisen Bank International AG. These tables yielded 613 annotated Q&A pairs. The remaining 236 tables were obtained from publicly available governmental data provided via the DESTATIS platform. This portion contributed an additional 1,036 annotated question–answer pairs. The final dataset thus combines both general-purpose and domain-specific tabular content, supporting diverse evaluation scenarios in German-language TQA.

Notably, the tables in the dataset are generally of modest size, which is consistent with the typical structure found in sustainability reports (cf. Fig. 1). This also aligns with the practical limitations of the TAPAS model, which operates within constraints related to input size and transformer-based encodings. While the model can technically handle up to 512 cells, prior work has shown that larger tables can result in performance degradation, or even failure during training and conversion, due to format incompatibilities (Kowieski et al., 2024).

	GovDat	SusRep	Total
# Tables	236	124	360
# Q&A pairs	1036	613	1649
Percentage	62.8%	37.2%	100%

Table 1: Distribution of tables and question–answer (Q&A) pairs obtained by source domain: Governmental data (GovDat) and Sustainability Reports (SusRep).

4 Annotation Tool

To streamline the creation of training data for Tabular Question Answering (TQA) models, particularly TAPASGO, a custom annotation tool was developed. This tool was designed with a focus on ease of use, domain-specific adaptability, and seamless integration of annotated data into the fine-tuning process.

4.1 Design Goals and Architecture

The primary goal of the annotation tool was to ensure usability for non-technical users, enabling them to create high-quality question–answer pairs without requiring programming skills or prior experience in data annotation. The tool was used in this work for both sustainability and ESG-related content as well as general-purpose tabular data, demonstrating its flexibility and effectiveness across domains, provided the input follows the required format.

The system is built with separate frontend and backend components. The frontend provides an intuitive and interactive interface for annotators, while the backend manages data ingestion, storage, and annotation tracking. Upon initialization, the tool reads a metadata CSV file containing table identifiers, filenames, and file paths. Using this metadata, it loads individual CSV tables into a PostgreSQL database, storing each cell along with its row and column index and corresponding column headers. This structure ensures that each table cell is stored with sufficient context to support meaningful question generation.

All annotations created through the tool are stored in a dedicated PostgreSQL table. Once the annotation process is complete, the resulting dataset is exported as a CSV file, which contains natural-language questions, the corresponding answer cell coordinates, answer text, and other relevant metadata. This exported file serves as the basis for subsequent preprocessing and model training.

The annotation tool can also be found in the GitHub repository associated with the TQA dataset (Karapandžić and Hellwig, 2025).

4.2 Features and Extensibility

Once initialized, the tool presents annotators with five randomly selected rows from five different tables, each accompanied by the relevant column headers for context. Before beginning the annotation process, annotators are shown clear guidelines,

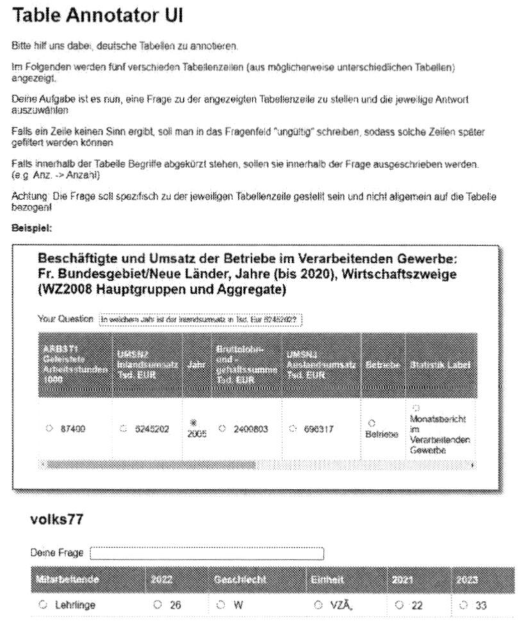

Figure 2: Illustration of the Annotation Tool interface and the introductory guidelines.

suggestions, and examples to help them understand what is expected and how to formulate valid questions[1]. This initial explanation ensures consistency and improves annotation quality, especially for non-expert users. Annotators are then prompted to write a natural-language question for each row and select the appropriate answer by clicking on the corresponding cell. Due to this design, only single-cell answers are supported. Each annotation includes the question, the selected cell value, and metadata such as table ID, answer coordinates, and file name. A screenshot of the interface is shown in Figure 2.

In case that either the question or the selected answer is missing, the tool alerts the annotator and prevents submission until the input is complete. If the annotator is unsure how to formulate a question or notices an issue with the presented data that makes it unclear or unusable, they are instructed to enter "ungültig" (invalid), so that these cases can be reviewed and processed separately afterward. After submitting, all data is stored centrally in a PostgreSQL database table designed for annotation management. A sample of the annotated entries is displayed Figure 3.

Although current functionality is limited to single-cell span selection, the tool architecture al-

[1] As the tool is primarily designed to support the creation of German question annotation, so far the guidelines are displayed in German language only.

	id	annotator	position	question	table_file	answer_coordinates	answer_text
0	56	0	0	Wie viele Frauen wurden in den Mitarbeiterkennzahlen (nach Köpfen) an den Berichtsstichtagen im Jahr 2021 in der Bank erfasst?	hypo54.csv	[(1, 6)]	['0']
1	23	0	0	Wie hoch ist die Gesamtanzahl der Vollzeitäquivalente (VZÄ) für männliche Mitarbeitende in Osteuropa?	table24.csv	[(1, 3)]	['0']
2	2	0	0	Wie hoch ist das Kreditrisiko von physischen Risikoarten?	table3.csv	[(1, 2)]	['mittel']
3	6	0	0	Wie hoch sind die direkten THG-Emissionen für Scope 1 für den Immobiliensektor?	table7.csv	[(0, 3)]	['212']
4	56	1	0	Wie viele Frauen arbeiten im Bankensektor im Jahr 2022?	hypo54.csv	[(7, 4)]	['408']
...	...	...	...	...	...	...	...
605	122	7	0	Wie Viele weibliche Mitarbeitende in Teilzeit gab es im Jahr 2023?	volks77teil3.csv	[(0, 3)]	['1248']
606	124	5	0	Wieviele männliche Betriebsräte hatte die Volksbank Salzburg eG im Jahr 2023?	volks87teil2.csv	[(0, 4)]	['3']
607	13	2	0	Wie viele männliche Mitarbeitende im Durchschnitt gibt es im Immobiliensektor?	table14.csv	[(2, 3)]	['227.26']
608	53	4	0	Welchen Anteil am Umsatz hatte Österreich im Jahr 2022?	hypo27.csv	[(0, 2)]	['90.76%']
...	...	...	...	...	...	...	...

Figure 3: Illustration of a sample of annotated dataset entries.

lows for future extensibility. Features such as text highlighting, multi-span selection, and abstractive answer support could be added with minor frontend and backend extensions. Similarly, the tool could incorporate automatic question suggestions, user roles for collaborative annotation, and quality control mechanisms like annotator agreement metrics.

The system also allows for scalable expansion of the dataset with domain-specific questions, supporting future iterations of fine-tuning and evaluation. Although no formal annotation guidelines were enforced in the current version, the simplicity of the interface and the constrained question type ensured consistent and high-quality annotations across users.

5 Use Case and Evaluation

5.1 Domain Adaptation Scenarios

The dataset introduced in this work supports domain-specific question answering over tabular data in German. Two TAPAS-based models were fine-tuned using this dataset: one on governmental data and the other on sustainability reports.

The first model, TAPASGO, was obtained by fine-tuning the original TAPAS architecture on a newly created corpus of German-language governmental tables. This resulted in a German-adapted variant capable of understanding and extracting information from structured public-sector data, as documented in Kowieski et al. (2024). While TAPASGO performed well on general tabular content, it showed limitations when applied to domain-specific contexts such as sustainability reporting.

To address this, TAPASGO was further fine-tuned on a set of annotated tables extracted from sustainability reports published by major European banking institutions. This phase used 80% of the sustainability-specific QA pairs to adapt the model to the specialized terminology, structures, and question patterns typical of ESG-related data. As discussed next, the remaining 20% of the annotated examples were reserved for evaluation. Fine-tuning followed the same hyperparameter configuration as the original TAPASGO setup (Kowieski et al., 2024), using a learning rate of $5e-5$, a batch size of 13, and training for 100 epochs.

5.2 Evaluation and Test Results

The held-out test set was used to evaluate the performance of the fine-tuned TAPASGO model in comparison to both the original TAPAS and the initial TAPASGO baseline trained only on governmental data.

The primary evaluation metric was Exact Match (EM) accuracy, which measures whether the predicted answer cell content exactly matches the ground-truth text. Results demonstrate a substantial improvement in domain-specific accuracy following fine-tuning on the sustainability dataset. The adapted TAPASGO model showed significantly better precision in identifying the correct cell and understanding the semantics of domain-specific questions.

These results highlight the effectiveness of domain-specific fine-tuning in enhancing TQA performance on specialized corpora. They also reinforce the importance of aligning QA models with the structural and linguistic characteristics of the target domain to achieve high accuracy and practical utility.

5.3 Annotation Efficiency

To evaluate the efficiency of the annotation process using the custom annotation tool, the time required for creating question–answer pairs was analyzed. The annotators, a mix of employees and researchers from the research institution, interacted with the tool to generate questions and select the corresponding answers.

Due to the simplicity of the interface, annotators quickly adapted to the tool's functionality. However, the initial phase of question formulation proved challenging. For first-time users, understanding the structure of the presented tables, reading through them, and formulating valid questions took approximately 10 minutes for the first three questions. This steep initial learning curve was primarily due to the need to familiarize themselves with the table structure and identify patterns for meaningful question generation.

Once annotators became accustomed to the process, their efficiency improved significantly. They could generate five high-quality question–answer pairs in approximately 5 to 6 minutes. This indicates a marked improvement in annotation speed after overcoming the initial adjustment period.

The tool's intuitive design and the simplicity of its requirements, such as single-cell answer selection, contributed to this efficiency. By ensuring ease of use, the annotation process became streamlined, enabling annotators to focus on question quality rather than tool navigation.

6 Conclusion and Future Work

The present work presents a German-language dataset and a custom-built annotation tool for Tabular Question Answering. While 2/3 of it is based on general governmental tabular data, a third of the data focuses on sustainability reporting. By combining structured data from governmental sources and the complex, structured data found in ESG-related disclosures, the dataset offers both thematic depth and generalizability, addressing a gap in existing non-Englisch TQA resources.

TQA Model	EM accuracy
TAPAS	17.9%
TAPASGO baseline	28.5%
TAPASGO fine-tuned	94.3%

Table 2: Exact Match (EM) accuracy of different TQA models on the held-out sustainability test set.

The annotation tool enabled efficient, high-precision span-based question–answer creation, even by non-technical users, though it currently lacks support for complex annotations. Its simple, constraint-driven interface allowed for the efficient creation of factoid question–answer pairs based on single-table cell selection. The decision to enforce a span-based answer format, despite being a limitation, ensured a high degree of answer precision, which is particularly relevant in regulatory and technical contexts such as sustainability reporting. While the tool currently lacks support for more complex annotations like multi-span or abstractive answers, its modular design allows for potential extensions in this direction.

Fine-tuning experiments demonstrated that domain-specific data significantly improves model performance, highlighting the value of tailored datasets. While the original TAPAS and a version fine-tuned on governmental data alone yielded modest results, the model adapted with sustainability-specific examples achieved a significant performance boost.

Looking forward, the project aims to foster community-driven development through public release and enhancements such as semi-automated annotation, broader answer formats, and active learning strategies, laying the groundwork for robust, domain-aware TQA in German language. Lessons learned during the annotation process included that providing clear, concise examples and task definitions for annotators significantly improved consistency. Additionally, domain-specific knowledge, while helpful, was not essential due to the limited question types and structure of the tool. User feedback was generally positive, particularly regarding the clarity and ease of use of the tool. However, commentators expressed a desire for features such as automatic question suggestions or better handling of ambiguous table entries, which could be important for future revisions of the tool.

Acknowledgments

We would like to thank our former team member Dominik Kowieski for his excellent contributions and valuable discussions.

Further, the financial support from the Austrian Federal Ministry of Labour and Economy, the National Foundation for Research, Technology and Development and the Christian Doppler Research Association is gratefully acknowledged.

References

Wenhu Chen, Hongmin Wang, Jianshu Chen, Yunkai Zhang, Hong Wang, Shiyang Li, Xiyou Zhou, and William Yang Wang. 2020. Tabfact: A large-scale dataset for table-based fact verification. *Preprint*, arXiv:1909.02164.

Ferderal Office of Statistics Germany DESTATIS. 2013. German tabular data.

Jacob Devlin and *et al.* 2019. Bert: Pre-training of deep bidirectional transformers for language understanding. *arXiv:1810.04805*, arXiv:1810.04805.

Julian Martin Eisenschlos, Syrine Krichene, and Thomas Müller. 2020. Understanding tables with intermediate pre-training. *Preprint*, arXiv:2010.00571.

Romina Etezadi and Mehrnoush Shamsfard. 2022. The state of the art in open domain complex question answering: a survey. *Applied Intelligence*, 53.

European Banking Authority (EBA). 2021. Report on management and supvervision of ESG risks for credit institutions and investment firms EBA/REP/2021/18.

European Commission. 2022. Directive (EU) 2022/2464. `http://data.europa.eu/eli/dir/2022/2464/oj`. Accessed: 01.03.2024.

European Union. 2022. Directive (EU) 2022/2464 of the European Parliament and of the Council of 14 December 2022 amending Regulation (EU) No 537/2014, Directive 2004/109/EC, Directive 2006/43/EC and Directive 2013/34/EU, as regards corporate sustainability reporting. European Union, L 322, 16.12.2022, p. 15–80.

Google Research. 2020. Tapas limitation issue.

Jonathan Herzig, Pawel Krzysztof Nowak, Thomas Müller, Francesco Piccinno, and Julian Martin Eisenschlos. 2020. Tapas: Weakly supervised table parsing via pre-training. *Preprint*, arXiv:2004.02349.

Hypo Vorarlberg Bank AG. 2023. Achtsam Wirtschaften - Nachhaltigkeitsbericht 2023.

Konrad Höffner, Sebastian Walter, Edgard Marx, Ricardo Usbeck, Jens Lehmann, and Axel-Cyrille Ngonga Ngomo. 2016. Survey on challenges of question answering in the semantic web. *Semantic Web*, 8.

Mohit Iyyer, Wen-tau Yih, and Ming-Wei Chang. 2017. Search-based neural structured learning for sequential question answering. In *Proceedings of the 55th Annual Meeting of the Association for Computational Linguistics (Volume 1: Long Papers)*, pages 1821–1831, Vancouver, Canada. Association for Computational Linguistics.

Nengzheng Jin, Joanna Siebert, Dongfang Li, and Qingcai Chen. 2022. A survey on table question answering: Recent advances. *Preprint*, arXiv:2207.05270.

Staša Karapandžić and Michael Hellwig. 2025. German Language Dataset and Annotation Tool for Tabular Question Answering. GitHub.com. `https://github.com/jrc-rodec/GermanTQAdataset`.

Dominik Andreas Kowieski, Michael Hellwig, and Thomas Feilhauer. 2024. TAPASGO: Transfer learning towards a German-language tabular question answering model. In *Proceedings of the 2024 Joint International Conference on Computational Linguistics, Language Resources and Evaluation (LREC-COLING 2024)*, pages 15579–15584, Torino, Italia. ELRA and ICCL.

OpenAI. 2023. Gpt-4 technical report. *Preprint*, arXiv:2303.08774.

Panupong Pasupat and Percy Liang. 2015. Compositional semantic parsing on semi-structured tables. In *Proceedings of the 53rd Annual Meeting of the Association for Computational Linguistics and the 7th International Joint Conference on Natural Language Processing (Volume 1: Long Papers)*, pages 1470–1480, Beijing, China. Association for Computational Linguistics.

Hugo Touvron, Thibaut Lavril, Gautier Izacard, Xavier Martinet, Marie-Anne Lachaux, Timothée Lacroix, Baptiste Rozière, Naman Goyal, Eric Hambro, Faisal Azhar, Aurelien Rodriguez, Armand Joulin, Edouard Grave, and Guillaume Lample. 2023. Llama: Open and efficient foundation language models. *Preprint*, arXiv:2302.13971.

Haifeng Wang, Jiwei Li, Hua Wu, Eduard Hovy, and Yu Sun. 2022. Pre-Trained Language Models and Their Applications. *Engineering*.

Zhen Wang. 2022. Modern Question Answering Datasets and Benchmarks: A Survey. *Preprint*, arXiv:2206.15030.

Frank F. Xu, Yufan Song, Boxuan Li, Yuxuan Tang, Kritanjali Jain, Mengxue Bao, Zora Z. Wang, Xuhui Zhou, Zhitong Guo, Murong Cao, Mingyang Yang, Hao Yang Lu, Amaad Martin, Zhe Su, Leander Maben, Raj Mehta, Wayne Chi, Lawrence Jang, Yiqing Xie, and 2 others. 2025. Theagentcompany: Benchmarking llm agents on consequential real world tasks. *Preprint*, arXiv:2412.14161.

Peng Yang, Wenjun Li, Guangzhen Zhao, and Xianyu Zha. 2023. Row-based hierarchical graph network for multi-hop question answering over textual and tabular data. *J. Supercomput.*, 79(9):9795–9818.

Mingyu Zheng, Yang Hao, Wenbin Jiang, Zheng Lin, Yajuan Lyu, QiaoQiao She, and Weiping Wang. 2023a. IM-TQA: A Chinese table question answering dataset with implicit and multi-type table structures. In *Proceedings of the 61st Annual Meeting of the Association for Computational Linguistics (Volume 1: Long Papers)*, pages 5074–5094, Toronto, Canada. Association for Computational Linguistics.

Mingyu Zheng, Yang Hao, Wenbin Jiang, Zheng Lin, Yajuan Lyu, QiaoQiao She, and Weiping Wang. 2023b. IM-TQA: A Chinese table question answering dataset with implicit and multi-type table structures. In *Proceedings of the 61st Annual Meeting of the Association for Computational Linguistics (Volume 1: Long Papers)*, pages 5074–5094, Toronto, Canada. Association for Computational Linguistics.

Victor Zhong, Caiming Xiong, and Richard Socher. 2017. Seq2sql: Generating structured queries from natural language using reinforcement learning. *Preprint*, arXiv:1709.00103.

Gap in pagination due to formatting issues.

Pages 301-305

Overview of the GermEval 2025 Shared Task on Harmful Content Detection

Jenny Felser and Michael Spranger
Mittweida University of Applied Sciences
Technikumplatz 17
09648 Mittweida

Melanie Siegel
Darmstadt University of Applied Sciences
Schöfferstr. 3
64295 Darmstadt

Abstract

Social media is not only a channel for the appropriate sharing of personal opinions and enriching discussions, but also facilitates the dissemination of inappropriate and aggressive statements. Those are especially concerning when they actively incite harmful actions such as violence or attacks on the government. Against this background, this paper presents the GermEval Shared Task for Harmful Content Detection, which addresses three subtasks that have been largely neglected in previous competitions and research projects: the detection of 1) calls to action, 2) attacks against the liberal democratic basic order and 3) violence-supporting statements. For this pilot task, 11,551 tweets from a German Twitter network belonging to an extremist group were annotated. A total of eleven teams participated in at least one of the three subtasks, with nine teams submitting a system paper. Overall, macro-average F_1-scores of up to 87% were achieved for subtasks 1 and 3 and up to 71% for subtask 2.

Content warning: We show illustrative examples of harmful content.

1 Introduction

Social media allows users to express their opinions, views and perceptions freely. However, the downside of freedom of expression is that increasingly toxic, hateful and aggressive content is being spread. That does not only include the mere expression of hurtful comments but goes so far as to incite other people to hate or even call for violent action. One of the best-known examples is the murder of Walter Lübcke, in which hate comments were posted by those involved in the crime in advance, which also contained calls for murder and incitement to overthrow the government violently (Thorwarth, 2023). From a prevention perspective, it is therefore essential to recognise incitement, advocacy of violence, and even incitement of violence in good time to take countermeasures. In this way, for example, moderators of online social networks may be assisted in removing harmful content.

Another focus in connection with current political developments is (verbal) attacks on the liberal Democratic Basic Order (DBO) by subversive movements. In 2024, the German Federal Office for the Protection of the Constitution warned that right-wing extremists, for example, are using microblogging services such as X (formerly Twitter) to spread propaganda, mobilise supporters and even announce attacks (Bundesamt für Verfassungsschutz, 2024). In this context, the detection of harmful content such as incitement to violence and subversive tendencies is not only essential from a preventive perspective, but also supports law enforcement authorities in analysing mass communication in social networks during criminal investigations.

Against this background, we are introducing the GermEval Shared Task on Harmful Content Detection. This shared task aims to initiate and promote research into the detection of three particularly worrying types of harmful content in German social media posts: 1) so-called calls to action, 2) attacks on the DBO and 3) worryingly positive statements about violence. For this purpose, three new German-language Twitter datasets were created, each based on the annotation of more than 11,500 tweets from the network of a right-wing extremist group. The eleven teams participating in the competition made an initial contribution to addressing the three tasks, which have hardly been tackled to date.

The remainder of this overview paper is structured as follows: section 2 provides an overview of related work, and section 3 presents the three subtasks addressed. The dataset and its creation are described in section 4. Section 5 presents the evaluation and the baseline systems, before section 6 discusses the approaches and results of the participants. Finally, we conclude in section 7.

Proceedings of the 21st Conference on Natural Language Processing (KONVENS), Volume 2: Workshops, pages 306–319, 2025

Objective/ task	Competition	Language
offensive language detection	GermEval 2018 (Wiegand et al., 2018) GermEval 2019 (Struß et al., 2019) GermEval 2021 (Risch et al., 2021)	German German German
hate speech detection	HASOC 2020 (Mandl et al., 2020) HASOC 2022 (Satapara et al., 2022)	German, English, Hindi German, Hinglish
sexism and/or misogyny detection	GermEval 2024 (Gross et al., 2024) EXIST 2025	German English, Spanish
classification of conspiracy theories	PAN 2024 (Korenčić et al., 2024)	English, Spanish
political bias detection	SemEval 2019 (Kiesel et al., 2019)	English
	CheckThat! 2023 (Barrón-Cedeño et al., 2023)	English
classification of violence incitements	BLP-2023 (Saha et al., 2023)	Bangla

Table 1: Overview of previous shared tasks in the area of detecting harmful, hartful or problematic content

2 Related Work

Harmful content in general has already been addressed by numerous shared tasks, with some examples listed in Table 1. However, earlier GermEval shared tasks focused mainly on the detection of offensive (toxic) language (e.g. Wiegand et al., 2018). Closely related to this task is the detection of hate speech and sexism, for which German-language resources have also been developed as part of shared tasks (e.g. Mandl et al., 2020). However, the focus has not yet been on detecting calls to action, attacks on the DBO, and incitement to violence:

Detection of calls to action. To our knowledge, calls to action detection has not been addressed by any previous shared tasks, and only a few datasets have been created in a small number of research projects in this area (e.g. Siskou et al., 2022). However, those did not focus on the German language and only considered a specific type of call to action, such as calls for harmful actions against a particular ethnic group (Pérez et al., 2023) or for the mobilisation of voters during an election in Spanish social media (Siskou et al., 2022). One of the few studies based on a German-language dataset of 1,388 Instagram posts aimed to identify calls to action in the context of the 2021 German federal elections (Achmann-Denkler et al., 2024). In contrast, subtask 1 of our shared task encompasses not only the mobilisation of voters, but also the identification of all calls to action, including those for rallies, demonstrations and protests.

The identification of calls for protests and gatherings has previously been investigated by Rogers et al. (2019), for example, using Russian tweets. However, as the authors themselves point out, the problem is that authoritarian regimes could abuse such methods to track down and suppress legitimate protests. The motivation behind the first subtask of the shared task, by contrast, is to identify and manually check calls with the express aim of distinguishing legitimate calls for protest from those inciting violent acts, and to support security force decision-makers in planning resources for potentially dangerous situations.

Detection of attacks on the DBO. Furthermore, there have been no shared tasks or other research projects to date that deal with the detection of subversive intentions and further attacks on the DBO. Instead, some shared tasks addressed the classification of conspiracy theories (Korenčić et al., 2024) and political bias (e.g. Kiesel et al., 2019) (see Table 1), which may also be expressed in anti-government tweets attacking the DBO. However, the data used for these shared tasks did not include German texts and, in some cases, consisted of newspaper articles (Kiesel et al., 2019; Barrón-Cedeño et al., 2023), which differ greatly from social media posts in terms of language and length.

In addition, research projects have focused on identifying verbal accusations against the government (e.g. Lemmens et al., 2022; Corral et al.,

2024), such as allegations of hypocrisy against politicians (Corral et al., 2024). Furthermore, efforts have been made to identify extremist views (e.g. Gaikwad et al., 2022). However, this work differs from our second subtask in that the latter involves deciding whether concrete actions against the government are planned, which is particularly important in terms of timely preventive measures.

Violence detection The only shared task dedicated to the announcement of violence uses YouTube comments in Bangla as its data source, with transformer models explicitly developed for Bangla achieving the best results (Saha et al., 2023). Another interesting study aimed to use a convolutional neural network to detect calls for violence in Urdu tweets (Khan et al., 2024). In addition to the fact that these studies did not address the German language, the third subtask stands out in that it is not only a matter of recognising incitements of violence, but also other types of questionable statements about violence, such as the glorification of violence. The task of recognising whether violence is being discussed in social media has already been addressed by Cano Basave et al. (2013) for English. However, they did not evaluate the authors' attitudes towards violent events.

In summary, the new shared task makes an essential contribution to research into the detection of harmful content, particularly concerning the German language, by providing new data sets.

3 Task Description

Participants were allowed to take part in one, two or all three subtasks, with up to three runs per subtask. All subtasks were designed as open tracks, where participants can use external datasets that have been annotated for the subtasks or related tasks (e.g. Gross et al., 2024). This decision was made to encourage data enrichment strategies that may be promising given the imbalance of the dataset described in section 4. Specifically, the shared task comprised the following subtasks:

Subtask 1: Detection of Calls to Action The first subtask was a binary decision as to whether a tweet contained a call to action (TRUE) or not (FALSE). According to the Oxford Dictionary definition, a call to action is defined as a command or request to perform a specific action or behaviour (Oxford University Press, 2024). This action may be criminally relevant if it is incited or encouraged, but this is not necessarily the case. It could also be a call for a legitimate demonstration. Examples[1] of calls to action are:

- AWO abschaffen. (engl. Abolish AWO)
- Ihr müsst schnell handeln ,sonst ist es zu spät.Ansonsten haben die uns schon überrannt. (engl. You have to act quickly, otherwise it will be too late. Otherwise, they will have overrun us.)

Subtask 2: Classification of attacks on the DBO The second subtask consists of a fine-grained classification in four categories (subversive, agitation, criticism, nothing) concerning various harmless and harmful forms of *attacks on the DBO of the Federal Republic of Germany*:

- **subversive:** Based on the definition in the Duden dictionary, a subversive tweet expresses the desire to overthrow the current government or state order violently, e.g. through militant action or paralysing the power grid (Duden, 2025).
- **agitation:** The tweet conveys inflammatory intentions against the DBO, such as the dissemination of propaganda by unconstitutional and terrorist organisations as defined in Section 86 of the German Criminal Code (StGB) or the defacement of state symbols such as the flag of the Federal Republic of Germany (§ 90a StGB).
- **criticism :** The tweet contains legal but negative criticism of the government, civil servants, government employees, authorities or political parties.
- **nothing:** The tweet does not contain any attacks on the DBO. Neutral or positive statements about government decisions also fall into this category.

Examples of tweets from each category in the training data set can be found in Table 2.

Subtask 3: Violence Detection The third task is determining whether the tweets express a disturbingly positive attitude towards violence (TRUE,

[1]All examples shown in this paper are taken from the newly created training dataset. Spelling mistakes were not corrected. An English translation is provided for each tweet.

Label	Example
subversive	...dieser Wahnsinn muss aufhören...weg mit dieser VolksVerräterVerrücktenRegierung...!!!
	...this madness must stop...away with this traitorous, crazy government...!!!
agitation	was für gesetze machen die eigentlich ‚EU ??? ‚kassieren 20.000 im Monat und lassen uns untergehen , EUROPA - Asoziale Politik .
	What kind of laws are they making, EU??? They earn 20,000 a month and let us go under, EUROPE – anti-social politics.
criticism	Die Polizei wird nur unnötig unter Druck gesetzt, wenn ständig irgendwelche Gegendemos genehmigt werden.
	The police are only put under unnecessary pressure if counter-demonstrations are constantly being authorised.
nothing	Sachsen ist Deutschland und Deutschland ist Sachsen
	Saxony is Germany, and Germany is Saxony.

Table 2: Examples of tweets from the categories *subversive*, *agitation*, *criticism* and *nothing* of the second subtask, each with an English translation.

FALSE). Such disturbing statements include trivialisation, support, glorification, incitement or announcement of violent acts, such as:

- *jo TOT gefallen sie mir auch am besten :)* (engl. *Yes, I like them best dead too :)*)
- *Der Schießbefehl muss unverzüglich gegeben werden* (engl. *The order to shoot must be given immediately.*)

4 Data Set

The primary source of data was previously collected, unannotated German tweets, which were annotated for the three subtasks. Underrepresented categories were supplemented with tweets from existing German datasets on hate speech detection (Demus et al., 2022; Kums et al., 2025).

4.1 Initial data collection

The bulk of the training and test data for the three subtasks is based on public German Twitter posts and comments in the context of a group considered as right-wing extremist. This data source was chosen because the Shared Task focuses on the German language, and content from the group's environment was expected to frequently serve mobilisation purposes, including calls for high-risk actions and actions against the government. The posts and comments were initially collected by members of Mittweida University of Applied Sciences from December 2014 to July 2016. For the annotation, a sample of posts and corresponding comments was selected from over 800,000 tweets, linking them via their respective post IDs. The sample comprised a total of 11,551 tweets to be annotated, including 54 posts.

To ensure anonymity, user mentions were semi-automatically replaced by [@PRE] for mentions of the press, [@POL] for the police, [@GRP] for groups and [@IND] for individuals. In this way, the information about who the tweet is addressed to can still be used to develop the models.

4.2 Data annotation

Members of Mittweida University of Applied Sciences annotated the 11,551 tweets. A total of 88 people were involved in the annotation process. The dataset was split into samples of around 500 tweets, each of which was annotated independently by four annotators, i.e., each annotator labelled approximately 500 tweets. The annotators were either students or research assistants in digital forensics and had expertise in identifying the characteristics of harmful textual content. They had confirmed their consent to the publication of the data in writing. The annotators were provided with comprehensive annotation guidelines and allowed to use external resources, such as dictionaries for unknown terms, in the comments.

Subtask 3 was originally annotated at a fine granularity, categorising worrying positive statements about violence into five subtypes (propensity, call to violence, support, glorification, other forms). However, since initial analyses showed that some categories were severely underrepresented, this task was converted into a binary classification.

For the binary detection of calls to action, the annotators could also indicate that they were unable to judge this. In addition to the annotations required for this shared task, the data set was annotated for hate speech, toxicity, target and emotions to support the classification tasks.

The final data sets for each subtask contained all tweets on which a majority decision was reached among the four annotators. In the case of the first subtask, tweets were also sorted out where the majority of annotators stated that they were unable to evaluate the tweet. The resulting datasets comprised 9,822 tweets for the first subtask, 9,307 for the second subtask, and 10,933 for the third subtask. The Fleiss kappa coefficient (Fleiss, 1971) was calculated for these data sets. The agreement between the four annotators was $\kappa = 0.391$ for the first subtask, $\kappa = 0.416$ for the second subtask, and $\kappa = 0.376$ for the third subtask. According to Landis and Koch (1977), these results correspond to a fair agreement for subtasks 1 and 3 and a moderate agreement for subtask 2, with the values for subtasks 1 and 2 close to the threshold of above 0.4 for moderate agreement. The relatively low level of agreement, even when compared to annotations of other types of harmful content, such as offensive language (e.g. Wiegand et al., 2018; Demus et al., 2022), can be attributed not only to the lack of annotation experience of the majority of annotators, but also to the complexity of the tasks and subjective differences in assessment. For example, when deciding at what point statements relating to violence should be classified as problematic. The following tweet, for instance, was assigned to the violence category by the majority of annotators.

> Baut das Ding. Am besten aus Asbest... (engl. Build that thing. Preferably out of asbestos...)

Although it seems likely that the tweet expresses a desire to cause someone physical harm, without knowing what kind of building is being referred to, it is difficult to assess whether there is a connection to violence.

4.3 Data augmentation

An initial analysis of the data sets revealed that the relevant categories were significantly underrepresented, particularly in subtasks 2 and 3. For subtask 2, for example, the data set contained only 29 subversive posts and 49 tweets with inflammatory content. In subtask 3, the proportion of violence-related statements was only 5.67%. Therefore, the data sets for the two subtasks were enriched as follows:

Subtask 2: For subtask 2, another annotator identified comments from the two German-language X (formely Twitter) datasets Detox (Demus et al., 2022) and the dataset described by Kums et al. (2025) from the field of hate speech that could be assigned to the four subclasses. The focus was particularly on enriching the two categories, subversive and agitation. Overall, the original dataset for the second subtask was expanded by 1,341 tweets.

Subtask 3: For the third subtask, the TRUE category (violence-related statements) was enriched using the hate speech dataset by Kums et al. (2025). In this dataset, the comments were manually classified relating to different offences under the Criminal Code. Only the 211 comments assigned to the category *Public Incitement to Commit Crimes and Disturbing the Public Peace*[2] were considered for enrichment, which were most likely to contain problematic, violence-related statements. These comments were re-annotated by a shared task organiser. 185 comments could be added to the violence category. The remaining comments were highly racist but did not directly refer to violence and were therefore not relevant to subtask 3.

Details about the composition of the data sets after augmentation are listed in subsection A.1.

4.4 Data splitting

The resulting data sets for the three subtasks comprised approximately 9,000 to 11,000 tweets, with a high degree of overlap of 7,708 tweets. The data sets for each subtask were split into training and test data using stratified sampling in a ratio of 70:30. In addition, a stratified sample of approximately 1,000 tweets was taken from the annotated training data and used as trial data. Those were published prior to the training data so that participants could familiarise themselves with the data format. All data sets were made available as semicolon-separated

[2] This category includes offences that are punishable under §111 StGB, §126 StGB, §130 StGB, §131 StGB, §140 StGB (Kums et al., 2025).

CSV files on GitHub[3]. For each tweet, only the ID was provided in addition to its text content; no other metadata was included. An example of the data format can be found in subsection A.2.

4.5 Description of the resulting data sets

Class distribution The size and class distribution of the training and test data for the three subtasks are given in Table 3. All data sets were highly unbalanced, with a low proportion of relevant and harmful content. This observation is consistent with the class distribution of data sets that have been annotated for the detection of other hurtful content, such as offensive language (Struß et al., 2019). The problem of imbalance is most evident in the fine-grained classification in subtask 2 for detecting attacks on the DBO (see second row in Table 3). The category subversive is particularly underrepresented, which presumably – and in a way fortunately – also reflects the actual, rare occurrence of such tweets in social media.

Linguistic properties Aside from the considerable imbalance in the data sets, another challenge is the linguistic characteristics of the tweets. To illustrate this, Table 4 presents the average usage of some token types in the tweets of the training data sets for the three subtasks.

Property	Subtask		
	(1)	(2)	(3)
∅ tokens	29.35	27.44	29.64
∅ chars	158.40	150.20	161.50
∅ emoticons	0.19	0.19	0.20
∅ capslock	0.33	0.33	0.36
∅ hashtags	0.02	0.09	0.03
∅ mentions	0.01	0.13	0.01

Table 4: Statistical description of the trainining data sets for (1) call to action detection, (2) detection of attacks on the DBO, (3) detection of worrying violence-related statements.

The tweets all have a small number of tokens (words, but also other units such as punctuation marks, symbols, etc.), which poses a challenge for text classification (Alsmadi and Gan, 2019). In addition, they contain components typical of social media, such as emoticons and caps lock[4]. The differences between the datasets were mostly minor, which can be explained by the high degree of overlap. However, the dataset from subtask 2 contains more hashtags and mentions than the other two datasets. A detailed analysis of the hashtags and mentions in the individual categories would go beyond the scope of this paper. An initial analysis showed that @IND mentions were most common in the dataset for subtask 2, mostly in response to another tweet and using hashtags referring to politicians, for instance *#Merkel* and *#MerkelMussWeg* or using the Hitler salute *#SiegHeil*.

5 Evaluation metrics and baselines

As with previous shared tasks by GermEval (e.g. Gross et al., 2024; Schomacker et al., 2024), the Codabench platform[5] was used for evaluation. The competition submissions were ranked using the macro-average F_1-score. This evaluation metric is an obvious choice, as all classes are treated equally instead of giving greater importance to the detection of harmless, overrepresented content. Accordingly, the macro-average F_1-score has already been used as the primary evaluation metric in previous shared tasks for detecting harmful content (Wiegand et al., 2018; Struß et al., 2019; Risch et al., 2021). Apart from that, the macro-average precision and recall were calculated.

A simple baseline system was developed for each subtask (classical methods, embeddings, large language models (LLMs)), and the code was published on GitHub[6]. The baselines represent obvious approaches and are intended to encourage participants to try out alternative, more innovative methods:

Subtask 1: For the first subtask, a gradient boosting classifier (Friedman, 2001) was used, whereby the tweets were represented as dense vectors using a pre-trained Sentence BERT model (Reimers and Gurevych, 2019). As an additional feature, the polarity score of the tweet was used, which was determined with a lexicon-based method using the TextBlob library (Loria, 2018). The underrepresentation of calls to action was addressed by random

[3]https://github.com/Communication-Forensics-Lab/harmful-content-detection/tree/main/data

[4]words written entirely in capital letters

[5]https://www.codabench.org/competitions/4963/

[6]https://github.com/Communication-Forensics-Lab/harmful-content-detection/tree/main/baseline

Subtask	Class Label	Training Data Freq	Training Data %	Test Data Freq	Test Data %
(1) Calls to action	TRUE	663	9.69	289	9.69
	FALSE	6177	90.31	2693	90.31
	Total	6840	100.00	2982	100.00
(2) Attacks on the DBO	subversive	60	0.80	25	0.78
	agitation	313	4.20	134	4.20
	criticism	804	10.79	345	10.80
	nothing	6277	84.21	2690	84.22
	Total	7454	100.00	3194	100.00
(3) Violence-related statements	TRUE	564	7.25	241	7.23
	FALSE	7219	92.75	3094	92.77
	Total	7783	100.00	3335	100.00

Table 3: Class distribution of training and test data in the three subtasks.

undersampling, after which the two categories contained the same number of tweets.

Subtask 2: A simple classification approach based on a linear Support Vector Machine (SVM) (Chang and Lin, 2011) with TF-IDF-weighted bag-of-phrases (unigrams and bigrams) was chosen as the baseline system. The vocabulary was limited to the 5000 most frequent phrases in the training data set. The class imbalance was taken into account by a cost-sensitive (weighted) SVM, in which misclassifications of instances from underrepresented classes are more penalised.

Subtask 3: For the third subtask, classification was performed by the generative open source large language model Qwen2.5 (Bai et al., 2023) with 32 billion parameters. In-context learning was chosen as the prompting strategy, which has already proven promising in the detection of related harmful content such as hate speech (Assis et al., 2024; Sahin et al., 2023). Details on prompt engineering can be found in Appendix A.

6 Results

A total of eleven teams participated in at least one subtask of the shared task, with six teams participating in all three subtasks. A summarised statistic of the macro-average F_1-score achieved in the individual tasks can be found in Table 5. As the table shows, the results achieved by the individual teams vary greatly. In the second task in particular, the range of scores was approximately 41%. The macro-average F_1-score for this subtask also showed the highest standard deviation, indicating that the effectiveness of the systems varied greatly. On average, higher values were achieved for subtasks 1 and 3 than for subtask 2. Possible causes can be found in the strong imbalance of the training data set for subtask 2.

Subtask 1: Participation was highest in the detection of calls to action: a total of 20 valid runs were submitted by nine teams, with the results listed in Table 6. In this subtask, F_1 scores of up to 86.98% were achieved, with the two highest results being obtained by *SuperGLEBer*. This team fine-tuned the ModernGBERT 1B model (Ehrmanntraut et al., 2025) for their third run, the best-performing run, and an LLäMmlein 7B model (Pfister et al., 2025) for their second run. In addition, all but one run outperformed the baseline, the gradient boosting classifier.

Subtask 2: We received a total of 16 valid runs from seven teams for the classification of attacks on the DBO, with the results shown in Table 7. The run submitted by the *munich_z* team during the competition phase was invalid. After the end of the competition, the team submitted three valid runs, which are marked in grey in Table 7 for assessment of system performance, but were not included in the summary statistics in Table 5. Considering the results, it is apparent that the macro-average F_1 values achieved were lower than those of the other

Subtask	# Teams	# Valid Runs	Min	Max	Median	Mean	SD
(1) call to action	9	20	53.93	86.98	78.81	76.27	8.94
(2) DBO	7	16	29.86	71.22	64.63	59.09	14.56
(3) violence	8	17	67.12	86.76	79.10	77.19	5.64

Table 5: Summary statistics of the macro-average F_1-scores achieved in the three subtasks.

two subtasks, with the team *nymera* achieving the best value of 71.22% with an ensemble of three different finely tuned BERT variants. Six teams were able to exceed the SVM baseline.

Subtask 3: The results achieved for the detection of worrying, violence-related statements, are illustrated in Table 8. A total of 17 valid runs were submitted by eight teams, with the best macro-average F_1-score of 86.76% again achieved by *SuperGLEBer*, this time with the LLäMmlein 7B model (Pfister et al., 2025) (run two by *SuperGLEBer*) outperforming the ModernGBERT 1B (Ehrmanntraut et al., 2025) (run 3) model. Furthermore, almost all teams except one exceeded the baseline using the Qwen2.5 model (Bai et al., 2023).

team	run	P	R	F_1
SuperGLEBer	**3**	**86.70**	**87.26**	**86.98**
SuperGLEBer	2	85.70	85.15	85.42
nymera	2	84.99	82.26	83.56
HSH;-)	2	82.97	84.09	83.52
nymera	3	84.65	81.40	82.92
nymera	1	84.30	80.86	82.46
abullardUR	3	79.36	86.12	82.25
abullardUR	2	81.60	82.57	82.08
HSH;-)	1	80.82	83.08	81.89
FI-CODE	2	81.33	77.70	79.37
LabelLords	1	79.35	77.25	78.25
NLPeace	2	81.44	75.77	78.23
mzb	2	73.77	82.08	77.01
FI-CODE	1	78.73	72.53	75.13
mzb	1	77.19	68.35	71.63
tweetbusters	3	68.02	64.54	66.01
tweetbusters	1	68.57	63.03	65.10
tweetbusters	2	68.57	63.03	65.10
LabelLords	2	62.39	71.60	64.64
baseline	-	*59.88*	*74.75*	*59.13*
NLPeace	1	54.98	61.37	53.93

Table 6: Results of subtask 1: the detection of calls to action. The macro-average of the precision (P), recall (R) and F_1 measures are given respectively.

team	run	P	R	F_1
nymera	**3**	**72.81**	**70.54**	**71.22**
SuperGLEBer	3	74.50	65.78	69.21
nymera	2	72.43	66.81	69.21
TheDBOs	2	72.94	66.02	68.59
TheDBOs	3	66.14	74.93	68.07
TheDBOs	1	68.37	66.48	67.34
HSH;-)	2	68.92	66.46	66.49
nymera	1	67.89	65.49	66.25
SuperGLEBer	2	68.07	59.98	63.01
FI-CODE	1	68.21	63.15	62.77
abullardUR	2	58.30	69.14	62.60
FI-CODE	2	63.82	62.04	62.36
abullardUR	3	53.81	61.08	56.38
baseline	-	*54.75*	*51.35*	*47.44*
munich_z	2	37.42	47.19	38.11
munich_z	1	36.88	55.50	37.41
munich_z	3	34.70	46.01	32.68
mzb	2	35.62	48.58	31.52
mzb	1	33.66	46.08	30.64
mzb	3	32.84	46.51	29.86

Table 7: Results of subtask 2: classification of different attacks on the DBO. The macro-average of the precision (P), recall (R) and F_1 values are specified.

General Conclusions: The following discussion focuses on the approaches of nine of the eleven participating teams for which a system description was available[7]. Eight of these nine teams used a neural (large) language model for at least one of their runs, with fine-tuning of German or multilingual variants of BERT such as $\text{GBERT}_{\text{Base}}$ (Chan et al., 2020) and XLM-RoBERTa (Conneau et al., 2020) on the training data of the shared task being a particularly popular approach (e.g., *FI-Code*, *HSH;-)*). ModernGBERT 1B ranked among the top three performing systems in all three subtasks (see *SuperGLEBer* run 3 in all subtasks). The smaller ModernGBERT 134M (e.g., *abullardUR*) yielded

[7]The systems used by the mzb and LabelLords teams are not covered here.

team	run	P	R	F_1
SuperGLEBer	**2**	**89.02**	**84.80**	**86.76**
SuperGLEBer	3	86.13	82.93	84.44
mzb	2	81.85	81.49	81.67
abullardUR	2	82.16	80.93	81.53
abullardUR	3	81.36	80.64	81.00
nymera	3	87.01	75.96	80.33
HSH;-)	2	84.04	76.74	79.86
nymera	1	82.64	76.42	79.13
nymera	2	88.40	73.82	79.10
HSH;-)	1	80.29	73.43	76.33
NLPeace	2	82.02	72.59	76.32
FI-CODE	1	73.62	75.51	74.52
FI-CODE	2	73.62	75.51	74.52
NLPeace	1	67.38	81.16	71.44
mzb	1	71.79	69.94	70.81
baseline	*1*	*65.32*	*88.36*	*68.97*
LabelLords	2	64.43	73.64	67.38
LabelLords	1	64.36	72.61	67.12

Table 8: Results of subtask 3: Detection of worrying, violent statements. The macro-average of the precision (P), recall (R) and F_1 values are listed.

more modest results, especially in the first two subtasks, illustrating that model size has a crucial influence on performance, alongside training data and architecture. Another promising approach was the use of a soft voting ensemble consisting of various German (Chan et al., 2020), multilingual (Conneau et al., 2020) and English (He et al., 2021) BERT-based models (Conneau et al., 2020) (e.g., *nymera*), even achieving the best result for subtask 2.

Some teams used modern open-source LLMs, including Mixtral-8x7B-Instruct-v0.1 (Jiang et al., 2024), Qwen-3 32B (Yang et al., 2025) and LLäMmlein 7B (Pfister et al., 2025) (e.g., *NLPeace, munich_z, SuperGLEBer*). Remarkably, LLäMmlein achieved second place in subtask 1 and first place in subtask 3, while other LLM-based approaches mostly failed to exceed the baseline (e.g., *NLPeace* in subtask 1, *munich_z* in subtask 2). One explanation is probably that LLäMmlein was trained exclusively on German-language texts. In systematic comparisons of over 30 models, the *SuperGLEBer* team also demonstrated that models optimised for German outperform multilingual LLMs such as Qwen. Furthermore, SuperGLEBer was the only team to fine-tune an LLM, while the other teams (i.e., *NLPeace, Munich_z*) used zero-/few-shot prompting. Although they found that choosing suitable prompts improved the results, LLMs not specifically optimised for German still lagged behind the fine-tuned, smaller BERT-based models. Similarly, the LLM-based baseline system for subtask 3 performed poorly.

None of the top ten systems used classic machine learning methods, which were only investigated in isolated cases (e.g. by *NLPeace, tweetbusters*). Nevertheless, *tweetbusters* achieved a macro-average F_1-score of 66.01% in subtask 1 using extensive feature engineering and a soft voting ensemble, outperforming a few-shot mixtral system (i.e. *NLPeace*) by approximately 12%, indicating that classical approaches can still be competitive.

Finally, six teams explicitly addressed the underrepresentation of harmful content in the training data through approaches such as re-sampling (e.g., *NLPeace, nymera*), suitable loss functions *nymera*, or data augmentation with LLM-generated examples (e.g., *TheDBOs, nymera, abullardUR*), including style changes, e.g., *FI-Code*. Since these strategies were combined with different classification models, it is not easy to assess which method is particularly effective. Nevertheless, it is noteworthy that *TheDBOs* achieved one of the best results in subtask 2. Their approach involved iteratively adding high-quality synthetic tweets generated with an LLM (Dubey et al., 2024), concluding that the quality of the synthetic examples is particularly crucial for success.

Error analysis: We further investigated which examples in the test dataset were easy or difficult for participants. In the first subtask, 51.5% of all examples were correctly classified in all runs, in the second subtask, only 25.6%, and in the third subtask, 68.9%. This observation highlights apparent differences between the subtasks in terms of 'easily classifiable' tweets.

Furthermore, for all subtasks, there were a few tweets in the test dataset that were misclassified in every submitted run (8 tweets in the first, 35 in the second and 6 in the third subtask). These often prove difficult for humans to classify as well. For example, the following tweet was classified by the majority of annotators as subversive in the second subtask, but it is questionable whether it expresses a desire for serious violent overthrow.

> Was für Fachkräfte, wenn die im eigenem Land arbeitslos sind, einfach lächerlich die Politik hier in Deutschland absetzen und von ihren Sesseln schubsen da oben.

pfui ? (engl. What kind of skilled workers are they if they are unemployed in their own country, simply dismissing the politics here in Germany as ridiculous and pushing them out of their seats up there? Disgraceful!)

A detailed error analysis of the individual systems is beyond the scope of this overview paper. However, looking at the best runs for each subtask reveals recurring difficulties. Those include implicit or subtly formulated content, which is consistent with the findings of previous shared tasks for detecting harmful content (e.g. Wiegand et al., 2018). For example, the following tweet was annotated as a call to action, but it does not contain any classic syntactic markers of a call to action, such as the imperative form:

Im Interesse des Weltfrieden hat niemand der IS zu überleben! So wäre das zu händeln! (engl. In the interest of world peace, no one should survive the IS! That is how it should be handled!)

Further cynical or sarcastic tweets make correct classification difficult without general knowledge, such as the following tweet in the criticism category of the second subtask.

DDR 2.0 läßt grüßen (engl. Greetings from DDR 2.0)

Moreover, the following tweet, which is assigned to the violence category of subtask 3, is difficult to classify without further context.

Spende Steakmesserset.... (engl. Donate a steak knife set...)

Very short posts also pose a problem when, for example, calls to action consist of only a few words, e.g. *schießen !!!* (engl. *shoot!!!*) and *einfach nur drüberfahren* (engl. *just run them over*).

7 Conclusion

This paper presents the pilot edition of the GermEval shared task for harmful content detection. This shared task comprised three subtasks: the detection of (1) calls to action, (2) various attacks on the DBO, and (3) worrying violence-related statements. For this purpose, new German-language Twitter datasets (approx. 9k–11k tweets) were constructed, most of which originate from the environment of a right-wing extremist group. A total of eleven teams participated, mainly using German-language or multilingual BERT models. The best systems achieved macro-average F_1-scores of up to 87% in subtasks 1 and 3 and up to 71% in subtask 2. German BERT variants, ensembles of various BERT-based models and modern open-source LLMs developed specifically for German, some of which were fine-tuned using training data supplemented with synthetic examples, were particularly successful.

Despite promising results, there is still room for improvement. For example, multi-task learning was not tested by any team, although it has already shown success for related classification problems (e.g. Kancharla et al., 2025). In addition, the datasets have limitations in terms of low inter-annotator agreement and a substantial under-representation of harmful content. For a possible second edition of the shared task, the annotation of further data is therefore planned, which should also enable the third task to be aligned as a fine-grained classification in the sense of a finer differentiation of different types of violent statements.

References

Michael Achmann-Denkler, Jakob Fehle, Mario Haim, and Christian Wolff. 2024. Detecting calls to action in multimodal content: Analysis of the 2021 German federal election campaign on Instagram. In *Proceedings of the 4th Workshop on Computational Linguistics for the Political and Social Sciences: Long and Short Papers*, pages 1–13, Vienna, Austria. Association for Computational Linguistics.

Issa Alsmadi and Keng Hoon Gan. 2019. Review of short-text classification. *International Journal of Web Information Systems*, 15(2):155–182.

Gabriel Assis, Annie Amorim, Jonnathan Carvalho, Daniel de Oliveira, Daniela Vianna, and Aline Paes. 2024. Exploring Portuguese Hate Speech Detection in Low-Resource Settings: Lightly Tuning Encoder Models or In-Context Learning of Large Models? In *Proceedings of the 16th International Conference on Computational Processing of Portuguese*, volume 1, pages 301–311, Santiago de Compostela, Galicia/Spain. Association for Computational Lingustics.

Jinze Bai, Shuai Bai, Yunfei Chu, Zeyu Cui, Kai Dang, Xiaodong Deng, Yang Fan, Wenbin Ge, Yu Han, Fei Huang, Binyuan Hui, Luo Ji, Mei Li, Junyang Lin, Runji Lin, Dayiheng Liu, Gao Liu, Chengqiang Lu, Keming Lu, and 29 others. 2023. Qwen Technical Report. *arXiv preprint*.

Alberto Barrón-Cedeño, Firoj Alam, Tommaso Caselli, Giovanni Da San Martino, Tamer Elsayed, Andrea Galassi, Fatima Haouari, Federico Ruggeri, Julia Maria Struß, Rabindra Nath Nandi, Gullal S. Cheema, Dilshod Azizov, and Preslav Nakov. 2023. The CLEF-2023 CheckThat! Lab: Checkworthiness, Subjectivity, Political Bias, Factuality, and Authority. In Jaap Kamps, Lorraine Goeuriot, Fabio Crestani, Maria Maistro, Hideo Joho, Brian Davis, Cathal Gurrin, Udo Kruschwitz, and Annalina Caputo, editors, *Advances in Information Retrieval*, volume 13982, pages 506–517. Springer Nature Switzerland, Cham.

Bundesamt für Verfassungsschutz. 2024. Rechtsextremismus im Internet: Gefahren digitaler Agitation und Radikalisierung. Retrieved 29 August 2025.

Amparo Elizabeth Cano Basave, Yulan He, Kang Liu, and Jun Zhao. 2013. A weakly supervised Bayesian model for violence detection in social media. In *Proceedings of the Sixth International Joint Conference on Natural Language Processing*, pages 109–117, Nagoya, Japan. Asian Federation of Natural Language Processing.

Branden Chan, Stefan Schweter, and Timo Möller. 2020. German's next language model. In *Proceedings of the 28th International Conference on Computational Linguistics*, pages 6788–6796, Barcelona, Spain (Online). International Committee on Computational Linguistics.

Chih-Chung Chang and Chih-Jen Lin. 2011. LIBSVM: A library for support vector machines. *ACM Transactions on Intelligent Systems and Technology*, 2(3):1–27.

Alexis Conneau, Kartikay Khandelwal, Naman Goyal, Vishrav Chaudhary, Guillaume Wenzek, Francisco Guzmán, Edouard Grave, Myle Ott, Luke Zettlemoyer, and Veselin Stoyanov. 2020. Unsupervised cross-lingual representation learning at scale. In *Proceedings of the 58th Annual Meeting of the Association for Computational Linguistics*, pages 8440–8451, Online. Association for Computational Linguistics.

Paulina Garcia Corral, Avishai Green, Hendrik Meyer, Anke Stoll, Xiaoyue Yan, and Myrthe Reuver. 2024. A Few Hypocrites: Few-Shot Learning and Subtype Definitions for Detecting Hypocrisy Accusations in Online Climate Change Debates. In *Proceedings of the 4th Workshop on Computational Linguistics for the Political and Social Sciences: Long and Short Papers*, pages 45–60, Vienna, Austria. Association for Computational Linguistics.

Christoph Demus, Jonas Pitz, Mina Schütz, Nadine Probol, Melanie Siegel, and Dirk Labudde. 2022. DeTox: A Comprehensive Dataset for German Offensive Language and Conversation Analysis. In *Proceedings of the Sixth Workshop on Online Abuse and Harms (WOAH)*, pages 143–153, Seattle, Washington (Hybrid). Association for Computational Linguistics.

Abhimanyu Dubey, Abhinav Jauhri, Abhinav Pandey, Abhishek Kadian, Ahmad Al-Dahle, Aiesha Letman, Akhil Mathur, Alan Schelten, Amy Yang, Angela Fan, and 1 others. 2024. The Llama 3 Herd of Models. *arXiv e-prints*, pages arXiv–2407.

Duden. 2025. Subversion. Retrieved 29 August 2025.

Anton Ehrmanntraut, Julia Wunderle, Jan Pfister, Fotis Jannidis, and Andreas Hotho. 2025. ModernGBERT: German-only 1B Encoder Model Trained from Scratch. *arXiv preprint*.

Joseph L. Fleiss. 1971. Measuring nominal scale agreement among many raters. *Psychological Bulletin*, 76(5):378–382.

Jerome H. Friedman. 2001. Greedy function approximation: A gradient boosting machine. *The Annals of Statistics*, 29(5):1189–1232.

Mayur Gaikwad, Swati Ahirrao, Ketan Kotecha, and Ajith Abraham. 2022. Multi-Ideology Multi-Class Extremism Classification Using Deep Learning Techniques. *IEEE access : practical innovations, open solutions*, 10:104829–104843.

Stephanie Gross, Johann Petrak, Louisa Venhoff, and Brigitte Krenn. 2024. GermEval2024 shared task: GerMS-detect – sexism detection in German online news fora. In *Proceedings of GermEval 2024 Task 1 GerMS-detect Workshop on Sexism Detection in German Online News Fora (GerMS-detect 2024)*, pages 1–9, Vienna, Austria. Association for Computational Lingustics.

Pengcheng He, Xiaodong Liu, Jianfeng Gao, and Weizhu Chen. 2021. DeBERTa: Decoding-enhanced BERT with Disentangled Attention. *Preprint*, arXiv:2006.03654.

Albert Q. Jiang, Alexandre Sablayrolles, Antoine Roux, Arthur Mensch, Blanche Savary, Chris Bamford, Devendra Singh Chaplot, Diego de las Casas, Emma Bou Hanna, Florian Bressand, Gianna Lengyel, Guillaume Bour, Guillaume Lample, Lélio Renard Lavaud, Lucile Saulnier, Marie-Anne Lachaux, Pierre Stock, Sandeep Subramanian, Sophia Yang, and 7 others. 2024. Mixtral of Experts. *arXiv preprint*.

Bharath Kancharla, Prabhjot Singh, Lohith Bhagavan Kancharla, Yashita Chama, and Raksha Sharma. 2025. Identifying aggression and offensive language in code-mixed tweets: A multi-task transfer learning approach. In *Proceedings of the First Workshop on Natural Language Processing for Indo-Aryan and Dravidian Languages*, pages 122–128, Abu Dhabi. Association for Computational Linguistics.

Muhammad Shahid Khan, Muhammad Shahid Iqbal Malik, and Aamer Nadeem. 2024. Detection of violence incitation expressions in Urdu tweets using convolutional neural network. *Expert Systems with Applications*, 245:123174.

Johannes Kiesel, Maria Mestre, Rishabh Shukla, Emmanuel Vincent, Payam Adineh, David Corney, Benno Stein, and Martin Potthast. 2019. SemEval-2019 task 4: Hyperpartisan news detection. In *Proceedings of the 13th International Workshop on Semantic Evaluation*, pages 829–839, Minneapolis, Minnesota, USA. Association for Computational Linguistics.

Damir Korenčić, Berta Chulvi, X Bonet Casals, Mariona Taulé, Paolo Rosso, and Francisco Rangel. 2024. Overview of the oppositional thinking analysis pan task at clef 2024. In *Working Notes of CLEF*, pages 2462–2485, Grenoble, France. CLEF.

Vincent Kums, Florian Meyer, Luisa Pivit, Uliana Vedenina, Jonas Wortmann, Melanie Siegel, and Dirk Labudde. 2025. A novel dataset for classifying German hate speech comments with criminal relevance. In *Proceedings of the the 9th Workshop on Online Abuse and Harms (WOAH)*, pages 41–52, Vienna, Austria. Association for Computational Linguistics.

J. Richard Landis and Gary G. Koch. 1977. The Measurement of Observer Agreement for Categorical Data. *Biometrics*, 33(1):159.

Jens Lemmens, Jens Van Nooten, Tim Kreutz, and Walter Daelemans. 2022. CoNTACT: A Dutch COVID-19 adapted BERT for vaccine hesitancy and argumentation detection. In *Proceedings of the 29th International Conference on Computational Linguistics*, pages 6837–6845, Gyeongju, Republic of Korea. International Committee on Computational Linguistics.

Steven Loria. 2018. Textblob Documentation. Retrieved 29 August 2025.

Thomas Mandl, Sandip Modha, Anand Kumar M, and Bharathi Raja Chakravarthi. 2020. Overview of the HASOC Track at FIRE 2020: Hate Speech and Offensive Language Identification in Tamil, Malayalam, Hindi, English and German. In *Forum for Information Retrieval Evaluation*, pages 29–32, Hyderabad India. ACM.

Oxford University Press. 2024. Call to action. Retrieved 29 August 2025.

Juan Manuel Pérez, Franco M. Luque, Demian Zayat, Martín Kondratzky, Agustín Moro, Pablo Santiago Serrati, Joaquín Zajac, Paula Miguel, Natalia Debandi, Agustín Gravano, and Viviana Cotik. 2023. Assessing the Impact of Contextual Information in Hate Speech Detection. *IEEE access : practical innovations, open solutions*, 11:30575–30590.

Jan Pfister, Julia Wunderle, and Andreas Hotho. 2025. LLäMmlein: Transparent, compact and competitive German-only language models from scratch. In *Proceedings of the 63rd Annual Meeting of the Association for Computational Linguistics (Volume 1: Long Papers)*, pages 2227–2246, Vienna, Austria. Association for Computational Linguistics.

Nils Reimers and Iryna Gurevych. 2019. Sentence-BERT: Sentence Embeddings using Siamese BERT-Networks. In *Proceedings of the 2019 Conference on Empirical Methods in Natural Language Processing and the 9th International Joint Conference on Natural Language Processing (EMNLP-IJCNLP)*, pages 3980–3990, Hong Kong, China. Association for Computational Linguistics.

Julian Risch, Anke Stoll, Lena Wilms, and Michael Wiegand. 2021. Overview of the GermEval 2021 Shared Task on the Identification of Toxic, Engaging, and Fact-Claiming Comments. In *Proceedings of the GermEval 2021 Shared Task on the Identification of Toxic, Engaging, and Fact-Claiming Comments*, pages 1–12, Duesseldorf, Germany. Association for Computational Linguistics.

Anna Rogers, Olga Kovaleva, and Anna Rumshisky. 2019. Calls to Action on Social Media: Potential for Censorship and Social Impact. In *Proceedings of the 2nd Workshop on NLP for Internet Freedom: Censorship, Disinformation, and Propaganda*, pages 36–44, Stroudsburg, PA. Association for Computational Linguistics.

Sourav Saha, Jahedul Alam Junaed, Maryam Saleki, Mohamed Rahouti, Nabeel Mohammed, and Mohammad Ruhul Amin. 2023. BLP-2023 task 1: Violence inciting text detection (VITD). In *Proceedings of the First Workshop on Bangla Language Processing (BLP-2023)*, pages 255–265, Singapore. Association for Computational Linguistics.

Umitcan Sahin, Izzet Emre Kucukkaya, Oguzhan Ozcelik, and Cagri Toraman. 2023. Zero and Few-Shot Hate Speech Detection in Social Media Messages Related to Earthquake Disaster. In *Proceedings of the 31st Signal Processing and Communications Applications Conference (SIU)*, pages 1–4, Istanbul, Turkiye. IEEE.

Shrey Satapara, Prasenjit Majumder, Thomas Mandl, Sandip Modha, Hiren Madhu, Tharindu Ranasinghe, Marcos Zampieri, Kai North, and Damith Premasiri. 2022. Overview of the HASOC Subtrack at FIRE 2022: Hate Speech and Offensive Content Identification in English and Indo-Aryan Languages. In *Proceedings of the 14th Annual Meeting of the Forum for Information Retrieval Evaluation*, pages 4–7, Kolkata India. ACM.

Thorben Schomacker, Miriam Anschütz, Regina Stodden, Georg Groh, and Marina Tropmann-Frick. 2024. Overview of the GermEval 2024 shared task on statement segmentation in German easy language (StaGE). In *Proceedings of GermEval 2024 Shared Task on Statement Segmentation in German Easy Language (StaGE)*, pages 1–14, Vienna, Austria. Association for Computational Lingustics.

Wassiliki Siskou, Clara Giralt Mirón, Sarah Molina-Raith, and Miriam Butt. 2022. Automatized detection and annotation for calls to action in Latin-American social media postings. In *Proceedings of the 6th Joint SIGHUM Workshop on Computational Linguistics for Cultural Heritage, Social Sciences, Humanities and Literature*, pages 65–69, Gyeongju, Republic of Korea. International Conference on Computational Linguistics.

Julia Maria Struß, Melanie Siegel, Josef Ruppenhofer, Michael Wiegand, and Manfred Klenner. 2019. Overview of GermEval Task 2, 2019 Shared Task on the Identification of Offensive Language. In *Proceedings of the 15th Conference on Natural Language Processing (KONVENS)*, pages 354–365, Nürnberg/Erlangen, Deutschland. German Society for Computational Linguistics.

Katja Thorwarth. 2023. „Wir schießen den Weg frei“ - bereitet die AfD-Sprache den Boden für rechten Terror mit? *Frankfurter Rundschau*. Retrieved 29 August 2025.

Michael Wiegand, Melanie Siegel, and Josef Ruppenhofer. 2018. Overview of the GermEval 2018 Shared Task on the Identification of Offensive Language. In *Proceedings of GermEval 2018, 14th Conference on Natural Language Processing (KONVENS 2018)*, pages 1–8, Vienna, Austria. German Society for Computational Linguistics.

An Yang, Anfeng Li, Baosong Yang, Beichen Zhang, Binyuan Hui, Bo Zheng, Bowen Yu, Chang Gao, Chengen Huang, Chenxu Lv, Chujie Zheng, Dayiheng Liu, Fan Zhou, Fei Huang, Feng Hu, Hao Ge, Haoran Wei, Huan Lin, Jialong Tang, and 41 others. 2025. Qwen3 Technical Report. *arXiv preprint*.

A Appendix

A.1 Details about class distribution after data augmentation

The dataset used in the shared task for the second subtask, the detection of attacks on the DBO, consisted of tweets from the German Twitter network of a right-wing extremist group as well as additional tweets from the datasets by Demus et al. (2022) and Kums et al. (2025). The data augmentation led to an increase in the number of tweets in all four categories. The number of tweets before and after data enrichment for the second subtask can be found in Table 9. The data for the third subtask, the detection of problematic, violence-related statements, was only enriched with data by Kums et al. (2025), which increased the number of tweets in the TRUE category.

A.2 Details about the data format

An example of a row from the training data set for the first subtask, the detection of calls to action, can be found in Table 10.

A.3 Prompt engineering for the baseline of subtask 3

For classification in subtask 3, a system prompt and a user prompt were fed into the model Qwen2.5. The system prompt consisted of a role assignment, a task description, a definition of worrying violence-related statements, and a description of the desired output:

System Prompt

Instruction: You are a filter system in a social network that specialises in monitoring German tweets. Your task is to detect worrying positive attitudes towards violence. Consider the following definitions: A tweet contains a worrying violence-related statement if it trivialises, advocates, glorifies, incites violence or announces the use of violence. Violence is understood to mean active, aggressive behaviour, i.e. the infliction of physical, sexual or psychological violence. If you predict a violence-related statement, your response is “true”. If you predict a no-violence-related statement, you respond with “false”. You only respond with one single word and not more!

The user prompt was composed of the following components: repetition of the task description, repetition of the desired output, examples of the classification task for in-context learning and the tweet to be classified.

User Prompt

Determine whether the input tweet contains a worrying violence-related statement. Respond with a single word. Do not provide explanations or notes. Your only possible responses, regarding if the provided text contains a worrying violence-related statement are true and false. Examples of classification are: <Examples> Input: <Tweet>

The following six tweets, which had been presented to the annotators, were provided as examples:

- @UserXY Wenn ich diesen Typ schon sehe, könnte ich ihn an die Wand stellen response: “true”
- Knallt das ganze linksgrün Dumme Antifa

Table 9: Class distribution in the total data set for subtasks 2 and 3 before and after data augmentation.

Subtask	categories	Newly collected tweets	After data augmentation
Subtask 2: Attacks on DBO	subversive	29 (0.31)	85 (0.80)
	agitation	48 (0.52)	447 (4.2)
	criticism	1072 (11.52)	1149 (10.79)
	nothing	8158 (87.65)	8967 (84.21)
	total	9307 (100)	10648 (100)
Subtask 3: Violence Detection	true	620 (5.67)	805 (7.24)
	false	10313 (94.339)	10313 (92.76)
	total	10933 (100)	11118 (100)

Table 10: Example row from the training data set for the first subtask, the detection of calls to action.

id	description	C2A
1096188353752920	Einfach überfahren wo ist das Problem ?	TRUE

Gesindel einfach ab! #LinksfaschistenStoppen *response: "true"*

- Man stelle sich vor, eine Gruppe on 40 jungen MÄNNERN [...], teilweise BEWAFFNET [...], versucht ILLEGAL eine Grenze zu übertreten, [...] und dann wundert man sich, wenn das Feuer gerechtfertigterweise eröffnet wird. *response: "true"*

- @UserXY endlich hat jemand den Mut ergriffen und dem Mistkerl die Fresse poliert. Der hat alles schlimme der Welt und mehr verdient dieser erbärmliche Perverse und geistig Behinderte #Volksverräter *response: "true"*

- @UserXY DU BIST TEIL dieser ganz GEZIELT INSZENIERTEN LÜGE über Lynchjustiz und Aufruf zu Mord und versuchst alle durch FREI ERFUNDENE HORRORGeschichten in PANIK zu VERSETZEN! #Lügenpresse *response: "true"*

- [...] Der 27- jährige Syrer wird verdächtigt, zwischen 2011 und 2014 als Mitglied von Jabhat al- Nusra bzw. Kataib Al Faroug im syrischen Bürgerkrieg gegen Anhänger bzw. Truppen des Assad- Regimes gekämpft und auf diese geschossen zu haben, sagte Peter Oehm, der Leiter des Landesamtes für Verfassungsschutz. *response: "false"*

abullardUR@GermEval Shared Task 2025: Fine-tuning ModernGBERT on Highly Imbalanced German Social Media for Harmful Content Detection

Samuel Bullard
Information Science Faculty
University of Regensburg
Regensburg, Germany
Samuel.Bullard@stud.uni-regensburg.de

Abstract

We present a system for the GermEval 2025 Shared Task on harmful content detection in German social media, addressing three tasks: Call to Action (C2A), Attacks on Democratic Basic Order (DBO), and Violence Detection (VIO). We fine-tune ModernGBERT on a dataset of German tweets from right-wing extremist networks (2014-2016) with severe class imbalance: 9.7% (C2A), 15.8% (DBO harmful), and 7.2% (VIO) positive ratios. Our experiments reveal that class-weighted cross-entropy loss outperforms the combined approach with Focal Loss, achieving macro-F1 scores of 0.82, 0.63, and 0.82 for C2A, DBO, and VIO respectively - improvements of +39%, +34%, and +19% over baselines. This suggests frequency imbalance, not hard example mining, is the primary challenge. While our models rank 4th/9 (C2A), 6th/9 (DBO), and 2nd/8 (VIO) on the leaderboard, nuanced categorization tasks requiring deep contextual understanding remain challenging, particularly for multi-class tasks.

1 Introduction

Harmful content detection is essential for online safety and democratic discourse in Germany. Three specific phenomena can pose societal risks: calls to action (C2A) can mobilize offline violence or criminal activity, attacks on democratic basic order (DBO) undermine constitutional principles and institutional legitimacy, while violence-related statements (VIO) normalize aggression and threaten individual safety. Each requires specialized detection approaches given their varied linguistic patterns and contextual markers.

This paper describes our system for the GermEval 2025 Shared Task (Communication Forensics Lab Mittweida, 2025; Felser et al., 2025), focusing on fine-tuning ModernGBERT with systematic loss function design for severe class imbalance. Our methodology centers on controlled comparison of class-weighted approaches and thorough dataset analysis to inform our modeling decisions.

Our contributions are threefold: (i) dataset characteristic analysis informing architectural choices, (ii) controlled comparison of class-weighted cross-entropy versus combined class-weights with focal loss, and (iii) competitive performance using a compact German encoder.

The papers' further structure is as follows: Section 2 surveys relevant work in the field of harmful content detection and class imbalance. Section 3 analyzes dataset properties that motivate our design choices. Section 4 details our system architecture and methodology. Section 5 presents results and discusses findings, limitations, and future directions. Section 6 concludes the paper.

2 Related Work

We summarize prior work on harmful content detection, German transformer models, and techniques for class imbalance that motivate our approach.

2.1 Early Approaches to Harmful Content Detection

Automated harmful-speech detection has progressed from rule-based filters to modern neural architectures. One of the earliest prototypes, *Smokey*, relied on manually crafted patterns to flag e-mail "flames" (Spertus, 1997). Traditional bag-of-words classifiers such as SVMs and logistic regression improved portability but still failed on creative orthography and implicit abuse (Davidson et al., 2017). Deep neural networks introduced convolutional and recurrent models that learn features directly from data; Collobert *et al.* demonstrated this paradigm on multiple NLP tasks and inspired early CNN-based hate-speech systems (Collobert et al., 2011). Nevertheless, limited context windows and vocabulary size constrained performance on nuanced, code-switched harmful speech (Kalchbrenner et al.,

Proceedings of the 21st Conference on Natural Language Processing (KONVENS), Volume 2: Workshops, pages 320–326, 2025

2014; Magu and Luo, 2018).

2.2 Harmful Speech Detection in the German Social Media Context

In Germany the *Netzwerkdurchsetzungsgesetz* (NetzDG) mandates swift removal of illegal content, motivating research into reliable German-language detectors (Bundesministerium der Justiz und Bundesamt für Justiz, 2017). Initial resources were scarce: Ross et al. (2016) introduced one of the first publicly available German hate-speech corpora, a set of 541 refugee-related tweets. Community benchmarks filled this gap. The GermEval shared-task series supplies steadily larger corpora: the 2018 pilot on offensive tweets (Wiegand et al., 2019), its 2019 extension with implicit/explicit labels (Struß et al., 2019), and the 2021 task on toxic, engaging and fact-claiming comments (Risch et al., 2021) and finally the 2025 GermEval shared task on harmful-content detection (Communication Forensics Lab Mittweida, 2025). At the same time, specialised extremist resources emerged. Hartung et al. (2017) compiled a profile-level dataset of right-wing extremist Twitter users and identified symbolic codes such as "d18," a numeric reference to Adolf Hitler, among many others. The subsequent *Right-Wing Hate Speech Twitter corpus* (RWHN) enlarged coverage to 50k tweets and documents ciphers like "88" (standing for "Heil Hitler") alongside other evasive euphemisms (Jaki and Smedt, 2019). Together, research, legislation and shared tasks have contributed to driving a shift from lexicon-based heuristics to context-aware neural models in German NLP.

2.3 Transformer-Based Language Models for German

The highly parallelisable self-attention architecture of transformers has enabled BERT-style encoders to reach billions of parameters and to power moderation at an industrial scale. Flipkart's Unified BERT (Nayak and Garera, 2022) filters millions of user reviews for hate speech and policy violations in real time. Since self-attention allows every token to attend to every other token (Vaswani et al., 2017), BERT's bidirectional encoder (Devlin et al., 2019) captures the nuanced context required to detect implicit abuse.

Monolingual German transformers soon outperformed multilingual baselines: GBERT and its sibling GELECTRA (Chan et al., 2020) improved downstream accuracy on classification and sequence-tagging tasks. Yet the 512-token context limit inherited from BERT hinders the analysis of long snippets of text. Long-context adaptations addressed this gap. Longformer introduced sliding-window attention for inputs beyond 4000 tokens (Beltagy et al., 2020), while the ModernBERT architecture replaced absolute positions with rotary embeddings and paired them with sparse 128-token windows, scaling sequence length to 8192 tokens without quadratic memory growth (Warner et al., 2024). These advances are crucial for German content moderation, where a single post can now stretch to 25,000 characters on X (X Corp., 2025), exceeding the 512-token window and requiring long-range attention.

Building on this progress, *ModernGBERT* provides 134M to 1B-parameter German-only models trained on roughly 470 billion tokens and sets new state-of-the-art scores on German benchmarks (Ehrmanntraut et al., 2025). Large multilingual encoders such as EuroBERT narrow the monolingual advantage on general German natural language understanding (Boizard et al., 2025), yet on the public SUPERGLEBER Toxicity leaderboard (Pfister and Hotho, 2024) ModernGBERT-1B is among the strongest openly released encoder models for German hate-speech detection. Its compact 134M-parameter variant, which we fine-tune in our experiments, still achieves a competitive macro-F1 of 0.526 while requiring an order of magnitude fewer parameters.

2.4 Addressing Class Imbalance in Text Classification

Harmful-content corpora are oftentimes highly skewed. Offensive or toxic instances constitute roughly one third of the tweets in GERMEVAL 2018 (34%) and 2019 (32%), and 35% of the Facebook comments in the GERMEVAL2021 toxic-comment task (Wiegand et al., 2019; Struß et al., 2019; Risch et al., 2021). For the 2025 GERMEVAL shared task we measured 9.7% Call-to-Action, 15.8% Democratic Basic Order and 7.2% Violence in the released training data.

Such imbalance biases models toward the majority class, so recent shared tasks rank systems by macro-F1 instead of accuracy (Sokolova and Lapalme, 2009; Risch et al., 2021).

Mitigation methods fall into three families:

1. **Data-centric re-balancing.** Random over- or undersampling, SMOTE (Chawla et al.,

2002) and its variants, back-translation or lexicon-guided augmentation (for example *AbusiveLexiconAug*) alter the training distribution (Krawczyk, 2016; Fernández et al., 2018; Zhang et al., 2024).

2. **Loss-centric re-weighting and margin tuning.** Inverse-frequency class weights are a common baseline; the winning *hpi-DEDIS* run at GermEval 2019 used weighted cross-entropy with weights {6.57, 1.96, 1.56, 0.37} for PROFANITY, ABUSE, INSULT and OTHER, respectively (Risch et al., 2019). Focal Loss (Lin et al., 2017), Label-Distribution-Aware Margin (LDAM) loss (Cao et al., 2019), Class-Balanced Loss (Cui et al., 2019) and Logit-Adjusted Loss (Menon et al., 2021) further reduce majority bias.

3. **Prediction-centric calibration and ensembling.** Threshold moving, cost-sensitive bagging or boosting, and majority-vote ensembles (used by several GermEval 2021 teams (Bornheim et al., 2021; Risch et al., 2021)) correct residual bias during or immediately after training.

A cross-corpus study covering eight abusive-language datasets finds weighted cross-entropy and Focal Loss to be the most robust single-model choices (Zhang et al., 2024). We therefore benchmark both losses within the ModernGBERT framework and the confines of the GermEval 2025 shared task.

3 Dataset Analysis

This section summarizes dataset properties that inform our modeling choices. The class distributions for the three subtasks are shown in Table 1.

3.1 Basic Dataset Statistics

3.2 Text Length Characteristics

Tweets are short on average but with long outliers. Approximately 75% of posts are under 180 characters, yet outliers up to 10k characters motivate a long-context encoder to avoid truncation.

3.3 Cross-Dataset Overlap

Substantial content overlap exists across subtasks (e.g., >60% of unique descriptions appearing in at least two subtasks), reinforcing the potential of shared representations and the need for careful split design to avoid leakage when experimenting with joint models and splitting datasets into train/validation/(test) splits.

Task / Class	Count	Share
C2A		
False	6,177	90.3%
True	663	9.7%
DBO		
Nothing	6,277	84.2%
Criticism	804	10.8%
Agitation	313	4.2%
Subversive	60	0.8%
VIO		
False	7,219	92.8%
True	564	7.2%

Table 1: Class distributions in the training data.

3.4 Linguistic Characteristics

German compounds, social-media artifacts (hashtags, mentions, URLs), and coded language (e.g., numeric ciphers) occur frequently and influence our model choice and preprocessing rationale.

4 System Architecture and Methodology

4.1 Model Architecture

We fine-tune ModernGBERT-134M (Ehrmanntraut et al., 2025; Warner et al., 2024) for each subtask with a mean-pooled classification head. ModernGBERT's 8192 token context length accommodates the vast majority of lengths in our dataset. We train separate models for each subtask end-to-end.

4.2 Loss Design for Class Imbalance

The dataset is severely imbalanced across all subtasks (see Section 3). We implement two strategies:

4.2.1 Class-Weighted Cross-Entropy Loss

We apply inverse frequency weighting to the cross-entropy loss function (King and Zeng, 2001):

$$w_i = \frac{n}{n_i \cdot k} \quad (1)$$

where w_i is the weight for class i, n is the total number of samples, n_i is the number of samples in class i, and k is the number of classes. The weighted loss becomes:

$$\mathcal{L}_{WCE} = -w_y \log(p_y) \quad (2)$$

This weighting ensures that mistakes on minority classes incur proportionally higher penalties during training.

4.2.2 Combined Approach: Class Weights with Focal Loss

In our second approach, we combine class weighting with Focal Loss (Lin et al., 2017) to address both frequency imbalance and hard example mining:

$$\mathcal{L}_{FL} = -\alpha_t(1 - p_t)^\gamma \log(p_t) \qquad (3)$$

where p_t is the predicted probability for the true class, α_t is the class-specific weight (equivalent to w_y above), and γ is the focusing parameter. The term $(1 - p_t)^\gamma$ acts as a difficulty multiplier: when the model is confident and correct ($p_t \approx 1$), this term approaches zero, effectively down-weighting easy examples. Conversely, for hard examples where the model assigns low probability to the correct class, this term remains significant.

We optimize γ in the range $[0.5, 3.0]$ using Bayesian hyperparameter optimization (Snoek et al., 2012) via Weights & Biases (Biewald, 2020) sweeps.

4.3 Preprocessing and Tokenization

The dataset undergoes minimal preprocessing to preserve the authentic characteristics of social media text and leverage the contextual understanding capabilities of transformer models:

- **Existing anonymization tokens** from the dataset are retained: `[@POL]` (police/police authorities), `[@GRP]` (groups/organisations/associations), `[@IND]` (individuals), and `[@PRE]` (press/press offices/news portals)
- **Additional anonymization** is performed: URLs are replaced with `[@URL]` and email addresses with `[@EMAIL]` using the `cleantext` library
- **Data leakage prevention:** We remove validation samples with exact text duplicates from the training set to prevent inflated validation metrics, thereby misguiding the training process. This removed 2.7% (C2A), 6.1% (DBO), and 4.6% (VIO) of validation samples.
- Text is tokenized using ModernGBERT's tokenizer.
- No additional normalization, lowercasing, or cleaning is applied to maintain the original linguistic characteristics

We preserve anonymization tokens as they carry contextual information - e.g., `[@POL]` references may be more relevant for detecting attacks on democratic order than `[@IND]` references.

4.4 Training Configuration

We optimize hyperparameters using Bayesian search over learning rate $\{1 \times 10^{-5}, 2 \times 10^{-5}, 3 \times 10^{-5}, 5 \times 10^{-5}, 1 \times 10^{-4}\}$ (discrete), weight decay $[0.01, 0.1]$ (continuous), batch size $\{8, 16\}$ (discrete), warmup steps $\{100, 300, 500\}$ (discrete), and focal loss gamma $[0.5, 3.0]$ (continuous). Models use AdamW with linear scheduling, early stopping (patience=5), and are selected based on validation macro-F1.

4.5 Evaluation Metrics

We use macro-F1 as the primary evaluation metric (as used by the shared task leaderboard on the hidden test set). On the validation split we report macro-F1, accuracy, macro-precision, macro-recall, and Matthews correlation (MCC). For binary tasks we additionally report ROC-AUC and Average Precision, and we include per-class precision/recall/F1 and support. Please note, that these validation-based metrics are optimistically biased since they steered the training process. For C2A and VIO, we will also report zero-shot results on the external GermEval-2018 (coarse) test set. These per-model metrics will be provided in the GitHub repository (see Section 6). Metrics are reported on the validation split, as the hidden test set for the GermEval2025 shared task was not publicly released by the organizers, post-competition.

5 Results and Discussion

This section first presents the overall results and loss-design comparison, then discusses key findings and limitations.

5.1 Results

Main Results. Our main results on the competition organizers' hidden test set are presented in Table 2.

Leaderboard. We achieved 4/9 (C2A), 6/9 (DBO), and 2/8 (VIO) by macro-F1.

Hyperparameter Search and Loss Comparison. We conducted limited Bayesian hyperparameter sweeps (10 iterations per subtask) using Weights & Biases (Biewald, 2020). Full sweep configurations

Method	C2A	DBO	VIO
Official Baselines			
Gradient Boosting + SBERT	0.59	–	–
Cost-Sensitive Linear SVM	–	0.47	–
Qwen2.5 LLM Few-Shot	–	–	0.69
Our Approaches			
ModernGBERT + Class Weights	**0.82**	**0.63**	**0.82**
ModernGBERT + Weights + Focal	0.82	0.56	0.81

Table 2: macro-F1 on hidden test set data. Official baseline per subtask from the shared task overview (Felser et al., 2025).

and run artifacts will be provided alongside the code and models. Class-weighted cross-entropy consistently matched or outperformed the combined focal-loss variant across subtasks.

5.2 Discussion

Key Findings. Class-weighted cross-entropy is sufficient for this dataset and choice of model. Focal loss did not improve performance and seems to down-weight scarce correctly classified minority examples.

Limitations and Future Directions. Results derive from a single dataset and time period, which makes generalization to other domains less effective. Future work should include methods of data augmentation for extreme minorities and exploring multi-task learning, given the substantial overlap across tweet descriptions in all three subtasks.

6 Conclusion

We presented a system for the GermEval 2025 shared task, focusing on handling the severe class imbalance present in the data. Our primary finding is that class-weighted cross-entropy is more effective than a combined approach with Focal Loss. Our results suggest that more complex, combined techniques are not always superior for real-world NLP tasks. The success of class weighting over Focal Loss demonstrates the importance of understanding problem-specific characteristics, dataset characteristics and the likely impact a specific technique has on the performance of a model rather than applying state-of-the-art methods uncritically.

For practitioners deploying harmful content detection systems, our findings indicate that ModernGBERT with appropriate class weighting can achieve competitive performance on German social media text. However, the 63% macro-F1 on the nuanced DBO task underscores that automated systems should augment rather than replace human moderation, particularly for legally sensitive categorizations requiring contextual understanding.

Acknowledgments

I thank Prof. Dr. Udo Kruschwitz for supervision and guidance throughout this research. I also acknowledge the GermEval 2025 organizers from the Communication Forensics Lab at Mittweida University of Applied Sciences for providing the dataset and organizing the shared task.

Code, Metrics and Model Availability

The code, trained models, evaluation metrics, sweep artifacts, and detailed analyses will be made available at: `https://github.com/abullard1/abullardUR-GermEval-Shared-Task-2025`

References

Iz Beltagy, Matthew E. Peters, and Arman Cohan. 2020. Longformer: The long-document transformer. In *Findings of the Association for Computational Linguistics: EMNLP 2020*, pages 152–168, Online. Association for Computational Linguistics.

Lukas Biewald. 2020. Experiment tracking with weights and biases. Software available from wandb.com.

Nicolas Boizard, Hippolyte Gisserot-Boukhlef, Duarte M. Alves, André Martins, and 1 others. 2025. Eurobert: Scaling multilingual encoders for european languages. *Preprint*, arXiv:2503.05500.

Tobias Bornheim, Niklas Grieger, and Stephan Bialonski. 2021. FHAC at GermEval 2021: Identifying German toxic, engaging, and fact-claiming comments with ensemble learning. In *Proceedings of the GermEval 2021 Shared Task on the Identification of Toxic, Engaging, and Fact-Claiming Comments*, pages 105–111, Duesseldorf, Germany. Association for Computational Linguistics.

Bundesministerium der Justiz und Bundesamt für Justiz. 2017. Gesetz zur verbesserung der rechtsdurchsetzung in sozialen netzwerken (netzwerkdurchsetzungsgesetz – netzdg). Bundesgesetzblatt Jahrgang 2017 Teil I Nr. 61, S. 3352. Ausfertigungsdatum 1. September 2017, verkündet am 7. September 2017.

Kaidi Cao, Colin Wei, Adrien Gaidon, Nikos Arechiga, and Tengyu Ma. 2019. Learning imbalanced datasets with label-distribution-aware margin loss. *Preprint*, arXiv:1906.07413.

Branden Chan, Stefan Schweter, and Timo Möller. 2020. German's next language model. In *Proceedings of the 28th International Conference on Computational*

Linguistics, pages 6788–6796, Barcelona, Spain (Online). International Committee on Computational Linguistics.

N. V. Chawla, K. W. Bowyer, L. O. Hall, and W. P. Kegelmeyer. 2002. Smote: Synthetic minority oversampling technique. *Journal of Artificial Intelligence Research*, 16:321–357.

Ronan Collobert, Jason Weston, Leon Bottou, Michael Karlen, Koray Kavukcuoglu, and Pavel Kuksa. 2011. Natural language processing (almost) from scratch. *Preprint*, arXiv:1103.0398.

Communication Forensics Lab Mittweida. 2025. Germeval 2025 shared task: Harmful content detection. Organised by the Communication Forensics Lab, Mittweida.

Yin Cui, Menglin Jia, Tsung-Yi Lin, Yang Song, and Serge Belongie. 2019. Class-balanced loss based on effective number of samples. *Preprint*, arXiv:1901.05555.

Thomas Davidson, Dana Warmsley, Michael Macy, and Ingmar Weber. 2017. Automated hate speech detection and the problem of offensive language. *Preprint*, arXiv:1703.04009.

Jacob Devlin, Ming-Wei Chang, Kenton Lee, and Kristina Toutanova. 2019. Bert: Pre-training of deep bidirectional transformers for language understanding. *Preprint*, arXiv:1810.04805.

Anton Ehrmanntraut, Julia Wunderle, Jan Pfister, Fotis Jannidis, and Andreas Hotho. 2025. Moderngbert: German-only 1b encoder model trained from scratch. *Preprint*, arXiv:2505.13136.

Jenny Felser, Michael Spranger, and Melanie Siegel. 2025. Overview of the germeval 2025 shared task on harmful content detection. In *Proceedings of the 21st Conference on Natural Language Processing (KONVENS 2025): Workshops*, Hildesheim, Germany.

Alberto Fernández, Salvador García, Mikel Galar, Ronaldo C Prati, Bartosz Krawczyk, and Francisco Herrera. 2018. Learning from imbalanced data sets. *IEEE Transactions on Knowledge and Data Engineering*, 30(4):657–675.

Matthias Hartung, Roman Klinger, Franziska Schmidtke, and Lars Vogel. 2017. Ranking right-wing extremist social media profiles by similarity to democratic and extremist groups. In *Proceedings of the 8th Workshop on Computational Approaches to Subjectivity, Sentiment and Social Media Analysis*, pages 24–33, Copenhagen, Denmark. Association for Computational Linguistics.

Sylvia Jaki and Tom De Smedt. 2019. Right-wing german hate speech on twitter: Analysis and automatic detection. *CoRR*, abs/1910.07518.

Nal Kalchbrenner, Edward Grefenstette, and Phil Blunsom. 2014. A convolutional neural network for modelling sentences. *Preprint*, arXiv:1404.2188.

Gary King and Langche Zeng. 2001. Logistic regression in rare events data. *Political Analysis*, 9:137–163.

Bartosz Krawczyk. 2016. Learning from imbalanced data: Open challenges and future directions. *Progress in Artificial Intelligence*, 5(4):221–232.

Tsung-Yi Lin, Priya Goyal, Ross Girshick, Kaiming He, and Piotr Dollar. 2017. Focal loss for dense object detection. In *Proceedings of the IEEE International Conference on Computer Vision*, pages 2980–2988. IEEE.

Rijul Magu and Jiebo Luo. 2018. Determining code words in euphemistic hate speech using word embedding networks. In *Proceedings of the 2nd Workshop on Abusive Language Online (ALW2)*, pages 93–100, Brussels, Belgium. Association for Computational Linguistics.

Aditya Krishna Menon, Sadeep Jayasumana, Ankit Singh Rawat, Himanshu Jain, Andreas Veit, and Sanjiv Kumar. 2021. Long-tail learning via logit adjustment. *Preprint*, arXiv:2007.07314.

Ravindra Nayak and Nikesh Garera. 2022. Deploying unified BERT moderation model for E-commerce reviews. In *Proceedings of the 2022 Conference on Empirical Methods in Natural Language Processing: Industry Track*, pages 540–547, Abu Dhabi, UAE. Association for Computational Linguistics.

Jan Pfister and Andreas Hotho. 2024. SuperGLEBer: German language understanding evaluation benchmark. In *Proceedings of the 2024 Conference of the North American Chapter of the Association for Computational Linguistics: Human Language Technologies (Volume 1: Long Papers)*, pages 7904–7923, Mexico City, Mexico. Association for Computational Linguistics.

Julian Risch, Anke Stoll, Lena Wilms, and Michael Wiegand. 2021. Overview of the GermEval 2021 shared task on the identification of toxic, engaging, and fact-claiming comments. In *Proceedings of the GermEval 2021 Shared Task on the Identification of Toxic, Engaging, and Fact-Claiming Comments*, pages 1–12, Duesseldorf, Germany. Association for Computational Linguistics.

Julian Risch, Anke Stoll, Marc Ziegele, and Ralf Krestel. 2019. hpidedis at germeval 2019: Offensive language identification using a german bert model. In *Conference on Natural Language Processing*, pages 251–257.

Bjoern Ross, Michael Rist, Guillermo Carbonell, Benjamin Cabrera, Nils Kurowsky, and Michael Wojatzki. 2016. Measuring the reliability of hate speech annotations: The case of the european refugee crisis. Preprint. University of Duisburg-Essen repository.

Jasper Snoek, Hugo Larochelle, and Ryan P. Adams. 2012. Practical bayesian optimization of machine learning algorithms. *Preprint*, arXiv:1206.2944.

Marina Sokolova and Guy Lapalme. 2009. A systematic analysis of performance measures for classification tasks. *Information Processing Management*, 45(4):427–437.

Ellen Spertus. 1997. Smokey: automatic recognition of hostile messages. In *Proceedings of the Fourteenth National Conference on Artificial Intelligence and Ninth Conference on Innovative Applications of Artificial Intelligence*, AAAI'97/IAAI'97, page 1058–1065. AAAI Press.

Julia Maria Struß, Melanie Siegel, Josef Ruppenhofer, Michael Wiegand, and Manfred Klenner. 2019. Overview of germeval task 2, 2019 shared task on the identification of offensive language. In German Society for Computational Linguistics, editor, *Proceedings of the 15th Conference on Natural Language Processing (KONVENS) 2019*, pages 354–365. s.a., Nürnberg/Erlangen.

Ashish Vaswani, Noam Shazeer, Niki Parmar, Jakob Uszkoreit, Llion Jones, Aidan N. Gomez, Lukasz Kaiser, and Illia Polosukhin. 2017. Attention is all you need. *Preprint*, arXiv:1706.03762.

Benjamin Warner, Antoine Chaffin, Benjamin Clavié, Orion Weller, Oskar Hallström, Said Taghadouini, Alexis Gallagher, Raja Biswas, Faisal Ladhak, Tom Aarsen, Nathan Cooper, Griffin Adams, Jeremy Howard, and Iacopo Poli. 2024. Smarter, better, faster, longer: A modern bidirectional encoder for fast, memory efficient, and long context finetuning and inference. *Preprint*, arXiv:2412.13663.

Michael Wiegand, Melanie Siegel, and Josef Ruppenhofer. 2019. Overview of the germeval 2018 shared task on the identification of offensive language. In Josef Ruppenhofer, Melanie Siegel, and Michael Wiegand, editors, *Proceedings of GermEval 2018, 14th Conference on Natural Language Processing (KONVENS 2018), Vienna, Austria - September 21, 2018*, pages 1 – 10. Austrian Academy of Sciences Press.

X Corp. 2025. About different types of posts. X Help Center. Accessed 20 Jul 2025.

Yaqi Zhang, Viktor Hangya, and Alexander Fraser. 2024. A study of the class imbalance problem in abusive language detection. In *Proceedings of the 8th Workshop on Online Abuse and Harms (WOAH 2024)*, pages 38–51, Mexico City, Mexico. Association for Computational Linguistics.

FI-CODE@GermEval Shared Task 2025: LLM Prompting for Augmentation of Underrepresented Classes

Nina Seemann, Yeong Su Lee, Hendrik Bothe, Michaela Geierhos
University of the Bundeswehr Munich, Research Institute CODE
Werner-Heisenberg-Weg 39, 85579 Neubiberg, Germany
{nina.seemann,yeongsu.lee,hendrik.bothe,michaela.geierhos}@unibw.de

Abstract

This paper summarizes our participation in the Harmful Content Detection in Social Media shared task. The task is divided into three subtasks: Call2Action (C2A), Attacks on the Democratic Basic Order (DBO), and Violence Detection (VIO). Following the organizers' recommendation, we used data augmentation to create more instances of each underrepresented category. To this end, we asked three large language models to rewrite a tweet in six different styles. We used a German BERT model for classification. The macro F1 scores obtained for the three subtasks were 79 % for C2A, 62 % for DBO, and 75 % for VIO.

1 Introduction

Social media platforms have become essential spaces for political communication and public discourse (Stieglitz and Dang-Xuan, 2013; Sapar et al., 2023), as evidenced by the frequent posting of many politicians who use platforms like Twitter (now X) and Instagram to communicate daily with voters and influence media cycles. However, these platforms also facilitate the rapid dissemination of hate speech. Political actors, interest groups, and polarized communities may exploit these platforms to spread harmful, discriminatory, or extremist content – often under the guise of opinion or satire. The virality and reach of such messages can undermine democratic dialogue, fuel polarization, and marginalize vulnerable groups. The volume and speed of online content makes it difficult for manual moderation to keep pace, so there is a growing demand for automated hate speech detection systems. These tools are crucial for safeguarding users, fostering respectful discourse, and upholding the integrity of democratic processes, particularly during election campaigns and times of heightened political tension. However, developing robust models remains challenging due to the implicit, context-dependent, and culturally varied nature of online hate speech.

In this Harmful Content Detection shared task, researchers focus on modeling three subtasks of such applications (Felser et al., 2025). Shared tasks on harmful content detection typically provide datasets containing normal and harmful content to differentiate between these two categories. These datasets primarily contain content from far-right extremist groups, as well as comments from non-supporters criticizing that content. Furthermore, not every tweet by a follower of an extremist group is automatically extremist. Hence, the goal is to identify content of the following three subtasks. Call2Action (C2A) aims to automatically identify calls to action on social media. This subtask involves a coarse-grained, binary classification. Attacks on the Democratic Basic Order (DBO) aims to automatically detect whether a tweet constitutes an attack on the free democratic basic order and involves classifying tweets into one of four categories. Violence Detection (VIO) aims to automatically determine if a tweet expresses an overly positive attitude toward violence. This subtask involves a coarse-grained, binary classification. For more details on each subtask, see Felser et al. (2025).

Harmful content on the internet is typically less numerous than normal content. This fact is reflected in the datasets provided for this shared task. Therefore, the organizers explicitly encouraged participants to use data augmentation, which we achieved by leveraging large language models (LLMs). Using LLMs for data augmentation is not a new idea (Ding et al., 2024; Jahan et al., 2024). However, in the context of this shared task, this approach may be ineffective due to the offensive and disturbing nature of the tweets. LLMs are trained on online texts containing harmful content[1], so cre-

[1] https://research.ibm.com/blog/efficient-llm-hap-detector (2025-07-15)

Proceedings of the 21st Conference on Natural Language Processing (KONVENS), Volume 2: Workshops, pages 327–336, 2025

ators are concerned about teaching their LLMs not to replicate or filter this content. Nevertheless, to obtain more instances for each underrepresented class, we asked three LLMs to rewrite a given tweet in six different styles.

In our experiments, we focus on two things. First, we examine the ability of LLMs to rewrite disturbing texts. Second, we examine how synthetic data can be helpful. Our goal is not to obtain the best F1 scores. This paper is organized as follows: Section 2 provides an overview of related work. In Section 3, we present the overview of the datasets provided by the organizers. Section 4 shows the process of data augmentation, while Section 5 details our experimental setups and results, and discusses related issues. Finally, we conclude our research and present future work in Section 6.

2 Related Work

Data augmentation is an established technique for improving the performancc of machine learning models when working with limited or imbalanced datasets. Traditional methods, such as SMOTE, generate synthetic samples by interpolating between existing data points in the feature space (Chawla et al., 2002). However, they often fail to capture the semantic complexity of textual data. More recent approaches use language-based techniques, such as synonym replacement, back-translation, and contextual embeddings, to introduce linguistic variation (Wei and Zou, 2019; Ciolino et al., 2022; Pantelidou et al., 2022; Jahan et al., 2024). Thanks to powerful LLMs, a new approach has emerged that generates semantically coherent augmented data.

Studies have shown that text generated by LLMs can significantly improve classification performance in scenarios involving short texts (Balkus and Yan, 2023). Compared to traditional augmentation methods, LLMs offer more linguistic diversity and are better at capturing domain-specific nuances (Ding et al., 2024). This is particularly important for classifying posts on platforms such as Twitter (now X), where informal language, irony, and brevity present additional challenges. The same applies to hate speech detection. The effectiveness of these models is closely related to the quality and diversity of their training data. However, recent studies have revealed that commonly used hate speech datasets exhibit systematic issues in their composition, such as imbalanced label distributions, platform-specific sampling biases, and inconsistent annotations (Jaf and Barakat, 2024). Models based on these biased datasets can learn biased patterns and produce unreliable results.

Therefore, recent research addresses these challenges by focusing on context-aware data augmentation strategies aimed at improving the representation of minority classes. The GAHD dataset, a new collection of approximately 11,000 instances of adversarial hate speech in German, was introduced to evaluate model robustness (Goldzycher et al., 2024). Experiments demonstrate that GAHD poses a significant challenge, even to state-of-the-art detection models. Incorporating GAHD into the training process notably enhances classification stability and generalization.

Other researchers have used different augmentation approaches to improve hate speech detection performance. A combination of synonym and token replacement, paraphrasing, and back-translation has been shown to significantly improve model performance when used as data augmentation techniques (Aljawazeri and Jasim, 2025). Jahan et al. (2024) evaluated several data augmentation techniques for hate speech detection, with a particular focus on LLM generation. Among these techniques, GPT-3-based augmentation was shown to generate syntactically rich and semantically coherent samples, thereby improving model performance. Unlike traditional methods, such as back-translation or synonym substitution, LLM-based augmentation enriches the diversity of the training distribution. The findings suggest that incorporating augmented data substantially improves classification accuracy and generalization, especially in low-resource scenarios.

Others explored the automated classification of Calls to Action in Instagram content from the 2021 German federal election campaign (Achmann-Denkler et al., 2024). They combined fine-tuned BERT (Devlin et al., 2019) models with synthetic training data generated via LLMs, specifically GPT-4. Using augmented data enabled them to achieve high classification accuracy and revealed distinct mobilization strategies across content types (posts vs. stories) and political parties. These results highlight the importance of LLM-driven augmentation in improving the robustness and generalization of real-world social media classification tasks.

3 Datasets

The organizers provided a newly annotated dataset for the aforementioned tasks (Felser et al., 2025). Tweets were collected between 2014 and 2016 and annotated by students or research assistants who are experts in identifying the characteristics of harmful textual content. The dataset consists of training and trial data. The trial data itself is included in the training data, hence we removed the trial part from the training data for our experiments (see Section 5). Table 1 gives a detailed overview of the dataset sizes per label for each subtask after excluding trial from training data.

As the table shows, there is significant imbalance in label distribution. Therefore, we augment each underrepresented class with LLMs.

		# Instances	
Subtask	**Label**	**Train**	**Trial**
C2A	true	561	102
	false	5,228	949
DBO	subversive	56	4
	agitation	307	6
	criticism	683	122
	nothing	5,653	921
VIO	true	504	60
	false	6,228	991

Table 1: An overview of the sizes of the training and trial data for each subtask.

4 Data Augmentation

Below, we describe the LLMs we used for data augmentation and the rewriting styles we selected. The augmented data was generated on a single Nvidia A100 80GB GPU, with a processing time of approximately 5 seconds per tweet.

4.1 Large Language Models

We utilized the following three state-of-the-art language models: Llama 3.3 with 70 billion parameters (Grattafiori et al., 2024), Gemma 3 with 27 billion parameters (Team et al., 2025) and Phi-4 with 14 billion parameters (Abdin et al., 2024) for data augmentation, as they represent diverse architectural paradigms and parameter scales, enabling the generation of robust, varied, and semantically coherent synthetic data.

The rewritten tweets are generated via the Ollama Python library[2], which provides a common interface for many published LLMs. A new model is initialized for each LLM and writing style using the same Ollama procedure, where only the LLM and writing style names are changed. First, we specify the LLM and the task that the model should perform. This task instructs the model to interpret all subsequent inputs as tweets to be rewritten in the specified tone. In addition to the tone, the LLMs were instructed to exchange entities. For example, the entity 'floor' could be exchanged for 'carpet'. This exchange should further diversify the dataset. LLMs typically refuse to answer questions about specific tasks involving harmful speech. Therefore, the instructions include a sentence stating that the task is for research purposes only, to minimize refusals to answer. If an LLM cannot interpret a tweet, it was instructed to return the word 'None'. The chosen parameters, including the prompt, can be found in Appendix A. After initialization, each tweet from an underrepresented class is fed into the LLM. These responses represent the augmented data. Depending on the LLM, some tweets were rejected or misinterpreted, rendering the responses unusable as augmented data. The cleaning of the created datasets is discussed in Section 4.3.

4.2 Rewriting Styles

The styles of social media posts have been widely studied. On Twitter (now X), for example, styles range from formal to casual and intimate (Sani et al., 2025). Their analysis revealed that the casual style was the most prevalent among Twitter users, accounting for approximately 40 % of the sampled tweets. This style characterizes the informal and conversational nature of the Twitter platform. Hu (2023) analyzed political tweets and identified six language styles: mobilizing, self-expressive, argumentative, narrative, analytical, and informative. The study examined how these styles relate to users' online characteristics, such as social connections or gender. Thus, we asked LLMs to identify the speech styles from a range of predefined styles in the tweets of the provided dataset. We selected these styles without conducting any theoretical analysis. Table 2 shows the prompt with the parameters.

The overall results are shown in Table 3, separated by class. However, it is worth noting the

[2] https://www.ollama.com (2025-07-15)

request	
role:	system
content:	Your task is to guess the speech style for the input text. Give only the guessed speech style without any comments or explanation. You have the following choices. Give one of these choices as answer back: {Neutral, Formal, Polemical, Sarcastic, Satirical, Aggressive, Polite, Colloquial, Ironic, Poetic, Biting, None}. If you do not have any text to analyze the style, give just None as answer back!
parameter:	{temperature: 0.9, top_p: 0.9}
role:	user
content:	Ist das nicht die Bürgermeisterin, die gegen den Drogenhandel im Görlitzer Park die Büsche abholzen liess? Durch solche Leute können diese Zustände erst entstehen.
response	
role:	Assistant
content:	Polemical

Table 2: Example of a prompt request and the response returned for a style guess.

difference in distribution between the negative and positive classes for all tasks. The colloquial style is most prevalent in negative tweets, while the aggressive style clearly dominates in positive tweets. We chose six of the returned guessed styles for data augmentation for the underrepresented classes: *bissig*, *formell*, *ironisch*, *neutral*, *polemisch*, and *sarkastisch* (The English translations are: *biting, formal, ironic, neutral, polemic,* and *sarcastic*). The following examples show the rewritten texts from Llama3.3:70b for the example text in Table 2.

(1) Die selbsternannte Heldin des Görlitzer Parks, welche glaubt, dass das Abholzen von Büschen den Drogenhandel bekämpft, trägt mit ihrem unzureichenden Handeln direkt zu solchen katastrophalen Zuständen bei! [*biting*]

(2) Die Entscheidung der zuständigen Kommunalbehörde, die Vegetation in einem bestimmten öffentlichen Park zu entfernen, um den Drogenhandel zu bekämpfen, wurde von einigen als maßgeblicher Faktor für das Entstehen bestimmter sozialer Probleme angesehen. [*formal*]

(3) Die Heldin des Görlitzer Parks, die mit ihrem genialen Plan, die Büsche abzuholzen, den Drogenhandel sicherlich ausgerottet hat - ein perfektes Beispiel dafür, wie man Probleme wirklich löst. [*ironic*]

(4) Eine lokale Politikerin hat Maßnahmen ergriffen, um den Drogenhandel in einem bestimmten Park zu bekämpfen. Kritiker sind der Meinung, dass solche Aktionen dazu beitragen könnten, Probleme zu verschärfen. [*neutral*]

(5) Die Verantwortliche für die Rodung der Büsche im Görlitzer Park, um den Drogenhandel zu bekämpfen, trägt selbst zur Entstehung dieser abscheulichen Verhältnisse bei! [*polemic*]

(6) Das ist bestimmt dieselbe Bürgermeisterin, die so clever war, die Büsche im Görlitzer Park abzuholzen, um den Drogenhandel zu bekämpfen - als ob das Problem einfach durch Entfernen von Pflanzen gelöst werden könnte. Es ist wirklich erstaunlich, wie solche Visionäre dazu beitragen, dass solche Zustände überhaupt entstehen können! [*sarcastic*]

In the dataset, the example in Table 2 is annotated as 'criticism'. Rewriting such an example as 'neutral', might change the tone of the tweet and would be annotated as 'nothing'. We ignore this fact and leave the original label as it is. We will discuss the effects at the end of Section 5.3.

4.3 Cleaning of Synthetic Data

As explained in Section 4.1 and demonstrated in the prompt in Appendix A, we instructed each LLM to output either the rewritten tweet or 'None' if rewriting was not possible. All answers containing 'None' were filtered out before training. Additionally, we manually inspected the answers to ensure the instruction was followed. During this process, we noticed that the LLMs handled our instruction very differently, as discussed further in this section.

Gemma 3. This LLM followed the instructions incredibly well. It either provided a rewritten tweet or answered 'None'. For some tweets, it stated that they could not be rewritten due to their hateful content. These instances could easily have been filtered out beforehand. Additionally, there are only a few exceptions in which it began its response with "Here is the rewritten tweet" or something similar. In these cases, we removed that part of the answer and only added the rewritten tweet to the dataset.

Llama 3.3. Llama understood the instructions well and most of the time answered with either a rewritten tweet or 'None'. There were some exceptions when it answered that it could not rewrite the tweet, providing an explanation for its decision. In these cases, the tweet either did not contain text (e.g., tweets containing only a URL) or

	C2A		DBO		VIO	
	False	True	Nothing	Others	False	True
Colloquial	**2,179**	126	**2,285**	90	**2,417**	90
Aggressive	1,247	**317**	1,542	**490**	1,507	**353**
Polemical	1,220	161	930	436	1,561	56
Sarcastic	958	34	818	135	1,009	54
Formal	82	8	116	5	114	4
Neutral	78	0	79	2	90	0
Polite	74	6	85	0	88	0
Satirical	67	4	52	10	67	6
Poetic	35	2	43	2	39	0
Ironic	19	0	20	3	21	0
Biting	4	1	2	1	3	0

Table 3: Results of the style guess per class for each subtask. Numbers in bold indicate the most prevalent style. Answers with 'None' are omitted.

the textual content was too disturbing, thus violating the LLM's principles. All of these exceptions were filtered out before training. For some tweets, Llama provided a rewritten version but stated at the beginning of its answer that the tweet was of questionable character. We removed that part of the answer and added only the rewritten tweet to the augmented dataset.

Phi-4. A visual inspection of this LLM's answers revealed that it completely ignored the instruction. One could describe it as "very chatty" with a lot of unnecessary output. Like the other two LLMs, it would sometimes answer that it could not rewrite a given tweet due to its hateful nature. However, even when it provided a rewritten tweet, Phi-4 also provided extensive additional information. For example, it provided an English translation of the tweet, the entities it replaced, the reasons for the replacements, a restatement of the task, and notes. Unfortunately, the additional output was not structured. Sometimes this output was marked with a star (*), and other times with a hashtag (#). Furthermore, the additional information was not always in the same position, i.e., at the beginning or end of the answer. During our inspection, the list of phrases to be filtered out became so long that we decided against using Phi-4's augmented data.

Summary. Although LLMs are trained to avoid repeating harmful content, we were able to bypass this behavior by informing each LLM that the task was scientific in nature. Still, there were some instances in which they refused to rewrite a tweet, though most of the time they complied. Gemma, in particular, rewrote more tweets than Llama. Table 4 illustrates this, showing the number of synthetic instances after cleaning. For DBO, we accumulated the numbers for each label. For a detailed overview of the synthetic instances per label for this subtask, see Table 10 in Appendix C.

5 Experiments & Results

In the following sections, we first describe the model that we used in our experiments. Then, we will describe the different setups that we evaluated. Lastly, we present the results for each subtask and setup.

5.1 Architecture & Model

For all experiments, we used the pre-trained GBERT base language model (Chan et al., 2020) from Huggingface[3]. The model was collaboratively trained by the creators of the original German BERT and dbmdz BERT models[4]. The following hyperparameters were applied: batch size = 8, learning rate = $2e^{-5}$, epochs = 3, and maximum sequence length = 128. Apart from the required preprocessing steps for BERT (adding [CLS] and [SEP] tokens, as well as tokenization with the BERT tokenizer), no other steps were implemented.

As mentioned in the introduction, our focus is on the ability of LLMs to rewrite harmful content and

[3]https://huggingface.co/deepset/gbert-base (2025-07-15)

[4]https://github.com/dbmdz/berts

Subtask	LLM	Style						Total
		bissig	*formell*	*ironisch*	*neutral*	*polemisch*	*sarkastisch*	
C2A	Gemma	657	661	658	660	657	659	3,952
	Llama	564	627	607	651	524	622	3,595
DBO	Gemma	1,167	1,169	1,174	1,170	867	1,174	6,721
	Llama	998	1,061	1,046	1,146	925	1,074	6,250
VIO	Gemma	555	558	561	559	560	561	3,354
	Llama	410	507	455	548	350	481	2,751

Table 4: Overview of the synthetic instances for each subtask, broken down by LLM and style.

the extent to which synthetic data is helpful in this shared task. Therefore, instead of training the 39 models on a GPU, we conducted all experiments on a MacBook Pro with an Apple M3 chip and 36 GB of RAM.

5.2 Experimental Setups

For each subtask, we first obtained baseline results using the provided training data (excluding the trial data as explained in Section 3). Then, we conducted preliminary experiments to determine the optimal combination of training data and LLM. We evaluated four different setups, which we will explain in greater detail. Section 5.3 provides details about the outcomes.

0 Baseline. To contextualize our results obtained by adding augmented data from LLMs, we first trained a baseline model. For training, we only used the provided datasets for each subtask.

1 Effectiveness of all styles from each LLM. In our initial setup, we evaluated the effectiveness of the instances generated with all six rewriting styles by each LLM. To this end, we added the augmented data created by one LLM to the original training datasets.

2 Effectiveness of combined LLMs. In our second setup, we evaluated whether more data would lead to better results. Therefore, we combined the augmented data from both LLMs in all six styles and added it to the provided datasets.

3 Effectiveness of each style from both LLMs. In our third setup, we conducted experiments on the usefulness of the different rewriting styles. Therefore, we combined the augmented data for each style from both LLMs before adding it to the provided datasets.

4 Effectiveness of combined styles. For our final setup, we first examined the F1 scores obtained by each rewriting style. Then, we combined the styles that obtained the best scores and added them to the provided training data.

5.3 Experimental Results

The following sections present the results obtained for the different setups. Each model was trained on the augmented training data and evaluated using the provided trial data (see Section 3). Due to the large number of models, we have summarized the scores where appropriate. The complete results can be found in Appendix B. For the submitted models, we report the macro F1 scores calculated by the organizers of the shared task on the official test set. See Table 5 for these results.

Subtask	Submission 1	Submission 2
C2A	75 %	79 %
DBO	63 %	62 %
VIO	75 %	75 %

Table 5: Official macro F1 scores obtained on the test set as computed by the organizers.

Subtask 1: C2A. Our baseline model, which was trained using the provided dataset, obtained a macro F1 score of 71 %. Augmenting the dataset with the instances from Gemma 3 increased the F1 score by 5 percentage points, while additional instances from Llama 3.3 only increased the score by 1 percentage point. Combining the synthetic instances from both LLMs resulted in an F1 score of 76 %. Using one style as additional data yielded measurable positive effects, with F1 scores ranging from 72 % to 79 %. The best results were obtained with the styles *bissig, ironisch, sarkastisch,* and *formell* and we experimented with different combinations of these styles. A complete overview of the results for Subtask 1 can be found in Table 7 in Appendix B.

For the first submission, we selected a model that was trained using synthetic data from Gemma, achieving an F1 score of 75 % on the test set. For the second submission, we chose the model trained with the styles *bissig+ironisch+sarkastisch* resulting in an F1 score of 79 % on the test set.

Subtask 2: DBO. Our baseline achieved a macro F1 score of 38 % and did not make a single correct prediction for the labels 'subversive' and 'agitation'. Adding synthetic data from Gemma increased the F1 score to 52 %, but it still did not predict any instances of 'agitation' correctly. Synthetic data from Llama increased the F1 score to 56 %, but it also failed to predict any 'agitation' instances correctly. Evaluating each style revealed that only *bissig* and *polemisch* made correct predictions for the labels 'subversive' and 'agitation'. The styles *formell* and *ironisch* could not make one correct prediction for 'agitation', while the styles *formell* and *sarkastisch* could not make any correct predictions for 'subversive' and 'agitation'. See Table 8 in Appendix B for a complete overview of the results for Subtask 2.

For the first submission, we submitted the model's predictions trained with additional data using the style *bissig*, which resulted in an F1 score of 63 % on the test set. For the second submission, we submitted the model's predictions trained with the *bissig+polemisch* styles, resulting in an F1 score of 62 %.

Subtask 3: VIO. Our baseline achieved a macro F1 score of 62 %. Adding the augmented data from Gemma increased the score by 16 percentage points, while adding the data from Llama increased the score by 10 percentage points. Interestingly, combining the augmented data from both LLMs resulted in only a 7 percent increase. Adding synthetic data for each style yielded F1 scores ranging from 60 % to 70 %. We experimented with different combinations of the highest-valued styles – namely, *bissig*, *ironisch*, and *sarkastisch* – but could not achieve a higher F1 score than with data augmented by Gemma's output. Since Gemma's scores were higher than Llama's, we experimented with the styles *bissig+ironisch+sarkastisch* only from Gemma, but this did not increase the F1 score. A complete overview of the results for Subtask 3 can be found in Table 9 in Appendix B.

For both submissions, we selected the model that was trained using augmented data from Gemma because no better results could be obtained on the trial dataset. This model achieved an F1 score of 75 % on the test set.

Discussion on the rewriting styles. As mentioned in Section 4.2, rewriting a tweet with either a 'neutral' or a 'formell' tone may alter the label an annotator would assign. Below, we discuss the results of the experimental setup in which we evaluated the effectiveness of each rewriting style from both LLMs (experimental setup *3 Effectiveness of each style from both LLMs*) with a focus on the aforementioned two styles.

For C2A, the style 'formell' had a decreased F1 score of four percentage points which was nevertheless higher than the scores for 'polemisch' and 'sarkastisch'. But the style 'neutral' scored the worst of all styles with a decrease of seven percentage points. Interestingly, the style 'formell' had the highest F1 score for DBO, while 'neutral' obtained the second worst score. For VIO, 'formell' obtained the second best result of all styles, while 'neutral' achieved the highest one.

These results suggest that rewriting a tweet in a 'formell' tone still conveys the message of harmful content that can be detected by a classifier. The same is not true for a 'neutral' style. Such rewritings lack the wording necessary for a classifier to detect, though this was not the case for the VIO subtask. Overall, the rewriting styles may be dependent on the task to be performed and would need tailoring for the specific (classification) task at hand. Furthermore, there might be an interaction between styles.

6 Conclusion & Future Work

In this work, we presented our participation in the shared task of Harmful Content Detection in Social Media. The organizers provided us with annotated datasets that exhibit a heavily skewed class imbalance toward harmless content. For this reason, we employed data augmentation. To this end, we asked three LLMs to rewrite harmful tweets in six different styles. Although LLMs should not replicate harmful content, we designed the prompt so that the LLMs would comply with our request most of the time. They only refused to answer for the most disturbing tweets. Gemma and Llama understood our request to respond with either a rewritten tweet or 'None', Phi-4 did not. It was not possible to remove all unnecessary information from Phi-4's output, and we could not evaluate its usefulness for this task.

Furthermore, we analyzed the writing styles of the original tweets in the dataset. The analysis revealed that instances from the 'false' (C2A/VIO) and 'nothing' (DBO) classes were written in a *colloquial* style, while the 'true' (C2A/VIO) and 'subversive'/'agitation'/'criticism' (DBO) classes are mostly categorized as written with an aggressive tone. These results suggest that balancing the writing styles may be important.

In our experimental setup, we evaluated the effectiveness of synthetic data generated by (i) each LLM, (ii) combined LLMs, (iii) one rewriting style, and (iv) combined rewriting styles. Different setups were shown to be more useful for each subtask. For C2A, we submitted predictions from a model trained with the additional synthetic data from Gemma (75 % on the test set) and those predicted by the styles *bissig+ironisch+sarkastisch* (79 % on the test set). For DBO, many of our models struggled to make correct predictions for the most underrepresented classes, i.e., 'subversive' and 'agitation'. Predicting all classes on the trial dataset was managed by the model trained with the additional data with style *bissig* – obtaining a macro F1 score of 63 % on the test set – and the model trained with the additional data with styles *bissig+polemisch*, resulting in a macro F1 score of 62 % on the test set. For VIO, no setup performed better on the trial dataset than the augmented Gemma data, which received a macro F1 score of 75 % on the test set.

Future research could examine how writing styles influence hate speech detection, focusing on the impact of tone, formality, punctuation, and rhetorical strategies on model performance. Subtle stylistic forms – such as irony, sarcasm, or variation in register – may obscure hateful intent and challenge standard classifiers. While this study did not account for coded language, i.e., veiled or context-dependent expressions that implicitly convey hate, addressing such phenomena is crucial for capturing more covert forms of abuse. LLMs offer promising capabilities to model and generate stylistically diverse, context-aware training data. Future work could leverage LLMs to identify, cluster, or synthesize stylistic and coded variations, thereby improving the robustness of classifiers across sociolinguistic boundaries and communicative contexts.

Acknowledgments. This work is partially funded by dtec.bw – Digitalization and Technology Research Center of the Bundeswehr, which is funded by the European Union – NextGenerationEU.

References

Marah Abdin, Jyoti Aneja, Harkirat Behl, Sébastien Bubeck, and et. al. 2024. Phi-4 Technical Report. *Preprint*, arXiv:2412.08905.

Michael Achmann-Denkler, Jakob Fehle, Mario Haim, and Christian Wolff. 2024. Detecting Calls to Action in Multimodal Content: Analysis of the 2021 German Federal Election Campaign on Instagram. In *Proceedings of the 4th Workshop on Computational Linguistics for the Political and Social Sciences: Long and short papers*, pages 1–13, Vienna, Austria. Association for Computational Linguistics.

Jinan Ali Aljawazeri and Mahdi Nsaif Jasim. 2025. Enhancing Hate-Speech Detection Using Data-Augmentation Techniques: A Multi-label Dataset Approach. In *Data Science and Applications*, pages 103–113, Singapore. Springer Nature Singapore.

Salvador V. Balkus and Donghui Yan. 2023. Improving short text classification with augmented data using GPT-3. *Natural Language Engineering*, 30(5):943–972.

Branden Chan, Stefan Schweter, and Timo Möller. 2020. German's Next Language Model. In *Proceedings of the 28th International Conference on Computational Linguistics*, pages 6788–6796, Barcelona, Spain (Online). International Committee on Computational Linguistics.

N. V. Chawla, K. W. Bowyer, L. O. Hall, and W. P. Kegelmeyer. 2002. SMOTE: Synthetic Minority Over-sampling Technique. *Journal of Artificial Intelligence Research*, 16:321–357.

Matthew Ciolino, David Noever, and Josh Kalin. 2022. Back translation survey for improving text augmentation. *Preprint*, arXiv:2102.09708.

Jacob Devlin, Ming-Wei Chang, Kenton Lee, and Kristina Toutanova. 2019. BERT: Pre-training of Deep Bidirectional Transformers for Language Understanding. In *Proceedings of the 2019 Conference of the North American Chapter of the Association for Computational Linguistics: Human Language Technologies, Volume 1 (Long and Short Papers)*, pages 4171–4186, Minneapolis, Minnesota. ACL.

Bosheng Ding, Chengwei Qin, Ruochen Zhao, Tianze Luo, Xinze Li, Guizhen Chen, Wenhan Xia, Junjie Hu, Anh Tuan Luu, and Shafiq Joty. 2024. Data Augmentation using Large Language Models: Data Perspectives, Learning Paradigms and Challenges. *Preprint*, arXiv:2403.02990.

Jenny Felser, Michael Spranger, and Melanie Siegel. 2025. Overview of the GermEval 2025 Shared Task on Harmful Content Detection. In *Proceedings of the 21st Conference on Natural Language Processing (KONVENS 2025): Workshops*.

Janis Goldzycher, Paul Röttger, and Gerold Schneider. 2024. Improving Adversarial Data Collection by Supporting Annotators: Lessons from GAHD, a German Hate Speech Dataset. In *Proceedings of the 2024 Conference of the North American Chapter of the Association for Computational Linguistics: Human Language Technologies (Volume 1: Long Papers)*, pages 4405–4424, Mexico City, Mexico. Association for Computational Linguistics.

Aaron Grattafiori, Abhimanyu Dubey, Abhinav Jauhri, and et. al. 2024. The Llama 3 Herd of Models. *Preprint*, arXiv:2407.21783.

Lingshu Hu. 2023. Mobilization, self-expression or argument? A computational method for identifying language styles in political discussion on Twitter. *Online Information Review*, 48(4):783–802.

Sadar Jaf and Basel Barakat. 2024. Empirical Evaluation of Public HateSpeech Datasets. *Preprint*, arXiv:2407.12018.

Md Saroar Jahan, Mourad Oussalah, Djamila Romaissa Beddiar, Jhuma Kabir Mim, and Nabil Arhab. 2024. A Comprehensive Study on NLP Data Augmentation for Hate Speech Detection: Legacy Methods, BERT, and LLMs. *CoRR*, abs/2404.00303.

Kyriaki Pantelidou, Despoina Chatzakou, Theodora Tsikrika, Stefanos Vrochidis, and Ioannis Kompatsiaris. 2022. Selective word substitution for contextualized data augmentation. In *Natural Language Processing and Information Systems*, pages 508–516, Cham. Springer International Publishing.

Nur Balqies Sani, Novia Lestari P. A., Ronny Ahmad Fauzi Pane, Anisa Novita Sari, and Rakhmat Wahyudin Sagala. 2025. An Analysis of Language Styles on Social Media: Twitter Case Study. *ALTERA: Journal of Applied Linguistics, English Education, and Literature*, 1(01):12–20.

Norman Sapar, Ab Razak Che Hussin, and Nadhmi A. Gazem. 2023. A New Landscape of Political Engagement Through Social Media: How Can We Map It? In *Advances on Intelligent Computing and Data Science*, pages 544–552, Cham. Springer International Publishing.

Stefan Stieglitz and Linh Dang-Xuan. 2013. Social media and political communication: a social media analytics framework. *Social Network Analysis and Mining*, pages 1277–1291.

Gemma Team, Aishwarya Kamath, Johan Ferret, and et. al. 2025. Gemma 3 Technical Report. *Preprint*, arXiv:2503.19786.

Jason Wei and Kai Zou. 2019. EDA: Easy data augmentation techniques for boosting performance on text classification tasks. In *Proceedings of the 2019 Conference on Empirical Methods in Natural Language Processing and the 9th International Joint Conference on Natural Language Processing (EMNLP-IJCNLP)*, pages 6382–6388, Hong Kong, China. Association for Computational Linguistics.

A Prompt

The `create` function of Ollama was used to initialize different LLMs and to instruct them on their task. The variable **rephStyle** written in bold stands for one of the six writing styles and is therefore substituted by the words *bissig*, *formell*, *ironisch*, *neutral*, *polemisch*, or *sarkastisch* (in English: *biting*, *formal*, *ironic*, *neutral*, *polemic*, and *sarcastic*). Table 6 shows the important parameters for the `create` function.

	Ollama `create` function
from_:	llama3.3:70b *or* gemma3:27b *or* phi4:latest
system:	Im Anschluss werden ausschließlich Tweets genannt, welche bitte umgeschrieben werden sollen. Die Tweets sollen so umgeschrieben werden, dass sie **rephStyle** klingen. Ersetze zudem bitte die Entitäten durch semantisch vergleichbare. Beachte bitte, dass es sich bei der Aufgabe um eine wissenschafltiche Aufgabe handelt. Die Inhalte der Tweets können teils verstörend sein, nichtsdestotrotz führe die Aufgabe bitte so präzise wie möglich aus. Gebe als Antwort ausschließlich den umgeschriebenen Tweet zurück. Beschreibungen sind nicht nötig! Solltest du Probleme mit dem Lesen bzw. Interpretieren des Tweets haben, dann gebe ausschließlich das Wort 'None' zurück.
parameters:	{temperature: 0.9, top_p: 0.9}

Table 6: Parameters used to initialize the LLM.

As the provided datasets contain German text samples, the system prompt was also provided in German. An English translation of the prompt would be: "In the following only tweets will be listed that need to be rewritten. The tweets should be rewritten so that they sound in the style of *rephStyle*. Also, please replace the entities with semantically comparable ones. Please note that this is a scientific task. The content of the tweets may be disturbing; nevertheless, please carry out the task as precisely as possible. Respond only with the rewritten tweet. No descriptions are necessary. If you have trouble reading or interpreting the tweet, respond only with the word 'None''."

B Complete Experimental Results

Tables 7, 8, and 9 list all experimental results conducted for each subtask. Reported F1 scores were obtained by evaluating each model on the trial data.

LLM/Style	Macro F1
Baseline	71 %
Gemma	76 %
Llama	72 %
Gemma+Llama	76 %
bissig	75 %
formell	75 %
ironisch	79 %
neutral	72 %
polemisch	73 %
sarkastisch	74 %
bissig+ironisch	71 %
bissig+sarkastisch	76 %
bissig+ironisch+sarkastisch	79 %
bissig+ironisch+formell	76 %

Table 7: All experimental results on the trial dataset for the subtask 'Call2Action'.

LLM/Style	Macro F1
Baseline	38 %
Gemma	52 %
Llama	56 %
Gemma+Llama	—∗
bissig	55 %
formell	58 %
ironisch	43 %
neutral	39 %
polemisch	56 %
sarkastisch	38 %
bissig+polemisch	67 %
bissig+polemisch+sarkastisch	60 %

Table 8: All experimental results on the trial dataset for the subtask 'Attack on the Democratic Basic Order'. (∗: The full dataset was too large to fit in a laptop's RAM.)

LLM/Style	Macro F1
Baseline	62 %
Gemma	78 %
Llama	72 %
Gemma+Llama	69 %
bissig	66 %
formell	69 %
ironisch	70 %
neutral	70 %
polemisch	60 %
sarkastisch	69 %
bissig+ironisch	68 %
ironisch+sarkastisch	67 %
Gemma *bissig+ironisch+sarkastisch*	68 %

Table 9: All experimental results on the trial dataset for the subtask 'Violence Detection'.

C Augmented Data for Subtask 2

Table 10 provides a detailed breakdown of the number of instances generated for each label and LLM for Subtask 2 (DBO).

		Label			
LLM	**Style**	subversive	agitation	criticism	**Total**
Gemma	bissig	60	305	802	1,167
	formell	61	306	802	1,169
	ironisch	60	312	802	1,174
	neutral	59	309	802	1,170
	polemisch	43	226	598	867
	sarkastisch	61	311	802	1,174
Llama	bissig	49	195	754	998
	formell	51	223	787	1,061
	ironisch	54	210	782	1,046
	neutral	58	287	801	1,146
	polemisch	45	159	721	925
	sarkastisch	55	231	788	1,074

Table 10: Detailed overview of the generated instances per label and per LLM for Subtask 2.

Munich_Z@GermEval Shared Task 2025:When Prompting Is Not Enough: The Limits of Large Language Models in GermEval's 2025 Harmful Content Detection Task

Florian Ludwig
ZITiS
Zamdorfer Straße 88, 81677 Munich
florian.ludwig@zitis.bund.de

Dr. Stefan Altmann
ZITiS
Zamdorfer Straße 88, 81677 Munich
stefan.altmann@zitis.bund.de

Abstract

In the context of automatic hate speech detection, effective methods for low-data scenarios are crucial due to the dynamic and evolving nature of harmful language, which demands frequent model retraining. Large Language Models (LLMs) are promising for this task because they can generalize tasks solely from task descriptions and thus reduce the need for extensive data annotation. We evaluate prompting strategies for subtask 2 of the *GermEval 2025 Harmful Content Detection* challenge, which involves classifying whether a tweet attacks the free democratic basic order. We show that techniques such as *Chain-of-Thought*, *In-Context Learning* or *Task Decomposition* outperform approaches like *Task Description*. However, a significant performance gap remains between our prompting-based strategies and the top-performing systems in the competition. These findings indicate that, under current conditions, prompting with open-source LLMs alone is insufficient to achieve state-of-the-art results in complex hate speech related classification tasks.

OFFENSIVE CONTENT WARNING: This work contains examples of hateful content. This is strictly for the purpose of enabling this research. Please be aware that this content could be offensive and cause you distress.

1 Introduction

Data annotation is considered a critical bottleneck in many machine learning projects, as it is resource intensive and time-consuming (Neves and Ševa, 2021; Anglin et al., 2022; Madukwe et al., 2020). This limitation is even more demanding in scenarios of low-resource data and of fast-paced dynamic changes, as is the case of hate speech, where the expression and targets of hate can constitute a small proportion of the material to be analyzed and change quickly. Thus, in automatic hate speech detection, it is crucial to explore methods that perform well with limited data and reduce the need for model retraining (Lupu et al., 2023; Florio et al., 2020). Employing LLMs for this task is appealing, since these models can use their inherent knowledge and linguistic skills to generalize to various tasks based on task descriptions. Hence, these models are potentially able to adapt to different tasks without the need for extensive annotation of data (Ludwig et al., 2025).

In this work, we investigate different zero-shot and few-shot prompting methods to solve the second subtask of the *GermEval 2025* shared task, *Harmful Content Detection in Social Media* (Felser et al., 2025). The goal of this is to classify whether a tweet constitutes an attack on the free democratic basic order. Our contributions are as follows:

- We propose prompting strategies for analyzing different attacks on the basic democratic order
- We analyze the suitability and limitations of these strategies across various Large Language Models

Section 2 presents an overview of related works relevant to the study. Section 3 details the methodology, including data collection, the models applied, prompting strategies used, and the evaluation procedures. In Section 4, the results are provided along with their analysis and discussion. Finally, Section 5 concludes the work by summarizing the key findings and implications.

2 Related Works

The application of LLMs for hate speech detection has been investigated in several studies (Del Arco et al., 2023; Han and Tang, 2022; Chiu et al., 2021). The authors Kumarage et al. (2024) reported strong classification results using *GPT 3.5* and *Llama 2* (Touvron et al., 2023) for the task of recognizing hate speech. In contrast to our work, they applied

Task Description

Subversive:
Subversive posts express the aim of overthrowing the government [...]

Agitational:
Posts in the "Agitational" category aim to incite others aggressively against the liberal democratic order. This involves concrete actions such as spreading propaganda [...]

Instruction:
Classify the following post into exactly one of the above categories.

Post:
<Post to classify>

Figure 1: In the **Task Description** approach, we include the class definitions, provided by the *GermEval* challenge organizers, as context in the prompt.

In-Context Learning

Subversive:
Subversive posts express the aim of overthrowing the government [...]

Agitational:
[...]

Instruction:
Classify the following post into exactly one of the above categories.

Post:
<Example Post 1>

[Example Answer 1]

Post:
<Example Post 2>

[Example Answer 2]

[...]

Post:
<Post to classify>

Figure 2: In **In-Context Learning** we provide few-shot examples in addition to the task descriptions in the prompt.

Chain of Thought

Subversive:
Subversive posts express the aim of overthrowing the government [...]

Agitational:
[...]

Instruction:
Classify the following post into exactly one of the above categories. Think step by step how you can solve this task. Think about which characteristics the individual classes require, how they differ from each other and which of these characteristics are present in the post.

Post:
<Post to classify>

Figure 3: In the **Chain of Thought** approach, the model is guided to reason through how the task can be broken down into subtasks before solving it.

Task Decomposition

Does the following post contain negative attitudes towards state institutions [...] ?

Post:
<Post to classify>

[Model Answer]

Does the post call for violence against state actors? This includes [...]

[Model Answer]

Does this post incite other anti-state but non-violent acts or does it spread propaganda or anti-constitutional symbols? [...]

[Model Answer]

Figure 4: In the **Task Decomposition** approach, we divide the overall problem into subtasks, which are made available to the model as a chain of prompts.

these models to the HateCheck corpus (Röttger et al., 2021), which consists of rather simple, handcrafted examples. Alkhamissi et al. (2022) investigated how hate speech recognition tasks can be prepared for large language models. The authors propose to split the task into simpler subtasks. They conducted task preparation for fine-tuning a BART model (Lewis et al., 2020). According to the authors the robustness of the classification depends on the prompt, its wording and the context provided. In contrast, our work employed inference-based approaches, such as *Task Decomposition*, *Chain-of-Thought* prompting and *In-Context Learning*. Morbidoni and Sarra (2023) investigated how GPT 3.5 can be made to recognize misogyny. The authors formulated the task as a simple yes/no question and experimented with additional prompt context.

In our previous work (Ludwig et al., 2025) we investigated how LLMs can be used to detect criminally relevant hate speech. We investigated how these models can be conditioned at different levels of abstraction in legal systems to accomplish this task. A remarkable difference in performance between LLMs and legal experts was reported. While this work addressed how general legal knowledge can be brought into LLMs to recognize criminally-relevant posts, the current work focuses on the sub-

Approach	Model	Pre.	Rec.	F1
Uniform Rand.	*Dummy*	.29	.29	.29
Description	*Phi 4*	.43	.39	.41
	Cmd-R+	.34	.30	.31
	Qwen	.48	.43	.41
CoT	*Phi 4*	.67	.54	.53
	Cmd-R+	.58	.56	.56
	Qwen	.62	.54	.51
In-Context	*Phi 4*	.59	.52	.50
	Cmd-R+	.59	.57	**.57**
	Qwen	.67	.56	.55
Decomposition	*Phi 4*	.58	.50	.49
	Cmd-R+	.40	.44	.44
	Qwen	.56	.51	.49

Table 1: Classification metrics with respect to different approaches and models.

jective definitions of attacks on the free democratic basic order.

3 Methods and Experiments

In this section, we introduce the dataset, language models and prompting strategies, employed in our experiments.

3.1 Data

The training data of the harmful content detection task (Felser et al., 2025) consists of $7,454$ German posts, containing different types of attacks on the free democratic basic order. The classes include (1) calling to overthrow the government (*Subversive*), (2) spreading propaganda (*Agitation*), (3) legitimate criticism of the government (*Criticism*) and (4) other posts, without any type of attack on the democratic order (*Nothing*). Data statistics and examples for each class can be seen in Appendix A, Table 5.

3.2 Models

For our experiments, we selected the following models due to their strong reasoning capabilities and state-of-the-art performance on a range of benchmarks, and demonstrated proficiency in multilingual tasks: *Phi-4 14B* (Abdin et al., 2024), known for its efficient scaling and reasoning depth; *Qwen-3 32B* (Yang et al., 2025), which excels in both language understanding and generation across diverse languages; and *Command-R+*[1], a model optimized for instruction following and retrieval-augmented generation.

[1]https://cohere.com/blog/command-r-plus-microsoft-azure

Approach	Noth.	Crit.	Agit.	Subv.	Avg.
Description	.57	.67	.48	.26	.49
CoT	.60	.77	.56	.27	.55
In-Context	.58	.68	.67	.27	.55
Decomposition	.66	.59	.47	.24	.49
Average	.62	.68	.54	.26	.52

Table 2: Proportion of correctly classified posts by approach and class label, averaged over all models.

3.3 Prompting Strategies

We investigated and compared four different prompting strategies. For the **Task Description** approach (Figure 1 and Appendix B.1), we used the definitions provided by the *GermEval* challenge organizers and incorporated them into the prompt as contextual information. Our second approach (Figure 2, Appendix B.2) focuses on **In-Context Learning**. This is done by extending the first approach with examples selected from the trial set. Example answers to these prompts were formulated by the authors based on the provided class labels. Our third approach is **Chain-of-Thought (CoT)** prompting (Wei et al., 2022). In this approach (Figure 3, Appendix B.3), the model is explicitly encouraged to engage in intermediate reasoning by decomposing a complex task into a sequence of smaller and more manageable subtasks to be solved step by step. *CoT* prompting was shown to enhance the model's accuracy on reasoning-intensive problems (Wang et al., 2023; Zhang et al., 2025; Yu et al., 2023). The fourth approach is based on **Task Decomposition** (Figure 4), in which the whole classification problem is manually divided into smaller sub-problems. In this case, the answers to the sub-problems are combined to provide the final answer to the complete problem (see Appendix B.4 for more details).

Similar to Ludwig et al. (2025), we used a two-step approach for retrieving the model answers. First, we let the language models freely generate their responses. Second, we prompted the models to format their responses in JSON format, which allowed us to analyze the answers automatically (see Appendix B.5 for further details).

3.4 Model Assessment

A balanced subset of the provided training data, consisting of 50 samples from each class, was extracted and used as a development set to test our prompting strategies. We optimized our prompts using the training set and then evaluated their final

Misclass. Models %	Noth.	Crit.	Agit.	Subv.
80%	.21	.11	.08	.67
100%	.10	.00	.02	.18

Table 3: Proportion of misclassified posts per class, averaged across models.

versions on this separate development set.

4 Results and Discussion

Table 1 presents classification results across various prompting strategies and language models on our development set. Almost all configurations significantly outperform the random baseline. Unlike Ludwig et al. (2025), we found that advanced prompting strategies (*Chain-of-Thought*, *In-Context Learning*, and *Task Decomposition*) outperformed the simpler *Task Description* approach. Notably, *Chain-of-Thought* surpassed manual *Task Decomposition*. No single model consistently outperformed others across all strategies. Our best approach achieved an F1-score of .57 on the development set, substantially lower than the competition winner's F1-score of .71. This suggests that LLMs cannot yet be reliably or robustly prompted to solve complex classification tasks, such as those related to hate speech detection.

Table 2 reports the proportion of correctly classified samples on the development set across prompting strategies and class labels, averaged over all three models. The models performed worst on the Subversive class, with only 26% of samples correctly classified, which is substantially lower than for the other classes. We further present statistics on posts that were particularly challenging for LLMs to classify (Table 3). The table shows the proportion of posts misclassified by at least 80% of models (first row) or by all models (second row) across all strategies, highlighting that the *Nothing* class and, in line with previous results, especially the *Subversive* class, contained samples most challenging for the models. While 10% of examples of the *Nothing* class were misclassified by all models and approaches, 18% were misclassified for the *Subversive* class.

We manually analyzed these posts and the corresponding language model responses. We observed that 50% of the normal posts, which were misclassified by all models and approaches, contained a call for violent action. These posts were, however, annotated as normal, because the call for violence is not clearly directed towards the government or its officials. This indicates that models struggle to grasp the task's fine-grained nuances, in line with previous findings (Ludwig et al., 2025). As for the posts misclassified as belonging to the *Subversive* class we observed that about 64% of these posts contain a call to dismiss the chancellor or the governing party. However, it is not clear from the posts that this action is to be carried out by force, as required to classify the posts as being subversive. These posts might be considered as borderline cases, which are evaluated differently by language models due to their inherent biases and conceptual understanding. The subjectivity and difficulty of hate speech annotation (Dehghan et al., 2025; Fleisig et al., 2023; Poletto et al., 2019) and inherent biases in language models (Navigli et al., 2023; Liang et al., 2021; Ferrara, 2023) are well-known problems in the research community. Examples of the discussed cases are shown in Table 4. [2]

Post	Label
Cut off his stumps and hang him by the feet 😡😡😡 ... far too little, great justice!	Nothing
Carry them? Better to have them flogged under Islamic law. 🕌	Nothing
Someone should shoot him! 💀	Nothing
[...] Enough of that 😠 #refugeesnotwelcome [...] #MerkelMustGo	Subversive
Merkel must go, and every asylum seeker who doesn't behave follow ...	Subversive
Encourage family and friends to vote nationalist in the elections! #MerkelMustGo #PartyBlocMustGo #Islamization	Subversive

Table 4: Example posts, which were misclassified by all models across all prompting schemes.

5 Conclusion

In this work, we examined various prompting strategies for language models aimed at classifying tweets according to different forms of attacks on the free democratic basic order. Our findings suggest that while LLMs are generally effective in classifying these attacks, their inherent conceptual biases can limit prompt-based control, resulting in suboptimal performances on the second subtask of the *GermEval's 2025 Harmful Content Detection* (Felser et al., 2025). In contrast, smaller models like BERT (Devlin et al., 2019) may offer greater adaptability through fine-tuning for highly specific tasks. Due to their strong linguistic abilities, LLMs

[2]These are English translations of posts; original posts were written in German.

are well suited for challenging tasks such as analyzing hate speech - provided that their internalized concepts required for their analyses are properly aligned with the intended goals of the task. Consequently, future work should focus on methods, which are able to achieve language model alignment for hate speech related tasks in a data- and annotation-efficient manner to combine the best of both worlds: strong linguistic capabilities and rapid model adaptation.

Limitations

Our study has some limitations. First, we focus exclusively on subtask 2 of the *GermEval 2025* challenge. While this allows for a more targeted evaluation, it limits the generalizability of our findings to other subtasks or related tasks. Second, we restrict our experiments to three open-source language models. This choice ensures transparency and reproducibility but excludes stronger proprietary models such as *GPT-4*, which could potentially yield better results. Third, we evaluate only a subset of existing prompting strategies. Although we include widely used techniques such as *Chain-of-Thought* and *In-Context Learning*, other recent approaches remain unexplored due to computational and scope constraints. Future work should address these limitations by expanding the range of tasks, models, and prompting methods.

Ethics Statement

We use publicly available, anonymized data from the *GermEval 2025* shared task. While this ensures reproducibility, we acknowledge that the dataset may contain biases and harmful content. Hate speech detection remains a subjective and context-dependent task, and automated systems may produce false positives or negatives. Our models are intended solely for research and should not be deployed in real-world applications without careful consideration of fairness, societal impact, and the need for human oversight.

References

Marah Abdin, Jyoti Aneja, Harkirat Behl, Sébastien Bubeck, Ronen Eldan, Suriya Gunasekar, Michael Harrison, Russell J. Hewett, Mojan Javaheripi, Piero Kauffmann, James R. Lee, Yin Tat Lee, Yuanzhi Li, Weishung Liu, Caio C. T. Mendes, Anh Nguyen, Eric Price, Gustavo de Rosa, Olli Saarikivi, and 8 others. 2024. Phi-4 technical report. *arXiv preprint arXiv:2412.08905*.

Badr Alkhamissi, Faisal Ladhak, Srinivasan Iyer, Veselin Stoyanov, Zornitsa Kozareva, Xian Li, Pascale Fung, Lambert Mathias, Asli Celikyilmaz, and Mona Diab. 2022. Token: Task decomposition and knowledge infusion for few-shot hate speech detection. In *Proceedings of the 2022 Conference on Empirical Methods in Natural Language Processing*, pages 2109–2120.

Kylie Anglin, Arielle Boguslav, and Todd Hall. 2022. Improving the science of annotation for natural language processing: The use of the single-case study for piloting annotation projects. *Journal of Data Science*, 20(3).

Ke-Li Chiu, Annie Collins, and Rohan Alexander. 2021. Detecting hate speech with gpt-3. *arXiv preprint arXiv:2103.12407*.

Somaiyeh Dehghan, Mehmet Umut Sen, and Berrin Yanikoglu. 2025. Dealing with annotator disagreement in hate speech classification. *arXiv preprint arXiv:2502.08266*.

Flor Miriam Plaza Del Arco, Debora Nozza, and Dirk Hovy. 2023. Respectful or toxic? using zero-shot learning with language models to detect hate speech. In *The 7th Workshop on Online Abuse and Harms (WOAH)*, pages 60–68.

Jacob Devlin, Ming-Wei Chang, Kenton Lee, and Kristina Toutanova. 2019. Bert: Pre-training of deep bidirectional transformers for language understanding. In *Proceedings of the 2019 conference of the North American chapter of the association for computational linguistics: human language technologies, volume 1 (long and short papers)*, pages 4171–4186.

Jenny Felser, Michael Spranger, and Melanie Siegel. 2025. Overview of the germeval 2025 shared task on harmful content detection. In *Proceedings of the 21st Conference on Natural Language Processing (KONVENS 2025): Workshops*.

Emilio Ferrara. 2023. Should chatgpt be biased? challenges and risks of bias in large language models. *arXiv preprint arXiv:2304.03738*.

Eve Fleisig, Rediet Abebe, and Dan Klein. 2023. When the majority is wrong: Modeling annotator disagreement for subjective tasks. In *Proceedings of the 2023 Conference on Empirical Methods in Natural Language Processing*, pages 6715–6726.

Komal Florio, Valerio Basile, Marco Polignano, Pierpaolo Basile, and Viviana Patti. 2020. Time of your hate: The challenge of time in hate speech detection on social media. *Applied Sciences*, 10(12):4180.

Lawrence Han and Hao Tang. 2022. Designing of prompts for hate speech recognition with in-context learning. In *2022 International Conference on Computational Science and Computational Intelligence (CSCI)*, pages 319–320. IEEE.

Tharindu Kumarage, Amrita Bhattacharjee, and Joshua Garland. 2024. Harnessing artificial intelligence to combat online hate: Exploring the challenges and opportunities of large language models in hate speech detection. *arXiv preprint arXiv:2403.08035*.

Mike Lewis, Yinhan Liu, Naman Goyal, Marjan Ghazvininejad, Abdelrahman Mohamed, Omer Levy, Veselin Stoyanov, and Luke Zettlemoyer. 2020. Bart: Denoising sequence-to-sequence pre-training for natural language generation, translation, and comprehension. In *Proceedings of the 58th Annual Meeting of the Association for Computational Linguistics*, pages 7871–7880.

Paul Pu Liang, Chiyu Wu, Louis-Philippe Morency, and Ruslan Salakhutdinov. 2021. Towards understanding and mitigating social biases in language models. In *International conference on machine learning*, pages 6565–6576. PMLR.

Florian Ludwig, Torsten Zesch, and Frederike Zufall. 2025. Conditioning large language models on legal systems? detecting punishable hate speech. *arXiv preprint arXiv:2506.03009*.

Yonatan Lupu, Richard Sear, Nicolas Velásquez, Rhys Leahy, Nicholas Johnson Restrepo, Beth Goldberg, and Neil F Johnson. 2023. Offline events and online hate. *PLoS one*, 18(1):e0278511.

Kosisochukwu Madukwe, Xiaoying Gao, and Bing Xue. 2020. In data we trust: A critical analysis of hate speech detection datasets. In *Proceedings of the fourth workshop on online abuse and harms*, pages 150–161.

Christian Morbidoni and Annalina Sarra. 2023. Can llms assist humans in assessing online misogyny? experiments with gpt-3.5. In *GENERALE Workshop @ CHItaly 2023*.

Roberto Navigli, Simone Conia, and Björn Ross. 2023. Biases in large language models: origins, inventory, and discussion. *ACM Journal of Data and Information Quality*, 15(2):1–21.

Mariana Neves and Jurica Ševa. 2021. An extensive review of tools for manual annotation of documents. *Briefings in bioinformatics*, 22(1):146–163.

Fabio Poletto, Valerio Basile, Cristina Bosco, Viviana Patti, and Marco Stranisci. 2019. Annotating hate speech: Three schemes at comparison. In *CEUR WORKSHOP PROCEEDINGS*, volume 2481, pages 1–8. CEUR-WS.

Paul Röttger, Bertie Vidgen, Dong Nguyen, Zeerak Waseem, Helen Margetts, and Janet Pierrehumbert. 2021. Hatecheck: Functional tests for hate speech detection models. In *Proceedings of the 59th Annual Meeting of the Association for Computational Linguistics and the 11th International Joint Conference on Natural Language Processing (Volume 1: Long Papers)*, pages 41–58.

Hugo Touvron, Louis Martin, Kevin Stone, Peter Albert, Amjad Almahairi, Yasmine Babaei, Nikolay Bashlykov, Soumya Batra, Prajjwal Bhargava, Shruti Bhosale, Dan Bikel, Lukas Blecher, Cristian Canton Ferrer, Moya Chen, Guillem Cucurull, David Esiobu, Jude Fernandes, Jeremy Fu, Wenyin Fu, and 49 others. 2023. Llama 2: Open foundation and fine-tuned chat models. *arXiv preprint arXiv:2307.09288*.

Boshi Wang, Sewon Min, Xiang Deng, Jiaming Shen, You Wu, Luke Zettlemoyer, and Huan Sun. 2023. Towards understanding chain-of-thought prompting: An empirical study of what matters. In *Proceedings of the 61st Annual Meeting of the Association for Computational Linguistics (Volume 1: Long Papers)*, pages 2717–2739.

Jason Wei, Xuezhi Wang, Dale Schuurmans, Maarten Bosma, Brian Ichter, Fei Xia, Ed Chi, Quoc V. Le, and Denny Zhou. 2022. Chain-of-thought prompting elicits reasoning in large language models. *Advances in neural information processing systems*, 35:24824–24837.

An Yang, Anfeng Li, Baosong Yang, Beichen Zhang, Binyuan Hui, Bo Zheng, Bowen Yu, Chang Gao, Chengen Huang, Chenxu Lv, Chujie Zheng, Dayiheng Liu, Fan Zhou, Fei Huang, Feng Hu, Hao Ge, Haoran Wei, Huan Lin, Jialong Tang, and 41 others. 2025. Qwen3 technical report. *arXiv preprint arXiv:2505.09388*.

Zihan Yu, Liang He, Zhen Wu, Xinyu Dai, and Jiajun Chen. 2023. Towards better chain-of-thought prompting strategies: A survey. *arXiv preprint arXiv:2310.04959*.

Yufeng Zhang, Xuepeng Wang, Lingxiang Wu, and Jinqiao Wang. 2025. Enhancing chain of thought prompting in large language models via reasoning patterns. In *Proceedings of the AAAI Conference on Artificial Intelligence*, volume 39, pages 25985–25993.

Appendix

A Data

Class	Counts	Original Examples	Translated Examples
Nothing	6, 277	Erwache Deutschland 🇩🇪	Awaken, Germany 🇩🇪
		Heil Deutschland !	Hail Germany!
		Es wäre traurig wenn man PEGIDA nur auf die unkontrollierte Zuwanderung reduzieren würde.	It would be sad if PEGIDA were reduced only to uncontrolled immigration.
Criticism	804	Dämonisierung des Gegners ist immer ein notwendiger Teil der Strategie. Jetzt sind wir an der Reihe.	Demonizing the opponent is always a necessary part of the strategy. Now it's our turn.
		wobei die ochsen und Esel in Berlin im Bundestag sitzen und zwar alle	where the oxen and donkeys sit in Berlin in the Bundestag, all of them.
		Gar kein Geld sollten die bekommen, wozu auch, die bekommen doch eh schon alles in den Arsch geschoben.	They shouldn't get any money at all, why should they, they already have everything shoved up their ass anyway.
Agitation	313	1488 ⚡⚡	1488 ⚡⚡
		Heil Hitler! Wir werden uns nicht erweichen lassen! #Vorwärts #SiegHeil #1488	Heil Hitler! We will not be softened! #Forward #SiegHeil #1488
		Blut und Ehre, Hakenkreuz über Europa!	Blood and Honor, swastika over Europe!
Subversive	60	Ihr werdet Frau Merkel stürzen, Die Welt schaut auf euch .....super	You will overthrow Mrs. Merkel, the world is watching you... great
		Kann den nicht einer erschießen - so mit Auftragskiller - am besten vielleicht die komplette Regierung???	Can't someone shoot him – like with a hitman – maybe even the entire government???
		RT @name: @name @news Die EU spaltet Europa. Merkel spaltet die EU. Merkel muss weg. Die EU muss weg. Damit Europa wieder atmen kann.	RT @name: @name @news The EU is dividing Europe. Merkel is dividing the EU. Merkel must go. The EU must go. So that Europe can breathe again.

Table 5: Examples of the provided training data of the *GermEval's 2025 Harmful Content Detection* Task.

B Language Model prompts

B.1 Task Description

Original prompt, written in German.

Task Description

A: „Subversive“
Posts der Kategorie „Subversive“ drücken das Ziel aus, die Regierung durch gewaltsame Handlungen zu stürzen und somit die staatliche Ordnung zu beseitigen. Dies kann in Form von Ankündigungen, Drohungen oder Aufrufen zum Handeln geschehen.

B: „Agitational“
Posts der Kategorie „Agitational“ haben das Ziel, andere Personen in aggressiver Art und Weise gegen die freiheitlich-demokratische Grundordnung aufzuhetzen. Dabei werden konkrete Maßnahmen wie beispielsweise die Verbreitung von Propaganda oder Beschädigung von Staatssymbolen ergriffen.

C: „Critical“
Der Tweet äußert Kritik an der Regierung, an Amtsträgern, Beamten, Behörden oder politischen Parteien, ohne konkrete Absichten gegen die freiheitlich-demokratische Grundordnung anzudeuten.

D: „Nothing“
Posts der Kategorie „Nothing“ richten sich weder gegen die Regierung noch gegen die freiheitlich demokratische Grundordnung.

Instruction:
Ordne den nachfolgenden Post in eine der oben genannte Kategorien (A-D) ein. Entscheide dich immer für genau eine Kategorie. Stelle deine Argumente in kurzer Form dar.

Post:
<Post to classify>

English translation of the original prompt.

Aufgabenbeschreibung

A: „Subversive“
Posts in the "Subversive" category express the goal of overthrowing the government through violent actions and thereby eliminating the state order. This can take the form of announcements, threats, or calls to action.

B: „Agitational“
Posts in the "Agitational" category aim to incite others aggressively against the liberal democratic order. This involves concrete actions such as spreading propaganda or damaging state symbols.

C: „Critical“
The tweet expresses criticism of the government, officials, civil servants, authorities, or political parties without indicating any concrete intentions against the free democratic basic order.

D: „Nothing“
Posts in the "Nothing" category are directed neither against the government nor against the liberal democratic order.

Instruction:
Classify the following post into one of the categories (A–D) mentioned above. Always choose exactly one category. Briefly explain your reasoning.

Post:
<Post to classify>

B.2 In-Context Learning

B.2.1 Example Answers

Original *In-Context Learning* examples and corresponding answers, written in German.

In-Context Learning Example	Manually Crafted Answer
Unsere ehre heisst treue, Kameraden!	Der Post verwendet eine verbotene Phrase (unsere ehre heisst treue) und verbreitet somit verfassungsfeindliche Symbole. Dementsprechend ist der Post als unter der Kategorie Agitational einzuordnen.
Es gibt immer noch eine Alternative, die man wählen kann ...	Der Post drückt Unzufriedenheit mit der Regierung aus und weist darauf hin, eine andere Partei zu wählen. Somit handelt es sich um legale Regierungskritik. Der Post ist dementsprechend unter der Kategorie Critical einzuordnen.
Mal sehen wann wir an der Erderwärmung schuld sind ;)	Der post enthält keine Kommentare, die sich gegen die Regierung wenden. Somit ist dieser Post unter der Kategorie Nothing einzuordnen.
Wir sollten unsere Fahne vor der Regierung schützen und gegen sie kämpfen!	Dieser Post spricht von eine Kampf gegen die Regierung, was einem Aufruf zur gewaltsamen Handlung entspricht. Somit ist der Post als Subversive einzustufen.
Alles für Deutschland! Wir werden die Demokraten vernichten! #Hammerskins88 #HH18	Die Phrase „Alles für Deutschland" zählt in Deutschland zu verbotener Symbolik. Somit ist dieser Post als Agitational einzustufen.
Danke allen Patrioten!	In diesem Post wird keine Regierungskritik oder negative Einstellung gegen über der demokratischen Grundordnung deutlich. Somit ist der Post der Kategorie Nothing zuzuordnen.
Wenn wir nicht bald handeln, werden wir noch mehr Schaden erleiden. Zeit für einen Aufstand!	Dieser Post ruft zu einem Aufstand gegenüber der Regierung auf. Somit ist der Post der Kategorie Subversive zuzuordnen.
Die schädliche Arbeitsagentur soll mal in den Spiegel schauen.	Der Post drückt Unzufriedenheit gegenüber der Agentur für Arbeit aus. Der Ausdruck wird somit als legitime Kritik verstanden, wodurch der Post der Klasse Critical zugeordnet werden kann.

In-Context Learning examples and corresponding answers, translated into English.

In-Context Learning Example	Manually Crafted Answer
Our honor is loyalty, comrades!	The post uses a banned phrase ("Our honor is loyalty") and thus disseminates unconstitutional symbols. Accordingly, the post should be classified under the category of agitational content.
There is still an alternative one can vote for...	The post expresses dissatisfaction with the government and suggests voting for another party. Therefore, it constitutes legal government criticism. Accordingly, the post should be classified under the category Critical.
Let's see when we'll be blamed for global warming ;)	The post does not contain any comments directed against the government. Therefore, this post should be classified under the category Nothing.
We should protect our flag from the government and fight against them!	This post talks about a fight against the government, which corresponds to a call for violent action. Therefore, the post should be classified as Subversive.
Everything for Germany! We will destroy the Democrats! #Hammerskins88 #HH18	The phrase "Alles für Deutschland" is considered banned symbolism in Germany. Therefore, this post should be classified as Agitational.
Thanks to all patriots!	This post does not express any government criticism or negative attitude towards the democratic constitutional order. Therefore, the post should be assigned to the category Nothing.
If we don't act soon, we will suffer even more damage. Time for an uprising!	This post calls for an uprising against the government. Therefore, the post should be assigned to the category Subversive.
The harmful employment agency should look in the mirror.	The post expresses dissatisfaction with the Employment Agency. The statement is therefore understood as legitimate criticism, allowing the post to be assigned to the category Critical.

B.2.2 Prompt Design

Original prompt, written in German.

In-Context Learning

A: „Subversive“
Posts der Kategorie „Subversive“ drücken das Ziel aus, die Regierung durch gewaltsame Handlungen zu stürzen und somit die staatliche Ordnung zu beseitigen. Dies kann in Form von Ankündigungen, Drohungen oder Aufrufen zum Handeln geschehen.

B: „Agitational“
Posts der Kategorie „Agitational“ haben das Ziel, andere Personen in aggressiver Art und Weise gegen die freiheitlich-demokratische Grundordnung aufzuhetzen. Dabei werden konkrete Maßnahmen wie beispielsweise die Verbreitung von Propaganda oder Beschädigung von Staatssymbolen ergriffen.

C: „Critical“
Der Tweet äußert Kritik an der Regierung, an Amtsträgern, Beamten, Behörden oder politischen Parteien, ohne konkrete Absichten gegen die freiheitlich-demokratische Grundordnung anzudeuten.

D: „Nothing“
Posts der Kategorie „Nothing“ richten sich weder gegen die Regierung noch gegen die freiheitlich demokratische Grundordnung.

Instruction:
Ordne den nachfolgenden Post in eine der oben genannte Kategorien (A-D) ein. Entscheide dich immer für genau eine Kategorie. Stelle deine Argumente in kurzer Form dar.

Post:
<Example 1>

[Example Answer 1]

Post:
<Example Post 2>

[Example Answer 2]

Post:
<Example Post 3>

[Example Answer 3]

[...]

Post:
<Example Post 7>

[Example Answer 7]

Post:
<Example Post 8>

[Example Answer 8]

Post:
<Post to classify>

English translation of the original prompt.

In-Context Learning

A: „Subversive“
Posts in the "Subversive" category express the goal of overthrowing the government through violent actions and thereby eliminating the state order. This can take the form of announcements, threats, or calls to action.

B: „Agitational“
Posts in the "Agitational" category aim to incite others aggressively against the liberal democratic order. This involves concrete actions such as spreading propaganda or damaging state symbols.

C: „Critical“
The tweet expresses criticism of the government, officials, civil servants, authorities, or political parties without indicating any concrete intentions against the free democratic basic order.

D: „Nothing“
Posts in the "Nothing" category are directed neither against the government nor against the liberal democratic order.

Instruction:
Classify the following post into one of the categories (A–D) mentioned above. Always choose exactly one category. Briefly explain your reasoning.

Post:
<Example 1>

[Example Answer 1]

Post:
<Example Post 2>

[Example Answer 2]

Post:
<Example Post 3>

[Example Answer 3]

[...]

Post:
<Example Post 7>

[Example Answer 7]

Post:
<Example Post 8>

[Example Answer 8]

Post:
<Post to classify>

B.3 Chain of Thought Prompting

Original prompt, written in German.

Chain of Thought

A: „Subversive“
Posts der Kategorie „Subversive“ drücken das Ziel aus, die Regierung durch gewaltsame Handlungen zu stürzen und somit die staatliche Ordnung zu beseitigen. Dies kann in Form von Ankündigungen, Drohungen oder Aufrufen zum Handeln geschehen.

B: „Agitational“
Posts der Kategorie „Agitational“ haben das Ziel, andere Personen in aggressiver Art und Weise gegen die freiheitlich-demokratische Grundordnung aufzuhetzen. Dabei werden konkrete Maßnahmen wie beispielsweise die Verbreitung von Propaganda oder Beschädigung von Staatssymbolen ergriffen.

C: „Critical“
Der Tweet äußert Kritik an der Regierung, an Amtsträgern, Beamten, Behörden oder politischen Parteien, ohne konkrete Absichten gegen die freiheitlich-demokratische Grundordnung anzudeuten.

D: „Nothing“
Posts der Kategorie „Nothing“ richten sich weder gegen die Regierung noch gegen die freiheitlich demokratische Grundordnung.

Instruction:
Ordne den nachfolgenden Post in eine der oben genannte Kategorien (A-D) ein. Entscheide dich immer für genau eine Kategorie. Denke dabei Schritt für Schritt, wie man diese Aufgabe lösen kann. Denke darüber nach, welche Merkmale die einzelnen Klassen erfordern, wie sie sich voneinander unterscheiden und welche dieser Merkmale im Post vorhanden sind.

Post:
<Post to classify>

English translation of the original prompt.

Chain of Thought

A: „Subversive“
Posts in the "Subversive" category express the goal of overthrowing the government through violent actions and thereby eliminating the state order. This can take the form of announcements, threats, or calls to action.

B: „Agitational“
Posts in the "Agitational" category aim to incite others aggressively against the liberal democratic order. This involves concrete actions such as spreading propaganda or damaging state symbols.

C: „Critical“
The tweet expresses criticism of the government, officials, civil servants, authorities, or political parties without indicating any concrete intentions against the free democratic basic order.

D: „Nothing“
Posts in the "Nothing" category are directed neither against the government nor against the liberal democratic order.

Instruction:
Classify the following post into one of the categories (A–D) mentioned above. Always choose exactly one category. Think through the task step by step. Consider what characteristics each category requires, how they differ from one another, and which of these characteristics are present in the post.

Post:
<Post to classify>

B.4 Task Decomposition

B.4.1 Prompt Design

Original prompt, written in German.

Task Decomposition

Enthält der Beitrag eine negative Einstellung, Handlungen oder Kritik gegenüber staatlichen Institutionen, staatlichen Akteuren oder gegen die demokratische Grundordnung? Antworte kurz mit Ja oder Nein.

Post:
<Post to classify>

[Model Answer 1]

Wird durch den Post zu Gewalt gegen staatliche Akteure oder deren Vertreter aufgerufen? Dies kann beispielsweise die gewaltsame Absetzung von Politikern beinhalten. Antworte kurz mit Ja oder Nein.

[Model Answer 2]

Wird durch diesen Post zu anderen staatsfeindlichen, aber gewaltfreien, Handlungen aufgerufen oder wird durch den Post Propaganda beziehungsweise verfassungsfeindliche Symbole verbreitet? Dazu zählen beispielsweise Hakenkreuze oder bestimmte Aussagen aus der NS-Zeit. Antworte kurz mit Ja oder Nein.

[Model Answer 3]

English translation of the original prompt.

Task Decomposition

Does the post contain a negative attitude, actions, or criticism toward state institutions, state actors, or the democratic constitutional order? Answer briefly with Yes or No.

Post:
<Post to classify>

[Model Answer 1]

Does the post call for violence against state actors or their representatives? This may include, for example, the violent removal of politicians. Answer briefly with Yes or No.

[Model Answer 2]

Does this post call for other anti-government but non-violent actions, or does it spread propaganda or unconstitutional symbols? This includes, for example, swastikas or specific statements from the Nazi era. Answer briefly with Yes or No.

[Model Answer 3]

B.4.2 Label Assignment

Answer 1	Answer 2	Answer 3	Class Label
No	No	No	Nothing
No	No	Yes	Criticism
No	yes	No	Subversive
No	yes	yes	Subversive
yes	No	No	Agitation
yes	No	yes	Agitation
yes	yes	No	Subversive
yes	yes	yes	Subversive

Table 6: Label assignment for the *Task Decomposition* approach for all combinations of model answers.

Post
[...] Genug davon 😠 #refugeesnotwelcome [...] #MerkelMussWeg
Merkel muss gehen, und jeder Asylbewerber, der sich nicht benimmt, muss folgen ...
Ermutigen Sie Familie und Freunde, bei den Wahlen nationalistisch zu wählen! #MerkelMussWeg #Islamisierung

B.5 Answer Formatting

Original prompt, written in German.

Multi-Step JSON Formatierung

Fasse deine Antwort in JSON-Format zusammen. Nutze dabei folgendes Format:

{
"Antwort": <Klasse>
}

Wobei für <Klasse> entweder „Nothing“, „Critical“, „Agitational“ oder „Subversive“ eingesetzt werden können.

Multi-Step JSON Formatierung

Fasse deine Antworten in JSON-Format zusammen. Nutze dabei folgendes Format:

{
'negative Einstellung': <Antwort 1>
'Gewalt': <Antwort 2>
'andere Handlungen': <Antwort 3>
}

Wobei für <Antwort 1>, <Antwort 2> und <Antwort 3> entweder Ja oder Nein eingesetzt werden können.

English translation of the original prompt.

Multi-Step JSON Formatting

Summarize your answer in JSON format. Use the following structure:

{
"Answer": <Class>
}

Whereby either "Nothing", "Critical", 'Agitational' or "Subversive" can be used for <Class>.

Multi-Step JSON Formatting

Summarize your answers in JSON format. Use the following structure:

{
'negative attitude': <Answer 1>
'Violence': <Answer 2>
'other Actions': <Answer 3>
}

Either Yes or No can be used for <Answer 1>, <Answer 2> and <Answer 3>.

NLPeace@GermEval Shared Task 2025: Fine-Tuned BERT vs. Prompted LLMs for German Hate Speech Detection

Patrick Göttfert
University of Augsburg
patrick.goettfert@uni-a.de

Raphael Huber
University of Augsburg
raphael.huber@uni-a.de

Fabio Mariani
University of Augsburg
fabio.mariani@uni-a.de

Abstract

We present our participation in the GermEval 2025 Shared Task on Harmful Content Detection in German social media, focusing on binary classification of calls to action (C2A) and violent content (VIO). We compare fine-tuned BERT models with prompting-based approaches using large language models (Mixtral, Qwen) in zero-shot and few-shot settings. Our results show that supervised BERT classifiers clearly outperform prompting methods, reaching macro-F1 scores up to 0.78 on the test set. While LLM prompting was competitive in some cases, it suffered from inconsistent outputs and high sensitivity to prompt wording. Overall, our findings highlight the reliability of fine-tuning for this task and the need for improved prompt design and strict separation between training and trial data.

1 Introduction

The proliferation of harmful content on social media, including hate speech, extremist propaganda, and incitement to violence, poses significant societal and technological challenges. Prior research shows that abusive language is frequent on platforms such as **X** (formerly Twitter) and can cause psychological harm and escalate to real-world violence (Waseem and Hovy, 2016). While hate speech is an important subset, other forms—such as calls to action and attacks on democratic institutions—are equally critical to detect and moderate.

To advance research in this area, the **Harmful Content Detection in Social Media** shared task[1] was organized on Codabench, comprising three subtasks evaluated via macro-F1 score (Felser et al., 2025). We focused on the two binary classification subtasks: **Call to Action (C2A)** and **Violence Detection (VIO)**. In C2A, the goal is to detect statements encouraging specific behavior. For example:

> "Jeder bringt zur morgigen Demonstration mindestens 10 Leute mit, denn eine Bürgerbewegung ist nur so stark wie ihre Anhänger!!!"

The VIO subtask targets tweets expressing a disturbingly positive attitude towards violence:

> "Knallt das ganze linksgrün dumme Antifa-Gesindel einfach ab! #LinksfaschistenStoppen"

Both subtasks are framed as binary classification problems, labeling each tweet as `True` (harmful) or `False` (not harmful). A newly constructed dataset and baseline models were provided for evaluation.

In this work, we explore these tasks by fine-tuning BERT (Devlin et al., 2019) models and experimenting with prompting techniques using state-of-the-art large language models (LLMs). Our main contribution is a comparative evaluation of both approaches on the shared task dataset.

The remainder of this paper is structured as follows: Section 2 reviews related work, Section 3 describes our methodology, Section 4 reports results, and Section 5 concludes with directions for future work.

2 Related Work

Li et al. (2024) evaluate ChatGPT's performance in annotating hateful, offensive, and toxic comments. They report high agreement with human annotators on non-harmful texts but substantially lower consistency for harmful content. Moreover, the study highlights the model's strong prompt sensitivity and tendency to produce extreme probability estimates. These findings underscore the importance of careful prompt engineering and class design, an aspect we also encountered when prompting LLMs for binary classification.

Alatawi et al. (2023) show that a BiLSTM classifier trained on embeddings derived from a large

[1] `https://www.codabench.org/competitions/4963/#/pages-tab`

Proceedings of the 21st Conference on Natural Language Processing (KONVENS), Volume 2: Workshops, pages 350–356, 2025

hate speech corpus achieves strong results, while fine-tuning BERT further increases F1-scores to 96%. However, the authors note that BERT struggles with intentionally misspelled or coded hate terms, underlining the need for domain-adapted representations.

In addition, Fillies et al. (2025) present the first German-language TikTok dataset focusing on far-right extremist discourse. Their dataset comprises over 10,000 comments annotated with a fine-grained taxonomy of 32 labels, capturing diverse targets, intensities, and types of hate speech. This work highlights the importance of platform-specific resources and the challenges of moderating content in dynamic environments like TikTok, which shows notable differences compared to the German Twitter data we used.

Beyond text-only approaches, multimodal research addresses the growing challenge of harmful content embedded in images and memes. Arya et al. (2024) propose a detection method based on Contrastive Language-Image Pre-Training (CLIP) combined with prompt engineering. Their model achieves an accuracy of 87.42%, demonstrating the effectiveness of joint vision-language reasoning. While our work focuses on textual classification, such multimodal strategies are likely to become increasingly important as harmful content diversifies in form and medium.

Furthermore Piot et al. (2024) present MetaHate, a unified hate speech dataset combining 36 existing corpora into a harmonized binary classification scheme with over 1.2 million labeled instances. Their benchmarks show that transformer-based models, particularly BERT, achieve the strongest performance (Macro-F1 ≈ 0.80), underlining the value of large, diverse datasets for robust and generalizable hate speech detection.

Moreover, Awal et al. (2021) propose AngryBERT, a multitask learning model for hate speech detection. It jointly learns the primary task of hate speech classification alongside two related secondary tasks: emotion classification and target identification. Using BERT as a shared layer, the model leverages features learned across tasks to improve overall performance. AngryBERT is evaluated on three public hate speech datasets (WZ-LS, DT, and FOUNTA), achieving higher F1-scores than both single-task BERT models and other multitask baselines. These results highlight the benefit of incorporating sentiment and target information for more robust hate speech detection. While our approach focuses on single-task BERT fine-tuning for C2A and VIO, the multitask strategy explored in AngryBERT suggests a promising direction for future work.

3 Methodology

In this section, we describe the dataset and models used in our approach to the shared task, including the experimental setup for each subtask.

3.1 Data

All subtasks rely on a newly annotated dataset derived from the German Twitter network of an extremist group, collected between 2014 and 2016.[2] The corpus comprises approximately 11,500 tweets annotated by trained coders with expertise in harmful content. To ensure privacy, all mentions of other users were anonymized.

The data is split into training, trial, and test sets. The test set labels were withheld for final evaluation. Each entry contains an ID, the tweet text, and a binary label indicating whether the tweet is harmful.

For subtask C2A, the training set contains 6,840 tweets and the trial set ~1,000. For VIO, there are 7,783 training tweets and ~1,000 trial examples. The trial set was used during development to compare and fine-tune approaches, while the test set served exclusively for final submission. Crucially, we discovered only after the submission deadline that the trial set overlapped with the training data, which likely led to inflated evaluation scores during development.

3.2 Subtask 1: C2A

We evaluated both traditional machine learning classifiers and transformer-based models for the C2A subtask.

Baseline Classifiers As reference systems, we adapted the baseline provided for the C2A subtask, which originally employed a Gradient Boosting Classifier for evaluation on the trial set. We further experimented with Logistic Regression, Gaussian Naive Bayes, and K-Nearest Neighbors, all trained on sentence embeddings generated by the `distiluse-base-multilingual-cased-v2` encoder.[3] This model is a distilled version of

[2] https://github.com/Communication-Forensics-Lab/harmful-content-detection

[3] https://huggingface.co/sentence-transformers/distiluse-base-multilingual-cased-v2

the multilingual Universal Sentence Encoder, optimized for producing sentence-level embeddings. Preprocessing included lemmatization and tokenization with SpaCy[4] and polarity feature extraction using TextBlobDE[5]. This variant was not fine-tuned.

BERT-based Classifiers We fine-tuned two BERT variants:

- `bert-base-uncased`[6]: implemented in PyTorch as a sequence classifier with a linear layer and sigmoid activation. Trained for 3 epochs with a batch size of 8 and a learning rate of 1e-5, validating on the trial set.
- `bert-base-german-cased`[7]: a cased German BERT pretrained on large German text corpora, fine-tuned using the Hugging Face `transformers` library, trained for 3 epochs (learning rate 2e-5, batch size 8, AdamW optimizer), also validating on the trial set.

LLM-based Classifiers We tested `Mixtral-8x7B-Instruct-v0.1` (Jiang et al., 2024)[8], an instruction-following LLM capable of processing German prompts without additional task-specific fine-tuning, in zero-shot and few-shot prompting (4 examples), following its instruction format, with inference via the Hugging Face pipeline (16-bit quantization). Outputs were post-processed to extract labels.

We also evaluated `Qwen2.5-32B-Instruct` (Bai et al., 2023)[9], a large multilingual instruction-following LLM supporting German input, with the same zero-shot prompt, including a variant with a minor spelling error. Qwen allows separate system and user prompts, which we leveraged to structure inputs.

3.3 Subtask 2: VIO

Due to structural similarity, we reused the C2A scripts with minimal changes for VIO labels. For LLMs, we introduced a dedicated prompt (see Appendix A.2) and evaluated both zero-shot and few-shot settings.

We also explored zero-shot chain-of-thought prompting with Qwen by adding the instruction:

```
The last TRUE or FALSE should be
the answer. Let's think step by
step.
```

This prompted step-by-step reasoning. Due to longer processing time, we reduced the batch size to 1. Additionally, we evaluated the official baseline prompt using our Qwen inference script.

4 Results

Table 1 presents the Macro-F1 scores for both subtasks —C2A and VIO — evaluated on the trial set. We compare several classification techniques, including baselines, transformer-based models, and LLM prompting methods.

For both subtasks, the provided official baseline based on a Gradient Boosting Classifier serves as a strong starting point, achieving F1-scores of 0.65 (C2A) and 0.59 (VIO). However, when experimenting with alternative classifiers using the same sentence embeddings, we observed lower performance across the board. Logistic Regression yielded the strongest results among these alternatives, with scores of 0.61 for C2A and 0.55 for VIO.

Our BERT-based models substantially outperformed the baselines. The best-performing model on C2A was the fine-tuned `bert-base-uncased` variant, achieving an F1-score of 0.92. For the VIO subtask, the fine-tuned `bert-base-german-cased` produced the highest score of 0.98, marking the best result overall across all configurations.

Prompt-based classification using LLMs showed mixed results. The `Mixtral-8x7B-Instruct` model, both in zero-shot and few-shot setups, achieved F1-scores around 0.52–0.53 for C2A and 0.70 for VIO. The `Qwen2.5-32B-Instruct` model generally performed slightly lower on C2A (with scores ranging from 0.46 to 0.52), but matched or surpassed Mixtral on VIO, reaching up to 0.76 using the prompt from the official baseline.

Furthermore, correcting a minor spelling error in the prompt improved the F1 score by 0.06, as seen in the table, showing that even small prompt changes can significantly affect LLM performance.

Overall, transformer-based fine-tuned models clearly outperform prompt-based approaches in this setting, especially for the C2A task. Nonetheless,

[4]https://spacy.io/

[5]https://textblob.readthedocs.io/

[6]https://huggingface.co/google-bert/bert-base-uncased

[7]https://huggingface.co/google-bert/bert-base-german-cased

[8]https://huggingface.co/mistralai/Mixtral-8x7B-Instruct-v0.1

[9]https://huggingface.co/Qwen/Qwen2.5-32B-Instruct

Technique	C2A	VIO
Baseline from C2A (using Gradient Boosting Classifier)	0.65	0.59
Adapted Baseline using K-Neighbours	0.55	0.39
Adapted Baseline using Gaussian Naive Bayes	0.53	0.50
Adapted Baseline using Logistic Regression	0.61	0.55
Fine-tuned bert-base-uncased	**0.92**	0.71
Fine-tuned bert-base-german-cased	0.85	**0.98**
Mixtral	0.52	0.70
Mixtral with few-shot	0.53	0.70
Qwen with faulty spelling	0.46	-
Qwen with corrected spelling	0.52	0.69
Qwen with prompt from baseline	-	0.76
Qwen with zero-shot chain-of-thought	-	0.70

Table 1: All Macro-F1 scores evaluated on the Trial Set (rounded to two decimal places). For each subtask and model category, the best score is underlined, while the overall best score per subtask is highlighted in **bold**.

Technique	C2A	VIO
Fine-tuned bert-base-german-cased	**0.78**	**0.76**
Mixtral with few-shot	0.54	0.71

Table 2: All F1-scores were evaluated on the test set. The overall best score per subtask is highlighted in **bold**.

few-shot prompting remains a promising alternative for zero-resource or multilingual transfer scenarios.

Finally, Table 2 summarizes the results obtained on the official test set using our final submitted systems. As expected, our fine-tuned BERT model consistently achieved the highest F1-scores across both subtasks, with 0.78 for C2A and 0.76 for VIO. In contrast, the best-performing LLM-based method (Mixtral in few-shot mode) yielded competitive but lower scores, particularly in the VIO subtask with 0.71.

We selected these two systems for final submission to Codabench in order to directly compare transformer-based fine-tuning with prompting-based LLM approaches. Among all our BERT-based experiments, the custom script consistently delivered the strongest results, while among LLM-based runs, the few-shot Mixtral model performed best—except for a single run using the baseline prompt provided in the task documentation. However, we opted not to use that baseline prompt in our final submission, as we aimed to showcase the effectiveness of our own prompt design and modeling choices.

After our experiments, we discovered that the trial set was actually a subset of the training set, a fact that became apparent only after the experimentation phase. This overlap introduces a risk of overfitting when evaluating models on the trial set, as the models may have already seen this data during training. Consequently, the trial set scores likely overestimate real-world performance, and the lower scores on the unseen test set are consistent with this expectation.

Additionally, we observed that prompting-based approaches using LLMs did not always follow our explicit instruction to return only the binary labels "TRUE" or "FALSE." Despite phrasing the prompts clearly (e.g., "Respond only with 'TRUE' or 'FALSE'. No explanation."), the models occasionally produced additional output such as punctuation (e.g., ", TRUE") or full sentences requiring further parsing to extract only the labels.

5 Conclusion and Future Work

In this work, we participated in the GermEval 2025 Shared Task on Harmful Content Detection, focusing on binary classification subtasks C2A and VIO. We compared fine-tuned transformer models and prompting-based approaches with LLMs.

Our experiments showed that transformer models, particularly our fine-tuned BERT, outperformed prompting methods in classification accuracy. While LLMs like Mixtral and Qwen delivered competitive results in few-shot and chain-of-thought configurations, they remained less reliable overall. However, LLMs offered advantages in development speed and required no additional training, albeit with challenges such as inconsistent output formatting.

Overall, our findings suggest that for small- to medium-sized datasets, supervised fine-tuning remains the most effective approach. Prompting with LLMs requires further refinement to improve reliability.

In the following, we outline directions for future work and improvements based on our experimental findings. For prompting methods, more systematic prompt engineering such as testing different templates and incorporating domain-relevant few-shot examples is needed to improve reliability.

On the supervised side, future work could explore alternative transformer architectures like RoBERTa (Liu et al., 2019) or DeBERTa (He et al., 2021). Addressing class imbalance and refining loss functions may reduce performance variability.

Ensuring clear separation of training, development, and trial data is crucial for fair evaluation. Future error analysis is needed to better understand the notably different performance of the two BERT models, particularly whether the variation stems from differences in language coverage, sensitivity to domain-specific patterns, or divergent handling of implicit harmful language.

References

Hind Saleh Alatawi, Areej Alhothali, and Kawthar Moria. 2023. Detection of hate speech using BERT and hate speech word embedding with deep model. *Appl. Artif. Intell.*, 37(1).

Greeshma Arya, Mohammad Kamrul Hasan, Ashish Bagwari, Nurhizam Safie, Shayla Islam, Fatima Rayan Awad Ahmed, Aaishani De, Muhammad Attique Khan, and Taher M. Ghazal. 2024. Multimodal hate speech detection in memes using contrastive language-image pre-training. *IEEE Access*, 12:22359–22375.

Md Rabiul Awal, Rui Cao, Roy Ka-Wei Lee, and Sandra Mitrovic. 2021. Angrybert: Joint learning target and emotion for hate speech detection. *Preprint*, arXiv:2103.11800.

Jinze Bai, Shuai Bai, Yunfei Chu, Zeyu Cui, Kai Dang, Xiaodong Deng, Yang Fan, Wenbin Ge, Yu Han, Fei Huang, Binyuan Hui, Luo Ji, Mei Li, Junyang Lin, Runji Lin, Dayiheng Liu, Gao Liu, Chengqiang Lu, Keming Lu, and 29 others. 2023. Qwen technical report. *Preprint*, arXiv:2309.16609.

Jacob Devlin, Ming-Wei Chang, Kenton Lee, and Kristina Toutanova. 2019. BERT: Pre-training of deep bidirectional transformers for language understanding. In *Proceedings of the 2019 Conference of the North American Chapter of the Association for Computational Linguistics: Human Language Technologies, Volume 1 (Long and Short Papers)*, pages 4171–4186, Minneapolis, Minnesota. Association for Computational Linguistics.

Jenny Felser, Michael Spranger, and Melanie Siegel. 2025. Overview of the germeval 2025 shared task on harmful content detection. In *Proceedings of the 21st Conference on Natural Language Processing (KONVENS 2025): Workshops*, Hildesheim, Germany.

Jan Fillies, Esther Theisen, Michael Hoffmann, Robert Jung, Elena Jung, Nele Fischer, and Adrian Paschke. 2025. A novel german tiktok hate speech dataset: far-right comments against politicians, women, and others. *Discover Data*, 3.

Pengcheng He, Xiaodong Liu, Jianfeng Gao, and Weizhu Chen. 2021. Deberta: Decoding-enhanced bert with disentangled attention. *Preprint*, arXiv:2006.03654.

Albert Q. Jiang, Alexandre Sablayrolles, Antoine Roux, Arthur Mensch, Blanche Savary, Chris Bamford, Devendra Singh Chaplot, Diego de Las Casas, Emma Bou Hanna, Florian Bressand, Gianna Lengyel, Guillaume Bour, Guillaume Lample, Lélio Renard Lavaud, Lucile Saulnier, Marie-Anne Lachaux, Pierre Stock, Sandeep Subramanian, Sophia Yang, and 7 others. 2024. Mixtral of experts. *CoRR*, abs/2401.04088.

Lingyao Li, Lizhou Fan, Shubham Atreja, and Libby Hemphill. 2024. "hot" chatgpt: The promise of chatgpt in detecting and discriminating hateful, offensive, and toxic comments on social media. *ACM Trans. Web*, 18(2):30:1–30:36.

Yinhan Liu, Myle Ott, Naman Goyal, Jingfei Du, Mandar Joshi, Danqi Chen, Omer Levy, Mike Lewis, Luke Zettlemoyer, and Veselin Stoyanov. 2019. Roberta: A robustly optimized bert pretraining approach. *Preprint*, arXiv:1907.11692.

Paloma Piot, Patricia Martín-Rodilla, and Javier Parapar. 2024. Metahate: A dataset for unifying efforts on hate speech detection. *Proceedings of the International AAAI Conference on Web and Social Media*, 18:2025–2039.

Zeerak Waseem and Dirk Hovy. 2016. Hateful symbols or hateful people? predictive features for hate speech detection on Twitter. In *Proceedings of the NAACL Student Research Workshop*, pages 88–93, San Diego, California. Association for Computational Linguistics.

A Appendix

This appendix provides supplementary materials, including our changes after the submission deadline and our prompt templates.

A.1 Experiments Conducted After the Codabench Phase

After the official Codabench phase ended, we conducted a few additional experiments. We added a few-shot script and corresponding result for the C2A task. In this context, the result for the baseline with the gradient boosting classifier and the results for the K-Nearest Neighbors classifier was updated due to a correction.

A.2 Prompt Templates

A.2.1 C2A: Zero-shot Prompt Mixtral

```
<s>[INST] You are a classification model. The input text is in German.
Output only 'TRUE' if it contains hate speech, otherwise 'FALSE'.
Respond only with 'TRUE' or 'FALSE'. Nothing else! [/INST]
```

A.2.2 C2A: Zero-shot Prompt Qwen with correct spelling

```
 [{"role": "system", "content": "You are a classification model."},
{"role": "user", "content": f"The input text is in German. Output only 'TRUE' if it
    contains hate speech, otherwise 'FALSE'. Respond only with 'TRUE' or 'FALSE'.
    Nothing else!{text}"}]
```

A.2.3 C2A: Zero-shot Prompt Qwen with faulty spelling

```
[{"role": "system", "content": "You are a classification model."},
{"role": "user", "content": f"The input text is in German. Output only 'TRUE' if it
    contains hate speech, otherwise 'FARLSE'. Respond only with 'TRUE' or 'FALSE'.
    Nothing else!{text}"}]
```

A.2.4 C2A: Few-shot Prompt Mixtral

```
[INST] You are a classification model. The input text is in German.
Output only 'TRUE' or 'FALSE'. No explanation. If the following text contains hate
    speech, output 'TRUE'.
Otherwise output 'FALSE'.

Text: die aus sicheren herkunftsländern nach hause schicken.
Label: TRUE
Text: Tja, wohl etwas schwierig, jetzt das Geld per Chip in die Heimat zu überweisen
Label: FALSE
Text: vergrabt ein totes Schwein, hat in Spanien auch den Bau der Moschee verhindert
    .
Label: TRUE
Text: In der Regierung haben doch schon alle das sonnenkönigsyndrom, lol.
Label: FALSE
```

A.2.5 VIO: Zero-shot Prompt Mixtral

```
[INST] You are a classification model. The input text is in German.
Output only 'TRUE' if it expresses a disturbingly positive attitude towards violence
(e.g., support, incitement, glorification, or willingness to commit violence).
Otherwise output 'FALSE'. Respond only with 'TRUE' or 'FALSE'. No explanation. [/
    INST]
```

A.2.6 VIO: Few-shot Prompt Mixtral

```
[INST] You are a classification model. The input text is in German.
Output only 'TRUE' or 'FALSE'. No explanation. If the following text expresses a
    disturbingly positive
attitude towards violence (e.g. glorification, incitement, support, or personal
    willingness), output 'TRUE'.
Otherwise, output 'FALSE'.
```

```
Text: schau Dir die Kinder an. Die werden benutzt! Die sollte man rausholen, aber
    die Eltern dort lassen
Label: TRUE
Text: Karl Valentin hat es auf den Punkt gebracht: "... und das Ritterfräulein
    Annerl ward von einem Neger schwanger. Doch der Ritter sagt nur: Scheiß,
    Hauptsach is, es wird ka Preiß!"
Label: FALSE
Text: Oh Graus!!! Vom Gehöft Sollte man Diese Jenigen jagen!!!??????
Label: TRUE
Text: Yeah Überraschungen - verkündet ihr endlich die Abtrennung von Deutschland?
Label: FALSE
```

A.2.7 VIO: Zero-shot Prompt Qwen

```
[{"role": "system", "content": "You are a classification model."},
{"role": "user", "content": f"The input text is in German. Output only 'TRUE' if it
    expresses a disturbingly positive attitude towards violence (e.g., support,
    incitement, glorification, or willingness to commit violence). Otherwise output
    'FALSE'. Respond only with 'TRUE' or 'FALSE'. No explanation. {text}"}]
```

A.2.8 VIO: Zero-shot chain-of-thought Prompt Qwen

```
[{"role": "system", "content": "You are a classification model."},
{"role": "user", "content": f"The input text is in German. Output only 'TRUE' if it
    expresses a disturbingly positive attitude towards violence (e.g., support,
    incitement, glorification, or willingness to commit violence). Otherwise output
    'FALSE'. The last TRUE or FALSE should be the answer. Let's think step by step.{
    text}"}]
```

A.2.9 VIO: Zero-shot with baseline prompt

```
[{"role": "system", "content": "You are a filter system in a social network that
    specialises in monitoring German tweets. Your task is to detect worrying
    positive attitudes towards violence.\nConsider the following definitions: A
    tweet contains a worrying violence-related statement if it trivialises,
    advocates, glorifies, incites violence or announces the use of violence.
    Violence is understood to mean active, aggressive behaviour, i.e. the infliction
     of physical, sexual or psychological violence. If you predict a violence-
    related statement, your response is \"true\". If you predict a no-violence-
    related statement, you respond with \"false\". You only respond with one single
    word and not more!"},
{"role": "user", "content": f"Determine whether the input tweet contains a worrying
    violence-related statement. Respond with a single word. Do not provide
    explanations or notes. Your only possible responses, regarding if the provided
    text contains a worrying violence-related statement are true and false. \
    nExamples of classification are:\n@UserXY Wenn ich diesen Typ schon sehe, könnte
     ich ihn an die Wand stellen response: \"true\"\nKnallt das ganze linksgrün
    Dumme Antifa Gesindel einfach ab! #LinksfaschistenStoppen  response: \"true\"\
    nMan stelle sich vor, eine Gruppe on 40 jungen MÄNNERN .[. ], teilweise BEWAFFNET
    .[. ], versucht ILLEGAL eine Grenze zu übertreten, .[. ] und dann wundert man sich,
    wenn das Feuer gerechtfertigterweise eröffnet wird.  response: \"true\"\n@UserXY
     endlich hat jemand den Mut ergriffen und dem Mistkerl die Fresse poliert. Der
    hat alles schlimme der Welt und mehr verdient dieser erbärmliche Perverse und
    geistig Behinderte #Volksverräter response: \"true\"\n@UserXY DU BIST TEIL
    dieser ganz GEZIELT INSZENIERTEN LÜGE über Lynchjustiz und Aufruf zu Mord und
    versuchst alle durch FREI ERFUNDENE HORRORGeschichten in PANIK zu VERSETZEN! #Lü
    genpresse  response: \"true\"\n\".[. ] Der 27- jährige Syrer wird verdächtigt,
    zwischen 2011 und 2014 als Mitglied von Jabhat al- Nusra bzw. Kataib Al Faroug
    im syrischen Bürgerkrieg gegen Anhänger bzw. Truppen des Assad- Regimes gekämpft
     und auf diese geschossen zu haben\", sagte Peter Oehm, der Leiter des
    Landesamtes für Verfassungsschutz.  response: \"false\" Input: {text}"}]
```

A.3 Parameter of the Baseline-Classifier

All classifiers were used with the default parameters of the Python library `scikit-learn`. For `LogisticRegression`, we set `max_iter` to 10000 and `random_state` to 42.

nymera@GermEval Shared Task 2025: One Ensemble, Many Harms: A Unified Transformer Approach to Harmful Content Detection in German Social Media

Hanna Köpcke
University of Applied Sciences Mittweida
Mittweida, Germany
koepcke@hs-mittweida.de

Abstract

We present a unified approach to detecting harmful content in German social media, developed for the GermEval 2025 Shared Task: Harmful Content Detection in Social Media (Felser et al., 2025). Our system addresses all three subtasks—(1) calls to action inciting harmful acts (C2A), (2) violence glorification (VIO), and (3) attacks on the free democratic basic order (DBO)—using a single ensemble-based framework. We fine-tuned a three-model ensemble (GBERT-large, XLM-RoBERTa-base, and DeBERTa) for each subtask and aggregated their predictions through soft-voting. To mitigate severe class imbalance in the training data, we augmented the dataset with synthetic examples and manually relabeled instances for minority classes, and applied oversampling during training. This unified modeling approach achieved strong performance in the official evaluation: our system obtained macro-F1 scores up to 0.83, ranking 1st in the DBO subtask, 3rd in C2A, and 4th in VIO.

1 Introduction

Harmful online content has evolved beyond generic hate speech to include nuanced categories such as explicit calls to action (incitements), violence glorification, and attacks on democratic institutions. These forms of content pose serious risks: direct calls to violence can spur real-world harm, and anti-democratic narratives erode public trust in societal structures. In response, the GermEval 2025 Shared Task on Harmful Content Detection in Social Media (Felser et al., 2025) introduced three focused subtasks for German: detecting calls to action inciting harmful acts (C2A), violence glorification (VIO), and attacks on the free democratic basic order (DBO). All task datasets consist of German Twitter posts from an extremist network collected in 2014–2016, providing a realistic testbed for these phenomena. Each subtask targets a distinct semantic layer of harmful discourse: C2A detection hinges on recognizing illocutionary intent (when users urge others to act), VIO involves identifying rhetoric that praises or justifies violent acts, and DBO requires spotting ideological content that undermines fundamental democratic values. These phenomena are often subtle; for example, a post may implicitly praise violence via humor or historical reference, making them challenging to identify automatically.

A key difficulty across all three categories is extreme class imbalance. In these datasets, harmful posts are vastly outnumbered by benign content (only $\sim$7–10% of instances are positive in C2A and VIO, and under 1% in the most severe DBO category). This imbalance can lead classifiers to overlook the rare but critical positive instances. Another challenge is pragmatic ambiguity: whether a message is a dangerous incitement or merely hyperbolic sarcasm often depends on subtle context and connotation. Effective solutions thus need to capture context, intent, and domain-specific cues without being overwhelmed by the majority class.

In this paper, we propose a unified ensemble-based method to tackle all three subtasks. Our approach fine-tunes three complementary Transformer models (GBERT-large, XLM-RoBERTa-base, and DeBERTa) for each task and combines their outputs through soft-voting (probability averaging) to produce robust predictions. By leveraging a monolingual German model alongside a multilingual model and an advanced Transformer architecture, the ensemble captures both language-specific nuances and generalizable patterns. We also address the class imbalance via targeted data augmentation and resampling: generating synthetic minority-class examples and adding a handful of manually relabeled misclassified posts, then oversampling the minority classes during training. Using this strategy, our unified system achieved strong

Proceedings of the 21st Conference on Natural Language Processing (KONVENS), Volume 2: Workshops, pages 357–365, 2025

performance across all three GermEval 2025 subtasks. To support reproducibility, we have made the full implementation publicly available in a GitHub repository.[1]

After presenting the current state of the literature on harmful content detection in Section 2, Section 3 introduces the dataset used in this work. Section 4 then details our unified transformer ensemble methodology and the data augmentation strategies employed. Section 5 presents and discusses the experimental results, and Section 6 concludes the paper with a summary of our findings and some directions for future work.

2 Related Work

Ensemble Methods for Harmful Content Detection: Ensemble classifiers have become standard in hate speech detection, as combining multiple models helps capture diverse abusive language cues and improves robustness. Transformer-based ensembles in particular have achieved state-of-the-art results in hate/offensive content tasks (e.g., winning entries in HASOC and SemEval challenges (Glazkova et al., 2021; Wiedemann et al., 2020)). Recent studies show that ensembling models emphasizing different facets of toxic content can yield further gains over single models (Kucukkaya and Toraman, 2025). Hybrid architectures mixing transformers with other classifiers likewise enhance performance by leveraging complementary strengths (Mazari et al., 2024). These findings establish ensembling as an effective strategy for complex content moderation tasks.

Handling Class Imbalance: Harmful content datasets are typically highly imbalanced, with genuine toxic instances vastly outnumbered by benign content. Without mitigation, classifiers tend to predict the majority class, missing rare but critical cases. Data-level solutions such as oversampling minority classes or generating synthetic examples have been shown to improve the learning of under-represented classes (Yuan and Rizoiu, 2025; Achmann-Denkler et al., 2024). Algorithm-level techniques like class weighting or focal loss (Zhang et al., 2024) also help by biasing the model toward rare categories. In practice, top systems often combine these approaches: for example, the winning GermEval 2021 toxicity system applied aggressive upsampling and cost-sensitive training to boost minority-class recall (Risch et al., 2021). Guided by these insights, we employ oversampling and weighted loss to counter class imbalance in our models.

[1] https://github.com/hannakoepcke/germeval2025

Multilingual and Multi-Task Modeling: Cross-lingual approaches leverage multilingual transformers (e.g., mBERT (Devlin et al., 2019), XLM-RoBERTa (Conneau et al., 2020)) to transfer knowledge from high- resource language corpora to lower-resource languages like German, improving toxic content classification (Muller et al., 2021; Calizzano et al., 2021). At the same time, language-specific models often better capture cultural nuances in abusive content (Zeinert et al., 2021). Multi- task learning across related content moderation tasks can also boost performance by sharing representations of "harmfulness" between tasks (Morgan et al., 2021; Ghosh et al., 2023). In this work, we opt for a simpler unified framework: we fine-tune separate models for each subtask and ensemble their predictions, avoiding the complexity of a multi-task model.

Datasets and Evaluation: The research community has developed numerous datasets and benchmarks for harmful content, though resources for fine-grained categories such as DBO or violence glorification are still limited. For German, the GermEval 2018 shared task (Wiegand et al., 2019) released a corpus of approximately 5,000 tweets annotated for offensive language in both coarse- and fine-grained categories, establishing the first German benchmark for hate speech and profanity detection. The GermEval 2019 shared task (Struß et al., 2019) extended this resource substantially by providing a corpus of about 18,000 similarly annotated tweets. The HASOC (Hate Speech and Offensive Content) track further provided German data in 2019–2022, covering hate, offensive, and profane content in a multilingual setting (Modha et al., 2019; Mandl et al., 2020, 2021; Modha et al., 2022). More recently, specialized datasets have emerged for specific harmful facets: (Krenn et al., 2024) compiled GERMS-AT, ∼8k German news comments annotated for sexism, to enable research on misogyny detection in German. The VioLence corpus (Saha et al., 2023) targets violence-inciting texts. The GermEval 2025 shared task fills an important gap by providing focused datasets for incitement (C2A), violence glorification (VIO), and anti-democratic content (DBO) in German.

Subtask	Train	Trial	Test
C2A	6,840	1,051	2,982
DBO	7,454	1,053	3,194
VIO	7,783	1,051	3,335

Table 1: Number of instances in the GermEval 2025 dataset per subtask. Test labels were not provided during the competition.

3 Dataset

For a detailed description of the tasks and datasets, see (Felser et al., 2025). The shared task provided three datasets corresponding to the subtasks C2A, DBO, and VIO, each split into training, trial (development), and test sets, as shown in Table 1. The training sets contain roughly 7–8 k posts each, the trial sets around 1 k posts, and the test sets about 3 k posts with labels withheld for evaluation. All data consists of German tweets from a far-right extremist network collected between 2014 and 2016, written in informal style with frequent slang, spelling variations, emojis, and social-media markers such as hashtags, @mentions, and URLs. C2A and VIO are binary classification tasks, with positive instances being very scarce – only about 9–10% of training posts in C2A and around 7% in VIO are labeled TRUE. DBO is a four-class task with the labels *nothing*, *criticism*, *agitation*, and *subversive* and is extremely skewed: the majority *nothing* class comprises roughly 84% of training examples, while the rare *subversive* class accounts for less than 1%. Figure 1 illustrates the class distribution in the training set for each subtask, highlighting these imbalances. The trial sets were constructed as stratified samples of the training data to give participants insight into the data structure, so their class proportions mirror those of the training set and are therefore not shown separately.

4 Methodology

Our approach consists of fine-tuning transformer-based classifiers for each subtask and then combining their predictions through a soft-voting ensemble. We address the severe class imbalance in all three subtasks by a combination of oversampling and data augmentation. Below, we detail our training pipeline and the iterative refinement steps we took to improve performance:

4.1 Baseline Model Training

For each task (C2A, DBO, VIO), we fine-tuned pre-trained transformer models on the task's training data. Each model contributes unique advantages in terms of language coverage or architecture:

- **GBERT-large (Chan et al., 2020):** a BERT-large model trained exclusively on extensive German corpora. As a monolingual German language model, GBERT-large captures German-specific linguistic nuances, leading to state-of-the-art performance on German-language NLP tasks (e.g., document classification and NER).
- **XLM-RoBERTa-base (Conneau et al., 2020):** a multilingual Transformer model based on RoBERTa, pre-trained on text from 100 languages. XLM-RoBERTa offers a broad linguistic scope, enabling effective cross-lingual representations. Notably, it outperforms the original multilingual BERT on various cross-lingual benchmarks, with especially strong gains for low-resource languages. This wide language coverage makes it well-suited for tasks involving diverse or non-English text.
- **DeBERTa (He et al., 2021):** an advanced Transformer architecture (Decoding-enhanced BERT with Disentangled Attention) that introduces novel improvements over BERT/RoBERTa. DeBERTa employs a disentangled attention mechanism, where each token is represented by separate content and position embeddings, and an enhanced mask decoder that incorporates positional information more effectively during pre-training. These architectural innovations boost model performance and efficiency, enabling DeBERTa to achieve state-of-the-art results on numerous NLP benchmarks.

Each model in the ensemble brings complementary strengths: GBERT-large provides deep coverage of German linguistic phenomena, XLM-RoBERTa-base contributes robust cross-lingual understanding, and DeBERTa offers cutting-edge architectural enhancements. By combining these models, our ensemble is able to leverage both language-specific knowledge and generalizable representations, improving overall predictive performance.

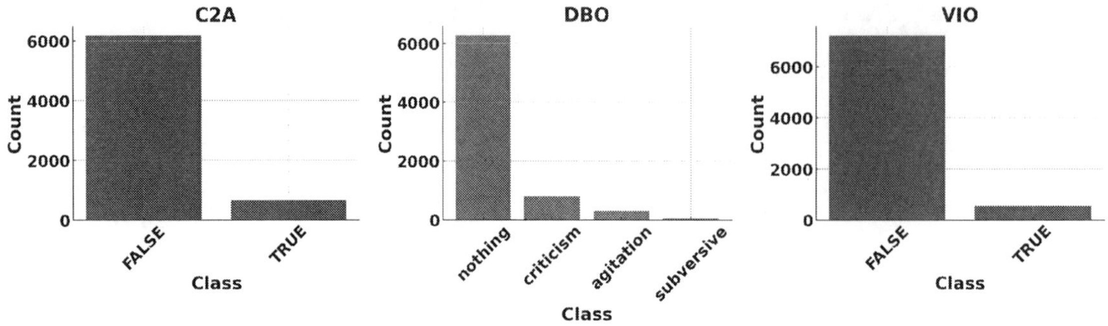

Figure 1: Class distributions across training splits for each subtask

Each model was trained with binary or multi-class cross-entropy as appropriate. We used early stopping on the validation (trial) set to prevent over-fitting. The outputs of these individual models were later combined in an ensemble by averaging their predicted probabilities (soft voting), leveraging the complementary strengths of different model architectures. This ensemble strategy is lightweight yet robust, and ensemble methods have proven effective in prior hate speech tasks (Kucukkaya and Toraman, 2025).

4.2 Handling Class Imbalance

The training data for all subtasks was highly skewed (e.g. only 7–10% positives in C2A and VIO, and <1% for the subversive class in DBO). To ensure the models learned minority classes, we applied random oversampling of the minority class instances. Additionally, we employed a class-weighted loss function to further bias training toward the minority classes. In practice, we duplicated examples from the under-represented classes until approximately balancing the class distribution. Importantly, any additional data (described next) was added before oversampling was performed, so that the oversampling procedure could incorporate these new examples as well. By oversampling after augmentation, we ensured the final effective training set had a more balanced mix of classes, mitigating the bias toward predicting the majority class.

4.3 Iterative Data Augmentation

After the initial training run, we analyzed the model's predictions on the test set to identify patterns of errors or obvious gaps in the training data. We found that the models struggled with some subtle positive instances due to the paucity of examples. To address this, we augmented the training set with additional examples for each subtask, using two strategies:

Synthetic examples via ChatGPT: For the binary subtasks C2A and VIO (calls-to-action and violence glorification), we generated new positive examples to enrich the minority class. We prompted ChatGPT (GPT-4o) (OpenAI et al., 2024) in German to create 100 artificial training instances labeled TRUE for each task, instructing it to mimic the style and format of our data. The prompts used for data generation were:

- **VIO:** *„Könntest du bitte basierend auf den Trainingsbeispielen in der angehängten Datei 100 neue Trainingsbeispiele für die Klasse VIO = TRUE generieren? Die neuen Beispiele sollten denselben Aufbau wie die Originaldatei haben und im CSV-Format vorliegen.“*
- **C2A:** *„Könntest du bitte basierend auf den Trainingsbeispielen in der angehängten Datei 100 neue Trainingsbeispiele für die Klasse C2A = TRUE generieren? Die neuen Beispiele sollten denselben Aufbau wie die Originaldatei haben und im CSV-Format vorliegen.“*

The synthetic examples produced by ChatGPT were then reviewed for plausibility and correctness (to ensure they indeed reflected genuine calls-to-action or violence-glorifying content). Once vetted, we appended these 100 generated samples for VIO and 100 for C2A to the respective training sets. This approach of leveraging GPT-generated data is inspired by recent studies which showed that incorporating synthetic examples can boost performance on hate speech detection (Khullar et al., 2024; Schmidhuber and Kruschwitz, 2024; Girón et al., 2025). By expanding the positive class with diverse, machine-generated samples, we aimed to expose the model to a wider variety of subtle harmful content phrases that were missing from the original data.

Manual addition of misclassified case: For the DBO task the model was sometimes too lenient. Some posts that were actually clear attacks on the democratic order (either agitational or subversive in nature) were wrongly classified by the model as mere "criticism." In other words, the model failed to recognize the extreme nature of these comments, treating them as if they were just normal policy critique. Through error analysis of the results on the test set, we identified 13 such misclassified instances.

These 13 posts contained strong anti-democratic sentiment (for example, calls to vote out all established parties or even references to a "revolution" with pitchforks), yet the model had placed them in the mild criticism category. To address this, we manually labeled each of these posts to its appropriate class (e.g. reassigning them from criticism to "agitation" or "subversive" as warranted) and added them to the DBO training set as additional examples. By including these cases, we reinforced the model's understanding of what truly constitutes an attack on the democratic order versus what is acceptable criticism, helping it draw a clearer line between normal dissent and dangerous subversive speech.

4.4 Training with Augmented Data

After augmenting the datasets as described, we retrained our models on the expanded training sets. All new examples (the 100 ChatGPT-generated positives for VIO, 100 for C2A, and 13 manually-added DBO criticism examples) were used alongside the original data in training. We then applied the same oversampling procedure on this combined set – oversampling the minority classes in the augmented training data. This ensured that the synthetic and newly added real examples were included in the oversampling, effectively amplifying their presence during training. The final models therefore learned from a balanced dataset that was both larger and more diverse than the original. We found this iterative enhancement of training data to be crucial: it allowed the models to correct some of their earlier mistakes by exposing them to informative new examples (both generated and hand-labeled) in the next training round.

4.5 Ensembling and Prediction

For each task, we fine-tuned multiple augmented models, as described above, and then used a soft-voting ensemble to make the final predictions. Each model in the ensemble outputs a probability distribution over classes, and we average these probabilities to determine the predicted label. This ensemble prediction was applied to the test set. The combination of data augmentation, oversampling, and ensembling yielded a noticeable improvement in capturing the minority classes without being overwhelmed by the majority class. In particular, augmenting with GPT-generated positives helped our classifiers detect subtle incitement and violence-glorifying cues they previously missed, and the additional criticism examples in DBO reduced false positives where the model had over-reacted to benign critiques.

Each team could submit a maximum of three runs. Our second run used the same ensemble configuration but without any data enrichment, relying solely on oversampling of the original training data. This variant achieved official F1-scores of 0.84 on C2A, 0.69 on DBO, and 0.79 on VIO. By comparison, our final ensemble with data enrichment obtained 0.83, 0.71, and 0.80 on the respective tasks. While the score for C2A showed a slight decrease of 0.01, detailed analysis of the predictions revealed the reason: between the two runs, 73 instances in the C2A test set changed predicted labels, with 34 switching from `FALSE` to `TRUE` and 39 from `TRUE` to `FALSE`. The enrichment thus helped to identify additional subtle calls to action but also led to some previously correct positive predictions being flipped to negative, which slightly reduced recall and thereby the overall F1-score. Table 2 shows representative examples of these shifts.

Overall, our methodology exemplifies an iterative refinement process: we start with a base trained model, analyze its weaknesses on the data, then address those weaknesses by expanding and rebalancing the training data before retraining. By doing so, we align our system with the nuanced nature of the GermEval 2025 tasks, ensuring that each classifier receives sufficient signal to recognize the rare but crucial harmful content, while not mislabeling innocuous content as dangerous.

5 Results and Discussion

The official leaderboard results for the GermEval 2025 shared task are presented in (Felser et al.,

Comment Text (translated excerpt)	Without Enrich.	With Enrich.
"... Dann wird gekämpft!" ("... then there will be fighting!")	FALSE	TRUE
"Schaut sie mal in Hamburg an." ("Just look at them in Hamburg.")	TRUE	FALSE
"Vielleicht die Leute von der Arbeitsagentur mal ARBEITEN lassen!" ("Maybe let the employment agency staff actually work!")	TRUE	FALSE

Table 2: Examples of C2A predictions that switched between the ensemble without data enrichment and the ensemble with data enrichment.

2025). Our system **nymera** delivered strong performance across all three subtasks: it ranked 3rd in the **C2A** task (Call-to-Action identification), 1st in **DBO** (detection of content attacking the free democratic basic order), and 4th in **VIO** (recognition of disturbingly positive statements towards violence). Notably, **nymera** achieved the *highest* score in the DBO subtask with an F1-score of 0.71, outperforming the second-place system by a margin of 0.02 . In the C2A task, **nymera** attained an F1-score of 0.83, narrowly behind the top two entries (0.87 and 0.84 by teams *SuperGLEBer* and *HSH;-)*, respectively). Similarly, for VIO our system reached 0.80 F1 , which, while competitive, trailed the best result (0.84) by 0.04. These outcomes confirm that **nymera** was among the leading systems in all categories, with an exceptional result in DBO and solid standings in C2A and VIO.

These results highlight the strengths of our approach. In particular, the first- place finish on DBO suggests that **nymera** excels at detecting content that targets the free democratic basic order. This strength may stem from the model's ability to capture domain-specific cues (e.g. terminology or hostile narratives) that characterize attacks on the free democratic basic order. Furthermore, **nymera**'s top-tier performance across all three tasks (ranking within the top four for each) demonstrates the system's robust generalization to different manifestations of harmful content. The architecture and training regimen we employed appear to transfer well between identifying overt incitement (C2A), anti-democratic rhetoric (DBO), and even subtle positive references to violence (VIO), underlining the versatility of the system.

Despite this strong overall performance, the areas where **nymera** did not secure the very top rank point to opportunities for improvement. In the C2A subtask, our system's third-place result indicates that at least two competing systems were better at recognizing calls to action. Similarly, the fourth-place outcome in VIO shows that a few systems surpassed **nymera** in detecting disturbingly positive or encouraging statements about violence. These relative gaps suggest that **nymera** may have missed certain linguistic cues or context nuances that are critical for these categories. For instance, calls to action can be implied indirectly or phrased in subtle ways (e.g., polite requests or coded language inciting action), and our model might not capture all such subtleties. In the case of VIO, distinguishing genuinely positive references to violence from sarcastic or context-dependent statements is challenging; the fact that other teams achieved higher scores implies that they may have incorporated more effective strategies for modeling such context or sarcasm. Thus, while **nymera** was competitive, missing the top-2 in C2A and VIO suggests room for refinement in handling the more nuanced or implicit instances of harmful content.

Several limitations of the current system could underlie these observations. One potential issue is overfitting. Our model was fine-tuned extensively on the provided training data for each subtask. This intensive fine-tuning, especially with limited training examples, raises the risk that **nymera** learned patterns too specific to the training set. If the model latched onto superficial cues that do not generalize (e.g., particular keywords or idiosyncratic patterns present in the training data), its performance on some unseen examples would be suboptimal. Although the system performed well on the official test sets, overfitting may still limit its robustness, particularly if deployed on content from different platforms or contexts not covered by the competition data.

Another limitation is the lack of deeper linguistic modeling in our approach. **nymera** relies on a transformer-based classifier without explicit incorporation of higher-level linguistic or world knowledge. It treats each input largely as a sequence of tokens, without modeling discourse-level information (such as conversation context or speaker intention) or leveraging linguistic features (such as syntax or semantic roles). As a result, the system might not fully grasp cases where understanding pragmatics or context is necessary – for example, differentiating a genuine call to action from a figurative statement can require understanding the surrounding discourse or the speaker's intent. Similarly, recognizing a "positive" statement about violence may require understanding sarcasm or cultural references that go beyond surface text patterns. The absence of such enriched linguistic handling could have contributed to **nymera**'s slight underperformance in the more nuanced C2A and VIO tasks.

Additionally, our solution made use of synthetic data augmentation, which comes with its own trade-offs. We expanded the training set by generating or paraphrasing examples of harmful content to cover a wider range of expressions (especially for under-represented classes). While this strategy can improve recall and make the model more resilient to rare phrasings, it can also introduce distributional biases. If the synthetic examples are not perfectly reflective of real-world data, the model may learn artifacts specific to the artificially generated data. There is also a risk of the model over-relying on synthetic patterns at the expense of real data patterns. This reliance may have contributed to certain inconsistencies—for example, if some subtle forms of calls to action were underrepresented or inaccurately captured in the synthetic data, **nymera** might have struggled with those cases in the test set, while competing systems employing alternative strategies may have handled them more effectively.

6 Summary and Future Work

In summary, our unified system delivered strong, consistent performance across all three GermEval 2025 subtasks. It ranked 1st in the **DBO** task, 3rd in **C2A**, and 4th in **VIO**, confirming its effectiveness in detecting a diverse range of harmful content. These high rankings across the board underscore the versatility of our approach and its ability to generalize well to different manifestations of incitement, violent rhetoric, and anti-democratic speech.

This success can be attributed to several key strengths of our approach. First, the transformer-based ensemble (combining multiple fine-tuned models via soft-voting) enabled the system to capture complementary cues and improved its overall robustness. Second, extensive class balancing and data augmentation were critical: by oversampling minority classes and introducing synthetic examples, we mitigated severe class imbalance and exposed the models to a wider variety of rare but important patterns. Third, careful manual refinement—such as adding real misclassified examples for the DBO "criticism" class—helped correct systematic errors and sharpen the decision boundaries for under-represented categories. Together, these techniques enabled the system to reliably detect subtle forms of harmful content while minimizing false positives on benign inputs.

Looking ahead, we identify several avenues for further improvement. One direction is to explore a multi-task learning framework across the three subtasks, which could enable the model to leverage shared representations and cross-task signals (e.g., learning a general notion of "harmfulness" applicable to all categories). Another priority is to improve model calibration and decision threshold tuning to ensure optimal precision–recall trade-offs—especially important in high-stakes content moderation scenarios where false alarms and misses carry different costs. Finally, we aim to reduce reliance on synthetic data by incorporating additional real-world examples or external corpora into training. Expanding the training set with more authentic harmful content (drawn from varied sources) would help align the model with real-world distributions and mitigate any biases introduced by artificial examples. Pursuing these future directions should further enhance the robustness and generalizability of our system, paving the way for even more effective harmful content detection in German social media.

References

Michael Achmann-Denkler, Jakob Fehle, Mario Haim, and Christian Wolff. 2024. Detecting calls to action in multimodal content: Analysis of the 2021 German federal election campaign on Instagram. In *Proceedings of the 4th Workshop on Computational Linguistics for the Political and Social Sciences: Long and short papers*, pages 1–13, Vienna, Austria. Association for Computational Linguistics.

Remi Calizzano, Malte Ostendorff, and Georg Rehm. 2021. DFKI SLT at GermEval 2021: Multilingual pre-training and data augmentation for the classification of toxicity in social media comments. In *Proceedings of the GermEval 2021 Shared Task on the Identification of Toxic, Engaging, and Fact-Claiming Comments*, pages 25–31, Duesseldorf, Germany. Association for Computational Linguistics.

Branden Chan, Stefan Schweter, and Timo Möller. 2020. German's next language model. In *Proceedings of the 28th International Conference on Computational Linguistics, COLING 2020, Barcelona, Spain (Online), December 8-13, 2020*, pages 6788–6796. International Committee on Computational Linguistics.

Alexis Conneau, Kartikay Khandelwal, Naman Goyal, Vishrav Chaudhary, Guillaume Wenzek, Francisco Guzmán, Edouard Grave, Myle Ott, Luke Zettlemoyer, and Veselin Stoyanov. 2020. Unsupervised cross-lingual representation learning at scale. In *Proceedings of the 58th Annual Meeting of the Association for Computational Linguistics, ACL 2020, Online, July 5-10, 2020*, pages 8440–8451. Association for Computational Linguistics.

Jacob Devlin, Ming-Wei Chang, Kenton Lee, and Kristina Toutanova. 2019. BERT: pre-training of deep bidirectional transformers for language understanding. In *Proceedings of the 2019 Conference of the North American Chapter of the Association for Computational Linguistics (NAACL-HLT 2019)*, pages 4171–4186. Association for Computational Linguistics.

Jenny Felser, Michael Spranger, and Melanie Siegel. 2025. Overview of the GermEval 2025 Shared Task on Harmful Content Detection. In *Proceedings of the 21st Conference on Natural Language Processing (KONVENS 2025): Workshops*, Hildesheim, Germany.

Soumitra Ghosh, Amit Priyankar, Asif Ekbal, and Pushpak Bhattacharyya. 2023. A transformer-based multitask framework for joint detection of aggression and hate on social media data. *Nat. Lang. Eng.*, 29(6):1495–1515.

Adrián Girón, Javier Huertas-Tato, and David Camacho. 2025. Llm synthetic generation to enhance online content moderation generalization in hate speech scenarios. *Computing*, 107:164.

Anna V. Glazkova, Michael Kadantsev, and Maksim Glazkov. 2021. Fine-tuning of pre-trained transformers for hate offensive and profane content detection in english and marathi. In *Working Notes of FIRE 2021 - Forum for Information Retrieval Evaluation, Gandhinagar, India, December 13-17, 2021*, volume 3159 of *CEUR Workshop Proceedings*, pages 52–62. CEUR-WS.org.

Pengcheng He, Xiaodong Liu, Jianfeng Gao, and Weizhu Chen. 2021. Deberta: decoding-enhanced bert with disentangled attention. In *9th International Conference on Learning Representations, ICLR 2021, Virtual Event, Austria, May 3-7, 2021*. OpenReview.net.

Aman Khullar, Daniel Nkemelu, V. Cuong Nguyen, and Michael L. Best. 2024. Hate speech detection in limited data contexts using synthetic data generation. *ACM J. Comput. Sustain. Soc.*, 2(1).

Brigitte Krenn, Johann Petrak, Marina Kubina, and Christian Burger. 2024. GERMS-AT: A sexism/misogyny dataset of forum comments from an Austrian online newspaper. In *Proceedings of the 2024 Joint International Conference on Computational Linguistics, Language Resources and Evaluation (LREC-COLING 2024)*, pages 7728–7739, Torino, Italia. ELRA and ICCL.

Izzet Emre Kucukkaya and Cagri Toraman. 2025. Constructing ensembles for hate speech detection. *Natural Language Processing*, 31(3):745–770.

Thomas Mandl, Sandip Modha, Gautam Kishore Shahi, Amit Kumar Jaiswal, Durgesh Nandini, Daksh Patel, Prasenjit Majumder, and Johannes Schäfer. 2020. Overview of the HASOC track at FIRE 2020: Hate speech and offensive content identification in indo-european languages. In *Working Notes of FIRE 2020 - Forum for Information Retrieval Evaluation, Hyderabad, India, December 16-20, 2020*, volume 2826 of *CEUR Workshop Proceedings*, pages 87–111. CEUR-WS.org.

Thomas Mandl, Sandip Modha, Gautam Kishore Shahi, Hiren Madhu, Shrey Satapara, Prasenjit Majumder, Johannes Schäfer, Tharindu Ranasinghe, Marcos Zampieri, Durgesh Nandini, and Amit Kumar Jaiswal. 2021. Overview of the HASOC subtrack at FIRE 2021: Hatespeech and offensive content identification in english and indo-aryan languages. In *Working Notes of FIRE 2021 - Forum for Information Retrieval Evaluation, Gandhinagar, India, December 13-17, 2021*, volume 3159 of *CEUR Workshop Proceedings*, pages 1–19. CEUR-WS.org.

Ahmed Cherif Mazari, Nesrine Boudoukhani, and Abdelhamid Djeffal. 2024. Bert-based ensemble learning for multi-aspect hate speech detection. *Clust. Comput.*, 27(1):325–339.

Sandip Modha, Thomas Mandl, Prasenjit Majumder, and Daksh Patel. 2019. Overview of the HASOC track at FIRE 2019: Hate speech and offensive content identification in indo-european languages. In *Working Notes of FIRE 2019 - Forum for Information Retrieval Evaluation, Kolkata, India, December 12-15, 2019*, volume 2517 of *CEUR Workshop Proceedings*, pages 167–190. CEUR-WS.org.

Sandip Modha, Thomas Mandl, Prasenjit Majumder, Shrey Satapara, Tithi Patel, and Hiren Madhu. 2022. Overview of the HASOC subtrack at FIRE 2022: Identification of conversational hate-speech in hindi-english code-mixed and german language. In *Working Notes of FIRE 2022 - Forum for Information Retrieval Evaluation, Kolkata, India, December 9-13, 2022*, volume 3395 of *CEUR Workshop Proceedings*, pages 475–488. CEUR-WS.org.

Skye Morgan, Tharindu Ranasinghe, and Marcos Zampieri. 2021. WLV-RIT at GermEval 2021: Multitask learning with transformers to detect toxic, engaging, and fact-claiming comments. In *Proceedings of the GermEval 2021 Shared Task on the Identification of Toxic, Engaging, and Fact-Claiming Comments*, pages 32–38, Duesseldorf, Germany. Association for Computational Linguistics.

Benjamin Muller, Yanai Elazar, Benoît Sagot, and Djamé Seddah. 2021. First align, then predict: Understanding the cross-lingual ability of multilingual BERT. In *Proceedings of the 16th Conference of the European Chapter of the Association for Computational Linguistics: Main Volume*, pages 2214–2231, Online. Association for Computational Linguistics.

OpenAI, :, Aaron Hurst, Adam Lerer, Adam P. Goucher, Adam Perelman, Aditya Ramesh, Aidan Clark, AJ Ostrow, Akila Welihinda, Alan Hayes, Alec Radford, Aleksander Mądry, Alex Baker-Whitcomb, Alex Beutel, Alex Borzunov, Alex Carney, Alex Chow, Alex Kirillov, and 401 others. 2024. Gpt-4o system card. *Preprint*, arXiv:2410.21276.

Julian Risch, Anke Stoll, Lena Wilms, and Michael Wiegand. 2021. Overview of the GermEval 2021 shared task on the identification of toxic, engaging, and fact-claiming comments. In *Proceedings of the GermEval 2021 Shared Task on the Identification of Toxic, Engaging, and Fact-Claiming Comments*, pages 1–12. Association for Computational Linguistics.

Sourav Saha, Jahedul Alam Junaed, Maryam Saleki, Arnab Sen Sharma, Mohammad Rashidujjaman Rifat, Mohamed Rahouti, Syed Ishtiaque Ahmed, Nabeel Mohammed, and Mohammad Ruhul Amin. 2023. Vio-lens: A novel dataset of annotated social network posts leading to different forms of communal violence and its evaluation. In *Proceedings of the First Workshop on Bangla Language Processing (BLP-2023)*, pages 72–84, Singapore. Association for Computational Linguistics.

Maximilian Schmidhuber and Udo Kruschwitz. 2024. LLM-based synthetic datasets: Applications and limitations in toxicity detection. In *Proceedings of the Fourth Workshop on Threat, Aggression & Cyberbullying @ LREC-COLING-2024*, pages 37–51, Torino, Italia. ELRA and ICCL.

Julia Maria Struß, Melanie Siegel, Josef Ruppenhofer, Michael Wiegand, and Manfred Klenner. 2019. Overview of germeval task 2, 2019 shared task on the identification of offensive language. In *Preliminary proceedings of the 15th Conference on Natural Language Processing (KONVENS 2019), October 9 - 11, 2019 at Friedrich-Alexander-Universität Erlangen-Nürnberg*, pages 352 – 363.

Gregor Wiedemann, Seid Muhie Yimam, and Chris Biemann. 2020. UHH-LT & LT2 at semeval-2020 task 12: Fine-tuning of pre-trained transformer networks for offensive language detection. *CoRR*, abs/2004.11493.

Michael Wiegand, Melanie Siegel, and Josef Ruppenhofer. 2019. Overview of the germeval 2018 shared task on the identification of offensive language. In Josef Ruppenhofer, Melanie Siegel, and Michael Wiegand, editors, *Proceedings of GermEval 2018, 14th Conference on Natural Language Processing (KONVENS 2018), Vienna, Austria - September 21, 2018*, pages 1 – 10.

Lanqin Yuan and Marian-Andrei Rizoiu. 2025. Generalizing hate speech detection using multi-task learning: A case study of political public figures. *Comput. Speech Lang.*, 89:101690.

Philine Zeinert, Nanna Inie, and Leon Derczynski. 2021. Annotating online misogyny. In *Proceedings of the 59th Annual Meeting of the Association for Computational Linguistics and the 11th International Joint Conference on Natural Language Processing (Volume 1: Long Papers)*, pages 3181–3197, Online. Association for Computational Linguistics.

Yaqi Zhang, Viktor Hangya, and Alexander Fraser. 2024. A study of the class imbalance problem in abusive language detection. In *Proceedings of the 8th Workshop on Online Abuse and Harms (WOAH 2024)*, pages 38–51, Mexico City, Mexico. Association for Computational Linguistics.

TheDBOs@GermEval Shared Task 2025: Supporting BERT Model Training with LLM-Based Synthetic Tweets for Harmful Content Detection

Christoph Papadatos and **Claudia Grote** and **Florian Ludwig**
ZITiS
Zamdorfer Straße 88, 81677 Munich
christoph.papadatos@zitis.bund.de
claudia.grote@zitis.bund.de
florian.ludwig@zitis.bund.de

Abstract

Imbalanced and limited data poses significant challenges in the context of harmful content detection. By participating in subtask 2 of the GermEval's 2025 Harmful Content Detection challenge, we investigate the potential of Large Language Models (LLMs) in generating synthetic data to address this issue. We propose a four-step approach to generate and validate a synthetic dataset, which is then used to train BERT-based classification models for detecting tweets containing potential attacks on the democratic basic order (DBO). Our experiments demonstrate that incorporating synthetic data can significantly enhance model recall and precision, leading to improved overall performance. Crucially, our results highlight that careful selection of high-quality synthetic samples is essential for achieving these gains.

1 Introduction

Despite notable progress in automatic detection of hate speech, grasping the subliminal expressions of harmful content remains a challenge to natural language processing (NLP) systems (Albladi et al., 2025). The difficulty of recognition is grounded in the language of hateful content, which is variant in context and takes advantage of pernicious stylistic and rhetorical devices (Kennedy et al., 2022).

Reliably labelled harmful textual content is rare, causing data of interest and variation to form minority classes and unfavourable class imbalance (Zhang et al., 2024; Madukwe et al., 2020; Rathpisey and Adji, 2019). The impact of class imbalance on performance in NLP tasks cannot be underestimated and should be addressed according to the respective task (Henning et al., 2023). Due to the expense of intellectually annotating data, generating additional high-quality and variant training data is a current and important topic in research.

For our solution to Subtask 2 of the GermEval 2025 "Harmful Content Detection" competition (Felser et al., 2025), we developed a sophisticated method for generating synthetic training data. This generated data was designed to augment the provided dataset for classifying attacks on the free democratic basic order (DBO).[1] With our work, we make the following contributions:

- We propose a four-step approach for generating and evaluating synthetic data samples to support the training of machine learning models in detecting attacks on the democratic basic order.
- We investigate the suitability of different strategies for selecting synthetic samples for machine learning model training.
- We show the competitiveness of our solution for the GermEval 2025 "Harmful Content Detection" Shared Task.

An overview of related work relevant to the present study is provided in Section 2, followed by a brief description of the task and data in Section 3. The details of our methodological framework are presented in Section 4: We describe the prompts used and the few-shot examples selected using three different methods. Furthermore, we outline the process of synthetic tweet generation and the subsequent filtering of the generated tweets using validation models, resulting in the final synthetic corpus. Section 5 describes the baseline, the experimental setup and the datasets consisting of different subsets of the synthetic data used for three experiments. We discuss the results in Section 6,

[1] in German "Freiheitliche Demokratische Grundordnung", refers to the unalterable key values and principles constituting the core of the German democratic system, cp. https://www.verfassungsschutz.de/EN/about-us/mission-and-working-methods/protecting-the-constitution/protecting-the-constitution_article.html

Proceedings of the 21st Conference on Natural Language Processing (KONVENS), Volume 2: Workshops, pages 366–374, 2025

Label	Count	Proportion
Nothing	6,277	.84
Criticism	804	.11
Agitation	313	.042
Subversive	60	.008
Total	7,454	1

Table 1: Distribution of the training data according to their labels.

and in Section 7, we conclude the study by highlighting the most important findings.

2 Related Work

Struß et al. (2019) reports on the success of BERT-based classification models, shortly after the introduction of BERT by Devlin et al. (2019), at the GermEval 2019 "Identification of Offensive Language" challenge in the same year. As Albladi et al. (2025) shows in their review, several approaches to improve the performance of encoder models on the classification of harmful content have been introduced, but the problems of data scarcity and lack of variance in the data continue to negatively affect performance. Our approach addresses these causes and aims to improve the classification performance of BERT classifiers by providing additional and variant synthetic training data.

In order to generate annotated training data on a large scale to classify punishable offensive content, the decompositional approach described in Zufall et al. (2019) breaks down a jurisprudential annotation guideline into consecutive binary decisions that are comprehensible for legal laypeople to be followed as instructions for annotation. We apply a similar strategy to guide an LLM, using class descriptions instead, to generate appropriate data using few-shot prompting.

Variant toxic-data augmentation using LLMs has already proven successful. Juuti et al. (2020) compares different data augmentation approaches on several toxic language classifiers. Their binary BERT classifier gained best performance with additional training data generated by an LLM after fine-tuning on minority-class content, in combination with other data. Instead of resource-consuming fine-tuning of an LLM, we rely on the inherent language-understanding capabilities of the LLM with few-shot prompting.

Casula et al. (2024) describes the generation of

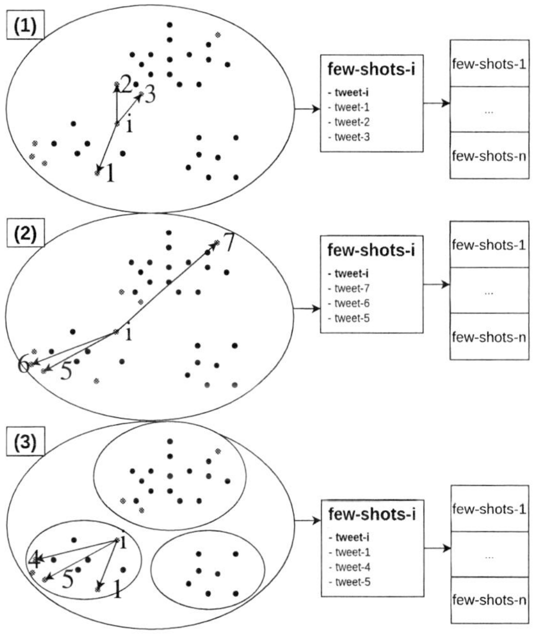

Figure 1: Illustration of the three methods for selecting few-shot examples from tweets that share the same class label l as a reference tweet i. Tweets of class l are shown as red dots. All methods use semantic similarity, measured by cosine similarity in the embedding space, to identify suitable candidates. (1) selects the k most similar tweets, (2) the k most dissimilar tweets. (3) uses topic clustering and selects the k most similar tweets within the same cluster. After selection, the tweets are ordered by their cosine similarity to i. The reference tweet and the selected tweets form a list of view shot examples.

additional training data by prompting an LLM to paraphrase original data and subsequent filtering to remove low-quality data. This differs from our approach, as we create novel synthetic data based on few-shot examples using an LLM and rank these through majority voting afterwards.

3 Description of the Task and Data

The GermEval 2025 competition on "Harmful Content Detection" (Felser et al., 2025) concerned the classification of German-language social media posts. Subtask 2 addressed the challenge of identifying attacks on the free democratic basic order (DBO) by predicting the membership to one of these four categories for each tweet: (1) *nothing* (no attack on the DBO), (2) *criticism* (legitimate verbal criticism of the government or parties), (3) *agitation* (worrying attacks expressing agitative aspirations), or (4) *subversive* (calls for or support of the overthrow of the government). For this reason, a new dataset, consisting of annotated 7,454 tweets for training purposes and 3,194 tweets for testing purposes, was introduced. This dataset comprises tweets from a German group considered extremist posted from December 2014 to July 2016 and was annotated by members of Mittweida University of Applied Sciences. The tweets were anonymised with respect to the mentions of usernames. The training data is quantitatively distributed as shown in Table 1.

The unmarked class, *nothing*, holds 84% of the training data, and the size of the smallest minor class, *subversive*, is less than 1% of the cardinality of the majority class, such that the distribution of the training data across the classes is extremely unbalanced.

4 Methods

In this work, we propose a four-step approach for generating suitable synthetic data samples. We start with the selection of few-shot examples, which are used to guide the generation of appropriate synthetic data samples with a LLM (Section 4.1). Next, we generate synthetic data samples with the help of class-specific prompts and the few-shot samples, which were selected in the first step (Section 4.2). We then train an ensemble of classifiers to assess the reliability of the generated synthetic data (Section 4.3). Each sample is assigned an agreement score based on the number of models that correctly predict its intended class. Samples with higher scores are considered more reliable. In the final step, we employ the previously trained classifiers to validate and pre-filter the synthetic data (Section 4.4).

4.1 Few-Shot Selection

In the first step, we prepare few-shot examples for the LLM to guide the generation of synthetic data. We propose three different strategies to select lists of few-shot examples from the training data. The common idea of all three methods is to consider each tweet of the training data as a reference for the selection of k additional tweets of the same class and from the same training set. The reference tweet, together with these additional selected tweets, forms a list of few-shot examples. The additional tweets are arranged in descending order according to their similarity to the reference tweet. For each method, n of these few-shot lists are collected in advance, one list for each of the n tweets in the training set. Figure 1 visualises the following strategies.

(1) Semantic Similarity-Based Selection: The first selection strategy aims to group semantically similar tweets as few-shot examples. For each reference tweet, this is done by considering the similarities to all tweets of the same class in the training corpus. In order to compute the similarities, all tweets were embedded using the embedding model proposed in (Mohr et al., 2024). The k nearest tweets are selected based on cosine similarity on these embeddings and form, together with the reference tweet, the list of few-shot examples.

(2) Semantic Dissimilarity-Based Selection: The second selection strategy selects the k most dissimilar tweets of the same class in order to form the few-shot list. As for the previous selection strategy, similarity is measured using cosine similarity on tweet embeddings. The goal of this selection strategy is to provide the LLM with few-shot examples that cover diverse semantic content, thus encouraging the generation of synthetic tweets that span a broad range of topics.

(3) Topic-Based Selection: We use a BERTopic model (Grootendorst, 2022) to cluster the training data into topics. We assume that tweets, which share the same topic cluster and the same class label, are contextually related, making them suitable as few-shot examples. To select these examples, we retrieve the k nearest tweets to a reference tweet within the same cluster using cosine similarity on tweet embeddings, ensuring topical alignment.

4.2 Synthetic Tweet Generation

The next step of the proposed approach involves the generation of a synthetic training dataset. For this reason, over 200,000 synthetic tweets were generated using the previously constructed few-shot examples and class-specific prompts.

4.2.1 Prompt Design

Synthetic data generation is guided by class-specific prompts, each following a standardised template consisting of up to five components (an exemplary prompt is shown in Appendix A).

(1) Introduction: The first part of the prompt serves as an introduction, outlining the task, and offering guidance on the characteristics of those tweets that belong to the desired class.

(2) Definition: The second part of the prompt provides the German translations of the class definitions. This is intended to describe the scope of the tweets the LLM should follow.

(3) Instruction: The third part defines the expected output: it specifies the characteristics of the synthetic tweets to be generated for a given class. This includes a short description of the class as well as the number of tweets to generate.

(4) Few-Shot Examples: This part provides class-specific few-shot examples (see Section 4.1) that the LLM should use as a reference. These examples serve to guide the model in generating tweets that match their style and semantics.

(5) Additional Topic: To address the limited number of available examples in the *subversive* and *agitation* classes, we extended the previous parts of the prompts for these classes by an additional component. This component introduces a topic placeholder, allowing the LLM to generate synthetic tweets on a specified topic, potentially increasing topical diversity within the synthetic dataset.

4.2.2 Generation Pipeline

We treat each tweet in the training data as a reference tweet. For each reference tweet, we identify its class label and use its corresponding class-specific Introductions and Instructions (see Section 4.2.1). For each few-shot selection strategy (Section 4.1), a list of few-shot examples is selected based on the current reference tweet and class label. For the *agitation* and *subversive* classes, the prompts are further extended with a specific topic (see Section 4.2.1), resulting in separate prompts for each topic. The composed prompts are used by a large language model (LLM) during inference to generate synthetic data (see Section 5.5 for details on the LLM used).

4.3 Training of Validation Models

To evaluate the reliability of the generated synthetic tweets, we classify each tweet using an ensemble of German BERT-based models. Since the prompts are class-specific, generated synthetic tweets are considered to belong to their associated classes. For each tweet, we define its reliability score as the number of models in the ensemble that correctly predict its assigned class. Tweets that receive higher reliability scores are regarded as more reliable.

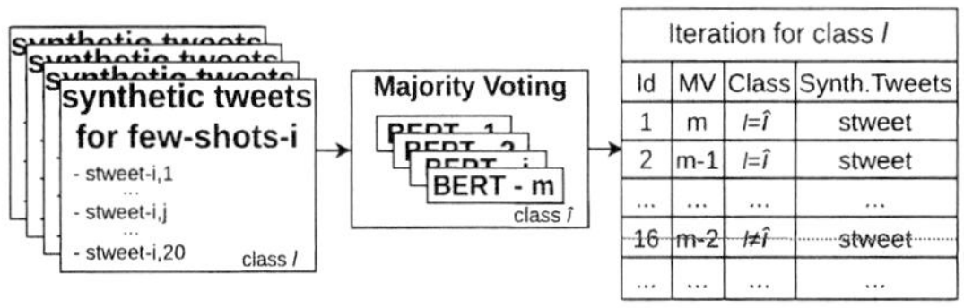

Figure 2: Reliability scoring of synthetic tweets using an ensemble of BERT-based classifiers. Each tweet is assigned a reliability score based on how many models correctly predict its associated class. Higher scores indicate greater reliability. Tweets with a low reliability score are discarded.

All validation models in the ensemble are trained using different variations of the training data. These variations include the following label aggregations and subsets of class labels.

- The original training dataset containing all four classes: *nothing*, *criticism*, *agitation*, and *subversive*
- A modified dataset with two aggregated classes: *nothing* vs. the combined class of *criticism*, *agitation*, and *subversive*
- A filtered dataset excluding the *nothing* class, containing only tweets labeled as *criticism*, *agitation*, or *subversive*

For a detailed overview of the models used, we refer to Section 5.5.

4.4 Pre-Filtering of the Synthetic Data

In the final step of our approach, we use the reliability scores assigned to the synthetic tweets to pre-filter the dataset (see Figure 2). Tweets with reliability scores below half the size of the model ensemble were discarded. The tweets that remain after this filtering process form the final synthetic corpus.

5 Experiments

This section presents an overview of our experimental setup. Model evaluation was conducted on the provided training set using 4-fold cross-validation.

5.1 Baseline Experiment

For our baseline experiment $E0$, we trained German BERT models (Chan et al., 2020) on the training dataset provided by the competition organisers, without including any synthetic data.

	$E1$	$E2$	$E3$
Nothing	$14,672$	0	0
Criticism	$14,672$	$1,299$	686
Agitation	$14,672$	$1,545$	1101
Subversive	$10,593$	$1,513$	$1,398$
Aggregate	$54,609$	$4,357$	$3,185$

Table 2: Counts of synthetic tweets with respect to each class label and experiment ($E1$ - $E3$).

5.2 Automatic Selection of Synthetic Data

For experiment $E1$, synthetic tweets were automatically selected based on their reliability scores. We identified the two highest reliability scores within each class and selected all tweets with scores matching these top two values. Due to the disproportionately large number of available examples for the classes *criticism* and *nothing* in the provided training dataset, a correspondingly larger number of synthetic tweets were generated for these classes. As a result, these classes also have a much higher number of synthetic samples with top reliability scores. To prevent class imbalance in the synthetic training set, we randomly sub-selected samples from these high-resource classes to roughly match the number selected for the other classes. The final counts of synthetic samples per class are detailed in Table 2 ($E1$). The synthetic samples were used to enhance the training data. As in the previous experiment, this dataset is then used to train German BERT models.

5.3 Manual Selection of Synthetic Data

In the second experiment $E2$, we drew a random sample from the synthetic dataset. Because the *nothing* class was already sufficiently represented in the original training set, we limited the sampling to the classes *criticism*, *agitation*, and *subversive*. Each synthetic tweet, along with its assigned class label, was manually reviewed, and only those judged to be correctly classified were retained for model training. Due to time constraints imposed by the competition timeline, we were unable to manually review as many samples as had been automatically selected in Experiment $E1$. The resulting number of synthetic training samples chosen for this experiment are shown in Table 2 ($E2$). As in the previous experiments, the selected synthetic data samples were used to enhance the provided training dataset for BERT model training.

5.4 Combining Manual and Automatic Selection of Synthetic Data

In this experiment, we filter the synthetic data, used in the previous experiment $E2$, according to their reliability scores. We selected all tweets whose scores matched the top two reliability scores within their respective class. This procedure resulted in the smallest number of samples, as shown in Table 2 ($E3$), which, however, were considered to be of the highest quality.

5.5 Experimental Parameters

In this section, we briefly describe the base models used and the parameters we chose for our approaches.

Topic Modelling: The BERTopic (Grootendorst, 2022) model was trained with the embeddings based on the embedding model proposed in (Mohr et al., 2024). To obtain fine-grained topic clusters, we applied `UMAP` and `HDBSCAN` with the following parameters: $n\_neighbors = 5$, $n\_components = 50$, and $min\_topic\_size = 5$. Additionally, we configured the `CountVectoriser` to use uni-, bi-, and trigrams, and to ignore all German stop words, to improve the quality of the topic representations.

Validation Models: The following list shows the models chosen as validation models (Section 4.3).

- `google-bert/bert-base-german-cased`[2]
- `EuroBERT/EuroBERT-610m` (Boizard et al., 2025)
- `deepset/gbert-base` (Chan et al., 2020)
- `deepset/gbert-large` (Chan et al., 2020)
- `deepset/gelectra-large` (Chan et al., 2020)
- `deepset/gbert-large-sts`[3]
- `answerdotai/ModernBERT-large` (Warner et al., 2024)

Setup for Generation Pipeline: The synthetic tweets were generated using an uncensored version of the `LLaMA 3.0 70B` model deployed via Ollama[4].

[2]Released by deepset.ai (June 2019) https://www.deepset.ai/, downloaded at https://huggingface.co/google-bert/bert-base-german-cased

[3]Released by deepset.ai (August 2021) https://www.deepset.ai/, downloaded at https://huggingface.co/deepset/gbert-large-sts

[4]https://ollama.com/taozhiyuai/llama-3-uncensored-lumi-tess-gradient:70b-q8_0

	Precision	Recall	F1-Score	F1-Score
	Cross-Validation			*Testset*
$E0$	.69	.68	.68	-
$E1$	.61	**.80**	.67	.67
$E2$	.73	.73	.72	.68
$E3$	**.74**	.73	**.73**	**.69**

Table 3: Classification metrics for different experiments *E0 - E3*. Columns 2–4 show the average results of 4-fold cross-validation on the provided training dataset. The final column reports the F1-score on the provided test set, calculated using the best-performing model selected from each experiment.

Final Models: For our experiments $E0$ $E1$, $E2$ and $E3$, we finetuned a pre-trained German BERT model (Chan et al., 2020). The models were trained for 20 epochs with a batch size of 16, using a fused AdamW optimizer (Loshchilov and Hutter, 2019) with a learning rate of 2×10^{-5}.

6 Results and Discussion

The classification results (see Table 3) highlight the critical role of data quality in achieving strong model performance. Synthetic samples selected solely through the automatic selection method appear to be of the lowest quality. This is indicated by the models trained in Experiment $E1$, which achieved the lowest F1-Score despite being trained on the largest amount of data. Although they achieved high recall, likely due to greater data variance, these models suffered from low precision due to frequently and incorrectly classifying *nothing* cases as relevant instances. In contrast, models trained on a moderate amount of manually selected synthetic data (experiment $E2$) outperformed both the baseline models (experiment $E0$) and those trained on a large quantity of lower-quality data (experiment $E1$). These models achieved significantly higher precision with only a slight decrease in recall, resulting in a higher overall F1-Score. This improvement can be attributed to the improved data quality, despite using considerably fewer synthetic data samples than the models in $E1$. The best performance was achieved by models trained exclusively on highest-quality synthetic data, which was ensured by both manual and automatic filtering of the synthetic data (experiment $E3$). While these models were trained with the least amount of data, these models not only maintained the recall observed in the previous experiment $E2$, but also further improved its precision. As a result, these models recorded the best overall F1-Score. The results obtained on the competition's test data support these findings (see Table 3, last column). The best-performing model from experiment $E3$ achieved the best performance overall, while the best-performing model from experiment $E1$ performed the worst.

Overall, we observed that the most reliable data samples were obtained by combining human judgment with automated filtering, leveraging the strengths of both approaches. While increasing the volume of data can improve recall, it does not necessarily lead to better overall results if the data quality is poor. In contrast, training with higher-quality data consistently enhances precision and overall model effectiveness. Consequently, we propose that future research focus on developing automated selection strategies to filter high-quality synthetic data for model training, thus reducing the effort of manual data inspection.

7 Conclusion

In this paper, we demonstrated that generating high-quality synthetic data samples is a suitable approach to address data scarcity and class imbalance in the GermEval 2025 Shared Task on Harmful Content Detection (Felser et al., 2025). Our findings, based on cross-validation results on the provided training dataset, highlight that careful selection of synthetic examples significantly impacts model performance and robustness. The best-performing models were then evaluated on the competition's unseen testset, where they maintained strong performance consistent with the development results. These outcomes positioned our approach among the top three teams in the competition, validating the effectiveness and generalizability of our method. Future work will focus on automating the selection of synthetic data to further improve model accuracy and reliability.

Limitations

This system description has certain limitations. Most notably, we applied our approach exclusively on subtask 2 of the GermEval 2025 challenge. Furthermore, we only investigate one model for synthetic tweet generation.

Ethics Statement

We use publicly available, anonymised data from the GermEval 2025 shared task. While this ensures reproducibility, we acknowledge that the dataset may contain biases and harmful content. Hate speech detection remains a subjective and context-dependent task, and automated systems may produce false positives or negatives. The tweet generation methods and the resulting synthetic tweets are intended solely to support model training in the detection of harmful content. Our models are intended solely for research and should not be deployed in real-world applications without careful consideration of fairness, societal impact, and the need for human oversight.

References

Aish Albladi, Minarul Islam, Amit Das, Maryam Bigonah, Zheng Zhang, Fatemeh Jamshidi, Mostafa Rahgouy, Nilanjana Raychawdhary, Daniela Marghitu, and Cheryl Seals. 2025. Hate speech detection using large language models: A comprehensive review. *IEEE Access*, 13:20871–20892.

Nicolas Boizard, Hippolyte Gisserot-Boukhlef, Duarte M Alves, André Martins, Ayoub Hammal, Caio Corro, Céline Hudelot, Emmanuel Malherbe, Etienne Malaboeuf, Fanny Jourdan, and 1 others. 2025. Eurobert: scaling multilingual encoders for european languages. *arXiv preprint arXiv:2503.05500*.

Camilla Casula, Sebastiano Vecellio Salto, Alan Ramponi, and Sara Tonelli. 2024. Delving into qualitative implications of synthetic data for hate speech detection. In *Proceedings of the 2024 Conference on Empirical Methods in Natural Language Processing*, pages 19709–19726, Miami, Florida, USA. Association for Computational Linguistics.

Branden Chan, Stefan Schweter, and Timo Möller. 2020. German's next language model. *arXiv preprint arXiv:2010.10906*.

Jacob Devlin, Ming-Wei Chang, Kenton Lee, and Kristina Toutanova. 2019. BERT: Pre-training of deep bidirectional transformers for language understanding. In *Proceedings of the 2019 Conference of the North American Chapter of the Association for Computational Linguistics: Human Language Technologies, Volume 1 (Long and Short Papers)*, pages 4171–4186, Minneapolis, Minnesota. Association for Computational Linguistics.

Jenny Felser, Michael Spranger, and Melanie Siegel. 2025. Overview of the germeval 2025 shared task on harmful content detection. In *Proceedings of the 21st Conference on Natural Language Processing (KONVENS 2025): Workshops*.

Maarten Grootendorst. 2022. Bertopic: Neural topic modeling with a class-based tf-idf procedure. *arXiv preprint arXiv:2203.05794*.

Sophie Henning, William Beluch, Alexander Fraser, and Annemarie Friedrich. 2023. A survey of methods for addressing class imbalance in deep-learning based natural language processing. In *Proceedings of the 17th Conference of the European Chapter of the Association for Computational Linguistics*, pages 523–540, Dubrovnik, Croatia. Association for Computational Linguistics.

Mika Juuti, Tommi Gröndahl, Adrian Flanagan, and N. Asokan. 2020. A little goes a long way: Improving toxic language classification despite data scarcity. In *Findings of the Association for Computational Linguistics: EMNLP 2020*, pages 2991–3009, Online. Association for Computational Linguistics.

Brendan Kennedy, Mohammad Atari, Aida Mostafazadeh Davani, Leigh Yeh, Ali Omrani, Yehsong Kim, Kris Coombs, Shreya Havaldar, Gwenyth Portillo-Wightman, Elaine Gonzalez, Joe Hoover, Aida Azatian, Alyzeh Hussain, Austin Lara, Gabriel Cardenas, Adam Omary, Christina Park, Xin Wang, Clarisa Wijaya, and 3 others. 2022. Introducing the gab hate corpus: defining and applying hate-based rhetoric to social media posts at scale. *Lang. Resour. Eval.*, 56(1):79–108.

Ilya Loshchilov and Frank Hutter. 2019. Decoupled weight decay regularization. *Preprint*, arXiv:1711.05101.

Kosisochukwu Madukwe, Xiaoying Gao, and Bing Xue. 2020. In data we trust: A critical analysis of hate speech detection datasets. In *Proceedings of the fourth workshop on online abuse and harms*, pages 150–161.

Isabelle Mohr, Markus Krimmel, Saba Sturua, Mohammad Kalim Akram, Andreas Koukounas, Michael Günther, Georgios Mastrapas, Vinit Ravishankar, Joan Fontanals Martínez, Feng Wang, and 1 others. 2024. Multi-task contrastive learning for 8192-token bilingual text embeddings. *arXiv preprint arXiv:2402.17016*.

Heng Rathpisey and Teguh Bharata Adji. 2019. Handling imbalance issue in hate speech classification using sampling-based methods. In *2019 5th International Conference on Science in Information Technology (ICSITech)*, pages 193–198. IEEE.

Julia Maria Struß, Melanie Siegel, Josep Ruppenhofer, Michael Wiegand, and Manfred Klenner. 2019. Overview of germeval task 2, 2019 shared task on the identification of offensive language. In *Proceedings of the 15th Conference on Natural Language Processing (KONVENS 2019)*, pages 354–365, Erlangen, Germany. German Society for Computational Linguistics & Language Technology.

Benjamin Warner, Antoine Chaffin, Benjamin Clavié, Orion Weller, Oskar Hallström, Said Taghadouini, Alexis Gallagher, Raja Biswas, Faisal Ladhak, Tom Aarsen, and 1 others. 2024. Smarter, better, faster, longer: A modern bidirectional encoder for fast, memory efficient, and long context finetuning and inference. *arXiv preprint arXiv:2412.13663*.

Yaqi Zhang, Viktor Hangya, and Alexander Fraser. 2024. A study of the class imbalance problem in abusive language detection. In *Proceedings of the 8th Workshop on Online Abuse and Harms (WOAH 2024)*, pages 38–51, Mexico City, Mexico. Association for Computational Linguistics.

Frederike Zufall, Tobias Horsmann, and Torsten Zesch. 2019. From legal to technical concept: Towards an automated classification of German political Twitter postings as criminal offenses. In *Proceedings of the 2019 Conference of the North American Chapter of the Association for Computational Linguistics: Human Language Technologies, Volume 1 (Long and Short Papers)*, pages 1337–1347, Minneapolis, Minnesota. Association for Computational Linguistics.

A Prompts

This section contains the prompts used for generating synthetic data.

Prompt Part 1

Gebe mir Beispiele von Tweets, die in einer der Kategorien sind, die unten aufgelistet sind. Sie sollen keine Angriffe auf die freiheitliche und demokratische Grundordnung der Bundesrepublik Deutschland beinhalten.

Prompt Part 2

subversive: Ein Wille wird geäußert, die bestehende Regierung mit Gewalt zu stürzen und zu zerstören (z.B. durch militanten Einsatz, Störung des Stromnetzes usw.).

agitation: Agitative Bemühungen werden geäußert. Dazu gehören die Bekanntgabe von Aktionen wie der Verbreitung von Propagandamaterial unkonstitutioneller und terroristischer Organisationen oder die Beschädigung von Staatsymbolen wie der Fahne der Bundesrepublik Deutschland.

criticism: Tweets, in denen legitime Kritik an der Regierung, Amtsträgern, Regierungsangestellten, Behörden oder Parteien geäußert wurde, wurden dieser Klasse zugeordnet.

nothing (kein Angriff auf die freiheitlich-demokratische Grundordnung): Der Tweet enthält keinen Angriff auf die freiheitliche demokratische Grundordnung. Auch neutrale oder positive Aussagen über Regierungsentscheidungen fallen in diese Kategorie. Generell alle Tweets, die nicht in die Kategorie subversive, agitation oder criticism fallen.

Prompt Part 3

Liste mir 20 Beispiel-Tweets auf in deutscher Sprache der Kategorie nothing. Formuliere Tweets und achte darauf, dass ein paar wenige Tweets auch neutrale oder positive Aussagen über Regierungsentscheidungen beinhalten. Schreibe in den übrigen Tweets über die Themen, die in den Beispielen vorkommen!

Prompt Part 4

Orientiere dich dabei an folgenden Beispielen: {few_shots}

Prompt 1: Prompting to obtain completions of class *nothing*. Each prompt is composed of four parts. Part 1 consists of a general prefix to describe the task of proposing examples of tweets belonging to one of the categories described in part 2, in this case, class *nothing* is addressed. Part 2 describes die four classes of the multi-class scheme using unambiguous formulations. Part 3 states the desired quantity of completions, language and category label. It also contains a piece of advice to include neutral or positive mentions of governmental decisions, whereas the other completions have to adopt the topics found in the examples in part 4. Part 4 lists examples operating as few-shots.

tweetbusters@GermEval Shared Task 2025: Comprehensive Feature Engineering for Call to Action detection

Anastasia Schwichtenberg
Mittweida University of Applied Sciences
Technikumplatz 17
09648 Mittweida

Abstract

In previous GermEval Shared Tasks, deep learning methods, particularly the fine-tuning of transformer models, were frequently employed to detect harmful content in social media. However, this trend should not overshadow the fact that traditional approaches, especially when combined with comprehensive feature engineering, remain promising. Against this backdrop, we report on our participation in the GermEval Shared Task 2025, where we are pursuing an approach based on traditional machine learning for the first subtask, the detection of calls to action. Our system utilises a variety of linguistic, word list-based, and statistical features, as well as pre-trained sentence embeddings. A soft voting ensemble of established machine learning methods, including random forest, gradient boosting, logistic regression and a support vector machine (SVM), was used as the classifier. On the official test data set, our system achieved a macro-F_1 score of 66.01%.

1 Introduction

The dissemination of harmful content via social media poses a significant risk. Calls for violence or other harmful acts are particularly worrying. Recent examples illustrate the potential danger: in July 2025, video messages called for violence against Druze in the run-up to an Islamist demonstration (Meischen, 2025); in the United Kingdom, the term 'keyboard warriors' has even been coined to describe people who incite violence or hatred on social media, such as blowing up mosques (Riecke, 2024).

Early detection of such content is therefore crucial for security. Since manual analysis is not feasible on a large scale, automated procedures are required. The first subtask of the GermEval Shared Task on Harmful Content Detection (Felser et al., 2025), which involves identifying calls to action (CTA), addresses this problem. The aim is to capture all forms of linguistic appeals intended to elicit specific reactions from the audience – from harmless examples, such as "Share this post!" or "Support us!", to more serious calls, such as "Shoot!". Detecting these calls enables moderators to be supported by an early warning system for prioritising potentially dangerous content. It allows security authorities to plan resources for protests and demonstrations with potential for escalation.

This paper describes our approach to detecting CTA in the context of the first subtask. Our focus is on constructing a precise feature representation and using a soft-voting ensemble classifier to achieve good classification performance.

The remainder of the paper is structured as follows: section 2 provides an overview of existing literature on CTA and harmful content detection, highlighting the specific research gap addressed by our work. Section 3 details our proposed pipeline, covering data preprocessing, extensive feature engineering, and the ensemble model architecture. Section 4 presents a thorough evaluation of our system's performance, including a detailed analysis of results on both training and validation sets. Section 5 discusses the constraints and potential biases of our approach. Finally, section 5 summarises our findings and outlines promising directions for future research.

2 Related Work

The problem of detecting CTA has only been investigated in a few studies to date, with Achmann-Denkler et al. (2024) being the only one to focus on German-language social media posts. As part of the 2021 German federal election campaign, they analysed around 1,400 Instagram posts from candidate accounts. When comparing Bidirectional Encoder Representations from Transformers (BERT) (Devlin et al., 2019) and Generative Pre-trained Transformer (GPT-4) (Achiam et al., 2022) in the detection of CTA in Instagram posts, both models

Proceedings of the 21st Conference on Natural Language Processing (KONVENS), Volume 2: Workshops, pages 375–384, 2025

achieved macro-F_1 scores above 0.9, with BERT performing slightly better.

BERT and its variants have also proven successful with other types of CTA, such as detecting CTAs for protest in Russian-language social media posts (Rogers et al., 2019), requests for help in tweets after a hurricane (Zhou et al., 2022), and distinguishing whether Spanish-language hate speech tweets contained explicit calls for violence (Pérez et al., 2023). However, it should also be noted that Pérez et al. (2023) in particular had access to contextual information in the form of newspaper articles related to the posts to be classified. The lack of such information for the first task of the shared task makes it more difficult.

Although BERT models were also particularly popular in previous GermEval Shared Tasks in the area of detecting harmful content (Bornheim et al., 2021; Gawron and Schmidt, 2021), such as toxic language (Risch et al., 2021), the potential of traditional classification approaches should not be overlooked, especially when computational resources are scarce. For example, as part of the GerMS-Detect task in GermEval 2024 (Gross et al., 2024), Donabauer (2024) found that traditional methods, such as XGBoost, even outperformed BERT-based models in the binary detection of sexism in German comments on online forums. This result already indicates that state-of-the-art standard language models do not necessarily outperform traditional classification approaches in every case.

Even more relevant to our work are approaches focusing on traditional learning and/or feature engineering in the detection of CTA (e.g., Siskou et al., 2022; Ullah et al., 2021). Lampert et al. (2010) aimed to identify requests in emails using the Enron dataset (Klimt and Yang, 2004) to assign them a higher priority. Lampert et al. (2010) employed a Support Vector Machine (SVM) with extensive feature engineering, including bag-of-words (BoW) features as well as structural features such as message length. Although their results were promising, some of the features used are highly email-specific – such as a binary feature for the presence of sender or recipient information – so the approach cannot be directly transferred to subtask 1.

In contrast, Siskou et al. (2022) examined CTA in the social media context of Latin American elections using tweets and Facebook posts. They developed a rule-based system that classifies posts as CTA using keywords and grammatical structures such as imperative forms. However, generalisability is limited because many rules are specifically tailored to the election context. Nevertheless, some word- and grammar-based features could also be of interest for machine learning.

Mathur et al. (2018) demonstrated that machine learning, combined with comprehensive feature engineering, can achieve high performance in detecting blood donation appeals on Twitter, even though the features are based on metadata such as user follower counts, which were not available in the dataset for subtask 1. Finally, Ullah et al. (2021) focused less on feature engineering and more on the classification algorithm when detecting requests for help in English-language disaster tweets. Of the seven methods tested, logistic regression with N-grams and regular expressions performed best. However, like the studies presented so far, this study also refrains from using ensemble learning. Studies on the detection of hate speech in social media (e.g., Raza and Chatrath, 2024) and the GermEval workshops on the detection of offensive tweets (Wiegand et al., 2018; Struß et al., 2019; Risch et al., 2021) have both found that ensemble methods achieve better results overall than their individual components.

To close this research gap, we are investigating the use of a soft voting classifier for detecting CTAs. Moreover, the particular challenge compared to previous work lies in developing features that are fundamentally suitable for any CTA and are not limited to calls in the context of particular events.

3 Methodology

We utilised the annotated dataset provided by the organisers of the Shared Task for subtask 1 (Felser et al., 2025). This dataset comprised German-language tweets from the context of a right-wing extremist group as the primary data source, with each tweet labelled as either CTA (TRUE) or non-CTA (FALSE). The organisers had previously split the dataset into training and test data, with the training dataset containing 6,840 tweets and the test dataset containing 2,982 tweets. The training data was highly unbalanced, where the number of tweets per category can be taken from the training data in Table 1. For a more detailed description, please refer to the overview paper by Felser et al. (2025).

Before feature extraction, the tweets were subjected to a standardised pre-processing pipeline using spaCy (Honnibal et al., 2020) for the reduction to content-bearing words and for normalisation

Class Label	Freq	%
TRUE	663	9.69
FALSE	6177	90.31
Total	6840	100.00

Table 1: Absolute and percentage number of tweets in the categories TRUE (CTA) and FALSE (no CTA) in the training data set.

purposes.

Lowercasing All tweets were converted to lowercase to reduce vocabulary size and treat words identically regardless of their capitalisation.

Punctuation Removal Punctuation marks were removed to focus on the lexical content.

Lemmatisation Words were reduced to their dictionary form (lemma) to group inflected forms (e.g., "gehen", "ging", "geht" all become "gehen").

Stopword Filtering Common function words (e.g., "und", "der", "ein") were removed as they typically carry little semantic information for classification.

3.1 Feature Engineering

To reliably detect CTA, we designed an extensive feature engineering process that extracts a diverse set of linguistic, semantic, and surface-level features from each text. The features are grouped as follows:

Linguistic Features These features capture grammatical structures that can be considered as indications of commands or requests. To extract these features, part of speech (POS) tagging was first performed. To this end, the tweets were tokenised according to defined rules, taking into account exceptions such as contractions and abbreviations, as described by Honnibal et al. (2020). POS tagging was performed using a model trained on the TIGER corpus (Brants et al., 2004) and provided by the Python library spaCy (Honnibal et al., 2020).

The following features were then extracted:

- Number of verbs, nouns and adjectives in the tweet to capture characteristic patterns such as missing nouns in elliptical exclamations, which, according to Blühdorn (2023), can serve as CTA (e.g. "Jetzt mal aufgepasst!", engl. "Now pay attention!").
- Ratio of verbs, nouns and adjectives to the total number of words to obtain normalised measures.
- Binary indicator of whether the tweet begins with a verb – as is typical for German imperative sentences (e.g. "Geh!", engl. "Go!"). According to Siskou et al. (2022), imperative sentences often express CTA.
- Fragment detection: Binary indicator of whether the tweet is very short (i.e. less than four words) and either begins with a verb or consists only of characters such as exclamation marks – often characteristic of direct requests (e.g., "Ergreift die Initiative!", engl. "Take the initiative!")

Semantic and Content-based Features As in previous work on the detection of CTA (e.g. Siskou et al., 2022; Ullah et al., 2021), we defined features based on specific words and patterns that are frequently associated with CTAs. For this purpose, we created two lists: *CTA-KW* with CTA character-specific keywords and *CTA-PAT* with regular expressions that describe phrases typical for CTA. To generate both lists, Perplexity AI (Perplexity AI, Inc., 2024) was prompted in a zero-shot scenario and the resulting lists were then supplemented manually. The CTA-KW list contained a total of 327 words, such as:

- imperative form, e.g., "geh wählen" (engl. "go vote")
- words that express urgency, e.g., "unbedingt" (engl. "absolutely")
- words associated with resistance, e.g., "boykottieren" (engl. "boycott") or "kämpfen" (engl. "fight")

The CTA-PAT list comprised 35 regular expressions that include common imperative forms and phrases to activate readers, such as:

- `komm\s+\w+` to capture expressions such as "komm mit!" (engl. "come on!")
- `mach\s+dich\s+\w+` to describe expressions such as "mach dich stark" (engl. "Be strong!")

Based on the lists of keywords and regular expressions, the following features were implemented:

- Binary indicator indicating whether the tweet contains any word from the CTA-KW list
- Number of words in the tweet that appear in the CTA-KW list
- Binary indicator whether any regular expression from the CTA-PAT list matches the tweet
- Number of regular expressions from CTA-PAT that match the tweet
- A binary feature *cta_boost* that indicates whether at least two different CTA patterns have been detected, which indicates a higher probability of CTA.
- An indicator if the text starts or ends with a CTA keyword, which can emphasise urgency

Additionally, we added two more features to ensure that most forms of CTA were covered:

- Binary feature indicating whether one of the word stems "geh" (engl. "go"), "mach" (engl. "do"), "sollt" (engl. "should"), "müss" (engl. "must"), "komm" (engl. "come"), "stell" (engl. "put") or "nehm" (engl. "take") is part of a word in the tweet. In particular, according to Siskou et al. (2022), modal verbs such as "müssen" and "sollen" imply obligations, which is why they can be part of a CTA.
- Binary feature indicating whether the tweet contains the common informal construction "mal" + "verb" (e.g., "schau mal", engl. "just look") and "probier mal", engl. "just try"), which, by experience, are often used for casual suggestions or soft commands in German.

Structural and Surface Features These features capture non-linguistic but informative text characteristics.

- Text length (in characters) and word count, as it is obvious that calls such as "Wake up!" can be considerably shorter than factual, explanatory statements.
- Average word length, which can be related to the informativeness of words (Levshina, 2022), making it likely that CTAs will tend to use simple language with short words such as "Los!" (engl. "go")
- Number of exclamation and question marks, which can indicate strong emotions or direct address.
- Number of emojis (using Unicode detection), relevant in social media context for expressing intent or tone.
- A binary feature indicating whether a hashtag appears in the tweet, as a brief analysis of the tweets in the training data set showed that these alone can constitute a CTA (e.g., #allesdichtmachen, #niewiederaufmachen).
- Four binary features, each indicating whether a specific mention type occurred (i.e. [@PRE], [@POL], [@GRP], [@IND]), as it seems likely that mentions are used to direct a call to a specific person/group.
- An indicator for very short tweets (fewer than four words), which might be direct, imperative statements.

All of these features are either numerical (e.g., numbers, ratios) or categorical (e.g., binary indicators). This comprehensive set of features forms the basis for the subsequent modelling and ensemble steps, enabling the model to capture the diverse expressions of CTAs in German texts.

3.2 Text Representation

The tweet was represented in two ways to capture its textual content.

- **TF-IDF Features**: Term Frequency-Inverse Document Frequency (TF-IDF) was applied to extract up to 500 features, considering 1-gram and 2-gram word combinations. TF-IDF assigns weights to words based on their importance in a document relative to the corpus (Sparck Jones, 1972).
- **Sentence Embeddings:** We utilised pretrained SentenceTransformer models, specifically paraphrase-multilingual-MiniLM-L12-v2 (Reimers and Gurevych, 2019), to generate dense, fixed-size vector representations for each sentence. These embeddings captured the semantic meaning and context of the text, providing a powerful complement to the handcrafted features.

To comprehensively describe the characteristics of a tweet, the linguistic, content-related and superficial text features described in subsection 3.1 were first extracted from the pre-processed tweets. Numerical features (e.g., numbers, ratios) were standardised using Z-score normalisation, and categorical features (e.g., binary indicators) were converted using one-hot encoding (Pedregosa et al., 2011). All features were combined into a feature vector.

In addition, the pre-processed tweets were converted into TF-IDF vectors and sentence embeddings. These three vector representations were ultimately combined into a single feature vector that represents the tweet.

3.3 Data Splitting and Balancing

The dataset was partitioned into training and validation sets with an 80/20 split, respectively. To ensure that both sets retain the original class distribution, stratified sampling was employed. To address the inherent class imbalance (where non-CTA samples typically outnumber CTA samples), we applied the Synthetic Minority Over-sampling Technique (SMOTE) (Chawla et al., 2002) to the training data. The minority class (CTA) was oversampled to achieve 50% of the majority class's size, thereby providing a more balanced training environment without generating redundant exact duplicates. The number of tweets per category in the training dataset (excluding validation data) before and after applying SMOTE is presented in Table 2.

	Class Label	Freq	%
Before SMOTE	TRUE	530	9.69
	FALSE	4942	90.31
	Total	5472	100.0
After SMOTE	TRUE	2471	33.33
	FALSE	4942	66.67
	Total	7413	100.0

Table 2: Absolute and relative number of tweets in the two classes in the training data set (without validation data) before and after applying SMOTE.

3.4 Model Architecture

Our final classification model is a soft-voting ensemble, which combines the predictions of four diverse machine learning algorithms. Each individual model is chosen for its complementary strengths, aiming to capture different patterns in the data:

- **Random Forest:** An ensemble method that builds multiple decision trees and merges their predictions (Breiman, 2001). Random Forest was configured with 100 trees. The weights associated with the classes were chosen inversely proportional to the class frequencies in the training data to deal with the problem of high imbalance, as described by Pedregosa et al. (2011).

- **Gradient Boosting:** A powerful ensemble technique that builds models sequentially, with each new model correcting errors made by previous ones (Friedman, 2001). One hundred boosting stages were carried out.

- **Logistic Regression:** A linear model widely used for binary classification, providing interpretable probability estimates (Yu et al., 2011). The maximum number of iterations that a solver can take to converge to a solution has been limited to 100 iterations. Similar to Random Forest, the class weights were again set inversely proportional to the class frequency.

- **SVM:** A non-linear model with a Radial Basis Function (RBF) kernel, capable of capturing complex relationships (Cortes and Vapnik, 1995). The class weights were specified in the same way as in Random Forest and logistic regression to minimise the problem of imbalance. To make the SVM output suitable for subsequent soft voting, the class membership probabilities were estimated using Platt scaling (Platt, 1999).

The predicted probabilities from these four models were combined using a soft voting procedure, whereby the predicted probabilities of the four classifiers are averaged for each class (Kyriakides, 2019). This approach aggregates the strengths of individual classifiers, typically leading to improved generalisation performance compared to any single model.

3.5 Threshold Optimization

The default probability threshold for binary classification is typically 0.5 (Nikolov and Radivchev, 2019). However, especially with unbalanced data sets, this threshold value may not necessarily be the best choice (Iguazio Ltd., 2025). Therefore, we explicitly optimised the probability value for the F_1 measure for the first two runs submitted on the validation data set. The third run differed from these only in that it was optimised according to the macro-F_1 measure instead of the F_1 measure. This process involved searching a range of thresholds (from 0.1 to 0.9 with a step of 0.02) and selecting the one that yields the highest F_1 and macro-F_1 scores, respectively. That ensured that our model's final predictions are optimally tuned for the evaluation metric. We refer to the determined optimal threshold value as θ_{opt} in the following.

3.6 Evaluation and Submission

We evaluated our approach on the validation dataset using macro-F_1, the official competition metric. This metric weights precision and recall equally for both classes and is therefore robust against imbalanced datasets (Zhou, 2021). The probability threshold for classification was explicitly optimised on the validation data, as described in subsection 3.5.

To submit predictions on the test data in the competition phase, we then trained the model on the entire training dataset provided, i.e. on all 6,840 tweets (including the data previously used for validation). To obtain the binary label for the test data after the trained ensemble model made its prediction, the previously optimised threshold θ_{opt} was applied: if the mean probability of the four classifiers was above θ_{opt}, the tweet was assigned to the positive class (*TRUE*).

4 Results and Discussion

This section describes and discusses the results achieved by the proposed ensemble approach on the validation and test data. In addition, the performance of the ensemble approach is compared with that of the individual models.

4.1 Results of the proposed ensemble approach

Hyperparameter tuning yielded a result showing that the best macro-F_1 score of 64.3% could be achieved on the validation data when the threshold for classifying a tweet as CTA was set to 0.48.

Using this threshold, the model trained on the complete training data achieved a slightly improved macro-F_1 score of 66.01% on the test data. The results of our other two runs were slightly worse, as noted in all references to Felser et al. (2025).

Compared to the results of the other participants, our best run yielded poor results. For better comparability, Table 3 lists the macro-F_1 scores of our best run on the test data, together with the result of the best performing system of the SuperGLEBER team for subtask 1. The baseline is a gradient boosting classifier based on polarity features and pre-trained sentence embeddings, as described in detail by (Felser et al., 2025). As can be seen from Table 3, our system outperformed this by more than 6%. Whether this improvement is primarily due to the extended feature engineering or the use of the ensemble approach cannot be clearly determined without an ablation study. However, such an investigation is beyond the scope of this work.

Team	Run	Macro-F_1
SuperGLEBer	3	86.98
tweetbusters	**3**	**66.01**
baseline	-	59.13

Table 3: Macro-F_1 scores achieved by the best system, our approach (tweetbusters) and the baseline system on the test data.

4.2 Discussion and Error Analysis

The low ranking of the submitted run illustrates that the approach presented needs to be further improved. One possible reason for the limited performance could be redundant features. For example, it is questionable whether the parallel use of the same feature as a binary indicator and as a frequency feature actually provides additional information for the classifier (e.g. whether a word from the CTA keyword list occurs versus how often it occurs). Here, the use of feature selection methods that were developed not only to select distinctive features for a category, but also specifically to avoid redundancy, as proposed by Hussain et al. (2020), for example, appears promising, but this must remain the subject of future work.

To better understand which examples were particularly challenging for the classification approach, the misclassified tweets were analysed. Several recurring patterns can be identified that the system has problems with:

- **Very Short Texts or Fragments:** Short, ambiguous phrases (e.g., "Feuer frei!", engl. "Fire at will!") often lack sufficient context for accurate classification without prior knowledge.

- **Ironically Phrased or Ambiguous CTAs:** Sarcasm, irony, or subtle implications are challenging for automated systems, leading to misinterpretations (e.g., "Go on, make my day", which is an imperative but might be ironic).
- **Rare or Creative CTA Formulations:** CTA patterns that deviate significantly from common templates or established keyword lists (e.g., newly emerging slang, highly metaphorical language) are difficult to capture solely through rule-based or frequency-based features.
- **Contextual Dependency:** Some phrases only become a CTA in a specific dialogue or discourse context, which is not fully captured by analysing isolated sentences.

While expanding keyword and pattern lists during development improved recall for some of these challenging cases, these categories remain areas for further improvement.

4.3 Performance of the individual models

After completion of the competition phase, further analysis was conducted to determine the extent to which the ensemble approach is actually superior to the individual models. To this end, the optimal threshold value was determined for each of the probabilistic classifiers using the macro-F_1 measure on the validation data, analogous to the procedure described in subsection 3.5. Table 4 presents the determined threshold values and the resulting macro-F_1 scores on the validation data.

Method	Threshold	Macro F_1
Random Forest	0.16	58.15
Gradient Boosting	0.18	62.68
Logistic Regression	0.76	**67.08**
SVM	0.24	62.64

Table 4: Individual performance of the four classification methods combined for the soft voting classifier on the validation data, with the best result highlighted in bold.

When analysing the results, it is immediately apparent that all methods – except logistic regression – favour very low thresholds below 0.25. However, the problem is that the classifiers in question then exhibit a high degree of uncertainty when assigning to the positive class, which argues against the robustness of the system. For future investigations, it is therefore essential to calculate additional evaluation metrics, such as the precision and recall of the positive class. It cannot be ruled out that a higher macro-F_1 measure is primarily due to high recall but low precision, i.e. many tweets incorrectly classified as CTA.

In contrast, logistic regression prefers a significantly higher threshold and also slightly outperforms the ensemble classifier by about 3.3%. The fact that the ensemble approach performs poorly suggests that logistic regression should be combined with other, possibly more advanced methods and that a weighted voting approach should be used to assign a higher weight to high-performance models.

5 Conclusion

This paper presents a soft voting ensemble approach combined with comprehensive feature engineering for detecting calls to action (CTAs) in German social media texts as part of the first subtask of the GermEval 2025 Shared Tasks for detecting harmful content. SMOTE was used to address the severe class imbalance in the provided training dataset. In addition, the threshold at which the voting classifier classifies a tweet as a CTA was optimised using hyperparameter tuning. Our best submitted system achieved a macro-F_1 score of 66.01%. This result is below the performance of other participants and may be due, in particular, to a high degree of feature redundancy.

Future work should therefore focus more on the use of feature selection methods to reduce redundancy and systematically investigate the contribution of individual features and their combinations to overall performance. It is also necessary to question whether optimising the threshold based solely on the macro-F_1 score actually produces a reliable system. A targeted analysis of different threshold values could help to achieve a more balanced compromise between precision and recall for the positive CTA class. Furthermore, the question arises as to what extent the integration of deep learning methods into the ensemble model can further improve classification performance compared to the traditional approaches used to date.

Limitations

Our current approach has several limitations:

- **Language and Domain Specificity:** The extensive keyword and pattern lists are tailored explicitly for German social media texts. Adapting the system to other languages or very different domains would require significant re-engineering of these handcrafted features.
- **Dependency on spaCy:** The preprocessing pipeline relies heavily on spaCy's linguistic capabilities for German (lemmatisation, POS tagging). Changes or limitations in spaCy's performance could directly impact the system's accuracy.
- **Lack of End-to-End Deep Learning Exploration:** This research focuses on combining traditional features with neural sentence embeddings and classical ML ensembles as classifiers. Pure deep learning approaches, such as BERT, have not been systematically investigated or evaluated, despite their potential to enable further performance improvements and eliminate the need for complex feature engineering.
- **No Multi-label/Intent Classification:** The system is designed for binary CTA detection. It does not distinguish between different types of CTAs (e.g. call to vote vs. call to share) or other intents.

Ethical Statement

This work aims to support research on mobilisation and intent detection, contributing to understanding communication patterns in social media. We are fully aware of the potential for misuse, such as aiding surveillance, targeted manipulation, or censorship, and strongly recommend the responsible, transparent, and ethical application of such technologies. Our goal is to empower researchers and platform providers to identify and mitigate harmful content, rather than facilitating its creation or suppressing legitimate speech.

References

Josh Achiam, Steven Adler, Sandhini Agarwal, Lama Ahmad, Ilge Akkaya, Florencia Leoni Aleman, Diogo Almeida, Janko Altenschmidt, Sam Altman, Shyamal Anadkat, Red Avila, Igor Babuschkin, Suchir Balaji, Valerie Balcom, Paul Baltescu, Haiming Bao, Mohammad Bavarian, Jeff Belgum, Irwan Bello, and 261 others. 2022. GPT-4 technical report. Technical report, OpenAI, San Francisco.

Michael Achmann-Denkler, Jakob Fehle, Mario Haim, and Christian Wolff. 2024. Detecting calls to action in multimodal content: Analysis of the 2021 German federal election campaign on Instagram. In *Proceedings of the 4th Workshop on Computational Linguistics for the Political and Social Sciences: Long and Short Papers*, pages 1–13, Vienna, Austria. Association for Computational Linguistics.

Hardarik Blühdorn. 2023. Imperative und Aufforderungssätze im Deutschen. *Deutsche Sprache*, 51(2):120–149.

Tobias Bornheim, Niklas Grieger, and Stephan Bialonski. 2021. FHAC at GermEval 2021: Identifying German toxic, engaging, and fact-claiming comments with ensemble learning. In *Proceedings of the GermEval 2021 Shared Task on the Identification of Toxic, Engaging, and Fact-Claiming Comments*, pages 105–111, Duesseldorf, Germany. Association for Computational Linguistics.

Sabine Brants, Stefanie Dipper, Peter Eisenberg, Silvia Hansen-Schirra, Esther König, Wolfgang Lezius, Christian Rohrer, George Smith, and Hans Uszkoreit. 2004. TIGER: Linguistic Interpretation of a German Corpus. *Research on Language and Computation*, 2(4):597–620.

Leo Breiman. 2001. Random Forests. *Machine Learning*, 45(1):5–32.

Nitesh V. Chawla, Kevin W. Bowyer, Lawrence O. Hall, and W. Philip Kegelmeyer. 2002. SMOTE: Synthetic Minority Over-sampling Technique. *Journal of Artificial Intelligence Research*, 16(1):321–357.

Corinna Cortes and Vladimir Vapnik. 1995. Support-vector networks. *Machine Learning*, 20(3):273–297.

Jacob Devlin, Ming-Wei Chang, Kenton Lee, and Kristina Toutanova. 2019. BERT: Pre-training of deep bidirectional transformers for language understanding. In *Proceedings of the 2019 Conference of the North American Chapter of the Association for Computational Linguistics: Human Language Technologies*, volume 1, pages 4171–4186, Minneapolis, Minnesota. Association for Computational Linguistics.

Pia Donabauer. 2024. Pd2904 at GermEval2024 (Shared Task 1: GerMS-Detect): Exploring the Effectiveness of Multi-Task Transformers vs. Traditional Models for Sexism Detection (Closed Tracks of Subtasks 1 and 2). In *Proceedings of GermEval 2024 Task 1 GerMS-detect Workshop on Sexism Detection in German Online News Fora (GerMS-detect 2024)*, pages 39–47, Vienna, Austria. Association for Computational Lingustics.

Jenny Felser, Michael Spranger, and Melanie Siegel. 2025. Overview of the GermEval 2025 Shared Task on Harmful Content Detection. In *Proceedings of the 21st Conference on Natural Language Processing (KONVENS 2025): Workshops*, Hildesheim, Germany.

Jerome H. Friedman. 2001. Greedy Function Approximation: A Gradient Boosting Machine. *The Annals of Statistics*, 29(5):1189–1232.

Christian Gawron and Sebastian Schmidt. 2021. FH-SWF SG at GermEval 2021: Using transformer-based language models to identify toxic, engaging, & fact-claiming comments. In *Proceedings of the GermEval 2021 Shared Task on the Identification of Toxic, Engaging, and Fact-Claiming Comments*, pages 19–24, Duesseldorf, Germany. Association for Computational Linguistics.

Stephanie Gross, Johann Petrak, Louisa Venhoff, and Brigitte Krenn. 2024. GermEval2024 shared task: GerMS-detect – sexism detection in German online news fora. In *Proceedings of GermEval 2024 Task 1 GerMS-detect Workshop on Sexism Detection in German Online News Fora (GerMS-detect 2024)*, pages 1–9, Vienna, Austria. Association for Computational Lingustics.

Matthew Honnibal, Ines Montani, Sofie Van Landeghem, and Adriane Boyd. 2020. spaCy: Industrial-strength Natural Language Processing in Python.

Syed Fawad Hussain, Hafiz Zaheer-Ud-Din Babar, Akhtar Khalil, Rashad M. Jillani, Muhammad Hanif, and Khurram Khurshid. 2020. A Fast Non-Redundant Feature Selection Technique for Text Data. *IEEE Access*, 8:181763–181781.

Iguazio Ltd. 2025. What is Classification Threshold. Retrieved 29 August 2025.

Bryan Klimt and Yiming Yang. 2004. The Enron Corpus: A New Dataset for Email Classification Research. In *Machine Learning: ECML 2004*, volume 3201, pages 217–226, Berlin, Heidelberg. Springer Berlin Heidelberg.

George Kyriakides. 2019. *Hands-On Ensemble Learning with Python: Build Highly Optimized Ensemble Machine Learning Models Using Scikit-Learn and Keras*, 1 edition. Packt Publishing Limited, Birmingham.

Andrew Lampert, Robert Dale, and Cecile Paris. 2010. Detecting emails containing requests for action. In *Human Language Technologies: The 2010 Annual Conference of the North American Chapter of the Association for Computational Linguistics*, pages 984–992, Los Angeles, California. Association for Computational Linguistics.

Natalia Levshina. 2022. Frequency, Informativity and Word Length: Insights from Typologically Diverse Corpora. *Entropy*, 24(2):280.

Puneet Mathur, Meghna Ayyar, Sahil Chopra, Simra Shahid, Laiba Mehnaz, and Rajiv Shah. 2018. Identification of emergency blood donation request on Twitter. In *Proceedings of the 2018 EMNLP Workshop SMM4H: The 3rd Social Media Mining for Health Applications Workshop & Shared Task*, pages 27–31, Brussels, Belgium. Association for Computational Linguistics.

Dennis Meischen. 2025. Islamistische Demo vor Rotem Rathaus: Polizei ohne Dolmetscher. *Berliner Morgenpost*.

Alex Nikolov and Victor Radivchev. 2019. Nikolov-Radivchev at SemEval-2019 Task 6: Offensive Tweet Classification with BERT and Ensembles. In *Proceedings of the 13th International Workshop on Semantic Evaluation*, pages 691–695, Minneapolis, Minnesota, USA. Association for Computational Linguistics.

Fabian Pedregosa, Fabian Pedregosa, Gael Varoquaux, Gael Varoquaux, Normalesup Org, Alexandre Gramfort, Alexandre Gramfort, Vincent Michel, Vincent Michel, Logilab Fr, Bertrand Thirion, Bertrand Thirion, Olivier Grisel, Olivier Grisel, Mathieu Blondel, Peter Prettenhofer, Peter Prettenhofer, Ron Weiss, Vincent Dubourg, and 5 others. 2011. Scikit-learn: Machine Learning in Python. *Machine Learning in Python*, 10(11):2825–2830.

Juan Manuel Pérez, Franco M. Luque, Demian Zayat, Martín Kondratzky, Agustín Moro, Pablo Santiago Serrati, Joaquín Zajac, Paula Miguel, Natalia Debandi, Agustín Gravano, and Viviana Cotik. 2023. Assessing the Impact of Contextual Information in Hate Speech Detection. *IEEE access : practical innovations, open solutions*, 11:30575–30590.

Perplexity AI, Inc. 2024. Perplexity. Retrieved 29 August 2025.

John Platt. 1999. Probabilistic Outputs for Support Vector Machines and Comparisons to Regularized Likelihood Methods.

Shaina Raza and Veronica Chatrath. 2024. HarmonyNet: Navigating hate speech detection. *Natural Language Processing Journal*, 8:100098.

Nils Reimers and Iryna Gurevych. 2019. Sentence-BERT: Sentence embeddings using Siamese BERT-networks. In *Proceedings of the 2019 Conference on Empirical Methods in Natural Language Processing and the 9th International Joint Conference on Natural Language Processing (EMNLP-IJCNLP)*, pages 3982–3992, Hong Kong, China. Association for Computational Linguistics.

Torsten Riecke. 2024. Regierung will härter gegen Online-Hass und Fake News vorgehen. *Handelsblatt*. Retrieved August 29, 2025.

Julian Risch, Anke Stoll, Lena Wilms, and Michael Wiegand. 2021. Overview of the GermEval 2021 Shared Task on the Identification of Toxic, Engaging, and Fact-Claiming Comments. In *Proceedings of the GermEval 2021 Shared Task on the Identification of Toxic, Engaging, and Fact-Claiming Comments*, pages 1–12, Duesseldorf, Germany. Association for Computational Linguistics.

Anna Rogers, Olga Kovaleva, and Anna Rumshisky. 2019. Calls to Action on Social Media: Potential for Censorship and Social Impact. In *Proceedings of the 2nd Workshop on NLP for Internet Freedom: Censorship, Disinformation, and Propaganda*, pages 36–44, Stroudsburg, PA. Association for Computational Linguistics.

Wassiliki Siskou, Clara Giralt Mirón, Sarah Molina-Raith, and Miriam Butt. 2022. Automatized detection and annotation for calls to action in Latin-American social media postings. In *Proceedings of the 6th Joint SIGHUM Workshop on Computational Linguistics for Cultural Heritage, Social Sciences, Humanities and Literature*, pages 65–69, Gyeongju, Republic of Korea. International Conference on Computational Linguistics.

Karen Sparck Jones. 1972. A statistical interpretation of term specificity and its application in retrieval. *Journal of Documentation*, 28(1):11–21.

Julia Maria Struß, Melanie Siegel, Josef Ruppenhofer, Michael Wiegand, and Manfred Klenner. 2019. Overview of GermEval Task 2, 2019 Shared Task on the Identification of Offensive Language. In *Proceedings of the 15th Conference on Natural Language Processing (KONVENS)*, pages 354–365, Nürnberg/ Erlangen, Deutschland. German Society for Computational Linguistics.

Irfan Ullah, Sharifullah Khan, Muhammad Imran, and Young-Koo Lee. 2021. RweetMiner: Automatic identification and categorization of help requests on twitter during disasters. *Expert Systems with Applications*, 176:114787.

Michael Wiegand, Melanie Siegel, and Josef Ruppenhofer. 2018. Overview of the GermEval 2018 Shared Task on the Identification of Offensive Language. In *Proceedings of GermEval 2018, 14th Conference on Natural Language Processing (KONVENS 2018)*, pages 1–8, Vienna, Austria. German Society for Computational Linguistics.

Hsiang-Fu Yu, Fang-Lan Huang, and Chih-Jen Lin. 2011. Dual coordinate descent methods for logistic regression and maximum entropy models. *Machine Learning*, 85(1-2):41–75.

Bing Zhou, Lei Zou, Ali Mostafavi, Binbin Lin, Mingzheng Yang, Nasir Gharaibeh, Heng Cai, Joynal Abedin, and Debayan Mandal. 2022. VictimFinder: Harvesting rescue requests in disaster response from social media with BERT. *Computers, Environment and Urban Systems*, 95:101824.

Zhi-Hua Zhou. 2021. *Machine Learning*. Springer, Singapore.

Gap in pagination due to formatting issues.

Pages 385-387

Overview of the GermEval 2025 Shared Task on Candy Speech Detection

Yulia Clausen
CRC 1567 Virtual Lifeworlds
Ruhr University Bochum
44801 Bochum, Germany
yulia.clausen@rub.de

Tatjana Scheffler
CRC 1567 Virtual Lifeworlds
Ruhr University Bochum
44801 Bochum, Germany
tatjana.scheffler@rub.de

Michael Wiegand
Digital Philology
Faculty of Philological and Cultural Studies
University of Vienna
AT-1010 Vienna, Austria
michael.wiegand@univie.ac.at

Abstract

We present the pilot edition of the GermEval 2025 Shared Task on Candy Speech Detection in German YouTube comments. This shared task includes two subtasks which aim to identify the presence of candy speech in a given YouTube comment (Subtask 1), and determine the exact types and spans of candy speech expressions (Subtask 2). The dataset consists of 46,286 comments extracted from a corpus of German YouTube comments (Cotgrove, 2018). The shared task had 11 participating teams submitting 20 runs for Subtask 1 and 16 for Subtask 2. The shared task website can be found at https://yuliacl.github.io/GermEval2025-Flausch-Erkennung.

1 Introduction

Candy speech refers to expressions of positive attitudes on social media toward individuals or their output, such as videos, comments and other content (Clausen and Scheffler, 2025). The purpose of candy speech is to encourage, cheer up, support, and empower others. It can be seen as the counterpart to hate speech (Schmidt and Wiegand, 2017), as it similarly seeks to influence the self-image of the target person or group, but in a positive manner. Beyond this, candy speech can serve as a valuable resource for fine-grained sentiment analysis, representing a specific subtype of positive sentiment, which is directed at giving support for specific people. It may also have applications in computational social science, such as identifying group membership or fandom affiliation.

Numerous methods have been developed for detecting and censoring negative speech (e.g., hate speech or offensive or harmful language) on social media platforms. However, there is much less focus on identifying and promoting positive supportive discourse in online communities, even though the importance of the automatic detection of positive online language has already been acknowledged, for example, in shared tasks on hope speech detection (Chakravarthi and Muralidaran, 2021; Chakravarthi et al., 2022; Jiménez-Zafra et al., 2023; García-Baena et al., 2024) and the identification of empowering language (Njoo et al., 2023). However, there exists no systematic approach to identifying such utterances, specifically with respect to clear definitions and standardized annotation procedures. The GermEval 2025 Shared Task on Candy Speech Detection aims to address this gap and encourage researchers to focus more closely on the identification and analysis of positive expressions in digital media. This is a task of identifying the presence of candy speech (on the span level) in German YouTube comments and classifying each such expression in one of the predefined categories. The annotations are based on a theoretically grounded definition of candy speech and follow clearly defined annotation guidelines (Clausen and Scheffler, 2025).

This shared task is part of GermEval, a series of evaluation campaigns that focus on natural language processing for the German language, which has been held since 2014. The topics of the previous shared tasks range from named entity recogni-

Proceedings of the 21st Conference on Natural Language Processing (KONVENS), Volume 2: Workshops, pages 388–397, 2025

tion, lexical substitution, sentiment analysis, and hierarchical classification of blurbs, text complexity classification, speaker attribution, easy language detection to the identification of offensive language. Teams from both academia and industry are invited to develop and evaluate their approaches on datasets provided by the organizers. The shared tasks are run informally by self-organized groups of interested researchers. Our Shared Task on Candy Speech Detection was endorsed by the Special Interest Groups for German Sentiment Analysis (IG-GSA) within the German Society for Computational Linguistics (GSCL).

The remainder of this paper is structured as follows. We describe the task in Section 2 and give an overview of related work addressing the subtasks in Section 3. The dataset is described in detail in Section 4. In Section 5, we briefly comment on the evaluation we conducted, while in Section 6, we discuss the results. Section 7 concludes the paper.

2 Task Description

Teams could participate in both or only one of the following subtasks. Every team was allowed at most three submissions per subtask.

Subtask 1: Coarse-Grained Classification. The goal of Subtask 1 was to identify whether a given YouTube comment contains candy speech or not (a binary classification task). The dataset has been manually annotated for the presence of candy speech (see Section 4).

Subtask 2: Fine-Grained Classification. The goal of Subtask 2 was to identify the exact span of each candy speech expression in a given comment and classify it into one of the predefined categories. The dataset has been manually annotated for ten different types of candy speech expressions, such as positive feedback, compliment, and group membership; see Table 1 for the full list of types along with examples. This task is a multilabel span detection task at the character level, similar to named entity recognition, since individual phrases expressing candy speech can overlap.

3 Related Work

The automatic detection of hate speech and various forms of offensive language in social media data has become one of the most active research areas in natural language processing (see, e.g., Vidgen and Derczynski, 2020; Risch et al., 2021a). Since 2018, the detection and classification of offensive content have been the focus of several shared tasks. For the German language in particular, three editions of the GermEval shared task series have addressed this challenge (Struß et al., 2019; Wiegand et al., 2019; Risch et al., 2021b). Other shared task initiatives that include German-language data have also contributed to advancements in this field (Mandl et al., 2020, 2021).

In contrast, efforts on the identification of positive online language remain relatively limited. Recent initiatives have begun addressing this gap, but are typically limited to specific types of positive speech, specific data types, and few languages. These include the identification of empowering language in English Reddit posts (Njoo et al., 2023) and shared tasks on hope speech detection in various languages. The shared task on Hope Speech Detection for Equality, Diversity, and Inclusion focuses on the binary classification (hope speech vs. non-hope speech) of YouTube comments and tweets in English, Tamil, Malayalam, Kannada, Spanish, Bulgarian and Hindi (Chakravarthi and Muralidaran, 2021; Chakravarthi et al., 2022; Kumaresan et al., 2023). The HOPE: Multilingual Hope Speech Detection Shared Task comprises binary (hope vs. non-hope) and multiclass (generalized, realistic or unrealistic hope) classification tasks in English and Spanish YouTube comments and tweets (Jiménez-Zafra et al., 2023; García-Baena et al., 2024).

To further promote awareness and understanding of positive, supportive online language, we introduce a novel task on candy speech detection in German, which involves both binary classification (candy speech vs. non-candy speech) and fine-grained detection of distinct candy speech types.

4 Data and Resources

The data for the shared task is sourced from the NottDeuYTSch corpus (Cotgrove, 2018), which contains over 33 million words drawn from approximately 3 million YouTube comments published between 2008 and 2018 by a young German-speaking audience. For this task, 16 videos, together with all associated user comments, were randomly selected from the corpus. These videos were authored by seven different creators representing diverse sectors, such as music, lifestyle and fitness. The comments were labeled by two annotators with linguistic background. The inter-annotator agreement is

Type	Short Definition	Example (orig. + Engl. translation)
affection declaration	admiration, love and affection towards others	*ich mag euch XD* 'I like you XD'
compliment	acknowledgment of skills, personal characteristics or achievements of others	*Ihr macht echt tolle videos!* 'You create really great videos!'
encouragement	comments that aim to encourage others	*Bleibt dran!* 'Keep at it!'
gratitude	sincere gratitude expressed unprompted	*Danke, dass du mich motivierst!* 'Thanks for motivating me!'
group membership	markers of group membership, e.g., belonging to a fan community	*ich bin ein #lochinator* 'I am a #lochinator'
positive feedback	positive attitude toward a post, video, comment etc.	*Das Lied ist mega mega cool.* 'The song is mega mega cool.'
sympathy	words of compassion and understanding	*die neuen haben doch mal auch ne chanche verdient!* 'the new ones are worth a chance, too!'
agreement	agreement with an opinion or statement that represents candy speech	*Jaa so krass* 'Yeaah so amazing'
implicit	indirect expression of candy speech	*Wieso geht ihr nicht zum Supertalent?* 'Why don't you go to Supertalent?'
ambiguous	unclear whether candy speech or not	*OMG*

Table 1: Types of candy speech expressions.

above 70% (Cohen's κ) for the coarse-grained annotation, i.e., determining whether a comment contains candy speech or not. For the fine-grained annotation, i.e., identification of candy speech types and their exact spans in a comment, agreement reaches an F1-score of at least 51% (for details on the annotation procedure, see Clausen and Scheffler, 2025).

Data format. The dataset for the shared task was provided in CSV format. The YouTube comments in the dataset had already been pre-tokenized using the SoMaJo tokenizer.[1] For the training set, three separate files were released. One file contained the comments along with their corresponding document and comment IDs, as illustrated below:

```
document,comment_id,comment
NDY-274,93,ich will mehr buch reviews :D
NDY-274,94,gute review !!
NDY-274,95,200 Seiten in 1,5 h ?
```

Two additional files provided labels for these comments. The file for Subtask 1 contained labels for the same set of comments, indicating whether each comment contains candy speech ('yes') or not ('no'):

```
document,comment_id,flausch
NDY-274,93,yes
NDY-274,94,yes
NDY-274,95,no
```

The file for Subtask 2 contained labels only for the comments that included candy speech, specifying both the type and the start and end character indices of each candy speech expression, as illustrated below:

```
document,comment_id,type,start,end
NDY-274,93,encouragement,0,29
NDY-274,94,positive feedback,0,14
```

For the test set, only the file containing the comment texts was released.

The dataset, including both the training and test data, as well as the annotation guidelines, and evaluation scripts are publicly available under the following link: `https://osf.io/4g8zb/`.

[1] `https://github.com/tsproisl/SoMaJo`

Dataset statistics. The final annotated dataset for the shared task contains 46,286 comments (training data = 37,057, test data = 9,229). The basic statistics on the dataset are given in Table 2.

Total # of tokens in the dataset:	553,701
Average # of tokens per comment:	11.96
Shortest comment (tokens):	1
Longest comment (tokens):	1,880
Type-token ratio:	0.08

Table 2: Basic statistics on the dataset.

The binary class distribution in the dataset, i.e., the annotations relevant for Subtask 1, is imbalanced, with the 'yes' class (indicating the presence of candy speech) being the minority (Table 3).

	Train		Test		Total	
	#	%	#	%	#	%
yes	10,773	29.1	3,807	41.3	14,580	31.5
no	26,284	70.9	5,422	58.7	31,706	68.5

Table 3: Binary class distribution in the dataset.

In total, the dataset contains 21,785 candy speech expressions. The comments containing candy speech have a minimum of 1, a maximum of 26, and an average of 3.76 expressions per comment. The average length of a candy speech expression is 28.09 characters, with a minimum of 1 and a maximum of 533 characters. The number of unique types per comment ranges from 1 to 6, with an average of 1.27. A total of 3,176 comments (21.78%) contain more than one unique type. The most frequent co-occurring type pair is affection declaration and positive feedback (7.4%; 1,082 instances). Other common pairs include compliment with positive feedback (7.1%; 1,028) and encouragement with positive feedback (4.0%; 587). Less frequent but notable are affection declaration with compliment (2.8%; 414) and gratitude with positive feedback (1.9%; 270). The distribution of the annotated candy speech types in the dataset is shown in Table 4.

5 Evaluation

Following in the footsteps of previous GermEval shared tasks (Remus et al., 2019; Johannßen et al., 2020; Risch et al., 2021b), we use the platform Codabench for the evaluation of submissions.[2] We used F1-score as the primary evaluation metric, and reported precision and recall for additional reference. In Subtask 1, which was a binary classification task, submissions were ranked based on the F1-score for the positive class ('yes', i.e., comment contains candy speech). Subtask 2 involved the exact identification of candy speech expression spans in the input text and their classification into predefined categories. Notably, individual candy speech expressions may be nested or overlapping, and each expression must be identified independently. We investigated a range of classification and span-based evaluation metrics for clarity and feasibility, and arrived at per-span F1-score as the final metric. We computed precision, recall and F1-score for three custom evaluation metrics: *strict match*, *type match* and *span match*. The overall ranking of submissions was based on the F1-score for *strict match*. The other two metrics were included to differentiate between distinct methodological approaches, such as the use of different models by participants. The details on these metrics are provided below.

Strict match requires an exact match between both the type and the character-based span of each candy speech expression in a comment. Strict match recall measures the number of span-type tuples in the manually annotated gold data which were recovered by the automatic system. Strict match precision measures the number of span-type candy speech expression tuples identified by the system which were also present in the gold data. F1-score is the harmonic mean between these two measures as usual. To achieve a perfect score, the system must identify all candy speech expressions in a comment with their correct type labels and exact spans. Note that one comment may contain multiple instances of the same type of candy speech (e.g., two compliments), which is taken into account by this metric.

Type match evaluates whether the candy speech types present in a given comment were correctly identified by the system, regardless of their spans. To achieve a perfect score, the predicted candy speech types for a comment must exactly match those and only those present in our gold standard. This metric also accounts for the fact that one com-

[2]The competition pages for the two respective subtasks are `https://www.codabench.org/competitions/6120` and `https://www.codabench.org/competitions/7921`.

Type	Total #	Total %	Train #	Train %	Test #	Test %
positive feedback	11,403	52.3	8,417	53.3	2,986	49.9
affection declaration	3,933	18.1	2,720	17.2	1,213	20.3
compliment	3,504	16.1	2,773	17.6	731	12.2
encouragement	1,009	4.6	769	4.9	240	4
group membership	558	2.6	167	1.1	391	6.5
gratitude	474	2.2	236	1.5	238	4
ambiguous	279	1.3	213	1.3	66	1.1
agreement	269	1.2	224	1.4	45	0.8
implicit	255	1.2	183	1.2	72	1.2
sympathy	101	0.5	97	0.6	4	0.1
Total	21,785	100	15,799	100	5,986	100

Table 4: Distribution of candy speech types in the dataset.

ment may contain multiple instances of the same candy speech type (e.g., two compliments).

Span match ignores the type label of candy speech expressions but is otherwise strict regarding the span boundaries. An expression is counted as correctly identified only if its exact character span matches that in the gold standard.

6 Results

A high-level summary of the participants' results for the two subtasks is presented in Table 5. This table provides statistics for the F1-score, which was used as the official ranking metric in the shared task. Compared to Subtask 1, the results for Subtask 2 are more diverse, as indicated by the higher standard deviation. Furthermore, the best F1-score for Subtask 1 (89.06) is considerably higher than for Subtask 2 (63.07), and the median for Subtask 2 is much lower and farther from the best system score than in Subtask 1. These numbers suggest that Subtask 2 is substantially more challenging, indicating that there is still considerable room for improvement in fine-grained detection of candy speech expressions.

Coarse-grained classification. We received 20 submissions from 10 teams for Subtask 1. The results are presented in Table 6. The highest score was obtained by team AIxcellent Vibes (F1 = 89.06), closely followed by teams HHUflauschig and Die SuperGLEBer. As a baseline, we report the performance of a random classifier that predicts labels on the test data based on the class distribution observed in the training set. All systems achieved F-scores well above the random baseline.

Fine-grained classification. We received 16 submissions from 7 teams for Subtask 2. The results are shown in Table 7. In this subtask, team AIxcellent Vibes achieved the highest score (F1 = 63.07), followed again by team HHUflauschig and, with a large distance, by team Coling-UniA.

To capture the complexity of the fine-grained classification task, we include three baselines that reflect its multi-step nature. The first baseline (*random spans and labels*) performs random prediction of both spans and their corresponding labels, representing the most challenging scenario. The second baseline assumes perfect knowledge of the gold-standard spans but assigns labels randomly (*random labels*), while the third baseline assumes perfect knowledge of the gold-standard labels but predicts spans randomly (*random spans*). All baseline predictions are made on the test set, with labels assigned according to the distribution observed in the training data. Since only very few comments contain overlapping spans (126; 0.86%), the baselines are designed to generate only non-overlapping spans. The baseline results show that predicting types when spans are known is more straightforward than the more challenging tasks of assigning spans to gold labels or randomly guessing both spans and types. The teams' results range from levels similar to the baselines to substantially outperforming them, highlighting both the diversity of approaches and the complexity of the task.

Subtask	# Teams	# Runs	Min	Max	Median	Mean	SD
(1) Coarse-Grained Classification	10	20	68.42	89.06	85.44	81.89	7.36
(2) Fine-Grained Classification	7	16	0.00	63.07	14.32	25.37	24.09

Table 5: Summary statistics for overall F1-scores in the two subtasks.

Team ID	Submission Number	F1	P	R
AIxcellent Vibes	submission 2	**89.06**	92.67	85.71
HHUflauschig	submission 1	**88.72**	90.00	87.47
Die SuperGLEBer	submission 2	**88.27**	91.49	85.26
Die SuperGLEBer	submission 3	88.03	92.33	84.11
NLPSuedwestfalen	submission 1	**87.96**	91.11	85.03
TUM NLP Group	submission 2	**87.85**	88.66	87.05
NLPSuedwestfalen	submission 3	87.78	90.24	85.45
AIxcellent Vibes	submission 1	87.50	93.31	82.37
Die SuperGLEBer	submission 1	87.43	91.43	83.77
NLPSuedwestfalen	submission 2	87.28	89.99	84.74
NLP_Augsburg_04	submission 1	**83.60**	90.33	77.80
ANON-A*	submission 1	**81.90**	86.77	77.54
ANON-A*	submission 2	81.79	86.77	77.36
TUM NLP Group	submission 3	77.15	84.42	71.03
TUM NLP Group	submission 1	76.68	86.87	68.64
Quabynar	submission 1	**75.42**	70.99	80.43
ANON-B*	submission 1	**74.63**	81.69	68.69
Flauschgummi	submission 3	**69.72**	88.79	57.39
Flauschgummi	submission 1	68.52	68.29	68.74
Flauschgummi	submission 2	68.42	87.65	56.11
random baseline		34.44	41.12	29.63

Table 6: Results of Subtask 1: coarse-grained classification. The best submission of each team is shown in **bold**. Teams marked with * withdrew from further participation.

General conclusions drawn from the evaluation. Participants in the shared task completed a survey designed to gather essential information about their submissions. Based on their responses and the submitted papers, we draw the following conclusions. Most submissions focused on the machine learning aspects of the task. In particular, the use of transformer-based language models was by far the most common approach, with 7 out of 9 teams that completed the survey employing this method. The remaining teams primarily used supervised learning with traditional algorithms such as logistic regression or SVM. Notably, among the various ways to utilize transformers, fine-tuning was the predominant strategy (all teams that used transformers at least experimented with fine-tuning), whereas zero-shot and few-shot approaches were much less common (two teams explored zero-shot or few-shot classification (Coling-UniA and Quabynar), while one team used few-shot prompting for data augmentation (TUM NLP Group). This also explains why prompt engineering played only a minor role in the task. Similarly, only one team employed some form of pre-training (TUM NLP Group).

Although the methodological approach was similar, primarily fine-tuning transformers, there was considerable variation in system performance across both tasks (see Table 5). This may be attributed to the use of a wide range of language models: approximately 50 (!) distinct models were experimented with, and only a few were used by more than one team (e.g., `bert-base-german-cased` was used by four

Team ID	Sub	Strict			Type			Span		
		F1	P	R	F1	P	R	F1	P	R
AIxcellent Vibes	sub 2	**63.07**	65.84	60.52	76.91	80.28	73.81	67.56	70.53	64.83
AIxcellent Vibes	sub 1	62.33	68.78	56.98	75.58	83.40	69.09	66.19	73.04	60.51
HHUflauschig	sub 1	**61.46**	62.92	60.07	76.64	78.46	74.91	66.80	68.38	65.29
Coling-UniA	sub 2	**49.80**	47.48	52.36	67.98	64.82	71.47	56.68	54.05	59.59
Coling-UniA	sub 3	46.26	42.36	50.95	64.63	59.18	71.18	52.74	48.29	58.09
NLP_Augsburg_04	sub 1	**33.38**	24.09	54.31	49.24	35.54	80.12	36.50	26.35	59.39
Coling-UniA	sub 1	31.96	29.26	35.20	64.63	59.18	71.18	35.90	32.88	39.54
Quabynar	sub 3	**15.90**	14.87	17.09	40.79	38.14	43.84	25.65	23.98	27.56
Die SuperGLEBer	sub 3	**12.74**	13.63	11.96	17.28	18.48	16.22	57.99	62.03	54.44
Die SuperGLEBer	sub 1	8.87	9.26	8.52	15.66	16.33	15.04	46.47	48.48	44.62
Die SuperGLEBer	sub 2	8.66	9.65	7.85	16.27	18.13	14.75	42.77	47.67	38.79
ANON-A*	sub 2	**3.94**	4.41	3.56	56.16	62.88	50.74	4.97	5.57	4.49
ANON-A*	sub 3	3.57	4.05	3.19	53.82	61.10	48.10	4.58	5.20	4.09
ANON-A*	sub 1	2.32	2.61	2.09	45.77	51.50	41.18	2.91	3.28	2.62
Quabynar	sub 1	1.67	1.30	2.36	38.12	29.56	53.64	2.30	1.79	3.24
Quabynar	sub 2	0.00	0.00	0.00	0.00	0.00	0.00	0.00	0.00	0.00
random spans and labels		3.01	3.97	2.42	12.43	16.40	10.01	8.76	11.55	7.05
random spans		–	–	–	–	–	–	8.10	8.10	8.10
random labels		–	–	–	40.93	40.93	40.93	–	–	–

Table 7: Results of Subtask 2: fine-grained classification. The best submission (sub) of each team is shown in **bold**. Teams marked with * withdrew from further participation.

teams, and deepset/gbert-large by three). Still, more than half of the participants tested some form of BERT (Devlin et al., 2019).

Team AIxcellent Vibes (the winning team in both subtasks) used hybrid methods combining pretrained language models with traditional or lightweight classifiers, adapting them to the specific structure of each subtask.

In terms of training data, only one team (Flauschgummi) used additional data beyond what was provided by the organizers of the shared task, incorporating the GoEmotions dataset (Demszky et al., 2020). In addition, team TUM NLP Group experimented with data augmentation employing techniques such as synonym replacement, back translation (via English), and LLM-based synthetic data generation. In their approach, only LLM-based augmentation with a small amount of synthetic data (10%) showed an improvement. Team AIxcellent Vibes applied oversampling to the candy speech class via sampling with replacement to balance the ratio with the non-candy speech class.

Linguistic pre-processing was generally rare and mostly limited to basic forms of text normalization, such as stemming or lemmatization. Only two teams applied domain-specific normalization to account for the social media origin of the data, such as removing non-alphanumeric characters, e.g., emojis (team Flauschgummi), or applying spelling correction (team HHUflauschig).

Only a few participants made use of additional (linguistic) tools or resources. One team used spaCy[3] (HHUflauschig), and another team used NLTK[4] (Flauschgummi). Furthermore, one team utilized a sentiment lexicon (Palanisamy et al., 2013) and employed Doc2Vec (Le and Mikolov, 2014) (Flauschgummi), and a different team incorporated German spelling correction and machine translation (HHUflauschig).

Despite the popularity of ensemble methods in other shared tasks (Wiegand et al., 2019; Struß et al., 2019; Risch et al., 2021b), only two teams in this competition used ensemble approaches (again teams Flauschgummi and HHUflauschig).

Nearly half of the participants focused on proper hyperparameter tuning. According to responses in the shared task survey, most teams considered the choice of language model to be the most impor-

[3]https://spacy.io

[4]www.nltk.org

tant and effective aspect of system development. Interestingly, not a single team relied exclusively on large language models offered by subscription-based platforms, such as OpenAI's GPT-4o.

Hardware resources also played a significant role. Only one team conducted experiments without access to a compute cluster (either via Colab or an institutional cluster). Consequently, it is perhaps unsurprising that around 75% of participants viewed improvements in hardware resources (e.g., more powerful GPUs) as a realistic avenue for enhancing system performance.

Notable insights to mention in this overview paper, as reported by the participants in the shared task survey, include the following: tagging (i.e., Subtask 2) exhibits much greater variance in results across models than classification (i.e., Subtask 1) (team Die SuperGLEBer), linguistic techniques substantially improve a model's understanding of sarcasm (team NLP_Augsburg_04), and two-step stacking outperforms direct modeling (team HHUflauschig).

Team AIxcellent Vibes found that token-level span annotations provide a richer training signal than comment-level labels, resulting in models leveraging the former outperforming those trained with the latter in Subtask 1.

7 Conclusion

In this paper, we presented the GermEval 2025 Shared Task on Candy Speech Detection. As part of this task, we introduced a manually annotated dataset consisting of 46,286 German YouTube comments. The results for the two offered subtasks show that state-of-the-art classification approaches perform well on Subtask 1, with many systems achieving F-scores in the high 80s. However, performance on Subtask 2 still lags notably behind, indicating that this subtask remains far from solved. Regarding methodology, most participants employed transformer-based neural networks. Due to the complexity of these methods, there is a large number of degrees of freedom, such as the choice of language models and hyperparameter settings. These choices continue to have a significant impact on the overall classification performance. Notably, we cannot identify a clear winning approach, particularly for Subtask 1, as several systems achieved similarly strong results.

Acknowledgments

We are grateful to the large number of teams whose enthusiastic participation made the GermEval 2025 shared task on candy speech detection a great success. We would also like to thank Dennis Reisloh for help with the annotations and Geraldine Baumann for the nice flyer design.

This work was partially funded by the Deutsche Forschungsgemeinschaft (DFG, German Research Foundation), CRC 1567, Project ID 470106373.

References

Bharathi Raja Chakravarthi and Vigneshwaran Muralidaran. 2021. Findings of the Shared Task on Hope Speech Detection for Equality, Diversity, and Inclusion. In *Proceedings of the First Workshop on Language Technology for Equality, Diversity and Inclusion*, pages 61–72, Kyiv. Association for Computational Linguistics.

Bharathi Raja Chakravarthi, Vigneshwaran Muralidaran, Ruba Priyadharshini, Subalalitha Chinnaudayar Navaneethakrishnan, John McCrae, Miguel Ángel García, Salud María Jiménez-Zafra, Rafael Valencia-García, Prasanna Kumaresan, Rahul Ponnusamy, Daniel García-Baena, and José García-Díaz. 2022. Overview of the Shared Task on Hope Speech Detection for Equality, Diversity, and Inclusion. In *Proceedings of the Second Workshop on Language Technology for Equality, Diversity and Inclusion*, pages 378–388, Dublin, Ireland. Association for Computational Linguistics.

Yulia Clausen and Tatjana Scheffler. 2025. Annotating candy speech in German YouTube comments. In *Proceedings of the 19th Linguistic Annotation Workshop (LAW-XIX-2025)*, pages 264–269, Vienna, Austria. Association for Computational Linguistics.

Louis A. Cotgrove. 2018. Nottinghamer Korpus Deutscher YouTube-Sprache (The NottDeuYTSch Corpus) (2022-07-27). LINDAT/CLARIAH-CZ digital library at the Institute of Formal and Applied Linguistics (ÚFAL), Faculty of Mathematics and Physics, Charles University.

Dorottya Demszky, Dana Movshovitz-Attias, Jeongwoo Ko, Alan Cowen, Gaurav Nemade, and Sujith Ravi. 2020. GoEmotions: A dataset of fine-grained emotions. In *Proceedings of the 58th Annual Meeting of the Association for Computational Linguistics*, pages 4040–4054, Online. Association for Computational Linguistics.

Jacob Devlin, Ming-Wei Chang, Kenton Lee, and Kristina Toutanova. 2019. BERT: Pre-training of Deep Bidirectional Transformers for Language Understanding. In *Proceedings of the Human Language Technology Conference of the North American Chapter of the ACL (HLT/NAACL)*, pages 4171–4186, Minneapolis, MN, USA.

Daniel García-Baena, Fazlourrahman Balouchzahi, Sabur Butt, Miguel Ángel García Cumbreras, Atnafu Lambebo Tonja, José Antonio García-Díaz, Selen Bozkurt, Bharathi Raja Chakravarthi, Hector G. Ceballos, Rafael Valencia-García, Grigori Sidorov, Luis Alfonso Ureña López, Alexander F. Gelbukh, and Salud María Jiménez-Zafra. 2024. Overview of HOPE at IberLEF 2024: Approaching Hope Speech Detection in Social Media from Two Perspectives, for Equality, Diversity and Inclusion and as Expectations. In *Procesamiento del Lenguaje Natural*, volume 73, pages 407–419.

Salud María Jiménez-Zafra, Miguel Ángel Garcia-Cumbreras, Daniel García-Baena, José Antonio Garcia-Díaz, Bharathi Raja Chakravarthi, Rafael Valencia-García, and Luis Alfonso Ureña-López. 2023. Overview of HOPE at IberLEF 2023: Multilingual hope speech detection. In *Procesamiento del Lenguaje Natural, Revista*, 71, pages 371–381.

Dirk Johannßen, Chris Biemann, Steffen Remus, Timo Baumann, and David Scheffer. 2020. GermEval 2020 Task 1 on the Classification and Regression of Cognitive and Motivational Style from Text: Companion Paper. In *KONVENS*, pages 1–10. CEUR-WS.org.

Prasanna Kumar Kumaresan, Bharathi Raja Chakravarthi, Subalalitha Cn, Miguel Ángel García-Cumbreras, Salud María Jiménez Zafra, José Antonio García-Díaz, Rafael Valencia-García, Momchil Hardalov, Ivan Koychev, Preslav Nakov, Daniel García-Baena, and Kishore Kumar Ponnusamy. 2023. Overview of the Shared Task on Hope Speech Detection for Equality, Diversity, and Inclusion. In *Proceedings of the Third Workshop on Language Technology for Equality, Diversity and Inclusion*, pages 47–53, Varna, Bulgaria. INCOMA Ltd., Shoumen, Bulgaria.

Quoc Le and Tomas Mikolov. 2014. Distributed Representations of Sentences and Documents. In *Proceedings of the International Conference on Machine Learning (JMLR)*.

Thomas Mandl, Sandip Modha, Anand Kumar M, and Bharathi Raja Chakravarthi. 2021. Overview of the HASOC Track at FIRE 2020: Hate Speech and Offensive Language Identification in Tamil, Malayalam, Hindi, English and German. In *Proceedings of the 12th Annual Meeting of the Forum for Information Retrieval Evaluation*, FIRE '20, pages 29–32, New York, NY, USA. Association for Computing Machinery.

Thomas Mandl, Sandip Modha, Gautam Kishore Shahi, Amit Kumar Jaiswal, Durgesh Nandini, Daksh Patel, Prasenjit Majumder, and Johannes Schäfer. 2020. Overview of the HASOC track at FIRE 2020: Hate speech and offensive content identification in indo-european languages. In *Working Notes of FIRE 2020 - Forum for Information Retrieval Evaluation, Hyderabad, India, December 16-20, 2020*, volume 2826 of *CEUR Workshop Proceedings*, pages 87–111. CEUR-WS.org.

Lucille Njoo, Chan Park, Octavia Stappart, Marvin Thielk, Yi Chu, and Yulia Tsvetkov. 2023. TalkUp: Paving the way for understanding empowering language. In *Findings of the Association for Computational Linguistics: EMNLP 2023*, pages 9334–9354, Singapore. Association for Computational Linguistics.

Prabu Palanisamy, Vineet Yadav, and Harsha Elchuri. 2013. Serendio: Simple and practical lexicon based approach to sentiment analysis. In *Second Joint Conference on Lexical and Computational Semantics (*SEM), Volume 2: Proceedings of the Seventh International Workshop on Semantic Evaluation (SemEval 2013)*, pages 543–548, Atlanta, Georgia, USA. Association for Computational Linguistics.

Steffen Remus, Rami Aly, and Chris Biemann. 2019. GermEval 2019 Task 1: Hierarchical Classification of Blurbs. In *KONVENS*, pages 280–292. German Society for Computational Linguistics and Language Technology (GSCL).

Julian Risch, Philipp Schmidt, and Ralf Krestel. 2021a. Data Integration for Toxic Comment Classification: Making More Than 40 Datasets Easily Accessible in One Unified Format. In *Proceedings of the 5th Workshop on Online Abuse and Harms (WOAH 2021)*, pages 157–163, Online. Association for Computational Linguistics.

Julian Risch, Anke Stoll, Lena Wilms, and Michael Wiegand. 2021b. Overview of the GermEval 2021 Shared Task on the Identification of Toxic, Engaging, and Fact-Claiming Comments. In *Proceedings of the GermEval 2021 Shared Task on the Identification of Toxic, Engaging, and Fact-Claiming Comments*, pages 1–12, Online.

Anna Schmidt and Michael Wiegand. 2017. A Survey on Hate Speech Detection using Natural Language Processing. In *Proceedings of the EACL-Workshop on Natural Language Processing for Social Media (SocialNLP)*, pages 1–10, Valencia, Spain.

Julia Maria Struß, Melanie Siegel, Josef Ruppenhofer, Michael Wiegand, and Manfred Klenner. 2019. Overview of GermEval Task 2, 2019 Shared Task on the Identification of Offensive Language. In *Proceedings of the 15th Conference on Natural Language Processing (KONVENS 2019)*, pages 354–365.

Bertie Vidgen and Leon Derczynski. 2020. Directions in abusive language training data, a systematic review: Garbage in, garbage out. *PLoS ONE*, 15(12).

Michael Wiegand, Melanie Siegel, and Josef Ruppenhofer. 2019. Overview of the GermEval 2018 Shared Task on the Identification of Offensive Language. In *Proceedings of GermEval 2018, 14th Conference on Natural Language Processing (KONVENS 2018), Vienna, Austria - September 21, 2018*, pages 1 – 10.

Appendix

Team ID	Affiliation	Paper Title
AIxcellent Vibes	FH Aachen University of Applied Sciences / ORDIX AG	AIxcellent Vibes at GermEval 2025 Shared Task on Candy Speech Detection: Improving Model Performance by Span-Level Training
Coling-UniA	University of Augsburg	Coling-UniA at GermEval 2025 Shared Task on Candy Speech Detection: Retrieval Augmented Generation for Identifying Expressions of Positive Attitudes in German YouTube Comments
Die SuperGLEBer	Julius Maximilian University of Würzburg	Die SuperGLEBer at GermEval 2025 Shared Tasks: Growing Pains - When More Isn't Always Better
Flauschgummi	University of Regensburg	Flauschgummi at GermEval 2025 Shared Task on Candy Speech Detection: Sentiment Analysis and Classification of Online Comments
HHUflauschig	Heinrich Heine University of Düsseldorf	HHUflauschig at GermEval 2025 Shared Task on Candy Speech Detection: Hybrid Approaches for Binary Classification and Span Typing
NLP_Augsburg_04	University of Augsburg	NLP_Augsburg_04 at GermEval 2025 Shared Task on Candy Speech Detection: The Role of Surface Cues in Candy Speech Classification
NLPSuedwestfalen	The South Westphalia University of Applied Sciences	NLPSuedwestfalen at GermEval 2025 Shared Task on Candy Speech Detection: Binary Classification of German YouTube Comments using Transformer Models
Quabynar	University of Regensburg	Quabynar at GermEval 2025 Candy Speech Detection: Zero-shot Approach for Detecting Candy Speech
TUM NLP Group	Technical University of Munich	TUM NLP Group at GermEval 2025 Shared Task on Candy Speech Detection: Small Dose, Big Effect: Leveraging Synthetic Data for Candy Speech Detection

Table 8: Overview of the participating teams, their affiliations and papers (2 of 11 submitting teams withdrew from further participation).

AIxcellent Vibes at GermEval 2025 Shared Task on Candy Speech Detection: Improving Model Performance by Span-Level Training

Christian Rene Thelen[1,3], Patrick Gustav Blaneck[1,4], Tobias Bornheim[5], Niklas Grieger[1,2,6], Stephan Bialonski[1,2]

[1]Department of Medical Engineering and Technomathematics
[2]Institute for Data-Driven Technologies
FH Aachen University of Applied Sciences, Jülich, Germany

[3]Academic and Research Department Engineering Hydrology
[4]IT Center
RWTH Aachen University, Aachen, Germany

[5]Department for Data Science and AI
ORDIX AG, Paderborn, Germany

[6]Department of Information and Computing Sciences
Utrecht University, Utrecht, The Netherlands

Correspondence: bialonski@fh-aachen.de

Abstract

Positive, supportive online communication in social media ("candy speech") has the potential to foster civility, yet automated detection of such language remains underexplored, limiting systematic analysis of its impact. We investigate how candy speech can be reliably detected in a 46k-comment German YouTube corpus by monolingual and multilingual language models, including GBERT, Qwen3 Embedding, and XLM-RoBERTa. We find that a multilingual XLM-RoBERTa-Large model trained to detect candy speech at the span level outperforms other approaches, ranking first in both binary (positive F1: 0.8906) and categorized span-based detection (strict F1: 0.6307) subtasks at the *GermEval 2025 Shared Task on Candy Speech Detection*. We speculate that span-based training, multilingual capabilities, and emoji-aware tokenizers improved detection performance. Our results demonstrate the effectiveness of multilingual models in identifying positive, supportive language.

1 Introduction

User comments on social media can significantly shape the perceptions of discourse participants and alter the trajectory of debates (Kubin et al., 2024). While research has been dedicated to detecting negative user contributions, such as hate speech (Albladi et al., 2025), corresponding mitigation strategies like counterspeech (Bonaldi et al., 2024), positive and empowering expressions, known as candy speech (German: "Flausch"; lit. "fluff" (Clausen et al., 2025)) or hope speech (Chakravarthi et al., 2022) remain underexplored. To facilitate systematic analysis of candy speech, automated annotation tools are desirable that allow the detection of such speech events in large datasets at a level of granularity that would be impractical for human annotators to achieve at scale.

Detection methods for candy speech can build upon established natural language processing (NLP) techniques, ranging from traditional rule-based systems to contemporary data-driven approaches based on transformer models pretrained on large text corpora (Tucudean et al., 2024). Encoder-only transformer architectures, such as BERT (Devlin et al., 2019) or XLM-RoBERTa (Conneau et al., 2020), transform text tokens into embedding vectors and have demonstrated strong performance across various NLP classification and regression tasks. Specifically, monolingual variants like the German BERT model GBERT (Chan et al., 2020) have achieved competitive results on German-language NLP tasks (Bornheim et al., 2021; Blaneck et al., 2022). Decoder-only transformers, including GPT-4o (OpenAI, 2023), DeepSeek-V3 (DeepSeek-AI et al., 2024), and

Proceedings of the 21st Conference on Natural Language Processing (KONVENS), Volume 2: Workshops, pages 398–403, 2025

Qwen3 (Yang et al., 2025), traditionally used for text generation, have also shown promise in annotation tasks through zero-shot, few-shot, and fine-tuning approaches (Bornheim et al., 2024). Recent advancements, such as GPT-based embedding models like Qwen3 Embedding, further enhance these capabilities by generating embeddings conditioned on specific task-related instructions (Zhang et al., 2025).

In this contribution, we investigate the performance of monolingual (GBERT) and multilingual (Qwen3 Embedding, XLM-RoBERTa) language models in detecting candy speech within a novel dataset of German YouTube comments (Clausen et al., 2025). Our experiments demonstrate that XLM-RoBERTa-Large, when trained to detect spans of various candy speech types using the BIO tagging scheme (Ramshaw and Marcus, 1995), outperforms all other approaches, including binary classifiers designed solely to distinguish candy from non-candy speech. We share our implementation online.[1]

2 Data and Tasks

The *GermEval 2025 Shared Task on Candy Speech Detection* consisted of two subtasks. For the first subtask, participants developed a binary classification model to predict whether a YouTube comment contained candy speech. The second subtask required developing a model that could identify candy speech spans of different types (i.e., *positive feedback*, *compliment*, *affection declaration*, *encouragement*, *gratitude*, *agreement*, *ambiguous*, *implicit*, *group membership*, *sympathy*).

The provided dataset was split into a public training set and a blind test set used to evaluate the final Shared Task submissions. The training set contained 37,057 annotated comments from the comment threads of eleven YouTube videos. In contrast, the test set contained 9,229 comments from the comment threads of five YouTube videos not included in the training set. Each comment included a `document` referencing its source video, a `comment_id` that was incremented for each comment, and the comment's text. The training set also included annotations on whether a comment was candy speech, as well as the spans of different candy speech types as triplets for each span (start character index, end character index, type). See Figure 1 for examples of span annotations in the

Example 1: (document: NDY-252, comment_id: 792)

"Du sieht in dem Video mal wieder Mega hübsch aus! [compliment] Kannst du ein Video zur Frisur machen?"

(Trans.: "You look super pretty in the video! [compliment] Can you make a video about the hairstyle?")

Example 2: (document: NDY-179, comment_id: 4917)

"ich bin dein Grölsta fen seit 2010" [group membership]

(Trans.: I have been your biggest fan since 2010) [group membership]

Example 3: (document: NDY-252, comment_id: 195)

"Die Tipps in dem Video sind echt hilfreich. [positive feedback] ich werde auf jeden fall einige davon ausprobieren! Danke dafür! :)" [gratitude]

(Trans.: The tips in the video are really helpful. [positive feedback] I will definitely try some of them! Thanks! :)) [gratitude]

Figure 1: Examples of span annotations in the training data. Each comment is identified by a `document` and a `comment_id`. The spans are color-coded and labeled with the corresponding candy speech type.

training data. Although many comments included multiple spans (an average of 1.47 per comment), there were only 301 instances of overlapping spans, accounting for roughly 1.9 % of all spans.

3 Methods

3.1 Preprocessing and Data Split

We removed 3,829 comments from the training data as duplicates with identical text and labels. Furthermore, we identified 99 comments with identical text but differing labels, which we chose to retain.

We used two different data splits for model exploration and final training, respectively. During model exploration, we split the provided training dataset into five folds for cross-validation, which were stratified by the binary candy speech label or first span type for Subtask 1 and Subtask 2, respectively. For our submissions to the competition, we recombined the cross-validation folds and retrained the final models on the entire training dataset. In both model exploration and final training, if not otherwise specified, we reserved 10 % of the training data for early stopping.

3.2 Models

We based our detection systems on three different open-source pretrained language models (LMs), each extended with task-specific classifiers to address the two Subtasks.

[1] `https://github.com/dslaborg/germeval2025`

Qwen3 Embedding (Zhang et al., 2025) is a family of text embedding models derived from the Qwen3 foundation models (Yang et al., 2025). This model family contains models of various sizes (0.6B, 4B, 8B) and achieves state-of-the-art performance on tasks like multilingual retrieval. Their multilingual capabilities and ability to handle a broad range of input tokens (e.g., emojis) make the models well suited for processing internet-style text corpora, such as the dataset used in the GermEval 2025 Shared Task.

GBERT (Chan et al., 2020) is a German-language transformer model developed by deepset, based on the BERT architecture (Devlin et al., 2019), and pretrained on a large corpus of German text. The model is optimized for a variety of downstream NLP tasks in German, including classification, named entity recognition, and semantic similarity. Its monolingual training makes GBERT particularly effective for domain-specific or informal German texts and has been a popular architecture in previous GermEval Shared Tasks (Bornheim et al., 2021; Blaneck et al., 2022; Geiss and Zarcone, 2024).

XLM-RoBERTa (Conneau et al., 2020) is a multilingual transformer model developed by Facebook AI, built upon the RoBERTa architecture and trained on over 2 TB of filtered CommonCrawl data across 100 languages. It achieves strong cross-lingual performance, often on par with, and in some cases even surpassing, monolingual models on language-specific tasks.

For Subtask 1, a binary classification task, we explored two approaches: (i) using Qwen3-Embedding-8B[2] as a feature extractor in combination with a support vector machine (SVM) classifier, and (ii) extending GBERT-Large[3] with a multilayer perceptron (MLP) classifier. In the latter approach, the MLP was applied to the last hidden state of the CLS token and consisted of a linear layer with hidden size 1024, followed by a Tanh activation function, dropout with a rate of 0.1, and a final linear layer with two output units and a Softmax activation function for classification.

We addressed the span detection task in Subtask 2 with a token-wise BIO tagging approach (Ramshaw and Marcus, 1995). Since the dataset contained spans for ten different candy speech types, we defined separate B (beginning) and I (inside) labels for each type, resulting in a total of 21 labels (including the O (outside) label for non-candy speech). In our approach, we appended a linear classification layer with 21 output units to both GBERT-Large and XLM-RoBERTa-Large[4]. The linear layer was applied to the last hidden state of each token to predict whether the token was part of a span of a specific candy speech type.

3.3 Training

In our first approach to Subtask 1, we extracted embeddings from a frozen Qwen3-Embedding-8B model and used them as input features for an SVM with a radial basis function (RBF) kernel. The SVM hyperparameters were selected using the cross-validation setup described in Section 3.1 with a grid search over $C \in [1, 100]$ and $\gamma \in [10^{-8}, 6 \cdot 10^{-4}]$. Calculating the F1 score of the positive candy speech class (*positive F1*), we found the optimal hyperparameters of the SVM to be $C = 5$ and $\gamma = 2 \cdot 10^{-4}$. Since the SVM does not require early stopping, we trained the model on the entire training dataset without the need for a separate early stopping set.

Our second approach to Subtask 1 involved fine-tuning a GBERT-Large model together with an MLP classifier. Different from our first approach, we oversampled the candy speech class in the training data up to a ratio of 1:1 with the non-candy speech class by sampling with replacement from the candy speech class. Using the resampled data, we trained the model for five epochs to minimize the cross-entropy loss with the AdamW optimizer, a batch size of 32, a weight decay of 0.01, and gradient clipping to an L2 norm of 1.0. The learning rate increased from 0 to $5 \cdot 10^{-5}$ during a warmup phase spanning the first 30 % of the total gradient steps, after which it declined linearly back to 0. We evaluated the model on the early stopping set using the positive F1-score every 44 gradient steps, and stopped training if the score did not improve for 64 consecutive evaluations.

In Subtask 2, we fine-tuned both GBERT-Large and XLM-RoBERTa-Large models, each extended with a linear layer as classification head. The training setup was similar to the one used for our second approach in Subtask 1, except for the peak learning rate of $2 \cdot 10^{-5}$, the training duration of 20 epochs with evaluations every 40 gradient steps, an early stopping patience of 87 evaluations, and

[2]https://huggingface.co/Qwen/Qwen3-Embedding-8B

[3]https://huggingface.co/deepset/gbert-large

[4]https://huggingface.co/FacebookAI/xlm-roberta-large

Approach	Subtask 1 Positive F1	Subtask 2 Strict F1
Fine-tuning LMs for Spans		
Basic Postprocessing		
GBERT-Large	0.903 (0.004)	0.731
XLM-RoBERTa-Large*	**0.913** (0.002)	**0.747**
Extended Postprocessing		
GBERT-Large*	–	0.739
XLM-RoBERTa-Large	–	0.742
Training SVM for Binary Classification		
Qwen3-Embedding-8B*	0.901 (0.006)	–
Fine-tuning LMs for Binary Classification		
GBERT-Large	0.887 (0.004)	–

Table 1: Validation scores obtained for different modeling approaches. For Subtask 1, scores are reported as average (standard deviation) over the cross-validation folds. For Subtask 2, scores were obtained on the early stopping set of the final retraining before submission. Approaches marked with * denote those submitted to the Shared Task.

the length of the warmup phase of 200 and 500 gradient steps for GBERT and XLM-RoBERTa, respectively. To evaluate model performance, we calculated the strict match F1-score (*strict F1*), which counts two spans as matching if they have the same start and end position and the same label.

3.4 Postprocessing

For Subtask 2, we defined two sets of postprocessing steps to parse predicted BIO-tokens into the required span format. In the first, *basic* set of postprocessing steps, we parsed all valid spans consisting of a B-token and optional following I-tokens of the same candy speech type into a span start, span end, and span label. Spans that began with an I-token instead of a B-token were discarded. Additionally, I-tokens whose types did not match the preceding B- or I-token were also discarded.

The second, *extended* set of postprocessing steps included the basic set and ensured that spans did not begin or end within a word (e.g., before a subword token like "##en"). In such cases, we included the subword token in the span and did not initiate a new span, even if it was marked as a B-token.

4 Results

Among the approaches developed for Subtask 1, the Qwen3 Embedding model performed better than GBERT, with an average positive F1-score of 0.901 compared to 0.887 for GBERT (see lower part of Table 1). In addition to these approaches, we investigated whether the span detection models trained for Subtask 2 could be leveraged to indirectly identify candy speech comments in Subtask 1. To this end, we applied the Subtask 2 models to the data, postprocessed the predicted spans, and classified a comment as candy speech if it included at least one detected span of any type. We observed this approach to slightly outperform the dedicated binary classification models on the validation folds of the cross-validation setup, achieving an average positive F1-score of 0.903 and 0.913 for GBERT and XLM-RoBERTa, respectively (see upper part of Table 1).

Based on the results obtained during model exploration, our Subtask 1 submissions consisted of the Qwen3 Embedding model with the SVM classifier and the predictions derived from the XLM-RoBERTa model fine-tuned for span detection. Both models were retrained on the entire training dataset and evaluated on the test set by the Shared Task organizers. Consistent with our validation findings, the XLM-RoBERTa derivate outperformed the Qwen3 Embedding model on the test set, achieving positive F1-scores of 0.891 and 0.875 and earning first and 8th place, respectively (see Table 2).

For Subtask 2, we explored the fine-tuning of GBERT and XLM-RoBERTa model architectures and the set of postprocessing steps used to parse BIO-tokens into spans. We trained both models on the entire training dataset and evaluated them on the early stopping set, finding that XLM-RoBERTa slightly outperformed GBERT, regardless of the postprocessing steps used. Interestingly, GBERT seemed to benefit from the more advanced postprocessing steps, slightly increasing the strict F1-score from 0.731 to 0.739, while XLM-RoBERTa's scores declined from 0.747 to 0.742.

For our submissions to Subtask 2, we retrained the GBERT model with the advanced set of postprocessing steps and the XLM-RoBERTa model

Approach	Subtask 1 Positive F1	Subtask 2 Strict F1
Fine-tuning LMs for Spans		
Basic Postprocessing		
XLM-RoBERTa-Large	**0.891**	**0.631**
Extended Postprocessing		
GBERT-Large	–	0.623
Training SVM for Binary Classification		
Qwen3-Embedding-8B	0.875	–

Table 2: Performance scores on the test set for models submitted to the Shared Task.

with the basic set of postprocessing steps. XLM-RoBERTa achieved a strict F1-score of 0.631 on the test data, earning first place in Subtask 2, while GBERT achieved a strict F1-score of 0.623, earning second place.

5 Conclusion

In our study, we demonstrated that even in the era of generalist LLMs, fine-tuning smaller, specialized models remains a competitive strategy for specific tasks, such as the identification of candy speech in German YouTube comments. Using a single fine-tuned XLM-RoBERTa model, our top submissions to the *GermEval 2025 Shared Task on Candy Speech Detection* secured first place in both Subtasks. Although the model was trained for span detection in Subtask 2, it was able to identify candy speech comments in Subtask 1 by predicting a comment as containing candy speech whenever a span was detected. It even outperformed models trained specifically for binary classification in Subtask 1, which we hypothesize is due to the richer training signal provided by token-level (span) annotations, as opposed to the comment-level binary labels of Subtask 1.

We consider several directions as promising to further improve our model's performance: (i) fine-tuning larger models like the Qwen3 Embedding model, (ii) creating ensembles similar to previous GermEval contributions (Bornheim et al., 2021; Blaneck et al., 2022), and (iii) expanding the context of each comment (e.g., by including previous comments or video content). Future work should address our model's current inability to handle overlapping spans, which was a trade-off we accepted for the sake of simplicity in the GermEval 2025 Shared Task, given the low prevalence of overlapping spans in the training data. This limitation may be overcome by reframing the problem as a multi-label task, as demonstrated by the winning submission to the GermEval 2023 Shared Task (Ehrmantraut, 2023). Finally, we recommend evaluating our model on data from different media platforms before deploying it in real-world applications. We anticipate that candy speech detection models, such as those presented in this paper, will be valuable not only in social media moderation but also as essential components of control mechanisms in generative LLMs, where they could help to monitor sycophancy and other forms of user manipulation.

Acknowledgements

We are grateful to M. Reißel and V. Sander for providing us with computing resources.

References

Aish Albladi, Minarul Islam, Amit Das, Maryam Bigonah, Zheng Zhang, Fatemeh Jamshidi, Mostafa Rahgouy, Nilanjana Raychawdhary, Daniela Marghitu, and Cheryl D. Seals. 2025. Hate Speech Detection Using Large Language Models: A Comprehensive Review. *IEEE Access*, 13:20871–20892.

Patrick Gustav Blaneck, Tobias Bornheim, Niklas Grieger, and Stephan Bialonski. 2022. Automatic Readability Assessment of German Sentences with Transformer Ensembles. In *Proceedings of the GermEval 2022 Workshop on Text Complexity Assessment of German Text, GermEval@KONVENS 2022*, pages 57–62, Potsdam, Germany. Association for Computational Linguistics.

Helena Bonaldi, Yi-Ling Chung, Gavin Abercrombie, and Marco Guerini. 2024. NLP for Counterspeech against Hate: A Survey and How-To Guide. In *Findings of the Association for Computational Linguistics: NAACL 2024, Mexico City, Mexico, June 16-21, 2024*, pages 3480–3499. Association for Computational Linguistics.

Tobias Bornheim, Niklas Grieger, and Stephan Bialonski. 2021. FHAC at GermEval 2021: Identifying German toxic, engaging, and fact-claiming comments with ensemble learning. In *Proceedings of the GermEval 2021 Shared Task on the Identification of Toxic, Engaging, and Fact-Claiming Comments, GermEval@KONVENS 2021*, pages 105–111, Düsseldorf, Germany. Association for Computational Linguistics.

Tobias Bornheim, Niklas Grieger, Patrick Gustav Blaneck, and Stephan Bialonski. 2024. Speaker Attribution in German Parliamentary Debates with QLoRA-adapted Large Language Models. *Journal for Language Technology and Computational Linguistics*, 37(1):1–13.

Bharathi Raja Chakravarthi, Vigneshwaran Muralidaran, Ruba Priyadharshini, Subalalitha Chinnaudayar Navaneethakrishnan, John P. McCrae, Miguel Ángel García, Salud María Jiménez-Zafra, Rafael Valencia-García, Prasanna Kumar Kumaresan, Rahul Ponnusamy, Daniel García-Baena, and José Antonio García-Díaz. 2022. Overview of the Shared Task on Hope Speech Detection for Equality, Diversity, and Inclusion. In *Proceedings of the Second Workshop on Language Technology for Equality, Diversity and Inclusion, LT-EDI 2022, Dublin, Ireland, May 27, 2022*, pages 378–388. Association for Computational Linguistics.

Branden Chan, Stefan Schweter, and Timo Möller. 2020. German's Next Language Model. In *Proc. 28th Int. Conf. on Computational Linguistics, COLING 2020*, pages 6788–6796, Barcelona, Spain (Online). International Committee on Computational Linguistics.

Yulia Clausen, Tatjana Scheffler, and Michael Wiegand. 2025. Overview of the GermEval 2025 Shared Task on Candy Speech Detection. In *Proceedings of the 21st Conference on Natural Language Processing (KONVENS 2025): Workshops*, Hildesheim, Germany. ACL.

Alexis Conneau, Kartikay Khandelwal, Naman Goyal, Vishrav Chaudhary, Guillaume Wenzek, Francisco Guzmán, Edouard Grave, Myle Ott, Luke Zettlemoyer, and Veselin Stoyanov. 2020. Unsupervised Cross-lingual Representation Learning at Scale. In *Proceedings of the 58th Annual Meeting of the Association for Computational Linguistics, ACL 2020, Online, July 5-10, 2020*, pages 8440–8451. Association for Computational Linguistics.

DeepSeek-AI, Aixin Liu, Bei Feng, Bing Xue, Bingxuan Wang, Bochao Wu, Chengda Lu, Chenggang Zhao, Chengqi Deng, Chenyu Zhang, Chong Ruan, Damai Dai, Daya Guo, Dejian Yang, Deli Chen, Dongjie Ji, Erhang Li, Fangyun Lin, Fucong Dai, and 81 others. 2024. DeepSeek-V3 Technical Report. *CoRR*, abs/2412.19437.

Jacob Devlin, Ming-Wei Chang, Kenton Lee, and Kristina Toutanova. 2019. BERT: Pre-training of Deep Bidirectional Transformers for Language Understanding. In *Proc. 2019 Conf. North American Chapter of the Association for Computational Linguistics: Human Language Technologies, NAACL-HLT 2019*, volume 1, pages 4171–4186, Minneapolis, MN, USA. Association for Computational Linguistics.

Anton Ehrmanntraut. 2023. Politics, BERTed: Automatic Attribution of Speech Events in German Parliamentary Debates. In *Proceedings of the GermEval 2023 Shared Task on Speaker Attribution in Newswire and Parliamentary Debates (SpkAtt-2023)*, pages 22–30.

Corsin Geiss and Alessandra Zarcone. 2024. THAugs at GermEval 2024 (Shared Task 1: GerMS-Detect): Predicting the Severity of Misogyny/Sexism in Forum Comments with BERT Models (Subtask 1, Closed Track and Additional Experiments). In *Proceedings of GermEval 2024 Task 1 GerMS-Detect Workshop on Sexism Detection in German Online News Fora (GerMS-Detect 2024)*, pages 10–20, Vienna, Austria. Association for Computational Linguistics.

Emily Kubin, Pascal Merz, Mariam Wahba, Cate Davis, Kurt Gray, and Christian von Sikorski. 2024. Understanding news-related user comments and their effects: A systematic review. *Frontiers in Communication*, 9:1447457.

OpenAI. 2023. GPT-4 Technical Report. *CoRR*, abs/2303.08774.

Lance A. Ramshaw and Mitch Marcus. 1995. Text Chunking using Transformation-Based Learning. In *Third Workshop on Very Large Corpora, VLC@ACL 1995, Cambridge, Massachusetts, USA, June 30, 1995*.

Georgiana Tucudean, Marian Bucos, Bogdan Dragulescu, and Catalin-Daniel Caleanu. 2024. Natural language processing with transformers: A review. *PeerJ Comput. Sci.*, 10:e2222.

An Yang, Anfeng Li, Baosong Yang, Beichen Zhang, Binyuan Hui, Bo Zheng, Bowen Yu, Chang Gao, Chengen Huang, Chenxu Lv, Chujie Zheng, Dayiheng Liu, Fan Zhou, Fei Huang, Feng Hu, Hao Ge, Haoran Wei, Huan Lin, Jialong Tang, and 41 others. 2025. Qwen3 Technical Report. *CoRR*, abs/2505.09388.

Yanzhao Zhang, Mingxin Li, Dingkun Long, Xin Zhang, Huan Lin, Baosong Yang, Pengjun Xie, An Yang, Dayiheng Liu, Junyang Lin, Fei Huang, and Jingren Zhou. 2025. Qwen3 Embedding: Advancing Text Embedding and Reranking Through Foundation Models. *CoRR*, abs/2506.05176.

Coling-UniA at GermEval 2025 Shared Task on Candy Speech Detection: Retrieval Augmented Generation for Identifying Expressions of Positive Attitudes in German YouTube Comments

Georg Hofmann **Annemarie Friedrich**
University of Augsburg, Germany
{georg.hofmann|annemarie.friedrich}@uni-a.de

Abstract

We present our system for the GermEval 2025 Shared Task on Candy Speech Detection, which focuses on identifying and categorizing positive expressions in German YouTube comments. To address the task, we apply a Retrieval-Augmented Generation approach using large language models, experimenting with two target output formats, an XML-style and a CoNLL-style format. Our few-shot setup, which selects relevant training examples as demonstrations using dense encoders, enables the model to predict labeled spans effectively. Among all configurations, the XML-style prompt with the Qwen model achieved the best performance. Our system ranked third in the official evaluation, highlighting the potential of few-shot prompting of large language models for fine-grained span classification tasks, especially in low-resource scenarios.

1 Introduction

While many methods have been developed to detect and moderate negative speech, such as hate speech or offensive language on social media, much less attention has been paid to identifying *candy speech*, i.e., supporting, positive, or encouraging messages. In this work, we describe our system for participating in the GermEval 2025 Shared Task on Candy Speech Detection (Clausen et al., 2025),[1] which seeks to address this gap by encouraging research on positive expressions in online communication. The task focuses on identifying and labeling instances of candy speech in German YouTube comments. Specifically, it involves span-level detection, requiring systems to mark the exact text segments that contain candy speech and classify each span into one of ten predefined categories.

To tackle the task, we apply a Retrieval-Augmented Generation (RAG) method using a large language model (LLM), as shown in Figure 1. For each test instance, our system retrieves similar examples from the training data, using dense encoders and cosine similarity, to help the LLM to accurately identify candy speech spans and their categories. We test various specifications of output formats for performing span detection as a sequence labeling task with nested spans, finding that an XML-like style outperformed a CoNLL-based format. Our system ranks third in the official evaluation, demonstrating that our method to prompt LLMs for this task is promising.

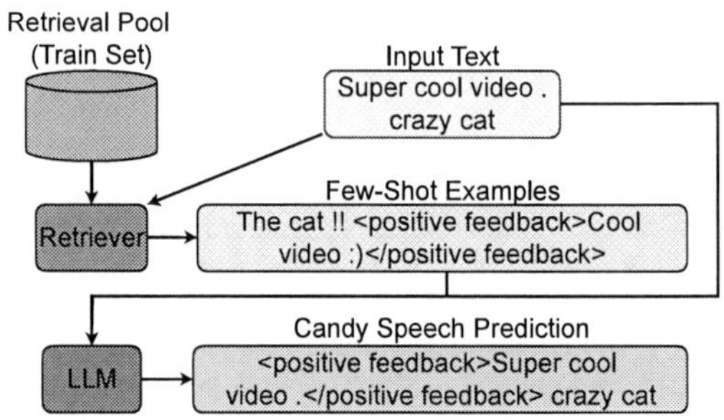

Figure 1: Overview of the proposed Retrieval-Augmented Generation (RAG) pipeline. (Input Text and Few-Shot Example are translated to English.)

2 Related Work

The task of candy speech detection is closely related to sentiment analysis and sequence labeling, as it involves identifying both the emotional tone and the exact spans of expressions in user-generated text.

LLMs have recently been explored for sentiment analysis (e.g., Deng et al., 2023; Zhong et al., 2023; Wang et al., 2023). Building on these efforts, Zhang et al. (2024) provide a comprehensive evaluation of LLMs across 13 sentiment analysis tasks and 26 datasets, including standard, aspect-based, and multifaceted sentiment classification. While LLMs perform competitively on simpler tasks in a zero-

[1] https://yuliacl.github.io/GermEval2025-Flausch-Erkennung/

Proceedings of the 21st Conference on Natural Language Processing (KONVENS), Volume 2: Workshops, pages 404–410, 2025

shot setting, they struggle with more complex ones. In few-shot scenarios, however, LLMs significantly outperform smaller domain-specific models, showing strong potential for low-resource settings.

In recent years, LLMs have also been applied to sequence labeling tasks, such as named entity recognition (NER). Although LLMs have advanced significantly, their performance in NER tasks remains substantially lower than fully supervised BERT-based models (Xie et al., 2023; Kim et al., 2024). Wang et al. (2025) proposed using special tokens to mark entities for extraction in NER tasks. These special tokens act as clear delimiters around the target entity to help the model identify it precisely. For example, when extracting a location, the entity is wrapped with special tokens like "@@China##". Their approach achieved performance comparable to fully supervised baselines, marking a notable first in effectively leveraging LLMs for NER.

We build on recent progress in sentiment classification and NER using LLMs to tackle candy speech detection in German user-generated text.

3 Task and Data

We participate in Subtask 2: Fine-Grained Classification, which involves identifying the exact spans of candy speech expressions in German YouTube comments and classifying each into one of ten predefined categories, such as `positive feedback`, `compliment`, and `group membership`. Notably, spans can overlap, and even spans of the same category may be nested within each other. The dataset comprises complete written comment threads from a variety of YouTube creators and communities, with no overlap between the videos used for training and testing. This setup guarantees diversity in topics, styles, and audience demographics between the training and test sets. The input texts were pre-tokenized: tokens are separated by whitespace e.g., "Viele Leute fühlen sich cool , wenn sie haten ." (English: "Many people feel cool when they hate ."). All annotations are span-based and refer to these tokenized forms. For a more detailed description of the task and data, we refer the reader to the shared task overview by Clausen et al. (2025).

4 Method

We propose a RAG approach for fine-grained candy speech detection and classification that combines a dense retrieval model with an LLM, as shown in Figure 1. During inference, the retriever first selects similar text documents from a predefined pool, i.e., the training set. The *top-k* documents with a similarity score above a threshold t are included as demonstrations in the prompt to guide the LLM in both span detection and classification. The selected demonstrations, their spans, and associated candy speech categories are combined with the current test instance text to create a prompt that guides the LLM in predicting candy speech spans and categories. After the LLM generates its prediction, any spans that have been assigned categories not included in the predefined set are discarded to ensure that only valid categories are retained.

4.1 Retrieval of Few-Shot Examples

For the retriever, we use a Sentence-BERT model (Reimers and Gurevych, 2019) to convert texts into embeddings. These embeddings are stored and searched using the FAISS library (Douze et al., 2024), which allows for fast and efficient retrieval of semantically similar texts using cosine similarity. The specific Sentence-BERT model we use is *all-mpnet-base-v2*,[2] intended for encoding sentences and short paragraphs. This model is applied without further fine-tuning in all experiments.

4.2 Prompting and Span Labeling

We use the instruction-tuned LLMs Llama-3.3-70B-Instruct[3] and Qwen2.5-72B-Instruct[4] for our experiments. These large models were chosen because their size and instruction tuning make them particularly capable of following complex prompts. We used two different prompts, which are illustrated in Figure 2.

XML-style prompting. The first prompt instructed the LLM to mark spans directly within the text using XML-style tags. Each span was enclosed by an opening and closing tag corresponding to one of the ten predefined candy speech categories. For example, a model output might contain a phrase like `<compliment>you sing really well :)</compliment>` to indicate that the expression "you sing really well :)" belongs to the compliment category. In this format, the model is supposed to explicitly identify both the boundaries and the

[2]https://huggingface.co/sentence-transformers/all-mpnet-base-v2

[3]https://huggingface.co/meta-llama/Llama-3.3-70B-Instruct

[4]https://huggingface.co/Qwen/Qwen2.5-72B-Instruct

(a) XML-style prompt

system: You are a helpful assistant for detecting Candy Speech...<Further details on the task and the desired output format.>

user: Text: you sing really well :)
Insert the appropriate tags into the text.

assistant:

```
<compliment>you sing really well :)</compliment>
```

(b) CoNLL/BIO-style prompt

system: You are a helpful assistant for detecting Candy Speech...<Further details on the task and the desired output format.>

user: Text: you sing really well :)
Output the text with the appropriate categories in CoNLL format. Tokenize by whitespace.

assistant:

```
you     B-compliment
sing    I-compliment
really  I-compliment
well    I-compliment
:)      I-compliment
```

Figure 2: Two prompt formats used to guide the LLM (translated to English). (a) In the XML-style prompt, the assistant annotates positive spans directly using opening and closing tags for one of the predefined Candy Speech categories. (b) In the CoNLL-style prompt, the assistant returns a token-per-line output using the BIO tagging scheme, indicating span boundaries with prefix codes (B- for beginning, I- for inside, or O for outside tokens not part of any span) and appending the corresponding category.

type of each positive span within the original input. The XML-style format also made it possible to represent overlapping spans or even nested spans with the same category, both of which occur in the dataset. In the case of overlapping spans, however, the structure is no longer valid XML, as valid XML does not support overlapping tags.

The input texts are already provided in a tokenized format by the shared task organizers, as mentioned in Section 3. When using Llama with the XML-style prompt, we observed that the model almost consistently removed whitespaces, typically before punctuation marks that are not likely present in the original YouTube comments, despite explicit instructions in the prompt to not change the input text. This led to incorrect span boundaries when constructing the annotations from the LLM output. To mitigate this issue, we applied a simple postprocessing step to restore the original spacing.

CoNLL-style prompting. The second prompt follows a more structured sequence labeling approach. We instructed the LLM to tokenize the input text using whitespace and apply the BIO tagging scheme (also known as IOB: Inside, Outside, Beginning). This format assigns a label to each token indicating whether it is part of a candy speech span and, whether it appears at the beginning (B-), inside (I-), or outside (O) of that span. The specific candy speech category is appended to the prefix, forming labels such as B-compliment, I-gratitude, or simply O if the token is not part of any span. The output is structured in a CoNLL-style format, where each token appears on a separate line alongside its BIO tag, separated by a tab character. This format is commonly used in sequence labeling tasks such as NER. This format makes it possible to handle overlapping or adjacent spans. However, it cannot represent nested spans of the same category, which is a known limitation of the BIO scheme. This type of nesting appears once in the training set and three times in the test set.

5 Experiments

We test different combinations of LLMs and prompt formats in both few-shot and zero-shot settings.

Hyperparameters. To tune our hyperparameters, we split the original training set into a reduced training set and a separate development set. The development set corresponds to the official trial set provided with the dataset. We conduct a series of preliminary experiments on the development set. Based on these experiments, we set the number of retrieved demonstrations *top-k* to 50 and the similarity threshold t to 0.25 for the few-shot setting.

Evaluation metrics. The primary metric for the shared task is *strict match*, which requires systems to correctly identify both the type and the exact character span of each candy speech expression in a comment. In addition, *type match* evaluates whether the correct candy speech types are predicted for each comment regardless of their spans. Both metrics account for multiple instances of the same type in a single comment. *Span match*, assesses whether the character spans are identified correctly, ignoring the type labels.

Results. Table 1 presents the results for five different model and prompt format combinations, evaluated in the zero-shot and few-shot settings. When considering strict match, the XML-style prompt

		Zero-Shot			Few-Shot								
		Strict Match			Strict Match			Type Match			Span Match		
LLM	**Prompt**	P	R	F1	P	R	F1	P	R	F1	P	R	F1
Llama	CoNLL	2.10	3.88	2.72	43.96	42.77	43.36	66.12	64.32	65.20	50.68	49.30	49.98
Llama	XML	2.02	4.14	2.71	29.26	35.20	31.96	59.18	71.18	64.63	32.88	39.54	35.90
Llama	XML (fw*)	2.71	5.58	3.65	42.36	50.95	46.26	59.18	71.18	64.63	48.29	58.09	52.74
Qwen	CoNLL	4.15	11.08	6.03	44.34	43.48	43.91	**67.02**	65.74	66.37	50.20	49.23	49.71
Qwen	XML	**8.44**	**14.18**	**10.58**	**47.48**	**52.36**	**49.80**	64.82	**71.47**	**67.98**	**54.05**	**59.59**	**56.68**

Table 1: Performance results on the test set across LLMs, prompt formats and match types. For each metric, the highest value per column is shown in **bold**, and the second highest is underlined. P stands for Precision, R for Recall, and F1 for F1-score. *fw = fixed whitespaces. Only the few-shot systems using the XML-style prompt were submitted to the official evaluation.

consistently outperforms the CoNLL-style prompt for both Qwen and Llama (with fixed whitespaces) in terms of recall and F1-score. Notably in the few-shot setting, the precision for Llama is slightly higher when using the CoNLL-style (43.96 vs. 42.36 for XML), making it the only metric where the BIO tagging format shows a small advantage. Comparing across models, Qwen outperforms Llama on all three metrics when using the same prompt format, indicating stronger span prediction capabilities.

Correcting the whitespace issues ("Llama XML (fw*)") resulted in a substantial improvement across all metrics, highlighting the sensitivity of generative models to formatting consistency. Notably, this issue did not occur with Qwen, which preserved spacing as instructed. However, both models occasionally altered the original input text in both prompt formats, for example, by correcting spelling or making small grammatical adjustments and other times by making unrelated changes, which can also negatively affect span predictions. More details on how often the LLMs changed the original input text across different settings are provided in the Appendix A.2.

Overall, performance in the zero-shot setting is substantially lower compared to the few-shot setting. We find that in this setting, both Llama and Qwen sometimes fail to follow the CoNLL format producing malformed outputs that could not be evaluated (see Appendix A.1 for more details).

To better understand model performance beyond strict match metrics, we examine the type match and span match metrics the few-shot setting. For Qwen, the XML-style prompt overall yields better results for the type and span match. For Llama, the picture is less clear—while type match performance is slightly better with the CoNLL-style prompt, the XML-style prompt appears more robust overall when considering both match types.

For type match, both Qwen and Llama achieve higher precision with the CoNLL-style prompt and higher recall with the XML-style prompt, meaning the XML-style prompt results in more predicted labels overall, at the cost of moderately reduced precision. For span match, the XML-style prompt performs better for both LLMs across all metrics, with one exception: for Llama, the CoNLL-style prompt results in slightly higher precision. This suggests that XML formatting helps both models better localize relevant spans, while Llama may benefit from the more structured CoNLL format when it comes to making precise span boundary decisions. Overall, however, Qwen with the XML-style prompt achieves the best performance. Notably, only the few-shot systems using the XML-style prompt were submitted to the official evaluation.

The span match metrics also reflects that Llama's original XML output without whitespace correction results in substantially lower span match performance. After applying a simple postprocessing step to fix spacing, the span-level metrics improve clearly, showing that consistent formatting plays an important role in structured prediction tasks using LLMs.

6 Discussion

Despite achieving strong results in the shared task, we have observed several challenges with using LLMs for span prediction. Both Llama and Qwen occasionally change the original input text, even when explicitly instructed not to do so. This included Llama removing whitespaces in the XML-style prompt, and both models occasionally correcting spelling or grammar and at other times making unrelated changes. These seemingly harmless edits often led to incorrect span boundaries and reduced performance, particularly for strict match and span match metrics. However, our system ranks third in the official evaluation, showing that prompting LLMs, especially in a few-shot setup that retrieves similar examples from the training data, can be a highly effective strategy. This makes it a promising approach for tasks where annotated training data is scarce.

7 Conclusion and Future Work

Our experiments show that prompting LLMs can effectively identify and classify candy speech spans. The best performance was achieved by Qwen using the XML-style prompt in the few-shot setting. Future work could explore category-specific prompting, asking the model to find only one candy speech category at a time, which might improve performance at the cost of increased computation time.

References

Yulia Clausen, Tatjana Scheffler, and Michael Wiegand. 2025. Overview of the GermEval 2025 Shared Task on Candy Speech Detection. In *Proceedings of the 21st Conference on Natural Language Processing (KONVENS 2025): Workshops*, Hildesheim, Germany. ACL.

Xiang Deng, Vasilisa Bashlovkina, Feng Han, Simon Baumgartner, and Michael Bendersky. 2023. LLMs to the Moon? Reddit Market Sentiment Analysis with Large Language Models. In *Companion Proceedings of the ACM Web Conference 2023*, WWW '23 Companion, page 1014–1019, New York, NY, USA. Association for Computing Machinery.

Matthijs Douze, Alexandr Guzhva, Chengqi Deng, Jeff Johnson, Gergely Szilvasy, Pierre-Emmanuel Mazaré, Maria Lomeli, Lucas Hosseini, and Hervé Jégou. 2024. The Faiss library. *CoRR*, abs/2401.08281.

Hongjin Kim, Jai-Eun Kim, and Harksoo Kim. 2024. Exploring Nested Named Entity Recognition with Large Language Models: Methods, Challenges, and Insights. In *Proceedings of the 2024 Conference on Empirical Methods in Natural Language Processing*, pages 8653–8670, Miami, Florida, USA. Association for Computational Linguistics.

Nils Reimers and Iryna Gurevych. 2019. Sentence-BERT: Sentence Embeddings using Siamese BERT-Networks. In *Proceedings of the 2019 Conference on Empirical Methods in Natural Language Processing and the 9th International Joint Conference on Natural Language Processing (EMNLP-IJCNLP)*, pages 3982–3992, Hong Kong, China. Association for Computational Linguistics.

Shuhe Wang, Xiaofei Sun, Xiaoya Li, Rongbin Ouyang, Fei Wu, Tianwei Zhang, Jiwei Li, Guoyin Wang, and Chen Guo. 2025. GPT-NER: Named Entity Recognition via Large Language Models. In *Findings of the Association for Computational Linguistics: NAACL 2025*, pages 4257–4275, Albuquerque, New Mexico. Association for Computational Linguistics.

Zengzhi Wang, Qiming Xie, Zixiang Ding, Yi Feng, and Rui Xia. 2023. Is ChatGPT a Good Sentiment Analyzer? A Preliminary Study. *CoRR*, abs/2304.04339.

Tingyu Xie, Qi Li, Jian Zhang, Yan Zhang, Zuozhu Liu, and Hongwei Wang. 2023. Empirical Study of Zero-Shot NER with ChatGPT. In *Proceedings of the 2023 Conference on Empirical Methods in Natural Language Processing*, pages 7935–7956, Singapore. Association for Computational Linguistics.

Wenxuan Zhang, Yue Deng, Bing Liu, Sinno Pan, and Lidong Bing. 2024. Sentiment Analysis in the Era of Large Language Models: A Reality Check. In *Findings of the Association for Computational Linguistics: NAACL 2024*, pages 3881–3906, Mexico City, Mexico. Association for Computational Linguistics.

Qihuang Zhong, Liang Ding, Juhua Liu, Bo Du, and Dacheng Tao. 2023. Can ChatGPT Understand Too? A Comparative Study on ChatGPT and Fine-tuned BERT. *CoRR*, abs/2302.10198.

A Evaluation of LLM Output Quality

A.1 How Often LLMs Failed to Follow the CoNLL-Format

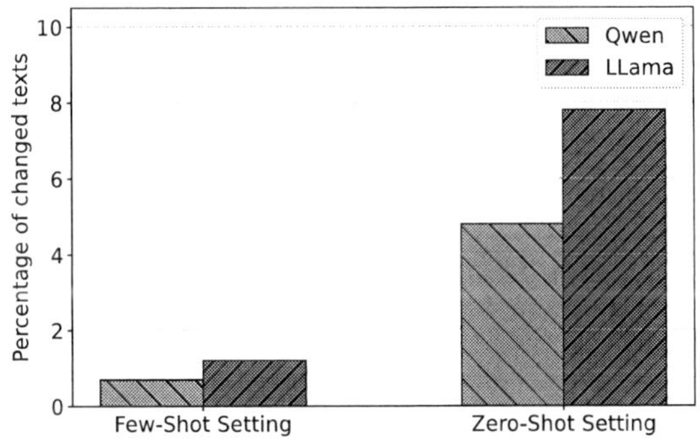

Figure 3: Percentage of LLM outputs instructed to use the CoNLL-format that did not follow the format on the test set.

Figure 3 shows the percentage of LLM outputs that were instructed to use the CoNLL-format, but did not follow it. In both the few-shot and zero-shot settings, Llama struggles more to adhere to the CoNLL-format. Additionally, LLMs generally perform worse in the zero-shot setting, with a higher rate of format violations compared to the few-shot setting.

A.2 How Often LLMs Changed the Original Input Texts

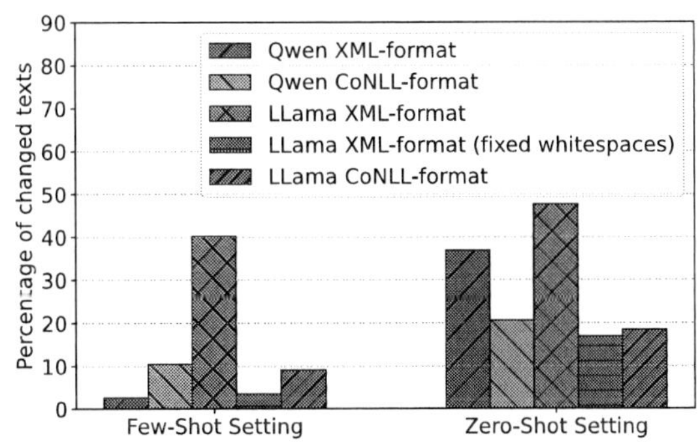

Figure 4: Percentage of input texts altered by the LLM on the test set. (For the CoNLL-format we only considered LLM outputs conforming to the instructed format.)

In both the few-shot and zero-shot settings, Figure 4 shows how the whitespace removal issue of Llama in the XML-style prompt leads to a high percentage of altered texts when span predictions are inserted directly into the original input text. Once these whitespace inconsistencies are corrected through post-processing, the percentage of changed texts drops significantly ("Llama XML-format (fixed whitespaces)"). In the few-shot setting, both LLMs tend to modify the original input text more when using the CoNLL-format (when accounting for missing whitespaces in the case of Llama).

In the zero-shot setting, we observe the same pattern for Llama, but Qwen struggles more when using the XML-format. Overall, both LLMs find it more difficult to maintain the original input text in the zero-shot setting.

In the following, we list a few test instances for which the LLM changed the original input text using Llama and the XML-type format in the few-shot setting. For better comparison, we show the original input, the LLM output, the output without XML-style tags, and highlight the part that was changed:

- **Original input text:** `Löslich liebe diesen song`
  LLM output: `<positive feedback>Ich liebe diesen song</positive feedback>`
  LLM output without XML-type tags: `Ich liebe diesen song`
  Changed part: <u>`Löslich`</u> → <u>`Ich`</u>

- **Original input text:** `schönes Lied`
  LLM output: `<positive feedback>schoenes Lied</positive feedback>`
  LLM output without XML-type tags: `schoenes Lied`
  Changed part: <u>`schönes`</u> → <u>`schoenes`</u>

- **Original input text:** `Ihr seit so cool . Ich liebe eure parodie . Hab es mir sogar runtergeladen . :-)`
  LLM output: `affection declaration>Ihr seit so cool</affection declaration>. <affection declaration>Ich liebe eure parodie</affection declaration>. <positive feedback>Hab es mir sogar runtergeladen</positive feedback>. :-)`
  LLM output without XML-type tags: `Ihr seit so cool. Ich liebe eure parodie. Hab es mir sogar runtergeladen. :-)`
  Changed part: `whitespaces`

Figure 5: Examples of input text, LLM outputs with and without XML-type tags, and the corresponding differences.

Flauschgummi at GermEval 2025 Shared Task on Candy Speech Detection: Sentiment Analysis and Classification of Online Comments

Björn Kießwetter and **Christoph Lukas** and **Tim Sieber**
University of Regensburg
{Bjoern.Kiesswetter|Christoph1.Lukas|Tim.Sieber}@stud.uni-regensburg.de

Abstract

There has been a noticeable increase in the use of offensive language across user-generated content on social media platforms. Such language can target, harm, or marginalize individuals or entire communities. In contrast to this negative trend, we focus on the identification and classification of candy speech – supportive and emotionally positive statements. We examine the effectiveness of stacking traditional machine learning techniques like Logistic Regression, k-Nearest Neighbors, Random Forest, Multi-Layer Perceptron, Support Vector Classifier and simple word counting, and compare them to BERT, a powerful pre-trained language model. The study evaluates both individual and ensemble methods to determine the most effective strategy. Our results indicate that traditional stacking methods used without BERT achieve the highest accuracy, followed by the hybrid approach, while BERT alone performs the worst on this specific task.

1 Introduction

Anyone who visited a social media platform like Facebook, Instagram or YouTube has most likely encountered offensive posts from users in the comment section, also known as hate speech. What if we could not only remove negativity, but also actively promote and spread positivity? To explore this idea, we participate in Subtask 1 of the GermEval 2025 Shared Task on Candy Speech Detection, where we focus on identification of candy speech in YouTube comments. Candy speech refers to expression of positive attitudes on social media toward individuals or their output, e.g. videos or comments (Clausen et al., 2025).

Detecting candy speech is a very complex task, as it depends not only on sentiment but also on contextual understanding. While langue models like GPT (OpenAI, 2024) or BERT (Devlin et al., 2019) have gained enormous influence in today's era, they also come with major limitations like high computational costs and a significant carbon footprint (Li et al., 2021). To evaluate the trade-off between computational efficiency and classification performance, we compare three modeling approaches: a classical stacking model as a lightweight baseline, a BERT-based model to assess the potential accuracy gains from deep contextual embeddings, and a hybrid model combining both approaches.

2 Related Work

2.1 Offensive Language Detection

Previous studies have explored the detection of hate speech using classical machine learning methods (Ayo et al., 2020; Davidson et al., 2017). Their findings suggest that traditional approaches, such as SVMs or Logistic Regression, can achieve performance comparable to that of deep learning models, particularly in the context of hate speech recognition on Twitter (Mercan et al., 2021).

2.2 Emotion Classification in Text

In recent years, language models like GPT, BERT and RoBERTa (Liu et al., 2019) proved to be very powerful in tasks such as emotion and sentiment classification (Zian et al., 2021). Automatic recognition of emotions in text is an active research field in natural language processing. Traditional approaches often use classical machine learning methods, such as SVMs or Random Forest. With the emergence of large pretrained language models, the precision and robustness of emotion classification have improved significantly (Stigall et al., 2024).

3 Methodology

This section introduces the steps taken to obtain additional training data, clean and prepare the data sets, as well as conducting the experiments.

Proceedings of the 21st Conference on Natural Language Processing (KONVENS), Volume 2: Workshops, pages 411–415, 2025

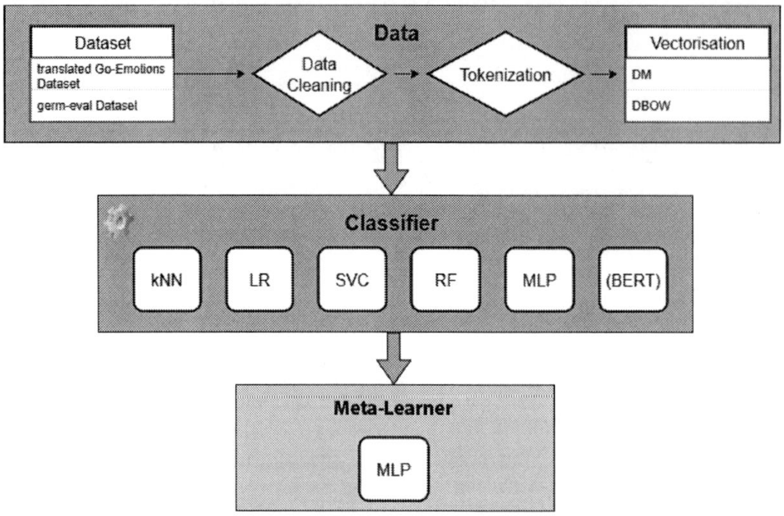

Figure 1: Pipeline

Figure 1 shows the execution flow of our code in the form of a pipeline, illustrating each step and how data is processed sequentially. First we clean the data, then tokenize it and apply our two vectorization methods: Distributed Memory (DM) and Distributed-Bag-of-Words (DBOW). These vectors are then passed on to our 5 different classifiers: k-Nearest Neighbors (kNN), Logistic Regression (LR), Support Vector Classifier (SVC), Random Forest (RF), and Multi-Layer Perceptron (MLP). The BERT model, in contrast, directly processes the raw comments, instead of vectors. The last station is the MLP. With help of the 6-dimensional vector, from the models mentioned above, it predicts whether a given comment contains candy speech or not.

3.1 Data Preparation

In an initial test, we trained our models on the official data provided by the shared task organizers, but our models did not achieve satisfactory results. Therefore, we decided to extend the training data by including additional comments from external sources (Demszky et al., 2020). Details are described in the following section. Since these comments were in English, we translated them into German using Helsinki-NLP/opus-mt-en-de (Tiedemann and Thottingal, 2020).

Data Cleaning The importance of preprocessing data in form of data cleaning is essential for improving the models' performance and ensuring consistent input for our classifier (Kalra and Aggarwal, 2018). Therefore, we performed a series of data cleaning steps. The effectiveness of this approach was also demonstrated by Lee et al. (2021) and further supported by Li et al. (2021).

Given the noisy and unstructured nature of YouTube comments, we deleted usernames, links, emojis, and excessive punctuation, which further improved model accuracy (see Figure 3).

Tokenization Since classical machine learning algorithms cannot process text directly, we converted it into numerical vectors using Doc2Vec (Le and Mikolov, 2014). This required an initial tokenization, for which we used NLTK's tokenization algorithm (Bird et al., 2009). The outcome of this procedure is a list of tokens that serve as input to Doc2Vec.

Vectorization of Comments For vectorisation, the Doc2Vec algorithm offers two main variants: DM and DBOW. Both approaches aim to learn fixed-length vector representations of given text. DM learns from word sequences and context, while DBOW focuses on predicting document words without considering word order. Both aim to produce meaningful representations of documents for downstream tasks (Le and Mikolov, 2014).

4 Models

4.1 Stacking without BERT

For a classification task, there are different approaches. We decided to use a stacking variant that combines five different machine learning algorithms. Stacking is a method in which multiple classifiers perform the same task in parallel. Their results are then combined, via a Meta-Learner reclassified, which allows them to compensate for each other's weaknesses and reinforce their strengths. This technique has shown its effectiveness in terms of accuracy and robustness (Zian et al., 2021).

For our stacking ensemble, we used the following traditional machine learning models: LR, kNN, SVC, MLP and RF. Since each of these classifiers uses random seeds, we performed the classification for each comment 10 times and returned the mean of the outcome to ensure stability and reduce variance. This resulted in a 5-dimensional vector with values ranging from 0 to 1.

4.2 Stacking with BERT

To leverage deeper semantic context, we repeated the same classification pipeline, i.e., LR, kNN, SVC, MLP, and RF, but added BERT. As before, we ran 10 iterations for every classification, resulting in a 6-dimensional vector with values again ranging from 0 to 1.

4.3 Simple Word Counting

An additional dimension for our classifier was to "rate" a comment based on present words. We used a collection of "bad", "good" and "intensifier" words to obtain a very easy semantic understanding of the given comment, inspired by the approach in (Palanisamy et al., 2013). This dictionary was manually curated from the comments in our dataset and includes several categories of words: positive and negative sentiment words, intensifiers that amplify the sentiment strength, negation words that can reverse sentiment polarity, and positive/negative emojis to capture emotional expressions.

4.4 Meta-Learner

Our main prediction model, the meta-learner, is a Multi-Layer Perceptron, which we trained with BERT on 6–7 dimensional vectors. These vectors were generated by the methods previously described to determine the semantics of each comment. The MLP was trained on 4,000 comments that were cleaned and preprocessed and not part of the comments we used to train our classifiers above. This means that our main prediction model comes into contact only with new and unseen data.

4.5 BERT

For comparison, we evaluated the classification performance of a pre-trained German BERT model (Guhr et al., 2020) applied directly to the task, without any additional stacking or feature engineering.

5 Results

5.1 Meta-Learner Performance

Model	F1	Precision	Recall
stacking without BERT	0.6972	0.8879	0.5739
stacking with BERT	0.6842	0.8765	0.5611
BERT alone	0.6852	0.6829	0.6874

Table 1: Performance comparison of the models submitted to Subtask 1.

As shown in Table 1, stacking without BERT outperforms the other approaches in terms of precision. However, when it comes to recall, BERT alone achieves the highest performance.

5.2 Model comparison

In this section, we present a comparison of all models based on the following metrics: accuracy, F1-score, Precision, and Recall.

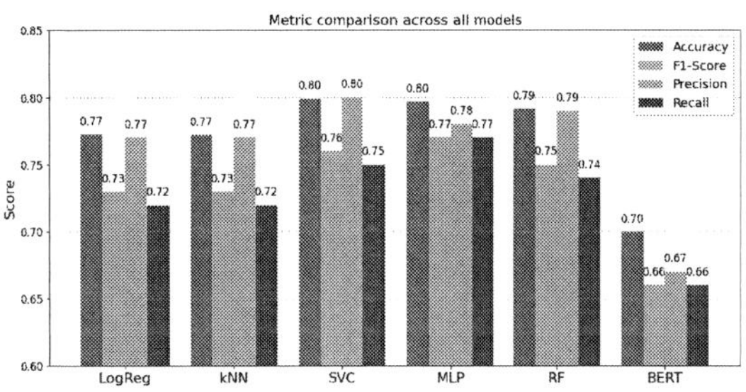

Figure 2: Metric comparison across all models.

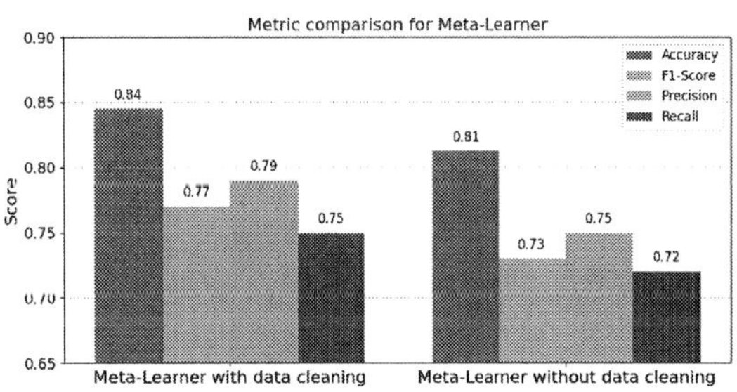

Figure 3: Metric comparison for Meta-Learner.

6 Discussion

We explored to what extent classical machine learning algorithms can remain relevant in an era increasingly shaped by the use of large language models, as discussed in (Miah et al., 2024; Zhan et al., 2024; Zhang et al., 2023). While we did not achieve state-of-the-art results with our model, it is important to note that GPT-3.5 obtains a precision score of 0.87, compared to 0.96 for GPT-4 and 0.91 for Llama 2 in a related study that analyzes sentiment of text via large language models (Krugmann and Hartmann, 2024). Nonetheless, our findings highlight that relatively simple techniques, when combined thoughtfully, can still achieve competitive performance.

The overall accuracy, F1-score, Precision, and Recall of our model improved substantially, after we cleaned and preprocessed the training data. A direct comparison shows that our model trained on the unchanged data performed worse in classifying candy speech than the one trained on preprocessed data, as shown in Figure 3. A possible explanation could be that in the case of unchanged data, the model was trained with vectors that were distorted or semantically meaningless.

The improvements in accuracy, F1-score, Precision, and Recall can likely be attributed to preprocessing, which helped produce more consistent and informative input patterns, thereby enhancing classification performance. This trend has already been demonstrated by earlier research (Lee et al., 2021; Li et al., 2021) and appears consistent with the current findings.

A critical aspect in evaluating our model lies in the choice of the vectorization method. Although we used Paragraph Vector - Distributed Memory (PV-DM) and Paragraph Vector - Distributed Bag of Words (PV-DBOW), it remains an open question how our results might have improved, if we had used an alternative method, such as Term Frequency-Inverse Document Frequency (TF-IDF). The latter represents text by weighting each term based on its relative importance within a comment and across the entire dataset.

In related work on hate speech detection (Mercan et al., 2021), TF-IDF has proven its effectiveness by recognizing the relevance of a single word and reducing the influence of common but uninformative terms. This approach achieved higher accuracy scores using classifiers such as SVM, which is closely related to the SVC, RF, and LR models we used (Table 2).

Accuracy comparison	SVM/SVC	LR	RF
our study	0.76	0.73	0.75
related study	0.94	0.94	0.95

Table 2: Accuracy comparison of different classifiers in our study and a related study by Mercan et al. (2021).

As Table 2 shows, alternative vectorization methods led to noticeably better performance. This suggests that to improve our results, we should consider replacing PV-DM and PV-DBOW with TF-IDF.

Surprisingly, the best-performing model in our experiments did not include any LLM components. Instead, it relied solely on traditional ML algorithms and supervised stacking. This suggests that in tasks with strong lexical or stylistic signals, such as detecting emotionally supportive candy speech comments, deep contextual understanding may not be necessary. Simpler models can exploit these surface-level patterns effectively.

Moreover, while BERT is a powerful and general-purpose model, its embeddings did not considerably boost performance in our hybrid approaches.

7 Conclusion

In summary, with regard to candy speech detection, our results support the idea, that classical stacking ensembles can outperform both the standalone BERT-classifier as well as a hybrid model that incorporates deep contextual embeddings. We achieved substantial gains in accuracy, Precision, Recall, and F1-score trough data cleaning. Our cleaning process was tailored to the characteristics of the vectorization algorithm, which appeared to struggle with non-German words, emojis, and fragmented inputs. Moving forward, exploring alternative vectorization methods such as TF-IDF, employing data-augmentation strategies, and investigating model-distillation techniques could further enhance both performance and efficiency. Overall, our results support the idea that classical ML methods should not be dismissed outright in modern NLP workflows. They remain accessible, interpretable and surprisingly powerful.

References

Femi Emmanuel Ayo, Olusegun Folorunso, Friday Thomas Ibharalu, and Idowu Ademola Osinuga. 2020. Machine learning techniques for hate speech classification of twitter data: State-of-the-art, future challenges and research directions. *Computer Science Review*, 38:100311.

Steven Bird, Ewan Klein, and Edward Loper. 2009. Natural Language Processing with Python: Analyzing Text with the Natural Language Toolkit. Original-date: 2009-09-07T10:53:58Z.

Yulia Clausen, Tatjana Scheffler, and Michael Wiegand. 2025. Overview of the GermEval 2025 Shared Task on Candy Speech Detection. In *Proceedings of the 21st Conference on Natural Language Processing (KONVENS 2025): Workshops*, Hildesheim, Germany. ACL.

Thomas Davidson, Dana Warmsley, Michael Macy, and Ingmar Weber. 2017. Automated Hate Speech Detection and the Problem of Offensive Language. In *Proceedings of the 11th International AAAI Conference on Web and Social Media*, ICWSM '17, pages 512–515.

Dorottya Demszky, Dana Movshovitz-Attias, Jeongwoo Ko, Alan Cowen, Gaurav Nemade, and Sujith Ravi. 2020. GoEmotions: A Dataset of Fine-Grained Emotions. In *Proceedings of the 58th Annual Meeting of the Association for Computational Linguistics*, pages 4040–4054, Online. Association for Computational Linguistics.

Jacob Devlin, Ming-Wei Chang, Kenton Lee, and Kristina Toutanova. 2019. BERT: Pre-training of Deep Bidirectional Transformers for Language Understanding. In *Proceedings of the 2019 Conference of the North American Chapter of the Association for Computational Linguistics: Human Language Technologies, Volume 1 (Long and Short Papers)*, pages 4171–4186, Minneapolis, Minnesota. Association for Computational Linguistics.

Oliver Guhr, Anne-Kathrin Schumann, Frank Bahrmann, and Hans Joachim Böhme. 2020. Training a Broad-Coverage German Sentiment Classification Model for Dialog Systems. In *Proceedings of The 12th Language Resources and Evaluation Conference*, pages 1620–1625, Marseille, France. European Language Resources Association.

Vaishali Kalra and Rashmi Aggarwal. 2018. Importance of Text Data Preprocessing & Implementation in RapidMiner. In *Proceedings of the First International Conference on Information Technology and Knowledge Management*, page 71–75.

Jan Ole Krugmann and Jochen Hartmann. 2024. Sentiment Analysis in the Age of Generative AI. *Customer Needs and Solutions*, 11(1):3.

Quoc Le and Tomas Mikolov. 2014. Distributed Representations of Sentences and Documents. In *Proceedings of the 31st International Conference on Machine Learning (ICML)*, pages 1188–1196, Beijing, China. PMLR.

Ga Young Lee, Lubna Alzamil, Bakhtiyar Doskenov, and Arash Termehchy. 2021. A Survey on Data Cleaning Methods for Improved Machine Learning Model Performance.

Peng Li, Xi Rao, Jennifer Blase, Yue Zhang, Xu Chu, and Ce Zhang. 2021. CleanML: A Study for Evaluating the Impact of Data Cleaning on ML Classification Tasks. In *2021 IEEE 37th International Conference on Data Engineering (ICDE)*, pages 13–24.

Yinhan Liu, Myle Ott, Naman Goyal, Jingfei Du, Mandar Joshi, Danqi Chen, Omer Levy, Mike Lewis, Luke Zettlemoyer, and Veselin Stoyanov. 2019. Roberta: A robustly optimized bert pretraining approach. *arXiv preprint arXiv:1907.11692*.

Vildan Mercan, Akhtar Jamil, Alaa Ali Hameed, Irfan Ahmed Magsi, Sibghatullah Bazai, and Syed Attique Shah. 2021. Hate Speech and Offensive Language Detection from Social Media. In *2021 International Conference on Computing, Electronic and Electrical Engineering (ICE Cube)*, pages 1–5. IEEE.

Md Saef Ullah Miah, Md Mohsin Kabir, Talha Bin Sarwar, Mejdl Safran, Sultan Alfarhood, and M. F. Mridha. 2024. A multimodal approach to cross-lingual sentiment analysis with ensemble of transformer and LLM. *Scientific Reports*, 14(1):9603.

OpenAI. 2024. GPT-4 Technical Report.

Prabu Palanisamy, Vineet Yadav, and Harsha Elchuri. 2013. Serendio: Simple and Practical lexicon based approach to Sentiment Analysis. In *Second Joint Conference on Lexical and Computational Semantics (*SEM), Volume 2: Proceedings of the Seventh International Workshop on Semantic Evaluation (SemEval 2013)*, pages 543–548, Atlanta, Georgia, USA. Association for Computational Linguistics.

William Stigall, Md Abdullah Al Hafiz Khan, Dinesh Attota, Francis Nweke, and Yong Pei. 2024. Large Language Models Performance Comparison of Emotion and Sentiment Classification. In *Proceedings of the 2024 ACM Southeast Conference on ZZZ*, pages 60–68, Marietta GA USA. ACM.

Jörg Tiedemann and Santhosh Thottingal. 2020. OPUS-MT – Building open translation services for the World. In *Proceedings of the 22nd Annual Conference of the European Association for Machine Translation*, pages 479–480, Lisboa, Portugal. European Association for Machine Translation.

Tong Zhan, Chenxi Shi, Yadong Shi, Huixiang Li, and Yiyu Lin. 2024. Optimization Techniques for Sentiment Analysis Based on LLM (GPT-3).

Wenxuan Zhang, Yue Deng, Bing Liu, Sinno Jialin Pan, and Lidong Bing. 2023. Sentiment Analysis in the Era of Large Language Models: A Reality Check.

Seng Zian, Sameem Abdul Kareem, and Kasturi Dewi Varathan. 2021. An Empirical Evaluation of Stacked Ensembles With Different Meta-Learners in Imbalanced Classification. *IEEE Access*, 9:87434–87452.

HHUflauschig at GermEval 2025 Shared Task on Candy Speech Detection: Hybrid Approaches for Binary Classification and Span Typing

Wiebke Petersen, Lara Eulenpesch
Heinrich Heine Universität
Düsseldorf, Germany
{wiebke.petersen, lara.eulenpesch}@hhu.de

Abstract

We present our submission to the GermEval 2025 Shared Task on *Candy Speech Detection*, which focuses on identifying and analyzing affectionate language ('Flausch') in German social media comments. For Subtask 1 (binary classification of comments), our approach combines linguistically motivated features with large language models (LLMs). For Subtask 2 (fine-grained span-level detection and categorization), we employ a stacked architecture integrating specialized models for span identification and type classification. Our system achieves second place in Subtask 1 (out of 20 submitted models) and third in Subtask 2 (out of 16 models).

1 Introduction

While the detection of harmful language such as hate speech has received considerable attention in recent years, its positive counterpart remains largely unexplored. The *Candy Speech Detection Shared Task* by Clausen et al. (2025) addresses this gap by introducing the concept of *Flausch* (candy speech), i.e. positive, supportive expressions in online discourse, particularly in German-language YouTube comments.

The task comprises two subtasks: (1) binary classification of whether a comment contains candy speech, and (2) fine-grained span-level detection and categorization of candy speech expressions into one of ten predefined classes.

For Subtask 1, we combined finetuned BERT-based language models with linguistically motivated features such as sentiment and positive word counts. These were fed into a meta-classifier to leverage both learned representations and interpretable features.

For Subtask 2, we compared two strategies: (1) direct fine-tuning of a BERT token classifier with BIO labels, and (2) a two-step pipeline separating span detection and classification. Span detection was implemented via either a fine-tuned BERT model or a rule-based segmentation using dependency parses.

All models were evaluated on a held-out portion of the training data, with only the top-performing system for each subtask submitted to the competition. Our model ranked 2nd in Subtask 1 (out of 20 submissions) and 3rd in Subtask 2 (16 submissions).

2 Related Work

The detection and classification of harmful or toxic content on social media, particularly hate speech, has been extensively studied across multiple languages, including German (e.g., Struß et al., 2019). A wide range of methods have been applied to this task, from keyword-based and tf-idf approaches to shallow classifiers such as logistic regression, support vector machines (SVM), and multi-layer perceptrons. More recently, deep learning and especially transformer-based models have consistently achieved state-of-the-art results (Alkomah and Ma, 2022; Geetanjali and Kumar, 2025; Yin and Zubiaga, 2021).

The SemEval shared task on toxicity span detection (Pavlopoulos et al., 2021) extended toxicity detection and classification to span-level identification, which is closely related to Subtask 2 in our work. As in hate speech detection on the comment or sentence level, transformer models proved most effective for accurately locating toxic spans.

Compared to hate speech, positive or encouraging language such as the *Flausch* or *candy speech* targeted in this shared task has received considerably less attention in NLP. It has been the focus of shared tasks on *hope speech* for multilingual social media content (Chakravarthi et al., 2022; Kumaresan et al., 2023). In those tasks as well, transformer-based models, in combination with tf-idf, SVM and ensemble methods, achieved the strongest results.

Proceedings of the 21st Conference on Natural Language Processing (KONVENS), Volume 2: Workshops, pages 416–423, 2025

3 Data

The dataset released by the task organizers comprises 37,057 German-language social media comments annotated for Flausch-content. We used 90% of this data (33,351 comments) as our training set and held out 10% (3,706 comments) for internal evaluation across all experiments. Throughout the paper, we refer to this set as the *held-out test data*. The official test set provided during the competition consists of 9,229 comments.

For Subtask 1, each comment is labeled with a binary Flausch-label. In Subtask 2, fine-grained span annotations are provided for Flausch-expressing comments, using ten specific categories (e.g., *positive feedback*, *encouragement*, etc.). The official competition test set differs substantially from the training data. On average, comments in the test set are longer (68.6 vs. 58.3 tokens), contain a higher proportion of comments labeled as Flausch (41.3% vs. 29.1%), and include more annotated spans per comment (0.65 vs. 0.43). In addition, the distribution of span types in the test data diverges noticeably from that in the training set (see Appendix A for details).

4 Subtask 1

4.1 System Overview

Our approach to Subtask 1 combines transformer-based models with linguistic feature extraction and a meta-classification step. The following sections describe the key components of our system.

Data Preprocessing. To improve robustness and feature quality, we applied two preprocessing steps to the original German YouTube comments:
Spelling correction: Since YouTube comments often contain numerous typos, non-standard spelling, and informal language, we used a publicly available BART-based spelling correction model[1] to normalize spelling variants and reduce noise in the input data.
English translation: As many NLP models perform better in English or are only available for English, we translated the comments using the German-English model[2] by Tiedemann and Thottingal (2020) to enable cross-lingual feature extraction.

[1]oliverguhr/spelling-correction-german-base
[2]Helsinki-NLP/opus-mt-de-en

Fine-tuning BERT Models. We fine-tuned several transformer-based models for binary classification of candy speech across different comment variants. For the German data, we used the large German BERT model[3] by Chan et al. (2020) and the base German BERT model[4] by the dbmdz team and trained each on both the original and the spelling-corrected comments. In addition, we fine-tuned the large English RoBERTa model[5] by Liu et al. (2019) on the translated versions of the comments to leverage the potential of high-performing English-language models.

For fine-tuning, 15% from our internal training data (see Section 3) were set aside as validation set. All models were fine-tuned for 3 epochs using the Huggingface `Trainer` framework with a batch size of 16, a learning rate of $2 \cdot 10^{-5}$, and weight decay of 0.01. Model selection was based on the best evaluation F1 score on the validation set, with evaluation and logging performed every 500 training steps. All fine-tuned models are publicly available on Huggingface (see Appendix B.1).

Linguistic Features To complement our transformer-based models, we incorporated a set of linguistically motivated features. These include sentiment polarity and emotion scores, as well as various count-based surface indicators. Polarity scores, ranging from -1.0 (most negative) to 1.0 (most positive), were computed using `TextBlobDE` for the German comments (both original and spelling-corrected) and `TextBlob` for their English translations.[6]

Emotion probabilities for Ekman's six basic emotions (*joy*, *sadness*, *anger*, etc.) plus a *neutral* class were derived from the English translations using the RoBERTa-based model by Hartmann (2022).[7]

As a reference for common surface elements in candy speech, lists of positive words (and some short phrases), emojis, and emoticons were generated using ChatGPT-4o.[8] To derive a list of positive tokens, the word list was tokenized using the uncased base German BERT tokenizer.[9] Tokens occurring in more than 2% of non-Flausch-comments

[3]deepset/gbert-large
[4]dbmdz/bert-base-german-cased
[5]FacebookAI/roberta-large
[6]https://github.com/sloria/textblob
[7]j-hartmann/emotion-english-distilroberta-base
[8]Prompt used: "Gib mir drei sehr ausführliche Listen im csv Format für Wörter, Emoticons und Emojis, die häufig in positiven deutschen YouTube Kommentaren vorkommen. Keine Erklärungen oder ähnliches hinzufügen."
[9]dbmdz/bert-base-german-uncased

were excluded to improve specificity.

These resources were used to compute additional features: counts of positive words, positive tokens, emojis, and emoticons per comment. We also computed the ratio of positive tokens relative to total tokens. Finally, two additional surface-level features were included: the number of fully capitalized words and the number of characters repeated three or more times, both of which can be indicative of emphatic or emotionally expressive language often found in candy speech.

Meta-Classifier Finally, we experimented with several meta-classifiers from the `scikit-learn` library to combine the softmax outputs of the fine-tuned BERT models with the extracted linguistic features. To evaluate different combinations of input features and classifiers (e.g., logistic regression, random forest, SVM), we internally split our held-out test set into a training portion and a separate evaluation portion. Since differences in performance were marginal across classifier types, we opted for logistic regression due to its simplicity and interpretability.

4.2 Results

Table 1 summarizes the results of our fine-tuned transformer models on the held-out test data. The best model, `gbert-large` trained on original (uncorrected) comments, achieved an F1 score of 0.906. Performance trends show that (1) models trained on original input outperform those using corrected text, (2) large models outperform base models, and (3) German models perform better on original comments than the English model on translated ones.

Model	Input	Prec.	Recall	F1
`gbert-large`	orig.	0.881	**0.932**	**0.906**
`gbert-large`	corr.	**0.887**	0.906	0.896
`bert-base-german`	orig.	0.885	0.884	0.885
`bert-base-german`	corr.	0.881	0.879	0.880
`roberta-large`	transl.	0.885	0.865	0.875

Table 1: Precision, recall, and F1-score of fine-tuned transformer models on different input variants (original comment, spelling corrected, translated) on held-out test data (Subtask 1).

To enhance performance, we trained a logistic regression meta-classifier combining BERT softmax scores with linguistic features (Table 2). It turns out that combining BERT softmax scores with the additional features yields a clear improvement over using the linguistic features alone, and also outperforms the best individual BERT model. The strongest performance was achieved using only the softmax scores of the best-performing BERT model (`gbert-large`), all sentiment scores (polarity and Ekman's emotions), and positive word/token statistics. This feature configuration was used in our final competition submission.

Features	Prec.	Rec.	F1
all sentiments (Ekman + polar.)	0.754	0.519	0.615
all non-BERT features	0.785	0.621	0.694
all features (incl. BERT)	0.936	0.927	0.932
all BERT features	**0.944**	0.908	0.926
`gbert-large` comment + all non-BERT features	0.920	**0.947**	0.933
`gbert-large` comment + all sentiments + positive word count + positive token count + positive token ratio (∗)	0.929	**0.947**	**0.938**

Table 2: Performance of logistic regression meta-classifier with different feature combinations on our held-out test data. Submitted model marked with (∗).

On the official competition test set, the final model achieved a precision of 0.900, recall of 0.875, and F1 score of 0.887 – slightly below our held-out results but still strong. Our system ranked second out of 20 submissions for Subtask 1. The drop in performance likely reflects distributional differences between training and competition data (see Section 3) and a non-ideal selection of held-out test data (see Section 6).

5 Subtask 2

5.1 System Overview

We approach Subtask 2 by a single-step model that performs joint span detection and classification with a token classifier as well as by two-step approaches that decouple span detection and classification.

1-step model (`flausch-span-end-to-end`). This model is based on `gbert-large` and fine-tuned using the BIO tagging scheme with type-specific labels (`B-type`, `I-type`, `O`), where `type` corresponds to one of the ten Flausch-categories. Training and evaluation are performed on the same splits as in Subtask 1, with 15% of the internal training data held out for validation. The model is optimized for the F1-score using standard parameters and an evaluation frequency of 500 steps. Performance scores of this model are given in Table 3.

Dependency-based 2-step model (`spacy 2-step`). Our first two-step model combines rule-based span segmentation based on dependency parsing with a learned classifier for span categorization. In the first step, each comment is parsed using spaCy's dependency parser. Span segmentation is then performed by assigning each token to the root of its syntactic subtree. A token is considered a span root if it is either the sentence's syntactic root or has a dependency relation such as 'reported speech' (rs), 'coordinating conjunction' (cd), or 'junctor' (ju). For each token, we recursively follow its syntactic head until a span root is reached.[10] Tokens sharing the same span root and occurring consecutively in the comment are grouped into a span.

In the second step, the extracted spans are classified using a `gbert-large`-based sequence classifier (`span-classifier-with-none`), trained to assign one of ten fine-grained Flausch categories or the additional `not-flausch` class. The training and validation data are based on the same split used in Subtask 1 and are constructed as follows: (1) For comments annotated as containing Flausch (`flausch: yes`), we label the gold Flausch spans with their respective subtype. The remaining contiguous sequences of tokens between these gold spans are treated as separate spans and labeled `not-flausch`. (2) For comments labeled as not containing Flausch, we apply our spaCy-based span segmentation method and label all resulting spans as `not-flausch`.

The classifier is fine-tuned to optimize macro-F1, using standard hyperparameters and an evaluation interval of 1000 steps. On our held-out test set, the model achieves a weighted F1 score of 0.95, but a substantially lower macro F1 score of 0.66. This discrepancy reflects the extreme label imbalance in the training data (e.g., 92 *sympathy*-spans and 55,501 *not-flausch*-spans).

BERT-based 2-step model (1st variant, `gbert 2-step`). In this approach, Flausch-spans are detected in the first step using a dedicated span detector model (`span-detector`). The model is fine-tuned with BIO labels indicating generic span boundaries: `B-span`, `I-span`, and `O`. The training and validation data are the same as in the single-step model, with labels converted accordingly. The span detector is fine-tuned with the same hyperparameters as the single-step model, except for a longer evaluation interval. It reaches an F1 score of 0.77 on our held-out test data.

In the second step, detected Flausch-spans are classified by a multinomial sequence classifier (`span-classifier`) into one of the ten Flausch-types. This classifier is trained on gold spans from the training data and uses the same hyperparameters as the classifier `span-classifier-with-none` in the previous paragraph, but with an evaluation every 500 steps. On our held-out test data it achieves a weighted average F1 score of 0.92 and a macro F1 score of 0.78.

BERT-based 2-step model (2nd variant, `gbert 2-step + not-flausch`). This model combines the previous two-step variants. Span detection is performed using the trained Flausch-span detector `span-detector`, and classification is done using the more general span classifier `span-classifier-with-none`, which is able to assign the label `not-flausch`. The rationale is that the classifier can correct for Flausch-span detection errors by rejecting non-Flausch-spans.

5.2 Results

For Subtask 2, we evaluated both end-to-end models and two-step pipelines. Table 3 summarizes the global results on our held-out evaluation set using three metrics:[11] *Strict* (exact match of span and type), *Span* (correct span regardless of type), and *Type* (correct type regardless of span boundaries).[12]

System	Strict	Span	Type
`flausch-span-end-to-end`	0.647	0.682	0.792
`gbert 2-step` (∗)	**0.728**	**0.769**	**0.833**
`gbert 2-step + not-flausch`	0.693	**0.769**	0.785
`spacy 2-step`	0.370	0.389	0.733

Table 3: Global evaluation results (Strict, Span, and Type-level F1) for Subtask 2 on held-out data. Submitted marked with (∗).

Our best performing system was a two-step BERT-based pipeline (`gbert 2-step`) with sep-

[10] In pseudo code:

```
function ROOT(token)
    if token.dep in ["ROOT", "rs", "cd", "ju"] then
        return token
    else
        return ROOT(token.head)
```

[11] Appendix C provides detailed per Flausch-type label results.

[12] Detailed results for the individual span detector and classifier models are provided in Appendix B.2.

arate span detection and classification modules. It achieved a strict F1 score of 0.728 on our held-out data, outperforming the end-to-end baseline (`flausch-span-end-to-end`) by 8 points. Submitted to the official competition, this model attained a strict F1 of 0.615, a type F1 of 0.766, and a span F1 of 0.668, ranking third among 16 submissions. The drop in performance can be attributed to considerable differences in the Flausch-type distribution between training and test data (see Section A), as well as to the lack of video-level stratification in the held-out test set (see Section 6).

Introducing an additional `not-flausch` label for rejecting non-Flausch spans (`gbert 2-step + not-flausch`) did not improve span-level results and even degraded type-level accuracy. The unbalanced training data, with an overrepresentation of `not-flausch` examples, reduced the model's ability to assign correct Flausch subtypes, without yielding gains in span detection accuracy.

Finally, a rule-based approach using SpaCy dependency parsing for span segmentation produced comparatively weaker results. While conceptually appealing, we believe this method could be enhanced through a more detailed error analysis and by refining the set of rules used for decomposition of the dependency trees.

6 Limitations

Our approach faces several limitations that affect generalization and evaluation reliability:

First, the class distributions in the official training and test sets differ substantially, particularly in the proportion and type of Flausch-comments (see Appendix A). This mismatch limits comparability between held-out and final test performance and likely contributed to the performance drop on the competition set in both subtasks.

Second, our held-out evaluation set was created by randomly sampling 10% of annotated comments without stratifying by video. As a result, comments from the same YouTube videos may appear in both training and evaluation sets, enabling models to exploit video-specific associations (e.g., linking certain creators such as "Die Lochis" to higher probabilities of Flausch-speech) rather than learning generalizable patterns. This setup introduces a form of data leakage and may lead to overly optimistic performance estimates. A more robust design would reserve entire videos for evaluation.

Third, we did not perform a systematic error analysis across models, which limits our understanding of typical failure modes. This is particularly critical for the rule-based span segmentation using SpaCy dependency parsing. The current rule set is heuristic and lacks empirical validation. A detailed qualitative analysis of typical errors (e.g., oversegmentation, incorrect boundary detection) could inform improvements. While we believe this linguistically motivated method holds promise, it currently lacks empirical tuning and optimization.

7 Conclusion

Our submission[13] demonstrates the value of combining linguistic features with LLMs and of structuring the problem into modular components. For Subtask 1, integrating linguistically motivated features led to clear improvements over LLMs alone. For Subtask 2, a two-step pipeline separating span detection and classification outperformed the end-to-end approach. While rule-based span detection using dependency structures showed limited success, we believe that this line of work holds promise and could benefit substantially from more targeted error analysis and refined heuristics.

References

Fatimah Alkomah and Xiaogang Ma. 2022. A literature review of textual hate speech detection methods and datasets. *Information*, 13(6).

Bharathi Raja Chakravarthi, Vigneshwaran Muralidaran, Ruba Priyadharshini, Subalalitha Cn, John McCrae, Miguel Ángel García, Salud María Jiménez-Zafra, Rafael Valencia-García, Prasanna Kumaresan, Rahul Ponnusamy, Daniel García-Baena, and José García-Díaz. 2022. Overview of the shared task on hope speech detection for equality, diversity, and inclusion. In *Proceedings of the Second Workshop on Language Technology for Equality, Diversity and Inclusion*, pages 378–388, Dublin, Ireland. Association for Computational Linguistics.

Branden Chan, Stefan Schweter, and Timo Möller. 2020. German's next language model. In *Proceedings of the 28th International Conference on Computational Linguistics*, pages 6788–6796, Barcelona, Spain (Online). International Committee on Computational Linguistics.

Yulia Clausen, Tatjana Scheffler, and Michael Wiegand. 2025. Overview of the GermEval 2025 Shared Task on Candy Speech Detection. In *Proceedings of the 21st Conference on Natural Language Processing*

[13]Code available at https://github.com/WiebkePetersen/GermevalFlausch

(*KONVENS 2025*): *Workshops*, Hildesheim, Germany. ACL.

Geetanjali and Mohit Kumar. 2025. Exploring hate speech detection: challenges, resources, current research and future directions. *Multimedia Tools and Applications*.

Jochen Hartmann. 2022. Emotion English DistilRoBERTa-base. https://huggingface.co/j-hartmann/emotion-english-distilroberta-base/.

Prasanna Kumar Kumaresan, Bharathi Raja Chakravarthi, Subalalitha Cn, Miguel Ángel García-Cumbreras, Salud María Jiménez Zafra, José Antonio García-Díaz, Rafael Valencia-García, Momchil Hardalov, Ivan Koychev, Preslav Nakov, Daniel García-Baena, and Kishore Kumar Ponnusamy. 2023. Overview of the shared task on hope speech detection for equality, diversity, and inclusion. In *Proceedings of the Third Workshop on Language Technology for Equality, Diversity and Inclusion*, pages 47–53, Varna, Bulgaria. INCOMA Ltd., Shoumen, Bulgaria.

Yinhan Liu, Myle Ott, Naman Goyal, Jingfei Du, Mandar Joshi, Danqi Chen, Omer Levy, Mike Lewis, Luke Zettlemoyer, and Veselin Stoyanov. 2019. RoBERTa: A robustly optimized bert pretraining approach.

John Pavlopoulos, Jeffrey Sorensen, Léo Laugier, and Ion Androutsopoulos. 2021. SemEval-2021 task 5: Toxic spans detection. In *Proceedings of the 15th International Workshop on Semantic Evaluation (SemEval-2021)*, pages 59–69, Online. Association for Computational Linguistics.

Julia Maria Struß, Melanie Siegel, Josef Ruppenhofer, Michael Wiegand, and Manfred Klenner. 2019. Overview of GermEval task 2, 2019 shared task on the identification of offensive language. In German Society for Computational Linguistics, editor, *Proceedings of the 15th Conference on Natural Language Processing (KONVENS) 2019*, pages 354–365. s.a., Nürnberg/Erlangen.

Jörg Tiedemann and Santhosh Thottingal. 2020. OPUS-MT — Building open translation services for the world. In *Proceedings of the 22nd Annual Conferenec of the European Association for Machine Translation (EAMT)*, Lisbon, Portugal.

Wenjie Yin and Arkaitz Zubiaga. 2021. Towards generalisable hate speech detection: a review on obstacles and solutions. *PeerJ Computer Science*, 7:e598.

A Data Statistics

This section provides detailed statistics on the training, held-out test, and competition test sets used in our experiments.

Comment Statistics (Task 1)

Dataset	Flausch Ratio	Avg. Length
Own Train	29.2%	58.3 tokens
Own Test	28.2%	59.0 tokens
Competition Test	41.3%	68.6 tokens

Table 4: Flausch ratios and comment lengths across datasets (Task 1).

Span Statistics (Task 2)

Dataset	Spans per Comment	Avg. Length
Own Train	0.43	28.84 tokens
Own Test	0.41	28.14 tokens
Competition Test	0.65	26.30 tokens

Table 5: Span frequency and average span length per dataset (Task 2).

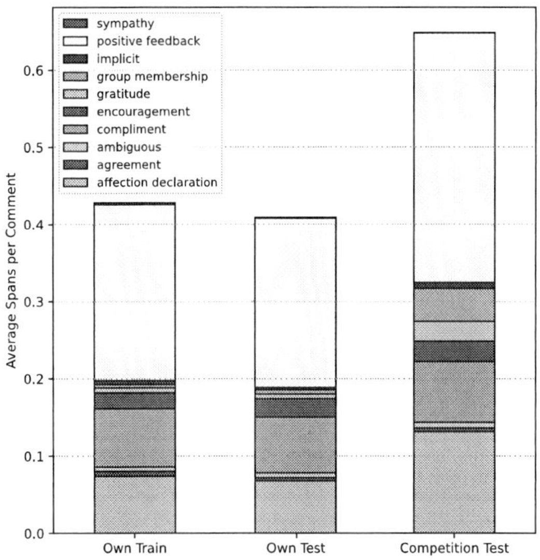

Figure 1: Distribution of fine-grained span types in each dataset. The total height of each bar corresponds to the number of spans per comment.

B Fine-tuned LLMs

B.1 LLMs for Subtask 1

The LLMs finetuned for Subtask 1 are binary classifiers for Flausch-comments. The performances are given in Table 1.

bert-base-german original https://huggingface.co/Wiebke/results_flausch_classification_bert-base-german-cased_comment

bert-base-german spelling corrected https://huggingface.co/Wiebke/results_flausch_classification_bert-base-german-cased_spelling_corrected

gbert-large original https://huggingface.co/Wiebke/results_flausch_classification_gbert-large_comment

gbert-large spelling corrected https://huggingface.co/Wiebke/results_flausch_classification_gbert-large_spelling_corrected

roberta-large translated https://huggingface.co/Wiebke/results_flausch_classification_roberta-large_translated

B.2 LLMs for Subtask 2

flausch-span-end-to-end The `flausch-span-end-to-end` model jointly predicts Flausch-span boundaries and their corresponding types in a single step. It performs reasonably well on all metrics, achieving an F1 of 0.647 (strict), 0.682 (span), and 0.792 (type) on the held-out set. However, performance degrades substantially on the competition test set (strict: 0.544), likely due to domain differences. https://huggingface.co/Wiebke/flausch_span_gbert-large_all

span-detector The `span-detector` model identifies Flausch-span locations. It reaches an F1 of 0.769 (span) and 0.768 (strict) on the held-out data, and 0.668 strict F1 on the competition test set. https://huggingface.co/Wiebke/flausch_span_gbert-large_non_labeled_spans

span-classifier The `span-classifier` takes gold Flausch-span boundaries and classifies each span into one of the ten fine-grained types. It achieves a macro F1 of 0.78 on the held-out set and 0.71 on the competition test set. Table 6 shows per-class results on both datasets. https://huggingface.co/Wiebke/results_flausch_classification_gbert-large_span_classifier

span-classifier-with-none The `span-classifier-with-none` variant includes an explicit `not` class for negative examples and operates on a mixture of annotated and non-annotated spans. While it performs lower overall (macro F1: 0.66), it allows for end-to-end inference when no gold spans are given. Table 7 shows per-class results. https://huggingface.co/Wiebke/task2_flausch_classification_gbert-large_span_classifier_with_nonspan

Label	Held-out F1	Comp. F1
affection declaration	0.91	0.88
agreement	0.94	0.82
ambiguous	0.57	0.61
compliment	0.90	0.83
encouragement	0.92	0.90
gratitude	0.93	0.98
group membership	0.88	0.63
implicit	0.36	0.29
positive feedback	0.95	0.92
sympathy	0.44	0.22

Table 6: Per-label F1 scores for the `span-classifier` model on held-out and competition test sets.

Label	F1 Score	Support
affection declaration	0.85	252
agreement	0.27	16
ambiguous	0.34	22
compliment	0.84	267
encouragement	0.88	87
gratitude	0.75	23
group membership	0.76	21
implicit	0.47	11
not	0.98	6494
positive feedback	0.85	813
sympathy	0.31	5

Table 7: Per-label F1 scores and support counts for the `span-classifier-with-none` model on span data derived from held-out test data.

C Subtask 2: per Flausch-type label results

Label	flausch-span-end-to-end	gbert 2-step	gbert 2-step + not	spacy 2-step
positive feedback	0.700	**0.760**	0.756	0.403
affection declaration	0.631	0.734	**0.747**	0.441
group membership	0.421	**0.615**	**0.615**	0.171
encouragement	0.605	0.728	**0.754**	0.239
compliment	0.597	**0.718**	0.710	0.317
ambiguous	0.383	**0.419**	0.387	0.324
implicit	0.125	**0.182**	0.133	0.133
sympathy	0.000	0.143	**0.182**	0.154
agreement	0.091	0.138	**0.174**	0.000
gratitude	0.744	0.800	**0.837**	0.235

Table 8: Strict-level F1 scores per Flausch-type label for Subtask 2 on held-out test data.

Label	flausch-span-end-to-end	gbert 2-step	gbert 2-step + not	spacy 2-step
positive feedback	0.877	**0.890**	0.877	0.781
affection declaration	0.843	**0.870**	0.866	0.784
group membership	0.788	**0.800**	0.765	0.581
encouragement	0.875	0.859	**0.893**	0.874
compliment	0.856	**0.877**	0.867	0.800
ambiguous	**0.550**	0.465	0.387	0.324
implicit	0.250	0.364	**0.400**	0.267
sympathy	**0.222**	0.154	0.182	0.154
agreement	**0.182**	0.138	0.174	0.000
gratitude	0.900	0.884	**0.905**	0.720

Table 9: Type-level F1 scores per Flausch-type label for Subtask 2 on held-out test data.

NLP_Augsburg_04 at GermEval 2025 Shared Task on Candy Speech Detection: The Role of Surface Cues in Candy Speech Classification

Evren Ataş* **Malika Abitova*** **Fabio Mariani**
evren.atas@uni-a.de malika.abitova@uni-a.de fabio.mariani@uni-a.de
University of Augsburg

Abstract

With the rise of social media, the automatic detection of affective or candy speech—defined as language expressing affection, support, or positivity—has gained increasing relevance. This project investigates the identification of candy speech in German YouTube comments as part of the GermEval shared task on Candy Speech Detection, which comprises two subtasks: (1) Coarse-Grained Classification and (2) Fine-Grained Classification. We fine-tune a German BERT model for both tasks, enabling classification at the comment level and span identification at the token level. Our analysis indicates that the binary classification model (subtask 1) performs particularly well on comments featuring surface-level cues, such as emojis and hashtags. Nonetheless, both models exhibit limitations when processing bilingual content, non-standard orthography, and sarcastic language.

1 Introduction

With the rise of social networks, the detection of affective or candy speech—language expressing affection, support, or positivity—has become increasingly relevant (Clausen and Scheffler, 2025). Such detection plays a critical role in sentiment analysis, content moderation, and the development of emotionally intelligent systems.

This paper describes our submission to the GermEval 2025 Shared Task on Candy Speech Detection, which focuses on identifying candy speech in German YouTube comments (Clausen et al., 2025), conducted as part of an introductory course on natural language processing (NLP). The shared task consists of two subtasks:

- **Subtask 1**: Coarse-Grained Classification (whether a given comment is candy speech or not)
- **Subtask 2**: Fine-Grained Classification (identifying the span of each candy speech expression in a comment and assigning it to one of the ten predefined categories)

As participants in this challenge, we fine-tuned German BERT-based models tailored to each subtask and submitted our results under the group name nlp-augsburg-04. Our models rank 12th in Subtask 1 and 7th in Subtask 2 of the shared task. Notably, the binary classifier demonstrates particularly strong performance on comments featuring surface-level affective cues such as emojis, heart symbols, and expressive hashtags, which emerge as highly predictive indicators of candy speech. At the same time, both models struggle with more nuanced or unconventional expressions, including bilingual content, non-standard orthography, and sarcastic language.

2 Related Work

Understanding emotions and opinions in text is a central task in NLP, with applications in social media analysis, customer feedback, and online discourse. Early approaches relied on sentiment lexicons, which are predefined lists of positive and negative terms. However, these methods often fall short when faced with context-dependent language, figurative expressions, or sarcasm (Liu, 2012).

Transformer-based models such as BERT (Devlin et al., 2019) have been widely adopted for tasks such as hate speech detection. This area of research has gained importance due to the growing need to automatically moderate harmful content on social media platforms, where toxicity can escalate into broader

*Equal contribution.

Proceedings of the 21st Conference on Natural Language Processing (KONVENS), Volume 2: Workshops, pages 424–428, 2025

social or political tensions (Mnassri et al., 2022). For example, (Mazari et al., 2023) proposes a multi-class framework that distinguishes among six types of hate speech, including threats, insults, and identity-based abuse. Their findings underscore the complexity of automatically detecting nuanced forms of hate speech.

GermEval 2021 (Risch et al., 2021) introduced a subtask focused on classifying engaging comments, expanding the scope of sentiment analysis beyond the identification of harmful content. Candy speech detection continues in this direction by targeting emotionally supportive language, such as expressions of affection, praise, or encouragement. Unlike conventional sentiment classification based on positive or negative polarity, this task demands a more nuanced and context-aware understanding of affective intent.

3 Dataset and Annotation

The annotated data for training and evaluation originate from the GermEval 2025 Shared Task on Candy Speech Detection, which provided a corpus of German YouTube comments partitioned into three subsets

- Training set: Contains 37,058 manually labeled comments per subtask, representing approximately 80% of the full dataset.
- Trial set: Comprises 306 manually labelled comments per subtask (approximately 0.8% of the training set), intended for small-scale experiments and preliminary testing.
- Test set: Contains 9,230 comments (approximately 20% of the total dataset). This set is used for blind evaluation, with predictions submitted to the organizers for assessment.

Subtask 1 is framed as a binary classification problem, where each comment is labeled as either containing candy speech or not. Subtask 2 requires identifying the exact span of each candy speech expression and assigning it to one of ten predefined categories. For this purpose, we convert the provided span annotations into token-level labels using the BIO tagging scheme, which assigns each token a label indicating whether it marks the **B**eginning, **I**nside, or **O**utside of a candy speech span, along with the corresponding span type (Fritzler et al., 2019). For example, in the sentence "Das ist ein super Kommentar!", the token "super" would be labelled as B-positive feedback, and "Kommentar" as I-positive feedback, while the other tokens would receive O.[1]

4 Models

For both subtasks, we employ the `bert-base-german-cased` model, accessed through the Hugging Face Transformers library (Wolf et al., 2020).[2] The model is pre-trained on large-scale German corpora.

Subtask 1 is implemented as a sequence classification task, where BERT is fine-tuned with a classification head to assign a binary label indicating the presence or absence of candy speech in each comment.

Subtask 2 is implemented as a token classification task, where BERT is fine-tuned with a token-level classification head to identify and label spans of candy speech using BIO-encoded tags corresponding to ten fine-grained categories.

The training data are split into 90% for training and 10% for evaluation. Both models are trained using a batch size of 16. Based on initial development experiments with varying training durations, we select the final models after three epochs of training for each subtask. All models are trained and evaluated using the `Trainer` API provided by Hugging Face, and inference is performed via the `pipeline` interface.[3]

5 Experiments and Results

This section presents the performance of our models during development and on the official test set, evaluated using standard classification metrics: precision, recall, and F1

[1] Translated into English as: "That is a super comment!".

[2] `https://huggingface.co/google-bert/bert-base-german-cased`

[3] Trained models available on the Hugging Face Model Hub: Subtask 1 (Coarse-Grained Classification) `https://huggingface.co/mmllk/uni_a_nlp_model_t1_v2_group04`; Subtask 2 (Fine-Grained Classification) `https://huggingface.co/mmllk/uni_a_nlp_model_t2_v2_group04`.

score. During development, we initially evaluated model performance using the provided trial set. However, we later discovered that this set overlaps with the training data, rendering it unsuitable for unbiased validation. As a result, the development results reported below likely overestimate true generalization performance. We include them here for completeness, but rely on the official test set for conclusive evaluation.

5.1 Subtask 1: Coarse-Grained Classification

Subtask 1 addresses on a binary classification task, aiming to determine whether a comment contains candy speech. Table 1 reports the performance of our model on both the trial set and the blind test set released by the task organizers.

Data	Recall	Precision	F1
Trial set	66.5%	96.5%	78.7%
Test set	77.8%	90.3%	83.6%

Table 1: Performance of the Subtask 1 model on the trial and test sets.

Surprisingly, although the trial set was partially seen during training and therefore biased, the model performs better on the official test set. Precision decreases slightly, which is expected on unseen data, but recall increases sharply, meaning the model identifies a larger proportion of candy speech instances in the test set, at only a small cost to precision.

5.2 Subtask 2: Fine-Grained Classification

Subtask 2 focuses on a sequence labeling task, where the goal is to identify and annotate spans of candy speech within each comment. Table 2 shows the model's performance on the trial and test sets, evaluated using strict metrics that require both the correct label and exact span boundaries.

Data	Recall	Precision	F1
Trial set	77.4%	46.1%	57.8%
Test set	54.3%	24.0%	33.4%

Table 2: Strict evaluation results for Subtask 2 on the trial and test sets.

To better understand the model's strengths and weaknesses on the test set, Table 3 reports separate results for span boundaries detection (ignoring label correctness) and type classification (ignoring span boundaries).

Aspect	Recall	Precision	F1
Type	80.1%	35.5%	49.2%
Span	59.4%	26.3%	36.5%

Table 3: Evaluation results on Subtask 2 test set, showing separate performance for type classification and span detection.

The results for Subtask 2 highlight low precision in both span detection and type classification, indicating that the model frequently over-predicts candy speech spans. Despite this, recall remains high for type classification, suggesting the model is often correct in recognizing the presence of candy speech, even if it fails to localize it precisely.

6 Analysis and Insights

Candy speech detection appears as a nuanced challenge. While our BERT-based models successfully capture many lexical and surface-level patterns, they exhibit persistent difficulties with ambiguity, sarcasm, and informal language.

We observed two recurring types of classification errors. False positives often occurred in humorous or sarcastic comments, such as "XD," where features like emojis or exaggerated punctuation led the model to incorrectly predict candy speech. In contrast, false negatives were more frequent in comments expressing affection through informal or creatively spelled language, such as "lieeebbbe dicchh." Linguistic elements commonly found in comments labeled as candy speech include personal pronouns (e.g., "ich," "du," "ihr") and intensifiers (e.g., "mehr," "voll").

To examine the impact of surface-level cues, Table 4 reports Subtask 1 test set performance across comments containing emojis, heart emojis, or hashtags. The "Plain" category includes comments that lack these explicit markers.

Among the 1,437 comments in the test set that included emojis, 990 were labeled as candy speech, and the model correctly identi-

Category	Total	Candy Speech	Candy S. %	True Pos.	Rec.	Prec.	F1
Emoji	1437	990	68.9%	751	75.9%	93.6%	83.8%
Heart	539	487	90.4%	374	76.8%	97.9%	86.1%
Hashtag	316	294	93.0%	173	58.8%	99.4%	73.9%
Plain	7676	2721	35.4%	2175	79.9%	89.1%	84.3%

Table 4: Model performance across different comment types in Subtask 1 (binary classification, test set).

fied 751 of them, yielding a precision of 93.6%. This indicates that the model is highly responsive to this feature when detecting emotional content. In particular, the model shows strong sensitivity to heart emojis, where candy speech occurs in 90.4% of the comments containing at least one such emoji, and the model achieves its highest F1 score (86.1%) with near-perfect precision (97.9%). In contrast, for comments containing hashtags, where candy speech is also common (93.0%), recall drops to 58.8% despite a precision of 99.4%, suggesting that while hashtags are a strong indicator of candy speech, the model remains highly selective in such cases.

Overall, these findings reinforce the view that candy speech detection is shaped by a tension between surface cues and linguistic subtlety. The model performs reliably when explicit emotional markers are present but remains cautious in their absence, sometimes failing to capture more implicit or creatively expressed forms of affection.

7 Conclusion and Outlook

Candy speech detection presents a complex challenge that combines lexical patterns with contextual subtlety. In Subtask 1 (ranked 12th), surface-level cues such as emojis and heart symbols had a clear positive impact on model performance. In Subtask 2 (ranked 7th), despite difficulties with precise span boundaries, the model achieved notably high recall in identifying the types of candy speech spans.

These findings suggest that while surface markers are useful, a deeper understanding of informal, bilingual, and implicit expressions is essential. Future work should focus on more diverse data, better handling of linguistic variability, and improved span localization.

Tackling this task further will require models that not only recognize patterns but also grasp the fluid, playful, and often ambiguous ways people express emotion online.

References

Yulia Clausen and Tatjana Scheffler. 2025. Annotating candy speech in German YouTube comments. In *Proceedings of the 19th Linguistic Annotation Workshop (LAW-XIX-2025)*, pages 264–269, Vienna, Austria. Association for Computational Linguistics.

Yulia Clausen, Tatjana Scheffler, and Michael Wiegand. 2025. Overview of the germeval 2025 shared task on candy speech detection. In *Proceedings of the GermEval 2025 Shared Task on Candy Speech Detection*, Konvens, Hildesheim, Germany.

Jacob Devlin, Ming-Wei Chang, Kenton Lee, and Kristina Toutanova. 2019. BERT: Pre-training of deep bidirectional transformers for language understanding. In *Proceedings of the 2019 Conference of the North American Chapter of the Association for Computational Linguistics: Human Language Technologies, Volume 1 (Long and Short Papers)*, pages 4171–4186, Minneapolis, Minnesota. Association for Computational Linguistics.

Alexander Fritzler, Varvara Logacheva, and Maksim Kretov. 2019. Few-shot classification in named entity recognition task. In *Proceedings of the 34th ACM/SIGAPP Symposium on Applied Computing*, SAC '19, page 993–1000. ACM.

Bing Liu. 2012. *Sentiment Analysis and Opinion Mining*. Morgan & Claypool Publishers.

Ahmed Cherif Mazari, Nesrine Boudoukhani, and Abdelhamid Djeffal. 2023. Bert-based ensemble learning for multi-aspect hate speech detection. *Cluster Computing*, 27(1):325–339.

Khouloud Mnassri, Praboda Rajapaksha, Reza Farahbakhsh, and Noel Crespi. 2022. Bert-based ensemble approaches for hate speech detection. In *GLOBECOM 2022 - 2022 IEEE Global Communications Conference*, pages 4649–4654.

Julian Risch, Anke Stoll, Lena Wilms, and Michael Wiegand. 2021. Overview of the GermEval 2021 shared task on the identification of toxic, engaging, and fact-claiming comments. In *Proceedings of the GermEval 2021 Shared Task on the Identification of Toxic, Engaging, and Fact-Claiming Comments*, pages 1–12, Duesseldorf, Germany. Association for Computational Linguistics.

Thomas Wolf, Lysandre Debut, Victor Sanh, Julien Chaumond, Clement Delangue, Anthony Moi, Pierric Cistac, Tim Rault, Remi Louf, Morgan Funtowicz, Joe Davison, Sam Shleifer, Patrick von Platen, Clara Ma, Yacine Jernite, Julien Plu, Canwen Xu, Teven Le Scao, Sylvain Gugger, and 3 others. 2020. Transformers: State-of-the-art natural language processing. In *Proceedings of the 2020 Conference on Empirical Methods in Natural Language Processing: System Demonstrations*, pages 38–45. Association for Computational Linguistics.

NLPSuedwestfalen at GermEval 2025 Shared Task on Candy Speech Detection: Binary Classification of German YouTube Comments using Transformer Models

Emir Bradaric
bradaric.emir@fh-swf.de

Manuel-Alexander Falk
falk.manuel-alexander@fh-swf.de

Anna Hoff
hoff.anna@fh-swf.de

University of Applied Sciences Suedwestfalen

Abstract

This paper presents our solution to Subtask 1 of the GermEval 2025 Candy Speech Detection shared task, focusing on binary classification for identifying the presence of candy speech in German YouTube comments. The given comments were preprocessed, tokenized and then used so we could fine-tune multiple pretrained models (Logistic Regression, BiLSTM, German BERT, and German RoBERTa) using the Hugging Face Trainer API. We systematically evaluated traditional and advanced NLP models, including logistic regression, recurrent neural networks, and transformer-based models such as German BERT and RoBERTa. Our final model, based on fine-tuned German RoBERTa with targeted data augmentation and class-balanced loss, achieved a top F1 score of 0.93. We discuss the impact of emojis and outline future directions for further improving candy speech detection.

1 Introduction

To classify user text is a critical task in natural language processing. Transformer models like BERT have emerged as state of the art for these problems. Especially for binary classification task like detecting candy speech a well working model can be quickly generated out of a German BERT base model, given a good data sample set to train on, as shown in this paper. Candy speech refers to positive, supportive, and uplifting expressions frequently used within online communities. Unlike hate speech, candy speech enhances user interactions positively, promoting supportive digital environments. This task is crucial for automatic moderation, user engagement analysis, and understanding online behavior dynamics.

The GermEval 2025 shared subtask 1 introduced a specific binary classification problem, requiring systems to determine the presence of candy speech in YouTube comments (Clausen et al., 2025). This paper summarizes our comparative evaluation of various machine learning approaches, detailing preprocessing methods, model selection, and result analyses.

2 Related Work

The area of candy speech detection, a relatively new subfield, complements existing research on hate speech detection and sentiment analysis. Sentiment analysis historically used simpler machine learning models such as bag-of-words and logistic regression (Pang and Lee, 2008). More recent approaches have successfully applied neural network architectures, such as CNNs and BiLSTMs, for sentiment classification (Kim, 2014; Hochreiter and Schmidhuber, 1997).

Transformer models, particularly BERT and RoBERTa, have significantly improved NLP benchmarks across various text classification tasks. For German language tasks, German BERT and multilingual RoBERTa models have achieved state-of-the-art results in sentiment analysis and hate speech detection tasks (Krause et al., 2020; de Vries et al., 2019; Conneau et al., 2020).

Proceedings of the 21st Conference on Natural Language Processing (KONVENS), Volume 2: Workshops, pages 429–432, 2025

3 Task and Data

The provided dataset consists of German YouTube comments, which are categorized into two classes indicating the presence or absence of candy speech. The dataset is divided into training (10,000 comments), development (2,000 comments), and test sets (3,000 comments), with approximately 30% candy speech prevalence. All files are .cvs files.

The training data itself is split into two parts: first, the file comments.csv, which contains comments from the users and unique identifiers; second, the file task1.csv, which contains the same unique identifiers and the ground truth indicating whether a given text is considered candy speech.

4 Methodology

Our preprocessing approach included:

- Text normalization (lowercasing, removing elongated words, labeling blank comments)
- Emoji conversion to textual descriptions
- Punctuation normalization

As all blank comments are considered not candy speech according to the ground truth, we have decided to keep them in, since this presents a clear pattern, our classifier can pick up on.

While there were some outliers in terms of length most comments were very short with a mean length of 11.59 characters.

After exploration of the dataset was finished, we tokenized the dataset, though we limited the length of each comment to a maximum of 512 tokens, which would fit most comments. We executed a stratified split of the dataset, reserving 80 % for training and 20 % for testing, while maintaining equal class proportions.

We tested the following models:

- Logistic Regression: Using TF-IDF vectorization with n-grams (unigrams, bigrams).
- Bidirectional LSTM (BiLSTM): Implemented with pretrained fastText embeddings.
- German BERT: fine-tuned transformer-based model with an additional fully connected classification layer.
- German RoBERTa: like German BERT but leveraging RoBERTa's optimized pre-training and fine-tuning protocols.

Hyperparameters such as learning rates (1e-5 to 3e-5), batch size (16), and weight decay (0.01) were optimized via grid search. Additionally, focal loss was integrated to handle class imbalance more effectively.

The training of the models themselves was done using the hugging face trainer API. A batch size of 256 was selected given GPU memory constraints and 500 warmup_steps were made. The weight decay was set to 0.01. The number of epochs we trained the models on was also part of our experimentation and not limited to a fixed number.

5 Experiments and Results

For the first run, the model bert-base-german-case and its tokenizer was used. One problem with this approach was that emojis, which are featured quite heavily in the comments are all tokenized into the same token therefore, some meaning is lost to the classifier. The "emoji" library in python to turn emojis into emoji description and tokenizing those was also tried out. A further experiment was freezing the upper layers of bert model and only letting the head classifier be trained instead of the entire model. In the end none of these methods seemed to yield any significant improvements over just letting the model train for a short time without any changes or additions. The exact F1 scores for each different version of model, with and without, freezing and extra tokenization of emojis were not kept, so our results focus only on the stronger base versions.

The results on our self-compiled dataset are summarized below (see Table 1):

Model	Precision	Recall	F1
Logistic Regression	0.89	0.81	0.85
BiLSTM	0.90	0.84	0.87
German BERT (submission 2)	0.92	0.88	0.90
German RoBERTa (submission 1)	0.93	0.90	0.91
RoBERTa + augmentation + focal loss	0.92	0.95	0.93

Table 1: Results self-compiled dataset.

The logistic regression baseline offered simplicity and speed but struggled with recall. The BiLSTM improved generalization to informal language, while transformer models significantly advanced overall performance. The RoBERTa model with data augmentation and focal loss optimization provided the best precision-recall trade-off, ultimately reaching an F1 score of 0.93 on the test dataset.

6 Discussion

The error analysis highlighted challenges posed by colloquial expressions, informal language, and emoji usage, often resulting in false negatives. False positives typically emerged from neutral comments with mildly supportive tones. Implementing data augmentation and focal loss notably improved model sensitivity towards nuanced candy speech expressions.

Potentially part of the problem with changing emojis into multi-character strings is that this produces multiple tokens instead of single tokens which are hard to interpret for the classifier.

There should still be a lot of meaning to be gained from the further integration of emojis into the classifier.

Model efficiency varied considerably, with logistic regression offering fast CPU-based predictions and transformers requiring GPU resources. Practical applications might benefit from hybrid systems combining fast pre-filtering models with transformer-based models for ambiguous cases.

Our results demonstrate that even with minimal fine tuning, a BERT model can be quickly trained as a classifier.

7 Conclusion and Future Work

Our study systematically evaluated several machine learning approaches to coarse-grained candy speech detection, identifying the RoBERTa transformer model as most effective. Achieving a final F1 score of 0.93 demonstrated the robustness of transformer models in informal text classification tasks. Future work includes extending these approaches to cross-platform applications, fine-grained candy speech span detection, and multilingual modeling.

Acknowledgments

We thank the GermEval organizers for the dataset and evaluation framework provided. Support from NLPSuedwestfalen was essential to this project's success.

References

Balahur, A., & Turchi, M. (2014). Comparative experiments using supervised learning and machine translation for multilingual sentiment analysis. *COLING.*

Bojanowski, P., Grave, E., Joulin, A., & Mikolov, T. (2017). Enriching word vectors with subword information. *TACL.*

Clausen, Y., Scheffler,T., Wiegand, M. (2025). Overview of the GermEval 2025 Shared Task on Candy Speech Detection, in Ulrich Heid and Christian Wartena (eds.): Proceedings of the 21st Conference on Natural Language Processing (KONVENS 2025): Workshops, Hildesheim, Germany, 2025.

Conneau, A., Khandelwal, K., Goyal, N., et al. (2020). Unsupervised cross-lingual representation learning at scale. *ACL.*

de Vries, T., Roth, M., & Gurevych, I. (2019). German BERT: pretraining and evaluation. *LREC.*

Hochreiter, S., & Schmidhuber, J. (1997). Long short-term memory. *Neural Computation.*

Kim, Y. (2014). Convolutional neural networks for sentence classification. *EMNLP.*

Krause, B., et al. (2020). Hate speech detection in German. *LREC.*

Lin, T.-Y., et al. (2017). Focal loss for dense object detection. *ICCV.*

Pang, B., & Lee, L. (2008). Opinion mining and sentiment analysis. *Foundations and Trends in Information Retrieval.*

Quabynar at GermEval 2025 Candy Speech Detection: Zero-shot Approach For Detecting Candy Speech

Kwabena Odame Akomeah
University of Regensburg, Germany
kwabena-odame.akomeah@ur.de

Udo Kruschwitz
University of Regensburg, Germany
udo.kruschwitz@ur.de

Bernd Ludwig
University of Regensburg, Germany
bernd.ludwig@ur.de

Kwame Boateng Akomeah
Lewis University, IL, USA
kwameboatengakomea@lewisu.edu

Abstract

While content moderation typically focuses on harmful language, identifying positive expressions such as encouragement and appreciation remains underexplored. This work addresses the novel task of detecting *candy speech* in German YouTube comments through two subtasks: binary classification and span-level label extraction. We employ prompt-based large language models (Mistral-8x7B and Mistral-NEMO) with asynchronous inference and post-processing for Subtask 1, achieving an F1 score of 0.75. For Subtask 2, we apply zero-shot span extraction using Mistral-8x7B with regex-based offset alignment. Results highlight both the effectiveness of LLMs for classification and the challenges of span-level extraction due to hallucinations and formatting inconsistencies. We discuss prompt design, model alignment, and propose a scalable pipeline for affective content analysis in social computing.

1 Introduction

Content moderation traditionally centers on detecting harmful language such as hate speech or harassment (Schomacker et al., 2024; Akomeah et al., 2024), while positive expressions remain underexplored. **Candy speech**, encompassing encouragement, appreciation, and empowerment directed at individuals or their contributions, represents this positive discourse spectrum (Clausen et al., 2025). It plays a vital role in fostering affirming online communities and offers a constructive complement to harmful content detection.

This shared task addresses candy speech annotation in German YouTube comments defining two subtasks: (1) binary classification of comments containing candy speech and (2) span-level extraction of labeled phrases across ten predefined categories (Clausen et al., 2025). Systematic identification of such language not only enables computational modeling of supportive discourse but also facilitates contrastive learning, where unlabeled or contrary expressions can inform harmful content detection (Rosenthal et al., 2021).

We employed two large language models: Mistral-8x7B[1] and Mistral-NEMO[2], both released in mid-2024. Mistral-8x7B uses a mixture-of-experts design for efficient zero-shot multilingual tasks. Mistral-NEMO is optimized for distributed, mixed-precision training. Final submissions included zero-shot predictions for Subtask 1 and span extraction with regex-based offsets for Subtask 2.

Inference was deployed via **RunPod GPU instances** (RTX 4000 Ada, 9 vCPUs, 50 GB RAM) combined with the **OpenRouter API**[3], allowing asynchronous batch processing over large datasets. We used mistralai/mistral-8x7b (33K context, $0.08/M input, $0.24/M output tokens) and Mistral-Nemo (131K context, $0.008/M input, $0.001/M output) for cost-effective alternatives.

OpenRouter provides unified API access to multiple hosted models, requiring structured prompts compatible with SDK formats. The system remains portable across modern CPU/GPU setups due to batch learning. Code, models, and configurations are available on GitHub[4] for reproducibility.

2 Subtask 1: LLM-Based Binary Classification of Candy Speech

To address Subtask 1, which requires binary classification of German YouTube comments for the

[1] https://mistral.ai/news/announcing-mistral-7b
[2] https://mistral.ai/news/mistral-nemo
[3] https://openrouter.ai/
[4] https://github.com/kaodamie/Germeval-2025

Proceedings of the 21st Conference on Natural Language Processing (KONVENS), Volume 2: Workshops, pages 433–437, 2025

Model	Dataset	F1 Score	Precision	Recall
`Mistral-8x7B`	Training	0.4921	0.3339	0.9355
`Mistral-NEMO`	Training	0.7655	0.7810	0.8740
`Mistral-NEMO`	Test (Codabench)	0.7542	0.7099	0.8043

Table 1: Performance for Mistral models on Subtask 1 evaluated on both training and test data

presence of candy speech, we employed a scalable and prompt-based approach using a large language model (LLM). Specifically, we utilized the **Mistral-NEMO** model, accessed via the OpenRouter API. Mistral's mixture-of-experts architecture activates only a subset of its parameters per inference, enabling efficient, high-quality responses that are well suited to our domain of short, context-poor comments.

2.1 Prompt Design

We designed a task-specific system prompt to frame the model's behavior as a strict binary classifier. The model receives each comment in isolation and must decide whether it qualifies as candy speech defined as respectful, encouraging, or positive language. The exact prompt is as follows:

> *You are a strict binary classifier for short German comments. Each comment is provided in isolation and may be a word or a phrase.*
> *Your task is to decide whether the comment contains **candy speech** — defined as positive, respectful, or encouraging language.*
> *Respond with only: **yes** or **no**. If uncertain, choose 'no'.*

2.2 Asynchronous Inference Pipeline

To classify thousands of comments efficiently, we implemented an asynchronous processing pipeline using Python's `asyncio` and `aiohttp` libraries.

Comments were processed in batches and submitted in parallel to the API endpoint. Model responses were parsed using regular expressions to extract standardized binary decisions. Responses containing "yes" were mapped to a positive label, while "no" and all ambiguous or non-standard outputs were mapped to a negative label. This setup enables: rapid and scalable parallel inference without local model hosting, transparent and reproducible classification logic via prompt engineering and robustness against model output variability through post-processing filters.

This LLM-based classifier served as the backbone of our Subtask 1 solution and laid the groundwork for selective fine-grained analysis in Subtask 2.

3 Subtask 2: Candy Speech Span Extraction Using LLMs with Character-Level Offset Resolution

The goal of this task is to detect and extract subphrases (spans) that express *candy speech* defined as positive, encouraging, or affectionate language from user-generated German comments. Each span must be assigned one of ten predefined semantic classes and located precisely within the original text using character-level offsets. These spans enable fine-grained linguistic and affective analysis of online communication.

3.1 Model and Inference Setup

The dataset consisted of user comments from various German Youtube Channels, each identified by a document or video ID, a unique comment ID, and the comment text. For Subtask 1, we applied a binary classifier to label each comment as either `yes` or `no`, indicating the presence of candy speech. Only comments labeled as `yes` were passed to Subtask 2 for span-level extraction. This filtering step helped focus model inference efforts on relevant data while reducing unnecessary computation.

Similar to Subtask 1, we employed the Mistral-8x7B model, accessed via the OpenRouter API in a zero-shot setting without fine-tuning. To handle inference over thousands of comments efficiently, asynchronous HTTP requests were issued using Python's `aiohttp` and `asyncio` libraries.

Comments were processed in batches of 10 with concurrent API calls, ensuring high-throughput span extraction across the filtered dataset.

3.2 Prompt Engineering

Each comment was paired with a fixed instruction prompt that clearly defined the task (Choi et al., 2023). The system prompt explicitly listed the ten permissible candy speech categories:

positive feedback, compliment, affection declaration, encouragement, gratitude, agreement, ambiguous, implicit, group membership, sympathy

The model was instructed to return only a JSON list of dictionaries, where each dictionary contained: **label**: the assigned candy speech category, **phrase**: the exact phrase extracted from the comment.

The LLM model was instructed to use the exact labels and specific output format (see Listing 2).

3.3 Span Matching and Character Offset Extraction

While LLMs can return character offsets, our experiments showed these were often inaccurate, malformed, or misaligned with the input text. To ensure reliability, we extracted only the labeled phrases and computed offsets post hoc using re.finditer() to locate all exact matches within the original comment in 2 of the 3 submissions made. Each match yielded a (start, end) tuple of character indices, and all occurrences were recorded.

Final outputs were structured as flat tables containing document ID, comment ID, label, phrase, and computed offsets. Labels were cross-checked against a predefined schema, and malformed outputs were discarded. This regex-based resolution ensured robust span alignment and enabled scalable, lightweight annotation from zero-shot LLM predictions (Phukan et al., 2025).

3.4 Three Submissions for Subtask 2

This section outlines our three submission strategies for Subtask 2 (span-level extraction), analyzing the trade-offs in model prompting and offset alignment.

Across all submissions, separating span identification from offset computation improved robustness. Nevertheless, hallucinated labels and ambiguous phrase boundaries persisted, especially in complex or implicit comments. To address this, all wrongly labeled comments and hallucinated labels where discarded. Future iterations will explore few-shot examples, active learning on ambiguous inputs, and filtering strategies based on model confidence and response consistency.

3.4.1 Submission 1: Direct Offset Extraction (Mistral-NEMO)

Our first approach used Mistral-NEMO to generate both label and character offsets directly via structured JSON prompts (Listing 1). This method suffered from severe hallucinations, with outputs frequently containing: invalid or out-of-scope labels, incorrect or missing character positions and format violations (e.g., broken JSON or non-integer offsets)

```
PROMPT = f'''You are a precise label span extractor...
- "label": the flausch category
- "start": start character index (inclusive)
- "end": end character index (exclusive)
Strictly output only a JSON list like this:
[{{"label": "compliment", "start": 0, "end": 10}}, ...]
'''
```

Listing 1: Prompt requesting both labels and character offsets from the LLM (note that the term *flausch* represents the German equivalent of *candy*).

Despite explicit instructions, this submission failed to produce any valid extractions, resulting in zero scores across all evaluation metrics on the test set on Codabench (see Table 2).

3.4.2 Submission 2: Phrase Extraction with Regex Offsets (Mistral-NEMO)

```
PROMPT = f'''You are a precise label extractor...
- "label": the flausch category
- "phrase": the exact words or phrase from the comment
Return a list of dicts like:
[{{"label": "compliment", "phrase": "Toll gemacht"}}, ...]
'''
```

Listing 2: Improved prompt instructing LLM to return label and phrase only.

```
def find_phrase_offsets(comment, phrase):
    matches = list(re.finditer(re.escape(phrase), comment))
    return [(m.start(), m.end()) for m in matches]
```

Listing 3: Post-processing function for finding character offsets using regex.

To improve reliability, Submission 2 modified the prompt to request only label and phrase text, omitting offsets. Character positions were computed post hoc using regular expressions (See Listings 2 and 3 above). This reduced structural errors and enabled offset recovery for many phrases. However, hallucinations in label generation remained frequent, and span alignment was still suboptimal, yielding limited improvements in strict F1.

Submission	F1 (Strict)	Prec. (Strict)	Rec. (Strict)	F1 (Type)	Prec. (Type)	Rec. (Type)	F1 (Span)	Prec. (Span)	Rec. (Span)
3 (Mistral-7B + Regex)	**0.1590**	**0.1487**	**0.1709**	**0.4079**	**0.3814**	**0.4384**	**0.2565**	**0.2398**	**0.2756**
2 (NEMO + Regex)	0.0167	0.0130	0.0236	0.3812	0.2956	0.5364	0.0230	0.0179	0.0324
1 (NEMO + Prompt Offsets)	0.0000	0.0000	0.0000	0.0000	0.0000	0.0000	0.0000	0.0000	0.0000

Table 2: Subtask 2 results on the Codabench test set. Evaluation includes strict label-span match, label-type match (ignoring span), and span overlap (ignoring label type). The best results are in bold.

3.4.3 Submission 3: Phrase Extraction with Regex Offsets (Mistral-8x7B)

Our third and final submission switched to the Mistral-8x7B model, retaining the same regex-based offset resolution strategy. This configuration achieved the highest performance across all metrics as seen in Table 2. These gains reflect improved generation quality and improved phrase consistency from Mistral-8x7B, as well as better compatibility with post-processing routines.

4 Results

For Subtask 1, only Mistral-NEMO was submitted, achieving a strong F1 score of 0.75 on the test set (see Table 1) though in training, we used both Mistral-NEMO and 8x7B. The decision to continue with Mistral-NEMO for the test set was influenced by its performance in training as seen Table 1. Subtask 2 involved three submissions: (1) Mistral-NEMO with prompt-based character offsets which failed due to formatting errors, (2) Mistral-NEMO with regex and (3) Mistral-8x7B with regex which yielded the highest scores across all metrics (see Table 2). While all models demonstrated zero-shot capability, results show that precise prompt formatting and robust post-processing particularly regex-based span alignment are critical. Despite Submission 3's relative success, overall performance suggests future gains require few-shot or fine-tuning learning.

5 Conclusion and Future Work

We explored LLM-based methods for binary classification and span-level label extraction of candy speech in German comments. Mistral-NEMO gave better results than Mistral-8x7B in Subtask 1 with an F1 score of 0.76 to 0.49 in training, demonstrating the impact of model choice for the test set. Subtask 2 remained challenging, with our best setup (Mistral-8x7B combined with regex extraction) yielding limited absolute performance, reflecting zero-shot prompting constraints. Our findings emphasize the need for refined post-processing, prompt design, and guided sampling to enhance structured LLM outputs.

While zero-shot prompting with LLMs shows promise, our results highlight its limitations for span-level extraction tasks due to label hallucinations and formatting inconsistencies. To address this, we plan to integrate active learning to identify informative examples for few-shot prompting, aiming to guide the model more reliably. Future efforts will also focus on optimizing prompt structure, instruction clarity, and robust response parsing to further enhance output quality and consistency.

References

Kwabena Odame Akomeah, Udo Kruschwitz, and Bernd Ludwig. 2024. Team quabynar at the GermEval 2024 shared task 1 GerMS-detect (subtasks 1 and 2) on sexism detection. In *Proceedings of GermEval 2024 Task 1 GerMS-Detect Workshop on Sexism Detection in German Online News Fora (GerMS-Detect 2024)*, pages 26–32, Vienna, Austria. Association for Computational Lingustics.

Eunbi Choi, Yongrae Jo, Joel Jang, Joonwon Jang, and Minjoon Seo. 2023. Fixed input parameterization for efficient prompting. In *Findings of the Association for Computational Linguistics: ACL 2023*, pages 8428–8441, Toronto, Canada. Association for Computational Linguistics.

Yulia Clausen, Tatjana Scheffler, and Michael Wiegand. 2025. Overview of the GermEval 2025 Shared Task on Candy Speech Detection. In *Proceedings of the 21st Conference on Natural Language Processing (KONVENS 2025): Workshops*, Hildesheim, Germany. ACL.

Anirudh Phukan, Divyansh Divyansh, Harshit Kumar Morj, Vaishnavi Vaishnavi, Apoorv Saxena, and Koustava Goswami. 2025. Beyond logit lens: Contextual embeddings for robust hallucination detection & grounding in VLMs. In *Proceedings of the 2025 Conference of the Nations of the Americas Chapter of the Association for Computational Linguistics: Human Language Technologies (Volume 1: Long Papers)*, pages 9661–9675, Albuquerque, New Mexico. Association for Computational Linguistics.

Sara Rosenthal and 1 others. 2021. Detecting constructive online comments. In *Proceedings of the Workshop on Online Abuse and Harms (WOAH)*.

Thorben Schomacker, Miriam Anschütz, and Regina Stodden, editors. 2024. *Proceedings of GermEval 2024 Shared Task on Statement Segmentation in German Easy Language (StaGE)*. Association for Computational Lingustics, Vienna, Austria.

TUM NLP Group at GermEval 2025 Shared Task on Candy Speech Detection: Small Dose, Big Effect: Leveraging Synthetic Data for Candy Speech Detection

Sophie Luise Opheiden, Elisei Shushpanov, Faeze Ghorbanpour
Department of Informatics
Technical University of Munich
{sophie.opheiden, e.shushpanov, faeze.ghorbanpour}@tum.de

Abstract

This paper presents our submission to the GermEval 2025 Shared Task on Candy Speech Detection. We fine-tune a multilingual transformer model (mDeBERTa-v3) on original and LLM-augmented data using prompt-based dual-class generation. Our best model, trained with 10% synthetic data per class, achieved an F1-score of 0.8785 on the test set, ranking 6th out of 20 submissions. Further augmentation did not improve performance, underlining the need for carefully targeted augmentation.

1 Introduction

Over the past two decades, social media platforms have risen to be one of the main communication channels across generations. With the increasing number of users, the need to monitor online discourse has grown — particularly to prevent the misuse of anonymity that these platforms provide. Consequently, numerous methods for detecting and censoring negative speech (e.g., hate speech or harmful language) on social media have been developed, allowing social media platform providers to enforce community guidelines.

In contrast, less attention has been given to identifying and promoting positive and supportive discourse in online communities (Clausen et al., 2025). Yet, this research field holds relevance for practical applications and academia: Candy speech detection complements negative speech detection by actively identifying and promoting positive communication. This can help foster a more welcoming and empathetic online culture, especially on platforms like YouTube, where comments can significantly impact both creators and viewers.

Sentiment detection in social media is complex: The nature of social media content, such as YouTube video comments, is informal and may intentionally deviate from standard orthography to enhance expressiveness and convey hyperbolic sentiment beyond the literal meaning of the word. This makes processing of the input text data not trivial, potentially negatively impacting downstream model performance.

The GermEval Shared Task 2025 on Candy Speech Detection (Clausen et al., 2025) invited researchers to detect candy speech in YouTube comments. We participated in Subtask 1: Coarse-Grained Classification, which targets the identification of *"Flausch"* speech in German YouTube comments as a whole. Our best approach fine-tuned a transformer-based model on a dataset augmented by 10%. Notably, our experiments showed that increasing the amount of synthetic data beyond this point did not lead to further improvements.

2 Dataset

The dataset consists of German-language YouTube comments. The source videos vary widely in content, style, audience, and creators, resulting in diverse topic distributions. Notably, the final test set includes previously unseen topics, highlighting the importance of robust model generalization.

The dataset is imbalanced, with only 29% of the comments labeled as *"Flausch"* and 71% as *"not Flausch"*. It also contains highly informal language, including intentional spelling deviations (e.g., "suuuuper") to express emphasis or hyperbole. Most comments are short: Fifty percent contain six words or fewer and 32 characters or fewer.

3 Methodology

This section introduces a formal problem definition of the GermEval Challenge Task 1 (Coarse-Grained Classification). Subsequently, we discuss experiment design and utilized methods with justifications for the steps taken in the experiment.

3.1 Problem Definition

Candy speech, also known by its German name *"Flausch"*, has been formally defined by the

Proceedings of the 21st Conference on Natural Language Processing (KONVENS), Volume 2: Workshops, pages 438–443, 2025

GermEval 2025 organizing committee as an "expression of positive attitudes on social media toward individuals or their output (videos, comments, etc.)" (Clausen et al., 2025).

Subtask 1 (Coarse-Grained Classification) is framed as a binary classification problem: given a YouTube comment $c \in C$, the goal is to learn a function

$$f : C \to \{0, 1\}$$

that predicts whether c contains candy speech ($f(c) = 1$) or not ($f(c) = 0$).

A labeled training set is provided in the form:

$$D_{\text{train}} = \{(c_i, y_i)\}_{i=1}^{N}, \quad y_i \in \{0, 1\} \tag{1}$$

The classifier f is trained on D_{train} and evaluated on an unseen test set $D_{\text{test}} = \{(c_j, y_j)\}_{j=1}^{M}$.

3.2 Model Selection

We conducted an exploratory comparison of popular transformer models to identify the strongest baseline. The models include: mBERT[1] (Devlin et al., 2018), a multilingual bidirectional encoder representation from transformers; XLM-RoBERTa[2] (Conneau et al., 2019), a robustly optimized BERT pretraining model; and mDeBERTaV3[3], a multilingual version of DeBERTaV3(He et al., 2021a) which pretrain DeBERTa(He et al., 2021b) using gradient-disentangled embedding sharing. DeBERTa itself is a decoding-enhanced BERT architecture with disentangled attention.

Grid search and Optuna[4] (Akiba et al., 2019) were utilized to find the best hyperparameters. Table 1 compares the performance of all models across various hyperparameter settings. We used macro-averaged metrics for the exploration, as this allowed us to assess the performance across all classes, regardless of class imbalance. Choosing the best model, we employed mDeBERTaV3, a transformer-based encoder architecture developed by Microsoft.

mDeBERTaV3 is pretrained across 100+ languages. Known for its strong performance in multilingual natural language processing (NLP) tasks, it is able to capture fine-grained syntactic and semantic patterns—an important property for detecting certain sentiment in stylistically distorted social media comments.

Our final baseline model was fine-tuned with a learning rate of `3e-5`, batch size `16`, `3` epochs, and weight decay `0.01`. All textual inputs were tokenized with the model's associated tokenizer.

3.3 Data Augmentation

Data augmentation is used to artificially expand a training dataset by creating modified versions of existing data. Using this technique, generalization to unseen data may be improved as the size of the training set is increased. Three methods were implemented:

Synonym Replacement is a lexical data augmentation technique, in which randomly selected words in a sentence are replaced with semantically similar alternatives using word embedding models.

Back translation involves translating a sentence into an intermediate language (e.g., English) and then translating it back to the original language. It is particularly useful for creating diverse training examples that differ in structure and phrasing but convey the same semantic content.

Large Language Model (LLM) based Dual-Class Augmentation is a prompt-based generative approach. In contrast to single-class augmentation, it includes examples from both classes in the prompt, allowing the model to better learn the decision boundary between classes (Ibrahim et al., 2025). Each prompt combined five random examples from each class, and the model was instructed to generate a new German comment for a given label (Table 2). We introduced the classification labels and their definitions in the prompt to provide clearer context for the generation task and explicitly associate the label *"Flausch"* with its meaning. This approach was intended to help the model better understand the task requirements while also reducing prompt length, as it eliminated the need to repeatedly replace *"Flausch"* with its full definition in each instruction. We augmented both *"Flausch"* and *"not Flausch"* classes equally to preserve the original class distribution.

To study the effect of class imbalance on model performance, we created training sets with different *"not Flausch"/"Flausch"* ratios (70/30, 65/35, 60/40, 50/50) utilizing synonym replacement and back translation. Synonym replacement was implemented leveraging a pre-trained

[1] https://huggingface.co/google-bert/bert-base-multilingual-cased

[2] https://huggingface.co/FacebookAI/xlm-roberta-base

[3] https://huggingface.co/microsoft/mdeberta-v3-base

[4] https://github.com/optuna/optuna

Model	Method	Accuracy	F1	Precision	Recall	Hyperparameters
mBERT	Grid Search	0.8779	0.8392	0.8714	0.8093	LR=2e-5, BS=16, Epochs=3, WD=0.01
mBERT	Grid Search	0.8781	0.8410	0.8504	0.8318	LR=3e-5, BS=16, Epochs=3, WD=0.01
mBERT	Grid Search	0.7910	0.7635	0.6798	0.8707	LR=5e-5, BS=8, Epochs=4, WD=0.01
mBERT	Grid Search	0.8763	0.8411	0.8370	0.8453	LR=1e-5, BS=32, Epochs=5, WD=0.01
mBERT	Optuna	0.8308	0.8385	0.8589	0.8308	LR=4.28e-5, BS=8, Epochs=5, WD=0.0706, WR=0.167
mBERT	Optuna	0.8171	0.8275	0.8624	0.8171	LR=4.35e-5, BS=16, Epochs=2, WD=0.0551, WR=0.174
XLM-RoBERTa	Grid Search	0.8790	0.8445	0.8414	0.8477	LR=2e-5, BS=16, Epochs=3, WD=0.01
XLM-RoBERTa	Grid Search	0.8789	0.8431	0.8467	0.8396	LR=3e-5, BS=16, Epochs=3, WD=0.01
XLM-RoBERTa	Grid Search	0.8844	0.8513	0.8482	0.8545	LR=1e-5, BS=32, Epochs=5, WD=0.01
XLM-RoBERTa	Optuna	0.8051	0.8135	0.8325	0.8051	LR=4.60e-5, BS=8, Epochs=5, WD=0.2592, WR=0.0197
XLM-RoBERTa	Optuna	0.8161	0.8265	0.8610	0.8161	LR=1.21e-5, BS=8, Epochs=2, WD=0.0267, WR=0.0238
mDeBERTa	Grid Search	0.8664	0.8381	0.7901	0.8922	LR=2e-5, BS=16, Epochs=3, WD=0.01
mDeBERTa	Grid Search	0.8882	0.8594	0.8383	0.8815	LR=3e-5, BS=16, Epochs=3, WD=0.01
mDeBERTa	Grid Search	0.8771	0.8367	0.8619	0.8129	LR=5e-5, BS=8, Epochs=4, WD=0.01
mDeBERTa	Grid Search	0.8888	0.8579	0.8497	0.8662	LR=1e-5, BS=32, Epochs=5, WD=0.01
mDeBERTa	Optuna	0.7812	0.7961	0.8585	0.7812	LR=3.91e-5, BS=8, Epochs=4, WD=0.0942, WR=0.1508

Table 1: Performance of transformer models across different hyperparameter configurations. Both grid search and Optuna were used to explore learning rate (LR), batch size (BS), weight decay (WD), warmup ratio (WR), and number of epochs. The goal was to identify the best-performing setup for each model. All reported metrics are macro-averaged across both classes. The chosen baseline model is indicated in grey.

German Word2Vec model[5] (Müller, 2015). Each word had a 20% chance of being replaced. Replacement candidates were drawn from the top 5 most similar embeddings and randomly chosen. For back translation, we used the Hugging Face MarianMT [6] (Junczys-Dowmunt et al., 2018) models `Helsinki-NLP/opus-mt-de-en` and `Helsinki-NLP/opus-mt-en-de` to perform German → English → German translation.

Before applying augmentation, we performed standard preprocessing steps, including stopword removal and lemmatization. These methods were applied to improve the matching rate against the Word2Vec vocabulary by reducing the inflected forms to their base forms. The removal of stop words ensured that the replacement of synonyms focused only on meaningful content words, avoiding unnecessary substitutions of function words.

Approximately 20% of the augmented samples were created via back translation and 80% via synonym replacement. The low back translation ratio was chosen deliberately as a portion of the input texts—often short, grammatically incorrect, or containing emoji tokens—could not be meaningfully translated, leading to empty outputs.

Prompt-based dual-class augmentation was applied using the instruction-tuned model `tiiuae/falcon-7b-instruct`[7] (Almazrouei et al., 2023; Penedo et al., 2023), generating new samples via nucleus sampling ($p = 0.9$) with a temperature of 0.7. The synthetic data was added to the training set in increments of 10%, 20%, and 30% data increase per class. We augmented and trained without text-preprocessing, as we observed during a first round of experiments with dual-class data augmentation, that our model performed better without it, likely because such operations removed stylistic and informal features important for classifying *"Flausch"* content.

3.4 Final Submission

All submissions were based on our baseline model, but differed in training datasets: Our first submission was our baseline model paired with our normal training data. After receiving the submission results, we observed a steep performance decline in contrast to our test results. Our assumption is that our model had a problem generalizing the trained patterns to the new data, as the unseen test set has other topics than the training data. Thus, we decided to pursue two different approaches for the next submissions: For the second submission, we merged the 10% augmented training dataset, the evaluation, and the test data to increase the training sample size. For the third submission, we incorporated tweets from the SB10k dataset[8] (Cieliebak et al., 2017) into our training data, in addition to the augmented samples. The SB10k corpus is a German Twitter dataset that provides sentiment annotations for each tweet. From this resource, we

[5]https://github.com/devmount/GermanWordEmbeddings

[6]`https://github.com/huggingface/transformers/blob/main/docs/source/en/model_doc/marian.md`

[7]`https://huggingface.co/tiiuae/falcon-7b-instruct`

[8]`https://huggingface.co/datasets/Alienmaster/SB10k`

reduzieren

Label	Prompt
Flausch	*I will give you 10 examples of YouTube comments: 5 flausch (overtly positive, encouraging) and 5 not flausch (neutral or critical). Based on these, generate a realistic, stylistically natural flausch tweet that differs from the examples.* *Flausch examples: [5 random examples]* *Not flausch examples: [5 random examples]* *Now generate a new flausch tweet in German.*
Not Flausch	*I will give you 10 examples of YouTube comments: 5 flausch (overtly positive, encouraging) and 5 not flausch (neutral or critical). Based on these, generate a realistic, stylistically natural not flausch tweet that differs from the examples.* *Flausch examples: [5 random examples]* *Not flausch examples: [5 random examples]* *Now generate a new not flausch tweet in German.*

Table 2: Prompts used for dual-class tweet generation with `tiiuae/falcon-7b-instruct`.

extracted 1,193 tweets labeled as *positive* and 794 labeled as *negative*. To make it easier for our model to distinguish between the two target classes, we included only the *negative* and not the *neutral* samples for the *"not Flausch"* category.

4 Results

We evaluate model performance using Accuracy as well as Precision, Recall, and F1-score for the positive class (*"Flausch"*). The *"Flausch"* F1-score served as the primary metric for model selection and final ranking in the GermEval Shared Task 2025 (Clausen et al., 2025).

We first explored the effect of altering the class distribution by increasing the proportion of *"Flausch"* comments using synonym replacement and back translation. However, as shown in Table 3, these adjustments led to a decline in performance compared to the baseline. Even the 70/30 ratio—closest to the original—performed worse, motivating us to retain the natural class distribution in further experiments.

To understand the drop in performance from synonym replacement and backtranslation, we examined several augmented examples. We observed some decline in the data input quality: In some cases, synonym replacement led to semantic errors—for instance, "voll cool wer hören 2017" became "ordentlich doof wer hören 2017", reversing the intended sentiment. Backtranslation produced awkward literal translations, e.g., "cool Parodie Loch" became "Kühles Parodienloch". Additionally, stylistic exaggerations were inconsistently translated, such as "voll süüüüüüüß" becoming simply "voll süß". These stylistic and semantic degradations likely weakened the signal that distinguishes *"Flausch"* comments, confusing the model during training.

Based on these qualitative insights, we concluded that neither synonym replacement nor backtranslation preserved the stylistic patterns of the original data. As a result, we opted not to include augmented samples of both methods in subsequent experiments. Since the adjusted class distribution might have negatively impacted performance, as the true distribution in the test data is likely skewed, we chose to retain the original class balance in further experiments.

Next, we evaluated LLM-based augmentation techniques. Augmenting the dataset by 10% per class produced the best results, achieving an F1-score of 0.8888. Increasing the augmentation to 20% or 30% did not yield further improvements, highlighting that more augmentation is not always beneficial, but careful tuning is essential for tweaking model performance.

The final predictions of our submissions were generated on the unseen test set provided by the GermEval organizers. From the results, we observe that increasing the amount of training data in both subsequent submissions led to a performance improvement over the baseline model trained solely on the original training set. However, training on (artificial and original) data that is native to the challenge appears to yield a greater performance gain than incorporating sentiment data from a different domain. By merging the original training set with the evaluation and test splits, we exposed the model to the same distribution and topical variety it would face at inference time, thereby effectively reducing domain shift. This likely enabled the model to learn more representative features and generalize more effectively to the unseen test data. In contrast, the first submission lacked this exposure, while the third submission—although enriched with SB10k sentiment data—introduced out-of-domain content

Model	Accuracy	F1	Precision	Recall
Development Results				
MDeBERTa (base model)	0.8781	0.8594	0.8383	0.8815
Synonym/Back Translation with Class Distribution Variants				
class distr. 70/30	0.8771	0.8496	0.8172	0.8847
class distr. 65/35	0.8701	0.8454	0.7935	0.9045
class distr. 60/40	0.8707	0.8448	0.7990	0.8961
class distr. 50/50	0.8561	0.8331	0.7647	0.9150
LLM-Based Augmentation (Falcon-7B)				
10% augmentation	0.9101	0.8888	0.8639	0.9150
20% augmentation	0.9077	0.8853	0.8642	0.9075
30% augmentation	0.9090	0.8829	0.8926	0.8733
Official Submission (Test Set)				
submission-1	–	0.7668	0.8687	0.6864
submission-2	–	**0.8785**	**0.8866**	**0.8705**
submission-3	–	0.7715	0.8442	0.7103

Table 3: Performance of different mDeberta-based model configurations during development and final evaluation. Synonym/back translation and LLM-based augmentation results are shown separately. The table highlights the F1-score as the official competition metric.

(general Twitter sentiment) that may not align well with the specific tone, structure, or subject matter of the challenge data.

Our best submission achieved an F1-score of **0.8785** for the *"Flausch"* class, placing 6th out of 20 submissions. Since the hidden test set was drawn from a different thematic domain than the provided dataset, the model's ability to maintain its performance on unseen data indicates strong generalization capabilities across varying comment contexts. This suggests that our approach captures underlying linguistic patterns of candy speech that extend beyond topic-specific cues.

5 Conclusion

In this paper, we present our approach to Subtask 1 of the GermEval 2025 Shared Task on Candy Speech Detection (Clausen et al., 2025), addressing the challenge of detecting *Flausch* comments in German YouTube discussions—a task complicated by informal language, class imbalance, and topic diversity between training and test sets.

We established a strong transformer-based baseline using mDeBERTa-v3, selected through comparative evaluation against other transformer models. To improve generalization, we investigated several data augmentation strategies. Synonym replacement and backtranslation expanded the dataset but likely degraded its semantic and stylistic quality. Combined with changes to the class distribution, these factors likely contributed to the observed drop in model performance. In contrast, prompt-based dual-class augmentation using a large language model proved highly effective. Augmenting each class with only 10% additional data resulted in notable performance improvements. Further increases led to diminishing returns. In-domain augmentation via evaluation and test splits proved more effective than external data (e.g., SB10k), emphasizing the importance of domain alignment in contextual classification.

Our best submission achieved an F1-score of **0.8785** on the *Flausch* class, ranking 6th out of 20 submissions. The model's ability to generalize to unseen topics in the hidden test set suggests that it successfully learned domain-independent patterns of positive discourse. This outcome reinforces the potential of using generative augmentation techniques and task-specific prompt engineering for improving NLP models on subtle, affective language detection tasks.

Ethics Statement

This work makes use of publicly available datasets provided by the GermEval Shared Task 2025, which were collected and annotated under ethical and legal considerations outlined by the task organizers (Clausen et al., 2025).

Acknowledgements

We would like to thank the organizers of the GermEval 2025 Shared Task for providing the dataset and creating a well-structured and challenging benchmark for German-language social media analysis.

References

Takuya Akiba, Shotaro Sano, Toshihiko Yanase, Takeru Ohta, and Masanori Koyama. 2019. Optuna: A next-generation hyperparameter optimization framework. In *The 25th ACM SIGKDD International Conference on Knowledge Discovery & Data Mining*, pages 2623–2631. https://doi.org/10.48550/arXiv.1907.10902.

Ebtesam Almazrouei, Hamza Alobeidli, Abdulaziz Alshamsi, Alessandro Cappelli, Ruxandra Cojocaru, Merouane Debbah, Etienne Goffinet, Daniel Heslow, Julien Launay, Quentin Malartic, Badreddine Noune, Baptiste Pannier, and Guilherme Penedo. 2023. Falcon-40B: an open large language model with state-of-the-art performance. https://huggingface.co/tiiuae/falcon-7b-instruct.

Mark Cieliebak, Jan Deriu, Dominic Egger, and Fatih Uzdilli. 2017. A twitter corpus and benchmark resources for german sentiment analysis. In *Proceedings of the Fifth International Workshop on Natural Language Processing for Social Media*, pages 45–51, Valencia, Spain. Association for Computational Linguistics. https://aclanthology.org/W17-1106.

Yulia Clausen, Tatjana Scheffler, and Michael Wiegand. 2025. Overview of the GermEval 2025 Shared Task on Candy Speech Detection. In *Proceedings of the 21st Conference on Natural Language Processing (KONVENS 2025): Workshops*, Hildesheim, Germany. ACL.

Alexis Conneau, Kartikay Khandelwal, Naman Goyal, Vishrav Chaudhary, Guillaume Wenzek, Francisco Guzmán, Edouard Grave, Myle Ott, Luke Zettlemoyer, and Veselin Stoyanov. 2019. Unsupervised cross-lingual representation learning at scale. *CoRR*, abs/1911.02116. http://arxiv.org/abs/1911.02116.

Jacob Devlin, Ming-Wei Chang, Kenton Lee, and Kristina Toutanova. 2018. BERT: pre-training of deep bidirectional transformers for language understanding. *CoRR*, abs/1810.04805. http://arxiv.org/abs/1810.04805.

Pengcheng He, Jianfeng Gao, and Weizhu Chen. 2021a. Debertav3: Improving deberta using electra-style pre-training with gradient-disentangled embedding sharing. https://doi.org/10.48550/arXiv.2111.09543.

Pengcheng He, Xiaodong Liu, Jianfeng Gao, and Weizhu Chen. 2021b. Deberta: Decoding-enhanced bert with disentangled attention. In *International Conference on Learning Representations*. https://doi.org/10.48550/arXiv.2006.03654.

Muhammad Amien Ibrahim, Faisal, Tora Sangputra Yopie Winarto, and Zefanya Delvin Sulistiya. 2025. Dual-class prompt generation: Enhancing indonesian gender-based hate speech detection through data augmentation. https://doi.org/10.48550/arXiv.2503.04279.

Marcin Junczys-Dowmunt, Roman Grundkiewicz, Tomasz Dwojak, Hieu Hoang, Kenneth Heafield, Tom Neckermann, Frank Seide, Ulrich Germann, Alham Fikri Aji, Nikolay Bogoychev, André F. T. Martins, and Alexandra Birch. 2018. Marian: Fast neural machine translation in C++. In *Proceedings of ACL 2018, System Demonstrations*, pages 116–121, Melbourne, Australia. Association for Computational Linguistics. https://doi.org/10.48550/arXiv.1804.00344.

Andreas Müller. 2015. Analyse von Wort-Vektoren deutscher Textkorpora. Bachelor's thesis, Technische Universität Berlin. https://devmount.github.io/GermanWordEmbeddings.

Guilherme Penedo, Quentin Malartic, Daniel Hesslow, Ruxandra Cojocaru, Alessandro Cappelli, Hamza Alobeidli, Baptiste Pannier, Ebtesam Almazrouei, and Julien Launay. 2023. The RefinedWeb dataset for Falcon LLM: outperforming curated corpora with web data, and web data only. *arXiv preprint arXiv:2306.01116*. https://arxiv.org/abs/2306.01116.

Gap in pagination due to formatting issues.

Pages 444-446

Annif at the GermEval-2025 LLMs4Subjects Task: Traditional XMTC Augmented by Efficient LLMs

Osma Suominen and **Juho Inkinen** and **Mona Lehtinen**
National Library of Finland, University of Helsinki
firstname.lastname@helsinki.fi

Abstract

This paper presents the Annif system in the LLMs4Subjects shared task (Subtask 2) at GermEval-2025. The task required creating subject predictions for bibliographic records using large language models, with a special focus on computational efficiency. Our system, based on the Annif automated subject indexing toolkit, refines our previous system from the first LLMs4Subjects shared task, which produced excellent results. We further improved the system by using many small and efficient language models for translation and synthetic data generation and by using LLMs for ranking candidate subjects. Our system ranked 1st in the overall quantitative evaluation of and 1st in the qualitative evaluation of Subtask 2.

1 Introduction

Subject indexing is an important aspect of improving the discoverability of bibliographic databases and digital collections. The LLMs4Subjects Shared Task at GermEval-2025 invited teams to produce innovative systems for the application of large language models (LLMs) to the task of automated subject indexing.

We participated in the shared task (D'Souza et al., 2025) with an Annif[1]-based system, as we have been developing the Annif automated subject indexing toolkit since 2017 (Suominen et al., 2022). Our system is a more refined version of the one we used in the first LLMs4Subjects shared task at SemEval-2025 (Suominen et al., 2025). The novel aspects of our work are 1) translation of metadata records using many different LLMs and choosing an optimal compromise between throughput and quality, 2) generation of synthetic training data using different LLMs in combination, 3) a fusion approach involving optimised weights and exponents, and 4) using a LLM for ranking candidate subjects in an ensemble.

[1] https://annif.org

Our system ranked first within Subtask 2 in both quantitative and qualitative evaluations. We demonstrated that our approach that combines LLMs with traditional natural language processing and machine learning remains competitive against other systems that use LLMs more heavily, and allows for different compromises between efficiency and quality - finding the best ones is important in and as of itself.

Our code, configuration files and customised data sets are available on GitHub[2]. The models we trained are available on Hugging Face Hub[3].

2 Background

We only participated in Subtask 2: Subject Indexing. The task involved developing LLM-based systems that recommend the most relevant subjects from the GND subject vocabulary (200,035 subjects) to tag a given TIBKAT record based on its title and abstract. This is an extreme multi-label text classification (XMTC) problem.

The organisers provided bibliographic records from the TIBKAT database as a data set (D'Souza et al., 2025) divided into train (n=90452), development (n=19949), and test (n=27998) subsets. Subsets were further split by document type (e.g. Article or Book) and language (German or English). GND subjects were included for the train and development records.

As in our previous work, our system relied mainly on the traditional XMTC algorithms in Annif. However, we used LLMs to pre-process the data sets, to generate additional synthetic training data, and for the final ranking of candidate subjects.

[2] https://github.com/NatLibFi/Annif-LLMs4Subjects-GermEval2025/

[3] https://huggingface.co/NatLibFi/Annif-LLMs4Subjects-GermEval2025-data

Proceedings of the 21st Conference on Natural Language Processing (KONVENS), Volume 2: Workshops, pages 447–454, 2025

3 System overview

As in our previous work, we based our system on the Annif automated subject indexing toolkit that provides a selection of XMTC algorithms. We set up base projects using three Annif backends: 1) **Omikuji**[4], an implementation of a family of efficient machine learning algorithms for multilabel classification based on the idea of partitioned label trees, including Parabel (Prabhu et al., 2018) and Bonsai (Khandagale et al., 2020). We used the Bonsai-style configuration. 2) **MLLM**[5] (Maui-like Lexical Matching), a lexical algorithm for matching words and expressions in document text to terms in a subject vocabulary. It is a reimplementation of the ideas behind Maui (Medelyan, 2009). 3) **XTransformer**, an XMTC and ranking algorithm based on fine-tuned BERT-style Transformer models that is part of the PECOS framework (Yu et al., 2022). We used **FacebookAI/xlm-roberta-base** as the base model.

ID	HuggingFace ID	Size
A8	CohereLabs/aya-expanse-8b	8
E9	utter-project/EuroLLM-9B-Instruct	9
G4	google/gemma-3-4b-it	4
G12	google/gemma-3-12b-it	12
H3	NousResearch/Hermes-3-Llama-3.2-3B	3
H8	NousResearch/Hermes-3-Llama-3.1-8B	8
I8	ibm-granite/granite-3.3-8b-instruct	8
L3	meta-llama/Llama-3.2-3B-Instruct	3
L8	meta-llama/Llama-3.1-8B-Instruct	8
M8	mistralai/Ministral-8B-Instruct-2410	8
M12	mistralai/Mistral-Nemo-Instruct-2407	12
Q4	Qwen/Qwen3-4B	4
Q8	Qwen/Qwen3-8B	8
S8	VAGOsolutions/Llama-3-SauerkrautLM-8b-Instruct	8
S12	VAGOsolutions/SauerkrautLM-Nemo-12b-Instruct	12
G27	google/gemma-3-27b-it	27
M24	mistralai/Mistral-Small-3.1-24B-Instruct-2503	24
Q30	Qwen/Qwen3-30B-A3B	30

Table 1: LLMs used in our system.

Since a special theme for this shared task was **energy- and compute-efficient LLMs**, we specifically looked at opportunities to reduce computational costs while maintaining high performance. Thus, we mainly applied smaller, locally run (see Appendix C) language models and evaluated their relative performance. We selected recently published open-weight LLMs, ranging in size from 3B to 12B parameters, with support for both English and German language, including models specifically fine-tuned for improved support of German (SauerkrautLM) as well as general purpose finetunes (Hermes 3). We also included three models in a larger size category (24B to 30B) for comparison. The language models we used are shown in Table 1; we use the mnemonic model IDs listed in the table in the remainder of the paper.

We combined the base backends into two types of ensembles: *simple ensembles* that merge subject suggestions from two or more backends by averaging their scores and a new *LLM ranking ensemble*. The simple ensemble was improved from our previous work by adding support for weighting exponents (see Appendix A for details). The LLM ranking ensemble, in addition to averaging scores, also uses an external LLM to rank candidate subjects similar to the DNB-AI-Project system (Kluge and Kähler, 2025) in the first LLMs4Subjects Shared Task (see Appendix B for details).

For evaluation during system development, we used common XMTC metrics built in to the Annif toolkit: *F1@5* (F1 score calculated using the top 5 suggestions from the system) and *nDCG@20* (Järvelin and Kekäläinen, 2002), a ranking metric calculated using the top 20 suggestions from the system. We used the Data Version Control[6] tool to manage the data sets, project configurations and the training and evaluation processes.

4 Experimental setup

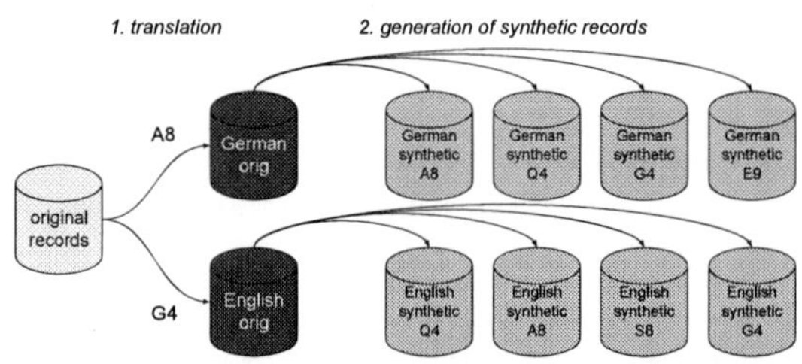

Figure 1: LLM pre-processing steps for the data sets.

4.1 Translation of data sets

For the vocabulary, we reused the bilingual English-German SKOS version of GND that was produced in our earlier work by translating the preferred terms into English using the **GPT-4o-mini** LLM.

To translate the titles and abstracts of the TIBKAT records into a consistent target language, we tested many different LLMs, aiming to find

[4] https://github.com/tomtung/omikuji

[5] https://github.com/NatLibFi/Annif/wiki/Backend%3A-MLLM

[6] https://dvc.org/

a good balance between computational efficiency and subject indexing quality. We translated each record from the train and development sets separately into German-only and English-only variants (step 1 in Figure 1). We then trained Omikuji Bonsai models on the translated train records and evaluated the results against the corresponding development set. We scored the LLMs separately for English and German target languages using the formula $score = nDCG@20 + \alpha \cdot throughput$, which combines quality and efficiency into a single metric, selecting $\alpha = 0.003$ as the balancing factor. The value for the factor α was chosen based on experimentation and the results are shown in Figure 3 in Appendix D. Continuing the work based on these scores, we selected the models to use for translation of TIBKAT records: G4 (Gemma 3 4B) for English and A8 (Aya 8B) for German. These were not the absolute best models in translation quality (Q30 and M24 were), but they provided the best compromise between quality and efficiency.

4.2 Synthetic training data

The number of training records was relatively small, so we generated additional synthetic data. For each language, we used the four top-ranking LLMs from the translation task to generate synthetic training records (titles and abstracts) in the same language. Using a one-shot approach, we presented the LLM with each of the train records (its title and abstract) at a time along with its manually assigned subject labels (GND preferred terms in either German or English, matching the language of the document). We then prompted the LLM to generate a similar record with the same set of subjects plus one additional, randomly chosen preferred term from the GND (step 2 in Figure 1) that had been the subject of at least one record in the original train subset. We recognise that this process may cause seemingly unrelated subjects to appear together, but did not want to place too much constraint here; this could be the subject of further work. The result of this process was four sets of synthetic training records per language, each having the same number of records (90,452) as the original train subset.

4.3 Base projects

We first set up, trained and evaluated the three kinds of base projects: (Omikuji) Bonsai, MLLM and XTransformer. We aimed to maximise their evaluation scores against the development set by exploring various approaches and settings. Once satisfied with the performance of the base projects, we combined them into ensembles that were used to produce our system output.

We trained each project on the LLM-translated monolingual records from the train set (German-only or English-only, matching the project language) and tested different hyperparameters. For the Bonsai projects, we enabled bigram features using the *ngram=2* setting and set a *min_df* value of 5 to filter features that occur rarely in the training data. For the XTransformer projects, we reused the model-specific hyperparameters from our previous work. The final hyperparameters can be seen in the project configuration files on GitHub[7].

4.4 Adding synthetic data

We evaluated the quality of the eight synthetic training record sets (2 languages $\times$ 4 LLMs) by training Bonsai models using the original training data plus each of the synthetic sets in turn and evaluated the resulting models against the development set. The evaluation scores are shown in Table 4 in Appendix E. We ranked the synthetic data sets by descending nDCG score and trained models with the original training records plus 2, 3 and 4 sets of synthetic records. The nDCG scores started to plateau after the 3rd set of synthetic data, as shown in Figure 4 in Appendix E. The best nDCG score was achieved using two sets of the original data (each record was used twice) and all four sets of synthetic records. We chose this setup for our final Bonsai models.

For XTransformer, we performed similar experiments. The evaluation results did not improve much after two sets of synthetic data, so we chose to use only the original records plus two sets of synthetic records for the final XTransformer models. We did not use synthetic data for MLLM because the original records were sufficient.

The final evaluation scores for the base projects are shown in Table 5 in Appendix F. The Bonsai projects achieved the best scores in all cases, followed by XTransformer and MLLM.

4.5 Ensemble projects

We set up three kinds of ensemble projects that combined the base projects in different ways: a "BM" simple ensemble combining Bonsai and MLLM, and two "BMX" ensembles (simple + LLM ranking) that combine all three base projects

[7]https://github.com/NatLibFi/Annif-LLMs4Subjects-GermEval2025/blob/main/projects.toml

System	Ensemble type	development set / de		development set / en		test set / de+en		Rank
		F1@5	nDCG@20	F1@5	nDCG@20	F1@5	nDCG@20	
Annif (ours)	BM simple	0.3344	0.5923	0.3345	0.6101	0.3200	0.5496	
	BMX simple	0.3386	0.6012	0.3479	0.6162	0.3200	0.5507	
	BMX LLM Q4	0.3507	0.6259	0.3547	0.6329	0.3251	0.5631	
	BMX LLM M24	**0.3587**	**0.6375**	**0.3600**	**0.6412**	**0.3288**	**0.5697**	1st
Annif (ours)						**0.3288**	**0.5697**	1st
DNB-AI-Project						0.2466	0.4180	2nd
ubffm						0.0742	0.1465	3rd

Table 2: Quantitative evaluation results for the ensemble projects measured against the development and test sets. Other participating systems included for comparison. Development set results are split by language of the Annif project (de/en), while the test set results were produced using bilingual predictions.

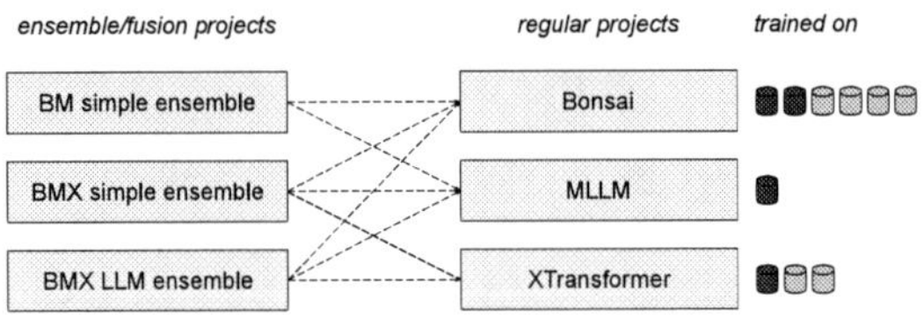

Figure 2: Annif base projects and ensembles.

(see Figure 2). We then tuned the simple ensembles using the `annif hyperopt` command to try 400 different combinations of weights and exponents per project, choosing hyperparameters that maximised the nDCG scores against the development set (see Table 6 in Appendix G).

In the BM ensembles, the Bonsai model contributed 85–90% while MLLM had a minor role. In the BMX ensembles, the Bonsai model contributed the most for English (46%), while XTransformer was the most important model for German (44%). The weighting exponents ranged from 0.63 to 1.17. We reused the optimised weights and exponents of the BMX simple ensembles also for the corresponding BMX LLM ensembles. The weighting exponents are intended to account for the differing scoring scales of the backends, as the relative relevance of the algorithms can vary depending on the score range. We set up two variants of the LLM ensembles: 1) using the smaller Q4 LLM and 2) using the larger M24 LLM. The results of evaluating the ensembles against the development set are shown in Table 2.

Teams were allowed to submit up to 10 different system outputs (up to 20 subject predictions per test set record) to the Codabench system[8] used for evaluation. We translated the test records to produce German-only and English-only versions of each record using the same LLM choices as for the train and development records. For each of the ensemble types, we first produced 100 predictions each using the German and English versions of the ensembles, then merged the predictions by summing the scores of the predicted subjects and choosing the top 20 subjects by score. We submitted these bilingual predictions.

[8] `https://www.codabench.org/competitions/8373/`

5 Results

The main quantitative metric used for ranking systems was nDCG@20, but other metrics such as precision, recall, F1 score and R-precision were also provided by the Codabench system. The bilingual predictions of our LLM ranking ensemble using the M24 LLM ranked 1st with a nDCG@20 score of 0.5697 (see Table 2).

System	nDCG@20 C1	nDCG@20 C2	Rank
Annif (ours)	**0.8787**	**0.7699**	1st
DNB-AI-Project	0.6545	0.5837	2nd
ubffm	0.3454	0.2471	3rd

Table 3: Qualitative evaluation results for systems in cases 1 (C1) and 2 (C2)

Subject librarians conducted a qualitative evaluation as well: five different subject classification categories were considered, each containing 10 records, within which the top 20 GND codes for each submission were assessed as correct (Y), technically correct but irrelevant (I), or incorrect (N or blank). Two types qualitative results were calculated: one considering both Y and I as correct (Case 1), and another considering only Y as correct (Case 2). The results are detailed in Table 3. Annif was ranked first in both cases with the overall nDCG@20 being 0.8787 in the first and 0.7699 in the second case.

6 Conclusions

We experimented with different local LLMs and found that some models, including A8 (Aya 8B), G4 (Gemma3 4B) and Q4 (Qwen3 4B) have a particularly good balance of quality and efficiency. By using LLM-generated synthetic training data, we could improve the results of traditional XMTC models: Bonsai improved a lot, while the improvements for XTransformer were less dramatic. The new LLM ranking ensemble approach improved the nDCG scores of topic suggestions by 0.01-0.03 compared to simple ensembles. The four different ensembles allow different compromises to be made between quality and computational efficiency, with the best scores achieved using a larger M24 LLM and somewhat lower scores for the smaller Q4 LLM and the simpler ensembles that do not require an LLM at all.

Acknowledgments

The authors wish to thank the Finnish Computing Competence Infrastructure (FCCI) for supporting this project with computational and data storage resources.

References

Jennifer D'Souza, Sameer Sadruddin, Holger Israel, Mathias Begoin, and Diana Slawig. 2025. SemEval-2025 task 5: LLMs4Subjects - LLM-based automated subject tagging for a national technical library's open-access catalog. In *Proceedings of the 19th International Workshop on Semantic Evaluation (SemEval-2025)*, pages 2570–2583, Vienna, Austria. Association for Computational Linguistics.

Jennifer D'Souza, Sameer Sadruddin, Holger Israel, Mathias Begoin, and Diana Slawig. 2025. The GermEval 2025 2nd LLMs4Subjects Shared Task Dataset.

Kalervo Järvelin and Jaana Kekäläinen. 2002. Cumulated gain-based evaluation of IR techniques. *ACM Trans. Inf. Syst.*, 20(4):422–446.

Sujay Khandagale, Han Xiao, and Rohit Babbar. 2020. Bonsai: Diverse and shallow trees for extreme multi-label classification. *Machine Learning*, 109(11):2099–2119.

Lisa Kluge and Maximilian Kähler. 2025. DNB-AI-Project at SemEval-2025 task 5: An LLM-Ensemble approach for automated subject indexing. In *Proceedings of the 19th International Workshop on Semantic Evaluation (SemEval-2025)*, pages 1114–1124, Vienna, Austria. Association for Computational Linguistics.

Olena Medelyan. 2009. *Human-competitive automatic topic indexing*. Ph.D. thesis, The University of Waikato.

Yashoteja Prabhu, Anil Kag, Shrutendra Harsola, Rahul Agrawal, and Manik Varma. 2018. Parabel: Partitioned label trees for extreme classification with application to dynamic search advertising. WWW '18, page 993–1002, Republic and Canton of Geneva, CHE. International World Wide Web Conferences Steering Committee.

Osma Suominen, Juho Inkinen, and Mona Lehtinen. 2022. Annif and Finto AI: Developing and implementing automated subject indexing. *JLIS.it*, 13(1):265–282.

Osma Suominen, Juho Inkinen, and Mona Lehtinen. 2025. Annif at SemEval-2025 task 5: Traditional XMTC augmented by LLMs. In *Proceedings of the 19th International Workshop on Semantic Evaluation (SemEval-2025)*, pages 2395–2402, Vienna, Austria. Association for Computational Linguistics.

Hsiang-Fu Yu, Kai Zhong, Jiong Zhang, Wei-Cheng Chang, and Inderjit S. Dhillon. 2022. PECOS: Prediction for enormous and correlated output spaces. *Preprint*, arXiv:2010.05878.

A Ensemble with weighting exponents

Annif supports a simple ensemble approach that performs weighted averaging of prediction scores from multiple projects. Automated hyperparameter optimisation can be used to discover the weight values that maximise the evaluation results measured against a development set.

For this task, we enhanced the Annif simple ensemble by adding support for weighting exponents. The concept-specific prediction scores of the simple ensemble are calculated using the formula

$$f = \sum_{k=1}^{n} w_k \cdot x_k^{p_k}$$

where f is the final combined prediction score, x_k is the prediction score from the k-th project, w_k is the weight coefficient for the k-th project (weights add up to 1.0), p_k is the power exponent for the k-th project and n is the total number of projects in the ensemble. Along with the weights, the optimal exponents can be found using hyperparameter optimisation.

B LLM ranking ensemble

We implemented a new type of ensemble in Annif based on the idea of an LLM that ranks candidate subjects based on how well they describe a given text. As in the simple ensemble, the subject predictions from multiple projects are first combined using configurable weights and exponents. The top K combined predictions (we chose $K = 100$) are then given to an LLM along with the document text, and the LLM is prompted to respond with relevance scores (from 0 to 100) for each candidate subject. The final subject predictions of the LLM ranking ensemble are calculated using the formula

$$f = w \cdot r^p + (1 - w)x$$

where x is the combined prediction from the source projects (calculated as in the simple ensemble above), r is the relevance score given by the LLM (rescaled to the interval $[0.0, 1.0]$), w is the weight (0.0 to 1.0) and p is the weighting exponent given to the LLM prediction. The optimal weights and exponents for the LLM ranking can be found using hyperparameter optimisation.

C Details about LLM usage

We used the vLLM[9] inference engine to translate and synthesise records and to rank candidate subjects. For the processing, we used a single NVIDIA A100 GPU with 80GB VRAM from the University of Helsinki HPC cluster Turso.

C.1 Prompt templates

In the following prompt templates, the system prompt is set in *italics*. Tags in the template were replaced with relevant information from the records. The prompt templates are the same as in our earlier work (Suominen et al., 2025), except for the ranking prompt, which is new to this system.

C.1.1 Record translation

This prompt was used to translate records:

You are a professional translator specialized in translating bibliographic metadata.

Your task is to ensure that the given document title and description are in <LANGUAGE> language, translating the text if necessary. If the text is already in <LANGUAGE>, do not change or summarize it, keep it all as it is.

Respond with only the text, nothing else.

Give this title and description in <LANGUAGE>:

<TITLE>

<DESCRIPTION>

---

[9] https://docs.vllm.ai

C.1.2 Record synthesis

This prompt was used to synthesise new records:

You are a professional metadata manager.

Your task is to create new bibliographic metadata: document titles and descriptions.

Here is an example document title and description in <LANGUAGE> with the following subject keywords: <OLD_KEYWORDS>

<TITLE_DESC>

Generate a new document title and description in <LANGUAGE>. Respond with only the title and description, nothing else. Create a new title and description that match the following subject keywords: <NEW_KEYWORDS>

C.1.3 Ranking of candidate concepts

This prompt was used to rank candidate concepts:

You will be given text and a list of keywords to describe it. Your task is to score the keywords with a value between 0 and 100. The score value should depend on how well the keyword represents the text: a perfect keyword should have score 100 and completely unrelated keyword score 0. You must output JSON with keywords as field names and add their scores as field values. There must be the same number of objects in the JSON as there are lines in the intput keyword list; do not skip scoring any keywords.

D LLMs for translating metadata

The evaluation results of different LLMs for translating metadata are shown in Figure 3.

E Evaluation results for synthetic data

Lang	Train data	nDCG@20
de	orig	0.5122
	orig+A8	**0.5513**
	orig+Q4	0.5492
	orig+G4	0.5488
	orig+E9	0.5469
en	orig	0.5595
	orig+Q4	**0.5896**
	orig+A8	0.5889
	orig+S8	0.5845
	orig+G4	0.5845

Table 4: Evaluation scores when evaluating Omikuji Bonsai trained using various combinations of original and synthetic data against the development set.

The evaluation results of different LLMs for producing synthetic records are shown in Table 4. All

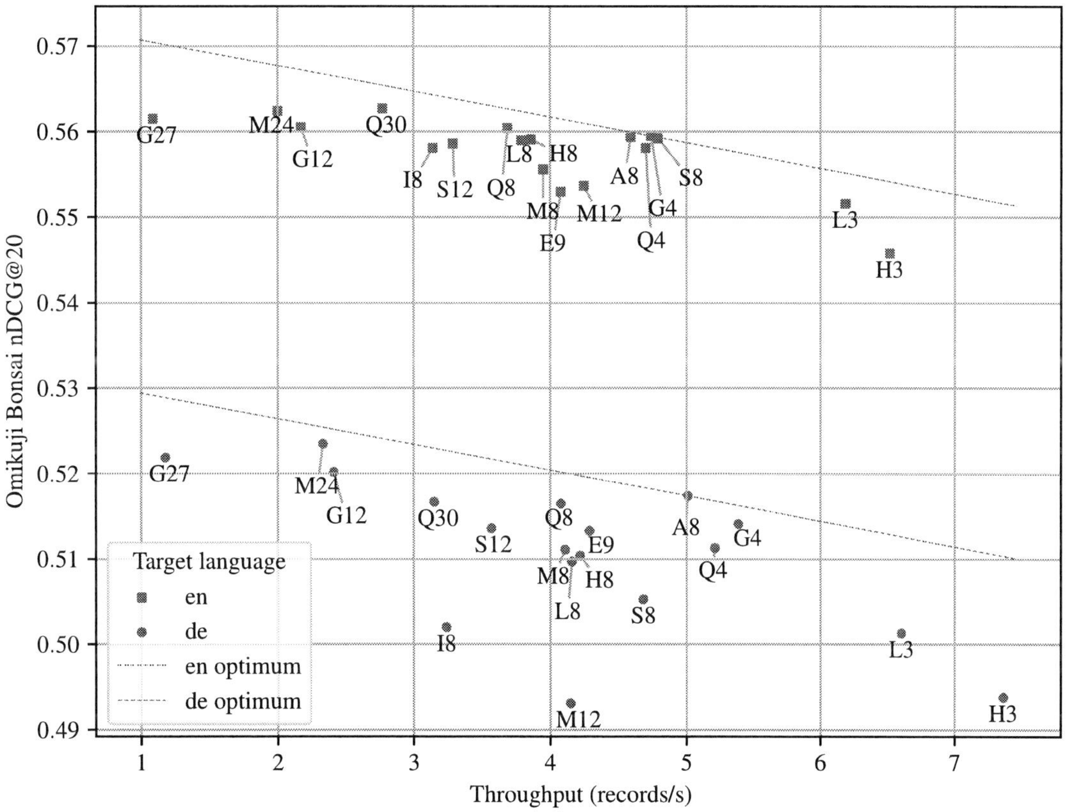

Figure 3: Evaluation of different LLMs for translating metadata records into English and German. The lines indicate the maximum value for the combined quality and efficiency score; the best models are located near the lines.

the tested models produced similar levels of improvement in terms of nDCG score. Figure 4 shows the improvement in nDCG scores after adding multiple sets of synthetic data to the original data.

F Results for base projects

Backend	Lang	F1@5	nDCG@20
Bonsai	de	**0.3229**	**0.5701**
	en	**0.3401**	**0.5985**
MLLM	de	0.2487	0.4437
	en	0.2304	0.4180
XTransformer	de	0.3189	0.5609
	en	0.3122	0.5517

Table 5: Evaluation scores of the base projects measured against the development set. The best scores for each language have been set in **bold**.

The evaluation results of the final base projects are shown in Table 5.

G Ensemble overview, weights and exponents

Type	Bonsai	MLLM	XTransformer
BM/de	0.8523:1.1119	0.1477:1.1611	-
BM/en	0.9015:1.0342	0.0985:0.8483	-
BMX/de	0.3823:1.0457	0.1734:1.1675	0.4443:1.0794
BMX/en	0.4608:0.6855	0.2403:0.8567	0.2989:0.6290

Table 6: Optimised weights and exponents (given as *weight* : *exponent*) of the base projects in the BM and BMX ensembles.

An overview of the configurations of the BM and BMX ensembles with optimised weights and exponents is shown in Table 6. For the LLM ranking ensemble, we used an LLM weight of 0.1592 (exponent 7.898) for English and 0.0921 (exponent 9.328) for German. Thus, the LLM ranking had only a relatively small effect on individual prediction scores, but overall output quality improved, as shown in the evaluation results.

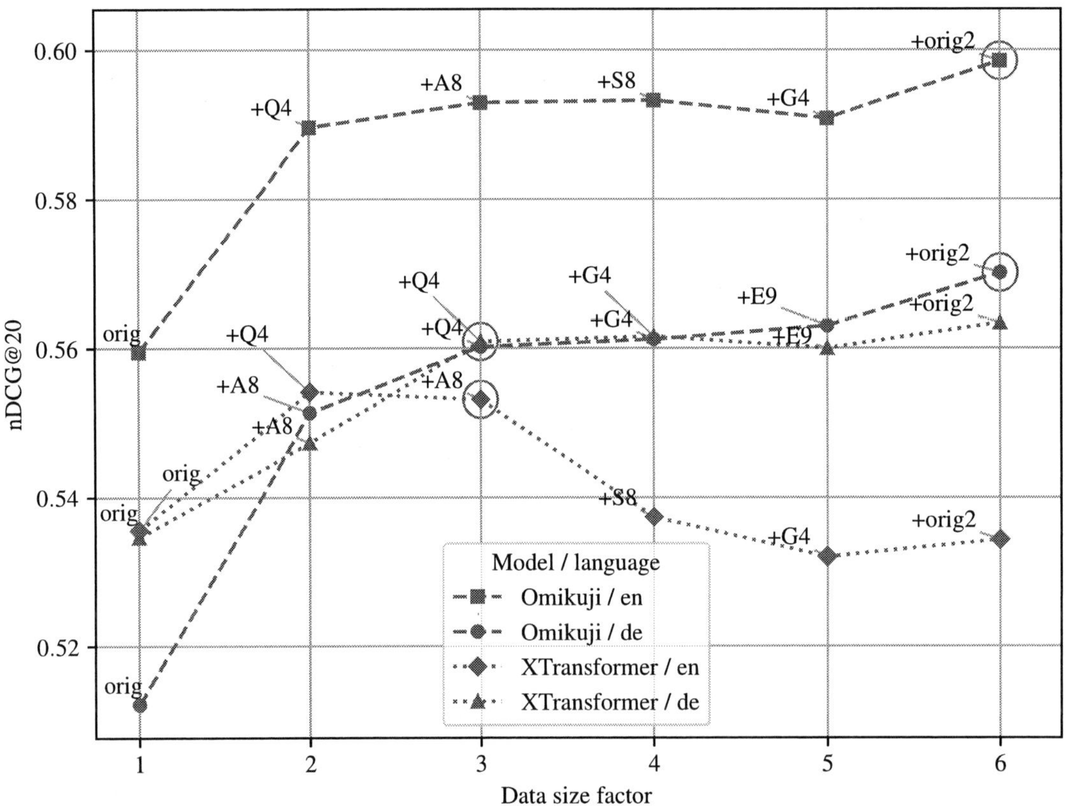

Figure 4: Effect of adding synthetic training data for Omikuji Bonsai and XTransformer models. The models were evaluated against the development set. The circles indicate our final choice of synthetic data: four sets of synthetic data and a doubling of the original records for Omikuji Bonsai, and two sets of synthetic data for XTransformer.

DNB-AI-Project at the GermEval-2025 LLMs4Subjects Task: KIFSPrompt - Knowledge-Injected Few-Shot Prompting

Maximilian Kähler and **Katja Konermann** and **Lisa Kluge**
Deutsche Nationalbibliothek
Leipzig/ Frankfurt am Main, Germany

Correspondence: m.kaehler@dnb.de

Abstract

This work-in-progress report presents our system, KIFSPrompt, developed for the second phase of the shared task LLMs4Subjects at GermEval'25. The primary focus of this phase is the development of energy- and compute-efficient large language model (LLM) systems for subject tagging in library cataloging systems. A key challenge in this task is the requirement to select keywords from a large, normed vocabulary, the Integrated Authority File (GND). Building on our previous work ([12] and [13]), our system leverages few-shot prompting, where a generative LLM is presented with a limited number of examples of texts annotated with subject terms, and prompted to identify the most relevant subject terms for a new input text. To ensure alignment with the library's normed subject terms, we employ a mapping approach based on embedding similarity. We extend our previous work by incorporating a retrieval stage, which selects relevant few-shot examples from the training set to create knowledge-injected prompts, enabling the LLM to provide more specific and accurate keyword suggestions. This enhancement allows the LLM to adapt to the input text, resulting in improved performance in a single prompt.

1 Motivation

LLMs4Subjects [6, 7] is a shared task organized by TIB[1] aiming at utilising large language models (LLMs) for the task of automated subject indexing. In the previous round for LLMs4Subjects, the DNB-AI-Project submitted a prototype that employed a multitude of LLMs in a Few-Shot-Prompting ensemble to solve the subject tagging problem. While results did not outperform other methods when directly compared to the gold-standard subject terms that were intellectually annotated following the German rules for subject headings (RSKW[2]), our approach was ranked first in the qualitative ratings conducted by TIB's subject librarians. However, a major drawback of our previous work is the computational complexity involved in generating keywords from multiple LLMs with multiple prompts. During keyword generation, each test document would undergo a series of 20 LLM-calls with LLMs of varying size. With our on-premise hardware, generating subject terms for the LLMs4Subjects test set took 234 GPUh in total. While showing an increase in quality, this immense resource consumption disqualifies our previous system from being of practical relevance for (usually poorly equipped) library systems. In line with the main theme of developing compute- and energy-efficient systems in this second phase of the shared task, we aim at reducing the cost of the system by restricting ourselves to two LLM-calls per document: (*complete* and *rank*) complemented by two similarity search stages (*retrieve* and *map*).

Inspired by the work on analogical reasoning of LA²I²F [21] in the first round of LLMs4Subjects, our main advance in this second round is to add a similar retrieval step to our system pipeline. For any test document, the retrieval stage extracts the top L documents from the training set most similar to the test document. The LLM prompt is then assembled from these most similar training examples, along with their annotated GND labels. This dynamic assembling of few-shot examples directly injects knowledge of related documents and the relevant GND subject terms into the prompt, bridging the problem that a pre-trained LLM would have no knowledge of relevant subject terms in the GND.

2 Related Work

One established perspective on subject tagging with a normed vocabulary is to approach the prob-

[1] TIB: German National Library of Science and Technology

[2] Regeln für die Schlagwortkatalogisierung, cf. https://d-nb.info/1126513032/34

Proceedings of the 21st Conference on Natural Language Processing (KONVENS), Volume 2: Workshops, pages 455–464, 2025

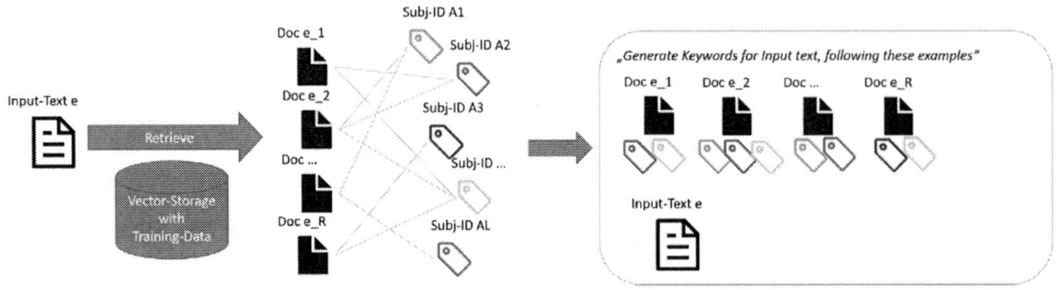

Figure 1: Assembling the knowledge injected few-shot prompt from training data. Training data is processed with an embedding model and indexed in a vector storage. Hybrid search enables retrieval of documents similar to the input document. A few-shot prompt is dynamically assembled using the retrieved training documents and their known subject terms.

lem as an extreme multilabel classification problem (XMLC). Dasgupta et al. [5] gives a recent overview of developments in XMLC algorithms. Using backends of the Annif toolkit, Poley et al. [19] used a combination of XMLC algorithms and classical lexical matching [18, 9] to address the problem of extracting subject terms from the GND in a productive library system.

Pushing forward the capabilities of Annif, Suominen et al. [22] extended Annif with another XMLC backend [3, 24] and used LLMs for translation as well as generation of synthetic data to achieve top performance in the first phase of LLMs4Subjects.

Combining retrieval techniques with generative language models goes back to Lewis et al. [15]'s work on retrieval augmented generation (RAG). The first phase of LLMs4Subjects [6] has stimulated many contributions to the field, that follow RAG-like approaches. Besides the work of Salfinger et al. [21], which directly inspired this new adaptation of our system, team Tian et al. [23] used a multi-stage LLM approach, including data synthesis, knowledge distillation, fine-tuning, retrieval, and re-ranking, which achieved high marks in quantitative and qualitative scores of LLMs4Subjects.

3 System Description

3.1 Stage Design

Our system can be described as a sequential process of four stages. We start with an input text e:

1. Retrieve: Based on embedding similarity, a vector search among the training documents is performed, retrieving the top L documents most similar to the input text e. Based on the language of the input text, which is recorded in each documents metadata, only training documents of the same language are selected.

2. Complete: A prompt is assembled containing the retrieved top L documents and their annotated subject terms as few-shot examples, as well as the input text. An LLM generates keyword suggestions from this prompt.

3. Map: Generated keywords are mapped to subject terms in the target vocabulary using hybrid search [2] based on embedding similarity and BM25 [20].

4. Rank: An LLM ranks the suggested subject terms according to their relevance to the input text.

Figure 1 illustrates how the few-shot prompt is assembled from similar training documents and the input text. The system instruction and an example prompt for the *complete* stage is displayed in Table 1. Note, the translation in the table is only for readability. We did not translate texts or subject terms in our system. In particular, English examples would be presented with German subject terms inside a prompt. However, we restricted the retrieved examples to fit the language of the input text using the language metadata of the record. The example demonstrates how the retrieval stage selects few-shot examples that are highly similar to the input text.

The stages *Map* and *Rank* work as in our previous system, cf. [13]. Instructions for the rank stage can be found in appendix A.1. The system does not involve any fine-tuning and works with off-the-shelf open-weight models from Hugging Face[3].

[3] `https://huggingface.co/`

	German Prompt	English Translation
INSTRUCTION	<|im_start|>system Dies ist eine Unterhaltung zwischen einem intelligenten, hilfsbereitem KI-Assistenten und einem Nutzer. Der Assistent antwortet mit Schlagwörtern auf den Text des Nutzers. <|im_end|>	<|im_start|>system This is a conversation between an intelligent, helpful AI assistant and a user. The assistant responds with keywords to the user's text. <|im_end|>
RETRIEVED EXAMPLE 1	<|im_start|>user Gleitende Übergänge in den Ruhestand: Wirkung auf die Erwerbsbeteiligung und das Humankapital Älterer in Deutschland ... <|im_end|> <|im_start|>assistant Altersteilzeitarbeit, Arbeitsangebot, Humankapital, Wirkungsanalyse <|im_end|>	<|im_start|>user Gradual transitions into retirement: Effects on labor force participation and human capital of older people in Germany ... <|im_end|> <|im_start|>assistant Partial retirement, labor supply, human capital, impact analysis <|im_end|>
RETRIEVED EXAMPLE 2	<|im_start|>user Eingliedern statt ausmustern: Möglichkeiten und Strategien zur Sicherung der Erwerbstätigkeit älterer Arbeitnehmer ... <|im_end|> <|im_start|>assistant Älterer Arbeitnehmer, Erwerbsfähigkeit, Gesundheitspolitik, Personalpolitik <|im_end|>	<|im_start|>user Integrate instead of discarding: Options and strategies to secure employment of older workers ... <|im_end|> <|im_start|>assistant Older worker, employability, health policy, personnel policy <|im_end|>
FURTHER RETRIEVED EXAMPLES	...	...
TEST-TEXT	<|im_start|>user Arbeit im Alter: Zur Bedeutung bezahlter und unbezahlter Tätigkeiten in der Lebensphase Ruhestand ... <|im_end|> <|im_start|>assistant	<|im_start|>user Work in old age: On the importance of paid and unpaid activities in the retirement phase of life ... <|im_end|> <|im_start|>assistant
GENERATED KEYWORDS	'Ruhestand', 'Gesundheit', 'Arbeit', 'Geschlecht', 'Alter'	'Retirement', 'Health', 'Work', 'Gender', 'Age'

Table 1: Example for a dynamically created few-shot prompt used for the *complete* stage. Input text is displayed in green. Generated keywords are printed in red.

3.2 Implementation Details

As embedding model for the *Retrieve* and *Map* stages, we used Chen et al. [4]'s BGE-M3-embeddings, for their good benchmark results and multilingual capabilities. Our vector search is powered by a local Weaviate[4] vector storage, enabling efficient HNSW-Search [16] in the target vocabulary (*Map*) and the training data set (*Retrieve*). The hybrid search is configured with a weight-value of $\alpha = 0.7$ between HNSW-Search and BM25. The number of retrieved documents was set to $L = 8$.[5] However, if the concatenation of the examples in the few-shot prompt exceeded the total length of 15,000 tokens, the number of examples was automatically reduced accordingly. For the generation stage (*Complete*) we used Mistral AI's `Ministral-8B-Instruct-2410`[6] instruction-tuned eight billion parameter model. The ranking was conducted with Dubey et al. [8]'s `Llama-3.1-8B-Instruct`[7] of similar size. The models were chosen as large as possible, such that each model would fit a single NVIDIA A100 GPU with 80 GB GPU RAM at 16-bit floating point precision for the model weights and still allow for a prompt length of up to 15 000 tokens. To have some independence between *Complete* and *Rank* we selected the models to stem from distinct base models and model providers. All stage processes were synchronized in a data processing pipeline using DVC [14]. Calculations were performed with on-premise hardware consisting of a 2 x Intel(R) Xeon(R) Gold 6338T CPU @ 2.10GHz (48 cores) architecture equipped with two NVIDIA A100 GPU processors.

[4] `https://weaviate.io/`

[5] See section A.3 in the appendix for a sensitivity analysis on the choice of L

[6] `https://huggingface.co/mistralai/Ministral-8B-Instruct-2410`

[7] `https://huggingface.co/meta-llama/Llama-3.1-8B-Instruct`

4 Metrics

The shared task evaluates results according to standard information retrieval metrics: Precision, Recall, F1-Measure and NDCG. These are computed as document averages with varying limits $k = 5, 10, 15, 20$ on the system's ranked output. As our system produces varying numbers of predicted subject terms per record, we added another metric, called R-Precision [17]:

$$\text{R-Prec} := \frac{\text{tp}}{\min(\text{tp} + \text{fp}, \text{tp} + \text{fn})} \quad (1)$$

with the usual notion of fp for false positives, tp for true positives, and fn for false negatives. R-Precision does not penalize a system if it produces fewer than k subject terms per record, provided that the gold standard also assigns fewer subject terms.

5 Results

5.1 Quantitative Results

When comparing suggested subject terms with intellectually annotated subject terms on the shared task's test set, we find the following results (Table 2). We restrict ourselves to the upper part of the ranking ($k = 5$), as our system does not usually produce more than 5 suggested subject terms.[8] Appendix A.4 analyzes our system's behaviour in terms of varying numbers of predicted subject terms per record. We hypothesize that our system is adapting the number of predicted subject terms per record from related training examples.

Team	Prec@5	Recall@5	F1@5	R-Prec@5
annif	0.272	0.513	0.323	0.525
DNB-AI-Project	0.202	0.395	0.247	0.466
ubffm	0.059	0.128	0.119	0.074

Table 2: Quantitative evaluation leaderboard on *Test-Set* ($n = 27,998$). The table contains only a selection of the official results, restricted to $k = 5$.

Our system is placed second out of three in this quantitative evaluation, with a significant margin to both contending teams. Notably, recall@5 is much higher than precision@5, indicating that a limit of $k = 5$ presumably does not strike an ideal precision-recall balance, in terms of F1-Score.

5.2 Qualitative Results

Opposed to the binary relevance rating of section 5.1, where a suggested subject term is either right or wrong according to the gold standard, the qualitative evaluation by TIB's subject experts assesses the correctness of suggestions, regardless of the gold standard that was actually assigned. Subject terms counted as false positives in the quantitative evaluation can be marked as correct in the qualitative rating. This evaluation is titled *Case 1*. Table 3 shows the qualitative leaderboard for Case 1. Ratings were conducted for a full ranking of theoretically $k = 20$ suggested subject terms per record. As our system is not designed to produce suggestions of arbitrary length, again, we only include the results at $k = 5$.

Team	Prec@5	Recall@5	NDCG@5	F1@5
Annif	0.820	0.353	0.871	0.494
DNB-AI-Project	0.520	0.580	0.707	0.548
ubffm	0.256	0.180	0.273	0.211

Table 3: Qualitative leaderboard Case 1 ($n = 50$)

In a second scenario, *Case 2*, subject librarians rated the usefulness of suggested subjects for retrieval purposes, which is more strict. General subject terms that are technically correct (and might even occur in the gold standard), but are irrelevant for retrieval from a user perspective, are ignored in this scenario. Table 4 summarizes the results for Case 2.

Team	Prec@5	Recall@5	NDCG@5	F1@5
Annif	0.604	0.428	0.712	0.501
DNB-AI-Project	0.392	0.522	0.617	0.448
ubffm	0.160	0.151	0.192	0.155

Table 4: Qualitative leaderboard Case 2 ($n = 50$)

In the Case 1 evaluation, KIFSPrompt achieves the best results in terms of F1@5 among the three teams. However, Team Annif still outperforms our system in terms of NDCG@5 and higher-rank metrics, as well as in the Case 2 scenario. In both qualitative evaluation scenarios KIFSPrompt scores highest in terms of recall@5. Further results containing scores by subject group can be found in the appendix A.5.

5.3 Error Analysis

In our development cycle on a small dev-set subsample, our `KIFSPrompt` system was able to perform on par with our previous `llm-ensemble` approach. However, transferring the results to the shared task's test set did not work equally well. Table 5 compares the performance of our two systems `llm-ensemble` and `KIFSPrompt` on our dev-sample as well as the test set. `KIFSPrompt`

[8] Visit the official task site for the full leaderboard.

has a large drop in recall@5 and also loses a significant amount of precision, whereas the `llm-ensemble` has a smaller performance deterioration. One reason for this behaviour could be a data distribution shift between the training set and the test set. The `llm-ensemble` does not draw any knowledge from the training set, so its performance does not depend on the training data distribution. However, `KIFSPrompt` relies on similarity of training and test data. The more similar the training documents are to the test documents, the more likely it is that `KIFSPrompt` will find correct subject terms in the examples.

Name	Prec@5	Recall@5	F1@5	R-Prec@5
Test-Set (n = 27,998)				
KIFSPrompt	0.202	0.395	0.247	0.466
llm-ensemble	0.247	0.473	0.301	0.485
Dev-Set-Subsample (n = 1,000)				
KIFSPrompt	0.237	0.467	0.311	0.517
llm-ensemble	0.247	0.500	0.328	0.510

Table 5: Comparison of system performance of our two approaches on Test and Dev sets.

Further system comparison of `KIFSPrompt` with our `llm-ensemble` can be found in the appendix section A.2.

5.4 Saved Resources

With the rapid development of the field, it is difficult to make an explicit comparison with our previous system. For example, we found that already an upgrade to the latest version of our inference engine vLLM[9] significantly improved speed in the generation steps. Also, there is a constant time-overhead for loading a model. Averaged over the test set of 27,998 documents, the completion stage for our llm-ensemble approach was at 30.1 s/*it*, whereas our `KIFSPrompt` system is at 0.5 s/*it*. Thus, our system uses less than two percent of the resources, in contrast to our previous approach. This saving in resources can be attributed to two facts: Firstly, during the completion step we only need one LLM call (in contrast to 20 previously). Secondly, we restrict to the smaller model `Ministral-8B-Instruct-2410`, rather than invoking large models such as `Meta-Llama-3.1-70B-Instruct` or `Mixtral-8x7B-Instruct-v0.1` in the LLM-Ensemble.

[9] version 0.6.4 → 0.9.0.1

6 Conclusion and Future Work

The introduction of Knowledge-Injected Few-Shot Prompting yields a significant reduction in costs compared to our previous approach, making it a viable option for resource-constrained institutions. Notably, `KIFSPrompt` can be seamlessly integrated with off-the-shelf language models, eliminating the need for costly training or fine-tuning. This makes it an attractive solution for libraries or institutions with limited hardware budgets. However, the optimal balance between quality and resources may vary depending on the specific use case and circumstances. The qualitative ranking shows, that our system can outperform even sophisticated ensemble approaches, such as Annif, in the $k <= 5$ part of the ranking, which is most relevant for practical library systems. As such, `KIFSPrompt` presents a valuable alternative for certain institutions, further expanding the quality-resource landscape of subject indexing systems and providing a useful benchmark for future developments. Using LLMs for subject indexing remains a promising road. There are ample opportunities to enhance such systems. Combining `KIFSPrompt` with our previous `llm-ensemble` approach could be a promising way to further improve quality. Additionally, evaluating `KIFSPrompt` with smaller language models may lead to further resource savings.

In the shared Task LLMs4Subjects, keywords are organized in a knowledge graph-like structure. Future research could explore how to leverage the relationships between keywords as an additional source of information for subject indexing using LLMs, cf. [11, 25, 1]. Moreover, fine-tuning a generative model specifically for this task may yield further performance improvements by adapting its parameters to the domain. Investigating parameter-efficient fine-tuning methods (cf. [10]) which reduce training time and memory consumption could also be advantageous in this context.

Acknowledgements

We thank the anonymous reviewers for their helpful feedback. This work is a result of a research project at the German National Library (DNB)[10]. The project is funded by the German Minister of State for Culture and the Media as part of the national AI strategy.

[10] `https://www.dnb.de/ki-projekt`

References

[1] Kriti Bhattarai, Inez Y. Oh, Zachary B. Abrams, and Albert M. Lai. 2024. Document-level clinical entity and relation extraction via knowledge base-guided generation. In *Proceedings of the 23rd Workshop on Biomedical Natural Language Processing*, pages 318–327, Bangkok, Thailand. Association for Computational Linguistics.

[2] Erika Cardenas. Hybrid search explained [online]. 2025.

[3] Wei-Cheng Chang, Hsiang-Fu Yu, Kai Zhong, Yiming Yang, and Inderjit S. Dhillon. 2020. Taming pretrained transformers for extreme multi-label text classification. In *Proceedings of the 26th ACM SIGKDD International Conference on Knowledge Discovery & Data Mining*, pages 3163–3171. ACM.

[4] Jianlv Chen, Shitao Xiao, Peitian Zhang, Kun Luo, Defu Lian, and Zheng Liu. 2024. Bge m3-embedding: Multi-lingual, multi-functionality, multi-granularity text embeddings through self-knowledge distillation. *arXiv e-prints*, page arXiv:2402.03216.

[5] Arpan Dasgupta, Siddhant Katyan, Shrutimoy Das, and Pawan Kumar. 2023. Review of extreme multilabel classification.

[6] Jennifer D'souza, Sameer Sadruddin, Holger Israel, Mathias Begoin, and Diana Slawig. 2025. SemEval-2025 task 5: LLMs4Subjects - LLM-based automated subject tagging for a national technical library's open-access catalog. In *Proceedings of the 19th International Workshop on Semantic Evaluation (SemEval-2025)*, pages 2570–2583, Vienna, Austria. Association for Computational Linguistics.

[7] Jennifer D'Souza, Sameer Sadruddin, Holger Israel, Mathias Begoin, and Diana Slawig. 2025. The GermEval 2025 2nd LLMs4Subjects Shared Task Dataset.

[8] Abhimanyu Dubey, Abhinav Jauhri, Abhinav Pandey, Abhishek Kadian, Ahmad Al-Dahle, Aiesha Letman, Akhil Mathur, Alan Schelten, Amy Yang, Angela Fan, et al. 2024. The llama 3 herd of models. *arXiv preprint arXiv:2407.21783*.

[9] Eibe Frank, Gordon W Paynter, Ian H Witten, Carl Gutwin, and Craig G Nevill-Manning. 1999. Domain-specific keyphrase extraction. In *Proceedings of the 16 th International Joint Conference on Arti Intelligence (IJCAI99*, pages 668–673. Morgan Kaufmann.

[10] Zeyu Han, Chao Gao, Jinyang Liu, Jeff Zhang, and Sai Qian Zhang. 2024. Parameter-efficient fine-tuning for large models: A comprehensive survey. *Transactions on Machine Learning Research*.

[11] Jinhao Jiang, Kun Zhou, Zican Dong, Keming Ye, Xin Zhao, and Ji-Rong Wen. 2023. StructGPT: A general framework for large language model to reason over structured data. In *Proceedings of the 2023 Conference on Empirical Methods in Natural Language Processing*, pages 9237–9251, Singapore. Association for Computational Linguistics.

[12] Lisa Kluge and Maximilian Kähler. 2024. Few-shot prompting for subject indexing of German medical book titles. In *Proceedings of the 20th Conference on Natural Language Processing (KONVENS 2024)*, pages 141–148, Vienna, Austria. Association for Computational Linguistics.

[13] Lisa Kluge and Maximilian Kähler. 2025. Dnb-ai-project at semeval-2025 task 5: An llm-ensemble approach for automated subject indexing. In *Proceedings of the 19th International Workshop on Semantic Evaluation (SemEval-2025)*, page 1114–1124, Vienna, Austria. Association for Computational Linguistics.

[14] Ruslan Kuprieiev, skshetry, Peter Rowlands, Dmitry Petrov, Paweł Redzyński, Casper da Costa-Luis, David de la Iglesia Castro, Alexander Schepanovski, Ivan Shcheklein, Gao, Batuhan Taskaya, Jorge Orpinel, Fábio Santos, Daniele, Ronan Lamy, Aman Sharma, Zhanibek Kaimuldenov, Dani Hodovic, Nikita Kodenko, Andrew Grigorev, Earl, Nabanita Dash, George Vyshnya, Dave Berenbaum, maykulkarni, Max Hora, Vera, and Sanidhya Mangal. 2025. Dvc: Data version control - git for data & models.

[15] Patrick Lewis, Ethan Perez, Aleksandra Piktus, Fabio Petroni, Vladimir Karpukhin, Naman Goyal, Heinrich Küttler, Mike Lewis, Wen-tau Yih, Tim Rocktäschel, Sebastian Riedel, and Douwe Kiela. 2020. Retrieval-augmented generation for knowledge-intensive nlp tasks. In *Advances in Neural Information Processing Systems*, volume 33, pages 9459–9474. Curran Associates, Inc.

[16] Yu A. Malkov and D. A. Yashunin. 2016. Efficient and robust approximate nearest neighbor search using hierarchical navigable small world graphs. *IEEE Transactions on Pattern Analysis and Machine Intelligence*, 42:824–836.

[17] Christopher D. Manning, Prabhakar Raghavan, and Hinrich Schütze. 2012. *Introduction to Information Retrieval*. Cambridge University Press.

[18] Olena Medelyan, Eibe Frank, and Ian H Witten. 2009. Human-competitive tagging using automatic keyphrase extraction. *ACL and AFNLP*, pages 6–7.

[19] Christoph Poley, Sandro Uhlmann, Frank Busse, Jan-Helge Jacobs, Maximilian Kähler, Matthias Nagelschmidt, and Markus Schumacher. 2025. Automatic subject cataloguing at the german national library. *LIBER Quarterly: The Journal of the Association of European Research Libraries*, 35:1–29.

[20] Stephen Robertson and Hugo Zaragoza. 2009. The probabilistic relevance framework: Bm25 and beyond. *Foundations and Trends® in Information Retrieval*, 3(4):333–389.

[21] Andrea Salfinger, Luca Zaccagna, Francesca Incitti, Gianluca G. M. De Nardi, Lorenzo Dal Fabbro, and Lauro Snidaro. 2025. LA^2I^2F at semeval-2025 task 5: Reasoning in embedding space – fusing analogical and ontology-based reasoning for document subject tagging. In *Proceedings of the 19th International Workshop on Semantic Evaluation (SemEval-2025)*, page 2384–2394, Vienna, Austria. Association for Computational Linguistics.

[22] Osma Suominen, Juho Inkinen, and Mona Lehtinen. 2025. Annif at semeval-2025 task 5: Traditional xmtc augmented by llms. In *Proceedings of the 19th International Workshop on Semantic Evaluation (SemEval-2025)*, pages 2395–2402, Vienna, Austria. Association for Computational Linguistics.

[23] Yicen Tian, Erchen Yu, Yanan Wang, Dailin Li, Jiaqi Yao, Hongfei Lin, Linlin Zong, and Bo Xu. 2025. Dutir831 at semeval-2025 task 5: A multi-stage llm approach to gnd subject assignment for tibkat records. In *Proceedings of the 19th International Workshop on Semantic Evaluation (SemEval-2025)*, pages 367–376, Vienna, Austria. Association for Computational Linguistics.

[24] Jiong Zhang, Wei cheng Chang, Hsiang fu Yu, and Inderjit S. Dhillon. 2021. Fast multi-resolution transformer fine-tuning for extreme multi-label text classification.

[25] Qinggang Zhang, Junnan Dong, Hao Chen, Daochen Zha, Zailiang Yu, and Xiao Huang. 2024. Knowgpt: Knowledge graph based prompting for large language models.

A Appendix

A.1 Instructions for *rank*

Figure 2 shows the instructions used for the ranking stage, also used in our previous system. We found that best results are achieved by presenting keywords individually and not as a set of keywords for each input text.

> Du erhälst einen Text und ein Schlagwort. Bewerte auf einer Skala von 0 bis 10, wie gut das Schlagwort zu dem Text passt. Nenne keine Begründungen. Gib nur die Zahl zwischen 0 und 10 zurück.
> *You receive a text and a keyword. Rate on a scale from 0 to 10 how well the keyword fits the text. Do not provide any explanations. Return only the number between 0 and 10.*

Figure 2: Instruction used for the *rank* stage.

A.2 System comparison KIFSPrompt vs. llm-ensemble

We include a precision-recall analysis on our dev-sample[11] ($n = 1,000$ documents), comparing `KIFSPrompt` with our previous `llm-ensemble` approach, cf. Figure 3. As a baseline, we also include the best results achieved with our single best hard-prompt (no dynamic few-shot examples) and best LLM (`Mixtral-8x7B-Instruct-v0.1`) from the previous study. All three curves include the LLM-ranking stage with `Llama-3.1-8B-Instruct` as post-processing. Table 6 shows point estimates for precision and recall that achieve optimal F1-score on the PR-curves. The optimal calibration is achieved by varying thresholds on confidence levels and limits (i.e. number of subject suggestions). We conclude that, with optimal calibration, `KIFSPrompt` can outperform the `llm-ensemble` in terms of optimal precision-recall balance, whereas the `llm-ensemble` achieves the best results in terms of PR-AUC.

Ensemble Type	Precision	Recall	F1	PR AUC
KIFSPrompt	0.582	0.396	0.431	0.308
llm-ensemble	0.488	0.459	0.421	0.412
one-model-one-prompt	0.461	0.384	0.380	0.235

Table 6: Comparison of systems on dev-sample ($n = 1,000$). Point estimates for precision, recall and F1-score correspond to the F1-optimal calibration, displayed as cross-marks in figure 3.

[11] a subsample of the official LLMs4Subjects dev set

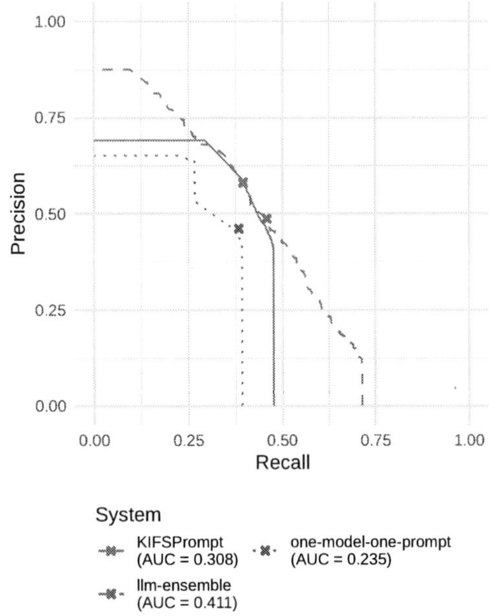

Figure 3: Precision-Recall curves for `KIFSPrompt`, `llm-ensemble` and baseline evaluated as doc-averages over our dev-sample. Cross-marks indicate the point of F1-optimal calibration for each curve, cf. Table 6 for point estimates.

A.3 Sensitivity Analysis: Number of Retrieved Documents L

Investigating our system in the post-submission phase, we conducted a sensitivity analysis regarding the fluctuation of results with respect to the parameter L. Figure 4 shows F1@5 for various values of L. We see some variation in scores, however, there is no strong correlation with L.

A.4 Distribution of Label-Numbers

A feature of `KIFSPrompt` seems to be its ability to learn the number of expected subject terms from the examples. On our dev set of $n = 1,000$ documents we compared the number of gold standard labels per document with the number of predicted labels and found that the dynamically selected examples seem to provide the LLM with a measure of how many labels to expect.

Figure 5 compares the distributions in the number of predicted subject terms.

The jitter plot in figure 6 demonstrates how KIFSPrompt produces varying numbers of predicted subject terms per Document.

The number of suggested subject terms may also depend on the sampling parameters for the LLM inference engine. Table 7 lists the settings for the

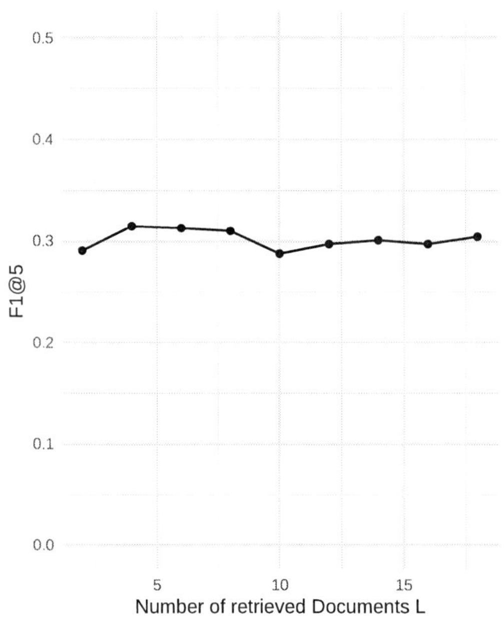

Figure 4: Sensitivity analysis: F1@5 as a function of the number of retrieved documents L used in the few-shot prompt. Metrics are computed on dev-sample ($n = 1,000$).

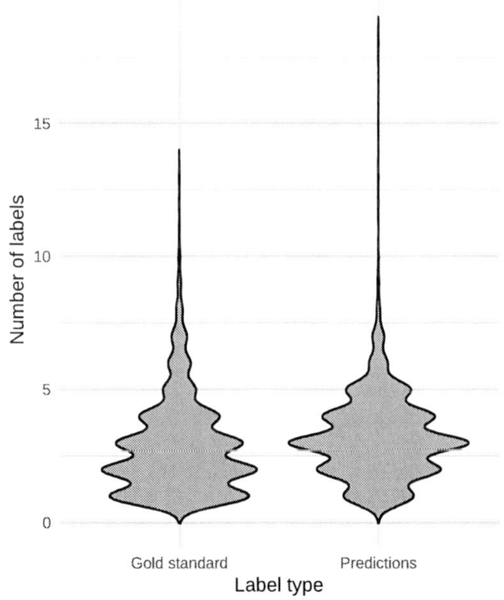

Figure 5: Distribution of the number of predicted subject terms per document compared to the gold standard, visualized as a violin plot.

sampling parameters used in our experiments.

A.5 Qualitative Results per Subject Group

Figure 7 shows the qualitative results per subject group and team for evaluation scenario *Case 1*.

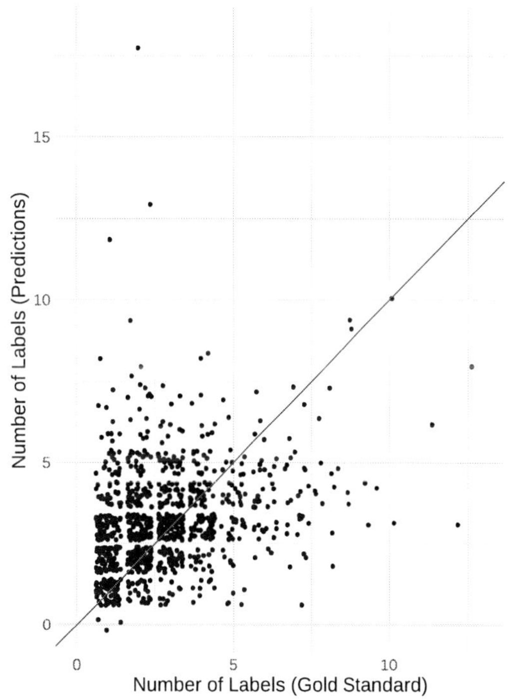

Figure 6: Jitter plot showing the number of predicted subject terms per document compared to the gold standard.

Parameter	Value
`max_tokens`	100
`min_tokens`	36
`temperature`	0
`presence_penalty`	0
`frequency_penalty`	0
`repetition_penalty`	1
`top_p`	1

Table 7: LLM sampling parameters for keyword generation using vLLM during the *Complete* stage.

In each subject group suggested subject terms for $n = 10$ records were evaluated by subject librarians of the TIB. `KIFSPrompt` performs best in economics and worst in literature studies.

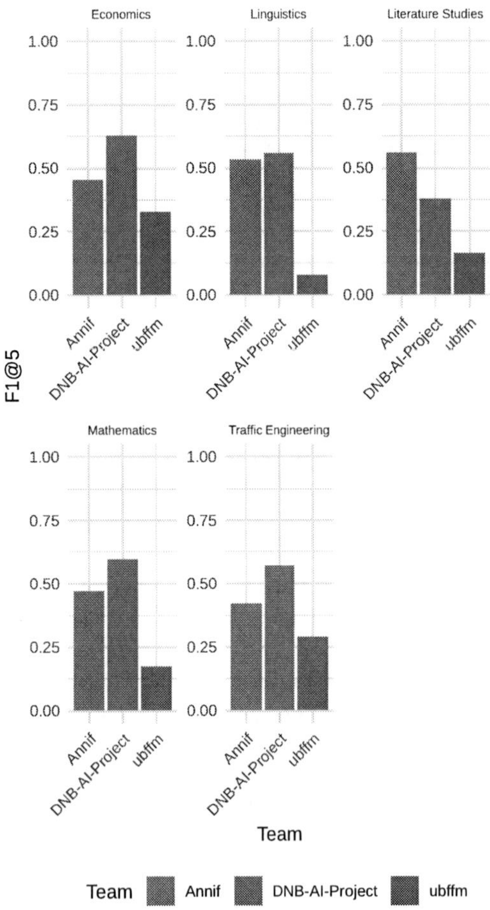

Figure 7: Qualitative F1@5 results per subject group. Evaluation scenario *Case 1*.

Last Minute at the GermEval-2025 LLMs4Subjects Task: Few-Shot Contrastive Learning for Multilingual Multi-Label Classification

Parisa Shirali*, **Zahra Sarlak***, **Ebrahim Ansari**
Institute for Advanced Studies in Basic Sciences (IASBS), Zanjan, Iran
p.shirali@iasbs.ac.ir, z.sarlak@iasbs.ac.ir, ansari@iasbs.ac.ir

Abstract

This paper addresses the challenges and recent advancements in automated domain classification for digital libraries, with a focus on integrating multilingual text embeddings to improve the classification of bilingual technical records. We employed the FastFit package to fine-tune a model capable of performing multi-label classification on the TIBKAT dataset, which presents a highly skewed distribution of subject categories. To enhance label interpretability, we generated detailed class descriptions using GPT-4-o Mini. Our method combines few-shot learning with a modified score calculation to ensure comparability across labels, enabling effective and scalable classification without extensive fine-tuning.

1 Introduction

Digital libraries are changing the ways we access and share scholarly and cultural resources by bringing together various information formats. As technology advances, our strategies for utilizing these evolving information technologies must adapt to support lifelong learning. This shift underscores the increasing need to explore automated methods for subject indexing and classification, which are vital for managing the growing volume of digital documents (Greenstein, 2000).

Models trained on extensive datasets can effectively capture complex interdisciplinary subjects, provide cohesive text, and produce useful annotations across various natural language processing (NLP) contexts (Dale, 2021). While these models promise speed and scalability, questions regarding their ability to produce high-quality annotations still remain. For example, what limitations do LLMs encounter in generating human-like annotations? Can they match or exceed the quality of annotations created by humans in bilingual subject tagging? In what manner does training data influence their ability to accurately capture intricate sentiment relationships in complex topics without inaccuracies or generalizations? These queries are central to the LLMs4Subject task (D'souza et al., 2025).

This challenge invited researchers to develop LLM-based systems that improve domain classification and semantic indexing of bilingual technical records at the TIB (Leibniz Information Centre for Science and Technology). The second LLMs4Subjects task highlights the importance of efficiency in LLMs while focusing on better model performance, reduced energy consumption, and faster inference speed.

In sub-task 1, our aim was to create an efficient model by using few-shot fine-tuning combined with synthetically generated data from readily available instruction-tuned LLMs. The model categorizes human-readable records into one or more of the 28 predefined subject domains from TIB's LinSearch Subject Classification System. Our findings show that few-shot fine-tuning with synthetic data can achieve strong performance without the need for extensive task-specific fine-tuning, providing insights into its potential and limitations for domain-specific classification tasks.

The rest of this article is organized as follows: Section 2 (Related Works) reviews key principles and existing methods in automated subject tagging. Section 3 (Methodology) outlines our approach, Section 4 (Results) presents our findings, and Section 5 (Future Work) discusses implications and future research directions.

2 Related Works

Automatic classification of scholarly literature is a critical yet challenging task, particularly in multi-label settings. Prior work has approached this problem using either supervised or unsupervised methods (Gialitsis et al., 2022); (Sadat and Caragea,

*These authors contributed equally to this work

Proceedings of the 21st Conference on Natural Language Processing (KONVENS), Volume 2: Workshops, pages 465–470, 2025

2022); (Liu et al., 2021); (Toney and Dunham, 2022); (Salatino et al., 2019); (Mustafa et al., 2021); (Kandimalla et al., 2020). However, Generative LLMs like GPT and BERT offer more powerful and flexible few-shot classification capabilities, reducing reliance on large labeled data.

Niraula et al. (Niraula et al., 2024) confirm this ability and show that fine-tuned LLM models trained on a relatively small amount of human-labeled data outperform baseline models. A particularly efficient approach is SetFit (Tunstall et al., 2022) which finetunes a sentence transformer in a contrastive manner without the need for prompt engineering or full fine-tuning. FusionSent (Schopf et al., 2024) is also a few-shot multi-label classification method that fine-tunes dual sentence embedding models from the same PLM checkpoint. One model optimizes intra-class similarity using cosine similarity loss, while the other focuses on aligning instances with labels using contrastive loss (Hadsell et al., 2006). The models are then combined using Spherical Linear Interpolation (SLERP) (Shoemake, 1985) to address limitations such as catastrophic forgetting (Biesialska et al., 2020) then frozen and employed as a logistic regression classification head (Cox, 1958). However, their approach introduces a trade-off in higher computational costs than lightweight alternatives like SetFit.

In this study, we adapt the FastFit package[1], which offers notable improvements in both training speed and classification accuracy compared to existing few-shot learning methods (Yehudai and Bendel, 2024). To improve robustness, FastFit augments the training batch by including the class name as an additional example and repeating each text r times (where r is a positive integer) while applying dropout, a minimal representation-level augmentation inspired by (Gao et al., 2022).

3 Methodology

For Subtask 1—Multi-Domain Classification of Library Records—we used the FastFit package (Yehudai and Bendel, 2024) to fine-tune an open-source embedding model.

The TIBKAT collection shows a significantly skewed distribution across its subject domain categories, as represented in Figure 1. If we train a model on this dataset, it will likely become heavily biased toward the majority classes. To mitigate it and regarding FastFit's ability in few-shot learning,

[1]https://github.com/IBM/fastfit

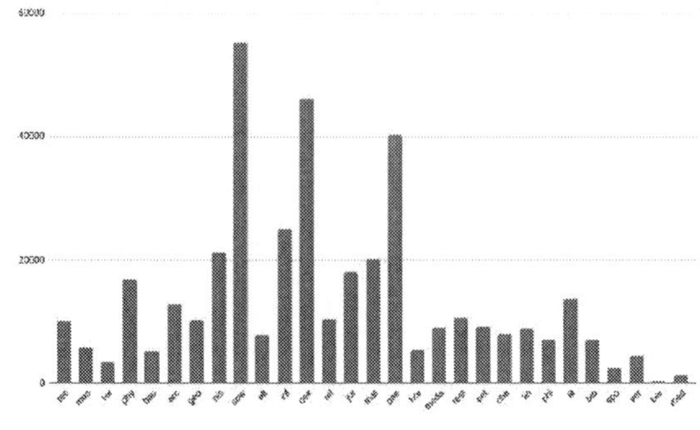

Figure 1: Distribution of domain categories within the dataset. The distribution is notably skewed, with some categories significantly outnumbering others, indicating a potential bias that may impact classification performance.

we randomly selected a fixed number of 100 samples from each subject category. FastFit encodes labels as positive pairs with their corresponding inputs, mapping them into a shared embedding space. It uses in-batch contrastive learning to bring the documents closer to their labels while simultaneously pushing all other texts apart based on their token-level similarity metric. This approach has a more pronounced effect for smaller models and less data, which makes the choice of 100 examples per subject category, a balanced choice. It is sufficient to capture intra-class variation while small enough to equalize representation across categories. Furthermore, its augmentation strategy, which includes class names and repeated examples, further compensates for reduced data volume. However, the domain labels in the TIBKAT dataset are single-word labels, which are often too general to capture the necessary semantic nuances in the embedding vectors. To enhance label clarity, we leveraged GPT-4-o Mini (see Appendix B for prompt) to generate detailed class descriptions for each category, providing one or two sentences for better context[2]. On average, each output contained approximately ±104 tokens, as measured with the OpenAI Playground[3].

Since our classification problem is a multi-label problem, we adjusted how scores are calculated in FastFit. In the original version (Yehudai and Bendel, 2024), FastFit sums the maximum token-level similarity between the input and the label description, which can result in different score scales depending on the number of tokens. This is not an

[2]The generated descriptions is available *here*.

[3]https://platform.openai.com/tokenizer

issue for single-label problems, where we simply choose the label with the highest score. However, when selecting multiple labels based on a threshold, we need all scores to be on the same scale. To address this, we normalized the FastFit scores.

We chose the Multilingual-E5 large-instruct[4] (Wang et al., 2024) model to fine-tune, which has performed well on the MTEB (Muennighoff et al., 2023) German benchmark (Wehrli et al., 2024) at the time. The Multilingual E5 Text Embeddings series is recognized for generating high-quality and dense embeddings and exhibits strong multilingual capabilities for encoding and understanding German and English texts.

For each document, we extracted the title, abstract, and classification label from TIBKAT records and saved them in the following format:

- **Query:** The combined title and abstract text, prefixed with "retrieval.query" as the model's text column.
- **Label:** The document's classification label, mapped to its corresponding descriptor (from GPT-4 definitions) and prefixed with "retrieval.passage" as the model label column.

Each query was then organized into separate pairs with its labels as follows:

$(query_1, label_1)$,
$(query_1, label_2)$,
...
$(query_i, label_k)$

And finally, we fine-tuned the model using the table 1 parameters:

Training Prameters	Value
Optimizer	AdamW
Training Epochs	4
Number of Repeats	3
Training Batch	16
Evaluation Batch	16
Learning Rate	1.5e-04
Weight Decay	0.02
Mask Probability	0.1
Gradient Accumulation Steps	2

Table 1: Training parameters utilized for fine-tuning the model.

After fine-tuning the model, we calculated the normalized similarity score for each test sample by comparing the concatenated title and abstract with each label description. Labels were assigned based on a selection threshold that was determined to yield the best results in comparison with a limited collection of other thresholds in a range during the evaluation phase, which was set at 0.90.

To track the environmental impact of our training, we used the CodeCarbon package[5]. The CodeCarbon package, monitors CPU, GPU, and RAM consumption and converts the energy consumed into CO_2 emissions. As can be seen in table 2

Training Metrics	Value
Energy consumed for RAM	1.242 Wh
RAM Power	10.0 W
Delta energy consumed for CPU with constant	0.143 Wh
CPU power	42.5 W
Energy consumed for All CPU	5.279 Wh
Energy consumed for all GPUs	8.344 Wh
Total GPU Power	67.95 W
Electricity used since the beginning	14.865 Wh

Table 2: Training metrics detailing energy consumption and performance statistics for 4 epochs and 2800 training samples taking 8 minutes and 48 seconds.

4 Results

The GermEval team evaluated our subject tagging system. Table 3 shows the overall results, including Macro and Micro precision, recall, and F1 scores and Table 4 shows the overall results grouped by language.

Detailed results for different record types and languages can be found in appendix A Table 5.

The findings reveal a balanced performance across both macro and micro metrics, indicating that our approach effectively handles bilingual classification tasks. The consistency between these metrics is significant because it shows that the model performs well across all categories, avoiding bias towards any specific class. This is important in multi-label situations, where we want to ensure strong performance across all subject categories in the dataset.

Additionally, the strong scores achieved in both languages highlight the model's multilingual abilities, suggesting that using few-shot classification

[4]https://huggingface.co/intfloat/multilingual-e5-large-instruct

[5]https://mlco2.github.io/codecarbon/

and effective label representation allows for accurate classification without requiring extensive fine-tuning. This is especially important in situations with limited resources, where creating large annotated datasets is difficult. The low resource usage highlighted in Table 2, combined with the strong results, shows that employing an efficient framework that includes data augmentation and in-batch contrastive learning can optimize performance even with a minimal dataset. By reducing the amount of data required to achieve high performance, we also decrease the training time and resources needed for the process leading to a significantly more energy-efficient method.

Metric	value
macro-precision	0.4683
macro-recall	0.4683
macro-f1	0.4683
micro-precision	0.4725
micro-recall	0.4725
micro-f1	0.4725

Table 3: Overall result of the proposed approach: This table presents the evaluation metrics related to the performance of the model. These metrics provide a comprehensive assessment of the model's effectiveness in classifying bilingual technical records, indicating its ability to balance precision and recall across different classes.

Metric	de	en
macro-precision	0.4649	0.4745
macro-recall	0.4649	0.4745
macro-f1	0.4649	0.4745
micro-precision	0.4690	0.4787
micro-recall	0.4690	0.4787
micro-f1	0.4690	0.4787

Table 4: Overall result of the proposed approach by language: This table summarizes the performance metrics for the model's classification of bilingual technical records, presented separately for German (de) and English (en).

5 Future Works

While the results demonstrate a solid foundation, there remains a clear opportunity for refinement. Identifying the areas where performance—especially in cases with lower scoring—will be vital for future research.

One challenge we encountered was defining negative pairs for our multi-labeled classification problem. Due to the nature of multi-label classification, we need to manage negative pairs carefully within a batch, which limits our ability to use techniques like Multiple Negative Ranking Loss (Henderson et al., 2017) that consider all other samples in the batch as negatives. Improving the handling of negative pairs will be important for enhancing the quality of our embeddings in future work.

Another challenge was the equal contribution of each token in sentence embedding and similarity score, which can introduce some noise. On the other hand, extracting important keywords may add additional computational costs. While FastFit's token-level similarity partially addresses this issue by focusing on the most similar token from one sentence to each token in another, we may not capture the importance of all relevant tokens. Considering the top K most similar tokens could help emulate keyword extraction and potentially improve the model's performance.

Another promising direction is the replacement or combination of FastFit's loss function with a more dynamic alternative, such as Adaptive Thresholding Loss (ATL)(Zhou et al., 2020) or its variants. ATL introduces a learnable "threshold class," which allows the model to dynamically adjust the decision boundary for each positive and negative pair. This would enable the model to learn instance-specific thresholds during training, which could lead to better generalization on unseen data.

6 Conclusion

In this paper, we explored the capabilities of large language models (LLMs) in the context of automated multi-label domain classification for bilingual technical records. By leveraging the FastFit package and generating synthetic data, we developed a model that effectively classifies records from the TIBKAT dataset.

Our results demonstrate that the proposed approach has the potential for enhanced classification performance across both German and English, highlighting the model's robustness in handling multi-label scenarios. While the findings are promising, they also reveal areas for improvement.

In summary, the results validate the effectiveness of our approach in automated subject classification while also signaling critical areas for further investigation.

References

Magdalena Biesialska, Katarzyna Biesialska, and Marta R. Costa-jussà. 2020. Continual lifelong learn-

Record Type	LANG	macro-precision	macro-recall	macro-f1	micro-precision	micro-recall	micro-f1
Article	de	0.3333	0.3333	0.3333	0.5000	0.5000	0.5000
	en	0.4460	0.4460	0.4460	0.4539	0.4539	0.4539
Book	de	0.4610	0.4610	0.4610	0.4652	0.4652	0.4652
	en	0.4813	0.4813	0.4813	0.4853	0.4853	0.4853
Conference	de	0.4516	0.4516	0.4516	0.4542	0.4542	0.4542
	en	0.4806	0.4806	0.4806	0.4853	0.4853	0.4853
Report	de	0.4835	0.4835	0.4835	0.4879	0.4879	0.4879
	en	0.3865	0.3865	0.3865	0.3901	0.3901	0.3901
Thesis	de	0.4834	0.4834	0.4834	0.4872	0.4872	0.4872
	en	0.4568	0.4568	0.4568	0.4598	0.4598	0.4598

Table 5: This table presents the quantitative results for Subtask 1, organized by record type and language. It includes key performance metrics that reflect the model's classification accuracy and effectiveness for different types of records, enabling a comprehensive analysis of how language and record type influence overall performance.

ing in natural language processing: A survey. In *Proceedings of the 28th International Conference on Computational Linguistics*. International Committee on Computational Linguistics.

D. R. Cox. 1958. The regression analysis of binary sequences. *Journal of the Royal Statistical Society: Series B (Methodological)*, 20(2):215–232.

Robert Dale. 2021. Gpt-3: What's it good for? *Natural Language Engineering*, 27:113–118.

Jennifer D'souza, Sameer Sadruddin, Holger Israel, Mathias Begoin, and Diana Slawig. 2025. SemEval-2025 task 5: LLMs4Subjects - LLM-based automated subject tagging for a national technical library's open-access catalog. In *Proceedings of the 19th International Workshop on Semantic Evaluation (SemEval-2025)*, pages 2570–2583, Vienna, Austria. Association for Computational Linguistics.

Tianyu Gao, Xingcheng Yao, and Danqi Chen. 2022. Simcse: Simple contrastive learning of sentence embeddings. *Preprint*, arXiv:2104.08821.

Nikolaos Gialitsis, Sotiris Kotitsas, and Haris Papageorgiou. 2022. Scinobo: A hierarchical multi-label classifier of scientific publications. In *Companion Proceedings of the Web Conference 2022*, WWW '22, page 800–809. ACM.

Daniel Greenstein. 2000. Digital libraries and their challenges. *Library Trend*, 49.

R. Hadsell, S. Chopra, and Y. LeCun. 2006. Dimensionality reduction by learning an invariant mapping. In *2006 IEEE Computer Society Conference on Computer Vision and Pattern Recognition (CVPR'06)*, volume 2, pages 1735–1742.

Matthew Henderson, Rami Al-Rfou, Brian Strope, Yun hsuan Sung, Laszlo Lukacs, Ruiqi Guo, Sanjiv Kumar, Balint Miklos, and Ray Kurzweil. 2017. Efficient natural language response suggestion for smart reply. *Preprint*, arXiv:1705.00652.

Bharath Kandimalla, Shaurya Rohatgi, Jian Wu, and C Giles. 2020. Large scale subject category classification of scholarly papers with deep attentive neural networks. *Frontiers in research metrics and analytics*.

Yonghao Liu, Renchu Guan, Fausto Giunchiglia, Yanchun Liang, and Xiaoyue Feng. 2021. Deep attention diffusion graph neural networks for text classification. In *Proceedings of the 2021 Conference on Empirical Methods in Natural Language Processing*, pages 8142–8152, Online and Punta Cana, Dominican Republic. Association for Computational Linguistics.

Niklas Muennighoff, Nouamane Tazi, Loïc Magne, and Nils Reimers. 2023. Mteb: Massive text embedding benchmark. *Preprint*, arXiv:2210.07316.

Ghulam Mustafa, Muhammad Usman, Lisu Yu, Muhammad Tanvir Afzal, Muhammad Sulaiman, and Abdul Shahid. 2021. Multi-label classification of research articles using word2vec and identification of similarity threshold. *Scientific Reports*, 11.

Nobal Niraula, Samet Ayhan, Balaguruna Chidambaram, and Daniel Whyatt. 2024. Multi-label classification with generative large language models. In *2024 AIAA DATC/IEEE 43rd Digital Avionics Systems Conference (DASC)*, pages 1–7.

Mobashir Sadat and Cornelia Caragea. 2022. Hierarchical multi-label classification of scientific documents. *Preprint*, arXiv:2211.02810.

Angelo Salatino, Francesco Osborne, Thiviyan Thanapalasingam, and Enrico Motta. 2019. The cso classifier: Ontology-driven detection of research topics in scholarly articles. In *International Conference on Theory and Practice of Digital Libraries*.

Tim Schopf, Alexander Blatzheim, Nektarios Machner, and Florian Matthes. 2024. Efficient few-shot learning for multi-label classification of scientific documents with many classes. *Preprint*, arXiv:2410.05770.

Ken Shoemake. 1985. Animating rotation with quaternion curves. In *Proceedings of the 12th Annual Conference on Computer Graphics and Interactive Techniques*, SIGGRAPH '85, page 245–254, New York, NY, USA. Association for Computing Machinery.

Autumn Toney and James Dunham. 2022. Multi-label classification of scientific research documents across domains and languages. In *Proceedings of the Third Workshop on Scholarly Document Processing*, pages 105–114, Gyeongju, Republic of Korea. Association for Computational Linguistics.

Lewis Tunstall, Nils Reimers, Unso Eun Seo Jo, Luke Bates, Daniel Korat, Moshe Wasserblat, and Oren Pereg. 2022. Efficient few-shot learning without prompts. *Preprint*, arXiv:2209.11055.

Liang Wang, Nan Yang, Xiaolong Huang, Linjun Yang, Rangan Majumder, and Furu Wei. 2024. Multilingual e5 text embeddings: A technical report. *arXiv preprint arXiv:2402.05672*.

Silvan Wehrli, Bert Arnrich, and Christopher Irrgang. 2024. German text embedding clustering benchmark. *Preprint*, arXiv:2401.02709.

Asaf Yehudai and Elron Bendel. 2024. When llms are unfit use fastfit: Fast and effective text classification with many classes. *Preprint*, arXiv:2404.12365.

Wenxuan Zhou, Kevin Huang, Tengyu Ma, and Jing Huang. 2020. Document-level relation extraction with adaptive thresholding and localized context pooling. *Preprint*, arXiv:2010.11304.

A Appendix A: Detailed Result

The Germval team evaluated our subject tagging system. Table 5 shows the detailed quantitative results, including Macro and Micro precision, recall, and F1 scores grouped by record type and language, on the TIBKAT dataset.

B Appendix B: Prompts to generate domain class description

- English: *Generate a single, comprehensive paragraph that provides a detailed overview of the field of [LABEL] suitable for a classification label. The tone should be informative and encyclopedic.*

- German: *Erstellen Sie einen einzelnen, umfassenden Absatz, der einen detaillierten Überblick über das Gebiet von [LABEL] bietet und für ein Klassifikationslabel geeignet ist. Der Ton sollte informativ und enzyklopädisch sein.*

UBFFM at the GermEval-2025 LLMs4Subjects Task: What if we take "You are an expert in subject indexing" seriously?

Clara Wan Ching Ho
Universitätsbibliothek Johann Christian Senckenberg, Goethe-Universität Frankfurt
c.ho@ub.uni-frankfurt.de

Abstract

This paper presents two contributions in subject classification and subject indexing of the UBFFM team at the GermEval shared task LLMs4Subjects. In Subtask 1, a fine-tune multilingual classifier is developed to assign LinSearch subject domains, achieving consistent performance across record types. For Subtask 2, an innovative generative approach is introduced by prompting to produce GND-like subject labels enriched with metadata. The pseudo-subjects are mapped to official GND terms via embedding-based similarity matching.

1 Introduction

Subject indexing and classification are key to organizing knowledge in digital libraries, enabling effective information retrieval and access. As scholarly content increases, automated methods have become crucial for scalable metadata generation.

Subject classification assigns documents to broad domains. LinSearch, developed by the Leibniz Information Centre for Science and Technology and University Library (TIB), categorizes publications into 28 scientific fields using text and metadata features (Technische Informationsbibliothek (TIB), 2023a), serving as a benchmark for automated classification.

Subject indexing uses specific descriptors to capture detailed content. The Gemeinsame Normdatei (GND) provides a standardized vocabulary widely used in German-speaking academia (Deutsche Nationalbibliothek, 2023). While indexing was traditionally manual, advances since the past decade have started exploring automatic approaches such as statistical machine learning, and more recently, using large language models (LLMs) for this complex task.

An initial iteration of LLMs4Subjects was previously conducted at SemEval 2025 (D'Souza et al., 2025a), where subject indexing using the GND served as the sole task. At the first phase, various LLM-based subject indexing methods were proposed and evaluated by the participating teams. The Annif team (Suominen et al., 2025) used LLMs for translation and synthetic data generation for training data, then performed subject indexing with three Annif-based submodels, Omikuji, Maui-like Lexical Matching (MLLM) and XTransformer. Ranking was performed by the Annif-based XMTC algorithms in the toolkit. The DNB team (Kluge and Kähler, 2025) took an ensemble prompt-based approach to extract keywords from documents by prompting multiple LLMs, and then aggregating the keywords and mapping them to the GND subject headings by a nearest neighbour search. The labels were ranked by employing an LLM to rank the relevance of each label. The La2I2F team (Salfinger et al., 2025) approached the task with vector space matching supported by analogical reasoning and ontology-based retrieval. After mapping the queried document's title and abstract onto the vector space, they are compared to the , finally fused the candidates retrieved as the output. The Homa team (Tekanlou et al., 2025) approached subject indexing as an alignment task. They used OntoAligner, a toolkit for ontology alignment, along with retrieval-augmented generation (RAG) technique for the task.

Our attempt at the task in this second phase by prompting an instruct model directly for the subject indexing task explores the possibilities in integrating external knowledge such as the GND taxonomy into LLMs, handling ambiguity in polysemous terms in different technical contexts and mitigating hallucinations from generative models.

2 Task Background

At the second phase of LLMs4Subjects (D'Souza et al., 2025b), two subtasks are released to challenge participants to develop LLM-based ap-

Proceedings of the 21st Conference on Natural Language Processing (KONVENS), Volume 2: Workshops, pages 471–478, 2025

proaches for domain classification and subject indexing, using the dataset of technical records from the TIBKAT open-access catalog, maintained by the Leibniz Information Centre for Science and Technology (TIB) (Deutsche Nationalbibliothek, 2023). Predictions of the subject domains and subject headings should be based on the semantic relationship between the subject, title, and abstract of the record.

Subtask 1 is a multi-label subject domain classification task, where systems are developed to classify a given document into one of more of 28 predefined subject domains according to Subject Classification System LinSearch from the TIB terminology service.

Subtask 2 is a subject indexing task, where systems are expected to tag up to 20 labels for a given document according to the set of over 200,000 subject headings in the GND subjects taxonomy (Deutsche Nationalbibliothek, 2023). The subject tagging capability of systems is expected to align with the annotations in TIBKAT (Technische Informationsbibliothek (TIB), 2023b).

3 System Overview

Two systems were developed for the two subtasks, where the system for Subtask 2 utilises predictions from Subtask 1 as a part of its input. For subtask 1, a simple approach of fine-tuning a multi-class classifier is taken to predict LinSearch classes. For subtask 2, we have taken a daring generative approach in attempt to instruct a model to directly generate subject headings despite its hallucinations. Then map the hallucinated pseudo-subjects into the set of labels existing in the GND.

3.1 Subtask 1: Multi-Domain Classification of Library Record

A multi-class classifier was fine-tuned with the TIBKAT dataset for the subtask, where titles and abstracts serve as inputs and LinSearch categories as outputs. Since each document can be labelled with multiple LinSearch labels, a threshold on prediction confidence is employed to filter predicted classes in returning final outputs.

The fine-tuned model[1] and training datasets [2] [3] are available on Huggingface.

[1] https://huggingface.co/ubffm/xlm_roberta_large_linsearch_classification

[2] https://huggingface.co/datasets/ubffm/linsearch_train_data

[3] https://huggingface.co/datasets/ubffm/linsearch_dev_data

3.2 Subtask 2: Subject Indexing

Since the set of subject headings is too large to be taken as a regular classification task, and there is not enough training data for each subject class, we decided to take a generative approach for this subtask. We have taken a three-step process of 1) classifying with LinSearch domains (Subtask 1), 2) generating GND-like subject headings with metadata by prompting a fine-tuned model, and 3) mapping the pseudo-subjects to the set of existing subjects.

3.2.1 Prompt-embedded dataset

In order to assist the model in learning the semantic relationships and conventional uses of the GND and LinSearch classes, as well as to contextualise the task to be given later at inference, a prompt-embedded dataset with labeled data is created. The dataset does not differentiate the language of the record, which has the advantage of simplicity in structure, as well as the disadvantage that all LLMs used in the pipeline are limited to multilingual pre-trained models. Training data of the instruct model is formatted with the role the agent should act as when performing the task, task description, document title and abstract, LinSearch classes and GND subject IDs and Names. The template format is illustrated in Appendix B. At inference, LinSearch labels predicted from Subtask 1 are integrated into the prompt, sample outputs in JSON are also provided. The template format is illustrated in Appendix C. A slight discrepancy exists between the prompts used during training and those employed at inference, resulting from modifications introduced through subsequent prompt experimentation. These adjustments were intended to enhance output quality and minimize formatting errors.

3.2.2 Generating Pseudo-classes

We employ a Llama instruct model fine-tuned with the prompt-embedded dataset and prompt it directly with a subject indexing task to generate the foundation of the subject headings. Fine-tuning is performed to enable the model to learn the patterns and conventions associated with subject indexing using the GND and specifically the TIBKAT dataset. While the model might have learnt the implicit relations between texts and some phrases that are repetitively used as subject headings, it does not have explicit knowledge of the set of predefined labels in the GND dataset and is prone to hallucination. We thus address this limitation by prompting the model to produce supplementary contextual information.

The model is given a document with a title, an abstract and a list of LinSearch labels predicted from Subtask 1, and prompted to label it with exactly 20 GND subjects in the sample JSON format. It is asked to provide not only the subject index name but also associated metadata, such as a unique "Code" (e.g., gnd:XXXXXXX-X), "Alternate Name" (synonyms), and "Related Subjects" (connected topics). An example of the sample output format is displayed in Appendix D. This structure replicates the GND dataset format, maintaining consistency with professional cataloging standards. This additional information enables the post-processing step, where hallucinated or inconsistent classes can be mapped back to the correct GND labels by taking the extra metadata as context, ensuring alignment with the structured dataset.

3.2.3 Fallback: Keywords Extraction

A significant limitation of relying on generative models to perform complex tasks is the increased unpredictability of outputs. Empirical observations demonstrate instances where the generated text fails to be parsed as a valid JSON object, speculated to be due to two primary factors. Firstly, the generated output may exceed the token limit, causing truncation. Secondly, the model may drift into generating repetitive content over extended sequences, reducing output utility.

Therefore, in instances where the model output cannot be extracted as a JSON object after simple postprocessing, a fallback strategy based on keyword extraction is employed to ensure essential information is retained. Specifically, KeyBERT (Grootendorst, 2020) is used to extract up to 10 keywords, each comprising 1-3 tokens. These keywords are derived from the concatenated text of the title and abstract, enabling downstream processing despite structural limitations in the model's output. This approach serves as a robust mechanism to handle edge cases while maintaining the utility of the extracted information for subsequent computational tasks.

3.2.4 Mapping to GND Subject Headings

The hallucinated pseudo-classes are mapped to subject headings in the GND set by comparing their respective encodings. By encoding the subject headings with the classes they are relevant to, the extra context given provides the model with the technical context each subject belongs to, to assist disambiguation for polysemous terms. Prior to mapping, the "Name," "Alternate Name," and "Related Subjects" fields of each GND subject are concatenated and encoded using a sentence-BERT model. Similarly, for each model-generated pseudo-class, the fields "Name," "Alternate Name," and "Related Subjects" are extracted, concatenated, and encoded using the same sentence-BERT model. The resulting embeddings from the pseudo-classes are then compared with the GND set encodings to establish the mapping. This approach utilises the creative output of the generative model, while ensuring the final outputs are constrained to align with the predefined set.

While the full pipeline remains unpublished, the fine-tuned instruct model is accessible on Huggingface[4]. Training datasets[5] [6] are also publicly accessible.

4 Experimental Setup

4.1 Subtask 1

A dataset is created by extracting the document title, abstract and LinSearch labels of each document in the TIBKAT dataset. It is further populated by splitting entires with more than one LinSearch tags into multiple entries. The resulting training and validation set have approximately 78,900 and 13,200 entries, where each of the entries has one LinSearch label.

The large XLM-RoBERTa model (Conneau et al., 2020) is chosen for the task for its balance between performance and model size. With 561M parameters, it delivers competitive multilingual classification accuracy without excessive computational cost. This makes it a practical and powerful choice across a wide range of real-world multilingual NLP tasks, especially with a lower complexity. The model is fine-tuned as a classifier with the Huggingface trainer module. It processes input text strings and returns a list of predicted LinSearch class with their corresponding confidence scores. In order to return multiple classes in the final output, a threshold of 0.05 in confidence score is applied to filter

[4]https://huggingface.co/ubffm/llama-3.2-3b-instruct-unsloth-bnb-4bit-gnd-subjects

[5]https://huggingface.co/datasets/ubffm/prompt_gnd_with_linsearch_train_data

[6]https://huggingface.co/datasets/ubffm/prompt_gnd_with_linsearch_dev_data

out unlikely predictions. The remaining classes are then ranked in descending order based on their confidence scores. Considering that the confidence scores of all classes add up to 1, the threshold is set so that 1 to 3 classes will be returned in most cases, to better resemble the number of LinSearch classes labeled in the majority of TIB records. Appendix A presents some sample predictions and scores to demonstrate the usefulness of the threshold.

4.2 Subtask 2

A dataset is created as in Subtask 1, then transform into a prompt-embedded task description, as described in 3.2.1. The dataset is then used to fine-tune a Llama 3.2 3B instruct model (Meta, 2024) with Unsloth (Unsloth, 2025) to include compute-efficient measures. The model is trained using Unsloth with 4-bit quantisation and rank-stabilized LoRA. As a result, only 32.5% of all trainable parameters, which is 982,515,712 parameters, are updated during training. Although GPU access at a high-performance data center was granted at a later stage by collaboration, initially the project was developed with one RTX 4080 GPU at our local institute. Therefore, we decided to stick to the decision with using Unsloth and a quantised model as we initially started, with the limited access to GPUs in most academic libraries in mind, as well as to align with the shared task's highlight on developing energy- and compute-efficient LLM systems in this phase.

The fine-tuned model is prompted with a subject assignment task, as described in 3.2.2 with a maximum token count of 2000 tokens, to obtain GND-like subject classes with extra information on top of the names of the classes. When the returned text is truncated due to the token limit, a simple postprocessing step is applied to cut off the output at the last complete class for which the full set of metadata can be extracted. When no information at all from the generated text can be extracted, mostly due to malformatted JSON text, a fallback measure is employed to extract keywords from the title and abstract, as described earlier in 3.2.3.

Since there is no guarantee that exactly 20 classes will be generated from the model, another postprocessing step ensures that there will be 20 classes at the output. Where $n \cdot p$ is the number of pseudo-classes extracted and l is the number of labels each pseudo-class would be mapped to, $n \cdot p \cdot l > 20$ is calculated for the minimum number of labels needed from each generated pseudo-class. Subsequently, l GND subject headings are extracted from each pseudo-class by comparing the n most similar subject labels with cosine similarity, as described in 3.2.4. In the output, ranking of the classes follows the order they are generated from the model. For example, when 3 pseudo-classes in the order of p_1, p_2 and p_3 are extracted, l will be 7. Seven labels mapped from p_1 will be placed at the top of the list, followed by 7 labels from p_2, then 7 from p_3. When the number of labels returned are over 20, the final output will be cut off at 20.

	Precision	Recall	F1
	macro / micro	macro / micro	macro / micro
Overall	0.65 / 0.66	0.65 / 0.66	0.65 / 0.66
Article	0.72 / 0.73	0.72 / 0.73	0.72 / 0.73
Book	0.65 / 0.66	0.65 / 0.66	0.65 / 0.66
Confer.	0.65 / 0.66	0.65 / 0.66	0.65 / 0.66
Report	0.62 / 0.63	0.62 / 0.63	0.62 / 0.63
Thesis	0.67 / 0.68	0.67 / 0.68	0.67 / 0.68

Table 1: Subtask 1 quantitative evaluation results by record type

5 Results and Limitations

5.1 Subtask 1

Performance in Subtask 1 is overall at 65% for precision, recall and F1, which placed us at 1st place due to low participation, but in the greater picture it is not particularly impressive as a classifier.

Table 1 presents the quantitative evaluation results for Subtask 1, broken down by record type. The model achieves consistent performance across all metrics, with overall macro and micro scores for precision, recall, and F1 hovering around 0.65–0.66. Among the individual categories, articles yield the highest performance, with an F1 score of 0.73, indicating that the model is especially effective at classifying this record type. Theses and books also show relatively strong performance, with F1 scores of 0.67 and 0.66, respectively. On the other hand, reports are the most challenging category, receiving the lowest F1 score (0.63), suggesting some ambiguity or variability in this class's metadata features. The small difference between macro and micro scores further indicates balanced performance across classes, with no severe class imbalance or overfitting to dominant types.

5.2 Subtask 2

Figure 1 presents the performance of the subject indexing system across different record types and cut-off values $K \in \{5, 10, 15, 20\}$. Overall, the system shows a linear and gradual improvement in ranking metrics as K increases. For instance, overall NDCG improves from 0.1193 at K@5 to 0.1465 at K@20, and recall increases correspondingly from 0.1282 to 0.2003.

Performance varies significantly by record type. *Book*, with the most training data, consistently outperform other categories across all metrics, achieving the highest NDCG (0.1549) and recall (0.2145) at K@20. *Conference* and *Report* records also demonstrate competitive performance, with F1 scores comparable to that of books. In contrast, *Articles* show the weakest performance, particularly in precision (e.g., 0.0138 at K@20) and F1 (0.024), suggesting difficulty in identifying relevant GND subjects for this type. *Thesis* fall in the mid-range, with moderate gains across K levels but overall lower recall and F1 compared to books and reports.

The results highlight both the general scalability of the system across increasing K values and the variability in performance across document types, likely due to differences in metadata richness, language structure, and topical consistency.

At test output generation, approximately one third of the cases triggered the fallback measure and their outputs were replaced by keywords. We speculate that this behavior is primarily due to the model's limited capacity, as it is a relatively small 3B parameter model quantised to 4 bits, which may contribute to instability in its outputs. There were attempts to adjust the temperature and repetition penalty to reduce invalid JSON formats. However, as both parameters severely interfere with the creativity of the generative model, we decided to settle on the trade-off between creative outputs and formatting correctness at the final model. Another challenge arising from the model's instability is the generation of unusually short or long outputs (e.g., fewer than 5 words or more than 50), particularly during phases of repetitive output. These length deviations lead to inconsistencies when such outputs are compared to embeddings derived from texts with typical lengths (10–20 words), which negatively impacts the reliability of embedding-based similarity matching.

6 Conclusion and Proposed Extensions

We present two systems for bilingual subject classification and indexing using fine-tuned LLMs and structured knowledge integration. The system developed for subtask 1 achieved consistent F1 scores above 0.65 across domains and was placed at the first place. For Subtask 2, an innovative approach utilising model hallucinated outputs mapped to GND labels was proposed. Although results were not comparable to the two best teams, we have attempted to push the limits of prompting to directly tackle the subject indexing task as is, and to address challenges such as polysemy, hallucination, and context ambiguity.

To further improve the performance of the subject indexing pipeline, we propose 3 potential extensions for the second subtask based on the current structure. Firstly, JSON could be opted out for other machine-readable formats to reduce output formatting issues, thus maximise the utility of the generative model. Secondly, implementing a more sophisticated fallback mechanism or integrating an alternative tool could enhance the alignment between extracted keywords and the structure of GND subject classes, thereby improving the accuracy of embedding-based similarity matching. Thirdly and similarly, post-processing generated texts from the instruct model to constrain the length of text used for encoding pseudo-classes may also facilitate more effective mapping to GND subjects.

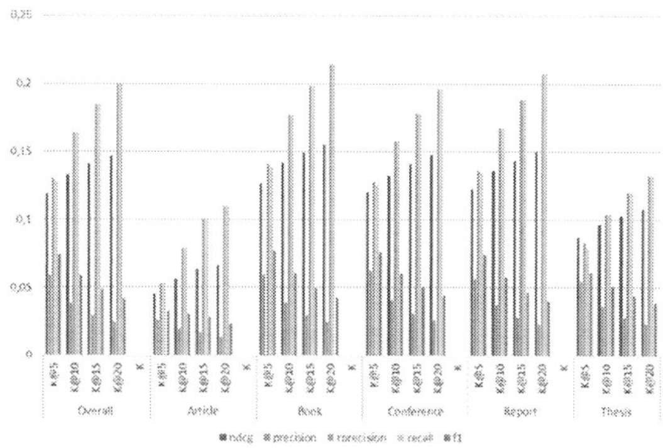

Figure 1: Subtask 2 quantitative evaluation results by record type

Acknowledgments

This work was partially funded by the DFG under FID Linguistik (326024153). We gratefully acknowledge support from the hessian.AI Service Center (funded by the Federal Ministry of Education and Research, BMBF, grant no. 01IS22091) and the hessian.AI Innovation Lab (funded by the Hessian Ministry for Digital Strategy and Innovation, grant no. S-DIW04/0013/003).

References

Alexis Conneau, Kartik Khandelwal, Naman Goyal, Vishrav Chaudhary, Guillaume Wenzek, Francisco Guzmán, Edouard Grave, Myle Ott, Luke Zettlemoyer, and Veselin Stoyanov. 2020. Unsupervised cross-lingual representation learning at scale. In *Proceedings of the 58th Annual Meeting of the Association for Computational Linguistics (ACL)*, Online. Association for Computational Linguistics.

Deutsche Nationalbibliothek. 2023. Gemeinsame normdatei (gnd). Accessed: 2025-07-11.

Jennifer D'Souza, Sameer Sadruddin, Holger Israel, Mathias Begoin, and Diana Slawig. 2025a. Semeval-2025 task 5: Llms4subjects - llm-based automated subject tagging for a national technical library's open-access catalog. In *Proceedings of the 19th International Workshop on Semantic Evaluation (SemEval-2025)*, pages 1082–1095, Vienna, Austria. Association for Computational Linguistics.

Jennifer D'Souza, Sameer Sadruddin, Holger Israel, Mathias Begoin, and Diana Slawig. 2025b. The GermEval 2025 2nd LLMs4Subjects Shared Task Dataset.

Maarten Grootendorst. 2020. KeyBERT: Minimal keyword extraction with BERT. Accessed: 2025-07-11.

Lisa Kluge and Maximilian Kähler. 2025. Dnb-ai-project at semeval-2025 task 5: An llm-ensemble approach for automated subject indexing. *Preprint*, arXiv:2504.21589.

Meta. 2024. Llama 3. https://www.llama.com/models/llama-3/. Accessed: 2025-07-11.

Andrea Salfinger, Luca Zaccagna, Francesca Incitti, Gianluca De Nardi, Lorenzo Dal Fabbro, and Lauro Snidaro. 2025. LA²I²F at SemEval-2025 task 5: Reasoning in embedding space – fusing analogical and ontology-based reasoning for document subject tagging. In *Proceedings of the 19th International Workshop on Semantic Evaluation (SemEval-2025)*, pages 2413–2423, Vienna, Austria. Association for Computational Linguistics.

Osma Suominen, Juho Inkinen, and Mona Lehtinen. 2025. Annif at semeval-2025 task 5: Traditional xmtc augmented by llms. *Preprint*, arXiv:2504.19675.

Technische Informationsbibliothek (TIB). 2023a. Linsearch: Klassifikation wissenschaftlicher publikationen. Accessed: 2025-07-11.

Technische Informationsbibliothek (TIB). 2023b. Tibkat: Katalog der tib – open-access-bibliographische daten.

Hadi Bayrami Asl Tekanlou, Jafar Razmara, Mahsa Sanaei, Mostafa Rahgouy, and Hamed Babaei Giglou. 2025. Homa at semeval-2025 task 5: Aligning librarian records with ontoaligner for subject tagging. *Preprint*, arXiv:2504.21474.

Unsloth. 2025. Unsloth: Efficient low-bit fine-tuning of large language models. https://github.com/unslothai/unsloth. Accessed: 2025-07-11.

A Sample LinSearch classification results

Record ID	Gold label	Prediction	Score (Pred)
3A371288258	mat	mat	0.99773
		phy	0.00053
		oek	0.00035
		elt	0.00022
		bio	0.00021
3A46120360X	lit	sow	0.78562
	lin	phi	0.14748
		his	0.05145
		lit	0.00785
		oek	0.00310
3A873554329	sow	oek	0.38645
	oek	sow	0.36542
	pae	pae	0.24364
		tec	0.00201
		phi	0.00077

Table 2: Top 5 LinSearch classification results for 3 records in the development set

B Template of prompt-embedded training data

```
### Act as:
Act as an expert librarian, who is
familiar with the GND (the integrated
authority files) and text processing.

### Task:
You are now tasked to assign subject titles
to documents according to the database of
GND subject titles. Given the document
title and abstract, assign the 10 most
suitable GND subject titles for the
document with no repetition.
Annotate GND Subjects in JSON format based
on document title, abstract and its class
in the subject classification system
LinSearch. You have been trained on a
dataset of GND and LinSearch annotated
documents.
Use your knowledge to match new documents
with GND subject data as closely as
possible to the style in the training
dataset. For each of the GND subject titles,
provide the name of the subject titles,
its names and related subjects.
```

~~~
Make sure all the information you provide
are as listed on the GND database and rank
your results by the likelihood they would
be assigned by an expert librarian.

### Title:
{title}

### Abstract:
{abstract}

### GND ID:
{list of GND codes}

### GND Class:
{list of GND classes}

### LIN Search class:
{list of LinSearch Classes}
~~~

C Template of prompt at inference

~~~
You are a librarian and an expert in the
GND (the integrated authority files):
{truncated GND subject headings
in dataframe}

You also have the knowledge of
LIN Search classification:
- arc Architecture
- bau Civil engineering
- ber Mining
... (content omitted)

### Given the following details:
- Document Title: {title}
- Document Abstract: {abstract}
- Document LIN Search class:
{list of predicted LinSearch classes}

### Your task:
Using your expert knowledge in the
conventional use of the GND, you are
now tasked to assign **exactly 20**
subject titles to documents according
to the database of GND subject titles.
Your task is to annotate documents
with GND subjects in JSON format based
on their content (title and abstract).
Use your knowledge of GND annotations
and follow the established patterns
from past training data.
1. Analyze the title, abstract and
LIN Search class of a document and
infer GND subject annotations.
2. Produce the output in structured
JSON format, maintaining consistency
with examples provided.

Rules:
- Always extract subjects from the
core concepts mentioned in the title/abstract.
- Include synonyms, variant names,
and related subjects in arrays.
- Follow the structure exactly as shown
in the examples.
- Always quote the JSON format output
between ```json and ```.
- No more than 20 alternate names is
allowed for each subject.
- No more than 20 related subjects is
allowed for each subject.

### Instructions:
1. Analyze the provided document to
identify its core themes, topics, and
concepts.
2. Select the most appropriate **20 unique
GND subject titles** that align with the
content, in the same style as the dataset
you were trained on.
3. Rank the GND subject titles according to
the relevance to the document, and the
likelihood they would be assigned by an
expert librarian.
4. Format the output as JSON, adhering to
the structure provided below. For each of
the subject titles, reply with the name of
the subject titles, its names and related
subjects in a list.
5. Make sure to complete the JSON output
before you hit the maximum token limit,
to ensure the correctness of the JSON format.

### Output example:
```json
{
"document_title": "Energie- und
Lademanagement für eine CO2-neutralen
Beladung von batterieelektrisch betriebenen
Service-Fahrzeugen auf dem Flughafenvorfeld",
"assigned_subject_titles": [
{
"Code": "gnd-4014736-8",
~~~

````
"Name": "Energieversorgung",
"Alternate Name": ["Energie",
"Energieversorgungssystem", "Energiesystem"],
"Related Subjects": ["Versorgung",
"Energieerzeugung", "Energiewirtschaft"]
},
{
"Code": "gnd-4068598-6",
"Name": "Erneuerbare Energien",
"Alternate Name": ["Sanfte Energie",
"Erneuerbare Energiequelle", "Regenerative
Energiequelle", "Regenerative Energie",
"Erneuerbare Energie", "Alternativenergie",
"Alternativenergien", "Regenerative Energien",
"Alternative Energiequelle", "Grüne Energie",
"Green energy"],
"Related Subjects": ["Energiequelle",
"Erneuerbare Ressourcen"]
},
...
]
}
```
````

D Output example at model inference (partial content omitted)

````
```json
{
  "document_title": "Probability matching
  priors : higher order asymptotics",
  "assigned_subject_titles": [
    {
      "Code": "gnd-4000000-9",
      "Name": "Statistik",
      "Alternate Name": ["Statistics",
      "Statisztika", "Statistiche",
      "Statistique", "Estimation",
      "Analyse statistique"],
      "Related Subjects": ["Inferenz",
    "Schätzung", "Methodik der Statistik",
      "Theorie der Wahrscheinlichkeit",
      "Wahrscheinlichkeitsrechnung"]
    },
    {
      "Code": "gnd-4021000-7",
      "Name": "Bayesische Statistik",
    "Alternate Name": ["Bayesian statistics",
      "Bayésienne statistique",
      "Bayes'che Methode",
      "Méthodologie bayésienne",
      "Théorie des Bayes"],
      "Related Subjects":
      ["Konditionalisierung",
      "Unsicherheit", "Vorkalkulation",
      "Prioritäten", "Schatzungen"]
    },
    ... (content omitted)
  ]
}
```
````
````

# Die SuperGLEBer at GermEval 2025 Shared Tasks: Growing Pains - When More Isn't Always Better

**Julia Wunderle** and **Jan Pfister** and **Andreas Hotho**
Data Science Chair
Center for Artificial Intelligence and Data Science (CAIDAS)
Julius-Maximilians-Universität Würzburg (JMU)
{lastname}@informatik.uni-wuerzburg.de

## Abstract

We participate in this year's GermEval 2025 Shared Tasks by extending SuperGLEBer, a comprehensive benchmark for evaluating German language understanding to the new tasks. Rather than focusing on optimizing task-specific performance, we adopt a complementary strategy: applying simple methods across 38 diverse (L)LMs (100M to 9B parameters) to analyze the tasks themselves, revealing that most models perform similarly on this year's tasks compared to existing SuperGLEBer tasks. Notably, the regression-based verifiability rating task diverges from this trend, emerging as substantially more difficult and methodologically distinct. Through our comprehensive analysis, we find that three new tasks, including Flausch-Erkennung subtask 2, rank among the top 10 most discriminating tasks of the benchmark, effectively distinguishing between model capabilities. Most remarkably, we demonstrate that just 2-3 strategically selected tasks can approximate the complete benchmark rankings with 97-99% correlation, potentially enabling more efficient large-scale model evaluation while maintaining ranking accuracy. Overall, our submissions achieved competitive results, placing 1st (out of one)-6th across different tasks, i.e. for Flausch-Erkennung subtask 1 and 2 we placed 3rd and 6th respectively.

## 1 Introduction

In an earlier work we introduced the first comprehensive benchmark for German language understanding models called SuperGLEBer (Pfister and Hotho, 2024). It contains 29 diverse tasks such as document classification, sequence tagging, sentence similarity, and question answering. This allowed us to systematically evaluate the performance of any existing HuggingFace model on German language understanding tasks.

In this work, we extend SuperGLEBer with all four shared tasks from GermEval 2025 to provide a comprehensive evaluation of current German models on all shared tasks: (**1**) **Flausch-/Candy Speech Detection** (Clausen et al.), which identifies "candy speech" in YouTube comments through coarse–grained binary classification and fine-grained span detection with category assignment (10 categories); (**2**) **SustainEval** (Prange et al.), which analyzes German sustainability reports through content classification of text snippets to predefined reporting criteria and verifiability rating of sentences on a 0.0-1.0 scale; (**3**) **Harmful Content Detection in Social Media** (Felser et al.), which detects harmful content in German social media posts through three binary/multi-class classifications: calls to action, stance toward democratic order (4 categories), and positive attitudes toward violence; and (**4**) **LLMs4Subjects** (D'Souza et al.), a multi-label classification task that assigns library records to subject domains (28 categories) using the GND taxonomy. We participate in all subtasks, except for LLMs4Subjects, where we only benchmark on subtask 1. However, we did not officially submit a run due to limitations requiring participation in both subtasks, and subtask 2 was not trivial to implement into the existing SuperGLEBer framework[1].

Our approach is partly inverse to traditional shared task participations, following the spirit of van der Goot (2022, 2023) at SemEval: we participate in multiple shared tasks at once, and rather than focusing solely on optimizing model performance, we aim to learn more about the tasks themselves by applying simple methods across a wide range of models. This systematic evaluation allows us not only to assess model performance but also to analyze the complexity and discriminative power of the new tasks in comparison to existing SuperGLEBer benchmark tasks.

These authors contributed equally to this work.

[1] https://github.com/LSX-UniWue/SuperGLEBer

*Proceedings of the 21st Conference on Natural Language Processing (KONVENS), Volume 2: Workshops, pages 479–493, 2025*

## 2 Modelling the tasks in SuperGLEBer

SuperGLEBer is an open-source benchmark suite designed to evaluate German language understanding of language models across a wide range of tasks (Pfister and Hotho, 2024). It includes 29 diverse tasks such as document classification, sequence tagging, sentence similarity, and question answering, reflecting the breadth of natural language understanding challenges in German. We add the shared tasks to the SuperGLEBer framework, which already supports most task types. Following flair's implementation (Akbik et al., 2019) we finetune the text classification tasks using the standard approach of adding a linear layer on top of the output representation of the CLS token, while for sequence tagging tasks we use the same approach, but train the linear layer to predict the correct class on top of the output representation of each input token individually.

**Flausch-Erkennung** For the binary classification in subtask 1, the input sentence: *"ihr seid die Besten"* has to be classified as `yes`. For the span prediction in subtask 2, each token's class is predicted individually using a BIO-label scheme:

| Token | Label |
|---|---|
| *ihr* | `B-affection_declaration` |
| *seid* | `I-affection_declaration` |
| *die* | `I-affection_declaration` |
| *Besten* | `I-affection_declaration` |

**SustainEval** The multi-class classification subtask 1 is solved by assigning text snippets to predefined reporting criteria: *"Prävention Über das Kerngeschäft „Versicherung" hinaus fühlt sich ..."* and *"Die [ORG] arbeitet hier eng mit den relevanten Institutionen und Einrichtungen..."* the model has to classify this as class `18`, i.e `Corporate Citizenship`. For the regression subtask 2 the verifiability of the last sentence given the previous context has to be predicted, in this case `0.667`. Here, we also follow flair's standard setup, using a simple linear layer on top of the model's hidden states. As we found that this can be unstable during training, we add two stabilizing measures:

1. An RMS-Norm before the linear layer, as some hidden state features can be very large, leading to training instabilities.
2. A sigmoid activation function after the linear layer, constraining outputs to the value range of the task: between 0 and 1.

**Harmful Content Detection** For harmful content detection, we perform binary or multi-class classification across three subtasks to detect harmful content in German social media posts: C2A and VIO use binary classification to detect calls to action and positive attitudes toward violence respectively. For example, given the input: *"In 300 Jahren sind dann alle wieder daheim"* the model classifies this as `False` for the violence subtask. DBO performs multi-class classification (4 categories) to determine stance toward democratic order. For example, given: *"Die schädliche Arbeitsagentur soll mal in den Spiegel schauen."* the correct label would be `criticism`.

**LLMs4Subjects Subtask 1** Here, we perform multi-label classification (28 categories) to assign library records to subject domains. For example, given the input describing a cultural heritage site: *"Der Löhrerhof in Hürth : Denkmalgerechte Planung und Sanierung "Der Löhrerhof ist eine bäuerliche Hofanlage aus dem 19. Jh. im Stadtteil Alt-Hürth, die zuletzt hauptsächlich als Kunst- und Kulturzentrum genutzt wurde."* the model assigns the labels `arc ; bau`.

## 3 Experiments

We evaluate the performance of all models from the original SuperGLEBer benchmark, as well as models added after its official release using the flair internal default metric: F1-score for classification and sequence tagging, and mean squared error for regression.

### 3.1 Models

This results in evaluating 38 models, all of which are listed alongside their results in Table 5. As SuperGLEBer is a model-architecture-agnostic framework, which allows us to evaluate most HuggingFace compatible models, we refer to these models using their HuggingFace identifiers, often omitting the leading organization name for simplicity (i.e. "(LSX-UniWue/)ModernGBERT_1B"). The models vary in size (from 100M to 9B parameters), and architecture (encoder and decoder), including recent multilingual models, German-specific models and models pretrained in languages other than German and later fine-tuned on German data (see Table 6 for more details).

### 3.2 Training Setup

For each of the task type, we follow SuperGLEBer (Pfister and Hotho, 2024) in implementing the training routine. For text classification, regression and sequence tagging we use flair (Akbik et al., 2019), applying consistent training procedures across all models: a batch size of 8 (without gradient accumulation), a learning rate of 5e-5, 5 epochs and a seed set to 42. In addition, we introduce a maximum input sequence length of 512 tokens, to enable fair comparisons for all models regardless of their individual context size and class weighting for all classification tasks during training.

**Efficient Training with (Q)LoRA** We consequently opt to use QLoRA-training (Dettmers et al., 2023) for all models where it is supported by the HuggingFace library, falling back to LoRA (Hu et al., 2022) for the GBERT family where quantization is not supported. Enabling (Q)LoRA for all models where possible ensures comparability between different models and rules out the possibility that the performance difference between models stems from different training procedures. Following the hyperparameters given by Dettmers et al. (2023) we use 4-bit quantization, double quantization and NormalFloat4, with a default LoRA rank of 8 and a dropout rate of 0.1. All models are trained on H100 GPUs.

## 4 Results

### 4.1 How does our simple approach perform?

Our full evaluation on the development datasets is presented in Table 5. For datasets without a predefined development split, we randomly split the training set into new train and dev subsets using an 80:20 ratio.

**Flausch-Erkennung** For Flausch-Erkennung, the binary classification subtask 1 proves relatively straightforward, with leo-hessian-7b achieving the highest performance (0.953), closely followed by DOSMo-7B-v0.2 (0.952). However, the span detection subtask 2 emerges as significantly more challenging, with ModernGBERT_1B leading at only 0.662, followed by LLäMmlein2Vec_7B (0.657) according to our metric. This substantial performance drop highlights the complexity of fine-grained span detection with category assignment compared to coarse-grained binary classification.

**SustainEval** Both SustainEval subtasks present considerable challenges for current models. The content classification subtask achieves moderate performance with ModernGBERT_1B leading (0.659) and LLäMmlein_7B following (0.633). The verifiability rating regression subtask proves particularly difficult, with even the best-performing Meta-Llama-3.1-8B reaching only 0.454, while Llama3-German-8B achieves 0.430. This regression task's low scores across all models suggest it requires fundamentally different capabilities than traditional classification tasks.

**Harmful Content Detection** The harmful content detection tasks show varied difficulty levels across subtasks. Call-to-action detection (c2a) achieves high performance with ModernGBERT_1B (0.953) and LLäMmlein_7B (0.952) performing similarly well. Stance detection toward democratic order (dbo) proves moderately more challenging, with LLäMmlein2Vec_7B leading (0.900), followed closely by ModernGBERT_1B and leo-hessian-7b (both 0.897). Violence detection (vio) represents the easiest subtask overall, with LLäMmlein_7B achieving the highest score (0.956) and EuroLLM-9B close behind (0.954).

**LLMs4Subjects** The multi-label subject classification task shows competitive performance between top models, with ModernGBERT_1B (0.787) and Llama3-German-8B (0.786) achieving nearly identical results. This close performance suggests that both encoder and decoder architectures can effectively handle this taxonomic classification challenge.

**Overall Performance Patterns** Remarkably, the German-only encoder ModernGBERT_1B demonstrates exceptional consistency, achieving best or second-best performance in 6 out of 8 subtasks despite being up to 9 times smaller than competing models. This pattern reinforces that specialized German training outweighs raw parameter count for these tasks. The performance hierarchy generally follows with decoder models leo-hessian-7b, LLäMmlein variants, and Meta-Llama-3.1-8B, most of which received explicit German fine-tuning, while even recent SotA model families like Qwen stay behind, highlighting the importance of specialized training for German. Despite this, many overall well performing models do not perform as well on SustainEval-Regression, with scores ranging from 0.029 to 0.454. This suggests that verifiability rating and the regression task present different challenges than the other SuperGLEBer tasks.

**Our official submissions** Overall, we submitted the three best overall performers according to our analyses - "ModernGBERT_1B", 'LLaMmlein_7B", and "Llama-3.1-8B" (details in Table 6) - to all official leaderboards except for LLMs4Subjects. Our simple SuperGLEBer framework approach achieved competitive results across most tasks: 3rd place out of 11 teams for Flausch-Erkennung subtask 1, with an F1 score of 0.883 (Table 1), 6th place out of 7 teams for Flausch-Erkennung subtask 2, with a strict F1 of 0.127, type F1 of 0.173, and span F1 score of 0.580 (Table 2). Notably, for subtask 2 we observed a significant discrepancy between the official span-based evaluations vs. our BIO-label token classification-based evaluation, which we aim to analyze in the future. For the SustainEval classification subtask we achieved 4th place out of 6 teams, with an accuracy score of 0.573 and 1st place out of 1 team for SustainEval regression subtask, with an kendall's tau score of 0.402 (see Table 3). Official Harmful-Content results have not yet been published[2]. For subtask 1 (c2a) we achieved a F1 score of 0.870, subtask 2 (dbo) 0.690 and subtask 3 vio (0.840).

### 4.2 How do models perform on the new tasks, compared to the old tasks?

As we augmented the SuperGLEBer benchmark with new tasks, we want to understand the performance relationship between the new shared tasks from this year and the already existing tasks. To shed light on this, we analyze the ranking consistency between tasks using Spearman rank correlation. Figure 1 shows the correlation matrix between all new tasks (rows) and existing tasks (columns) based on model performance rankings.

What we find is that most new tasks exhibit strong positive correlations (0.7-0.9) with many existing tasks, suggesting that models performing well on existing SuperGLEBer tasks also excel on these new tasks. In contrast, SE-Regression shows weak or inverse correlations, highlighting it as a distinct challenge that deviates from existing performance patterns. Interestingly, for the existing up-dep and up-pos tasks, we find a (strong) inverse correlation to most new tasks - except for Flausch-Erkennung Tagging and Harmful Content c2a, indicating that models that perform well on these tasks do not perform well on the new tasks. We assume up-dep and up-pos are special, because they are the only syntactic tasks in SuperGLEBer, focusing on predicting dependency parse labels and POS tags respectively, while all other tasks are semantic/pragmatic in nature, focusing on extracting meaning and content such as named entity recognition or text classification. This also becomes visible when embedding each task by interpreting each model's performance on a task as a "feature" (Figure 5) and subsequently calculating a principal component analysis (PCA) on the resulting space: as anticipatable the previously already discussed up-pos, up-dep and SE-Regression are most "out-of-distribution".

### 4.3 How well do the tasks discriminate between models?

Inspired by these insights, we reverse the process by interpreting task performance as embedding features for the models in Figure 4. We observe distinct clustering patterns: smaller multilingual models without a German focus (i.e., "bloomz-560m" and "Qwen2.5-0.5B") group in the lower-left quadrant, while high-performing models like ModernGBERTs and larger LLäMmlein variants tend to place in the upper-right region. Smaller German-focused encoder models (e.g., gbert variants and gelectra models) cluster together in the upper-center area, suggesting similar performance profiles despite architectural differences. On the other hand, decoder models (e.g. "bueble-lm-2b", EuroLLM, "leo-hessianai-7b") are grouped in the lower-right area. This pattern suggests that model architecture families and language-specific training create recognizable performance signatures that transcend individual task results.

In this figure the first two principal components already capture 74.7% of the total variance (PC1: 61.9%, PC2: 12.8%), indicating that model performance can be largely characterized by these two dominant factors, each resembling an axis in the "task performance space". Similarly, when we color the models in this graph according to the performance of the subtasks in Figure 3, we can identify a clear "gradient" in this PCA space along which the performance evolves rather monotonously. This is an indicator that most of the model performance discrimination might be driven by a small subset of tasks in the SuperGLEBer.

To further analyze this behavior we calculate

[2]although it looks like atleast a Top-3 finish at the moment

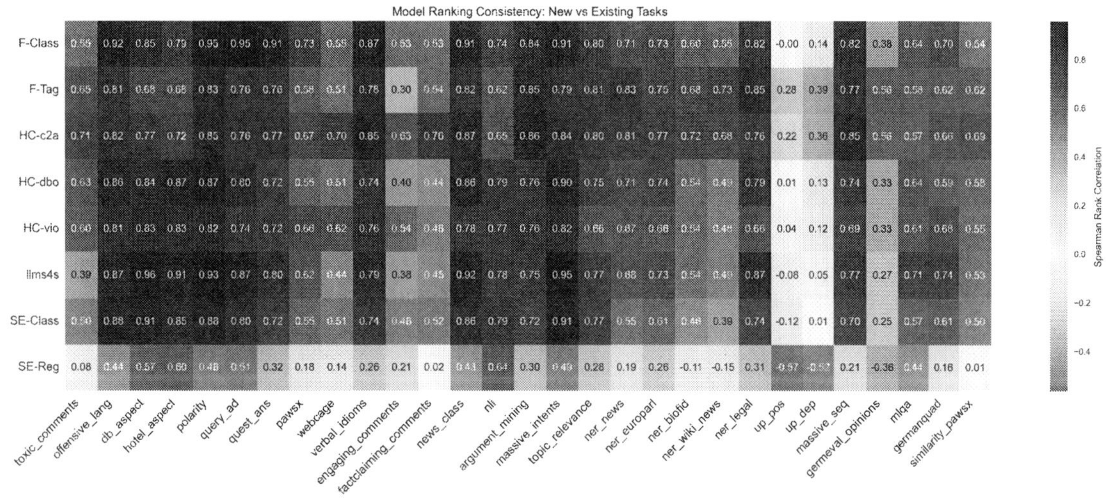


Figure 1: Model ranking consistency between new GermEval 2025 tasks and existing SuperGLEBer tasks. Each cell shows the Spearman rank correlation coefficient between model rankings on the corresponding task pair. Darker red indicates higher positive correlation (similar model rankings), while blue indicates negative correlations. The analysis reveals which new tasks are most predictive of performance on the existing tasks.

the standard deviation of model performances for each task. Tasks with higher deviation in model performance scores are more effective at distinguishing between models, while tasks where all models perform similarly provide less discriminative power (Figure 2). We find that three of the new tasks (SE-Class, Flausch-Tagging and SE-Regression) are able to create a standard deviation across models of about 0.1 or more, placing them in the top 10 most discriminating tasks overall. A more detailed list of task discrimination for new and existing tasks separately is provided in Figure 6. When examining these most discriminative tasks, we identify a common characteristic: most of these tasks have many target classes, like for the existing tasks "hotel_aspect" (15 labels, one for each combination of an aspect-class and sentiment class) or "massive_intents" (60 labels). A similar pattern holds for the new tasks: "SE-class" (20 labels), and "Flausch-tagging" (21 labels).

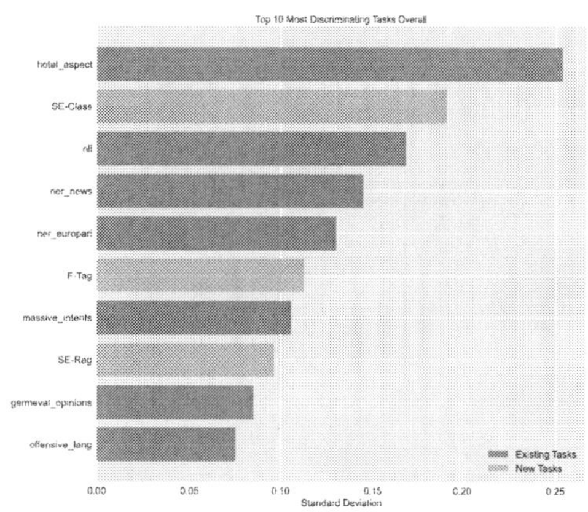


Figure 2: Top 10 most discriminating tasks, performance score standard deviation across all 38 evaluated models. Higher deviation indicates better discrimination between model capabilities: three of the new tasks from this year rank among the most discriminating overall.

### 4.4 Do we need the entire SuperGLEBer benchmark to reproduce the rankings?

Motivated by the findings in Sections 4.2 and 4.3, we investigate whether a smaller, carefully chosen subset of tasks can approximate the full benchmark's model rankings. This could greatly reduce evaluation costs while maintaining ranking accuracy. Using a greedy selection strategy, we construct subsets of increasing size by iteratively adding tasks that maximize alignment with the full 37-task ranking across all 38 models. We measure the subset quality using Spearman rank correlation, mean absolute rank difference (MAD), exact rank matches (number of models that keep their rank), and the number of models involved in ranking ties.

As shown in Table 4, remarkably few tasks are needed to approximate the full benchmark rankings. Starting with a single task ("massive_intents"), we achieve 96.9% correlation with the complete 37-task ranking, though this results in 10 models having identical performance scores and thus being tied for the same rank position.

When we expand to two selected existing SuperGLEBer tasks - "verbal_idioms" and "massive_intents" - the correlation improves to 97.8% while reducing ranking ambiguity: only 2 models remain tied in placement, compared to 10 with a single task. This means that 36 out of 38 models can be clearly distinguished and ranked using these two tasks. Expanding further to three tasks ("toxic_comments", "db_aspect", and "ner_legal") achieves 99.0% correlation with the full benchmark. The MAD, which measures the average difference in rank positions between the subset and full rankings, drops to 1.21 ranks. This means that on average, a model's rank using these three tasks differs by only about one position from its rank using all 37 tasks. Importantly, this subset eliminates all ties, providing a clear ranking for all models.

A four-task subset maintains similar correlation (99.2%) with slightly better rank precision (MAD of 1.16), while a five-task subset that includes one of this year's new tasks ("HC-dbo") achieves 99.4% correlation with a MAD of just 0.68 ranks. At this point, 22 out of 38 models maintain their exact rank positions compared to the full benchmark.

These results demonstrate that comprehensive model evaluation can be effectively approximated using a small, strategically chosen subset of tasks, making large-scale model comparison more computationally efficient - confirming that more isn't always better when it comes to benchmark design.

## 5 Related Work

GLUE (Wang et al., 2018) and SuperGLUE (Wang et al., 2019) established the paradigm of comprehensive language understanding benchmarks with 11 and 10 diverse NLU tasks respectively. The English-only nature of these benchmarks led to the development of similar multilingual efforts for e.g. Russian (Shavrina et al., 2020), Persian (Khashabi et al., 2021), and Bulgarian (Hardalov et al., 2023).

While cross-lingual benchmarks like XTREME (Hu et al., 2020) and XGLUE (Liang et al., 2020) include German tasks, their focus on cross-lingual transfer rather than monolingual capabilities makes them less suitable for comprehensive German model evaluation. Previous German evaluation efforts have been task-specific, focusing on individual capabilities like sentiment analysis (Cieliebak et al., 2017) or coreference resolution (Schröder et al., 2021), rather than providing comprehensive benchmarking frameworks.

## 6 Conclusion

We successfully extended SuperGLEBer with four new GermEval 2025 shared tasks, providing comprehensive evaluation of 38 models ranging from 100M to 9B parameters. Our simple approach achieved competitive results across tasks, placing 1st-6th in the shared task rankings, and on average performed best when using a "small" 1B model.

The analysis reveals that most new tasks correlate well with existing SuperGLEBer tasks (0.7-0.9 correlation), except for the regression-based verifiability rating which presents distinct challenges. Three new tasks rank among the top 10 most discriminating tasks, effectively distinguishing between model capabilities. We demonstrate that strategic task selection can reduce model benchmarking costs: just a small subset of 2-3 carefully chosen tasks approximate complete benchmark rankings consisting of 37 tasks with 97-99% correlation, enabling efficient large-scale model evaluation while maintaining ranking accuracy.

Regarding the Flausch-Erkennung (Candy Speech Detection) task specifically, we achieved solid performance with 3rd place in the binary classification subtask but found the span detection subtask more challenging, placing 6th with notable discrepancies between span-based and BIO-token evaluation approaches. Interestingly, the Flausch-Erkennung tagging subtask emerged as one of the top 10 most discriminating tasks in our benchmark, effectively distinguishing between model capabilities across the 38 evaluated models, suggesting its value for comprehensive model evaluation beyond just detecting candy speech in social media.

## Limitations

Our evaluation relies on a simple approach that may (likely) not capture the full potential of more sophisticated methods for these tasks. The regression task implementation required additional stabilization measures, indicating potential challenges in the dataset or our approach - as no other team participated in this subtask, we lack points of comparison for further investigations.

## Acknowledgements

The authors gratefully acknowledge the scientific support and HPC resources provided by the Erlangen National High Performance Computing Center (NHR@FAU) of the Friedrich Alexander-Universität Erlangen-Nürnberg (FAU) under the

NHR project b185cb. NHR funding is provided by federal and Bavarian state authorities. NHR@FAU hardware is partially funded by the German Research Foundation (DFG) – 440719683. Furthermore, we gratefully acknowledge the HPC resources provided by the JuliaV2 cluster at the Universität Würzburg (JMU), which was funded as DFG project as "Forschungsgroßgerät nach Art 91b GG" under INST 93/1145-1 FUGG. The project staff is partially funded by the DFG – 529659926. The data science chair is part of the CAIDAS, the Center for Artificial Intelligence and Data Science, and is supported by the Bavarian High-Tech Agenda, which made this research possible. This publication was partially funded by the Deutsche Forschungsgemeinschaft (DFG, German Research Foundation) under the project LitBERT, project no. 529659926. Furthermore, we would like to thank the task hosts for organizing the shared tasks and providing the data.

## References

Alan Akbik, Tanja Bergmann, Duncan Blythe, Kashif Rasul, Stefan Schweter, and Roland Vollgraf. 2019. FLAIR: An easy-to-use framework for state-of-the-art NLP. In *NAACL 2019, 2019 Annual Conference of the North American Chapter of the Association for Computational Linguistics (Demonstrations)*, pages 54–59.

Nicolas Boizard, Hippolyte Gisserot-Boukhlef, Duarte M. Alves, André Martins, Ayoub Hammal, Caio Corro, Céline Hudelot, Emmanuel Malherbe, Etienne Malaboeuf, Fanny Jourdan, Gabriel Hautreux, João Alves, Kevin El-Haddad, Manuel Faysse, Maxime Peyrard, Nuno M. Guerreiro, Patrick Fernandes, Ricardo Rei, and Pierre Colombo. 2025. Eurobert: Scaling multilingual encoders for european languages. *Preprint*, arXiv:2503.05500.

Branden Chan, Stefan Schweter, and Timo Möller. 2020. German's next language model. In *Proceedings of the 28th International Conference on Computational Linguistics*, pages 6788–6796, Barcelona, Spain (Online). International Committee on Computational Linguistics.

Mark Cieliebak, Jan Milan Deriu, Dominic Egger, and Fatih Uzdilli. 2017. A Twitter corpus and benchmark resources for German sentiment analysis. In *Proceedings of the Fifth International Workshop on Natural Language Processing for Social Media*, pages 45–51, Valencia, Spain. Association for Computational Linguistics.

Yulia Clausen, Tatjana Scheffler, and Michael Wiegand. 2025. Overview of the GermEval 2025 Shared Task on Candy Speech Detection. In *Proceedings of the 21st Conference on Natural Language Processing (KONVENS 2025): Workshops*, Hildesheim, Germany. ACL.

Alexis Conneau, Kartikay Khandelwal, Naman Goyal, Vishrav Chaudhary, Guillaume Wenzek, Francisco Guzmán, Edouard Grave, Myle Ott, Luke Zettlemoyer, and Veselin Stoyanov. 2019. Unsupervised cross-lingual representation learning at scale. *CoRR*, abs/1911.02116.

Pieter Delobelle, Alan Akbik, and 1 others. 2024. Büblelm: A small german lm.

Tim Dettmers, Artidoro Pagnoni, Ari Holtzman, and Luke Zettlemoyer. 2023. Qlora: Efficient finetuning of quantized llms. In *Advances in Neural Information Processing Systems*, volume 36, pages 10088–10115. Curran Associates, Inc.

DiscoResearch and Occiglot. 2024. Llama3-discoleo-instruct-8b-v0.1. Instruction-tuned German language model developed with support from DFKI and hessian.AI.

Jennifer D'Souza, Sameer Sadruddin, Holger Israel, Mathias Begoin, and Diana Slawig. 2025. The GermEval 2025 2nd LLMs4Subjects Shared Task Dataset.

Anton Ehrmanntraut, Julia Wunderle, Jan Pfister, Fotis Jannidis, and Andreas Hotho. 2025. Moderngbert: German-only 1b encoder model trained from scratch. *Preprint*, arXiv:2505.13136.

Jenny Felser, Michael Spranger, and Melanie Siegel. 2025. Overview of the GermEval 2025 Shared Task on harmful content detection. In *Proceedings of the 21st Conference on Natural Language Processing (KONVENS 2025): Workshops*, Hildesheim, Germany. HsH Applied Academics.

GERTuraX. 2025a. gerturax-1 (revision 18de094).

GERTuraX. 2025b. gerturax-2 (revision 50ede60).

GERTuraX. 2025c. gerturax-3 (revision e0f62ac).

Aaron Grattafiori, Abhimanyu Dubey, Abhinav Jauhri, Abhinav Pandey, Abhishek Kadian, Ahmad Al-Dahle, Aiesha Letman, Akhil Mathur, Alan Schelten, Alex Vaughan, Amy Yang, Angela Fan, Anirudh Goyal, Anthony Hartshorn, Aobo Yang, Archi Mitra, Archie Sravankumar, Artem Korenev, Arthur Hinsvark, and 542 others. 2024. The llama 3 herd of models. *Preprint*, arXiv:2407.21783.

Momchil Hardalov, Pepa Atanasova, Todor Mihaylov, Galia Angelova, Kiril Simov, Petya Osenova, Veselin Stoyanov, Ivan Koychev, Preslav Nakov, and Dragomir Radev. 2023. bgGLUE: A Bulgarian general language understanding evaluation benchmark. In *Proceedings of the 61st Annual Meeting of the Association for Computational Linguistics (Volume 1: Long Papers)*, pages 8733–8759, Toronto, Canada. Association for Computational Linguistics.

Edward J Hu, yelong shen, Phillip Wallis, Zeyuan Allen-Zhu, Yuanzhi Li, Shean Wang, Lu Wang, and Weizhu Chen. 2022. LoRA: Low-rank adaptation of large language models. In *International Conference on Learning Representations*.

Junjie Hu, Sebastian Ruder, Aditya Siddhant, Graham Neubig, Orhan Firat, and Melvin Johnson. 2020. Xtreme: A massively multilingual multi-task benchmark for evaluating cross-lingual generalization. *CoRR*, abs/2003.11080.

Maximilian Idahl. 2024. DOSMo-7B: A Large Language Model Trained Exclusively on German Text. In *Proceedings of the Konferenz der deutschen KI-Servicezentren 2024 (KonKIS 24)*. Accessed: 2024-12-10.

Daniel Khashabi, Arman Cohan, Siamak Shakeri, Pedram Hosseini, Pouya Pezeshkpour, Malihe Alikhani, Moin Aminnaseri, Marzieh Bitaab, Faeze Brahman, Sarik Ghazarian, Mozhdeh Gheini, Arman Kabiri, Rabeeh Karimi Mahabagdi, Omid Memarrast, Ahmadreza Mosallanezhad, Erfan Noury, Shahab Raji, Mohammad Sadegh Rasooli, Sepideh Sadeghi, and 6 others. 2021. ParsiNLU: A suite of language understanding challenges for Persian. *Transactions of the Association for Computational Linguistics*, 9:1147–1162.

Yaobo Liang, Nan Duan, Yeyun Gong, Ning Wu, Fenfei Guo, Weizhen Qi, Ming Gong, Linjun Shou, Daxin Jiang, Guihong Cao, Xiaodong Fan, Ruofei Zhang, Rahul Agrawal, Edward Cui, Sining Wei, Taroon Bharti, Ying Qiao, Jiun-Hung Chen, Winnie Wu, and 5 others. 2020. XGLUE: A new benchmark dataset for cross-lingual pre-training, understanding and generation. In *Proceedings of the 2020 Conference on Empirical Methods in Natural Language Processing (EMNLP)*, pages 6008–6018, Online. Association for Computational Linguistics.

Yinhan Liu, Jiatao Gu, Naman Goyal, Xian Li, Sergey Edunov, Marjan Ghazvininejad, Mike Lewis, and Luke Zettlemoyer. 2020. Multilingual denoising pre-training for neural machine translation. *Transactions of the Association for Computational Linguistics*, 8:726–742.

Pedro Henrique Martins, Patrick Fernandes, João Alves, Nuno M. Guerreiro, Ricardo Rei, Duarte M. Alves, José Pombal, Amin Farajian, Manuel Faysse, Mateusz Klimaszewski, Pierre Colombo, Barry Haddow, José G. C. de Souza, Alexandra Birch, and André F. T. Martins. 2024. Eurollm: Multilingual language models for europe. *Preprint*, arXiv:2409.16235.

Benjamin Minixhofer. 2020. GerPT2: German large and small versions of GPT2.

Niklas Muennighoff, Thomas Wang, Lintang Sutawika, Adam Roberts, Stella Biderman, Teven Le Scao, M Saiful Bari, Sheng Shen, Zheng Xin Yong, Hailey Schoelkopf, Xiangru Tang, Dragomir Radev, Alham Fikri Aji, Khalid Almubarak, Samuel Albanie, Zaid Alyafeai, Albert Webson, Edward Raff, and Colin Raffel. 2023. Crosslingual generalization through multitask finetuning. In *Proceedings of the 61st Annual Meeting of the Association for Computational Linguistics (Volume 1: Long Papers)*, pages 15991–16111, Toronto, Canada. Association for Computational Linguistics.

Malte Ostendorff and Georg Rehm. 2023. Efficient language model training through cross-lingual and progressive transfer learning. *arXiv preprint*.

Jan Pfister and Andreas Hotho. 2024. SuperGLEBer: German language understanding evaluation benchmark. In *Proceedings of the 2024 Conference of the North American Chapter of the Association for Computational Linguistics: Human Language Technologies (Volume 1: Long Papers)*, pages 7904–7923, Mexico City, Mexico. Association for Computational Linguistics.

Jan Pfister, Julia Wunderle, and Andreas Hotho. 2025. LLäMmlein: Transparent, compact and competitive German-only language models from scratch. In *Proceedings of the 63rd Annual Meeting of the Association for Computational Linguistics (Volume 1: Long Papers)*, pages 2227–2246, Vienna, Austria. Association for Computational Linguistics.

Björn Plüster. 2023. LeoLM: Igniting German-Language LLM Research. Accessed: 2024-11-15.

Jakob Prange, Charlott Jakob, Patrick Göttfert, Raphael Huber, Pia Wenzel Neves, and Annemarie Friedrich. 2025. Overview of the SustainEval 2025 Shared Task: Identifying the topic and verifiability of sustainability report excerpts. In *Proceedings of the 21st Conference on Natural Language Processing (KONVENS 2025): Workshops*, Hildesheim, Germany. HsH Applied Academics.

Raphael Scheible, Johann Frei, Fabian Thomczyk, Henry He, Patric Tippmann, Jochen Knaus, Victor Jaravine, Frank Kramer, and Martin Boeker. 2024. GottBERT: a pure German language model. In *Proceedings of the 2024 Conference on Empirical Methods in Natural Language Processing*, pages 21237–21250, Miami, Florida, USA. Association for Computational Linguistics.

Raphael Scheible-Schmitt and Johann Frei. 2025. Geistbert: Breathing life into german nlp. *Preprint*, arXiv:2506.11903.

Fynn Schröder, Hans Ole Hatzel, and Chris Biemann. 2021. Neural end-to-end coreference resolution for German in different domains. In *Proceedings of the 17th Conference on Natural Language Processing (KONVENS 2021)*, pages 170–181, Düsseldorf, Germany. KONVENS 2021 Organizers.

Tatiana Shavrina, Alena Fenogenova, Emelyanov Anton, Denis Shevelev, Ekaterina Artemova, Valentin Malykh, Vladislav Mikhailov, Maria Tikhonova, Andrey Chertok, and Andrey Evlampiev. 2020. RussianSuperGLUE: A Russian language understanding evaluation benchmark. In *Proceedings of the*

2020 Conference on Empirical Methods in Natural Language Processing (EMNLP), pages 4717–4726, Online. Association for Computational Linguistics.

Bayerische Staatsbibliothek. 2025. bert-base-german-cased (revision 43cce13).

Bayerische Staatsbibliothek and Stefan Schweter. 2025. german-gpt2 (revision ab6efd0).

Qwen Team. 2024. Qwen2.5: A party of foundation models.

Qwen Team. 2025. Qwen3 technical report. *Preprint*, arXiv:2505.09388.

Rob van der Goot. 2022. MaChAmp at SemEval-2022 tasks 2, 3, 4, 6, 10, 11, and 12: Multi-task multilingual learning for a pre-selected set of semantic datasets. In *Proceedings of the 16th International Workshop on Semantic Evaluation (SemEval-2022)*, pages 1695–1703, Seattle, United States. Association for Computational Linguistics.

Rob van der Goot. 2023. MaChAmp at SemEval-2023 tasks 2, 3, 4, 5, 7, 8, 9, 10, 11, and 12: On the effectiveness of intermediate training on an uncurated collection of datasets. In *Proceedings of the 17th International Workshop on Semantic Evaluation (SemEval-2023)*, pages 230–245, Toronto, Canada. Association for Computational Linguistics.

Alex Wang, Yada Pruksachatkun, Nikita Nangia, Amanpreet Singh, Julian Michael, Felix Hill, Omer Levy, and Samuel R. Bowman. 2019. *SuperGLUE: A Stickier Benchmark for General-Purpose Language Understanding Systems*. Curran Associates Inc., Red Hook, NY, USA.

Alex Wang, Amanpreet Singh, Julian Michael, Felix Hill, Omer Levy, and Samuel Bowman. 2018. GLUE: A multi-task benchmark and analysis platform for natural language understanding. In *Proceedings of the 2018 EMNLP Workshop BlackboxNLP: Analyzing and Interpreting Neural Networks for NLP*, pages 353–355, Brussels, Belgium. Association for Computational Linguistics.

Benjamin Warner, Antoine Chaffin, Benjamin Clavié, Orion Weller, Oskar Hallström, Said Taghadouini, Alexis Gallagher, Raja Biswas, Faisal Ladhak, Tom Aarsen, Griffin Thomas Adams, Jeremy Howard, and Iacopo Poli. 2025. Smarter, better, faster, longer: A modern bidirectional encoder for fast, memory efficient, and long context finetuning and inference. In *Proceedings of the 63rd Annual Meeting of the Association for Computational Linguistics (Volume 1: Long Papers)*, pages 2526–2547, Vienna, Austria. Association for Computational Linguistics.

Maurice Weber, Daniel Y. Fu, Quentin Anthony, Yonatan Oren, Shane Adams, Anton Alexandrov, Xiaozhong Lyu, Huu Nguyen, Xiaozhe Yao, Virginia Adams, Ben Athiwaratkun, Rahul Chalamala, Kezhen Chen, Max Ryabinin, Tri Dao, Percy Liang, Christopher Ré, Irina Rish, and Ce Zhang. 2024. RedPajama: an open dataset for training large language models. In *Advances in Neural Information Processing Systems*, volume 37, pages 116462–116492. Curran Associates, Inc.

| Team | F1 | Precision | Recall |
|---|---|---|---|
| AIxcellent Vibes | 0.891 | 0.927 | 0.857 |
| HHUflauschig | 0.887 | 0.900 | 0,875 |
| **Die SuperGLEBer** | 0.883 | 0.915 | 0.853 |
| NLPSuedwestfalen | 0.880 | 0.911 | 0.850 |
| TUM NLP Group | 0.879 | 0.887 | 0.871 |
| nlp-augsburg-04 | 0.836 | 0.903 | 0.778 |
| StickyBeardAux | 0.819 | 0.868 | 0.775 |
| Quabynar | 0.754 | 0.710 | 0.804 |
| Robert-Dennis-UniAugsburg03 | 0.746 | 0.817 | 0.687 |
| Flauschgummi | 0.697 | 0.888 | 0.574 |

Table 1: Leaderboard of Flausch-Erkennung subtask 1

| Team | F1 (strict) | P (strict) | R (strict) | F1 (type) | P (type) | R (type) | F1 (span) | P (span) | R (span) |
|---|---|---|---|---|---|---|---|---|---|
| AIxcellent Vibes | 0.631 | 0.658 | 0.605 | 0.769 | 0.803 | 0.738 | 0.676 | 0.705 | 0.648 |
| HHUflauschig | 0.615 | 0.629 | 0.601 | 0.766 | 0.785 | 0.749 | 0.668 | 0.684 | 0.653 |
| Georg Hofmann | 0.498 | 0.475 | 0.524 | 0.680 | 0.648 | 0.715 | 0.567 | 0.541 | 0.596 |
| nlp-augsburg-04 | 0.334 | 0.241 | 0.543 | 0.492 | 0.355 | 0.801 | 0.365 | 0.264 | 0.594 |
| Quabynar | 0.159 | 0.149 | 0.171 | 0.408 | 0.381 | 0.438 | 0.257 | 0.240 | 0.276 |
| **Die SuperGLEBer** | 0.127 | 0.136 | 0.120 | 0.173 | 0.185 | 0.162 | 0.580 | 0.620 | 0.544 |
| StickyBeardAux | 0.039 | 0.044 | 0.036 | 0.562 | 0.629 | 0.507 | 0.050 | 0.056 | 0.045 |

Table 2: Leaderboard of Flausch-Erkennung subtask 2

| Team | Subtask 1 Accuracy | Subtask 2 Kendall's Tau |
|---|---|---|
| 22520474 | 0.626 | - |
| 1234566 | 0.586 | - |
| s1nbo | 0.579 | - |
| **janpf (our)** | 0.573 | 0.402 |
| wangkongqiang | 0.505 | - |
| supachoke | 0.486 | - |

Table 3: Leaderboard of SustainEval subtask 1 - Content Classification and subtask 2 - Verifiability Rating

| Size | Task Subset | Correlation | MAD$^\dagger$ | Exact Rank Matches | Models in Ties |
|---|---|---|---|---|---|
| 1 | existing_massive_intents | 0.969 | 2.00 | 3/38 | 10 |
| 2 | existing_verbal_idioms<br>existing_massive_intents | 0.978 | 1.71 | 8/38 | 2 |
| 3 | existing_toxic_comments<br>existing_db_aspect<br>existing_ner_legal | 0.990 | 1.21 | 8/38 | 0 |
| 4 | existing_toxic_comments<br>existing_db_aspect<br>existing_verbal_idioms<br>existing_ner_legal | 0.992 | 1.16 | 6/38 | 0 |
| 5 | existing_offensive_lang<br>existing_db_aspect<br>existing_ner_news<br>existing_germanquad<br>new_HC-dbo | 0.994 | 0.68 | 22/38 | 0 |
| Full | All 37 tasks (29 existing + 8 new) | 1.000 | 0.00 | 38/38 | 0 |

Table 4: Minimal task subsets for reproducing SuperGLEBer model rankings. We evaluate the correlation between subset-based rankings and the full 37-task ranking across 38 models. Results show that just 2 tasks ("existing_verbal_idioms" + "existing_massive_intents") achieve 97.8% correlation with the complete benchmark while reducing ties from 10 to 2 models. This demonstrates that comprehensive model evaluation can be approximated with carefully selected task subsets. $^\dagger$MAD = Mean Absolute Rank Difference.

| model | Flausch Class | Flausch Tag | Harmful Content c2a | Harmful Content dbo | Harmful Content vio | Llms4s Class | SustainEval Class | SustainEval Reg | SuperGLEBer Old Avg |
|---|---|---|---|---|---|---|---|---|---|
| LLäMmlein_120M [Pfister et al.] | 0.924 | 0.433 | 0.920 | 0.845 | 0.943 | 0.728 | 0.225 | 0.330 | 0.676 |
| LLäMmlein_1B [Pfister et al.] | 0.941 | 0.541 | 0.936 | 0.886 | 0.945 | 0.773 | 0.449 | 0.321 | 0.733 |
| LLäMmlein_7B [Pfister et al.] | 0.950 | 0.575 | 0.952 | 0.887 | **0.956** | 0.784 | 0.633 | 0.357 | 0.747 |
| LLäMmlein2Vec_120M [Ehrmanntraut et al.] | 0.918 | 0.419 | 0.905 | 0.832 | 0.936 | 0.712 | 0.161 | 0.368 | 0.684 |
| LLäMmlein2Vec_1B [Ehrmanntraut et al.] | 0.940 | 0.609 | 0.943 | 0.874 | 0.951 | 0.765 | 0.251 | 0.270 | 0.762 |
| LLäMmlein2Vec_7B [Ehrmanntraut et al.] | 0.947 | 0.657 | 0.943 | **0.900** | 0.947 | 0.780 | 0.614 | 0.350 | 0.787 |
| ModernGBERT_134M [Ehrmanntraut et al.] | 0.932 | 0.520 | 0.932 | 0.865 | 0.936 | 0.753 | 0.210 | 0.243 | 0.749 |
| ModernGBERT_1B [Ehrmanntraut et al.] | 0.948 | **0.662** | **0.953** | 0.897 | 0.952 | **0.787** | **0.659** | 0.118 | **0.808** |
| german-gpt2 [Staatsbibliothek and Schweter] | 0.917 | 0.318 | 0.916 | 0.747 | 0.934 | 0.636 | 0.135 | 0.151 | 0.642 |
| gerpt2 [Minixhofer] | 0.913 | 0.237 | 0.923 | 0.779 | 0.932 | 0.702 | 0.094 | 0.281 | 0.619 |
| gerpt2-large [Minixhofer] | 0.935 | 0.450 | 0.935 | 0.858 | 0.941 | 0.749 | 0.382 | 0.321 | 0.708 |
| gbert-base [Chan et al.] | 0.924 | 0.386 | 0.929 | 0.843 | 0.933 | 0.729 | 0.292 | 0.222 | 0.718 |
| gbert-large [Chan et al.] | 0.937 | 0.567 | 0.948 | 0.878 | 0.943 | 0.753 | 0.378 | 0.307 | 0.768 |
| gelectra-base [Chan et al.] | 0.921 | 0.291 | 0.906 | 0.798 | 0.936 | 0.659 | 0.082 | 0.148 | 0.666 |
| gelectra-large [Chan et al.] | 0.936 | 0.536 | 0.928 | 0.858 | 0.940 | 0.726 | 0.191 | 0.248 | 0.734 |
| bert-base-german-cased [Staatsbibliothek] | 0.911 | 0.300 | 0.915 | 0.852 | 0.938 | 0.717 | 0.273 | 0.309 | 0.700 |
| gottbert-base [Scheible et al.] | 0.926 | 0.387 | 0.907 | 0.856 | 0.936 | 0.722 | 0.157 | 0.131 | 0.708 |
| GeistBERT-base [Scheible-Schmitt and Frei] | 0.933 | 0.481 | 0.927 | 0.842 | 0.935 | 0.656 | 0.277 | 0.228 | 0.703 |
| GottBERT-large [Scheible et al.] | 0.936 | 0.419 | 0.927 | 0.811 | 0.932 | 0.751 | 0.288 | 0.154 | 0.724 |
| gerturax-1 [GERTuraX] | 0.930 | 0.433 | 0.932 | 0.836 | 0.949 | 0.714 | 0.176 | 0.281 | 0.740 |
| gerturax-2 [GERTuraX] | 0.935 | 0.444 | 0.937 | 0.855 | 0.943 | 0.716 | 0.232 | 0.214 | 0.744 |
| gerturax-3 [GERTuraX] | 0.934 | 0.428 | 0.937 | 0.843 | 0.946 | 0.713 | 0.184 | 0.222 | 0.740 |
| DOSMo-7B-v0.2 [Idahl] | 0.952 | 0.577 | 0.945 | 0.891 | 0.947 | 0.783 | 0.580 | 0.401 | 0.759 |
| bueble-lm-2b [Delobelle et al.] | 0.935 | 0.553 | 0.932 | 0.873 | 0.944 | 0.764 | 0.438 | 0.358 | 0.741 |
| bloom-6b4-clp-german [Ostendorff and Rehm] | 0.948 | 0.427 | 0.947 | 0.884 | 0.949 | 0.778 | 0.502 | 0.391 | 0.752 |
| leo-hessianai-7b [Plüster] | **0.953** | 0.521 | 0.952 | 0.897 | 0.949 | 0.784 | 0.622 | 0.349 | 0.758 |
| Llama3-German-8B [DiscoResearch and Occiglot] | 0.949 | 0.527 | 0.944 | 0.871 | 0.950 | 0.786 | 0.626 | 0.430 | 0.746 |
| Llama-3.2-1B [Grattafiori et al.] | 0.934 | 0.342 | 0.910 | 0.872 | 0.938 | 0.760 | 0.371 | 0.357 | 0.710 |
| Llama-3.2-3B [Grattafiori et al.] | 0.939 | 0.455 | 0.923 | 0.867 | 0.938 | 0.776 | 0.494 | 0.390 | 0.733 |
| Meta-Llama-3.1-8B [Grattafiori et al.] | 0.948 | 0.510 | 0.936 | 0.873 | 0.949 | 0.785 | 0.584 | **0.454** | 0.744 |
| EuroBERT-210m [Boizard et al.] | 0.906 | 0.296 | 0.888 | 0.785 | 0.931 | 0.711 | 0.120 | 0.122 | - |
| EuroBERT-610m [Boizard et al.] | 0.907 | 0.494 | 0.878 | 0.817 | 0.931 | 0.753 | 0.101 | 0.209 | - |
| EuroBERT-2.1B [Boizard et al.] | 0.898 | 0.389 | 0.894 | 0.773 | 0.931 | 0.770 | 0.127 | 0.151 | - |
| EuroLLM-1.7B [Martins et al.] | 0.940 | 0.496 | 0.934 | 0.896 | 0.949 | 0.764 | 0.528 | 0.410 | 0.728 |
| EuroLLM-9B [Martins et al.] | 0.950 | 0.504 | 0.949 | 0.892 | 0.954 | 0.775 | 0.513 | 0.395 | 0.753 |
| xlm-roberta-base [Conneau et al.] | 0.923 | 0.313 | 0.913 | 0.839 | 0.931 | 0.672 | 0.139 | 0.271 | 0.689 |
| xlm-roberta-large [Conneau et al.] | 0.933 | 0.465 | 0.933 | 0.830 | 0.937 | 0.733 | 0.101 | 0.029 | 0.730 |
| Qwen2.5-0.5B [Team] | 0.917 | 0.205 | 0.888 | 0.832 | 0.931 | 0.703 | 0.086 | 0.305 | 0.661 |
| Qwen2.5-7B [Team] | 0.940 | 0.441 | 0.930 | 0.865 | 0.947 | 0.772 | 0.498 | 0.308 | 0.728 |
| Qwen3-0.6B [Team] | 0.924 | 0.344 | 0.905 | 0.848 | 0.928 | 0.745 | 0.172 | 0.253 | - |
| Qwen3-1.7B [Team] | 0.932 | 0.390 | 0.904 | 0.866 | 0.931 | 0.768 | 0.191 | 0.393 | - |
| Qwen3-4B [Team] | 0.941 | 0.441 | 0.922 | 0.864 | 0.938 | 0.774 | 0.412 | 0.358 | - |
| bloomz-560m [Muennighoff et al.] | 0.914 | 0.242 | 0.883 | 0.780 | 0.929 | 0.638 | 0.109 | 0.288 | 0.622 |
| mbart-large-50 [Liu et al.] | 0.935 | 0.438 | 0.922 | 0.826 | 0.932 | 0.705 | 0.090 | 0.262 | 0.651 |

Table 5: Model performance across tasks and a single, seeded run (Pfister and Hotho (2024) show SuperGLEBer to produce stable results even across seeds). Where no development set was available, we split the train set 80/20 into a new train and dev set. Best models in bold. "Old Avg" contains the overall average score on the old, already existing SuperGLEBer tasks, a dash here means this model is missing from the official SuperGLEBer rankings. This table can be viewed as an addition to the offical leaderboard: `https://lsx-uniwue.github.io/SuperGLEBer-site/leaderboard_v1`. Contained in this table are the 38 models mentioned in the paper, and an additional 6 models which are not yet contained in the official SuperGLEBer. Details for these models in Table 6.

| | Model | Parameters | Description |
|---|---|---|---|
| German only | LLäMmlein 120M, 1B & 7B | 100M I 1.036B I 6.612B | German-only decoder models based on LLaMA2 architecture trained entirely from scratch, on the further deduplicated and filtered German portion of RedPajama V2 (Weber et al., 2024). |
| | ModernGBERT 134M & 1B | 136M I 1.068B | German-only encoder models based on ModernBERT (Warner et al., 2025), trained from scratch, on German-only using the same dataset as the LLäMmlein models. Native context length up to 8192 tokens. |
| | LLäMmlein2Vec 120M, 1B & 7B | 100M I 1.036B I 6.612B | Encoder versions of the LLäMmlein decoder models, created via LLM2Vec and additional context extension to up to 8192 tokens. |
| | DOSMo-7B | 7.114B | German-only decoder built from scratch using the Mistral architecture. Trained on approximately 1 trillion German samples from RedPajama V2, MADLAD-400, OSCAR, mC4, Wikipedia, textbooks, and YouTube subtitles. |
| | german-gpt2 | 125M | German-only decoder based on GPT-2 architecture, trained from scratch on 16 GB of German subtitles CommonCrawl web crawls. |
| | gbert-base/-large | 110M I 337M | German-only encoder models based on BERT architecture trained on 163.4 GB of German text, consisting of OSCAR, OPUS, Wikipedia, legal documents. |
| | bert-base-german-cased | 109M | German-only encoder model based on BERT architecture trained from scratch on a 12GB dataset of wikipedia, legal documents and news. |
| | gelectra-base/-large | 110M I 335M | German-only encoder family based on Electra architecture trained from scratch, on the same 163.4GB dataset as gbert-base and gbert-large. |
| | gottbert-base | 126M | German-only encoders based on the RoBERTa architecture, trained on 145 GB of text from OSCAR, Wikipedia and a book corpus. |
| | GottBERT-large | 358M | German-only encoder model based on RoBERTa architecture, trained on 121GB of filtered texts sourced from the first released OSCAR dataset. |
| | GeistBERT-base | 126M | German-only encoder model family building on GottBERT trained on 1.3 trillion tokens sourced from OSCAR23, OPUS, MC4, German Wikipedia, OpenLegalData, Europarl, EUbookshop, ECB, and EuroPat, OpenSubtitles and TildeMODEL. |
| | gerturax-1/-2/-3 | 135M | German-only encoder family based on Electra architecture trained on 147GB to 1.1TB of texts from the CulturaX corpus. |
| German Finetune | gerpt2(-large) | 125M I 776M | German-only GPT-2-style decoder family trained from scratch/ with weights initialized from the english GPT2 model on data from the CC-100 corpus. |
| | bloom-6b4-clp-german | 6.251B | Decoder model preinitialized from multilingual bloom 7b checkpoint transfer learned to German using CLIP-Transfer. |
| | bueble-lm-2b | 2.072B | Decoder-only model preinitialized from multilingual gemma checkpoint trans-tokenized to German. Trained on 3.8B tokens from Occiglot-FineWeb. |
| | leo-hessianai-7b | 6.611B | Decoder-only model preinitialized from LLaMA2 checkpoint finetuned using German texts mostly sourced from OSCAR. |
| | Llama-German-8b | 7.508B | Decoder-only model preinitialized from the multilingual Llama3 8B and finetuned on German via continual pretraining on 65 billion tokens, sourced from occiglot-fineweb-0.5. |
| Multilingual | EuroBERT-210m/-610m/-2.1B | 212M I 609M I 2.110B | Multilingual encoder family based on EuroBERT architecture, supporting 15 languages. |
| | EuroLLM-1.7B/-9B | 1.396B I 8.633B | Multilingual decoder family based on LLaMa architecture, supporting 35 languages. |
| | xlm-roberta-base/-large | 278M I 561M | Multilingual encoder model family pretrained on 2.5TB of CommonCrawl data in 100 languages. |
| | mbart-large-50 | 612M | Multilingual encoder model trained on 50 languages, including German using a sequence-to-sequence translation objective. |
| | bloomz-560m | 560M | Multilingual decoder model initially trained on a 1.5 TB corpus spanning 45 natural and 12 programming languages, followed by supervised multitask fine-tuning across multiple languages. |
| Other Models | Qwen2.5-0.5B/-7B | 495M I 7.073B | Multilingual decoder model family trained on 18 trillion tokens supporting 29 languages. |
| | Qwen3-0.6B/-1.7B/-4B | 597M I 1.722B I 4.025B | Multilingual decoder model family trained on approximately 26 trillion tokens supporting over 100 languages and dialects |
| | Llama-3.2-1B/-3B | 1.237B I 3.215B | Multilingual decoder only model family trained on up to 9 trillion tokens of multilingual text and code. |
| | Meta-Llama-3.1-8B | 7.508B | Multilingual decoder only model trained on over 15 trillion tokens including multilingual text. |

Table 6: Short description of the models mentioned in Table 5. Parameter counts reflect total number of parameters after applying (Q)LoRA.

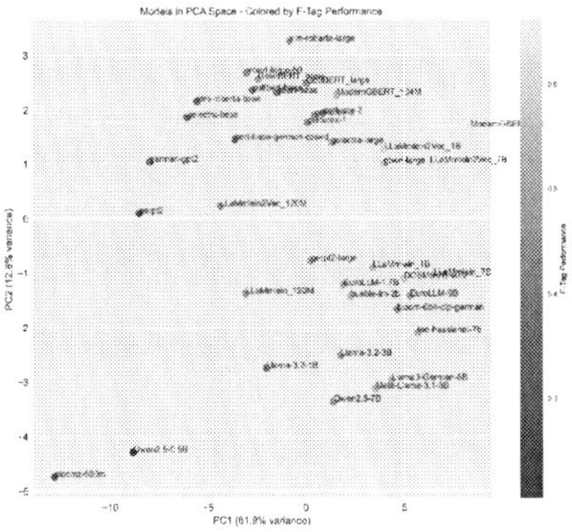


(a) F-Tag Performance

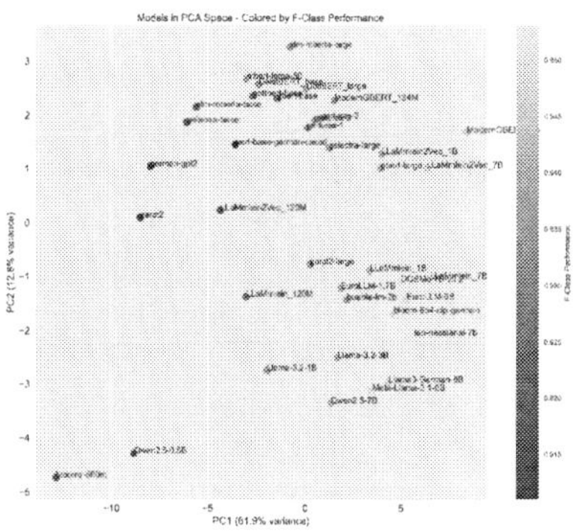


(b) F-Class Performance

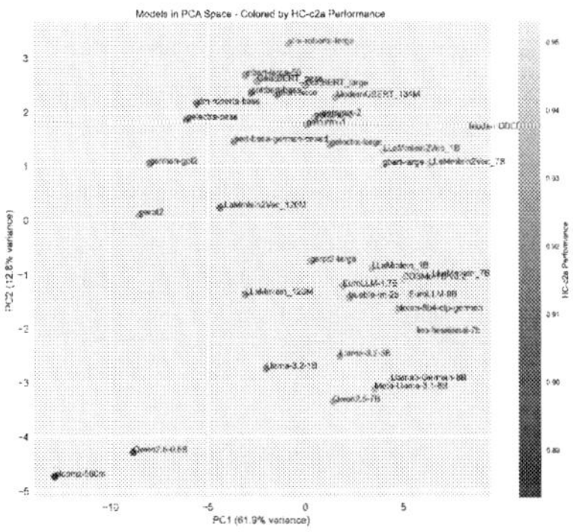


(c) HC-c2a Performance

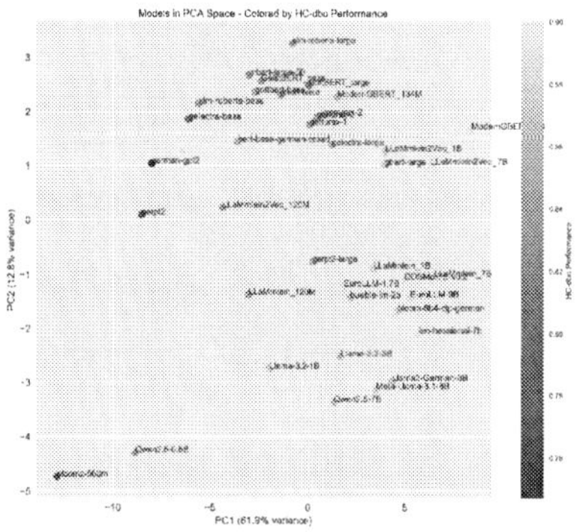


(d) HC-dbo Performance

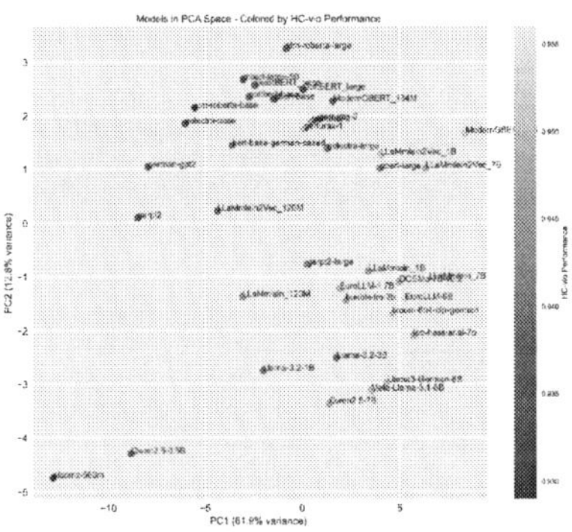


(e) HC-vio Performance

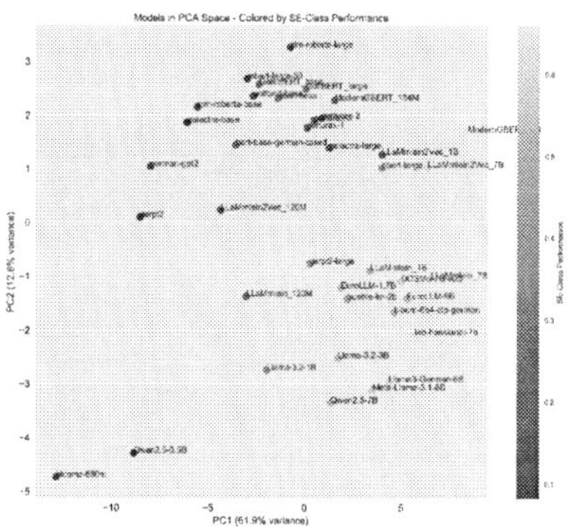


(f) SE-Class Performance

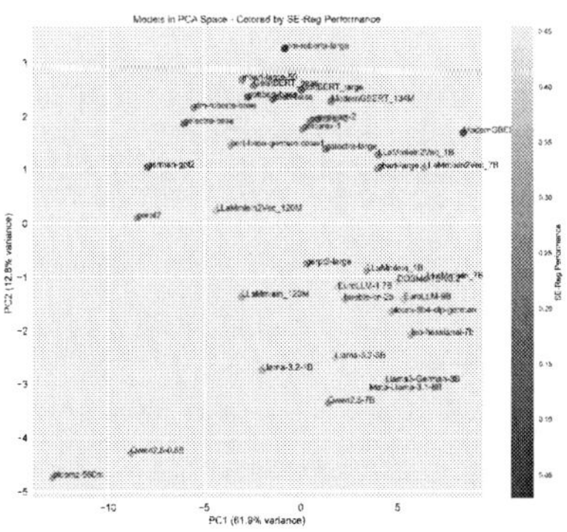


(g) SE-Reg Performance

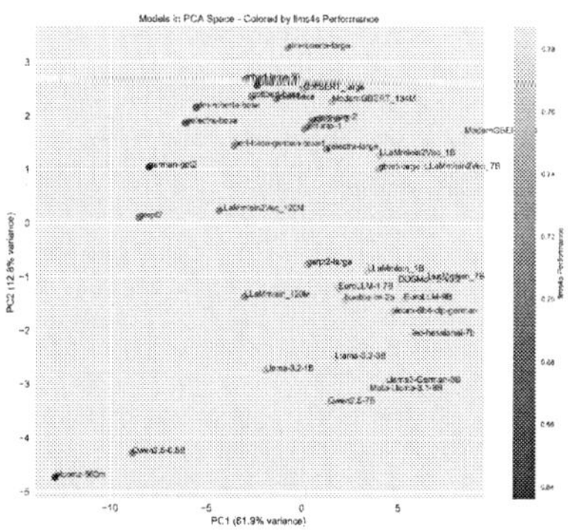


(h) LLMs4s Performance

Figure 3: Models in PCA space colored by performance on individual GermEval 2025 tasks. Each subplot shows the same PCA projection of models but colored by their performance on different tasks: (a) Flausch-Erkennung tagging, (b) Flausch-Erkennung classification, (c-e) Harmful content detection subtasks, (f) SustainEval classification, (g) SustainEval regression, and (h) LLMs4Subjects classification. The visualization reveals task-specific performance patterns and model clustering behaviors across different evaluation metrics. Model placement is identical to fig. 4.

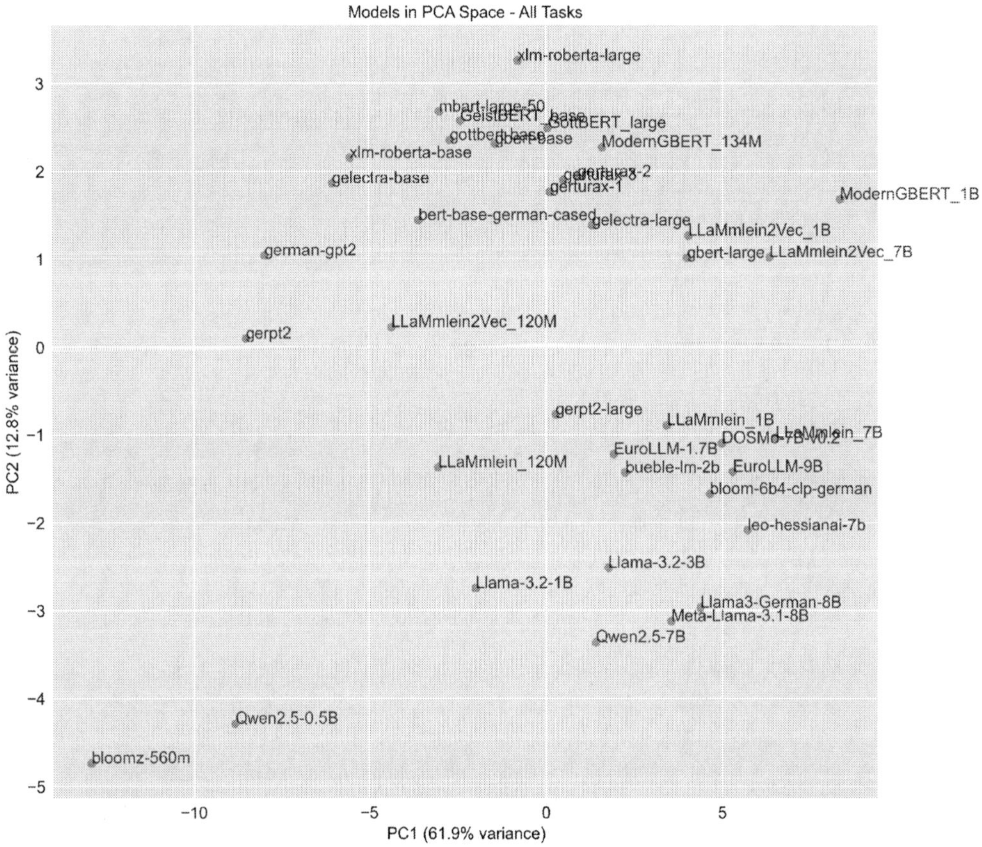


Figure 4: PCA visualization of model performance. Models positioned in PCA space based on their performance vectors across all tasks, showing clustering patterns of similar performing models. The visualization uses the complete set of 37 tasks (29 existing + 8 new GermEval 2025 tasks). Inspired by this plot, we also plotted the inverse loadings in Figure 5.

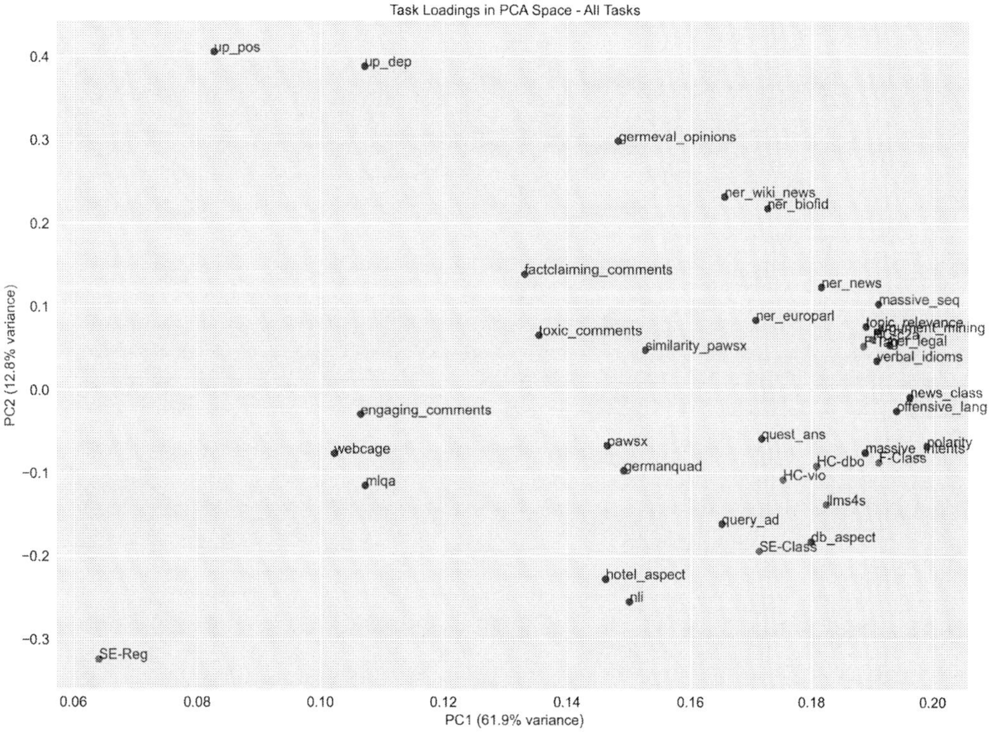


Figure 5: PCA visualization of task performance. Tasks positioned in PCA space based on each model's performance showing clustering patterns of tasks, where models perform similar. The visualization is based on the complete set of models, older SuperGLEBer tasks are blue, new ones from GermEval 2025 are red.

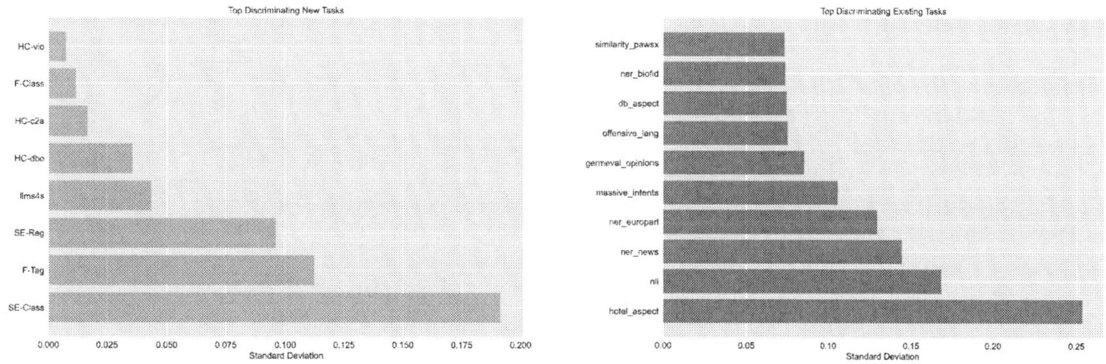


(a) New GermEval 2025 tasks

(b) Existing SuperGLEBer tasks

Figure 6: Task discrimination analysis showing standard deviation of model performance across tasks. (6a) New GermEval 2025 tasks ranked by their ability to discriminate between models. (6b) Top 10 most discriminating existing SuperGLEBer tasks. Higher standard deviation indicates better discrimination between model capabilities, making these tasks valuable for benchmark evaluation.

**Association for Computational Linguistics**
209 N. Eighth Street
Stroudsburg, Pennsylvania 18360

ISBN 979-8-3313-2676-0

CURRAN ASSOCIATES INC.
proceedings.com